Advanced Financial Accounting

Second Edition

Ronald J. Huefner, Ph.D., CMA, CPA
Professor of Accounting
State University of New York at Buffalo

James A. Largay III, Ph.D., CPA
Arthur Andersen & Co. Alumni Professor of Accounting
Lehigh University

The Dryden Press
Chicago   New York   Philadelphia   San Francisco
Montreal   Toronto   London   Sydney
Tokyo   Mexico City   Rio de Janeiro   Madrid

Acquisitions Editor: Larry Armstrong
Project Editor: Nancy Shanahan, Anne Knowles
Managing Editor: Jane Perkins
Design Director: Alan Wendt
Production Manager: Diane Tenzi, Claire Roth
Permissions Editor: Doris Milligan

Text and Cover Designer: Vargas Williams Design
Copy Editor: Mary Englehart
Compositor: The Clarinda Company
Text Type: 10/12 Times Roman

Library of Congress Cataloging-in-Publication Data

Huefner, Ronald J.
  Advanced financial accounting.

  Includes index.
  1. Accounting.   I. Largay, James A.   II. Title.
HF5635.H883   1986   657'.046   85-16165
ISBN: 0-03-001489-1

Address orders:
383 Madison Avenue
New York, NY 10017

Address editorial correspondence:
One Salt Creek Lane
Hinsdale, IL 60521

CBS COLLEGE PUBLISHING
The Dryden Press
Holt, Rinehart and Winston
Saunders College Publishing

To Our Families

For, as we know, there are three things needed by anyone who wishes to carry on business carefully.

The most important of these is cash or any equivalent, according to the saying *Unum aliquid necessarium est substantia*. Without this, business can hardly be carried on.

The second thing necessary in business is to be a good bookkeeper and ready mathematician. . . . .

The third and last thing is to arrange all transactions in such a systematic way that one may understand each one of them at a glance, i.e., by the debit (*debito*—owed to) and credit (*credito*—owed by) method. This is very essential to merchants, because, without making the entries systematically, it would be impossible to conduct their business, for they would have no rest and their minds would be troubled.

—Luca Pacioli, *Double Entry Bookkeeping* (1494)

The Dryden Press
Series in Accounting

Belkaoui
Cost Accounting: A Multidimensional Emphasis

Davidson, Stickney, and Weil
Financial Accounting: An Introduction to Concepts, Methods, and Uses, Fourth Edition

Davidson, Hanouille, Stickney, and Weil
Intermediate Accounting: Concepts, Methods, and Uses, Fourth Edition

Davidson, Maher, Stickney, and Weil
Managerial Accounting: An Introduction to Concepts, Methods, and Uses, Second Edition

Huefner and Largay
Advanced Financial Accounting, Second Edition

Lee
Elementary Accounting

Mueller and Smith
Accounting: A Book of Readings, Second Edition

Reynolds, Sanders, and Hillman
Principles of Accounting, Third Edition

Reynolds, Sanders, and Hillman
Financial Accounting, Second Edition

Titard
Managerial Accounting: An Introduction

Preface

This book is written with three major objectives in mind. First, we seek to reflect the changing topical emphasis and content in the advanced financial accounting course. Second, we write from the perspective of enhancing teachability. Third, we identify a unifying theme—the accounting entity—underlying many of the apparently diverse advanced accounting topics and use it as a focal point throughout the text.

In organizing the text, our goal is to provide a reasonably coherent flow of topics, beginning with relatively easy subjects and progressing to more complex ones. Our desire to focus on the accounting entity meshes with this approach. We start with simple entities—individuals and partnerships—and progress through fiduciary entities and home office and branch relationships until we reach the complex area of multiple corporations and consolidated financial statements. We then move to some special topics in financial reporting of profit-oriented entities and also address the accounting issues present when an entity's activities span national boundaries. The book ends with an examination of accounting and reporting in governmental and other nonprofit entities.

Topical Coverage

Chapter 1 deals with the **entity concept and personal financial statements,** introducing the unifying theme for the book and discussing many of the interesting accounting issues related to reporting the financial affairs of individual, family, or proprietorship entities. This material is typically not covered in depth anywhere in the accounting curriculum; it serves as a useful introduction to the diverse entities considered in advanced accounting.

Chapters 2 and 3 discuss **partnership accounting;** the partnership is viewed as an entity composed of several individuals. Several of the concepts relating to individual entities are seen also to be applicable to partnerships. Income determination and allocation and various forms of capital changes—formation, admission and resignation of a partner, and liquidation—are the major topics discussed.

Chapter 4, on **fiduciary accounting,** incorporates the accounting both for estates and trusts and for corporate bankruptcies. Various aspects of fiduciary accounting are related and presented in a manner which minimizes burdensome details and illuminates basic principles.

The chapter on **home office and branch accounting** (Chapter 5) turns to the familiar corporate entity and begins the consideration of multiple-entity accounting. Working papers and eliminating entries are introduced to prepare the student for the subsequent chapters on consolidations.

Business combinations and consolidated financial statements constitute a major topic in advanced accounting. We have streamlined the coverage and offer but six chapters in the area (Chapters 6–11). At the same time, however, we have provided expanded coverage of accounting for business combinations, accounting for income taxes in consolidated statements, and the consolidated statement of changes in financial position.

Following the material on consolidated statements, there are two chapters on special topics in financial reporting. Chapter 12 succinctly stresses theoretical issues and accounting standards related to **segment and interim reporting.** Generally accepted accounting principles are critically analyzed, and examples from actual annual reports are presented. Chapter 13 examines **the Securities and Exchange Commission (SEC) and its role in financial accounting and reporting.** Although the SEC has delegated the principal responsibility for the setting of accounting standards to the private sector (currently the FASB), it nevertheless exerts a direct influence on financial reporting. SEC reporting and disclosure requirements are discussed in conjunction with accounting issues of special interest to the SEC.

Accounting for international operations is a complex, controversial subject. It can best be understood within the context of the changing economic environment which has influenced current and previous accounting standards in the area. We have developed background material that reviews elements of the international economic system and have included a section on international accounting standards. Chapters 14 and 15 present this increasingly important material.

The expanding role of all types of **government and nonprofit organizations** in our society led us to devote three chapters to fund accounting. Chapter 16 introduces the basic principles of governmental accounting and applies them to accounting and reporting for routine activities of local government units. Coverage of accounting and reporting for nonroutine activities of local government is provided in Chapter 17. Finally, Chapter 18 discusses accounting and reporting for various types of nonprofit, nongovernmental organizations.

Certain complex and perhaps optional topics are covered in the following six chapter appendices, providing the instructor with additional flexibility:

1. Tax aspects of partnerships (Appendix to Chapter 2).
2. Estate planning and taxation (Appendix to Chapter 4).
3. Determining the price in a business combination when the constituent companies are publicly traded (Appendix to Chapter 6).
4. Accounting for futures contracts, other than foreign currency futures (Appendix to Chapter 14).

5. The relationship between foreign currency translation and constant-dollar accounting (Appendix to Chapter 15).
6. Accounting by state and federal governments (Appendix to Chapter 17).

Major Changes in the Second Edition

While the basic organization and entity-oriented theme of the first edition remain unchanged, numerous improvements to the teachability and topical coverage of the text have been made, and recently promulgated accounting standards have been thoroughly integrated. Major changes from the first edition include:

1. Approximately 144 new questions, exercises, and problems have been added—an average increase of 8 per chapter.
2. Chapter 1 is updated to incorporate the AICPA's *Statement of Position 82-1*, dealing with personal financial statements.
3. Chapter 3 describes how the partnership form of business organization is being applied in a variety of contexts and discusses accounting for joint ventures.
4. Chapter 7 includes an expanded discussion of alternative consolidation theories. The chapter also examines "push-down accounting" and illustrates its application.
5. Chapter 8 contains a more thorough discussion of the cash-based consolidated statement of changes in financial position.
6. Chapter 10 offers coverage of consolidation procedures related to intercompany leases.
7. Chapter 11 now includes a section on conversion to the equity method and expanded treatment of the eliminating entries needed when preparing consolidated statements after a change in the parent's ownership percentage in a subsidiary.
8. Chapter 13—an entirely new chapter—discusses the SEC and its accounting and reporting requirements.
9. Chapters 14 and 15 have been updated for the provisions of *SFAS 52*. An appendix on accounting for futures contracts incorporating *SFAS 80* has been added to Chapter 14. A new detailed illustration of the consolidation process under *SFAS 52* is now included in Chapter 15 and the coverage of international accounting standards has been condensed.
10. Chapters 16 and 17 reflect a reorganization of the governmental accounting material into two chapters, allowing more efficient presentation of the material as compared with the first edition. The lengthy appendix on consolidated financial statements of the United States government included in the first edition has been deleted, and the material on state and federal government accounting has been condensed into an appendix to Chapter 17. Pronouncements of the National Council on Governmental Accounting and the new Governmental Accounting Standards Board (GASB) are referenced as needed to enhance the authoritativeness of the text material.

11. Chapter 18 now contains an expanded discussion of accounting and reporting by colleges and universities and by hospitals.

Citations to professional literature are cross-referenced from the original pronouncement to the related section in the FASB volume, *Accounting Standards: Current Text,* whenever possible. For example, allocation of "negative goodwill" is discussed in paragraph 91 of *APBO 16.* The cross-reference to the appropriate section of the FASB current text volume is CT § B50.160. The original pronouncements themselves are identified as follows:

APBO: Accounting Principles Board Opinion

APBS: Accounting Principles Board Statement

ARB: Accounting Research Bulletin

ASR: Accounting Series Release (SEC)

FRR: Financial Reporting Release (SEC)

IFAS: Interpretation of Financial Accounting Standards

NCGA: National Council on Governmental Accounting

SFAS: Statement of Financial Accounting Standards

SGAS: Statement of Government Accounting Standards

Each chapter contains approximately 36 questions, exercises, and problems. Many of the questions can be used to review topics in the chapter, while others are more thought-provoking and challenging. Exercises and problems vary in level of difficulty and are frequently designed to reinforce and deepen the student's understanding of a topic by introducing a new element or complexity beyond the examples in the text. Numerous questions and problems have been adapted from the Uniform CPA Examination and the Certificate of Management Accounting Examination with the permission of the American Institute of Certified Public Accountants and the National Association of Accountants, respectively. In many cases, these materials are revised to conform with our text presentation of particular subjects.

Instructor's Support Materials

The authors have prepared two manuals available to adopters of the text. The first is a *Solutions Manual,* suitable for making transparency masters, which contains detailed solutions to all questions, exercises, and problems as well as a summary of the topics covered, level of difficulty and estimated times for working the exercises and problems in each chapter. The second is an *Instructor's Manual and Test Bank,* which includes lecture notes and suggestions for each chapter, true-false and multiple choice questions, and exercises suitable for examination use, and a list of check figures.

A few selected problems in consolidations and foreign operations are available on a computer diskette prepared by Professor Frank Luh of Lehigh University.

Student Support Materials

A student *Study Guide and Selected Working Papers* for *Advanced Financial Accounting,* second edition has been prepared by Professor Charles Fazzi of Bucknell University, Professor Eugene Rozanski and Professor Harlan Fuller, both of Illinois State University. These supplementary materials have been combined in one volume for convenience and cost savings to the student.

Acknowledgments

Many individuals were helpful in making this book what it is. While we gratefully acknowledge this assistance, we accept responsibility for the errors which remain. Several faculty members reviewed all or part of the manuscript or used it in their classes. In addition to our continuing appreciation for those who helped with the first edition, we recognize below, in alphabetical order, those who worked with us on the second edition.

J. Robert Barnhart   *Ball State University*
Walter G. Blacconiere   *University of Washington*
James R. Boatsman   *Oklahoma State University*
Richard Campbell   *SUNY College at Fredonia*
Gregory P. Cermignano   *Widener University*
Rosita S. Chen   *California State University, Fresno*
Lane A. Daley   *University of Minnesota*
Robert K. Eskew   *Purdue University*
Paul Frishkoff   *University of Oregon*
Mohamed E. Ghobashy   *Indiana University of Pennsylvania*
Samuel P. Graci   *Northern Michigan University*
Leon E. Hay   *University of Arkansas*
Robert E. Hoskin   *Duke University*
Jiuun C. Huang   *Villanova University*
Earl C. Keller   *University of Michigan*
Stanley H. Kratchman   *Texas A & M University*
Arlyn L. Lindskog   *Purdue University, Calumet*
Jimmy W. Martin   *University of Montevallo*
Charles W. Mulford   *Georgia Institute of Technology*
Jane F. Mutchler   *Ohio State University*
James A. Ohlson   *University of California, Berkeley*
William E. Paxton   *Case Western Reserve University*
G. Edward Philips   *University of New Mexico*
Gary John Previts   *Case Western Reserve University*
Jack C. Robertson   *University of Texas, Austin*
Norlin G. Rueschhoff   *University of Notre Dame*
Richard H. Simpson   *University of Massachusetts*
John Sweeney   *Eastern Oregon State College*
Charles A. Tritschler   *Purdue University*
Mark E. Zmijewski   *University of Chicago*

Special thanks are due to Professors Daley and Zmijewski, listed above, for their exceptionally thorough reviews and many constructive suggestions made at several stages during development of the second edition. Mr. Frederick E. Schea, Controller and Assistant Treasurer, Independence Bancorp, Inc., carefully reviewed the appendix to Chapter 14 and made many useful suggestions. Two students—Deborah Birke of the State University of New York at Buffalo and Jay Goffin of Lehigh University—also deserve recognition. Ms. Birke rendered editorial assistance and Mr. Goffin checked the assignment material and solutions for accuracy. Sharon Murawski and Janice Schaeffer are commended for their outstanding manuscript typing. Finally, our thanks go to Larry Armstrong and Nancy Shanahan of The Dryden Press for the care and encouragement they provided during development and production of the second edition.

The permission granted by the AICPA and FASB to quote from their documents in the text is appreciated. Documents issued by the AICPA are copyright © by the American Institute of Certified Public Accountants, Inc. FASB documents are copyright © by the Financial Accounting Standards Board, High Ridge Park, Stamford, Connecticut, 06905, U.S.A. Copies of the complete FASB documents are available from the FASB.

We express our appreciation for the support of the School of Management, State University of New York at Buffalo and the Department of Accounting, Lehigh University. Professor Largay also wishes to gratefully acknowledge the support which Arthur Andersen & Co. provides for his work; it greatly facilitated preparation of the second edition.

Comments from users are invited and will be welcomed.

Ronald J. Huefner
James A. Largay III

About the Authors

Ronald J. Huefner, Ph.D. (Cornell University), CMA, CPA, is Professor of Accounting and Director of Accounting Programs in the School of Management, State University of New York at Buffalo. He is a member of the American Accounting Association, the American Institute of Certified Public Accountants, the National Association of Accountants, and other professional organizations. Articles by Professor Huefner have appeared in *The Accounting Review,* the *Journal of Accounting Research,* the *Bell Journal of Economics and Management Science, Management Accounting,* and other journals. He is the author of *An Introduction to New York State Income Taxation* (Horton, 1983) and is a contributor to the *Handbook of Modern Accounting,* the *Handbook of Cost Accounting,* and the *Accountant's Cost Handbook.* Professor Huefner currently teaches undergraduate and graduate courses in financial accounting. He has received the Chancellor's Award of the State University of New York for Excellence in Teaching.

James A. Largay III, Ph.D. (Cornell University), CPA, is Arthur Andersen & Co. Alumni Professor of Accounting in the College of Business and Economics, Lehigh University. He previously served on the faculties of the Amos Tuck School of Business Administration at Dartmouth College, Georgia Institute of Technology, and Rice University. Professor Largay is a member of the American Accounting Association, the American Institute of Certified Public Accountants, the Financial Executives Institute, and other professional organizations. He has public accounting experience with Arthur Andersen & Co. Articles by Professor Largay have appeared in *The Accounting Review,* the *Journal of Finance,* the *Journal of Political Economy,* the *Financial Analysts Journal,* and other journals. He is co-author of *Accounting for Changing Prices* (Wiley, 1976) and is a contributor to the *Handbook of Modern Accounting* and the *Handbook of Cost Accounting.* Professor Largay currently teaches undergraduate and graduate courses in financial accounting and taxation.

Contents

Part FIVE
Governmental and Nonprofit Entities   812

Part ONE **Simple Entities**

The entity concept is the theme which links the diverse topics of an advanced accounting text. This section of the text describes the entity concept and several relatively simple entities. Chapter 1 discusses individuals. It covers reporting for business activities of sole proprietorships and comprehensive reporting for individuals in the form of personal financial statements. The latter topic involves several accounting issues, including current value reporting. Chapters 2 and 3 discuss accounting for partnerships. Here the difficulty in separating the business entity from its individual partners leads to several accounting practices that differ significantly from corporate accounting. These differences affect the determination of income and accounting for capital changes. Chapter 4 covers fiduciary accounting. Fiduciaries are entities which hold and manage assets on behalf of others. Some common fiduciary entities are estates of deceased individuals, estates of bankrupt firms, and trusts of various types. Accounting and reporting are designed to show clearly how the responsibilities to the beneficiaries have been carried out. Financial statements for fiduciaries therefore differ significantly from those for other entities.

Most of the study of accounting prior to this course has been limited to the corporate business entity. Advanced accounting will introduce a variety of other entities as well as expanding the corporate entity. These first four chapters emphasize how the purposes and characteristics of each entity influence the accounting procedures and the design of financial statements.

Chapter 1 Introduction to Entity Concept and Personal Financial Statements

Advanced accounting courses cover a variety of topics in financial accounting, including accounting for individuals; partnerships; trusts, estates, and bankrupt firms; business combinations; parent–subsidiary corporate structures; reporting to the SEC; multinational corporations; governmental units; and nonprofit organizations.

At first glance, this appears to be a list of unrelated topics. There is, however, a unifying theme which connects them—the concept of **entity.** This concept, first encountered in basic accounting courses, concerns the definition of the unit for which accounting data are accumulated and reported. Up to this point in the study of accounting, the most frequently covered entity has been the business corporation. For this entity, the affairs of the business are distinguished from the affairs of the owners by definition. The separate legal existence of the corporation facilitates this view of the reporting entity. The view may change, however, when organizations other than the simple corporation are examined. When we contemplate individuals and partnerships, we find that we cannot separate the business from the owners as easily as we can for corporations. In analyzing multiple corporations under common ownership, we shall see that the fact of separate legal entities is overcome by the existence of common economic control. Thus consolidated statements are prepared for the group on the basis of a single economic entity. When we study government accounting, we shall see that the reporting emphasis shifts away from an organizational unit and toward groups of resources to be expended for certain purposes. These groups of resources, known as *funds,* become the accounting and reporting entities. As a result, several reporting entities and several sets of financial statements may exist for a single government unit.

Thus, as we progress through this book, we shall see how the question of defining the entity is always a basic issue. Once the entity is defined, different accounting techniques will follow from the differing entity definitions.

We begin our study of these entities and their accounting problems by considering the entity concept and its role in accounting. Later in the chapter, we shall proceed to a discussion of a fundamental accounting entity—the individual—and some of the interesting reporting problems encountered in the preparation of personal financial statements.

The Entity Concept in Accounting

In its 1964 report on the business entity concept, a committee of the American Accounting Association concluded:

> In accounting, the entity with which we are concerned may be defined as *an area of economic interest to a particular individual or group.* The boundaries of such an economic entity are identifiable (1) by determining the interested individual or group, and (2) by determining the nature of that individual's or that group's interest.[1]

Several points contained in this definition of **entity concept** need to be emphasized.

1. An *accounting entity* is an area of economic activity. This is a much narrower concept than the more general notions of separate identity and distinctness applied to entity in the abstract. A faculty committee, for example, is generally considered an entity, but it can become an accounting entity only if it has a budget. An accounting entity can stand alone or be included in the accounts and reports of another entity. Thus, for managerial accounting purposes, a product line, branch, or division represents an area of economic activity. Yet, for public reporting purposes, the area of economic activity is the firm, a more inclusive entity. This latter contrast leads to the next point.

2. An accounting entity is of interest to a particular individual or group. Although there are many possible areas of economic activity, the nature of an individual's or group's interest helps delimit the accounting entity. Hence a division of a firm, which is an area of economic activity, becomes an accounting entity because of the interest of both divisional and corporate management in its performance. The corporation's stockholders, however, are more interested in the accounting entity known as the firm than in its smaller pieces. Since the focus of the stockholders' interest is on the firm, divisional data need not be reported to them. Yet, divisional or segment data are reported publicly (as will be discussed in Chapter 12), primarily because of the interests of another group—security analysts.

   The Internal Revenue Service is another interested group. Its concerns include determination of *taxable entities,* accounting entities which may have different boundaries than those of interest to other groups. For example, a partnership is generally considered to be an accounting entity, but it is not a taxable entity. An accounting entity may consist of a group of

---

[1]American Accounting Association, 1964 Concepts and Standards Research Study Committee—the Business Entity Concept, "The Entity Concept," *The Accounting Review,* April 1965: 358.

affiliated corporations; yet, each individual corporation—an accounting entity—rather than the group may be a taxable entity because of the size of minority interests.

3. Theoretically, all the financial information gathered for an economic activity of interest to some group could be disclosed in reports to that group. The nature of the group's interest is important in deciding on the subset of information possibilities to be reported. For what purposes will the interested group—the users—use the reported information? What decisions will be made by members of the group? Corporate management may use manufacturing data prepared on a direct or variable cost basis in their decision models while full or absorption costing data may be of interest to stockholders.

   Defining the boundaries of an accounting entity is helpful in determining the totality of information relevant to that entity which is eligible for disclosure. It also assists in identifying the information needs of users. Yet the entity concept itself provides no detailed guidance for deciding which of the available information is to be disclosed, how it is to be reported, what accounting principles are to be emphasized, and so forth.[2] In the case of the Internal Revenue Service, however, identification of accounting entities of relevance to it (that is, taxable entities) also serves to define the information and disclosure requirements of those taxable entities.

4. Note the stress on the economic aspect of the accounting entity. Legal aspects play a secondary role, although they can be helpful in identifying an area of economic activity, and, in the case of corporations, legal entities and accounting entities are often one and the same. The entity concept stresses substance over form, thereby leading to the identification of partnerships and groups of related but legally separate corporations as accounting entities. Similarly, the sole proprietorship can be a legitimate accounting entity, separate from the proprietor's personal financial affairs. Of course, for other purposes, such as taxation and personal financial reporting, the individual proprietor's business and personal affairs are combined. Other entity-related considerations relevant to individuals are discussed later in the chapter.

The Relationship between the Entity Concept and the Entity Theory in Accounting

The entity concept is central to accounting. Without it, one is hard pressed to discern any mission for accounting to perform. The entity concept cannot be employed as justification for particular accounting principles, but the nature of the accounting entity and those having interests in it do influence the type of information disclosed in financial reports. This will be especially evident in the mate-

---

[2]A general, though abstract, approach to the level of detail appropriate in financial reports designed to be responsive to the needs of users is given in John E. Butterworth, "The Accounting System as an Information Function," *Journal of Accounting Research,* Spring 1972: 11–27.

rials on individuals, estates and trusts (fiduciaries), and governmental organizations.

In contrast to the *entity concept* is the *entity theory,* which takes as given the existence of accounting entities and offers a particular view of the entity and the interests therein. The entity theory and its alternatives are philosophies of the nature of the entity and the interests in its assets. In essence, the entity theory, the proprietary theory, and the fund theory[3] are alternative approaches to understanding the nature of the relationships expressed on the right-hand side of the fundamental accounting equation: Assets = Liabilities + Owners' Equity. They are briefly discussed in the following paragraphs.

Entity Theory. The **entity theory** holds that the accounting entity has an existence separate from its owners and creditors. The entity owns or controls its assets, while various individuals and organizations have claims on those assets or equities in them. The equities of creditors (that is, liabilities) are viewed as the specific obligations of the entity subject to independent valuation, while the equities of owners consist of recorded amounts of paid-in capital and invested earnings with no particular valuation interpretation. Earnings are said to accrue to the entity rather than to the stockholders directly. Dividends represent distributions of the entity's income and at that point become income to owners.

When applied to consolidated financial statements, the entity theory implies equivalence between the majority and minority stockholders and the valuations assigned to their proportionate equities in the consolidated entity. This is discussed in Chapter 7.

Proprietary Theory. The **proprietary theory** stresses the importance of the proprietor or owner of an accounting entity and views the accounting entity itself as being coincident with the proprietor's area of economic activity. The ownership interest and income of the proprietor are of paramount importance, and accounting reports focus on the information needs of the proprietor, not the needs of other interests in the firm as is the case with the entity theory.

Thus the right-hand side of the accounting equation clearly differentiates between the liabilities of the proprietor and the proprietor's net worth. Assets are presumed to belong to the proprietor, and the earnings resulting from revenues and expenses directly affect the proprietor's net worth. In the corporate context, dividends paid to the proprietors (stockholders) represent withdrawals of capital by the owners.

A version of the proprietary theory surfaces in Chapter 7 as the parent theory of consolidated financial statements. In this setting, the parent company's shareholders emerge as the center of interest or proprietors. A clear distinction is drawn between the interests of majority and minority shareholders and the valuation of their interests. Consolidated net income accrues only to the parent company's

---

[3]These theories and others of lesser importance are contrasted in more detail in Eldon S. Hendriksen, *Accounting Theory,* 4th ed. (Homewood, IL: Irwin, 1982), 452–461.

shareholders, and only dividends paid to parent company shareholders are shown as distributions to owners.

Fund Theory. The **fund theory** offers an alternative view of the accounting entity. It forsakes the personal aspects of the proprietor's interest in the proprietary theory and the separateness of the entity and its equity holders in the entity theory. Rather, the fund theory views the accounting entity in a more operational or goal-oriented context. In short, the entity is viewed as a **fund,** a collection of resources assembled for a particular economic purpose and constrained by a set of restrictions. The right-hand side of the accounting equation specifies the types and quanities of restrictions placed on the assets of the fund. Liabilities are viewed as contractual restrictions on the assets, and "owners' equity" or "invested capital" implies legal or statutory restrictions. Financial statements describe the activities of the fund and are not oriented toward any particular interests. The focus is on sources and dispositions of cash and other resources as they relate to the activities of the fund.

Despite the effort by Vatter[4] to flesh out the fund theory and argue its applicability to accounting in general, it has not caught on in corporate accounting. Today, fund accounting is used extensively only in government and other organizations with nonprofit activities, such as colleges and universities, hospitals, and so forth. Many of these applications are studied in Chapters 16, 17, and 18 of this book.

Thus the entity concept is essential to accounting, while the entity theory and its alternatives are philosophies of the nature of the entity and the interests in its assets. The entity concept cannot be employed as justification for particular accounting principles, but the nature of the accounting entity and those having interests in it do influence the type of information disclosed in financial reports. This will be especially evident in the material on individuals, estates and trusts (fiduciaries), and government organizations.

The definition of the entity can also have accounting implications. When an accounting entity includes two or more smaller entities, as in the cases of home office/branch and parent/subsidiary accounting, certain accounting procedures become necessary to correctly reflect the affairs of the smaller entities in the reports of the larger one.

Individuals and Personal Financial Statements

An individual engaged in economic activity can be viewed as the fundamental accounting entity. Yet, if the individual is also a **proprietor,** the sole owner of a business, the individual's economic activities may encompass two or more accounting entities. Categorizing the individual's financial affairs along entity lines

---

[4]A comprehensive examination of the fund theory is given in William J. Vatter, *The Fund Theory of Accounting and Its Implications for Financial Reports* (Chicago: University of Chicago Press, 1947).

is affected by the nature of his or her interests in those entities. A typical problem where individuals are concerned involves determining the boundaries of their proprietorship and personal activities. Such matters are discussed in the remainder of the chapter, beginning with consideration of entity and accounting issues related to proprietorships.

Proprietorships

The **proprietorship** is a common form of organization for small businesses having a sole owner. In general, proprietorship accounting is not a difficult topic. Most of the accounting procedures applicable to corporate business entities also apply to proprietorships. However, a few topics merit special discussion.

Entity. As we have seen, identification of the accounting entity in a business enterprise is a basic need. For corporations and partnerships, this identification is aided by their legal recognition as separate entities. For the proprietorship, however, legal recognition of the firm as distinct from the individual owner is lacking. While a proprietorship may have a legally recognized trade name, virtually no other legal recognition exists. Thus, identification of the business entity in accounting requires judgment in separating the affairs of the business from the personal affairs of the owner. In many cases, this distinction is clear; in others, it is difficult to make. To illustrate this difficulty, consider the following situations:

1. Mr. Adams owns a building. The first floor houses a grocery store, which Mr. Adams operates as a proprietorship. The second floor contains an apartment, which he rents to tenants. Should the building and the rental income be included in the financial statements of the proprietorship?
2. Mr. Townsend is a successful attorney. He frequently receives advance fees from clients, which he invests in short-term securities. He also invests the profits of his practice in long-term securities. Should either of the investments and the related interest income be included in the financial statements of the proprietorship?
3. Ms. Segrist is a self-employed CPA. Each year, she contributes a percentage of her profits to a tax-qualified retirement plan for the self-employed *(Keogh plan)*. Should this expense and the value of the accumulation in the retirement plan be included in the financial statements of the proprietorship?

Generally accepted accounting principles provide little guidance in dealing with these questions. The logic of the entity concept suggests that an attempt must be made to view the business separately and to ask how the transactions would be treated if the business were a legally distinct entity. Applying this logic, we would answer the above questions as follows:

1. Assuming the primary purpose of owning the building is to house the grocery store, the building should be reported as a proprietorship asset and the rental income as proprietorship income. Other rental properties owned by Mr. Adams, however, should not be included in proprietorship financial statements.

2. The short-term investment of advance fees and the associated income should be reported by the proprietorship, on the basis that the earning process is not yet complete (that is, the services have not yet been rendered). It is reasonable, therefore, to view the short-term securities as an asset of the business. Once the services are complete, the profits of Mr. Townsend's practice are his to spend as he wishes. Thus the long-term securities in which he invests the profits would be considered personal assets.

3. The contribution to the retirement plan appears to be a business-related expense, analogous to pension expense of a corporation. In a proprietorship, however, compensation of the owner is viewed as an element of profit, not an expense. It would be appropriate, therefore, to treat indirect compensation in the same manner. Thus we would not include the expense in the proprietorship statements. The treatment of the accumulation in the retirement plan is clear. This asset belongs to Ms. Segrist, not to the business (that is, if she sold her practice, this asset would clearly not be transferred to the buyer).

Special accounting issues and the lack of a distinct legal entity create difficulty in separating, for accounting purposes, the business affairs of the proprietorship and the personal affairs of the owner. The logic of the entity concept guides the accountant in achieving this separation.

Income Reporting. Net income of a proprietorship differs in definition from net income of a corporation. Corporate net income calculations include deductions for salary expense of *all* employees, including those who are also owners (stockholders). The net income of a proprietorship, however, reflects both profit and compensation for the owner's services in that compensation of the owner is not deducted as an expense. While the absence of compensation as an expense of the business is at variance with the entity concept, the lack of an arm's-length transaction hinders objective determination of compensation. Admittedly, this same situation exists in the closely held corporation. There, the Internal Revenue Service acts as a modifying force, insisting that compensation must be "reasonable in amount" in order to be deductible. No such constraint exists for the proprietorship because no tax deduction for the owner's compensation is allowed.

No provision for federal income taxes is made in determining the net income of a proprietorship. The Internal Revenue Code does not impose a distinct tax on proprietorship income; rather, the income is included on the owner's personal income tax return. Allocation of a portion of the individual's total income tax to the business for financial reporting purposes is not attempted.

As a result of the above differences, the income statement of a proprietorship would have the following general format:

```
Sales and Other Revenues  . . . . . . . . . . . . . . . . . . . . . . . .        $XXX
Costs and Expenses:
   Materials and Supplies. . . . . . . . . . . . . . . . . . . . . . . . .  $XX
```

```
Salaries and Wages of Employees
    (Excluding any Salary to Proprietor) . . . . . . . . . . . . . . .  XX
Depreciation . . . . . . . . . . . . . . . . . . . . . . . . . . . . . . .  XX
Other Expenses . . . . . . . . . . . . . . . . . . . . . . . . . . . .   XX      XXX
Net Income  . . . . . . . . . . . . . . . . . . . . . . . . . . . . . .          $ XX
```

Cash to Accrual Conversions. In very small businesses (including many proprietorships), records are often maintained on a cash basis. This system may be adequate for the owner's information needs and for tax reporting. Moreover, there may not exist on a regular basis a need to have formal financial statements prepared for external parties. If cash basis records are maintained and the need arises for financial statements suitable for external use (for example, an application for a bank loan), a conversion from cash basis to accrual basis will be needed. The process of conversion from cash basis to accrual basis is typically covered in introductory or intermediate-level accounting courses, and hence will only be reviewed here. The basic approach is to adjust the cash basis data for the accruals, deferrals, and prepayments present under accrual basis accounting. The effect is to change the *timing* of revenue and expense recognition, not the ultimate amount.

For example, consider the conversion from cash basis sales (collections from customers) to accrual sales (total billings during the period). If accounts receivable (uncollected billings) have *increased* during the period, then total billings exceed collections from customers and the increase is *added* to cash basis sales. Conversely, if accounts receivable have *decreased,* then collections from customers exceed total billings and the decrease is *subtracted* from cash basis sales. In this case, the decrease in accounts receivable represents collection of *prior period* billings. These relationships may be summarized as follows:

Accrual sales = Cash sales + Ending accounts receivable − Beginning accounts
            receivable,

or alternatively:

Accrual sales = Cash sales + (−) Increase (decrease) in accounts receivable.

Other revenue accounts, such as interest, would be handled in the same way.

Similarly, conversion of an expense account from cash basis to accrual basis is calculated as:

Accrual expense = Cash expense + (−) Increase (decrease) in related accounts
            payable and/or accrued liability account(s).

If accounts payable or accrued liabilities related to a given expense item have *increased* during the period, then total accrual basis expense exceeds cash basis expense (the amount paid to vendors) and the increase is *added* to cash basis expense. A decrease in accounts payable and accrued expenses indicates that amounts paid to vendors are greater than accrual expense incurred this period, i.e., some prior period expenses were paid in the current period.

If inventories are significant to the business operation, the accrual method is generally used, since this is required for tax purposes. However, should a conversion from cash purchases to accrual cost of goods sold be required, the relationship is:

Accrual cost of goods sold = Cash purchases $+(-)$ Increase (decrease) in related accounts payable $+(-)$ Decrease (increase) in inventories.

Here an *increase* in accounts payable for merchandise signifies that more merchandise was purchased this period than was paid for—the increase in payables is *added* to cash purchases—and an *increase* in inventories indicates that not all merchandise purchases were sold—the increase in inventories is *subtracted* from cash purchases.

The approach used above for cost of goods sold also applies to other expenses which involve prepayments. For example, accrual basis insurance expense consists of insurance payments paid plus (minus) the decrease (increase) in prepaid insurance.

As a final illustration of converting from the cash basis to the accrual basis, consider the establishment of an allowance for doubtful accounts. Periodic bad debt expense under the allowance method is subtracted from cash basis income to obtain accrual basis income. If the allowance should have been established in a prior period, the pro forma allowance account must be reconstructed and analyzed to determine the effect on cash basis income. This relationship is:

Accrual basis income = Cash basis income $+(-)$ decrease (increase) in the allowance for doubtful accounts.

If the pro forma allowance *increased* in a given year, bad debt expense exceeded net accounts written off and a *subtraction* results. If the pro forma allowance *decreased*, then net accounts written off exceeded bad debt expense and an *addition* to cash basis income is needed.

Personal Financial Statements

Financial statements of a proprietorship focus only on the business activity of an individual. For certain purposes, it may be necessary to prepare financial statements covering *all* assets and liabilities of an individual (or group of individuals), including business interests as well as nonbusiness items. We refer to such statements as **personal financial statements.** The need for personal financial statements may arise on an ad hoc basis—for example, in connection with an application for a bank loan, a major investment in a business activity (such as formation of a partnership), or election or appointment to public office. Alternatively, personal financial statements may be required on a more regular basis as part of an individual's personal financial planning. Whatever the case, personal financial statements may be viewed as financial reporting for the most basic entity—the individual.

Personal Financial Planning. Personal financial planning is an activity that has received increased attention in recent years, and for which a group of specialized professionals has emerged, combining skills in accounting, taxation, investments, and insurance. **Personal financial planning** is a process that begins with an assessment of an individual's resources, income, financial requirements, and goals, and then develops strategies to meet these requirements and goals. Personal financial statements are useful in the assessment of resources and income, as they provide a framework for collection, valuation, and presentation of this information. Financial goals and requirements are then considered: wealth accumulation for education, investment, or retirement; general financial security; and eventual wealth transfer to others.[5] A financial plan is then developed which may involve investment strategies, insurance policies, interim wealth transfers (e.g., creation of trusts), and use of tax-saving devices (e.g., tax shelters). The plan should be monitored on a regular basis—again, personal financial statements are useful here—and revised as appropriate.

Because of the growing importance of personal financial planning, familiarity with personal financial statements is desirable. In addition, study of this subject offers exposure to complete use of a current value, rather than historical cost, approach.

Accounting Principles. Accounting principles for personal financial statements were initially established in *Audits of Personal Financial Statements,* an audit guide issued by the AICPA in 1968.[6] This guide recommended a dual presentation of assets and liabilities, along with the change in net assets, on both a historical cost and current value basis. This guide was amended in 1982, by *Statement of Position 82–1,*[7] which specified current value as the sole basis for the presentation of assets and liabilities. This conclusion was based on the belief that the uses of personal financial statements (such as loan applications, financial planning, and information about candidates for public office) were better served by current value data than by historical cost data.

The Entity. Normally, personal financial statements are prepared for an individual or for a husband and wife jointly. Occasionally, it may be appropriate for a larger family group to constitute the reporting entity. The purposes for which the statements will be used and the ownership status of major assets are important considerations in defining the reporting entity.

Multiple ownership of assets may complicate the definition of the reporting entity. Several forms of multiple ownership exist:

---

[5]See the Appendix to Chapter 4 on estate planning and taxation for a brief discussion of this aspect of financial planning.

[6]American Institute of Certified Public Accountants, *Audits of Personal Financial Statements* (New York: AICPA, 1968).

[7]American Institute of Certified Public Accountants, *Statement of Position 82–1: Accounting and Financial Reporting for Personal Financial Statements* (New York: AICPA, 1982). Further details on the compilation, review, and audit of personal financial statements are provided in the *Personal Financial Statements Guide* (New York: AICPA Accounting Standards Division, 1983).

1. *Tenancy in common* means that two or more persons own undivided interests in an asset. These interests need not be equal and may be transferred to others.
2. *Joint tenancy* means that two or more persons own equal interests in an asset, with *rights of survivorship* (at death, the interest of the decedent passes to the other owners). A joint tenant may transfer the interest to a third party, in which case the joint tenancy ceases and a tenancy in common is created.
3. *Tenancy by the entireties* is a joint tenancy involving a husband and wife, in which neither party can eliminate the right of survivorship by transferring the interest to a third party.
4. *Community property laws,* which exist in some states, provide for joint ownership in any asset acquired by either spouse during a marriage, even if title is in one spouse's name, unless the asset was acquired with resources possessed by that spouse prior to the marriage.

State laws generally define the rights of multiple owners; not all of the above forms exist in all states. Where the reporting entity does not correspond to the ownership of assets or liabilities, the appropriate proportionate share should be reported in the financial statements, with full disclosure of the details of ownership in the notes. For example, if statements are being prepared for an individual who holds a one-third interest in a parcel of land as a tenant in common, one-third of the value of the land would be presented with a footnote explaining the ownership.

Types of Financial Statements. A **statement of financial condition** is the primary financial statement for individuals. Assets are presented at estimated current values, in order of liquidity. Liabilities are presented at estimated current amounts, in order of maturity. Current/noncurrent classifications are not used, as the concept of working capital is not particularly meaningful in the individual (nonbusiness) context. Comparative statements may be presented if desired. Exhibit 1.1 presents an illustration of comparative statements of financial condition. Several items in this statement will be discussed in more detail in subsequent sections.

In addition to the statement of financial condition, a **statement of changes in net worth** *may be presented, but is not required.* This statement is generally omitted if a beginning-of-year balance sheet is not available, or if detailed records of transactions have not been maintained. As illustrated in Exhibit 1.2, this statement presents major sources of increases and decreases in net worth: income, expenses, changes in current values of assets (distinguished as to realized versus unrealized), and changes in liabilities. The statement of changes in net worth is similar to the business statement of changes in financial position, except that it deals with changes in *net assets* rather than a short-term definition of funds, such as cash or working capital.

Disclosures in personal financial statements, typically found in the **notes to financial statements,** include information on valuation methods, ownership of major assets, descriptive details concerning assets and liabilities, and tax information. Exhibit 1.3 presents an illustration of such notes.

Exhibit 1.1   **Illustrative Statements of Financial Condition**

JAMES AND JANE PERSON
STATEMENTS OF FINANCIAL CONDITION
DECEMBER 31, 19X3 AND 19X2

	December 31	
	19X3	**19X2**
ASSETS		
Cash	$ 3,700	$ 15,600
Bonus Receivable	20,000	10,000
Investments		
Marketable Securities (Note 2)	160,500	140,700
Stock Options (Note 3)	28,000	24,000
Kenbruce Associates (Note 4)	48,000	42,000
Davekar Company, Inc. (Note 5)	550,000	475,000
Vested Interest in Deferred Profit-Sharing Plan	111,400	98,900
Remainder Interest in Testamentary Trust (Note 6)	171,900	128,800
Cash Value of Life Insurance ($43,600 and $42,900), Less		
Loans Payable to Insurance Companies ($38,100 and		
$37,700) (Note 7)	5,500	5,200
Residence (Note 8)	190,000	180,000
Personal Effects (Excluding Jewelry) (Note 9)	55,000	50,000
Jewelry (Note 9)	40,000	36,500
	$1,384,000	$1,206,700
LIABILITIES		
Income Taxes—Current Year Balance	$ 8,800	$ 400
Demand 10.5% Note Payable to Bank	25,000	26,000
Mortgage Payable (Note 10)	98,200	99,000
Contingent Liabilities (Note 11)	—	—
	$132,000	$125,400
Estimated Income Taxes on the Differences between the		
Estimated Current Values of Assets and the Estimated		
Current Amounts of Liabilities and Their Tax Bases		
(Note 12)	239,000	160,000
Net Worth	1,013,000	921,300
	$1,384,000	$1,206,700

The notes to financial statements are an integral part of these statements.

Source: The illustrative statements and notes in Exhibits 1.1, 1.2, and 1.3 are taken from *Statement of Position 82–1: Accounting and Financial Reporting for Personal Financial Statements* (New York: AICPA, 1982), Appendix A. Copyright © 1982 by the American Institute of Certified Public Accountants, Inc.; reprinted with permission.

Valuation of Assets and Liabilities. As mentioned earlier, assets are to be reported at their estimated current values and liabilities at their estimated current amounts. Current value of an asset follows the standard definition of fair market value: The price at which an item could be exchanged between a buyer and a seller, each of whom is well informed and neither of whom is compelled to buy or sell. Converting this definition into practice, however, will often pose difficul-

Exhibit 1.2	Illustrative Statements of Changes in Net Worth

JAMES AND JANE PERSON
STATEMENTS OF CHANGES IN NET WORTH
FOR THE YEARS ENDED DECEMBER 31, 19X3 AND 19X2

	Year Ended December 31	
	19X3	19X2
Realized Increases in Net Worth		
Salary and Bonus	$ 95,000	$ 85,000
Dividends and Interest Income	2,300	1,800
Distribution from Limited Partnership	5,000	4,000
Gains on Sales of Marketable Securities	1,000	500
	$ 103,300	$ 91,300
Realized Decreases in Net Worth		
Income Taxes	$ 26,000	$ 22,000
Interest Expense	13,000	14,000
Real Estate Taxes	4,000	3,000
Personal Expenditures	36,700	32,500
	$ 79,700	$ 71,500
Net Realized Increase in Net Worth	$ 23,600	$ 19,800
Unrealized Increases in Net Worth		
Marketable Securities (Net of Realized Gains on Securities Sold)	$ 3,000	$ 500
Stock Options	4,000	500
Davekar Company, Inc.	75,000	25,000
Kenbruce Associates	6,000	
Deferred Profit-Sharing Plan	12,500	9,500
Remainder Interest in Testamentary Trust	43,100	25,000
Jewelry	3,500	
	$ 147,100	$ 60,500
Unrealized Decrease in Net Worth		
Estimated Income Taxes on the Differences between the Estimated Current Values of Assets and the Estimated Current Amounts of Liabilities and Their Tax Bases	79,000	22,000
Net Unrealized Increase in Net Worth	$ 68,100	$ 38,500
Net Increase in Net Worth	$ 91,700	$ 58,300
Net Worth at the Beginning of Year	921,300	863,000
Net Worth at the End of Year	$1,013,000	$921,300

The notes to financial statements are an integral part of these statements.

ties. It is recognized that the resulting current amounts will be estimates with varying reliability. Several techniques for estimating current values exist; it is the accountant's task to select the most appropriate in each particular case. These techniques include:

1. Inference of value from recent transactions involving similar assets.
2. Appraisal by experts.

Exhibit 1.3	Illustrative Notes to Financial Statements

JAMES AND JANE PERSON
NOTES TO FINANCIAL STATEMENTS

Note 1. The accompanying financial statements include the assets and liabilities of James and Jane Person. Assets are stated at their estimated current values, and liabilities at their estimated current amounts.

Note 2. The estimated current values of marketable securities are either (a) their quoted closing prices or (b) for securities not traded on the financial statement date, amounts that fall within the range of quoted bid and asked prices.

Marketable securities consist of the following:

	December 31, 19X3		December 31, 19X2	
	Number of Shares or Bonds	Estimated Current Values	Number of Shares or Bonds	Estimated Current Values
STOCKS				
Jaiven Jewels, Inc.	1,500	$ 98,813		
McRae Motors, Ltd.	800	11,000	600	$ 4,750
Parker Sisters, Inc.	400	13,875	200	5,200
Rosenfield Rug Co.			1,200	96,000
Rubin Paint Company	300	9,750	100	2,875
Weiss Potato Chips, Inc.	200	20,337	300	25,075
		$153,775		$133,900
BONDS				
Jackson Van Lines, Ltd.				
(12% Due 7/1/X9)	5	$ 5,225	5	$ 5,100
United Garvey, Inc.				
(7% Due 11/15/X6)	2	1,500	2	1,700
		$ 6,725		$ 6,800
		$160,500		$140,700

Note 3. Jane Person owns options to acquire 4,000 shares of stock of Winner Corp. at an option price of $5 per share. The option expires on June 30, 19X5. The estimated current value is its published selling price.

Note 4. The investment in Kenbruce Associates is an 8 percent interest in a real estate limited partnership. The estimated current value is determined by the projected annual cash receipts and payments capitalized at a 12 percent rate.

Note 5. James Person owns 50 percent of the common stock of Davekar Company, Inc., a retail mail order business. The estimated current value of the investment is determined by the provisions of a shareholders' agreement, which restricts the sale of the stock and, under certain conditions, requires the company to repurchase the stock based on a price equal to the book value of the net assets plus an agreed amount for goodwill. At December 31, 19X3, the agreed amount for goodwill was $112,500, and at December 31, 19X2, it was $100,000.

A condensed balance sheet of Davekar Company, Inc., prepared in conformity with generally accepted accounting principles, is summarized on following page:

Exhibit 1.3 **Continued**

	December 31	
	19X3	**19X2**
Current Assets	$3,147,000	$2,975,000
Plant, Property, and Equipment—net	165,000	145,000
Other Assets	120,000	110,000
Total Assets	$3,432,000	$3,230,000
Current Liabilities	$2,157,000	$2,030,000
Long-Term Liabilities	400,000	450,000
Total Liabilities	$2,557,000	$2,480,000
Equity	$ 875,000	$ 750,000

The sales and net income for 19X3 were $10,500,000 and $125,000 and for 19X2 were $9,700,000 and $80,000.

Note 6. Jane Person is the beneficiary of a remainder interest in a testamentary trust under the will of the late Joseph Jones. The amount included in the accompanying statements is her remainder interest in the estimated current value of the trust assets, discounted at 10 percent.

Note 7. At December 31, 19X3 and 19X2, James Person owned a $300,000 whole life insurance policy.

Note 8. The estimated current value of the residence is its purchase price plus the cost of improvements. The residence was purchased in December 19X1, and improvements were made in 19X2 and 19X3.

Note 9. The estimated current values of personal effects and jewelry are the appraised values of those assets, determined by an independent appraiser for insurance purposes.

Note 10. The mortgage (collateralized by the residence) is payable in monthly installments of $815 a month, including interest at 10 percent a year through 20Y8.

Note 11. James Person has guaranteed the payment of loans of Davekar Company, Inc., under a $500,000 line of credit. The loan balance was $300,000 at December 31, 19X3, and $400,000 at December 31, 19X2.

Note 12. The estimated current amounts of liabilities at December 31, 19X3, and December 31, 19X2, equaled their tax bases. Estimated income taxes have been provided on the excess of the estimated current values of assets over their tax bases as if the estimated current values of the assets had been realized on the statement date, using applicable tax laws and regulations. The provision will probably differ from the amounts of income taxes that eventually might be paid because those amounts are determined by the timing and the method of disposal or realization and the tax laws and regulations in effect at the time of disposal or realization.

The estimated current values of assets exceeded their tax bases by $850,000 at December 31, 19X3, and by $770,300 at December 31, 19X2. The excess of estimated current values of major assets over their tax bases are:

	December 31	
	19X3	**19X2**
Investment in Davekar Company, Inc.	$430,500	$355,500
Vested Interest in Deferred Profit-Sharing Plan	111,400	98,900
Investment in Marketable Securities	104,100	100,000
Remainder Interest in Testamentary Trust	97,000	53,900

3. Calculation by present value of future cash flows, using an appropriate discount rate.
4. Use of an earnings–capitalization formula.
5. Historical cost adjusted by an appropriate price index.

The following sections discuss the application of these techniques to several types of assets.

For liabilities, *estimated current amount* means the discounted amount of cash to be paid. Hence, an appropriate discount rate must be selected. If the debt can be discharged currently at an amount lower than the calculated present value, the lower amount should be presented.

Receivables and Payables. Personal financial statements must reflect the accrual basis of accounting. Hence, receivables and payables are to be recognized. Discounted present value of future cash flows is typically used to value receivables and payables. Included in liabilities are definite obligations, such as alimony, which are noncancelable and have known amounts and durations.

Investments. Investments, of various types, constitute a significant portion of assets for many individuals. Estimates of current value range from very precise to very imprecise.

Investments in publicly held companies have market quotations which serve as current values. However, if the individual holds a large block of a given stock, question may be raised as to whether current market quotations are the best estimate of the stock's current value. On the one hand, a large block may be difficult to sell. If the market for the stock is thin, a large block might be salable only at lower prices. On the other hand, a large block might be worth more than current prices to a buyer interested in achieving control. Thus, some judgment is required to estimate current value.

Individuals may also have investments in closely held (nonpublic) companies, including proprietorships, general and limited partnerships, and corporations. The lack of market quotations makes the estimation of current value difficult. Earnings–capitalization formulas are often used; these range from simple formulas (such as "four times average earnings for the last three years") to more complex relationships (such as "excess earnings over the average industry rate of return, discounted at 20 percent"). Other approaches that may be used include appraisals by business brokers, estimates of reproduction cost of assets, or adjusted book value. The nature of the business activity and the character of its assets may, in part, determine the method to be used. For example, a law practice might be valued at a multiple of earnings, while an appraised value of land, buildings, and equipment might be used for a farm. On the statement of financial condition, investment in a business is presented as a single net item; various assets and liabilities are not shown separately on the statement. In other words, investment in a business is presented in the same way as an equity investee or unconsolidated subsidiary on a corporate balance sheet.

Life insurance is also viewed as an investment. Its current value is the cash surrender value of the policy (not the face value) less any outstanding loans against the policy.

Real Estate. Valuation of real estate may also prove difficult. Among the factors that may be considered are recent sales of similar property, appraisals by real estate brokers, and assessed values for property tax purposes (taking into account the relationship between assessed value and market value). Often a clear and consistent relationship between assessed value and market value does not in fact exist, making assessed value a weak indicator of current value. In the case of rental property, a discounted cash flow approach might also be considered. In presenting real estate on the statement of financial condition, any related mortgage liabilities are presented in the liability section, not netted against the asset.

Future Interests. An individual may have several assets in the form of nonforfeitable rights to receive known amounts of future cash payments, such as deferred compensation, guaranteed or vested benefits from pension or profit-sharing plans, individual retirement accounts (IRAs), annuities, alimony, or interests in trust funds. These assets should be presented at their current values, which may be known directly (e.g., current balance in profit-sharing plan or IRA) or may be calculated by discounting future cash flows.

Income Taxes. There are two income tax liabilities presented on the statement of financial condition. *Income taxes payable* includes the estimated income taxes for the current year, net of any payments, as well as any unpaid balances for prior years.

The second account is formally called *estimated income taxes on the differences between the estimated current values of assets and the estimated current amounts of liabilities and their tax bases*. While this title is very descriptive, it is also very long. For short, we shall call this liability *estimated income taxes on unrealized appreciation* (for this purpose, appreciation may be positive or negative). Because assets and liabilities are presented at current values on the statement of financial condition, this estimated tax liability is needed to demonstrate that the full current value may not in fact be realizable. Taxes may be incurred when the current value is realized. Thus the true net worth of the individual is current value of net assets minus estimated taxes on the unrealized appreciation in asset value.

Calculation of estimated income taxes on unrealized appreciation requires knowledge of applicable tax laws, and it also requires data on the tax basis of each asset and liability. For each asset and liability, the difference between current value and tax basis (which may be positive or negative) must be evaluated along the following lines:

Is the gain taxable, or the loss deductible? (For example, losses on assets held for personal use are not deductible.)

Are there any special tax provisions? (An example is the $125,000 exclusion of gain on sale of personal residence for taxpayers over age 55.)

Does the gain or loss constitute ordinary income or capital gain?

To answer questions such as these, current income tax rules should be followed.

To illustrate the calculation of estimated income taxes on unrealized appreciation, assume an individual has the following assets:

Investments in securities having current value of $200,000 and tax basis of $70,000, all long term.

Residence with current value of $210,000 and tax basis of $50,000; individual is over age 55 and qualifies for the special exclusion.

Pension plan rights having a current value of $150,000 and zero tax basis (fully funded by employer).

Household furnishings with current value of $8,000 and tax basis of $15,000.

Investment in rental property (long term) with current value of $80,000 and tax basis of $90,000 (assume no depreciation recapture).

Assume further that the individual is subject to a 40 percent marginal tax rate on ordinary income. The estimated income tax on unrealized appreciation is calculated as follows:

Description	Current Value	Tax Basis	Unrealized Appreciation	Taxable Amount	Effective Tax Rate	Estimated Income Tax
Securities	$200,000	$ 70,000	$130,000	$130,000	16%	$20,800
Residence	210,000	50,000	160,000	35,000	16	5,600
Pension	150,000	—	150,000	150,000	40	60,000
Furnishings	8,000	15,000	(7,000)	—		—
Rental Property	80,000	90,000	(10,000)	(10,000)	16	(1,600)
	$648,000	$225,000	$423,000	$305,000		$84,800

The appreciation on the residence is only partially taxable because the $125,000 exclusion applies. The loss on the household furnishings, as a personal use item, is nondeductible. The pension will be taxed as ordinary income and hence is subject to the full 40 percent rate. The securities, residence (after exclusion), and rental property all constitute long-term capital gains or losses. Under current tax law, there is a long-term capital gain deduction of 60 percent; hence only 40 percent of the net gain is subject to tax. The effective tax rate is therefore 16 percent (16 percent effective tax rate = 40 percent × 40 percent marginal rate).

On the statement of changes in net worth, the *change* in the estimated income tax on unrealized appreciation is shown as an unrealized decrease in net worth (assuming the estimated income tax increased during the year). For convenience, the change may be calculated as ending balance minus beginning balance; there is no need to trace the effect of each asset value change.

Preparation of Personal Financial Statements. In practice, the preparation of personal financial statements may be somewhat difficult. Most individuals do not maintain a comprehensive set of accounting records. In the preparation of statements, the individual's assets and liabilities must first be identified. Data sources may include income tax returns, checkbooks, statements from security brokers, property tax bills, loan statements, and similar items. Once the assets and liabilities have been identified, the second step is to estimate current value, as discussed in the preceding sections. Finally, all the information must be presented in the proper format. Textbook problems emphasize the last (and easiest) step—preparing statements given a set of information; they cannot adequately represent the difficulty of the two preceding steps—identification and valuation of assets and liabilities.

Summary of Key Concepts

The **entity** is the organizational unit for which accounting data are accumulated and reported. Definition of the entity is an important aspect of the various areas of accounting discussed in this book.

The **entity theory, proprietary theory,** and **fund theory** are different explanations of the nature of the accounting entity and the interests in its assets. Each of these three theories will be encountered in the topics covered in this book.

A **proprietorship** is an unincorporated business entity having a single owner. Although most aspects of corporate accounting apply to proprietorships, the definition of **net income** is different.

Personal financial statements consist of a **statement of financial condition,** an optional **statement of changes in net worth,** and **notes to financial statements.** Data are presented on a **current value basis.**

Questions

Q1.1 Explain the difference between the terms *entity concept* and *entity theory* in accounting.

Q1.2 Millie Watson converted her garage to a beauty salon, which she operates as a sole proprietorship. Watson has a practice of collecting tips in a glass jar. Periodically she empties the jar and buys magazines, which she reads before setting them out for customers.

   1. In preparing the financial statements for the proprietorship, how would the tips be reported?
   2. In preparing the financial statements for the proprietorship, how would the cost of the magazines be reported? (Assume the cost is a material amount.)
   3. Would either item be reported on Watson's personal financial statements? If so, how?

Q1.3 Kyle Johnson lives on the second floor of a three-story house which he owns. He rents the top floor to local university students. A home-decorating business which Johnson owns and operates occupies the ground floor of the house. Should the house and the rental income be included in the financial statements of the proprietorship?

Q1.4 E. A. Grimes owns an insurance agency, which is operated as a sole proprietorship. Because of the substantial amount of travel connected with the business, Grimes owns two automobiles. One, a compact car, is used almost exclusively for business (about 10 percent of the use of the compact car is for personal rather than business purposes). The other, a station wagon, is used exclusively for family (personal) purposes.

In preparing a financial statement for the insurance agency only, how would you recommend that the two cars be treated?

Q1.5 In what ways do the financial statements of a proprietorship differ from the financial statements of a corporation?

Q1.6 Why are items on the statement of financial condition of an individual not separated into current and noncurrent categories?

Q1.7 The statement of financial condition is always prepared when presenting financial statements for an individual or group. The statement of changes in net worth, however, is optional. Under what circumstances might a statement of changes in net worth *not* be presented?

Q1.8 Personal financial statements are being prepared for an individual who owns and operates a grocery store as a sole proprietorship. What information concerning the grocery store would appear on the personal financial statements? What are the likely sources of that information?

Q1.9 What are future interests, and how are they presented on personal financial statements?

Q1.10 Current values of material items are presented on personal financial statements. How could the current value of the following assets be determined?

1. Postage stamp collection.
2. Vacant lot in a housing development.
3. Antique furniture.
4. Life insurance policy.

5. Household appliances.
6. Inventory of a proprietorship.
7. Jewelry.
8. Minority interest in a closely held corporation.

Exercises

E1.1 The following unadjusted trial balance has been prepared from the books of the Aston Refinishing Company:

```
Cash . . . . . . . . . . . . . . . . . . . . . . . . . . . . . . . . . . . . . . . . $ 9,000
Equipment . . . . . . . . . . . . . . . . . . . . . . . . . . . . . . . . . . . .   12,000
Supplies . . . . . . . . . . . . . . . . . . . . . . . . . . . . . . . . . . . . .    4,000
```

```
Prepaid Rent . . . . . . . . . . . . . . . . . . . . . . . . . . . . . . . . .     3,000
Accounts Payable. . . . . . . . . . . . . . . . . . . . . . . . . . . . . .    (4,460)
Notes Payable . . . . . . . . . . . . . . . . . . . . . . . . . . . . . . .   (10,000)
Capital . . . . . . . . . . . . . . . . . . . . . . . . . . . . . . . . . . .    (6,160)
Revenues. . . . . . . . . . . . . . . . . . . . . . . . . . . . . . . . . .   (59,840)
Supplies Expense. . . . . . . . . . . . . . . . . . . . . . . . . . . . .     9,500
Labor Expense . . . . . . . . . . . . . . . . . . . . . . . . . . . . . . .     8,000
Salary Expense (Aston). . . . . . . . . . . . . . . . . . . . . . . . . .    34,000
Interest Expense . . . . . . . . . . . . . . . . . . . . . . . . . . . . . .       960
```

Additional information:

1. Wages owed on December 31, 19X1, are $600.
2. Daniel Aston, sole owner of the company, earned a salary of $35,000 in 19X1. Of this amount, $1,000 remains to be paid as of December 31.
3. Prepaid rent as of December 31 should be $1,000.
4. Semiannual interest on the note of $720 is due on February 28. The note has been outstanding all year.
5. The corporate tax rate is assumed to be 17 percent; Aston's personal tax rate is 21 percent. The accrual basis is used.

Required: Prepare income statements for the Aston Refinishing Company, assuming the company is:

1. A proprietorship.
2. A corporation.

E1.2 Moretti Auto Repair maintains its books on a cash basis. Selected account balances for 19X2 show:

```
Sales Revenue. . . . . . . . . . . . . . . . . . . . . . . . . . . . . . . .  $71,600
Wages Paid to Employees. . . . . . . . . . . . . . . . . . . . . . . . . .   11,000
Parts and Supplies Purchased. . . . . . . . . . . . . . . . . . . . . . .   21,300
Insurance Expense . . . . . . . . . . . . . . . . . . . . . . . . . . . . .    1,500
```

At the end of each year, Mr. Moretti makes a note of (but does not record) various information:

	12/31/X2	12/31/X1
Owed to Suppliers.	$2,200	$1,800
Owed to Employees.	600	800
Owed by Customers.	3,700	1,400
Unexpired Insurance	200	100
Parts and Supplies on Hand.	900	1,200

Required: Calculate sales revenue, wages expense, parts and supplies expense, and insurance expense, using an accrual basis.

E1.3 James Cromwell, age 45, is employed as an engineer. He participates in his employer's pension plan, which requires that he contribute 4 percent of his annual salary to the plan. To date, he has contributed $8,947 to the plan. His benefits, which are vested, will be based on his past and future salary levels. Given reasonable assumptions about his future salary growth, he anticipates benefits of approximately $10,500 per year upon retirement at age 65 (at which time his life expectancy will be 12 years).

Required: Assuming that a 10 percent discount rate and a 40 percent tax rate are appropriate, indicate the amounts that would be presented for pension rights and for estimated income tax on unrealized appreciation on Cromwell's personal statement of financial condition.

E1.4 James and Elaine Vincent are preparing a personal statement of financial condition. They are attempting to estimate a current value for their personal residence. The residence was acquired 15 years ago at a cost of $40,000. At the time, it was assessed for local property tax purposes at $13,000 (the locality assesses at about 30 percent of market value). Eight years ago, the house was reassessed at $16,000; there has been no further change in the assessed value.

Over the years, the Vincents have made improvements to the house (beyond routine painting, redecorating, etc.) costing about $8,000. Fire insurance carried on the house (exclusive of contents) is currently $75,000 (this amount was last revised 3 years ago to reflect then-current replacement cost).

Within the past year, two homes in the neighborhood were sold at prices of $86,000 and $91,000. All houses in the neighborhood are of approximately the same age and size, but vary as to design, condition, and amenities. A friend who is a real estate agent estimated that the Vincent house would have an asking price of $90,000 to $95,000, and that houses sell for about 93 percent of the asking price.

Required: On the basis of the above information, recommend a single figure which the Vincents should present as the current value of their residence. Justify your selection.

E1.5 Ann Laurence is preparing a personal statement of financial condition as of December 31, 19X3, which will include the following assets:

1. A bonus of $9,000 receivable from her employer for services performed in 19X3; the bonus will be paid in March 19X4.
2. Investment in stocks and bonds having a current value of $38,000. Cost (tax basis) is $27,500, and all have been held for the long-term holding period.

3. An IRA account having a current balance (including accumulated interest) of $7,300. In each of the last three years, $2,000 has been deposited in this account.
4. A recreational vehicle purchased 2 years ago for $18,000, with a current value of $14,000.

Laurence's marginal tax rate is 40 percent on ordinary income and 16 percent on long-term capital gains.

Required: Calculate the estimated income tax on unrealized appreciation which should be included in the statement of financial condition.

E1.6 Prepare a statement of financial condition for Michael Fenway as of December 31, 19X3, given the following information:

1. Fenway's unincorporated business yielded a profit of $42,000 on the cash basis and $50,000 on the accrual basis.
2. The book value of Fenway's equity in the business is $30,000 at year-end. However, the market value of the business is estimated to be $100,000. The books are kept on the accrual basis.
3. Fenway, a cash basis taxpayer, is subject to a tax rate of 40 percent on all income. During the year, estimated tax payments of $12,000 were made.
4. Fenway's only income is derived from the business. His only other asset is cash of $15,000.

E1.7 Arthur Randolf owns 75 percent of the Granitville Services Company. The book value of the firm's total assets is $700,000; liabilities are $300,000. The normal rate of return on total assets for similar firms in the same industry is 15 percent. Because of its long-standing reputation for quality service, Granitville has repeatedly enjoyed excess earnings. Net income before extraordinary items for the last 6 years is shown below:

19X4.	$140,000	19X7.	$132,500
19X5.	$130,000	19X8.	$120,000
19X6.	$127,500	19X9.	$130,000

A capitalization rate of 10 percent for excess earnings is considered appropriate.

Required: Calculate the values of the investment to be shown on Randolf's personal statement of financial condition under each of the following assumptions:

1. Excess earnings will continue indefinitely.
2. Excess earnings will continue for 15 years.

E1.8 Comparative statements of financial condition are given below for Jonathan Flanders, along with additional information.

JONATHAN FLANDERS
COMPARATIVE STATEMENTS OF FINANCIAL CONDITON

| | 12/31/X4 | | 12/31/X5 | |
	Cost	Current Value	Cost	Current Value
ASSETS				
Cash.	$ 4,000	$ 4,000	$ 3,500	$ 3,500
Marketable Securities (Note 1)	10,000	12,000	8,500	13,600
Total Assets	$14,000	$16,000	$12,000	$17,100
LIABILITIES				
Accrued Income Taxes.	$ 600	$ 600	$ 450	$ 450
Estimated Income Taxes on				
Unrealized Asset Appreciation				
(Note 2)	—	300	—	765
Total Liabilities.	$ 600	$ 900	$ 450	$ 1,215
EXCESS OF ASSETS OVER				
LIABILITIES	$13,400	$15,100	$11,550	$15,885

Note 1: Marketable securities are 100 shares in Weber Company at 12/31/X4.

Note 2: Taxes on unrealized appreciation are accrued at a rate of 15 percent.

Additional information:

1. During 19X5, Flanders sold 15 shares of Weber Company for $195 each. He paid $125 in taxes on the sale. No other sale or purchase of marketable securities occurred in 19X5.
2. Dividends of $238 on Weber stock were received during 19X5.
3. Flanders's salary during 19X5 was $14,000. He paid income taxes totaling $3,700 (not including taxes on sale of stock).

Required: Prepare a statement of changes in net worth for Jonathan Flanders for 19X5.

Problems

P1.1 **Discussion and Applications of Entity Concept**   The concept of the accounting entity often is considered to be the most fundamental of accounting concepts—one that pervades all of accounting.

Required:

1. **a.** What is an accounting entity? Explain.
   b. Explain why the accounting entity concept is so fundamental that it pervades all of accounting.
2. For each of the following, indicate whether the accounting concept of entity is applicable. Discuss and give illustrations.
   a. A unit created by or under law.

b. The product line segment of an enterprise.

c. A combination of legal units and product line segments.

d. All of the activities of an owner or a group of owners.

e. An industry.

f. The economy of the United States.

   (AICPA adapted)

P1.2 Proprietorship Accounting—Simple Peter Becker started repairing watches in his spare time several years ago. The hobby has evolved into a business, and Becker is considering resigning from his maintenance job and opening a watch repair shop. Before taking such a drastic step, Becker wants to know how profitable the repair business will be. For tax purposes, Becker kept receipts for repair work. He did not report any expenses related to the business.

Becker's expenditures during the past year, 19X0, were recorded in his checkbook. He made no purchases for the business with cash.

Because the demand for Becker's work far exceeds the time he can currently spend, he has turned away many customers in the past year. Becker estimates he can triple 19X0 cash receipts in his first year of operation. Other clock and watch repairers in the area make $15 an hour. Becker plans to use this number in determining his salary based on a 50-week, 40-hours-a-week, work year.

A local jewelry store has agreed to rent Becker a back room for $300 a month including utilities. Phone bills for the first year are expected to be $350.

Data from Becker's checkbook are as follows:

Groceries and Other Living Expenses	$8,500
Clothing	1,000
Payment of Taxes	250
Purchases of Watch Parts	500
House Payments	3,720
Miscellaneous Personal Expenditures	2,000

Becker's tax return shows that he received $8,000 cash from repairing watches and $15,000 in salary from his maintenance job. He paid $5,700 in taxes.

Required:

1. Prepare a projected income statement for the first year of Becker's watch repair shop.
2. What other factors should Becker consider before opening the repair shop?

P1.3 Proprietorship Statements—Cash to Accrual Jacob Peterson owns a warehouse which he operates as a sole proprietorship. Jacob has applied for a bank loan to expand the facilities. Jacob maintains his accounting records on a cash basis. The lending institution has requested a balance sheet and income statement for the proprietorship prepared on the accrual basis. Below are trial balances of accounts in the general ledger as of December 31, 19X5.

GENERAL LEDGER TRIAL BALANCE
DECEMBER 31, 19X5

	Debit	Credit
Cash.	$ 170,000	
Investments	425,000	
Property, Plant, and Equipment	1,200,000	
Accumulated Depreciation		$ 350,000
Payroll Taxes Withheld.		12,000
Capital, Jacob Peterson		1,318,000
Rental and Service Income		400,000
Operating Expense	220,000	
Insurance Expense	30,000	
Administrative Expense	70,000	
Investment Income.		35,000
Totals	$2,115,000	$2,115,000

Details of unrecorded accruals and other information follow:

	December 31	
	19X4	19X5
Accounts Receivable—Rents and Services (includes doubtful accounts totaling $700 at December 31, 19X5; all doubtful accounts were for 19X5 services)	$ 27,000	$ 37,000
Rental Deposits from Lessees ($7,500 of 19X5 amount was received in 19X5 and recorded in Rental and Service Income; $600 of the 19X4 amount was applied to final month's rentals in 19X5)	2,100	9,000
Interest Income Receivable from Investments	1,000	2,600
Market Value of Investments (all investments are corporate bonds)	460,000	475,000
Accounts Payable (Operating Expenses)	8,000	9,700

The amount in the Insurance account is a February 1 payment for insurance premiums: $6,000 for a one-year liability insurance policy and $24,000 for a 3-year fire insurance policy. The coverage under both policies commenced on January 1.

Payroll Taxes Withheld includes employees' FICA taxes of $800. Administrative Expenses includes a payment of $300 for 19X4 employer FICA taxes.

Required: Prepare a work sheet for the preparation of financial statements on the accrual basis. The work sheet should have debit and credit columns for each of the following: (1) trial balance (cash basis); (2) adjustments; (3) income statement (accrual basis); (4) balance sheet (accrual basis). *(AICPA adapted)*

P1.4 Preparation of Statement of Financial Condition Marilyn Gray is sole owner and operator of Gray's Art Shop. The balance sheet and income statement for the current year are presented below:

GRAY'S ART SHOP
BALANCE SHEET
DECEMBER 31, 19X9

ASSETS		LIABILITIES AND CAPITAL	
Cash.	$ 10,000	Accounts Payable	$ 5,000
Accounts Receivable	20,000	Short-Term Loan	30,000
Inventory	130,000	Loan on Automobile	800
Automobile (Net).	1,800		$ 35,800
Equipment, Fixtures (Net)	20,000	Capital—Marilyn Gray	150,200
Prepaid Expenses	4,200		
Total Assets	$186,000	Total Liabilities and Capital	$186,000

GRAY'S ART SHOP
INCOME STATEMENT
FOR THE YEAR ENDED DECEMBER 31, 19X9

Sales		$250,000
Cost of Goods Sold		150,000
Gross Profit.		$100,000
Other Expenses		
Rent	$24,000	
Car Expense	3,800	
Insurance and Security	10,000	
Interest	3,500	
Depreciation	5,000	
Miscellaneous	2,300	
Total Expenses.		48,600
Net Income		$ 51,400

Gray has been renting space in a building since she began business. The owner has offered to sell her the building if she can raise the necessary money. As her accountant, you instructed Marilyn to assemble both personal and business financial information so that you can prepare a personal financial statement to be included with her loan application. The information received is as follows:

1. The mortgage on her house, which she owns jointly with her husband Neil, has a current balance of $17,500. The Grays purchased the house 10 years ago for $50,000. A real estate broker estimates current market value to be $70,000.
2. Their joint checking account shows a balance of $2,000 on the last statement date. Since then, the Grays have written checks totaling $1,400 and deposited $230 up to December 31.
3. A joint savings account shows a balance of $25,000, including interest, at December 31.

4. Outstanding charge accounts (joint) total $5,000 from the purchase of personal items.
5. Marilyn estimates that household effects purchased at various times at a cost of $30,000 now have a resale value of $10,000 (jointly owned).
6. Data on securities held in Marilyn's name are as follows:

Security	Purchase Date	Shares	Cost	Market Value
A	2/1/X6	300	$ 3.83	$ 5.60
B	4/1/X8	250	15.80	35.20
C	10/1/X8	1,500	.35	.50
D	5/1/X9	150	2.34	2.00

7. The automobile Marilyn uses only for business purposes is in her name. It cost $5,400 and has a market value of $1,000. Balance due on the loan for the car is $800. The Grays use Neil's car for personal purposes. He owes $4,000 on the principal of the car loan. Neil paid $5,900 for the car. He estimates it to be worth $3,500 now.
8. Recently a local art gallery offered to purchase Gray's Art Shop for $200,000.
9. Income taxes owed on December 31, 19X9, which are attributable to Marilyn's income are $1,200. The effective tax rate on unrealized appreciation of assets is 20 percent.

Required: Prepare a personal statement of financial position for Marilyn Gray, with accompanying notes.

P1.5 **Statement of Changes in Net Worth**   Janice Tucker graduated in May 19X1 from Great Lakes University and accepted a position as a staff accountant at a CPA firm. At the end of 19X1, she summarized her personal transactions for the year as follows:

CASH RECEIPTS

Student Loan	$ 2,000
Salary—CPA Firm.	9,800
Salary—Part-Time Job While Student	1,750
Gifts	800
Proceeds from Sale of Old Car.	950
	$15,300

CASH DISBURSEMENTS

Living Expenses	$10,200
Tuition	3,000
Payment on Student Loan . . .	300
Purchase of Furniture	2,100
Down Payment on New Car . .	1,000
Income Taxes Paid	1,200
	$17,800

Additional information:

1. Tucker's bank account balance declined from $4,100 to $1,600 during the year.
2. Following graduation, Tucker bought furniture for her apartment at a cost of $3,000; she still owes the store $900 (no interest is accrued). Current value of the furniture is estimated to be 80 percent of its cost.

3. In December, Tucker sold her old car, which had a current value of $1,300 at the beginning of 19X1. She bought a new car for $8,800, making a $1,000 down payment and financing the balance. She estimates the current value of the new car at December 31 to be $8,000.

4. A preliminary calculation of her 19X1 income tax indicates an expected refund of $250. Tucker is subject to a marginal rate of 20 percent on any unrealized appreciation.

5. The student loan had a balance of $6,200 at the beginning of the year. Interest at 7 percent begins to accrue on January 1, 19X2.

Required: Prepare a statement of changes in net worth for 19X1.

P1.6   Statement of Financial Condition—Comprehensive James Bolan, M.D., and Louis Scott, M.D., are applying for a $115,000 loan to purchase additional equipment for their medical practice. The bank has requested a personal statement of financial condition as of June 30, 19X3, from James Bolan and his wife, Frances. Pertinent facts about the Bolans follow. Unless stated otherwise, all facts are presented as of June 30, 19X3.

1. The Bolans have $8,000 in a checking account and $30,000, including interest through June 30, 19X3, in a savings account.

2. The Bolans paid $7,500 in 19X1 for a 15 percent interest in Crown Corporation, which has 100,000 shares outstanding. The stock is traded on a Midwestern exchange. In recent months, the stock has traded in blocks of 100 shares or less at $1.50 per share. Dr. Bolan was recently offered $1.10 per share for all his shares. The offer is still outstanding.

3. Dr. Bolan and Dr. Scott each own a 50 percent interest in the Suburban Medical Group, a partnership. The balance sheet of the Suburban Medical Group, prepared on a cash basis, is presented below.

ASSETS		LIABILITIES	
Cash (in Non-Interest-Bearing Account)	$ 10,400	6% Notes Payable (Principal and Interest Payable Monthly until 19Y0)	$ 39,000
30-day Treasury Bills (Maturing July 30, 19X3)	11,000	Capital	120,300
Drugs and Supplies Inventory	6,100		
Equipment and Office Furniture (Net of $14,000 Accumulated Depreciation)	66,000		
Automobiles (Net of $1,150 Accumulated Depreciation)	10,800		
Building (Purchased June 28, 19X3)	55,000		
Total	$159,300	Total	$159,300

4. As of June 30, 19X3, the Suburban Medical Group had unrecorded accounts receivable of $12,451 and unrecorded accounts payable of $1,327. Payments on the notes are current. The partnership prepares its tax returns on the accrual basis.

5. Dr. Bolan and Dr. Scott were offered $260,000 for their practice by the Rural Medical Center. The offer is still outstanding. Counsel has advised that if the offer is accepted, any difference between the proceeds and the partners' tax bases in the partnership will be taxed as ordinary income.

6. The Bolans purchased their residence in 19X0 for $85,000. The balance of the 30-year, 10 percent mortgage is $64,498. The current rate charged on similar mortgages is 10 percent. Payments on the mortgage are current. Similar homes in the area have increased in value approximately 30 percent since 19X0. The assessed real estate value was determined in March 19X3 to be $108,500 based on fair value.

7. Frances Bolan owns a 19X0 automobile which cost $7,100. Current newspaper advertisements indicate that her car could be sold for $4,800.

8. Fifteen years ago the Bolans bought a painting by an artist who has since become internationally famous. The Bolans paid $6,000 for the painting. In June 19X3, the painting was appraised at $16,000.

9. The Bolans have maintained cost records on their major household effects. The costs aggregate $27,500. A local business which specializes in auctioning this type of merchandise estimated in July 19X3 that the household effects have a net realizable value of $12,000. Other household effects are of nominal value.

10. Dr. Bolan has a vested interest of $14,175 in a group-participating pension plan. The present value of the vested benefits is $6,818. Dr. Bolan's contributions to the plan (tax basis) have been $5,432.

11. On July 1, 19X0, Dr. Bolan paid $9,000 for 25 percent of the capital stock of Medical Instruments, Inc., a closely held business which designs medical instruments. A summary of financial data of the corporation follows:

Balance Sheet at June 30, 19X2		Earnings Summary for the Years Ended June 30		Dividends Paid	
Assets	$112,800				
Liabilities	$ 46,650	19X1	$12,050		
Equity.	66,150	19X2	18,100		
	$112,800	19X3	28,050	$6,200	June 10

Similar businesses in the area have been sold recently for 10 times the average of the last 3 years' earnings.

12. The Bolans owed $810 on charge accounts and $220 on a national credit card account at June 30, 19X3.

13. In early July 19X3, the Bolans estimated their federal income tax for their 19X3 return to be $26,000. Estimated tax payments of $8,000 had been made as of June 30, 19X3. A tax rate of 40 percent is assumed for all tax considerations, with capital gains subject to a 60 percent deduction.

Required:

1. Prepare for James and Frances Bolan a statement of financial condition in good form as of June 30, 19X3. Do not prepare accompanying notes.
2. Identify the items of the statement of financial condition that require explanatory and disclosure notes. Do not prepare the notes. (AICPA adapted)

P1.7 Personal Financial Statements Howard Schulman is retired. At the beginning of 19X4, his personal statement of financial condition was as follows:

Cash.	$ 73,000	Accounts Payable	$ 1,500
Pension Receivable		Mortgage Payable	38,000
(Present Value)	81,400	Estimated Income Tax on	
Marketable Securities—		Unrealized Appreciation . .	58,200
Stocks.	157,500	Net Worth	500,200
Marketable Securities—			
Bonds	120,000		
Investment in Real Estate . .	143,000		
Automobile	8,000		
Household and Personal			
Items	15,000		
		Total Liabilities	
Total Assets	$597,900	and Net Worth	$597,900

During 19X4, the following transactions occurred:

1. Schulman received $18,000 from his pension (the present value is calculated using a 10 percent discount rate), $5,000 from Social Security, $10,000 in dividends, $12,500 in bond interest, and $8,300 net rental income from his real estate investments.
2. Schulman's cash disbursements included $26,000 for living expenses (his accounts payable increased to $1,800), $16,000 for income taxes (this should cover his 1984 tax liability), and $7,000 for gifts to his grandchildren.
   'ocks with a current value of $32,000 at January 1 were sold for ،35,500. New stocks were purchased at a cost of $40,000. His total stock portfolio had a value of $191,000 at December 31.
4. There were no transactions involving the bonds other than the receipt of interest noted above. However, due to increasing interest

rates in the economy, the value of his bond holdings dropped to $105,000.

5. Real estate owned at January 1 was estimated to have increased in value by 10 percent during 19X4. The mortgage principal was reduced by $6,000 due to payments (interest payments are reflected in the net income from rental). In October, Schulman bought an additional property for $70,000, financing $55,000 via a new mortgage. By year-end, $700 of principal had been paid, and there was no change in the value of the property.

6. The values of the automobile and the household and personal items are estimated to have decreased by 10 percent during 19X4. Their tax bases exceed their current values.

7. Schulman is subject to an average tax rate of 30 percent on asset appreciation.

Required: Prepare a statement of changes in net worth for 19X4, and a statement of financial condition as of December 31, 19X4.

P1.8 Personal Financial Statements Z. D. Sanberry, who practices dentistry as a sole proprietor, recently filed as a candidate for mayor of his city. He has requested your assistance in preparing combined personal financial statements for himself and his wife, June. Your firm rendered an unqualified opinion on similar statements last year in connection with an examination conducted to support Sanberry's application for a bank loan. Last year's statement of financial condition (based on current values) is shown below:

Z. D. AND JUNE SANBERRY
STATEMENT OF FINANCIAL CONDITION
APRIL 30, 19X0

Cash.	$ 6,120	Accounts Payable	$ 2,850
Marketable Securities	21,400	Income Taxes—Current	1,900
Cash Value of Life		Mortgage Payable	35,300
Insurance	3,900		$40,050
Dental Practice	27,000	Estimated Income Taxes on	
Interest in Dental Supply,		Unrealized Appreciation	10,970
Inc.	8,600	Net Worth	136,300
Residence	94,000		
Automobile	5,800		
Paintings	12,700		
Household Furnishings	7,800		
		Total Liabilities	
Total Assets	$187,320	and Net Worth	$187,320

Sanberry's bookkeeper has provided you with a trial balance listing the Sanberrys' assets and liabilities on the *cost basis* at April 30, 19X1, as follows:

Cash.	$ 3,300	Accounts Payable	$ 3,100
Marketable Securities	23,000	Income Taxes Payable—	
Cash Value of Life		Current	2,225
Insurance	4,250	Mortgage Payable	34,000
Net Assets of Dental		Net Worth	118,225
Practice	19,500		
Interest in Dental Supply,			
Inc.	6,100		
Residence	65,000		
Automobile	11,300		
Paintings	11,000		
Household Furnishings . . .	14,100		
Total Assets	$157,550	Total Liabilities and Net Worth	$157,550

Additional information:

1. A summary of cash receipts and disbursements for the year ended April 30, 19X1, follows:

DISBURSEMENTS

Personal Expenditures, Including Personal Life Insurance		
Premium	$16,000	
Purchase of Kindred Company 6% Bonds at Par	8,000	
Income Taxes	4,100	
Interest on Mortgage	1,400	
Mortgage Principal Amortization	1,300	
Real Estate Taxes.	900	$31,700

RECEIPTS

Withdrawals from Sanberry's Dental Practice	$21,000	
Sale of Inco Stock (Purchased 6/1/W8 for $3,200; Market		
Value on 4/30/X0, $4,500)	6,100	
Dividends on Stock	1,540	
Interest on Bonds	240	28,880
DECREASE IN CASH		$ 2,820

2. The bonds were purchased on July 31, 19X0. Interest is payable semi-annually on January 31 and July 31.
3. In 19W4, Sanberry invested $10,000 to begin his dentistry practice and since has made additional investments. On April 2, 19X1, Sanberry was offered $31,000 for the net assets of his dental practice.
4. Sanberry owns 25 percent of the outstanding stock of the closely held corporation, Dental Supply, Inc.
5. The April 30, 19X1, statements of net assets of Sanberry's dental practice and Dental Supply, Inc., both accompanied by unqualified opinions rendered by a CPA, were composed of the assets and liabilities shown below:

	Sanberry's Dental Practice	Dental Supply, Inc.
Current Assets.	$ 6,000	$30,000
Noncurrent Assets	36,000	70,000
Current Liabilities	3,650	17,000
Long-Term Liabilities.	16,350	35,000
Deferred Credits	2,500	4,000

6. Investments in marketable securities on April 30, 19X1, were composed of the following:

	April 30, 19X1, Bid	Latest Prices Asked
STOCKS		
Steele, Inc.	$15,100	$15,500
Gilliam Corp.	4,000	4,200
BONDS		
Kindred Company 6% Bonds	7,800	7,900
	$26,900	$27,600

7. The valuation (at 100 percent of fair market value) of other property owned by the Sanberrys on April 30, 19X1, was as follows:

Residence	$100,000
Automobile.	4,300
Paintings.	14,500
Household Furnishings.	7,600

8. The accounts payable as of April 30, 19X0, and April 30, 19X1, represent liabilities for personal living costs.
9. The Sanberrys would have to pay a capital gains tax at an effective rate of 25 percent if the assets were sold.
10. Accrued income taxes payable of $2,225 as of April 30, 19X1, represent the Sanberry's appropriate tax liability for the current year to date.

Required: Prepare a statement of financial condition and a statement of changes in net worth for Z. D. and June Sanberry at April 30, 19X1.

Chapter 2 Partnerships: Formation, Operation, and Expansion

Despite the apparent popularity of the corporate form of business organization, most businesses in the United States are organized as sole proprietorships or partnerships rather than as corporations. We discussed sole proprietorships in Chapter 1. In Chapters 2 and 3, we consider partnerships. In this chapter, we discuss the characteristics of a partnership and the accounting issues relating to its formation, operation, and expansion.

Characteristics of a Partnership

The organizational and operational rules for partnerships derive from two sources: *law* (the Uniform Partnership Act) and *contract* (the partnership agreement).

Legal Provisions

Partnerships are subject to the laws of the particular state in which they are organized. Many states have adopted the provisions of the Uniform Partnership Act. This act has sections dealing with:

1. The nature of a partnership.
2. Relations of partners to others.
3. Relations among partners.
4. Partners' property rights.
5. Termination and dissolution of the partnership.

We shall briefly discuss the major provisions of these sections.

The Nature of a Partnership. The act defines a **partnership** as ''an association of two or more persons to carry on as co-owners a business for profit.'' Thus the actions of individuals as they jointly conduct a business activity and share profits and losses legally create a partnership even if no formal agreement among the individuals exists. The term *persons* in the foregoing definition is not limited to individuals. Corporations or other legal entities may be partners. An association of two or more corporations is often called a *joint venture;* this topic is discussed in Chapter 3.

Relations of Partners to Others. Each partner is considered an agent of the partnership. That is, for most transactions, any one partner can act for the entire partnership and can legally enter into binding contracts, representing other partners as well. Only a few transactions, such as disposing of the goodwill of the business or confessing a judgment in court, require authorization of all the partners. This characteristic, known as **mutual agency,** is of great convenience to partners in transacting business. One partner may act for the entire partnership, and outsiders know that any partner with whom they deal legally represents the entire partnership.

There is another significant aspect to this section of the act. Although any one partner may enter into transactions on behalf of the partnership, all partners are liable for the partnership's obligations. The partners are said to be liable *jointly and severally.* This means that as a group they are liable for the obligations of the partnership, and also that each partner has personal liability which could extend to the entire partnership obligation. In other words, creditors of the partnership could seek to collect from a single partner. Since the partners' obligations are not limited to their investments in the partnership, personal assets are also at risk. Partners are thus said to assume **unlimited liability.** We consider this matter more fully in the next chapter, in the discussion of partnership liquidations.

Relations among Partners. This section of the act deals with the rights and duties of partners, setting forth the following:

The rights and duties of the partners in relation to the partnership shall be determined, subject to any agreement between them, by the following rules:

a. Each partner shall be repaid his contributions, whether by way of capital or advances to the partnership property and share equally in the profits and surplus remaining after all liabilities, including those to partners, are satisfied; and must contribute toward the losses, whether of capital or otherwise, sustained by the partnership according to his share in the profits.

b. The partnership must indemnify every partner in respect of payments made and personal liabilities reasonably incurred by him in the ordinary and proper conduct of its business, or for the preservation of its business or property.

c. A partner, who in aid of the partnership makes any payment or advance beyond the amount of capital which he agreed to contribute, shall be paid interest from the date of payment or advance.

d. A partner shall receive interest on the capital contributed by him only from the date when repayment should be made.

e. All partners have equal rights in the management and conduct of the partnership business.

f. No partner is entitled to remuneration for acting in the partnership business, except that a surviving partner is entitled to reasonable compensation for his services in winding up the partnership affairs.

g. No person can become a member of a partnership without the consent of all the partners.

h. Any difference arising as to ordinary matters connected with the partnership business may be decided by a majority of the partners; but no act in contravention of any agreement between the partners may be done rightfully without the consent of all the partners.[1]

Note that any of the above rules are subject to modification by the partnership agreement. For example, the partners may agree to a division of profits and losses in unequal shares. However, if no specific agreement exists, then the provision of the act regarding equal sharing applies.

Partners' Property Rights. The act defines three specific property rights which a partner possesses:

1. The partner is a co-owner of all property held by the partnership and has no claim on specific assets.
2. The partner possesses a partnership interest (that is, a right to a share of the capital and profits).
3. The partner has a right to participate in the management of the partnership.

Termination and Dissolution of the Partnership. The act deals extensively with the dissolution of partnerships, covering ways in which dissolution occurs, impact of dissolution on the rights of various parties, and the rules for distribution of partnership assets. These issues are discussed in Chapter 3.

Contractual Provisions

The **partnership agreement** (sometimes referred to as the **articles of partnership**) is a contract among the partners. On certain matters, such as the distribution of income among partners, the contractual agreement takes precedence over the provisions of the Uniform Partnership Act. On other matters, such as the rights of outside parties, the contract cannot be at variance with the law. In general, the partnership agreement deals with the following matters:

1. Characteristics of the partnership—its name, nature, location of its business activity, duration, fiscal year, and so on.
2. Methods of allocating partnership income to the partners.
3. Procedures for admitting new partners and for settling a partner's interest upon withdrawal or death, including life insurance to be carried on partners, buy–sell agreements, and so on.

Thus the partnership agreement generally addresses the various aspects of the relationship among the partners. It will have little if anything to say about the relationship of the partnership to outside parties.

---

[1]Uniform Partnership Act, Part IV, Section 18.

Limited Partnerships

The above discussion has focused on general partnerships, in which all partners can participate in the management of the firm and all are liable for the partnership's obligations.

Another type of partnership, the **limited partnership,** has both general partners and limited partners. The *general partners* (of whom there must be at least one) manage the firm and have all the rights and obligations previously discussed. The *limited partners* invest capital and have the right to a specified share of income or loss but have no right to participate in management. Moreover, their liability for the partnership's obligations is limited to their investment in the partnership. In other words, limited partners have *no personal liability* for partnership obligations, as general partners do.

Limited partnerships have often been used in situations where investment capital is desired. A general partner may initiate the project, such as a real estate development or an oil well, and finance it by selling limited partnership interests to a number of investors. The general partner acquires the needed capital without relinquishing management control, and investors acquire a right to share in income without bearing any personal responsibility for partnership liabilities. Limited partnerships are discussed further in Chapter 3.

Comparison of Partnership and Corporation Forms of Business Organization

Exhibit 2.1 presents a detailed comparison of general partnerships, limited partnerships, and corporations, summarizing characteristics of each form of business organization.

Major Accounting Issues

Because it is a business entity, a partnership uses many of the same accounting principles used by corporations. For example, general topics such as revenue and expense recognition and asset valuation are given the same treatment. There are, however, a few important areas where partnership accounting differs from corporate accounting. Most of these differences are due to the particular nature of the partnership entity.

Like a corporation, a partnership is an entity distinct from the individual partners. However, the partners typically are actively involved in the firm; they are not absentee owners. This fact influences the concept of net income for a partnership as well as the treatment of owners' equity. Corporate equity is reflected in several accounts (Common Stock, Paid-In Capital, and Retained Earnings) but no attempt is made to maintain equity accounts for each stockholder. Partnership equity, on the other hand, is recorded in a single **capital account,** which reflects both invested capital and accumulated earnings. A capital account is maintained for each partner.

Exhibit 2.1	A Comparison of General Partnership, Limited Partnership, and Corporate Forms of Business Organization		
Aspect	**General Partnership**	**Limited Partnership**	**Corporation**
Creation	By contract between two or more parties.	By contract between two or more parties, under statutory enabling legislation, with recording of certificate in prescribed office.	Under statutory enabling legislation with charter granted by a governmental entity.
Legal status	Governed by state partnership law, commonly the Uniform Partnership Act or variant thereof. Each partner has authority to bind the partnership when dealing with outsiders in the usual manner.	Governed by state partnership law, commonly the Uniform Limited Partnership Act or variant thereof. Only general partners (not limited partners) deal with outsiders on partnership business.	A legal entity that may carry out all activities authorized by the charter issued by the governmental unit.
Life of organization	Ceases at death, withdrawal, or addition of a partner, or earlier by contractual provision. Business operation may continue by contractual arrangement.	Ceases at death, withdrawal, or addition of general partner, or earlier by contractual provision. Withdrawal or addition of limited partners need not terminate the partnership. When all limited partners cease to be such, partnership is terminated.	Perpetual, unless limited by charter.
Ownership share transferability	Only with consent of all other partners.	General partner interests may be changed only with consent of all partners. Limited partner interests may be assigned; assignees may become substituted limited partners with consent of all other partners or by action of assignor if certificate gives assignor such authority.	Freely transferable, unless limited by a contractual arrangement.
Management	Each partner is entitled to an equal voice unless the partnership agreement provides otherwise.	Only general partners have rights to manage.	Responsibility is vested in a board of directors who commonly employ the chief executive officer.
Status of owners	Each partner is a principal and an agent of the other partners.	Each general partner is principal and agent of the other general partners. Limited partners do not serve as principal or agent for other partners.	Shareholder is neither principal nor agent, but has contractual rights only.
Liability of owners	Unlimited liability for debts of the partnership and torts of partners, unless limited by contract (subject to limitations).	Limited partners not liable to creditors unless they take part in management of the business. General partners have liability similar to that of partners in a general partnership.	Shareholders not liable for debts of corporation.

Exhibit 2.1   Continued

| Additional owners | Creates new partnership. All current partners must consent. | Additional limited partners may be admitted upon filing amendment to original certificate, subject to rights of original partners. | Limited by charter and preemptive rights of current shareholders. |

Source: From *Handbook of Modern Accounting*, 3rd ed., edited by S. Davidson and R. L. Weil. Copyright © 1983 McGraw-Hill Book Company, New York, pp. 30–4 and 30–5. Used with the permission of the McGraw-Hill Book Company.

Allocations versus Payments to Partners

In discussing the flow of income from the partnership to the individual partners, we must distinguish two steps. First are the *allocations* to partners, which are the credits to the partners' capital accounts reflecting the sharing of income (or debits reflecting the sharing of loss). Much of the following discussion is devoted to these allocations. Second are the *payments* to partners (debits to capital accounts) reflecting the transfer of resources from the partnership to the partners. These payments (also called *drawings*) involve no special accounting problems, except in cases where the partnership is being liquidated. Partnership liquidations are discussed in Chapter 3.

Income Determination

We must define *net income* as it applies to the special distinctions of the partnership form. There are several differences between income determination for partnerships and corporations. There are several similarities between income determination for proprietorships and for partnerships.

In corporate accounting, net income signifies the return to the owners (stockholders) of the corporation. In partnership accounting, net income also should signify the return to the owners (partners). A practical problem arises, however, in that in most cases partners are actually involved in the operation of the firm. In addition to being investors, partners may also render personal services in the day-to-day conduct of business and may loan money to the partnership. Stockholders of a corporation may also be employees of, or lenders to, that corporation, but no problem of income determination arises. Accounting and tax requirements necessitate a careful distinction between the corporate entity and the individual, along with a distinction among the individual's possible roles as stockholder, employee, and lender. These constraints are much weaker in the case of a partnership because a partnership does not have the distinct legal status of a corporation, nor is it a taxable entity. As a result, when partners have multiple involvement in the financial affairs of the partnership—as investors, employees, and lenders—it is difficult to distinguish among: (1) compensation for services performed, (2) interest on loans, and (3) return on capital invested. Certain allocations may be called salaries, other allocations interest, and still others distribution of profit. The lack of an arm's-length transaction in establishing the amounts causes these distinctions to be disregarded and *all* allocations to partners to be considered as divisions of profit. In other words, in determining the net income of a partnership, salaries to partners and interest to partners are excluded from expenses.

A second area of difference between corporation and partnership net income is the treatment of income taxes. A corporation is a taxable entity, but a partnership is not. A partnership is considered a conduit, whereby income flows to the individual partners. Thus *no federal income tax is imposed directly on the partnership;* rather, the individual partners include their share of income on their personal income tax returns. The income statement of the partnership, therefore, does not provide for income tax expense.

Allocation of Net Income to Partners

After the partnership's net income is determined, the next concern is allocation of the net income among the individual partners. As discussed above, all allocations to partners are viewed as divisions of net income. It is not surprising, therefore, that in dividing net income, attention may be given to the various roles (investor, employee, lender) which each partner may hold.

The partnership agreement should specify the rules for the allocation of income. These rules may be simple or complex. Should the partnership agreement be silent as to the allocation of income, then it must be assumed that income is to be divided equally among all partners. Various approaches to allocation are discussed and illustrated in a subsequent section.

Capital Changes

The third major accounting issue is changes in the capital structure of the partnership. Such changes occur for many reasons. In this chapter and the next, we consider the formation of the partnership, the subsequent entry and exit of individual partners, and the eventual liquidation of the partnership.

Formation of the Partnership

Accounting for the formation of a partnership requires the valuation of assets contributed by the partners and determination of each partner's capital account. Following GAAP (Generally Accepted Accounting Principles), assets contributed to a partnership in exchange for a capital interest should be valued at fair market value.[2] This often creates a difference between the accounting basis and the tax basis of particular assets. Our main concern in this chapter is the accounting basis. The tax basis is briefly examined in the appendix to this chapter.

---

[2]Accounting Principles Board, *Opinion No. 29,* "Accounting for Nonmonetary Transactions" (New York: AICPA, 1973).

Bonus and Goodwill Approaches

The determination of each partner's capital account is somewhat more complex than the valuation of assets. One straightforward approach is to set each partner's capital account equal to the fair market value of net assets invested. For example, assume that Prince and Quinn form a partnership. Prince invests $30,000 cash, and Quinn invests land and a building having a combined fair market value of $75,000, subject to a mortage of $35,000, which the partnership assumes. Thus Quinn has invested net assets with fair market value of $40,000. If each partner's capital is to equal net assets invested at fair market value, the entry to record partnership formation would be:

Cash	30,000	
Land and Building	75,000	
Mortgage Payable		35,000
Capital—Prince		30,000
Capital—Quinn		40,000
To record formation of partnership.		

An alternative possibility is that the partners might specify that a predetermined percentage interest in total partnership capital is to apply to each partner. This approach could generate several alternative entries for recording the partnership's formation, depending on the details of the agreement between Prince and Quinn. For example, assume that Prince and Quinn decide that each is to have a 50 percent interest in partnership capital. How can this be accomplished, given that Prince invested $30,000 and Quinn invested $40,000? Two approaches are possible: One is simply to divide the total capital of $70,000 equally, crediting each with $35,000. Thus, there is an implied transfer of $5,000 of capital from Quinn to Prince. The entry recording the formation of the partnership would then be:

Cash	30,000	
Land and Building	75,000	
Mortgage Payable		35,000
Capital—Prince		35,000
Capital—Quinn		35,000
To record formation of partnership.		

This is called the **bonus approach to partnership formation.** Quinn is assumed to be paying Prince a bonus of $5,000.

A second approach is to assume that intangible assets exist which will bring the investments (and hence the capital balances) into the desired relationship. We may argue, for example, that the reason the partners agreed on equal capital balances while making apparently unequal investments is that one partner, Prince in this case, brings certain talents, contacts, or other intangible benefits to the partnership. We may record this intangible asset, called *goodwill*, in an amount sufficient to achieve the desired relationship among the capital accounts. In our example, we would need to record $10,000 of goodwill in order to make Prince's investment equal to Quinn's. Our entry to record formation of the partnership would then be:

```
Cash. . . . . . . . . . . . . . . . . . . . . . . . . . . . . . . .   30,000
Land and Building . . . . . . . . . . . . . . . . . . . . . . . .   75,000
Goodwill . . . . . . . . . . . . . . . . . . . . . . . . . . . . .   10,000
    Mortgage Payable. . . . . . . . . . . . . . . . . . . . . .              35,000
    Capital—Prince . . . . . . . . . . . . . . . . . . . . . . .              40,000
    Capital—Quinn . . . . . . . . . . . . . . . . . . . . . . .              40,000
To record formation of partnership.
```

This approach is called the **goodwill approach to partnership formation.** In forming the partnership, the partners must specify which accounting approach is to be used.

The bonus and goodwill methods will be examined more thoroughly in connection with the admission of a new partner, which is discussed later in the chapter.

Investment of an Existing Business

Rather than investing individual assets, a partner may have an existing business entity (a proprietorship) which becomes that partner's investment in the partnership. This does not cause any substantial accounting problem.

The main question is whether the books of the existing proprietorship will be retained to serve as the books of the partnership or a new set of books will be established. If the existing books are retained, two steps are necessary:

1. Revaluations of assets may be necessary to reflect the fair market value of assets being transferred to the partnership, and intangible assets may need to be recognized.
2. Investments by partners must be recorded.

If a new set of books is to be established, each asset of the business must be recorded at its fair market value. The entry is made in the same manner as described in the preceding section. Whichever of these two approaches is followed, the asset values and capital accounts which result should be the same.

Accounting for Partnership Operations

Rules covered in introductory and intermediate accounting courses regarding corporate revenue and expense recognition and asset and liability valuation apply in general to partnerships. Thus the special accounting considerations for partnerships focus primarily on the capital accounts representing the owners' equity.

A capital account for each partner serves as the set of owners' equity accounts. This account combines invested capital and undistributed income. Three types of events affect capital account balances:

1. *Investment of capital.* An individual partner's capital account may be affected not only by the partner's own investment (as illustrated in discussing partnership formation above) but also by the investments of new partners (as will be illustrated later in discussing the admission of partners).

2. *Distribution of net income.* Upon allocation of net income to the partners, the appropriate share is credited (or debited if there is a loss) to each partner's capital account.

3. *Withdrawal of capital* (including withdrawal of net income). Amounts withdrawn are debited to each partner's capital account. Often, withdrawals are made in anticipation of net income and are debited to a separate **drawing account** for each partner. This account is then closed at year-end to the capital account. For example, if partner Burns withdraws $500 per month, the following entry could be made monthly:

```
Drawing—Burns . . . . . . . . . . . . . . . . . . . . . . . . . . . . 500
    Cash. . . . . . . . . . . . . . . . . . . . . . . . . . . . . . . . .         500
To record monthly withdrawal.
```

At year-end, the balance in the drawing account would be closed, as follows:

```
Capital—Burns. . . . . . . . . . . . . . . . . . . . . . . . . . . . 6,000
    Drawing—Burns . . . . . . . . . . . . . . . . . . . . . . . . .        6,000
To close drawing account to capital.
```

Use of the drawing account is optional; withdrawals may be directly debited to capital.

Allocation of Net Income to Partners

As was discussed above, partners' salaries or interest are not considered expenses in determining the partnership's net income. Rather, all such allocations to partners are considered divisions of net income.

In allocating partnership net income to the individual partners, therefore, a multifactor allocation procedure may be used. While partners may agree to use any factors they wish, three common ones are:

1. A salary factor, reflecting personal services which each partner provides to the operations of the partnership.
2. An interest factor, reflecting the capital which each partner has invested.
3. A percentage factor, reflecting an agreed **income-sharing ratio** to be used after provision has been made for any salaries and interest.

We shall discuss and illustrate each of these.

Salaries to Partners

Allocations of net income to partners in the form of salary allowances are typically established by formal agreement among the partners. This agreement usually specifies the amount each partner is to receive or the formula for calculating the amount (for example, a bonus formula). The amounts can be based on the time, effort, or experience that each partner contributes to the business. For example, the DEF partnership might agree that D is to receive an annual salary of $20,000, E is to receive an annual salary of $6,000, and F is to receive no salary. Any remaining income or loss is to be divided equally among the partners. If partnership net income for the year is $38,000, the allocation would first provide for the $26,000 in salaries and then allocate the remaining $12,000 by the income-sharing ratio. This yields the following allocations:

	D	E	F	Total
Salaries	$20,000	$ 6,000	$ 0	$26,000
Balance	4,000	4,000	4,000	12,000
	$24,000	$10,000	$4,000	$38,000

The salary allocation may be *fully implemented,* even if it exceeds the partnership net income.[3] In the example above, assume that net income is $17,000 and salaries are to be fully implemented. The salary allocation of $26,000 exceeds net income by $9,000. This $9,000 ''loss'' is then allocated by the income-sharing ratio, producing the following allocations:

	D	E	F	Total
Salaries	$20,000	$ 6,000	$ 0	$26,000
Balance	(3,000)	(3,000)	(3,000)	(9,000)
	$17,000	$ 3,000	$(3,000)	$17,000

Bonus to Partners

Allocation of net income to partners for services rendered might be described in terms of a bonus formula. In discussing various bonus relationships, we use the following symbols:

$$X = \text{Net income before bonus.}$$

$$B = \text{Amount of bonus.}$$

$$Y = \text{Net income after bonus } (Y = X - B).$$

$$R = \text{Percentage rate of bonus.}$$

If the bonus is defined as a percentage of net income before bonus, its calculation is simply:

$$B = RX.$$

Sometimes the bonus is defined as a percentage of the net income which will remain after the bonus. This involves a somewhat more complex formula:

---

[3]The partnership agreement should specify whether salary (and interest) allocations are to be fully implemented if they exceed total net income. We assume such a provision in our discussion.

$$B = RY$$
$$B = R(X - B)$$
$$(1 + R)B = RX$$
$$B = \frac{RX}{1 + R}.$$

For example, assume net income before the bonus is $30,000, and the bonus is to be 25 percent of net income after the bonus (a figure which is presently unknown). Using the above formula, we would calculate the bonus as:

$$B = \frac{RX}{1 + R}$$
$$B = \frac{.25(30,000)}{1.25}$$
$$B = \frac{7,500}{1.25}$$
$$B = 6,000.$$

We can then easily verify that the $6,000 bonus is indeed 25 percent of the net income after bonus of $24,000(= $30,000 - $6,000).

Interest to Partners

Allocations of net income may also be made on the basis of interest allowances on partners' capital accounts. An interest rate is specified, which usually applies to weighted average capital balances.[4] We calculate the *weighted average capital balance* by multiplying each level of a partner's capital balance by the fraction of the year during which that amount existed. For example, assume that a partner's capital account has a balance of $6,000 on January 1. On March 1, additional capital of $20,000 is invested, and on September 1, $2,000 is withdrawn. The weighted average capital balance for the year would be calculated as follows:

Period	Capital Balance	Fraction of Year	Weighted Average
1/1–2/28	$ 6,000	2/12	$ 1,000
3/1–8/31	26,000	6/12	13,000
9/1–12/31	24,000	4/12	8,000
			$22,000

If an interest rate of 8 percent were specified, net income of $1,760 (= .08 × $22,000) would be allocated to this partner.

---

[4] The partnership agreement should specify the base for the calculation of interest. For example, beginning-of-year capital balance or a simple average of beginning and ending balances could be used.

As was the case with salaries to partners, any allocation of net income in the form of interest may be made fully, even if it exceeds total net income. Again, any remaining loss would be allocated by the income-sharing ratio.

Percentage Allocation

A percentage allocation formula (income-sharing ratio) is always assumed to exist for a partnership. The entire net income of the partnership may be allocated by a percentage formula. Alternatively, some income may be allocated by a salary formula, an interest formula, or both. In the latter case, the balance of net income after salaries and interest, whether positive or negative, is allocated by a percentage formula.

The partnership agreement sets forth the income-sharing ratio. Normally, a single set of percentages is applied to all forms of income. The partners may, however, agree that different types of income (or expense) will be divided in different ways. Should the partnership agreement be silent as to an income-sharing ratio, then it is automatically assumed that all partners share *equally*.

Illustration of Allocation of Partnership Income

Thomas, Underwood, and Vickers are partners in a printing firm. Their partnership agreement contains the following provisions regarding income allocation:

1. Thomas is to devote 2 days per week to partnership business and receive an annual salary of $15,000. Underwood and Vickers are to work full time and receive annual salaries of $35,000 and $30,000, respectively.
2. Vickers, who is responsible for sales, is to receive a bonus of 10 percent of any net income in excess of $100,000.
3. The partners are to receive 10 percent interest on their weighted average capital balances. Payments of salaries and bonus are ignored for purposes of this calculation.
4. After the above allocations are implemented, any remaining income or loss is to be allocated 50 percent to Thomas, 30 percent to Underwood, and 20 percent to Vickers.

Assume that net income for 19X6 was $150,000. The partners' capital balances at the beginning of the year were: Thomas, $69,000; Underwood, $40,000; and Vickers, $40,000. Underwood invested an additional $10,000 on March 31, 19X6. At the end of each quarter, the partners withdrew a total of $6,000, divided according to the percentages in Provision 4 above (that is, Thomas withdrew $3,000, Underwood $1,800, and Vickers $1,200). Thomas withdrew an additional $18,000 on October 31, 19X6.

The allocation of income for 19X6 is shown in Exhibit 2.2.

Exhibit 2.2   **Illustration of Income Allocation**

	Thomas	Underwood	Vickers	Total
Salaries	$15,000	$35,000	$30,000	$ 80,000
Bonus[a]	—	—	5,000	5,000
Interest[b]	6,150	4,480	3,820	14,450
				$ 99,450
Balance[c]	25,275	15,165	10,110	50,550
	$46,425	$54,645	$48,930	$150,000

[a]Bonus is 10 percent of $50,000 (= $150,000 − $100,000).
[b]Weighted average capital is calculated as follows:

	Thomas	Underwood	Vickers
1/1–3/31	$69,000 × 3/12 = $17,250	$40,000 × 3/12 = $10,000	$40,000 × 3/12 = $10,000
4/1–6/30	66,000 × 3/12 = 16,500	48,200 × 3/12 = 12,050	38,800 × 3/12 = 9,700
7/1–9/30	63,000 × 3/12 = 15,750	46,400 × 3/12 = 11,600	37,600 × 3/12 = 9,400
10/1–10/31	60,000 × 1/12 = 5,000	{44,600 × 3/12 = 11,150	{36,400 × 3/12 = 9,100
11/1–12/31	42,000 × 2/12 = 7,000		
Weighted average . . .	$61,500	$44,800	$38,200

Ten percent of the weighted average capital is the amount of interest.
[c]The balance of $50,550 is allocated 50 percent to Thomas, 30 percent to Underwood, and 20 percent to Vickers.

Admission of a New Partner

The admission of a new partner gives rise to another important accounting problem for partnerships. Technically, there is no such thing as "the admission of a new partner." If a new partner is admitted, the old partnership legally ends, and a new partnership is created. For practical purposes, however, business operations are likely to continue without interruption. As is often the case in accounting, the economic substance (of a continuing business activity) takes precedence over the legal form (the termination of the old partnership and the creation of a new one). It is in this economic sense, therefore, that we speak of the admission of a new partner.

In the illustrations which follow, assume the partnership of Arthur Associates has a balance sheet at June 30, 19X2, as follows:

Various Assets	$140,000	Liabilities		$ 50,000
		Capital:		
		Arthur.	$31,000	
		Bradley	26,000	
		Crowe	33,000	90,000
	$140,000			$140,000

Assume further that the partners share income in the following ratio: Arthur, 50 percent; Bradley, 20 percent; and Crowe, 30 percent.

Admission by Purchase of an Existing Partnership Interest

One manner in which a new partner may enter an existing partnership is by purchasing the interest of one or more existing partners. Such a transaction occurs between the old and new partners as *individuals* and usually has no direct effect on the partnership accounts. This is parallel to the case in which one individual sells shares of stock in a corporation to another individual. Only those two are involved in the transaction; the corporation makes no entry other than to update its stockholder records. In a similar manner, when one individual buys an existing partnership interest, the only entry usually needed is a transfer of the capital account from the old partner to the new.

Transfer of Capital Interests. The usual method of accounting for a purchase of a partnership interest is to transfer the capital balance of the selling partner to a new capital account which is established for the buyer. The amount of the entry is the existing capital balance of the selling partner, which may be different from the selling price.

Purchase from One Partner. In the case of Arthur Associates, assume that on July 1, 19X2, Findley purchases Crowe's entire partnership interest for $45,000. The partnership would record the following entry to show transfer of the interest from Crowe to Findley:

```
Capital—Crowe . . . . . . . . . . . . . . . . . . . . . . . . . . . .  33,000
     Capital—Findley. . . . . . . . . . . . . . . . . . . . . . . . . .           33,000
     To record transfer of partnership interest from Crowe to Findley.
```

Note that the purchase price of $45,000 has no bearing on the entry. The $45,000 was received by Crowe directly, not by the partnership. Crowe has realized a gain of $12,000 on the sale of the partnership interest, assuming Crowe's basis is the book figure of $33,000. The cost (tax basis) of Findley's partnership interest is $45,000, despite the fact that the partnership books show the capital account as $33,000. Findley's cost of $45,000 will have no effect on any capital-based distributions which the partnership may make. In contrast, the $45,000 cost will affect the subsequent recognition of gain or loss by Findley when the partnership interest is sold.

Purchase from Several Partners. A new partner may purchase a portion of the interest of several partners. For example, assume that Grogan buys a 25 percent interest in Arthur Associates by purchasing 25 percent of each partner's interest for a total of $28,000. Following the procedure illustrated in the preceding section, we could simply record the transfer of capital interests. By this method, 25 percent of each partner's capital at the date of entry would be transferred to the new partner, Grogan. The entry would be:

```
Capital—Arthur . . . . . . . . . . . . . . . . . . . . . . . . . . . . .  7,750
Capital—Bradley . . . . . . . . . . . . . . . . . . . . . . . . . . . .  6,500
Capital—Crowe . . . . . . . . . . . . . . . . . . . . . . . . . . . . .  8,250
   Capital—Grogan . . . . . . . . . . . . . . . . . . . . . . . . .              22,500
To record transfer of 25 percent interest to Grogan.
```

The debits to the capital accounts of the three existing partners represent 25 percent of their respective capital balances, and Grogan's capital of $22,500 is 25 percent of the total capital of $90,000. Note that, as before, the $28,000 purchase price has no bearing on the entry. The three existing partners will recognize gains or losses as individuals on the sale of part of their partnership interests.

Recognition of Implied Goodwill. The admission of a new partner by purchase of an existing partnership interest is usually recorded by the transfer of capital accounts described above. Another possible method involves the recognition of *implied goodwill*. Under this approach, the purchase price is used to infer the value of the entire partnership. To illustrate, again assume the case where Grogan buys 25 percent of each partner's interest for a total of $28,000.

If Grogan is willing to pay $28,000 to buy a 25 percent interest in the partnership, the entire partnership capital must be worth $112,000 ($= $28,000/.25$). But the partnership books show only $90,000, the total capital of Arthur, Bradley, and Crowe. This implies that $22,000 ($= $112,000$ implied total value $- $90,000$ recorded capital) of unrecorded assets exist. For convenience, we call these unrecorded assets **goodwill.** We first record the goodwill, apportioning a share to each partner according to the established income-sharing ratio of 50 percent for Arthur, 20 percent for Bradley, and 30 percent for Crowe. The entry to record implied goodwill is:

```
Goodwill . . . . . . . . . . . . . . . . . . . . . . . . . . . . . . . 22,000
   Capital—Arthur . . . . . . . . . . . . . . . . . . . . . . . . . .            11,000
   Capital—Bradley . . . . . . . . . . . . . . . . . . . . . . . . .             4,400
   Capital—Crowe . . . . . . . . . . . . . . . . . . . . . . . . . .             6,600
To record implied goodwill.
```

We now make an entry to transfer 25 percent of each partner's capital to Grogan:

```
Capital—Arthur (25% × 42,000) . . . . . . . . . . . . . . . . 10,500
Capital—Bradley (25% × 30,400) . . . . . . . . . . . . . . . .  7,600
Capital—Crowe (25% × 39,600) . . . . . . . . . . . . . . . . .  9,900
   Capital—Grogan . . . . . . . . . . . . . . . . . . . . . . . . .             28,000
To record transfer of 25 percent interest to Grogan.
```

Note that when this approach is used the credit to the new partner's capital account equals the amount paid to acquire the interest.

A new income-sharing ratio must be established for the four partners. For convenience, we typically assume that the contract for the new partnership specifies that (1) the new partner's percentages of income and of the initial capital balance are equal and (2) the old partners maintain their income-sharing relationship. After Grogan joins the firm, therefore, the partners share as follows: Arthur, 37.5 percent; Bradley, 15 percent; Crowe, 22.5 percent; and Grogan, 25 percent. These percentages are based on the fact that the old partners now own 75 percent of the partnership—Arthur has 50 percent of 75 percent, or 37.5 percent; Bradley has 20 percent of 75 percent; and Crowe has 30 percent of 75 percent.

Unless the agreement covering the purchase of partners' interests specifically provides for the recognition of implied goodwill on the partnership books, the transfer of capital accounts method should be used. Moreover, suppose the implied value of the partnership, as calculated by capitalizing the purchase price, is *less* than total capital. If specific assets are deemed to be overvalued, they should be written down. If this is done, and the implied value is still less than total capital, the transfer of capital accounts method should be used to eliminate the difference. Negative goodwill should not be recorded. Alternatively, an argument may be made in some cases that goodwill should be attributed to the new partner. The capital credit to the new partner would be increased, and additional assets recorded, so that the implied value of the partnership equals total capital.

Admission by Investment of New Capital

The second way in which a new partner may enter an existing partnership is by investing directly in the partnership. In this case, the new partner contributes an agreed-upon amount of assets, which may be cash, property, or services, to the partnership. The new partner receives an agreed-upon share of capital at the date of entry and a specified share of subsequent income. The capital percentage is used primarily to establish the new partner's initial capital balance. Thereafter, the income percentage is of primary importance, because this guides the division of subsequent profits and losses among the partners. In many cases, the capital percentage and income percentage are equal. If they are not equal, their use is guided by the following rule:

Capital percentage (capital-sharing ratio) is used to establish the value of the firm and hence the total amount of goodwill.
Income percentage (income-sharing ratio) is used to allocate goodwill or bonus to partners as well as income.

The partnership must record the investment of assets by the new partner, the capital account of the new partner, and, perhaps, some further adjustments to reconcile the two. If the investment by the new partner happens to equal the new partner's capital percentage times the new net assets (old net assets plus assets invested), then no accounting problem exists. For example, assume that on July 1, 19X2, Edwards invests $10,000 in Arthur Associates in exchange for a 10 percent interest in capital (hereafter referred to simply as a 10 percent interest). We have:

1. Investment by Edwards = $10,000.
2. Edwards's share of new net assets = 10% × ($90,000 old net assets + $10,000 invested by Edwards) = 10%($100,000) = $10,000.

Since Items 1 and 2 are equal, we simply record:

Assets 10,000
    Capital—Edwards   10,000
To record investment by Edwards.

Suppose, however, that Edwards has invested $9,000 for a 10 percent interest. We would then have:

Case A
1. Investment = $9,000.
2. Share of new net assets = 10%($90,000 + $9,000) = $9,900.

Alternatively, suppose Delano invests $12,000 for a 10 percent interest, giving:

Case B
1. Investment = $12,000.
2. Share of new net assets = 10%($90,000 + $12,000) = $10,200.

In each of the two preceding cases, the investment differs from the computed share of net assets. When this situation occurs, the disparity must be reconciled before the entry recording the investment can be made. Reconciliation can be achieved in one of two ways:

1. Consider the share of assets amount (Item 2 above) to be the correct entry to the new partner's capital account. The difference between this amount and the amount invested is considered to be a capital adjustment of the existing partners. This is known as the **bonus method of admission.**
2. Bring the investment (Item 1) and the share of net assets (Item 2) amounts into agreement by assuming the existence of intangible assets and adding these either to the investment of the new partner or to the existing net assets of the partnership. This is known as the **goodwill method of admission.**

The agreement accepting the new partner generally specifies which of these methods is to be used. In the following sections, both are discussed and illustrated.

Bonus Method. Under the bonus method, the total net assets of the new partnership after admission of the new partner equal the net assets before admission plus the investment of the new partner. The new partner's capital account is credited with the appropriate share of these net assets.

Say that the new partner's investment is *less* than the computed share of net assets, as in Case A above, where Edwards invests $9,000 but receives a $9,900 share in net assets. In such a case, the existing partners have some reason for admitting Edwards at this less-than-fair-share price. Perhaps Edwards brings some important talents or resources to the firm, and to obtain these the existing partners are willing to subsidize Edwards's admission by giving a $9,900 share for only

$9,000.[5] The $900 difference is charged against the existing partners' capital accounts in their income-sharing ratio. In effect, each existing partner is transferring a portion of capital to Edwards. The entry to record Edwards's admission for a 10 percent interest with an investment of $9,000 is:

Cash	9,000	
Capital—Arthur.	450	
Capital—Bradley	180	
Capital—Crowe	270	
Capital—Edwards		9,900

To record Edwards's admission under the bonus method.

This situation results in a **bonus to the new partner.**

The second possibility is that the new partner's investment is *more* than the computed share of net assets, as in Case B above, where Delano invests $12,000 but has a $10,200 share in net assets. We assume that the existing partners are able to command a premium when admitting a new partner. Perhaps the assets of the partnership are worth more than their book value. Perhaps the partnership has above-average earning potential. Or perhaps the existing partners wish to be compensated for the risk and effort they incurred in establishing the firm. In any event, to gain admittance Delano must contribute not only a fair share of assets, $10,200, but also an additional $1,800, which will be credited to the capital accounts of the existing partners in their income-sharing ratio. The entry to record Delano's admission, reflecting an investment of $12,000 in exchange for a 10 percent interest, would be:

Cash	12,000	
Capital—Arthur		900
Capital—Bradley		360
Capital—Crowe		540
Capital—Delano		10,200

To record Delano's admission under the bonus method.

This situation results in a **bonus to the existing partners.**

We may summarize the bonus method in formula terms. We calculate the amount to be credited to the new partner's capital account (NC) as follows:

$$NC = S(OC + I),$$

where

OC = Total capital of the old partners,

I = Amount invested by the new partner,

S = New partner's percentage share in the partnership capital.

---

[5]Another possible reason for the low price is that the partnership's assets are overvalued. However, we generally ignore this possibility. If generally accepted accounting principles have been followed, write-downs to market for current assets such as marketable securities and inventories should have been made as losses occurred. Fixed assets are generally not written down, unless there is evidence that their utility value has permanently and materially declined.

For example, if two existing partners each have capital balances of $43,000, and a new partner invests $50,000 for a 25 percent interest in the partnership, the balance of the new partner's capital account would be calculated as follows:

$$NC = S(OC + I)$$
$$= 25\%(86,000 + 50,000)$$
$$= 25\%(136,000)$$
$$= 34,000.$$

The difference between the credit to the new partner's capital account and the amount invested $(NC - I)$ would be divided among the old partners in accordance with their income-sharing ratio, and debited or credited to their capital accounts, depending on whether the new investment was less than or greater than the balance in the new partner's capital account.

Goodwill Method. Under the goodwill method, the discrepancy between the amount invested by the new partner and the share of net assets initially calculated is attributed to the presence of unrecorded intangible assets. To reconcile the discrepancy, these unrecorded assets must be recorded.

For example, say that the new partner's investment of tangible assets is less than the computed share of net assets, as in Case A above, where Edwards invests $9,000 cash but has a $9,900 share in net assets. To explain this imbalance, we assume that Edwards must be bringing something more to the firm than $9,000 cash—perhaps some special skills or talents—such that the existing partners are willing to admit Edwards as a 10 percent partner. Thus we conclude that Edwards is also investing some intangible assets or *goodwill* in the partnership. We determine this amount in such a way that the investment (cash plus goodwill) and the share of net assets will be brought into balance. Note that as we add assets in the form of goodwill, Edwards's share of net assets will increase. The calculation proceeds as follows:

1. Determine the total value of the new firm as implied by the net assets of the existing partners. In our example, existing net assets are $90,000, and the existing partners will have a 90 percent interest in the new partnership. This implies a total value of the new partnership of $100,000 (= $90,000/.9).
2. Calculate the new partner's share of this total value. In our example, Edwards's share is $10,000 (10 percent of $100,000).
3. The goodwill invested by the new partner is the difference between the calculated share of the value of the firm and the amount of tangible assets invested. In our example, Edwards is assumed to invest $1,000 of goodwill (= $10,000 share of firm's value − $9,000 cash invested).

The entry to record Edwards' admission would be:

```
Cash . . . . . . . . . . . . . . . . . . . . . . . . . . . . . . . . . . . .  9,000
Goodwill . . . . . . . . . . . . . . . . . . . . . . . . . . . . . . . . . .  1,000
   Capital—Edwards . . . . . . . . . . . . . . . . . . . . . . . . . .          10,000
To record Edwards's admission under goodwill method.
```

This situation is referred to as **goodwill to the new partner.**

The second possibility is that the new partner's investment of tangible assets is more than the initially computed share of net assets, as in Case B above, where Delano invests $12,000 cash for only a $10,200 share in net assets. To explain this imbalance, the net assets of the existing partnership are assumed to be understated. Perhaps some of the firm's tangible assets have market values in excess of their book values. Or perhaps the firm has unrecorded goodwill in the form of established customers, product recognition, and skillful management. The fact that a new partner is willing to pay more than book value for a partnership interest gives credence to the idea that undervalued or unrecorded assets exist. To bring the new partner's investment into balance with the share of net assets, we must acknowledge these unrecorded asset amounts. We proceed as follows:

1. Determine the total value of the new firm as implied by the investment of the new partner. In our example, Delano invests $12,000 for a 10 percent interest. This implies a total value of the new partnership of $120,000 ($= \$12,000/.10$).

2. Calculate the amount by which assets are understated. In our example, present net assets are recorded at $90,000. Delano will invest an additional $12,000, bringing the total to $102,000. But we have calculated the value of the new firm to be $120,000. Thus assets are understated by $18,000 ($= \$120,000 - \$102,000$).

3. Correct the understatement of assets by recognizing the existence of an intangible asset, with offsetting credits to the capital accounts of the existing partners in their income-sharing ratio. In this way, recognition is given to the fact that the unrecorded increase in net assets occurred in the past and is attributable to the old partners. Revaluation of tangible assets to remove the understatement is generally not proper unless objective evidence—for example, a quoted market value of securities—substantiates the revaluation.

The entry to record Delano's admission would be:

Cash	12,000	
Goodwill	18,000	
Capital—Arthur		9,000
Capital—Bradley		3,600
Capital—Crowe		5,400
Capital—Delano		12,000
To record Delano's admission under the goodwill method.		

This situation is referred to as **goodwill to the existing partners.**

Any goodwill recorded in admitting a new partner should be amortized over its estimated life. According to *APBO 17,* this life should not exceed 40 years.[6]

Comparison of Bonus and Goodwill Methods. The mechanics of the bonus and goodwill methods may be expressed in formulas, using the following notation:

---

[6]Accounting Principles Board, *Opinion No. 17,* "Intangible Assets" (New York: AICPA, 1970), par. 29; CT § I60.110.

I = Amount invested by new partner.

S = New partner's percentage share in the partnership capital.

$(1 - S)$ = Percentage share in the partnership capital which will be held by the existing partners.

OC = Total capital of the existing partners ("old capital").

TV = Calculated total value of the partnership.

G = Goodwill to be recorded.

B = Total amount of bonus to be recorded.

First determine whether bonus or goodwill will apply to the new partner or to the existing partners. We may identify two general cases, which correspond to the Edwards (Case A) and Delano (Case B) illustrations in the preceding section.

Case A: $I < S(OC + I)$. If the investment by the new partner is *less* than that partner's share in the firm's total capital, the difference is accounted for by recording either a bonus or goodwill to the *new* partner. Under the bonus method, the bonus to the new partner is the difference between the new partner's capital share and investment:

$$B = S(OC + I) - I.$$

Under the goodwill method, we first calculate the implied total value of the firm:

$$TV = OC/(1 - S).$$

The total amount of goodwill to be associated with the new partner is the difference between the calculated total value and the new capital (old capital plus investment):

$$G = TV - (OC + I).$$

The relationship between the amount of goodwill and the amount of bonus can be seen by expanding and rearranging the above goodwill formula:

$$G = TV - (OC + I)$$

$$G = \frac{OC}{(1 - S)} - (OC + I).$$

This simplifies to:

$$(1 - S)G = S(OC + I) - I.$$

Recall that the bonus formula is:

$$B = S(OC + I) - I.$$

Thus we see that:

$$B = (1 - S)G.$$

Case B: $I > S(OC + I)$. If the investment by the new partner *exceeds* that partner's share in the firm's total capital, we record either a bonus or goodwill to the *existing* partners. Under the bonus method, the total bonus to the existing partners is the difference between the new partner's investment and capital share:

$$B = I - S(OC + I).$$

Under the goodwill method, we first calculate the implied total value of the firm:

$$TV = I/S.$$

The total amount of goodwill to be allocated to the existing partners is the difference between the calculated total value and the new capital:

$$G = TV - (OC + I).$$

Again, the relationship between the amount of goodwill and the amount of bonus can be seen by expanding and rearranging the above goodwill formula:

$$G = TV - (OC + I)$$

$$G = \frac{I}{S} - (OC + I)$$

$$SG = I - S(OC + I).$$

Recall that the bonus formula is:

$$B = I - S(OC + I)$$

and thus:

$$B = SG.$$

These results may be summarized as shown in Exhibit 2.3. The formulas relating bonus and goodwill may be useful in problem solving. If the bonus has already been calculated for a given situation, the goodwill can be readily determined by use of a formula, and vice versa.

Exhibit 2.3	Summary of Bonus and Goodwill Formulas	
	Relation of New Partner's Investment to Capital Share	
	$I < S(OC + I)$	$I > S(OC + I)$
Bonus Method	$B = S(OC + I) - I$ (Bonus to new partner)	$B = I - S(OC + I)$ (Bonus to existing partners)
Goodwill Method	$G = \dfrac{OC}{(1 - S)} - (OC + I)$ (Goodwill to new partner)	$G = \dfrac{I}{S} - (OC + I)$ (Goodwill to existing partners)
Relationship of Bonus to Goodwill	$B = (1 - S)G$	$B = SG$

Comparison of Results. In general, the bonus and goodwill methods will *not* yield the same capital balances for the individual partners nor the same total capital for the partnership. The total capital of the partnership after admission of a new partner is as follows:

Bonus Method	Goodwill Method
Total capital before admission + Amount invested by new partner	Total capital before admission + Amount invested by new partner + Goodwill recorded

Compare the results obtained in the previous illustrations for Arthur Associates. The total capital before admission was $90,000. Edwards invested $9,000 and was admitted as a partner. Under the goodwill method, $1,000 of goodwill was attributed to Edwards. The capital balances after admission are:

	Bonus Method	Goodwill Method
Arthur	$30,550	$ 31,000
Bradley	25,820	26,000
Crowe	32,730	33,000
Edwards	9,900	10,000
Total	$99,000	$100,000

In our other illustration, Delano invested $12,000 and was admitted as a partner. Under the goodwill method, $18,000 of goodwill was attributed to the existing partners. The capital balances after admission are:

	Bonus Method	Goodwill Method
Arthur	$ 31,900	$ 40,000
Bradley	26,360	29,600
Crowe	33,540	38,400
Delano	10,200	12,000
Total	$102,000	$120,000

In only one case do the bonus and goodwill approaches lead to the same initial result. This happens when the amount invested equals the new partner's capital share $[I = S(OC + I)]$. In this case, the amount of bonus is zero and the amount of goodwill is zero, and the capital balances are the same, both individually and in total, under either method.

While the bonus and goodwill methods lead to the same initial result only in the limited case where goodwill and bonus are zero, they lead to the same ultimate result in a broader set of cases. Consider the situation where goodwill is initially recorded and is subsequently written off, either all at once or by the process of amortization. After write-off, the goodwill method will yield the same capital balances as the bonus method in cases where two conditions are met:

1. The new partner's initial capital percentage and income percentage are equal, and
2. The existing partners retain their relative income-sharing ratios.

Both conditions are met in our examples above. Observe that under each method, Edwards's capital percentage and income percentage are both 10 percent. The same holds for Delano in the second example. Arthur, Bradley, and Crowe retain their $5:2:3$ relationship for sharing income. Originally, their percentages were 50, 20, and 30 percent, respectively; after admitting a new partner with a 10 percent share, their percentages become 45, 18, and 27 percent.

The ultimate equivalence of the two methods is demonstrated below for the Edwards example. The far right column reflects the bonuses recorded on page 59.

	Goodwill Method before Write-Off	Write-Off of Goodwill	Goodwill Method after Write-Off	Bonus Method
Arthur	$ 31,000	$ 450 (= $1,000 × 45%)	$30,550	$30,550
Bradley	26,000	180 (= $1,000 × 18%)	25,820	25,820
Crowe	33,000	270 (= $1,000 × 27%)	32,730	32,730
Edwards	10,000	100 (= $1,000 × 10%)	9,900	9,900
	$100,000	$1,000	$99,000	$99,000

Similar results would be obtained in the Delano example.

Evaluation of Bonus and Goodwill Methods. In comparing the bonus and goodwill methods, we find that the rationales for the discrepancy between investment and share of net assets are similar, but that the accounting conclusions are different. An investment which is less than the computed share of net assets (Case A in our preceding illustrations) is explained in terms of the intangible benefits which the new partner brings to the firm. The goodwill method records these as an asset, while the bonus method leaves them unrecorded but shows side payments by the existing partners, in the form of a capital transfer to the new partner, in order to obtain these intangible benefits for the firm. An investment which is more than the computed share of net assets (Case B in our preceding illustrations) is explained in terms of understated asset values presently existing in the partnership. The goodwill method records these increases in asset values. The bonus method leaves them unrecorded, but shows side payments by the new partner, in the form of capital transfers to the existing partners, in order to obtain an interest in these assets.

Comparison with Corporate Accounting Practices. The admission of a new partner to a partnership is conceptually similar to the acquisition of one firm by another. Thus we may compare the bonus and goodwill approaches used in partnership accounting to the purchase and pooling approaches used in corporate accounting (to be discussed in detail in Chapter 6).

The bonus approach uses methods roughly comparable to pooling-of-interests accounting. The assets of the combining entities (the acquiring and acquired corporations of the existing partnership and new partner) are simply added together. No revaluation of assets occurs in a pooling; under the bonus method, assets may be revalued to market, but no goodwill is ever recognized. The equity accounts are then adjusted in such a way that the new equity relationships are reflected. Under pooling, transfers may occur among the Capital Stock, Paid-In Capital, and Retained Earnings accounts. Under the bonus method, transfers may occur among the capital accounts of the old and new partners.

The goodwill approach shares some similarities with purchase accounting. Under both methods, assets may be revalued based on the amount of the investment. The purchase–goodwill analogy is not perfect, however. In corporate acquisitions under the purchase method, goodwill is recorded only with respect to the *acquired* firm's assets (comparable to goodwill to the new partner). This recognizes that the value of the ownership interest given exceeds the value of tangible assets acquired, and so goodwill is recorded to make up the difference. In corporate accounting, goodwill is *not* recognized with respect to the assets of the *acquiring* (existing) firm, whereas in partnership accounting, goodwill may be recognized on the existing firm's assets (goodwill to the old partners). We should, however, note an important difference in circumstances. In the corporate case, the acquiring firm continues to exist, while in the partnership case, the old partnership is terminated and a new one created. Therefore, the corporate and partnership approaches share the following results:

1. Goodwill may be recognized with respect to an addition to the firm (an acquired corporation or a new partner).
2. A new basis of accountability may be established when a new entity is created. (The new partnership is a new entity; the acquiring corporation is not.)

Why Adjust at All? Before evaluating the two approaches to reconciling imbalances between investment and share of net assets, we should ask why any adjustment is needed. What does it matter if the capital accounts per books do not properly reflect the actual shares in net partnership assets? Granted, the capital accounts are important for capital-based income distribution and for liquidation. However, income distribution formulas and liquidation rights could be recognized by the partners even if not recorded on the books. The only arguments for recording the adjustments are convenience (to avoid maintaining two sets of books) and better disclosure (readers of financial statements will be aware of the true capital relationship among the partners). While these arguments are compelling, we should note that partnership accounting could be carried on without either the bonus or goodwill method.

Conclusions. The bonus approach is conservative in that it avoids recording intangible assets whose presence and value are difficult to verify and which are likely to have little, if any, realizable value upon liquidation. However, the going concern principle should lead us to have little concern for liquidation situations. The bonus approach follows the accounting convention that economic substance often takes precedence over legal form. Since in substance the partnership continues upon admission of a new partner, no new accountability basis for assets is provided. On the other hand, the implied side payments that are part of the bonus method are unusual accounting procedures. In short, the bonus method is consistent with several accounting conventions, but it is difficult to defend in terms of accounting theory.

The goodwill approach, on the other hand, has a better theoretical foundation. Since the admission of a new partner creates a new legal entity, a new basis of asset accountability is appropriate. The transaction which occurs (the investment by the new partner) forms the basis for the valuation of assets. As discussed above, the goodwill method for a partnership admission is roughly analogous to the purchase method for a corporate acquisition (which is usually viewed as a method superior to pooling of interests). The goodwill approach is also consistent with the general principles set forth in *APBO 29* dealing with nonmonetary transactions. While the *Opinion* does not specifically deal with partnerships, it sets forth the general principle that "accounting for nonmonetary transactions should be based on the fair values of the assets involved."[7] It would be logical to extend this principle to the investment of the existing interests of the old partners, and any noncash assets of the new partner, into the new partnership.

Summary of Key Concepts

Partnership law provides the general conditions under which partnerships operate. Many specific details are subject to the terms established by the partners in the **partnership agreement.**

Net income of a partnership does not include deductions for salaries to partners or interest to partners. Salaries, bonus, interest, and percentage formulas all may be used to **allocate net income to partners.** Full implementation of such allocation is commonly used.

In the **formation of a partnership,** assets are recorded at **fair market value.** Initial capital balances may be based on amounts actually invested or on a preestablished capital ratio. In the latter case, either the **bonus** or **goodwill** approach is applied.

Admission of a new partner may occur by **purchase** or **investment.** In the case of a purchase, **transfer of capital accounts** is the usual accounting method. In the case of investment, either the **bonus** or **goodwill** approach is applied.

The bonus and goodwill approaches are based on different conceptual views of the nature of admission. The two approaches may be related by formula. The bonus method recognizes transfers of capital among partners, while the goodwill method recognizes intangible assets.

---

[7]APB, *Opinion No. 29*, par. 18; CT § N35.105.

Appendix to Chapter 2

Tax Aspects of Partnerships

A partnership is not a taxable entity, merely a conduit through which taxable income flows to individual partners. A partnership files an information return (Form 1065), but pays no tax. However, certain tax aspects of partnership activity are worthy of discussion. We shall focus primarily on differences between tax and accounting figures with respect to the basis of partnership assets and the basis of partners' capital accounts.

Tax Basis of Partnership Assets

When an individual transfers assets to a partnership in exchange for an interest in that partnership, no gain or loss is recognized on the transfer for tax purposes. Thus the tax basis of the asset carries over from the individual to the partnership. Recall, however, that for accounting purposes the asset would be recorded at its fair market value. As an example, assume that a machine having a tax basis to Partner A of $6,000 has a fair market value of $15,000 when it is transferred to the AB Partnership. For accounting purposes, the machine would be recorded at $15,000, and depreciation for income statement purposes would be based on this amount. The asset would retain its tax basis of $6,000, however, and for purposes of calculating taxable income, depreciation would be based on the $6,000 amount. Similarly, if the machine were subsequently sold, the accounting gain or loss would differ from the tax gain or loss.

When differences between accounting basis and tax basis exist, dual records must be kept with respect to basis, depreciation, and income. A question arises as to how the difference between accounting income and taxable income should be allocated to the partners. Assume, for simplicity of discussion, that the machine mentioned above has a useful life of 3 years, that A and B share income equally, and that income before depreciation on the machine is $20,000. For accounting purposes, net income (using straight-line depreciation with zero salvage value) would be:

Income before Depreciation	$20,000
Depreciation (Book)	5,000
Net Income per Books	$15,000

and $7,500 would be allocated to each partner. For tax purposes, however, the partnership would report:

Income before Depreciation	$20,000
Depreciation (Tax)	2,000
Taxable Income	$18,000

How much income should each partner report for tax purposes? One possibility is $9,000 each, reflecting an equal division. In this case, however, Partner B is being taxed on A's previously unrecognized gain. (Recall that A had an economic gain of $9,000 when the machine was transferred to the partnership, but the gain was not taxed.) Thus the partners may specify that taxable income should be allocated as follows:

	A	B	Total
Accounting Income Divided Equally	$ 7,500	$7,500	$15,000
Adjustment Resulting from Lower Tax Basis of Machine—			
Allocated to Partner A	3,000	—	3,000
Taxable Income	$10,500	$7,500	$18,000

In this way, the $9,000 gain that went untaxed when A transferred the machine to the partnership would be included in A's taxable income over 3 years.

Tax Basis of Partnership Interest

The tax basis of each partner's interest begins with the tax basis of property contributed to the partnership, is increased by the partner's share of taxable income, and is decreased by the partner's share of losses and by amounts withdrawn from the partnership. In addition, *each partner's share of partnership liabilities* is considered to constitute a part of the tax basis of the partner's interest. Because of unlimited liability to partners, the capital account plus liabilities indicates the total amount the partner has at risk. This provision is very important and is clearly different from the accounting definition of partner's capital. The tax law permits partners to deduct their share of partnership losses up to the tax basis of their partnership interest. Suppose that Keller and Lehman are equal partners whose partnership interests, excluding liabilities, have tax bases of $4,000 and $2,800, respectively. Assume that the partnership has liabilities of $6,000, and that there is a net loss for the year of $15,000. While each partner's share of the loss would be $7,500, the loss claimed on their income tax returns would be limited to $7,000 for Keller (= $4,000 capital + $3,000 liabilities) and $5,800 for Lehman (= $2,800 + $3,000).

In an illustration presented earlier in the chapter, Prince and Quinn formed a partnership. Prince contributed $30,000 in cash, while Quinn contributed land and a building having a fair market value of $75,000, subject to a mortgage of $35,000 which was assumed by the partnership. Recall the three ways of determining the partners' initial capital for accounting purposes:

Capital Accounts Based on:	Prince	Quinn
Net Assets Invested	$30,000	$40,000
Equal Interests, Bonus Method	35,000	35,000
Equal Interests, Goodwill Method	40,000	40,000

Regardless of the method used for accounting purposes, the tax basis of their partnership interests would be calculated as follows:

Individual's basis in assets transferred

+ Share of liabilities assumed from others

− Share of liabilities assumed by others

= Tax basis of partnership interest.

If the tax basis of the land and building is equal to the fair market value of $75,000, we get:

	Prince	**Quinn**
Individual's Basis in Assets Transferred	$30,000	$ 75,000
Liabilities Assumed from (by) Others	17,500	(17,500)
Tax Basis of Partnership Interest.	$47,500	$ 57,500

These figures result from the assumption that, by having the partnership assume the $35,000 mortgage, Prince in effect assumes half of Quinn's previous obligation. We may view these same figures in another manner, which may more clearly indicate the fact that the tax basis of a partnership interest includes the partner's share of partnership liabilities:

	Prince	**Quinn**
Basis in Net Assets Transferred	$30,000	$40,000
Share of Partnership Liabilities.	17,500	17,500
Tax Basis of Partnership Interest.	$47,500	$57,500

If the tax basis of the land and building was different than $75,000, then the basis of Quinn's interest (but not Prince's) would be affected accordingly. Suppose Quinn's tax basis in the land and building was $52,000. The tax basis of each partner's interest would be:

	Prince	**Quinn**
Individual's Basis in Assets Transferred	$30,000	$ 52,000
Liabilities Assumed from (by) Others	17,500	(17,500)
Tax Basis of Partnership Interest.	$47,500	$ 34,500

As the partnership paid off the $35,000 mortgage, the tax basis of the partners' interests would be correspondingly reduced. Similarly, as the partnership incurred new liabilities, the tax bases would be increased. In effect, incurring liabilities is treated as an investment by the partners, and repaying liabilities is treated as a distribution to partners. Partnership liabilities can logically be viewed as individual partners' liabilities, since the partners are legally liable for them.

The tax basis of the partner's interest is particularly important when there is a loss. Tax law permits a partner to deduct a loss only to the extent of the tax basis (in other words, the tax basis cannot become negative). Note, however, that even if the partner's capital account for accounting purposes is negative, the partner's **tax basis** (capital account for tax purposes plus the partner's share of partnership liabilities) may be positive.

Questions

Q2.1 Define *partnership* and identify the information that a partnership agreement contains.

Q2.2 From what two sources are the organizational and operational rules for partnerships derived? Discuss the situations in which one source takes precedence over the other.

Q2.3 What major issues does the Uniform Partnership Act address?

Q2.4 Describe briefly the power of a partner to bind fellow partners in business contracts. What is meant by saying that all partners are liable jointly and severally?

Q2.5 What are the rules of partnership law with respect to:
1. Specific property rights which a partner possesses.
2. Sharing of profits and losses by partners.
3. Partners' rights to compensation for services performed for the firm.

Q2.6
1. X and Y are forming a partnership. X invests assets worth $100,000, and Y invests assets worth $120,000. Prepare the journal entry to record the formation.
2. If X and Y agree that each is to have a 50 percent interest in partnership capital, discuss two ways to record the investments described in No. 1.

Q2.7
1. Identify the three types of events that affect capital account balances.
2. Identify three ways of allocating partnership net income to the individual partners.

Q2.8 Explain the difference between the terms *partners' salary* and *partners' drawings*.

Q2.9 Select the best answer for each of the following multiple choice questions:
1. Partners Cox and Kaler share profits and losses equally after each has been credited in all circumstances with annual salary allowances of $15,000 and $12,000, respectively. Under this arrangement, Cox will benefit by $3,000 more than Kaler in which of the following circumstances?
   a. Only if the partnership has earnings of $27,000 or more for the year.
   b. Only if the partnership does not incur a loss for the year.
   c. In all earnings or loss situations.
   d. Only if the partnership has earnings of at least $3,000 for the year.

2. Partners Hutton and Elbert share profits in a $2:1$ ratio, respectively. Each partner receives an annual salary allowance of $6,000. If the salaries are recorded in the accounts of the partnership as an expense rather than treated as a division of net income, the total amount allocated to each partner for salaries and net income would be:

   a. Less for both Hutton and Elbert.

   b. Unchanged for both Hutton and Elbert.

   c. More for Hutton and less for Elbert.

   d. More for Elbert and less for Hutton.

3. If A is the total capital of a partnership before the admission of a new partner, B is the total capital of the partnership after the admission of a new partner, C is the amount of the new partner's investment, and D is the amount of capital credited to the new partner, then there is:

   a. A bonus to the new partner if $B = A + C$ and $D < C$.

   b. Goodwill to the old partners if $B > (A + C)$ and $D = C$.

   c. Neither bonus nor goodwill if $B = A - C$ and $D > C$.

   d. Goodwill to the new partner if $B > (A + C)$ and $D < C$.

4. If E is the total capital of a partnership before the admission of a new partner, F is the total capital of the partnership after the admission of the new partner, G is the amount of the new partner's investment, and H is the amount of capital credited to the new partner, then there is:

   a. Goodwill to the new partner if $F > (E + G)$ and $H < G$.

   b. Goodwill to the old partners if $F = E + G$ and $H > G$.

   c. A bonus to the new partner if $F = E + G$ and $H > G$.

   d. Neither bonus nor goodwill if $F > (E + G)$ and $H > G$. *(AICPA adapted)*

Q2.10 Identify and briefly discuss two ways a new partner can enter an existing partnership.

Q2.11 Alice, Thelma, and Dee are partners with capital balances of $50,000, $30,000, and $20,000, respectively. The partners share profits and losses equally. For an investment of $50,000 cash, Mary is to be admitted as a partner with a one-fourth interest in capital and profits. Based on this information, the amount of Mary's investment can best be justified by which of the following?

1. Mary will receive a bonus from the other partners upon her admission to the partnership.

2. Assets of the partnership were overvalued immediately prior to Mary's investment.

3. The book value of the partnership's net assets was less than their fair market value immediately prior to Mary's investment.

4. Mary is apparently bringing goodwill into the partnership, and her capital account will be credited for the appropriate amount.

If Mary invested $20,000 (rather than $50,000) for a one-fourth interest in capital and profits, how could you justify the amount of her investment using (1) the bonus method and (2) the goodwill method?

Q2.12 *(Appendix)* Eisenman is investing securities worth $15,000 in a new partnership. She purchased these securities several years ago for $6,000, which became her tax basis. Corman, the other (equal) partner, does not suggest any change in the terms of the proposed partnership agreement which provide that the partnership's allocation of taxable income shall be identical to its allocation of accounting income. Assuming Corman is subject to a 40 percent tax rate, what is the impact of this decision on Corman?

Exercises

E2.1 On March 1, 19X7, Rowen and Evans formed a partnership with each contributing assets having the following fair market values:

	Rowen	Evans
Cash.	$70,000	$ 70,000
Machinery and Equipment	25,000	75,000
Building	0	225,000
Furniture and Fixtures	10,000	0

The building is subject to a mortgage loan of $180,000, which is to be assumed by the partnership. The partnership agreement provides that Rowen and Evans share profits and losses 30 percent and 70 percent, respectively.

Required:

1. Compute the balances in each partner's capital account on March 1, 19X7, if the partners do not specify any capital relationship.
2. Compute the balances in each partner's capital account if the partners agree that each is to have a 50 percent interest in partnership capital, and they specify the bonus approach to recording the formation.
3. Compute the balances as for No. 2, except the partners specify the goodwill approach. *(AICPA adapted)*

E2.2 On January 1, 19X6, Kurley, Lary, and Meau form an accounting services firm. Kurley, who had operated an individual CPA practice, invested cash of $10,000, office equipment worth $21,000, and an unvalued clientele. Lary, who had been a corporate tax accountant, invested $18,000 cash. Meau, a recent graduate with good computer skills, had no money to invest currently, but signs a note agreeing to pay the firm $12,000 (plus interest) as a capital contribution. They agree to a 2:2:1 capital and income ratio.

Required:

1. Record the formation using the bonus approach.
2. Record the formation using the goodwill approach.

E2.3 Ralph Greene, a partner in the Brite Partnership, has a 30 percent participation in partnership profits and losses. Greene's capital account had a net decrease of $60,000 during the calendar year 19X4. During 19X4, Greene withdrew $130,000 (charged against his capital account) and contributed property valued at $25,000 to the partnership.

Required: Compute the net income of the Brite Partnership for 19X4. *(AICPA adapted)*

E2.4 On January 1, 19X7, Melvin and Lacey formed a partnership with each contributing $75,000 cash. The partnership agreement provided that Melvin would receive a guaranteed salary of $20,000 and that partnership profits and losses (computed after deducting Melvin's salary) would be shared equally for the year ended December 31, 19X7. The partnership's operations resulted in a net income of $2,000; Melvin's entire salary was paid in cash during 19X7.

Required:

1. Compute the amount of Melvin's partnership capital as of December 31, 19X7.
2. Compute the amount of Melvin's partnership capital as of December 31, 19X7, assuming there is net income of $42,000. *(AICPA adapted)*

E2.5 The January 1, 19X0, balance sheet of the partnership of Linda Kingston and Jeannette Allen is shown below. The partnership reported revenues of $80,000 and expenses of $55,000 for 19X0. Neither partner withdrew funds from the partnership during the year. Kingston invested $8,000 in the firm on June 28, 19X0.

ASSETS		LIABILITIES AND CAPITAL	
Cash.	$ 20,000	Liabilities	$ 60,000
Other Assets.	180,000	Capital—Kingston	56,000
		Capital—Allen	84,000
	$200,000		$200,000

Required: Compute the December 31, 19X0, capital balance for each partner under each of the following assumptions:

1. The partnership agreement does not specify how income is to be divided.
2. The partnership agreement specifies that Kingston receives 65 percent of income and Allen 35 percent.
3. The partnership agreement specifies that income is divided equally after paying each partner 10 percent interest on her average capital balance.
4. The partnership agreement specifies that Kingston and Allen receive

salaries of $12,000 and $8,000, respectively, and that each partner receives 5 percent interest on her capital balance at the beginning of the year. Salary and interest allocations are to be fully implemented if they exceed total income. Any remaining income is to be divided equally.

E2.6 Lancer and Day are partners with capital balances of $80,000 and $40,000, respectively. The partners share profits and losses in the ratio of 6:4, respectively. The partners agree to admit Corey, upon his investment of $30,000, as a partner with a one-third interest in capital and profits and losses.

Required: Compute the balances in the capital accounts of Lancer, Day, and Corey after Corey's admission, assuming that the parties agree that the admission is to be recorded without recognizing goodwill *(AICPA adapted)*

E2.7 The following balance sheet is for the Amos, Grant, and Derrick partnership. The partners share profits and losses in the ratio of 5:3:2, respectively.

Cash.	$ 30,000	Liabilities	$ 70,000
Other Assets.	270,000	Capital—Amos	140,000
		Capital—Grant.	80,000
		Capital—Derrick.	10,000
	$300,000		$300,000

The partnership wishes to admit Martin as a new partner with a one-fifth interest. Compute the amount of cash or other assets Martin should contribute if the partners agree that the admission is to be recorded without recognizing goodwill or bonus. *(AICPA adapted)*

E2.8 Felix and Hubert are partners who share profits and losses equally in a highly successful partnership. The capital accounts of Felix and Hubert are currently $90,000 and $60,000, respectively. Taylor wishes to join the firm and offers to invest $70,000 for a one-fourth interest in the capital and profits and losses of the firm.

Required: Compute the balances in the capital accounts of Felix, Hubert, and Taylor after Taylor's admission, assuming:

1. The parties agree that the admission is to be recorded by recognizing goodwill.
2. The parties agree that the admission is to be recorded without recognition of goodwill. *(AICPA adapted)*

E2.9 Graham and Hyde are partners who share income in a 3:1 ratio. Their respective capital balances are $50,000 and $30,000. Ingalls proposes to invest $40,000 in the firm in exchange for a 20 percent interest.

Required:

1. How would Ingalls's admission be recorded using the goodwill method?
2. How would Ingalls's admission be recorded using the bonus method?
3. Suppose instead that Ingalls purchased 20 percent of Graham's interest for $30,000 and 20 percent of Hyde's interest for $10,000 (paying these amounts directly to the individuals). How would this transaction be recorded by the partnership, assuming use of the implied goodwill approach?

E2.10 Each of the following independent situations shows either a bonus or goodwill recognized upon admission of a new partner to an existing partnership. In each case, calculate the amount of bonus or goodwill that would have been recognized if the alternative accounting treatment had been followed. That is, if the bonus method was used, calculate the goodwill to be recognized under the goodwill method and vice versa.

1. D and E admit F as an equal partner. A bonus to F of $3,000 is recorded.
2. O, P, and Q admit R as a new partner. R is to have a one-third interest in the new partnership. Goodwill of $6,000 is attributed to R.
3. H purchases a one-fifth interest in the partnership of I, J, and K. Goodwill to the existing partners ($6,000) is recorded.
4. L and M admit N as an equal partner for $10,000. No goodwill is recognized under the goodwill method.

E2.11 Presented below is the condensed balance sheet of the partnership of Kane, Clark, and Lane, who share profits or losses in the ratio of $6:3:1$, respectively:

Cash.	$ 85,000	Liabilities	$ 80,000
Other Assets.	415,000	Capital—Kane.	252,000
		Capital—Clark.	126,000
		Capital—Lane.	42,000
	$500,000		$500,000

Required:

1. The assets and liabilities on the above balance sheet are fairly valued, and the partnership wishes to admit Bayer with a 25 percent interest in the capital and profits and losses without recording goodwill or bonus. How much should Bayer contribute in cash or other assets?
2. Assume that the partners agree instead to sell Bayer 20 percent of their respective capital and profit and loss interests for a total payment of $90,000. The payment by Bayer is to be made directly to the individual partners. The partners agree that implied goodwill is to be recorded prior to the acquisition by Bayer. What are the capital balances of

Kane, Clark, and Lane, respectively, after the acquisition by Bayer? *(AICPA adapted)*

E2.12 *(Appendix)* Burriss, Culpepper, and Downstreet formed a partnership with each individual contributing assets as shown here:

	Cost	Fair Value
Burriss—Cash.	$15,000	$15,000
Culpepper—Equipment	13,000	15,000
Accumulated Depreciation	(3,000)	
Downstreet—Land	30,000	30,000

The equipment had an original life of 13 years, no salvage value, and has been depreciated on a straight-line basis for 3 years. The land has an outstanding mortgage of $15,000, which the partnership assumes.

The partners agreed to share profits and losses equally. Profit for the first year was $6,000 before depreciation.

Required:

1. Compute the tax basis of each partner's interest in the partnership at the date of formation.
2. Compute the taxable income of each partner, assuming Culpepper is to bear any tax related to the equipment appreciation.

Problems

P2.1 Partnerships versus Corporations—Discussion Case Twenty years ago a new partnership purchased land in Midville, erected a building, and opened a furniture and appliance merchandising store under the name of Furniture Fair. The partnership agreement specified that profits or losses would be shared equally after the allocation of partners' salary allowances and interest on average capital balances.

Midville has grown considerably, and the store is now the most prominent in a fashionable suburban area. Good management, imaginative merchandising, and the general improvement in the economy have made Furniture Fair the leading and most profitable firm of its type in Midville's trade area.

Now the partners wish to admit an investor and incorporate the business, and they have obtained a charter for Furniture Fair, Inc. Each partner will purchase at par an amount of preferred stock equal to the book value of the partner's interest in the partnership and common stock equal to that portion of the fair market value which exceeds the book value. The investor will purchase at a 10 percent premium over par value common and preferred stock equal to one-third the number of shares of each purchased by the partners. The corporation will then purchase the Furniture Fair partnership at its fair market value from the partners. After the consummation of the partners' plan, the corporation will own the partnership's assets, assume its liabilities, and employ the partners as the management of the corporation.

Required:

1. List and explain the differences in items and valuations that you would expect to find between the assets to appear on the balance sheet of the proposed corporation and the assets which appear on the partnership's balance sheet.
2. List and explain the differences that would be expected in a comparison of an income statement prepared for the proposed corporation and an income statement prepared for the partnership. *(AICPA adapted)*

P2.2 **Formation of Partnership** The partnership of Frank and Keller was formed on February 28, 19X3. At that date, Frank invested $25,000 cash and furniture and equipment valued at $15,000. Keller invested $35,000 cash, merchandise valued at $55,000, and a building valued at $100,000, subject to a mortgage of $30,000 (which the partnership assumes). The partnership agreement provides that Frank and Keller share profits or losses 25 percent and 75 percent, respectively.

Required:

1. Compute the amount of each partner's capital account at February 28, assuming that each partner is credited for the full amount of net assets invested.
2. Compute the amount of Frank's capital account at February 28, assuming that the partnership agreement provides that Frank and Keller should have, initially, an equal interest in partnership capital, using the bonus method.
3. Given the facts stated in No. 2, compute the amount of Keller's capital account at February 28, using the goodwill method. *(AICPA adapted)*

P2.3 **Formation of Partnership** Augustus Berrini, the sole proprietor of the Berrini Company, is planning to expand the company and establish a partnership with Fiedler and Wade. The partners plan to share profits and losses as follows: Berrini, 50 percent; Fiedler, 25 percent; Wade 25 percent. They also agree that the beginning capital balances of the partnership will reflect this same relationship.

Berrini asked Fiedler to join the partnership because his many business contacts are expected to be valuable during the expansion. Fiedler is also contributing $28,000. Wade is contributing $11,000 and a block of marketable securities which the partnership expects to liquidate as needed during the expansion. The securities, which cost Wade $42,000, are currently worth $57,500.

Berrini's investment in the partnership is the Berrini Company. He plans to pay off the notes with his personal assets. The other partners have agreed that the partnership will assume the accounts payable and the mortgage. The balance sheet for the Berrini Company follows. The three partners agree that the inventory is worth $85,000, the equipment is worth half its original cost, the building and land are worth $65,000 and $25,000, respectively, and the allowance established for doubtful accounts is correct.

BERRINI COMPANY
BALANCE SHEET
DATE OF PARTNERSHIP FORMATION

ASSETS		LIABILITIES	
Cash.	$ 7,000	Accounts Payable	$ 53,000
Accounts Receivable (Net). .	48,000	Notes Payable.	7,000
Inventory	72,000	Mortgage Payable	55,000
Equipment (Net of $12,000			$115,000
Accumulated			
Depreciation)	18,000	**OWNER'S EQUITY**	
Building (Net of $20,000			
Accumulated		Capital, Berrini.	85,000
Depreciation)	40,000		
Land.	15,000		
		Total Liabilities and Owner's	
Total Assets	$200,000	Equity	$200,000

Required: Prepare the balance sheet of the partnership on the date of formation under each of the following independent assumptions:

1. The partners agree to follow the bonus method to record the formation.
2. The partners agree to follow the goodwill approach to record the formation.

P2.4 Partnership Income Allocation Grandis and Hayley formed a partnership on January 2, 19X4, and agreed to share profits 90 percent and 10 percent, respectively. Grandis contributed capital of $25,000. Hayley contributed no capital but has a specialized expertise and manages the firm full time. There were no withdrawals during the year, except for Hayley's salary. The partnership agreement provides for the following:

1. Capital accounts are to be credited annually with interest at 5 percent of beginning capital.
2. Hayley is to be paid a salary of $1,000 a month.
3. Hayley is to receive a bonus of 20 percent of income calculated before deducting Hayley's salary, Hayley's bonus, and interest on both capital accounts.

Income to be allocated on December 31, 19X4, after deduction of partners' interest and Hayley's salary and bonus, was $46,750.

Required:

1. Assume that the partners had initial capital interests equal to their income-sharing ratios and that no goodwill was recognized on the

formation of the partnership. Determine the original capital for each partner.

2. Compute Hayley's 19X4 bonus.
3. Calculate the balances in the capital accounts at year-end.

P2.5 Partnership Income Allocation   A December 31, 19X5 balance sheet for the Silverstone Partnership is shown below:

SILVERSTONE PARTNERSHIP
BALANCE SHEET
DECEMBER 31, 19X5

ASSETS		LIABILITIES AND CAPITAL	
Cash.	$ 10,000	Accounts Payable	$ 60,000
Accounts Receivable	50,000	Long-Term Liabilities.	100,000
Equipment	85,000	Capital—Lamke	55,000
Buildings.	125,000	Capital—Perez	80,000
Land.	30,000	Capital—Sills	5,000
Total Assets	$300,000	Total Liabilities and Capital .	$300,000

Additional information:

1. The partners have agreed that each will be paid 5 percent interest on the capital balance as of the beginning of the year.
2. Salaries are as follows: Lamke, $15,000; Perez, $20,000; and Sills, $10,000.
3. Sills is to receive a bonus of 10 percent of income before salaries, bonus, and interest to partners.
4. Any income remaining after salaries, bonus, and interest to partners is to be allocated equally.
5. During 19X5, Lamke withdrew $3,300 from the firm. All other allocations to Lamke for salary, interest, and profit were retained in the business.
6. Perez withdrew all but $10,000 of 19X5 allocations.
7. In 19X5 Sills withdrew $15,000 and all salary, bonus, interest, and profit allocations.
8. Total capital investment at the beginning of the year was $120,000.
9. Income for 19X5 after deducting interest to partners but before deductions for salaries and bonus was $90,000.

Required: Prepare a schedule showing all allocations to and withdrawals by the partners in the Silverstone Partnership. The schedule should begin with capital balances as of January 1, 19X5.

P2.6 Admission by Direct Purchase   Williams wishes to purchase a one-fourth capital and profit and loss interest in the partnership of Cob, Howards, and Lee. The three partners agree to sell Williams one-fourth of their respective capital and profit and loss interests in exchange for a total payment of $40,000. The capital accounts and the respective percentage interests in profit and losses immediately before the sale to Williams follow:

	Capital Accounts	Percentage Interests in Profits and Losses
Cob	$80,000	60%
Howards	40,000	30
Lee	20,000	10

All other assets and liabilities are fairly valued.

Required:

1. Compute the amount of the capital balances of Cob, Howards, Lee, and Williams immediately after Williams's acquisition, assuming *no* recognition of implied goodwill.
2. Compute the amount of the capital balances of Cob, Howard, Lee, and Williams immediately after Williams's acquisition, assuming there *is* recognition of implied goodwill. *(AICPA adapted)*

P2.7 Admission—Goodwill Approach Wright and Koehler formed a partnership on January 1, 19X6. They have agreed to admit Robertson as a partner on January 1, 19X9. The books for the year ending December 31, 19X8, are closed. The following additional information is available:

1. Wright and Koehler shared profits equally until January 1, 19X8, when they agreed to share profits 40 percent and 60 percent, respectively. The profit-sharing ratio after Robertson is admitted will be 32 percent to Wright, 48 percent to Koehler, and 20 percent to Robertson.
2. Robertson will invest $25,000 cash for a one-fifth interest in the capital of the partnership.
3. The partnership reported earnings of $22,000 in 19X6, $35,000 in 19X7, and $32,000 in 19X8.
4. The partnership of Wright and Koehler did not use accrual accounting for some items. It was agreed that before Robertson's admission is recorded, adjustments should be made in the accounts retroactively to report properly on the accrual method of accounting.
5. Use of a modified cash basis of accounting led to net overstatements of income of $7,000 in 19X6 and $6,000 in 19X7 and a net understatement of income of $1,000 in 19X8.

Required:

1. Prepare a schedule presenting computation of the adjustments necessary to report Wright's and Koehler's correct capital account balances at December 31, 19X6, 19X7, and 19X8.
2. Assume the capital balances as originally reported on December 31, 19X8, were Wright, $66,100 and Koehler, $81,900. Adjust these capital balances to reflect accrual accounting and determine (a) Robertson's capital balance if admission is recorded under the goodwill ap-

proach and (b) the amount of goodwill to be recognized. *(AICPA adapted)*

P2.8 Admission—Various Cases Given below are account balances for the partnership of Simpson and Scott before the admission of a new partner, Lansing. Each case presents account balances of the partnership immediately after the admission of Lansing. The cases are independent of each other.

Balance Sheet Accounts	Balances before Lansing's Admission	Balances after Lansing's Admission				
		Case 1	Case 2	Case 3	Case 4	Case 5
Cash.	$ 10,000	$ 10,000	$ 10,000	$ 20,000	$ 10,000	$ 30,000
Other Assets.	80,000	130,000	80,000	80,000	170,000	80,000
Goodwill	10,000	10,000	10,000	10,000	30,000	20,000
Liabilities.	(30,000)	(30,000)	(30,000)	(30,000)	(80,000)	(30,000)
Capital—Simpson	(35,000)	(42,500)	(35,000)	(30,000)	(35,000)	(40,000)
Capital—Scott	(35,000)	(42,500)	—	(30,000)	(35,000)	(40,000)
Capital—Lansing.	—	(35,000)	(35,000)	(20,000)	(60,000)	(20,000)

Required: For each independent case, answer the following questions. Show supporting computations.

1. What method of accounting was used to record the admission (bonus, goodwill, neither)?
2. How much did Lansing invest in the partnership?
3. What percentage of ownership does Lansing have in the new partnership?

P2.9 Cash to Accrual Basis—Admission of Partner The partnership of Kraft, Mills, and Farmer engaged you to adjust its accounting records and convert them uniformly to the accrual basis in anticipation of admitting Ward as a new partner. Some accounts are on the accrual basis and others are on the cash basis. The partnership's books were closed at December 31, 19X6, by the bookkeeper, who prepared the general ledger trial balance that appears below.

KRAFT, MILLS, AND FARMER
GENERAL LEDGER TRIAL BALANCE
DECEMBER 31, 19X6

	Debit	Credit
Cash.	$ 10,000	
Accounts Receivable.	40,000	
Inventory.	26,000	
Land	9,000	
Buildings	50,000	
Allowance for Depreciation of Buildings		$ 2,000
Equipment	56,000	
Allowance for Depreciation of Equipment.		6,000

Goodwill	5,000	
Accounts Payable		55,000
Allowance for Future Inventory Losses		3,000
Capital—Kraft		40,000
Capital—Mills		60,000
Capital—Farmer		30,000
Totals	$196,000	$196,000

Your inquiries disclosed the following:

1. The partnership was organized on January 1, 19X5, with no provision in the partnership agreement for the distribution of partnership profits and losses. During 19X5, profits were distributed equally among the partners. The partnership agreement was amended effective January 1, 19X6, to provide for the following profit-and-loss-sharing ratio: Kraft, 50 percent; Mills, 30 percent; and Farmer, 20 percent. The amended partnership agreement also stated that the accounting records were to be maintained on the accrual basis and that any adjustments necessary for 19X5 should be allocated according to the 19X5 distribution of profits.

2. The following amounts were not recorded as prepayments or accruals:

	December 31	
	19X6	**19X5**
Prepaid Insurance	$700	$ 650
Advances from Customers	200	1,100
Accrued Interest Expense	—	450

The advances from customers were recorded as sales in the year the cash was received.

3. In 19X6 the partnership recorded a provision of $3,000 for anticipated declines in inventory prices. You convinced the partners that the provision was unnecessary and the provision and related allowance should be removed from the books.

4. The partnership charged equipment purchased for $4,400 on January 3, 19X6, to expense. The equipment has an estimated life of 10 years and an estimated salvage value of $400. The partnership depreciates its capitalized equipment under the double-declining-balance method.

5. The partners agreed to establish an allowance for doubtful accounts at 2 percent of current accounts receivable and 5 percent of past due accounts. At December 31, 19X5, the partnership had $54,000 of accounts receivable, of which only $4,000 was past due. At December 31, 19X6, 15 percent of accounts receivable was past due, of which $4,000 represented sales made in 19X5, and was generally considered collectible. The partnership had written off uncollectible accounts in the year the accounts became worthless as follows:

	Accounts Written Off	
	19X6	**19X5**
19X6 Accounts	$ 800	—
19X5 Accounts	1,000	$250

6. Goodwill was recorded on the books in 19X6 and credited to the partners' capital accounts in the profit-and-loss-sharing ratio in recognition of an increase in the value of the business resulting from improved sales volume. No amortization of goodwill was recorded. The partners agreed to write off the goodwill before admitting the new partner.

Required:

1. Prepare the journal entries to convert the accounting records to the accrual basis and to correct the books before admitting the new partner.

2. Without prejudice to your solution to No. 1 above, assume the assets were properly valued and that the adjusted total of the partners' capital account balances at December 31, 19X6, was $140,000. On that date, Ward invested $55,000 in the partnership. Record the admission of Ward using the goodwill method. Ward is to be granted a one-fourth interest in the partnership. The other partners will retain their 50:30:20 income-sharing ratio for the remaining three-fourths interest. *(AICPA adapted)*

P2.10 Formula Relationships   Use the formulas presented in the chapter to solve each of the following independent cases:

1. Existing capital of a partnership is $100,000. A new partner, having a 10 percent interest, is admitted. Total value of the partnership is calculated to be $120,000, and goodwill of $8,000 is recorded. Had the bonus method been used, how much bonus would have been recorded and who would have received it?

2. A new partner invests $15,000 for a 30 percent interest in a partnership. A bonus of $21,000 to the new partner is recorded. Had the goodwill method been used, how much goodwill would have been recorded and to whom?

3. Admission of a new partner, having a 25 percent interest, would result in recording an $8,000 bonus or $32,000 of goodwill. If the capital of the existing partners is $28,000, how much is to be invested by the new partner?

P2.11 Partnership Accounting—Comprehensive   You have been engaged to prepare financial statements for the partnership of Allison, Reed, and Werner as of June 30, 19X2. You have obtained the following information from the partnership agreement as amended and from the accounting records:

1. The partnership was formed originally by Allison and Bailey on July 1, 19X1. At that date:
   a. Bailey contributed $400,000 cash.
   b. Allison contributed land, building, and equipment with fair market values of $110,000, $520,000, and $185,000, respectively. The land and building were subject to a mortgage securing an 8 percent per annum note (interest rate of similar notes at July 1, 19X1, was 8 percent). Quarterly payments of $5,000 plus interest are due on the note on January 1, April 1, July 1, and October 1 of each year. Allison made the July 1, 19X1, principal and interest payment personally. The partnership then assumed the obligation for the remaining $300,000 balance.
   c. The agreement further provided that Allison had contributed a certain intangible benefit to the partnership due to his many years of business activity in the area to be serviced by the new partnership. The assigned value of this intangible asset plus the net tangible assets he contributed gave Allison a 60 percent initial capital interest in the partnership. The intangible asset is amortized over 10 years.
   d. Allison was designated the only active partner at an annual salary of $24,000 plus an annual bonus of 4 percent of net income after deducting his salary but before deducting the bonus and interest on partners' capital investments.
   e. Each partner is to receive a 6 percent return on his average capital investment. The average is based on the capital balances at the beginning of each month.
   f. All remaining profits or losses are to be shared equally.
2. On October 1, 19X1, Bailey sold his partnership interest and rights as of July 1, 19X1, to Werner for $370,000. Allison agreed to accept Werner as a partner if he would contribute sufficient cash to meet the October 1, 19X1, principal and interest payment on the mortgage note. Werner made the payment from personal funds.
3. On January 1, 19X2, Allison and Werner admitted a new partner, Reed. Reed invested $150,000 cash and received a 10 percent capital interest based on the July 1, 19X1, original investments of Allison and Bailey. The January 1, 19X2, capital balances of Allison and Werner were ignored for this calculation. At January 1, 19X2, the book value of the partnership's assets and liabilities approximated their fair market values. Reed contributed no intangible benefit to the partnership.

   Similar to the other partners, Reed is to receive a 6 percent return on his average capital investment. His investment also entitles him to 20 percent of the partnership's profits or losses as defined above. However, for the year ended June 30, 19X2, Reed would receive one-half of his pro rata share of the profits or losses.
4. The accounting records show that on February 1, 19X2, miscellaneous Expenses had been charged $3,600 in payment of hospital expenses incurred by Allison's 8-year-old daughter.

5. Allison's salary was paid in one lump sum on June 29, 19X2, and charged to his drawing account. On June 1, 19X2, Werner made a $33,000 withdrawal. These are the only transactions recorded in the partners' drawing accounts.

6. Presented below is a trial balance summarizing the partnership's general ledger balances at June 30, 19X2. The general ledger has not been closed.

	Debit	Credit
Current Assets.	$ 307,100	
Fixed Assets, Net	1,285,800	
Current Liabilities		$157,000
8% Mortgage Note Payable		290,000
Capital—Allison		515,000
Capital—Reed.		150,000
Capital—Werner.		400,000
Drawing—Allison	24,000	
Drawing—Reed	0	
Drawing—Werner	33,000	
Sales		872,600
Cost of Sales	695,000	
Administrative Expenses.	16,900	
Miscellaneous Expenses.	11,100	
Interest Expense.	11,700	

Required: Compute the ending balances of the partners' capital accounts. Show supporting calculations. *(AICPA adapted)*

P2.12 Partner's Tax Basis and Taxable Income *(Appendix)* Refer to the data in P2.3 concerning the formation of a partnership by Berrini, Fiedler, and Wade.

The equipment had an original life of 5 years with no salvage value. The building had an original life of 30 years, also with no salvage value. The straight-line method of depreciation is used.

Accounting net income for the first year of operations is $30,000. All of the inventory transferred from the Berrini Company was charged to cost of goods sold under the FIFO method. The marketable securities contributed by Wade were sold during the year for $65,000 (the $7,500 accounting gain is included in the net income figure cited above).

The partners have agreed that accounting income will be divided according to the 50:25:25 percentage ratio. As the partnership realizes the gains or losses which were unrecognized at the time of the original transfer of assets, these will be included in the taxable income of the partner(s) who invested the assets.

Required:

1. Compute the tax basis of each partner's interest in the partnership at the date of formation.
2. Compute the taxable income to be reported by each partner.

Chapter 3 Partnerships: Contraction, Termination, and Liquidation

A partnership terminates legally whenever the composition of the partnership changes, as in the admission of a new partner or the retirement or death of an existing partner. Accounting, however, is concerned with the economic entity rather than the legal entity. This chapter addresses one legal situation—legal dissolution of a partnership—with two economic interpretations. The partnership may continue as an economic entity or may cease to exist.

When a partnership terminates legally but the business activities are maintained by a successor partnership, the economic entity is intact. This can occur when a partner leaves the business due to retirement, resignation, or death.

On the other hand, if the assets of a partnership are liquidated and distributed, the partnership ceases to exist as an economic entity. There are several possible reasons for this type of termination. Bankruptcy of the partnership will lead to termination. Or the partners may have initially specified that the partnership would exist for only a limited time or until a certain purpose was accomplished. For example, a partnership may be created to buy a tract of land and develop and sell subdivision lots. When all lots are sold and paid for, the partnership may be dissolved. In other cases, partners may mutually agree to terminate a partnership because it is unsuccessful or because they wish to pursue other activities.

Retirement of a Partner

Ownership composition of a partnership changes when a partner withdraws. Accounting for such changes varies, depending on whether the interest of the withdrawing partner is purchased by one or more remaining partners with their personal assets or by the partnership with partnership assets. Because the accounting treatment is similar regardless of the reason for withdrawal (resignation, retirement, or death), we discuss only the case of retirement.

Purchase with Individual Assets

We first consider the situation in which the remaining partners, as individuals, purchase the interest of the retiring partner. Since the transaction—between the retiring partner and remaining partner(s)—occurs outside the partnership, the only entry necessary on the partnership books is a transfer of capital balances. Assume, for example, that KLM Associates shows the following information:

Partner	Capital Balance	Income Share
Keenan.	$ 75,000	45%
Ludlow	60,000	30
Morris	30,000	25
Total	$165,000	100%

If Keenan and Ludlow buy Morris's interest for $60,000, Morris's $30,000 capital account must be transferred to Keenan and Ludlow. If the purchasers retain their relative shares (45:30, or 3:2), $18,000 would be credited to Keenan and $12,000 to Ludlow. The transfer of capital would be recorded as:

Capital—Morris	30,000	
Capital—Keenan		18,000
Capital—Ludlow		12,000
To record Morris' retirement.		

This treatment is similar to procedures discussed in Chapter 2 for admission of a new partner by purchase of an existing interest. In that case, however, the purchase transaction with an outside party could lead to recognition of implied goodwill on the partnership books. In this retirement case, no outside party is involved. Without the presence of an arm's-length transaction, the argument that market value has been determined and goodwill can be recognized is weak.

Purchase with Partnership Assets

The second possibility is that the retiring partner will receive assets directly from the partnership in settlement of that individual's capital interest. In effect, the partnership will buy out the retiring partner. The remainder of this section explains procedures for dealing with this situation.

Determination of Payment to Retiring Partner. The settlement with a retiring partner should be based on the *fair value* of the partner's interest. There is no reason to expect that this value is equal to the balance in the partner's capital account at time of retirement. Some equitable manner of determining the value of the retiring partner's interest, and hence the payment to the retiring partner, is needed. In general, we would expect the partnership agreement to answer the question. When forming the partnership, the partners should have considered and agreed upon a method of valuing a partner's interest in the event of resignation, retirement, or death. They might have agreed on a formula, such as ''5 times the partner's average share of income over the preceding 3 years, plus the balance in the capital account''. Or they might have agreed to base the value on an outside appraisal of the partnership's assets, both tangible and intangible. Whatever the partnership agreement specifies will be used to determine the value of the retiring partner's interest. If no provision was made in the agreement, the parties will have to agree on valuation procedures at the time of retirement.

Accounting for Retirement. As stated above, payment of partnership assets to a retiring partner is not necessarily based on the balance in the retiring partner's capital account. Upon retirement, however, the capital account must be eliminated from the books, and any differences between the payment and the capital balance must be considered.

In the illustrations that follow, we assume that the retiring partner is paid with partnership cash. If part or all of the payment is made with other partnership assets, then the assets should be adjusted on the books to fair market value before their distribution to the retiring partner is recorded. Any difference between fair market value and book value should be entered in the partners' capital accounts according to their income-sharing ratio.

Accounting for the retirement of a partner via distribution of partnership assets is similar to accounting for the admission of a new partner via investment. In the simplest case, where payment to the retiring partner *does* equal that partner's capital balance, the retirement is recorded as follows:

```
Capital—Retiring Partner . . . . . . . . . . . . . . . . . . . . . . . . . . .   XX
    Cash (or other assets) . . . . . . . . . . . . . . . . . . . . . . . . . .        XX
```

If, however, the payment does *not* equal the capital balance, we must account for the difference by either the bonus or goodwill method. To discuss these, we return to the data for KLM Associates:

Partner	Capital Balance	Income Share
Keenan.	$ 75,000	45%
Ludlow	60,000	30
Morris	30,000	25
Total	$165,000	100%

Bonus Method. To illustrate the **bonus method of recording a partner's retirement,** assume the partners determine that Morris, the retiring partner, will receive $55,000. Under the bonus method, the $25,000 difference between the payment ($55,000) and the balance in Morris's capital account ($30,000) is treated as a bonus from Keenan and Ludlow to Morris:

```
Capital—Keenan  . . . . . . . . . . . . . . . . . . . . . . . . . . . . . .  15,000
Capital—Ludlow. . . . . . . . . . . . . . . . . . . . . . . . . . . . . . .  10,000
Capital—Morris . . . . . . . . . . . . . . . . . . . . . . . . . . . . . . .  30,000
    Cash . . . . . . . . . . . . . . . . . . . . . . . . . . . . . . . . . .            55,000
To record Morris's retirement under the bonus method.
```

Note that the bonus is divided between Keenan and Ludlow in relation to their respective income shares (45:30, or 3:2).

If, instead, Morris is to receive less than the $30,000 capital balance, the difference is treated as a bonus from Morris to Keenan and Ludlow. For example, if Morris receives $22,000, we record:

Capital—Morris	30,000	
Capital—Keenan		4,800
Capital—Ludlow		3,200
Cash		22,000

To record Morris's retirement under the bonus method.

Again, the bonus is divided between the remaining partners according to their income-sharing relationship.

Goodwill Method. The assumption underlying the bonus method of recording a partner's retirement is that a bonus is being paid either by or to the retiring partner. The bonus accounts for the difference between the settlement price and the retiring partner's capital balance. In contrast, the general logic of the **goodwill method of recording a partner's retirement** is that such differences, in either positive or negative directions, signify that asset revaluations are appropriate. Existing assets may be written up, intangible assets (goodwill) recorded, or both. Or, if revaluations downward are indicated, assets may be written down. In some circumstances, therefore, retirement can be recorded under the goodwill method without making an entry to an account entitled Goodwill.

Two interpretations of the goodwill method exist: the partial goodwill approach and the total goodwill approach. Either can be applied to asset revaluations upward or downward. As noted earlier, use of the transaction price to justify asset revaluations is less supportable in the retirement case than in the admission case. In the retirement case, the transaction is with one of the partners and cannot be viewed as arm's-length.

Under the **partial goodwill approach,** the revaluations of asset book values that are triggered by a partner's retirement are limited to the difference between the settlement price and the retiring partner's capital account. If the payment is greater than the capital balance, then undervaluations of existing assets should be corrected, with any remaining difference being attributed to goodwill. If the payment is less than the capital balance, then asset values are reduced only to the extent of the difference—even though evidence indicates that additional asset overvaluations exist. These asset revaluations are charged or credited only to the capital account of the retiring partner; the capital accounts of other partners are unaffected.

The **total goodwill approach** specifies that *all* asset revaluations apparent at the time of retirement should be recorded. These revaluations are charged or credited to the capital accounts of all partners according to their income-sharing ratio.

An illustration may help clarify the differences between these two approaches. Returning to the example of Morris's retirement from KLM Associates, assume that Morris receives $55,000, that the capital account balance is $30,000, and that the partners determine that existing assets are appropriately valued. The partial goodwill approach calls for recognition of $25,000 of goodwill—the difference between the settlement price and the capital balance. The total goodwill approach follows the logic that if $25,000 of goodwill is attributable to Morris's 25 percent interest, then total goodwill of the firm is $100,000 (= $25,000/.25), and this entire amount should be recognized and allocated to the partners according to their income-sharing percentages. Note that the income percentage, rather than the capital percentage, is used here. Capital percentages are useful for recording partnership formation but are generally meaningless thereafter, as different patterns of additions to and withdrawals from capital disturb any constant relationship among capital accounts.

The total goodwill approach yields total partnership capital, before Morris's retirement, of $265,000 (the original $165,000 plus $100,000 goodwill). Note that, in general, this result cannot be obtained by capitalizing the total payment to Morris ($55,000/.25, or $220,000). This latter procedure yields correct results only in the case where the dollar balance in the retiring partner's capital account is exactly equal to that partner's income-sharing percentage times total capital.[1] Thus, in general, total goodwill is determined from the goodwill attributable to the retiring partner rather than from the payment made to the retiring partner.

Exhibit 3.1 illustrates application of the two approaches of the goodwill method under three independent assumptions regarding Morris's retirement from KLM Associates. The usual arguments exist with respect to the choice between the two approaches. Proponents of the partial goodwill approach argue that the partnership should record goodwill only to the extent that it is purchased or paid for. Total goodwill advocates argue that the transaction provides evidence of the total value of the partnership, and that the accounts of the new entity (the successor partnership) should be based on fair market value. In essence, the argument comes down to an entity question. If we view the successor partnership as a continuation of the old entity, then partial goodwill is reasonable. If we view the successor partnership as a new entity, then total goodwill should be used. Following the concept of economic entity advocated in this text, we believe the partial goodwill approach is superior.

Termination and Liquidation of the Partnership

Previous discussion addressed situations in which a partnership continued as an economic entity despite legal dissolution through retirement of a partner. Now we turn to cases where a partnership terminates economically as well as legally. The business ceases operation and liquidates its assets.

---

[1] To see this, suppose that A, B, and C have capital balances of $40,000, $40,000, and $20,000, respectively, and have income-sharing percentages in the ratio 5:3:2. C is retiring and will receive a $30,000 payment from the partnership. Partial goodwill is $10,000 (= $30,000 − $20,000), and total goodwill is $50,000 (= 5 × $10,000), giving total capital of $150,000. Capitalizing the $30,000 payment to C also gives total capital of $150,000 (= $30,000/.2).

Exhibit 3.1   Comparison of the Partial and Total Goodwill Approaches: KLM Associates

Assumption	Partial Goodwill Approach			Total Goodwill Approach		

Morris's capital balance = $30,000. Payment upon retirement = $55,000. Excess payment is attributable to goodwill.	Goodwill
	  Capital—Morris
	Capital—Morris
	  Cash
		25,000
		
		55,000
			
			25,000
			
			55,000
				Goodwill
				  Capital—Keenan
				  Capital—Ludlow
				  Capital—Morris
				Capital—Morris
				  Cash
					100,000
					
					55,000
						
						45,000
						30,000
						25,000
						
						55,000

Morris's capital balance = $30,000. Payment upon retirement = $55,000. Excess payment is attributable to undervalued existing assets ($15,000) and to goodwill.	Assets
	  Capital—Morris
	Goodwill
	  Capital—Morris
	
	Capital—Morris
	  Cash
		15,000
		
		10,000
		
		55,000
			
			15,000
			
			10,000
			
			55,000
				Assets
				  Capital—Keenan
				  Capital—Ludlow
				  Capital—Morris
				Goodwill
				  Capital—Keenan
				  Capital—Ludlow
				  Capital—Morris
				Capital—Morris
				  Cash
					15,000
					
					85,000
					
					55,000
						
						6,750
						4,500
						3,750
						
						38,250
						25,500
						21,250
						
						55,000

Morris's capital balance = $30,000. Payment upon retirement = $22,000. Difference is attributable to overvalued assets.	Capital—Morris
	  Assets
	Capital—Morris
	  Cash
		8,000
		
		22,000
			
			8,000
			
			22,000
				Capital—Keenan
				Capital—Ludlow
				Capital—Morris
				  Assets
				Capital—Morris
				  Cash
					14,400
					9,600
					8,000
					
					22,000
						
						32,000
						
						22,000

Priorities for Payments

One issue central to the study of liquidations is the sequence in which the proceeds of liquidation are distributed. Outside creditors have claims against partnership assets. Partners have claims on partnership assets resulting from loans of personal assets to the partnership, investments in the partnership, and the right to share in undistributed income of the partnership.

Simply stated, liquidation distributions go first to outside creditors and then to partners. Technically, the sequence of liquidation distributions can be much more complicated than this.[2] With respect to partners' claims, the law identifies three subcategories: partners' loans, partners' invested capital, and partners' undistributed income.

As a practical matter, however, there is little difference between partners' invested capital and undistributed income, which is closed annually to the capital accounts. Drawings by partners are typically not differentiated as to withdrawals of capital or income. Similarly, there is little practical difference between partners' loans or partners' invested capital. Liquidation often involves a loss on sale of assets, and the balance of a partner's capital account could become negative when the loss is allocated. One of the provisions of partnership law requires partners to contribute sufficient capital to cover a **capital deficiency** (debit balance in the capital account). If a partner with a capital deficiency has made loans from personal assets to the partnership, then the **right of offset** allows the loan balance to be applied to the deficiency. For example, if Partner A has a capital deficiency of $8,000 (that is, the individual owes the partnership $8,000) and has a loan account of $10,000 (that is, the partnership owes the individual $10,000), then the net effect is that Partner A is entitled to receive $2,000 of the liquidation proceeds.

While recognizing that more complexity may exist in particular cases, we shall use the two-step sequence for distribution of liquidation proceeds:

1. Outside creditors.
2. Partners' combined loans and capital.

In partnership liquidations, therefore, the first concern is to meet obligations to outside creditors. Next we focus on determining the proper distribution to partners of any remaining proceeds from liquidation.

Rights of Creditors

Both the creditors of the partnership and the creditors of the individual partners have legal rights regarding partnership liquidation. These rights influence the accounting procedures.

---

[2]The first priority of distribution to outside creditors is subdivided among fully secured, partially secured, and unsecured creditors. Such distinctions are discussed in the section on bankruptcy accounting in Chapter 4. For purposes of illustrating partnership liquidation, we treat all outside creditors as a single category.

Creditors of the partnership must first seek payment of their claims from partnership assets. If the partnership is insolvent, the partnership creditors may then seek payment from *any* partner. Thus a partner can be individually liable for any and all claims against the partnership. If an individual partner pays partnership creditors, this payment is recorded as an investment of capital in the partnership.

Creditors of an individual partner must first seek payment of their claims from the individual. If the individual is insolvent, the creditors then have a claim against partnership assets remaining after satisfaction of partnership creditors. This claim is limited to the amount of that partner's equity in the partnership.

The above provisions may be restated from an asset viewpoint. In this form, they are often referred to as the **marshaling of assets rule.**

Assets of the partnership are applied in the following order:
1. Partnership creditors.
2. Creditors of individual partners, but only to the extent of each partner's capital balance.

Assets of the individual partner are applied in the following order:
1. Creditors of the individual partner.
2. Partnership creditors.
3. Other partners (to remedy a capital deficiency).

These priorities agree with the provisions of the Uniform Partnership Act. Under common law and federal bankruptcy law, however, other partners have the same standing as the partner's creditors. In this case, liquidated assets of the individual partner would be applied in the following order:

1. The partner's creditors, including other partners.
2. Partnership creditors.

This sequence is likely to apply in states which have not adopted the Uniform Partnership Act.

Under the *right of offset,* mentioned earlier, loans payable to a partner are offset against a capital deficiency. This effectively gives the other partners first claim on this asset of the deficient partner.[3] As seen above, under either the marshaling of assets rule or federal bankruptcy law, other creditors may rank ahead of the other partners. In cases where the deficient partner is personally insolvent and higher-ranking creditors exist, the above rights of creditors would supersede the other partners' right of offset. Court cases on this matter have not clearly settled the question of the relative standing of creditors. For purposes of our subsequent illustrations and problems, we shall assume that the right of offset is operable.

---

[3]See Stephen A. Zeff, "Right of Offset vs. Partnership Act in Winding-Up Process," *The Accounting Review,* January 1957: 68–70.

Simple versus Installment Liquidations

Liquidation of a partnership may be carried out in several ways. All assets might be sold in a single transaction at a going-business price to a competitor or to others wishing to continue the business. All assets might be sold in a single transaction at distress prices (for example, at a bankruptcy auction). Some assets might be sold individually over a period of time as buyers for specific items are found, while other assets such as receivables and prepayments are liquidated by means other than sale. In this last case, the partners may request distribution of the cash as it becomes available.

The timing of cash distributions to partners influences the accounting procedures. In a **simple liquidation,** all assets are sold before any cash is distributed to partners. An **installment liquidation** occurs if cash is distributed to partners before the sale of assets is complete. Some assets are sold and cash is distributed, then additional assets are sold and more cash is distributed, and so on. The following sections consider first simple liquidations and then installment liquidations.

Simple Liquidations

Determining the distribution of cash to partners of a liquidating partnership can be a straightforward task or a complex one. Liquidation involving sales and payments by installments complicates distribution. Settlement becomes more complex, too, when any partners have capital deficiencies or develop them during the liquidation.

Successful Liquidating Partnerships. We may view a liquidating partnership as "successful" if, in the process of liquidation, all partners receive a return of capital. In other words, the sale of assets results in either a gain or a loss small enough that no capital deficiencies result. In this circumstance, the distribution of cash to outside creditors and to partners is easy to determine.

To illustrate, assume that the JKL partnership has the following balance sheet.

Cash	$12,000	Liabilities	$17,000
All Other Assets	48,000	Capital—J.	21,000
		Capital—K	6,000
		Capital—L	16,000
	$60,000		$60,000

The partners share income in a 2:1:1 ratio (that is, J has a 50 percent share; K and L, 25 percent each). If the other assets are sold for $64,000 and the resulting $16,000 gain is allocated to the partners, the accounts would show:

Cash	$76,000	Liabilities	$17,000
		Capital—J.	29,000
		Capital—K	10,000
		Capital—L	20,000
	$76,000		$76,000

The distribution of the $76,000 would therefore be $17,000 to the outside creditors, $29,000 to J, $10,000 to K, and $20,000 to L.

Unsuccessful Liquidating Partnerships. We may view a liquidating partnership as "unsuccessful" if the losses from the sale of assets result in one or more capital deficiencies. If a partner still has a capital deficiency after offsetting any loans payable to that partner against the capital account, two possibilities exist. One is that the partner is able to contribute sufficient resources to remedy the deficiency. Enough assets would then be available to pay the creditors and the other partners. The other possibility is that the deficient partner is unable to contribute any resources or cannot contribute enough to eliminate the deficiency. In this case, the deficiency must be allocated to the other partners before the assets are distributed.

To illustrate, suppose that the balance sheet of the XYZ partnership appears as follows:

Cash	$ 10,000	Liabilities	$ 20,000
All Other Assets.	100,000	Loan—X	6,000
		Loan—Y	4,000
		Capital—X	41,000
		Capital—Y	10,000
		Capital—Z	29,000
	$110,000		$110,000

The partners share income in a 5:3:2 ratio, respectively. Assume now that the other assets are sold for $30,000. The loss on the sale of $70,000 must be allocated to capital balances:

	Capital Accounts Before Loss	Loss Allocation			Capital Accounts After Loss
Partner X	$41,000	−	(.5 × 70,000)	=	$ 6,000
Partner Y	10,000	−	(.3 × 70,000)	=	(11,000)
Partner Z	29,000	−	(.2 × 70,000)	=	15,000
	$80,000				$10,000

Thus Y has a capital deficiency of $11,000.

First consider the case in which Y is able to contribute additional resources. Since the partnership owes Y $4,000, Y's net deficiency is $7,000. If Y contributes $7,000, and we offset Y's loan against the capital account, the accounts would appear as follows (the cash balance of $47,000 includes the original $10,000, the $30,000 sale proceeds, and Y's investment of $7,000):

Cash	$47,000	Liabilities	$20,000
		Loan—X	6,000
		Capital—X	6,000
		Capital—Y	0
		Capital—Z	15,000
	$47,000		$47,000

The cash should be distributed as follows:

Outside Creditors	$20,000
Partner X	12,000
Partner Y	0
Partner Z	15,000
	$47,000

In contrast, assume that Y is personally insolvent. Recall that the capital accounts after allocation of the loss are: X, $6,000; Y, ($11,000); and Z, $15,000. Y is unable to contribute any resources to remedy the deficiency. The $4,000 owed to Y by the partnership is offset against Y's capital account, reducing the deficiency to $7,000. The accounts now show:

Cash	$40,000	Liabilities	$20,000
		Loan—X	6,000
		Capital—X	6,000
		Capital—Y	(7,000)
		Capital—Z	15,000
	$40,000		$40,000

Since Y is unable to contribute, X and Z must bear this loss. We allocate Y's $7,000 deficiency to X and Z according to their income-sharing ratio (5:2). Thus X bears $5,000 of the loss and Z bears $2,000, and the new account balances are:

Cash	$40,000	Liabilities	$20,000
		Loan—X	6,000
		Capital—X	1,000
		Capital—Y	0
		Capital—Z	13,000
	$40,000		$40,000

The $40,000 cash should be distributed as follows:

Outside Creditors	$20,000
Partner X	7,000
Partner Y	0
Partner Z	13,000
	$40,000

In summary, to account for simple partnership liquidations, we use the following sequence of accounting procedures:

1. Determine the gain or loss on the sale of assets.
2. Allocate the gain or loss to the partners' capital accounts according to the income-sharing ratio.
3. Offset loans against capital accounts in cases where a capital deficiency exists.
4. Record any investments by partners in response to capital deficiencies.

5. Allocate any remaining deficiencies to partners with positive capital account balances. (If this step produces new deficiencies, repeat Steps 3 through 5.)
6. Distribute the cash.

Installment Liquidations

In the preceding sections, we discussed liquidations in which the sale of all assets is completed before any cash is distributed to the partners. In such cases, all gains and losses can be determined and allocated to the partners' capital accounts prior to determining the distribution of cash.

Suppose, however, that the partners request cash distributions before all assets are sold. Since the amount of gains and losses on future sales is unknown, it is not immediately evident how to distribute cash. Clearly, outside creditors have the first claim; they must be paid before any cash is distributed to the partners. We then require a method for determining an equitable plan for distributing cash to the partners. Two general approaches are available: determination of safe payments and preparation of a cash distribution plan.

Safe Payment Approach. The **safe payment approach** is a way of determining how a given amount of cash is to be distributed. The calculation is repeated prior to each distribution. The calculation is based on two simple assumptions—that *all remaining assets will be a total loss* (that is, no more cash will be realized), and that *deficient partners will not contribute additional resources.*

To illustrate, assume that the ABC partnership has decided to terminate business and liquidate its assets. The assets will be sold or otherwise converted into cash over a period of time, and the partners plan to distribute cash as it becomes available. Assume that the balance sheet presently appears as follows:

Cash	$ 3,000	Liabilities	$ 30,000
Receivables	30,000	Loan—A	20,000
Inventory	47,000	Capital—A	86,000
Land	25,000	Capital—B	140,000
Building (Net)	72,000	Capital—C	41,000
Equipment (Net)	140,000		
	$317,000		$317,000

The partners share income in a $4:4:2$ ratio.

Suppose that half of the receivables are collected and that the entire inventory is sold for $35,000. The accounts now show:

Cash	$ 53,000	Liabilities	$ 30,000
Receivables	15,000	Loan—A	20,000
Land	25,000	Capital—A	81,200
Building (Net)	72,000	Capital—B	135,200
Equipment (Net)	140,000	Capital—C	38,600
	$305,000		$305,000

The decrease in the capital accounts represents the allocation of the $12,000 loss on the sale of inventory. If the partners wish to distribute the $53,000, then $30,000 will go to the outside creditors, and $23,000 will be available for the partners. How is this $23,000 to be distributed?

First, we combine the partners' loans with the partners' capital. In this example, the $20,000 loan payable to A is combined with A's capital balance of $81,200. For convenience, we refer to the total of $101,200 as *capital*. Second, we assume that all remaining assets will be a total loss, which is allocated by the income-sharing ratio. These remaining assets—receivables, land, building, and equipment—amount to $252,000. If these do produce a total loss, the partners' capital accounts would be affected as follows:

	Capital Accounts Before Loss	Loss Allocation	Capital Accounts After Loss
Partner A (Includes $20,000 Loan)	$101,200	− (.4 × 252,000) =	$ 400
Partner B	135,200	− (.4 × 252,000) =	34,400
Partner C	38,600	− (.2 × 252,000) =	(11,800)
	$275,000		$23,000

Next, we make the assumption that Partner C is unable to contribute additional capital. We allocate C's deficiency to A and B equally since they have equal income shares. We now have:

	Capital Accounts Before Loss	Loss Allocation	Capital Accounts After Loss
Partner A	$ 400	− (.5 × 11,800) =	$ (5,500)
Partner B	34,400	− (.5 × 11,800) =	28,500
Partner C	(11,800)		0
	$23,000		$23,000

We also make the assumption that A is also unable to contribute additional capital, and we allocate the entire deficiency to B, leading to the following capital balances:

Partner A	$ 0
Partner B	23,000
Partner C	0
	$23,000

The $23,000 will therefore be distributed entirely to Partner B. This is called a **safe payment** because it is based on the worst possible circumstances, namely that no more cash will be generated by the sale of assets and that deficient partners will be unable to contribute additional capital. If additional expenses are anticipated as part of the liquidation process, these should also be included in the loss allocation.

Following distribution of the $53,000 to the creditors and to Partner B, the accounts show:

Receivables.	$ 15,000	Loan—A	$ 20,000
Land	25,000	Capital—A	81,200
Building (Net)	72,000	Capital—B	112,200
Equipment (Net).	140,000	Capital—C	38,600
	$252,000		$252,000

When the next stage in the liquidation is complete and more cash becomes available for distribution, the next safe payment can be computed. Assume that receivables of $6,000 are collected, the remaining receivables are deemed uncollectible, and the equipment is sold for $90,000. Recording these transactions, including allocation to the partners of the $9,000 loss on receivables and the $50,000 loss on sale of equipment, yields:

Cash	$ 96,000	Loan—A	$ 20,000
Land	25,000	Capital—A	57,600
Building (Net)	72,000	Capital—B	88,600
		Capital—C	26,800
	$193,000		$193,000

As before, assume no recovery of the remaining assets and allocate this potential loss to the partners as shown below:

	Capital Accounts Before Loss	Loss Allocation		Capital Accounts After Loss
Partner A (Includes $20,000 Loan).	$ 77,600	− (.4 × 97,000)	=	$38,800
Partner B.	88,600	− (.4 × 97,000)	=	49,800
Partner C.	26,800	− (.2 × 97,000)	=	7,400
	$193,000			$96,000

Since no capital deficiencies result, the $96,000 is distributed thus: $38,800 to A, $49,800 to B, and $7,400 to C. This process would continue until the liquidation is complete.

The safe payment approach to cash distribution is a fairly easy procedure. Its main disadvantages are that (1) new calculations must be made for each distribution and (2) no information on future distributions is provided. The cash distribution plan remedies these disadvantages.

Cash Distribution Plan. Rather than recalculating payments during the liquidation process, we can develop a comprehensive **cash distribution plan.** Once this plan is prepared, we merely refer to it to determine how available cash is to be distributed.

The balances of the partners' capital accounts continue to be the focus for determining cash distributions. Throughout partnership accounting, we have noted that partners' shares of net assets and profit shares are not necessarily the same. Development of a cash distribution plan is based on the concept of adjusting capital balances to the income-sharing ratio.

We can illustrate this concept with a simple example. Suppose Black and Jones share profits and losses equally, but Black's capital account has a balance of $45,000, while Jones's has a balance of $30,000. Despite the fact that they are equal partners, Black has more capital, due to Black's either investing more or withdrawing less than Jones. Fairness suggests that when liquidating the partnership Black should receive $15,000 before Jones receives anything so as to equalize their capital positions. Once Black's capital is reduced to $30,000, they should share any remaining cash equally. Thus we have developed a cash distribution plan for this simple situation:

1. All liabilities are paid.
2. Black receives the next $15,000.
3. Any further distributions are divided equally between Black and Jones.

Where several partners with different income shares are liquidating their partnership by installments, derivation of the cash distribution plan requires a more formal approach. The logic is the same as in the simple example above: cash should be distributed so as to bring the capital accounts of the partners into proper alignment with respect to each other. This means that the partner having the largest capital balance relative to his or her income percentage will be the first to receive cash. In the preceding example, Black, with a 60 percent capital share and a 50 percent income percentage, received the first distribution. After all the imbalances in relative capital have been remedied, subsequent distributions are made to *all* partners in proportion to their income percentages. The approach we shall follow is:

1. Standardize the capital relationship among the partners by dividing each capital balance by that partner's income-sharing ratio. The standardized capital balance is an indicator of each partner's ability to absorb losses that may occur during liquidation. The bigger the standardized capital balance, the greater is that partner's ability to absorb losses before his or her capital balance is eliminated.
2. Equalize the standardized capital figures in steps. Begin with the largest, and determine the adjustment (subtraction) necessary to equalize it with the next largest. Continue this process until all standardized capital figures are equal. The equalization adjustments signify the *incremental* amount of loss which can be absorbed by partners with larger standardized capital balances over and above what can be absorbed by partners with smaller balances.
3. Convert the equalization adjustments back into terms of the respective partners' capital accounts by multiplying each adjustment by that partner's income-sharing ratio. This gives the amounts and priorities of cash distributions to the partners.
4. Organize the results of Step 3 into a cash distribution plan. Remember to provide first for the payment of amounts due to all outside creditors.

To illustrate the preparation of a cash distribution plan, consider again the ABC partnership discussed in the previous section. At the beginning of the liquidation process, the right-hand side of the balance sheet showed:

Liabilities	$ 30,000
Loan—A.	20,000
Capital—A.	86,000
Capital—B.	140,000
Capital—C.	41,000
	$317,000

The partners share income in a $4:4:2$ ratio. As before, A's capital of $86,000 and loan of $20,000 will be combined.

First, standardize the capital accounts by dividing actual capital by the income-sharing ratio:

	Actual Capital	Income Ratio	Standardized Capital
Partner A.	$106,000	.4	$265,000
Partner B.	140,000	.4	350,000
Partner C.	41,000	.2	205,000

This calculation tells us that when we standardize for the different income shares, Partner B has the greatest amount of capital, and Partner C has the least. In other words, Partner B can absorb the greatest amount of loss, and Partner C the least amount. It is reasonable to expect that B will receive money first, then A, then finally C.

Second, equalize the standardized capital figures, starting with the largest:

	Partner A	Partner B	Partner C
Standardized Capital.	$265,000	$350,000	$205,000
a. Equalize A with B .		(85,000)	
	$265,000	$265,000	$205,000
b. Equalize A and B with C	(60,000)	(60,000)	
	$205,000	$205,000	$205,000

This process is repeated in steps, noted a and b above, until all partners are equalized. The number of steps will be, at most, one less than the number of partners.

Third, convert these adjustments back into terms of the capital accounts as follows:

	Partner A	Partner B	Partner C
Step a.		$85,000 × .4 = $34,000	—
Step b.	$60,000 × .4 = $24,000	$60,000 × .4 = $24,000	—

This calculation indicates that after the $30,000 of liabilities are paid, Partner B should receive $34,000, and then Partners A and B should each receive $24,000. At this point, the relative capital balances of each partner would be equal, and any further distributions of cash should be made according to the partners' profit-sharing ratios $(4:4:2)$.

A worksheet combining the second and third steps is shown in Exhibit 3.2. The left side of the worksheet shows the equalization of standardized capital. The

Exhibit 3.2   Worksheet for Cash Distribution Plan

	Equalization of Standardized Capital				Actual Capital Accounts and Cash Distributions		
	Partner A	**Partner B**	**Partner C**		**Partner A (40%)**	**Partner B (40%)**	**Partner C (20%)**
Standardized Capital	$265,000	$350,000	$205,000	Actual Capital	$106,000	$140,000	$41,000
a. Equalize A with B		(85,000)				(34,000)	
	$265,000	$265,000	$205,000		$106,000	$106,000	$41,000
b. Equalize A and B with C	(60,000)	(60,000)			(24,000)	(24,000)	
	$205,000	$205,000	$205,000		$ 82,000	$ 82,000	$41,000
				Capital Share	40%	40%	20%

right side shows the conversion back into terms of the partners' actual capital account balances. The figures on the left side are multiplied by the respective income percentages to get the figures on the right side. Note that the adjustments which equalize the standardized capital translate into cash distributions that bring the partners' capital accounts into line with the income-sharing ratio.

Fourth, organize the results into a formal cash distribution plan, such as that shown in Exhibit 3.3. The plan shows how to distribute any amount of cash which becomes available. Remember that distributions are cumulative; that is, each distribution starts where the previous one ended.

To illustrate application of the plan, recall that we previously calculated the proper distribution of $53,000 and $96,000, proceeds from the liquidation of the ABC Partnership, using the safe payment approach. We now apply the cash distribution plan to these amounts to verify the results.

First, the $53,000 is considered. The cash distribution plan states that the first $30,000 is paid to creditors and the next $34,000 is paid to Partner B. A distribution of $53,000 permits us to complete the first step (to pay the creditors $30,000) and to partially complete the second step (to pay Partner B $23,000 of the required $34,000). Thus the $53,000 would be distributed:

Creditors.	$30,000
Partner B	23,000
	$53,000

Exhibit 3.3   ABC Partnership Cash Distribution Plan

Step	Amount	Distribution
1	First $30,000	Creditors
2	Next $34,000	Partner B
3	Next $48,000	Partners A and B in equal amounts
4	Any further amount	Partners A, B, and C in 4:4:2 ratio

Next, we had $96,000 to distribute. We must complete the second step of the plan (to pay Partner B an additional $11,000) before moving on to the third step. Following the cash distribution plan, we get:

1. Pay $11,000 to Partner B to complete the second step, leaving $85,000 (= $96,000 − $11,000) available to distribute.
2. Divide the next $48,000 equally between A and B, thus completing the third step of the plan. Left to distribute is $37,000.
3. Divide the $37,000 among A, B, and C in a 4:4:2 ratio, as specified by the fourth and final step of the plan.

The proper distribution of the $96,000 is summarized here:

			Distribution	
Step	Amount	Partner A	Partner B	Partner C
2	$11,000	$ 0	$11,000	$ 0
3	48,000	24,000	24,000	0
4	37,000	14,800	14,800	7,400
	$96,000	$38,800	$49,800	$7,400

Observe that this result is identical to that achieved by the safe payment approach.

Not all available cash need be distributed. Cash may be retained for anticipated liquidation expenses or other purposes. The approach discussed above would be applied to the amount of cash to be distributed. Occasionally, temporary deviations from the cash distribution plan may occur. For example, a specific asset may be distributed to a partner in lieu of cash, and the value of the asset may exceed the amount to which that partner is entitled. Subsequent distributions must be adjusted in favor of other partners until the excess is absorbed. For example, assume the following cash distribution plan:

Step	Amount	Distribution
1	First $10,000	Creditors
2	Next $16,000	Partner A
3	Next $30,000	Partners A and B in 2:1 ratio
4	Any further amount	Partners A, B, and C in 6:3:1 ratio

Suppose that at Step 3, in lieu of $10,000 cash, B receives a truck worth $14,200. In effect, B has received an advance of the Step 4 distribution, and appropriate distributions to A and C in a 6:1 ratio must be made before continuing the 6:3:1 distribution in step 4. The excess distribution of $4,200 (= 3 × $1,400) to B must be remedied in Step 4 by distributing $8,400 (= 6 × $1,400) to A and $1,400 (= 1 × $1,400) to C before B receives any further payment.

The derivation of the cash distribution plan has been described in terms of standardizing the capital accounts of the various partners and then distributing cash in such a way as to equalize their relative capital. The derivation may also be described in terms of **loss-absorption ability.** The procedures remain the same, but the numbers take on an alternative meaning. Exhibit 3.2 indicates that the result of dividing each partner's capital balance by the appropriate income share is the maximum loss that the partnership could incur without an individual partner's capital becoming negative. For example, Partner A has capital of $106,000 and an income share of 40 percent. Dividing yields $265,000. If the partnership incurred a $265,000 loss, A's share would be 40 percent or $106,000, which would wipe out A's capital. Thus the $265,000 may be viewed as A's maximum ability to absorb losses. The partner whose ability to absorb losses is largest is in the strongest position and should receive the first distribution. We proceed to equalize the loss absorption abilities in the same manner as described earlier.

In accounting for partnership liquidations, the accountant must ensure an equitable distribution of partnership assets. Consideration must be given to actual and prospective losses on the sale of assets and to the potential inability of partners to remedy capital deficiencies. These factors are considered, either directly or indirectly, in the two procedures discussed for installment liquidations—the safe payment approach and the cash distribution plan.

Use of the Partnership Form of Business Organization

The partnership form of business organization is usually associated with small business. One typically thinks of a partnership as an association of a very small number of individuals (often two or three) operating a relatively small firm. In some professions—especially accounting and law—we find large firms organized as partnerships, largely because of historical impediments to organizing these activities as corporations. In other areas of endeavor—such as manufacturing or retailing—it is rare to find a large firm organized as a partnership. While the image of the partnership as being almost exclusively related to small business is generally correct, recent years have seen the partnership form of business organization increasingly used in other contexts. In this section, we briefly discuss joint ventures and limited partnerships.

Joint Ventures

A **joint venture** is an entity formed by two or more other entities to carry out a single transaction or activity, usually over a limited period of time. Frequently, the partners in a joint venture are themselves large firms; they may be either partnerships or corporations. They form the joint venture for some activity wherein it is mutually desirable to combine expertise, special technology, capital, and/or access to certain markets. Examples include research projects, or development of new products, in which two areas of technology must be joined, or large-scale construction projects, in which the capital and facilities of two or more contractors may be needed. In many cases, the joint venture is relatively short lived, although in some cases an initial project may lead to an ongoing business activity.

No particular accounting problems are posed by joint ventures. A joint venture may have the legal form of a partnership or a corporation; in either case, partnership accounting principles are relevant. The agreement between the parties should clearly specify how costs or profits are to be shared, and how any remaining assets are to be distributed upon termination. Owners of the joint venture usually account for their investments by the equity method. In most cases, the number of owners is small (often two or three), and the 20 percent ownership threshold for use of the equity method is easily met. *APBO 18* specifies use of the equity method for investments in joint ventures organized as corporations;[4] it is commonly also used for joint ventures organized as partnerships.

Limited Partnerships

A **limited partnership** consists of at least one general partner who has all the usual characteristics of a partner, and one or more limited partners who are essentially investors only. The limited partners have no role in management, and their liability is limited to their capital balances. The limited partnership interests are typically freely transferable in the same manner as shares of stock, assuming a market exists. Limited partnerships are often used for investment programs, especially tax shelters. **Tax shelters** are investments which usually possess one or more of the following characteristics:

1. Creation of tax-deductible losses by various tax-accounting rules, such as fast depreciation write-offs, immediate expensing of costs having long-term benefit (research and development, intangible drilling costs for oil and gas), or creation of tax credits (investment tax credit, rehabilitation credits).
2. Concentration of tax losses in the early years of the investment.
3. Aggregate tax losses possibly exceeding the amount invested. (Recall, from the Appendix to Chapter 2, that a partner's tax basis is the capital account plus the partner's share of liabilities.) Ability to deduct excess losses has been restricted in recent years to the amount for which the partner is economically ''at risk.''
4. Eventual profit from the investment qualifying for favorable tax treatment as a capital gain.

To illustrate, assume that a real estate investment is structured as a limited partnership. A **promoter,** who typically also serves as the general partner, enters into a contract to buy a property—for example, a shopping center. As with most real estate, much of the purchase is to be financed by mortgage debt. For the equity portion, the promoter sells a number of limited partnership interests. Money received from the investors is used for the down payment, closing costs on the property (legal fees, commissions, and so on), working capital to meet initial operating costs, and compensation of the promoter. The partnership agreement typically provides (1) that virtually all of the annual profits or losses (usually losses, because of the relatively short depreciable lives available under current tax law) are allocated to the limited partners, and (2) that the eventual gain on the sale of the property is shared in some way by the general partner and the limited partners.

---

[4]Accounting Principles Board, *Opinion No. 18,* par. 16; CT § 182.103, 182.508–512.

The limited partnership form has several attractions as a vehicle for investment programs. The investor's risk is limited, and the partnership form allows the pass-through of tax losses to the individual partners to be offset against other sources of taxable income. Also, many limited partnerships fall under the "small offering" provisions of the SEC, exempting them from the full SEC registration process. Limited partnerships have long been used for investments in real estate, oil and gas exploration, and farming (e.g., cattle breeding). In recent years, new areas such as research and development have emerged as investments in limited partnership form.

Again, no new accounting problems are introduced by limited partnerships. Note that there are two classes of partners—general and limited. Formation of the partnership is typically recorded on the basis of amounts invested. Because limited partners generally invest cash in equal amounts, there are no valuation or bonus/goodwill adjustments needed. The general partner often makes little or no tangible investment; possibly goodwill may be recorded to reflect the general partner's intangible services in organizing the venture. Income allocation is governed by the partnership agreement, which may provide any one of a variety of possibilities of how income is to be divided between the general partner and the limited partners. The agreement further governs how liquidation proceeds are to be allocated between the general partner and the limited partners.

Summary of Key Concepts

The interest of a **retiring partner** may be purchased with the **individual assets of one or more of the remaining partners** or with **partnership assets.** In the latter case, the **bonus, partial goodwill,** or **total goodwill** approach is used to account for any difference between the payment to the retiring partner and the amount of the retiring partner's capital account.

If the partnership is to be **liquidated,** the rights of creditors are usually based on the **marshaling of assets rule.** Partners' loans and capital balances may be combined under the **right of offset.** If an individual partner has a **capital deficiency,** that partner is obligated to contribute additional assets to the partnership to remedy the deficiency; if this is impossible, the deficiency is allocated to the other partners.

In a **simple liquidation,** all assets are sold before any cash is distributed to the partners. In an **installment liquidation,** cash distributions occur before the sale of assets is complete. Under an installment liquidation, the equitable division of each cash distribution among the partners may be based on either the **safe payment approach** or the **cash distribution plan.**

Questions

Q3.1 How do the concepts of legal and economic entity relate to a partnership that continues after the retirement of one partner?

Q3.2 Identify the differences in accounting for retirement of a partner when the retiree's partnership interest is purchased (1) with personal assets of one or more existing partners and (2) with partnership assets.

Q3.3 Cite several techniques for valuing a retiring partner's interest in the partnership.

Q3.4 Upon what assumption is the goodwill method of accounting for partnership retirements based? How does this reasoning apply to the partial and total goodwill approaches?

Q3.5 What is meant by *right of offset* in accounting for partnership liquidations?

Q3.6 Assume that a partnership is being liquidated and that the obligations to creditors exceed the assets of the partnership. What, if any, rights do the creditors have in attempting to collect the full amount owed them?

Q3.7 In partnership accounting, what is the difference between a simple liquidation and an installment liquidation?

Q3.8 Discuss the procedure followed in accounting for simple partnership liquidations.

Q3.9 What advantage does the cash distribution plan have over the safe payment approach in determining cash payments to partners during liquidation? How do the results of the two approaches differ?

Q3.10 What purpose do the safe payment approach and the cash distribution plan serve during partnership liquidation? Why is this important?

Q3.11 A large company is developing a new product involving an area of technology in which it has little experience. Why might this company consider forming a joint venture with another (noncompeting) company having expertise in that technology?

Q3.12 Why is the limited partnership form, rather than the regular partnership form or the corporate form, often used for real estate investments?

Exercises

E3.1 On June 30, 19X8, the balance sheet for the partnership of Winston, Barker, and Langley, together with the partners' respective income-sharing ratios, was as follows:

Assets, at Cost	$300,000
Loan—Winston	$ 15,000
Capital—Winston (20%)	70,000
Capital—Barker (20%)	65,000
Capital—Langley (60%)	150,000
	$300,000

Winston has decided to retire from the partnership, and by mutual agreement the assets are to be adjusted to their fair value of $360,000 at June 30,

19X8. It was agreed that the partnership would pay Winston $102,000 cash for his partnership interest exclusive of his loan, which is to be repaid in full. *No* goodwill is to be recorded in this transaction.

Required: After Winston's retirement, what are the capital account balances of Barker and Langley, respectively? *(AICPA adapted)*

E3.2 James Dixon, a partner in an accounting firm, decided to withdraw from the partnership. Dixon's share of the partnership profits or losses was 20 percent. Upon withdrawing from the partnership, he was paid $74,000 in final settlement for his interest. The total of the partners' capital accounts before recognition of partnership goodwill prior to Dixon's withdrawal was $210,000. After his withdrawal, the remaining partners' capital accounts, excluding their share of goodwill, totaled $160,000.

Required: What was the total agreed-upon goodwill of the firm? *(AICPA adapted)*

E3.3 Baxter is planning to retire from the partnership of Baxter, Helman, and Caines. The partners' income-sharing ratio is $2:1:1$. Helman and Caines will continue as a partnership, sharing profits and losses equally. The partners are considering various ways to pay Baxter $90,000, which is the fair market value of her interest in the business. Prior to retirement, Baxter's capital account balance is $70,000.

Required: Prepare the journal entry to record Baxter's retirement on the partnership books under each of the following assumptions:

1. Helman and Caines each pay Baxter $45,000 from personal funds.
2. Partnership cash is used to pay Baxter. The bonus method is followed.
3. Partnership cash is used to pay Baxter. The total goodwill approach is followed.
4. Partnership cash is used to pay Baxter. The partial goodwill approach is followed.
5. Helman and Caines each pay Baxter $10,000 from personal funds; the rest is paid with partnership cash.

E3.4 The following balance sheet is for the LMN partnership. The partners (L, M, and N) share profits and losses in the ratio of $5:3:2$, respectively.

Cash.	$ 30,000	Liabilities	$ 70,000
Other Assets.	270,000	Capital—L.	140,000
		Capital—M	80,000
		Capital—N.	10,000
	$300,000		$300,000

Assume that L, M, and N have agreed to liquidate the partnership by selling the other assets.

Required: What should each of the partners receive if the other assets are sold for $200,000? *(AICPA adapted)*

E3.5 The following condensed balance sheet is presented for the partnership of Bond, Whit, and Tell, who share profits and losses in the ratio of 5:3:2, respectively:

Cash.	$120,000	Liabilities	$240,000
Other Assets.	600,000	Capital—Bond.	300,000
		Capital—Whit	160,000
		Capital—Tell.	20,000
	$720,000		$720,000

Required:

1. Assume that the assets and liabilities are fairly valued on the balance sheet, and that the partnership decided to admit Eller as a new partner with a one-fifth interest. No goodwill or bonus is to be recorded. How much should Eller contribute?
2. Assume that instead of admitting a new partner, the partners decided to liquidate the partnership. If the other assets are sold for $460,000, how much of the available cash should be distributed to Bond? *(AICPA adapted)*

E3.6 The following condensed balance sheet is presented for the partnership of Cooke, Dorry, and Evans, who share profits and losses in the ratio of 4:3:3, respectively:

Cash.	$ 90,000	Accounts Payable	$210,000
Other Assets.	820,000	Loan—Evans	40,000
Loan—Cooke	30,000	Capital—Cooke	300,000
		Capital—Dorry.	200,000
		Capital—Evans	190,000
	$940,000		$940,000

Required:

1. Assume that the assets and liabilities are fairly valued on the balance sheet and the partnership decides to admit Fisher as a new partner with a one-fourth interest. No goodwill or bonus is to be recorded. How much should Fisher contribute in cash or other assets?
2. Assume that instead of admitting a new partner, the partners decide to liquidate the partnership. If the other assets are sold for $600,000, how much of the available cash should be distributed to Cooke? *(AICPA adapted)*

E3.7 The following are data for the AB Partnership and for A and B as individuals. Assume that A and B are equal partners.

AB Partnership	Case 1	Case 2
Assets.	$48,000	$ 31,000
Liabilities	42,000	51,000
Capital—A	3,000	(8,000)
Capital—B	3,000	(12,000)
Partner A		
Assets.	10,000	30,000
Liabilities	17,000	17,000
Partner B		
Assets.	50,000	15,000
Liabilities	9,000	16,000

Required: For each case, following the marshaling of assets rule, indicate how the assets of the partnership and the assets of each partner would be applied if creditor claims were to be satisfied as fully as possible.

E3.8 Partners James, Storm, and Hadley share profits and losses in the ratio of 5:3:2, respectively. The partners vote to dissolve the partnership when its assets, liabilities, and capital are as follows:

Cash.	$ 40,000	Liabilities	$ 60,000
Other Assets.	210,000	Capital—James	48,000
		Capital—Storm	72,000
		Capital—Hadley.	70,000
	$250,000		$250,000

The partnership will be liquidated over a prolonged period of time. As cash becomes available, it will be distributed to the partners. The first sale of noncash assets having a book value of $120,000 realizes $90,000.

Required: How much cash should be distributed to each partner after this sale? *(AICPA adapted)*

E3.9 Conley, Lewis, and Miller have decided to liquidate their partnership. The records show the following balances:

Cash.	$ 10,000	Liabilities	$ 30,000
Receivables	50,000	Capital—Conley.	270,000
Inventory	130,000	Capital—Lewis	80,000
Equipment (Net).	200,000	Capital—Miller.	10,000
	$390,000		$390,000

The partners share income in a 7:2:1 ratio, respectively. Assume that the entire inventory is sold for $90,000 and that the partners wish to distribute the $100,000 which is now available.

Required: Determine how the $100,000 should be divided among the three partners.

E3.10 The partnership of Jones, Brown, and Smith is to be liquidated. The partners share income equally. Each partner has a capital balance of $15,000, and the balance sheet shows liabilities of the partnership as $25,000.

Required: Devise a plan for distribution of cash as it becomes available during the liquidation.

E3.11 Partners Whitehead, Ellis, and Riley had capital accounts of $72,000, $60,000, and $65,000, respectively, on the date liquidation proceedings for their partnership began. Liabilities at that date were $32,000. The partners had shared income in a 3:5:2 ratio.

Required: Prepare a plan for distribution of cash received during liquidation.

E3.12 1368 Main Associates is formed as a limited partnership to acquire and operate an apartment building. A promoter/general partner, who makes a $2,000 investment, sells 15 limited partnership interests for $10,000 each. The building costs $850,000; a down payment of $100,000 is made, with the remaining $750,000 financed via a 20-year mortgage. The general partner is paid $40,000 for services; this amount is to be expensed. Net loss for the first year, exclusive of the payment to the general partner, is $14,000; all items except depreciation of $37,500 are assumed to be cash transactions. Also, a payment of $20,000 is made on the principal of the mortgage. The partnership agreement provides that income is to be allocated 10 percent to the general partner and 90 percent to the limited partners.

Required: Prepare a balance sheet for the partnership at the end of its first year of operation.

Problems

P3.1 Retirement of Partner   Horton, Fischer, and Walker are partners in a trucking firm. They share income in a 3:4:2 ratio, respectively. On March 8, the date of Fischer's retirement from the partnership, the balances of the partners' capital accounts are Horton, $35,000; Fischer, $15,000; and Walker, $21,000. Fischer has agreed to surrender his interest to Horton and Walker (who plan to continue the business) for $18,000 and a pick-up truck owned by the partnership. The cash payment is to be made from partnership funds. The truck cost $8,000 and has accumulated depreciation of $5,000. Fair value of the used truck is $3,900.

Required: Make the entries to record Fischer's retirement and compute the capital balances for Horton and Walker after the retirement (1) under the bonus approach and (2) under the partial goodwill approach.

P3.2 Retirement of Two Partners   Thirty years ago, five mechanics formed a partnership and established an automobile repair shop. Two of the partners,

Dewitt and Galax, are now retiring. The other three partners, Farber, Wayne, and Lane, are continuing the partnership. The original agreement called for an equal division of income. The remaining partners plan to continue this arrangement.

The following balance sheet has been prepared for the partnership as of the date of retirement:

Cash.	$ 65,000	Accounts Payable	$ 90,000
Accounts Receivable	80,000	Loan Payable	40,000
Inventory of Parts	40,000	Capital—Dewitt	50,000
Equipment (Net)	90,000	Capital—Galax	40,000
Building (Net)	30,000	Capital—Farber	70,000
Land.	25,000	Capital—Wayne	7,500
		Capital—Lane	32,500
	$330,000		$330,000

All partners have agreed that Dewitt should receive $62,500 for his interest in the business and Galax should receive $50,000. Farber has proposed the bonus method for recording the retirements. Wayne objects to this method and has suggested the partial goodwill approach.

Required:

1. Prepare the journal entry to record the retirements under the bonus method.
2. Prepare the journal entry to record the retirements under the partial goodwill approach.
3. Why is Wayne objecting to the bonus method of accounting?
4. Regardless of the accounting method employed, what immediate problem for the business can you identify at the time of retirement? Propose a solution to this problem.

P3.3 Retirement—Various Cases Given below are account balances for the partnership of Flint, Yancy, and Goldsmith before the retirement of Goldsmith. Each case presents account balances of the Flint and Yancy partnership immediately after Goldsmith's retirement. The cases are independent of each other. In Case 4, no bonus was recorded.

Balance Sheet Accounts	Balances before Goldsmith's Retirement	Balances after Goldsmith's Retirement				
		Case 1	Case 2	Case 3	Case 4	Case 5
Cash	$ 50,000	$ 20,000	$ 0	$ 50,000	$ 50,000	$ 0
Other Assets	130,000	130,000	130,000	130,000	100,000	130,000
Goodwill	10,000	10,000	20,000	10,000	10,000	40,000
Liabilities	(70,000)	(70,000)	(70,000)	(70,000)	(70,000)	(70,000)
Capital—Flint	(40,000)	(45,000)	(40,000)	(80,000)	(45,000)	(50,000)
Capital—Yancy	(40,000)	(45,000)	(40,000)	(40,000)	(45,000)	(50,000)
Capital—Goldsmith	(40,000)	—	—	—	—	—

Required: For each independent case, answer the following questions. Show supporting calculations.

1. What method of accounting was used to record the retirement (bonus, goodwill, neither)?
2. How much did Goldsmith receive upon retirement?

P3.4 Partnership Agreement—Payments to Estates of Deceased Partners
The partnership agreement of Lee, Perng, Quinn, Robin, and Schwartz contained a buy and sell agreement, among numerous other provisions, which would become operative in case of the death of any partner. Some provisions contained in the buy and sell agreement were as follows:

1. Purposes of the Buy and Sell Agreement
   a. The partners mutually desire that the business shall be continued by the survivors without interruption or liquidation upon the death of one of the partners.
   b. The partners also mutually desire that the deceased partner's estate shall receive the full value of the deceased partner's interest in the partnership and that the estate shall share in the earnings of the partnership until the deceased partner's interest shall be fully purchased by the surviving partners.
2. Purchase and Sale of Deceased Partner's Interest
   a. Upon the death of the partner first to die, the partnership shall continue to operate without dissolution.
   b. Upon the decedent's death, the survivors shall purchase and the executor or administrator of the deceased partner's estate shall sell to the surviving partners the deceased partner's interest in the partnership for the price and upon the terms and conditions hereinafter set forth.
   c. The deceased partner's estate shall retain the deceased partner's interest until the amount specified in the next paragraph shall be paid in full by the surviving partners.
   d. The parties agree that the purchase price for the partnership interest shall be an amount equal to the deceased partner's capital account at the date of death. Said amount shall be paid to the legal representative of decedent as follows:
      i. The first installment of 30 percent of said capital account shall be paid within 60 days from the date of death of the partner or within 30 days from the date on which the personal representative of decedent becomes qualified by law, whichever date is later, and
      ii. The balance shall be due in four equal installments, which shall be due and payable annually on the anniversary date of said death.
3. Deceased Partner's Estate's Share of the Earnings
   a. The partners mutually desire that the deceased partner's estate shall be guaranteed a share in the earnings of the partnership over the period said estate retains an interest in the partnership. Said estate shall not be deemed to have an interest in the partnership after the final installment for the deceased partner's capital account is paid, even though a portion of the guaranteed payments specified below may be unpaid and may be due and owing.

b. The deceased partner's estate's guaranteed share of the earnings of the partnership shall be determined from two items and shall be paid at different times as follows:

 i. First, interest shall be paid on the unpaid balance of the deceased partner's capital account at the same date the installment on the purchase price is paid. The amount to be paid shall be an amount equal to accrued interest at the rate of 6 percent per annum on the unpaid balance of the purchase price for the deceased partner's capital account.

 ii. Second, the parties agree that the balance of the guaranteed payment from the partnership earnings shall be an amount equal to 25 percent of the deceased partner's share of the aggregate gross receipts of the partnership for the full 36 months preceding the month of the partner's death. Said amount shall be payable in 48 equal monthly installments without interest, and the first payment shall be made within 60 days following the death of the partner or within 30 days from the date on which the personal representative of deceased becomes qualified, whichever date is later; provided, however, that the payments so made under this provision during any 12-month period shall not exceed the highest annual salary on a calendar-year basis received by the partner for the 3 calendar years immediately preceding the date of his death. In the event that said payment would exceed said salary, then an amount per month shall be paid which does not so exceed said highest monthly salary, and the term over which payments shall be paid to the beneficiary shall be lengthened out beyond the said 48 months in order to complete said payment.

Lee and Schwartz were both killed simultaneously in an automobile accident on January 10, 19X6. The surviving partners notified the executors of both estates that the first payment due under the buy and sell agreement would be paid on March 10, 19X6, and that subsequent payments would be paid on the tenth day of each month as due.

The following information was determined from the partnership's records:

Partner	Income-Sharing Ratio	Capital Account on January 10, 19X6	Annual Salaries to Partners by Years		
			19X3	19X4	19X5
Lee	30	$25,140	$16,500	$17,000	$17,400
Perng	25	21,970	15,000	15,750	16,500
Quinn	20	4,780	12,000	13,000	14,000
Robin	15	5,860	9,600	10,800	12,000
Schwartz . . .	10	2,540	8,400	9,600	10,800

The partnership's gross receipts for the 3 prior years were:

19X3	$296,470
19X4	325,310
19X5	363,220

Required: Prepare a schedule of the amounts to be paid to the Lee estate and to the Schwartz estate in March 19X6, December 19X6, and January 19X7. The schedule should identify the amounts attributable to earnings and to interest in the guaranteed payments and to capital. Supporting computations should be in good form. *(AICPA adapted)*

P3.5 Partnership Admission and Liquidation The following balance sheet is for the partnership of Alex, Stanley, and George (figures shown parenthetically reflect agreed income-sharing ratio):

Cash.	$ 20,000	Liabilities	$ 50,000
Other Assets.	180,000	Capital—Alex (40%).	37,000
		Capital—Stanley (40%)	65,000
		Capital—George (20%)	48,000
	$200,000		$200,000

Required:

1. If the assets are fairly valued on the balance sheet and the partnership wishes to admit Day as a new partner having a one-sixth interest without recording goodwill or bonus, how much cash or other assets should Day contribute?

2. If assets on the initial balance sheet are fairly valued, Alex and Stanley consent, and Day pays George $51,000 for his interest, what would the revised capital balances of the partners be?

3. If the firm, as shown on the original balance sheet, is dissolved and liquidated by selling assets in installments, the first sale of noncash assets, having a book value of $90,000, realized $50,000, and all cash available after settlement with creditors is distributed, how much cash would the respective partners receive (to the nearest dollar)?

4. If the facts are as in No. 3 above, except that $3,000 cash is to be withheld for expenses of liquidation, the respective partners would then receive how much cash (to the nearest dollar)?

5. Assume that each partner properly received some cash in the distribution after the second sale, the cash to be distributed amounts to $12,000 from the third sale, and unsold assets with an $8,000 book value remain. Ignoring Nos. 3 and 4 above, which of the following would the respective partners receive?
   a. Alex, $4,800; Stanley, $4,800; George, $2,400.
   b. Alex, $4,000; Stanley, $4,000; George, $4,000.
   c. Alex, 37/150 of $12,000; Stanley, 65/150 of $12,000; George, 48/150 of $12,000.
   d. Alex, $0; Stanley, $8,000; George, $4,000.
   (AICPA adapted)

P3.6 Partnership Liquidation—Safe Payment Several years ago, Judith Able, Leslie Bowen, Janice Cratz, and Donna Ogleby formed a partnership to operate the Abco Delicatessen. Rerouting of bus lines caused declines in patronage to the extent that the partners have agreed to dissolve the partnership and liquidate the assets.

The November 2, 19X0, balance sheet of the Abco Delicatessen and other data are given below. The partnership agreement did not specify how profits and losses were to be shared.

ABCO DELICATESSEN
BALANCE SHEET
NOVEMBER 2, 19X0

Cash	$30,000	Liabilities	$40,000
Supplies	14,000	Loan—Ogleby	13,000
Equipment	35,000	Capital—Able	16,000
Fixtures	15,000	Capital—Bowen	7,000
		Capital—Cratz	3,000
		Capital—Ogleby	15,000
	$94,000		$94,000

Additional information:

1. During November, half of the fixtures were sold for $4,000. Equipment with a book value of $9,000 was sold for $4,000.
2. During December, all outside creditors were paid. A neighboring restaurant bought Abco Delicatessen's supplies at 85 percent of cost. The remaining fixtures were sold for $3,100.
3. During January, equipment with a book value of $6,000 was sold for $4,500.

Required: Following the safe payment approach, specify how cash is to be distributed at the end of November, December, and January.

P3.7 Partnership Liquidation—Cash Distribution Plan Using the data in P3.6, develop a cash distribution plan for the liquidation of Abco Delicatessen. Show each step in the development of the plan.

P3.8 Safe Payment Plan On January 1, 19X2, the partners of Allen, Brown, and Cox, who share income in the ratio of $5:3:2$, respectively, decide to liquidate their partnership. The partnership trial balance at this date is as follows:

	Debit	Credit
Cash	$ 18,000	
Accounts Receivable	66,000	
Inventory	52,000	
Machinery and Equipment (Net)	189,000	
Loan—Allen	30,000	
Accounts Payable		$ 53,000
Loan—Brown		20,000
Capital—Allen		118,000
Capital—Brown		90,000
Capital—Cox		74,000
	$355,000	$355,000

The partners plan a program of piecemeal conversion of assets in order to minimize liquidation losses. All available cash, less an amount retained to provide for future expenses, is to be distributed to the partners at the end of each month. A summary of the liquidation transactions is as follows:

January 19X2

a. $51,000 was collected on accounts receivable; the balance is uncollectible.
b. $38,000 was received for the entire inventory.
c. $2,000 liquidation expenses were paid.
d. $50,000 was paid to outside creditors, after offset of a $3,000 credit memorandum received on January 11, 19X2.
e. $10,000 cash was retained in the business at the end of the month for potential unrecorded liabilities and anticipated expenses.

February 19X2

f. $4,000 liquidation expenses were paid.
g. $6,000 cash was retained in the business at the end of the month for potential unrecorded liabilities and anticipated expenses.

March 19X2

h. $146,000 was received on sale of all items of machinery and equipment.
i. $5,000 liquidation expenses were paid.
j. No cash was retained in the business.

Required: Prepare a schedule to compute safe installment payments to the partners at the end of January, February, and March. *(AICPA adapted)*

P3.9 Safe Payment Plan After several heated disputes over management of their business, Tinsley and Shields decided to liquidate their partnership. The partnership agreement specified that the partners share profits and losses equally despite their original unequal investment of capital. Liquidation proceedings began in April, and final cash distributions to partners were made on June 30. The partners received cash as follows:

	Tinsley	Shields
April 30.	$ 0	$ 0
May 31.	5,000	0
June 30	47,500	22,500

The accountant followed the safe payment plan in making the distributions. During the 3-month liquidation period, the following occurred:

1. Accounts receivable collections: April, $25,000; May, $10,000; June, $10,000. At the end of June, remaining receivables of $5,000 were written off. No new receivables were added during the liquidation period.
2. Equipment was sold in June.
3. Inventory was sold for cash at three-fourths its book value; half was

sold in April and half in May. Total cash received for inventory was $60,000.

4. Starting in April, liabilities were paid at the end of each month with all available cash. Total liabilities paid equaled $110,000.

5. Total assets on March 31, including $20,000 cash, had a book value of $200,000.

6. Calculation of the safe payment in May created a potential deficit in Shields's account of $12,500.

Required:

1. Prepare the balance sheets for the partnership of Tinsley and Shields on March 31, April 30, and May 31.

2. What was the gain or loss on the sale of equipment?

P3.10 Cash Distribution Plan The Five-Star Partnership is liquidating because of a series of disagreements among its members. Each partner has an equal income interest; however, their respective capital accounts are:

Allison	$40,000
Brockway	15,000
Carswell	7,000
Danti	21,000
Erdman	2,000

Additionally, the partnership has a loan payable to Allison of $30,000 and a loan receivable from Erdman of $10,000. Erdman refuses to repay the loan, and the other partners have elected to offset it against capital and forego legal action to collect payment.

Required:

1. Prepare a cash distribution plan.

2. Assume that after all outside creditors are paid, two successive distributions of $35,000 each are made to the partners. How is each distribution to be allocated?

P3.11 Cash Distribution Plan for Partnership Liquidation On August 25, 19X5, Pinson, Howards, and Ropp entered into a partnership agreement to acquire a speculative second mortgage on undeveloped real estate. They invested $55,500, $32,000, and $12,500, respectively. They agreed on an income-sharing ratio of 4:2:1, respectively.

On September 1, 19X5, they purchased for $100,000 a mortgage note with an unpaid balance of $120,000. The amount paid included interest accrued from June 30, 19X5. The note principal matures at the rate of $2,000 each quarter. Interest at the annual rate of 8 percent computed on the unpaid balance is also due quarterly.

Regular interest and principal payments were received on September 30 and December 31, 19X5. A working capital imprest fund of $150 was established, and collection expenses of $70 were paid in December.

In addition to the regular September payment, on September 30 the mortgagor made a lump-sum principal reduction payment of $10,000 plus a penalty of 2 percent for prepayment.

Because of the speculative nature of the note, the partners agree to defer recognition of the discount until their cost has been fully recovered.

Required:

1. Assuming that no cash distributions were made to the partners, prepare a schedule computing the cash balance available for distribution to the partners on December 31, 19X5.
2. After payment of collection expenses, the partners expect to have cash in the total amount of $170,000 available for distribution to themselves for interest and return of principal. They plan to distribute the cash as soon as possible so that they can individually reinvest it. Prepare a schedule showing how the total cash of $170,000 should be distributed to the individual partners by installments as it becomes available. *(AICPA adapted)*

P3.12 Limited Partnership Judith Jamison formed Suburban Properties IX as a limited partnership to acquire a shopping center. Jamison, who serves as general partner, made a $5,000 investment. Nineteen limited partnership interests were sold at $25,000 each.

The shopping center was purchased for $3,600,000. A down payment of $250,000 was made, with the balance financed by a mortgage. In addition, $200,000 was paid to Jamison as a commission on the transaction; this amount is to be capitalized as part of the cost of the shopping center. The center is to be depreciated straight-line over 20 years, with zero salvage value.

The limited partnership agreement contains the following terms:

1. Operating profit or loss is to be allocated 95 percent to the limited partners and 5 percent to the general partner.
2. If cash flow from operations in any year exceeds $10,000, a distribution of $10,000 is to be made, 95 percent to the limited partners and 5 percent to the general partner. If cash flow in a given year does not exceed $10,000, no distribution is to be made that year. For this purpose, principal payments on the mortgage count as operating disbursements.
3. Upon sale of the property, sale proceeds net of mortgage repayment are to be distributed as follows:
   a. One hundred percent to limited partners until they have received their original investment net of any distributions received to date.
   b. Thereafter, 57 percent to the limited partners and 43 percent to the general partner.
4. Any remaining operating cash shall be distributed 95 percent to the limited partners and 5 percent to the general partner.

Operating results were as follows:

	Year 1	Year 2	Year 3	Year 4
Revenues (Cash)	$700,000	$720,000	$735,000	$740,000
Cash Expenses (Including Interest)	610,000	610,000	600,000	605,000
Principal Payments	100,000	110,000	120,000	130,000

The shopping center was sold at the end of Year 4 for $4,500,000, and the partnership was terminated in accordance with the limited partnership agreement.

Required:

1. Determine, by year, the cash distributions to:
   a. The limited partners.
   b. The general partner.
2. Calculate the discounted rate of return earned by a limited partner on this investment.

Chapter 4   Fiduciary Accounting

Proprietorships, partnerships, and corporations are entities created to conduct business activities. Entities may be created for another purpose—the management of certain assets. Two such entities are estates and trusts. Their special purpose results in unique accounting treatment which merits attention. Estates and trusts are considered in a single chapter because the mechanics of accounting for them are similar; the differences between the two lie in the different reasons for which the assets are being managed. In both cases, the assets are managed by someone other than the owner. Estates are entities which hold and manage the assets of a deceased person until they can be properly distributed to creditors and heirs. Estates are also used to manage the assets of a "deceased" firm—one in bankruptcy or receivership—until the assets can be properly distributed to creditors, bondholders, and stockholders. Trusts may be established to manage a pool of assets on behalf of a group of people, as in the case of a pension trust or an investment trust. Trusts may also be established to manage assets for a beneficiary upon direction of the *donor* (creator of the trust), as in the case of a trust set up for a minor child by parents. In all these cases, the stewardship function of accounting dominates. Thus the responsibility of the accountant is to report on the management of the assets to the concerned parties.

One important aspect which distinguishes an estate or trust from a corporation is the responsibility of management. The corporate manager has a considerable amount of discretion in managing the assets of the firm, and the focus is on the manager's performance as measured in terms of income or other statistics. The manager of a trust or estate has much less flexibility, being subject to legal restrictions such as wills, bankruptcy laws, and trust agreements in the management and disposition of assets. Since assets are managed on behalf of beneficiaries, the focus is on the manager's **fiduciary responsibility**—the custodial or stewardship responsibility for property belonging to others. Thus the executor of an estate, the receiver of a firm in bankruptcy, or the trustee of a trust is commonly called a **fiduciary.** Fiduciary accounting is the subject of this chapter.

Adherence to laws affecting estates and trusts is an important part of accounting for these entities. As laws exist to protect those incapable of self-protection, laws have been created to safeguard the interests of beneficiaries while their assets are managed by others. Thus the accountant must be aware of the legal framework within which estates and trusts operate. This issue is addressed throughout the chapter.

The assets of estates and trusts are viewed legally as belonging to two categories:

1. **Principal** (also called **corpus**) consists of the property and rights to property (such as receivables) existing at the date the entity is created. Examples are buildings, marketable securities, and interest receivable.
2. **Income** consists of the additional assets generated from the investment or use of principal assets. Examples are rental revenue from buildings and interest or dividends from securities.

Because laws often dictate that this division be maintained and because the beneficiaries of principal and income assets may be different, accounting for estates and trusts recognizes this distinction. Accounts for the entities are classified as to principal or income. Financial statements of estates and trusts report on the two elements separately.

Estates of Individuals

An **estate** is an entity which holds, manages, and accounts for the real and personal property of a deceased person, the **decedent,** until the property can be properly distributed to the appropriate beneficiaries. These beneficiaries and their rights to property are specified in the decedent's will or in the law if the individual died **intestate** (without a valid will). The estate is managed by a personal representative: a representative named by the will is an **executor** or **executrix;** a court-appointed representative is called an **administrator.** The personal representative of an estate has numerous duties and responsibilities and may become personally liable if lax in performance of these functions. Therefore, most states require an accounting by the fiduciary in order to enforce these duties. Interim accountings allow the court to oversee and review the fiduciary's actions, while the final accounting provides beneficiaries the opportunity to object to the representative's actions. However, once the final accounting is approved by all interested parties, the representative is released from further liability.

The estate may exist as an entity for a few months or several years. Note that the going-concern assumption underlying most business entities is absent. An estate is created with the assumption of a limited life; it ends when the assets are distributed. In this respect, it resembles a limited-life partnership created to accomplish a specific purpose.

Legal Aspects of Estates

Since accounting for estates is influenced by law, understanding the legal proceedings surrounding the creation and operation of an estate is essential for the accountant. First, it must be determined if the decedent had a will. Once validated, a will governs the distribution of the decedent's property. The process of validating a will is called **probate.** Probate involves court hearings at which parties may question the validity of the will. Early in the probate proceedings, the personal representative takes possession and control of the decedent's assets to manage them until final distribution to the beneficiaries. Even if there is no will and the laws of intestacy govern the ultimate property distribution, there is a lapse of time between the death and distribution during which the property must be managed. In either case, the time period is at least 6 months. A longer period is not unusual, since it may be neither practical nor desirable to distribute the assets quickly.

Once the claims are settled and the beneficiaries are determined through probate, the personal representative can distribute the assets and close the estate. Beneficiaries of real property are called **devisees;** of personal property, **legatees.** The gift of property, either a **devise** or **legacy,** can be *specific* (an identified object), *general* (an indicated quantity of something, usually an amount of cash), or *residuary* (property remaining after specific and general gifts are met). The legal classification of the beneficiaries as well as the legal classification of assets is important for the distribution of estate assets.

Following are some responsibilities of the personal representative:

1. *Notify the decedent's heirs* of the appointment as personal representative.
2. *Establish a family allowance* for the decedent's surviving spouse and dependent children. The Uniform Probate Code specifies the amount and timing of payment. The allowance is exempt from claims against the estate.
3. *Prepare an inventory of the assets.* The basis for the inventory is the fair value of property or rights owned at the date of death.
4. *List any liens* against the property.
5. *Publish a notice requesting creditors to present claims* against the estate of the decedent. The law dictates the appropriate vehicle and timing of such publication. Creditors have 4 months to present claims.
6. *Manage the decedent's business and investments.* If the decedent was a sole proprietor, then the personal representative has the right to manage the business for 4 months after the appointment.
7. *Establish an accounting system* which classifies the property as to principal or income assets. All assets existing at the date of death are principal. As income assets are generated, the personal representative must maintain records so as to retain the distinction between principal and income.
8. *Pay claims* against the estate.
9. *Distribute the assets* to the beneficiaries.

Several of these responsibilities require further discussion.

Preparing the Inventory. The fiduciary should prepare a complete inventory of the assets of the estate as soon as possible after the decedent's death. The Uniform Probate Code stipulates that within 3 months after appointment, the personal representative must prepare an inventory of property owned by the decedent at the time of death together with a listing of any liens against the property. If the representative anticipates a delay in appointment (for example, due to a will contest), he or she may have an objective party, such as an attorney, prepare the inventory. A prompt inventory of assets should be made in order to prevent any losses or misunderstanding which may arise regarding the existence, valuation, and location of the decedent's assets.

When preparing the inventory, the following information should be recorded:

1. Type of asset.
2. How the asset was held by the decedent (for example, outright or in trust).
3. Location of the asset.
4. Fair value of the asset at date of death.
5. The income tax basis of the asset to the decedent.
6. Date the asset was brought under the control of the fiduciary.
7. Any other distinguishing features (for example, description of jewelry and antiques).

The services of a professional appraiser may be required to estimate the value of assets for which markets are not readily available.

Along with the inventory of assets, the representative should obtain any pertinent documents such as stock certificates, bankbooks, deeds, life insurance policies, and tax returns. Once the inventory is completed, it is filed with the probate court and copies may be provided to interested parties. If other assets are subsequently discovered by the representative, they should be listed on a separate schedule to be filed with the court.

Claims against the Estate. The fiduciary has the duty of satisfying all claims against the estate. However, the representative also has the authority to allow or disallow a claim. The holder of a disallowed claim can bring action to establish the validity of the claim, but the burden of proof lies with the holder of the claim. The fiduciary can also negotiate compromise settlements of claims.

As a general rule, the personal representative should publish notice to creditors in a newspaper with general circulation. The Uniform Probate Code requires that a notice be published at least once a week for 3 consecutive weeks. Creditors must then respond within 4 months from the date of first publication, or forever be barred from asserting their claims.

When the estate's assets are sufficient to cover all claims, the order of debt payment is irrelevant. However, if assets are insufficient to pay all claims in full, the following is a generally accepted order of payment, closely following that prescribed by the Uniform Probate Code:

1. Debts secured by liens on assets (for example, mortgage on residence).
2. Expenses of administering the estate.
3. Funeral expenses and expenses of last illness.
4. Debts given preference under federal or state law.
5. Taxes assessed on decedent's property prior to death.
6. Bonds and notes issued by the decedent.
7. All other claims.

If the will is silent as to the assets to be used for debt payment, assets should be used in the following order:

1. Personal property not bequeathed.
2. Personal property bequeathed generally.
3. Personal property bequeathed specifically.
4. Real property not devised.
5. Real property devised generally.
6. Real property devised specifically.

Distributions to Beneficiaries. Another duty of the personal representative is to distribute the estate assets to the beneficiaries named in the will. The fiduciary should, if possible and if so specified in the will, distribute the assets in kind rather than converting them into cash before distribution.

When the estate assets are insufficient to cover both creditors' claims and devises or legacies, then the devises (or legacies) are reduced (or abated) according to the sequence provided for in the will. The Uniform Probate Code provides an order of abatement for the occasions when the will does not specify an order. This order is the same as that listed above for the use of assets to pay debts.

Accounting and Reporting. The personal representative must maintain proper accounting records for the estate. It is usually desirable for the representative to open a checking account in the name of the estate so that the cash transactions of the estate are kept separate from the fiduciary's personal transactions. The primary financial statement presented for estates is the **charge and discharge statement.** This statement, illustrated in Exhibit 4.1, identifies what assets were placed under the control of the personal representative and any distributions made of such property. The financial report for the estate is subject to court review in the interest of the beneficiaries. Note that the legal division of principal and income is carried into the accounting report. The accounting system for an estate must maintain this distinction to ensure legal compliance and facilitate statement preparation.

The charge and discharge statement is usually accompanied by a number of supporting schedules, which provide details of various items on the statement. For example, the assets comprising the initial inventory, the gains and losses on disposal of principal assets, and the distributions made to beneficiaries would each be detailed on supporting schedules. These schedules are illustrated in the example presented in a subsequent section.

The financial report for a small estate may be prepared only once, at the time of final distribution of estate assets. For a more complex estate, several interim reports may be made. Since an estate is a limited-life entity, reports are usually cumulative, covering the estate from the date of death to the date of the report.

Closing the Estate. Under the Uniform Probate Code, the fiduciary must file a petition with the probate court to close the estate. This may be done no earlier than 6 months after appointment and not until the time for presenting claims against the estate has expired. In the petition, the personal representative must state that he or she has:

Exhibit 4.1	Format of Charge and Discharge Statement

IDENTIFICATION OF ESTATE
IDENTIFICATION OF EXECUTOR
CHARGE AND DISCHARGE STATEMENT
FOR THE PERIOD ———

FIRST, AS TO PRINCIPAL

I charge myself as follows:
Inventory of Assets . . . . $XX
Assets Subsequently Discovered. XX
Gain on Disposal of Principal Assets. . . . . XX $XXX
I credit myself as follows:
Debts of Decedent Paid . . . . $XX
Administrative Expenses Paid XX
Loss on Disposal of Principal Assets. XX
Distributions to Beneficiaries XX   XXX
Balance, End of Period. . . . . $ XX

SECOND, AS TO INCOME

I charge myself as follows:
Revenues . . . . $ XX
I credit myself as follows:
Expenses . . . . $XX
Distributions to Beneficiaries XX   XX
Balance, End of Period. . . . . $ XX

1. Published notice to creditors at least 4 months prior to the date of the petition.
2. Fully administered the decedent's estate—paid all claims, administration expenses, and taxes (and perhaps distributed certain assets to beneficiaries).
3. Distributed a copy of the petition to all beneficiaries, creditors, and unpaid or barred claimants.

A charge and discharge statement must accompany the petition. Having collected all the decedent's assets, paid the debts, and carried out the appropriate tax duties and responsibilities, the personal representative is ready to prepare the final estate accounting and make the final distribution of the decedent's assets.

Accounting for Principal and Income

Since the personal representative is charged with the responsibility of managing the assets, the accounting system must be based on the concept of accountability for the assets. A significant aspect of estate accounting is the distinction between principal and income.

The Revised Uniform Principal and Income Act, drafted in 1962 and since adopted by 20 states, defines **principal** as the property which has been set aside by the owner or the person legally empowered so that it is held in trust eventually

Exhibit 4.2 | **Treatment of Some Common Estate Transactions as They Affect Principal or Income**

Increases in Principal

Subsequent discovery of assets existing at date of death (not included in original inventory)
Gain resulting from disposition of principal assets

Charges Against Principal

Cost of investing and reinvesting principal
Expenditures incurred in preparing principal property for sale or rent
Costs of administering and preserving the non-income-producing property of the estate (for example, property taxes, repairs, and maintenance)
Extraordinary repairs or permanent improvements
Income taxes on profit, gains, or other receipts allocable to principal (for example, capital gains tax)
Decedent's debts, expenses of last illness, funeral expenses
Fees of executor, estate attorney, accountant, and other administrative costs
Federal estate tax and state inheritance tax
Payment of devises and other distributions of principal
Loss resulting from any change in the form of principal (for example, sale or destruction)

Increases in Income

Rent on real or personal property
Interest (but premium or discount on debt securities is generally not amortized)
Cash dividends
Business profits
Annuities
Other income earned during administration of decedent's estate

Charges Against Income

Expenses of administering and preserving the income-producing property of the estate (for example, property taxes, utilities, wages, office expenses, repairs, and maintenance)
Depreciation on assets subject to depreciation under GAAP
Interest on mortgage and other indebtedness
Income taxes on profit, gains, or other receipts allocable to income
Fees of executor, estate attorney, accountant, and other administrative costs
Distributions of income

---

to be delivered to a beneficiary. As a general rule, principal includes any property or rights which the decedent had at date of death. For example, wages earned prior to death, interest receivable at date of death, and dividends receivable declared prior to death are all included in principal, even though payment is not received until later. The act defines **income** as "the return in money or property derived from the use of principal." Thus any earnings on principal assets which arise after the date of death are income. Each transaction of the estate must be analyzed to determine if it affects principal or income. Exhibit 4.2 shows the treatment of various common transactions. Note that certain administrative costs (such as executor's fee, attorney and accountant fees, income taxes) must be allocated between principal and income.

Principal is viewed, according to the Revised Uniform Principal and Income Act, "not as a certain amount of monetary value, but . . . as a certain group of assets which must be capable of isolation from the assets which compose the undistributed net income." Once an item is classified as a principal asset, its character is unaffected by subsequent transactions involving the item. For example, if a principal asset is sold, all proceeds are considered to be part of principal. In other words, gains and losses on sales of principal assets are recorded as principal, *not* as income.

A special aspect of estate accounting is that liabilities are generally not recorded in the accounts. In practice, this rule may be followed literally (i.e., record no liabilities at all), or an exception may be made to record those liabilities which constitute a lien on specific property, such as a mortgage and accrued interest thereon. The illustrations in this chapter follow the second practice.

Estate accounting follows an unusual pattern with respect to the use of cash versus accrual accounting. Assets are accrued at date of death so that the principal of the estate is correctly established. Accruals are also recognized at the final settlement of the estate so that the rights of income beneficiaries are not affected by timing of receipts and payments. During the life of the estate, however, accruals are not recorded; interim charge and discharge statements are presented on a cash basis.

Other than the special accounting characteristics addressed above, estate accounting follows generally accepted accounting principles common to other entities.

Illustration of Estate Accounting. Helen Corbett, a widow with two children (Janice Nelson and William Corbett), died on June 28, 19X1. Helen was 75 at the time of her death. In her will, she named her daughter as executrix and specified that she receive 2 percent of the gross estate at time of death as compensation for administering the estate. This compensation was to be in addition to the following specifications in the will:

Janice is to receive the residence. The estate is to pay off the mortgage.

The Society for the Prevention of Cruelty to Animals is to receive $5,000 and all income of the estate earned between the date of death and the settlement of the estate.

William is to receive all other assets remaining after the payment of administrative expenses, claims against the estate, mortgage, and the bequest to charity.

The will entered probate proceedings. Janice notified her brother and the Society for the Prevention of Cruelty to Animals of her appointment as executrix.

Soon after Helen Corbett's death, Janice took an inventory of her mother's assets. She valued marketable securities at their quoted prices. The residence and her mother's art collection were appraised to establish value at the date of death. Current values of other items were estimated by Janice.

The entry that follows shows the recording of the inventory. Note (1) that the only liabilities recorded are those with liens against the property and (2) that the cash account is specifically labeled "Principal Cash."

Principal Cash	25,700	
Marketable Securities	22,000	
Accrued Interest Receivable	250	
Residence	84,000	
Automobile	2,800	
Furniture	3,200	
Personal Effects	3,500	
Art Collection	12,000	
Mortgage Payable (Secured)		23,000
Accrued Interest Payable on Mortgage		140
Estate Principal Balance		130,310
To record inventory.		

The Estate Principal Balance account reflects the excess of assets over liens against them. At the time of inventory, all assets are classified as principal assets. The gross estate (total assets) is $153,450.

According to the law, Janice published a notice requesting that claims against her mother's estate be filed. She received the following bills: funeral expenses, $2,000; utility bills, $91; charges at a local clothing store, $150; charges at a book store, $30. No entry was made to the accounts of the estate upon receipt of the bills.

Two months after taking the inventory, Janice discovered a cache of commemorative coins worth $6,000 at her mother's home. The discovery increased the gross estate to $159,450. The discovery was recorded as follows:

Coin Collection	6,000	
Assets Subsequently Discovered		6,000
To record discovered assets.		

It is important to note that postinventory discoveries of assets do not affect the Estate Principal Balance. The balance in that account remains intact until closing entries are made after court acceptance of the charge and discharge statement. This treatment enhances the accountability function of the records.

During the period of administration, $320 of dividends and $850 in interest were received by the estate and recorded as follows:

Principal Cash	250	
Accrued Interest Receivable		250
To record receipt of interest.		
Income Cash	920	
Dividend Revenue		320
Interest Revenue		600
To record receipt of interest and dividends.		

Janice then paid off the mortgage as indicated below:

```
Mortgage Payable. . . . . . . . . . . . . . . . . . . . . . . . .    23,000
Accrued Interest Payable on Mortgage . . . . . . . . . . . . .       140
   Principal Cash  . . . . . . . . . . . . . . . . . . . . . . . .            23,140
To record settlement of mortgage.
```

To generate cash needed to meet the remaining claims against the estate and to pay the general devise to the SPCA, marketable securities with a recorded value of $7,000 and the car were sold. Despite its estimated value of $2,800, the car sold for only $2,500. The marketable securities yielded $7,150.

```
Principal Cash. . . . . . . . . . . . . . . . . . . . . . . . . .     2,500
Loss on Disposal of Principal Assets . . . . . . . . . . . . . .       300
   Automobile . . . . . . . . . . . . . . . . . . . . . . . . . .             2,800
To record sale of automobile.

Principal Cash. . . . . . . . . . . . . . . . . . . . . . . . . .     7,150
   Marketable Securities . . . . . . . . . . . . . . . . . . . . .            7,000
   Gain on Disposal of Principal Assets . . . . . . . . . . . . .               150
To record sale of securities.
```

Note that any gains or losses on disposals of assets are identified as to the type of asset (principal versus income) involved.

Claims against the estate, including Janice's fee for administering the estate, were paid. Since the coin collection was part of the estate at date of death, its value was included in the calculation of the administrative fee.

```
Administrative Expenses  . . . . . . . . . . . . . . . . . . . . .   3,189
Debts of Decedent Paid . . . . . . . . . . . . . . . . . . . . . .   2,271
   Principal Cash  . . . . . . . . . . . . . . . . . . . . . . . .            5,460
To record payment of:
   Administrative expenses (2% of $159,450). . . . . . $3,189
   Funeral expenses . . . . . . . . . . . . . . . . .   2,000
   Various charge accounts. . . . . . . . . . . . .      180
   Utility bills . . . . . . . . . . . . . . . . . . . .      91
```

After all claims were paid, Janice distributed the assets to the beneficiaries. The entries below record those distributions:

```
Distributions to Principal Beneficiaries. . . . . . . . . . . . . .   5,000
   Principal Cash . . . . . . . . . . . . . . . . . . . . . . . .             5,000
To record distribution of principal cash to the SPCA according to
the specifications of the will.

Distributions to Income Beneficiaries . . . . . . . . . . . . . .      920
   Income Cash . . . . . . . . . . . . . . . . . . . . . . . . . .              920
To record distribution of income cash to the SPCA according to
the specifications of the will.

Distributions to Principal Beneficiaries. . . . . . . . . . . . . .  84,000
   Residence . . . . . . . . . . . . . . . . . . . . . . . . . . .           84,000
To record distribution of residence to Janice Nelson according to
the specifications of the will.
```

Distributions to Principal Beneficiaries. 41,700	
Principal Cash	2,000
Marketable Securities.	15,000
Furniture	3,200
Personal Effects	3,500
Art Collection	12,000
Coin Collection	6,000

To record distribution of residuary principal assets to William
Corbett according to the specifications of the will.

The books of the estate were closed on December 28, 19X1, as follows:

Estate Principal Balance 130,310	
Assets Subsequently Discovered 6,000	
Gain on Disposal of Principal Assets 150	
Dividend Revenue. 320	
Interest Revenue 600	
Loss on Disposal of Principal Assets	300
Debts of Decedent Paid.	2,271
Administrative Expenses	3,189
Distributions to Principal Beneficiaries	130,700
Distributions to Income Beneficiaries	920

To close estate.

The charge and discharge statement for Janice Nelson, executrix, appears in
Exhibit 4.3; the supporting schedules are shown in Exhibit 4.4.

Exhibit 4.3   **Charge and Discharge Statement**

ESTATE OF HELEN CORBETT
JANICE NELSON, EXECUTRIX
CHARGE AND DISCHARGE STATEMENT
FOR THE PERIOD JUNE 28 THROUGH DECEMBER 28, 19X1

FIRST, AS TO PRINCIPAL

I charge myself as follows:		
Inventory (Schedule 1)	$130,310	
Assets Subsequently Discovered (Schedule 2)	6,000	
Gain on Disposal of Principal Assets (Schedule 3)	150	$136,460
I credit myself as follows:		
Debts of Decedent Paid (Schedule 4).	$ 2,271	
Administrative Expenses	3,189	
Loss on Disposal of Principal Assets (Schedule 5)	300	
Distributions to Beneficiaries (Schedule 6)	130,700	136,460
Balance, Dec. 28, 19X1		$ 0

SECOND, AS TO INCOME

I charge myself as follows:		
Dividend Revenue.	$ 320	
Interest Revenue	600	$ 920
I credit myself as follows:		
Distributions to Beneficiaries (Schedule 6)		920
Balance, Dec. 28, 19X1		$ 0

Exhibit 4.4	Schedules for Charge and Discharge Statement

SCHEDULE 1: INVENTORY OF ASSETS

Cash	$25,700	
Marketable Securities	22,000	
Accrued Interest Receivable	250	
Residence	84,000	
Automobile	2,800	
Furniture	3,200	
Personal Effects	3,500	
Art Collection	12,000	$153,450
Less:		
Mortgage Payable	$23,000	
Accrued Interest Payable	140	23,140
Total Net Assets		$130,310

SCHEDULE 2: ASSETS SUBSEQUENTLY DISCOVERED

Coin Collection	$ 6,000

SCHEDULE 3: GAIN ON DISPOSAL OF PRINCIPAL ASSETS

Marketable Securities:	
Proceeds of Sale	$ 7,150
Value per Inventory	7,000
Gain on Disposal	$ 150

SCHEDULE 4: DEBTS OF DECEDENT PAID

Funeral Expenses	$ 2,000
Charge Accounts	180
Utility Bills	91
Total Debts Paid	$ 2,271

SCHEDULE 5: LOSS ON DISPOSAL OF PRINCIPAL ASSETS

Automobile:	
Proceeds of Sale	$ 2,500
Value per Inventory	2,800
Loss on Disposal	$ 300

SCHEDULE 6: DISTRIBUTIONS TO BENEFICIARIES

Principal:	
Janice Nelson	$ 84,000
William Corbett	41,700
SPCA	5,000
Total Principal Distributed	$130,700
Income:	
SPCA	$ 920

Trusts

A **trust** is an entity established by a legal process to hold and manage assets on behalf of beneficiaries. Trusts are widely used for a variety of purposes. All have certain common characteristics:

1. A *donor* or *grantor* transfers assets to the trust.
2. A *trust agreement* sets forth the purposes of the trust, the duration of the trust, the identification of the beneficiaries, the identification of (or the process for appointing) the trustee, and other relevant matters.
3. A *trustee* is appointed to take possession of the assets, to manage the assets, and to make distributions to the beneficiaries.
4. One or more *beneficiaries,* who are entitled to receive the income and the principal of the trust, are identified.

Types of Trusts

Despite the variety of origins and purposes for trusts, three major types of trusts can be identified. Each type has special accounting characteristics. For convenience, they are labeled personal trusts, public trusts, and group trusts.

Personal Trusts. Individuals create **personal trusts** for the benefit of other individuals. For example, an individual's will may provide for the establishment of a trust for the spouse, children, or others. Such a trust, created by will to be effective at the grantor's death, is known as a *testamentary trust.* Another example is a *living trust,* also called an *inter vivos trust,* which takes effect while the grantor is living. In both cases, the trust usually has a limited life (for example, for a spouse's lifetime or until a child reaches age 21). The individual(s) who will periodically receive the trust's income is known as an *income beneficiary* or *life tenant.* The individual(s) who will receive the trust's principal, typically at the end of the trust's life, is known as a *principal beneficiary or remainderman.* In some cases, the income beneficiary and principal beneficiary are different individuals. For example, a man may create a testamentary trust, providing that his widow receive the income of the trust during her lifetime, and upon her death the principal be distributed to their children.

Personal trusts follow principles of fiduciary accounting similar to those discussed earlier for estates of individuals. The distinction between principal and income is important, since different beneficiaries may exist. The financial report of the trustee may take the form of a charge and discharge statement, as was illustrated earlier. Alternatively, a **statement of trust principal** and a **statement of trust income** may be presented. The formats of these two statements are shown in Exhibits 4.5 and 4.6 respectively.

Public Trusts. Public trusts are established for the benefit of a public beneficiary, that is, an institution, a group, an activity, or a cause, not one or more specific individuals. Some examples of public trusts include:

Exhibit 4.5   **Format of Statement of Trust Principal**

IDENTIFICATION OF TRUST
NAME OF TRUSTEE
STATEMENT OF TRUST PRINCIPAL
FOR THE PERIOD JANUARY 1, 19X1, to DECEMBER 31, 19X1

Trust Principal, Jan. 1, 19X1
  (Detailed list) . . . . $ XX
Increases
  (Detailed list)   XX
                                                                                                 $XXX
Decreases
  (Detailed list)   XX
Trust Principal, Dec. 31, 19X1 . . . . $ XX

(A schedule showing the assets which make up the ending balance would be attached.)

Exhibit 4.6   **Format of Statement of Trust Income**

IDENTIFICATION OF TRUST
NAME OF TRUSTEE
STATEMENT OF TRUST INCOME
FOR THE PERIOD JANUARY 1, 19X1, to DECEMBER 31, 19X1

Undistributed Trust Income, Jan. 1, 19X1 . . . . $ X
Revenues
  (Detailed list)   X
                                                                                $XX
Expenses and Distributions
  (Detailed list)   X
Undistributed Trust Income, Dec. 31, 19X1 . . . . $ X

(A schedule showing the assets which make up the ending balance would be attached.)

---

1. A wealthy alumnus of a university establishes a trust which provides annual income to support the university's athletic programs.
2. An individual establishes a trust which provides funds to be spent for scientific research on solar energy.
3. An individual establishes a trust which provides funds to be spent in support of wildlife preservation in Alaska.

These trusts are often known as *charitable trusts* or *foundations*. While typically created and endowed by individuals, these entities sometimes expand in size and scope, generating additional resources from public contributions, government grants, and other sources.

Public trusts differ from personal trusts in several ways. A public trust usually has an indefinite life, whereas the life of a personal trust is limited. A public trust is likely to be managed by a board of directors rather than a single trustee. And, as mentioned above, a public trust benefits a group, an activity, or a cause, whereas a personal trust has specific individual beneficiaries selected by the grantor.

Public trusts may follow principles of fiduciary accounting. The distinction between principal and income continues to be important, but not for the reason that different beneficiaries are likely to exist. Rather, the trust agreement may provide for the principal to be maintained indefinitely and for only the income to be expended. In the case of public trusts which expand into larger, broadly supported entities, the accounting practices and reports are likely to be similar to those for nonprofit organizations (a topic discussed in Chapter 18).

Group Trusts. Group trusts are established by firms or other entities for the benefit of individuals who belong to a specified group. Some examples include:

1. A professional association establishes an insurance trust for its members. The association collects premiums from its members who desire coverage and purchases group policies from insurance companies.
2. A brokerage firm establishes an investment trust. It solicits investments and acquires a particular type of assets. Municipal bond trusts and real estate investment trusts are common examples.
3. A firm establishes a pension trust for its employees. The firm contributes an amount (usually specified by a complex formula) to the trust each year. Contributions from the employees may also be required or permitted. The trust invests these resources and pays benefits to retired employees in accord with the provisions of the pension plan.

Group trusts typically have an unlimited life, and the trustee is often an institution (a bank, an insurance company, a brokerage house, or a professional association) rather than one or more individuals.

In accounting for group trusts, the distinction between principal and income is usually not important. All resources are combined and used for the specific purpose of the trust. A balance sheet and a statement of increases and decreases in the total capital of the trust are the common financial statements.

The pension plan is a major example of a group trust, and one where much attention has been given to accounting and reporting requirements. Under the provisions of *SFAS 35,* financial statements should provide information that is useful in assessing the plan's ability (both present and future) to pay promised benefits.[1] To achieve this objective, investments are to be presented at *fair value,* and benefits payable to participants are presented at *actuarial present value.* Actuarial assumptions include expectations about mortality, disability, departure before retirement, early retirement, and the like. Financial statements present data on accumulated benefits, assets available, and resulting underfunded (or overfunded) balance, and on changes in these amounts during the year. Illustrative statements are shown in Exhibits 4.7 and 4.8.

---

[1]*Statement of Financial Accounting Standards No. 35,* "Accounting and Reporting by Defined Benefit Pension Plans" (Stamford, CT: FASB, 1980). CT § Pe 5.104.

Exhibit 4.7 **Balance Sheet for Pension Plan**

C&H COMPANY PENSION PLAN
STATEMENT OF ACCUMULATED PLAN BENEFITS
AND NET ASSETS AVAILABLE FOR BENEFITS
DECEMBER 31, 19X1

Accumulated Plan Benefits

Actuarial Present Value of Vested Benefits:
Participants Currently Receiving Payments . . . . $ 3,040,000
Other Participants. 8,120,000
$11,160,000
Actuarial Present Value of Nonvested Benefits 2,720,000
Total Actuarial Present Value of Accumulated Plan Benefits $13,880,000

Net Assets Available for Benefits

Investments at Fair Value:
U.S. Government Securities . . . . $ 350,000
Corporate Bonds and Debentures 3,500,000
Common Stock:
C&H Company 690,000
Other 2,250,000
Mortgages 480,000
Real Estate 270,000
$ 7,540,000
Deposit Administration Contract, at Contract Value 1,000,000
Total Investments. . . . . $ 8,540,000
Receivables:
Employees' Contributions 40,000
Securities Sold 310,000
Accrued Interest and Dividends 77,000
$ 427,000
Cash . . . . $ 200,000
Total Assets . . . . $ 9,167,000
Accounts Payable 70,000
Accrued Expenses 85,000
Total Liabilities . . . . $ 155,000
Net Assets Available for Benefits . . . . $ 9,012,000
Excess of Actuarial Present Value of Accumulated Plan Benefits over Net
Assets Available for Benefits . . . . $ 4,868,000

Source: *SFAS No. 35*, Exhibit D-6 CT § Pe 5.131 (Exhibit 131F). Used with permission of the Financial Accounting Standards Board.

Estates of Bankrupt Firms

For the purposes of accounting, the bankruptcy of a firm is similar to the death of an individual. In both cases, an estate is created, and a representative is appointed via a legal process to administer the estate on behalf of the beneficiaries. In the case of a deceased individual, an executor or administrator is responsible for dis-

Exhibit 4.8	Statement of Changes for Pension Plan

C&H COMPANY PENSION PLAN
STATEMENT OF CHANGES IN ACCUMULATED PLAN BENEFITS
AND NET ASSETS AVAILABLE FOR BENEFITS
YEAR ENDED DECEMBER 31, 19X1

Net Increase in Actuarial Present Value of Accumulated Plan Benefits

Increase (Decrease) during the Year Attributable to:

Plan Amendment	$ 2,410,000
Change in Actuarial Assumptions	(1,050,500)
Benefits Accumulated	895,000
Increase for Interest Due to the Decrease in the Discount Period	742,500
Benefits Paid	(997,000)
Net Increase	$ 2,000,000

Net Increase in Net Assets Available for Benefits

Investment income:

Net Appreciation in Fair Value of Investments	207,000
Interest	345,000
Dividends	130,000
Rents	55,000
	$ 737,000
Less: Investment Expenses	39,000
	$ 698,000
Contributions:	
Employer	780,000
Employees	450,000
	$ 1,230,000
Total Additions	$ 1,928,000
Benefits Paid Directly to Participants	740,000
Purchases of Annuity Contracts	257,000
	$ 997,000
Administrative expenses	65,000
Total deductions	$ 1,062,000
Net increase	$ 866,000
Increase in Excess of Actuarial Present Value of Accumulated Plan Benefits over Net Assets Available for Benefits	1,134,000
Excess of Actuarial Present Value of Accumulated Plan Benefits over Net Assets Available for Benefits:	
Beginning of Year	3,734,000
End of Year	$ 4,868,000

Source: *SFAS No. 35*, Exhibit D-6 CT § Pe 5.131 (Exhibit 131F). Used with permission of the Financial Accounting Standards Board.

tributing assets to heirs in accord with the provisions of a will or intestacy law. In the case of a bankrupt firm, a trustee or receiver is responsible for distributing assets to creditors in accord with the provisions of contracts (security agreements) and bankruptcy law. In both cases, a fiduciary relationship is created, and the accounting procedures and statements are designed to show how the fiduciary responsibilities are met.

Legal Aspects of Bankruptcy

For the firm in financial difficulty, several possible actions exist; formal actions may be taken under the provisions of federal bankruptcy law, or less formal actions may be taken. Least formal of the various actions is a **composition** (or **creditors' composition agreement**), whereby the creditors agree that the firm may settle its debts at less than full payment. A somewhat more formal procedure is an **assignment for the benefit of creditors.** The firm voluntarily transfers its assets to a trustee, who sells or otherwise liquidates the assets and who offers partial payment to the creditors on a pro rata basis. Creditors may accept the offer, discharging the remaining debt, or they may reject the offer and initiate proceedings to force the firm into involuntary bankruptcy.

Federal bankruptcy law provides the legal process and remedies for cases of **bankruptcy,** that is, cases where individuals or business firms are unable to meet their debts and where either the debtor or the creditors initiate the legal process. The bankruptcy process is designed to provide relief and protection to debtors, and also to provide a fair means of distributing the debtor's assets to its creditors.

Three different situations are covered in the law. Chapter 7 of the Bankruptcy Reform Act of 1978, which applies to both individuals and firms, provides for liquidation of the debtor's assets in order to pay the creditors. The firm turns its assets over to a trustee, who sells the assets and distributes the proceeds to creditors on a pro rata basis. When this process is complete, most remaining debts are discharged (exceptions include certain taxes, alimony and child support, and certain student loans). Chapter 7 proceedings may be *voluntary* (initiated by the debtor) or *involuntary* (initiated by one or more creditors). Chapter 11, the provision most commonly used by business firms, relates to reorganization. **Reorganization** permits the firm to continue to exist, without liquidation of its assets, via a fair plan to modify the rights and interests of both the creditors and the stockholders of the firm. Chapter 11 proceedings may also be voluntary or involuntary. A plan is formulated under which the firm continues to operate, pays a portion of its debts, and has the remainder discharged. This plan must be approved by two-thirds of the creditors (measured in dollar value of claims); its administration is supervised by a creditors' committee. The continued operation of the firm may be under the direction of management (referred to as a *debtor in possession*), or a trustee may be appointed. Creditors may prefer reorganization to liquidation because their prospects of collecting what is due them may be better if the company continues to operate than if its assets are sold. Chapter 13 of the Bankruptcy Reform Act is analogous to reorganization but applies only to an individual debtor having a regular income. Rather than liquidating the debtor's assets, a repayment plan is worked out with creditors. Of these three provisions, the liquidation process of Chapter 7 of the law is what is commonly referred to as *bankruptcy,* and this process is the focus of the remainder of this section.

The Legal Process. The legal process begins with the filing of a petition with the federal bankruptcy court, stating that the debtor is unable to meet obligations and requesting that the provisions of the bankruptcy law be applied. If the petition is filed by the debtor, it is called a *voluntary petition;* if filed by creditors, it is called an *involuntary petition*. The law specifies the number of creditors and the amount of obligation to them that is required in order to file an involuntary petition.

The filing of a proper petition imposes an orderly process on the debtor's situation. Individual creditors cannot enforce liens or judgments, or repossess assets of the debtor. Rather, the claims of all creditors will be processed and satisfied, to the extent possible, according to the provisions of the law. The desire to be subject to this orderly process rather than subject to the lawsuits, repossessions, and liens of individual creditors explains why debtors may choose to file a voluntary petition.

The court appoints an interim trustee, who may subsequently be replaced by a permanent trustee elected by the creditors. The trustee takes possession of the debtor's assets, converts them to cash, and distributes cash to creditors in accord with their legal rights and priorities. Usually, the cash is insufficient to pay all debts fully. When all available assets are distributed, the debtor is *discharged,* that is, the debtor is released from all remaining debts except those explicitly not discharged by law.

Financial Reports for a Bankruptcy

The financial reports for a bankruptcy situation fall into two categories. First is an initial report which shows the debts and available asset values of the debtor. This report, known as a **statement of affairs,** is analogous to the initial inventory in estate accounting. Both present assets at fair market value; however, the statement of affairs also includes information on liabilities. The second category is the periodic report of the fiduciary. In estate accounting, the charge and discharge statement showed how the executor had managed the estate assets on behalf of the heirs. In bankruptcy accounting, a **realization and liquidation statement** shows how the **trustee in bankruptcy,** or **receiver,** has managed the assets of the bankrupt firm on behalf of the creditors. These statements are discussed in subsequent sections.

Statement of Affairs. The statement of affairs is a statement of financial condition of a company entering bankruptcy. Because such a company is no longer a going concern, the usual means of balance sheet valuation are not applicable. Estimated realizable values replace historical costs as the relevant measure of assets.

One purpose of the statement of affairs is to present the liabilities of the firm according to their legal preference. Liabilities are organized into four categories:

1. *Fully secured liabilities.* For these liabilities, the creditor has a lien on specific assets, and the estimated realizable value of those assets equals or exceeds the amount of the liability. For example, a bank holds a $50,000 mortgage on a building of a bankrupt firm, and the building has an estimated realizable value of $82,000. The mortgage is, therefore, fully secured, and the bank is referred to as a fully secured creditor.

2. *Partially secured liabilities.* In other cases, the creditor has a lien on specific assets, but the estimated realizable value of those assets is less than the amount of the liability. For example, a finance company holds a $20,000 note secured by equipment of a bankrupt firm, but the equipment has an estimated realizable value of only $13,000. This note is partially secured, and the finance company is referred to as a partially secured creditor.

3. *Unsecured liabilities with priority.* When the creditor has no lien on any specific assets of the bankrupt firm, but its claims rank ahead of other unsecured liabilities in order of payment, the claims are considered unsecured liabilities with priority. These liabilities, in order of priority, are:
   a. Administrative expenses of the trustee.
   b. Unpaid wages, up to $2,000 per employee, earned within 90 days prior to the bankruptcy petition.
   c. Obligations to employee benefit plans, up to $2,000 per employee, accrued within 180 days prior to the bankruptcy petition.
   d. Deposits made with the bankrupt firm by consumers for the purchase, lease, or rental of property or services, up to $900 per claimant.
   e. Taxes.

4. *Unsecured liabilities.* All other liabilities for which the creditor has no lien on any specific assets of the bankrupt firm are unsecured. This category includes the unsecured portion of the liability to partially secured creditors. In the example above, there is a note payable to the finance company for $20,000 secured by equipment worth $13,000; the difference of $7,000 is added to the unsecured liabilities.

A second purpose of the statement of affairs is to present the assets of the firm according to any specific claims against them, and to indicate amounts expected to be available for the unsecured creditors. As mentioned earlier, all assets are valued at their estimated realizable value rather than historical cost. Assets are organized into three categories:

1. *Assets pledged to fully secured creditors.* Certain assets may be pledged as security for a particular liability, and the estimated realizable value of the assets equals or exceeds the amount of the liability. Such assets may also yield resources to cover unsecured liabilities. The building with an estimated realizable value of $82,000, which secures a $50,000 mortgage liability, is an example of an asset pledged to a fully secured creditor. After the mortgage is paid, $32,000 remains for unsecured creditors.

2. *Assets pledged to partially secured creditors.* Other assets that are pledged as security for a particular liability may have estimated realizable value less than the amount of the liability. Partial satisfaction of the liability will consume the entire asset value; nothing will be left for the unsecured liabilities. The equipment with an estimated realizable value of $13,000, which secures a $20,000 note payable, is an example of an asset pledged to a partially secured creditor.

3. *Free assets.* Assets that are not pledged as security for any particular liability, and thus are available to meet the claims of unsecured creditors, are labeled free assets. This category also includes the value of assets pledged

to fully secured creditors in excess of the related liability. In the example in No. 1, $32,000 of the value of the building is included in free assets.

Format of the Statement. The statement of affairs presents assets and liabilities organized into the categories discussed in the preceding section. Secured claims and corresponding assets are offset so that the statement shows the total amount of free assets and the total amount of unsecured liabilities. These two amounts are then compared to show the **estimated deficiency to unsecured creditors**—the amount by which the unsecured liabilities exceed the assets available to pay them.

The liability section of the statement of affairs is structured as follows:

	Creditors' Claims	Unsecured Liabilities
Fully Secured Creditors:		
(List).	$XX	
Partially Secured Creditors:		
(List).	$XX	
Less: Value of Pledged Assets	X	$ X
Unsecured Creditors with Priority:		
(List).	$XX	
Unsecured Creditors:		
(List).		X
Total Unsecured Liabilities.		$XX

Note that the total of the unsecured liabilities consists of the obligations to unsecured creditors plus the obligations to partially secured creditors in excess of the value of pledged assets. Observe also that the unsecured liabilities with priority are included under Creditors' Claims but not in the total of Unsecured Liabilities.

The asset section of the statement of affairs is structured as follows:

	Estimated Realizable Value	Free Assets
Assets Pledged to Fully Secured Creditors:		
(List)	$XX	
Less: Amount of Liability	X	$ X
Assets Pledged to Partially Secured Creditors:		
(List)	$XX	
Free Assets:		
(List)		X
Total Free Assets.		$XX
Less: Unsecured Liabilities with Priority		XX
Net Free Assets		$ X
Estimated Deficiency to Unsecured Creditors		X
Total Unsecured Liabilities.		$XX

We see that the total free assets consist of the value of unpledged assets plus the value of assets pledged to fully secured creditors in excess of the amount of the related liability. The estimated deficiency to unsecured creditors reconciles the difference between the amount of net free assets and the amount of unsecured liabilities, making the statement balance.

This simple format focuses on the key aspects of bankruptcy reporting. In practice, somewhat more complex formats may be employed. For example, book values are generally presented on the statement of affairs along with the estimated realizable values. As previously discussed, estimated realizable values are most important because the company is no longer a going concern and we wish to present information relating to the status of the various classes of creditors. However, book values are also useful, since they tie the statement of affairs to the balance sheet and, when compared to the estimated realizable values, indicate the expected gains or losses upon liquidation. Thus the statement of affairs commonly appears in the format shown in Exhibit 4.9.

Illustration of Statement of Affairs. Bristol Corporation is entering bankruptcy proceedings on October 31, 19X4. Its balance sheet on that date shows the information given below:

BRISTOL CORPORATION
BALANCE SHEET
OCTOBER 31, 19X4

ASSETS		LIABILITIES AND STOCKHOLDERS' EQUITY	
Cash	$ 4,000	Accounts Payable	$134,000
Marketable Securities	7,000	Loan Payable	100,000
Accounts Receivable	27,000	Equipment Note Payable	30,000
Inventory	63,000	Accrued Wages	41,000
Land	15,000	Taxes Payable	12,000
Building	135,000	Mortgage Payable	94,000
Equipment	163,000	Stockholders' Equity	14,000
Deferred Charges	11,000		
		Total Liabilities and Stockholders'	
Total Assets	$425,000	Equity	$425,000

Note that, as in this example, a firm may enter into bankruptcy even though it has positive stockholders' equity. The key factor is that the firm is unable to meet its debt obligations. For example, when the Penn Central Railroad entered bankruptcy proceedings in 1970, its last annual report showed retained earnings of $495 million, and stockholders' equity of $1.8 billion. Nevertheless, the company's liquid assets were inadequate to meet its current obligations, and bankruptcy resulted.

It is estimated that Bristol's assets have the following realizable values:

Cash	$ 4,000
Marketable Securities	9,000
Accounts Receivable	20,000
Inventory	44,000
Land and Building	190,000
Equipment	63,900
Deferred Charges	0
	$330,900

Exhibit 4.9   Format of Statement of Affairs

X CORPORATION
STATEMENT OF AFFAIRS
DATE

Book Value		Estimated Realizable Value	Free Assets	Book Value		Creditors' Claims	Unsecured Liabilities
	Assets Pledged to Fully Secured Creditors:				Fully Secured Creditors:		
$ XX	(List)	$XX		$ XX	(List)	$XX	
	Less: Liabilities to Fully Secured				Partially Secured Creditors:		
	Creditors	XX	$ X	XX	(List)	$XX	
	Assets Pledged to Partially Secured				Less: Value of Pledged Assets . .	XX	$ X
	Creditors:			X	Unsecured Creditors with Priority:		
XX	(List)	$XX			(List)	$ X	
	Free Assets:			XX	Unsecured Creditors:		
XX	(List)	XX	XX	XX	(List)		XX
	Total Free Assets		$XX		Stockholders' Equity		—
	Less: Unsecured Liabilities with						
	Priority		X				
	Net Free Assets		$XX				
	Estimated Deficiency to Unsecured						
	Creditors		X				
$XXX	Total Unsecured Liabilities		$XX	$XXX	Total Unsecured Liabilities		$XX

The receivables and inventory are pledged as security for the $100,000 loan; the land and building are pledged as security for the mortgage. The $30,000 equipment note payable is secured by a machine having an estimated realizable value of $22,000 (and a book value of $20,000).

Exhibit 4.10	Statement of Affairs for Bristol Corporation

BRISTOL CORPORATION
STATEMENT OF AFFAIRS
OCTOBER 31, 19X4

Book Value		Estimated Realizable Value	Free Assets
	Assets Pledged to Fully Secured Creditors:		
$150,000	Land and Building	$190,000	
	Less: Mortgage Payable	94,000	$ 96,000
	Assets Pledged to Partially Secured Creditors:		
27,000	Accounts Receivable.	$ 20,000	
63,000	Inventory.	44,000	
20,000	Equipment	22,000	
		$ 86,000	
	Free Assets:		
4,000	Cash.	$ 4,000	
7,000	Marketable Securities	9,000	
143,000	Equipment	41,900	
11,000	Deferred Charges	0	54,900
	Total Free Assets		$150,900
	Less: Unsecured Liabilities with Priority		53,000
	Net Free Assets		$ 97,900
	Estimated Deficiency to Unsecured Creditors . . .		80,100
$425,000	Total Unsecured Liabilities		$178,000

Book Value		Creditors' Claims	Unsecured Liabilities
	Fully Secured Creditors:		
$ 94,000	Mortgage Payable	$ 94,000	
	Partially Secured Creditors:		
100,000	Loan Payable	$100,000	
	Less: Value of Accounts Receivable and		
	Inventory	64,000	$ 36,000
30,000	Equipment Note Payable.	$ 30,000	
	Less: Value of Machine	22,000	8,000
	Unsecured Creditors with Priority:		
41,000	Accrued Wages	$ 41,000	
12,000	Taxes Payable.	12,000	
		$ 53,000	
	Unsecured Creditors:		
134,000	Accounts Payable		134,000
14,000	Stockholders' Equity		
$425,000	Total Unsecured Liabilities		$178,000

The statement of affairs for Bristol is shown in Exhibit 4.10. The statement shows net free assets of $97,900 and unsecured liabilities of $178,000, resulting in an estimated deficiency to unsecured creditors of $80,100. This information can be converted into an **expected recovery percentage** for unsecured creditors:

$$\text{Expected recovery percentage} = \frac{\text{Net free assets}}{\text{Unsecured liabilities}}$$

$$= \frac{\$97,900}{\$178,000}$$

$$= 55\%.$$

In other words, unsecured creditors can expect to receive 55 cents per dollar owed to them by the bankrupt firm. Fully secured creditors, of course, receive the full amount owed them, as do (typically) the unsecured creditors with priority. The partially secured creditors receive less than 100 percent, but more than the percentage received by unsecured creditors. For the two partially secured creditors in this example, the recovery is calculated as follows:

```
Loan Payable of $100,000:
  Secured Portion (Full Recovery)
    Value of Pledged Assets . . . . . . . . . . . . . . . . . . . . . . . . $64,000
  Unsecured Portion (Partial Recovery)
    $36,000 × 55%. . . . . . . . . . . . . . . . . . . . . . . . . . . .    19,800
Total Recovery . . . . . . . . . . . . . . . . . . . . . . . . . . . . . . $83,800

Equipment Note Payable of $30,000:
  Secured Portion (Full Recovery)
    Value of Pledged Asset . . . . . . . . . . . . . . . . . . . . . . . . $22,000
  Unsecured Portion (Partial Recovery)
    $8,000 × 55% . . . . . . . . . . . . . . . . . . . . . . . . . . . .     4,400
Total Recovery . . . . . . . . . . . . . . . . . . . . . . . . . . . . . . $26,400
```

Thus the loan creditor will recover 83.8 percent (= $83,800/$100,000), and the equipment note creditor will recover 88 percent (= $26,400/$30,000).

Realization and Liquidation Statement. The realization and liquidation statement provides a complete record of the transactions of the receiver for a period of time. Its structure is similar to a T account, and it is composed of three elements: asset transactions, liability transactions, and income/loss transactions. First, consider the structure of T accounts for assets and liabilities. A completed and balanced T account appears as follows:

Asset Account

Beginning balance	100	70	Decreases
Increases	50	80	Ending balance
	150	150	

Liability Account

Decreases	40	60	Beginning balance
Ending balance	50	30	Increases
	90	90	

We now apply this structure to the activities of the receiver. One task of the receiver is to **realize the assets,** that is, to convert the noncash assets into cash so that creditors may be paid. The process of realization may take several forms. Certain activities of the firm may continue in operation, providing cash or other assets. Some assets may be realized via normal business operations, such as the continuing collection of receivables from customers. Other assets may be realized via sale. Since the receiver is to act in the interest of the creditors, he or she must select the means of realization which will provide the best return to the creditors. As a result, the realization process may extend over a considerable period of time. During this time, gains and losses on asset sales may occur, expenses may be incurred, and revenues may be earned. The realization activities may be described in T account format as follows:

Assets (Other than Cash)

Beginning Balance: Assets to be realized	Decreases: Assets realized
Increases: Assets acquired	Ending Balance: Assets not realized

Income Effect of Realization

Expenses and losses	Revenues and gains

The second task of the receiver is to **liquidate the liabilities,** that is, to arrange full or partial settlement with the creditors. Again, gains or losses may occur in the process of liquidation, as may expenses or revenues. The liquidation activities may also be described in T account format as follows:

Liabilities

Decreases: Liabilities liquidated	Beginning Balance: Liabilities to be liquidated
Ending Balance: Liabilities not liquidated	Increases: Liabilities incurred

Income Effect of Liquidation

Expenses and losses	Revenues and gains

Accounting for Realization and Liquidation Activities. To prepare a realization and liquidation statement, the asset and liability accounts must be structured in a way that segregates the gain or loss. Consider first an asset account, which is structured as follows:

Assets (Other than Cash)

Assets to be realized	Assets realized
Assets acquired	Assets not realized

Suppose that inventory having a book value of $100,000 is to be realized. Assume that a portion of the inventory, having a book value of $30,000, is sold for $12,000. Following the above format, the account would indicate that $30,000 of inventory has been realized, and $70,000 remains to be realized.

Inventory

Assets to be realized	100,000	30,000	Assets realized
Assets acquired	0	70,000	Assets not realized
	100,000	100,000	

In addition, there would be a debit to Cash of $12,000 and a debit to Loss of $18,000.

The inventory account could be restructured to show that the $30,000 of inventory that was realized resulted in $12,000 of cash and an $18,000 loss. In this case, the account would appear as follows:

Inventory

Assets to be realized	100,000	12,000	Assets realized (proceeds)
Assets acquired	0	18,000	Assets realized (loss)
		70,000	Assets not realized
	100,000	100,000	

If the inventory with a book value of $30,000 had been sold for $35,000, the $30,000 of assets realized would be shown as $35,000 of proceeds and a $5,000 gain as follows:

Inventory

Assets to be realized	100,000	35,000	Assets realized (proceeds)
Assets acquired	0		
Assets realized (gain)	5,000	70,000	Assets not realized
	105,000	105,000	

Note that the gain appears on the debit side, and that the balance in the account is maintained. In other words, the $30,000 realization of inventory appears as $35,000 of proceeds less the $5,000 gain. In addition, there would be a debit to Cash of $35,000 and a credit to Gain of $5,000.

Similar considerations exist for the liability accounts. The general structure is:

Liabilities

Liabilities liquidated	Liabilities to be liquidated
Liabilities not liquidated	Liabilities incurred

Suppose that notes payable of $73,000 exist, and that the holder of a $20,000 note accepts $16,000 in full settlement. Following the above format, we have:

Notes Payable

Liabilities liquidated	20,000	73,000	Liabilities to be liquidated
Liabilities not liquidated	53,000		
		0	Liabilities incurred
	73,000	73,000	

We may replace the $20,000 book value of liabilities liquidated with the information that this liability was settled for an actual payment of $16,000, resulting in a $4,000 gain. We then have:

Notes Payable

Liabilities liquidated (payment)	16,000	73,000	Liabilities to be liquidated
Liabilities liquidated (gain)	4,000	0	Liabilities incurred
Liabilities not liquidated	53,000		
	73,000	73,000	

There would also be a credit to Cash of $16,000 and a credit to Gain of $4,000. It would be rare for a liability to be liquidated at a loss. Should this occur, however, the loss would appear on the credit side of the account.

Revenues and expenses (as distinct from gains and losses) usually arise from acquisition of assets or incurrence of liabilities. For example, if interest of $500 is accrued on notes receivable, the following entries would be recorded (the revenue and expense T accounts are presented in conventional, rather than balance, format):

Interest Receivable

Assets acquired	500	500	Assets not realized

Revenues

	500	Interest

Similarly, if administrative expenses of $1,800 were incurred by the receiver but not paid, we record:

Accrued Administrative Expenses

Liabilities not liquidated	1,800	1,800	Liabilities incurred

Expenses

Administrative	1,800

The Realization and Liquidation Statement Format. The general structure of the realization and liquidation statement follows from the expanded format of the asset and liability accounts discussed in the preceding section. Various formats are found in practice; Exhibit 4.11 shows one possibility. Note that certain accounts are excluded from the statement:

1. The Cash account.
2. Revenues and Expenses.
3. The income accounts for gains and losses.
4. The Equity account.

Exhibit 4.11　　**Format of Realization and Liquidation Statement**

X CORPORATION
(NAME OF RECEIVER OR TRUSTEE)
REALIZATION AND LIQUIDATION STATEMENT
(TIME PERIOD COVERED)

Assets to Be Realized:	Assets Realized:
(List and amounts)	(List and amounts)
Assets Acquired:	Assets Not Realized:
(List and amounts)	(List and amounts)
Liabilities Liquidated:	Liabilities to Be Liquidated:
(List and amounts)	(List and amounts)
Liabilities Not Liquidated:	Liabilities Incurred:
(List and amounts)	(List and amounts)
Gain on Realization or Liquidation	Loss on Realization or Liquidation:
Combined Total	Combined Total

A balance sheet and a statement of estate deficit should accompany the realization and liquidation statement. The balance sheet of the trustee has the following format:

BALANCE SHEET

Cash	Liabilities Not Liquidated
Assets Not Realized	Estate Deficit

The statement of estate deficit shows the revenues, expenses, gains, and losses for a period, resulting in a net change in the estate deficit. It is analogous to a statement of income and retained earnings of a going concern. One possible format of this statement is shown below:

STATEMENT OF ESTATE DEFICIT

Revenues	$X	
Gains	X	$XX
Expenses	$X	
Losses	X	XX
Net Change in Estate Deficit		$ X
Estate Deficit—Beginning of Period		X
Estate Deficit—End of Period		$XX

One question which arises for a firm in receivership or bankruptcy is whether depreciation should be recognized. A reasonable answer is that if the firm is continuing to carry on operations, recognition of depreciation is appropriate to measure the results of operations. If few or no operating activities are being conducted—that is, the assets are being sold and liabilities settled—no depreciation charges should be made.

Illustration. Joanne Willis is appointed trustee of the Weeks Corporation, which is in bankruptcy. Her responsibilities are to administer the firm's estate, to realize the assets, and to liquidate the liabilities. At the time of her appointment, the company's balance sheet appears as follows:

WEEKS CORPORATION
BALANCE SHEET
MARCH 31, 19X3

Cash	$ 1,000	Accounts Payable	$27,000
Accounts Receivable	6,000	Accrued Wages	5,000
Inventories	11,000	Notes Payable	40,000
Equipment, Net	35,000	Stockholders' Equity	(19,000)
	$53,000		$53,000

The accounts payable and notes payable are unsecured.

Willis takes custody of the company's assets. A statement of affairs would be prepared to show the estimated realizable values of the company's assets, and the estimated recovery by each class of creditors. Willis must then establish accounting records for herself as trustee. Her initial entry records, at book value, the assets and liabilities which she is administering:

Cash	1,000	
Accounts Receivable	6,000	
Inventories	11,000	
Equipment	35,000	
Estate Deficit	19,000	
Accounts Payable		27,000
Accrued Wages		5,000
Notes Payable		40,000

To record assets and liabilities of Weeks Corporation.

Suppose that during the next 3 months, the following transactions occur:

1. A total of $3,300 is received in settlement of $5,000 of accounts receivable; the remaining $1,000 is expected to be collectible.
2. Inventory items having a book value of $8,000 are sold for $6,400.
3. A machine with a book value of $7,000 is sold for $12,000.
4. The accrued wages are paid.
5. Administrative expenses of $4,000 are accrued.
6. An initial payment of 20 cents per dollar of indebtedness is made to the unsecured creditors.

The trustee records these transactions as follows:

1. Cash	3,300	
Loss on Realization	1,700	
Accounts Receivable		5,000

To record collection of receivables.

2. Cash   6,400
   Loss on Realization   1,600
      Inventory.   8,000
   To record sale of inventory.

3. Cash   12,000
   Equipment   7,000
   Gain on Realization   5,000
   To record sale of machine.

4. Accrued Wages.   5,000
   Cash.   5,000
   To record payment of wages.

5. Administrative Expenses   4,000
   Accrued Expenses   4,000
   To accrue expenses of trustee.

6. Accounts Payable.   5,400
   Notes Payable   8,000
   Cash.   13,400
   To record partial payment of 20 percent of amount due to
   unsecured creditors.

T accounts reflecting the initial entry and the six transaction entries are shown in Exhibit 4.12. The credits for assets realized are broken down between proceeds (coded P) and gain or loss (coded G or L). The T accounts enclosed in the box represent the information which will appear on the realization and liquidation statement. This statement is presented in Exhibit 4.13 on page 149.

The trustee's balance sheet and statement of estate deficit at June 30, 19X3, would appear as follows:

WEEKS CORPORATION
JOANNE WILLIS, TRUSTEE
BALANCE SHEET
JUNE 30, 19X3

Cash	$ 4,300	Accounts Payable.	$21,600
Accounts Receivable	1,000	Notes Payable	32,000
Inventory	3,000	Accrued Expenses	4,000
Equipment	28,000	Estate Deficit	(21,300)
	$36,300		$36,300

WEEKS CORPORATION
JOANNE WILLIS, TRUSTEE
STATEMENT OF ESTATE DEFICIT
JUNE 30, 19X3

Gain on Realization		$ 5,000
Loss on Realization	$3,300	
Administrative Expenses	4,000	7,300
Net Change in Estate Deficit		$ (2,300)
Estate Deficit—March 31, 19X3		(19,000)
Estate Deficit—June 30, 19X3		$(21,300)

Exhibit 4.12	**Accounts for Realization and Liquidation Activities**

Cash

B	1,000	5,000	(4)
(1)	3,300	13,400	(6)
(2)	6,400		
(3)	12,000		

ASSETS TO BE REALIZED

Accounts Receivable

B	6,000	3,300	P	(1)
		1,700	L	(1)
		1,000	E	
	6,000	6,000		

Inventory

B	11,000	6,400	P	(2)
		1,600	L	(2)
		3,000	E	
	11,000	11,000		

Equipment

B		35,000	12,000	P	(3)
G	(3)	5,000	28,000	E	
		40,000	40,000		

LIABILITIES TO BE LIQUIDATED

Accounts Payable

(6)	5,400	27,000	B
E	21,600		
	27,000	27,000	

Accrued Wages

(4)	5,000	5,000	B
E	0		
	5,000	5,000	

Notes Payable

(6)	8,000	40,000	B
E	32,000		
	40,000	40,000	

Accrued Expenses

E	4,000	4,000	(5)

Administrative Expenses

(5)	4,000	

Gain on Realization

		5,000	(3)

Loss on Realization

(1)	1,700	
(2)	1,600	

Estate Deficit

B	19,000	

Legend:

B = Beginning balance.
E = Ending balance.
P = Proceeds from realization.
G = Gain on realization.
L = Loss on realization.
Numbers in parentheses correspond to numbered journal entries in the text.

Summary of Key Concepts

Fiduciary accounting relates to entities which exist to hold and manage assets on behalf of others. **Estates of individuals, estates of bankrupt firms, and trusts** are the major entities to which fiduciary accounting applies.

Exhibit 4.13	Realization and Liquidation Statement

WEEKS CORPORATION
JOANNE WILLIS, TRUSTEE
REALIZATION AND LIQUIDATION STATEMENT
FOR THE 3 MONTHS ENDED JUNE 30, 19X3

Assets to Be Realized:			Assets Realized:		
Accounts Receivable	$ 6,000		Accounts Receivable	$ 3,300	
Inventory	11,000		Inventory	6,400	
Equipment	35,000	$ 52,000	Equipment	12,000	$ 21,700
Assets Acquired:			Assets Not Realized:		
None		0	Accounts Receivable	$ 1,000	
			Inventory	3,000	
			Equipment	28,000	32,000
Liabilities Liquidated:			Liabilities to Be Liquidated:		
Accounts Payable	$ 5,400		Accounts Payable	$27,000	
Accrued Wages	5,000		Accrued Wages	5,000	
Notes Payable	8,000	18,400	Notes Payable	40,000	72,000
Liabilities Not Liquidated:			Liabilities Incurred:		
Accounts Payable	$21,600		Accrued Expenses		4,000
Notes Payable	32,000				
Accrued Expenses	4,000	57,600			
Gain on Realization		5,000	Loss on Realization		3,300
Combined Total		$133,000	Combined Total		$133,000

Legal considerations, especially the distinction between **principal** and **income,** are important in fiduciary accounting.

In the case of **estates of individuals,** an **executor** or **administrator** takes charge of the decedent's assets, pays claims against the estate, and makes distributions to beneficiaries. The **charge and discharge statement** details, for both principal and income, the assets under the fiduciary's control and the disposition of those assets.

In the case of **trusts,** accounting and reporting depend on the nature of the trust. Accounting for **personal trusts** is similar to accounting for estates of individuals. Accounting for **public trusts** and **group trusts** is usually similar to accounting for nonprofit organizations.

In the case of **bankrupt firms,** a **statement of affairs** is prepared to show the financial condition of the company. Assets are valued at **estimated realizable value** and are classified according to any security interests held by creditors. Liabilities are classified according to their **legal preference.** The statement shows the **estimated deficiency to unsecured creditors.**

The **statement of realization and liquidation** details the activities of the **receiver** or **trustee** in administering the estate of the bankrupt firm.

Appendix to Chapter 4   Estate Planning and Taxation

In addition to accounting and reporting for estates, accountants also participate in estate planning and determination of estate taxes. Both are complex topics requiring considerable study; this appendix touches on only a few major aspects of these subjects.

Estate planning may be described as a process by which an individual (1) provides for the transfer of assets to desired beneficiaries and (2) attempts to reduce taxes on the transfers. The first objective—directing assets to desired beneficiaries—can be accomplished in several ways:

1. A *will* should be prepared which specifies the disposition of the individual's property at death. If no will exists, state intestacy laws govern the distribution of property.
2. *Gifts* may be made during the individual's lifetime.
3. *Trusts* may be established, either during the individual's lifetime or at death, to hold assets on behalf of beneficiaries. There are many forms of trusts, as will be discussed later in this appendix.

By these and other means, an individual's assets are transferred, either during life or at death, to desired beneficiaries.

The second objective of estate planning is to minimize the tax cost of this transfer of assets. **Gift taxes** apply to transfers of property during the individual's lifetime, and **estate taxes** apply to transfers at death. Minimizing gift and estate taxes involves planning the timing and form of the transfer of assets.

Estate and Gift Taxation

The federal estate tax and gift tax are both levied on the transfer of property from one individual to another. These taxes are imposed on the transferor, not on the recipient, of the property. That is, the giver is responsible for paying the gift tax, and the estate of a decedent is responsible for paying the estate tax. On the other hand, some states impose inheritance taxes on the recipient.

The estate and gift taxes are *unified,* that is, the same rate schedule applies to both types of transfers. The tax rates currently range from 18 to 55 percent, as shown in Exhibit 4.14. As of January 1, 1988, the maximum rate drops to 50 percent, on taxable amounts of $2,500,000 or more; other rates remain unchanged. The tax base is cumulative, that is, the tax is based on the aggregate amount of taxable transfers to date, including both taxable gifts (since 1976) and the amount of the taxable estate.

Exhibit 4.14	Federal Estate and Gift Tax Rates

Amount Subject to Tax

At Least	But Less than	Amount of Tax
$ 0	$ 10,000	18% of taxable amount
10,000	20,000	$ 1,800 + 20% of excess over $ 10,000
20,000	40,000	3,800 + 22% of excess over 20,000
40,000	60,000	8,200 + 24% of excess over 40,000
60,000	80,000	13,000 + 26% of excess over 60,000
80,000	100,000	18,200 + 28% of excess over 80,000
100,000	150,000	23,800 + 30% of excess over 100,000
150,000	250,000	38,800 + 32% of excess over 150,000
250,000	500,000	70,800 + 34% of excess over 250,000
500,000	750,000	155,800 + 37% of excess over 500,000
750,000	1,000,000	248,300 + 39% of excess over 750,000
1,000,000	1,250,000	345,800 + 41% of excess over 1,000,000
1,250,000	1,500,000	448,300 + 43% of excess over 1,250,000
1,500,000	2,000,000	555,800 + 45% of excess over 1,500,000
2,000,000	2,500,000	780,800 + 49% of excess over 2,000,000
2,500,000	3,000,000	1,025,800 + 53% of excess over 2,500,000
3,000,000		1,290,800 + 55% of excess over 3,000,000

Source: Internal Revenue Code, Section 2001(c).

Transfers Subject to Tax

Estate and gift taxes are generally based on the fair market value of the property at time of transfer. Transfers of property by gift are generally subject to the gift tax, with the following major exceptions:

1. Gifts to charity.
2. Gifts of $10,000 or less. This exclusion applies *annually* to each recipient. In other words, an individual may give up to $10,000 per year to each of an unlimited number of recipients without incurring a gift tax.
3. Gifts to a spouse are subject to an unlimited *marital deduction*.

Determining the amount of an estate subject to tax is considerably more complex. The gross estate consists of the value of all property which the decedent owned or possessed an interest in at time of death. Jointly owned property, such as real estate, is generally included to the extent of the decedent's interest (e.g., half the value of the property is included if there are two equal co-owners). In addition to property such as cash, securities, real estate, and automobiles, other property is also included in the decedent's gross estate, such as:

1. Life insurance, even though payable directly to a beneficiary, if the decedent possessed rights of ownership of the policy (for example, the right to cancel the policy or to change the beneficiary).
2. Value of decedent's pension and annuity benefits which will be paid to a beneficiary.

To determine the taxable amount of the estate, the gross estate is then reduced by the following deductions:

1. Funeral expenses.
2. Administrative expenses of the estate.
3. Debts of the decedent.
4. Losses of estate property due to casualty or theft during the period of administration.
5. A marital deduction for property which passes to the surviving spouse; this deduction has no maximum.
6. Transfers or bequests to qualified charitable organizations.

Calculation of Tax

The taxable amount of gifts or of the taxable estate is subject to the rates shown in Exhibit 4.14. As mentioned earlier, the tax base is the cumulative amount of transfers. To determine the tax on a current gift, the tax on all gifts to date (since 1976) is calculated, and the tax applicable to previous gifts is then deducted. For example, assume an individual who has previously made post-1976 taxable gifts of $470,000 now makes a taxable gift of $80,000 (in excess of the $10,000 annual exclusion). The tax on the current gift is calculated as follows, using the rates in Exhibit 4.14:

Tax on Cumulative Gifts of $550,000 [$155,800 + (37% × $50,000)].	$174,300
Tax on Prior Gifts of $470,000 [$70,800 + (34% × $220,000)]	145,600
Tax on Current Gift of $80,000	$ 28,700

A lifetime tax credit of $192,800 is available,[2] which is applied to gift and estate taxes until consumed. As can be verified from the rate schedule, this credit offsets the tax on the first $600,000 of taxable transfers.

The same process applies in calculating the estate tax. In schedule form, the calculation is as follows:

Gross estate

Less: Deductions

Equals: Taxable estate

Plus: Post-1976 taxable transfers (gifts)

Equals: Tax base (cumulative taxable transfers)

Tentative tax (tax base times appropriate rates from Exhibit 4.14)

Less: Taxes already paid on post-1976 gifts

Less: Lifetime credit

Equals: Estate tax due

---

[2]The $192,800 credit exists as of 1987; for 1986, the credit is $155,800 and for 1985 it was $121,800.

Illustration. George Johnson died on July 17, 19X5, leaving half of his adjusted gross estate to his wife. The gross estate amounted to $1,730,000. The estate paid funeral expenses, administrative costs, and debts of the decedent in the amount of $253,000. George had made taxable gifts of $75,000 five years ago but, by applying a portion of his lifetime credit, had paid no gift tax. The calculation of the estate tax is:

Gross Estate.	$1,730,000
Expenses	253,000
Adjusted Gross Estate	$1,477,000
Marital Deduction	738,500
Taxable Estate	$ 738,500
Previous Taxable Transfers	75,000
Cumulative Taxable Transfers	$ 813,500
Tentative Tax on Cumulative Transfers of $813,500 [$248,300 + (39% × $63,500)]	$ 273,065
Tax on Prior Transfers of $75,000 [$13,000 + (26% × $15,000)].	16,900
Estate Tax before Credit	$ 256,165
Less: Lifetime Credit ($192,800 less $16,900 applied to gift tax in prior years).	175,900
Estate Tax.	$ 77,265

Estate Planning

Estate planning is a process whereby an individual plans for the transfer of property to beneficiaries, either during life or at death, in a way that accomplishes a number of objectives, such as:

1. Providing sufficient availability of assets to meet the individual's lifetime needs.
2. Minimizing income taxes during the individual's lifetime.
3. Minimizing estate taxes, both at the time of the individual's death and at the time of beneficiaries' deaths.

In the following sections, a number of factors involved in estate planning are briefly discussed.

Transfers during Life

The transfer of assets to beneficiaries during an individual's lifetime may be desirable for several reasons. If the individual's expected future needs are well provided for, lifetime transfers may satisfy personal objectives such as helping one's children to buy a home or start a business. Income tax reductions will occur if the recipients are in lower tax brackets than the donor. Savings on gift and estate taxes may occur but are limited by the cumulative nature of the tax. However, the $10,000 annual exclusion does permit tax savings where transfers occur in small amounts over a period of time.

One form of transfer during life is outright gift, which permanently and irrevocably transfers ownership. Gifts are typically made to immediate family members, such as spouse or children. For example, if most of a couple's property is acquired and owned by the husband, gifts to his wife will reduce the disparity in their estates and may lead to lower total estate taxes.

Another form of transfer during life, which may be permanent or temporary, is the *inter vivos trust*. Various forms of inter vivos trusts exist. *Revocable trusts* exist at the pleasure of the grantor. There are no tax advantages to such trusts; the income is taxed to the grantor, and the trust property is included in the grantor's estate. Thus revocable trusts are usually created for nontax reasons, some of which are relevant to estate planning. The trust assets do not go through probate, thereby reducing delays and costs. Also, since wills are public documents when they are brought to probate court, while trusts are not, the use of a trust as a "will substitute" results in increased privacy. The trust assets are protected from creditors of the estate and may also be protected from control by a legal guardian should the donor become incapacitated. Finally, the trust (especially if in existance for some time) is less likely to be challenged by heirs, as a will might be. These nontax advantages, which apply to any form of inter vivos trust, are often desirable in an estate plan.

Irrevocable trusts are permanent dispositions of property. Once an irrevocable trust is established, the income is no longer taxed to the grantor, and the trust property is excluded from the grantor's estate. Transfer of property to an irrevocable trust constitutes a gift, and thus a gift tax obligation may be incurred. The advantage of transfer to an irrevocable trust over a direct gift to the beneficiary is that control is provided over the beneficiary's access to the principal.

An intermediate type of trust, which has some characteristics of both revocable and irrevocable trusts, is a trust for a fixed period of time. Commonly referred to as *Clifford trusts,* these have become popular in estate planning in recent years. The trust must be established for a fixed term of more than 10 years or for an indefinite term (for example, the lifetime of the beneficiary). A Clifford trust may be used to provide support for elderly parents or an educational fund for a child. It is like an irrevocable trust in that the grantor is not taxed on the income of the trust. The present value of the income constitutes a gift, but the principal does not. Like a revocable trust, the assets will ultimately revert to the grantor and be included in the grantor's estate.

Transfers at Death

Transfers of property at time of death are specified in the will. Before these transfers can occur, however, provision for estate taxes must be made. The marital deduction is a major factor in reducing estate taxes. Thus estate planning usually takes maximum advantage of the marital deduction by leaving much of the estate to the spouse. Note that, assuming no remarriage, the marital deduction is available only on the death of the first spouse. Consideration must be given to minimizing the estate tax upon the death of the surviving spouse. One common approach is for the first spouse to leave part of the estate to the surviving spouse, so as to qualify for the marital deduction, and to leave the other part to a trust where the surviving spouse is the income beneficiary but the children are the principal beneficiaries. In this way, the full amount of the estate will be available to provide support for the surviving spouse, but only part will be included in the surviving spouse's estate. There are some limitations on the use of trusts to minimize estate taxes. So-called *generation-skipping trusts,* in which the principal beneficiaries are grandchildren or subsequent generations but earlier generations (e.g., children) are the income beneficiaries, are subject to special estate tax rules to prevent abuse.

Joint Ownership

Property owned jointly with right of survivorship automatically passes, upon the death of one owner, to the surviving owners. While this eliminates the need to provide for disposition of the property via will, it also limits flexibility in that all owners must agree to any sale of the property. Joint ownership that seems appropriate at one point in time may later prove inappropriate, as in the case of divorce. Jointly owned property is included in each owner's estate in a proportionate manner.

Life Insurance

Life insurance is usually a significant part of an estate. While the proceeds are paid directly to the beneficiary, the face value of the policy is included in the estate if the decedent owned the policy. Ownership is measured in terms of possession of major rights, such as the right to cancel the policy or to change the beneficiary. To remove the insurance from the estate, the policy could be transferred as a gift to another individual or to an irrevocable trust. However, this involves loss of control over a major asset.

Liquidity

An important aspect of estate planning is the assurance that sufficient cash will be available in the estate to pay expenses, living costs of surviving family members, and estate taxes. Liquidity is a particular problem for individuals whose major asset is a business or a farm. The decedent's desire may have been to leave this asset intact for heirs, but often the asset must be sold to raise necessary cash. Various techniques are available to ensure the availability of cash to the estate. For example, life insurance may be purchased with the estate named as the beneficiary.

Summary

An estate plan is not fixed or absolute. Once established, it needs regular monitoring and revision as an individual's assets, needs, and circumstances change over time. Because of the complexities involved, estate planning is usually handled by a team of professionals, including accountants, attorneys, tax experts, and perhaps others, such as investment brokers and insurance agents.

Questions

Q4.1 Legal terminology is important in accounting for estates, trusts, and firms in bankruptcy. Explain the meaning of the following terms:

1. Executor.
2. Intestate.
3. Administrator.
4. Principal.
5. Receiver.
6. Probate.
7. Residuary devise.
8. Specific devise.

Q4.2 Valuation of assets under fiduciary accounting often differs from historical cost valuation. Indicate the basis of asset valuation used for each of the following financial statements:

1. Charge and discharge statement (estate).
2. Statement of affairs (bankruptcy).
3. Realization and liquidation statement (bankruptcy).
4. Charge and discharge statement (trust).
5. Balance sheet (trust).

Q4.3 When principal assets are sold, are gains and losses resulting from the sale treated as income or principal items? Can you offer any explanation for such treatment?

Q4.4 Does accounting for estates follow cash basis or accrual basis accounting? Discuss your answer.

Q4.5 What is meant by fully secured liabilities? By partially secured liabilities?

Q4.6 In fiduciary accounting, the fiduciary manages assets on behalf of some other party. Explain the role of the fiduciary in accounting for estates, trusts, and firms in bankruptcy.

Q4.7 Briefly explain the accounting procedures appropriate to each of the following:

1. Postinventory discovery of assets (estates).
2. Liabilities existing at date of death (estates).
3. Liabilities existing at date of declaration of bankruptcy (bankruptcy).
4. Involuntary conversion of principal assets (trusts).
5. Permanent improvements to principal assets (trusts).
6. Regular maintenance of principal assets (trusts).

Q4.8 Do firms entering bankruptcy always have a deficit in Retained Earnings? Explain.

Q4.9 Compare the role of the statement of realization and liquidation and the statement of affairs in bankruptcy with respect to (1) purpose of the statements, (2) timing of statement presentation, and (3) basis of asset valuation.

Q4.10 What role, if any, does depreciation play in accounting for the activities of a receiver (or trustee) in bankruptcy?

Q4.11 Complete each of the following statements:

1. An important aspect of fiduciary accounting is the distinction between _____ and _____.
2. The balance sheet of a bankrupt firm, which sets forth the estimated realizable value of assets and the legal priority of creditors, is known as _____.
3. In bankruptcy, a liability wherein the creditor has a security interest in a particular asset and wherein the amount of the liability is greater than the value of the asset, is known as _____.
4. The asset described in No. 3 is known as _____.
5. On a statement of realization and liquidation, assets to be realized plus assets acquired minus assets realized equals _____.

Q4.12 Complete each of the following statements:

1. The primary financial statement of the estate of a deceased person is known as _____.
2. The list of assets, and their values, owned by an individual at date of death is known in estate accounting as _____.
3. In bankruptcy, the estimated deficiency to unsecured creditors is the difference between the amount of _____ and the amount of _____.
4. In a bankruptcy, a liability which is paid or settled in some way by the fiduciary is said to be _____.
5. The financial statement that reports on the activities of a receiver in bankruptcy is known as _____.

Exercises

E4.1 In accounting for estates and trusts, there is a problem of separating the items that should be charged against principal from the items that should be charged against income. State whether each of the following items would be charged to principal or to income, assuming the case of a testamentary trust:

1. Taxes on vacant city lots.
2. Interest paid on mortgage on real estate.
3. Depreciation of real estate.
4. Legal fees for collection of rent.
5. Special assessment tax levied on real estate for street improvement.
6. Amortization of premium on bonds which had been purchased by the testator.

7. Loss on sale of trust investments.
(AICPA adapted)

E4.2 The numbered transactions below pertain to the accounts maintained by the executor of an estate. The decedent died on January 17, 19X0. The will and other documents revealed that the decedent's son had been specifically bequeathed the decedent's only rental property and bonds of the MT Corporation ($100,000 par value, 3 percent, due February 28, 19Z5); the decedent's daughter was the beneficiary of a life insurance policy (face amount $150,000), on which the decedent had paid the premiums; and his widow had been left the remainder of the estate in trust, with full powers of appointment.

For each numbered transaction below, indicate whether the amount in question should be: (a) allocated between principal and income, (b) attributed solely to principal, (c) attributed solely to income.

1. January 20, 19X0: $3,450 was collected in connection with the redemption of AB Corporation bonds, 3 percent, due January 15, 19X0, par value $3,000.
2. January 20, 19X0: $1,000 was collected from FG Corporation on account of a dividend of $1 per share on common stock declared December 1, 19W9, payable January 15, 19X0, to stockholders of record January 2, 19X0.
3. January 20, 19X0: $3,250.50 was paid to Smith & Company, brokers, for the purchase of income bonds of A.A.R.R., 5 percent, due June 30, 19Y2, face value $3,000.
4. January 21, 19X0: thirty shares of common stock were received from the DQ Corporation, constituting receipt of an ordinary 3 percent common stock dividend declared December 14, 19W9, payable January 20, 19X0, to holders of record January 15, 19X0.
5. February 1, 19X0: $400 quarterly interest was paid on a promissory note due January 31, 19X1.
6. February 1, 19X0: Dr. Mathews, the decedent's physician, was paid $1,000 for professional services rendered during the decedent's final illness.
7. February 1, 19X0: $1,600 was collected from TC Corporation on account of a cash dividend of $.50 per share on common stock, declared January 18, 19X0, payable January 30, 19X0, to holders of record January 27, 19X0.
8. February 1, 19X0: $400 rental income for February was deposited.
9. February 10, 19X0: $500 was paid for real estate taxes covering the period February 1–July 31, 19X0.
10. March 1, 19X0: $1,572 was paid on account of the decedent's state income tax for 19W9.

(AICPA adapted)

E4.3 On August 1, 19X3, Kevin Jackson, administrator of Susan Phoenix's will, distributed the following and closed the estate:

Distributed To	Amount
George Franklin.	$3,500
Carol Phoenix.	$95,000 (gross proceeds from sale of Susan Phoenix's residence)
Darrell Phoenix	$48,400 (cash and securities)
Linda Webster	Personal belongings valued at $30,000

Jackson's term as administrator commenced on December 1, 19X2, immediately after the death of Susan Phoenix. During the period of administration, the following events occurred:

1. Jackson invested some estate cash in securities (Group A).
2. Real estate fees on the sale of the house ($7,500) were paid. There was no mortgage remaining on the house.
3. Dividends on Group B securities (originally purchased by Susan Phoenix) of $1,000 were declared and received. Dividends and interest on Group A securities were received, totaling $2,500.
4. Legal and administrative fees (all charged to principal) of $3,000 were paid.
5. Jackson paid $800 brokerage fees on security transactions during his administration.
6. Group B securities increased in value $1,200.

Required:

1. Reconstruct the market value of Susan Phoenix's assets on December 1, 19X2.
2. Calculate the income of the estate during the administration period. What expenses were charged to income?
3. Briefly state the terms of Susan Phoenix's will.

E4.4 During the last few years of Maynard Crowley's life, he underwent expensive surgery and medical treatments. Back taxes and other overdue bills accumulated because Maynard was too ill to manage his financial affairs properly. After Felix Crowley, Maynard's son and executor of the estate, published notice to creditors of Maynard's death, the following bills were received:

Funeral Expenses	$ 2,500
Unpaid Medical Bills, Final Illness.	12,000
Taxes Due at Date of Death	10,000
Charges at Local Stores	7,000
Loan from Bank.	8,000

Maynard's will contained the following provisions:

1. Bequeathed to Felix Crowley, $30,000 plus residence and automobile (both fully owned by Maynard).
2. Bequeathed to St. Angela's High School, land (fully owned by Maynard) adjoining the school.

3. Bequeathed to Katherine Hutchinson, diamond and emerald brooch.
4. Bequeathed to St. Angela's High School, all property remaining after other distributions are complete.

Executor's fee was $2,000. Felix was also beneficiary of a $40,000 life insurance policy. The net realizable values of assets at date of death were as follows:

Residence	$60,000
Certificates of Deposit	30,000
Land Adjoining St. Angela's High School	15,000
Other Land	10,000
Diamond and Emerald Brooch	4,000
Automobile	1,500

Required: State the amount and nature of the assets received by Katherine Hutchinson, Felix Crowley, and St. Angela's High School upon settlement of Maynard Crowley's estate.

E4.5 The following information is available concerning Hopkins, Inc., on the date the company entered bankruptcy proceedings:

Account	Balance per Books
Cash	$ 2,860
Accounts Receivable	52,260
Inventory	28,000
Prepaid Expenses	430
Buildings, Net	59,000
Equipment, Net	5,600
Goodwill	5,650
Wages Payable	(2,500)
Taxes Payable	(1,810)
Accounts Payable	(79,000)
Notes Payable	(15,150)
Common Stock	(72,000)
Retained Earnings—Deficit	16,660

Inventory with a book value of $20,000 is security for notes of $10,100. The other notes are secured by the equipment.

Expected realizable value of the assets is:

Accounts Receivable	$44,100
Inventory	18,500
Buildings	22,000
Equipment	2,000

Required: Compute the estimated deficiency to unsecured creditors.

E4.6 Because of inability to pay its debts, the Fox Manufacturing Company has been forced into bankruptcy as of April 30, 19X3. The balance sheet on that date shows:

ASSETS		LIABILITIES	
Cash.	$ 2,700	Accounts Payable	$ 52,500
Accounts Receivable	39,350	Notes Payable (First Bank)	15,000
Notes Receivable	18,500	Notes Payable (Suppliers)	51,250
Inventories.	87,850	Accrued Wages	1,850
Prepaid Expenses	950	Accrued Taxes.	4,650
Land and Buildings	61,250	Mortgage Bonds Payable	90,000
Equipment.	48,800	Common Stock	
		($100 Par).	75,000
		Retained Earnings.	(30,850)
	$259,400		$259,400

Additional information:

1. Accounts receivable of $16,110 and notes receivable of $12,500 are expected to be collectible. The good notes are pledged to First Bank.
2. Inventories are expected to bring in $45,100 when sold under bankruptcy conditions.
3. Land and buildings have an appraised value of $95,000. They serve as security on the bonds.
4. The current value of the equipment, net of disposal costs, is $9,000.

Required: Compute the following:

1. Estimated loss on asset disposition.
2. Estimated gain on asset disposition.
3. Priority claims.
4. Estimated payments to secured creditors.
5. Expected recovery percentage.

(AICPA adapted)

E4.7 Dellwood Corporation is experiencing difficulty in paying its bills and is considering filing for bankruptcy. Current data show:

ASSETS	Book Value	Expected Realizable Value
Cash.	$ 4,000	$ 4,000
Accounts Receivable	40,000	30,000
Inventory—Materials.	36,000	27,000
Inventory—Finished Goods	50,000	55,000
Prepaid Expenses	1,000	0
Land.	10,000	42,000
Building	70,000	160,000
Trucks.	20,000	6,000
Equipment.	45,000	25,000
Intangibles.	16,000	0
	$292,000	

LIABILITIES		Secured by
Accounts Payable	$ 77,000	
Bank Loan.	25,000	80% of receivables
Wages Payable	12,000	
Taxes Payable.	8,000	
Truck Loan	5,000	Truck with $12,000 BV and $3,500 ERV
Mortgage Payable	43,000	Land and building
Loan Payable	50,000	Finished goods
Stockholder Loan	110,000	Not subordinated to other debt
Stockholders' Equity	(38,000)	
	$292,000	

Required: Prepare a statement of affairs.

E4.8 The balance sheet of the Binder Company immediately prior to entering bankruptcy proceedings and a balance sheet prepared during liquidation are shown below:

BINDER COMPANY
BALANCE SHEET
JUNE 30, 19X0

Cash		$ 2,000	Accounts Payable. . .	$ 40,000
Accounts			Accrued Wages	7,000
Receivable		10,000	Taxes Payable	8,000
Inventories		30,000	Notes Payable[a]	70,000
Equipment	$73,000		Stockholders'	
Less: Accumulated			Equity.	(15,000)
Depreciation	20,000	53,000		
Land		15,000		
		$110,000		$110,000

[a] Of the notes payable, $15,000 are secured with inventory having a book value of $15,000. The remaining notes payable and the accounts payable as unsecured.

BINDER COMPANY
ALFRED WADE, TRUSTEE
BALANCE SHEET
DECEMBER 31, 19X0

Cash		$10,000	Liabilities Not Liquidated:	
Assets Not Realized:			Accounts Payable . .	$32,000
Equipment	$73,000		Notes Payable	48,000
Less: Accumulated			Estate Deficit.	(17,000)
Depreciation	20,000	53,000		
		$63,000		$63,000

The inventory was sold at two-thirds its book value. Half of the accounts receivable were collected; the rest were written off.

Required: Reconstruct the journal entries for Binder from June 30 to December 31, 19X0.

E4.9 At January 1, 19X4, the records of Frederick McDonald, trustee in bankruptcy for VCM Corporation, showed the following:

Cash	$ 8,200
Assets Not Realized:	
Land	10,000
Building	43,000
Equipment	28,000
Patents	4,400
Liabilities Not Liquidated:	
Accounts Payable	80,000
Loans Payable	40,000
Estate Deficit	26,400

During January, McDonald sold equipment having a book value of $15,000 for $8,800, and sold the patents for $12,000. McDonald was paid $1,300 as a trustee's fee, and $21,000 was distributed proportionately to the creditors.

Required: Prepare a statement of realization and liquidation for January and a balance sheet and statement of estate deficit as of January 31, 19X4.

E4.10 A trustee's statement of realization and liquidation is presented below:

Assets to Be Realized:			Assets Realized:		
Accounts			Accounts		
Receivable	$15,000		Receivable	$ 9,000	
Inventory	41,000		Inventory	18,000	
Equipment	88,000	$144,000	Equipment	23,000	$ 50,000
Assets Acquired:			Assets Not Realized:		
None			Accounts		
			Receivable	$ 6,000	
			Inventory	20,000	
			Equipment	72,000	98,000
Liabilities Liquidated:			Liabilities to Be Liquidated:		
Notes Payable		45,000	Accounts		
			Payable	$ 90,000	
			Notes		
			Payable	160,000	250,000
Liabilities Not Liquidated:			Liabilities Incurred:		
Accounts			None		
Payable	$ 90,000				
Notes					
Payable	110,000	200,000			
Gain on Realization		7,000	Loss on Realization		3,000
Gain on Liquidation		5,000			
Combined Total		$401,000	Combined Total		$401,000

Required: Reconstruct, in journal entry form, the trustee's transactions for the period.

E4.11 When he was 66 years old and his grandson Vincent had just turned 18, Walter Dodson established a trust for Vincent. The principal was composed of 8 percent bonds (face and market value, $80,000) and common stock (market value, $30,000) in several companies. Merchant's Bank agreed to administer the trust for an annual fee of 6 percent of gross trust income. The stocks and bonds were to come under Vincent's control when he reached age 21. Until that time, the yearly net income of the trust was to be paid to Vincent on his birthday. Dividends received on the stock for the 3 years of the trust were $1,200, $1,800, and $2,000, respectively.

Required: Record all journal entries made by Merchant's Bank for the trust of Vincent Dodson.

E4.12 *(Appendix)* Edith Barnes died on July 17, 19X5, leaving one-half of her estate to her husband and one-half to a trust for the benefit of their children. The gross estate amounted to $1,930,000. The estate paid debts, funeral expenses, and administrative costs of $40,000. During her lifetime, Edith made no gifts exceeding the $10,000 exclusion. Assume a $192,800 lifetime credit.

Required:

1. Calculate the estate tax owed by the estate of Edith Barnes.
2. Calculate the estate tax assuming Edith had left her entire estate to her husband.
3. Calculate the estate tax assuming Edith had left her entire estate to the trust for the benefit of their children.

Problems

P4.1 Estate and Trust Accounting On May 2, 19X2, Theodosia Hale died in a boating accident. The will specified that Hale's residence was to be sold and the mortgage settled. Her personal belongings (furniture, jewelry, photographs, and so on) were bequeathed to Rosenelle Abernathy, Hale's sister and only living relative. Rosenelle Abernathy was also named beneficiary of income from the estate subject to the following limitations:

1. Maximum annual distribution is to be $18,000. Earnings of the estate in excess of that amount are to be added to principal.
2. Minimum annual distribution is to be $10,000. Any deficiency in earnings is to be met by principal.

The will also called for creation of a trust. Income from the trust was to be distributed to Rosenelle Abernathy subject to the same limitations established for income from the estate. Upon Abernathy's death, the holdings of the trust were to be given to the United Fund. Kevin Boylston was named as executor of the estate and trustee of the trust.

The following information is available:

1. Residence: estimated fair market value at date of death, $110,000; mortgage payment made on June 1, 19X2, $400, of which $180 was interest; selling price, $108,000; selling and closing expenses, $9,700; payment of remaining mortgage, $25,000; selling date, June 2, 19X2.
2. Personal belongings: estimated fair market value at date of death, $27,000.
3. Estate taxes: $66,000, paid in 19X2; funeral expenses: $3,000, paid in 19X2.
4. Assets other than residence and personal belongings: cash, $20,000; securities, $200,000; undeveloped land, $40,000. Values are stated as of May 2, 19X2.
5. Accrued interest receivable on May 2, 19X2: Security A, $100, and Security B, $900.
6. Creation of the trust: April 30, 19X3.
7. Administrative expenses: May 2, 19X2, to April 30, 19X3, $5,000; May 1, 19X3, to April 30, 19X4, $4,000; divided evenly between principal and income.
8. Security transactions: Security A, interest of $600 received on July 1, 19X2, and July 1, 19X3; Security B, interest of $1,200 received on February 2, 19X3, and February 2, 19X4; dividends and interest on other securities, $16,000 in the first year of administration and $24,000 in the second year; sale of Security W in August 19X3 yielded $42,000 compared to book value of $30,000, with proceeds invested in Security G.
9. All distributions to the beneficiary were made on April 30.
10. Contents of safe deposit box discovered on July 10, 19X2: jewelry worth $9,000 and Security E worth $15,000 (values as of May 2, 19X2).

Required:

1. Prepare the journal entries made by the fiduciary for the period May 2, 19X2, to April 30, 19X3.
2. Prepare a charge and discharge statement for Kevin Boylston as of April 30, 19X3.
3. Prepare the journal entries made by the fiduciary for the period May 1, 19X3, to April 30, 19X4.
4. Prepare a charge and discharge statement for Kevin Boylston as of April 30, 19X4.

P4.2 Estate Accounting The will of Albert Brown, deceased, directed that his executor, Charles Dawson, liquidate the entire estate within 2 years of the date of Mr. Brown's death and pay the net proceeds and income, if any, to the Sunnydale Orphanage. Mr. Brown, who was a bachelor, died on February 1, 19X4, after a brief illness.

An inventory of the decedent's property was prepared, and the fair market value of all items was determined. The preliminary inventory, before the computation of any appropriate income accruals on inventory items, follows:

	Fair Market Value
First National Bank Checking Account	$ 6,000
$60,000 City of Laguna School Bonds, Interest Rate 6% Payable Jan. 1 and July 1, Maturity Date 7/1/X8	59,000
2,000 Shares Jones Corporation Capital Stock	220,000
Term Life Insurance (Beneficiary—Estate of Albert Brown)	20,000
Personal Residence ($45,000) and Furnishings ($5,000)	50,000

During 19X4, the following transactions occurred:

1. The interest on the City of Laguna School bonds was collected. The bonds were sold on July 1 for $59,000, and the proceeds and interest were paid to the orphanage.
2. The Jones Corporation paid cash dividends of $1 per share on March 1 and December 1, as well as a 10 percent stock dividend on July 1. All dividends were declared 45 days before each payment date and were payable to holders of record as of 40 days before each payment date. On September 2, 1,000 shares were sold at $105 per share, and the proceeds were paid to the orphanage.
3. Because of a depressed real estate market, the personal residence was rented furnished at $300 per month commencing April 1. The rent is paid monthly, in advance. Real estate taxes of $900 for the calendar year of 19X4 were paid. The house and furnishings have estimated lives of 45 years and 10 years, respectively. The part-time gardener-handyman was paid 4 months' wages totaling $500 on April 30 for services performed, and he was released.
4. The First National Bank checking account was closed and the balance of $6,000 was transferred to an estate bank account.
5. The term life insurance was paid on March 1 and deposited in the estate bank account.
6. The following disbursements were made:
   a. Funeral expenses, $2,000.
   b. Expenses of final illness, $1,500.
   c. April 15 income tax remittance, $700.
   d. Attorney's and accountant's fees, $12,000.
7. On December 31, the balance of the undistributed income, except for $1,000, was paid to the beneficiary. The balance of the cash on hand derived from the principal of the estate was also paid to the beneficiary on December 31.

Required: As of December 31, 19X4, the executor resigned and waived all commissions. Prepare a charge and discharge statement separately stated as to principal and income, together with its supporting schedules, on behalf of the executor of the estate of Albert Brown for the period from February 1, 19X4, through December 31, 19X4. *(AICPA adapted)*

P4.3 Estate Accounting Arthur Taine died in an accident on May 31, 19X2. His will, dated February 28, 19X1, provided that all just debts and expenses be paid and that his property be disposed of as follows:

U.S. Treasury bonds and Puritan Company stock—to be placed in trust. All income to go to his wife, Bertha Taine, during her lifetime, with right of appointment upon her death.

Seneca Company mortgage notes—bequeathed to Wanda Taine Langer, daughter.

Cash—a bequest of $10,000 to David Taine, son.

Remainder of estate—to be divided equally between the two children, Wanda Taine Langer and David Taine.

The will further provided that during the administration period Bertha Taine was to be paid $300 a month out of estate income, and estate and inheritance taxes were to be paid out of principal. David Taine was named as executor and trustee.

Bertha and Arthur owned their personal residence jointly with rights of survivorship.

An inventory of the decedent's property was prepared. The fair market value of all items as of the date of death was determined. The preliminary inventory, before the computation of any appropriate income accruals on inventory items, follows:

Personal Residence Property	$ 95,000
Jewelry—Diamond Ring	9,600
York Life Insurance Co.—Term Life Insurance Policy on Life of Arthur Taine, Beneficiary—Bertha Taine, Widow	120,000
Granite Trust Co.—3% Savings Bank Account, Arthur Taine, in Trust for Philip Langer (Grandchild), Interest Credited Jan. and July 1; Balance May 31, 19X2	400
Fidelity National Bank—Checking Account; Balance May 31, 19X2	143,000
$100,000 U.S. Treasury Bonds, 3% (Maturing in 30 Years), Interest Payable Mar. 1 and Sept. 1	100,000
$9,700 Seneca Co. First Mortgage Notes, 6%, due 19X6, Interest Payable May 31 and Nov. 30	9,900
800 Shares Puritan Co. Common Stock	64,000
700 Shares Meta Mfg. Co. Common Stock	70,000

The executor opened an estate bank account to which he transferred the decedent's checking account balance. Other deposits, through July 1, 19X3, were as follows:

Interest Collected on Bonds:
$100,000 U.S. Treasury
Sept. 1, 19X2 . . . . $ 1,500
Mar. 1, 19X3   1,500
Dividends Received on Stock:
800 Shares Puritan Co.
June 15, 19X2, Declared May 7, 19X2, Payable to Holders of Record May
27, 19X2   800
Sept. 15, 19X2   800
Dec. 15, 19X2   1,200
Mar. 15, 19X3   800
June 15, 19X3   800
Net Proceeds of June 19, 19X2, Sale of 700 Shares Meta Mfg. Co. 68,810

Payments were made from the estate's checking account through July 1, 19X3, for the following:

Funeral Expenses . . . . $ 2,000
Assessments for Additional 19X0 Federal and State Income Tax ($1,700) plus
Interest ($110) to May 31, 19X2   1,810
19X2 Income Taxes of Arthur Taine for the Period Jan. 1, 19X2, through May
31, 19X2, in Excess of Amounts Paid by the Decedent on Declarations of
Estimated Tax   9,100
Federal and State Fiduciary Income Taxes, Fiscal Years Ending June 30,
19X2 ($75), and June 30, 19X3 ($1,400)   1,475
Federal and State Estate Taxes 58,000
Monthly Payments to Bertha Taine—13 payments of $300   3,900
Attorney's and Accountant's Fees. 25,000

The executor waived his commission. However, he desired to receive his father's diamond ring in lieu of the $10,000 specific legacy. All parties agreed to this in writing, and the court's approval was secured. All other specific legacies were delivered by July 15, 19X2.

Required: Prepare a charge and discharge statement as to principal and income, together with its supporting schedules, on behalf of the executor of the estate of Arthur Taine for the period from May 31, 19X2, through July 1, 19X3. *(AICPA adapted)*

P4.4 Statement of Affairs Statton Corporation is facing bankruptcy proceedings. The balance sheet of Statton Corporation at June 30, 19X6, and supplementary data are presented here:

ASSETS

Cash . . . . $ 2,000
Accounts Receivable, less Allowance for Doubtful Accounts   70,000
Inventory, Raw Materials   40,000
Inventory, Finished Goods   60,000
Marketable Securities   20,000
Land   13,000
Buildings, less Accumulated Depreciation 90,000
Machinery, less Accumulated Depreciation 120,000
Goodwill   20,000
Prepaid Expenses   5,000
Total Assets $440,000

LIABILITIES AND CAPITAL

Accounts Payable	$ 80,000
Notes Payable	135,000
Accrued Wages	15,000
Mortgages Payable	130,000
Common Stock	100,000
Retained Earnings (Deficit)	(20,000)
Total Liabilities and Capital	$440,000

Supplementary data:

1. Cash should be reduced by $500 for a travel advance which has been expended.
2. Accounts Receivable of $40,000 have been pledged in support of Notes Payable of $30,000. Credit balances of $5,000 are netted in the Accounts Receivable total.
3. Marketable Securities consist of government bonds costing $10,000 and 500 shares of Bartlett Company stock. The market value of the bonds is $10,000 and the stock is $18 per share. The bonds have accrued interest due of $200. The securities are collateral for a $20,000 bank loan.
4. Appraised value of raw materials is $30,000 and of finished goods is $50,000. For an additional cost of $10,000, the raw materials would realize $70,000 as finished goods.
5. The appraised values of fixed assets are: Land, $25,000; Buildings, $110,000; Machinery, $75,000.
6. Prepaid Expenses will be exhausted during the liquidation period.
7. Accounts Payable include $15,000 of withheld payroll taxes and $6,000 owed to creditors who had been reassured by the president they would be paid. There are unrecorded employer's payroll taxes in the amount of $500.
8. Accrued Wages are not subject to any limitations under bankruptcy laws.
9. Mortgages Payable consist of $100,000 on land and buildings and a $30,000 mortgage on machinery. Total unrecorded accrued interest for these mortgages amounts to $2,400.
10. Estimated legal fees and expenses in connection with the liquidation are $10,000.
11. Probable judgment on a pending damage suit is $50,000. This meets the accrual criteria of *SFAS 5*.
12. There is an unrecorded invoice for $5,000 for last year's audit, and it is estimated that the fee for liquidation work will be $1,000.

Required:

1. Prepare a statement of affairs.
2. Compute the estimated settlement per dollar of unsecured liabilities.

(AICPA adapted)

P4.5 Statement of Affairs   The Bellow Company, Inc., a furniture store, has been finding it more and more difficult to meet its obligations. Although its sales volume appeared to be satisfactory and it was showing a profit, the requirements for capital for inventory and payments on current liabilities were greater than the company could provide. Finally, after pledging all of its installment accounts, it found itself unable to meet the bills falling due on October 10, 19X4. Management feels that if the company could obtain an extension of time in which to pay its obligations it could meet its liabilities in full. The corporation has arranged for a meeting of creditors to determine if the company should be granted an extension or be forced into bankruptcy.

The trial balance for the current calendar year of the company on September 30, 19X4, is as follows:

	Debit	Credit
Cash on Hand	$ 500	
Cash in Bank	1,620	
Installment Contracts—Pledged	215,000	
Allowance for Bad Contracts		$ 13,440
Accounts Receivable—30-day	20,830	
Allowance for Doubtful Accounts		1,050
Inventories—Jan. 1, 19X4	151,150	
Prepaid Insurance	1,490	
Autos and Trucks	22,380	
Accumulated Depreciation (Autos and Trucks)		14,960
Furniture and Equipment	12,500	
Accumulated Depreciation (Furniture and Equipment)		2,140
Buildings	89,760	
Accumulated Depreciation (Buildings)		7,530
Land	10,240	
Organization Expense	880	
Trade Accounts Payable		132,100
Contract Payable (Furniture and Equipment)		5,800
Installment Note on Auto and Trucks		10,000
Bank Loan—Secured by Installment Contracts		161,250
Taxes Payable (Prior Years)		14,220
Accrued Salaries and Wages		4,680
Accrued Interest		10,990
Notes Payable—Stockholder		100,000
First Mortgage		49,000
Capital Stock		100,000
Retained Earnings	65,290	
Sales		708,900
Purchases	527,630	
Expenses and Miscellaneous Income, Net	216,790	
	$1,336,060	$1,336,060

From further investigation, the following additional data are obtained:

1. Depreciation, doubtful accounts, and prepaid and accrued items had all been adjusted as of September 30, 19X4.

2. All installment contracts had been pledged with the bank on September 30, 19X4; the bank had deducted its interest to date and had increased the company loan to equal 75 percent of face amount of the contracts, in accordance with a loan agreement. It was estimated that a forced liquidation would result in a loss of $40,000 from the face amount of the contracts.

3. Thirty-day accounts receivable were not pledged, and it was estimated that they would provide $16,500 on a liquidation basis.

4. It was estimated that since January 1, 19X4, the company had made a gross profit of $33\frac{1}{3}$ percent but that the inventory on hand would provide only $100,000 in a forced liquidation.

5. Cancellation of the insurance would provide $990.

6. All the autos and trucks were covered by an installment note, and their total market value was $8,000.

7. The store had been remodeled in 19X3, and the furniture and equipment had been acquired on contract. Because of its specialized nature, it was estimated that in a forced sale no more than $5,000 could be realized.

8. The land and buildings were subject to a 6 percent first mortgage, on which interest had been paid to July 30, 19X4. It was estimated the property could be sold for $75,000.

9. The notes payable to stockholders had not been subordinated to general creditors. The notes carried a 6 percent rate of interest, but no interest had been paid since December 31, 19X2.

10. Since prior income tax returns disclosed a large available net operating loss carryover, no current income tax need be considered.

11. The cost of liquidation proceedings was estimated to be $5,000.

12. There appeared to be no other realizable values on liquidation and no unrecorded liabilities.

Required:

1. Prepare a statement of affairs for the Bellow Company as of September 30, 19X4.

2. Compute the percentage of recovery by the unsecured creditors if the Bellow Company is forced into bankruptcy.

(AICPA adapted)

P4.6 Statement of Realization and Liquidation Barnwell Corporation, which has had a history of profitable operations, has recently encountered serious difficulty in paying its bills. Attempts to acquire bank financing have been unsuccessful, due to the advanced age and ill health of the firm's sole owner and manager, Amos Barnwell. Attempts to sell the company have also proven unsuccessful. Faced with the prospect of the firm's bankruptcy, Barnwell's creditors met and proposed the following terms to Mr. Barnwell:

1. Operations would be continued until the present raw materials and work-in-process inventories were used or completed and sold.

2. The creditors would advance $9,000 to finance the necessary operating costs.

3. A trustee would be appointed by the creditors to manage the remaining operations and subsequent liquidation.

Amos Barnwell agreed to these terms and on August 1, 19X1, Frank Carrington was appointed trustee. The company's balance sheet on that date showed the following:

Cash.	$ 397	Accounts Payable	$ 37,933
Accounts Receivable	6,093	Common Stock, $10 Par.	30,000
Raw Materials Inventory	24,000	Additional Paid-In Capital	60,000
Work-in-Process Inventory	51,600	Retained Earnings	12,783
Finished Goods	8,550		
Equipment, Net	50,076		
	$140,716		$140,716

During the first 6 months of Carrington's term as trustee, the following occurred:

1. The creditors advanced the company $9,000.
2. Additional raw materials were purchased on account for $9,450.
3. Expenses incurred on account were $22,500. Expenses paid with cash were $31,732, of which $24,937 was for labor. All expenses were charged to work in process.
4. Cash in the amount of $1,125 was expended for new equipment.
5. Of the accounts receivable outstanding on August 1, $570 was deemed uncollectible. The balance was collected.
6. Depreciation of $1,500 was recorded and charged to work in process.
7. Sales on account of $108,450 were collected during the 6-month period.
8. No equipment was sold.

On January 31, 19X2, account balances were as follows: Accounts Receivable (new), $5,073; Accounts Payable (new), $133; Raw Materials, $3,000; and Finished Goods, $45,000.

Required:

1. Prepare a schedule showing transactions affecting the cash account of Barnwell Corporation.
2. Prepare a statement of realization and liquidation for Barnwell Corporation for the 6-month period ending January 31, 19X2.

P4.7 Statement of Affairs The following items of information were taken from the statement of affairs of Brace Corporation:

1. Estimated deficiency to unsecured creditors—$35,000.
2. Unsecured liabilities with priority—$10,000.
3. Assets pledged to fully secured creditors ($100,000) exceed the related liabilities by $25,000.

4. Liabilities to partially secured creditors—$40,000.
5. Assets which are not pledged to any creditors—$80,000.
6. Total assets—book value $275,000, estimated realizable value $210,000.

Required: Determine the following amounts:

1. Assets pledged to partially secured creditors.
2. Total unsecured liabilities (excluding those with priority).
3. Total liabilities.
4. Total stockholders' equity.

P4.8 Statement of Affairs—Partnership The Adams-Story Partnership has had difficulty in meeting its obligations as its debts matured. If the business is dissolved, the process will take 6 months. Burke, the part-time book-keeper, prepared the following trial balance:

ADAMS-STORY PARTNERSHIP
TRIAL BALANCE
APRIL 15, 19X8

Cash in Banks	$ 20,000	
Accounts Receivable	100,000	
Allowance for Doubtful Accounts		$ 4,000
Notes Receivable	58,000	
Notes Receivable Discounted		12,000
Raw Materials	9,000	
Work in Process	20,000	
Finished Goods	15,000	
Prepaid Insurance	1,200	
Property Held in Trust	18,000	
Machinery and Equipment, Cost	9,000	
Building	33,000	
Land	12,000	
Accumulated Depreciation		6,000
Interest Receivable	700	
Payroll Taxes Payable		200
Real Estate Taxes Payable		1,200
Wages Payable		3,450
Notes Payable		60,000
Accounts Payable		125,700
Mortgage Payable—4%		40,000
Equipment Contract Payable (Purchased on a Conditional Sales Contract)		6,400
Interest Payable		1,000
Capital—Adams		15,975
Capital—Story		1,975
Trust Principal		18,000
	$295,900	$295,900

An analysis of the accounts revealed the following:

1. Cash in First Bank, $8,000; in Second Bank, $12,000.
2. Of the accounts receivable, 60 percent are good and fully collectible,

30 percent are doubtful and considered to be only 80 percent collectible, and the remaining 10 percent are worthless.

3. All notes are good and are pledged as security on notes payable to the Factor House of $50,000 with accrued interest of $500.

4. Of the notes which were discounted at the Manning Bank, it is estimated that one, amounting to $2,000, will not be paid at maturity or thereafter.

5. All finished goods will be sold for 20 percent less than their cost. Work in process cannot be sold until finished and can be completed by incurring labor and material costs of $9,000, of which $3,000 will be from raw material inventory. The balance of the raw material inventory will realize $5,000.

6. The prepaid insurance, which expires October 15, has a short-term cancellation value on April 15 of $900.

7. Property held in trust is in the form of stocks and bonds with realizable value of $24,000. The partnership is entitled to a fee of $600 per year, payable April 15, for its services. Because cash was not available in the trust for the payment, the fee was not recorded.

8. The machinery and equipment with a book value of $8,000 will realize $5,000.

9. The land and building may be sold for $38,000; however, the mortgage holder has indicated a willingness to cancel the debt and assume all encumbrances for the surrender of title to the real estate. Interest on the mortgage was paid on January 15.

10. The wages and commissions were last paid in full on January 31. Commission salesmen were dismissed on February 15. Accrued wages in the trial balance are:

Burke, Bookkeeper (to April 15)	$1,400
Maxwell, Commission Salesman (to February 15)	300
Josephs, Manager (to April 15)	1,750
	$3,450

11. The partnership owes Second Bank a note of $10,000. The note is secured by the balance in the Adams-Story account in Second Bank.

12. The estimated administrative expenses are $3,000.

13. While Adams has personal liabilities which are approximately equal to his personal assets, Story's personal assets exceed his personal liabilities by $2,800.

Required:

1. Prepare a statement of affairs for the Adams-Story Partnership as of April 15, 19X8.

2. What percentage of liabilities is expected to be recovered by each class of creditors?

(AICPA adapted)

P4.9 **Statement of Realization and Liquidation—Partnership** On March 1, 19X4, the balance sheet of Xavier & Company, a partnership, appeared as follows:

Cash.	$ 10,000	Accounts Payable	$ 80,000
Receivables	40,000	Notes Payable—Bank	50,000
Inventory	60,000	Mortgage Payable	120,000
Land.	30,000	Capital—Xavier	90,000
Building, Net.	150,000	Capital—Young	35,000
Equipment, Net	110,000	Capital—Zelman	25,000
	$400,000		$400,000

Xavier (who has a 60 percent interest) has operated the business; Young (30 percent) and Zelman (10 percent) are investors who are not active in the business.

Required:

1. On March 1, Xavier died; you are appointed a trustee to liquidate the partnership. As cash becomes available, you are to make distributions to Xavier's estate and to Young and Zelman. As a first step, prepare a cash distribution plan.

2. You decide to continue business operations on a limited scale for 2 months while you try to find a buyer for the entire business. During March and April, the following occur:

Sales on Account	$70,000
Collection of Receivables	60,000
Purchases for Cash	30,000
Operating Expenses (Paid)	20,000
Decrease in Inventory	10,000

Failing to find a buyer, you shut down operations and begin the liquidation process. During May and June, you achieve the following:

a. Sell equipment (book value $50,000) for $25,000 cash.

b. Sell the land and building for $240,000 cash.

c. Agree with the bank to pay off the mortgage for $105,000 rather than transfer it to the new buyer of the building.

d. Sell inventory (book value $20,000) for $14,000.

e. Collect $18,000 of accounts receivable.

f. Pay $2,000 rent for space to store the remaining inventory and equipment.

g. Pay yourself a $7,000 trustee's fee.

Prepare a realization and liquidation statement for the period March 1 through June 30, 19X4.

3. As a result of the above transactions, the cash account has a balance of $203,000. You plan to retain $13,000 for future transaction needs and distribute the balance. Indicate how the $190,000 will be distributed.

P4.10 Personal Trust Shortly before her death, Theresa Letterman established a $120,000 trust for the daughters of a friend. Emily and Janet Wallace, the beneficiaries of the trust, were each to receive half the income from the trust until their twenty-first birthdays. Upon reaching her majority, Emily was to receive $20,000. Janet (the younger sister) would continue to receive one-half of the trust income with the remainder being added to the principal. On Janet's twenty-first birthday, the remaining trust principal was to be divided equally and distributed to both women. Emily and Janet were 16 and 11 years old at the time Theresa Letterman made the arrangements.

Data concerning earnings and expenses of the trust are as follows:

	Total for First 5 years	Total for Second 5 Years
Gross Earnings.	$36,000	$43,000
Administrative Expenses (Allocated 60% to Principal and 40% to Income)	2,000	2,500
Gains (Losses) on Sales of Securities	(500)	3,000

Required:

1. Calculate the distribution of principal on Janet's twenty-first birthday.
2. Calculate the total dollar amount received by Janet from the trust. Calculate the total dollar amount received by Emily from the trust.
3. Calculate the distribution in the third year of the trust, assuming trust investment revenue was $7,000, administrative expenses were $400, and gains on sales of securities were $800 that year.

P4.11 Profit-Sharing Trust The Habler Company established a noncontributing profit-sharing trust for its employees, effective January 1, 1984. Contributions to the trust have been determined to be allowable as a deduction on the company tax return. The records of the trust have been kept by the company bookkeeper, who has computed prior years' distributions accurately. The following trial balance of the trust at December 31, 1986, is available:

HABLER EMPLOYEE PROFIT-SHARING TRUST
TRIAL BALANCE
DECEMBER 31, 1986

Cash in Bank.	$1,505	
Savings and Loan Shares	1,000	
Government Securities	2,000	
Stocks	1,095	
Loans to Members	500	
Accrued Interest Receivable	85	
Liability to Members		$6,000
Interest Earned.		260
Dividends.		50
Payment on Account to Separated Employee.	115	
Brokers' Fees.	10	
	$6,310	$6,310

Employee records and records of the trust show the following:

Name	Date Employed	1986 Salaries	Trust Account Balances December 31, 1985
John Jones	2/1/66	$ 40,000	$2,500
Mary Smith	12/10/81	10,000	500
Oscar Johnson	1/20/71	30,000	1,500
Wendell Davis (quit 8/31/86) . . .	8/10/80	11,800	500
James Saunders	6/2/78	20,000	1,000
Susan Jacobs.	8/10/84	10,000	0
Sam Dodd	10/20/85	10,000	0
		$131,800	$6,000

The profit-sharing trust agreement provides:

1. The annual company contribution to the trust is to be computed on the basis of income as determined for tax purposes but before deduction of the profit-sharing contribution. The contribution is to be made at the rate of 10 percent of the first $50,000 of such income and 15 percent of the excess over $50,000.
2. Company contributions and relinquishments (forfeitures) are to be distributed to members in the employ of the company at the close of each year on the basis of service and salary points—one point for each full year of company service and one point for each $200 of earnings for the year.
3. Annual earnings of the trust are to be distributed to members having balances in their membership accounts at the beginning of the year in the ratio that each such beginning balance bears to the total beginning balances.
4. An employee must have 2 full years of service to be eligible for participation in the trust. Eligibility for new members is to be determined as of the end of each fiscal year.
5. A member leaving the employ of the company for any reason other than at the instigation of the employer for cause is entitled to receive ten percent of his or her trust balance for each full year of service with the company. For example, a person with 3 full years of service receives 30% of his or her trust balance.

Employees do not participate in the company contribution for the year of separation. Income of the company for the year ended December 31, 1986, amounted to $60,666.67 before income taxes and deduction for its contribution to the plan.

Required:

1. Compute the profit-sharing contribution by the company for 1986.
2. Compute:
   a. The distribution of company contributions to members' accounts.

    b. The allocation of the trust income to members' accounts.

    c. The severance settlement and forfeiture of Wendell Davis.

3. Complete the chart illustrated below and compute the ending balance of liabilities of the trust to members and to the separated employee.

EMPLOYEE PROFIT-SHARING TRUST
STATEMENT OF CHANGES IN MEMBER ACCOUNTS
FOR YEAR ENDING DECEMBER 31, 1986

Members	Beginning Balance	Company Contributions	Trust Income	Relinquishments (Forfeitures)	Total	Payments during Year	Ending Balance
John Jones	$2,500						
Mary Smith	500						
Oscar Johnson . . .	1,500						
James Saunders . .	1,000						
Susan Jacobs . . .							
Wendell Davis . . .	500						
	$6,000						

4. Record the 1986 adjusting entries for the profit-sharing trust and prepare the balance sheet of the trust as of December 31, 1986.

(AICPA adapted)

P4.12 Estate Taxation *(Appendix)* Refer to P4.3, which relates to the estate of Arthur Taine. Arthur made two gifts during his lifetime that exceeded his $10,000 annual exclusion:

1. A $20,000 wedding gift given 5 years ago to his daughter, Wanda, for a down payment on a house.
2. A $15,000 sports car given to his son David upon his graduation from college 4 years ago.

Required: Calculate the estate tax owed by the estate of Arthur Taine (ignore the $58,000 figure for federal and state taxes given in P4.3). Assume that the lifetime credit at the time of Arthur's death was $47,000.

Part TWO Multiple Corporate Entities

Corporate financial accounting and reporting have long been the focus of much of accounting theory, standards, and practice. In this part of the book, we address accounting problems arising when multiple corporate entities are viewed as a single accounting entity or area of economic interest to shareholders. We look beyond legal and organizational distinctions to identify the inclusive accounting entity, which often consists of several subentities, to serve as the basis for reports on financial position, operations, and changes in financial position.

Chapters 5 through 11 deal with the aggregation of accounting information. Many business units are, in themselves, legitimate accounting entities. Yet such units are often parts of a larger collection of economic resources in which common ownership interests exist. Bringing together the accounts of these business units involves more than a simple summation.

Chapter 5 offers an introduction to this aggregation problem within the relatively simple framework of a single corporation organized around subfirm entities, called branches, which have separate financial accounting systems. In Chapter 6, the accounting problems arising when separate corporations are brought under common control are studied. When corporations under common control remain as separate legal entities, their accounts are normally consolidated for financial reports reflecting the status and performance of the commonly controlled economic resources. Chapters 7 through 11 provide comprehensive analyses of typical problems arising when consolidated statements are prepared and the aggregation problem is more complex.

Chapter 5 Home Office and Branch Accounting

Within a firm, there are various accounting or reporting entities. These entities range from production, service, and marketing *departments* to *branches, divisions,* and separately controlled corporations known as *subsidiaries*. The concept of *responsibility accounting* provides the basis for identifying departments as cost or profit centers; accordingly, expense and revenue data are accumulated for these units of activity in the firm's management accounting system. On a larger scale, divisions and subsidiaries of a firm often have considerable autonomy and may include many departments.

The degree of financial accounting responsibility varies among these business units. While individual departments normally do not have their own financial accounting systems, they are viewed as accounting entities because their activities are separately identified in the firm's management or cost accounting system. In contrast, the subsidiaries under common corporate control have complete financial accounting systems. Between departments on the one hand and subsidiaries on the other lie sales agencies, branches, and divisions. These subfirm entities have varying degrees of financial accounting responsibility. This chapter addresses the financial accounting procedures employed by such subfirm entities.

Sales Agencies

We begin with a discussion of accounting for sales agencies. A **sales agency** is a business unit physically removed from the firm's main or home office. Its limited functions include serving as a base for sales personnel in the field, processing customer orders, and maintaining limited inventories of the company's products. From an accounting standpoint, the sales agency's accounts are carried on the books of the home office. Transactions are recorded in accounts which identify the particular sales agency. An imprest fund is established to provide the agency with cash used for various small expenses. Since rent, payroll, utilities, and asset accounting are all handled by the home office, the agency's primary accounting responsibility relates to the imprest fund. Entries made by the home office to account for typical transactions of a sales agency are illustrated by Exhibit 5.1.

Exhibit 5.1	Accounting for the Operation of a Sales Agency by the Home Office

Oceanside Company decides to open a sales agency to promote its leisure-time products in Longport, a popular resort town. A $10,000 imprest fund is established for the Longport Agency:

Imprest Fund: Longport Agency	10,000	
Cash		10,000
To establish a $10,000 imprest fund for use of the Longport Agency.		

The following transactions related to the Longport agency are recorded by the Oceanside Company during the month of July:

Merchandise Samples: Longport Agency	25,000	
Inventory		25,000
To record the cost of samples shipped to the Longport Agency. Oceanside uses a perpetual inventory system. Under a periodic inventory system, an account such as Merchandise Shipments: Longport Agency rather than Inventory would be credited.		

Accounts Receivable	50,000	
Sales: Longport Agency.		50,000
To record sales generated by the Longport Agency.		

Operating Expenses: Longport Agency (details omitted).	7,000	
Cash		7,000
To reimburse the Longport Agency's imprest fund for various cash expenses.		

Operating Expenses: Longport Agency	9,000	
Depreciation Expense—Furniture and Fixtures:		
Longport Agency	1,500	
Accounts Payable.		9,000
Accumulated Depreciation—Furniture and Fixtures		1,500
To charge the Longport Agency for expenses incurred by Oceanside on behalf of the agency.		

Cost of Goods Sold: Longport Agency.	22,000	
Inventory		22,000
To charge the Longport Agency for the cost of merchandise sold by its personnel.		

Selling Expenses: Longport Agency	5,000	
Merchandise Samples: Longport Agency		5,000
To record use of sample merchandise by the Longport Agency; samples costing $20,000 are still on hand.		

At the end of July, Oceanside prepares an income statement for the Longport Agency and closes the revenue and expense accounts to Oceanside's income summary. The income statement is given as follows:

(continued on next page)

Exhibit 5.1 **Continued**

LONGPORT SALES AGENCY
INCOME STATEMENT FOR THE MONTH OF JULY

Sales	$50,000
Cost of Goods Sold	$22,000
Operating Expenses	16,000
Depreciation Expense	1,500
Selling Expenses	5,000
Total Expenses	$44,500
Net Income	$ 5,500

Note that the sales agency itself makes no entries because it has no financial
accounting system.

From Exhibit 5.1, we see that accounting for a sales agency creates no
special problems. Except for the imprest fund, the accounting identifies transactions made *by* or *for* the sales agency rather than *between* the sales agency and
the home office. The transfer of merchandise samples indicates their new physical
location. As an alternative to maintaining home office accounts identified by sales
agency, as in Exhibit 5.1, entries could be made in control accounts at the home
office with simultaneous updating of subsidiary records for the various sales agencies.

We now turn to consideration of accounting for home office/branch (or divisional) relationships. The major factors distinguishing these business units from
sales agencies for accounting purposes are (1) separate accounting systems and (2)
greater variety of transactions *between* the home office and its branches.

Branches and Divisions

In the world of practice, there is almost a continuous spectrum of subentities
ranging from sales agencies with almost no autonomy or accounting functions to
large divisions which can operate much like separate companies. *Branches and
divisions* are typical of the larger business units which perform many functions.
Accounting for such business units requires special consideration when a more
complete chart of accounts is maintained by the unit and numerous transactions
with the home office are recorded in the accounts of *both* the branch or division
and the home office. The equivalent of sales agency accounting could be used for
a division if the division has no financial accounting responsibility. Profitability
of such a division would be measured by the internal accounting system, and the
home office/branch accounting procedures which we describe below would not be
needed. To simplify the terminology, the term **branch** will be used to identify a
business unit (branch office or division) which has more than a minimal financial

accounting responsibility. Transactions between the home office and branch are recorded by *both* units in their separate accounts.

Reciprocal Accounts

A key element both in identifying home office/branch situations and in providing the needed accounting is the presence of *reciprocal accounts*.

> **Reciprocal accounts** have equal and offsetting balances on both the home office and branch books. They are used by both business units to record those transactions *between* the units or made *on behalf of* one unit by the other.

When a company's financial statements are prepared, all internal transactions among the units of the company are netted out so that the statements reflect only transactions with outside parties. The procedures for netting out the reciprocal accounts—which represent internal transactions—when combined financial statements for the home office and its branches are prepared are discussed later in the chapter.

Investment in Branch and Home Office Accounts. From the home office point of view, all resources transferred to the branch and earnings generated by the branch are included in the home office's investment in the branch. To keep track of its claim on branch assets, the home office uses an **Investment in Branch** account (sometimes called *Branch Office* or *Branch Current*). After periodic results of branch operations are recorded, Investment in Branch reflects the equity of the home office in the branch. Similarly, the branch uses an account called **Home Office** (or *Home Office Current*) to record transactions with the home office from the branch perspective. The balance in the Home Office account represents the dollar amount of the branch's obligations to the home office or, alternatively, may be viewed as an owners' equity account where the home office is the owner. In normal circumstances, the Investment in Branch account on the home office books has a debit balance, while the Home Office account on the branch books has a credit balance.

As an example, suppose the home office transfers the following items to a newly established branch:

Item	Amount per Home Office Books
Cash	$20,000
Unexpired Insurance	1,400
Office Supplies	800
Furniture and Fixtures	35,000
Accumulated Depreciation—Furniture and Fixtures	(10,000)
Net Book Value of Items Transferred	$47,200

These transfers would be recorded by the home office and branch as shown below:

RECORDING THE TRANSFER OF ASSETS
BETWEEN HOME OFFICE AND BRANCH

Account	Home Office Books		Branch Books	
	Dr.	Cr.	Dr.	Cr.
Investment in Branch	47,200		—	—
Cash		20,000	20,000	
Unexpired Insurance		1,400	1,400	
Office Supplies		800	800	
Furniture and Fixtures		35,000	35,000	
Accumulated Depreciation—Furniture and Fixtures	10,000			10,000
Home Office	—	—		47,200

Note that after the transfer has been recorded there is no difference in the firm's total assets or liabilities. Rather, the fact that assets have changed their location within the organization is recorded in the reciprocal accounts. In order to avoid overstatement of assets and liabilities when combined financial statements are prepared, the offsetting balances in both the Investment in Branch and Home Office accounts will be netted out.

Treatment of Start-Up Costs of New Branches. Establishing a new branch often requires that considerable start-up costs be incurred before revenues are generated. The matching principle might be invoked by some to justify deferring or capitalizing those costs pending the realization of revenue. *SFAS 7* offers some guidance in this area.[1] Technically, *SFAS 7* applies to development stage enterprises (as defined therein) which will issue separate financial statements; its thrust is given in the following excerpt:

> Generally accepted accounting principles that apply to established operating enterprises shall govern the recognition of revenue by a development stage enterprise and shall determine whether a cost incurred by a development stage enterprise is to be charged to expense when incurred or is to be capitalized or deferred. Accordingly, capitalization or deferral of costs shall be subject to the same assessment of recoverability that would be applicable in an established operating enterprise.[2]

Although separate financial statements are not issued externally for a branch, whether in a "development stage" or not, it seems clear that *future benefit* is the main criterion when capitalization is being considered. No special accounting principles apply. This means that conventional organization costs could be capitalized and amortized but that training costs or early operating losses must be expensed as incurred and not deferred.

---

[1] Financial Accounting Standards Board, *Statement of Financial Accounting Standards No. 7*, "Accounting and Reporting by Development Stage Enterprises" (Stamford, CT: FASB, 1975); CT § De4.

[2] Ibid., par. 10; CT § De4.105.

Merchandise Shipments to Branches

Branches are often established to serve as retail outlets for a company's products. Merchandise inventories carried at the branch locations are periodically replenished with shipments of merchandise from the home office. The internal transfer price used to bill shipments to branches affects the accounting for shipments and the procedures employed to combine the accounts of the home office and its branches when financial statements are prepared. Transfer prices may be based on any of the following:

1. Cost to the home office.
2. An amount in excess of cost:
   a. Cost plus an internal markup percentage.
   b. Retail or market value.

Merchandise Shipments Billed at Cost. The simplest practice is to bill shipments of merchandise to the branch at cost; it creates no special accounting problems and results in a branch income statement that provides management with a straightforward view of the results of branch operations. On the other hand, it has the effect of attributing the entire gross profit on merchandise sales to the branch, even though the home office may have played a substantial role in the manufacture or procurement of merchandise from outside sources or in the generation of sales. Evaluation of the performance of the branch relative to the home office may therefore be clouded—some of the ultimate gross profit attributed to the branch may legitimately have been attributable to operation of the home office.

Periodic Inventory System. When the home office and branch use periodic inventory accounting, shipments are recorded in two additional offsetting reciprocal accounts, as shown below:

HOME OFFICE BOOKS

Investment in Branch XXX
   Shipments to Branch   XXX
To record the shipment of inventory to the branch.

BRANCH BOOKS

Shipments from Home Office XXX
   Home Office   XXX
To record the receipt of inventory shipped from the home office.

If the branch pays the freight cost, it will charge Freight In and credit Cash. No entry need be made by the home office. In contrast, payment of the freight by the home office means that additional entries are required to assign the freight cost to the branch.

HOME OFFICE BOOKS

Investment in Branch XXX
   Cash   XXX
To record payment of shipping costs on behalf of the branch.

BRANCH BOOKS

Freight In XXX
    Home Office   XXX
To record freight expense on inventory paid by home office.

Perpetual Inventory System. When both the home office and branch employ perpetual inventory systems, the additional reciprocal accounts—Shipments to Branch and Shipments from Home Office—are unnecessary. Instead, the home office credits Inventory when shipments are made and the branch debits Inventory when the shipments are received. Cost of freight for the shipments is handled the same as under the periodic system.

Merchandise Shipments Billed above Cost. The billing of shipments at an amount above cost is often appropriate for performance evaluation and optimal decision making within the firm. It has the effect of attributing some, or all, of the gross profit on sales to the home office. The practice has also been motivated by the desire to conceal the true profitability of the branch operation from the branch manager. An added advantage arises when shipments are billed at *retail prices*. Even if a periodic inventory system is used, billing at retail has the effect of creating a perpetual system at the branch. If shipments are billed at retail, the branch inventory account will reflect retail prices. Sales made by the branch are, of course, made at retail. Therefore, the home office record of shipments to the branch at retail less sales reported by the branch tells the home office the branch inventory which should be on hand, at retail. Periodic physical inventory counts by home office personnel will reveal any shortages in the branch inventory with a high degree of accuracy. In this way, a system of billing shipments to the branch at retail prices enhances internal control over branch inventories.

These internal control benefits associated with billing intrafirm shipments at retail must be weighed against the possible distortion of branch operating results. When shipments are billed at retail, branch sales revenue will approximate its cost of goods sold. Consequently, the branch will consistently report an operating loss equal to its operating expenses. This is not an accurate picture of branch operations. It might impede proper managerial analysis of the branch and have a demoralizing effect on branch personnel.

Periodic Inventory System. Once a firm begins pricing merchandise shipments to branches at amounts in excess of cost, a new accounting problem arises. When the home office computes its own cost of goods sold for a reporting period, it reduces its own merchandise purchases from outside sources by the amount shown in the Shipments to Branch account. Similarly, if the home office manufactures the goods itself, the shipments to the branch go to reduce cost of goods manufactured.

For financial reporting purposes, the home office carries its inventory accounts at cost (or lower of cost or market). This cost basis will be disturbed if merchandise purchases are reduced by branch shipments measured at more than cost. To avoid this problem, the home office uses an account entitled **Overval-**

uation of Branch Inventory, sometimes called *Unrealized Profit in Branch Inventory,* together with the Shipments to Branch account, to record the intrafirm shipments. The markup on each shipment to the branch will be entered and accumulated in this account, which becomes another reciprocal account. The Shipments to Branch balance at cost plus the Overvaluation account balance on the home office books will equal the Shipments from Home Office balance at billed prices on the branch books. These accounts are used to record *intrafirm* (or *interoffice*) merchandise shipments, as shown below:

HOME OFFICE BOOKS

Investment in Branch	XXX	
Shipments to Branch		YYY
Overvaluation of Branch Inventory		ZZZ

To record the shipment of inventory costing $YYY to the branch at a
billed price of $XXX, reflecting intrafirm markup of $ZZZ.

BRANCH BOOKS

Shipments from Home Office	XXX	
Home Office		XXX

To record the receipt of inventory shipped from the home office at a
billed price of $XXX.

Although this overvaluation account relates to the *branch* inventory, the account cannot be viewed as deferred profit (as in installment sales) because no external sale has occurred. Rather, it reflects the fact that an internal transfer price in excess of cost has been used to record the movement of goods from the home office to the branch. When combined statements are prepared, the overvaluation account will be eliminated as discussed later in the chapter.

As an example, suppose the home office bills the branch $25,000 for a shipment of merchandise which cost the home office $15,000. The branch pays freight costs of $800. Journal entries made by the home office and branch are given next:

HOME OFFICE BOOKS

Investment in Branch	25,000	
Shipments to Branch		15,000
Overvaluation of Branch Inventory		10,000

To record the shipment of inventory costing $15,000 to the branch
at a billed price of $25,000.

BRANCH BOOKS

Shipments from the Home Office	25,000	
Freight In	800	
Home Office		25,000
Cash		800

To record the receipt of inventory shipped from the home office,
$25,000, and payment of the freight, $800.

Perpetual Inventory System. Again, when the home office and branch both have perpetual inventory systems, the shipments accounts are no longer needed—the Inventory accounts are debited and credited directly. The home office continues to account for the markup in the overvaluation account in order to avoid disturbing the cost basis of its inventory. Below are shown the entries needed in a perpetual inventory system to record the $25,000 shipment just mentioned:

HOME OFFICE BOOKS

Investment in Branch	25,000	
Inventory		15,000
Overvaluation of Branch Inventory		10,000

To record the shipment of inventory costing $15,000 to the branch at a billed price of $25,000.

BRANCH BOOKS

Inventory	25,000	
Freight In	800	
Home Office		25,000
Cash		800

To record the receipt of inventory shipped from the home office, $25,000, and payment of the freight, $800.

Over the course of the year, the overvaluation account grows. At year-end it includes the intrafirm markup reflected in (1) current year shipments and (2) the beginning inventory of the branch. Observe that the branch's inventory is carried on the branch books at prices billed by the home office, *not* at home office cost.

Treatment of Freight In. Freight costs on merchandise purchases or shipments from the home office attach to the merchandise and are inventoriable costs. When recording the ending inventory, the accountant must include either the actual freight costs on those goods or a pro rata share of total freight in. For example, if freight of $50 is incurred on a merchandise shipment costing $2,000, the goods should be inventoried at $2,050. Alternatively, suppose total freight in for the year is $20,000 on merchandise purchases of $600,000. If 10 percent of these goods remains in ending inventory, it should be priced at $62,000 [= .1($600,000 + $20,000)]. We assume throughout that the cost of merchandise to the home office includes the appropriate freight unless stated otherwise.

Charging the Branch with Expenses Incurred by the Home Office

Since the branch is not autonomous, the home office will incur various expenses on its behalf. This situation occurs for two major reasons:

1. Certain accounting records, such as those for plant assets and payroll, may be retained in the home office. As a result, depreciation expense, salaries and wages, and payroll taxes pertaining to the branch are initially recorded by the home office.

2. Various general and administrative overhead expenses as well as certain marketing expenses (such as advertising) are normally incurred at the home office. Such expenses are generally not separable, although some portion obviously relates to the branch operations.

How these expenses are accounted for varies across firms. Some companies may not charge expenses to their branches in formal accounting entries. Rather, they may simply make memorandum allocations for internal reporting purposes. In other situations, expenses incurred on behalf of branches are credited in the home office accounts and entered in the accounts of the branch. We briefly illustrate the latter case:

HOME OFFICE BOOKS

Investment in Branch XXX
    Various Credits (details omitted)   XXX
To charge the branch for expenses incurred on its behalf by the home office. Credits are to expenses such as advertising, assets such as prepayments, and accumulated depreciation.

BRANCH BOOKS

Various Expenses (details omitted) XXX
    Home Office   XXX
To record expenses attributable to the branch which were originally incurred by the home office.

Observe that these entries affect the reciprocal Home Office and Investment in Branch accounts. Incurrence of these expenses by the home office clearly increases the resources committed to the branch and, concurrently, increases the obligation of the branch to the home office.

Transactions among Branches

Although it is possible for a branch to have reciprocal accounts with other branches, there is little need to do so. As part of its control system, the home office coordinates and controls any transactions between branches through its investment in branch accounts. Branch offices record any transactions with other branches in their respective home office accounts.

Merchandise shipments between branches are probably the most common type of interbranch transaction. Excess inventory at one branch location is frequently moved to cover a shortage at another location. In considering such interbranch transactions, one must also address the treatment of freight costs. The freight cost associated with direct shipment of the merchandise from the home office to the branch where it is sold is properly inventoriable. Shipments between branches, however, may cause the total freight cost incurred in getting the merchandise to its ultimate destination to exceed the cost of direct shipment from the home office. This excess is not inventoriable and is an expense of the current period generally attributable to the home office, which usually makes decisions on shipments.

To illustrate, suppose that the Hanover branch had received $10,000 of merchandise at cost from its home office; the home office had paid the freight of $500. Subsequently, Hanover is instructed to ship these items to the Concord branch at an additional shipping cost of $200, also paid by the home office. *Had the items been shipped direct to Concord from the home office,* the freight cost would have been $600 and the following entries made:

HOME OFFICE BOOKS			CONCORD BRANCH BOOKS		
Investment in Concord	10,600		Shipments from Home Office	10,000	
Shipments to Concord		10,000	Freight In	600	
Cash		600	Home Office		10,600

To achieve this result, we now prepare journal entries recording the original shipment to Hanover and the interbranch shipment from Hanover to Concord:

Original Shipment to Hanover

Interbranch Shipment from Hanover to Concord

HOME OFFICE BOOKS			HOME OFFICE BOOKS		
Investment in Hanover	10,500		Investment in Concord	10,600	
Shipments to Hanover		10,000	Shipments to Hanover	10,000	
Cash		500	Excess Freight Expense	100	
			Investment in Hanover		10,500
			Shipments to Concord		10,000
			Cash		200

HANOVER BRANCH BOOKS			HANOVER BRANCH BOOKS		
Shipments from Home Office	10,000		Home Office	10,500	
Freight In	500		Shipments from Home Office		10,000
Home Office		10,500	Freight In		500

CONCORD BRANCH BOOKS			CONCORD BRANCH BOOKS		
No entry.			Shipments from Home Office	10,000	
			Freight In	600	
			Home Office		10,600

After these entries have been made, all reciprocal accounts have the proper offsetting balances. Moreover, the actual freight expense totaled $700 (= $500 + $200). Because it exceeded the cost of direct shipment by $100 (= $700 − $600), the excess freight represents a period expense to the home office.

End-of-Period Procedures

At the end of an accounting period, *three* types of procedures are required in home office/branch accounting. *First,* the accountant must determine that the offsetting balances in the reciprocal accounts are equal, as intended. If discrepancies exist, the reciprocal accounts must be reconciled and their balances adjusted accordingly. *Second,* to account for the operations of the period, conventional closing

entries must be made on the home office and branch books. *Third,* the accountant must prepare combined financial statements for the home office, often using a working paper to facilitate their preparation. We discuss each procedure in turn.

Reconciliation of Reciprocal Accounts. Reciprocal accounts must be reconciled, and any necessary adjustments must be made to bring these accounts into balance before end-of-period procedures can be continued. Differences in reciprocal account balances can result from errors but usually arise when intrafirm transactions occur near the end of an accounting period. Such transactions are normally recorded by *either* the home office *or* the branch, but not by both. Delays in shipping, mailing, or the processing of information can mean the second half of the transaction goes unrecorded until the next accounting period. Some common examples of these transactions include:

1. Shipments in transit at the end of a period, which are recorded by the home office but not by the branch.
2. Remittances from the branch mailed on the last day of an accounting period and therefore not yet received and recorded by the home office.
3. Collections of home office receivables by the branch close to the end of a period, which are not recorded in the home office records.
4. If all fixed asset records are maintained at the home office, a last-minute fixed asset purchase by the branch does not yet appear on the home office books at the end of the period.

All such transactions are recorded in only one reciprocal account by the end of the period. A reconciliation of reciprocal accounts and appropriate adjusting entries, which record the other half of all such transactions, are needed so that the offsetting account balances are brought into agreement.

Closing Entries. After the reciprocal accounts have been reconciled, closing entries are made on both the branch and home office books. When a periodic inventory system is used, these closing entries include the recognition of home office and branch ending inventories. The branch revenue and expense accounts are closed to the branch's income summary. If the branch had net income (loss), closing the branch's income summary generates a credit (debit) to the Home Office account. The home office records the income (loss) of the branch and increases (decreases) its Investment in Branch account accordingly. Similarly, home office revenue and expense accounts are closed to the home office income summary account. When shipments to the branch are billed at prices above cost, the overvaluation account must be reduced by the amount of intrafirm markup realized during the period through branch sales to external customers. Whether the realized intrafirm markup should be attributed to branch operations or home office operations is related to the previously discussed reasons for setting the transfer price above cost. The typical closing entries presented in Exhibit 5.2 reflect the realized intrafirm markup in home office operations by assigning it to an account entitled Realized Intrafirm Profit.

Exhibit 5.2	Typical Closing Entries Made on Branch and Home Office Books

BRANCH BOOKS

Sales	XXX	
Inventory, Dec. 31	XXX	
Shipments from Home Office		XXX
Freight In		XXX
Expenses (details omitted)		XXX
Inventory, Jan. 1		XXX
Income Summary		XXX

To close the branch revenue and expense accounts to Income Summary and record the net income for the period. Cost of goods sold for the branch equals Inventory, Jan. 1 + Shipments from Home + Freight In − Inventory, Dec. 31.

Income Summary	XXX	
Home Office		XXX

To close the net income for the period to the Home Office account.

HOME OFFICE BOOKS

Investment in Branch	XXX	
Income from Branch		XXX

To record the net income reported by the branch, thereby increasing the investment in the branch.

Overvaluation of Branch Inventory	XXX	
Realized Intrafirm Profit		XXX

To credit the home office for the markup on the intrafirm shipments realized on sales to external customers during the period.

Sales	XXX	
Shipments to Branch	XXX	
Inventory, Dec. 31	XXX	
Realized Intrafirm Profit	XXX	
Purchases		XXX
Freight In		XXX
Expenses (details omitted)		XXX
Inventory, Jan. 1		XXX
Income Summary		XXX

To close the home office revenue and expense accounts to Income Summary and record the net income from home office operations. Cost of goods sold for the home office equals Inventory, Jan. 1 + Purchases − Shipments to Branch + Freight In − Inventory, Dec. 31.

Income from Branch	XXX	
Income Summary		XXX

To close the branch's net income to Income Summary.

Income Summary	XXX	
Retained Earnings		XXX

To close combined net income for the period to Retained Earnings.

Adjustment of the Overvaluation Account. Treatment of the markup on interoffice merchandise shipments and the related overvaluation account is a complex subject and deserves some additional explanation here. Recall that the overvaluation account is used to record the markup when merchandise shipped from the home office to the branch is billed at a price higher than home office cost. This interoffice markup remains unrealized, pending realization through branch sales to outside customers. *During the year, the account balance consists of the markup in the branch's beginning inventory plus the markup on current period shipments.* At year-end, when total branch sales are known, the markup related to those sales is recognized as income by removing it from the overvaluation account during closing, as shown in Exhibit 5.2. After this entry, the remaining balance in the overvaluation account pertains to the markup in the branch's ending inventory.

To illustrate these points, suppose the branch acquires merchandise from the home office at 50 percent over home office cost. The branch's beginning inventory is $90,000, purchases from the home office are $300,000, and the branch's ending inventory is $75,000, all at the billed price of 50 percent over home office cost. On the assumption that the branch uses a *perpetual inventory system,* the following T accounts summarize the relationship between the home office Overvaluation and branch Inventory accounts.

OVERVALUATION OF BRANCH INVENTORY (HOME OFFICE)			INVENTORY (BRANCH)	
	30,000	Beginning Balances	90,000	
	100,000	Interoffice Shipments	300,000	
		Goods Sold		315,000
105,000		Markup Realized (Closing)		
	25,000	Ending Balances	75,000	

Working Papers for Combined Statements. Financial statements issued to external users report the financial position and operations of the home office and its branches as a *single business unit,* the firm. Preparation of these combined financial statements is facilitated by use of a **working paper** designed to organize the preclosing account balances and ending inventories of the home office and branch along income statement and balance sheet lines. As mentioned earlier, transactions between the home office and branch must be netted out (or **eliminated**) in combining the accounts to avoid overstating combined assets, liabilities, revenues, and expenses. These internal transactions are reflected in the offsetting reciprocal account balances on the home office and branch books. The Investment in Branch and Home Office reciprocal account balances are eliminated on the working paper as part of this netting-out or **elimination process.** If they are not eliminated, combined assets and equities will both be overstated by the balance in these accounts. This part of the elimination process is depicted graphically in Figure 5.1. Be aware, however, that the elimination process is a *working paper technique only.* Because the reciprocal accounts reflect bonafide transactions between the

Figure 5.1 | **Diagrammatic Approach to Eliminating Reciprocal Account Balances When Preparing Combined Statements for a Home Office and Branch**

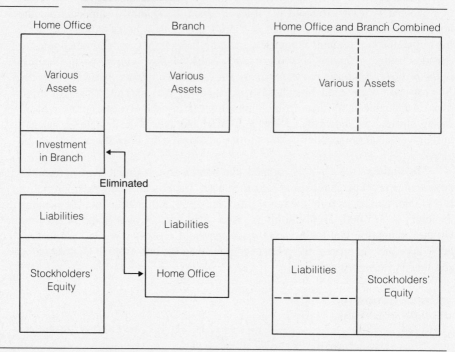

home office and branch, their balances are not eliminated on the two entities' books.

The shipments and overvaluation accounts also are reciprocal accounts and are eliminated on the working paper to avoid overstatement of revenues and cost of goods sold and to reduce the branch inventories to cost. Although the shipments accounts are closed and the overvaluation account adjusted as part of the normal closing procedures, their elimination on the working paper is not entered in the books of the home office and branch. They too reflect bonafide transactions between the home office and branch. In sum, *working paper eliminations are not posted to the books.*

Branch Inventories Priced above Cost. When the home office prices merchandise shipments to the branch above cost, it accounts for the excess in an account such as Overvaluation of Branch Inventory. This practice creates two problems when combined statements are prepared:

1. Since the branch's ending inventory includes an intrafirm markup, the markup must be removed before home office and branch inventories can be combined in the firm's balance sheet.
2. Markup in both the beginning and ending inventories of the branch distorts the firm's cost of goods sold and, accordingly, must be eliminated.

Since *preclosing* account balances are used in the combined financial statement working paper, the above problems necessitate working paper eliminations even though the formal closing entries achieve the same result on the books. To see how these complications are treated on the working paper, suppose we have the following set of account balances (a periodic inventory system is used):

HOME OFFICE BOOKS: (CR.)

Shipments to Branch . . . . $(100,000)
Overvaluation of Branch Inventory . . . .   (58,000)

BRANCH BOOKS: DR.

Inventory, Jan. 1 . . . . $ 24,000
Shipments from Home Office   150,000
Inventory, Dec. 31   30,000

Merchandise shipments to the branch are marked up 50 percent above cost by the home office. The balance of $58,000 in Overvaluation of Branch Inventory includes the $50,000 markup on current period shipments and the $8,000 markup reflected in the branch's January 1 inventory balance of $24,000. The objectives are to eliminate the reciprocal shipments accounts, to remove the markup from the beginning and ending inventories of the branch, and to reduce the branch's ending inventory to home office cost.

Our working paper (illustrated later, in Exhibit 5.7) has arranged the preclosing trial balance data in financial statement format. It includes the income statement, statement of retained earnings, and balance sheet. Furthermore, within the income statement separate lines are provided for beginning and ending inventories and merchandise purchases. These are the components of cost of goods sold. The ending inventory therefore appears on the working paper twice: (1) as a credit (reduction) to Cost of Goods Sold in the income statement and (2) as a debit in the balance sheet. Adding equal debits and credits for the ending inventory does not disturb the debit-credit equality in the preclosing trial balance.

Since removing the markup from ending inventory affects that ending inventory on both the balance sheet and the income statement, our working paper elimination must debit and credit Inventory by the same amount but in two different financial statements. The eliminating entries are given in Exhibit 5.3. If the working paper contains a single line for Cost of Goods Sold, instead of the individual components, the eliminations are made to Cost of Goods Sold (as shown in parentheses in Exhibit 5.3).

Accounting for Shipments to Branch as Sales. The preferred treatment for merchandise shipments to branches is to use a *shipments* account, which reduces home office purchases, and a separate overvaluation account to keep track of any markup. Some firms, however, may treat all shipments to branches as *sales* at billed prices. This practice requires that the interoffice sales be eliminated on the working paper against the branch's shipments account. As before, branch inventories are maintained at billed prices, and any markup must be removed on the combined financial statement working paper.

Exhibit 5.3	Illustration of End-of-Period Eliminating Entries Relating to Merchandise Shipments Priced above Cost

COMBINED FINANCIAL STATEMENT WORKING PAPER

Shipments to Branch (or Cost of Goods Sold).	100,000	
Overvaluation of Branch Inventory	50,000	
Shipments from Home Office (or Cost of Goods Sold)		150,000
To eliminate the offsetting reciprocal account balances relating to intrafirm merchandise shipments.		
Overvaluation of Branch Inventory	8,000	
Inventory, Jan. 1, Income Statement (or Cost of Goods Sold).		8,000
To reduce the branch beginning inventory to cost, thereby reducing cost of goods sold.		
Inventory, Dec. 31, Income Statement (or Cost of Goods Sold) .	10,000	
Inventory (Balance Sheet)		10,000
To reduce the branch ending inventory to cost, thereby increasing cost of goods sold.		

Markup in *ending inventory* is eliminated from the ending inventory on both the income statement and balance sheet in the way illustrated in Exhibit 5.3. If there is markup in *beginning inventory,* however, it is eliminated against beginning inventory on the income statement and against *beginning retained earnings.* In the normal closing procedures, home office ''sales'' to the branch are closed to the home office income summary and then to retained earnings. Thus the home office net income and retained earnings include the markup on the sales to the branch, even though some of it is reflected in the branch's inventory and is not realized. Since the markup reflected in last period's net income is in this period's beginning retained earnings, the elimination is against beginning retained earnings.

To contrast this sales treatment with the use of the shipments and overvaluation accounts, consider the following example. During Year 1, the home office bills a newly established branch $100,000 for merchandise shipped to it. The merchandise cost the home office $80,000. At year-end, $25,000 of this merchandise remains in the branch inventory, reflecting unrealized intrafirm markup of $5,000. The branch records sales of $130,000 in Year 1. In Year 2, $150,000 is billed to the branch for merchandise costing the home office $120,000. Branch sales during Year 2 amounted to $240,000, and there is *no ending inventory.* Total gross profit on branch sales over the two-year period is $170,000 [= ($130,000 + $240,000) − ($80,000 + $120,000)]. Comparative gross profit data under the two methods are presented in Exhibit 5.4.

The correct gross profits for the two years are computed in the top half of Exhibit 5.4, where the shipments and overvaluation accounts are used. After the normal closing procedures in Year 1, the unrealized intrafirm markup of $5,000 remains in the overvaluation account. It is counted as realized at the end of Year 2, when the overvaluation account is adjusted to reflect the external sale of all the inventory.

Exhibit 5.4 **Comparison of Gross Profits Reported under the Shipments and Sales Alternatives**

SHIPMENTS AND OVERVALUATION ACCOUNTS	Year 1	Year 2
Branch Sales	$130,000	$240,000
Branch Cost of Goods Sold	$(75,000)^a$	$(175,000)^c$
Branch Gross Profit on Sales	$ 55,000	$ 65,000
Intrafirm Markup Realized on External Sales.	$15,000^b$	$35,000^d$
Total Gross Profit on Branch Sales	$ 70,000	$100,000

RECORDING INTRAFIRM SHIPMENTS AS SALES	Year 1	Year 2
Branch Gross Profit (as above)	$ 55,000	$ 65,000
Home Office Sales to Branch	$100,000	$150,000
Cost of Goods Sold to Branch	(80,000)	(120,000)
Home Office Gross Profit on Sales to Branch	$ 20,000	$ 30,000
Total Reported Gross Profit on Branch Sales	$ 75,000	$ 95,000
Working Paper Elimination Needed	(5,000)	5,000
Corrected Total Gross Profit on Branch Sales (as above)	$ 70,000	$100,000

^{a}$75,000 = $100,000 - $25,000.$
^{b}$15,000 = ($100,000 - $80,000) - $5,000.$
^{c}$175,000 = $25,000 + $150,000.$
^{d}$35,000 = $5,000 + ($150,000 - $120,000).$

In contrast, when shipments to the branch are treated as sales, the results in the bottom half of Exhibit 5.4 occur. Although the $5,000 unrealized intrafirm markup is eliminated on the Year 1 working paper in both cases, as shown next, it remains in the home office reported net income for Year 1 and is closed to retained earnings.

COMBINED FINANCIAL STATEMENT WORKING PAPER

Inventory, Dec. 31 (Year 1) (Income Statement) 5,000
    Inventory, (Year 1) (Balance Sheet)   5,000
To reduce the branch ending inventory to cost, thereby increasing cost
of goods sold and decreasing combined net income in Year 1.

The $5,000 actually belongs in Year 2's net income, and the working paper entry that follows achieves the result. Note that the debit is to beginning retained earnings rather than the overvaluation account, as was illustrated in Exhibit 5.3.

COMBINED FINANCIAL STATEMENT WORKING PAPER

Retained Earnings, Jan. 1 (Year 2). 5,000
    Inventory, Jan. 1 (Year 2) (Income Statement).   5,000
To reduce the beginning inventory to cost and remove the markup
from beginning retained earnings. Recording intrafirm shipments as
sales led to inclusion of the unrealized markup in Year 1 income and
in retained earnings at the end of Year 1.

Comprehensive Illustration of Home Office and Branch Accounting

The Hardy Corporation established a branch office in Blockville on January 2, 19X1. Hardy bills all shipments of merchandise to Blockville at 25 percent over cost. Periodic inventory systems are used. At January 1, 19X4, the beginning of the current year, the condensed trial balance of the Blockville branch is as follows:

BLOCKVILLE BRANCH
TRIAL BALANCE AT JANUARY 1, 19X4

Account	Amount Dr. (Cr.)
Cash	$ 14,000
Accounts Receivable	65,000
Inventory	77,000
Furniture and Fixtures	100,000
Accumulated Depreciation	(49,090)
Accounts Payable	(8,000)
Salaries Payable	(5,000)
Home Office	(193,910)
	$ 0

The furniture and fixtures were acquired on January 2, 19X1. They are being depreciated by Blockville over ten years by the sum-of-the-years'-digits (SYD) method and have no salvage value. All other property accounts and prepayments are maintained at the home office. The branch's beginning inventory was $75,000 at billed prices and the applicable freight was $2,000, a total of $77,000. Home office and branch books are closed annually, and combined financial statements are prepared. A summary of transactions involving the branch during 19X4 follows:

1. Merchandise costing $300,000 was shipped to the branch; $8,000 was in transit at December 31, 19X4. Freight on the in-transit shipment to be paid by the branch is $100.
2. Freight costs on shipments received from the home office (excluding the shipment in transit) amounted to $9,000; $7,000 of this was paid in cash by the home office, $2,000 by the branch.
3. Sales of $500,000 were made by Blockville, including $125,000 of cash sales.
4. Collections on accounts receivable in the amount of $390,000 were received in the Blockville branch.
5. Operating expenses incurred by the branch amounted to $35,000; salaries were $50,000. Payments of $31,000 were made for operating expenses, and $53,000 was paid to employees (disregard payroll taxes).
6. Cash remittances to the home office were $410,000, of which $20,000 was in transit on December 31, 19X4.

7. On December 29, 19X4, a $7,800 payment from a home office customer was received in the branch. Branch personnel deposited the check but had not informed the home office by December 31, 19X4.
8. The home office allocated $27,000 of its operating expenses to the branch.
9. Depreciation expense of $12,727 [= (7/55) × $100,000] on furniture and fixtures was recorded by the branch on December 31, 19X4.
10. Ending inventory at the branch was $60,000 at billed prices and the applicable freight was $1,500, a total of $61,500; home office ending inventory, at cost, was $275,000.

Accounting entries made by the home office and branch during 19X4 are given in Exhibit 5.5. After the entries in Exhibit 5.5 are posted, preclosing trial balances for the home office and branch are prepared (Exhibit 5.6). Note that the overvaluation account balance of $90,000 includes the markup related to the branch's beginning inventory, $15,000 [= $75,000 (= $77,000 − $2,000 freight) − $75,000/1.25] plus the markup of $75,000 (= .25 × $300,000) on current period shipments.

Reconciliation of Reciprocal Accounts

Exhibit 5.6 (on page 204) shows a discrepancy between the Investment in Branch and Home Office reciprocal accounts. The Investment in Branch account has a debit balance of $212,910, while the Home Office account has a credit balance of $190,710. Before we can continue with our end-of-period procedures, these reciprocal accounts must be reconciled and brought into balance.

To accomplish this, we refer back to our summation of the year's transactions. *First,* we note from Transaction 1 that a merchandise shipment costing $8,000 with freight of $100 was in transit to the branch at December 31. At the 25 percent markup being used by the home office, this shipment has a billed value of $10,000. To record this shipment, the branch makes the following entry:

BLOCKVILLE BRANCH BOOKS
1(a)

Shipments from Home Office (in Transit)	10,000	
Home Office		10,000

To record the merchandise shipment in transit from the home office. *Note: This transaction increases the branch's ending physical inventory by $10,000 to $71,500, the amount to be recorded in the closing entries given in the next section.*

Freight In (in Transit)	100	
Accounts Payable		100

To accrue the freight cost on the merchandise shipment in transit. *Note: This transaction increases the branch's ending inventory by another $100, to $71,600.*

Second, Transaction 6 indicated that cash remittances to the home office of $20,000 were in transit at December 31. The home office will record this as shown:

Exhibit 5.5 Accounting Entries Made by Hardy Corporation and Its Blockville Branch to Record Transactions Involving the Branch in 19X4

HOME OFFICE BOOKS

Transaction		Debit	Credit
1	Investment in Branch	375,000	
	Shipments to Branch		300,000
	Overvaluation of Branch Inventory . . .		75,000
	To record merchandise shipped to the branch at 125 percent of cost. The markup of $75,000 is 25 percent of home office cost, $300,000.		
2	Investment in Branch	7,000	
	Cash		7,000
	To record freight cost paid on merchandise shipments to the branch.		

BLOCKVILLE BRANCH BOOKS

Transaction		Debit	Credit
1	Shipments from Home Office	365,000	
	Home Office		365,000
	To record merchandise received from the home office, at billed prices excluding the shipment in transit; $365,000 = $375,000 − $10,000.		
2	Freight In	9,000	
	Cash		2,000
	Home Office		7,000
	To record freight cost on merchandise shipments received, including that paid by the home office (except for the $100 freight on the shipment in transit).		
3	Cash	125,000	
	Accounts Receivable	375,000	
	Sales		500,000
	To record cash and credit sales made during the year.		
4	Cash	390,000	
	Accounts Receivable		390,000
	To record collection of receivables.		

5

Operating Expenses 35,000
Salaries Expense 50,000
Salaries Payable 3,000
  Accounts Payable 4,000
  Cash 84,000
To record operating expenses, salaries expense, and payments to employees and suppliers.

6

Home Office 410,000
  Cash 410,000
To record cash remitted to the home office during 19X4.

7

Cash 7,800
  Home Office 7,800
To record payment received from a home office customer and deposited (not recorded by home office).

8

Operating Expenses 27,000
  Home Office 27,000
To record expenses allocated by the home office.

9

Depreciation Expense 12,727
  Accumulated Depreciation 12,727
To record depreciation expense on furniture and fixtures in 19X4.

Cash 390,000
  Investment in Branch 390,000
To record cash received from the branch during 19X4 (excluding the cash in transit).

Investment in Branch 27,000
  Operating Expenses 27,000
To record allocation of home office expenses to the branch.

Exhibit 5.6	Hardy Corporation and Blockville Branch: Preclosing Trial Balances at December 31, 19X4

	Amount: Dr. (Cr.)	
Account	**Home Office**	**Branch**
Cash	$ 110,000	$ 40,800
Accounts Receivable	260,000	50,000
Inventory, Jan. 1, 19X4	280,000	77,000
Overvaluation of Branch Inventory	(90,000)	—
Prepayments	40,000	—
Property, Plant, and Equipment	750,000	100,000
Accumulated Depreciation	(200,000)	(61,817)
Investment in Branch	212,910	—
Accounts Payable	(162,000)	(12,000)
Salaries Payable	(18,000)	(2,000)
Other Liabilities	(300,000)	—
Capital Stock	(200,000)	—
Retained Earnings, Jan. 1, 19X4	(352,910)	—
Home Office	—	(190,710)
Sales	(1,700,000)	(500,000)
Shipments to Branch	(300,000)	—
Purchases	1,150,000	—
Shipments from Home Office	—	365,000
Freight In	25,000	9,000
Salaries Expense	250,000	50,000
Operating Expenses	195,000	62,000
Depreciation Expense	50,000	12,727
	$ 0	$ 0
Inventory, Dec. 31, 19X4 (excluding the shipment in transit)	$ 275,000	$ 61,500

HOME OFFICE BOOKS
6(a)

Cash (in Transit)	20,000	
Investment in Branch		20,000

To record the cash remittance in transit to the home office at Dec. 31.

Third, we see that in Transaction 7 the branch recorded the collection of a home office receivable but had not informed the home office. Since the receivable was not on the branch books, the credit was made to Home Office. Now, of course, the home office must recognize that this receivable has been collected.

HOME OFFICE BOOKS
7(a)

Investment in Branch	7,800	
Accounts Receivable		7,800

To record the collection of a home office receivable made by the branch.

These adjustments are posted to the reciprocal accounts and bring them into balance as shown next:

INVESTMENT IN BRANCH				HOME OFFICE		
Bal., 12/31/X4	212,910	6(a)	20,000		Bal., 12/31/X4	190,710
7(a)	7,800				1(a)	10,000
Adj. bal.	200,710				Adj. bal.	200,710

Closing Entries

After the above adjustments have been posted, both the home office and branch must record the typical closing entries at the end of the accounting period. These entries are posted to the accounts of the home office and branch. Be aware of the distinction, however, between the closing entries made here and the subsequent preparation of combined financial statements. In preparing the combined balance sheet and statements of income and retained earnings, we start with *preclosing trial balances* and make working paper eliminations that are *not* posted to the accounts of the home office or branch.

Branch Closing Entries. Branch personnel record the ending inventory and close all revenue and expense accounts, including Shipments from Home Office, first to an income summary account and then to the Home Office account. Any net income (loss) recorded by the branch increases (decreases) its obligation to the home office. After adjusting for the merchandise shipment in transit of $10,000 and the related freight of $100, the branch's ending inventory is $71,600, and Shipments from Home Office is $375,000.

BLOCKVILLE BRANCH BOOKS

Sales	500,000	
Inventory, Dec. 31.	71,600	
Income Summary	14,227	
Shipments from Home Office		375,000
Freight In		9,100
Salaries Expense		50,000
Operating Expenses		62,000
Depreciation Expense.		12,727
Inventory, Jan. 1		77,000

To close the revenue and expense accounts for 19X4 to Income Summary and record the net loss of $14,227.

Home Office	14,227	
Income Summary		14,227

To close the net loss for 19X4 to the Home Office account.

Home Office Closing Entries. In addition to recording its own ending inventory and closing its own revenue and expense accounts to Income Summary and then to Retained Earnings, the home office must accrue the net income (loss) of the branch and adjust the Overvaluation of Branch Inventory account. Ending inventory of the Blockville branch *at billed prices* (excluding freight in of $1,600) is $70,000, which is 25 percent or $14,000 [= $70,000 − ($70,000/1.25)] above cost. The overvaluation account must be reduced to $14,000; the other $76,000 (= $90,000 − $14,000) has been realized through sales by the branch to outsiders. Should the realization of this $76,000, which is now profit, be attributed to the branch or the home office? This question can only be answered by recalling the reasons for billing merchandise shipments at a markup.

If the markup in fact represents a profit element attributable to the home office, the home office could include it in income from its own operations. In contrast, when the markup is actually a portion of branch profit, the home office will increase the profit reported by the branch accordingly. As before, *assume that the home office attributes the markup to home office operations* and records it as Realized Intrafirm Profit. The home office closing entries appear below.

HOME OFFICE BOOKS

Income from Branch	14,227	
Investment in Branch		14,227

To record the operating loss reported for 19X4 by the Blockville branch, thereby reducing the investment in the branch.

Overvaluation of Branch Inventory	76,000	
Realized Intrafirm Profit		76,000

To credit the home office for the markup on merchandise shipments realized on sales to external customers during 19X4.

Sales	1,700,000	
Shipments to Branch	300,000	
Inventory, Dec. 31	275,000	
Realized Intrafirm Profit	76,000	
Purchases		1,150,000
Freight In		25,000
Salaries Expense		250,000
Operating Expenses		195,000
Depreciation Expense		50,000
Inventory, Jan. 1		280,000
Income Summary		401,000

To close the revenue and expense accounts for 19X4 to Income Summary and record net income from home office operations of $325,000(= $401,000 − $76,000).

Income Summary	14,227	
Income from Branch		14,227

To close the branch's net loss to Income Summary, thereby decreasing net income for 19X4 to $386,773(= $401,000 − $14,227).

Income Summary	386,773	
Retained Earnings		386,773

To close net income for 19X4 to Retained Earnings.

Note that neither the Investment in Branch nor the Home Office account has been closed out. The shipments accounts are closed because they are purchases to the branch and a reduction in purchases to the home office. As the next section makes evident, however, all reciprocal account balances are *eliminated* when combined financial statements are prepared.

Working Paper Preparation of Combined Financial Statements

Because the balances of certain of the reciprocal accounts are carried forward on the home office and branch books, combined financial statements are often prepared using a working paper. The working paper includes the preclosing trial balance data and ending inventory balances for the home office and branch as well as columns for adjustments and eliminations. The *columns for adjustments and eliminations* have two purposes:

1. To record any adjusting entries not reflected in the preclosing trial balances. In our example, the preclosing trial balances used in the working paper *do* reflect the adjustments made earlier to reconcile the reciprocal accounts.
2. To record eliminating entries whose purpose is to remove the offsetting balances in the intrafirm reciprocal accounts. *Eliminations are made on working papers only and are not posted to the accounts.*

Combined Financial Statement Working Paper. We have chosen a working paper format organized around three principal financial statements—the income statement, statement of retained earnings, and balance sheet. The *preclosing* trial balance data from Exhibit 5.6 have been *adjusted* to reconcile the reciprocal accounts and have been organized to fit under one of these three financial statements. This is a **combined financial statement working paper.** An alternative approach, illustrated later, is to use the trial balances themselves, generate a combined trial balance, and reorganize the combined accounts into the appropriate financial statement format.

We believe that the financial statement working paper format has some procedural advantages, including several total and subtotal points which help ensure accuracy. Furthermore, this format is used extensively in the chapters involving consolidated financial statements.

The completed working paper from which formal combined statements may be prepared appears in Exhibit 5.7. Note that the combined net income of $386,773 equals the total net income recorded by the home office in its closing entries, as it should.

Compare the closing entry that adjusted the overvaluation account down to $14,000 with the working paper eliminations that remove it entirely. In making our closing entries, we did not reduce the branch inventory to cost. The overvaluation account is actually a contra-asset account and, when subtracted from the marked-up inventory, provides us with inventory at cost. On the working paper, Entry 1 eliminates $75,000 of the overvaluation account balance in conjunction

Exhibit 5.7 **Hardy Corporation and Blockville Branch: Combined Financial Statement Working Paper for the Year Ended December 31, 19X4**

	Home Branch	Blockville Branch	Adjustments and Eliminations		Combined
INCOME STATEMENT			**Dr.**	**Cr.**	
Sales	1,700,000	500,000			2,200,000
Inventory, 12/31/X4	275,000	71,600[a]	(3) 14,000		332,600
Shipments to Branch.	300,000	—	(1) 300,000		—
Total Credits	2,275,000	571,600	314,000		2,532,600
Inventory, 1/1/X4	280,000	77,000		(2) 15,000	342,000
Purchases	1,150,000	—			1,150,000
Shipments from Home Office	—	375,000[a]		(1) 375,000	—
Freight In.	25,000	9,100[a]			34,100
Salaries Expense	250,000	50,000			300,000
Operating Expenses	195,000	62,000			257,000
Depreciation Exp.	50,000	12,727			62,727
Total Debits.	1,950,000	585,827		390,000	2,145,827
Net Income—to Ret. Earn. Stmt. . . .	325,000	(14,227)	314,000	390,000	386,773
RETAINED EARNINGS STATEMENT					
Retained Earnings, 1/1/X4	352,910	—			352,910
Net Income—from Income Stmt. . . .	325,000	(14,227)	314,000	390,000	386,773
Dividends.	—	—			—
Ret. Earn., 12/31/X4—to Balance Sheet	677,910	(14,227)	314,000	390,000	739,683
BALANCE SHEET					
Cash.	130,000[a]	40,800			170,800
Accounts Receivable.	252,200[a]	50,000			302,200
Inventory	275,000	71,600[a]		(3) 14,000	332,600
Overval. of Branch Inventory	(90,000)	—	(1) 75,000 (2) 15,000		—
Prepayments	40,000	—			40,000
Investment in Branch	200,710[a]	—		(4) 200,710	—
Property, Plant, & Equipment	750,000	100,000			850,000
Accumulated Depreciation	(200,000)	(61,817)			(261,817)
Total	1,357,910	200,583	90,000	214,710	1,433,783
Accounts Payable	162,000	12,100			174,100
Salaries Payable	18,000	2,000			20,000
Other Liabilities	300,000	—			300,000
Home Office	—	200,710[a]	(4) 200,710		—
Capital Stock	200,000	—			200,000
Ret. Earnings—from Ret. Earn. Stmt. .	677,910	(14,227)	314,000	390,000	739,683
Total	1,357,910	200,583	514,710	390,000	1,433,783
			604,710	604,710	

[a]These balances reflect adjustments 1(a), 6(a), and 7(a) made to reconcile the reciprocal accounts.

Exhibit 5.7   Continued

Explanations of Working Paper Entries

(1) To eliminate the balance in Shipments from Home Office against the reciprocal Shipments to Branch and the related portion of the overvaluation account.

(2) To eliminate the remaining portion of the overvaluation account and remove the markup in the beginning inventory of the branch.

(3) To remove the markup included in the ending inventory of the branch on both the income statement and balance sheet.

(4) To eliminate the Investment in Branch against the reciprocal Home Office account.

with eliminating the shipments accounts. The remaining $15,000 is the markup in the branch's *beginning inventory*. Entry 2 eliminates this markup and reduces the branch's beginning inventory to home office cost. The branch's *ending inventory* (at billed prices plus freight in) appears on the working paper in both the income statement and the balance sheet. In *both* places, it must be written down to home office cost by removing $14,000 of markup from the ending inventory. Entry 3 on the working paper accomplishes this and provides the same result given by offsetting the book balance of $14,000 in the overvaluation account against the branch's ending inventory at billed prices.

Combined Trial Balance Working Paper. Another approach to the preparation of combined financial statements for the home office and branch calls for a **combined trial balance working paper.** The combined accounts are then rearranged in financial statement format. Such a combined trial balance working paper is given in Exhibit 5.8 for the Hardy Corporation and its Blockville branch. In comparing it with the combined financial statement working paper in Exhibit 5.7, we make the following observations:

1. Adjusting entries 1(a), 6(a), and 7(a) made to reconcile the Investment in Branch and Home Office reciprocal accounts are entered on the combined trial balance working paper. Alternatively, adjusted trial balances could have been used, as in Exhibit 5.7.

2. Note the treatment of the ending inventory. The preclosing trial balance given in Exhibit 5.6 reflects only the beginning January 1 inventory. Ending inventory at December 31 is entered in the trial balance as *both* a debit and credit, thereby maintaining the integrity of the trial balance. The debit entry will be carried to the balance sheet while the credit entry and the January 1 inventory (a debit) will be carried to the income statement as the ending and beginning inventories used in computing cost of goods sold.

3. The eliminating entries made on the combined trial balance working paper are the same as those made on the combined financial statement working paper.

Formal Combined Statements. Using the data in the Combined column of Exhibit 5.7 or 5.8, we prepare formal financial statements for the Hardy Corporation, which include the accounts of the Blockville branch. These statements are presented in Exhibits 5.9 and 5.10.

Exhibit 5.8 Hardy Corporation and Blockville Branch: Combined Trial Balance Working Paper for the Year Ended December 31, 19X4

Account	Home Office Dr. (Cr.)	Branch Dr. (Cr.)	Adjustments and Eliminations Dr.	Cr.	Combined Dr. (Cr.)
Cash	110,000	40,800	6(a) 20,000		170,800
Accounts Receivable	260,000	50,000		7(a) 7,800	302,200
Inventory, Jan. 1, 19X4	280,000	77,000		(2) 15,000	342,000
Inventory, Dec. 31, 19X4 (Balance Sheet)	275,000^a	71,600^a		(3) 14,000	332,600
Prepayments	40,000	—			40,000
Property, Plant, and Equipment	750,000	100,000			850,000
Accumulated Depreciation	(200,000)	(61,817)			(261,817)
Investment in Branch	212,910	—	7(a) 7,800	6(a) 20,000 / (4) 200,710	—
Accounts Payable	(162,000)	(12,000)		1(a) 100	(174,100)
Salaries Payable	(18,000)	(2,000)			(20,000)
Other Liabilities	(300,000)	—			(300,000)
Capital Stock	(200,000)	—			(200,000)
Retained Earnings	(352,910)	—			(352,910)
Home Office	—	(190,710)	(4) 200,710	1(a) 10,000	—
Sales	(1,700,000)	(500,000)			(2,200,000)
Shipments to Branch	(300,000)	—	(1) 300,000		—
Inventory, Dec. 31, 19X4 (Income Statement)	(275,000)^a	(71,600)^a	(3) 14,000		(332,600)
Overvaluation of Branch Inventory	(90,000)	—	(1) 75,000 / (2) 15,000		—
Purchases	1,150,000	—			1,150,000
Shipments from Home Office	—	365,000	1(a) 10,000	(1) 375,000	—
Freight In	25,000	9,000	1(a) 100		34,100
Salaries Expense	250,000	50,000			300,000
Operating Expenses	195,000	62,000			257,000
Depreciation Expense	50,000	12,727			62,727
	0	0	642,610	642,610	0

^{a}The ending inventory of the home office and branch [reflecting adjustment 1(a)] is entered twice. The debit entry will be carried to the balance sheet and the credit is carried to the income statement as a component of cost of goods sold.

Exhibit 5.8   **Continued**

Explanations of Working Paper Entries

1(a) To record the merchandise shipment in transit from the home office and the related freight.
6(a) To record the cash remittance in transit to the home office.
7(a) To record the collection of a home office receivable made by the branch.
(1) To eliminate the balance in Shipments from Home Office against the reciprocal Shipments to Branch and the related portion of the overvaluation account.
(2) To eliminate the remaining portion of the overvaluation account and remove the markup in the beginning inventory of the branch.
(3) To remove the markup included in the ending inventory of the branch on both the income statement and the balance sheet.
(4) To eliminate the Investment in Branch against the reciprocal Home Office account.

Exhibit 5.9   **Hardy Corporation: Statement of Income and Retained Earnings for the Year Ended December 31, 19X4**

Sales	$2,200,000
Cost of Goods Sold	$1,193,500[a]
Salaries Expense	300,000
Operating Expenses	257,000
Depreciation Expense	62,727
Total Expenses	$1,813,227
Net Income	$ 386,773
Retained Earnings, Jan. 1, 19X4	352,910
Retained Earnings, Dec. 31, 19X4	$ 739,683

[a]$1,193,500 = $342,000 + $1,150,000 + $34,100 − $332,600.

Disposal of a Branch

As mentioned earlier, home office/branch accounting is used in a variety of intra-firm entity situations. Indeed, branch accounting can be used for business units significant enough for their activities to represent a *separate major line of business or class of customer*. When such business units are closed down or sold, the provisions of *APBO 30* relating to **discontinued operations** must be followed.[3] Closing down or selling a branch activity that is one of several similar branch activities does not constitute disposal of a separate identifiable business segment. On the other hand, discontinuing operation of a particular manufacturing division, accounted for as a branch, may be subject to the rules in *APBO 30*. The relevant sections of *APBO 30* have two principal objectives in connection with discontinued operations:

1. Separate disclosure of income or loss from discontinued operations, net of

---

[3]Accounting Principles Board, *Opinion No. 30*, "Reporting the Results of Operations" (New York: AICPA, 1973); CT § 113.

Exhibit 5.10	Hardy Corporation: Balance Sheet at December 31, 19X4

ASSETS

Cash.	$ 170,800
Accounts Receivable	302,200
Inventory	332,600
Prepayments	40,000
Total Current Assets	$ 845,600
Property, Plant, and Equipment	$ 850,000
Less Accumulated Depreciation	(261,817)
Total Noncurrent Assets.	$ 588,183
Total Assets	$1,433,783

LIABILITIES AND STOCKHOLDERS' EQUITY

Accounts Payable	$ 174,100
Salaries Payable.	20,000
Other Liabilities	300,000
Total Liabilities	$ 494,100
Capital Stock	$ 200,000
Retained Earnings.	739,683
Total Stockholders' Equity.	$ 939,683
Total Liabilities and Stockholders' Equity	$1,433,783

applicable income taxes, between income from continuing operations and extraordinary items.

2. Provide disclosure of gain or loss on disposal of the business segment, net of applicable income taxes, along with the income or loss from discontinued operations.

This information should first appear in the financial statements covering the **measurement date,** the date at which management formally adopts a plan leading to the termination of operations. Descriptive information regarding the disposal should be disclosed in the notes to the financial statements encompassing the measurement date and in subsequent reporting periods until disposal is complete.

Item 1 above will reflect income or loss generated by the discontinued operation during the current period up to the measurement date. Prior period financial statements should be revised to disclose the results of operating the discontinued segment in those periods, net of applicable income taxes, as a separate component of income before extraordinary items. Item 2 above will also be disclosed in the period covering the measurement date. If the actual disposal has not taken place during that period, any estimated *loss* from disposal, net of applicable taxes, must be provided as of the measurement date. This provision includes the anticipated loss from disposal itself and from operations of the discontinued unit between the measurement date and the **disposal date**—the date when the segment is actually disposed of. The treatment differs if the disposal itself and the remaining period of operations are expected to result in an overall gain. In this case, the estimated *gain* is not recognized at the measurement date and is deferred until actually realized at the disposal date.

As an example, suppose management of Amalgam Corporation decides to dispose of an unprofitable manufacturing operation, the Toy Branch. The branch is shut down shortly after the decision is made. It had incurred pretax losses of $300,000 in the current year and is sold at a pretax loss of $800,000. Toy's property and liability accounts are maintained at the branch and, after closing the books immediately prior to disposal, the Home Office account has a credit balance of $1,500,000, reflecting various branch assets of $3,000,000, accumulated depreciation of $1,000,000, and liabilities of $500,000. Entries made by the branch and home office to record the disposal follow:

TOY BRANCH BOOKS

Accumulated Depreciation.	1,000,000	
Liabilities	500,000	
Home Office	1,500,000	
Assets		3,000,000

To record termination of operations as a unit of Amalgam Corporation.

AMALGAM CORPORATION BOOKS

Cash	700,000	
Loss on Disposal to Toy Branch	800,000	
Investment in Branch		1,500,000

To record the sale of Toy Branch for $700,000 and to recognize the pretax loss of $800,000.

Assuming Amalgam's marginal income tax rate is 40 percent, Amalgam would disclose the following information in its income statement for the period in which the disposal occurred:

Income from Continuing Operations (after Taxes)		XXX
Discontinued Operations:		
Loss from Operation of Discontinued Toy Division (after Tax Savings of $120,000).	$180,000	
Loss on Disposal of Toy Division (after Taxes of $320,000)	480,000	$660,000
Income before Extraordinary Items		XXX

Concluding Remarks

Branches are integral units of a business firm which have varying degrees of autonomy and accounting responsibility, perform various functions, and are normally physically removed from the home office. The term **branch accounting** is used in this chapter to identify a type of internal accounting system characterized by the presence of offsetting **reciprocal accounts** at both the branch and home office. These reciprocal accounts enable the home office and branch to easily account for transactions between them or made on behalf of one unit by the other.

Since reciprocal accounts reflect internal and not external transactions, their balances must be eliminated when financial statements including the combined home office and branch accounts are prepared. Mastery of this elimination concept is critical, for it will be encountered repeatedly in the chapters describing the preparation of consolidated financial statements.

The chapter has stressed the accounting procedures for a branch that is a going concern. To round out the subject area, we have related generally accepted accounting principles for development-stage enterprises and discontinued operations to the start-up and termination phases of branch operations.

Summary of Key Concepts

Accounting for a **sales agency** generally entails only an imprest fund and subsidiary accounting records maintained at the home office.

Home office/branch accounting refers to the type of accounting system used when a business unit of a larger firm has substantial financial accounting responsibilities and engages in various kinds of transactions with the home office.

Criteria for assessing whether **capitalization of start-up costs** of new branches is appropriate are no different than those employed for any going concern.

Reciprocal accounts are accounts with equal and offsetting balances maintained by the home office and branch, which are used to record transactions between home office and branch or made by one business unit on behalf of the other.

Merchandise shipments by the home office to the branch may be billed at cost to the home office or at cost plus a markup (which may equal retail price). Such shipments are normally accounted for in reciprocal accounts established for that purpose. Any difference between home office cost and amount billed should be separately accounted for as **overvaluation of branch inventory.**

Adjusting and closing entries are made at the end of an accounting period to reconcile reciprocal accounts, record the branch closing entries, accrue the branch's reported net income on the home office books, and adjust the overvaluation account.

Preparation of **combined financial statements** for the home office and branch is facilitated by the use of a working paper designed for that purpose. A key working paper procedure involves *eliminating the offsetting reciprocal accounts* to avoid double counting and to remove intrafirm markup from branch inventories. **Working paper eliminations are not posted to the books.**

Closing down or selling a branch that represents a separate major line of business or class of customer may call for special disclosures on the combined income statement. Under *APBO 30*, both **income or loss from discontinued operations** and **gain or loss on disposal** must be separately disclosed.

Questions

Q5.1 The term *branch* is broad enough to include business organizations of varying complexity. In advising a client on the installation of an accounting system, what factors would have to be present for you to recommend the use of home office/branch accounting procedures?

Q5.2 Briefly discuss the major differences between accounting for a sales agency and accounting for a branch from the home office point of view.

Q5.3 Reciprocal accounts are a key characteristic of home office/branch accounting. Briefly explain why they are important and the ways in which they are used.

Q5.4 You have been engaged to audit the Clifford Company. When you arrive at the client's office to begin the preliminary audit work, you learn that several new branches have been opened by Clifford during the year. What principles should you use to decide the appropriateness of capitalizing the start-up costs of those branches? The costs are material to Clifford's overall operations.

Q5.5 Under what conditions will the reciprocal accounts Shipments to Branch and Shipments from Home Office not have equal and offsetting balances?

Q5.6 When the home office transfers merchandise to a branch at prices above home office cost, the difference between billed prices and cost is often accounted for in an ''overvaluation'' account. Briefly discuss two alternative interpretations of this overvaluation account.

Q5.7 The controller of Barret, Inc., decides that merchandise shipments to its branch are to be priced at an amount greater than cost. What advantage could be cited for setting the transfer price equal to Barret's external selling price?

Q5.8 The text treats excess freight cost incurred in interbranch merchandise shipments as a period expense (loss) rather than as a product cost. Criticize this position and explain how the two treatments can affect the financial statements.

Q5.9 In discussing the end-of-period accounting procedures employed in home office/branch accounting, a student makes the following objection: ''This is just so much hocus-pocus and duplication. I see no need for both closing entries and a combined financial statement working paper.'' Do you agree with the student's objection? Explain.

Q5.10 In preparing a combined financial statement working paper, we find it necessary to make eliminating entries. What is the purpose of such entries, and why are they made only on the working paper?

Q5.11 Reciprocal accounts must be reconciled and brought into balance before combined financial statement working papers can be prepared. List four common reasons reciprocal accounts may be out of balance.

Q5.12 Disposal of a branch may fall under the provisions of *APBO 30* for public reporting purposes. Under what condition is *APBO 30* relevant to disposal of a branch? Briefly describe and evaluate the principal disclosure requirements of the *Opinion*.

Exercises

E5.1 During 19X4 the following transactions occurred between the Elmhurst Corporation and its Rockford branch:

1. Cash advance was sent to branch, $10,000.
2. Goods which cost Elmhurst $150,000 were shipped to the branch. Billing for these goods amounted to $225,000 and the related freight of $1,750 was paid by the home office.
3. Depreciation on branch assets amounted to $15,000. Plant asset accounts are maintained at the home office.
4. Merchandise which the branch had purchased from the home office for $200,000 was sold for $250,000 (on account).
5. Collections on branch receivables amounted to $220,000 (of which $20,000 was paid directly to the home office by customers).
6. Cash of $180,000 was remitted by the branch to the home office.

Required: Assuming that Elmhurst uses shipments and overvaluation accounts for intrafirm merchandise shipments, prepare the journal entries made by both business units to record the above transactions during 19X4.

E5.2 The Morrissey Company established a branch office early this year. Merchandise is shipped to the branch from the home office at prices 25 percent over cost. Freight costs are inventoriable and are paid by the branch in cash and amount to 4 percent of billed prices. Transactions for the year are summarized here:

1. Merchandise was shipped to the branch at billed prices amounting to $200,000.
2. The branch recorded sales of $320,000, all in cash.
3. Operating expenses of the branch amounted to $75,000, paid in cash.
4. A physical inventory at year-end showed merchandise on hand of $50,000 at billed prices.

Required:

1. Prepare journal entries made by the home office and branch during the year for the above transactions. Periodic inventory systems are used, and the home office accounts for the markup in an overvaluation account.

2. Prepare closing entries made by the branch and by the home office related to branch operations. The home office attributes the realized markup to home office operations.

E5.3 At December 31, 19X6, the Kercsmar Corporation and its branch report the following trial balances:

Account	Home Office Dr. (Cr.)	Branch Dr. (Cr.)
Cash	$ 60,000	$ 30,000
Accounts Receivable, Net.	80,000	45,000
Inventory, Dec. 31 (Perpetual)	120,000	65,000
Overvaluation of Branch Inventory	(39,000)	—
Plant Assets	300,000	—
Accumulated Depreciation	(120,000)	—
Investment in Branch	85,000	—
Liabilities	(260,000)	(19,000)
Home Office	—	(85,000)
Capital Stock	(10,000)	—
Retained Earnings	(90,000)	—
Sales	(600,000)	(188,000)
Cost of Goods Sold.	350,000	104,000
Depreciation Expense.	40,000	18,000
Other Operating Expenses	84,000	30,000
	$ 0	$ 0

Required: Assuming that all intrafirm merchandise shipments are made at home office cost plus 30 percent and that both business units use perpetual inventory systems, prepare closing entries on both the branch and home office books. Realized intrafirm profit is attributed to home office operations.

E5.4 The Winery, seller of fine imported and domestic table wines, opened a branch office on December 20 of the current year. Not being familiar with the accounting procedures used in home office and branch operations, the firm's owner has asked your assistance in updating his accounting records and preparing combined statements at December 31. No entries have been made to record transactions involving the home and branch offices, but the following information is available:

1. Set-up costs of the branch: $30,000.
2. Shipments to branch (at 25 percent over cost): $10,000.
3. Sales by branch (at price billed from home office): $4,000.
4. Branch salaries paid by home office: $1,500.
5. Cash remitted by branch: $2,000.

Required:

1. Determine the balances in the Home Office and Investment in Branch reciprocal accounts at December 31.

2. What amount of inventory overvaluation must be recognized as income on December 31? Give the journal entry necessary to do this on the home office books.

3. Explain *how* the reciprocal accounts should be treated for combined statement purposes and *why* this treatment is necessary.

E5.5 The controller of the Paran Company recently resigned. You are engaged on July 1 to assist the new controller after it is discovered that several transactions relating to its branch have not been posted since the beginning of the year. After considerable work, the following data are assembled:

1. The Investment in Branch and Home Office accounts at January 1 are not in agreement. The Investment in Branch account shows a debit balance of $385,000 while the Home Office account has a credit balance of $340,000. The shipments accounts have zero balances.

2. Merchandise costing $160,000 has been shipped to the branch during the year. Such shipments are billed at cost.

3. Year-to-date depreciation expense is $40,000. One-fifth of all depreciable assets are located at the branch office. The home office had charged the branch for its share but had failed to notify the branch of the charge.

4. Cash remitted by the branch during the year totals $200,000.

5. A review of last year's working paper for combined statements revealed adjustments of $40,000 for inventory in transit to the branch and $5,000 for cash in transit from the branch to the home office at December 31.

6. Paran uses a periodic system to account for all inventories.

7. At July 1, the books show:

	Dr. (Cr.)
Investment in Branch.	$493,000
Home Office	(300,000)
Shipments from Home Office.	160,000
Shipments to Branch.	(100,000)

Required: Prepare a schedule to reconcile all reciprocal accounts.

E5.6 The Arriba Company has a branch office in another state. Given below are balances of the reciprocal accounts at the end of the current year and additional information.

	Home Office Dr. (Cr.)		Branch Dr. (Cr.)
Investment in Branch. . .	270,000	Home Office	(200,000)
Shipments to Branch. . .	(120,000)	Shipments from Home	
Overvaluation of Branch		Office.	140,000
Inventory.	(35,000)		

Additional information:

1. The branch acquires all of its merchandise from the home office at home office cost plus 25 percent.
2. On the last day of the current year, the home office billed the branch $10,000 for merchandise shipped that day.
3. Copy of a journal voucher charging the branch $25,000 for branch expenses paid by the home office has not yet been received at the branch office.
4. Just prior to year-end, the branch mailed a check for $35,000 to the home office.
5. Beginning and ending inventories of the branch amounted to $25,000 and $40,000, respectively, at billed prices, excluding the shipment in transit.

Required:

1. Prepare all adjusting entries relative to the reciprocal accounts given above. *Clearly identify which set of books your entries will appear in.*
2. Prepare all working paper eliminations needed in order to prepare combined statements from the adjusted data.

E5.7 Ajax, Inc., accounts for all its inventories under a perpetual system and bills all shipments to the branch at cost. The branch obtains all its merchandise from the home office. At year-end, a discrepancy appears to exist in the merchandise accounts. Aside from the transactions causing the discrepancy, all other transactions between the home office and branch have been recorded correctly. Merchandise purchased by the home office during the year amounted to $800,000. Relevant account balances at December 31 are shown here:

	Home Office Dr. (Cr.)	Branch Dr. (Cr.)
Investment in Branch	$430,000	
Home Office		($430,000)
Inventory, Jan. 1	100,000	70,000
Inventory, Dec. 31	120,000	40,000
Cost of Goods Sold	600,000	280,000

Required: Compute the amount of the discrepancy. Assuming that the home office records are correct and that all inventories have been verified by physical count, explain what must have happened.

E5.8 The Wicket Company bills merchandise to its branch at retail selling prices which represent a 100 percent markup over cost. Transportation costs on shipments amount to 5 percent of billed prices. The following data relate to Wicket's intrafirm merchandise transactions during the year:

Inventory, Jan. 1, Branch Office. $210,000
Home Office Shipments to the Branch 500,000
Freight Cost on Shipments 25,000
Branch Sales 546,000

Required:

1. Compute the cost of goods sold on the branch books.
2. Compute the amount of ending inventory on the branch books.
3. Give the closing entry made by the home office to adjust the overvaluation account.
4. If the ending inventory of the home office is $400,000 at cost, compute the ending inventory to be reported on a combined balance sheet.
5. Give the eliminating entries relative to inventories that must be made on the combined financial statement working paper.

E5.9 The following data have been taken from the adjusted preclosing trial balances at December 31, 19X6, of the Fawn Company and its branch:

	Home Office Dr. (Cr.)		**Branch** Dr. (Cr.)
Investment in Branch. . .	$ 360,000	Inventory, Jan. 1	$ 40,000
Shipments to Branch . . .	(200,000)	Shipments from Home	
Overvaluation of Branch		Office.	250,000
Inventory.	(58,000)	Home Office	(360,000)

The branch acquires all of its inventory from the home office at prices reflecting a markup of 25 percent over home office cost and maintains its Inventory account at billed prices. Ending inventory of the branch is $25,000 at billed prices. Home office ending inventory is $150,000 at cost.

Required: Prepare the eliminating entries which would appear on a combined financial statement working paper.

E5.10 The Marble Company operates several branches and records all merchandise shipments to those branches as sales. Freight costs are trivial. The branches acquire all of their merchandise from the home office at markups approximating 30 percent of home office cost. Intrafirm merchandise transactions are summarized here:

Inventory, Jan. 1 (All Branches at Billed Prices) . . . . $ 390,000
Inventory, Dec. 31 (All Branches at Billed Prices) 520,000
Sales (from Home Office to Branches) 1,950,000

Required: Give the necessary eliminating entries to be made on the combined financial statement working paper.

E5.11 On May 15, 19X1, Marine, Inc., shipped outboard motors costing $12,000 to its Seaport branch. Seaport was billed $18,000 plus freight (prepaid by

Marine) of $760. On June 22, 19X1, Marine directed Seaport to ship 25 percent of this merchandise to the Bayview branch, which was temporarily out of stock for certain models. Additional freight cost, paid by Bayview, was $200. Periodic inventory systems are used.

Required:

1. Prepare the journal entries made by Marine, Inc., and the Seaport branch relative to the shipment made on May 15, 19X1.
2. Prepare the journal entries made by all three business units relative to the June 22 shipment, assuming that transportation direct from Marine to Bayview cost $300.

E5.12 On September 30, 19X1, the board of directors of Mills Corporation decided to close down the Low Cost Branch, an unprofitable retailing unit of the firm. Shortly thereafter, Low Cost was sold to an optimistic buyer for $160,000, which is $20,000 over the postclosing balance in the Investment in Low Cost Branch account. Low Cost reported a pretax operating loss of $70,000 during the portion of the current year prior to the sale. Mills's marginal income tax rate is .45.

Required: Assuming that Mills reported pretax income of $600,000 from home office continuing operations and that *APBO 30* applies, prepare the section of Mills's 19X1 income statement in which the information required by *APBO 30* relative to the disposal of Low Cost is disclosed.

Problems

P5.1 Propriety of Capitalizing Start-Up Operating Losses You are engaged in the audit of the Willis Corporation, which opened its first branch office in 19X0. During the audit, Willis's president raises the question of the accounting treatment of the branch office operating loss for its first year—a material amount.

The president proposes to capitalize the operating loss as a starting-up expense to be amortized over a 5-year period. He states that branch offices of other firms engaged in the same field generally suffer a first-year operating loss which is invariably capitalized, and you are aware of this practice. He argues, therefore, that the loss should be capitalized so that the accounting will be conservative; further, he argues that the accounting must be consistent with established industry practice.

Required: Discuss the president's use of the words "conservative" and "consistent" from the standpoint of accounting terminology. Discuss the accounting treatment you would recommend. *(AICPA adapted)*

P5.2 Calculate Branch Inventory Loss The TOTO Company operates a branch in a small town in West Texas. During June of the current year, a tornado swept through the town and destroyed the warehouse in which the branch's inventory was stored. TOTO is self-insuring but needs to compute the amount of the loss for tax purposes. You have gathered the following information:

1. Goods are acquired from the home office and from outside suppliers. Historically, about 60 percent of the merchandise purchases, at billed prices, is acquired from the home office at prices 20 percent over home office cost; the balance is purchased from external sources. Freight charges on all merchandise purchases are 5 percent of billed prices. The branch's selling prices reflect a markup of 20 percent on purchases from the home office (at billed prices) and 30 percent on other purchases, excluding the freight costs.
2. Inventory at January 1 was $105,000 on the branch books.
3. Shipments from the home office received at the branch prior to the tornado amounted to $150,000.
4. Payments to outside suppliers made during the year and before the tornado were $125,000. No unpaid invoices existed at the time of the tornado, but accounts payable to suppliers at the previous year-end showed a balance of $25,000.
5. Sales made prior to the tornado amounted to $320,000, net of sales returns of $20,000.

Required:

1. Calculate the amount of the loss suffered by TOTO in connection with the destruction of its branch's inventory by the tornado. Show all computations in good form.
2. Prepare the journal entry to record the loss.

P5.3 Closing Entries and Working Paper Eliminations Shown below are condensed trial balances for the home office and southern branch of Marshall Corporation:

Account	Home Office Dr. (Cr.)	Branch Dr. (Cr.)
Inventory, Jan. 1	$ 60,000	$ 20,000
Overvaluation of Branch Inventory	(29,000)	—
Other Assets	185,000	90,000
Investment in Branch	70,000	—
Liabilities	(106,000)	(37,000)
Home Office	—	(70,000)
Capital Stock	(10,000)	—
Retained Earnings, Jan. 1	(140,000)	—
Sales	(300,000)	(150,000)
Shipments to Branch	(100,000)	—
Purchases	280,000	—
Shipments from Home Office	—	125,000
Expenses	90,000	22,000
	$ 0	$ 0

branch were purchased by the home office in 19X5. The physical inventories at December 31, 19X5, excluding the shipment in transit, were: home office, $55,000 (at cost); branch, $20,000 (comprised of $18,000 from home office and $2,000 from outside vendors).

7. The home office consistently bills shipments to the branch at 20 percent above cost. The Sales account is credited for the invoice price. Since the home office does not use an overvaluation account for shipments to the branch, the markup included in the branch's beginning inventory is reflected in beginning Retained Earnings.

Required:

1. Prepare a schedule to reconcile the Investment in Branch and Home Office reciprocal accounts.
2. Using a trial balance worksheet with columns for adjustments and eliminations, prepare a combined trial balance. Formal combined statements are not required. Supporting computations must be in good form.
3. Prepare formal adjusting and eliminating entries and indicate which are adjustments (A) and which are eliminations (E). *(AICPA adapted)*

P5.6 Combined Financial Statement Working Paper You are engaged to audit the records of the Pacific Import Company, which have not previously been audited. The trial balance at December 31, 19X6, follows:

DEBITS	Home Office	Branch
Cash	$ 15,000	$ 2,000
Accounts Receivable	20,000	17,000
Inventory, Dec. 31, 19X6	30,000	8,000
Fixed Assets, Net	150,000	
Investment in Branch	44,000	
Cost of Sales	220,000	93,000
Expenses	70,000	41,000
Total	$549,000	$161,000
CREDITS		
Accounts Payable	$ 23,000	
Mortgage Payable	50,000	
Capital Stock	100,000	
Retained Earnings, Jan. 1, 19X6	26,000	
Sales	350,000	$150,000
Accrued Expenses		2,000
Home Office		9,000
Total	$549,000	$161,000

Additional information:

1. The branch receives all of its merchandise from the home office. The home office bills goods to the branch at 125 percent of cost. During 19X6, the branch was billed for $105,000 on shipments from the home office.

2. The home office credits Sales for the invoice price of goods shipped to the branch.

3. On January 1, 19X6, the inventory of the home office was $25,000. The branch books showed a $6,000 inventory.

4. On December 31, 19X6, the home office billed the branch for $12,000—the branch's share of expenses paid by the home office. The branch has not recorded this billing.

5. All cash collections made by the branch are deposited in a local bank to the account of the home office. Deposits of this nature included the following:

Amount	Date Deposited by Branch	Date Recorded by Home Office
$5,000	Dec. 28, 19X6	Dec. 31, 19X6
3,000	Dec. 30, 19X6	Jan. 2, 19X7
7,000	Dec. 31, 19X6	Jan. 3, 19X7
2,000	Jan. 2, 19X7	Jan. 5, 19X7

6. Expenses incurred locally by the branch are paid from an imprest bank account, which is reimbursed periodically by the home office. Just prior to the end of the year, the home office forwarded a reimbursement check in the amount of $3,000, which was not received by the branch office until January 19X7.

Required:

1. Prepare a reconciliation of the Investment in Branch and Home Office accounts showing the corrected book balances. (Hint: Recompute the branch's cost of sales.)

2. Prepare a combined financial statement working paper for the Pacific Import Company. Rearrange the trial balance data given in the problem into financial statement format. Use the Adjustments and Eliminations columns to post the entries reconciling the reciprocal accounts as well as to make the eliminations. Formal journal entries and formal financial statements are not required. *(AICPA adapted)*

P5.7 Adjusting and Eliminating Entries—Formal Combined Statements
Trial balance data for the Azure Company and its branch at December 31, 19X3, prior to the annual audit, are as follows:

THE AZURE COMPANY
TRIAL BALANCES
DECEMBER 31, 19X3

DEBITS	Home	Branch
Cash	$ 17,000	$ 200
Inventory, Jan. 1 (at billed prices)	23,000	11,550
Other Assets	200,000	48,700

Investment in Branch	60,000	—
Purchases	190,000	—
Shipments from Home	—	105,000
Freight In from Home	—	5,250
Various Expenses	42,000	24,300
Totals	$532,000	$195,000

CREDITS

Various Liabilities	$ 35,000	$ 3,500
Home Office	—	51,500
Sales	155,000	140,000
Shipments to Branch	110,000	—
Overvaluation of Branch Inventory, Jan. 1	1,000	—
Capital Stock	200,000	—
Retained Earnings, Jan. 1	31,000	—
Totals	$532,000	$195,000

The audit at December 31, 19X3, disclosed the following:

1. The branch deposits all cash receipts in a local bank for the account of the home office. The audit worksheet for the cash cutoff revealed:

Amount	Date Deposited by Branch	Date Recorded by Home Office
$1,050	Dec. 27, 19X3	Dec. 31, 19X3
1,100	Dec. 30, 19X3	Jan. 2, 19X4
600	Dec. 31, 19X3	Jan. 3, 19X4
300	Jan. 2, 19X4	Jan. 6, 19X4

2. The branch pays expenses incurred locally from an imprest bank account that is maintained with a balance of $2,000. Checks are drawn once a week on this imprest account, and the home office is notified of the amount needed to replenish the account. At December 31, an $1,800 reimbursement check was mailed to the branch.

3. The branch receives all of its goods from the home office. The home office bills the goods at cost plus a markup of 10 percent of cost. At December 31, a shipment with a billing value of $5,000 was in transit to the branch. Freight costs are typically 5 percent of billed values, are considered to be inventoriable costs, and are paid by the branch.

4. The trial balance opening inventories are shown at their respective costs to the home office and the branch. The inventories at December 31, excluding the shipment in transit, are:

Home Office (at cost)	$30,000
Branch Office (at billing value)	10,400

Required:

1. Prepare a reconciliation of the Investment in Branch and Home Office reciprocal accounts.

2. Prepare the formal adjusting and eliminating entries needed on working papers for the preparation of combined financial statements. Entries should be identified as adjusting (A) or eliminating (E), and supporting computations should be in good form. Do not prepare closing entries.

3. Prepare a statement of income and retained earnings and a balance sheet for the Azure Company as of December 31, 19X3. *(AICPA adapted)*

P5.8 Combined Financial Statement Working Paper The Saffron Company has a branch located in Loadsville, 200 miles away. The branch purchases about 40 percent of its inventory for resale from local suppliers; the rest is acquired from Saffron at billed prices representing a markup equal to 20 percent of selling price. Freight on merchandise purchases and shipments to the branch is 2 percent of billed prices. Trial balances for both business units at December 31, 19X6, follow:

SAFFRON COMPANY AND BRANCH
PRECLOSING TRIAL BALANCES AT DECEMBER 31, 19X6

Account	Home Office Dr. (Cr.)	Branch Dr. (Cr.)
Cash	$ 263,200	$ 50,000
Accounts Receivable	300,000	158,000
Inventory, Jan. 1	90,000	81,600
Prepayments	60,000	10,400
Plant Assets	800,000	—
Accumulated Depreciation	(100,000)	—
Investment in Branch	182,000	—
Current Liabilities	(330,000)	(150,000)
Capital Stock	(400,000)	—
Retained Earnings, Jan. 1	(268,600)	—
Home Office	—	(138,000)
Sales	(2,100,000)	(800,000)
Shipments to Branch	(240,000)	—
Overvaluation of Branch Inventory	(69,600)	—
Purchases	1,300,000	200,000
Shipments from Home Office	—	290,000
Freight In	42,000	9,800
Operating Expenses	471,000	288,200
	$ 0	$ 0

The following information has been gathered by Saffron's controller:

1. On Friday, December 31, 19X6, the branch mailed a check for $27,000 to the home office.

2. Expenses incurred by Saffron on behalf of the branch and allocated to the branch amounted to $7,000. The branch was never notified.

3. The final merchandise shipment to the branch left Saffron on December 28; invoice amount was $10,000. Freight will be paid by the branch.

4. Ending inventories of the home office and branch amounted to

$98,000 and $76,500, respectively, at invoice prices plus applicable freight. Sixty percent of the branch beginning and ending inventory (excluding the shipment in transit) was acquired from the home office.

Required: Prepare a combined financial statement working paper for the Saffron Company and its branch at December 31, 19X6. Formal adjusting and eliminating entries and combined statements are not required.

P5.9 Two Branches—Reconciliation of Reciprocal Accounts and Making Adjusting and Closing Entries Following are the preclosing trial balances of the Wash Company and its two branches at June 30, 19X8, the end of the Wash Company's fiscal year:

Account	Amount: Dr. (Cr.)		
	Home Office	Branch A	Branch B
Cash and Receivables	$ 281,000	$214,000	$105,000
Inventory, July 1, 19X7.	560,000	180,000	80,000
Plant Assets	940,000	155,000	100,000
Accumulated Depreciation	(250,000)	(25,000)	(10,000)
Investment in Branch A.	470,000	—	—
Investment in Branch B.	300,000	—	—
Current Liabilities.	(580,000)	(130,600)	(60,000)
Capital Stock	(500,000)	—	—
Retained Earnings, July 1, 19X7	(750,000)	—	—
Home Office	—	(376,000)	(230,000)
Sales.	(2,800,000)	(790,000)	(430,000)
Shipments to Branch A	(280,000)	—	—
Shipments to Branch B	(190,000)	—	—
Overvaluation of Branch A Inventory . .	(180,000)	—	—
Overvaluation of Branch B Inventory . .	(115,000)	—	—
Purchases	2,400,000	180,000	70,000
Shipments from Home Office	—	380,000	255,000
Freight In on Merchandise	24,000	—	—
Operating Expenses	670,000	212,600	120,000
	$ 0	$ 0	$ 0

Additional information:

1. The home office ships merchandise to the branches at cost plus 50 percent. Of the beginning inventory of Branch A, $120,000 had been acquired from the home office; of Branch B, $60,000.
2. The following shipments of merchandise originally acquired by the home office were in transit at June 30, 19X8:

From	To	Amount[a]
Home	Branch A	$10,000
Home	Branch B	9,000
Branch B	Branch A	21,000[b]
Branch A	Home	30,000

[a]Billed prices.
[b]Not recorded by home office.

3. Cash payments in transit among the three business units at June 30, 19X8, are:

From	To	Amount
Branch B	Branch A	$40,000[a]
Branch A	Home	54,000

[a]Not recorded by home office.

4. Ending physical inventories of Branch A and Branch B on June 30, 19X8, at billed prices amounted to $150,000 and $110,000, respectively; about 60 percent of each had been acquired from the home office. The home office's ending inventory was $600,000.

Required:

1. Prepare a schedule to reconcile all reciprocal accounts, including the shipments and overvaluation accounts.
2. Prepare formal adjusting and closing entries, assuming that the realized intrafirm markup on merchandise sales is attributed to home office operations. A separate set of entries should be made for each of the three entities.

P5.10 Combined Trial Balance Working Paper   Refer to the data in P5.9 for the Wash Company.

Required: Prepare a combined trial balance working paper for the Wash Company and its branches.

P5.11 Work Sheet—Branch Treated as Sales Agency   You are examining the financial statements of the Conrad Sales Company for the year ended December 31, 19X7. Conrad has not had an audit before. Sales are made from Conrad's home office and a newly opened branch office.

A general ledger trial balance as of December 31, 19X7, is shown below.

CONRAD SALES COMPANY
GENERAL LEDGER TRIAL BALANCE
DECEMBER 31, 19X7

Account	Debit	Credit
Cash	$ 65,400	
Accounts Receivable—Home Office	311,500	
Allowance for Bad Debts		$ 9,000
Merchandise Inventory—Home Office	349,600	
Merchandise Inventory—Branch	100,000	
Investments	165,000	
Prepaid Incentive Bonus	20,000	
Prepaid Expenses	32,100	

Other Assets	164,000	
Accounts Payable		205,600
Accrued Incentive Bonus		35,000
Capital Stock, $1 Par Value		500,000
Retained Earnings, Jan. 1, 19X7		366,600
Sales—Home Office		1,043,800
Cost of Sales—Home Office	746,800	
Selling Expenses—Home Office	98,000	
Selling Expenses—Branch	9,600	
General and Administrative Expenses—Home Office	92,700	
General and Administrative Expenses—Branch	5,300	
Totals	$2,160,000	$2,160,000

Additional information:

1. An inventory taken at the home office on December 31, 19X7, showed merchandise costing $345,200 with a fair market value of $347,300. A perpetual inventory system is maintained.

2. The Investments account balance at December 31, 19X7, in the general ledger was composed of the following:

Cost of 40,000 Shares of Conrad Treasury Stock Purchased in 19X5	$ 68,000
Marketable Securities at Cost (Market Value December 31, 19X7, $82,000)	80,000
Cost of Exclusive Distribution Franchises with Unlimited Lives	17,000
Total	$165,000

3. Conrad paid $20,000 for an incentive bonus on December 22, 19X7, before the bonus was due on December 31, 19X7. The entire bonus of $35,000 was accrued at December 31, 19X7, and the balance of $15,000 was paid on January 15, 19X8.

4. Other assets included $10,000 of market survey costs for a sales project undertaken and abandoned in 19X7, $1,000 of deposits held by utility companies, and $153,000 of net fixed assets. Examination of fixed asset records revealed that Conrad deducted the correct amount of depreciation each year from the recorded cost of fixed assets. The $153,000 was comprised of original costs of $53,000 for land, $100,000 for a building, and $28,000 for furniture and equipment less accumulated depreciation of $22,000 on the building and $6,000 on the furniture and equipment.

5. On September 15, 19X7, Conrad established a branch and shipped it merchandise having a retail value of $140,000 (140 percent of Conrad's cost). At December 31, 19X7, the branch inventory was $56,000, priced at retail value. The branch reported 19X7 sales of $84,000, of which $50,400 had been collected by the branch and represented cash in transit to Conrad at December 31, and $33,600 was receivable from branch customers. This information on branch sales has not been recorded by the home office. The branch considered all

its accounts collectible at December 31, 19X7. Branch administrative expenses totaling $4,100 were paid by Conrad in 19X7 and charged to the General and Administrative Expenses—Branch account. Prepaid expenses of $1,200 related to the branch were also charged to this account.

6. Formal home office/branch accounting procedures have not yet been adopted by Conrad. In effect, the branch is being accounted for as if it were a sales agency. All branch accounts are to be identified as such and maintained on the home office books.

7. The home office accounts receivable consist of the following:

Various small 19X6 balances in dispute (not likely to be collected). .	$ 2,000
Account balances of bankrupt customers (uncollectible)	9,500
Remaining accounts (estimated 3 percent uncollectible)	300,000
Total.	$311,500

8. A bad debts expense of $4,000 was included in the General and Administrative Expenses—Home Office account at December 31, 19X7.

Required: Prepare a work sheet to adjust the accounts of the Conrad Sales Company at December 31, 19X7, and to provide the basis for preparation of financial statements. The work sheet should have columns labeled Trial Balance (Dr., Cr.), Adjustments (Dr., Cr.), Income Statement (Dr., Cr.), and Balance Sheet (Dr., Cr.). Formal adjusting and closing entries are not required. *(AICPA adapted)*

P5.12 Combined Statement of Changes in Financial Position Comparative balance sheets of the home office and branch of Overland, Inc., at the beginning and end of 19X7 are given below:

	Home Office		Branch	
ASSETS	**12/31/X7**	**12/31/X6**	**12/31/X7**	**12/31/X6**
Cash	$ 211,000	$ 190,000	$ 85,000	$ 87,000
Accounts Receivable . . .	300,000	320,000	160,000	145,000
Inventory	450,000	400,000	120,000	150,000
Overvaluation of Branch				
Inventory	(40,000)	(50,000)	—	—
Investment in Branch . . .	220,000	200,000	—	—
Other Assets, Net	869,000	760,000	80,000	70,000
Total Assets.	$2,010,000	$1,820,000	$445,000	$452,000
LIABILITIES AND OWNERS' EQUITY				
Current Liabilities	$ 550,000	$ 505,000	$225,000	$252,000
Long-Term Debt.	600,000	500,000		
Capital Stock	300,000	300,000		
Retained Earnings.	560,000	515,000		
Home Office.	—	—	220,000	200,000
Total Liabilities and				
Owners' Equity	$2,010,000	$1,820,000	$445,000	$452,000

Additional information:

1. Combined net income was $160,000 in 19X7; dividends of $115,000 were paid to Overland's stockholders.
2. Combined depreciation expense was $75,000 in 19X7.
3. Other assets with a net book value of $45,000 were sold for $32,000 during 19X7.
4. A new bond issue was sold at par, $100,000.

Required:

1. Prepare a combined statement of changes in financial position (working capital basis) for 19X7.
2. Prepare a schedule to convert working capital from operations to cash flow from operations.

Chapter 6 Business Combinations

Business combinations occur when two or more companies are brought under common control. They have long been present in the American economy and have occurred for many reasons. In the short run, a business combination leads to a larger single entity than previously existed; more transactions are controlled and more decisions are made by the combined firm than by either previous single entity. Outside an individual firm, price movements direct production through an exchange mechanism called the *market*. After a business combination, the combined firm has substituted its own decision-making apparatus for that of the market's in respect to the factors of production acquired in the combination. The acquiring firm initiates the combination because it believes that it can accomplish its objectives more efficiently and at lower cost than it could in dealing directly with the input and output markets. It follows that a primary motivating principle behind business combinations can be identified as follows.

> In general, a **business combination** will occur when management believes that the cost of achieving a set of objectives (for example, contracting for sources of supply, increasing sales volume, diversification) through the market exceeds the cost of acquiring existing firms and bypassing the market altogether.

This principle is reflected in the practical reasons typically cited to explain the business combination phenomenon. We now turn to these as we review the history of business combinations in the United States.

Business Combinations: Incentives, Incidence, and Insights

Growth is a major objective of most corporate enterprises and may take many forms. *Growth in sales* is needed to increase the firm's share of the market and solidify its position. *Growth in earnings and earnings per share* is seen as essential if the firm's securities are to become more attractive in the capital markets. *Growth in diversity* is pursued in order to reduce or spread business risk, insulate earnings from downturns in business, and decrease the cost of capital. Although growth in these areas can be achieved internally as well as externally, there are several reasons why combination with other existing firms may be preferred to expansion from within.

1. A going concern has its own historical records, experienced personnel, network of suppliers, customers, and creditors. Combination with such a firm eliminates the need to start from scratch. Although managerial and other changes may be necessary, the inescapable fact is that growth from within, whether for reasons of market share or diversification, would usually require duplication of many of the efforts already made by an existing firm. The cost of duplicating these efforts could exceed the cost of acquiring the firm outright.
2. Combination with an existing firm often leads to lower levels of actual or potential competition. If two competing firms combine, competition is actually reduced. Similarly, if a firm enters an industry by acquiring one of the firms currently competing, the number of competing firms remains unchanged. Entry via investment in a new firm, however, increases the number of competitors, thereby making it more difficult for the entering firm to succeed.
3. Desired expansion or entry into a new market may be achieved more quickly through combination with an existing firm.
4. The cost of growth may be cut substantially by combining with a firm possessing large tax loss carryforwards. A profitable firm may be able to combine with one that has generated losses and provide the taxable income needed to realize tax benefits from the losses.

Business Combinations in the American Economy

A large number of business combinations, or mergers, have taken place in the last hundred years, contributing significantly to the development of the American economy. Economic historians often identify three time periods coincidental with extensive ''merger movements.''

The first of these occurred around the turn of the century. During the period 1898–1902, there were some 360 business combinations per year. At that time, American companies were acquiring their competitors and expanding their geographic markets. This type of business combination is generally referred to as **horizontal integration.**

A second period of high merger activity took place during the 1920s. For the years 1920–1929, an average of 680 mergers per year took place, with an average of over 900 per year in 1925–1929. The characteristics of most mergers during this period differed from those of the earlier period. Whereas the earlier horizontal combinations meant that firms were expanding the scale of their activities by entering new markets and increasing productive capacity, **vertical integration** was far more common during the 1920s. Vertical combinations involved firms having a supplier/customer relationship. For example, a manufacturing firm would merge with a mining company to ensure the continued supply of raw materials. Or a manufacturing company might combine with a retailing firm in order to secure ready outlets for its products.

The third merger movement began during the late 1950s and reached its peak during the period 1965–1969. From 1955 to 1969, an average of 1,062 business combinations occurred each year, and an average of 1,642 occurred during each of the years from 1965 to 1969. The combining companies of this period often had fundamentally different characteristics, giving rise to a new type of merger—the **conglomerate merger.** Unlike traditional horizontal and vertical integration, in which the combining companies were engaged in similar or related activities, conglomerates were formed by groups of unrelated companies. Food companies and tobacco companies combined. Motion picture, mining, and manufacturing firms were brought under common management, and so on.

The motivation for conglomerate enterprises can be attributed to the desire to diversify business risks. As previously mentioned, such diversification may provide stability in earnings by insulating the combined firm against economic forces which affect different industries at different times. Furthermore, it was found during the ''go-go'' years of the 1960s that cleverly executed business combinations could provide instant growth in earnings per share.

Antitrust Law and Business Combinations. Business combinations often result in improved economic efficiency, particularly through achieving economies of scale. Nevertheless, the concentrations of economic power represented by large firms occasionally lead to abuses, such as anticompetitive behavior and monopolistic pricing. The antitrust statutes were enacted primarily to promote competition, restrict monopoly, and to serve as countervailing forces against the misuse of economic power often concentrated in large firms resulting from business combinations.

First among these statutes was the *Sherman Act,* passed by Congress in 1890. In Section 1, the act declared every contract, business combination, or conspiracy in restraint of trade or commerce to be illegal. This section prohibited ''unreasonable'' behavior such as predatory pricing and other practices aimed at coercing competitors and unfairly limiting their ability to compete effectively. Section 2 declared that those who monopolize, or attempt to monopolize, or combine or conspire to monopolize any part of trade or commerce are outside the law. Whereas Section 1 tended to emphasize market conduct and behavior, Section 2 became a vehicle for attacking market structure. That is, a dominant firm (or firms) may be found guilty under Section 2 even though it engaged in no unscrupulous practices and did not conspire to restrain trade.

Although in 1911 the Sherman Act was responsible for breaking up two giant trusts—Standard Oil and American Tobacco—it did not represent a wholly satisfactory solution to the abuses of the time. To complement and strengthen the Sherman Act, Congress enacted additional legislation in 1914.

One of these laws, the *Clayton Act,* attacks specific business policies which would substantially reduce competition or promote monopoly. Price discrimination, arrangements whereby sellers would force their customers not to buy from competitors, and mergers which would substantially lessen competition are among the activities forbidden by the Clayton Act. In 1936 the *Robinson-Patman Act* was enacted in order to strengthen the law against price discrimination. The *Celler-Kefauver Act* of 1950 further strengthened the prohibition against those mergers which would lead to reduced competition by broadening the scope of the relevant section in the Clayton Act.

A second statute, the *Federal Trade Commission Act,* was also passed in 1914. It created the Federal Trade Commission (FTC) and provided it with the potentially wide-ranging mandate to declare unfair methods of competition in commerce as unlawful, a role not substantively different from that of Section 1 of the Sherman Act. The *Wheeler-Lea Act* of 1938 authorized the FTC to prohibit unfair or deceptive acts or practices in commerce, thus establishing the basis for its action against unfounded or misleading advertising claims.[1]

Accounting for Business Combinations

At the outset of this section, it is important to recognize that *accounting for business combinations* and *preparation of consolidated financial statements are two separate and distinct topics in accounting theory and practice.* The rules governing accounting for business combinations are employed to determine how the combination should be recorded. Not all business combinations lead to the subsequent preparation of consolidated statements. When consolidated statements are prepared, however, the method used in accounting for the business combination will affect certain details in their preparation. These matters are discussed in Chapters 7 and 8.

In a business combination, two or more companies are joined as one under common control. The combination may occur in various ways, but to simplify and standardize the discussion, we define and use the following terms:

> An **acquiring company** is one whose shareholders as a group control the ownership interests in the combined enterprise. These ownership interests will also be referred to as the **controlling interest.**

Other companies involved in a business combination are considered to be acquired companies. Although some might argue that neither company in a particular business combination is being acquired, a distinction must be made between the relative status of the various ownership interests before and after a business combination. Therefore:

---

[1]For more on the subject of antitrust law, see Richard Caves, *American Industry: Structure, Conduct, Performance,* 4th ed. (Englewood Cliffs, NJ: Prentice-Hall, 1977), especially Chapter 6; and Richard A. Posner, *Economic Analysis of Law* (Boston: Little, Brown, 1973), especially Chapter 7.

> An **acquired company** is one whose ownership interests are substantially eliminated in the combined enterprise or whose ownership interests become part of the controlling interest in the combined enterprise.

A completed combination is typically the outcome of negotiations between the acquiring and acquired companies. An analytical approach to these negotiations when the constituent companies are publicly traded is discussed in the Appendix to this chapter.

Four types of business combinations can be identified from a legal and organizational point of view.

1. A **statutory merger** results when Company B is absorbed into Company A. Company B ceases to exist as a legal entity and its shares are retired. Only the surviving firm, Company A, remains as a legal entity.

2. A **statutory consolidation** takes place when a new corporation, Company C, is organized to absorb the activities of two or more existing corporations. Thus, if Company C is formed out of Companies A and B, the shares of A and B are retired and only Company C continues to exist as a legal entity.

   The above two types of combinations are *statutory* in the sense that the reorganization, issue and retirement of shares, and so forth are governed by the laws of a state. Even though the absorbed firms cease to exist as legal entities, their operations may continue undisturbed as divisions of the combined firm.

3. An **asset acquisition** reflects the acquisition by one firm of all or part of the assets (and liabilities) and business operations of another firm. The selling firm may continue to survive as a legal entity, perhaps with an equity interest in the buying firm, or it may liquidate entirely.

4. A **stock acquisition** occurs when the acquiring firm obtains all or most of the voting shares of another firm. Both firms continue as separate legal entities, and the investment in the acquired firm is treated as an intercorporate investment. Furthermore, a **parent/subsidiary relationship** is created between the two firms by virtue of the acquiring (parent) firm's controlling equity interest in the acquired (subsidiary) firm.

Note that in Items 1–3 above the surviving or acquiring firm records the assets and liabilities acquired on its books. A single legal entity with a single set of financial accounting records remains, and consolidated statements are not necessary. In contrast, a stock acquisition (Item 4) results in an intercorporate investment whereby the shares acquired are recorded in an *Investment in Subsidiary* account. Since both of the combining firms remain as separate legal entities, with their own financial accounting records, preparation of consolidated statements normally follows.

APBO 16 contains authoritative guidance relative to accounting for business combinations.[2] During the 3 years subsequent to the issue of *APBO 16* in August

---

[2] Accounting Principles Board, *Opinion No. 16*, "Business Combinations" (New York: AICPA, 1970); CT § B50.

1970, 39 unofficial interpretations were published by the AICPA.[3] Together, *APBO 16* and the unofficial interpretations represent the bulk of generally accepted accounting principles in the business combinations area. *SFAS 38* clarifies and amends *APBO 16* with respect to the accounting treatment of contingent assets, contingent liabilities, and contingent impairments of assets at date of business combination.[4] Additional technical issues are discussed in the following pronouncements:

1. *SFAS 10. APBO 16* had provided an exemption from some of the pooling conditions in certain situations for business combinations completed within 5 years of October 31, 1970. *SFAS 10* extends this exemption indefinitely by removing the 5-year limitation.[5]
2. *IFAS 4.* The general requirement of *SFAS 2* that research and development costs be expensed as incurred is not waived in a purchase combination. That is, the cost assigned to identifiable assets used in research and development is expensed unless the test of alternative future use is met.[6]
3. *IFAS 9.* The portion of this *Interpretation* relating to *APBO 16* indicates that the *individual* assets and liabilities of savings and loan associations or similar institutions acquired in purchase combinations are to be accounted for at their fair values. An aggregate or institution-wide valuation approach is not permitted.[7]
4. *SFAS 72.* This *Statement* deals with issues related to certain acquisitions of banking and thrift institutions, including allocation of cost to "identifiable" and "unidentifiable" intangible assets, and with issues related to treatment of financial assistance received from regulatory authorities.[8]
5. *SFAS 79.* In this *Statement,* the requirement for disclosure of pro forma results of operations following a purchase combination is waived for *nonpublic enterprises.*[9]

---

[3]American Institue of Certified Public Accountants, *Unofficial Interpretations of* APB Opinion No. 16 (New York: AICPA, 1970–1973); CT § B50.501–.650. Additional interpretations of *APBO 16* may be found in Arthur Andersen & Co., *Interpretations of* APB Opinion Nos. 16 and 17, 5th ed. (Chicago: Arthur Andersen & Co., 1981).

[4]Financial Accounting Standards Board, *Statement of Financial Accounting Standards No. 38,* "Accounting for Preacquisition Contingencies of Purchased Enterprises" (Stamford, CT: FASB, 1980); CT § B50.148–.150.

[5]Financial Accounting Standards Board, *Statement of Financial Accounting Standards No. 10,* "Extension of 'Grandfather' Provisions for Business Combinations" (Stamford, CT.: FASB, 1975).

[6]Financial Accounting Standards Board, *Interpretation of Financial Accounting Standards No. 4,* "Applicability of *FASB Statement No. 2* to Business Combinations Accounted for by the Purchase Method" (Stamford, CT: FASB, 1975); CT § B50.151–.152.

[7]Financial Accounting Standards Board, *Interpretation of Financial Accounting Standards No. 9,* "Applying *APB Opinions No. 16 and 17* When a Savings and Loan Association or a Similar Institution Is Acquired in a Business Combination Accounted for by the Purchase Method" (Stamford, CT.: FASB, 1976); CT § B50.155–.158.

[8]Financial Accounting Standards Board, *Statement of Financial Accounting Standards No. 72,* "Accounting for Certain Acquisitions of Banking or Thrift Institutions" (Stamford, CT: FASB, 1983); CT § B50.158–.158F.

[9]Financial Accounting Standards Board, *Statement of Financial Accounting Standards No. 79,* "Elimination of Certain Disclosures for Business Combinations by Nonpublic Enterprises" (Stamford, CT: FASB, 1984).

Further changes in accounting for business combinations are likely to occur. On August 19, 1976, the FASB published a massive Discussion Memorandum entitled "Accounting for Business Combinations and Purchased Intangibles." To date, however, this Discussion Memorandum has not generated any specific proposals.

The two generally accepted methods of accounting for a business combination are the *purchase* and *pooling of interests* methods. Technically, the method of accounting depends on the characteristics of the combination—only one of the two methods is acceptable for a particular combination. As we shall see, however, sufficient flexibility often exists to enable the parties to choose the accounting by tailoring the combination to conform with the requirements of the desired accounting method.

Purchase Method of Accounting for Business Combinations

The first generally accepted method of accounting for business combinations is the purchase method.

> Under the **purchase method** of accounting for business combinations, the business combination is accounted for as an *acquisition of assets or equity shares,* the outcome of a completed exchange transaction in the open market. The consideration surrendered by the acquiring firm provides the basis for valuing the assets or equities acquired.

Use of the purchase method normally assumes the presence of a dominant firm in the business combination. The acquiring firm engages in an arm's-length market transaction to obtain its interest in the assets or equity of the acquired firm. An exchange transaction has therefore occurred in the market, and, consistent with the principles of historical cost accounting, the assets and liabilities (or equities) acquired are recorded at their cost to the acquiring firm. Cost is measured by either the fair market value of the consideration surrendered or the fair market value of the property acquired, whichever is the more readily determinable.

The purchase method has several postcombination accounting implications. *First, a new basis of accountability for the property acquired is established when the purchase transaction is completed.* Subsequent depreciation and amortization is computed on this new basis. *Second,* property has been acquired; it only begins generating earnings for the new owners (the controlling interest) *after* the date of business combination. *Third,* any retained earnings of the acquired firm at the date of business combination relate to the previous stockholders; these *prior earnings are not included in postcombination retained earnings.* In sum, the purchase method of accounting for business combinations provides the shareholders of the acquiring firm with a new firm. Since the new firm can have neither earnings nor retained earnings until after it begins operations, the controlling shareholders' interest in the earnings of the new (acquired) firm begins at the date of acquisition.

Pooling of Interests Method of Accounting for Business Combinations

The second generally accepted method of accounting for business combinations is the pooling of interests method.

> Under the **pooling of interests method** of accounting for business combinations, the business combination is accounted for as a *union of previously separate ownership interests* achieved through the exchange of equity securities. Since these equity securities are neither purchased nor sold, no new basis of accountability arises out of this exchange.

This method also has some postcombination accounting implications. *First,* the assets and liabilities of the constituent firms are carried forward to the combined firm at their *existing book values.* If the separate companies used different accounting methods for similar assets and liabilities, the amounts may be adjusted to the same accounting basis so long as the change is appropriate for the separate company. Any such changes in accounting method should be applied retroactively, and prior period statements presented for comparative purposes should be restated to reflect the changes.[10] *Second,* all of the current period's earnings of the constituent firms attributable to the controlling interest are *added together,* regardless of when the pooling occurred. This follows from the fact that, in a pooling of interests, the previous ownership interests remain intact but are simply combined. Aggregate income remains the same because the total resources of the combined firm have not changed. Similarly, since the ownership interests in the combined firm are the same interests which existed in the constituent firms prior to combination, earnings of the current period prior to the date of combination are reflected in the net income attributable to the controlling interest. *Third,* retained earnings of the combined firm includes the controlling shareholders' interest in *all retained earnings* of the constituent firms. These accounting implications of the purchase and pooling of interests methods are summarized in Exhibit 6.1.

A short example will serve to illustrate how the postcombination accounting implications differ in the two methods. Suppose Park Corporation wishes to acquire all of the outstanding voting stock of Street Corporation and is evaluating the two accounting methods. The combination is scheduled for December 31. Street Corporation's books show net assets of $1,000,000, retained earnings of $250,000, and current net income of $30,000 at December 31.

1. *Purchase.* Park issues shares of its own stock for $1,500,000 cash and uses the proceeds to purchase Street's outstanding stock in the market. Combined or consolidated statements at December 31 include the assets and liabilities

---

[10]See Accounting Principles Board, *Opinion No. 20,* "Accounting Changes" (New York: AICPA, 1971), pars. 34 and 35; CT § A35.112–113. Such accounting changes are viewed as resulting in financial statements for a different reporting entity—the pooled companies.

Exhibit 6.1	Postcombination Accounting Implications of the Purchase and Pooling of Interests Methods	
Accounting Implication	**Purchase**	**Pooling of Interests**
1. Value of Property Acquired	Fair market value at date of combination, generally measured by the fair market value of the consideration given in the combination. Subsequent depreciation and amortization charges based on fair market value.	Book value as recorded in the accounts of the acquired company. Subsequent depreciation and amortization charges continue to be based on book value.
2. Combined Net Income in the Period of Acquisition	Includes the acquiring company's net income plus the controlling interest's share of the acquired company's earnings *after* date of combination.	Includes the acquiring company's net income plus the controlling interest's share of the acquired company's earnings for the *entire period*.
3. Combined Retained Earnings	Includes the acquiring company's retained earnings plus the controlling interest's share of the acquired company's earnings *after* date of combination.	Includes the acquiring company's retained earnings plus the controlling interest's share of the acquired company's retained earnings both *before* and *after* date of combination.

of Street valued at a net of $1,500,000. None of Street's retained earnings or current period income is included.

2. *Pooling of Interests.* Park exchanges additional shares of its own stock for the shares of Street owned by Street's shareholders. No cash changes hands. Combined or consolidated statements at December 31 now reflect Street's assets and liabilities valued at a net of $1,000,000 *and* Street's retained earnings of $250,000 *and* current period net income of $30,000.

Prior period financial statements and financial information of the constituent companies are to be restated to the combined basis to furnish information comparable to the current period which reflects the pooling. In contrast, prior period information presented after a purchase combination is disclosed on a pro forma combined basis only in the notes to the statements and only for the immediately preceding fiscal period.

These accounting implications suggest that, over the years, combined net income in a pooling is likely to exceed combined net income in a purchase. This phenomenon begins in the period of the combination. Companies which complete a pooling of interests combination at any time during a reporting period can include the acquired company's net income for the entire period in combined net income. Another factor contributes to this phenomenon in periods subsequent to

Exhibit 6.2 **Business Combinations Recorded as Purchases or Poolings of Interests by the 600 Companies Surveyed in *Accounting Trends and Techniques 1967–1982***

| | Business Combinations | | | | |
| | Purchase | | Pooling of Interests | | |
Year	Number	Percent	Number	Percent	Total
1982	145	86%	24	14%	169
1981	156	84	30	16	186
1980	159	82	34	18	193
1979	185	83	39	17	224
1978	149	73	56	27	205
1977	118	71	48	29	166
1976	103	71	43	29	146
1975	75	71	31	29	106
1974	143	74	50	26	193
1973	163	65	89	35	252
1972	160	61	102	39	262
1971	133	57	100	43	233
1970 *APBO 16, APBO 17*	155	53	139	47	294
1969	195	51	185	49	380
1968	190	51	184	49	374
1967	116	45	144	55	260

Source: American Institute of Certified Public Accountants, *Accounting Trends and Techniques,* various issues. Copyright © by the American Institute of Certified Public Accountants, Inc.

the combination. Recall that a purchase combination produces a new basis of accountability for depreciable and amortizable assets. If the new basis is higher than the original book value, the purchase method will result in larger charges for depreciation and amortization made against combined net income after the date of business combination.

Prior to the issuance of *APBO 16,* the search for companies capable of providing these kinds of benefits in a pooling of interests combination had almost become a national pastime. Abuses of pooling were common and will be discussed later in this chapter. While the rules enabled a company disappointed with its own profit prospects to improve net income by consummating a pooling of interests combination late in the reporting period, some companies went even further. For example, poolings completed between the end of the reporting period and the date that period's financial statements were issued were sometimes included in those statements.

In Exhibit 6.2, we tabulate purchase and pooling combinations reported by the 600 companies surveyed by *Accounting Trends and Techniques* from 1967 to 1982. The relative significance of poolings declined sharply after *APBO 16* was issued in 1970.

Recording the Business Combination

How a business combination is to be recorded depends primarily on two factors:

1. The nature of the business combination—whether it is a statutory merger, a statutory consolidation, an asset acquisition, or a stock acquisition.
2. The accounting method appropriate in the circumstances—purchase or pooling of interests.

The Nature of the Business Combination. *All assets acquired and all liabilities assumed in a business combination are recorded directly on the books of the acquired company in the statutory merger, statutory consolidation, and asset acquisition cases.* In a statutory merger, the acquired company is absorbed into the acquiring company, its stock is retired, and it ceases to exist as a legal entity. A statutory consolidation differs in degree only. Because the stock of two or more acquiring companies is retired, they too cease to exist as legal entities. In contrast, an asset acquisition does not involve the stock of the company from which the assets were acquired at all; the company may continue in business or liquidate in an unrelated transaction. For these reasons, the acquiring company will record the property acquired and the liabilities assumed directly on its own books; recording a statutory merger or consolidation is equivalent to recording an asset acquisition.

The method of recording a business combination which is a *stock acquisition* differs from the above. A parent/subsidiary relationship is created between the acquiring and the acquired companies. The acquired company remains as a separate legal entity and is treated as an intercorporate investment by the acquiring firm. Consequently, *the acquiring firm does not record the assets and liabilities of the acquired firm on its books.* Rather, the acquiring firm uses an **Investment in Subsidiary account** to record the shares of stock acquired. The Investment in Subsidiary account gives a one-line summation of the acquiring company's interest in the underlying assets and liabilities of the acquired company. As we shall see in subsequent chapters, this parent/subsidiary relationship normally calls for the preparation of consolidated financial statements. In a consolidated balance sheet, the Investment in Subsidiary account is replaced by the underlying assets and liabilities of the subsidiary.

The Method of Accounting. We have already indicated that a major difference between purchase and pooling of interests accounting involves the basis for recording the property acquired. Under purchase accounting, the fair value of the consideration given typically provides the total dollar amount used to record the assets or stock acquired. In contrast, the acquiring firm uses book values for recording the acquired company's assets or stock obtained in a pooling of interests. Other rules applicable to the recording of business combinations are discussed below in the context of the two allowable accounting methods. Although both methods are allowable in general, only one is appropriate for a particular business combination. Any business combination failing to satisfy *all* of the conditions for a pooling of interests (to be discussed later) *must be accounted for as a purchase.*

Application of the Purchase Method

The acquiring company's recorded cost of the stock or assets acquired in a purchase combination is normally based on the fair value of the consideration given. When securities are given, their fair market (trading) value measures the amount of consideration. *Costs of registering and issuing equity securities* are charged against Additional Paid-In Capital. For example, suppose that common stock with par value of $100,000 and fair market value of $1,000,000 is given in a purchase combination. Costs of registering and issuing these common shares amount to $26,000. The recorded cost of the investment in the acquired company is the fair market value of the issuing company's stock, in this case $1,000,000. The acquiring company will account for the common stock issued and the related registration and issue costs as follows:

Cost of the Investment (Fair Market Value of the Stock Given Up)	$1,000,000
Par Value of the Common Stock	$ 100,000
Additional Paid-In Capital ($1,000,000 − $100,000 − $26,000)	874,000
Cash Paid or Liabilities Incurred for the Registration and Issue Costs	26,000
	$1,000,000

If the registration and issue costs have not been paid when the securities are issued, a liability for them must be accrued and charged against Additional Paid-In Capital.

Expenses of a Purchase Combination. The investment cost is increased by certain *direct costs* associated with the combination, such as fees paid to accountants and consultants and the out-of-pocket cost of legal services related to the combination. In contrast, *indirect (internal) costs* and the recurring expenses of mergers and acquisitions departments within the acquiring company are treated as normal operating expenses of the period. They are *not* added to the investment cost. Thus, if $50,000 of direct costs were incurred in the preceding example where common stock worth $1,000,000 was given up, the total cost of the investment would be recorded as $1,050,000.

Accounting for Assets Acquired and Liabilities Assumed. In a purchase combination, the price paid represents the aggregate basis of accountability of the property acquired and liabilities assumed. Amounts recorded for individual items are based on the following principles from *APBO 16:*

> A portion of the total cost is then assigned to each individual asset acquired [and liability assumed] on the basis of its fair value. A difference between the sum of the assigned costs of the tangible and identifiable intangible assets less liabilities assumed and the cost of the group is evidence of unspecified intangible values [goodwill].[11]

---

[11] Accounting Principles Board, *Opinion No. 16,* par. 68; CT § B50.126; parenthetical phrases added by the authors.

While individual assets acquired and liabilities assumed will be recorded at their fair values, a systematic approach to allocating the total cost of the business combination which incorporates *differences between fair and book values* has been developed and is explained below. This approach is efficient when dealing with acquired companies that are less than wholly owned and will be used extensively in the chapters on consolidated financial statements.

The investment cost, as measured by the total fair value of consideration given in a purchase combination, is rarely equal to the book value of the assets acquired less liabilities assumed. To simplify dealing with this difference, we use the following terminology:[12]

A **purchase premium** is said to exist when the cost of the acquisition is *greater than* the total book value of the underlying assets acquired less the liabilities assumed. Similarly, a **purchase discount** arises when the cost of the acquisition is *less than* the total book value of the underlying assets acquired less the liabilities assumed.

Since a purchase premium or purchase discount is the *total difference* between the cost or fair value of the acquired company and its book value, it will be allocated among the assets acquired and liabilities assumed in accordance with the *individual differences* between their fair and book values. If the total cost of the acquired company exceeds the fair value of its net assets, the excess is a residual intangible asset called **goodwill.** Exhibit 6.3 illustrates the procedure for allocating investment cost to individual assets acquired and liabilities assumed in a hypothetical *purchase premium* case.

Since application of the purchase method results in a new basis of accountability for the property acquired, depreciation, amortization, and other asset expirations (costs) in subsequent years are to be based on the amounts assigned at date of combination. These amounts appear in the fourth column of Exhibit 6.3. *APBO 16* requires, however, that any *goodwill previously recorded* by the acquired company is to be ignored in allocating the investment cost among the assets and liabilities acquired. Such goodwill is not an "identifiable intangible asset" and is implicitly assigned a fair value of zero.[13]

Moreover, if the *income tax basis* of an asset acquired or liability assumed in a purchase combination differs from its fair market value, the cost assigned to this item must reflect any related **tax effects.** This situation will frequently occur when a purchase involves an exchange of common shares and is treated as a tax-free reorganization under federal income tax law. For example, suppose an acquired building's fair market value is appraised at $300,000 and its tax basis is

---

[12]Our thanks to Peter S.M. Wolcott, MBA 1979, the Amos Tuck School of Business Administration, Dartmouth College, for suggesting this terminology to us.

[13]Accounting Principles Board, *Opinion No. 16,* par. 88; CT § B50.146.

Exhibit 6.3   P and S Companies: Schedule for Determining and Allocating the Purchase Premium (Discount) Arising in the 100 Percent Purchase Acquisition on December 31, 19X1

Total Cost of Acquisition $1,000,000
Book Value of Net Assets or Stockholders' Equity Acquired.   800,000
Purchase Premium (Discount). . . . . $ 200,000

Assets and Liabilities of S Company	(1) Fair Value	(2) Book Value	(3) = (1) − (2) Fair Value Less Book Value	(4) = (2) + (3) Cost Assigned to P's Interest (100%)
Current Assets	$1,150,000	$1,125,000	$ 25,000	$1,150,000
Noncurrent Assets	1,080,000	1,030,000	50,000	1,080,000
Current Liabilities	(600,000)	(600,000)	—	(600,000)
Noncurrent Liabilities . . .	(700,000)	(755,000)	55,000	(700,000)
	$ 930,000	$ 800,000	$130,000	$ 930,000
Goodwill			70,000	70,000
Total Purchase Premium (Discount)			$200,000	
Total Cost.				$1,000,000

$200,000. The tax basis of $200,000 will carry over to the acquirer in the tax-free reorganization. The $100,000 excess is *not* eligible for tax depreciation (it is a *permanent difference*) and, at a 46 percent income tax rate, will *not* produce tax savings of $46,000. Thus the cost assigned to the building should be based on its adjusted fair value of $254,000 (= $300,000 − $46,000), its original estimated fair value reduced by the lost tax benefits. Adjustments for such tax effects should be considered before allocating any purchase premium or discount.

We now give an illustration of the purchase method of accounting for business combinations applied to a statutory merger with goodwill present.

Purchase Accounting—Statutory Merger, Goodwill. S Company is to be merged into P Company on December 31, 19X1, pursuant to the laws of the state in which P is incorporated. The condensed balance sheet of S Company at the date of combination appears in Exhibit 6.4, along with estimated fair values.

As consideration, P Company is issuing 12 percent bonds with par value and current market value of $900,000 to the shareholders of S in exchange for their entire equity interest in the net assets (that is, assets less liabilities) of S Company. Direct costs associated with the merger (consultants' and attorneys' fees) amount to $25,000. Since the stockholders' equity of S Company amounts to only $450,000, P Company has paid a *purchase premium*. In Exhibit 6.5, we compute this purchase premium and determine how it is to be allocated among the assets and liabilities of S Company.

Using the results in Exhibit 6.5, P Company makes the following journal entry on its books to record the merger with S Company:

Cash and Receivables	100,000	
Inventory	375,000	
Buildings and Equipment, Net	960,000	
Discount on 6% Bonds Payable	100,000[a]	
Goodwill	90,000[b]	
Current Liabilities		200,000
Cash		25,000[c]
Bonds Payable, 6%		500,000[a]
Bonds Payable, 12%		900,000

To record the acquisition of S Company, a statutory merger, accounted for as a purchase.

[a]The 6 percent bonds payable assumed by Company P are recorded at their current market value of $400,000 by entering the liability at par value, $500,000, and recording a discount on bonds payable of $100,000.
[b]Goodwill of $90,000 arises because the consideration given exceeded the fair values of the identifiable assets acquired reduced by liabilities assumed (see Exhibit 6.5).
[c]The $25,000 credit to Cash reflects payment of the direct costs of the merger.

Accounting for Accumulated Depreciation of the Acquired Company. In a purchase combination, the acquiring company has purchased the assets and liabilities of the acquired company either directly or indirectly through the purchase of

---

Exhibit 6.4   **Balance Sheet of S Company at December 31, 19X1**

S COMPANY
BALANCE SHEET AT DECEMBER 31, 19X1

ASSETS		Book Value	Fair Value
Cash and Receivables		$ 100,000	$100,000
Inventory		250,000	375,000
Buildings and Equipment	$1,000,000		
Less Accumulated Depreciation	(200,000)	800,000	960,000 (net)
Total Assets		$1,150,000	

LIABILITIES AND STOCKHOLDERS' EQUITY

Current Liabilities		$ 200,000	200,000
Bonds Payable, 6%, Par Value $500,000		500,000	400,000[a]
Common Stock, Par Value $1		100,000	
Additional Paid-In Capital		125,000	
Retained Earnings		225,000	
Total Liabilities and Stockholders' Equity		$1,150,000	

[a]With current interest rates approximating 12 percent, the market value of the debt has fallen since the bonds were initially issued.

Exhibit 6.5 **P and S Companies: Schedule for Determining and Allocating the Purchase Premium Arising in the Statutory Merger on December 31, 19X1**

Cost of Acquisition:
Market Value of Long-Term Debt Issued . . . . $ 900,000
Consultants' and Attorneys' Fees 25,000

Total Cost of Acquisition . . . . $ 925,000
Book Value of Net Assets or Stockholders' Equity Acquired:
Common Stock . . . . $ 100,000
Additional Paid-In Capital 125,000
Retained Earnings. 225,000

Total Book Value of S Company . . . . $ 450,000
Purchase Premium . . . . $ 475,000

Assets and Liabilities of S Company	(1) Fair Value	(2) Book Value	(3) = (1) − (2) Fair Value Less Book Value	(4) = (2) + (3) Cost Assigned to P's Interest (100%)
Cash and Receivables. .	$ 100,000	$ 100,000	—	$ 100,000
Inventory	375,000	250,000	$125,000	375,000
Buildings and Equipment, Net	960,000	800,000	160,000	960,000
Current Liabilities	(200,000)	(200,000)	—	(200,000)
Bonds Payable, 6%	(400,000)	(500,000)	100,000	(400,000)
	$ 835,000	$ 450,000	$385,000	$ 835,000

Goodwill 90,000   90,000
Total Purchase Premium $475,000
Total Cost . . . . $ 925,000

shares. Allocation of the purchase price is dependent on the fair values of the properties acquired, and any accumulated depreciation recorded by the acquired company becomes irrelevant after the combination. The fair values established for assets, whether new or used, become their carrying values after the combination. These new carrying values (net of any estimated salvage proceeds) are then depreciated over their remaining useful lives. In the statutory merger just recorded, only the net fair value of S Company's buildings and equipment, $960,000, is entered on P Company's books.

Bargain Purchases and Negative Goodwill. In the great majority of cases, a purchase combination involves consideration with fair value greater than the book value of the property acquired. Moreover, the cost of the acquisition often exceeds the fair value of the tangible assets and identifiable intangible assets acquired less liabilities assumed, thereby generating a residual intangible called *goodwill*. A problem arises, however, if the fair value of the property acquired less liabilities assumed *exceeds* the cost of the investment. Or, in other words, the problem occurs if the fair value of the consideration given up is less than the total fair value of the net assets acquired. When this occurs, we have what might be considered a *bargain purchase*. Yet the bargain purchase interpretation arises essentially because of a disagreement between estimates of the fair value of the consideration surrendered and the fair value of the property acquired. The fair value of the property acquired dominates the transaction only if it is more clearly evident than the fair value of the consideration given.

For example, cash or the market value of securities traded on the New York or American Stock Exchange would be more reliable evidence of the cost of an acquired company than appraisals of the acquired company's assets and liabilities. On the other hand, competent appraisals may have more validity in establishing cost than prices of thinly traded, over-the-counter securities. *If the fair value of the consideration given more clearly represents the actual combination cost, then the total of the amounts assigned to assets acquired less liabilities assumed cannot exceed that cost.* When the investment cost is *less* than the fair values of the net assets acquired, **negative goodwill** arises and a *two-stage allocation process* is called for to deal with the negative goodwill.

1. The first stage produces a *tentative* allocation of the investment cost to the assets acquired and liabilities assumed in accordance with their fair values. This procedure has already been illustrated in Exhibits 6.3 and 6.5. If the total of these tentative allocations exceeds the investment cost, however, negative goodwill is produced and we are led to the second stage.

2. *APBO 16* provides that any excess of fair value of assets over investment cost (negative goodwill) *must be allocated proportionately among noncurrent assets except long-term investments in marketable securities.*[14] This is the second stage of the allocation process. If there is sufficient negative goodwill to reduce the recorded fair values of eligible noncurrent assets to zero, any remaining (unallocated) amount is classified as a *deferred credit.* Under the provisions of *APBO 17,* both positive goodwill arising in a business combination and deferred credits arising from unallocated negative goodwill must be *systematically amortized to income over a period not to exceed 40 years. Straight-line amortization is required.*[15] If adjustment for tax effects is needed when negative goodwill is present, the tax effects are considered *before* the negative goodwill is allocated.

Observe that the existence of a purchase discount does not in itself guarantee that

---

[14] Accounting Principles Board, *Opinion No. 16,* par. 91; CT § B50.145.
[15] Accounting Principles Board, *Opinion No. 17,* "Intangible Assets" (New York: AICPA, 1970); CT § I60.

negative goodwill will arise. Nor will a purchase premium always mean that positive goodwill is present. In short, the *purchase premium or discount* determination is based on a comparison between the *investment cost* and the *book value* of the net assets acquired. Whether *positive or negative goodwill* exists follows from the relationship between investment cost and the *fair value* of the net assets acquired. For example, if investment cost exceeds book value, a purchase premium was paid. Yet negative goodwill will be present if investment cost is less than fair value. Similarly, if book value exceeds investment cost, a purchase discount exists, but positive goodwill will result if investment cost is more than fair value.

We now illustrate the treatment of negative goodwill in a statutory merger of P Company and T Company.

Purchase Accounting—Statutory Merger, Negative Goodwill. T Company is to be merged into P Company on December 31, 19X1, pursuant to the laws of the state in which P is incorporated. The balance sheet of T Company at the combination date appears in Exhibit 6.6, along with estimated fair values.

T Company's stockholders agreed to exchange all of their stock for 88,000 shares of P Company's $7.50 par value stock worth $880,000 and $120,000 cash.

Exhibit 6.6   **Balance Sheet of T Company at December 31, 19X1**

T COMPANY
BALANCE SHEET AT DECEMBER 31, 19X1

ASSETS		Book Value	Fair Value
Cash and Receivables		$ 150,000	$ 150,000
Marketable Equity Securities—Current .		100,000	120,000
Inventory		300,000	350,000
Marketable Equity Securities—Long-			
Term		500,000	600,000
Land.		200,000	400,000
Buildings and Equipment	$1,800,000		
Less Accumulated Depreciation	(600,000)	1,200,000	1,200,000 (net)
Total Assets.		$2,450,000	
LIABILITIES AND STOCKHOLDERS' EQUITY			
Current Liabilities		$ 500,000	500,000
Other Liabilities		800,000	1,200,000ª
Common Stock, Par Value $5.		250,000	
Additional Paid-In Capital		400,000	
Retained Earnings.		500,000	
Total Liabilities and Stockholders'			
Equity.		$2,450,000	

ªThe fair value of Other Liabilities exceeded their book value due to the recognition of certain pension obligations which, consistent with generally accepted accounting principles, had not been booked by T Company. See footnote 13 to par. 88(h) of *APBO 16* [CT § B50.146(h)].

P Company also incurred registration and issue costs in the amount of $20,000 and other direct costs of $40,000.

Prior to recording this merger on P Company's books, the accountant must allocate the purchase premium or discount among the assets acquired and liabilities assumed. Exhibit 6.7 demonstrates this allocation procedure for T Company. A similar procedure was illustrated for S Company in Exhibit 6.5.

The T Company acquisition, however, requires the *two-stage allocation process*. Specifically, it appears that the acquisition of T Company was a *bargain purchase*. Following paragraph 91 of *APBO 16*, we illustrate how the "excess of fair value over cost," or *negative goodwill*, of $80,000 is to be treated in allocating the overall purchase discount of $110,000 to the assets and liabilities of T Company. This is the second stage of the two-stage allocation process. Negative goodwill must be used to reduce the cost assigned to noncurrent assets exclusive

---

Exhibit 6.7 **P and T Companies: Schedule for Determining and Allocating the Purchase Discount Arising in the Statutory Merger on December 31, 19X1**

Cost of Acquisition
Fair Value of Stock Given	$ 880,000
Cash Given	120,000
Direct Costs Incurred	40,000
Total Cost of Acquisition	$ 1,040,000

Book Value of Net Assets or Stockholders' Equity Acquired:
Common Stock	$ 250,000
Additional Paid-In Capital	400,000
Retained Earnings	500,000
Total Book Value of T Company	$ 1,150,000
Purchase Discount	$ (110,000)

Assets and Liabilities of T Company	Fair Value	Book Value	Fair Value Less Book Value	Cost Tentatively Assigned to P's Interest (100%)
Cash and Receivables	$ 150,000	$ 150,000	—	$ 150,000
Marketable Equity Securities—Current	120,000	100,000	$ 20,000	120,000
Inventory	350,000	300,000	50,000	350,000
Marketable Equity Securities—Long-Term	600,000	500,000	100,000	600,000
Land	400,000	200,000	200,000	400,000
Buildings and Equipment, Net	1,200,000	1,200,000		1,200,000
Current Liabilities	(500,000)	(500,000)	—	(500,000)
Other Liabilities	(1,200,000)	(800,000)	(400,000)	(1,200,000)
	$ 1,120,000	$1,150,000	$ (30,000)	$ 1,120,000
Negative Goodwill			(80,000)	(80,000)
Total Purchase Discount			$(110,000)	
Total Cost				$ 1,040,000

of long-term investments in marketable securities. Current assets, long-term investments in marketable securities, and all liabilities are to be recorded at their fair values. From Exhibit 6.6, we see that the noncurrent assets eligible to absorb the negative goodwill are Land (fair value, $400,000) and Buildings and Equipment, Net (fair value, $1,200,000). Allocation of the negative goodwill in accordance with the relative fair values of the eligible noncurrent assets is shown next.

	(1)	(2)	(3)	(4) = (1) − (3)
			Allocation of	
	Fair Value		Negative Goodwill	
	Amount	Percent	[(2) × $80,000]	Cost Assigned
Land	$ 400,000	25%	$20,000	$ 380,000
Buildings and				
Equipment, Net . .	1,200,000	75	60,000	1,140,000
	$1,600,000	100%	$80,000	$1,520,000

P Company now makes the following entry on its books to record the merger with T Company. Most of the amounts appeared in Exhibit 6.7; the amounts assigned to Land and to Buildings and Equipment reflect the negative goodwill allocation.

Cash and Receivables	150,000	
Marketable Equity Securities—Current	120,000	
Inventory	350,000	
Marketable Equity Securities—Long-Term	600,000	
Land	380,000	
Buildings and Equipment, Net	1,140,000	
Current Liabilities		500,000
Other Liabilities		1,200,000
Cash		180,000^a
Capital Stock		660,000^b
Additional Paid-In Capital		200,000^c
To record the acquisition of T Company, a statutory merger,		
accounted for as a purchase.		

^{a} The $180,000 credit to Cash reflects $120,000 paid to the former stockholders of T Company, direct merger costs of $40,000, and registration and issue costs of $20,000.
^{b} $660,000 = 88,000 × $7.50.
^{c} $200,000 = $880,000 − $660,000 − $20,000 (registration and issue costs).

Purchase Accounting—Statutory Consolidations and Asset Acquisitions. The preceding two examples illustrated the principles of the purchase method of accounting for business combinations in statutory merger settings. These principles are no different for business combinations structured as statutory consolidations and asset acquisitions. If stock is given in the statutory consolidation case, however, the investment cost may be better represented by the fair value of the net assets acquired than by the market value of the stock. If Company C is formed expressly to acquire companies A and B, there may be no independent measure of the market value of C's stock and no basis for valuing the consideration given.

Purchase Accounting—Stock Acquisitions. Recall that from a legal and organizational point of view, a business combination may occur even though the combining companies remain as separate entities. A parent/subsidiary relationship may be established, in which the acquiring company accounts for its interest in the acquired company by means of an **Investment in Subsidiary** account ("Subsidiary" is generally referred to as "S"). The parent/subsidiary relationship is established when the acquiring company secures control of more than 50 percent of the voting shares of the acquired company. This controlling interest may be secured through a purchase of shares in the market, an exchange of equity shares, or some similar means.

When a stock acquisition is accounted for as a purchase, the cost of the investment is measured by the fair value of the consideration given if this amount is clearly more obvious than the fair value of the property underlying the equity shares. *If a purchase premium or discount exists,* it is not accounted for separately and *is allocated subsequently when consolidated statements are prepared.* To illustrate the accounting for stock acquisitions, we use companies S and T as previously introduced.

Consider first the acquisition of S Company. If S Company is to remain as a separate legal entity, the acquisition of its shares would be recorded on the books of P Company by the following journal entry:

Investment in S	925,000	
Cash		25,000
Bonds Payable, 12%		900,000

To record the acquisition of all the outstanding common stock of S Company. Consideration to the former shareholders of S consisted of $900,000 of P's 12 percent bonds. Direct costs associated with this acquisition were consultants' and attorneys' fees of $25,000, which were paid in cash and are part of the total investment cost of $925,000.

With respect to the acquisition of T Company, if a parent/subsidiary relationship is to be maintained, P Company makes a similar journal entry:

Investment in T	1,040,000	
Cash		180,000
Common Stock		660,000
Additional Paid-In Capital		200,000

To record the acquisition of all the outstanding common stock of T Company. Consideration to the former shareholders of T included cash of $120,000 and 88,000 shares of P Company $7.50 par value stock with a market value of $880,000. Registration and issue costs of $20,000, which were paid in cash, are netted against Additional Paid-In Capital. Direct costs associated with this acquisition were consultants' and attorneys' fees of $40,000, which were paid in cash and are part of the total investment cost of $1,040,000.

In Chapters 7 and 8, we discuss how the Investment in Subsidiary account is to be accounted for *after* the business combination. Whether the proper accounting requires consolidated statements or not, we still need to know both book values *and* fair values of the assets and liabilities of companies S and T.

A stock acquisition often involves less than 100 percent of the subsidiary's outstanding voting stock. Regardless of the percentage of ownership, the cost of the shares acquired is accounted for as an investment in subsidiary. Partially owned subsidiaries, however, generate additional problems for the accountant who must prepare consolidated financial statements. These problems will be studied in subsequent chapters.

Contingent Consideration in Purchase Accounting. Paragraphs 77–86 of *APBO 16* provide guidance for accounting for various types of **contingent consideration agreements** which often arise in a business combination. Such agreements call for the payment of additional cash or the issuance of additional securities in the future if specified events occur. The existence of a contingent consideration arrangement violates pooling condition (g) (shown later in Exhibit 6.8) and will therefore be dealt with only in the context of a purchase combination. These arrangements generally benefit the shareholders of the acquired company and are of two general types:

1. Contingencies based on earnings.
2. Contingencies based on security prices.

A **contingency based on earnings** typically derives from the beliefs of the former shareholders of the acquired company that they are entitled to more consideration for their shares because their company will substantially bolster postcombination earnings. Although there may be no evidence on this point, the acquiring company may agree that if earnings equal or exceed a given amount in a specified period of time, additional consideration will be paid to the former shareholders of the acquired company. Such payments, when they materialize, represent *an addition to the cost of the acquired company*. The parties are, in effect, agreeing that *the total cost will not be known until the contingency period elapses*. Accordingly, payments resulting from the resolution of an earnings contingency will increase a previously existing purchase premium or decrease a previously existing purchase discount. Any change in the purchase premium or discount is viewed as a change in accounting estimate. Allocation of the new amount to depreciable or amortizable assets simply increases the costs which must now be depreciated or amortized over the assets' remaining lives.

As an example, consider the merger of P Company and S Company. Suppose P Company agrees that if average postcombination earnings over the next 2 years exceed $250,000, payments of $100,000 in cash or stock will be made to former S Company shareholders. Footnote disclosure of the contingency is required in P's financial statements. If, at the close of the second year, average earnings for the 2-year period are $275,000, P Company may settle the contingency by issuing additional shares. P's shares have a par value of $7.50 and, assuming a per share market value of $20 at the end of the contingency period, the accountant will record the issuance of 5,000 (= $100,000/$20) shares. According to our initial allocation of the cost of the S Company acquisition in Exhibit 6.5, the additional market value of $100,000 (= 5,000 × $20) would be allocated in its entirety to goodwill. Had the business combination been accounted for as a stock acquisition, the earnings contingency payments would increase the Investment in Subsidiary account.

Goodwill 100,000
    Common Stock   37,500
    Additional Paid-In Capital   62,500
To record the issue of 5,000 shares of P Company's $7.50 par
value stock at their per share market value of $20 in settlement of
the earnings contingency arranged as part of the combination with
S Company.

In contrast, a **contingency based on security prices** does not affect the cost of the acquired company. Such a contingency guarantees the former shareholders of the acquired company that the market value of securities (stock or debt) issued to them in exchange for their stock will be at least a specified amount at a specified time. It is this *guaranteed amount* that *measures the cost of the acquired company*. Although additional consideration may be required in the future to restore the economic position of the acquired company's former shareholders, the cost of the acquired company has not changed.

To illustrate, suppose that, in acquiring T Company, P Company agreed to guarantee that the 88,000 P Company shares issued would be worth at least $10 per share in one year. If the closing market price was $8 per share at the end of one year, P must issue additional consideration worth $176,000 (= 88,000 shares issued $\times$ $2 per share). Whether more shares are now issued or cash is paid, the debit is to Additional Paid-In Capital. We assume that P Company satisfies the contingent consideration agreement by issuing more shares of its stock. At $8 per share, 22,000 (= $176,000/$8) new shares must be issued.

Additional Paid-In Capital 165,000
    Common Stock   165,000
To record the additional shares issued at their total par value of
$165,000 (= 22,000 $\times$ $7.50) in settlement of the contingent
consideration agreement made with the former shareholders of
S Company.

This entry has the effect of properly stating both the total par value of stock issued in the combination and the additional paid-in capital which, in the final analysis, resulted. We demonstrate this point by observing:

Agreed-Upon Value of Stock Given (88,000 $\times$ $10). . . . . $ 880,000
Total Par Value of 110,000 (= 88,000 + 22,000) Shares at $7.50
    per Share . . . . $ 825,000
Registration and Issue Costs 20,000
Net Additional Paid-In Capital   35,000
                                              $880,000

Amount Originally Credited to Additional Paid-In Capital. . . . . $ 200,000
Amount Debited to Additional Paid-In Capital When 22,000 Additional Shares
    Are Issued . . . . (165,000)
Net Additional Paid-In Capital . . . . $ 35,000

Accounting for Preacquisition Contingencies. In September 1980, the FASB issued *SFAS 38*.[16] This statement clarifies the application of *SFAS 5*[17] and *SFAS*

16^{18} to *APBO 16* as the valuation of **preacquisition contingencies** of purchased enterprises and subsequent adjustments generated by the resolution of those contingencies. More specifically, the issues are: What criteria should govern the allocation of investment cost to unrecorded (and perhaps unknown) contingent assets, contingent impairments of assets, or contingent liabilities existing at date of business combination? Should subsequent adjustments to or resolutions of such contingencies enter the income statement or be used to revise the original purchase price allocation?

SFAS 38 addresses these issues by identifying an **allocation period,** normally not to extend beyond one year after a business combination, during which the initial purchase price allocations may be revised as new information regarding preacquisition contingencies arises. After this allocation period expires, subsequent adjustments to recorded preacquisition contingencies enter the income statement.

Two criteria must be satisfied if the original purchase price allocation is to be revised during the *allocation period:*

1. Information which becomes available during the allocation period indicates that, at the date of business combination, it is probable that an unrecorded asset, liability, or asset impairment existed.
2. The amount of the asset, liability, or asset impairment can be reasonably estimated.

If the contingency is resolved (settled or withdrawn) during the allocation period, the original (or revised) purchase price allocation would be adjusted, if necessary, to reflect the resolution. In cases where the contingency remains unresolved at the end of the allocation period, all information then available should be analyzed to determine whether the allocation for the contingency should be increased or decreased. Once the allocation period has expired, however, any further increases or decreases in the contingent item are accounted for as gains or losses.

For example, suppose that on March 1, 19X2, P Company acquired S Company for $1,000,000 cash, an amount which exceeded the fair value of the assets acquired ($3,000,000) less liabilities assumed ($2,200,000) by $200,000. On March 20, an unanticipated lawsuit was filed against the combined company claiming damages of $120,000 from defective goods sold by S Company during 19X1. P Company's attorneys expect an unfavorable outcome from the lawsuit. In January 19X3, a similar case was decided against a competing firm and the estimate of probable damages rose to $150,000. The case was finally decided in December 19X4, with judgment for the plaintiffs in the amount of $220,000.

---

[16]Financial Accounting Standards Board, *Statement No. 38.*
[17]Financial Accounting Standards Board, *Statement of Financial Accounting Standards No. 5,* "Accounting for Contingencies" (Stamford, CT: FASB, 1975); CT § C59.
[18]Financial Accounting Standards Board, *Statement of Financial Accounting Standards No. 16,* "Prior Period Adjustments" (Stamford, CT: FASB, 1977); CT § A35.

Assuming that P Company reports on the calendar-year basis, application of *SFAS 38* produces the following financial statement effects at the relevant dates. Amortization has been ignored.

	3/1/X2	12/31/X2	12/31/X3	12/31/X4
Various Assets.	$ 3,000,000	$ 3,000,000	$ 3,000,000	$ 3,000,000
Goodwill	200,000	320,000	350,000	350,000
Loss (Income Statement)	—	—	—	70,000
Various Liabilities	(2,200,000)	(2,200,000)	(2,200,000)	(2,200,000)
Estimated Liability-Lawsuit	—	(120,000)	(150,000)	(220,000)

The filing of the lawsuit and the revision of probable damages occurred within one year of the business combination and are reflected in revised purchase price allocations at the end of 19X2 and 19X3, respectively. Since the case was decided after the allocation period ended, the additional $70,000 of loss not provided for is charged against 19X4 income.

Preacquisition contingencies can also relate to assets. Suppose that a patent was applied for prior to the combination and subsequently approved after the combination but during the allocation period. The original purchase price allocation would be adjusted to reflect the estimated fair value of the approved patent.

Application of the Pooling of Interests Method

We mentioned earlier in the chapter that *APBO 16* was issued in 1970 to improve accounting for business combinations in general and to curtail abuses of the pooling of interests method in particular. Several of these abuses will be discussed later in the chapter. For now, consider the restrictions imposed by *APBO 16* on the use of pooling.

APBO 16 **and the Conditions for Pooling of Interests.** The continued use of pooling was criticized by several members of the Accounting Principles Board in their dissents from *APBO 16*. Their sentiments were undoubtedly reflected in *APBO 16* because it acknowledged that pooling is appropriate only in certain circumstances. Then, to ensure that business combinations recorded as poolings faithfully reflected the pooling concept, *APBO 16* imposed 12 conditions; *all 12* must be satisfied if a given business combination is to be accounted for as a pooling of interests. These conditions are reproduced verbatim in Exhibit 6.8. We summarize their meaning in the following paragraphs.

Attributes of the Combining Companies. These conditions were designed to ensure that a pooling will reflect only a legitimate union of previously independent ownership interests undertaken to share the risks and rights of ownership in the combined enterprise. Precluded are piecemeal combinations (unless completed within one year of the initiation of a formal plan for the combination) and combinations between companies already holding more than a 10 percent interest in the outstanding voting shares of any combining company (the *"10 percent rule"*).

Exhibit 6.8 **Necessary and Sufficient Conditions for the Use of the Pooling of Interests Method**

Attributes of the Combining Companies

a. Each of the combining companies is autonomous and has not been a subsidiary or division of another corporation within two years before the plan of combination is initiated.

b. Each of the combining companies is independent of the other combining companies.

Manner of Combining Interests

a. The combination is effected in a single transaction or is completed in accordance with a specific plan within one year after the plan is initiated.

b. A corporation offers and issues only common stock with rights identical to those of the majority of its outstanding voting common stock in exchange for substantially all of the voting common stock interest of another company at the date the plan of combination is consummated.

c. None of the combining companies changes the equity interest of the voting common stock in contemplation of effecting the combination either within two years before the plan of combination is initiated or between the dates the combination is initiated and consummated; changes in contemplation of effecting the combination may include distributions to stockholders and additional issuances, exchanges, and retirements of securities.

d. Each of the combining companies reacquires shares of voting common stock only for purposes other than business combinations, and no company reacquires more than a normal number of shares between the dates the plan of combination is initiated and consummated.

e. The ratio of the interest of an individual common stockholder to those of other common stockholders in a combining company remains the same as a result of the exchange of stock to effect the combination.

f. The voting rights to which the common stock ownership interests in the resulting combined corporation are entitled are exercisable by the stockholders; the stockholders are neither deprived of nor restricted in exercising those rights for a period.

g. The combination is resolved at the date the plan is consummated and no provisions of the plan relating to the issue of securities or other consideration are pending.

Absence of Planned Transactions

a. The combined corporation does not agree directly or indirectly to retire or reacquire all or part of the common stock issued to effect the combination.

b. The combined corporation does not enter into other financial arrangements for the benefit of the former stockholders of a combining company, such as a guaranty of loans secured by stock issued in the combination, which in effect negates the exchange of equity securities.

c. The combined corporation does not intend or plan to dispose of a significant part of the assets of the combining companies within two years after the combination other than disposals in the ordinary course of business of the formerly separate companies and to eliminate duplicate facilities or excess capacity.

Source: Accounting Principles Board, *Opinion No. 16*, "Business Combinations" (New York: AICPA, 1970), pars. 46–48; CT § B50.104–107.) Copyright © 1970 by the American Institute of Certified Public Accountants, Inc.

Manner of Combining Interests. The conditions in this section have a bearing on the consummation of the combination. Fundamental to the concept of pooling is the notion that substantially all of the ownership interests in the combining companies continue as ownership interests in the combined companies. This can be achieved only through the exchange of voting common shares. The issue of cash, debt, or other nonvoting equity consideration in the combination would eliminate or alter some of the previously existing ownership interests. Moreover, the exchange of voting stock for "substantially all" of the voting stock of an acquired company means that at least 90 percent of the acquired company's voting stock is exchanged (the *"90 percent rule"*). Acquisition of part or all of the remaining stock (10 percent or less after the pooling) at a later date is accounted for by the purchase method. Note, however, that the issue of cash or debt for related expenses such as consultants' and attorneys' fees does not violate these conditions.

Conditions (c) and (d) (in Exhibit 6.8) prohibit the rearrangement of capital structures and the retirement or reacquisition of shares in contemplation of a business combination. Such changes in capital structure and shares outstanding could represent a buy-out of certain ownership interests, which would defeat the pooling concept. Condition (d) is known as the *"treasury stock rule."* It specifically precludes the application of pooling of interests accounting when combining companies acquire treasury stock in connection with a business combination. This condition does not apply to treasury stock acquired more than two years prior to the combination. Any such shares should first be retired and then treated as previously unissued shares.

Condition (g) indicates that future consideration contingent upon the occurrence of the specified events has no place in a pooling of interests because of its incompatibility with the mutual exchange of ownership interests fundamental to pooling.

Absence of Planned Transactions. These conditions emphasize the importance of substance over form in pooling of interests accounting. For example, a combination satisfying the "90 percent rule" in form would not satisfy it in substance if (1) former stockholders of a combining company also received contracts employing them as "consultants" at excessive "wages" or (2) the stock issued in a business combination was repurchased by the combined firm shortly after the combination occurred.

Packaging a Pooling as a Purchase. Before we turn to the process of recording a pooling of interests, one further observation on the 12 conditions for a pooling is appropriate. In their entirety, these conditions are restrictive and effectively limit the use of pooling of interests accounting to those combinations which faithfully reflect the pooling concept. Although it may be difficult to package a purchase transaction to meet the pooling criteria, the reverse is clearly not true. For example, management of the acquiring company may favor a purchase in order to bolster the resulting combined balance sheet. Yet the Internal Revenue Code provisions governing nontaxable corporate reorganizations often motivate the shareholders of the acquired firm to insist on a complete exchange of equity shares. To achieve the tax-free corporate reorganization *and* the purchase accounting treatment, the negotiating companies might agree to some contingent consideration in the plan of combination, thereby failing to conform to the pooling of interest conditions in their entirety.

Expenses of a Pooling of Interests Combination. Since a pooling reflects neither the cost of acquiring assets nor the obtaining of new capital, capitalization of any expenses related to the business combination is inappropriate. Paragraph 58 of *APBO 16* provides that *all direct or indirect costs of the pooling combination,* including costs of registering and issuing equity securities, *are to be treated as expenses of the period* and deducted from net income when incurred.

Accounting for Assets Acquired, Liabilities Assumed, and Stock Issued. In a pooling of interests, the assets and liabilities of the acquired company are carried forward in the business combination at their *book values*. No new basis of accountability arises, and, accordingly, information regarding the fair value of consideration given, assets acquired, or liabilities assumed is not considered in recording the combination. The primary problem encountered in recording a pooling of interests lies in combining the stockholders' equity accounts. Under the pooling concept, *the total contributed capital (that is, capital stock plus additional paid-in capital) of the combined firm should not be less than the sum of the contributed capital accounts of the combining firms.* The exchange of shares in a pooling implies that simply adding the contributed capital accounts together is not sufficient. Rather, the par or stated value of the acquiring company's shares which are issued in the combination must be properly accounted for. If the total contributed capital of the acquired company is greater than (less than) the par value of new shares issued, the difference is credited (debited) to the acquiring company's Additional Paid-In Capital (APIC) account. Retained earnings of the constituent companies are added together without adjustment unless the acquiring company's APIC would be driven below zero in recording the combination.

To systematically analyze how a pooling of interests combination is recorded, consider the following format for the journal entry to be made on the books of the acquiring company as it pools with an acquired company:

Net Assets (= Assets − Liabilities) . . . . . Book Value^a
    Common Stock . . . .   Par Value^b
    Additional Paid-In Capital . . . .   Contributed Capital of
                                                Acquired Company
                                                less Par Value of
                                                Stock Issued^c
    Retained Earnings . . . .   Book Value^a

^{a}Book Value refers to the appropriate account balances on the books of the acquired company.
^{b}Par Value is the total par or stated value of the shares issued by the acquiring company in the combination.
^{c}If the par value of the stock issued by the acquiring company *exceeds* the total contributed capital of the acquired comapny, the excess is *debited* to APIC. If the excess is greater than the acquiring company's credit balance in APIC, it is necessary to debit retained earnings for any amount remaining after the credit balance in APIC is exhausted.

To see how this journal entry would be used to record a particular pooling of interests combination, consider the following stockholders' equity data for P Company and S Company:

	P Company	S Company
Common Stock, Par Value $7.50, Authorized 300,000 Shares; Issued and Outstanding 135,000 Shares.	$1,012,500	—
Common Stock, Par Value $1, Authorized, Issued, and Outstanding 100,000 Shares	—	$100,000
Additional Paid-In Capital	50,000	125,000
Retained Earnings	2,000,000	225,000
Total Precombination Stockholders' Equity (= Net Assets)	$3,062,500	$450,000

In Exhibit 6.9, we record the pooling of interests of P and S under four different possible exchanges of equity shares.

Pooling of Interests—Statutory Mergers and Consolidations. Earlier in the chapter, we recorded the statutory merger of companies P and S under purchase accounting. We now assume that the combination will be accomplished as a pooling of interests solely through the exchange of equity shares. P Company is issuing 20,000 of its $7.50 par value shares for the 100,000 shares of S Company (Case 2 in Exhibit 6.9). Out-of-pocket costs for related expenses—consultants' and attorneys' fees, registration and issue costs—amount to $40,000. Using the balance sheet data (book values) for S Company from Exhibit 6.4, we record the statutory merger as a pooling with the following journal entry made on the books of P Company:

Cash and Receivables	100,000	
Inventory	250,000	
Buildings and Equipment	1,000,000	
Expenses of Business Combination	40,000	
Cash		40,000
Accumulated Depreciation		200,000
Current Liabilities		200,000
Bonds Payable, 6%		500,000
Common Stock		150,000
Additional Paid-In Capital (APIC)		75,000
Retained Earnings		225,000

To record the statutory merger of P Company and S Company, accounted for as a pooling of interests.

The $75,000 credit to APIC equals the difference between S's contributed capital of $225,000 and the par value of stock issued, $150,000. Note that, in contrast with purchase accounting, the Accumulated Depreciation balance of the "acquired" company is carried over in the combination. Moreover, had goodwill been recorded on the books of S Company, it also would be carried over in the pooling.

Exhibit 6.9 **Recording the Pooling of Interests of P and S Companies under Alternative Exchanges of Equity Shares**

	Case 1		Case 2		Case 3		Case 4	
	Dr.	Cr.	Dr.	Cr.	Dr.	Cr.	Dr.	Cr.
Net Assets	450,000		450,000		450,000		450,000	
Common Stock		75,000		150,000		240,000		375,000
Additional Paid-In								
Capital		150,000		75,000	15,000		50,000	
Retained Earnings . . .		225,000		225,000		225,000		125,000

Case 1: P exchanges 10,000 of its $7.50 par value shares for the 100,000 shares of S's outstanding stock.
Case 2: P exchanges 20,000 of its $7.50 par value shares for the 100,000 shares of S's outstanding stock.
Case 3: P exchanges 32,000 of its $7.50 par value shares for the 100,000 shares of S's outstanding stock.
Case 4: P exchanges 50,000 of its $7.50 par value shares for the 100,000 shares of S's outstanding stock.

Exhibit 6.10 **Recording the Statutory Consolidation of S and T Companies into P Company on the Books of P Company as a Pooling of Interests**

	Relative to S Company		Relative to T Company		Total Statutory Consolidation	
	Debit	Credit	Debit	Credit	Debit	Credit
Cash and Receivables	100,000		150,000		250,000	
Marketable Equity						
Securities—Current.	—		100,000		100,000	
Inventory	250,000		300,000		550,000	
Marketable Equity						
Securities—Long-Term	—		500,000		500,000	
Land	—		200,000		200,000	
Buildings and Equipment	1,000,000		1,800,000		2,800,000	
Expenses of Business						
Combination	40,000[a]		60,000[a]		100,000	
Cash		40,000[a]		60,000[a]		100,000
Accumulated Depreciation		200,000		600,000		800,000
Current Liabilities		200,000		500,000		700,000
Other Liabilities.		—		800,000		800,000
Bonds Payable, 6%.		500,000		—		500,000
Common Stock.		150,000[b]		375,000[b]		525,000
Additional Paid-In Capital		75,000[b]		275,000[b]		350,000
Retained Earnings.		225,000[c]		500,000[c]		725,000

[a]Following paragraph 58 of *APBO 16,* expenses incurred in connection with a pooling of interests are not capitalized but are charged directly against income.
[b]Common Stock is credited for the par value of P Company stock issued; the total credits to Common Stock and Additional Paid-In Capital equal the total contributed capital of companies S and T.
[c]In a pooling of interests, unlike the purchase case, the retained earnings of the acquired companies become part of the postcombination retained earnings.

If S Company and T Company were to pool their interests with P Company in a statutory consolidation, the pooling would be recorded as in Exhibit 6.10. Say that P Company issues 50,000 shares of its $7.50 par value common stock for all 50,000 shares of T Company stock issued and outstanding. Out-of-pocket costs amount to $60,000 and the balance sheet data for T Company (book values) are from Exhibit 6.6. The entry given above to record the pooling with S Company is also included as part of the statutory consolidation in Exhibit 6.10 on page 263. Given T Company's contributed capital of $650,000, a credit of $275,000 [= $650,000 − (50,000 × $7.50)] to APIC results.

Pooling of Interests—Stock Acquisition. Pooling of interests accounting may also be used to account for a stock acquisition, provided that the pooling conditions are satisfied. Since the acquired company survives as a separate legal entity, P Company records the acquisition on its books by debiting the Investment in Subsidiary account for its interest in the net assets (at book value) of S Company. The entries to the stockholders' equity accounts are identical to those just presented in connection with statutory mergers and consolidations. Therefore, to record the pooling of P Company and S Company as a stock acquisition, we give P Company's entry for the case in which P issues 20,000 shares of its $7.50 par value stock for all 100,000 outstanding shares of S Company. The out-of-pocket costs were $40,000.

Investment in S	450,000	
Expenses of Business Combination	40,000	
Cash		40,000
Common Stock		150,000
Additional Paid-In Capital		75,000
Retained Earnings		225,000

To record the pooling of P Company and S Company as a stock acquisition.

Recording a Less than 100 Percent Pooling. Stock acquisitions often involve the acquisition of less than 100 percent of the subsidiary's outstanding common shares. In a pooling of interests, at least 90 percent of these shares must be aquired. To facilitate this discussion, we define α as the percent of voting shares acquired by P Company.

> In a business combination, α refers to the percent of a subsidiary's outstanding voting shares acquired by the parent or controlling interest; α = number of shares of S acquired by P/total number of shares of S outstanding.

Our journal entry format for recording a stock acquisition may now be modified as follows:

```
Investment in S (= Assets −
   Liabilities). . . . . . . . . . α(Book Value)ᵃ
Common Stock . . . . . . . .            Par Valueᵇ
Additional Paid-In Capital . . . .      α(Contributed Capital of S)
                                           Less Par Value of Stock
                                           Issuedᶜ
Retained Earnings . . . . . . .         α(Book Value)ᵃ
To record a stock acquisition as a
pooling of interests, where
.9 ≤ α < 1.
```

ᵃ Book Value refers to the appropriate account balances on the books of S, the acquired company.
ᵇ Par Value is the total par or stated value of the shares issued by P in the combination.
ᶜ If the par value of stock issued by P exceeds P's share (α) of the total contributed capital of S, the excess is *debited* to APIC. If the excess is greater than P's credit balance in APIC, it is necessary to debit retained earnings for any amount remaining after the credit balance in APIC is exhausted.

As an example, consider the pooling with S Company. Suppose P Company exchanges 19,000 shares of its $7.50 par value stock for 95 percent of S Company's 100,000 shares. Ignoring any out-of-pocket costs, P Company records the stock acquisition as follows:

```
Investment in S (.95 × $450,000). . . . . . . . . . . . . . .  427,500
   Common Stock (19,000 × $7.50) . . . . . . . . . . . . . .            142,500
   Additional Paid-In Capital [.95($100,000 + $125,000) −
      $142,500]. . . . . . . . . . . . . . . . . . . . . . . .            71,250
   Retained Earnings (.95 × $225,000) . . . . . . . . . . . .            213,750
To record the pooling of P Company and S Company, in which
19,000 shares of P Company's stock were exchanged for 95
percent of S Company's outstanding shares.
```

Issue of Treasury Stock in a Pooling of Interests. Although the acquisition of treasury stock in contemplation of a business combination defeats the pooling concept [see Condition (d), Exhibit 6.8], it does not follow that treasury stock may never be used in a pooling. Specifically, there is no prohibition against the use of *treasury stock acquired more than 2 years prior* to initiating the business combination. Paragraph 54 of *APBO 16* instructs us to first account for these shares as retired, and then reissue them. Since the shares issued in a pooling are to be accounted for at the book value of the shares (or net assets) acquired, the basis of previously acquired treasury stock is not relevant.

If, in a pooling, P Company were issuing 20,000 shares of treasury stock previously acquired several years ago at a cost of $220,000, the stock (par value $7.50) would first be retired as shown below:

```
Common Stock . . . . . . . . . . . . . . . . . . . . . . . . .  150,000
Additional Paid-In Capital . . . . . . . . . . . . . . . . . . .   70,000
   Treasury Stock . . . . . . . . . . . . . . . . . . . . . . .            220,000
To record the retirement of 20,000 shares of $7.50 par value
common stock in contemplation of their reissue in a pooling of
interests combination. Total par value of the retired stock is
$150,000 (= 20,000 shares × $7.50).
```

The issue of such stock in a subsequent pooling of interests would now be treated as if the shares had been previously unissued, consistent with our other illustrations.

To assist the reader, a summary of the principal journal entries made by acquiring companies to record both purchase and pooling combinations is given in Exhibit 6.11. Note that an asset acquisition cannot be accounted for as a pooling of interests.

The Fall from Favor of Pooling of Interests Accounting. The pooling of interests concept in a business combination is not new;[19] it was incorporated as part of the authoritative literature in *ARB 40* published in September 1950 and was included in 1953 as Chapter 7-C of *ARB 43*.[20] Additional elaboration of the concept and discussion of the criteria governing its application were presented in *ARB 48*, issued in January 1957. The thrust of *ARB 48* with respect to the definition and propriety of pooling of interests accounting provided the basis for *APBO 16*. Unfortunately, *ARB 48* turned out to be an inadequate guide to practice because it permitted too much interpretation. Paragraph 7 (reproduced below) best sums up why *ARB 48* became virtually irrelevant as a guide to accounting for business combinations in the years following its publication. Its ambiguities are, we believe, obvious.

> 7. No one of the factors discussed in paragraphs 5 and 6 would necessarily be determinative and any one factor might have varying degrees of significance in different cases. However, their presence or absence would be cumulative in effect. Since the conclusions to be drawn from consideration of these different relevant circumstances may be in conflict or partially so, determination as to whether a particular combination is a purchase or a pooling of interests should be made in light of all such attendant circumstances.[21]

To fully appreciate how the thrust of *ARB 48* was twisted and distorted, one must examine some of the business combinations which were accounted for as poolings. Most combinations now viewed as abuses of the pooling concept took place during the 1960s. This was the decade when the conglomerate merger came of age. It was also a period known in investment circles as the "go-go" years on Wall Street.[22] Reported earnings per share were considered of paramount importance to investors and, correspondingly, to corporate managements. The achievement of robust, systematic growth in earnings per share (or, as we shall see, the *appearance* of such growth) became the overriding objective of many business

---

[19]See Arthur R. Wyatt, *Accounting Research Study No. 5*, "A Critical Study of Accounting for Business Combinations" (New York: AICPA, 1963).

[20]Committee on Accounting Procedure, *Accounting Research Bulletin No. 43*, "Restatement and Revision of Accounting Research Bulletins" (New York: AICPA, 1953).

[21]Committee on Accounting Procedure, *Accounting Research Bulletin No. 48*, "Business Combinations" (New York: AICPA, 1957), par. 7.

[22]For a colorful and entertaining view of this period, see Adam Smith [pseud.], *The Money Game* (New York: Random House, 1968).

Exhibit 6.11   **Summary of Journal Entries to Record Business Combinations**

PURCHASE

Statutory Merger, Consolidation, or Asset Acquisition			Stock Acquisition		
	Dr.	Cr.		Dr.	Cr.
Specific Assets Acquired	FMV		Investment in Subsidiary	FMV	
Goodwill[a]	Residual		Consideration Given[b]		FMV
Specific Liabilities Assumed		FMV			
Consideration Given[b]		FMV			

[a]If *negative goodwill* arises, it is offset against the FMV of noncurrent assets acquired, except long-term investments in marketable securities. Any remaining negative goodwill is recorded as a deferred credit.
[b]Includes fair value of the consideration given and related direct costs which are to be capitalized. Costs to register and issue securities are offset against additional paid-in capital; indirect costs are treated as recurring period expenses and need not be recorded separately in the acquisition entry.

POOLING OF INTERESTS

Statutory Merger or Consolidation			Stock Acquisition		
	Dr.	Cr.		Dr.	Cr.
Specific Assets Acquired	BV		Investment in Subsidiary[e]	BV	
Expenses of Business Combination[c] . . .	BV		Expenses of Business Combination[c] . . .	BV	
Specific Liabilities Assumed		BV	Cash[c]		BV
Cash[c]		BV	Common Stock (PV = Par or Stated Value)		PV
Common Stock (PV = Par or Stated Value).		PV	Additional Paid-In Capital[d, e]		Residual
Additional Paid-In Capital[d]		Residual	Retained Earnings[e] .		BV
Retained Earnings. .		BV			

[c] All expenses of a pooling—direct, indirect, and registration and issue costs—are expensed and not capitalized. Cash (or Liabilities) is credited for the actual amount incurred.
[d] Contributed capital of acquired company less par value of acquiring company's stock issued. If *negative*, it is debited to acquiring company's APIC; any excess over acquiring company's APIC is debited to retained earnings
[e] If less than 100 percent (but at least 90 percent) of the acquired company's voting shares is obtained in the pooling, the percentage obtained, α $(1 > \alpha \geq .9)$, is multiplied by the BV of the acquired company's net assets, contributed capital (to compute APIC), and retained earnings.

---

firms. Business combinations, and the pooling of interests method to account for them, were employed almost ruthlessly to promote growth in earnings per share by many companies during the 1960s.

As stated earlier, a major reason for the popularity of the pooling concept is its ability to create instant growth in earnings and earnings per share. This growth in earnings may arise in two ways. *First,* in the year of the pooling, the net incomes of the constituent companies for the whole year are combined, regardless of when the combination was completed. *Second,* by combining assets at their book values rather than at their generally higher fair values, any unrealized gains become a reservoir of potential income which may be recognized almost at will by the combined company. To accomplish this, the unrealized gains are gradually realized and recognized as income as the undervalued assets are sold or used. We now consider how some actual companies bent, twisted, or stretched the pooling concept to achieve these ends.

Retrospective Poolings—Western Equities, Inc. (Westec). The Westec case is a prominent example of the creative accounting practices which came to light during the 1960s. In September 1964, Westec's stock was selling for about $3.50 on the American Stock Exchange. Over the next 19 months, the price of Westec stock climbed to over $67 a share, while the financial statements were presenting a picture of incredible growth. On August 25, 1966, trading in Westec stock was halted by the exchange as certain manipulative securities transactions by Westec executives were revealed, and the bubble burst. The questionable pooling transactions which contributed to that growth are now discussed briefly. A complete account of the case can be found in *Accounting Series Release (ASR) 248,* issued by the SEC on May 31, 1978, following a lengthy investigation.

In order to bolster earnings for calendar year 1964, Westec acquired three companies at the end of March 1965 and retrospectively included the pooled income statements in 1964 earnings. These acquisitions contributed about 23 percent of Westec's total earnings for 1964. Westec's auditors approved of this accounting treatment.

In April 1966, a similar situation occurred. To maintain the growth pattern for calendar year 1965, Westec again retrospectively pooled two acquisitions, which contributed 32 percent of the 1965 earnings.

These and other transactions contributed to the increase in Westec's reported earnings per share from $.12 in 1963 to $.43 in 1964 (23 percent from poolings) to $1.10 in 1965 (32 percent from poolings).

Retrospective Poolings—National Student Marketing Corporation (NSMC). Although this case is famous primarily because of its improper revenue recognition practices (see *ASR 173*), it too had a number of retrospective poolings. Subsequent to NSMC's fiscal year ended August 31, 1969, eight major acquisitions were completed and their profits pooled with those of NSMC for fiscal 1969. These acquisitions contributed some $3,750,000 in earnings, thereby turning a loss into a substantial profit.[23]

Pooling via the Issue of Treasury Stock—American Tobacco Company and Sunshine Biscuits, Inc. *APBO 16* prohibits the use of pooling when substantial trans-

---

[23]See Abraham J. Briloff, *Unaccountable Accounting* (New York: Harper & Row, 1972), Chapter 3, "Dirty Pooling and Polluted Purchase," especially pp. 86–87.

actions in treasury stock are made in contemplation of a business combination. When American Tobacco Company acquired Sunshine Biscuits, Inc., in May 1966 (prior to *APBO 16*), almost 40 percent of the shares issued to effect the pooling were treasury shares acquired for about $30,000,000.[24] Not only did the acquisition of the treasury shares eliminate a component of American Tobacco's ownership interest, it also involved a cash payment which, although indirect, seems to violate the pooling concept. Furthermore, this $30,000,000 cash cost never entered subsequent income statements because, consistent with accounting for treasury stock, the excess of cost over par value of the shares was charged to stockholders' equity accounts.

Implications of Pooling of Interests—A Final Note. As mentioned earlier, pooling-of-interests accounting preserves the book values of the pooled firms' assets and liabilities. If the book values of assets acquired are far below their fair values, the unrealized gains are not recorded since zero cost is assigned to the appreciation in the assets' values. As the gains are realized in subsequent periods, they are attributed to the postcombination entity and flow through the income statement unreduced by the (suppressed) costs which were incurred to obtain them. Two examples follow.

1. The pooling of Paramount Pictures and Desilu into Gulf & Western (G & W) in 1967 enabled G & W to acquire many motion picture films having substantially amortized costs. By negotiating television distribution contracts which reflected the fair value of the films, G & W was able to recognize income on the unrealized gains attributable to the films.[25] Because of the pooling, G & W's statements never reflected the true cost of the films; the concurrent overstatement of income was hidden.

2. When International Telephone and Telegraph Corporation (ITT) acquired The Hartford Fire Insurance Company in 1969–1970, it also acquired a stock portfolio with total unrealized gains approximating $282 million. Starting with 1970, profits on the investment portfolio exceeding $260 million were realized over 5 years. As a comparison, total investment portfolio profits were a mere $2.5 million in the 5 years including 1964–1968, suggesting that the unrealized gains were systematically realized as income once ITT took over.[26]

    Overall, a number of ITT's poolings in the 1964–1970 period involved some $2.4 billion in consideration. Yet, the properties acquired were booked at $1.02 billion, indicating that, for these poolings, the cost of properties acquired was understated in ITT's financial statements by approximately $1.4 billion.

---

[24]Ibid., 94.
[25]Ibid., 65–67.
[26]See Abraham J. Briloff, *More Debits than Credits* (New York: Harper & Row, 1976), Chapter 8, "Of Pools and Fools," especially pp. 219–226.

Accounting for Business Combinations: The Future

Despite the publication of *APBO 16* and the interpretations that followed, considerable dissatisfaction with generally accepted accounting principles still exists. Prior to *APBO 16,* two *Accounting Research Studies (ARS's)* recommended elimination of the pooling of interests method. In *ARS 5,* Wyatt concluded that

> no basis exists in principle for a continuation of what is presently known as "pooling of interests" accounting *if* the business combination involves an exchange of assets and/or equities between independent parties.[27]

Five years later, in their conclusion to *ARS 10,* Catlett and Olson stated:

> Except in a few business combinations in which the combination is not a purchase transaction but creates a new enterprise, the proper accounting for business combinations is found in the general concepts underlying purchase accounting. Pooling of interests is not a valid method of accounting for business combinations.[28]

Concurrent with the APB's deliberations on the issues ultimately treated in *APBO 16* and *APBO 17,* Burton was conducting a research study on these subjects under the auspices of the Financial Executives Research Foundation.[29] This work focused on an evaluation of the exposure draft which preceded the above Opinions and a preliminary draft was provided to the board in June 1970, prior to its final deliberations. After reviewing the somewhat mixed results of his empirical work, Burton observed:

> A business combination is a significant economic event which involves the firm and not simply individual stockholders exchanging shares. The assets of the acquired firm undergo a majority change in ownership bargained by management and hence are no longer under the same economic control. . . . From these perceptions I conclude that purchase accounting is a better reflection of reality than is pooling.[30]

With respect to *APBO 16* itself, six of the eighteen board members dissented. In particular, the *Opinion* states that "Messrs. Davidson, Horngren and Seidman dissent to the Opinion because it seeks to patch up some of the abuses of pooling. The real abuse is pooling itself. On that, the only answer is to eliminate pooling."[31] Nevertheless, it appears that *APBO 16* had an impact on the incidence of business combinations recorded as poolings of interests (see Exhibit 6.2).

The obvious questions are: Why has pooling survived for so long, and can we forecast its demise? We shall attempt an answer. *First,* the pooling concept has some intuitive appeal. The notion of companies pooling their resources and

---

[27]Wyatt, op. cit., 105.

[28]George R. Catlett and Norman O. Olson, "Accounting for Goodwill," *Accounting Research Study No. 10* (New York: American Institute of Certified Public Accountants, 1968), 110.

[29]Burton, John C., *Accounting for Business Combinations* (New York: Financial Executives Research Foundation, 1970).

[30]Ibid., 87–88.

[31]Accounting Principles Board, *Opinion No. 16,* par. 99.

adopting a new form of business organization in which the previous ownership interests remain to share in the risks and rewards flowing from the combined enterprise cannot be condemned outright. Yet the pooling takes place not in a vacuum, but in a world in which securities having determinable economic value are exchanged. Can this exchange of value be safely ignored when financial statements are prepared? We think not. Formation of a partnership could be viewed as a sort of pooling of interests. Does it then follow that the fair value of property invested in a partnership is irrelevant, and that the partners' capital interests should be based on previous book values which may bear no relationship to the fair values of assets invested? Again, we think not.

Second, pooling of interests accounting does possess distinct potential for improving the *appearance of the income statement.* Many continue to value this potential. We question whether accounting principles should be based on this type of argument.

In sum, we acknowledge the intuitive and economic appeal of the pooling method but question the legitimacy of the pooling concept in a business combination. We believe that pooling will ultimately disappear from the scene. Its demise will be hastened if some form of current value accounting becomes more widely used.

Summary of Key Concepts

A business combination occurs when two or more companies are brought under common control. From a legal and organizational perspective, business combinations may be classified as **statutory mergers, statutory consolidations, asset acquisitions,** and **stock acquisitions.** In a stock acquisition, the combining companies remain as separate legal entities.

For simplicity, we define the surviving or controlling company in a business combination as the **acquiring company.** Similarly, the **acquired company** is one whose ownership interests are substantially eliminated in the combined enterprise or whose ownership interests become part of the controlling interest in the combined enterprise.

A given business combination is accounted for under either the purchase or pooling of interests method. In a **purchase** combination, an arm's-length exchange transaction has occurred, and the assets and liabilities of the acquired company are stated at their **fair market values** at the date of combination. A **pooling of interests** is viewed as a union of previously separate ownership interests, not as an arm's-length exchange transaction. Assets and liabilities of the "acquired" company in a pooling are stated at the **book values** to the acquired company.

If the investment cost in a purchase combination is greater than (less than) the book value of the net assets acquired, a **purchase premium (discount)** results. This premium or discount is allocated among the identifiable assets and liabilities acquired in order that they be stated at their fair values. Any **unallocated debit balance** is reclassified as **goodwill.** If the process of stating the assets and liabilities of the acquired company at their fair values produces an unallocated **credit balance,** it is viewed as **negative goodwill.** Negative goodwill must in turn be allocated among the noncurrent assets of the acquired company (except long-term investments in marketable securities) in proportion to their fair market values.

In a **pooling of interests,** the total contributed capital of the combined entity should not be less than the sum of the contributed capital accounts of the combining firms. To achieve this, capital stock is increased by the par value of the additional shares issued by the ''acquiring'' company. Combined additional paid-in capital is increased if the acquired company's contributed capital exceeds the par value of stock issued; otherwise it is decreased. The acquired company's retained earnings becomes part of combined retained earnings.

Contingent consideration is frequently part of a purchase combination. If the contingency is based on **future earnings,** any additional payments made at the end of the contingency period go to increase the cost of the acquired company. In contrast, a contingency based on **future security prices** does not result in a change to the cost of the acquired company when the contingency period ends, even if additional payments are required to satisfy the contingency clause.

Contingent liabilities, contingent assets, and contingent impairments of assets are often present when a business combination is consummated. Establishing valuations for these items in a purchase combination is often made difficult by uncertainty. *SFAS 38* allows adjustments to be made to these valuations during an **allocation period,** which generally expires one year after the combination. Subsequent adjustments enter the postcombination income statement and cannot be used to make retroactive changes in the purchase price allocation.

Appendix to
Chapter 6

Determining the Price in a Business Combination When the Constituent Companies Are Publicly Traded

As we have seen, merger and acquisition activities have been widespread in the American economy. The terms under which business combinations have taken place are varied. Whether publicly traded or privately held companies are involved, however, the parties must decide upon the amount of economic value to be exchanged and its composition. The *composition of the economic value transferred* in a business combination refers to that mix of cash, common stock, preferred stock, debt, and warrants which make up the agreed-upon economic value. Since the possible arrays of cash and securities are almost limitless, we cannot begin to explore them here. Indeed, such a comprehensive treatment of price and payment negotiations in business combinations is beyond the scope of this book.

To give an idea of the nature of merger negotiations and the role played by accounting data in these negotiations, we shall focus on companies whose shares are publicly traded. To further simplify the analysis, we shall assume that a single class of stock—voting common—will be exchanged. In this way, we can concentrate on determining the amount of economic value to be exchanged.[32]

A company analyzing a potential acquisition has, in effect, a capital budgeting problem. When the target company is privately held, its economic value must be estimated. A schedule of estimated future cash flows to be generated by the target company must be prepared, adjusted for applicable taxes, and discounted to its present value at the combination date. Because any such estimate of economic value will be sensitive to (1) the amounts and timing of the estimated cash flows and (2) the choice of discount rate, qualitative and subjective factors are likely to play large roles in the decision-making process.

The situation differs, however, when the target company is publicly held and its shares are traded on a major stock exchange. In this case, the market provides us with independently determined information regarding the economic value and risk of the target company. These data are:

1. The *per-share* value or *price (P)* of the target company's stock.
2. The target company's *price/earnings (P/E) ratio*.

Similar data relative to the acquiring company are also available, assuming that it too is publicly held and its shares are traded on a major stock exchange.

Just as the risk associated with the privately held company will usually be an important factor in the choice of discount rate, the *P/E* ratio gives us the market's estimate of the risk associated with the publicly held company. Literally, the P/E ratio is interpreted as the number of dollars investors are willing to pay for $1 of earnings. A low P/E ratio often means that investors view the company as risky and are not willing to pay much for its earnings. Alternatively, a low P/E ratio could indicate slow projected-earnings growth.

Stock Exchange Ratios

When a business combination is to be achieved solely through the exchange of common stock, a mutually acceptable price is set when a mutually acceptable *stock exchange ratio* (ER) is negotiated.

---

[32]For a more detailed and formal treatment of this approach, see Kermit D. Larson and Nicholas J. Gonedes, "Business Combinations: An Exchange Ratio Determination Model," *The Accounting Review,* October 1969, 720–728; also see Robert L. Conn and James F. Nieisen, "An Empirical Test of the Larson-Gonedes Exchange Ratio Determination Model," *The Journal of Finance,* June 1977, 749–759.

> A **stock exchange ratio** is defined as the number of shares of the acquiring company's stock to be exchanged for one share of the target company's stock.

Consider a business combination involving S Company and T Company. Since the value of ER will determine the total number of shares outstanding after the combination, it will also determine the postcombination earnings per share, E_{ST}. Given that the price of a share of stock, $P = E(P/E)$, and that we can compute postcombination E_{ST} for any exchange ratio, ER, the value of the stock after the combination will depend on the postcombination P/E ratio assigned by the market. We call this the *ex post* P/E ratio and emphasize that it is *unknown prior to completion of the combination*. Because of this, the best we can do is identify the boundaries of the range within which the final, mutually acceptable ER must be negotiated. Subjective factors continue to have importance. For example, the target company may have a large tax loss carryforward. If its eventual realization is uncertain, its potential value may only be partially reflected in the target company's stock price, if at all. Such a loss carryforward may have significant value to the acquiring company if consolidated tax returns are envisioned. It will surely have an impact on the acceptability of alternative exchange ratios to the acquiring company.

Thus we emphasize that the agreed-upon ER will typically not be the outcome of a mathematical model. Rather, it will fall within a range, but its precise determination will be based on managerial judgment, accounting and tax advice, and the relative bargaining positions of the constituent companies. We now illustrate the application of these concepts with a numerical example.

Stock Exchange Ratio Negotiating Range: An Example

S Company and T Company are planning to merge through an exchange of common stock if terms acceptable to the shareholders of both companies can be negotiated. Relevant data for companies S and T are given below:

	S Company	T Company
Net Income	$9,000,000	$2,000,000
Shares Outstanding	3,000,000	1,000,000
Earnings per Share	$ 3	$ 2
Market Price per Share	$ 30	$ 16
P/E Ratio	10	8

To introduce the method of analysis, a reasonable exchange ratio might simply be based on the inverse of the companies' share prices. That is, $ER = 1/(P_S/P_T) = P_T/P_S = \$16/\$30 = .5333$. S Company will exchange .5333 share for each share of T Company. Total shares of S Company outstanding increase to 3,533,300 [= 3,000,000 + .5333(1,000,000)]. Earnings per share for the combined firm, E_{ST}, will equal $3.1132 [= (\$9,000,000 + \$2,000,000)/3,533,300]$.

The value of S Company's shares will now reflect T Company and will depend on the ex post price/earnings ratio, P/E_{ST}. One might expect P/E_{ST} to accurately reflect the relative significance of companies S and T. If so, it would be a *weighted average* of the separate price/earnings ratios, which we shall denote $\overline{P/E}_{ST}$.

$$\overline{P/E}_{ST} = \left(\frac{\text{Net income of S}}{\text{Combined net income}}\right)P/E_S + \left(\frac{\text{Net income of T}}{\text{Combined net income}}\right)P/E_T.$$

For our example, then,

$$\overline{P/E}_{ST} = \left(\frac{\$9,000,000}{\$11,000,000}\right)10 + \left(\frac{\$2,000,000}{\$11,000,000}\right)8$$

$$\overline{P/E}_{ST} = 8.1818 + 1.4545$$

$$\overline{P/E}_{ST} = 9.6363.$$

Therefore, the per-share price for the combined firm, $P_{ST} = \$30$ [$= E_{ST}(P/E_{ST})$ $= \$3.1132(9.6363)$]. This is exactly what should be expected. Each shareholder is in precisely the same economic position as before. The original shareholders of S Company still own 3,000,000 shares worth $30 each for a total of $90,000,000. The former shareholders of T now own 533,300 shares of S stock worth $16,000,000, the same as the value of their 1,000,000 T shares surrendered. Under some combinations of ER and P/E_{ST}, however, the total market value of the 3,000,000 shares held by the original shareholders of S *would be less than* $90,000,000. Presumably, these original shareholders would not accept any ER which, at some P/E_{ST}, would reduce their wealth. We can therefore identify the upper boundary of the negotiating range by finding the *maximum* ER, denoted ER_S, which would be acceptable to S shareholders at any given P/E_{ST}. By allowing P/E_{ST} to vary, we can solve for the ER_S which maintains the market value of the 3,000,000 original S shares at $90,000,000.

Similarly, T Company's former shareholders would reject an exchange ratio which, at some potential P/E_{ST}, reduced the market value of the S shares they receive below $16,000,000. Thus the lower boundary of the negotiating range will consist of a set of *minimum* ER, denoted ER_T, which the T shareholders would find acceptable at any given P/E_{ST}.

To demonstrate how these exchange ratios are calculated, we use alternative postcombination price/earnings ratios of 9, 10, 12, and 15 and compute the maximum (minimum) ER acceptable to the shareholders of S(T) for each of these P/E_{ST}. *First,* we note that

$$3,000,000 + ER(1,000,000) = \text{Number of shares of S Company stock}$$
$$\text{outstanding after the combination.}$$

Second, with knowledge of the shares outstanding, E_{ST} may be written as

$$\frac{\$11,000,000}{3,000,000 + ER(1,000,000)} = \text{Earnings per share of the combined firm, ST.}$$

Third, the price of a share of postcombination S Company stock is

$$P_{ST} = E_{ST} \times P/E_{ST}$$

$$P_{ST} = \left[\frac{\$11,000,000}{3,000,000 + ER(1,000,000)} \right] P/E_{ST}.$$

Exhibit 6.12   **Determination of Maximum and Minimum Stock Exchange Ratios, $ER_S(ER_T)$, Acceptable to Shareholders of S(T) at Alternative Postcombination P/E Ratios**

	P/E_{ST}				
	9	9.6363	10	12	15
ER_S	.3000[1]	.5333	.6667	1.4000	2.5000
ER_T	.5783	.5333	.5106	.4138[2]	.3221

EXAMPLES OF THE CALCULATIONS

(1) $\$90,000,000 = 3,000,000 \left[\dfrac{\$11,000,000}{3,000,000 + ER_S(1,000,000)} \right] 9.$

Dropping 000,000, we have

$$\$90 = \frac{\$297}{3 + ER_S}$$

$$\$270 + \$90 ER_S = \$297$$

$$90 ER_S = 27$$

$$ER_S = 27/90$$

$$\boxed{ER_S = .3000.}$$

Note: If $P/E_{ST} = 9$, any $ER > .3$ will, by reducing E_{ST}, cause the market value of 3,000,000 shares of S to fall below \$90,000,000.

(2) $\$16,000,000 = ER_T(1,000,000) \left[\dfrac{\$11,000,000}{3,000,000 + ER_T(1,000,000)} \right] 12.$

Dropping 000,000, we have

$$\$16 = ER_T \left[\frac{\$132}{3 + ER_T} \right]$$

$$\$48 + \$16\ ER_T = \$132\ ER_T$$

$$116\ ER_T = 48$$

$$ER_T = 48/116$$

$$\boxed{ER_T = .4138.}$$

Note: If $P/E_{ST} = 12$, any $ER < .4138$ will, by reducing the number of shares going to the former shareholders of T, result in a total market value of the S shares received of less than \$16,000,000.

Figure 6.1 **Graphing ER_S, ER_T, and the Negotiating Range**

Panel 1 Graph of Maximum Stock Exchange Ratio (ER_S) Acceptable to the Original Shareholders of S Company

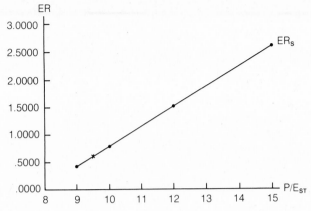

Panel 2 Graph of Minimum Stock Exchange Ratio (ER_T) Acceptable to the Original Shareholders of T Company

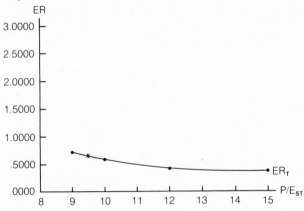

Panel 3 Graph of Stock Exchange Ratio Negotiating Range within Which All Shareholders Will Be at Least as Well Off as They Were before the Combination

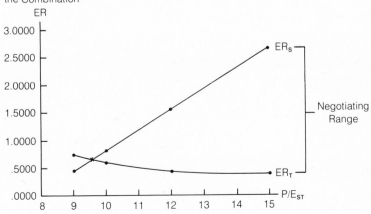

Fourth, the total market value of the original 3,000,000 shares of S Company stock after the combination is given by

$$3{,}000{,}000 \times P_{ST} = 3{,}000{,}000 \left[\frac{\$11{,}000{,}000}{3{,}000{,}000 + ER(1{,}000{,}000)} \right] P/E_{ST}.$$

Fifth, the total postcombination market value of the S Company shares now held by the former T Company shareholders is:

$$ER(1{,}000{,}000) \times P_{ST} = ER(1{,}000{,}000) \left[\frac{\$11{,}000{,}000}{3{,}000{,}000 + ER(1{,}000{,}000)} \right] P/E_{ST}.$$

We have already determined that at the weighted average price/earnings ratio, $\overline{P/E}_{ST} = 9.6363$, an $ER = .5333$ is acceptable to all shareholders. Indeed, we shall see that if $P/E_{ST} = 9.6363$, then $ER = .5333$ is the *only* acceptable stock exchange ratio. The calculations pertaining to the alternative values of P/E_{ST} of 9, 10, 12, and 15 are summarized in Exhibit 6.12 on page 276.

The *stock exchange ratio negotiating range* is graphed in Figure 6.1 on page 277. In the first panel, ER_S is graphed. The curve for ER_T appears in the second panel. Finally, in the third panel, the ER_S and ER_T curves are combined, thereby identifying the area between them as the negotiating range.

Conclusion

Accounting information can be of significant help in establishing the terms of a business combination. As we see in Figure 6.1, however, the final exchange ratio must be negotiated, for there are many that would injure neither group of stockholders. If one draws a horizontal line through $ER = .5333$, one has identified the only exchange ratio that will have an equivalent effect on both groups of stockholders at any P/E_{ST}. To the right of $P/E_{ST} = 9.6363$, exchange ratios between the curves will be such that all stockholders will be better off. Unless $ER = .5333$, however, either the original S shareholders or the former T shareholders will benefit disproportionately.

Questions

Q6.1 Describe the various motivating factors behind business combinations.

Q6.2 In discussing the history of authoritative pronouncements on accounting for business combinations, the text quotes a passage from *ARB 48*. Read *ARB 48*. Has the pooling concept changed substantially from *ARB 48* to *ARBO 16*? Why or why not?

Q6.3 See Q6.2 above. Why has *APBO 16* apparently succeeded in preventing abuses of pooling, whereas *ARB 48* failed? The two pronouncements seem to suggest a fundamentally different approach to accounting principles. What is the nature of this difference? Are you troubled by it?

Q6.4 A publishing company owns the copyrights to many books. The original cost of these copyrights has been substantially amortized, yet, due to the reissue of many books as paperbacks, the copyrights have high market values. The publishing company is about to be acquired by a conglomerate whose management insists on structuring the combination as a pooling. Why might management be so adamant about the choice of accounting method?

Q6.5 In a purchase combination, a purchase premium is to be allocated to the acquired company's identifiable assets and to goodwill. There is potential for some abuse here. Describe how it can occur.

Q6.6 Any negative goodwill arising in a purchase combination must be allocated among noncurrent assets, excluding long-term investments in marketable securities. Also, no negative goodwill is allocated among current assets and liabilities. Briefly discuss the apparent reason for these rules.

Q6.7 Describe the accounting rules governing the composition of combined stockholders' equity following a pooling. Briefly indicate the reasoning which led to these rules.

Q6.8 Suppose bonds are issued by the acquiring company as the consideration in a purchase combination. Former stockholders of the acquired company are guaranteed that the bonds they receive will be worth at least some minimum amount in 2 years. At the end of the 2 years, a substantial number of new bonds are issued under the terms of the guarantee. Explain what must have happened during the 2 years, the accounting treatment by the acquiring company when the new bonds are issued, and whether the accounting is sound.

Q6.9 The general prohibition against the use of treasury stock in a pooling of interests is waived when the treasury stock was acquired more than 2 years prior to initiating the business combination. What message is implied by this 2-year rule?

Q6.10 Suppose current value account were adopted. Would this defeat the pooling concept? How would the traditional advantages attributed to pooling be affected?

Q6.11 One of the conditions for pooling states that "the combined corporation does not enter into other financial arrangements for the benefit of the former stockholders of a combining company. . ." Explain how the pooling concept could easily be abused without such a condition.

Q6.12 Explain the accounting treatment of costs incurred to register and issue securities used as consideration in a purchase combination.

Exercises

E6.1 The Pen Company has agreed to acquire all of the outstanding common stock of the Simpson Company through an exchange of 55,000 shares of Pen Company stock. The stock has an aggregate fair market value of

$2,500,000. Since the method of accounting for this combination is not yet certain, you have been asked to reflect the contemplated combination both as a purchase and as a pooling of interests. Prior to the combination, the stockholders' equity accounts of both companies are as follows:

	Pen Company	Simpson Company
Common Stock Outstanding:		
530,000 Shares, Par Value $1	$ 530,000	—
40,000 Shares, Par Value $5	—	$ 200,000
Additional Paid-In Capital	5,665,000	1,350,000
Retained Earnings	12,373,000	378,000
Total Stockholders' Equity	$18,568,000	$1,928,000

Required: Give the postcombination components of Pen Company's stockholders' equity under both purchase and pooling. Show all calculations.

E6.2 The Nugget Company's balance sheet on December 31, 19X1, is as follows:

ASSETS

Cash	$ 100,000
Accounts Receivable	200,000
Inventories	500,000
Property, Plant, and Equipment, Net	900,000
	$1,700,000

LIABILITIES AND STOCKHOLDERS' EQUITY

Current Liabilities	$ 300,000
Long-Term Debt	500,000
Common Stock, Par Value $1	100,000
Additional Paid-In Capital	200,000
Retained Earnings	600,000
	$1,700,000

On December 31, 19X1, the Bronc Company purchases all of the assets and liabilities of Nugget for $1,500,000 cash. On that date, the fair (market) value of Nugget's inventories is $450,000 and the fair value of Nugget's property, plant, and equipment (net) is $1,000,000. The fair values of all other assets and liabilities of Nugget are equal to their book values.

Required:

1. As a result of the acquisition of Nugget by Bronc, the postcombination balance sheet of Bronc and Nugget should show goodwill in the amount of:
   a. $500,000.
   b. $550,000.
   c. $600,000.
   d. $650,000.

Current Assets	$ 850,000
Noncurrent Assets	1,600,000
Estimated Liability: Defective Product Lawsuits	(280,000)
Other Liabilities	(500,000)

The $280,000 estimated liability represented Step's best estimate of likely losses due to lawsuits pending as of January 3, 19X7. Later in 19X7, as favorable information regarding the defective products became available, the estimated liability was reduced to $200,000. Then, late in 19X8, after observing the large judgments awarded by courts in similar lawsuits against competitors, management revised the estimated liability upward to $350,000.

Required: Show how the original identifiable assets and liabilities of Step would be reflected in postcombination balance sheets as of January 3, 19X7, and the year-ends December 31, 19X7 and 19X8. Disregard amortization in 19X7 and 19X8.

E6.12 *(Appendix)* The Alpha Company and the Beta Company are contemplating a merger in which shares of Alpha will be exchanged for shares of Beta. Alpha earned $6,000,000 last year ($2.50 per share); its stock currently sells at $25. Beta earned $2,000,000 ($2.00 per share); its stock currently sells at $8. In negotiating the terms of the merger, managements of the two companies estimate that the ex post combined price/earnings ratio will be 9.

Required: Compute the upper and lower boundaries of the stock exchange ratio negotiating range for Alpha and Beta at the given ex post combined price/earnings ratio of 9.

Problems

P6.1 **Propriety of Purchase and Pooling under Various Conditions** The boards of directors of Kessler Corporation, Bar Company, Cohen, Inc., and Mason Corporation are meeting jointly to discuss plans for a business combination. Each of the corporations has one class of common stock outstanding; Bar also has one class of preferred stock outstanding. Although terms have not as yet been settled, Kessler will be the acquiring or issuing corporation. Because the directors want to conform to generally accepted accounting principles, they have asked you to attend the meeting as an advisor.

Required: Consider each of the following questions independently of the others and answer each in accordance with generally accepted accounting principles. Explain your answers.

1. Assume that the combination will be consummated August 31, 19X3. Explain the philosophy underlying the accounting and how the balance sheet accounts of each of the four corporations will appear on Kessler's consolidated balance sheet on September 1, 19X3, if the combination is accounted for as (a) a pooling of interests; (b) a purchase.

2. Assume that the combination will be consummated August 31, 19X3. Explain how the income statement accounts of each of the four corporations will be accounted for in preparing Kessler's consolidated income statement for the year ended December 31, 19X3, if the combination is accounted for as (a) a pooling of interests; (b) a purchase.

3. Some of the directors believe that the terms of the combination should be agreed upon immediately and that the method of accounting to be used (whether pooling of interests, purchase, or a mixture) may be chosen at some later date. Others believe that the terms of the combination and the method to be used are very closely related. Which position is correct?

4. Kessler and Mason are comparable in size; Cohen and Bar are much smaller. How do these facts affect the choice of accounting method?

5. Bar was formerly a subsidiary of Tucker Corporation, which has no other relationship to any of the four companies discussing combination. Eighteen months ago Tucker voluntarily spun off Bar. What effect, if any, do these facts have on the choice of accounting method?

6. Kessler holds 2,000 of Bar's 10,000 outstanding shares of preferred stock and 15,000 of Cohen's 100,000 outstanding shares of common stock. All of Kessler's holdings were acquired during the first 3 months of 19X3. What effect, if any, do these facts have on the choice of accounting method?

7. It is almost certain that Mrs. Victor Mason, Sr., who holds 5 percent of Mason's common stock, will object to the combination. Assume that Kessler is able to acquire only 95 percent (rather than 100 percent) of Mason's stock, issuing Kessler common stock in exchange.
   a. Which accounting method is applicable?
   b. If Kessler is able to acquire the remaining 5 percent at some future time—say in 5 years—in exchange for its own common stock, which accounting method will be applicable to this second acquisition?

8. Since the directors feel that one of Mason's major divisions will not be compatible with the operations of the combined company, they anticipate that the division will be sold as soon as possible after the combination is consummated. They expect to have no trouble in finding a buyer. What effect, if any, do these facts have on the choice of accounting method? *(AICPA adapted)*

P6.2 Multiple Choice Questions on Business Combinations

1. Pluto Corporation issued 100,000 shares of its $1 par (current fair value, $10) capital stock for all 1,000 shares of the issued and out-

standing capital stock of the Saturn Company. At the date of the business combination, the stockholders' equity of Saturn was as follows:

Capital Stock, Par Value $10	$ 10,000
Additional Paid-In Capital	82,300
Retained Earnings	60,900
Total Stockholders' Equity	$153,200

If the business combination is recorded as a pooling, the effect on Pluto's Additional Paid-In Capital account (precombination balance of $136,000) would be which of the following?

a. A credit of $900,000.   **d.** A debit of $7,700.

b. A credit of $82,300.   **e.** None of the above.

c. A debit of $10,000.

2. On May 17, 19X8, Port Corporation paid $600,000 cash for all of the outstanding common stock of the Short Company in a purchase combination. Short's assets and liabilities at May 17, 19X8, had the following book values:

Cash	$ 80,000
Inventories	320,000
Plant and Equipment, Net	260,000
Liabilities	(190,000)
	$ 470,000

Appraisals as of May 17, 19X8, indicated that Short's inventory had a fair value of $295,000 and that the fair value of Short's plant and equipment (net) was $300,000. If Port is to recognize goodwill in the combination, the amount is which of the following?

a. $0.   **d.** $130,000.

b. ($25,000).   **e.** None of the above.

c. $115,000.

3. P Company acquired all of the outstanding shares of S Company for a cost below the book value of S Company's identifiable net assets at the date of the business combination. The difference is related to the technological obsolescence of some of S Company's equipment. In a combined or consolidated balance sheet, this difference is accounted for by which of the following?

a. Decreasing the equipment account.

b. Increasing consolidated additional paid-in capital.

c. Recognizing an extraordinary loss.

d. Recording negative goodwill.

e. None of the above.

4. Which of the following is *not* a postcombination financial statement difference between the pooling and purchase methods?

a. Par value of postcombination capital stock.

b. The financial statements which are combined or consolidated in the year of the combination.

c. Composition of postcombination retained earnings.
d. Valuation of the acquired company's assets and liabilities.
e. None of the above.

Items 5, 6, and 7 are based on information presented in the following balance sheets of two companies prior to their combination.

	January 1, 19X0	
	P Company	S Company
Cash.	$ 3,000	$ 100
Inventory (af FIFO Cost, Which Approximates Fair Value)	2,000	200
Fixed Assets, Net	5,000	700ª
Total Assets	$10,000	$1,000
Current Liabilities	$ 600	$ 100
Common Stock, $1 Par Value	1,000	100
Additional Paid-In Capital	3,000	200
Retained Earnings	5,400	600
Total Equities	$10,000	$1,000

ªFair value at January 1, 19X0, is $1,500.

5. On January 1, 19X0, P Company acquires 100 percent of the common stock of S Company by issuing, in a tax-free exchange, 200 shares of its own common stock, which has a fair value of $10 per share on that date. The requirements for use of pooling of interests accounting are met and will be followed. A balance sheet of the two companies combined as of January 1, 19X0, is to be prepared. The amount of additional paid-in capital that would be shown on this combined balance sheet is which of the following?
   a. $3,000.   c. $3,200.
   b. $3,100.   d. $3,900.

6. On January 1, 19X0, P Company acquires 100 percent of the common stock of S Company in a taxable purchase by payment of $2,000 cash. The amount that would be shown as "goodwill" on the combined balance sheet as of January 1, 19X0, is which of the following?
   a. $200.   c. $1,100.
   b. $900.   d. $300.

7. On January 1, 19X0, P Company acquires 100 percent of the common stock of S Company in a taxable purchase by payment of $1,500 cash. The amount that would be shown as fixed assets in the combined balance sheet is which of the following?
   a. $5,700.   c. $6,300.
   b. $6,500.   d. $6,700.

8. During 19X8, the Henderson Company purchased the net assets of John Corporation for $800,000. On the date of the transaction, John had no long-term investments in marketable securities and had

$100,000 of liabilities. The fair values of John's assets when acquired were as follows:

Current Assets	$ 400,000
Noncurrent Assets	600,000
	$1,000,000

How should Henderson account for the $100,000 difference between the fair value of the net assets acquired ($900,000) and the cost ($800,000)?

a. The $100,000 difference should be credited to retained earnings.

b. The noncurrent assets should be recorded at $500,000.

c. The current assets should be recorded at $360,000, and the noncurrent assets should be recorded at $540,000.

d. A deferred credit of $100,000 should be set up and then amortized to income over a period not to exceed 40 years.

(Items 5–8, AICPA adapted)

P6.3 Purchase Entries: Statutory Merger Plastic Corporation is contemplating a business combination with Steel Corporation at December 31, 19X3. Steel's condensed balance sheet on that date appears below:

ASSETS	Book Value	Fair Value
Cash and Receivables	$ 35,000	$35,000
Inventory	35,000	45,000
Long-Term Investments in Marketable Securities	18,000	20,000
Land	8,000	11,000
Buildings and Equipment, Net	7,000	14,000
Patents	5,000	10,000
	$108,000	

LIABILITIES AND STOCKHOLDERS' EQUITY		
Liabilities	$ 22,000	$ 22,000
Common Stock	50,000	—
Retained Earnings	36,000	—
	$108,000	

Required: Give the journal entry to record the business combination of Plastic and Steel as a purchase for each of the following purchase prices and combination methods:

1. Plastic merges with Steel by acquiring all of Steel's stock for $100,000 cash. Other direct cash costs are $25,000.

2. Plastic merges with Steel by acquiring all of Steel's stock for $90,000 cash. Other direct cash costs are $10,000.

3. Plastic merges with Steel by acquiring all of Steel's stock for $50,000 cash. Other direct cash costs are $10,000.

4. Plastic acquires 80 percent of Steel's stock for $90,000 cash in a stock acquisition. Other direct cash costs are $15,000.

P6.4 Pooling: Statutory Consolidation On December 31, 19X2, the Cole Company and the Bond Company entered into a business combination appropriately accounted for as a pooling of interests. As a result of this combination, a new company, Gold Corporation, was formed with 500,000 authorized shares of no par, $1 stated value common stock. The management of Gold did not intend to retain either Cole or Bond as subsidiaries.

On December 31, 19X2, Gold issued its common stock in exchange for all of the outstanding common stock of Cole and Bond as follows:

Cole: 300,000 shares of Gold common stock for all 10,000 outstanding shares of Cole's $5 par value common stock.

Bond: 200,000 shares of Gold common stock for all 4,000 outstanding shares of Bond's $10 par value common stock.

Presented below are condensed financial statements of Cole and Bond for the year ended December 31, 19X2, prior to the pooling of interests.

BALANCE SHEETS AT DECEMBER 31, 19X2 (PRECOMBINATION)

ASSETS	Cole Company	Bond Company
Current Assets	$260,000	$235,000
Property, Plant, and Equipment, Net	410,000	320,000
Other Assets	90,000	65,000
Total Assets	$760,000	$620,000

LIABILITIES AND STOCKHOLDERS' EQUITY

	Cole Company	Bond Company
Current Liabilities	$167,000	$124,000
Long-Term Debt	300,000	—
Common Stock	50,000	40,000
Capital in Excess of Par Value	10,000	160,000
Retained Earnings	233,000	296,000
Total Liabilities and Stockholders' Equity	$760,000	$620,000

STATEMENTS OF INCOME AND RETAINED EARNINGS
FOR THE YEAR ENDED DECEMBER 31, 19X2

	Cole Company	Bond Company
Net Sales	$1,600,000	$2,200,000
Costs and Expenses:		
Cost of Sales	$1,120,000	$1,560,000
Operating and Other Expenses	330,000	480,000
	$1,450,000	$2,040,000
Net Income	$ 150,000	$ 160,000
Retained Earnings, January 1, 19X2	83,000	136,000
Retained Earnings, December 31, 19X2	$ 233,000	$ 296,000

Cole values its inventory using the FIFO method; Bond uses the LIFO method for its inventory. Bond agreed to change its method of inventory valuation from LIFO to FIFO prior to the business combination.

Bond began operations on January 1, 19X1, and data relevant to Bond's inventory are as follows:

	LIFO Method	FIFO Method
Inventory, Dec. 31, 19X1	$42,000	$62,000
Inventory, Dec. 31, 19X2	55,000	85,000

Required:

1. Prepare the adjusting journal entry with the appropriate explanation and supporting calculations to be made by the Bond Company on December 31, 19X2, to change its inventory from LIFO cost to FIFO cost. Income taxes should not be considered in your solution.
2. Prepare a schedule computing pooled retained earnings of Gold Corporation as of December 31, 19X2.
3. Prepare the December 31, 19X2, journal entry on the books of Gold Corporation to record the business combination as a pooling of interests.

P6.5 **Merger Entries: Pooling and Purchase** AMAX Corporation merged with BETAX Corporation on December 31, 19X8. Consultants' and attorneys' fees relating to the merger amounted to $50,000, and the costs of registering and issuing securities exchanged in the merger totaled $30,000. Condensed balance sheet data for AMAX and BETAX just prior to the combination and estimated fair values of BETAX properties and liabilities are given below:

	AMAX	BETAX	
Account		Book Value	Fair Value
Cash and Receivables	$2,000,000	$ 900,000	$850,000
Inventory	1,500,000	800,000	920,000
Plant Assets	1,800,000	1,100,000	700,000 (net)
Accumulated Depreciation	(500,000)	(600,000)	
Total Assets	$4,800,000	$2,200,000	
Current Liabilities	$1,600,000	$ 700,000	700,000
Long-Term Debt	2,100,000	1,000,000	980,000
Common Stock, $10 Par Value . . .	200,000	100,000	
Additional Paid-In Capital	300,000	100,000	
Retained Earnings	600,000	300,000	
Total Liabilities and Stockholders' Equity	$4,800,000	$2,200,000	

Required: Prepare journal entries to record the merger of AMAX and BETAX under each of the following sets of circumstances:

1. AMAX issues 10,000 shares with a market value of $800,000 for all the shares of BETAX in a purchase transaction.

2. AMAX exchanges 12,000 shares for all of the shares of BETAX in a pooling of interests.

3. AMAX exchanges 20,800 shares for all of the shares of BETAX in a pooling of interests.

P6.6 Postcombination Stockholders' Equity (Pooling) and Balance Sheet (Purchase) On December 31, 19X2, Miller Corporation and Fulton Corporation were merged into Milton Corporation, a newly organized corporation. Shareholders of Miller and Fulton exchanged all of their stock for 18,000 and 12,000 shares of Milton's $10 par value common stock, respectively. Prior to the merger, Milton's condensed balance sheet showed cash of $60,000, common stock (par value) of $20,000, and additional paid-in capital of $40,000. Milton will spend $50,000 in cash for expenses related to the business combination.

Condensed balance sheet data for Miller and Fulton prior to the merger are shown below:

	Miller	Fulton
Current Assets	$100,000	$100,000
Plant Assets	300,000	200,000
	$400,000	$300,000
Liabilities	$ 95,000	$110,000
Common Stock	50,000	40,000
Additional Paid-In Capital	140,000	60,000
Retained Earnings	115,000	90,000
	$400,000	$300,000

Required:

1. Assuming that the combination is to be accounted for as a pooling of interests, prepare the postcombination stockholders' equity section of Milton's balance sheet.

2. Assume that the constituent companies agree to an earnings contingency, thereby violating the pooling concept, and that the implied fair value of Milton's stock is $30 per share. Moreover, Miller's plant assets are *under*valued by $100,000 and Fulton's plant assets are *over*valued by $20,000. Prepare a condensed postcombination balance sheet for Milton.

P6.7 Postcombination Balance Sheets: Pooling and Purchase The Cooper family owns all of the outstanding stock of Cooper Corporation. Reynolds Corporation is planning to merge with Cooper by exchanging its common stock for all of the outstanding common stock of Cooper. In addition, Reynolds will issue $100,000 par value, 6 percent, cumulative, nonparticipating preferred stock to the holders of Cooper's long-term bonds. The Cooper family intends to sell 80 percent of its Reynolds shares through a prearranged secondary offering to the public shortly after the combination takes place. In order to keep the family name associated with the company, the Cooper family will continue to hold the remaining 20 percent of its interest in Reynolds Corporation.

The number of $10 par value Reynolds Corporation common shares given will be based on the relationship between the market value of the recorded net assets of Cooper and the market price of Reynolds' stock, which is currently $30 per share.

The following balance sheet data are obtained:

	Reynolds	Cooper	Cooper (Market Value)
Current Assets	$400,000	$100,000	$115,000
Plant Assets, Net	500,000	350,000	427,000
Total	$900,000	$450,000	
Current Liabilities	$200,000	$ 50,000	50,000
Long-Term Liabilities	300,000	100,000	90,000
Common Stock, $10 Par Value	60,000	100,000	
Additional Paid-In Capital	40,000	—	
Retained Earnings	300,000	200,000	
Total	$900,000	$450,000	

Required:

1. Should this combination be accounted for as a purchase or a pooling of interests? Support your response with reference to applicable provisions of *APBO 16* (CT § B50) and the related AICPA Accounting Interpretations, especially Interpretations Nos. 21 and 37 (CT § 350.569–.571, .638–.640).

2. Prepare postcombination balance sheets for the merged companies under the method selected in No. 1 and the alternative method. *(Adapted from a problem prepared by Clyde P. Stickney)*

P6.8 Postcombination Balance Sheets: Pooling and Purchase Blue Corporation was merged into Ace Corporation on August 31, 19X4, with Blue Corporation going out of existence. Both companies had fiscal years ending on August 31; this fiscal year will be retained after the merger. Immediately prior to the merger, the balance sheets of the two companies were as follows:

ASSETS	Ace	Blue
Current Assets	$ 4,350,000	$ 3,000,000
Plant and Equipment, Net	18,500,000	11,300,000
Patents	450,000	200,000
Plant Rearrangement Costs	150,000	—
	$23,450,000	$14,500,000

LIABILITIES AND STOCKHOLDERS' EQUITY

Liabilities.	$ 2,650,000	$ 2,100,000
Common Stock, $10 Par Value	12,000,000	—
Common Stock, $5 Par Value	—	3,750,000
Additional Paid-In Capital	4,200,000	3,200,000
Retained Earnings.	5,850,000	5,450,000
	$24,700,000	$14,500,000
Less: Treasury Stock at Cost, 100,000 Shares.	1,250,000	—
	$23,450,000	$14,500,000
Net Income	$ 2,450,000	$ 1,300,000

The fair values of the assets and liabilities on August 31, 19X4, of Ace and Blue were as follows:

	Ace	Blue
Current Assets.	$ 4,950,000	$ 3,400,000
Plant and Equipment, Net	22,000,000	14,000,000
Patents.	570,000	360,000
Plant Rearrangement Costs	150,000	40,000
Total Assets.	$27,670,000	$17,800,000
Liabilities.	(2,650,000)	(2,100,000)
Net Assets.	$25,020,000	$15,700,000

Ace capitalized its fiscal year 19X4 plant rearrangement costs and has always amortized them over 5 years beginning with the year of expenditure. All plant rearrangement costs of Ace have been appropriately capitalized and amortized for the current and preceding years. Blue incurred $50,000 of plant rearrangement costs which were expensed during the fiscal year ending August 31, 19X4. Blue did not have any plant rearrangement costs in any year before 19X4. Blue will adopt Ace's method of accounting for plant rearrangement costs.

Internally generated general expenses incurred because of the merger were $25,000 and are included in the current assets of Ace as a prepaid expense.

There were no intercompany transactions during the year.

Before the merger, Ace had 3,000,000 shares of common stock authorized, 1,200,000 shares issued, and 1,100,000 shares outstanding. Blue had 750,000 shares of common stock authorized, issued, and outstanding.

Required: Prepare the balance sheet and determine the amount of net income under each of the following independent situations. Show all calculations. Do not prepare formal journal entries.

1. Ace exchanged 400,000 shares of previously unissued common stock and 100,000 shares of treasury stock for all the outstanding common stock of Blue. All the conditions for pooling of interests accounting enumerated in APB *Opinion No. 16* were met.

2. Ace purchased the assets and assumed the liabilities of Blue by paying $3,100,000 cash and issuing debentures of $16,900,000 at face value. *(AICPA adapted)*

P6.9 Negative Goodwill, Preacquisition Contingency, and Tax Basis Less than Fair Value On January 2, 19X9, Fisher Corporation acquired all of the voting common stock of Grant Corporation for its own stock worth $10,000,000 in a tax-free statutory merger. The combination is accounted for as a purchase, and the fair values of assets acquired and liabilities assumed will be recorded by Fisher. Grant's assets and liabilities have tax bases equal to their recorded book values; future tax deductions taken by Fisher will be based on these book values and not on estimated fair values. Fisher's marginal income tax rate is 40 percent. Grant's condensed balance sheet on January 2, 19X9, appears below:

GRANT CORPORATION
CONDENSED BALANCE SHEET AT JANUARY 2, 19X9

ASSETS	Book Value	Fair Value
Cash and Receivables	$ 6,400,000	$6,400,000
Inventory	3,800,000	5,800,000
Depreciable Plant Assets, Net	4,000,000	6,500,000
Other (Nondepreciable) Assets	3,000,000	3,000,000
	$17,200,000	

LIABILITIES AND STOCKHOLDERS' EQUITY		
Current Liabilities	$ 5,000,000	$5,000,000
Long-Term Debt	1,800,000	1,800,000
Capital Stock	2,000,000	—
Retained Earnings	8,400,000	—
	$17,200,000	

Note: On December 27, 19X8, a lawsuit alleging defective products and claiming damages of $1,000,000 was filed against Grant. The estimated liability and related loss, believed to be $800,000, have not yet been accrued. Since the lawsuit had been anticipated, Fisher accepts responsibility for the liability.

Required:

1. Prepare the journal entry made by Fisher to record the acquisition of Grant. Support the entry with a schedule allocating the purchase premium or discount. Disregard income tax effects.

2. Assume that at the end of 19X9 the product liability lawsuit was settled out of court for $100,000. Prepare the journal entry needed to revise the original purchase price allocation determined in No. 1.

3. Same as No. 1 except that the income tax effects attributable to the difference between fair value and tax basis are to be considered.

4. Same as No. 2 except that the original purchase price allocation is to reflect the tax effects.

P6.10 Combining a Partnership and a Proprietorship to Form a Corporation
The Howard & Sanders Electrical Contracting Company, a partnership, and the Grover Wholesale Electricians' Hardware Company, a proprietorship, have agreed to transfer the assets and liabilities of their companies on November 1, 19X9, to a newly chartered corporation, Major Electrical, Inc., in exchange for Major's stock. In addition to specifying that the combination is to be accounted for as a purchase, the agreement provides the following:

1. Preferred stock shall be issued at par value of $100 per share to each of the parties in exchange for the individual's share of the net assets (assets minus liabilities) transferred to Major Electrical. John Grover shall receive at least 900 shares of preferred stock, and Bill Howard and Joe Sanders shall receive together a total of not more than 480 shares of preferred stock. Cash shall be contributed to the companies by the respective parties or distributed by the companies to the parties to accomplish the proper net asset transfers.

2. Common stock shall be issued in a total amount equal to the earnings expected to be contributed by the companies to Major Electrical for the next 5 years to the extent that the earnings of each company, based on the past 3 calendar years, exceed the average earnings of its respective industry. The common stock shall be issued at par value of $10 per share to the owners of the companies in the ratio of the amount that each company's average earnings are expected to exceed the average industry earnings of the company with the lesser earnings. The par value of the common stock issued shall represent goodwill.

Trial balances for the 10 months ended October 31, 19X9, for both companies are shown in Exhibit 6.13.

Additional information:

1. Howard & Sanders maintains the partnership books on the cash basis of accounting. Grover maintains his proprietorship books on the accrual basis. Major's books are to be maintained on the accrual basis. Items not recorded on the Howard & Sanders' books at October 31, 19X9, follow:

Accounts Receivable.	$20,300
Allowance for Bad Debts.	400
Unbilled Contract in Progress	8,000
Prepaid Expenses	1,200
Accounts Payable	6,200
Accrued Expenses Payable	2,400

Exhibit 6.13	Trial Balances for Grover Hardware Company and Howard & Sanders Company, to Be Used in P6.10

GROVER WHOLESALE ELECTRICIANS' HARDWARE COMPANY AND
HOWARD & SANDERS ELECTRICAL CONTRACTING COMPANY
TRIAL BALANCES
NOVEMBER 1, 19X9

Account	Grover Hardware		Howard & Sanders	
	Debit	Credit	Debit	Credit
Cash.	$ 17,000		$ 20,700	
Accounts Receivable . .	43,000			
Allowance for Bad Debts		$ 3,000		
Inventory	63,000		3,500	
Prepaid Expenses	2,000		1,300	
Land, Building, and				
Equipment.	44,000		26,000	
Allowance for Depreciation		27,000		$ 12,000
Accounts Payable		54,000		
Accrued Expenses				
Payable		4,000		
Deposit on Contract . . .				2,500
Capital—Grover		75,000		
Drawing—Grover	5,000			
Capital—Howard				11,300
Capital—Sanders				7,700
Revenues		200,000		70,000
Cost of Producing				
Revenues	160,000		31,000	
Partners' Salaries				
(Drawings).			7,000	
Operating Expenses . . .	29,000		14,000	
Totals	$363,000	$363,000	$103,500	$103,500

All accounts receivable are for jobs completed and billed. The unbilled contract in progress is for a $10,000 contract, which was 80 percent complete (to be recorded as revenue) and upon which a $2,500 deposit was paid to Howard & Sanders when the contract was signed. Cash payments by Howard & Sanders for work on the contract to October 31, 19X9, total $3,500 and were recorded on the partnership books as inventory. Accounts Payable includes $2,800 owed to Grover Hardware.

2. The partnership agreement specified that Bill Howard would receive a salary of $12,000 per year and share 60 percent of any profit or loss, and that Joe Sanders would receive a salary of $9,000 per year and share 40 percent of any profit or loss. Each partner will receive the

same annual salary from the corporation. In 19X9, each partner drew one-third of the annual salary.

3. John Grover withdraws an amount each month from his proprietorship equal to a normal salary. Grover's annual salary from the corporation will be $15,000.

4. Based on the past 3 years, John Grover could expect his proprietorship to earn an average of $39,000 per year for the next 5 years before any salary allowance, with average expected sales of $600,000 per year. The industry average net income (after deducting all salaries and income taxes) for electrical hardware wholesalers for the next 5 years is expected to be 1.35 percent of sales.

5. Based on the past 3 years, Bill Howard and Joe Sanders could expect their partnership to earn an average of $55,500 per year for the next 5 years before deducting partners' salaries, with average expected revenues of $240,000 per year. The industry average net income (after deducting all salaries and income tax) for electrical contractors for the next 5 years is expected to be 7.5 percent of sales.

6. The parties expect the corporation to pay income tax at an average rate of 40 percent during the next 5 years.

7. The final distribution of partnership income to Howard and Sanders is to reflect all accrual basis adjustments.

8. Net book values of assets approximate their current fair values.

Required: Prepare a work sheet to determine the pro forma opening account balances of Major Electrical, giving effect to the agreement to transfer the assets and liabilities and issue stock. The work sheet should have columns for Grover Hardware Trial Balance (Dr., Cr.), Howard & Sanders Trial Balance (Dr., Cr.), Grover Hardware Adjusting and Eliminating Entries (Dr., Cr.), Howard & Sanders Adjusting and Eliminating Entries (Dr., Cr.), and Major Electrical Opening Account Balances (Dr., Cr.). Prepare supporting schedules computing (1) any cash contributions or distributions necessary and preferred stock to be issued to each party and (2) the number of shares of common stock to be issued to each party. Formal adjusting and closing entries and formal financial statements are not required. *(AICPA adapted)*

P6.11 Combining a Partnership and a Corporation: Pooling and Purchase
The B & Q Company was organized on July 1, 19X1. Under the partnership agreement, $900,000 was provided by Beke and $600,000 by Quinn as initial capital; income and losses were to be shared in the same ratio as the initial capital contributions. No additional capital contributions have been made. The June 30, 19X6, balance sheet of the B & Q Company follows:

B & Q COMPANY
BALANCE SHEET AT JUNE 30, 19X6

ASSETS

Cash	$ 500,500
Accounts Receivable, Net	950,000
Inventory (LIFO Basis)	1,500,000
Prepaid Insurance	18,000
Land	58,000
Machinery and Equipment, Net	1,473,500
Total Assets	$4,500,000

LIABILITIES AND CAPITAL

Current Liabilities	$1,475,000
Capital—Beke	1,815,000
Capital—Quinn	1,210,000
Total Liabilities and Capital	$4,500,000

Assume that Beke and Quinn have engaged in lengthy discussions with the executives and directors of Preston Corporation during the past few months. With the permission of Beke and Quinn, the auditors of Preston conducted an examination and expressed an unqualified opinion on the historical cost financial statements of B & Q Company as of June 30, 19X6. The allowance for doubtful accounts and accumulated depreciation on June 30, 19X6, amounted to $300,000 and $536,500, respectively.

Beke agrees to accept 8,700 shares and Quinn agrees to accept 5,800 shares of Preston common stock in exchange for all partnership interests. During the month of June 19X6, the market value of a share of Preston was $265. The stockholders' equity account balances of Preston as of June 30, 19X6, follow:

Common Stock, Par Value $100	$2,000,000
Additional Paid-In Capital	580,000
Retained Earnings	2,496,000
	$5,076,000

Required:

1. Prepare the necessary journal entry (or entries) to record the business combination as a pooling of interests on July 1, 19X6, on the books of Preston.
2. Assume that the combination is to be recorded as a purchase. The assets and liabilities of Beke and Quinn are stated at their fair values except for inventory and land, with fair values of $1,800,000 and $100,000, respectively. Prepare the necessary journal entry (or entries) to record the combination as a purchase on July 1, 19X6, on the books of Preston. *(AICPA adapted)*

P6.12 Computation of Stock Exchange Ratios *(Appendix)*　The Bate Company and the Tate Company are planning a merger to be accounted for as a pooling of interests. Representatives of each company's board of directors are trying to work out a set of mutually acceptable stock exchange ratios. These stock exchange ratios are expressed in terms of the number of new shares of Bate's stock to be exchanged for one share of Tate's stock. Financial data for the two companies are given here:

	Bate	Tate
Net Income	$8,000,000	$4,000,000
Shares Outstanding.	4,000,000	1,000,000
Earnings per Share	$　　2	$　　4
Market Price per Share	$　30	$　40
P/E Ratio	15	10

Required:

1. Compute the stock exchange ratio and ex post combined price/earnings ratio which leave all shareholders in exactly the same economic position they had prior to the merger.
2. Assume the ex post combined price/earnings ratio is 15. Compute the *maximum* stock exchange ratio likely to be acceptable to the stockholders of Bate and the *minimum* stock exchange ratio likely to be acceptable to the stockholders of Tate.

Chapter 7   Introduction to Consolidated Financial Statements: The Balance Sheet

The Nature of Consolidated Statements

The preceding chapter discussed four types of business combinations: statutory mergers, statutory consolidations, asset acquisitions, and stock acquisitions. For the first three types of combinations, a single set of accounting records remained—those of the acquiring company. Moreover, only the acquiring company survived as a separate and distinct legal entity. In a *stock acquisition,* however, the combining companies remain as separate and distinct legal entities under common ownership control. That is, the shareholders of P Company control S Company by virtue of their ownership of more than 50 percent of S's outstanding voting shares. Furthermore, if P's control over S were 100 percent, financial statements for companies P and S together should not differ from those prepared if companies P and S had merged, with P Company the only surviving legal entity. With some refinements, of course, this is precisely the motivating force behind the preparation of consolidated financial statements.

Corporations which maintain a parent/subsidiary relationship are often referred to as **affiliated corporations.** Accordingly, we can state the following:

> The purpose of **consolidated financial statements** is to report the financial affairs of two or more affiliated corporations as if they were a single *unified economic entity.*

Consolidated statements stress substance over form. The mere fact that affiliated corporations remain as separate legal entities does not detract from the fact that they are under common ownership control. In *APBS 4,* the Accounting Principles Board pointed out:

> Consolidated financial statements present the financial position and results of operations of a parent company and its subsidiaries essentially as if the group were a single

enterprise comprised of branches or divisions. The resulting accounting entity is an economic rather than a legal unit, and its financial statements are considered to reflect the substance of the combined economic relationships to an extent not possible by merely providing the separate financial statements of the corporate entities comprising the group[1]

In this chapter, we begin consideration of the preparation of consolidated financial statements. Experience has shown that approaching this subject one step at a time is wise. Accordingly, our major emphasis in this chapter is on preparation of a consolidated balance sheet. To further simplify the presentation, we make the assumption that the balance sheet is being prepared *at the date of the business combination. This assumption is made for pedagogical reasons only—in the business world, a balance sheet is prepared at the end of the reporting period, not during the period to coincide with a merger or acquisition.* Consolidation at date of business combination offers the important advantage of focusing on the problems of consolidating balance sheets without the added complexities associated with consolidating income statements.

Criteria for Consolidation

When one company has a controlling interest in another, a presumption exists "that consolidated statements are more meaningful than separate statements and that they are usually necessary for a fair presentation."[2] A controlling interest generally exists when P Company owns, either directly or indirectly, a majority of the outstanding voting shares of S Company. Ownership of more than 50 percent of S Company's voting shares means that management of P Company can control 100 percent of S Company's assets and operations. The dividend and investment policies of S Company, as well as other tactical and strategic business decisions, are controlled by P Company. Although P Company may effectively control S Company with an ownership interest of less than 50 percent, consolidated statements are not prepared in such instances. Ownership of a unified block (say, 40 percent) of S Company's voting shares might enable P Company to dominate S's management. Yet the shares not held by P—the "minority" interest—would be larger than the "controlling" interest. Moreover, maintaining control under such circumstances is more uncertain than it would be if P actually owned (directly or indirectly) a majority of S Company's outstanding voting shares. It is hard to see how consolidated financial statements could provide a fair presentation to P's shareholders in these situations, where their equity in the subsidiary is smaller than that of the outside shareholders, the majority.

ARB 51 notes, however, that ownership of a majority of S's shares is *not a sufficient condition* for consolidation for the following reasons:

---

[1] Accounting Principles Board, *Statement No. 4*, "Basic Concepts and Accounting Principles Underlying Financial Statements of Business Enterprises" (New York: AICPA, 1970), par. 194.
[2] Committee on Accounting Procedure, *Accounting Research Bulletin No. 51*, "Consolidated Financial Statements" (New York: AICPA, 1959), par. 1; CT § C51.101.

1. Control may be temporary, or a long-term investment position may not be contemplated. That is, a majority interest may be acquired for the purpose of facilitating other business deals and not with a managerial commitment to the acquired company.
2. For companies in financial difficulty, effective control may rest not with the majority shareholders but with fiduciaries. Similarly, effective control of foreign subsidiaries may rest with foreign governments and not with the majority shareholders.
3. A subsidiary in a line of business unrelated to the parent's business may be excluded from consolidation. This frequently occurs when finance companies are owned by manufacturing companies. Even though control exists, consolidation of companies with significantly different asset and liability structures can result in a misleading presentation. The component companies are far different from the "average" portrayed in consolidation.

After evaluating its subsidiaries in terms of these criteria, a parent company must decide which of its subsidiaries are to be included in consolidated statements. This decision involves an **accounting policy** and is subject to *APBO 22*.[3] When investments in subsidiaries become a significant factor in the parent's overall financial picture, the **consolidation policy** followed by the parent must be disclosed in a note to the financial statements. Pursuant to this requirement, a recent annual report of the General Electric Company stated, in part:

> The financial statements consolidate the accounts of the parent General Electric Company and those of all majority-owned and controlled companies ("affiliated companies"), except finance companies whose operations are not similar to those of the consolidated group.

A summary of consolidation policies followed by the 600 companies surveyed in *Accounting Trends and Techniques* over the period 1980–1982 is shown in Exhibit 7.1. The types of subsidiaries which are not consolidated generally follow from Reasons 1 and 3 above.

Overview of Consolidation Procedures

When approaching the preparation of consolidated statements, the accountant must keep in mind the basic objective: to report the financial affairs of affiliated corporations as if they were those of a single unified economic entity. Thus the consolidated statements must reflect only the outcomes of transactions between firms within the affiliated group and *external* parties—individuals, corporations, and government agencies, for example. Financial relationships or transactions between the affiliates themselves—*intercompany transactions*—are not reflected. Achieving this state of affairs necessitates the use of eliminating entries.

---

[3] Accounting Principles Board, *Opinion No. 22*, "Disclosure of Accounting Policies" (New York: AICPA, 1972); CT § A10.

Exhibit 7.1	Consolidation Policies			

NATURE OF SUBSIDIARIES NOT CONSOLIDATED	1982	1981	1980
Finance Related:			
Credit	102	94	97
Insurance	60	53	49
Leasing	21	24	22
Banks	4	6	5
Real Estate	33	29	27
Foreign	20	19	28
NUMBER OF COMPANIES			
Consolidating All Significant Subsidiaries	414	423	422
Consolidating Certain Significant Subsidiaries	180	168	170
Not Presenting Consolidated Financial Statements	6	9	8
Total Companies	600	600	600

Source: American Institute of Certified Public Accountants, *Accounting Trends and Techniques* (New York: AICPA, 1983), 49. Copyright © 1983 by the American Institute of Certified Public Accountants, Inc.

> An **eliminating entry,** as made in the preparation of consolidated statements, *neutralizes, reverses,* or *removes* an existing intercompany financial relationship or transaction between two or more affiliated corporations.

Before proceeding to a discussion of the kinds of eliminating entries that are used, we must recognize that such entries are *not booked* or journalized by any of the affiliated companies and appear on consolidated statement working papers only.

> Because eliminating entries are used to prepare consolidated statements, they have *no substantive effect* on the economic or legal relationships between the *separate legal entities* comprising an affiliated group. Accordingly, they do not affect the internal accounting records of any of the affiliated companies and are *not booked*.

The preparation of consolidated financial statements consists of *combining* the trial balances or financial statements of the affiliates after any adjusting entries and the appropriate eliminating entries have been made. Adjusting entries involve no new concepts, so we shall focus on a description of the kinds of eliminating entries used and the rationale behind them. Subsequent examples in this and later chapters will thoroughly illustrate how these entries are developed in the consolidation process.

Types of Eliminating Entries

As was mentioned, the objective of consolidated statements is to provide financial statements for a group of affiliated companies as if they were a single company. Our use of eliminating entries accomplishes this objective in two fundamental ways:

1. Double counting of assets, liabilities, revenues, and expenses is avoided.
2. Gains and losses arising from transactions among the companies are removed when no transactions with external parties substantiate the realization of these gains and losses.

The various types of eliminating entries will be discussed. As part of this discussion, we mention several principles central to consolidated statements from which the reasoning behind the eliminations follows.

Eliminating the Investment in S Company and the Stockholders' Equity of S Company. In a stock acquisition, the *Investment in S account* reflects the cost of the net assets (= assets less liabilities) or stockholders' equity of S Company owned by the parent, P Company. Since it is carried as an asset on the books of P Company, *the Investment in S must be eliminated against the stockholders' equity of S Company* in consolidation to avoid double counting. The need for this elimination can be viewed from two perspectives.

First, note that the investment account reflects the cost of S Company's net assets to P Company. If we simply combined the balance sheets of P and S, without eliminating the investment account, S's net assets would be counted twice, once in the investment account and again in the asset and liability accounts themselves. This elimination accomplishes what we refer to as the **substitution principle,** in which the underlying assets and liabilities of S Company are substituted in consolidated statements for the Investment in S account in the parent's unconsolidated statements.

Second, observe that the stockholders' equity of S Company is embodied in the stockholders' equity of P Company. Because P Company owns S Company's stock, the stockholders of P become the stockholders of S. With respect to P and S consolidated, the shares of S are held *internally* in the Investment in S account. Failure to eliminate the Investment in S and the stockholders' equity of S would also overstate consolidated stockholders' equity. Thus the stockholders' equity of S would be duplicated—first by the stockholders' equity accounts of S and second by the stockholders' equity of P, which, by definition, includes the ownership interest in S.

To illustrate, suppose that P Company purchases 100 percent of S Company's outstanding voting shares for $1,000,000 cash, and that this amount equals the stockholders' equity of S Company. P uses the following journal entry to record the stock acquisition:

BOOKS OF P COMPANY

Investment in S 1,000,000
  Cash.   1,000,000
To record the acquisition of all of S Company's outstanding
voting shares at a cost of $1,000,000.

If a consolidated balance sheet is prepared at the date of acquisition, the working paper would include an eliminating entry:

CONSOLIDATED FINANCIAL STATEMENT WORKING PAPER

Stockholders' Equity—S Company. 1,000,000
  Investment in S   1,000,000
To eliminate the Investment in S against the stockholders'
equity (details omitted) of S Company.

The eliminating entry is posted to the condensed consolidated balance sheet working paper appearing in Exhibit 7.2.

Therefore, using the *substitution principle,* we substitute the underlying assets ($3,500,000) and liabilities ($2,500,000) of S Company for the Investment in S account ($1,000,000 = $3,500,000 − $2,500,000) when the consolidated balance sheet is prepared. Moreover, consolidated stockholders' equity now equals the stockholders' equity of the controlling interest, the stockholders of P Company.

Eliminating Intercompany Receivables and Payables. Since consolidated statements report the affairs of affiliated companies as those of one company, *amounts due to or from affiliated companies must be eliminated* in order to avoid overstatement of consolidated assets and liabilities. Intercompany obligations do not represent amounts due to or from external parties and thus are excluded from consolidated statements.

Exhibit 7.2 **P and S Companies:**
Condensed Consolidated Balance Sheet Working Paper

	P Company	S Company	Adjustments and Eliminations Dr.	Adjustments and Eliminations Cr.	Consolidated
Investment in S	1,000,000	—		(1) 1,000,000	—
Other Assets	5,000,000	3,500,000			8,500,000
	6,000,000	3,500,000		1,000,000	8,500,000
Liabilities	3,000,000	2,500,000			5,500,000
Stockholders' Equity	3,000,000	1,000,000	(1) 1,000,000		3,000,000
	6,000,000	3,500,000	1,000,000		8,500,000

Explanation of Working Paper Entry

(1) To eliminate the Investment in S against the Stockholders' Equity of S.

For example, if P Company loans $20,000 to S Company, have total consolidated assets and liabilities increased? Of course not. Yet P Company's books show a receivable of $20,000 due from S Company, and a payable of $20,000 to P Company is recorded on S Company's books. From a legal entity perspective, this is a valid $20,000 debt; from a consolidated statement point of view, the $20,000 debt does not exist. The cash has moved from P to S, but we eliminate the intercompany debt on the working paper:

CONSOLIDATED FINANCIAL STATEMENT WORKING PAPER

Loan Payable to P. 20,000
    Loan Receivable from S.   20,000
To eliminate the intercompany loan of $20,000 by P to S.

Although our introduction to consolidated statements begins with the balance sheet, we shall briefly mention two other types of eliminating entries, which will be used often in the preparation of a consolidated income statement.

Eliminating Intercompany Revenues and Expenses. Affiliated companies often sell merchandise to one another or perform services for each other, thereby generating revenue and expense entries on the books of the participating firms. Consolidated statements, however, show revenues and expenses that arise through transactions with parties *outside* the affiliation. Furthermore, there is a double counting problem. Suppose P Company purchases goods in the open market and sells them to S Company. S subsequently sells the goods outside. In this case, purchases and sales have each been recorded twice within the P and S affiliation. Elimination of the intercompany purchase and sale means the consolidated revenue and expense accounts reflect only the transactions with outside parties.

Eliminating Unconfirmed Intercompany Gains and Losses. We have just discussed why the amounts recorded as revenues and expenses generated by intercompany transactions must be eliminated in consolidated statements. Unfortunately, intercompany revenue and expense transactions often lead to a second problem requiring treatment in consolidated statements. Suppose S Company purchases merchandise from P Company for $9,000—150 percent of the cost to P Company. At year-end, S Company's inventory includes $3,000 of this merchandise. The original cost to P was $2,000. Realization of the gain of $1,000 is not confirmed—there has been no sale outside the P and S affiliation—and it must be eliminated. The elimination will reduce both consolidated net income and consolidated inventory. In this way, we recognize the important **confirmation principle:** Gains and losses arising out of intercompany transactions are not recognized in consolidated net income until they are confirmed by transactions outside the affiliated group. These matters are discussed in detail in Chapters 9 and 10.

A Note on Our "Principles" of Consolidation. The overriding objective in the preparation of consolidated statements is to report the affairs of a group of affiliated corporations as if it were a single economic entity. Hence, the eliminations are designed to remove the effects of reported transactions and relationships between components of the entity. In this way, the financial statements for the consolidated entity are guided by the same accounting principles that guide any financial statement—namely, that information (revenues, expenses, gains, assets, liabilities, and so on) is reported based on transactions with outside parties. Our principles—substitution, confirmation, and removal of intercompany assets, liabilities, and revenues and expenses—are simply specific applications of the single-entity approach underlying consolidated statements. We use them to provide some structure to the various eliminations and, accordingly, view them as a learning device to complement, but not substitute for, an understanding of this single-entity concept.

Consolidated Balance Sheet at Date of Business Combination

In this section, we discuss the preparation of a consolidated balance sheet on the date that the business combination occurs. There are several cases to be considered.

1. Investment cost *equals* book value of the amount of S Company's stockholders' equity acquired. Although the book values of individual assets and liabilities could differ from their fair values, in presenting this case *we assume there are no such differences*. This assumption provides a convenient starting point for discussing the preparation of a consolidated balance sheet following a purchase combination or a pooling of interests. In a pooling, fair values are irrelevant and investment cost equals the book value of S Company's stockholders' equity by definition.

2. Investment cost is *greater than* the book value of S Company's stockholders' equity. This case arises only in business combinations accounted for as purchases and is referred to as a **purchase premium.**

3. Investment cost is *less than* the book value of S Company's stockholders' equity. This case also arises only in business combinations accounted for as purchases and is referred to as a **purchase discount.**

Many business combinations include subsidiaries that are not wholly owned by their parents. Consolidated statements including such subsidiaries will reflect the separate interests of shareholders outside of the controlling interest in the subsidiaries' net assets. An account entitled **Minority Interest in Subsidiary** will be used to reflect the equity interest of these outside shareholders. Because the existence of a minority interest is a complicating factor, we defer considering the consolidation of partially owned subsidiaries until later in the chapter and address consolidation of wholly owned subsidiaries first.

We assume that the date of business combination is January 1, 19X2, the beginning of Year 1, so that income statement issues can be safely postponed. The balance sheet of P Company at January 1, 19X2, *prior to the combination*

Exhibit 7.3 | **Precombination Balance Sheet of P Company at January 1, 19X2**

P COMPANY
BALANCE SHEET AT JANUARY 1, 19X2
(PRECOMBINATION)

ASSETS

Cash and Receivables		$ 800,000
Inventory		600,000
Buildings and Equipment	$ 4,000,000	
Less Accumulated Depreciation	(1,700,000)	2,300,000
Total Assets.		$3,700,000

LIABILITIES AND STOCKHOLDERS' EQUITY

Current Liabilities	$ 400,000
Other Liabilities	300,000
Common Stock, Par Value $7.50, Authorized 1,000,000 Shares, Issued and Outstanding 200,000 Shares . . .	1,500,000
Additional Paid-In Capital	900,000
Retained Earnings	600,000
Total Liabilities and Stockholders' Equity	$3,700,000

Exhibit 7.4 | **Balance Sheet of S Company at January 1, 19X2**

S COMPANY
BALANCE SHEET AT JANUARY 1, 19X2

ASSETS

Cash and Receivables		$ 100,000
Inventory		250,000
Buildings and Equipment	$1,000,000	
Less Accumulated Depreciation	(200,000)	800,000
Total Assets		$1,150,000

LIABILITIES AND STOCKHOLDERS' EQUITY

Current Liabilities	$ 200,000
Bonds Payable, 6%, Par Value $500,000	500,000
Common Stock, Par Value $1	100,000
Additional Paid-In Capital	125,000
Retained Earnings	225,000
Total Liabilities and Stockholders' Equity	$1,150,000

with S Company, appears in Exhibit 7.3 on the previous page. The balance sheet of S Company at the same date is given in Exhibit 7.4 on the previous page. The data in these two exhibits provide the basis for our balance sheet consolidations until we reach the purchase discount case.

Consolidated Balance Sheet at Date of Business Combination: P's Investment Cost Equals S's Book Value

This case assumes that P Company's investment cost equals the book value of the S Company stock acquired. Given our additional assumption that the book values of S's individual assets and liabilities equal their fair values, we may encounter this case in either a purchase or pooling combination. In a purchase combination, the amount recorded by P in the Investment in S account depends on the fair value of the consideration given by P in the combination. We assume here that this fair value equals the book value of the acquired portion of S's stockholders' equity.

Figure 7.1 **Diagrammatic Approach to Consolidating the Balance Sheets of P and S Companies When Investment Cost Equals Book Value (Purchase and Pooling of Interests Combination)**

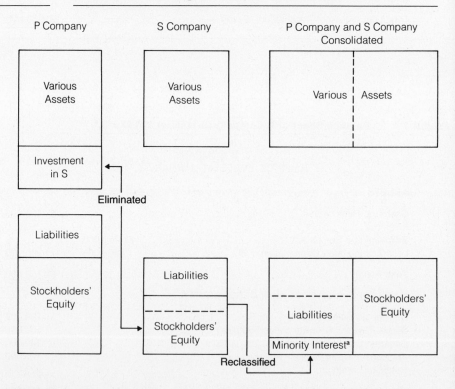

[a]If P owns 100 percent of the outstanding voting shares of S, the entire stockholders' equity of S is eliminated, and there is no minority interest.

In practice, such an equality is strictly coincidental. Under the pooling-of-interest rules, however, the amount recorded in the Investment in S account is *based* on the book value of the stockholders' equity of S acquired and will *always* be equal to it at date of combination.

Assuming no intercompany receivables and payables exist, consolidation requires a single eliminating entry. This entry applies the substitution principle and substitutes the underlying assets and liabilities of S for the Investment in S account. A diagram which visually portrays this process appears in Figure 7.1.

Purchase Combinations: S Company Wholly Owned. On January 1, 19X2, P Company acquires all the outstanding voting shares of S Company in an exchange of equity shares plus some contingent consideration based on postcombination earnings. The use of contingent consideration will cause this transaction to be accounted for as a purchase, *not* a pooling. P Company will issue 20,000 shares of its $7.50 par value stock to the *shareholders* of S Company in exchange for their 100,000 shares of S Company's outstanding stock. Market value of the 20,000 P Company shares is assumed to be $450,000. The stockholders' equity of S Company equals $450,000; we assume that the book values of S Company's assets and liabilities equal their fair values. It is important to recognize that the acquisition generates no entries on the books of S Company. The shares are acquired directly from S Company's shareholders and no resources flow in or out of S Company itself. P Company records the acquisition on its books with the following journal entry:

BOOKS OF P COMPANY

Investment in S	450,000	
Common Stock (20,000 × $7.50)		150,000
Additional Paid-In Capital		300,000

To record the acquisition of all 100,000 outstanding shares of S Company for 20,000 shares of P Company stock worth $450,000.

If a consolidated balance sheet is prepared immediately after the combination occurs, an eliminating entry is made on the consolidated financial statement working paper:

CONSOLIDATED FINANCIAL STATEMENT WORKING PAPER

Common Stock	100,000	
Additional Paid-In Capital	125,000	
Retained Earnings	225,000	
Investment in S		450,000

To eliminate the Investment in S account against the stockholders' equity accounts of S Company.

The resulting consolidated balance sheet is presented in Exhibit 7.5.

Pooling of Interests Combination: S Company Wholly Owned. Alternatively, P Company and S Company may decide against the contingent consideration and

| Exhibit 7.5 | P and S Companies: Consolidated Balance Sheet at January 1, 19X2 (Purchase Combination) |

P AND S COMPANIES
CONSOLIDATED BALANCE SHEET AT JANUARY 1, 19X2

ASSETS

Cash and Receivables		$ 900,000
Inventory		850,000
Plant and Equipment	$ 4,800,000	
Less Accumulated Depreciation	(1,700,000)	3,100,000
Total Assets.		$4,850,000

LIABILITIES AND STOCKHOLDERS' EQUITY

Current Liabilities	$ 600,000
Other Liabilities	300,000
Bonds Payable, 6%	500,000
Total Liabilities	$1,400,000
Common Stock, Par Value $7.50, Authorized 1,000,000 Shares, Issued and Outstanding 220,000 Shares	$1,650,000
Additional Paid-In Capital	1,200,000
Retained Earnings	600,000
Total Stockholders' Equity	$3,450,000
Total Liabilities and Stockholders' Equity	$4,850,000

pool their interests through the exchange of equity shares just described. P will issue 20,000 shares of its $7.50 par value stock to the shareholders of S. In recording this pooling combination, three items must be remembered:

1. The amount assigned to the Investment in S account reflects the book value of the stockholders' equity or net assets of S, $450,000 (the market value of the 20,000 shares of P Company stock is irrelevant).
2. The entries to paid-in capital (par value of common stock plus additional paid-in capital) should equal the total paid-in capital as recorded on the books of S Company, $225,000.
3. The retained earnings of S Company at date of combination ($225,000) become part of consolidated retained earnings and must be included when P Company records the combination.

Therefore, the journal entry we make on P Company's books to record the pooling is:

BOOKS OF P COMPANY

Investment in S	450,000	
Common Stock (20,000 × $7.50)		150,000
Additional Paid-In Capital ($225,000 − $150,000)		75,000
Retained Earnings		225,000

To record the acquisition of all the outstanding shares of S Company through the exchange of 20,000 P Company shares in a pooling of interests.

A consolidated balance sheet prepared for P Company and its new subsidiary, S Company, on January 1, 19X2, would require that the following eliminating entry be made on the consolidated financial statement working paper:

CONSOLIDATED FINANCIAL STATEMENT WORKING PAPER

Common Stock	100,000	
Additional Paid-In Capital	125,000	
Retained Earnings	225,000	
Investment in S		450,000

To eliminate the Investment in S account against the
stockholders' equity accounts of S Company.

In recording the pooling, the retained earnings of S are brought onto P's books. This procedure is consistent with the notion that a pooling unites previously separate stockholder interests. Since S's retained earnings are recorded by P, the working paper entry eliminates the retained earnings of S on S's separate statements. An alternative procedure is to record only the amount of S's paid-in capital accounts in the Investment in S account on P's books and sum the retained earnings of the two companies on the working paper. We do not use the alternative procedure in this book.

Observe that the investment elimination entries in the pooling and purchase cases are *identical*. Although this is coincidental in general, it is *not* coincidental here. *In both cases being examined,* the balance in the investment account *equals* the book value of S Company's stockholders' equity.

Consolidated Stockholders' Equity Accounts under Purchase and Pooling When S Company Is Wholly Owned. Even though the investment elimination entries made at date of business combination under purchase and pooling are the same, not all of the individual consolidated stockholders' equity accounts are. This is because the acquisition is recorded differently in the purchase and pooling cases. To see this, consider the comparison of the stockholders' equity accounts in Exhibit 7.6. We can make several observations:

1. Consolidated paid-in capital (par value of common stock plus additional paid-in capital) includes the market value of the shares issued in the purchase ($450,000) versus the book value of S's paid-in capital in the pooling ($225,000).
2. Consolidated retained earnings includes none of S Company's retained earnings in the purchase but all of S Company's retained earnings in the pooling.
3. Total consolidated stockholders' equity is the same in both the purchase and pooling cases because of our assumption that the investment cost equals the book value of the shares acquired. In general, total consolidated stockholders' equity differs under the two methods.
4. S Company's stockholders' equity accounts are unaffected by the acquisition in both cases.
5. Because S Company's stockholders' equity accounts are eliminated in consolidation, the consolidated stockholders' equity accounts are equal to P Company's stockholders' equity accounts after the acquisition.

Exhibit 7.6 **Comparison of Consolidated Stockholders' Equity Accounts in the Purchase and Pooling of Interests Cases**

PURCHASE: EXCHANGE OF SHARES

Stockholders' Equity Accounts	P before Acquisition	Acquisition Entry	P after Acquisition	S Company	Eliminations	Consolidated
Common Stock at Par .	$1,500,000	$150,000	$1,650,000	$100,000	$(100,000)	$1,650,000
Additional Paid-In Capital.	900,000	300,000	1,200,000	125,000	(125,000)	1,200,000
Retained Earnings. . .	600,000	—	600,000	225,000	(225,000)	600,000
Total.	$3,000,000	$450,000	$3,450,000	$450,000	$(450,000)	$3,450,000

POOLING: EXCHANGE OF SHARES

Stockholders' Equity Accounts	P before Acquisition	Acquisition Entry	P after Acquisition	S Company	Eliminations	Consolidated
Common Stock at Par .	$1,500,000	$150,000	$1,650,000	$100,000	$(100,000)	$1,650,000
Additional Paid-In Capital.	900,000	75,000	975,000	125,000	(125,000)	975,000
Retained Earnings. . .	600,000	225,000	825,000	225,000	(225,000)	825,000
Total.	$3,000,000	$450,000	$3,450,000	$450,000	$(450,000)	$3,450,000

Purchase Combination: S Company Partially Owned. As previously mentioned, failure to acquire all of S Company's outstanding shares means that a group of *minority shareholders,* separate from the controlling shareholders of P Company, continues to have an equity interest in S Company. In making the investment elimination entry, then, the entire stockholders' equity of S Company is not eliminated against the Investment in S account. Rather, the portion which pertains to the shares owned by the minority shareholders is reclassified and reported as **Minority Interest in Subsidiary** in the consolidated balance sheet. This latter point can be seen by referring to Figure 7.1; the portion of S Company's stockholders' equity *above* the dashed line represents the equity attributable to those shares not held by P Company and is appropriately reclassified as minority interest.

Suppose P Company acquires 90 percent ($\alpha = .9$) of S Company's outstanding shares by issuing 18,000 shares of its own stock (having a market value of $405,000) and agreeing to an earnings contingency. The journal entry made by P to record the acquisition is:

BOOKS OF P COMPANY

```
Investment in S . . . . . . . . . . . . . . . . . . . . . . . .  405,000
    Common Stock (18,000 × $7.50) . . . . . . . . . . . . .              135,000
    Additional Paid-In Capital . . . . . . . . . . . . . . . . .              270,000
To record the acquisition of 90,000 shares of S Company for
18,000 shares of P Company stock worth $405,000.
```

We begin by illustrating the investment elimination in this case with *two working paper entries*. The first entry *eliminates* the Investment in S account against P Company's share (90 percent) of S Company's stockholders' equity. The second entry *reclassifies* the remaining 10 percent of S's stockholders' equity as Minority Interest in S.

CONSOLIDATED FINANCIAL STATEMENT WORKING PAPER

Common Stock (.9 × $100,000)   90,000
Additional Paid-In Capital (.9 × $125,000)   112,500
Retained Earnings (.9 × $225,000).   202,500
    Investment in S.   405,000
To eliminate the Investment in S against 90 percent of the
stockholders' equity accounts of S Company.

Common Stock (.1 × $100,000)   10,000
Additional Paid-In Capital (.1 × $125,000)   12,500
Retained Earnings (.1 × $225,000).   22,500
    Minority Interest in S   45,000
To reclassify as minority interest the remaining balances in S
Company's stockholders' equity accounts which pertain to
outstanding shares not owned by P Company.

Throughout the subsequent consolidation material, however, we use a single entry to eliminate the investment account and establish the minority interest. Thus the above two entries are combined into the following single eliminating entry:

CONSOLIDATED FINANCIAL STATEMENT WORKING PAPER

Common Stock   100,000
Additional Paid-In Capital   125,000
Retained Earnings   225,000
    Investment in S.   405,000
    Minority Interest in S   45,000
To eliminate the Investment in S against 90 percent of the
stockholders' equity accounts of S Company and to reclassify
the remaining 10 percent as minority interest.

Pooling of Interests Combination: S Company Partially Owned. For the combination to qualify as a pooling, at least 90 percent of S Company's shares must be exchanged for shares of P Company. If we now assume that the earnings contingency is removed from the combination plan, we may proceed with a pooling in which 18,000 shares of P's stock are exchanged for 90,000 shares of S's stock.

BOOKS OF P COMPANY

Investment in S [.9($100,000 + $125,000 + $225,000)]   405,000
    Common Stock (18,000 × $7.50)   135,000
    Additional Paid-In Capital [.9($100,000 + $125,000) −
      $135,000].   67,500
    Retained Earnings (.9 × $225,000).   202,500
To record the acquisition of 90,000 shares of S Company stock
through the exchange of 18,000 shares of P Company stock in
a pooling of interests.

Moving to the consolidated financial statement working paper, we use a single entry to accomplish investment elimination and minority interest reclassification:

CONSOLIDATED FINANCIAL STATEMENT WORKING PAPER

Common Stock	100,000	
Additional Paid-In Capital	125,000	
Retained Earnings	225,000	
Investment in S		405,000
Minority Interest in S		45,000

To eliminate the Investment in S against 90 percent of the stockholders' equity accounts of S Company and to reclassify the remaining 10 percent as minority interest.

Nature and Disclosure of Minority Interest. The problem with **minority interest** arises, it seems to us, for two reasons. *First,* minority shareholders do not have a proportional interest in specific assets but rather in the subsidiary as a whole. In other words, the interests of the majority and minority shareholders in the subsidiary's net assets are *inseparable*. One cannot be factored out from the other, and the total net assets must equal all stockholders' equity. *Second,* the parent company controls 100 percent of the net assets of the subsidiary by virtue of its ownership of more than 50 percent of S's shares. Thus there exists an arithmetic gap between the net assets *controlled* and the net assets *owned*. This gap is filled by the minority interest, and its disclosure is important because it defines the extent of the stockholders' equity of the controlling interest.

Nevertheless, it may not be obvious where the minority interest is to be found in published consolidated balance sheets. Both theoretical issues and methods adopted in practice affect placement of the minority interest among the liabilities and stockholders' equity accounts. There seem to be three possibilities:

1. Report the minority interest as a noncurrent liability, perhaps of indeterminate term. According to *Accounting Trends and Techniques,* of 594 firms issuing consolidated statements in 1982, 137 included minority interest among the noncurrent liabilities; of 591 in 1981, 138 did so.[4]
2. Report the minority interest in a separate caption between noncurrent liabilities and stockholders' equity.
3. Report the minority interest as part of consolidated stockholders' equity.

Accounting Trends and Techniques does not indicate the proportions of its survey companies which treat minority interest in the manner suggested in No. 2 or No. 3 above. Nevertheless, approximately 77 percent of the companies surveyed did not report the minority interest as a noncurrent liability. We prefer to see minority interest clearly disclosed within consolidated stockholders' equity (No. 3 above). The reasons for our preference are discussed in detail later in this chapter, in the "Alternative Consolidation Theories" section.

---

[4]American Institute of Certified Public Accountants, *Accounting Trends and Techniques* (New York: AICPA, 1983), 49, 202.

Consolidated Balance Sheet at Date of Business Combination: Purchase Premium

In a purchase combination, the surrender of consideration which has a fair value in excess of the acquired stockholders' equity of S Company indicates that a *purchase premium* has been paid by P Company. We addressed the accounting treatment of this premium in the previous chapter as part of our discussion of statutory mergers accounted for as purchases. Our objective was to allocate the cost of the investment to the identifiable assets and liabilities of the acquired company. Any premium unallocated in this way is recorded as an unspecified intangible asset, goodwill.

Accounting for a stock acquisition differs from that for a statutory merger in that the acquired company does not lose its legal identity. Further, the cost of the investment is not directly allocated among the assets and liabilities of S Company by a journal entry on P Company's books. Rather, in a *stock acquisition, the allocation of investment cost* among the assets and liabilities of S Company generally takes place *only on the consolidated statement working paper*.[5] In this way, the new basis of accountability established by the fair value of the consideration given in the acquisition of S Company is reported on the consolidated balance sheet.

If a consolidated balance sheet is prepared immediately following the stock acquisition and a purchase premium exists, three working paper entries are required.

1. Remove the excess of investment cost over book value of S's shares from the Investment in S account and reclassify it as Purchase Premium.
2. Allocate the purchase premium among the identifiable assets and liabilities of S Company in accordance with their fair values, assigning any amount unallocated in this way to goodwill. If negative goodwill exists, it must be allocated using the two-stage allocation process discussed later.
3. Eliminate the Investment in S account, now adjusted to the book value of the S Company shares owned, against the stockholders' equity accounts of S Company and, if appropriate, recognize the existence of a minority interest by reclassifying the remaining stockholders' equity of S as Minority Interest in S.

These procedures are diagramed in Figure 7.2.

Purchase Premium: S Company Wholly Owned. When we dealt with recording the business combination of Companies P and S in the last chapter, we compared the estimated fair values of S Company's assets and liabilities with their book values, as shown in Exhibit 7.7.

---

[5]See the section " 'Push-Down' Accounting" later in this chapter for possible exceptions to this general rule.

Figure 7.2 **Diagrammatic Approach to Consolidating the Balance Sheets of P and S Companies When a Purchase Premium Exists (Purchase Combinations Only)**

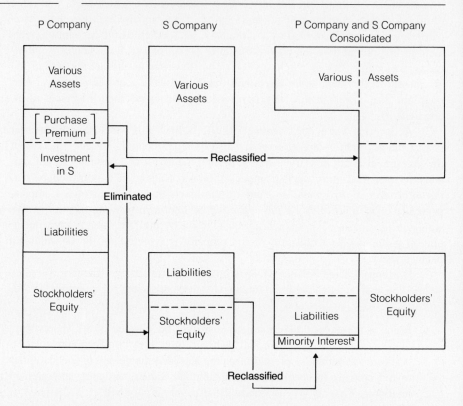

[a]If P owns 100 percent of the outstanding voting shares of S, the entire stockholders' equity of S is eliminated, and there is no minority interest.

P Company acquires all the outstanding shares of S Company through an exchange of equity shares and a cash payment. S Company shareholders receive $200,000 cash and 70,000 shares of P Company stock worth $700,000. Out-of-pocket costs incurred by P in connection with the stock acquisition amount to $40,000, as follows:

Registration and Issue Costs $15,000
Consultants' and Attorneys' Fees   25,000
Total Out-of-Pocket Costs of Stock Acquisition $40,000

In conformance to the rules stated in *APBO 16,* the registration and issue costs have no net effect on the cost of the acquisition. Their incurrence simply decreases the additional paid-in capital otherwise recorded. In contrast, the con-

Exhibit 7.9	**Working Paper Entries to Consolidate P and S Companies ($\alpha = 1$; Purchase Premium = \$475,000)**

CONSOLIDATED FINANCIAL STATEMENT WORKING PAPER

Purchase Premium	475,000	
Investment in S		475,000

To reclassify amount paid by P in excess of book value of S Company's shares as a purchase premium.

Inventory	125,000	
Buildings and Equipment, Net	160,000	
Discount on Bonds Payable	100,000	
Goodwill	90,000	
Purchase Premium		475,000

To allocate the purchase premium paid for S Company's shares among the assets and liabilities of S Company and goodwill according to Exhibit 7.8.

Common Stock	100,000	
Additional Paid-In Capital	125,000	
Retained Earnings	225,000	
Investment in S		450,000

To eliminate the Investment in S against the stockholders' equity accounts of S Company.

> Payment of a purchase premium in a less-than-100-percent stock acquisition results in reporting the *parent's share (α)* of S's assets and liabilities at their *fair values* in a consolidated balance sheet and the minority's share at book value. The amount of *minority interest* reported is derived from the *book value* of S's net assets and is not imputed from the purchase premium paid by P. Any unspecified intangibles *(goodwill)* established by the purchase premium relate solely to the *controlling interest*.

Before proceeding, we use a short numerical example to clarify this treatment. Suppose A pays \$800,000 for 80 percent of B's outstanding voting shares ($\alpha = .8$). The net assets of B Company have a book value of \$700,000 and a fair value of \$900,000. Therefore,

Purchase premium = Investment cost − α(Book value of B's net assets)

Purchase premium = \$800,000 − .8(\$700,000)

Purchase premium = \$240,000.

Of this \$240,000, \$160,000 [= .8(\$900,000 − \$700,000)] is allocated to the identifiable assets of B, and \$80,000 (= \$240,000 − \$160,000) to goodwill on the consolidated balance sheet. The minority interest is reported as \$140,000 (= .2 × \$700,000). *Only the controlling interest's portion* of the assets and liabilities of B included in consolidated totals *is recorded at fair value;* the minority interest's portion is recorded at book value.

Returning to the acquisition of S Company, we now assume that P Company acquired 80 percent of the outstanding voting shares at a total cost of $740,000. Stock worth $560,000 and $160,000 cash were given to the shareholders of S Company. Registration and issue costs amounted to $12,000; consultants' and attorneys' fees were $20,000.

BOOKS OF P COMPANY

Investment in S	740,000	
Cash		192,000
Common Stock (56,000 × $7.50)		420,000
Additional Paid-In Capital		128,000

To record the acquisition of 80 percent of the outstanding common stock of S Company. Consideration to the former shareholders of S Company included cash of $160,000 and 56,000 shares of P Company $7.50 par value stock with a market value of $560,000. Registration and issue costs of $12,000, which were paid in cash, are netted against Additional Paid-In Capital. Direct costs associated with this acquisition were consultants' and attorneys' fees of $20,000. They were paid in cash and are part of the total investment cost of $740,000.

Exhibit 7.10	**Determination and Allocation of the Purchase Premium Paid by P Company in the January 1, 19X2, Acquisition of S Company (80 Percent)**

Cost of the Acquisition:

Fair Value of Stock Given	$560,000
Cash Given	160,000
Direct Costs Incurred (Consultants' and Attorneys' Fees)	20,000
Total Cost of Acquisition.	$740,000

Book Value of the Net Assets or Stockholders' Equity Acquired (80%):

Common Stock	$80,000
Additional Paid-In Capital	100,000
Retained Earnings	180,000
Total Book Value of S Company (80%)	$360,000
Purchase Premium.	$380,000

Assets and Liabilities of S Company	Fair Value	Book Value	Fair Value Less Book Value	Allocation Based on P's Interest (80%)
Cash and Receivables.	$ 100,000	$ 100,000	—	—
Inventory.	375,000	250,000	$125,000	$100,000
Buildings and Equipment, Net	960,000	800,000	160,000	128,000
Current Liabilities	(200,000)	(200,000)	—	—
Bonds Payable, 6%	(400,000)	(500,000)	100,000	80,000
	$ 835,000	$ 450,000	$385,000	$308,000
Goodwill				72,000
Total Purchase Premium				$380,000

Exhibit 7.11	**Working Paper Entries to Consolidate P and S Companies** ($\alpha = .8$; Purchase Premium = \$380,000)

CONSOLIDATED FINANCIAL STATEMENT WORKING PAPER

Purchase Premium.	380,000	
Investment in S		380,000

To reclassify amount paid by P in excess of book value of the 80 percent of S Company's shares acquired as a purchase premium.

Inventory.	100,000	
Buildings and Equipment, Net	128,000	
Discount on Bonds Payable	80,000	
Goodwill	72,000	
Purchase Premium		380,000

To allocate the purchase premium paid for S Company's shares among the assets and liabilities of S Company and goodwill according to Exhibit 7.10.

Common Stock	100,000	
Additional Paid-In Capital	125,000	
Retained Earnings	225,000	
Investment in S		360,000
Minority Interest in S.		90,000

To eliminate the Investment in S against 80 percent of the stockholders' equity accounts of S Company and to reclassify the remaining 20 percent of the stockholders' equity accounts of S Company as minority interest.

Determination and allocation of the purchase premium is given in Exhibit 7.10. The working paper eliminations are presented in Exhibit 7.11.

Consolidated Balance Sheet at Date of Business Combination: Purchase Discount

A *purchase discount* exists when the cost of P's investment in S is less than the book value of the shares acquired. As in the case of a purchase premium, the discount must be allocated among the assets and liabilities of the subsidiary. While the discount allocation could imply the existence of positive goodwill (an unallocated debit balance), the more likely result is an unallocated credit balance, commonly referred to as *negative goodwill*. This negative goodwill must then be allocated among the subsidiary's noncurrent assets—except long-term investments in marketable securities—in accordance with their relative fair values. Thus the procedure for allocating a purchase discount with negative goodwill is somewhat more complex than the typical purchase premium allocation involving positive goodwill. In the premium case with positive goodwill, the goodwill remains and is amortized in subsequent periods. In contrast, none of the negative goodwill arising in a purchase discount (or occasionally in a purchase premium) remains unless the subsidiary has no noncurrent assets to which it can be allocated. Unallocated negative goodwill appears in the consolidated balance sheet as a deferred

| **Figure 7.3** | **Diagrammatic Approach to Consolidating the Balance Sheets of P and T Companies When a Purchase Discount Exists (Purchase Combinations Only)** |

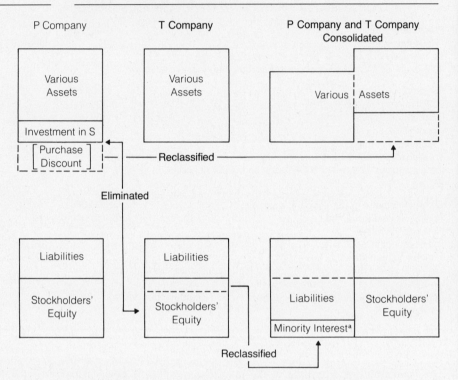

[a]If P owns 100 percent of the outstanding voting shares of T, the entire stockholders' equity of T is eliminated, and there is no minority interest.

credit and is amortized into income by the straight-line method over a period not to exceed 40 years.

We first encountered the purchase discount case with negative goodwill in Chapter 6, when the statutory merger of companies P and T took place; we followed the allocation among T's assets and liabilities in Exhibit 6.7 and related schedules. In the stock acquisition case which we are now addressing, however, the purchase discount is allocated only on the consolidated financial statement working paper. A diagram of this process appears in Figure 7.3.

Purchase Discount: T Company Wholly Owned. We now consider the acquisition of T Company at a purchase discount. The book value of T Company's stockholders' equity is $1,150,000. To acquire the shares of T, P Company issues stock worth $880,000 and pays cash of $120,000. Registration and issue costs were $20,000 and direct costs were $40,000; all were paid in cash. P makes the following journal entry on its books:

BOOKS OF P COMPANY

```
Investment in T . . . . . . . . . . . . . . . . . . . . . . . .    1,040,000
    Cash . . . . . . . . . . . . . . . . . . . . . . . . . . .                    180,000
    Common Stock (88,000 × $7.50)  . . . . . . . . . . . . .                      660,000
    Additional Paid-In Capital . . . . . . . . . . . . . . . .                    200,000
```
To record the acquisition of all the outstanding common stock
of T Company. Consideration to the former shareholders of T
included cash of $120,000 and 88,000 shares of P Company
$7.50 par value stock with a market value of $880,000.
Registration and issue costs of $20,000, which were paid in
cash, are netted against Additional Paid-In Capital. Direct
costs associated with this acquisition were consultants' and
attorneys' fees of $40,000. They were paid in cash and are
part of the total investment cost of $1,040,000.

Thus the shares of T are acquired at a purchase discount of $110,000 ($= \$1,150,000 - \$1,040,000$). The initial allocation of the purchase discount is illustrated in Exhibit 7.12. Following *APBO 16*,[7] we now allocate the negative goodwill to T Company's Land, and Buildings and Equipment. This is the second stage of the two-stage allocation process developed in Chapter 6. Exhibit 7.12 indicates that Land, and Buildings and Equipment, have book values of $200,000 and $1,200,000 and fair values of $400,000 and $1,200,000, respectively. The tentative fair value adjustment of $200,000 allocated to these two accounts in Exhibit 7.12 will be reduced to $120,000 by the negative goodwill of $80,000. This is discussed next.

Since preparation of consolidated statements starts with the book values of T's land, and buildings and equipment items, *only the final purchase premium or discount allocation is entered on the working paper*. The next schedule is used to compute this final allocation. This is somewhat different from the approach developed in Chapter 6, where we computed the total cost assigned to these items, which was recorded in a journal entry on P's books and did not separately identify the increment or decrement to book value. In the present case, we calculate this increment or decrement which is to be entered on the working paper.

	(1)	(2)	(3)	(4)	(5)
	Fair Value		**Allocation of Negative Goodwill**	**Tentative Purchase Discount Allocation**	**Final Allocation**
	Amount	**Percent**	**[(2) × $80,000]**	**(Ex. 7.12)**	**(4) − (3)**
Land	$ 400,000	25%	$20,000	$200,000	$180,000
Buildings and Equipment, Net	1,200,000	75	60,000	—	(60,000)
	$1,600,000	100%	$80,000	$200,000	$120,000

Consolidating P and T requires three working paper entries, given in Exhibit 7.13. The first entry, which reclassifies the purchase discount, deserves some ex-

---

[7]Accounting Principles Board, *Opinion No. 16*, "Business Combinations" (New York: AICPA, 1970), par. 91; CT § B50.145.

Exhibit 7.12	Determination and Allocation of the Purchase Discount Realized by P Company in the January 1, 19X2, Acquisition of T Company (100 Percent)

Cost of Acquisition:
Fair Value of Stock Given	$ 880,000
Cash Given.	120,000
Direct Costs Incurred	40,000
Total Cost of Acquisition	$1,040,000

Book Value of Net Assets or Stockholders' Equity Acquired:
Common Stock	$ 250,000
Additional Paid-In Capital	400,000
Retained Earnings	500,000
Total Book Value of T Company	$1,150,000
Purchase Discount	$ (110,000)

Assets and Liabilities of T Company	Fair Value	Book Value	Fair Value Less Book Value	Allocation Based on P's Interest (100%)
Cash and Receivables	$ 150,000	$ 150,000	—	—
Marketable Equity Securities—				
Current	120,000	100,000	$ 20,000	$ 20,000
Inventory	350,000	300,000	50,000	50,000
Marketable Equity Securities—				
Long-Term	600,000	500,000	100,000	100,000
Land	400,000	200,000	200,000	200,000
Buildings and Equipment, Net	1,200,000	1,200,000	—	—
Current Liabilities	(500,000)	(500,000)	—	—
Other Liabilities	(1,200,000)	(800,000)	(400,000)	(400,000)
	$ 1,120,000	$1,150,000	$ (30,000)	$ (30,000)
Negative Goodwill				(80,000)
Total Purchase Discount				$(110,000)

planation. Since the purchase discount has a credit balance, recording it on the working paper requires that some account be debited. The account to be debited is Investment in T. By so doing, the balance in the Investment in T is increased up to the book value of T Company's stockholders' equity so that it can be cleanly eliminated. In contrast, reclassification of a purchase premium decreases the balance in the Investment in T account so that it equals the book value of the subsidiary's stockholders' equity.

Purchase Discount: T Company Partially Owned. The final case of consolidation at date of acquisition involves companies P and T, with a minority interest present. The entries are familiar by now, so we shall illustrate this case using a consolidated balance sheet working paper. We assume that P has acquired 80 percent (α = .8) of the outstanding voting shares of T Company for stock and cash at a total cost of $832,000. The book value of 80 percent of T's stockholders'

Exhibit 7.13	**Working Paper Entries to Consolidate P and T Companies ($\alpha = 1$; Purchase Discount = \$110,000)**

CONSOLIDATED FINANCIAL STATEMENT WORKING PAPER

Investment in T	110,000	
Purchase Discount		110,000
To recognize the purchase discount implicit in the Investment in T by increasing the Investment in T to the book value of T Company's stockholders' equity.		
Marketable Equity Securities—Current	20,000	
Inventory	50,000	
Marketable Equity Securities—Long-Term	100,000	
Land	180,000	
Purchase Discount	110,000	
Buildings and Equipment (Net)		60,000
Other Liabilities		400,000
To allocate the purchase discount related to the acquisition of T Company among the assets and liabilities of T, in accordance with Exhibit 7.12 and the second stage of the allocation process applied to Buildings and Equipment, and Land.		
Common Stock	250,000	
Additional Paid-In Capital	400,000	
Retained Earnings	500,000	
Investment in T		1,150,000
To eliminate the Investment in T against the stockholders' equity accounts of T Company.		

equity is $920,000$ ($= .8 \times \$1,150,000$), implying a purchase discount of $88,000. P records the acquisition as follows:

BOOKS OF P COMPANY

Investment in T	832,000	
Cash		144,000
Common Stock (70,400 × \$7.50)		528,000
Additional Paid-In Capital		160,000
To record the acquisition of 80 percent of the outstanding common stock of T Company. The former shareholders of T received cash of \$96,000 and 70,400 shares of P Company \$7.50 par value stock with a market value of \$704,000. Registration and issue costs of \$16,000, which were paid in cash, are netted against Additional Paid-In Capital. Direct costs associated with this acquisition were consultants' and attorneys' fees of \$32,000. They were paid in cash and are part of the total investment cost of \$832,000.		

The \$88,000 purchase discount includes some negative goodwill. Accordingly, the allocation is handled in the two-stage process. The first stage, the analysis of book and fair values of T's assets and liabilities, appears below:

Assets and Liabilities of T Company	Fair Value	Book Value	Fair Value Less Book Value	Allocation Based on P's Interest (80%)
Cash and Receivables	$ 150,000	$ 150,000	—	—
Marketable Equity Securities—				
Current	120,000	100,000	$ 20,000	$ 16,000
Inventory	350,000	300,000	50,000	40,000
Marketable Equity Securities—				
Long-Term	600,000	500,000	100,000	80,000
Land	400,000	200,000	200,000	160,000
Buildings and Equipment, Net.	1,200,000	1,200,000	—	—
Current Liabilities	(500,000)	(500,000)	—	—
Other Liabilities	(1,200,000)	(800,000)	(400,000)	(320,000)
	$ 1,120,000	$1,150,000	$ (30,000)	$ (24,000)
Negative Goodwill				(64,000)
Total Purchase Discount				$ (88,000)

The negative goodwill of $64,000 is now allocated among Buildings and Equipment and Land, the components of T's Plant and Equipment account, in proportion to their relative fair values. This is the second stage of the purchase discount allocation process; it is shown below:

	(1) Percent of Fair Value	(2) Allocation of Negative Goodwill [(1) × $64,000]	(3) Tentative Purchase Discount Allocation	(4) Final Allocation [(3) − (2)]
Land	25%	$16,000	$160,000	$144,000
Buildings and Equipment .	75	48,000	—	(48,000)
Total	100%	$64,000	$160,000	$ 96,000

The consolidation of P and T appears in Exhibit 7.14. P Company's balance sheet data, drawn from those given in Exhibit 7.3, are updated in this exhibit for the acquisition entry just recorded. A formal consolidated balance sheet is shown in Exhibit 7.15.

Alternative Consolidation Theories

In this section we compare three alternative consolidation theories and apply them to a numerical example. This textbook's approach to consolidations is based on the parent theory of consolidated statements, which is discussed first.

Parent Theory of Consolidated Statements

Generally accepted consolidation practices are derived from the **parent theory of consolidated statements,** which considers consolidated statements to be nothing

Exhibit 7.14 P and T Companies:
Consolidated Balance Sheet Working Paper at January 1, 19X2
(80 Percent; Purchase Discount = $88,000)

ASSETS	P Company	T Company	Adjustments and Eliminations Dr.		Adjustments and Eliminations Cr.		P and T Consolidated
Cash and Receivables	656,000	150,000					806,000
Marketable Equity							
Securities—Current	—	100,000	(2)	16,000			116,000
Inventory	600,000	300,000	(2)	40,000			940,000
Marketable Equity							
Securities—Long-Term	—	500,000	(2)	80,000			580,000
Land	—	200,000	(2)	144,000			344,000
Buildings and Equipment	4,000,000	1,200,000			(2)	48,000	5,152,000
Accumulated							
Depreciation	(1,700,000)	—					(1,700,000)
Investment in T	832,000	—	(1)	88,000	(3)	920,000	—
Purchase Discount	—	—	(2)	88,000	(1)	88,000	—
Total Assets	4,388,000	2,450,000		456,000		1,056,000	6,238,000

LIABILITIES AND STOCKHOLDERS' EQUITY

	P Company	T Company	Dr.		Cr.		P and T Consolidated
Current Liabilities	400,000	500,000					900,000
Other Liabilities	300,000	800,000			(2)	320,000	1,420,000
Common Stock—P	2,028,000	—					2,028,000
Common Stock—T	—	250,000	(3)	250,000			—
APIC—P	1,060,000	—					1,060,000
APIC—T	—	400,000	(3)	400,000			—
Retained Earnings—P	600,000	—					600,000
Retained Earnings—T	—	500,000	(3)	500,000			—
Minority Interest in T	—	—			(3)	230,000	230,000
Total Liabilities and Stockholders' Equity	4,388,000	2,450,000		1,150,000		550,000	6,238,000

Explanations of Working Paper Entries

(1) To recognize the purchase discount implicit in the Investment in T by increasing the Investment in T to 80 percent of the book value of T Company's stockholders' equity.

(2) To allocate the purchase discount related to the acquisition of T Company among the assets and liabilities of T. The amounts allocated to Buildings and Equipment and to Land are from the second stage of the allocation process.

(3) To eliminate the Investment in T against 80 percent of the stockholders' equity accounts of T Company and to reclassify the remaining 20 percent of the stockholders' equity of T Company as minority interest.

Exhibit 7.15 **P and T Companies: Formal Consolidated Balance Sheet at January 1, 19X2 (80 Percent)**

P AND T COMPANIES
CONSOLIDATED BALANCE SHEET AT JANUARY 1, 19X2
$(\alpha = .8)$

ASSETS

Cash and Receivables		$ 806,000
Marketable Equity Securities—Current		116,000
Inventory		940,000
Total Current Assets		$1,862,000
Marketable Equity Securities—Long-Term		$ 580,000
Land		344,000
Buildings and Equipment	$ 5,152,000	
Less Accumulated Depreciation	(1,700,000)	3,452,000
Total Noncurrent Assets		$4,376,000
Total Assets		$6,238,000

LIABILITIES AND STOCKHOLDERS' EQUITY

Current Liabilities		$ 900,000
Other Liabilities		1,420,000
Total Liabilities		$2,320,000
Minority Interest in T		$ 230,000
Common Stock		2,028,000
Additional Paid-In Capital		1,060,000
Retained Earnings		600,000
Total Stockholders' Equity		$3,918,000
Total Liabilities and Stockholders' Equity		$6,238,000

more than an extension of parent company statements. The consolidated statements are not intended to be of significant benefit to minority shareholders, and the cost principle is followed in that only the parent's share of the assets acquired and liabilities assumed is reported at the fair value evidenced by the parent's cost. Minority shareholders are viewed more as creditors of the controlling interest than as part owners of the combined enterprise. Major characteristics of the *parent theory* are:

1. Fair values are assigned only to the portion (α) of the subsidiary's assets and liabilities owned by the parent. The minority interest's share of those assets and liabilities is carried at original book value in the consolidated statements.
2. Goodwill reported in consolidation pertains only to the controlling interest; none relates to the minority interest.

3. Minority Interest in S reflects the minority's share of the *book value* of the subsidiary's stockholders' equity.
4. Minority Interest in S will likely appear under the Noncurrent Liabilities heading in the consolidated balance sheet. Consolidated stockholders' equity relates only to the controlling interest.

Entity Theory of Consolidated Statements

The **entity theory of consolidated statements** is the most important theoretical alternative to the parent theory of consolidated statements. It holds that consolidated statements should reflect the viewpoint of the *total business entity*[8] and not overemphasize the controlling interest's perspective. The subsidiary's resources controlled by the consolidated entity relate to both the majority and minority shareholders and, in consolidated statements, both sets of interests must be valued consistently. Accordingly, the *total* fair value of the subsidiary implied by the cost of the parent's fractional interest is recognized. Under this view:

1. Fair values are assigned to *all* of the subsidiary's assets and liabilities, including the portion attributable to the minority shareholders.
2. Goodwill is derived from the *total fair value* of the subsidiary, which is inferred from the price paid by the parent for its fractional interest and pertains to both majority and minority shareholders.
3. Minority Interest in S reflects the minority's share of the *total fair value* of the subsidiary's stockholders' equity.
4. Minority Interest in S is separately disclosed and included within consolidated stockholders' equity.

Modified Entity Theory

A third approach to the measurement of the subsidiary's assets and liabilities and of the minority interest in a consolidated balance sheet focuses on the nature of goodwill. Under this approach, which we call the **modified entity theory,** the identifiable assets and liabilities of S are recorded at their total fair values in the consolidated balance sheet, and the appropriate portion is reflected in the minority interest. The existence of goodwill, however, is believed to be evidence of value which will accrue only to the parent by virtue of its control over the subsidiary. Thus the goodwill does not relate to the subsidiary standing alone and hence does not relate to the minority interest. In the consolidated balance sheet, Minority Interest in S is likely to be found either as part of noncurrent liabilities or as a separate caption between noncurrent liabilities and stockholders' equity.

Illustration of the Alternative Consolidation Theories

Consider the example in Exhibit 7.10 where P Company acquired 80 percent of S Company for a total cost of $740,000. Eighty percent of S's stockholders' equity

---

[8]A comprehensive development of this view of consolidated statements can be found in Maurice Moonitz, *The Entity Theory of Consolidated Statements,* American Accounting Association Monograph No. 4 (Evanston: American Accounting Association, 1944).

amounted to $360,000 (= .8 × $450,000), implying a purchase premium of $380,000 paid by P for the 80 percent interest. Since we use the *parent theory* in this textbook, the results in Exhibits 7.10 and 7.11 apply. S Company's identifiable assets and liabilities will be reported at a net of $758,000. This consists of S's book value of $450,000 plus 80 percent of the excess of fair value over book value, $308,000 (= .8 × $385,000); equivalently, it is 80 percent of the fair value of S Company's net assets, $668,000 (= .8 × $385,000) plus 20 percent of the book value, $90,000 (= .2 × $450,000). The goodwill of $72,000 pertains only to the controlling interest and the minority interest is $90,000 (= .2 × $450,000), 20 percent of the book value of S's net assets. Under the *entity theory,* the implied total fair value of S is computed by "grossing up" the price paid by P for its partial interest, α:

> Fair value of S Company = Price paid by P Company/α

Equivalently, P's purchase premium could be "grossed up" to compute the total premium implied if *all* of S's shares had been purchased:

> Total purchase premium = P's purchase premium/α

Thus the fair value of S Company as a whole is inferred to be $925,000 (= $740,000/.8) and the implied total purchase premium to be $475,000 (= $380,000/.8). S Company's identifiable assets and liabilities will be reported at their net fair value of $835,000 (see Exhibit 7.10). Goodwill of $90,000 is determined either by "grossing up" the controlling interest's goodwill ($90,000 = $72,000/.8) or by subtracting the fair value of S's identifiable net assets from the implied fair value of S Company as a whole ($90,000 = $925,000 − $835,000). Minority interest is stated at $185,000 (= .2 × $925,000).

Under the *modified entity theory,* the total fair value of S Company ($925,000) is irrelevant. Instead, the total fair value of S's net assets— $835,000—is reported, the minority interest is stated at $167,000 (= .2 × $835,000), and only the controlling interest's goodwill—$72,000—is reported.

With the use of the data from Exhibits 7.10 and 7.11 and the calculations above, the working paper entries and incremental consolidated balance sheet effects called for by the three consolidation theories are presented in Exhibit 7.16. Note that in the second entry in this exhibit the amount credited to Minority Interest in S under the entity and modified entity theories is the minority's share of the *excess* of fair value over book value. This excess relates to identifiable net assets and goodwill in the entity theory and only to identifiable net assets in the modified entity theory.

Exhibit 7.16 **Working Paper Eliminations to Consolidate P and S Companies and Incremental Effects on the Consolidated Balance Sheet under Alternative Consolidation Theories**

CONSOLIDATED FINANCIAL STATEMENT WORKING PAPER

	Parent Theory (Textbook Approach)		Entity Theory		Modified Entity Theory	
	Dr.	Cr.	Dr.	Cr.	Dr.	Cr.
Purchase Premium . .	380,000		380,000		380,000	
Investment in S . . .		380,000		380,000		380,000
Inventory	100,000		125,000		125,000	
Buildings and Equipment						
(Net)	128,000		160,000		160,000	
Discount on Bonds						
Payable.	80,000		100,000		100,000	
Goodwill.	72,000		90,000		72,000	
Purchase Premium		380,000		380,000		380,000
Minority Interest in S		—		95,000		77,000
Common Stock	100,000		100,000		100,000	
Additional Paid-In						
Capital	125,000		125,000		125,000	
Retained Earnings. . .	225,000		225,000		225,000	
Investment in S . . .		360,000		360,000		360,000
Minority Interest						
in S.		90,000		90,000		90,000

INCREMENTAL EFFECT OF INCLUDING S COMPANY IN CONSOLIDATED BALANCE SHEET

ASSETS	Parent Theory (Textbook Approach)	Entity Theory	Modified Entity Theory
Cash and Receivables	100,000	100,000	100,000
Inventory	350,000	375,000	375,000
Buildings and Equipment (Net) .	828,000	860,000	860,000
Goodwill	72,000	90,000	72,000

LIABILITIES AND STOCKHOLDERS' EQUITY

Current Liabilities	200,000	200,000	200,000
Bonds Payable, 6%	500,000	500,000	500,000
Discount on Bonds Payable . .	(80,000)	(100,000)	(100,000)
Minority Interest in S	90,000	185,000	167,000

Authors' Evaluation

While the *parent theory* predominates in practice today, the *modified entity theory* is also acceptable. When discussing the allocation of investment cost among assets acquired and liabilities assumed, *APBO 16* does not specifically refer to the fractional portion acquired by the parent in the partially owned subsidiary case. Indeed, the modified entity theory interpretation does remedy what we consider a flaw in the parent theory. Under the parent theory, the assets and liabilities of the subsidiary can be reported on two different bases in the same consolidated balance sheet—fair value (majority's portion) and book value (minority's portion).

Current accounting pronouncements provide no support for the pure *entity theory* concept of inferring the existence of goodwill attributable to minority shareholders. If accounting reports depart from historical cost and become more reliant on current values in the primary financial statements, however, the entity theory (or at least the modified version) could provide a more appropriate valuation basis for consolidated statements. The FASB is currently in the midst of a major project dealing with "Consolidations and the Equity Method." This project could lead to new accounting standards governing the acceptability of these alternative consolidation theories.

Although these alternative approaches to consolidation do occasionally appear in practice, we shall not use them in this text. Text examples and problem solutions reflect the method previously developed, unless a particular problem calls for alternatives. Our method, which is based on the *parent theory,* may be summarized as follows:

1. The consolidated balance sheet includes the identifiable assets and liabilities of companies P and S at book value *plus P's share* of the difference between the fair values and book values of S's identifiable assets and liabilities. Goodwill is a residual, attributable to P, and is the excess of investment cost over P's share of the fair value of S's assets and liabilities.
2. The minority interest is based on the book value of S Company's stockholders' equity. It does not include a pro rata share of asset and liability restatements to fair value or of goodwill.

Balance Sheet Classification of Minority Interest. As to the *balance sheet classification of minority interest,* we see no sound basis for the parent theory treatment of minority interest as a *noncurrent liability.* Although we acknowledge the parent theory view that consolidated statements are prepared primarily for the controlling interest and that the equity of controlling shareholders differs from the equity of minority shareholders, liability treatment does not follow. There is no obligation on the part of the controlling interest to pay a reasonably determinate amount at a reasonably determinate time to minority shareholders.

Classification *between noncurrent liabilities and stockholders' equity* is an improvement over the pure liability treatment. Nevertheless, we are uncomfortable with the notion of a special nonliability, nonstockholders' equity balance sheet caption.

We believe that the minority interest problem is one of *disclosure* of the fact that not all of S's shares are held internally. Since the resources controlled by the consolidated entity relate to both the majority and the minority shareholders, in consolidation both sets of interests must be treated consistently. In our view, minority shareholders may be viewed as shareholders in the consolidated entity even though their interest is limited to *part* of the consolidated entity. Therefore, the amount assigned to the minority interest should be *separately disclosed and included within consolidated stockholders' equity.*

Consolidated Balance Sheet at Date of Business Combination: Other Issues

Preparation of a consolidated balance sheet at date of business combination is often complicated by some other matters not yet addressed. We briefly discuss several of these in this section.

Dividends of Subsidiary Unpaid at Combination Date

When the parent company acquires the subsidiary's stock *after* a dividend declaration by the subsidiary but *before* the record date for payment, consolidated statements are affected in two ways:

1. The declared dividends which are attached to ownership of S Company's shares reduce the amount otherwise recorded as Investment in S. The Investment in S account is credited and Dividends Receivable is debited for the amount of the subsidiary's dividends to be received by P. Since the subsidiary's retained earnings has already been decreased by the dividend declaration, the credit to the Investment in S effectively recognizes the reduction in the subsidiary's stockholders' equity by the parent.
2. Establishment of a Dividends Receivable account generates an intercompany relationship with the Dividends Payable account recorded by S. Dividends Receivable is therefore eliminated against the portion of Dividends Payable relating to the shares owned by P on the consolidated balance sheet working paper.

Treasury Stock Held by Subsidiary

We have stressed the point that P's ownership interest in S is determined by the percentage of S's outstanding voting shares owned. Should S Company hold some of its own stock as treasury stock, this amount must be eliminated. This is done in recognition of the fact that treasury stock held by S is of no consequence in a consolidated balance sheet reporting the stockholders' equity of P Company.

The elimination would reflect the "retirement" of these treasury shares. How the shares were accounted for when reacquired affects the specifics of the elimination and readers are referred to any standard text in intermediate accounting for an explanation of the proper treatment.

Goodwill Previously Recorded by Subsidiary

In allocating purchase premiums and discounts among the identifiable assets and liabilities of a subsidiary, any goodwill previously recorded by a subsidiary is to be disregarded. *APBO 16* also states that "an acquiring corporation should not record as a separate asset the goodwill previously recorded by an acquired company."[9] Such goodwill is treated as having fair value equal to zero. This does not affect the minority interest, which is based on the book value of the subsidiary's stockholders' equity. Rather, the effect is to increase the otherwise determinable purchase premium (or decrease the purchase discount). Only one goodwill caption appears in a consolidated balance sheet, and it relates to the existence of *unspecified* intangible value established by the price paid in the business combination. In a pooling of interests, however, any goodwill recorded by the subsidiary is carried directly to the consolidated balance sheet at its book value.

Investment in Subsidiary Improperly Recorded

A minor technical problem arises if the Investment in S account is erroneously recorded. In a purchase combination, the accountant must ascertain that the investment account correctly measures the fair value of stock and other consideration given in exchange for the shares of S. If the investment account reflects only the book value of S's shares, fair values will not be properly reflected in the consolidated balance sheet.

In contrast, a pooling requires that the book value of S's shares provides the basis for the investment account balance. If the issue of P's shares is recorded at fair value, it is generally impossible to make a clean elimination of the investment account against the stockholders' equity of S. These problems are readily solved simply by recording the appropriate adjusting entry on P Company's books prior to consolidation.

Parent and Subsidiary with Different Fiscal Years

Financial statements of companies to be consolidated need not cover identical fiscal years. *ARB 51* indicates that if the fiscal years end on different dates, the separate statements may be consolidated if the difference is not much greater than 3 months.[10] If such is the case, the resulting consolidated statements, or the notes thereto, should reflect any intervening events which materially affect the financial position or results of operations of the constituent companies. Should the difference between the closing dates of the separate companies' fiscal years be much more than 3 months, separate statements conforming to a common fiscal year should be prepared and used in the consolidation.

"Push-Down" Accounting

We have indicated that fair value adjustments to a subsidiary's assets and liabilities acquired in a stock acquisition accounted for as a purchase are made on con-

---

[9]Accounting Principles Board, *Opinion No. 16,* par. 88; CT § B50.146.
[10]Committee on Accounting Procedure, *ARB No. 51,* par. 4; CT § C51.107.

solidation working papers only. Indeed, paragraph 17 of *APBO 6* prohibits an entity from writing up its plant assets "to reflect appraisal, market or current values which are above cost to the entity."[11] If separate financial statements are issued for the subsidiary, they report the subsidiary's original book values.

This long-standing practice is now being questioned, especially in the context of financial reports supplied to the SEC. In *Staff Accounting Bulletin (SAB) No. 54* (November 1983), a change in ownership involving substantially all (generally at least 95 percent) of an acquired company's stock is said to establish a new basis of accountability for the acquired company, equal to the cost of the acquisition. Under this rule, the new owners' cost of the acquired company is "pushed down" to the acquired company as the fair value adjustments appearing on consolidation working papers are booked by the acquired company. This procedure assures that the acquired company's separate statements report the same valuations reflected in the parent company's consolidated statements. At the same time, however, **push-down accounting** could be criticized because it permits an entity to revalue its assets and liabilities based on an ownership change rather than a purchase transaction made by the entity.

Push-down accounting continues to evolve.[12] While the SEC does not require it for subsidiaries that are less than substantially wholly owned or that have significant outstanding public debt or preferred stock (thereby limiting its applicability), push-down accounting is encouraged in those situations. If all of the subsidiary's shares have not been acquired, then the asset and liability revaluations and goodwill booked by the subsidiary under push-down accounting would represent the percentage owned (α) by the parent.

To implement push-down accounting, the subsidiary would record the purchase premium or discount allocation with the following entry:

BOOKS OF SUBSIDIARY

Various Assets (details omitted) XXX
Goodwill XXX
    Various Liabilities (details omitted)   XXX
    Push-Down Capital.   XXX
To impute the parent's acquisition cost to our identifiable assets and
liabilities based on the parent's percentage ownership and record any
goodwill implied by the parent's acquisition cost.

The *Push-Down Capital* (or *Appraisal Capital*) account becomes part of the subsidiary's stockholders' equity and is eliminated in consolidation, as shown next. Since the purchase premium is booked by the subsidiary under push-down accounting, there is no need to reclassify and allocate it on the working paper.

---

[11]Accounting Principles Board, *Opinion No. 6*, "Status of Accounting Research Bulletins" (New York: AICPA, 1965), par. 17; CT § D40.102.
[12]Michael E. Cunningham, "Push-Down Accounting: Pros and Cons," *Journal of Accountancy*, June 1984, 72–77.

CONSOLIDATED FINANCIAL STATEMENT WORKING PAPER

Common Stock—S	XXX	
Additional Paid-In Capital—S	XXX	
Retained Earnings—S	XXX	
Push-Down Capital—S	XXX	
Investment in S		XXX
Minority Interest in S		XXX

To eliminate the stockholders' equity of S, including the push-down capital, against the investment account (which *includes* the purchase premium or discount reflected in the push-down capital) and establish the minority interest, if any.

Summary of Key Concepts

When a business combination takes place as a **stock acquisition,** the acquired company remains as a separate legal entity. A parent/subsidiary relationship is established between these **affiliated corporations.** For reporting purposes, consolidated statements are prepared in order that the financial affairs of two or more affiliated corporations will be reported as if they were a single **unified economic entity.**

Preparation of consolidated statements requires that the separate statements of the affiliated corporations be brought together for reporting purposes and that the books of the individual affiliates not be disturbed by the consolidation process. The consolidation process entails removing all financial relationships between the affiliates in order that combined assets, liabilities, and revenues and expenses not be overstated. **Eliminating entries** recorded on a working paper specifically designed to facilitate the preparation of consolidated statements remove the various intercompany financial relationships. After the eliminations, the separate statements are combined.

Consolidated statements incorporating wholly owned subsidiaries should be the same as if the subsidiaries had been merged and their assets and liabilities recorded by the acquiring company as explained in Chapter 6. In parent/subsidiary relationships, the "combining" of the asset and liability balances occurs on the working paper instead of the books.

Any **purchase premium** or **discount** arising in a purchase stock acquisition is allocated among the identifiable assets and liabilities of the subsidiary. This has the effect of reporting the parent's portion of the subsidiary's assets and liabilities at their fair values. If the investment cost exceeds net fair value of the property acquired, the excess is reported as **goodwill** in the consolidated balance sheet. In contrast, **negative goodwill** is created if net fair value of the property acquired exceeds the investment cost. Negative goodwill is then allocated among the noncurrent assets of the subsidiary, except long-term investments in marketable securities, in accordance with their relative fair values.

Most present-day consolidation practice is based on the **parent theory of consolidated statements,** which calls for valuation of the minority interest (and the minority's related portion of the subsidiary's assets and liabilities) at **book value.** An alternative view, the **entity theory of consolidated statements,** would report all identifiable assets and liabilities acquired, including the minority's share, at **fair value** and would impute goodwill to the minority interest. The **modified entity theory** states all assets and liabilities acquired, including the minority's portion, at fair value but does *not* impute goodwill to the minority interest.

Consolidating a stock acquisition accounted for as a **pooling of interests** is procedurally much simpler. No determination and subsequent allocation of fair values is necessary. The investment account reflects book value of the subsidiary's shares owned and is eliminated directly and cleanly against the subsidiary's stockholders' equity. Book values of the subsidiary's assets and liabilities are then added to the parent's balance sheet in consolidation.

Questions

Q7.1 Consolidated statements are prepared so that the financial affairs of affiliated corporations are reported as a single, unified economic entity under common control. Given this, explain why, in certain situations, the financial affairs of affiliated corporations should *not* be consolidated.

Q7.2 Working paper eliminations are central to the consolidation process and are used in many situations to eliminate double counting. What is meant by double counting, and why must it be eliminated in consolidation?

Q7.3 To simplify the introduction to consolidated statements, we began with a situation in which no differences existed between (1) investment cost and book value of S Company's stockholders' equity and (2) fair values and book values of S Company's identifiable assets and liabilities. Suppose (1) were true and (2) were not. Explain the procedure needed to state S's identifiable assets and liabilities at their fair values in consolidation following a purchase combination.

Q7.4 Explain how a purchase premium *and* negative goodwill could both be present in a business combination.

Q7.5 In Chapter 6, a purchase premium or discount was allocated immediately among the assets and liabilities of S for all purchase combinations except stock acquisitions. Why is the allocation made only on a consolidated statement working paper in the stock acquisition case? Would the results be different if the combination were accounted for as a statutory merger?

Q7.6 Suppose P Company acquires 90 percent of S Company's stock for $600,000. The book value of S Company's stockholders' equity is $500,000, and all assets and liabilities are fairly valued except land, which is understated by $60,000. Compute the three alternative amounts for valuing minority interest. Which is preferred in practice?

Q7.7 On January 1, 19X8, the net assets of P Company and S Company were $350,000 and $150,000, respectively. On that date, P acquired an 80 percent interest in S for $140,000 cash. One accountant believes that, at date of acquisition, consolidated net assets should be reported as $380,000. Another accountant argues that $385,000 is the correct amount. Explain the basis for the difference of opinion.

Q7.8 P Company acquired 80 percent of S Company's 100,000 outstanding common shares on March 18, 19X2, for $1,700,000. S's board of directors had declared a per-share dividend of $1 on February 22, 19X2, payable to holders of record on April 4, 19X2. S Company reported stockholders' equity of $2,000,000 on March 18, 19X2. Compute the amount of the purchase premium. If the investment account is not properly stated at $1,700,000 for purposes of consolidation, give the necessary correcting entry.

Q7.9 S Company reports net assets of $790,000, including goodwill of $70,000, on January 31, 19X5. How much of the $790,000 is reported in consolidated assets if P acquires all of S's outstanding stock in (1) a pooling of interests and (2) a purchase for $720,000?

Q7.10 At a time when P's $5 par value shares were selling for $21 per share, 100,000 shares were exchanged for 80 percent of S Company's outstanding stock. S's stockholders' equity amounted to $2,000,000 on that date. P recorded the stock acquisition as follows:

```
Investment in S . . . . . . . . . . . . . . . . . . . . . . .   1,600,000
   Common Stock . . . . . . . . . . . . . . . . . . . . . . .               500,000
   Additional Paid-In Capital . . . . . . . . . . . . . . . .             1,100,000
```

Comment on the above entry and make a correcting entry if needed.

Q7.11 P Company acquired S Company at a time when S's stockholders' equity included treasury stock acquired at a cost of $5,000,000 (par value $1,000,000). When a consolidated balance sheet is prepared for P and S, how should the treasury stock be reported?

Q7.12 Briefly explain and evaluate the concept of push-down accounting.

Exercises

E7.1 Below are the condensed balance sheets of P and S Companies at December 31, 19X1. On January 1, 19X2, P acquired 90 percent of the voting shares of S by issuing 15,000 shares of its $1 par value common stock. P's stock is currently selling at $10 in an active over-the-counter market.

	P	S
Various Assets	$1,000,000	$200,000
Liabilities	$ 200,000	$ 60,000
Common Stock.	100,000	30,000
Additional Paid-In Capital.	400,000	70,000
Retained Earnings	300,000	40,000
	$1,000,000	$200,000

Required:

1. Give the journal entry to record the business combination as a *purchase* and give the eliminating entry that would be made if a consolidated balance sheet were prepared on January 1. Compute consolidated assets and consolidated retained earnings. Assume that the book values of S's assets and liabilities approximate their fair values.

2. Give the journal entry to record the business combination as a *pooling of interests* and give the eliminating entry that would be made if a consolidated balance sheet were prepared on January 1. Compute consolidated assets and consolidated retained earnings. Assume that S's net assets are undervalued by $10,000.

E7.2 The Pluto Company is acquiring shares of the Saturn Company's stock. At December 31, 19X3, selected account balances of Saturn are as follows:

Common Stock, Par Value $10	$1,000,000
Additional Paid-In Capital	300,000
Donated Capital.	100,000
Appropriation of Retained Earnings for Contingencies	150,000
Retained Earnings	350,000
Long-Term Debt	800,000

Required: Give the working paper entry which eliminates the investment account, establishes any purchase premium (discount), and records the minority interest, if appropriate, under each of the following sets of conditions.

1. Pluto acquires all 100,000 shares of Saturn in the open market for $20 a share.

2. Pluto acquires all 100,000 shares of Saturn in the open market for $19 a share.

3. Pluto acquires all 100,000 shares of Saturn in the open market for $16 a share.

4. Pluto acquires 80,000 shares of Saturn in the open market for $20 a share.

5. Pluto acquires 80,000 shares of Saturn in the open market for $19 a share.

6. Pluto acquires 80,000 shares of Saturn in the open market for $16 a share.

7. Pluto acquires 400,000 previously unissued shares directly from Saturn for $20 a share.

E7.3 Refer to the data in E7.2. Pluto and Saturn are now planning a pooling of interests. Pluto's stockholders' equity accounts are given next:

Common Stock, Par Value $5; 2,000,000 Shares Authorized,	
600,000 Issued and Outstanding	$3,000,000
Additional Paid-In Capital	200,000
Retained Earnings	2,200,000
Total Stockholders' Equity	$5,400,000

Required: In each of the following situations, prepare the consolidated stockholders' equity section and include the minority interest when appropriate:

1. Pluto exchanges 200,000 of its shares for all 100,000 shares of Saturn.
2. Pluto exchanges 300,000 of its shares for all 100,000 shares of Saturn.
3. Pluto exchanges 400,000 of its shares for all 100,000 shares of Saturn.
4. Pluto exchanges 200,000 of its shares for 90,000 shares of Saturn.
5. Pluto exchanges 300,000 of its shares for 90,000 shares of Saturn.
6. Pluto exchanges 400,000 of its shares for 90,000 shares of Saturn.

E7.4 Giant Corporation acquired 90 percent of Small Corporation's common stock in an exchange of common shares with a current market value of $2,000,000. Related accountants' and attorneys' fees were $100,000. The total book value of Small's stockholders' equity consists of capital stock of $400,000 and retained earnings of $1,600,000. Book values and fair values of Small's assets and liabilities are given below:

	Book Value	Fair Value
Cash and Receivables	$ 800,000	$ 800,000
Inventories	1,040,000	1,140,000
Plant Assets, Net	1,600,000	1,800,000
Long-Term Investments in Marketable Securities	60,000	80,000
Current Liabilities	(1,000,000)	(1,000,000)
Long-Term Debt	(500,000)	(600,000)
	$ 2,000,000	$ 2,220,000

Required:

1. Give the working paper entries necessary to prepare a consolidated balance sheet at date of business combination assuming the purchase method is used.
2. Give the working paper entries necessary to prepare a consolidated balance sheet at date of business combination assuming the pooling of interests method is used.

E7.5 P Company acquired 80 percent of S Company's common stock for $2,200,000 cash; fees paid to an outside firm to estimate the earning power of S and the fair values of its properties amounted to $40,000. Book value of S's net assets was $2,500,000. Book values of S's identifiable assets and liabilities approximated their fair values except as noted below:

	Book Value	Fair Value
Inventories	$1,500,000	$1,600,000
Land	100,000	200,000
Other Plant Assets, Net	600,000	800,000
Long-Term Investments in Marketable Securities	200,000	250,000
Long-Term Debt	(400,000)	(470,000)

Required: Give the working paper entries necessary to prepare a consolidated balance sheet at date of business combination.

E7.6 When Willis Corporation acquired 95 percent of Navalco's common stock, it was decided that push-down accounting would be applied to Navalco. A purchase premium of $400,000 was paid and Navalco's identifiable assets and liabilities had book values approximating their fair values, except as noted below:

	Book Value	Fair Value
Inventory	$270,000	$320,000
Land	160,000	130,000
Patents	20,000	220,000

Required:

1. Prepare the journal entry needed to implement push-down accounting on Navalco's books.
2. Assuming Navalco's stockholders' equity included capital stock of $700,000 and retained earnings of $1,300,000 prior to the push-down entry, give the working paper elimination to be made if a consolidated balance sheet is prepared immediately after the push-down entry is recorded.

E7.7 Cove Corporation owns 90 percent of Bay Corporation's common stock, acquired for $1,600,000 cash. Prior to the acquisition, Cove reported current assets of $5,200,000, noncurrent assets of $3,800,000, and liabilities of $3,500,000. After consolidating Cove and Bay, consolidated total assets of $13,000,000 were reported, including goodwill (related to the acquisition of Bay) of $340,000. The book values of Bay's identifiable assets and liabilities approximated their fair values.

Required:

1. Using only the information given, reconstruct the working paper entries made when Cove and Bay were consolidated.
2. Calculate the book value of Bay's total assets.

E7.8 Below are condensed balance sheet data for the Pitman Company and the Stone Company prior to their proposed business combination. Book values of Stone's assets and liabilities approximate their fair values.

ASSETS	Pitman	Stone
Current Assets	$2,000,000	$ 800,000
Noncurrent Assets	4,500,000	1,200,000
Total Assets	$6,500,000	$2,000,000
LIABILITIES AND STOCKHOLDERS' EQUITY		
Liabilities	$2,700,000	$1,200,000
Common Stock (Par Value $1)	500,000	100,000
Additional Paid-In Capital	1,500,000	300,000
Retained Earnings	1,800,000	400,000
Total Liabilities and Stockholders' Equity	$6,500,000	$2,000,000

Required: Assume that Pitman acquires 80,000 shares of Stone for cash of $240,000 and short-term notes payable of $400,000. Prepare a consolidated balance sheet working paper as of the date of the acquisition.

E7.9 On January 31, 19X0, Bates, Inc., acquired 90 percent of the outstanding common stock of Wilkens Corporation for $300,000 cash plus 20,000 shares of Bates's $10 par value common stock having a market value of $80 per share. Immediately prior to the acquisition, the trial balances of the two companies were as follows:

	Bates	Wilkens
Current Assets	$ 1,000,000	$ 200,000
Plant and Equipment, Net	3,500,000	700,000
Current Liabilities	(500,000)	(150,000)
Long-Term Liabilities	(2,000,000)	(300,000)
Common Stock	(300,000)	(100,000)
Additional Paid-In Capital	(600,000)	(50,000)
Retained Earnings	(1,100,000)	(300,000)

The acquisition is to be treated as a purchase. A review of the fair values of Wilkens's assets indicates that current assets are undervalued by $50,000 and plant and equipment is undervalued by $600,000.

Required:

1. Prepare a consolidated balance sheet immediately following the acquisition.
2. How would this consolidated balance sheet differ if the entity theory of consolidated statements is used? The modified entity theory?

E7.10 The Pond Company recently acquired 70 percent of the shares of Stream Corporation for $2,000,000 cash. After the acquisition, the net assets (assets

− liabilities) of Pond and Stream had book values of $10,000,000 and $2,500,000, respectively. Fair value of Stream's net assets is $2,600,000.

Required: Compute consolidated net assets, goodwill, and minority interest under each of the following alternatives:

1. The approach used in this book.
2. The entity theory of consolidated statements.
3. The modified entity theory.

E7.11 Stiles Corporation just acquired 80 percent of the outstanding stock of the Thom Company by issuing 200,000 shares of its $10 par common stock valued at $10,000,000. Immediately prior to the acquisition, condensed balance sheet data for the two companies appeared as follows:

ASSETS	Stiles	Thom
Current Assets.	$45,000,000	$12,000,000
Plant and Equipment, Net	19,000,000	11,000,000
Total Assets	$64,000,000	$23,000,000
LIABILITIES AND STOCKHOLDERS' EQUITY		
Liabilities.	$24,000,000	$ 8,000,000
Common Stock (Par Value $10)	5,000,000	1,000,000
Additional Paid-In Capital	20,000,000	4,000,000
Retained Earnings	15,000,000	10,000,000
Total Liabilities and Stockholders' Equity.	$64,000,000	$23,000,000

Although Thom's plant and equipment was fairly stated, Thom's current assets and liabilities had fair values of $13,000,000 and $12,000,000, respectively.

Required: Prepare a consolidated balance sheet for Stiles and Thom immediately after the acquisition.

E7.12 Refer to the data in P6.3 in Chapter 6. Assume that Plastic acquired 80 percent of Steel's outstanding stock for $90,000. Other direct cash costs incurred in the acquisition amounted to $15,000.

Required: Prepare a schedule allocating the purchase premium or discount, and compute the minority interest in Steel at December 31, 19X3.

Problems

P7.1 Preparation of Consolidated Balance Sheet—Purchase Premium On June 30, 19X3, Paul Corporation acquired for cash of $19 per share all of the outstanding voting common stock of Sand Corporation. Both companies continued to operate as separate entities. After closing the nominal accounts, Sand's condensed balance sheet on June 30, 19X3, was as follows:

SAND CORPORATION
BALANCE SHEET AT JUNE 30, 19X3

ASSETS

Cash	$ 700,000
Accounts Receivable, Net.	600,000
Inventories	1,400,000
Property, Plant, and Equipment, Net	3,300,000
Other Assets	500,000
Total Assets	$6,500,000

LIABILITIES AND STOCKHOLDERS' EQUITY

Current Liabilities	$ 700,000
Long-Term Debt	2,600,000
Other Liabilities	200,000
Common Stock, Par Value $1	1,000,000
Additional Paid-In Capital	400,000
Retained Earnings	1,600,000
Total Liabilities and Stockholders' Equity	$6,500,000

On June 30, 19X3, Sand's assets and liabilities having fair values different from book values were as follows:

	Fair value
Property, Plant, and Equipment, Net	$16,400,000
Other Assets	200,000
Long-Term Debt	2,200,000

The amount paid by Paul in excess of the fair value of the net assets of Sand is attributable to expected future earnings of Sand.

Paul's balance sheet immediately *after* the acquisition appears below:

PAUL CORPORATION
BALANCE SHEET AT JUNE 30,19X3

ASSETS

Cash	$ 3,500,000
Accounts Receivable, Net	1,400,000
Inventories	1,000,000
Property, Plant, and Equipment, Net	2,000,000
Investment in Sand.	19,000,000
Other Assets	100,000
Total Assets	$27,000,000

LIABILITIES AND STOCKHOLDERS' EQUITY

Current Liabilities.	$ 1,500,000
Long-Term Debt	4,000,000
Other Liabilities.	750,000
Common Stock, Par Value $1	10,000,000
Additional Paid-In Capital.	5,000,000
Retained Earnings	5,750,000
Total Liabilities and Stockholders' Equity	$27,000,000

Required:

1. Prepare a schedule to determine and allocate the purchase premium.
2. Give the eliminating entries that would appear on a consolidated balance sheet working paper.
3. Prepare a formal consolidated balance sheet for Paul Corporation and Sand Corporation at June 30, 19X3. *(AICPA adapted)*

P7.2 Consolidated Balance Sheet Working Paper—Purchase Premium, Minority Interest Pearson Corporation and Saunders Corporation have entered into negotiations leading to a possible business combination. At December 31, 19X4, Saunders's condensed balance sheet was as follows:

SAUNDERS CORPORATION
BALANCE SHEET AT DECEMBER 31, 19X4

ASSETS

Cash	$ 50,000
Receivables, Net	300,000
Inventories	1,600,000
Prepayments	47,000
Noncurrent Assets, Net	2,003,000
Total Assets.	$4,000,000

LIABILITIES AND STOCKHOLDERS' EQUITY

Current Liabilities	$2,200,000
Common Stock, Par Value $100	1,000,000
Retained Earnings.	800,000
Total Liabilities and Stockholders' Equity	$4,000,000

During the negotiations, it was determined that the fair value of Saunders's noncurrent assets, net of accumulated depreciation, approximated $3,203,000. Initially, Pearson offered to acquire all of Saunders's stock for $3,000,000. Forty percent of Saunders's stockholders objected, however, because they felt that the purchase price should reflect about $500,000 in goodwill. Ultimately, Pearson acquired 60 percent of Saunders's outstanding stock for $300 per share.

After the acquisition was completed on December 31, 19X4, the following balance sheet was prepared for Pearson:

PEARSON CORPORATION
BALANCE SHEET AT DECEMBER 31, 19X4

ASSETS

Cash	$ 5,200,000
Receivables, Net	2,400,000
Inventories	11,200,000
Prepayments	422,000
Investment in Saunders	1,800,000
Other Noncurrent Assets, Net	18,978,000
Total Assets	$40,000,000

LIABILITIES AND STOCKHOLDERS' EQUITY

Current Liabilities	$ 9,487,000
Common Stock, Par Value $100	10,000,000
Retained Earnings	20,513,000
Total Liabilities and Stockholders' Equity	$40,000,000

Required:

1. Prepare a consolidated balance sheet working paper at December 31, 19X4.
2. Prepare a formal consolidated balance sheet at December 31, 19X4. *(AICPA adapted)*

P7.3 Consolidated Balance Sheet Working Paper—Purchase Premium, Minority Interest Placid Corporation acquired 70 percent of the outstanding stock of the Stagnant Company on June 30, 19X0, by issuing 100,000 shares of its $1 par value common stock valued at $41.80 per share. Direct cash costs associated with the acquisition were $35,000, and the cost of registering and issuing the stock was $20,000. On June 15, 19X0, Stagnant's board of directors had declared $80,000 of cash dividends on its common stock to holders of record on July 15, 19X0, and recorded a liability for that amount. Condensed balance sheet data for the two companies immediately *prior* to the combination are given below:

		Stagnant	
ASSETS	**Placid**	**Book Value**	**Fair Value**
Cash and Receivables	$ 8,000,000	$2,000,000	$1,800,000
Marketable Equity Securities, Current	—	600,000	1,000,000
Inventory	7,000,000	2,400,000	2,600,000
Plant Assets, Net	10,000,000	3,600,000	3,600,000
Copyrights	1,000,000	200,000	2,000,000
Goodwill	—	500,000	100,000
Total Assets	$26,000,000	$9,300,000	

LIABILITIES AND STOCKHOLDERS' EQUITY

Current Liabilities	$ 6,000,000	$2,000,000	2,000,000
Noncurrent Liabilities	4,000,000	3,300,000	3,000,000
Common Stock, Par Value $1	100,000	100,000	—
Additional Paid-In Capital	900,000	400,000	—
Retained Earnings	15,000,000	3,500,000	—
Total Liabilities and Stockholders' Equity	$26,000,000	$9,300,000	

Required: Prepare a consolidated balance sheet working paper as of June 30, 19X0, for Placid and Stagnant.

P7.4 Consolidated Balance Sheet—Partially Owned Subsidiary and Negative Goodwill On December 31, 19X2, Paxon Corporation acquired 100 percent of the outstanding common stock of the Saxon Company for $1,800,000 cash. The balance sheets of Paxon and Saxon, immediately *prior* to the combination, are shown below:

BALANCE SHEETS AT DECEMBER 31, 19X2
(PRECOMBINATION)

ASSETS		Paxon	Saxon
Cash and Receivables		$2,860,000	$ 720,000
Inventory		1,700,000	900,000
Marketable Equity Securities—			
Long-Term		—	300,000
Land		650,000	175,000
Buildings and Equipment	$3,400,000		
Less Accumulated Depreciation	(1,000,000)	2,400,000	600,000 (net)
Total Assets		$7,610,000	$2,695,000

LIABILITIES AND STOCKHOLDERS' EQUITY

		Paxon	Saxon
Current Liabilities		$1,500,000	$1,000,000
Long-Term Debt		2,000,000	400,000
Common Stock, Par Value $1		500,000	100,000
Additional Paid-In Capital		1,200,000	350,000
Retained Earnings		2,410,000	845,000
Total Liabilities and Stockholders' Equity		$7,610,000	$2,695,000

Several of Saxon's assets and liabilities had fair values different from their book values. Estimates of the fair values of these items follow:

	Estimated Fair Value
Inventory	$1,000,000
Marketable Equity Securities—Long-Term	250,000
Land	420,000
Buildings and Equipment, Net	900,000
Long-Term Debt	(290,000)

Required:

1. Prepare a consolidated balance sheet at December 31, 19X2.
2. Prepare a consolidated balance sheet assuming that Paxon paid $1,620,000 for a 90 percent interest in Saxon.

P7.5 Allocation of Purchase Discount and Negative Goodwill Refer to the data in P7.4. Assume that Paxon paid $1,000,000 for an 80 percent interest in Saxon. Give the final allocation of the purchase premium or discount. Show all calculations.

P7.6 Consolidated Balance Sheet Working Paper—Purchase Discount Following a period of protracted negotiations, the Penn Company and the Stark Company have agreed on terms for a business combination, scheduled to occur on January 2, 19X6. On that date, the following condensed precombination balance sheet data are prepared:

		Stark	
ASSETS	**Penn**	**Book Value**	**Fair Value**
Cash and Receivables.	$ 8,000,000	$1,000,000	$ 900,000
Inventories.	10,000,000	3,000,000	3,200,000
Plant Assets, Net	12,000,000	5,000,000	4,500,000
Investment in Bonds.	1,000,000	500,000	300,000
Total Assets	$31,000,000	$9,500,000	
LIABILITIES AND STOCKHOLDERS' EQUITY			
Current Liabilities	$6,000,000	$2,500,000	2,500,000
Noncurrent Liabilities	8,000,000	3,000,000	(Note)
Common Stock, Par Value $10	4,000,000	1,000,000	—
Retained Earnings.	13,000,000	3,000,000	—
Total Liabilities and Stockholders' Equity	$31,000,000	$9,500,000	

Note: Noncurrent liabilities of Stark include $2,000,000 of bonds payable and $1,000,000 accrued pension liability. At January 2, 19X6, Stark's pension fund had assets of $500,000; the present value of vested benefits was $2,500,000.

Required: Assuming that Penn acquired all the outstanding stock of Stark for a cash payment of $3,500,000, prepare a consolidated balance sheet working paper as of January 2, 19X6.

P7.7 Consolidated Balance Sheet Working Paper; Purchase Discount, Minority Interest Refer to the data in P7.6. Assume that Penn acquired 80 percent of Stark's outstanding stock for a cash payment of $3,000,000 and that the fair value of Stark's plant assets is $6,500,000.

Required: Prepare a consolidated balance sheet working paper as of January 2, 19X6.

P7.8 Consolidated Balance Sheet—Pooling of Interests Refer to the data in P7.3. Assume that Placid exchanged 100,000 shares of its $1 par value common stock for 90 percent of Stagnant's outstanding capital stock in a business combination qualifying as a pooling of interests. Other data in P7.3 are unchanged.

Required: Prepare a consolidated balance sheet for the two companies as of June 30, 19X0.

P7.9 Consolidation Working Paper with Purchased and Pooled Subsidiaries At the end of 19X8, Frank Corporation acquired 90 percent of the outstanding common stock of George Corporation and Hal Corporation. The transaction with George was accounted for as a pooling of interests in which Frank exchanged 100,000 shares for the interest in George. Expenses of the pooling were $40,000. With respect to Hal, 10 percent bonds worth $3,500,000 were issued for the 90 percent interest. Direct costs of the purchase were $50,000. Condensed balance sheets of the three companies immediately after the combinations were consummated appear below. Book values of all assets and liabilities approximate their fair values.

ASSETS	Frank	George	Hal
Cash and Receivables	$ 8,900,000	$1,100,000	$1,680,000
Inventory	7,000,000	1,650,000	1,170,000
Investment in George	3,060,000	—	—
Investment in Hal	3,550,000	—	—
Other Assets	12,000,000	2,250,000	2,650,000
Total Assets	$34,510,000	$5,000,000	$5,500,000
LIABILITIES AND STOCKHOLDERS' EQUITY			
Liabilities	$15,000,000	$1,600,000	$2,300,000
Common Stock	3,000,000	500,000	400,000
Additional Paid-In Capital	7,000,000	1,100,000	800,000
Retained Earnings	9,510,000	1,800,000	2,000,000
Total Liabilities and Stockholders' Equity	$34,510,000	$5,000,000	$5,500,000

Required: Prepare a working paper at date of business combination to consolidate the balance sheets of the three companies.

P7.10 Consolidated Balance Sheet—Pooling, Investment Account Incorrect On December 31, 19X3, Ransom and Salvage Corporations exchanged common stock in a business combination to be accounted for as a pooling of interests. The stockholders of Ransom gave up 500,000 shares of $2.50 par value common stock worth $4,000,000 for 90 percent of Salvage's common shares. Attorneys' and consultants' fees were $26,000. Balance sheets for Ransom and Salvage immediately after the exchange of shares are given on the next page:

ASSETS	Ransom	Salvage
Cash and Receivables	$ 2,974,000	$ 800,000
Inventory	1,700,000	700,000
Plant Assets, Net	8,500,000	3,000,000
Investment in Salvage	4,026,000	—
Goodwill	—	500,000
Total Assets	$17,200,000	$5,000,000
LIABILITIES AND STOCKHOLDERS' EQUITY		
Liabilities	$ 3,200,000	$1,200,000
Common Stock, Par Value	3,250,000	400,000
Additional Paid-In Capital	4,750,000	1,600,000
Retained Earnings	6,000,000	1,800,000
Total Liabilities and Stockholders' Equity	$17,200,000	$5,000,000

Required:

1. Prepare any adjusting entries called for by the above information.
2. Prepare the working paper eliminations needed for a consolidated balance sheet after any adjusting entries in No. 1 are made.
3. Prepare a formal consolidated balance sheet for Ransom and Salvage at December 31, 19X3.

P7.11 Working Backwards—Eliminating Entries and Preparing Subsidiary's Separate Balance Sheet P Company acquired 80 percent of S Company on December 31, 19X7, for $10,000,000 cash. The book value of S's net assets on that date was $9,000,000. S's individual assets and liabilities were fairly valued except for Inventory, which was undervalued by $500,000, and Plant Assets, which were undervalued by $1,200,000. Given below are condensed balance sheets for P Company before and after consolidation. Inventory is included in Current Assets.

P COMPANY
CONDENSED BALANCE SHEETS
AT DECEMBER 31, 19X7

ASSETS	Prior to Consolidation	Consolidated
Current Assets	$15,000,000	$21,400,000
Plant Assets, Net	20,000,000	30,000,000
Investment in S	10,000,000	—
Goodwill	—	1,440,000
Total Assets	$45,000,000	$52,840,000
LIABILITIES AND STOCKHOLDERS' EQUITY		
Liabilities	$19,000,000	$25,040,000
Capital Stock	12,000,000	12,000,000
Retained Earnings	14,000,000	14,000,000
Minority Interest in S	—	1,800,000
Total Liabilities and Stockholders' Equity	$45,000,000	$52,840,000

Required:

1. Determine the working paper entries that were made in consolidation.
2. Prepare S Company's separate condensed balance sheet at December 31, 19X7.

P7.12 Alternative Consolidation Theories—Eliminations and Balance Sheets P Company purchased 80 percent of the shares of S Company for $1,000,000. Condensed balance sheets for the two companies immediately following the acquisition are given below, as are estimates of the fair values of S's identifiable assets and liabilities.

		S Company	
ASSETS	P Company	Book Value	Fair Value
Cash and Receivables	$ 850,000	$ 500,000	$500,000
Inventory	550,000	600,000	640,000
Plant Assets, Net	2,400,000	800,000	900,000
Investment in S	1,000,000	—	—
Total Assets	$4,800,000	$1,900,000	
LIABILITIES AND STOCKHOLDERS' EQUITY			
Liabilities	$2,000,000	$ 900,000	$950,000
Capital Stock	1,000,000	400,000	—
Retained Earnings	1,800,000	600,000	—
Total Liabilities and Stockholders' Equity	$4,800,000	$1,900,000	

Required: Prepare the working paper eliminations and a condensed consolidated balance sheet under each of the following alternatives:

1. The approach used in this book.
2. The entity theory of consolidated statements.
3. The modified entity theory.

Chapter 8   **Consolidated Financial Statements after Date of Business Combination**

We indicated in the last chapter that once a company acquires a controlling interest in a subsidiary, the preparation of consolidated financial statements generally follows. Consolidated statements were introduced in Chapter 7 under the assumption that a consolidated balance sheet is prepared on the effective date of a business combination. After that date, however, the full range of financial statements must be prepared at the regular reporting intervals. Thus the passage of time requires that consolidated statements of income, retained earnings, and changes in financial position be generated. Furthermore, subsequent consolidated balance sheets must reflect the financial activities of the affiliated companies since the combination occurred.

The presentation of consolidated financial statements is a *reporting requirement* and not an *accounting requirement* (recall that eliminations are made on working papers only). For accounting purposes, however, the Investment in Subsidiary is an intercorporate investment. Preparation of postcombination consolidated financial statements is influenced not only by transactions among the affiliates but also by the method the parent company uses to account for the Investment in Subsidiary on its books. We begin the chapter with a brief review of accounting for intercorporate investments and marketable equity securities before concentrating on the equity method used in most parent/subsidiary relationships. We then introduce the preparation of consolidated statements of income, retained earnings, and changes in financial position and end the chapter with a discussion of certain issues in accounting for income taxes which are germane to these subjects.

Accounting for Intercorporate Investments

Accounting for marketable equity securities carried as current assets is subject to the provisions of *SFAS 12*.[1] The *Statement* also covers the accounting for market-

---

[1]Financial Accounting Standards Board, *Statement of Financial Accounting Standards No. 12*, "Accounting for Certain Marketable Securities" (Stamford, CT: FASB, 1975); CT § I89.

able equity securities carried as noncurrent assets when the investor company owns a small portion—generally less than 20 percent—of the voting shares of the investee. The accounting for other nonconsolidated intercorporate investments follows the rules set down in *APBO 18*.[2] According to *APBO 18,* ownership of 20 percent or more of the voting shares of an investee leads to the presumption that the investor may exercise significant influence over the affairs of the investee. Absent evidence refuting the ability of an investor to significantly influence or control an investee, the *Opinion* requires that the *equity method* be used to account for such intercorporate investments. *IFAS 35* lists five examples of factors which, if present, may overcome the presumption that ownership of 20 percent or more of an investee's stock is sufficient for the investor to exercise significant influence.[3] These examples are:

1. There is opposition by the investee, in the form of litigation or complaints to regulatory agencies, which challenge the investor's influence.
2. There are agreements between investor and investee in which the investor relinquishes significant stockholder rights.
3. Majority ownership of the investee is concentrated among a few stockholders who control the investee and severely limit the investor's influence.
4. The investor is thwarted in its attempts to obtain information, not generally available to stockholders, which is needed to apply the equity method.
5. The investor is unable to obtain representation on the investee's board of directors.

As previously indicated, ownership of more than 50 percent of the investee's shares generally invokes the reporting requirement for presentation of consolidated statements. Because of this, the parent company has the option of accounting for its subsidiary investment with either the *equity method* or an alternative known as the *cost method*. Strictly speaking, however, neither method is an accounting requirement when consolidated statements are presented. A flowchart summarizing these matters appears in Figure 8.1.

As we shall see, the method used by an investor company to account for intercorporate investments has no effect on consolidated financial statements, although it does affect the *procedures* required to prepare these statements. For this reason, parent companies which consolidate their subsidiaries sometimes use the cost method to account for intercorporate investments which are to be consolidated, even though the equity method is otherwise required by *APBO 18*. The FASB project on "Consolidations and the Equity Method," mentioned in Chapter 7, may lead to changes affecting applicability of the equity method and should be monitored.

Since most parent companies which consolidate their subsidiaries use the equity method, it is emphasized throughout this book. Moreover, the parent com-

---

[2]Accounting Principles Board, *Opinion No. 18,* "The Equity Method of Accounting for Investments in Common Stock" (New York: AICPA, 1971); CT § 182.

[3]Financial Accounting Standards Board, *Interpretation of Financial Accounting Standards No. 35,* "Criteria for Applying the Equity Method of Accounting for Investments in Common Stock" (Stamford, CT: FASB, 1981), par. 4; CT § 182.108.

Figure 8.1 **Accounting for Intercorporate Investments[a]**

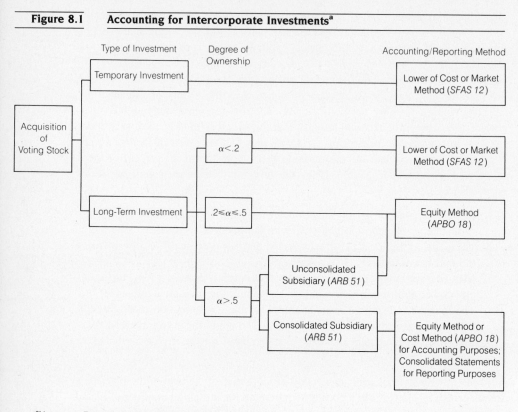

[a]Note: α = Percent of outstanding voting shares owned.

pany *must* use the equity method to account for its subsidiaries if it issues separate (unconsolidated) parent company statements. We do not, however, completely ignore the cost method. As we review the equity method in the next section, we contrast it with the cost method and, later in this chapter, we provide a comprehensive illustration of consolidation when the cost method is being used by the parent company.

Equity Method

Under the **equity method of accounting for intercorporate investments,** the parent increases (decreases) the Investment in S account for its share of the subsidiary's earnings (loss), and decreases the account by its share of the subsidiary's dividends. If there are no complicating factors—purchase premium or discount or intercompany gains or losses—application of the equity method simply means that the Investment in S account changes as the retained earnings of the subsidiary changes. Assuming no capital changes in the subsidiary's stockholders' equity, the balance in the investment account moves in tandem with the book value of the subsidiary's shares owned. Unfortunately, such a simple, straightforward situation seldom exists because of the complicating factors just mentioned. Before addressing these complications, however, we introduce the cost method and illustrate how it compares with the equity method.

Cost Method

The equity method need not be used by a parent company to account for subsidiaries which are to be consolidated. It becomes a factor in financial statements *only* when intercorporate investments of 20 percent or more are *not* consolidated. Because of this, some parent companies use the **cost method of accounting for intercorporate investments** which are to be consolidated. Under the cost method, the balance in the Investment in S account generally remains constant unless additional shares are bought or sold. Income is recorded by the parent only when dividends are declared by the subsidiary and only to the extent of the parent's share of those dividends. Accordingly, there is no relationship between the balance in P's investment account and changes in the book value of P's share of S Company's stockholders' equity. An exception arises when the subsidiary distributes dividends in excess of its earnings since the parent's acquisition by purchase (not pooling). Such dividends represent a return of capital and are credited to the investment account rather than being accounted for as income.

When consolidation occurs, however, it becomes necessary to make working paper entries which update P's investment account to reflect changes in S Company's stockholders' equity since date of combination in order that clean eliminations can be made. A **clean elimination** can be made when the balance in the investment account is equal to the dollar amount of S Company's stockholders' equity owned by P plus (minus) any unamortized purchase premium (discount).

Comparing the Cost and Equity Methods

The essence of the cost and equity methods can be grasped by working through a simple example. On January 1, 19X1, P Company acquires 90 percent of S Company's outstanding voting stock for $900,000 cash. The total book value of S Company's stockholders' equity is $1,000,000—P's share is $900,000—and the book values of S's assets and liabilities equal their fair values. The condensed stockholders' equity section of S Company follows:

Common Stock.	$ 100,000
Additional Paid-In Capital.	400,000
Retained Earnings	500,000
Total Stockholders' Equity	$1,000,000

During the year, S Company reports net income of $80,000 and pays dividends of $30,000 on June 30, 19X1. Rather than debiting Retained Earnings for

Exhibit 8.1	Comparison of Cost and Equity Methods

	Cost Method		Equity Method	
BOOKS OF P COMPANY	Debit	Credit	Debit	Credit
1/1/X1				
Investment in S	900,000		900,000	
Cash.		900,000		900,000
To record the acquisition of 90 percent of S's stock for $900,000.				
6/30/X1				
Cash.	27,000		—	
Dividend Income		27,000		—
Cash.	—		27,000	
Investment in S		—		27,000
To record the receipt of $27,000 ($= .9 \times \$30,000$) of dividends from S.				
12/31/X1				
Investment in S			72,000	
Income from S	No entry			72,000
To record P's share of S's net income; $72,000 ($= .9 \times \$80,000$).				
CONSOLIDATED FINANCIAL STATEMENT WORKING PAPER	Debit	Credit	Debit	Credit
Dividend Income	27,000		—	
Dividends—S		27,000		—
To eliminate intercompany dividends received from S.				
Income from S	—		72,000	
Dividends—S		—		27,000
Investment in S		—		45,000
To eliminate P's share of S's net income and intercompany dividends, thereby adjusting the Investment in S account to its beginning-of-year balance.				
Common Stock—S.	100,000		100,000	
Additional Paid-In Capital—S	400,000		400,000	
Retained Earnings—S, Jan. 1, 19X1	500,000		500,000	
Investment in S		900,000		900,000
Minority Interest in S.		100,000		100,000
To eliminate the Investment in S against 90 percent of S's stockholders' equity at the beginning of the year and reclassify the remaining 10 percent as minority interest.				

Exhibit 8.1   Continued

Minority Interest in Net Income	8,000		8,000
Dividends—S		3,000	3,000
Minority Interest in S		5,000	5,000

To establish the change in the
minority interest during the current
year—the minority's share of S's net
income less dividends paid by S
to the minority, $8,000
(= .1 × $80,000).

---

the dividends, S Company debits a Dividends account which effectively reduces retained earnings. Thus at December 31, 19X1, S Company's retained earnings of $550,000 consist of:

Retained Earnings, Jan. 1, 19X1	$500,000
Dividends	(30,000)
Net Income	80,000
Retained Earnings Dec. 31, 19X1	$550,000

The journal entries made on P Company's books, and the eliminating entries made on the working paper under the two methods appear in Exhibit 8.1. Note that when S Company's dividends are eliminated, the credit is to *Dividends—S,* rather than to Retained Earnings—S, January 1, 19X1. Furthermore, S Company's revenues and expenses are not eliminated; they flow into consolidated net income.

Before proceeding, we wish to clarify the elimination of intercompany dividends and P's share of S's net income illustrated in Exhibit 8.1. This is done in order to avoid *double counting.* When we consolidate the income statements of P and S, we add them together. Under the cost method, P's separate income statement includes dividend income from S, while under the equity method, P's separate income statement reflects P's share of S's net income. If we summed the income statements without eliminating these intercompany income components, they would be counted twice, once through inclusion in P's net income and again in S's net income. This process can be visualized by studying the diagram in Figure 8.2.

When the equity method is used, elimination of the entries recorded by P during the year adjusts the investment account to its balance at the *beginning* of the year. Assuming that retained earnings is the only component of S's stockholders' equity to have changed during the year, we can eliminate the investment account against S Company's beginning-of-year stockholders' equity. The change in S Company's retained earnings during the current year will be reflected in consolidated retained earnings and in the minority interest. The last working paper entry in Exhibit 8.1 records the minority's share of the current year change in S Company's retained earnings. It establishes the **Minority Interest in Net Income,**

Figure 8.2 **Diagrammatic Approach to Consolidating the Income Statements of P and S Companies When P Company Uses the Equity Method**

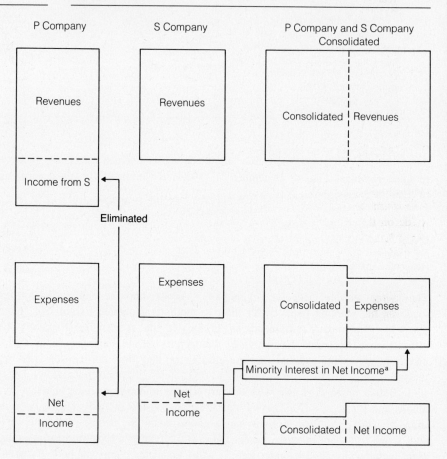

[a] If P owns 100 percent of the outstanding voting shares of S, then P's income from S and S's net income are the same, and there is no minority interest in net income.

eliminates the minority's share of S Company's dividends, and shows the difference as the *change in the minority interest* during the current year. At consolidation points more than one year after date of business combination, an additional working paper entry will be necessary under the cost method to permit a clean elimination. The purpose of this entry is to adjust the investment account to the equity basis. Without such an entry, a discrepancy will exist between S's stockholders' equity, which has changed since acquisition, and the investment account, which has not changed. This procedure is illustrated later in the chapter.

Complete Equity Method: A One-Line Consolidation

In most situations, application of the equity method is more complex than just described. The equity method is viewed as a **one-line consolidation.** Those events—amortization of purchase premium or discount and intercompany gains and losses—which affect consolidated net income must also be reflected in the parent's application of the equity method. *APBO 18* makes this quite clear:

> The difference between consolidation and the equity method lies in the details reported in the financial statements. Thus an investor's net income for the period and its stockholders' equity at the end of the period are the same whether an investment in a subsidiary is accounted for under the equity method or the subsidiary is consolidated.[4]

If the equity method is treated as a one-line consolidation, its use actually facilitates the consolidation process because many consolidation issues are addressed when the parent records its share of the subsidiary's periodic income or loss. To be consistent with the one-line consolidation concept, we present what might be termed the **complete equity method** in this text. *All* items—purchase premium or discount amortization and intercompany gains or losses—which affect consolidated net income are considered when the **equity method accrual** is made. Note, however, that the complete equity method does not extend to intercompany receivables/payables and revenues/expenses. While such items are eliminated in consolidation, they have no effect on consolidated net income. When the *equity method* is used in this text, it will be the *complete equity method* unless otherwise specified.

The complete equity method will not always be encountered in practice. If consolidated statements are prepared, the method used by the parent to account for its investments in subsidiaries is irrelevant. Details of the consolidation process differ, but the end result must be the same.

We now discuss how amortization of a purchase premium or discount affects the equity method; we defer consideration of intercompany gains and losses until Chapters 9 and 10.

Amortization of Purchase Premium (Discount)

In a purchase combination, the fair value of the consideration given for S Company's shares establishes the postcombination accounting basis of the underlying net assets and liabilities of S Company. The allocation of a purchase premium or discount to depreciable or amortizable assets or liabilities determines the amounts to be depreciated or amortized in subsequent consolidated financial statements. We now discuss this problem within the context of a purchase premium.

Suppose that the acquisition of S by P resulted in a purchase premium attributed entirely to goodwill. *APBO 17* requires that goodwill be amortized by the

---

[4]Accounting Principles Board, *Opinion No. 18,* par. 19; CT § 182.109.

straight-line method over a period of 40 years or less.[5] Furthermore, *APBO 18* provides that "a difference between the cost of an investment and the amount of underlying equity in net assets of an investee should be accounted for as if the investee were a consolidated subsidiary."[6] Therefore, the amortization of goodwill arising in a business combination must be reflected by P Company when it records its share of S Company's net income under the equity method. This is done by reducing the amount of S's income which otherwise would be accrued under the equity method by the amount of the goodwill amortization. Note, however, that no separate account for the goodwill appears on P's balance sheet and no separate expense account for goodwill amortization appears on P's income statement. Rather, the unamortized goodwill is shown separately as an asset only on the consolidated balance sheet, and the periodic amortization expense is reported only on the consolidated income statement. The working paper entry we make to allocate a purchase premium places the goodwill on the consolidated balance sheet. Another working paper entry is required to record the periodic amortization.

These principles are easily extended to cases in which the purchase premium allocation is more complex. Assume that P acquires a 90 percent interest in S on January 1, 19X1, for $1,200,000 cash. The stockholders' equity of S amounts to

---

Exhibit 8.2   **Determination and Allocation of the Purchase Premium Paid by P Company in Its 90 Percent Acquisition of S Company on January 1, 19X1**

Cost of Acquisition $1,200,000
Book Value of Net Assets or Stockholders' Equity Acquired (90%)   900,000
Purchase Premium . . . . $ 300,000

Assets and Liabilities of S Company	Fair Value	Book Value	Fair Value Less Book Value	Allocation Based on P's Interest (90%)
Cash and Receivables . . .	$ 300,000	$ 300,000	—	—
Inventory	450,000	400,000	$ 50,000	$ 45,000
Buildings and Equipment (Net)	1,000,000	800,000	200,000	180,000
Land	200,000	200,000	—	—
Liabilities	(700,000)	(700,000)	—	—
	$1,250,000	$1,000,000	$250,000	$225,000
Goodwill				75,000
Total Purchase Premium				$300,000

---

[5]Accounting Principles Board, *Opinion No. 17*, "Intangible Assets" (New York: AICPA, 1970), par. 29; CT § I60.110–111.
[6]Accounting Principles Board, *Opinion No. 18*, par. 19b; CT § I82.109b.

$1,000,000. Determination of the amount and allocation of the purchase premium is given in Exhibit 8.2, which shows that the purchase premium is allocated to inventory, buildings and equipment, and goodwill. Assume that these costs expire as follows:

1. The inventory is sold during 19X1.
2. Depreciation of buildings and equipment is straight-line, based on an average remaining life of 15 years.
3. Goodwill is amortized on the straight-line basis over 40 years.

Consolidation at End of First Year: Complete Equity Method

During 19X1, S Company reports net income of $350,000 and pays dividends of $100,000. As in the earlier illustration, S Company's dividends are debited to a dividends account rather than to retained earnings. To simplify the mechanics of applying the equity method, we use a schedule to determine the net amount of equity method income to be recorded by P. In this way, we keep the number of entries to a minimum.

**SCHEDULE TO DETERMINE THE EQUITY METHOD ACCRUAL
FOR THE YEAR ENDED DECEMBER 31, 19X1**

P's Share of S's Net Income (.9 × $350,000)	$315,000
Less Amortization of Purchase Premium:	
Sale of Revalued Inventory	$ 45,000
Additional Depreciation ($180,000/15)	12,000
Amortization of Goodwill ($75,000/40)	1,875
Total Amortization	$ 58,875
Net Equity Method Accrual for 19X1	$256,125

As P Company applies the equity method during 19X1, it records the following journal entries, including the January 1 acquisition entry:

BOOKS OF P COMPANY

Investment in S	1,200,000	
Cash		1,200,000
To record the acquisition of 90 percent of S's outstanding voting shares for $1,200,000 cash.		
Cash	90,000	
Investment in S		90,000
To record receipt of dividends from S.		
Investment in S	256,125	
Income from S		256,125
To record P's share of S's net income for 19X1, $315,000, less amortization of purchase premium amounting to $58,875.		

Consider the composition of the investment account at December 31, 19X1, after the above entries have been made:

INVESTMENT IN S

Total Acquisition Cost ($1,200,000)	1/1/X1	Book Value of 90 Percent Interest Acquired	900,000		
	1/1/X1	Purchase Premium	300,000		
				19X1 90 Percent of S Company's Dividends	90,⬚
Net Equity Method Accrual ($256,125)	12/31/X1	90 Percent of S's Net Income	315,000	12/31/X1 Purchase Premium Amortization	58,⬚
	12/31/X1	Balance	1,366,125		

The balance of $1,366,125 has two basic components: (1) an amount equal to 90 percent of S Company's stockholders' equity at December 31, 19X1, $1,125,000 [= .9($1,000,000 + $350,000 − $100,000)], and (2) the *unamortized purchase premium* of $241,125 (= $300,000 − $58,875). Completing this illustration are the working paper entries needed to consolidate P and S at the end of 19X1. They appear in Exhibit 8.3 and are numbered to tie in with the working paper in Exhibit 8.4.

Consolidated Statements of Income and Retained Earnings

The objectives of consolidated statements of income and retained earnings are to report consolidated net income and the changes in consolidated retained earnings. Both statements focus on those amounts relevant to the *controlling interest,* the shareholders of P Company. Indeed, when the equity method is used, consolidated net income equals the net income of P Company, and consolidated retained earnings equals P Company's retained earnings.

These interpretations of consolidated net income and retained earnings follow from the *parent theory of consolidated statements* by reason of their emphasis on the controlling interest. Under the *entity theory,* consolidated net income and retained earnings include the minority interest and relate to all shareholders of P and S, not just the majority. We support the emphasis on the controlling interest derived from the parent theory because it is consistent with current accounting practices and with the historical rationale for consolidated statements. Therefore, we offer the following definitions:

| Exhibit 8.3 | **Working Paper Entries to Consolidate P and S Companies at December 31, 19X1; Equity Method ($\alpha = .9$)** |

(1)

Income from S	256,125	
Dividends—S.		90,000
Investment in S.		166,125

To eliminate the equity method entries recorded by P, thereby adjusting the investment account to its balance on Jan. 1, 19X1.

(2)

Common Stock—S	100,000	
Additional Paid-In Capital—S	400,000	
Retained Earnings—S, Jan. 1, 19X1	500,000	
Purchase Premium	300,000	
Investment in S.		1,200,000
Minority Interest in S		100,000

To reclassify the purchase premium, eliminate the Investment in S against 90 percent of the stockholders' equity of S, and reclassify the remaining stockholders' equity as minority interest, all as of Jan. 1, 19X1.

(3)

Inventory, Balance Sheet	45,000	
Buildings and Equipment (Net)	180,000	
Goodwill.	75,000	
Purchase Premium		300,000

To allocate the purchase premium to the assets of S and goodwill as of Jan. 1, 19X1.

(4)

Inventory, Jan. 1, Income Statement (or Cost of Goods Sold).	45,000	
Depreciation Expense.	12,000	
Amortization Expense.	1,875	
Inventory, Balance Sheet		45,000
Accumulated Depreciation		12,000
Goodwill		1,875

To recognize current year amortization of the purchase premium (as reflected in the equity method accrual) in the consolidated income statement for 19X1.

(5)

Minority Interest in Net Income	35,000	
Dividends—S.		10,000
Minority Interest in S		25,000

To record the change in the minority interest during 19X1, consisting of the minority's interest in net income decreased by S's dividends paid to minority shareholders.

Exhibit 8.4　　**P and S Companies: Consolidated Financial Statement Working Paper for the Year Ended December 31, 19X1 (Equity Method)**

	P Company	S Company (90%)	Adjustments and Eliminations Dr.		Adjustments and Eliminations Cr.		Consolidated
INCOME STATEMENT							
Sales and Other Revenue . .	1,960,000	1,300,000					3,260,000
Income from S	256,125	—	(1)	256,125			—
Inventory, 12/31/X1.	75,000	390,000					465,000
Total Credits.	2,291,125	1,690,000		256,125			3,725,000
Inventory, 1/1/X1	100,000	400,000	(4)	45,000			545,000
Purchases.	900,000	600,000					1,500,000
Operating Expenses	480,000	340,000	(4)	13,875			833,875
Total Debits	1,480,000	1,340,000		58,875			2,878,875
Minority Interest in Net Income	—	—	(5)	35,000			(35,000)
Net Income—to Retained Earnings Statement. . . .	811,125	350,000		350,000			811,125
RETAINED EARNINGS STATEMENT							
Retained Earnings, 1/1/X1—P.	900,000	—					900,000
Retained Earnings, 1/1/X1—S.	—	500,000	(2)	500,000			—
Net Income—from Inc. Stmt .	811,125	350,000		350,000			811,125
Dividends—P	(200,000)	—					(200,000)
Dividends—S	—	(100,000)			(1)	90,000	—
					(5)	10,000	
Ret. Earn., 12/31/X1—to Balance Sheet.	1,511,125	750,000		850,000		100,000	1,511,125
BALANCE SHEET							
Cash and Receivables . . .	275,000	360,000					635,000
Inventory	75,000	390,000	(3)	45,000	(4)	45,000	465,000
Investment in S	1,366,125	—			(1)	166,125	—
					(2)	1,200,000	
Other Investments	100,000	—					100,000
Purchase Premium	—	—	(2)	300,000	(3)	300,000	—
Land	200,000	200,000					400,000
Buildings and Equipment . .	2,000,000	1,000,000	(3)	180,000			3,180,000
Accumulated Depreciation . .	(800,000)	—			(4)	12,000	(812,000)
Goodwill.	—	—	(3)	75,000	(4)	1,875	73,125
Total	3,216,125	1,950,000		600,000		1,725,000	4,041,125
Current Liabilities.	175,000	200,000					375,000
Other Liabilities	730,000	500,000					1,230,000
Capital Stock—P.	800,000	—					800,000
Capital Stock—S.	—	500,000	(2)	500,000			—
Ret. Earn.—from Ret. Earn. Stmt.	1,511,125	750,000		850,000		100,000	1,511,125
Minority Interest in S	—	—			(2)	100,000	125,000
					(5)	25,000	
Total	3,216,125	1,950,000		1,350,000		225,000	4,041,125
				1,950,000		1,950,000	

Explanations of Working Paper Entries

(1) To eliminate the equity method entries made by P during 19X1.
(2) To eliminate the investment account and reclassify the purchase premium and minority interest as of January 1, 19X1.
(3) To allocate the purchase premium as of January 1, 19X1.
(4) To recognize current year amortization of the purchase premium.
(5) To record the change in the minority interest during 19X1.

Consolidated net income is the net income of companies P and S attributable to the stockholders of P and, as such, includes the net income of P from its own operations plus P's share of S's net income, after adjustments for unconfirmed gains and losses on intercompany transactions and for amortization of any purchase premium or discount.

Consolidated retained earnings consist of P Company's retained earnings at date of business combination, increased (decreased) by consolidated net income (loss) in subsequent periods and decreased by dividends paid by P to its shareholders. In a pooling of interests, consolidated retained earnings also include any retained earnings of the subsidiary recorded by P when the pooling took place.

Consolidated Financial Statement Working Paper

All but the simplest consolidation situations require a systematic approach to the preparation of consolidated statements; otherwise the mechanics become unmanageable. An appropriately designed working paper provides such a systematic approach. A working paper incorporating the format of the consolidated financial statements to be prepared offers some clear advantages. One alternative is to use a trial balance working paper. (An example of this format appears later in the chapter, where consolidation under the cost method is illustrated.) Regardless of the working paper format selected, however, the working paper entries are basically the same.

The **consolidated financial statement working paper** is organized to accommodate the income statement, statement of retained earnings, and balance sheet data. It is not used for preparation of the consolidated statement of changes in financial position, which is derived from comparative consolidated balance sheets and the consolidated statements of income and retained earnings. An example of our consolidated financial statement working paper is given in Exhibit 8.4. It has been completely filled out and incorporates the information from our last example. Since this working paper format will be used again and again, spend the time necessary to become thoroughly familiar with it now. Note that there are numerous subtotals which can help locate errors. The *arrows* on the right side of the working paper indicate (1) the location of ending inventory on both the income statement and balance sheet and (2) the *carry-forward* (or roll-forward) of income statement totals to the retained earnings statement and retained earnings totals to the balance sheet, which *effectively replicates the closing process on the working paper*. The last line of the working paper—total debits and credits of $1,950,000—summarizes the adjustments and eliminations related to the balance sheet accounts.

There are four aspects of the consolidated financial statement working paper which we mention in order to link it to the working paper entries presented in Exhibits 8.1 and 8.3:

1. Consistent with our earlier discussion, since the statement of retained earnings discloses dividends declared or paid, we have *separate captions for the dividends of both companies,* which decrease (are debited to) retained earnings. Therefore, when P's share of S's dividends—the intercompany dividends—is eliminated and when the minority's share of S's dividends is charged to the minority interest, the credits are to Dividends—S rather than to Retained Earnings—S.

2. The income statement portion of the working paper has no Cost of Goods Sold caption. Rather, it includes captions for the components of cost of goods sold—*Beginning Inventory* plus *Purchases* less *Ending Inventory.* Allocation of a purchase premium to Inventory at January 1, 19X1—for inventory assumed sold during the year—has the desired effect of increasing the cost of goods sold. The advantage of this breakdown will become clear in the next chapter when we address intercompany transactions involving merchandise.

3. The *Operating Expenses* caption includes depreciation and amortization expense. Thus we debit Operating Expenses for the amount of extra depreciation and amortization expense resulting from the purchase premium.

4. The Capital Stock caption reflects *total* paid-in capital—par value of common stock plus additional paid-in capital. When the investment account is eliminated against the stockholders' equity of S and the minority interest is established, the debit to Capital Stock—S on the working paper serves to remove both components of paid-in capital.

Consolidating a Pooling of Interests. Recall that in a pooling of interests, the Investment in S account reflects the *book value* of S Company's net assets. Furthermore, the assets and liabilities of S Company are brought into the consolidated balance sheet at their book values. Application of the equity method by P Company is therefore not complicated by the need to amortize a purchase premium or discount, as there is none.

Consolidation procedures in a pooling differ from those we have described only in that the working paper entries made to reclassify, allocate, and amortize a purchase discount or premium are not used. The working paper entries to eliminate the equity method accrual, intercompany dividends, and the investment account and to establish the minority interest continue to be central to the consolidation process.

Consolidation in Subsequent Years: Complete Equity Method

Use of the complete equity method simplifies the consolidation process in later years because the Investment in S account continues to reflect (1) the book value of P's equity interest in S and (2) any unamortized purchase premium or discount. At each consolidation point we accomplish the following:

1. Eliminate the current year's equity method entries, thereby restoring the investment account to its balance at the beginning of the current year.
2. Eliminate the investment account and reclassify the unamortized purchase premium or discount and the minority interest, all as of the beginning of the current year.
3. Allocate the unamortized purchase premium or discount.
4. Record the additional expenses associated with current year amortization of the purchase premium or discount.
5. Recognize the change in minority interest during the year by recording the minority's share of S's net income and charging any remaining subsidiary dividends against the minority interest.

We now work through consolidation at the end of 19X2 using the equity method. This will provide us with a good basis for subsequent comparison to the cost method as well as giving us the opportunity to add a complication to the procedure.

During 19X2, S Company reported net income of $400,000. On November 30, 19X2, S Company declared dividends of $110,000, payable on January 5, 19X3. This produces an *intercompany receivable and payable* at December 31, 19X2, for the unpaid dividends. As we have seen, P's share of these dividends is recorded under the equity method, but *not* as income. Elimination of the intercompany receivable/payable, however, is accomplished only in consolidation.

P Company determines its equity method accrual as shown in the following schedule:

SCHEDULE TO DETERMINE THE EQUITY METHOD ACCRUAL FOR THE YEAR ENDED DECEMBER 31, 19X2

P's Share of S's Net Income (.9 × $400,000)	$360,000
Less Amortization of Purchase Premium:	
Additional Depreciation ($180,000/15)	$ 12,000
Amortization of Goodwill ($75,000/40)	1,875
Total Amortization	$ 13,875[a]
Net Equity Method Accrual for 19X2	$346,125

[a]Recall that $45,000 of the purchase premium was allocated to inventory of S Company that was sold during 19X1.

The entries made by P company in connection with these developments are shown next:

BOOKS OF P COMPANY

11/30/X2

Dividends Receivable	99,000	
Investment in S		99,000
To record P's share of dividends declared by S Company; (.9 × $110,000).		

12/31/X2

Investment in S 346,125
  Income from S 346,125
To record P's share of S's net income for 19X2, reduced by
purchase premium amortization for 19X2.

The balance in the Investment in S account at December 31, 19X2, reflects the equity method transactions which occurred during 19X1 and 19X2. These are summarized in the following T account:

INVESTMENT IN S

Total Acquisition Cost ($1,200,000)	1/1/X1	Book Value of 90 Percent Interest Acquired	900,000			
	1/1/X1	Purchase Premium	300,000			
				19X1	90 percent of S Company's Dividends	90,000
Net Equity Method Accrual: 19X1 ($256,125)	12/31/X1	90 Percent of S's Net Income	315,000	12/31/X1	Purchase Premium Amortization	58,875
	12/31/X1	Balance	1,366,125			
				19X2	90 percent of S Company's Dividends	99,000
Net Equity Method Accrual: 19X2 ($346,125)	12/31/X2	90 Percent of S's Net Income	360,000	12/31/X2	Purchase Premium Amortization	13,875
	12/31/X2	Balance	1,613,250			

Again, we see that the balance in the investment account reflects (1) the book value of P's 90 percent interest in S, $1,386,000 [= .9($1,000,000 + $350,000 − $100,000 + $400,000 − $110,000)], and (2) the *unamortized purchase premium* of $227,250 (= $300,000 − $58,875 − $13,875). After the unamortized purchase premium is reclassified and allocated on the working paper, the amount remaining in the investment account—the book value of P's 90 percent interest in S—can be cleanly eliminated against S's stockholders' equity.

The working paper entries needed to consolidate P and S at December 31, 19X2, are given in Exhibit 8.5. In Exhibit 8.6, the complete consolidated balance sheet, income statement, and statement of retained earnings data for P and S at December 31, 19X2, are given in our working paper format. The numbered entries in Exhibit 8.5 are posted to the working paper and the consolidated financial statement balances are computed.

Consolidation under the Cost Method in a Trial Balance Format

When P Company uses the *cost method* to account for an intercorporate investment, the Investment in S will *not* reflect changes in the book value of S Com-

Exhibit 8.5   Consolidated Financial Statement Working Paper Entries for the Year Ended December 31, 19X2 ($\alpha = .9$)

(1)

Income from S	346,125	
Dividends—S.		99,000
Investment in S.		247,125

To eliminate the equity method entries recorded by P, thereby adjusting the investment account to its balance on Jan. 1, 19X2.

(2)

Retained Earnings—S, Jan. 1, 19X2	750,000	
Capital Stock—S	500,000	
Purchase Premium ($300,000 − $45,000 − $12,000 − $1,875)	241,125	
Investment in S.		1,366,125
Minority Interest in S		125,000

To reclassify the purchase premium, now reduced by the amortization recorded at Dec. 31, 19X1, eliminate the Investment in S against 90 percent of the stockholders' equity of S, and reclassify the remaining stockholders' equity as minority interest, all as of Jan. 1, 19X2.

(3)

Buildings and Equipment	180,000	
Goodwill ($75,000 − $1,875)	73,125	
Accumulated Depreciation		12,000
Purchase Premium ($300,000 − $58,875)		241,125

To allocate the unamortized purchase premium at Jan. 1, 19X2, to the assets of S and goodwill. The original purchase premium allocations made at Jan. 1, 19X1, and the 19X1 amortization amounts are shown in parentheses (except for inventory of $45,000 that was sold during 19X1).

(4)

Operating Expenses	13,875	
Accumulated Depreciation		12,000
Goodwill		1,875

To recognize current year amortization of the purchase premium in the consolidated income statement for 19X2.

(5)

Minority Interest in Net Income	40,000	
Dividends—S.		11,000
Minority Interest in S		29,000

To record the change in the minority interest during 19X2, consisting of the minority's interest in net income decreased by S's dividends paid to minority shareholders.

(6)

Current Liabilities	99,000	
Cash and Receivables		99,000

To eliminate the intercompany receivable and payable related to P's share of S's dividends declared but unpaid at Dec. 31, 19X2.

Exhibit 8.6 **P and S Companies: Consolidated Financial Statement Working Paper for the Year Ended December 31, 19X2 (Equity Method)**

	P Company	S Company (90%)	Adjustments and Eliminations		Consolidated
INCOME STATEMENT			Dr.	Cr.	
Sales and Other Revenue. . . .	2,210,000	1,560,000			3,770,000
Income from S.	346,125	—	(1) 346,125		—
Inventory, 12/31/X2.	80,000	410,000			490,000
Total Credits.	2,636,125	1,970,000	346,125		4,260,000
Inventory, 1/1/X2.	75,000	390,000			465,000
Purchases.	1,120,000	740,000			1,860,000
Operating Expenses	520,000	440,000	(4) 13,875		973,875
Total Debits	1,715,000	1,570,000	13,875		3,298,875
Minority Interest in Net Income .	—	—	(5) 40,000		(40,000)
Net Income—to Ret. Earn. Stmt.	921,125	400,000	400,000		921,125
RETAINED EARNINGS STATEMENT					
Retained Earnings, 1/1/X2—P .	1,511,125	—			1,511,125
Retained Earnings, 1/1/X2—S .	—	750,000	(2) 750,000		—
Net Income—from Inc. Stmt. . .	921,125	400,000	400,000		921,125
Dividends—P	(230,000)	—			(230,000)
Dividends—S	—	(110,000)		(1) 99,000	—
				(5) 11,000	
Ret. Earn., 12/31/X2—to Balance Sheet.	2,202,250	1,040,000	1,150,000	110,000	2,202,250
BALANCE SHEET					
Cash and Receivables	399,000	436,000		(6) 99,000	736,000
Inventory	80,000	410,000			490,000
Investment in S	1,613,250	—		(1) 247,125	—
				(2) 1,366,125	
Other Investments	109,000	—			109,000
Purchase Premium.	—	—	(2) 241,125	(3) 241,125	—
Land	341,000	300,000			641,000
Buildings and Equipment	2,400,000	1,250,000	(3) 180,000		3,830,000
Accumulated Depreciation. . . .	(920,000)	(100,000)		(3) 12,000	(1,044,000)
				(4) 12,000	—
Goodwill	—	—	(3) 73,125	(4) 1,875	71,250
Total	4,022,250	2,296,000	494,250	1,979,250	4,833,250
Current Liabilities	320,000	256,000	(6) 99,000		477,000
Other Liabilities	700,000	500,000			1,200,000
Capital Stock—P.	800,000	—			800,000
Capital Stock—S.	—	500,000	(2) 500,000		—
Ret. Earn.—from Retained Earnings Statement.	2,202,250	1,040,000	1,150,000	110,000	2,202,250
Minority Interest in S	—	—		(2) 125,000	154,000
				(5) 29,000	
Total	4,022,250	2,296,000	1,749,000	264,000	4,833,250
			2,243,250	2,243,250	

Explanations of Working Paper Entries

(1) To eliminate the equity method entries made by P Company during 19X2.
(2) To eliminate the investment account and reclassify the purchase premium and minority interest as of January 1, 19X2.
(3) To allocate the purchase premium as of January 1, 19X2.
(4) To recognize current year amortization of the purchase premium.
(5) To record the change in the minority interest during 19X2.
(6) To eliminate intercompany receivables and payables.

pany's stockholders' equity. Similarly, P's retained earnings will include only the cumulative dividend income received from S but *not* P's equity in S's undistributed earnings since acquisition.

For these reasons, the investment account cannot be cleanly eliminated against S's stockholders' equity. If S's retained earnings have grown since acquisition, the growth would remain after the investment account, as recorded at date of acquisition, was eliminated. There are two ways to deal with this problem:

1. Prepare a working paper entry which would restate the Investment in S account and P's retained earnings to the equity basis at the beginning of the current year. After eliminating the dividend income recorded by P under the cost method against Dividends—S, proceed with the consolidation as before; *or*
2. Eliminate the Investment in S, as recorded at date of acquisition, against S's stockholders' equity at date of acquisition and allocate the purchase premium, charging any prior year amortization against P's retained earnings. Then after eliminating the intercompany dividends as in No. 1 above, allocate the growth in S's retained earnings between the retained earnings of P and the minority interest. This can be done with a working paper entry or by adding a Minority Interest column and extending the appropriate amounts to the Minority and Consolidated columns.

Of these two options, we prefer the first. We believe that this approach is more systematic in that it places all working paper manipulations in journal entry form.

To illustrate consolidation under the cost method, we use the data developed in our previous example for the year ended December 31, 19X2. The first step is to determine the amount needed to restate the investment account and P's retained earnings to the equity basis at January 1, 19X2. This is done in the schedule given in Exhibit 8.7.

In our example, an adjustment of $166,125 is required to bring both the investment account and the parent's retained earnings up to their balances at January 1, 19X2, under the equity method. An additional working paper entry must be made to reflect this restatement; it will be given shortly.

After this has been accomplished, the only remaining difference between the cost and equity methods involves intercompany dividends. Under the equity method, dividends received by P from S were credited to the investment account. In contrast, intercompany dividends are recorded by P as *Dividend Income* when the cost method is used. Therefore, the debit part of the eliminating entry which

Exhibit 8.7	**Determining the Needed Restatement of the Investment Account and the Retained Earnings of P Company at January 1, 19X2 (Cost Method Used by P Company)**

	Investment in S	Retained Earnings—P
Balance at Acquisition, Jan. 1, 19X1.	$1,200,000	$ 900,000
90 Percent of S's Net Income—Year 1	315,000	315,000
90 Percent of S's Dividends—Year 1	(90,000)	—
Amortization of Purchase Premium—Year 1.	(58,875)	(58,875)
P's Income from Its Own Operations—Year 1	—	555,000[a]
P's Dividends Declared—Year 1.	—	(200,000)
Equity Method Balances, Dec. 31, 19X1.	$1,366,125	$1,511,125
Balances per Books, Dec. 31, 19X1, Cost Method.	1,200,000	1,345,000[b]
Required Restatement.	$ 166,125	$ 166,125

[a]P's income from its own operations ($555,000) is simply its net income as recorded in Exhibit 8.4 ($811,125) less the equity method accrual of $256,125. Alternatively, $555,000 = $811,125 − ($315,000 − $58,875).
[b]This amount consists of P's retained earnings at January 1, 19X1 ($900,000), plus P's net income from its own operations ($555,000) plus dividend income from S ($90,000) less dividends declared by P ($200,000).

---

removes the intercompany dividends is to the Dividend Income account. Both of these entries appear below. All other working paper entries are the same as under the equity method.

CONSOLIDATED TRIAL BALANCE WORKING PAPER

Investment in S	166,125	
Retained Earnings—P		166,125

To restate the Investment in S and Retained Earnings—P, as carried under the cost method, to the equity method as of January 1, 19X2.

Dividend Income	99,000	
Dividends—S.		99,000

To eliminate the current year's intercompany dividends under the cost method.

Consolidated Trial Balance Working Paper. Consolidation procedures can readily be executed by using a working paper including the adjusted trial balances of P and S. The trial balance working paper is generally fashioned in one of two ways:

1. The final column (following the Adjustments and Eliminations columns) contains the consolidated trial balance. Once the consolidated trial balance is prepared, the resulting consolidated account balances are used in the formal consolidated financial statements.

2. Additional columns labeled "Balance Sheet," "Income Statement," and "Statement of Retained Earnings" may be included. Then, after the consolidation entries are recorded on the working paper, the consolidated account balances can be extended directly into the appropriate financial statement columns.

Our illustration incorporates both of the above. We provide a column for the consolidated trial balance and additional columns for the three financial statements. Having studied the consolidated financial statement working paper, the reader may wish to compare it with the trial balance working paper approach. The completed trial balance working paper for 19X2 appears in Exhibit 8.8.

Note that the trial balance working paper includes the same accounts as our financial statement working paper, although the format differs. As a result, under our system *working paper entries are the same whether the trial balance or financial statement format is being used*. Refer to Exhibits 8.5 and 8.6 to convince yourself of this. In doing so, remember that P's use of the cost method is being illustrated on this trial balance working paper, while the equity method was used previously. Had the financial statement working paper format been used to illustrate the cost method, it would include those working paper entries—(1) and (2) in Exhibit 8.8—which are specific to the cost method.

Business Combinations during an Accounting Period

Up to this point, our examples always involved business combinations at the beginning or end of an accounting period in order to avoid the minor technical problems caused by combination during an accounting period. When a purchase combination occurs *during* an accounting period, one must decide how to report the subsidiary's current period earnings *prior* to the combination when the consolidated statements are prepared at year-end. In a pooling, the consolidated income statement always includes the affiliate's revenues and expenses for the *entire year*. There are, however, two alternative treatments for the purchase case:

1. Include only the subsidiary's revenues and expenses arising *after* the date of acquisition in the consolidated income statement. Minority Interest in Net Income reflects the minority's share of the subsidiary's net income *after* acquisition. This follows from the fact that in purchase combinations the subsidiary's retained earnings at date of combination are eliminated. In effect, this treatment eliminates the subsidiary's revenues, expenses, and earnings prior to the business combination date.

2. Report the subsidiary's sales and expenses for the entire year but show a deduction for **preacquisition earnings**—the parent's share of the subsidiary's net income prior to date of combination—in the consolidated income statement. Here the Minority Interest in Net Income *includes the minority's pro forma share of the subsidiary's net income for the entire year. ARB 51* expresses a preference for this approach:

   One method, which usually is preferable . . . is to include the subsidiary in the consolidation as though it had been acquired at the beginning of the year, and to deduct at the bottom of the consolidated income statement the preacquisition earn-

Exhibit 8.8 P and S Companies: Consolidated Trial Balance Working Paper for the Year Ended December 31, 19X2 (Cost Method)

Account	P Company Dr. (Cr.)	S Company (90%) Dr. (Cr.)	Adjustments and Eliminations Dr.	Adjustments and Eliminations Cr.	Consolidated Trial Balance	Consolidated Income Statement	Consolidated Retained Earnings Statement	Consolidated Balance Sheet
Cash and Receivables	399,000	436,000		(7) 99,000	736,000			736,000
Inventory, 1/1/X2	75,000	390,000			465,000	465,000		
Inventory, 12/31/X2	80,000	410,000			490,000			490,000
Investment in S	1,200,000	—		(3) 1,366,125	—			
Purchase Premium	—	—	(1) 166,125 (3) 241,125	(4) 241,125	—			
Other Investments	109,000	—			109,000			109,000
Land	341,000	300,000			641,000			641,000
Buildings and Equipment	2,400,000	1,250,000	(4) 180,000		3,830,000			3,830,000
Accumulated Depreciation	(920,000)	(100,000)		(4) 12,000 (5) 12,000	(1,044,000)			(1,044,000)
Goodwill	—	—	(4) 73,125	(5) 1,875	71,250			71,250
Current Liabilities	(320,000)	(256,000)	(7) 99,000		(477,000)			(477,000)
Other Liabilities	(700,000)	(500,000)			(1,200,000)			(1,200,000)
Capital Stock—P	(800,000)	—			(800,000)			(800,000)
Capital Stock—S	—	(500,000)	(3) 500,000		—			
Retained Earnings—P, 1/1/X2	(1,345,000)	—		(1) 166,125	(1,511,125)		(1,511,125)	
Retained Earnings—S, 1/1/X2	—	(750,000)	(3) 750,000		—			
Dividends—P	230,000				230,000		230,000	
Dividends—S	—	110,000		(2) 99,000 (6) 11,000	—			
Minority Interest in S	—	—		(3) 125,000 (6) 29,000	(154,000)			(154,000)
Sales and Other Revenue	(2,210,000)	(1,560,000)			(3,770,000)	(3,770,000)		
Dividend Income from S	(99,000)	—	(2) 99,000		—			
Purchases	1,120,000	740,000			1,860,000	1,860,000		
Operating Expenses	520,000	440,000	(5) 13,875		973,875	973,875		
Inventory, 12/31/X2	(80,000)	(410,000)			(490,000)	(490,000)		
Minority Interest in Net Income	—	—	(6) 40,000		40,000	40,000		
Total	0	0	2,162,250	2,162,250	0			
Consolidated Net Income						(921,125)	(921,125)	
Consolidated Retained Earnings, 12/31/X2							(2,202,250)	(2,202,250)

Explanations of Working Paper Entries

(1) To adjust the Investment in S and retained Earnings of P to the equity basis as of January 1, 19X2.
(2) To eliminate the intercompany dividends.
(3) To eliminate the investment account and reclassify the purchase premium and minority interest as of January 1, 19X2.
(4) To allocate the purchase premium as of January 1, 19X2.
(5) To recognize current year amortization of the purchase premium.
(6) To record the change in the minority interest during 19X2.
(7) To eliminate intercompany receivables and payables.

ings. . . . This method presents results which are more indicative of the current status of the group, and facilitates future comparison with subsequent years.[7]

In our view, each method has advantages and disadvantages. Including only revenues and expenses generated by the subsidiary after date of acquisition (Method 1) seems more conceptually sound as long as some indication of the magnitude of the effect on consolidated net income is disclosed. Adopting the position favored by *ARB 51* (Method 2) does provide investors with a pro forma view of the entire year. Yet, when acquisition occurs late in the year, almost all of the subsidiary's net income would be deducted as preacquisition earnings, a somewhat odd treatment. We have a slight preference for including only the revenues and expenses generated by the subsidiary after acquisition—Method 1—but will illustrate both alternatives.

Suppose Praxon Corporation acquires 80 percent of the outstanding stock of the Sonnet Company on April 1, 19X2, at a cost of $40,000,000. Sonnet's contributed capital was recorded at $25,000,000 on January 1, 19X2, and has not changed. An analysis of Sonnet's retained earnings and 19X2 operations appears in Exhibit 8.9.

Exhibit 8.9 **Analysis of Changes in Sonnet's Retained Earnings Account during 19X2**

Retained Earnings, Jan. 1, 19X2	$ 10,400,000
Less Dividends Declared and Paid, Feb. 15, 19X2	(1,400,000)
Plus Revenue Realized, Jan. 1, 19X2–Mar. 31, 19X2	15,000,000
Less Operating Expenses, Jan. 1, 19X2–Mar. 31, 19X2	(11,000,000)
Retained Earnings If Books Closed on Mar. 31, 19X2	$ 13,000,000
Less Dividends Declared and Paid, Aug. 15, 19X2	(1,000,000)
Plus Revenue Realized, Apr. 1, 19X2–Dec. 31, 19X2	48,000,000
Less Operating Expenses, Apr. 1, 19X2–Dec. 31, 19X2	(34,000,000)
Retained Earnings after Closing on Dec. 31, 19X2	$ 26,000,000

[7]Committee on Accounting Procedure, *Accounting Research Bulletin No. 51,* "Consolidated Financial Statements" (New York: AICPA, 1959), par. 11; CT § C51.112.

Exhibit 8.10	Alternative Consolidated Income Statements in the Praxon and Sonnet Intraperiod Business Combination

	Praxon and Sonnet Consolidated	
	Method 1	Method 2
Sales	$ 198,000,000	$ 213,000,000
Operating Expenses	(144,000,000)	(155,000,000)
Goodwill Amortization	(180,000)[a]	(180,000)[a]
Minority Interest in Net Income	(2,800,000)[b]	(3,600,000)[c]
Preacquisition Earnings		(3,200,000)[d]
Consolidated Net Income	$ 51,020,000	$ 51,020,000

[a]$180,000 = .75($9,600,000/40).
[b]$2,800,000 = .2($48,000,000 − $34,000,000); based on Sonnet's net income during the postacquisition period only.
[c]$3,600,000 = .2[($15,000,000 + $48,000,000) − ($11,000,000 + $34,000,000)]; based on Sonnet's net income for the entire year.
[d]$3,200,000 = .8($15,000,000 − $11,000,000).

Praxon is paying a purchase premium of $9,600,000 [= $40,000,000 − .8($25,000,000 + $13,000,000)], which we assume is attributed entirely to goodwill. Given that Praxon had revenue of $150,000,000 and operating expenses of $110,000,000 from its own operations, we prepare consolidated income statements under the two methods in Exhibit 8.10.

Assuming that Praxon uses the equity method, it would record 80 percent of Sonnet's postacquisition income, $11,200,000 [= .8($48,000,000 − $34,000,000)], less goodwill amortization for three-fourths of the year, $180,000 [= ($9,600,000/40)(¾)], for a total of $11,020,000. Similarly, Praxon would reduce the investment account by 80 percent of Sonnet's postacquisition dividends, $800,000 (= .8 × $1,000,000). These entries are identical under Methods 1 and 2, and they will be reversed on the working paper in consolidation at December 31, 19X2.

If Method 1 is used, Sonnet's books should be closed as of April 1 so that in consolidation beginning retained earnings—now dated April 1—reflect net income and dividends for the first three months of the year. The usual eliminating entries are then made. Under Method 2, however, Sonnet's books are *not* closed as of April 1. Beginning retained earnings is dated January 1 and does *not* include net income and dividends through March 31. Therefore, both Sonnet's retained earnings at January 1 and the change (net income less dividends) during the preacquisition period must be eliminated. This is accomplished in two working paper entries:

1. The investment account balance at April 1 is eliminated against 80 percent of (a) Sonnet's stockholders' equity at January 1 and (b) Sonnet's earnings and dividends during the preacquisition period. The minority interest in Sonnet as of January 1 is also established in this entry.

2. The *change in the minority interest* is computed on a pro forma basis for the *entire year*. The working paper entry establishes 20 percent of Sonnet's

net income for the entire year as minority interest in net income and eliminates the remaining 20 percent of Sonnet's dividends for the entire year.

We now present the working paper entries made at December 31, 19X2, under *Method 2,* assuming that the investment account is carried at equity.

CONSOLIDATED FINANCIAL STATEMENT WORKING PAPER
(Method 2)

Income from Sonnet	11,020,000	
Dividends—Sonnet		800,000
Investment in Sonnet		10,220,000

To eliminate the investment income and intercompany dividends recorded under the equity method; $11,020,000 = .8($48,000,000 - $34,000,000) - $180,000.

Preacquisition Earnings	3,200,000	
Contributed Capital—Sonnet	25,000,000	
Retained Earnings—Sonnet	10,400,000	
Goodwill	9,600,000	
Dividends—Sonnet		1,120,000
Investment in Sonnet		40,000,000
Minority Interest in Sonnet		7,080,000

To eliminate the investment account against the stockholders' equity of Sonnet, establish the minority interest, eliminate Praxon's share of the preacquisition dividends, and record the preacquisition earnings. The minority interest is calculated as of Jan. 1, 19X2; $7,080,000 [= .2($25,000,000 + $10,400,000)].

Amortization Expense	180,000	
Goodwill		180,000

To record amortization of goodwill for three fourths of the year.

Minority Interest in Net Income	3,600,000	
Dividends—Sonnet		480,000
Minority Interest in Sonnet		3,120,000

To record the change in the minority interest during 19X2, consisting of the minority's interest in net income decreased by the minority's share of Sonnet's dividends; [$480,000 = .2($1,400,000 + $1,000,000)]. Minority interest in Sonnet at Dec. 31, 19X2, is $10,200,000 [= .2($25,000,000 + $26,000,000) = $7,080,000 + $3,120,000].

Three observations should be made about the working paper entries shown. *First,* the amount of Sonnet's net income for the year not included in consolidated net income is $6,800,000 [= ($15,000,000 - $11,000,000) + .2($48,000,000 - $34,000,000)]. The entries break this into two components: preacquisition earnings of $3,200,000 and minority interest in net income of $3,600,000. *Second,* $1,600,000 [= $1,400,000 + (.2 × $1,000,000)] of Sonnet's dividends were not paid to the controlling stockholders during the year. This amount also has two components: preacquisition dividends of $1,120,000 and 20 percent of Sonnet's total dividends, $480,000. *Third,* elimination of the portion of the investment account attributable to Praxon's share of the growth in Sonnet's retained earnings during the first three months of 19X2, $2,080,000 [= .8($13,000,000 − $10,400,000)], is reflected in the difference between the preacquisition earnings established ($3,200,000) and the preacquisition dividends eliminated ($1,120,000).

Consolidated Statement of Changes in Financial Position

Although the **statement of changes in financial position (SCFP),** or "funds" statement, is not a new disclosure device, it was not required as part of a firm's basic financial statements until 1971, when *APBO 19* was issued; it set forth the following requirement:

> When financial statements purporting to present both financial position (balance sheet) and results of operations (statement of income and retained earnings) are issued, a statement summarizing changes in financial position should also be presented as a basic financial statement for each period for which an income statement is presented.[8]

Nature of the Statement of Changes in Financial Position

The SCFP filled a significant gap in corporate reporting. It provided a much more complete link between successive balance sheets than statements of income and retained earnings alone. This linkage was established by the objectives of the SCFP, given in *APBO 19:*

> The objectives of a funds statement are (1) to summarize the financing and investing activities of the entity, including the extent to which the enterprise has generated funds from operations during the period, and (2) to complete the disclosure of changes in financial position during the period.[9]

The term **funds** refers to a short-term concept of net assets, typically **working capital** (current assets less current liabilities) or **cash.** In either case, the SCFP usually reports a computation of funds provided by operations and the other significant investing and financing activities which took place, even if they did not directly affect funds (for example, the issuance of common stock to retire bonds). If funds are defined as *working capital,* the SCFP may be viewed as an analysis of the change in working capital through reference to the changes in the *non-working-capital* accounts. If funds are defined as *cash,* the analysis explains the change in cash by referring to changes in the *noncash* accounts. An algebraic approach to understanding the SCFP is given in Exhibit 8.11.

---

[8]Accounting Principles Board, *Opinion No. 19,* "Reporting Changes in Financial Position" (New York: AICPA, 1971), par. 7; CT § F40.101.
[9]Ibid., par. 4; CT § F40.103.

Exhibit 8.11 **An Algebraic Approach to Understanding the Statement of Changes in Financial Position**

CA = Current assets. NCL = Noncurrent liabilities.

CL = Current liabilities. SE = Stockholders' equity.

NCA = Noncurrent assets. Δ = Greek letter *delta*, indicating *change in*.

The fundamental accounting equation provides that

$$Assets = Liabilities + Stockholders'\ Equity$$

$$CA + NCA = CL + NCL + SE,$$

which is the definition of a balance sheet. Since this equation holds for successive balance sheets, we can add the Δ to indicate change in the various balance sheet categories:

$$\Delta CA + \Delta NCA = \Delta CL + \Delta NCL + \Delta SE.$$

Using working capital as our definition of funds, we rearrange terms and have:

$$\Delta CA - \Delta CL = \Delta NCL + \Delta SE - \Delta NCA.$$

Thus our solution technique and the formal SCFP itself are based upon the concept of using changes in the *non-working-capital accounts* to explain the change in *working capital.* If funds are defined as cash (C), then the change in cash (ΔC) is explained through reference to changes in the *noncash accounts:*

$$\Delta C = \Delta CL - (\Delta CA - \Delta C) + \Delta NCL + \Delta SE - \Delta NCA.$$

Recent years have witnessed a dramatic increase in the number of companies defining funds as cash or cash plus short-term investments in their funds statements. Today, a majority of large companies no longer utilize working capital as the overall definition of funds in the funds statement. *Most companies, however, continue to report a line item representing working capital from operations, even in a cash-based SCFP.* Thus calculation of cash flow from operations in our illustration begins with the intermediate calculation of working capital from operations (see No. 6 in the next section).

We shall not duplicate the more complete discussions of the statement of changes in financial position found in intermediate accounting textbooks. Rather, we shall highlight the particular items that tend to show up on a consolidated SCFP and work through an example using the **T account solution method.**

Preparation of the Consolidated Statement of Changes in Financial Position

A consolidated statement of changes in financial position is prepared from comparative consolidated balance sheets, consolidated statements of income and retained earnings, and any necessary supplementary information. Attempts to prepare a consolidated SCFP from the unconsolidated SCFPs of companies P and S are relatively inefficient. Eliminations would have to be made both here and again when the other financial statements are consolidated. We now consider some items that are often encountered in a consolidated SCFP.

1. In determining funds provided by operations, *amortization of goodwill* arising in consolidation must be *added back to consolidated net income*. It is a deduction from net income which does not use funds—it decreases a noncurrent asset, goodwill.

2. *Minority interest in net income* is deducted in computing consolidated net income. Since it does not use funds—it increases a stockholders' equity account—it must be *added back* in computing funds provided by operations. Similarly, the *minority interest in a net loss* is added in computing consolidated net income. Since this does not provide funds—it decreases a stockholders' equity account—it must be *deducted* in computing funds provided by operations.

3. *Dividends paid to minority shareholders* are shown as a *nonoperating use of funds*. Payment of such dividends reduces Minority Interest in S, a stockholders' equity account.

4. *Purchase of additional subsidiary shares* in the open market constitutes a *nonoperating use of funds*. In contrast, if the shares are purchased directly from the subsidiary, there is no effect on consolidated funds or on the parent's capital stock account. Hence, no disclosure is needed on the funds statement.

5. *Undistributed equity method income (loss)* from *unconsolidated* subsidiaries or other equity method investments must be *subtracted (added)* in computing funds provided by operations. The accrual of such equity method income increases other noncurrent assets—long-term (unconsolidated) equity investments—and does not itself provide funds; it must be subtracted from consolidated net income. Dividends received from such investments, however, represent a realization of the equity method income and *do* increase funds. These dividends must be included in funds provided by operations. Therefore, the net effect is to subtract the undistributed equity method income (not received in dividends) in arriving at funds provided by operations.

6. As mentioned above, most companies report a line representing working capital from operations in their SCFP, regardless of their overall definition of "funds." If "funds" are defined as *cash* (or cash plus short-term investments), additional adjustments are needed to convert this measure of working capital from operations to an estimate of **cash flow from operations.** Known as the **indirect adjustment algorithm,**[10] this conversion method (a) *adds back* the changes in those current operating accounts (other than cash) which experienced a *credit change* (e.g., decrease in receivables, increase

---

[10]See James A. Largay III and Clyde P. Stickney, "Cash Flows, Ratio Analysis and the W. T. Grant Company Bankruptcy," *Financial Analysts Journal,* July/August 1980, 51–54, for a discussion and an interesting application of the indirect adjustment algorithm.

Consolidated Funds Statement Illustration

P COMPANY AND S COMPANY
COMPARATIVE CONSOLIDATED BALANCE SHEETS
AT DECEMBER 31, 19X2 AND 19X1

ASSETS		12/31/X2		12/31/X1
Cash		$ 305,000		$ 250,000
Receivables		380,000		385,000
Inventory		490,000		465,000
Total Current Assets		$1,175,000		$1,100,000
Other Investments		$ 109,000		$ 100,000
Land		641,000		400,000
Buildings and Equipment	$ 3,830,000		$3,180,000	
Less Accumulated Depreciation	(1,044,000)	2,786,000	(812,000)	2,368,000
Goodwill		71,250		73,125
Total Noncurrent Assets		$3,607,250		$2,941,125
Total Assets		$4,782,250		$4,041,125

LIABILITIES AND STOCKHOLDERS' EQUITY

		12/31/X2		12/31/X1
Current Liabilities		$ 427,250		$ 375,000
Other Liabilities		1,200,000		1,230,000
Total Liabilities		$1,627,250		$1,605,000
Capital Stock		$ 800,000		$ 800,000
Retained Earnings		2,201,000		1,511,125
Minority Interest in S		154,000		125,000
Total Stockholders' Equity		$3,155,000		$2,436,125
Total Liabilities and Stockholders' Equity		$4,782,250		$4,041,125

P COMPANY AND S COMPANY
CONSOLIDATED STATEMENT OF INCOME
AND RETAINED EARNINGS
FOR THE YEAR ENDED DECEMBER 31, 19X2

Sales and Other Revenue		$3,768,750
Cost of Goods Sold:		
Inventory, Jan. 1, 19X2	$ 465,000	
Purchases	1,860,000	
Inventory, Dec. 31, 19X2	(490,000)	$1,835,000
Operating Expenses		973,875
Minority Interest in Net Income		40,000
Total Expenses		$2,848,875
Net Income		$ 919,875
Retained Earnings, Jan. 1, 19X2		1,511,125
Dividends Declared		(230,000)
Retained Earnings, Dec. 31, 19X2		$2,201,000

Other Information:

1. Consolidated depreciation expense was $232,000.
2. Sales and Other Revenue includes $15,000 income from equity method investments; $6,000 in dividends was received.

in payables) and (b) *subtracts* the changes in those current operating accounts (other than cash) which experienced a *debit change* (e.g., increase in inventory, decrease in accrued liabilities).

Consolidated Funds Statement: An Illustration. Our illustration is based on the data previously developed for companies P and S. We now have comparative consolidated balance sheets for P and S at December 31, 19X1 and 19X2, and a consolidated statement of income and retained earnings for 19X2. These statements are presented in Exhibit 8.12 on page 383. The formal consolidated statement of changes in financial position (working capital basis) for 19X2 appears in Exhibit 8.13 and the T account work sheet used in its preparation appears in Exhibit 8.14.

When "funds" are defined as *cash,* we can apply the indirect adjustment

---

Exhibit 8.13   **P and S Companies: Consolidated Statement of Changes in Financial Position for the Year Ended December 31, 19X2 (Working Capital Basis)**

P COMPANY AND S COMPANY
CONSOLIDATED STATEMENT OF CHANGES IN FINANCIAL POSITION
FOR THE YEAR ENDED DECEMBER 31, 19X2

Working Capital Provided by Operations:
Net Income . . . . $ 919,875
Add (Subtract) Items Not Using (Providing) Working Capital:
  Depreciation Expense 232,000
  Goodwill Amortization 1,875
  Minority Interest in Net Income. 40,000
  Undistributed Equity Method Income. (9,000)

Working Capital Provided by Operations. $1,184,750

Working Capital Used for:
Payment of Dividends to P's Shareholders. . . . . $ 230,000
Payment of Dividends to Minority Shareholders 11,000
Purchase of Land 241,000
Purchase of Buildings and Equipment 650,000
Reduction in Other Liabilities. 30,000

Total Uses of Working Capital $1,162,000

Increase in Working Capital . . . . $ 22,750

SCHEDULE OF CHANGES IN WORKING CAPITAL ACCOUNTS

	12/31/X2	12/31/X1	Increase (Decrease) in Working Capital
Cash	$ 305,000	$ 250,000	$ 55,000
Receivables.	380,000	385,000	(5,000)
Inventory	490,000	465,000	25,000
Current Liabilities	(427,250)	(375,000)	(52,250)
Total	$ 747,750	$ 725,000	$ 22,750

Exhibit 8.14 **P and S Companies: T Account Work Sheet Used to Prepare Consolidated Statement of Changes in Financial Position (Working Capital Basis)**

WORKING CAPITAL

Balance, 1/1/X2   725,000

From Operations

(Net Income and Additions)			(Subtractions)		
Net Income	(1)	919,875	Equity Method Income from		
Depreciation Expense	(2)	232,000	Other Investments	(3)	15,000
Dividends from Other					
Investments	(4)	6,000			
Goodwill Amortization	(5)	1,875			
Minority Interest in Net Income	(6)	40,000			
		(15,000)			
W/C Provided by					
Operations		1,184,750			

Nonoperating

(Sources)		(Uses)		
		Purchase of Land	(7)	241,000
		Purchase of Buildings and		
		Equipment	(8)	650,000
		Decrease in Other Liabilities	(9)	30,000
		Parent Company Dividends	(10)	230,000
		Dividends Paid to Minority		
		Interest	(11)	11,000
		Total Nonoperating		
		Uses of W/C		1,162,000

Balance, 12/31/X2   747,750

Other Investments			
1/1	100,000		
(3)	15,000	(4)	6,000
12/31	109,000		

Land			
1/1	400,000		
(7)	241,000		
12/31	641,000		

Buildings and Equipment			
1/1	3,180,000		
(8)	650,000		
12/31	3,830,000		

Accumulated Depreciation			
		1/1	812,000
		(2)	232,000
		12/31	1,044,000

Goodwill			
1/1	73,125		
		(5)	1,875
12/31	71,250		

Other Liabilities			
		1/1	1,230,000
(9)	30,000		
		12/31	1,200,000

Capital Stock			
		1/1	800,000
		12/31	800,000

Retained Earnings			
		1/1	1,511,125
(10)	230,000	(1)	919,875
		12/31	2,201,000

Minority Interest in S			
		1/1	125,000
(11)	11,000	(6)	40,000
		12/31	154,000

Exhibit 8.15	**P and S Companies: Conversion of Consolidated Working Capital Provided by Operations to Consolidated Cash Flow from Operations**

Working Capital Provided by Operations (Exhibit 8.13) $1,184,750
Add (Subtract) Credit (Debit) Changes in Working Capital Accounts:
   Decrease in Receivables 5,000
   Increase in Inventory . . . . (25,000)
   Increase in Current Liabilities 52,250
Cash Flow from Operations $1,217,000

Note: Net increase in cash is $55,000 (= $1,217,000 − $1,162,000).

algorithm to convert Working Capital Provided by Operations to an estimate of Cash Flow from Operations, as shown in Exhibit 8.15. A formal cash-based SCFP would use the statement in Exhibit 8.13 and the conversion in Exhibit 8.15 and would arrive at a bottom line Increase in Cash of $55,000 (= $305,000 − $250,000). Moreover, there would be no need for the Schedule of Changes in Working Capital Accounts shown in the lower part of Exhibit 8.13.

Accounting for Income Taxes and Consolidated Statements

Intercorporate investments create some interesting complications in accounting for income taxes. We introduce certain of these issues now but defer considering the tax effects of unconfirmed intercompany gains and losses until Chapter 9.

Recall that *APBO 11* requires comprehensive interperiod income tax allocation.[11] Under this concept, a distinction is drawn between **income tax expense**—which accrues as income subject to tax is recognized in the accounting records—and **income tax liability**—which reflects taxes actually due to the government. The amount of income tax expense is based on pretax book income, while the amount of income tax liability is based on the income tax return. Most income tax accounting problems are traceable to differences between the firm's pretax book income and tax return income for a given reporting period. These differences are of two general types:

1. **Timing differences:** Some items affect book income and tax return income in different reporting periods, thereby creating temporary dissimilarities between book income and tax return income. In time, these dissimilarities *reverse*. When straight-line depreciation is used for book purposes and accelerated depreciation for tax purposes, tax depreciation will first exceed and

---

[11]Accounting Principles Board, *Opinion No. 11*, "Accounting for Income Taxes" (New York: AICPA, 1967); CT § 124.

then fall short of book depreciation over the asset's life. It is the existence of such timing differences that generated the perceived need for comprehensive interperiod tax allocation and the accrual of deferred income taxes.

2. **Permanent differences:** Some items affect *only* book income or tax return income, thereby creating lasting dissimilarities between book income and tax return income. The tax effect of such items does not reverse over time. For example, interest on municipal bonds is properly includable as book income but is permanently exempt from taxation under current law. Permanent differences do *not* give rise to deferred income taxes.

With these definitions in mind, we turn to their significance when intercorporate investments are concerned. Many groups of affiliated corporations issue consolidated income statements but do not file consolidated income tax returns. We defer discussion of consolidated tax returns to a later section and now examine how use of the equity method affects accounting for income taxes when consolidated returns are not filed.

Undistributed Equity Method Income

The rules governing provision of deferred taxes on undistributed equity method income depend on whether the investee is considered a *subsidiary* ($\alpha > .5$) or a *nonsubsidiary investment* ($.2 \leq \alpha \leq .5$). We discuss each in turn.

Subsidiary Equity Method Investments. Unless a consolidated income tax return is filed, an investor corporation is taxed only for dividends received from investees. Furthermore, these dividends are generally eligible for the 85 percent corporate deduction for dividends received. Therefore, if P Company carries its investment in S Company on the equity basis and separate income tax returns are filed, a difference arises. Recall that, under the equity method, the net income of P equals consolidated net income—the amount of the equity method accrual is reflected in each. In contrast, P's tax return includes the dividends received from S, net of the 85 percent dividends-received deduction; it does not include the equity method accrual.[12]

Accounting treatment of this difference was clarified in *APBO 23* superseding the conflicting positions which had appeared in *ARB 51, APBO 11,* and *APBO 18.* The general rule regarding undistributed earnings of subsidiaries is that they represent *timing differences* to the parent and are subject to interperiod tax allocation. Nevertheless, under certain conditions—known as the **indefinite reversal criteria**—a *permanent difference* results, and deferred taxes need not be provided. From *APBO 23,* we have:

---

[12]While the 85 percent dividends-received deduction is generally available to any domestic corporation, affiliated corporations (as defined in the Internal Revenue Code) are often able to elect to deduct 100 percent of any intercompany dividends from tax return income. A consolidated income tax return need not be filed. In such situations, equity method income—whether distributed or not—represents a permanent difference between pretax book income and tax return income; no deferred taxes need be provided.

Timing difference. The Board believes it should be presumed that all undistributed earnings of a subsidiary will be transferred to the parent company. Accordingly, the undistributed earnings of a subsidiary included in consolidated income (or in income of the parent company) should be accounted for as a timing difference, except. . . .[13]

Permanent difference: indefinite reversal criteria. The presumption that all undistributed earnings will be transferred to the parent company may be overcome, and no income taxes should be accrued by the parent company, if sufficient evidence shows that the subsidiary has invested or will invest the undistributed earnings indefinitely or that the earnings will be remitted in a tax-free liquidation.[14]

Since parent company management can effectively control the investment and dividend policies of its subsidiaries, it is often able to argue successfully that undistributed equity method income will be permanently invested by its subsidiaries. In such cases, the indefinite reversal criteria apply, and no deferred income taxes on the undistributed equity method income are accrued by the parent.

To summarize, if the parent's share of the subsidiary's earnings is expected to be received as dividends, 85 percent of this amount becomes a permanent difference due to the dividends received deduction. The remaining 15 percent, if undistributed, creates a timing difference unless the indefinite reversal criteria apply.

Nonsubsidiary Equity Method Investments. When $.2 \leqq \alpha \leqq .5$, the percentage of ownership is sufficient to require use of the equity method but not sufficient to justify preparation of consolidated statements. Use of the equity method in nonsubsidiary investments, then, will likely result in a difference between the equity method income reported in P Company's income statement and the dividend income included in the tax return. *APBO 24* concludes that the *undistributed equity method income of nonsubsidiary investments constitutes a timing difference* to the investor. The indefinite reversal criteria do not apply here.

The Board concludes that the *tax effects of differences between taxable income and pretax accounting income* attributable to an investor's share of earnings of investee companies (other than subsidiaries and corporate joint ventures). . .are related either to probable future distributions of dividends or to anticipated realization on disposal of the investment and therefore have the essential characteristics of *timing differences*. The Board believes that the ability of an investor to exercise significant influence over an investee differs significantly from the ability of a parent company to control investment policies of a subsidiary and that *only control can justify the conclusion that undistributed earnings may be invested for indefinite periods.*[15] [Emphasis added.]

---

[13] Accounting Principles Board, *Opinion No. 23,* "Accounting for Income Taxes—Special Areas" (New York: AICPA, 1972), par. 10; CT § I42.105.

[14] Ibid., par. 12; CT § I42.107.

[15] Accounting Principles Board, *Opinion No. 24,* "Accounting for Income Taxes—Investments in Common Stock Accounted For by the Equity Method" (New York: AICPA, 1972), par. 7; CT§I42.114.

Thus when $\alpha > .5$, the parent may be able to justify the indefinite reversal concept by virtue of its control over the subsidiary's dividend and investment policies. If $\alpha \leq .5$, however, this control is presumed not to exist and deferred taxes must be provided on undistributed equity method earnings.

Illustration of Interperiod Tax Allocation on Undistributed Equity Method Income. We continue to assume that a consolidated income tax return is not filed. Therefore, the investor corporation is taxed only on the dividends received from the investee. Unless indefinite reversal can be substantiated (in the case of subsidiary investments only), the investor must accrue deferred taxes on undistributed equity method income. In determining the income tax provision, the following two items are important:

1. The investor must decide the form in which the undistributed income will ultimately be realized. If dividends are expected, the tax is accrued on the undistributed income as if it were dividends subject to the 85 percent dividends-received deduction. In contrast, if the undistributed income is expected to be realized as a capital gain by virtue of the sale of the investment, the tax provision must be based on applicable capital gain tax rates.
2. Any adjustments to the investor's share of the investee's net income made under the one-line consolidation requirement of *APBO 18* are irrelevant in determining the tax provision. Such amounts are not allowable tax deductions against dividend income. Thus the equity method accrual must be cleansed of any purchase premium amortization. In addition, any intercompany gains or losses which normally would be eliminated in computing the equity method accrual must be reinstated for purposes of the tax provision. These issues will be discussed in Chapter 9.

Suppose that Paul Corporation owns 70 percent of the voting shares of Sam Corporation. Sam earned $90,000 after taxes during the current year and paid dividends of $20,000. A purchase premium of $100,000 was allocated as follows: $75,000 to depreciable equipment and $25,000 to goodwill. Paul faces a combined federal and state income tax rate of 60 percent. At year-end, Paul makes the following entry to provide for income taxes on its investment income from Sam; computation of tax amounts are shown in Exhibit 8.16. Management of Paul expects that the undistributed income will eventually be realized as dividends received from Sam.

BOOKS OF PAUL CORPORATION

Income Tax Expense.	5,670	
Income Taxes Payable.		1,260
Deferred Income Taxes		4,410
To provide for income taxes on income from Sam.		

Exhibit 8.16	Paul Corporation's Computation of Income Taxes on Investment Income from Sam Corporation

Paul's 70% Share of Sam's Aftertax Income of $90,000 (Expected to Be
  Realized as Dividends) . . . . $ 63,000
Less 85% Dividends-Received Deduction (Expected to Be Available When
  Dividends Are Distributed; a *permanent difference*) . . . . (53,550)
Income Subject to Tax When Distributed. . . . . $ 9,450
Income Tax Expense (.6 × $9,450) . . . . $ 5,670
Dividends Received during Current Year Subject to Income Tax
  [1 − .85)(.7)($20,000)] . . . . $ 2,100

Income Tax Currently Payable at 60% (.6 × $2,100)   1,260

Undistributed Income Subject to Tax in Future Years
  ($9,450 − $2,100; a *timing difference*)   7,350

Deferred Income Taxes at 60% (.6 × $7,350).   4,410

Income Tax Expense . . . . $ 5,670

Notes:
1. The purchase permium allocation (and amortization) has been disregarded in the income tax computations.
2. Even if consolidated financial statements are prepared and reflect the purchase premium amortization, the income tax provision remains as computed.

Consolidated Income Tax Returns

The set of corporate affiliations eligible to file consolidated income tax returns is substantially smaller than the set eligible to issue consolidated financial statements. Section 1501 of the Internal Revenue Code indicates that an **affiliated group of corporations** shall have the privilege of filing a consolidated return, subject to the Treasury regulations prescribed in Section 1502.

Section 1504 goes on to define an *affiliated group* as one or more chains of corporations connected through stock ownership with a common parent. The common parent must directly own stock possessing at least 80 percent of the voting power of all classes of stock and at least 80 percent of each class of the nonvoting stock of at least one of the other corporations. Furthermore, at least 80 percent of each class of nonvoting stock of each corporation, except the parent, must be owned directly by one or more of the corporations in the group. Certain corporations, such as tax-exempt corporations, foreign companies, and Domestic International Sales Corporations, are specifically excluded from filing consolidated returns. Criteria for issuing consolidated financial statements are far less restrictive than these.

Advantages of Filing a Consolidated Income Tax Return. An affiliated group of corporations benefits from the filing of a consolidated income tax return in the following ways:

1. Offsetting operating losses of one company against the operating profits of another provides immediate tax benefits, whereas the net operating loss provisions of the Code would defer those benefits to future periods if the tax return were not consolidated.

2. Offsetting capital losses of one company against the capital gains of another accelerates the deductibility of capital losses.
3. Taxes on intercompany dividends are completely eliminated.
4. The tax on unconfirmed gains resulting from intercompany sales or exchanges of property is deferred until the gains are ultimately realized.
5. A company's investment credit or foreign tax credit may be available for use in a consolidated return although it exceeds the limitation applying to a separate return.

Disadvantages of Filing a Consolidated Income Tax Return. On the other hand, the decision by an affiliated group to file a consolidated income tax return carries with it certain disadvantages:

1. The election to file a consolidated income tax return must be made with the consent of each affiliated corporation and is binding for future years. Permission must be obtained to revert to the filing of separate returns.
2. Deferral of unconfirmed losses resulting from intercompany sales or exchanges of property also defers their tax benefits.
3. Risk of increased minimum tax on preference items is greater.

Amortization of Purchase Premium or Discount in a Consolidated Income Tax Return. Many business combinations are treated as *tax-free* corporate reorganizations under Section 368 of the Internal Revenue Code. While these rules tend to result in the nonrecognition of gains and losses for tax purposes in eligible corporate reorganizations, they also provide for the carryover of existing tax bases of depreciable property. Thus, if purchase accounting is used for a business combination qualifying as a tax-free corporate reorganization, the existence and amortization of a purchase premium or discount is not considered for tax purposes and creates a *permanent difference* between the consolidated income statement and consolidated income tax return. Deferred taxes are not provided.

In contrast, if a purchase business combination is treated as a *taxable* exchange, with recognition of gain or loss for tax purposes, any purchase premium or discount must be allocated in conformity with Treasury regulations. Accordingly, consolidated tax depreciation may approximate consolidated book depreciation. *In no case, however, is amortization of goodwill an allowable tax deduction; it always creates a permanent difference.*

Concluding Comments

The major remaining problem of accounting for income taxes in consolidated financial statements arises when unconfirmed intercompany gains and losses exist and a consolidated income tax return is not filed. We deal with this situation in Chapter 9.

In order to concentrate on the major consolidation issues in subsequent chapters, we shall leave behind the interperiod tax allocation generally required under the equity method. To do so, we make the simplifying assumption that, unless otherwise stated, *undistributed equity method income is permanently reinvested and no tax allocation is necessary.*

Summary of Key Concepts

When a business combination is recorded as a **stock acquisition,** it is carried on the parent's books as an **intercorporate investment.** The parent accounts for such intercorporate investments using the equity or cost method. If the subsidiary is not consolidated, the equity method must be used for both accounting and reporting purposes. The **equity method** is stressed in this book.

Consolidated statements are prepared for reporting purposes only and do not represent accounting requirements. **Whether the equity or cost method is used** by the parent to account for its investments in subsidiaries, the **resulting consolidated statements are the same.** Only the procedures used to prepare them are affected by the choice of accounting method.

Under the **equity method,** the parent increases the investment account for its share of the subsidiary's net income and decreases the investment account for its share of the subsidiary's dividends. According to *APBO 18,* the equity method accrual is viewed as a **one-line consolidation** and must reflect all consolidation adjustments to net income. The only adjustment to the equity method accrual considered in this chapter is periodic purchase premium (discount) amortization. Other adjustments are considered in Chapters 9 and 10.

Consolidation under the equity method requires that the equity method entries made by the parent during the current year be eliminated on the working paper. By so doing, the parent's share of the subsidiary's net income is not counted twice—once in the equity method accrual and again when the revenue and expense accounts of the affiliates are combined.

Use of the **cost method** requires that the parent's share of the subsidiary's dividends be recognized as income when declared and the investment account balance **not** be periodically updated to reflect the subsidiary's net income. On the working paper, the investment account must be adjusted to the equity basis at the beginning of the year so it can be cleanly eliminated against the subsidiary's beginning stockholders' equity. Since the intercompany dividends were recorded by the parent as income, they must be eliminated in consolidation to avoid double counting of the parent's share of the subsidiary's net income.

A **consolidated financial statement working paper** is used to facilitate preparation of the consolidated balance sheet and statements of income and retained earnings. Preclosing trial balance data of the affiliates are rearranged in financial statement format on the working paper. Alternatively, a **consolidated trial balance working paper** may be used.

Preparation of the consolidated income statement for the year in which a **purchase combination** takes place can be complicated if the combination occurs **during** the year. The two alternatives are (1) to include only those revenues and expenses of the subsidiary arising **after** the date of combination and (2) to include the subsidiary's revenues and expenses for the **entire** year while deducting **preacquisition earnings.**

Consolidated net income covering the acquisition year should not include more than P's share of the subsidiary's earnings **after** date of acquisition. This result is achieved for the second alternative above in two steps. The first involves the deduction of the **minority interest in net income** for the **entire year.** The second concerns the deduction of **preacquisition earnings,** the parent's share of the subsidiary's earnings in the months prior to the intrayear combination. Observe that the deductions for preacquisition earnings and the portion of the minority interest in net income pertaining to the months prior to the intrayear combination add up to the subsidiary's total earnings in those prior months.

The **consolidated statement of changes in financial position (SCFP)** is prepared from comparative consolidated balance sheets, consolidated statements of income and retained earnings, and any necessary supplementary information. If this approach is followed, no further eliminations need be made when preparing the consolidated SCFP. Amortization of consolidated goodwill and the minority interest in net income must be added back to consolidated net income in determining funds provided by operations. Dividends paid to minority shareholders are shown as a nonoperating use of funds.

When the affiliates do not file a consolidated income tax return, undistributed equity method income normally represents a timing difference, and deferred taxes are provided. Under the **indefinite reversal criteria,** the parent may provide evidence that undistributed equity method income is permanently invested by the subsidiary and constitutes a **permanent difference.** In such situations, accrual of deferred taxes is not called for.

Questions

Q8.1 Proper application of the equity method by the parent results in the parent's net income and retained earnings being equal to consolidated net income and retained earnings, respectively. Explain why this happens.

Q8.2 "The parent's share of the subsidiary's dividends is recorded by the parent as dividend income under the cost method." Is this always true? Explain.

Q8.3 P Company owns 80 percent of S Company, acquired for $400,000 over book value. S's assets and liabilities are fairly stated at their book values. If S reports net income of $200,000 from its own operations in the current year, what is the maximum amount that P can accrue as income from S?

Q8.4 Minority Interest in Subsidiary appears on the consolidated balance sheet, and Minority Interest in Net Income appears on the consolidated income statement. Are they the same? What is the relationship between them?

Q8.5 How does the Minority Interest in Subsidiary change during the year? What working paper entries are made to record the change? Why are the entries necessary?

Q8.6 The consolidated financial statement working paper and the consolidated trial balance working paper presented in the chapter are set up so that the same working paper eliminations can be used in either format. Give the reason underlying this equivalence.

Q8.7 A pooling of interests combination recorded as a stock acquisition will normally lead to preparation of consolidated financial statements. In what significant way are the consolidation procedures different from those used in the purchase case?

Q8.8 When a purchase combination occurs *during* an accounting period, only that portion of S's net income earned *after* date of acquisition is eligible for inclusion in consolidated net income, and only to the extent of P's ownership of it. How do the consolidation procedures of Method 2 (including S's revenues and expenses for the entire year) described in the text achieve this result?

Q8.9 In reviewing a consolidated financial statement working paper, you notice the following entry:

Preacquisition Earnings	390,000	
Dividends—S		160,000
Investment in S		230,000

Interpret the entry and indicate what it accomplishes on the working paper.

Q8.10 How are the components of the change in minority interest during the current year treated on the consolidated statement of changes in financial position?

Q8.11 When affiliated companies *do not* file a consolidated income tax return, only intercompany dividends (after the 85 percent deduction) are included in tax return income. Yet pretax consolidated book income includes P's entire share of S's net income, whether distributed in dividends or not. How does this affect the computation of book consolidated income tax expense?

Q8.12 Explain why the indefinite reversal criteria are irrelevant to many equity method investments.

Exercises

E8.1 On January 2, 19X4, P Company acquired 90 percent of S Company's common stock for $1,900,000, an amount exceeding the book value of the shares acquired by $100,000. All of S's assets and liabilities are fairly stated; intangibles are amortized over a 10-year period. During the next 2 years, S reported the following:

	Net Income	Dividends
19X4.	$250,000	$150,000
19X5.	300,000	180,000

Required:

1. Prepare the journal entries made by P after acquisition relative to its investment in S during 19X4 and 19X5 and the eliminating entries at the end of the 2 years. Assume the equity method is used.
2. Repeat No. 1 assuming the cost method is used.

E8.2 During 19X2, P Company's 70-percent-owned subsidiary reported net income of $1,600,000 and declared dividends of $600,000. P had acquired its interest in the subsidiary on January 2, 19X2, at a cost of $5,200,000, which was $1,000,000 in excess of the net assets acquired. Of this $1,000,000, $500,000 was allocated to equipment with a 5-year life and $200,000 related to inventory—of which 40 percent was sold during 19X2. The remaining $300,000 could not be allocated to identifiable assets and liabilities. P Company amortizes its intangibles over the longest possible period.

Required: Give the journal entries recorded by P under the equity method in 19X2 and the working paper eliminations. Show all calculations.

E8.3 Refer to the data in E8.2. Assume that the remaining revalued inventory was sold during 19X3, and give all working paper entries made at December 31, 19X3, relative to the purchase premium.

E8.4 On December 31, 19X2, P Company acquired 80 percent of S Company's outstanding shares for $200,000, $40,000 more than their book value. S's assets and liabilities were fairly stated except for certain motor vehicles, which were appraised at $30,000 more than their book value. The vehicles' remaining life at December 31, 19X2, was 5 years. Any goodwill arising in consolidation is to be amortized over 20 years. P accounts for its investment in S using the cost method.

As of January 1, 19X5, the beginning of the current year, S had total earnings of $90,000 since the acquisition by P and had paid out dividends of $70,000. In 19X5, S reported net income of $32,000 and paid dividends of $20,000.

Required: Prepare the entries made by P during 19X5 relative to its investment in S and give the working paper eliminations. Compute the minority interest in S at December 31, 19X5.

E8.5 The separate income statements of the Parson and Soaper Companies for the year ended June 30, 19X7, are given below. When Parson acquired 80 percent of Soaper on July 1, 19X6, it was found that Soaper's inventory was undervalued by $160,000, plant assets with a 10-year life were overvalued by $200,000, and long-term debt which matures in 5 years was overvalued by $100,000. No goodwill arose in the combination. All Parson's depreciation and amortization charges are based on the straight-line method. The undervalued inventory was sold during the year ended June 30, 19X7.

	Parson	Soaper
Sales	$5,000,000	$2,000,000
Income from Soaper	112,000	—
Total Revenue	$5,112,000	$2,000,000
Cost of Goods Sold:		
Beginning Inventory.	$ 800,000	$ 300,000
Purchases	3,050,000	780,000
Ending Inventory	(850,000)	(280,000)
	$3,000,000	$ 800,000
Depreciation Expense.	500,000	140,000
Interest Expense	100,000	60,000
Other Expenses.	600,000	700,000
Total Expenses.	$4,200,000	$1,700,000
Net Income	$ 912,000	$ 300,000

Required: Prepare a consolidated income statement for Parson and Soaper for the year ended June 30, 19X7.

E8.6 P Company, a calendar-year corporation, acquired 90 percent of S Company's shares on September 30, 19X0, in a stock acquisition qualifying as a pooling of interests. S also reports on a calendar-year basis. Its business is nonseasonal. P accounts for the investment in S using the cost method. The separate income statements of the two companies for the year ended December 31, 19X0, follow:

	P Company	S Company
Sales	$10,000,000	$3,000,000
Dividend Income from S.	90,000	—
Total Revenue	$10,090,000	$3,000,000
Cost of Goods Sold:		
Beginning Inventory.	$ 1,140,000	$ 400,000
Purchases	6,360,000	1,970,000
Ending Inventory	(1,500,000)	(370,000)
	$ 6,000,000	$2,000,000
Selling and Administrative Expenses	1,500,000	400,000
Total Expenses.	$ 7,500,000	$2,400,000
Net Income	$ 2,590,000	$ 600,000

Required:

1. Prepare a consolidated income statement for the year ended December 31, 19X0.
2. Suppose P used the equity method. Compute the equity method accrual and consolidated net income.

E8.7 On June 30, 19X5, the Portly Company purchased 70 percent of the out-standing stock of Stout Corporation for $15,000,000 cash. Both companies report on a calendar-year basis. Portly earned $5,000,000 in 19X5 from its own operations and accounts for its investment in Stout by the equity meth-od. Stout's business is seasonal, and its controller determined that 30 per-cent of its net income of $2,000,000 was earned in the first 6 months of 19X5. Stout's dividend rate was increased late in 19X5, and, accordingly, 60 percent of its annual dividends of $1,200,000 were declared after June 30.

Assume that Stout's capital stock and retained earnings on June 30, 19X5, amounted to $7,000,000 and $13,000,000, respectively, and that its assets and liabilities are fairly stated. Portly amortizes intangibles over the maximum period allowed by *APBO 17*.

Required:

1. Compute consolidated net income for 19X5.
2. Prepare the working paper eliminations made in consolidation at De-cember 31, 19X5, under the preacquisition earnings approach.

E8.8 Following are the condensed income statements of P Company and its 80-percent-owned subsidiary, S Company, for the year ended December 31, 19X8. P acquired its interest in S on September 30, 19X8. The purchase discount of $1,900,000 on the acquisition was allocated entirely to assets of S being depreciated on the straight-line method over a remaining life of 10 years. Because of the nature of S's business, 50 percent of its revenues and expenses arose in the last quarter of 19X8.

	P Company	S Company
Sales	$10,000,000	$ 4,000,000
Cost of Goods Sold.	(6,000,000)	(3,000,000)
Other Operating Expenses	(3,200,000)	(900,000)
Net Income	$ 800,000	$ 100,000

Required: Prepare condensed consolidated income statements for P and S for 19X8 under *both* of the alternative presentations mentioned in the chapter.

E8.9 Using the following data, prepare the Working Capital Provided by Opera-tions section of a consolidated statement of changes in financial position.

Consolidated Net Income	$1,000,000
Purchase Premium Amortization: Goodwill ($30,000), Trademarks ($25,000), Inventory ($45,000)	100,000
Consolidated Depreciation Expense.	180,000
Net Income Reported by 80-Percent-Owned Consolidated Subsidiary. . .	200,000
Dividends Declared by 80-Percent-Owned Consolidated Subsidiary. . . .	60,000
Net Income Reported by 30-Percent-Owned Equity Investment	150,000
Dividends Declared by 30-Percent-Owned Equity Investment	90,000

E8.10 Prep Corporation has owned 80 percent of the Strep Company since Strep's inception. The condensed consolidated balance sheets of Prep and Strep at the beginning and end of the current year and other relevant information are presented below:

PREP CORPORATION AND SUBSIDIARY
CONDENSED CONSOLIDATED BALANCE SHEETS

ASSETS	End of Year	Beginning of Year
Cash	$ 600,000	$ 700,000
Other Current Assets	1,400,000	1,000,000
Plant Assets	4,000,000	4,200,000
Accumulated Depreciation	(1,500,000)	(1,600,000)
Goodwill	300,000	330,000
Total Assets	$ 4,800,000	$ 4,630,000
LIABILITIES AND STOCKHOLDERS' EQUITY		
Current Liabilities	$ 1,282,000	$ 1,550,000
Noncurrent Liabilities	1,800,000	1,700,000
Minority Interest in Strep	288,000	280,000
Stockholders' Equity	1,430,000	1,100,000
Total Liabilities and Stockholders' Equity	$ 4,800,000	$ 4,630,000

Additional information:

1. Consolidated net income for the year is $400,000.
2. Strep reported net income from its own operations of $120,000 and declared $80,000 in dividends.
3. Consolidated depreciation expense was $350,000.
4. Plant assets with an original cost of $500,000 and a net book value of $50,000 were retired from service and scrapped.
5. Prep declared $70,000 in dividends during the year.

Required:

1. Prepare, in good form, a consolidated statement of changes in financial position (working capital basis) for the current year.
2. Prepare a schedule to convert consolidated working capital from operations in No. 1 to consolidated cash flow from operations.

E8.11 The Press Company acquired 70 percent of the outstanding stock of the Stalwart Company several years ago and uses the equity method to account for its investment. Stalwart has paid no dividends (85 percent of which would be excluded from taxation under current law) and has net earnings of $840,000 since acquisition, including $120,000 in the current year. Press reported pretax book income of $500,000 from its own operations in the current year and has had no timing differences related to its own operations. Press expects that all of Stalwart's earnings will ultimately be distributed as dividends. Both companies face a combined federal and state income tax rate of 40 percent.

Required:

1. Prepare the journal entry made by Press to record its income tax expense for the year.
2. Compute the balance in Press's Deferred Income Taxes account at the end of the current year.
3. Repeat No. 1 assuming that the indefinite reversal criteria apply.

E8.12 The Plant Company owns 80 percent of the outstanding stock of the Seed Company. Seed reported net income of $200,000 after taxes during the current year and made dividend distributions of $80,000. In computing its equity method accrual, Plant recognized consolidated goodwill amortization of $20,000. Plant and Seed file separate federal income tax returns, and both companies face a marginal income tax rate of 40 percent. Current law provides for deduction of 85 percent of intercorporate dividends.

Required:

1. Give the journal entry made by Plant to provide for income taxes on its investment income in Seed. Show all supporting computations. Assume that Plant expects that Seed's undistributed income will eventually be received as dividends.
2. Repeat No. 1 assuming that the indefinite reversal criteria apply.

Problems

P8.1 Consolidated Balance Sheet—Purchase Premium Amortization Paul Corporation acquired all of the outstanding stock of Sand Corporation on June 30, 19X3, for $19,000,000. The Sand stock had a book value of $3,000,000, giving a purchase premium of $16,000,000, which was allocated as follows:

	Amount Dr.(Cr.)	Amortization Period (Straight-Line)
Property, Plant, and Equipment, Net	$13,100,000	13.1 years
Other Assets	(300,000)	15
Long-Term Debt	400,000	40
Goodwill	2,800,000	40
	$16,000,000	

During the 6-month period from July 1 to December 31, 19X3, Sand earned $1,250,000 and paid no dividends. Paul carries its Investment in Sand at equity. The balance sheets of Paul and Sand prior to consolidation at December 31, 19X3, are as follows:

ASSETS	Paul	Sand
Cash	$ 3,500,000	$ 600,000
Accounts Receivable, Net	1,400,000	1,500,000
Inventories	1,000,000	2,500,000
Property, Plant, and Equipment, Net.	2,000,000	3,100,000
Investment in Subsidiary, at Equity	19,720,000	—
Other Assets	100,000	500,000
Total Assets	$27,720,000	$8,200,000
LIABILITIES AND STOCKHOLDERS' EQUITY		
Current Liabilities	$ 1,500,000	$1,100,000
Long-Term Debt	4,000,000	2,600,000
Other Liabilities	750,000	250,000
Common Stock, Par Value $1 per Share	10,000,000	1,000,000
Additional Paid-In Capital	5,000,000	400,000
Retained Earnings	6,470,000	2,850,000
Total Liabilities and Stockholders' Equity	$27,720,000	$8,200,000

Required: Prepare a consolidated balance sheet of Paul Corporation and its wholly owned subsidiary, Sand Corporation, as of December 31, 19X3. Show supporting computations in good form. *(AICPA adapted)*

P8.2 Consolidated Financial Statement Working Paper and Purchase Premium Amortization   Padre Company, a wholesaler, purchased 80 percent of the issued and outstanding stock of Sun, Inc., a retailer, on December 31, 19X2, for $120,000. At that date, Sun had one class of common stock outstanding at a stated value of $100,000 and retained earnings of $25,000. Padre had a $50,000 deficit balance in retained earnings.

Padre purchased the Sun stock from Sun's major stockholder, primarily to acquire control of signboard leases owned by Sun. The leases will expire on December 31, 19X7, and Padre executives estimate the leases, which cannot be renewed, were worth at least $25,000 more than their book value when the stock was purchased.

Sun declared a $9,000 cash dividend on December 20, 19X6, payable on January 16, 19X7, to stockholders of record on January 2, 19X7. Padre carries its investment at equity but had not recorded this dividend on December 31, 19X6. No dividend payments occurred during 19X6.

The financial statements for both companies for the year ended December 31, 19X6, appear below:

BALANCE SHEETS

ASSETS	Padre	Sun
Other Current Assets	$117,200	$113,500
Inventories	54,800	85,600
Investment in Sun.	151,200	—
Signboard Leases, Net	—	12,000
Land	25,000	10,500
Plant and Equipment	200,000	40,000
Accumulated Depreciation.	(102,000)	(10,600)ᵃ
Total Assets.	$ 446,200	$251,000

LIABILITIES AND STOCKHOLDERS' EQUITY

Other Current Liabilities	$ 60,000	$ 67,000
Dividends Payable	—	9,000
Capital Stock	300,000	100,000
Retained Earnings	86,200	75,000
Total Liabilities and Stockholders' Equity	$ 446,200	$251,000

ᵃBalance allocated since acquisition on December 31, 19X2.

INCOME STATEMENTS

	Padre	Sun
Sales	$ 420,000	$300,000
Income from Sun	16,000	—
Total Revenue	$ 436,000	$300,000
Cost of Goods Sold:		
Beginning Inventory.	$ 52,300	$ 89,000
Purchases	317,500	236,600
Ending Inventory	(54,800)	(85,600)
	$ 315,000	$240,000
Other Expenses.	65,000	35,000
Total Expenses.	$ 380,000	$275,000
Net Income	$ 56,000	$ 25,000

Required:

1. Prepare a consolidated financial statement working paper for the Padre
   Company and its subsidiary, Sun, Inc., as of December 31, 19X6.
   Formal statements and journal entries are not required. You may assume that both companies made all the adjusting entries required for
   separate financial statements unless an obvious discrepancy exists.
2. Prepare a schedule explaining how the investment account balance
   changed between December 31, 19X2, and December 31, 19X6.
   (AICPA adapted)

P8.3 Equity Method Entries, Eliminations, and Consolidation Computations
On December 31, 19X0, P Company acquired 60 percent of S Company's

outstanding voting shares for $150,000—$30,000 more than their book value. S's assets and liabilities were all fairly stated at date of acquisition except for manufacturing equipment, which was appraised for $30,000 more than its book value. The equipment's remaining useful life at December 31, 19X0, was 10 years. Any goodwill arising in consolidation is to be amortized over 40 years.

As of January 1, 19X3, the beginning of the current year, S had total net income of $70,000 since the acquisition by P and had paid out dividends of $40,000. Aside from retained earnings, S's only other owners' equity account is capital stock of $100,000, unchanged since S was organized.

During 19X3, S had net income of $20,000 and paid dividends of $8,000. P accounts for its investment in S using the equity method. P's net income from its own operations was $36,000.

Required:

1. Give the journal entries made by P during 19X3 relative to its investment in S.
2. Give the eliminating entries which would appear on the consolidated working paper at December 31, 19X3.
3. Compute consolidated retained earnings and the minority interest in S at December 31, 19X3. P's retained earnings from its own operations are $220,000 at that date.
4. What is consolidated net income for 19X3?

P8.4 Analysis of Investment Account—Equity Method Entries and Eliminations On January 2, 19X6, P Company acquired 60 percent of S Company's outstanding voting common shares at a cost of $2,800,000. A purchase premium of $400,000 resulted; $50,000 was allocated to inventory (sold during 19X6), $150,000 to plant assets (10-year remaining life), and $200,000 to goodwill (20-year life). During 19X6 and 19X7, S reported total income from its own operations of $250,000 and paid total dividends of $120,000. P accounts for its investment in S by the equity method.

Required:

1. Prepare a schedule, with explanations, to determine the balance in the Investment in S account after the books are closed on December 31, 19X7.
2. Assuming that S reported income of $100,000 from its own operations and paid dividends of $40,000 during 19X8, give the journal entries made by P during 19X8 under the equity method and the working paper entries needed to prepare consolidated statements at December 31, 19X8.

P8.5 Consolidated Financial Statement Working Paper—Purchase Premium Paltry Corporation purchased all of the outstanding stock of the Slim Company on January 2, 19X7, for $2,000,000 cash. On that date,

Slim's inventory was undervalued by $100,000, plant assets with a 20-year life remaining were undervalued by $200,000, and, due to rising interest rates, the market value of its long-term debt stood at $400,000. The debt matures in 5 years. Paltry always uses straight-line amortization over the maximum period allowable. Inventories are accounted for using the FIFO cost-flow assumption.

Following are the separate financial statements for the two companies at December 31, 19X7:

STATEMENTS OF INCOME AND RETAINED EARNINGS

	Paltry	**Slim**
Sales	$12,780,000	$ 5,400,000
Income from Slim	470,000	—
Total Revenue	$13,250,000	$ 5,400,000
Cost of Goods Sold:		
Beginning Inventory	$ 3,000,000	$ 1,400,000
Purchases	8,000,000	3,000,000
Ending Inventory	(3,200,000)	(1,350,000)
	$ 7,800,000	$ 3,050,000
Operating Expenses	2,100,000	1,700,000
Interest Expense	160,000	40,000
Total Expenses	$10,060,000	$ 4,790,000
Net Income	$ 3,190,000	$ 610,000
Beginning Retained Earnings	4,200,000	1,000,000
Dividends	(300,000)	(80,000)
Ending Retained Earnings	$ 7,090,000	$ 1,530,000

BALANCE SHEETS

ASSETS	**Paltry**	**Slim**
Cash and Receivables	$ 2,800,000	$ 880,000
Inventory	3,200,000	1,350,000
Investment in Slim	2,390,000	—
Plant Assets	5,000,000	2,300,000 (net)
Accumulated Depreciation	(1,200,000)	—
Total Assets	$12,190,000	$ 4,530,000

LIABILITIES AND STOCKHOLDERS' EQUITY		
Current Liabilities	$ 2,600,000	$ 2,300,000
Long-Term Debt	1,700,000	500,000
Capital Stock	800,000	200,000
Retained Earnings	7,090,000	1,530,000
Total Liabilities and Stockholders' Equity	$12,190,000	$ 4,530,000

Required:

1. Prepare a schedule to show how the equity method accrual made by Paltry at December 31, 19X7, was calculated.

2. Prepare a consolidated financial statement working paper for Paltry and Slim at December 31, 19X7.

P8.6 Consolidated Financial Statement Working Paper—Purchase Discount P Company acquired 80 percent of the outstanding shares of S Company on January 2, 19X1, for $1,470,000 cash. Direct cash costs associated with the acquisition amounted to $50,000. S Company's stockholders' equity had a book value of $2,000,000 on that date; some of its assets and liabilities had fair values different from their book values, as shown below:

Accounts of S Company	Book Value	Fair Value
Inventory (LIFO Cost-Flow Assumption)	440,000	500,000
Notes Receivable, Noncurrent	110,000	130,000
Buildings and Equipment, Net (20-Year Life Remaining)	500,000	400,000
Long-Term Debt (Face Value $200,000)	(220,000)	(300,000)

All depreciation and amortization are allocated by the straight-line method. Preclosing trial balances for the two companies at December 31, 19X1, follow:

Account	P Company	S Company
Cash and Receivables	$ 1,000,000	$ 1,580,000
Inventory, Jan. 2, 19X1.	1,700,000	440,000
Notes Receivable, Noncurrent (Face Value $100,000)	—	108,000
Investment in S.	1,807,200	—
Land	600,000	330,000
Buildings and Equipment	2,200,000	600,000
Accumulated Depreciation	(700,000)	(50,000)[a]
Current Liabilities.	(1,400,000)	(500,000)
Long-Term Debt (10% Coupon Rate).	(600,000)	(218,000)
Capital Stock	(200,000)	(100,000)
Retained Earnings	(2,810,000)	(1,900,000)
Dividends.	120,000	50,000
Sales	(7,000,000)	(3,200,000)
Income from S	(327,200)	—
Interest Income.	—	(8,000)
Purchases	4,800,000	2,440,000
Operating Expenses	750,000	410,000
Interest Expense	60,000	18,000
	$ 0	$ 0
Inventory, Dec. 31, 19X1	$ 1,800,000	$ 500,000

[a]Amount allocated in 19X1.

Required:

1. Prepare a schedule to show how the equity method accrual made by P at December 31, 19X1, was calculated.
2. Prepare a consolidated financial statement working paper for P and S at December 31, 19X1.

P8.7 Investor Accounting and Consolidation—Cost and Equity Methods Compared On January 1, 19X1, Todd Corporation made the following investments:

1. Acquired 80 percent of the outstanding common stock of Meadow Corporation for cash at $70 per share. The stockholders' equity of Meadow on January 1, 19X1, consisted of the following:

Common Stock, Par Value $50 . . . . $50,000
Retained Earnings   20,000

2. Acquired 70 percent of the outstanding common stock of Van Corporation for cash at $40 per share. The stockholders' equity of Van on January 1, 19X1, consisted of the following:

Common Stock, Par Value $20 . . . . $60,000
Capital in Excess of Par Value.   20,000
Retained Earnings   40,000

An analysis of the retained earnings of each company for 19X1 is as follows:

	Todd	Meadow	Van
Balance, Jan. 1, 19X1.	$240,000	$20,000	$ 40,000
Net Income (Loss) from Own			
Operations	104,600	36,000	(12,000)
Cash Dividends Paid	(40,000)	(16,000)	(9,000)
Balance, Dec. 31, 19X1	$304,600	$ 40,000	$ 19,000

Required:

1. Assume Todd accounts for its investments in subsidiaries using the cost method. Give the entries made by Todd to record these investments and to account for them during 19X1. (Hint: Consider the nature of the "dividends" paid by Van.)
2. Again, assuming Todd uses the cost method, give the necessary working paper entries to consolidate Todd and its subsidiaries at December 31, 19X1.
3. Repeat No. 1, assuming that Todd uses the equity method.
4. Repeat No. 2, assuming that Todd uses the equity method.
5. Compute the amount of minority interest in each subsidiary's stockholders' equity at December 31, 19X1.
6. Compute consolidated net income for the year ended December 31, 19X1.
7. Compute consolidated retained earnings at December 31, 19X1. Show all calculations. *(AICPA adapted)*

P8.8 Investor Accounting—Cost and Equity Methods, Purchase Premium On December 31, 19X3, Paint Corporation acquired 90 percent of the stock of the Soil Company. During 19X4, Soil reported net income of $200,000 and paid dividends of $90,000. The market value of the consideration given by Paint was $3,200,000, which exceeded the book value of Paint's 90 percent interest by $500,000. Allocation of the purchase premium produced the following:

	Amount	Amortization Period
Inventory.	$ 75,000	Sold during 19X4
Depreciable Assets	225,000	Ten years
Goodwill	200,000	Maximum allowable
	$500,000	

Required:

1. Give the journal entries made by Paint during 19X4, assuming the equity method is used. Supporting computations must be in good form.
2. Same as No. 1 except that the cost method is used by Paint.
3. Give the working paper entries necessary to consolidate Paint and Soil at December 31, 19X4, under the equity method.
4. Same as No. 3 except that the cost method is used by Paint.
5. If Paint reports net income from its own operations in 19X4 of $500,000, compute consolidated net income.

P8.9 Consolidated Trial Balance Working Paper—Cost Method On January 2, 19X4, EON Corporation acquired 90 percent of NEO Corporation's voting common stock for $1,190,000. On that date, NEO's stockholders' equity consisted of capital stock of $400,000 and retained earnings of $600,000. All of NEO's identifiable assets and liabilities were fairly valued except for some land that was undervalued by $100,000. EON amortizes intangibles over a 20-year period and carries its investment in NEO at cost.

Preclosing trial balances for EON and NEO at December 31, 19X6, appear below:

	EON Dr. (Cr.)	NEO Dr. (Cr.)
Cash and Receivables	$ 2,610,000	$ 1,500,000
Inventory, Jan. 1, 19X6.	1,960,000	1,400,000
Land	200,000	150,000
Other Plant Assets, Net	3,170,000	1,450,000
Investment in Neo, Cost	1,190,000	—
Current Liabilities.	(2,300,000)	(1,500,000)
Noncurrent Liabilities.	(1,800,000)	(700,000)
Capital Stock.	(550,000)	(400,000)
Retained Earnings, Jan. 1, 19X6	(1,900,000)	(900,000)
Dividends	500,000	200,000
Sales.	(11,000,000)	(6,500,000)
Dividend Income	(180,000)	—
Purchases	6,200,000	4,000,000
Operating Expenses	1,900,000	1,300,000
	$ 0	$ 0
Inventory, Dec. 31, 19X6.	$ 2,030,000	$ 1,380,000

Required:

1. Prepare a consolidated trial balance working paper for EON and NEO at December 31, 19X6.
2. Explain how the consolidation process and consolidated results would differ if this business combination had been accounted for as a *pooling of interests.*

P8.10 Consolidated Funds Statements—Working Capital and Cash Bases Comparative consolidated balance sheets and the intervening consolidated income statement for P Company and S Company are shown below:

P COMPANY AND S COMPANY
COMPARATIVE CONSOLIDATED BALANCE SHEETS
AT DECEMBER 31, 19X7 AND 19X6

ASSETS	12/31/X7	12/31X6
Cash	$ 500,000	$ 200,000
Other Current Assets	900,000	800,000
Property, Plant, and Equipment	3,100,000	2,500,000
Accumulated Depreciation	(1,000,000)	(800,000)
Goodwill	275,000	300,000
Total Assets	$ 3,775,000	$3,000,000
LIABILITIES AND STOCKHOLDERS' EQUITY		
Current Liabilities	$ 900,000	$ 650,000
Other Liabilities	950,000	800,000
Capital Stock	700,000	500,000
Retained Earnings	1,065,000	900,000
Minority Interest in S	160,000	150,000
Total Liabilities and Stockholders' Equity	$ 3,775,000	$3,000,000

P COMPANY AND S COMPANY
CONSOLIDATED STATEMENT OF INCOME AND RETAINED EARNINGS
FOR THE YEAR ENDED DECEMBER 31, 19X7

Sales and Other Revenue	$3,555,000
Cost of Goods Sold	$1,700,000
Operating Expenses	1,243,000
Minority Interest in Net Income	12,000
Total Expenses	$2,955,000
Net Income	$ 600,000
Retained Earnings, Jan. 1, 19X7	900,000
Dividends Declared	(435,000)
Retained Earnings, Dec. 31, 19X7	$1,065,000

Additional information:

1. Consolidated depreciation expense was $250,000.
2. During the year, plant assets with an original cost of $75,000 and accumulated depreciation of $50,000 were sold for $25,000.

Required:

1. Prepare, in good form, a consolidated statement of changes in financial position (working capital basis) for the year ended December 31, 19X7.
2. Prepare, in good form, a consolidated statement of changes in financial position (cash basis) for the year ended December 31, 19X7.

P8.11 Consolidated Funds Statements—Working Capital and Cash Bases Comparative consolidated balance sheets for Parsimonious Corporation and subsidiaries appear below:

ASSETS	12/31/X6	12/31/X5
Cash	$ 70,000	$ 100,000
Receivables.	380,000	300,000
Inventory	500,000	520,000
Plant Assets, Net	1,000,000	950,000
Equity Investments (25%).	200,000	170,000
Goodwill	90,000	100,000
Total Assets	$2,240,000	$2,140,000
LIABILITIES AND STOCKHOLDERS' EQUITY		
Current Liabilities	$ 788,000	$ 775,000
Minority Interest in Subsidiaries.	82,000	75,000
Capital Stock	800,000	800,000
Retained Earnings	570,000	490,000
Total Liabilities	$2,240,000	$2,140,000

Additional information:

1. Consolidated net income for 19X6 was $130,000.
2. Consolidated depreciation expense was $100,000. No plant assets were sold during 19X6.
3. Parsimonious's unconsolidated equity investments reported net income of $200,000 and paid dividends of $80,000 during 19X6.
4. Minority interest in Parsimonious's consolidated subsidiaries' net income and dividends amounted to $20,000 and $13,000, respectively, during 19X6.

Required:

1. Prepare a consolidated statement of changes in financial position (working capital basis) for 19X6.
2. Prepare a consolidated statement of changes in financial position (cash basis) for 19X6.

P8.12 Various Consolidation Calculations, Including Taxes Presented below are selected items of information related to Pancho Corporation and its 80-percent-owned subsidiary, the Sisco Company, for the year ended December 31, 19X5. Pancho acquired its interest in Sisco on March 31, 19X5.

Net Income from Own Operations—Pancho	$4,000,000
Net Income from Own Operations—Sisco	1,000,000
Dividends—Sisco	400,000
Consolidated Depreciation Expense	600,000
Goodwill (Purchase Premium) Amortization	150,000
Income from Pancho's Equity Investments	60,000
Dividends Received from Equity Investees	40,000

Both companies face marginal income tax rates of 40 percent. Pancho expects to ultimately realize all undistributed equity method income in the form of dividends. Current tax law provides for a deduction of 85 percent of corporate dividends received. Sisco's earnings and dividends accrued evenly over the year.

Required: Determine the following and show all calculations:

1. Preacquisition earnings (ignore income tax implications).
2. Consolidated net income (ignore income tax implications).
3. Consolidated working capital provided by operations (ignore income tax implications).
4. The journal entry for income taxes related to Pancho's share of earnings and dividends from Sisco and the equity method investments. Pancho and Sisco do *not* file a consolidated income tax return.

Chapter 9 **Consolidated Financial Statements: Intercompany Transactions I**

This is the first of two chapters in which we study how **intercompany transactions**—transactions among affiliated corporations—affect the preparation of consolidated financial statements. Many of the intricacies common to the consolidation process are encountered in these two chapters.

Intercompany transactions are of two general types. The first type occurs when goods or services are sold between affiliated corporations. In consolidation, intercompany revenues and expenses are eliminated. Neither arose out of transactions with outside parties; both must be eliminated to avoid overstatement of consolidated revenues and expenses. Any related intercompany receivables and payables must also be eliminated. The second type of intercompany transaction requiring working paper eliminations arises when assets transferred among affiliates at a gain or loss to the selling company are still on hand at the end of an accounting period. Since such gains and losses have not yet been confirmed by transactions with outside parties, they too must be eliminated and the assets' balances adjusted in consolidation.

This chapter looks at intercompany revenues and expenses and the problems created by unconfirmed profits and losses arising out of intercompany transfers of land, merchandise inventory, and depreciable assets. These unconfirmed profits and losses are also related to the parent's equity method accrual and, where appropriate, to the minority interest in net income. Income tax effects of intercompany transactions and the computation of consolidated income tax expense are discussed at the end of the chapter.

In Chapter 10, the study of intercompany transactions is continued with emphasis on intercompany bondholdings, intercompany leasing, and a comprehensive numerical example involving a variety of intercompany transactions. Chapter 10 concludes with a discussion of situations in which the subsidiary has preferred stock *and* common stock outstanding.

As the problems created by intercompany transactions are addressed, the accountant is guided by the overriding objective in the preparation of consolidated statements: to report the affairs of a group of affiliated corporations as if it were a single economic entity. The **principles of confirmation** and **removal of inter-**

company assets, liabilities, and revenues and expenses, which follow from this overriding objective, are used over and over again in this chapter and the next.

Intercompany Revenues and Expenses

When affiliated corporations perform services or transfer merchandise to one another, the intercompany transaction causes one company to record revenues and the other to record expenses (or merchandise purchases). Because the companies have recorded (or will record) purchase and sales transactions with outside parties which incorporate these internally transferred goods or services, such *intercompany revenue and expense items are always eliminated in their entirety in consolidated statements*. The eliminating entry is:

CONSOLIDATED FINANCIAL STATEMENT WORKING PAPER

Revenues (Intercompany) XXX
    Expenses (Intercompany)   XXX
To eliminate the revenue and expense amounts recorded by the
affiliates on an intercompany sale of merchandise or services.

This removes the double counting of revenue and expense items which otherwise would exist without affecting the amount of consolidated net income. The effect of such an elimination can be seen in Figure 9.1. Notice that consolidated revenues and expenses are reduced by equal amounts and that the area labeled "Consolidated Net Income" is identical to the total area within the separate net incomes of P and S.

To illustrate, suppose that the Park Company performs some management services for the South Company. Personnel compensation, supplies, travel, and overhead result in out-of-pocket costs of $25,000 to Park, which have been recorded in Park's accounting records. The management services are billed to South at $40,000, thereby generating the following bookkeeping entries by Park and South:

BOOKS OF PARK COMPANY

Cash 40,000
    Service Revenue   40,000
To record the performance of services for South Company at a
price of $40,000.

BOOKS OF SOUTH COMPANY

General and Administrative Expenses 40,000
    Cash   40,000
To record the procurement of management services from Park
Company at a cost of $40,000.

We assume that the cost of these management services is, like all costs of being in business, reflected in the prices of goods and services sold to outside parties. While the intercompany revenues and expenses are bona fide transactions

Figure 9.1 **Effect of Eliminating Intercompany Revenues and Expenses**

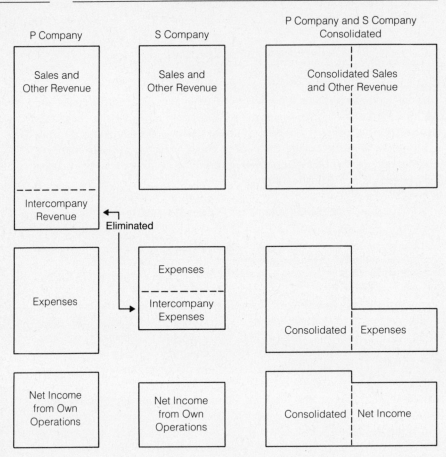

from the separate legal perspectives of both affiliates, when Park and South are consolidated we view them as a single economic entity. Therefore, from a consolidated point of view, we are interested in (1) the costs originally incurred by Park and (2) the revenue realized by South from external parties. The intercompany revenues and expenses are offsetting and have no effect on consolidated net income, but consolidated revenue and expenses will be overstated by $40,000 if these amounts are not eliminated. At the next consolidation point, then, the following eliminating entry is made on the working paper:

CONSOLIDATED FINANCIAL STATEMENT WORKING PAPER

Service Revenue 40,000
    General and Administrative Expenses.   40,000
To eliminate the intercompany revenue and expense resulting
from the management services provided by Park to South in the
amount of $40,000.

Note that this elimination reduces consolidated revenues and expenses by equal amounts and has no effect on consolidated net income. Moreover, neither P's equity method accrual nor the minority interest in net income is affected. As we shall see in the section on intercompany merchandise transactions, income of the affiliates is affected *only* if there are unconfirmed intercompany profits or losses. Eliminating intercompany sales and purchases is done to avoid double counting; removal of unconfirmed intercompany profits is a separate issue.

Intercompany Profits: Some Preliminaries

The intercompany profits that require elimination relate only to transfer of assets which remain inside the affiliated group at the end of the reporting period. These are the profits (or losses) which have not yet been confirmed by further sale to outside parties; confirmed profits require no elimination. Calculation of the intercompany profit is straightforward:

> **Intercompany profit** is the difference between the **intercompany transfer price** and the **cost** (or **net book value**) to the selling affiliate.

Suppose the parent had acquired a nondepreciable asset at a cost of $10,000. During the current year, the asset is sold to the subsidiary for $18,000. Prior to consolidation, a *gain* of $8,000 (= $18,000 − $10,000) appears on the parent's books, and the *asset* is carried at $18,000 on the subsidiary's books. The necessary eliminating entry made in consolidation is given next:

CONSOLIDATED FINANCIAL STATEMENT WORKING PAPER

Gain (Intercompany) 8,000
    Asset   8,000
To eliminate the unconfirmed intercompany profit and reduce the
asset to original acquisition cost.

After removing the effects of this transaction in consolidation, the asset is carried in the consolidated balance sheet at $10,000 (the original acquisition cost to the group) and the unconfirmed gain of $8,000 disappears. *From a consolidated point of view, the transaction is treated as if it never occurred.* The gain will be eliminated in consolidation each year until it is *confirmed* through use or sale to an outside party. This affects the *timing* of the ultimate recognition in consolidated net income but *not* the amount recognized.

To simplify the discussion, we distinguish between intercompany sales or transfers *from* parent *to* subsidiary and *to* parent *from* subsidiary, as follows:

> A **downstream sale** or **transfer** occurs when the *parent sells to a subsidiary*. An **upstream sale** or **transfer** indicates that a *subsidiary is selling to the parent*.

There are, of course, many complications to be addressed. We begin by discussing the controversy over how much intercompany profit is to be eliminated when a minority interest is present.

How Much Intercompany Profit Should be Eliminated?

Elimination of intercompany profits on asset transfers within an affiliated group derives from the fundamental argument that, since P Company and S Company are under common control, transactions between them are *not* the outcome of arm's-length bargaining. Therefore, any profits (or losses) recorded in such transactions are *tentative*, subject to confirmation via arm's-length transactions with external parties.

Total Elimination in Downstream Sales. There is general agreement that intercompany profits arising in downstream sales should be entirely eliminated against the controlling interest. This simply follows from the notion that no part of the unconfirmed intercompany profit benefits the controlling interest (P Company) until the assets are sold outside the affiliated group. Furthermore, the existence of a minority interest is irrelevant in downstream sales. Since elimination of the unconfirmed intercompany profit is entirely against the controlling interest, there is no effect on the minority interest in net income.

Total versus Partial Elimination in Upstream Sales. In cases where the subsidiary is selling to the parent, recorded unconfirmed intercompany profits show up first in the net income of S and then—by the equity method—in the net income of P. Clearly, if S is a wholly owned subsidiary, P has in effect made a sale to itself, and the distinction between downstream and upstream sales vanishes. P's net income should include none of these unconfirmed intercompany profits. The presence of a minority interest, however, complicates the issue.

Remember that P and S are separate legal entities. One could argue, with some merit, that the minority's share of intercompany profits on upstream sales needs no further confirmation. Indeed, once the upstream sale to P has occurred, the minority's share of the profit is fixed. Yet P may arbitrarily decide to void the sale and transfer the unsold items back to S, in which case the intercompany profit, along with the minority's share thereof, vanishes. This is the problem when non-arm's-length transactions occur between companies under common control. Nevertheless, some accountants believe that unconfirmed intercompany profits on upstream sales ought to be eliminated only to the extent of P's interest in S—the partial or fractional elimination position. The *parent theory of consolidated statements* supports partial elimination on upstream sales.

We believe that total elimination of all unconfirmed intercompany profits or losses is appropriate for consolidated statements. Whether upstream or downstream, intercompany sales are not likely to be arm's-length transactions, and recognition of any intercompany profits prior to sale outside the firm is premature. Furthermore, failure to remove the entire unconfirmed intercompany profit is inconsistent with reporting consolidated assets at cost to the consolidated entity.

This position is consistent with the *entity theory of consolidated statements* and with *ARB 51*, which states, in part:

> Accordingly, any intercompany profit or loss on assets remaining within the group should be eliminated; the concept usually applied for this purpose is *gross profit or loss*. . . .
>
> The amount of intercompany profit to be eliminated . . . is not affected by the existence of a minority interest. The complete elimination of the intercompany profit or loss . . . *may* be allocated proportionately between the majority and minority interests.[1] [Emphasis added]

The quotation indicates that elimination of the intercompany profit *may* be allocated proportionately between the controlling and minority interest. *ARB 51* seems to be suggesting that, when the subsidiary is partially owned, total elimination of the intercompany profit against the controlling interest is an acceptable alternative treatment. Such a procedure would have the unfortunate effect of reducing consolidated net income below what it would have been had the intercompany transaction not occurred at all!

To illustrate, suppose Post Corporation owns 80 percent of Staff Corporation. Net income of Post was $200,000. Staff earned $100,000 during the year, including $40,000 on sales to Post, as yet unconfirmed by external transactions. If Staff's upstream sales had not occurred at all, consolidated net income would be $248,000 [= $200,000 + (.8 × $60,000)]; minority interest in net income is $12,000 (= .2 × $60,000). The same result is obtained if the intercompany profit is eliminated proportionately against the controlling and minority interests [$248,000 = $200,000 + (.8 × $100,000) − (.8 × 40,000); $12,000 = (.2 × $100,000) − (.2 × $40,000)]. Elimination of the $40,000 intercompany profit against only the majority, however, leads to consolidated net income of $240,000 [= $200,000 + (.8 × $100,000) − $40,000] and minority interest in net income of $20,000 (= .2 × $100,000). In effect, the minority's share is recognized by charging the majority for $8,000 and shifting the $8,000 to the minority. We find no basis in principle for such a shift. Consistent application of this approach calls for crediting the majority for the same $40,000 when the intercompany profit is ultimately confirmed. Hence, consolidated net income is misstated by $8,000 in each of two accounting periods. Even though the misstatements cancel out, we see no justification for the first misstatement, let alone the second.

The treatment of unconfirmed intercompany gains and losses adopted throughout this book can be summarized as follows. We believe this treatment is theoretically sound and consistent with current practice.

---

[1]Committee on Accounting Procedure, *Accounting Research Bulletin No. 51*, "Consolidated Financial Statements" (New York: AICPA, 1959), pars. 6, 14; CT § C51.109,.115. Note that the *gross profit* on intercompany merchandise transfers is eliminated if unconfirmed. An alternative is to eliminate the *net profit*, gross profit reduced by selling and administrative expenses. Elimination of net profit only, however, would overstate consolidated inventories. The overstatement arises because the inventory account would include some period costs—selling and administrative expenses—which are not considered to be inventoriable costs. Therefore, we believe the elimination of net profit is *not* an acceptable alternative.

> Preparation of consolidated statements requires *total elimination* of unconfirmed intercompany gains and losses. Unconfirmed gains or losses on upstream sales are *eliminated proportionately* against the controlling and minority interests.

Impact on the Equity Method Accrual

As we have mentioned, *APBO 18* indicates that the equity method accrual is a *one-line consolidation*. Under this one-line consolidation concept, P's share of any unconfirmed intercompany gains (losses) is deducted from (added to) P's share of S's reported net income in computing the equity method accrual. Thus the equity method accrual is affected by unconfirmed intercompany gains and losses on upstream *and* downstream sales. Intuitively, P's unconfirmed intercompany profit on downstream sales would seem to have nothing to do with the income P accrues from S. Nevertheless, since these unconfirmed profits are eliminated in consolidation, they are also removed in determining the equity method accrual. This leads to the result called for in *APBO 18*—namely, that the reported net income of P equals consolidated net income and that P's retained earnings equal consolidated retained earnings.[2]

Intercompany Transfers of Land

Transfers of land between affiliated companies represent the most straightforward application of the concepts inherent in accounting for unconfirmed intercompany profits. Land is not depreciable and is not integrated into a cost-of-goods-sold computation.

While the purchasing affiliate records the purchase of land at the price paid, the intercompany sale of land generates a gain or loss to the selling affiliate. This gain or loss is included in the net income and ultimately in the retained earnings of the selling affiliate. Since an unconfirmed intercompany gain or loss affects consolidated net income and is eliminated in consolidation, an equivalent elimination is reflected in the parent's equity method accrual. If the sale is *downstream*, *all* of the unconfirmed gain is deducted from the equity accrual, thereby offsetting the gain reported in the parent's separate income statement. In the *upstream* case, the *parent's share* of the subsidiary's reported (unconfirmed) gain is deducted from the equity accrual. This offsets the parent's share of the gain reported in the subsidiary's separate income statement.

At each consolidation point, we prepare working paper entries to eliminate the effects of the intercompany land transfer until the land is sold externally. *In the year of intercompany sale*, the recorded intercompany gain is eliminated against the land account as shown below:

---

[2]Accounting Principles Board, *Opinion No. 18,* "The Equity Method of Accounting for Investments in Common Stock" (New York: AICPA, 1971), par. 19; CT § 182.109.

CONSOLIDATED FINANCIAL STATEMENT WORKING PAPER

Gain on Sale of Land XXX
    Land   XXX
To eliminate the unconfirmed gain on intercompany sale of land during
the current year and reduce the land account to original acquisition cost.

This working paper entry applies to both downstream and upstream sales in the
year of intercompany sale. If an upstream sale had occurred, calculation of the
Minority Interest in Net Income would reflect a deduction for the minority's share
of the eliminated gain.

Recall that consolidation elimination entries are *not* posted to the books.
Therefore, the gain remains on the seller's books, as part of retained earnings,
and the overvaluation of the land remains on the purchaser's books. Each year,
when consolidated statements are prepared, working paper entries must be made
to eliminate this transaction. We now consider these subsequent year eliminations
for both upstream and downstream sales.

Eliminations in Subsequent Years—Upstream Sales

If the land was sold *upstream* in a prior period, the unconfirmed gain must be
eliminated from the *beginning retained earnings of S*. Although it was eliminated
on the working paper, the gain remained intact on S's books and was closed to
S's retained earnings in the year of sale.

CONSOLIDATED FINANCIAL STATEMENT WORKING PAPER

Retained Earnings—S, Jan. 1 XXX
    Land   XXX
To eliminate the unconfirmed gain on an *upstream* intercompany sale of
land made in a prior year and to reduce the land account to original
acquisition cost.

To illustrate these concepts, consider the following transactions for Port Corporation and its 80-percent-owned subsidiary, Side Corporation:

1. On July 29, 19X1, Side sold a parcel of land to Port for $80,000. The land
   had originally cost Side $65,000.
2. Port continues to hold the land at December 31, 19X2.

Exhibit 9.1 shows the entries made by Port and Side to record these transactions
and the related working paper eliminations. In consolidation at December 31,
19X1, the $15,000 gain is eliminated, thereby removing it from consolidated net
income. Concurrently, however, it is closed to Side's separate net income and
then to Side's retained earnings. Now the unconfirmed gain must be eliminated in
consolidation at December 31, 19X2, by removing it from Side's retained earnings. This facilitates elimination of the investment account against Port's share of
Side's stockholders' equity and results in charging the minority interest for its
proportional share. To see this, suppose Port had acquired 80 percent of Side's
stock for $800,000 on January 1, 19X1, when the book value of Side's stockhold-

Exhibit 9.1	Intercompany Sale of Land Made Upstream: Journal Entries and Working Paper Eliminations

BOOKS OF SELLING OR PURCHASING AFFILIATE

July 29, 19X1 (Side Corporation)

```
Cash . . . . . . . . . . . . . . .   80,000
   Land. . . . . . . . . . . . . .              65,000
   Gain on Sale of Land . . . . . . .           15,000
To record sale of land to Port
Corporation.
```

(Port Corporation)

```
Land. . . . . . . . . . . . . . .   80,000
   Cash . . . . . . . . . . . . . .             80,000
To record purchase of land from Side
Corporation.
```

December 31, 19X1

Port's equity method accrual is reduced by $12,000 (= .8 × $15,000).

December 31, 19X2

No effect on equity method accrual.

CONSOLIDATED FINANCIAL STATEMENT WORKING PAPER

December 31, 19X1

```
Gain on Sale of Land . . . . . . . .  15,000
   Land. . . . . . . . . . . . . .              15,000
```
To eliminate the unconfirmed gain on intercompany sale of land and reduce the land account to original acquisition cost.

Note:

The minority interest in Side's *net income* for 19X1 is reduced by $3,000 (= .2 × $15,000).

December 31, 19X2

```
Retained Earnings—Side, Jan. 1,
19X2 . . . . . . . . . . . . . .  15,000
   Land. . . . . . . . . . . . . .              15,000
```
To eliminate the unconfirmed intercompany gain arising in 19X1 and reduce the land account to original acquisition cost.

Note:

The minority interest in Side at Jan. 1, 19X2, is reduced by $3,000 (= .2 × $15,000).

---

ers' equity was $1,000,000. Since $800,000 is .8 × $1,000,000, no purchase premium or discount was present. During 19X1, Side earned $200,000, including the gain of $15,000 on the intercompany sale of land. Port records an equity method accrual of $148,000 [= .8($200,000 − $15,000)] on December 31, 19X1. Thus the investment account is *reduced* by Port's share of the unconfirmed gain, $12,000 (= .8 × $15,000) via the equity method accrual, but Side's retained earnings *includes* the $15,000. Assuming Port continues to hold the land in 19X2, charging Side's retained earnings for $15,000 in the elimination made in consolidation at December 31, 19X2, restores the equivalence needed for a clean elimination. Consider the following T accounts:

INVESTMENT IN SIDE (80%)

Original acquisition cost	1/1/X1	800,000	
Net equity method accrual ($148,000)	12/31/X1	160,000	12,000
Balance	1/1/X2	948,000	

STOCKHOLDERS' EQUITY—SIDE

Balance: date of acquisition			1/1/X1	1,000,000
Net income			19X1	200,000
Balance			1/1/X2	1,200,000
Working paper elimination	12/31/X2	15,000		
				1,185,000

Now the Investment in Side can be cleanly eliminated against Side's Stockholders' Equity ($948,000 $=$ .8 $\times$ $1,185,000) as of January 1, 19X2. The Minority Interest in Side at that date is $237,000 ($=$ .2 $\times$ $1,185,000) and reflects proportionate (20 percent) elimination of the $15,000 gain on the upstream sale of land.

Eliminations in Subsequent Years—Downstream Sales

With *downstream* sales, in subsequent years the unconfirmed gain must be added to the *Investment in S* account. In this case, the total intercompany gain was originally charged against the accrual of equity method income from S Company, thereby reducing the investment account, but there was no corresponding effect on S's net income at time of consolidation. As before, a discrepancy exists between the investment account and S's stockholders' equity. Removal of this discrepancy is necessary for a clean elimination. We cannot adjust S's retained earnings, for this would imply proportionate elimination against the minority interest. Because the minority interest is *not* affected by downstream sales, the best approach is to adjust the investment account directly for the full amount of the intercompany gain. This simply means that, where unconfirmed downstream sales are concerned, we *debit or credit the investment account* at subsequent consolidation points instead of the beginning retained earnings of S. P's retained earnings were previously reduced when the unconfirmed intercompany gain was subtracted from the equity method accrual. P's retained earnings (and consolidated retained earnings) are therefore properly stated. This reduction in P's retained earnings is also reflected in the investment account. Elimination of the investment account against the stockholders' equity of S *without* adding back the unconfirmed gain would result in an incomplete elimination. A portion of S's stockholders' equity equal to the unconfirmed downstream gain would remain. An incomplete elimination would also result if the gain were charged against S's retained earnings (as in the upstream case) *unless* this charge is ignored when calculating the minority interest—an unnecessary computational inconvenience. The add-back to the investment account is needed to remedy this situation. No further working paper adjustments to P's retained earnings are necessary. In all other respects, the eliminations for downstream sales are the same as for upstream sales.

We return to the Port and Side example and use the following transactions to illustrate the entries for downstream sales. Recall that Port owns 80 percent of Side.

Exhibit 9.2   **Intercompany Sale of Land Made Downstream: Journal Entries and Working Paper Eliminations**

BOOKS OF SELLING OR PURCHASING AFFILIATE	CONSOLIDATED FINANCIAL STATEMENT WORKING PAPER

BOOKS OF SELLING OR PURCHASING AFFILIATE

March 15, 19X1   (Port Corporation)

```
Cash . . . . . . . . . . . . .   125,000
   Land . . . . . . . . . . . .            100,000
   Gain on Sale of Land . . . . .           25,000
To record sale of land to Side
Corporation.
```

(Side Corporation)

```
Land . . . . . . . . . . . . .   125,000
   Cash . . . . . . . . . . . .            125,000
To record the purchase of land
from Port Corporation.
```

December 31, 19X1

Port's equity method accrual is
reduced by $25,000.

December 31, 19X2

No effect on equity method accrual.

CONSOLIDATED FINANCIAL STATEMENT WORKING PAPER

December 31, 19X1

```
Gain on Sale of Land . . . . . .   25,000
   Land . . . . . . . . . . . .              25,000
To eliminate the unconfirmed gain
on the intercompany sale of land
and reduce the land account to
original acquisition cost.
```

Note: The minority interest in Side's net income for 19X1 is *not* affected.

December 31, 19X2

```
Investment in Side . . . . . . .   25,000
   Land . . . . . . . . . . . .              25,000
To add the unconfirmed
intercompany gain to the
investment account to maintain
equivalence with Side's retained
earnings and reduce land account
to original acquisition cost.
```

Note: The minority interest in Side Company at Jan. 1, 19X2, is *not* affected.

---

1. On March 15, 19X1, Port sold land to Side for $125,000. Port had purchased the land several years before for $100,000.
2. Side continued to hold the land at December 31, 19X2.

The entries made to record these transactions and the related working paper eliminations are given in Exhibit 9.2.

To understand the December 31, 19X2, elimination in the downstream case, let's redo the T account analysis used in the upstream case, recognizing that the intercompany gain is $25,000 (not $15,000) and resulted from a downstream sale.

		INVESTMENT IN SIDE (80%)	
Original acquisition cost	1/1/X1	800,000	
Net equity method accrual ($135,000)	12/31/X1	160,000	25,000
Balance	1/1/X2	935,000	
Working paper elimination	12/31/X2	25,000	
		960,000	

STOCKHOLDERS' EQUITY—SIDE

Balance: date of acquisition	1/1/X1	1,000,000
Net income	19X1	200,000
Balance	1/1/X2	1,200,000

Now the Investment in Side can be cleanly eliminated against Side's Stockholders' Equity ($960,000 $=$ .8 $\times$ $1,200,000) as of January 1, 19X2. The Minority Interest in Side at that date is $240,000 ($=$ .2 $\times$ $1,200,000) and reflects *none* of the eliminated gain on the downstream sale of land.

Treatment If Land Is Sold to Outside Party. Sale of the land to an outside party in a subsequent year requires that the original intercompany gain be recognized in consolidated net income in that subsequent year. If the original intercompany sale was *upstream,* the working paper entry transfers the original intercompany gain out of S Company's retained earnings and into current income. In the *downstream* case, the gain is added back to the investment account from which it had been previously deducted via the equity method accrual and is recognized as current income.

CONSOLIDATED FINANCIAL STATEMENT WORKING PAPER

Retained Earnings—S, Jan. 1 (*upstream* sale)
    or
Investment in S (*downstream* sale) XXX
    Gain on Sale of Land XXX
To include in current consolidated net income the previously recorded
gain on an intercompany sale of land, now confirmed through external
sale.

P Company's equity method accrual in the year of external sale includes all (part) of the now-confirmed downstream (upstream) intercompany gain. If the intercompany sale had been upstream, the minority interest in net income is increased by the minority's share of the now-confirmed intercompany gain. Often, the external sale results in a gain or loss *in addition to* the original intercompany gain or loss. This additional gain or loss is attributed entirely to the company selling the land externally (that is, the company which purchased the land internally).

To illustrate, refer to the Port and Side example and assume the following:

1. Port sells the land purchased from Side (for $80,000) outside for $78,000 on September 30, 19X3, and recognizes a $2,000 loss.
2. Side sells the land purchased from Port (for $125,000) outside for $165,000 on November 1, 19X3, and recognizes a $40,000 gain.

The entries made by Port and Side to record these transactions during 19X3 and the related working paper eliminations appear in Exhibit 9.3.

Exhibit 9.3	**External Sale of Land Acquired in Upstream and Downstream Intercompany Sales: Journal Entries and Working Paper Eliminations**

BOOKS OF SELLING AFFILIATE

September 30, 19X3   (Port Corporation)

```
Cash . . . . . . . . . . . .     78,000
Loss on Sale of Land . . . . .    2,000
  Land . . . . . . . . . . .              80,000
```
To record sale of land (acquired from Side in an *upstream* transfer) to outside party.

December 31, 19X3

Port's equity method accrual is increased by \$12,000 (= .8 × \$15,000) now that the upstream intercompany gain is confirmed.

November 1, 19X3   (Side Corporation)

```
Cash . . . . . . . . . . . .    165,000
  Land . . . . . . . . . . .              125,000
  Gain on Sale of Land . . . .            40,000
```
To record sale of land (acquired from Port in a *downstream* transfer) to outside party.

December 31, 19X3

Port's equity method accrual is increased by \$25,000, now that the downstream gain is confirmed.

CONSOLIDATED FINANCIAL STATEMENT WORKING PAPER

December 31, 19X3

```
Retained Earnings—Side
  Jan 1, 19X3 . . . . . . . . . .   15,000
  Gain on Sale of Land . . . . . .          15,000
```
To credit 19X3 income for the \$15,000 intercompany gain, which is now confirmed.

Note: The minority interest in Side's net income for 19X3 is increased by \$3,000 (= .2 × \$15,000).

December 31, 19X3

```
Investment in Side . . . . . . . .  25,000
  Gain on Sale of Land . . . . . .          25,000
```
To credit 19X3 income for the \$25,000 intercompany gain now confirmed and add to the investment account.

Note: The minority interest in Side's net income for 19X3 will reflect the minority's share of Side's external gain, \$8,000 (= .2 × \$40,000).

Intercompany Transfers of Merchandise

Transfers of merchandise inventory items between affiliated corporations are quite common. Component parts are often manufactured by one affiliate and assembled by another. Or finished goods may be produced by one affiliate and marketed by another. In all such cases, the preparation of consolidated statements requires elimination of intercompany revenues and expenses. If the intercompany transfer price differs from cost, an unconfirmed gain or loss results. When the merchandise is sold to outside customers during the same accounting period, the gain or loss is confirmed and no additional working paper entries are needed. If some merchandise remains in ending inventory, however, the unconfirmed gain or loss must be eliminated. Similarly, P Company's equity method accrual is reduced by the total amount of unconfirmed intercompany inventory profit on downstream sales and by a proportional amount of the unconfirmed profit on upstream sales. The minority interest in S Company's net income will be decreased by the minority's share of unconfirmed upstream gains.

Intercompany Sales: Unconfirmed Profit in Ending Inventory

The principles involved in intercompany inventory profit eliminations parallel those encountered in eliminations arising from land transfers among affiliates. Nevertheless, the procedures may seem more complex because merchandise inventory is reflected in the income statement through its inclusion in cost of goods sold. There is no gain on sale of merchandise indicated separately on the income statement. Rather, the unconfirmed gain is part of the ending (or beginning) inventory balance. Elimination of the unconfirmed gain in ending inventory results in an increase in consolidated cost of goods sold. Our consolidated financial statement working paper is set up to show the *components* of cost of goods sold in the income statement—beginning inventory + purchases − ending inventory—rather than cost of goods sold itself. Ending inventory *also appears* in the balance sheet section of the working paper. Since the amount of ending inventory reduces cost of goods sold, it is shown as a credit in the income statement. Removal of the gain, therefore, means debiting ending inventory (or cost of goods sold) on the income statement while crediting the inventory account on the balance sheet. At the same time, *total* intercompany merchandise sales (purchases) must also be eliminated so that consolidated revenues and expenses are not overstated. This entry *does not* affect consolidated net income, while the entry made to remove the unconfirmed profit on intercompany merchandise sales *does*. Both entries are now illustrated:

CONSOLIDATED FINANCIAL STATEMENT WORKING PAPER

```
Sales . . . . . . . . . . . . . . . . . . . . . . . . . . . . .   XXX
    Purchases (or Cost of Goods Sold)  . . . . . . . . . . .           XXX
    To eliminate intercompany merchandise sales by reducing
    consolidated sales and purchases (or cost of goods sold).


Inventory, Dec. 31, Income Statement (or Cost of Goods
    Sold) . . . . . . . . . . . . . . . . . . . . . . . . . .   XXX
    Inventory (Balance Sheet) . . . . . . . . . . . . . . .            XXX
    To eliminate unconfirmed intercompany profit in ending
    inventory by increasing cost of goods sold and decreasing
    the asset account to original acquisition cost.
```

As an example, consider Presento and Solento Corporations. Presento acquired 80 percent of Solento's voting stock several years ago. A summary of the intercompany inventory transactions between these affiliates in 19X2 is shown next:

	Presento	Solento	Total
Intercompany Sales of Merchandise Made to Affiliate during 19X2	$300,000	$80,000	$380,000
Intercompany Profits in Inventory Acquired from Affiliate, Dec. 31, 19X2	8,000	50,000	58,000

During 19X2, the affiliates recorded the intercompany sales as follows:

BOOKS OF PRESENTO CORPORATION

Cash 300,000
   Sales   300,000
To record sale of merchandise to Solento.

Purchases.   80,000
   Cash   80,000
To record purchase of merchandise from Solento.

BOOKS OF SOLENTO CORPORATION

Cash   80,000
   Sales   80,000
To record sale of merchandise to Presento.

Purchases. 300,000
   Cash   300,000
To record purchase of merchandise from Presento.

Presento's 19X2 equity method accrual will be decreased by P's share of the unconfirmed intercompany profits in ending inventory, $56,400 [= $50,000 + .8 ($8,000)].

We now show the working paper eliminations to be made when consolidated statements are prepared at the end of 19X2. Our eliminations deal with intercompany sales and intercompany profits in ending inventories, in that order.

CONSOLIDATED FINANCIAL STATEMENT WORKING PAPER

Sales 380,000
   Purchases   380,000
To eliminate intercompany sales and purchases made in 19X2.

Inventory, Dec. 31 (Income Statement)   58,000
   Inventory (Balance Sheet)   58,000
To eliminate unconfirmed intercompany profits in ending inventory by increasing cost of goods sold and reducing inventory to original acquisition cost.

The net effect of the elimination of intercompany profits on *upstream* merchandise sales is to decrease the minority interest in net income by $1,600 (= .2 × $8,000) in 19X2. This is the minority's share of unconfirmed profit in Presento's ending inventory, acquired from Solento in upstream sales.

Intercompany Sales: Unconfirmed Profit in Beginning Inventory

The existence of unconfirmed gains in the *ending* inventory of one period means that those gains are also reflected in the next period's *beginning* inventory. Working paper eliminations do not affect the companies' books, so at the next consolidation point the beginning inventory (or cost of goods sold) on the income statement is *overstated by the unconfirmed gain*. Another working paper elimination is needed so that these gains are transferred into current year income by reducing (crediting) beginning inventory (or cost of goods sold) on the income statement. (Of course, any such gains not actually confirmed during the current year will be included in unconfirmed gains removed from the ending inventory.) The offsetting *debit* is to Beginning Retained Earnings of S for *upstream sales* and to Investment in S for *downstream sales*. Since the unconfirmed gains on downstream sales were removed from P's equity method accrual made at the end of the last period, P's retained earnings are properly stated, while S's retained earnings are not affected. As in the land case, the increase to the Investment in S is necessary to restore equivalence with S's stockholders' equity.

The need to transfer unconfirmed intercompany gains in beginning inventory into current year income also extends to P's equity method accrual. Whereas unconfirmed intercompany gains in *ending* inventory were *deducted* from the equity accrual, unconfirmed intercompany gains in *beginning* inventory are *added* to the equity accrual. As before, such adjustments are total (for downstream sales) or proportional (for upstream sales). The needed working paper entries follow:

CONSOLIDATED FINANCIAL STATEMENT WORKING PAPER

Retained Earnings—S, Jan. 1 XXX
    Inventory, Jan. 1 (Income Statement)   XXX
To eliminate intercompany profit on *upstream* sales in the beginning inventory, assumed confirmed in the current year, by decreasing beginning retained earnings and cost of goods sold.

Investment in S. XXX
    Inventory, Jan. 1 (Income Statement)   XXX
To eliminate intercompany profit on *downstream* sales in the beginning inventory, assumed confirmed in the current year, by increasing the investment account and decreasing cost of goods sold.

Note that the elimination of both beginning and ending unconfirmed intercompany profits on *upstream* sales of merchandise affects the minority interest in net income. Under proportional allocation of eliminated intercompany profits, the eliminated amount affects consolidated net income and minority interest in net income in proportion to the interests of majority and minority shareholders.

Continuing with the Presento and Solento example, we present the working paper eliminations to be made in consolidation as of December 31, 19X3, relative to the intercompany profits in the affiliates' *beginning* inventories at January 1, 19X3. These are the same intercompany profits eliminated from ending inventory in consolidation as of December 31, 19X2. Remember that eliminations are *not booked* so that the 19X2 ending inventory (which includes the intercompany profit) becomes the 19X3 beginning inventory in the affiliates' separate accounting records.

CONSOLIDATED FINANCIAL STATEMENT WORKING PAPER

Retained Earnings—S, Jan. 1. 8,000
  Inventory, Jan. 1 (Income Statement) 8,000
To eliminate unconfirmed intercompany profits on *upstream* sales
from beginning inventory, assuming confirmation in 19X3, and
include them in 19X3 operations.

Investment in S 50,000
  Inventory, Jan. 1 (Income Statement) 50,000
To eliminate unconfirmed intercompany profits on *downstream*
sales from beginning inventory, assuming confirmation in 19X3,
and include them in 19X3 operations.

Assumed confirmation of these intercompany profits increases Presento's 19X3 equity method accrual by $56,400 [= $50,000 + .8($8,000)] and increases the minority interest in Solento's net income for 19X3 by $1,600 (= .2 × $8,000).

Intercompany Profits and Inventory Cost-Flow Assumptions

Most companies do not use specific identification when accounting for inventories and cost of goods sold. Rather, they employ a cost-flow assumption such as LIFO or FIFO. The reader should note that the intercompany profit elimination techniques discussed here are compatible with any cost-flow assumption. Our eliminations seem to imply a FIFO cost flow because any intercompany profit in beginning inventory is assumed confirmed and is added to current income. Then the intercompany profit in the ending inventory is eliminated.

Suppose, however, that LIFO was being used and, to simplify matters, that the ending LIFO inventory was unchanged from the beginning LIFO inventory Following our procedure, the beginning intercompany profit is added to current income, and the ending intercompany profit is deducted from current income. What is the effect on current income? Absolutely zero! Since the LIFO inventory is assumed constant, so is the unconfirmed intercompany profit, and its elimination from beginning and ending inventories on the income statement has no net effect on current period income. Moreover, in making the elimination from ending inventory on the income statement, we also remove the unconfirmed gain from the overstated inventory on the balance sheet.

Under FIFO, of course, our procedure shows as confirmed the old (beginning) intercompany profit and eliminates as unconfirmed the new (ending) intercompany profit—precisely what is needed.

Effect of Lower-of-Cost-or-Market Adjustments

Chapter 4 of *ARB 43* calls for inventories to be valued at *lower of cost or market (LCM)*. The "market value" to be compared with acquisition cost is presumed to be current replacement cost except that *market* cannot exceed net realizable value

(NRV, the "ceiling") or be less than NRV minus a normal profit margin (the "floor"). These considerations are reflected in the following expression which, when correctly evaluated, identifies the appropriate LCM inventory amount:

$$LCM = Min[OC, NRV, max(RC, NRV - \pi)],$$

where

OC = Original acquisition cost,

NRV = Net realizable value; selling price less estimated cost to complete and sell,

RC = Current replacement cost,

π = Normal profit margin.

At year-end, a member of an affiliated group may find it necessary to reduce to market the inventory acquired from another member of the group in order to conform to the LCM rule. How should this adjustment, which generates a loss to the purchasing affiliate, affect our intercompany profit eliminations? We see two possibilities:

1. Attribute the loss to the *purchasing* affiliate and use it to reduce the amount of intercompany profit to be eliminated. This treatment follows from the notion that the LCM adjustment is recognition of another economic event. Its effect is to confirm this portion of the intercompany profit to the selling affiliate.
2. Attribute the loss to the *selling* affiliate on the grounds that the write-down was necessitated by an artificially high transfer price determined in a non-arm's-length transaction. Under this interpretation, the LCM adjustment is considered as an exogenously determined reversal of the tentative intercompany profit, and none of the intercompany profit is confirmed to the selling affiliate.

Some accountants support the first treatment. It should certainly be used if the loss occurred *after* the intercompany transfer. If timing of the loss is uncertain, however, we believe that the first treatment is flawed because it allows affiliates to shift gains and losses among the members and to misstate consolidated net income. For example, suppose P Company owns 60 percent of S Company and sells inventory marked up $10,000 to S Company. Assume that S still owns the goods at year-end and, under the LCM rule, recognizes a loss of $10,000 by reducing the inventory to market. Under the first treatment above, the intercompany transaction increases consolidated net income by $4,000! The $10,000 intercompany profit assumed confirmed to P is not eliminated but is reduced by only $6,000, P's share of the LCM loss booked by S. In contrast, the second treatment effectively eliminates the entire $10,000 of intercompany profit, leaving consolidated net income unchanged.

The second treatment should certainly be used if the loss occurred *before* the intercompany transfer. Also, if timing of the loss is uncertain, it should be used in order to neutralize any short-term manipulative practices.

Shipping and Installation Costs

Frequently, intercompany transfers of merchandise and equipment result in shipping or installation costs. If these costs are paid by the purchasing affiliate, they represent valid costs to the affiliated group and do not affect the intercompany profit. In contrast, payment of such costs by the selling affiliate indicates a concession in the intercompany transfer price, and the intercompany profit is reduced accordingly. Observe that in both cases the resulting consolidated asset reflects original acquisition cost plus any shipping and installation costs incurred in the transaction, regardless of which company actually pays for the costs. To convince yourself of this point, consider the following data:

Intercompany Merchandise Transfer Price	$100
Cost to Selling Affiliate	80
Shipping Cost	5

If the *purchasing affiliate pays the shipping cost,* it records the inventory at $105. Assuming the inventory is unsold at consolidation, unconfirmed intercompany profit of $20 (= $100 − $80) would be eliminated, reducing consolidated inventory to $85 (= 105 − $20).

In contrast, *payment of the shipping cost by the selling affiliate* indicates that the transfer price is actually $95 (= $100 − $5), and the intercompany profit is $15 (= $95 − $80). The purchasing affiliate records the inventory at $100. Assuming it is unsold at consolidation, unconfirmed intercompany profit of $15 is eliminated, reducing consolidated inventory to $85 (= $100 − $15), as in the previous case.

Intercompany Transfers of Depreciable Assets

Though less common than intercompany merchandise sales, transfers of depreciable assets between members of an affiliated group also require special treatment when consolidated statements are prepared. The complication arises because of the way in which intercompany gains on depreciable assets are assumed confirmed. Recall that gains arising on intercompany transfers of land and merchandise are confirmed when the items are sold to outsiders. In contrast, *the confirmation or realization of intercompany gains on depreciable assets normally is linked to their depreciation.* As the book values of depreciable assets are written down, their services are assumed to be embodied in the goods and services sold externally by the purchasing affiliate. Hence recorded depreciation, which represents the expiration of assets' services, also represents their "sale" to outsiders. For reasons of simplicity and materiality, we typically assume that *all* of the annual depreciation is "sold" outside and an identical portion of the gain confirmed. This is, of course, not strictly true. If the purchasing affiliate is a manufacturing concern, a part of its annual depreciation is included in manufactured inventories under full or absorption costing. We may further complicate the issue by suggesting that some of the manufactured goods are sold to other affiliates and not to outsiders at all. Generally, however, the cost flows are not traced to their ultimate external disposition because the amounts involved are not material and the costs of tracing them would exceed the benefits. For this reason, we assume that recorded depreciation adequately measures the expiration of assets' services and their ''sale'' to outsiders, and we shall attempt no further investigation of actual cost flows.

Objectives of the Eliminations

When a depreciable asset is transferred from one affiliate to another, the amount recorded by the purchasing affiliate typically differs from the asset's net book value (original acquisition cost less accumulated depreciation) to the selling affiliate. Since the selling affiliate normally records a gain on the transfer, the resulting asset balance on the books of the purchaser exceeds the net book value of the asset. The general objective in consolidation is to remove the effects of the intercompany transaction, treating it as if it had never occurred. From this general objective, we derive three specific objectives for our working paper eliminations:

1. Eliminate the unconfirmed intercompany gain and reduce the asset account to its net book value at date of intercompany sale.
2. Eliminate the difference between the annual depreciation expense recorded by the purchasing affiliate and the amount based on original acquisition cost.
3. Restate the balances in the asset and accumulated depreciation accounts so that they are based on original acquisition cost.

The format of the necessary working paper entries follows.

Eliminations in the Year of Intercompany Sale. First, we consider the eliminations required in the *year of sale* when an intercompany gain has arisen on the transfer of a depreciable asset. Each working paper entry achieves one of the objectives just mentioned.

CONSOLIDATED FINANCIAL STATEMENT WORKING PAPER

Gain on Sale of Depreciable Assets XXX
    Depreciable Assets.   XXX
To eliminate the recorded intercompany gain. The amount remaining in the asset account is the net book value at date of intercompany sale.

Accumulated Depreciation XXX
    Depreciation Expense   XXX
To eliminate the excess annual depreciation expense recorded by the purchasing affiliate on the increased depreciable basis generated in the intercompany transaction. The remaining accumulated depreciation is based on original acquisition cost.

Depreciable Assets. XXX
    Accumulated Depreciation   XXX
To restate the asset and accumulated depreciation accounts to their original acquisition cost basis. *The amount of adjustment is equal to the accumulated depreciation at date of intercompany sale.* The *net book value* of the depreciable asset is not affected.

Taken together, the above entries restate the asset, accumulated depreciation, and depreciation expense accounts so that they reflect *original acquisition cost*. The reduction in depreciation expense is allocated to the *selling affiliate;* it represents *the amount of intercompany gain confirmed in the current year*. If the subsidiary was the selling affiliate, *minority interest in net income* is decreased by the minority's share of the total intercompany gain and increased by the minority's share of the portion confirmed during the year (that is, the excess depreciation expense).

Both the total intercompany gain and the portion assumed confirmed during the year through depreciation affect P's *equity method accrual,* proportionately if the sale was upstream. The accrual is decreased by the total gain and increased by the portion assumed confirmed.

To illustrate these concepts, consider the case of the Pump Company and the Slide Company. Pump owns 80 percent of Slide. On January 1, 19X1, Slide sells Pump a piece of machinery for $150,000. Slide had acquired the machinery 2 years before for $140,000 (useful life of 7 years) and had recorded accumulated depreciation of $40,000 (net book value = $100,000). The asset has a remaining useful life of 5 years, and use of straight-line depreciation will continue. No salvage value has been or is anticipated. We begin by showing the entries made by Slide and Pump on their own books during 19X1:

BOOKS OF SLIDE COMPANY

1/1/X1

Cash	150,000	
Accumulated Depreciation.	40,000	
Machinery		140,000
Gain on Sale of Machinery		50,000
To record the sale of machinery to Pump Company.		

BOOKS OF PUMP COMPANY

1/1/X1

Machinery.	150,000	
Cash		150,000
To record the purchase of machinery from Slide Company.		

12/31/X1

Depreciation Expense.	30,000	
Accumulated Depreciation		30,000
To record depreciation expense for 19X1;		
$30,000 = $150,000/5.		

An unconfirmed gain of $50,000 arose on January 1, 19X1, but $10,000 (= $50,000/5) is assumed confirmed during 19X1 via excess depreciation. Thus, at the end of 19X1, $40,000 (= $50,000 − $10,000) of the intercompany gain remains unconfirmed. Pump's 19X1 equity method accrual is *decreased* by $32,000 (= .8 × $40,000), the controlling interest's share of the unconfirmed gain. We now turn to the eliminations made at December 31, 19X1:

CONSOLIDATED FINANCIAL STATEMENT WORKING PAPER
12/31/X1

Gain on Sale of Machinery 50,000
    Machinery.   50,000
To eliminate the recorded intercompany gain and to reduce the
machinery account to net book value at date of intercompany
sale.

Accumulated Depreciation. 10,000
    Depreciation Expense.   10,000
To eliminate the annual excess depreciation recorded by Pump
Company. On the original acquisition cost basis, annual
depreciation expense is $20,000 ($= \$140,000/7$). The excess of
$10,000 is simply the difference between the $30,000 recorded
by Pump and the $20,000 based on original acquisition cost.
Equivalently, $10,000 = \$50,000/5$.

Machinery. 40,000
    Accumulated Depreciation.   40,000
To restate the machinery and accumulated depreciation accounts
to their original acquisition cost basis. This is the accumulated
depreciation recorded by Slide prior to the intercompany sale.

These eliminations effectively reduce the *minority interest in net income* by
$8,000. In consolidation, Slide's net income is first decreased by $50,000 (the
total intercompany gain) and then increased by $10,000 (the portion of the gain
realized through depreciation). The net effect on Slide's net income is a decrease
of $40,000 ($= \$50,000 - \$10,000$), of which the minority's share is $8,000 ($=
.2 \times \$40,000$).

If the intercompany transaction had not occurred, the machinery would be
reported at $140,000 and accumulated depreciation (after 3 years) at $60,000.
From the T accounts below, we see that our entries accomplish this.

	MACHINERY				ACCUMULATED DEPRECIATION		
/X1 (P)	150,000					12/31/X1 (P)	30,000
'31/X1 (E)	40,000	12/31/X1 (E)	50,000	12/31/X1 (E)	10,000	12/31/X1 (E)	40,000
'31/X1 (C)	140,000					12/31/X1 (C)	60,000

(P): Entry made by Pump Company.
(E): Working paper elimination.
(C): Consolidated balance.

Eliminations in Subsequent Years. At consolidation points subsequent to the
year of sale, eliminations must be made to achieve the three consolidation objectives previously discussed. Fortunately, only the entry made to eliminate the unconfirmed intercompany gain will differ. The same entries which were made in
the year of sale to eliminate the excess annual depreciation expense and accumulated depreciation and to restate the assets and accumulated depreciation accounts
to their original cost basis are also made at each subsequent consolidation point.
Of course, the excess depreciation expense eliminated each year will be different

if straight-line depreciation is not used. Recall that in the year of sale we first eliminated the entire gain and then recognized the amount confirmed through a reduction in depreciation expense. In subsequent years, however, the intercompany gain is included in the selling affiliate's retained earnings and we face a new set of conditions:

1. The original intercompany gain has been:
   a. Totally eliminated from the investment account in the year of sale under the one-line consolidation approach of the equity method if the transfer was *downstream,* with no offsetting effect on S's retained earnings, thereby creating a discrepancy between the investment account and P's interest in S's retained earnings; *or*
   b. Proportionately eliminated from the investment account in the year of sale under the one-line consolidation approach of the equity method if the transfer was *upstream.* The gain itself is included in S's retained earnings so that a discrepancy exists between the investment account and P's share of S's retained earnings.
2. Some portion of the gain has been confirmed through prior years' depreciation recorded on the purchasing company's books. The investment account includes all (part) of the confirmed portion in downstream (upstream) sales as these amounts have been added to P's equity method accruals made since the date of intercompany sale.
3. Accumulated depreciation is overstated by the total excess depreciation expense (= portion of gain confirmed) recorded since date of intercompany sale.

Taking these conditions into account, we now show the general form of the working paper entry needed to eliminate the unconfirmed portion of the intercompany gain and reduce the asset to its net book value at date of intercompany sale.

CONSOLIDATED FINANCIAL STATEMENT WORKING PAPER

Investment in S (*downstream* sale)
   or
Retained Earnings—S,
   Jan. 1 (*upstream* sale) . . .   Amount of gain *unconfirmed*
                                        in prior years

Accumulated Depreciation. . .   Amount of gain *confirmed*
                                    (= excess depreciation
                                    recorded) in prior years

   Depreciable Assets . . . . .   Total original
                                                                intercompany gain

To eliminate the amount of
intercompany gain
unconfirmed in prior years,
remove the excess
depreciation recorded in prior
years (the amount of gain
confirmed), and reduce the
asset to its net book value at
date of intercompany sale.

To illustrate, suppose a depreciable asset with a net book value of $40,000 was exchanged for $48,000 in an intercompany sale on January 1, 19X1. The purchasing affiliate depreciates the $48,000 asset by the straight-line method over its remaining life of 4 years. Excess depreciation of $2,000 [= ($48,000 − $40,000)/4] is recorded each year and represents the portion of the gain confirmed each year. In consolidation at December 31, 19X2, the eliminating entry below shows $6,000 of gain *unconfirmed* in prior years and $2,000 of gain *confirmed* in prior years (19X1).

CONSOLIDATED FINANCIAL STATEMENT WORKING PAPER

Investment in S (*downstream* sale) (3 × $2,000)
   or
Retained Earnings—S, Jan. 1 (*upstream* sale) (3 × $2,000) 6,000
Accumulated Depreciation (1 × $2,000) 2,000
   Depreciable Assets 8,000

If the depreciation method being used is not straight-line, calculation of the prior year unconfirmed and confirmed portions is more complex, but the principle remains unchanged. The confirmed portion is charged to Accumulated Depreciation. The total gain less the amount confirmed in prior years is the amount still unconfirmed. It is charged to Investment in S (downstream sale) or to Retained Earnings—S (upstream sale).

The portion of the gain assumed confirmed each year through depreciation increases P's *equity method accrual,* proportionately in upstream sales. Moreover, if the original sale was upstream, the *minority interest in net income* is also increased by the minority's share of the annual excess depreciation expense.

We continue with the Pump and Slide example, examining developments in 19X2. During 19X2, the only bookkeeping entry made is when Pump records the annual $30,000 depreciation expense. At December 31, 19X2, when the consolidated statements are prepared, the following eliminating entries are made:

CONSOLIDATED FINANCIAL STATEMENT WORKING PAPER

12/31/X2

Retained Earnings—Slide, Jan. 1, 19X2. 40,000
Accumulated Depreciation. 10,000
   Machinery. 50,000
To eliminate the intercompany gain unconfirmed in prior years
($40,000 = $50,000 − $10,000), remove the excess depreciation
recorded in prior years ($10,000), and reduce the machinery
account to its net book value at date of intercompany sale
($100,000 = $150,000 − $50,000).

Accumulated Depreciation. 10,000
   Depreciation Expense. 10,000
To eliminate the annual excess depreciation expense recorded by
Pump Company

Machinery 40,000
   Accumulated Depreciation. 40,000
To restate the machinery and accumulated depreciation accounts
to their acquisition cost basis.

The $10,000 gain confirmed in 19X2 through depreciation is allocated proportionately between the controlling and minority interests. The *equity method accrual* is increased by Pump's share, $8,000, and the *minority interest in net income* is increased by $2,000, the minority's share.

If the machine is sold outside the affiliated group before it is fully depreciated, the previously recorded intercompany gain is assumed fully confirmed and is allocated to the income of the original selling affiliate at the next consolidation point. Should Pump subsequently sell the machine externally, consolidated net income in that period would include (1) Pump's gain or loss on the external sale and Pump's share of (2) the remaining intercompany gain recorded by Slide not previously confirmed through depreciation. Item 2 would be reflected proportionately in Pump's equity method accrual and in the minority interest in net income in the period of external sale.

Computing the Equity Method Accrual and the Minority Interest in Net Income: An Example

We have now examined the procedures for dealing with several common types of intercompany transactions. In Chapter 10, additional intercompany transactions are analyzed, and a comprehensive numerical example complete with working paper is presented. Before moving to Chapter 10, however, it will be useful to summarize the effects of the transactions studied so far on the equity method accrual made by P Company, on the minority interest in net income, and on the consolidated financial statement working paper. Although the equity method accrual is eliminated in consolidation, it *does* become a component of the Investment in S and Retained Earnings accounts on P's books. Furthermore, we have seen that elimination of the unconfirmed intercompany gains and losses in the equity method accrual—under the one-line consolidation concept of *APBO 18*—influences the working paper entries needed at subsequent consolidation points.

This example is based on information which was discussed earlier in the chapter and is summarized below. Other financial statement data included on the working paper are assumed.

1. P owns 80 percent of S. S reported $200,000 of net income from its own operations and paid dividends of $50,000 in the current year, 19X2.
2. During the current year, S sold a parcel of land to P for $80,000. The land had originally cost S $65,000. P owns the land at year-end *(upstream)*.
3. S's ending inventory includes $50,000 of unconfirmed intercompany profits on $300,000 of merchandise purchased from P *(downstream)*.
4. On January 1 of the current year, S sold P a piece of machinery for $150,000. S had acquired the machinery 2 years ago for $140,000 (useful life of 7 years) and had recorded accumulated depreciation of $40,000 (net book value = $100,000). The equipment has a remaining life of 5 years, and straight-line depreciation will continue. Annual excess depreciation will be $10,000 [= ($150,000/5) − ($140,000/7)] *(upstream)*.

Exhibit 9.4 **Computation of P Company's Equity Method Accrual and the Minority Interest in Net Income, 19X2**

SCHEDULE TO COMPUTE THE EQUITY METHOD ACCRUAL

Share of S's Reported Net Income (.8 × $200,000)	$160,000
ss Amortization of Purchase Premium	(18,000)
ss P's Unconfirmed Intercompany Profit of $50,000 on Sale of Merchandise to S	(50,000)
ss 80% of S's Unconfirmed Intercompany Profit of $15,000 on Sale of Land to P	(12,000)
ss 80% of S's Unconfirmed Intercompany Gain of $40,000 on the Sale of Equipment to P:	
80% of the Total Intercompany Gain of $50,000 (= $150,000 − $100,000)	(40,000)
80% of the $10,000 Portion Confirmed (Excess Depreciation) in 19X2	8,000
t Equity Method Accrual	$ 48,000

SCHEDULE TO COMPUTE THE MINORITY INTEREST IN NET INCOME

nority's Share of S's Reported Net Income (.2 × $200,000)	$ 40,000
ss 20% of S's Unconfirmed Intercompany Profit of $15,000 on Sale of Land to P	(3,000)
ss 20% of S's Unconfirmed Intercompany Gain of $40,000 on the Sale of Equipment to P:	
20% of the Total Intercompany Gain of $50,000 (= $150,000 − $100,000)	(10,000)
20% of the $10,000 Portion Confirmed (Excess Depreciation) in 19X2	2,000
nority Interest in Net Income	$ 29,000

---

5. Current period amortization of P's purchase premium (goodwill) is assumed to be $18,000. The unamortized goodwill at the beginning of the year is $108,000.

Schedules to compute P's equity method accrual and the minority interest in net income for 19X2 are given in Exhibit 9.4. The completed consolidated financial statement working paper appears in Exhibit 9.5.

Income Tax Effects of Unconfirmed Intercompany Profits

When members of an affiliated group file separate income tax returns, unconfirmed intercompany gains and losses give rise to *timing differences* in consolidation. This happens because the eliminated items are removed only on the consolidated financial statement working paper; pretax book incomes of the affiliates are not affected. Therefore, elimination of unconfirmed intercompany gains in consolidation means that pretax consolidated book income is often smaller than the total unconsolidated pretax book income of all companies in the consolidated group. Similarly, consolidated income tax expense is often smaller than the sum of the unconsolidated separate companies' income tax expenses. In these cases, total income tax expense must be reduced in the working paper so that it bears the appropriate statutory relationship to pretax consolidated book income. This is achieved by reclassifying the income taxes pertaining to the unconfirmed intercompany gains on the working paper with the following entry on page 437.

Exhibit 9.5   **P and S Companies: Consolidated Financial Statement Working Paper for the Year Ended December 31, 19X2**

	P Company	S Company (80%)	Adjustments and Eliminations Dr.		Adjustments and Eliminations Cr.		Consolidated
INCOME STATEMENT							
Sales	3,000,000	1,000,000	(3)	300,000			3,700,000
Income from S	48,000	—	(1)	48,000			—
Gain on Sale of Land . . .	—	15,000	(2)	15,000			—
Gain on Sale of Machinery.	—	50,000	(5)	50,000			—
Inventory, 12/31/X2	420,000	200,000	(4)	50,000			570,000
Total Credits	3,468,000	1,265,000		463,000			4,270,000
Inventory, 1/1/X2	400,000	210,000					610,000
Purchases	2,000,000	600,000			(3)	300,000	2,300,000
Operating Expenses . . .	510,000	255,000	(9)	18,000	(6)	10,000	773,000
Total Debits	2,910,000	1,065,000		18,000		310,000	3,683,000
Minority Interest in Net Income			(10)	29,000			(29,000)
Net Inc.—to Ret. Earn. Stmt.	558,000	200,000		510,000		310,000	558,000
RETAINED EARNINGS STATEMENT							
Retained Earnings, 1/1/X2—P	1,500,000	—					1,500,000
Retained Earnings, 1/1/X2—S	—	750,000	(8)	750,000			—
Net Income—from Inc. Stmt.	558,000	200,000		510,000		310,000	558,000
Dividends—P	(250,000)	—					(250,000)
Dividends—S	—	(50,000)			(1)	40,000	—
					(10)	10,000	
Retained Earnings, 12/31/X2—to Balance Sheet	1,808,000	900,000		1,260,000		360,000	1,808,000
BALANCE SHEET							
Cash and Receivables . . .	547,000	300,000					847,000
Inventory	420,000	200,000			(4)	50,000	570,000
Investment in S	1,116,000	—			(1)	8,000	—
					(8)	1,108,000	
Land	400,000	140,000			(2)	15,000	525,000
Buildings and Machinery. .	2,600,000	1,600,000	(7)	40,000	(5)	50,000	4,190,000
Accumulated Depreciation.	(800,000)	(300,000)	(6)	10,000	(7)	40,000	(1,130,000)
Goodwill.			(8)	108,000	(9)	18,000	90,000
Total	4,283,000	1,940,000		158,000		1,289,000	5,092,000
Current Liabilities.	475,000	340,000					815,000
Other Liabilities	1,000,000	200,000					1,200,000
Capital Stock—P.	1,000,000	—					1,000,000
Capital Stock—S.	—	500,000	(8)	500,000			—
Ret. Earn.—from Retained Earnings Statement. . .	1,808,000	900,000		1,260,000		360,000	1,808,000
Minority Interest in S . . .	—	—			(8)	250,000	269,000
					(10)	19,000	
Total	4,283,000	1,940,000		1,760,000		629,000	5,092,000
				1,918,000		1,918,000	

Explanations of Working Paper Entries

(1) To eliminate the equity method entries recorded by P during the year.
(2) To eliminate the unconfirmed intercompany gain on the sale of land during the year and reduce the land account to original acquisition cost.
(3) To eliminate intercompany merchandise sales.
(4) To eliminate the unconfirmed intercompany profit in ending inventory.
(5) To eliminate the gain on intercompany sale of machinery and reduce the machinery to its net book value at date of intercompany sale.
(6) To eliminate the excess depreciation recorded by P during the current year.
(7) To restate the machinery and accumulated depreciation accounts to their original acquisition cost basis.
(8) To eliminate the Investment in S account against the stockholders' equity of S and establish the unamortized purchase premium (goodwill) and the minority interest in S, all as of the beginning of the year.
(9) To record current year amortization of the goodwill.
(10) To record the change in the minority interest during the year.

CONSOLIDATED FINANCIAL STATEMENT WORKING PAPER

Prepaid Income Taxes XXX
    Income Tax Expense.   XXX
To show as *prepaid* those taxes accrued or paid on current period
unconfirmed intercompany gains eliminated in consolidation.

In each subsequent year that these gains (or some portion of them) remain unconfirmed, a working paper entry must be made to reflect the appropriate amount of prepaid income taxes. The credit is made to the Investment in S (for downstream sales) or beginning Retained Earnings—S (for upstream sales), and it signifies that the original timing difference occurred in a prior year. When the gains are confirmed, the timing difference reverses and the related income tax expense must be reflected in the consolidated income statement. A working paper entry debiting Income Tax Expense and crediting the investment account or beginning retained earnings of S achieves this. Substantial reversals of these timing differences in a given period could lead to consolidated income tax expense greater than the sum of the separate companies' income tax expenses.

Impact of Taxes on the Equity Method Accrual

As mentioned previously, *APBO 18* indicates that the equity method accrual is a one-line consolidation, requiring that any unconfirmed intercompany gains (losses) be deducted from (added to) P's share of S's reported net income in computing the equity method accrual. With the introduction of income taxes, the equity method accrual is based on S's net income *after taxes*. Therefore, the removal of any unconfirmed intercompany gains must also be on an aftertax basis; the related taxes will be reclassified as *prepaid* in consolidation. We illustrate these procedures using the familiar schedular format for computing the equity method accrual.

Assume Pant Corporation owns 80 percent of Slack Corporation ($\alpha = .8$). Slack's reported net income, after income tax expense of $300,000, was $200,000. Slack had recorded $40,000 of unconfirmed profits on upstream merchandise sales, while Pant's net income of $350,000 (after income tax expense of

$525,000) included $10,000 of unconfirmed gain on a downstream sale of land. Both companies face combined state and federal income tax rates of 60 percent and file separate income tax returns. Purchase premium amortization of $15,000 is assumed. Computation of the equity method accrual follows:

PANT CORPORATION AND SLACK CORPORATION
SCHEDULE TO COMPUTE THE EQUITY METHOD ACCRUAL

Pant's Share of Slack's Net Income, after Taxes of 60 Percent (.8 × $200,000) $160,000
Less Amortization of Purchase Premium[a] . . . . (15,000)
Less Pant's Unconfirmed Intercompany Profits of $10,000, Net of Applicable Income Taxes of $6,000 (= .6 × $10,000). . . . . (4,000)
Less Pant's Share of Slack's Unconfirmed Intercompany Profits of $40,000, Net of Applicable Income Taxes of $24,000 (= .6 × $40,000); [.8($40,000 − $24,000) = $12,800] . . . . (12,800)
Net Equity Method Accrual $128,200

[a]Since purchase premium amortization is a permanent difference, there is no tax effect.

Using the same data, we see that the *minority interest in net income* will be:

Minority's Share of Slack's Net Income, after Taxes of 60 Percent (.2 × $200,000) $40,000
Less Minority's Share of Slack's Unconfirmed Intercompany Profits of $40,000, Net of Applicable Income Taxes of $24,000 (= .6 × $40,000); [.2($40,000 − $24,000) = $3,200] . . . . (3,200)
Minority Interest in Net Income. $36,800

If we also assume that Slack declared $55,000 in dividends during the year, the equity method requires the following entries:

BOOKS OF PANT CORPORATION

Cash 44,000
  Investment in Slack. 44,000
To record dividends received from Slack Company, $44,000 = (.8 × $55,000)

Investment in Slack 128,200
  Income from Slack 128,200
To record Pant's share of Slack's net income, net of purchase premium amortization, intercompany gains, and applicable taxes.

Computation of Consolidated Income Tax Expense

Consolidated income tax expense for P and S Companies has five basic components:

1. Income tax expense accrued by P on book income from its own operations.
2. Income tax expense accrued by S on book income from its own operations.

3. Adjustments for the taxes of both companies which relate to unconfirmed intercompany gains eliminated in consolidation.
4. Income tax expense related to P's income from S. This component consists of the taxes to be paid by P on dividends received from S.
5. Income tax expense accrued on undistributed equity method income not as-sumed to be permanently reinvested.

Item 5 was introduced at the end of Chapter 8. We bring it up again only for this example, to show how it would affect consolidated income tax expense.

We now return to the Pant and Slack example. Consolidated income tax expense for Pant and Slack is computed in Exhibit 9.6. We assume that the un-distributed equity method income will *not* be permanently reinvested, will ulti-mately be received by Pant as dividends, and that there are no other permanent or timing differences.

Exhibit 9.6   **Computation of Consolidated Income Tax Expense**

PANT CORPORATION AND SLACK CORPORATION
COMPUTATION OF CONSOLIDATED INCOME TAX EXPENSE
(α = .8; TAX RATE = .6; NO PERMANENT REINVESTMENT OF SLACK'S EARNINGS)

Income Tax Expense Recorded by Pant on Book Income from Its Own
Operations. $525,000
Income Tax Expense Recorded by Slack on Book Income from Its Own
Operations.   300,000

Total Income Tax Expense Recorded per Books. $825,000

Less Income Tax Expense on Pant's Unconfirmed Intercompany Profit on Sale of Land
($.6 \times$ $10,000). . . . . $ (6,000)
Less Income Tax Expense on Slack's Unconfirmed Intercompany Inventory Profits
($.6 \times$ $40,000)^a . . . .   (24,000)

Total Reduction for Income Tax Expense on Unconfirmed Intercompany Profits to Be
Eliminated . . . . $ (30,000)

Income Tax Currently Payable by Pant on Dividends Received from Slack
[.8 $\times$ .6 $\times$ (1 − .85) $\times$ $55,000]^b. . . . . $ 3,960
Deferred Income Taxes on Pant's Undistributed Equity Method Income from Slack
[.8 $\times$ .6 $\times$ (1 − .85) $\times$ ($200,000 − $55,000)]^b   10,440

Total Income Tax Expense on Pant's Equity Method Income Received or to
Be Received from Slack . . . . $ 14,400

Consolidated Income Tax Expense. $809,400

---

^{a} Recall that we eliminate 100 percent of the unconfirmed intercompany profit on upstream sales; 20 percent will be allo-cated to the minority interest. Similarly, by removing 100 percent of the tax expense attributable to intercompany profit, 20 percent of the tax reduction will be allocated to the minority interest.
^{b} When computing the tax on Pant's income from Slack that is or will be received as dividends, Pant's share of Slack's *reported income* is the critical amount. The adjustments which were made in determining the equity method accrual are not allowable tax deductions against dividend income. In particular, *purchase premium amortization* represents a *perma-*nent rather than a timing difference. It is ignored in the computation of consolidated income tax expense.

The following working paper entries are needed to reflect the tax effects computed in Exhibit 9.6 and the related intercompany profit eliminations:

CONSOLIDATED FINANCIAL STATEMENT WORKING PAPER

Gain on Sale of Land	10,000	
Land		10,000
To eliminate the unconfirmed intercompany gain on the *downstream* sale of land.		
Prepaid Income Taxes	6,000	
Income Tax Expense		6,000
To classify as prepaid the income taxes accrued or paid on the unconfirmed intercompany gain on sale of land eliminated in consolidation.		
Inventory, Dec. 31 (Income Statement)	40,000	
Inventory (Balance Sheet)		40,000
To eliminate the unconfirmed intercompany inventory profit on *upstream* sales.		
Prepaid Income Taxes	24,000	
Income Tax Expense		24,000
To classify as prepaid the income taxes accrued or paid on the unconfirmed intercompany inventory profit eliminated in consolidation.		
Income Tax Expense	14,400	
Income Tax Payable		3,960
Deferred Income Taxes		10,440
To record income taxes currently payable and deferred on P's share of S's net income received or to be received in dividends.		

Note that once the above entries are made, consolidated income tax expense—on the working paper—equals $809,400 (= $825,000 − $30,000 + $14,400).

Income Tax Effects in the Following Year

To complete the discussion of tax effects, consider the working paper entries made at the end of the following year. The gain on the land remains unconfirmed and Pant's ending inventory included $25,000 of intercompany profits recorded by Slack during the year. Intercompany profits of $40,000 in the beginning inventory are assumed confirmed this year. The entries relate only to the intercompany profits and related taxes.

The first two entries add the $4,000 aftertax gain on sale of land to the investment account; $4,000 (= $10,000 − $6,000) was removed in computing the prior year's equity method accrual. The third entry removes the aftertax intercompany inventory profit of $16,000 from S's retained earnings, transfers it to current operations, and reduces the beginning inventory to original acquisition cost. Minority interest in net income is then *increased* by $3,200 (= .2 × $16,000). The fourth entry eliminates the unconfirmed intercompany profit in ending inventory and reclassifies the related taxes. This results in a *decrease* in the minority interest in net income of $2,000 [= .2($25,000 − $15,000)].

CONSOLIDATED FINANCIAL STATEMENT WORKING PAPER

Investment in Slack	10,000	
Land		10,000

To add the unconfirmed intercompany gain to the investment
account and reduce the land account to original acquisition cost.

Prepaid Income Taxes	6,000	
Investment in Slack		6,000

To classify as prepaid the income taxes paid on the intercompany
gain which arose last year and to reduce the investment account
accordingly.

Income Tax Expense	24,000	
Retained Earnings—S, Jan. 1	16,000	
Inventory, Jan. 1 (Income Statement)		40,000

To eliminate unconfirmed intercompany inventory profits on
upstream sales from the beginning inventory, charge the related
income taxes against current income, and remove the net-of-tax
profit from S's beginning retained earnings.

Prepaid Income Taxes	15,000	
Inventory, Dec. 31 (Income Statement)	25,000	
Income Tax Expense		15,000
Inventory (Balance Sheet).		25,000

To eliminate unconfirmed intercompany inventory profits on
upstream sales from the ending inventory and classify the related
income taxes as prepaid.

Summary of Key Concepts

Transactions between affiliated companies often must be eliminated by working paper entries in consolidation. **Intercompany revenues and expenses** (for example, intercompany merchandise sales and purchases) and **intercompany assets and liabilities** (such as intercompany receivables and payables) are **eliminated to avoid double counting** in consolidation. In addition, any profits or losses recognized by the affiliates on intercompany transactions and **not confirmed** by transactions with external parties **are eliminated** in consolidation.

Intercompany profit refers to the difference between the **intercompany transfer price** and the **net book value** (acquisition cost plus capital inprovements minus accumulated depreciation, if applicable) to the selling affiliate. In consolidation, the entire amount of the unconfirmed intercompany profit is eliminated on the working paper. Elimination of unconfirmed intercompany profits on **upstream sales**—from subsidiary to parent—is **proportionate** between the controlling and minority interests. The minority interest in net income is affected by such elimination. Elimination of unconfirmed intercompany profit on **downstream sales**— from parent to subsidiary—is entirely against P's net income.

Following the one-line consolidation concept of *APBO 18,* the **equity method accrual reflects the same eliminations of unconfirmed intercompany profits as those made in computing consolidated net income.** P's share of S's reported net income is reduced by the total unconfirmed intercompany profits on downstream sales and by P's share (α) of the unconfirmed intercompany profits on upstream sales.

Elimination of unconfirmed intercompany profits in **beginning inventory** has the effect of **decreasing** current period **cost of goods sold.** On the other hand, elimination of unconfirmed intercompany profit in **ending inventory increases** consolidated cost of goods sold.

Intercompany profits or losses on transfers of inventory, land, and other **nondepreciable assets** are confirmed upon subsequent **sale to external parties.** In contrast, intercompany profits or losses on transfers of **depreciable or amortizable assets** are assumed confirmed as the assets's book values are written down by recording **depreciation or amortization expense.** This represents expiration of the assets' services which, in turn, are generally assumed reflected in the prices of goods and services sold to outsiders.

Intercompany transfers of depreciable or amortizable assets generally result in (1) confirmation of the gain over several accounting periods and (2) asset balances that differ from the original cost to the consolidated entity. Working paper entries deal with these facts by eliminating the amount of gain unconfirmed at the beginning of the year, recognizing the current period gain confirmation by eliminating "excess" depreciation expense, and restating the asset and related accumulated depreciation or amortization accounts to balances based on original cost to the consolidated entity.

When the affiliates **do not** file a consolidated tax return, elimination of unconfirmed intercompany profits on the working paper creates a timing difference between consolidated pretax book income and the combined tax return income of the affiliates. Thus the income taxes accrued separately by the affiliates are, to the extent that they relate to unconfirmed intercompany profits, reclassified as **prepaid** on the working paper. Similarly, the **aftertax** unconfirmed intercompany profits are removed in determining P's equity method accrual.

Intercompany profits often remain wholly or partially unconfirmed in years subsequent to the year in which the intercompany transfer occurred. When P uses the equity method, unconfirmed intercompany profits originating in prior years are eliminated against the Investment in S (for downstream sales) or the Retained Earnings—S (for upstream sales) account. Reclassification of the related income taxes as **prepaid** reduces the net amount of the elimination against Investment in S or Retained Earnings—S.

Proper application of the **one-line consolidation concept** to the equity method will assure that **P's net income equals consolidated net income** and **P's retained earnings equal consolidated retained earnings.**

Questions

Q9.1 What is the general objective of the consolidation process insofar as intercompany transactions are concerned?

Q9.2 The term *intercompany profit* generally refers to *gross profit* on intercompany transfers. An alternative view mentioned in the chapter suggests that *net profit* is the relevant intercompany profit concept. Discuss the difference between the two concepts and indicate the differential effects of applying them in consolidation.

Q9.3 Unconfirmed intercompany profits on *upstream* sales could be eliminated in three different ways: (1) elimination of the controlling interest's share only, (2) proportional elimination of the total amount against the majority and minority, and (3) elimination of the total amount against the majority. Evaluate these three possibilities.

Q9.4 The income tax effects of unconfirmed intercompany gains may seem unnecessarily complex, yet they represent a straightforward extension of the fact that taxable gains are reduced by income taxes. Explain how the working paper eliminations achieve this extension in consolidation.

Q9.5 The basis for charging P's equity method accrual with P's share of S's unconfirmed intercompany profits on upstream sales seems clear—in consolidation, S's income will be reduced as these gains are eliminated. What is the basis for charging the equity method accrual with *P's* unconfirmed intercompany gains on downstream sales?

Q9.6 Intercompany merchandise sales and purchases generate working paper entries in consolidation. Either one or two different types of eliminations might be needed. What are the purposes of the two types of eliminations? Identify the situations which call for either or both types of eliminations to be made. Ignore income taxes.

Q9.7 When P applies the equity method as prescribed in *APBO 18,* intercompany gains on downstream sales which remain unconfirmed in subsequent years are eliminated against the Investment in S account. Why is this necessary?

Q9.8 The following eliminating entry appears on a consolidated financial statement working paper:

```
Investment in S . . . . . . . . . . . . . . . . . . . . . . . .   60,000
Prepaid Income Taxes . . . . . . . . . . . . . . . . . . . . .   40,000
    Land . . . . . . . . . . . . . . . . . . . . . . . . . . . .          100,000
```

Carefully explain the circumstances lying behind such an entry.

Q9.9 Explain the following eliminating entry which appears on a consolidated financial statement working paper:

```
Retained Earnings—S. . . . . . . . . . . . . . . . . . . . .   20,000
Accumulated Depreciation. . . . . . . . . . . . . . . . . . .   30,000
    Buildings . . . . . . . . . . . . . . . . . . . . . . . . . .          50,000
```

Q9.10 If consolidated net income is \$960,000, P's equity method accrual is \$180,000, the minority interest in net income is \$45,000, and eliminated intercompany profits on upstream sales are $25,000, how much is P's income from its own operations? How much is S's income from its own operations?

Q9.11 The text recommends that lower of cost or market write-downs following intercompany merchandise sales be charged to the selling affiliate in consolidation, effectively reducing any intercompany profit. It has been suggested that this treatment might not be consistent with the general approach to recognizing gains and losses on intercompany transactions. Briefly discuss the basis for this objection.

Q9.12 In dealing with unconfirmed intercompany profits in inventories, we decrease the cost of goods sold by the amount in the beginning inventory and increase the cost of goods sold by the amount in the ending inventory. Will this approach work for all of the cost-flow assumptions? Why or why not?

Exercises

E9.1 S Company, a 90-percent-owned subsidiary of P Company, purchased a tract of land from P in 19X7 for $150,000. P had originally acquired the land for $100,000 and accounts for its investment in S under the equity method.

Required:

1. Assuming that S still owns the land, give the working paper eliminations needed when consolidated statements are prepared at the end of 19X7 and 19X8.
2. If S sells the land to a third party for $160,000 in 19X9, prepare the eliminations needed in consolidation at the end of 19X9.

E9.2 P Company acquired 90 percent of S Company's stock in a pooling of interests during 19X4. On June 15, 19X5, S transferred a parcel of land to P for $150,000 and recorded a gain of $25,000. P continues to hold the land. During the current year, 19X7, P sold $300,000 of merchandise to S, reflecting a markup of $60,000 over P's cost. S's inventory at December 31, 19X7, includes $50,000 of this merchandise. S reports net income of $225,000 in 19X7. P accounts for its investment in S under the equity method.

Required:

1. Compute the equity method accrual and give the working paper eliminations required when consolidated statements are prepared on December 31, 19X7.
2. How is the minority interest in S affected by the eliminations made in No. 1?

E9.3 Portland Corporation owns 80 percent of the outstanding stock of the Salem Company and carries the investment at equity. Portland sells merchandise to Salem at a 30 percent markup over cost and Salem sells to Portland at a markup of 25 percent over cost. Merchandise transactions between the affiliates during the year ended December 31, 19X4, are given below:

	Portland	Salem
Inventories at Jan. 1, 19X4, Acquired from Affiliate.	$ 50,000	$ 78,000
Sales Made to Affiliate during 19X4	460,000	380,000
Inventories at Dec. 31, 19X4, Acquired from Affiliate	40,000	91,000

Required: Prepare the working paper eliminations to be made at December 31, 19X4.

E9.4 P Company owns 80 percent of S Company's capital stock, acquired at par value at the date of organization in Year 1. At the beginning of Year 2, P purchased from S for $60,000 equipment which S had manufactured at a cost of $40,000. P has depreciated this equipment on a straight-line basis at the rate of 20 percent per year. (S had claimed no depreciation on this equipment.)

During Year 2, P sold to S merchandise for $40,000, reflecting a markup of $10,000; 30 percent of this merchandise remained in the ending inventory of S that year.

Required:

1. Give the eliminating entries to be made on the consolidated financial statement working papers at the end of Year 2 in respect to the intercompany sale of equipment. Disregard the reversal of the equity method entries made by P.

2. Give the eliminating entries to be made on the consolidated financial statement working papers at the end of Year 2 in respect to the intercompany sale of merchandise. Disregard the reversal of the equity method entries made by P.

3. Compute consolidated net income for Year 2, assuming P and S reported net income from their own operations of $50,000 and $40,000, respectively.

4. Using the data from No. 3, compute the minority interest in net income for Year 2.

E9.5 The Parker Company sold equipment to its wholly owned subsidiary, the Spencer Company, on January 2, 19X1. At the time of sale, Parker's books showed the equipment at a cost of $60,000 and accumulated depreciation of $15,000. Spencer bought the equipment for $50,000 and depreciated it over its remaining 5-year life (straight-line method, no salvage value).

Required:

1. Prepare the necessary consolidation elimination entries at December 31, 19X1.
2. Prepare the necessary consolidation elimination entries at December 31, 19X2.

E9.6 In consolidation of P and S Companies at December 31, 19X9, you assemble the following data related to unconfirmed intercompany profits:

	1/1/X9	12/31/X9
Land (One Parcel)	$25,000	$25,000
Merchandise Inventory	14,000	32,000
Equipment (One Item)	8,000	6,000

The equipment is carried on the purchasing affiliate's books at $72,000 with accumulated depreciation of $36,000 (straight-line, no salvage value) at December 31, 19X9. Accumulated depreciation at the date of intercompany sale was $20,000; the original intercompany gain was $12,000.

Required:

1. Assume that all of the above unconfirmed intercompany profits arose from *upstream* sales. Prepare the eliminating entries to be made in consolidation at December 31, 19X9.
2. Repeat No. 1 assuming that all of the above unconfirmed intercompany profits arose from *downstream* sales.

E9.7 P Company owns 80 percent of S Company and accounts for its investment in S under the equity method. The purchase premium of $100,000 originally paid by P was assigned to goodwill and is being amortized over 10 years. During the current year, the following intercompany transactions took place:

1. P sold land carried at $80,000 to S for $100,000; S still owns the land at year-end.
2. S sold merchandise costing $160,000 to P at a markup of 25 percent over cost. Half of this merchandise remains in P's inventory at year-end.
3. On January 2 of the current year, S sold equipment to P for $40,000. The equipment had a net book value of $30,000 and a remaining life of 5 years at the date of sale. Straight-line depreciation is being used.

Required:

1. Assuming S reported net income of $400,000, prepare a schedule computing P's equity method accrual.
2. Prepare a schedule computing the minority interest in S's net income.

E9.8 The Pin Company owns all of the outstanding stock of Stick Corporation. At the beginning of the current year, unconfirmed intercompany profits included in the inventories of Pin and Stick amounted to $42,000 and $17,000, respectively. During the year, Pin sold merchandise to Stick for $200,000 at an average markup equal to 20 percent of the selling price. Stick's physical inventory of goods purchased from Pin did not change during the year. In contrast, Pin's ending inventory of goods purchased from Stick was twice that of the beginning inventory. Pin purchased $600,000 worth of goods from Stick at an average markup equal to 20 percent over Stick's cost.

Required: Assume that the physical units in Pin's and Stick's beginning inventories equaled 40 percent of each company's intercompany purchases (in physical units) during the current year. Compute the net effect on consolidated net income of eliminating unconfirmed intercompany profit under LIFO and FIFO.

E9.9 P Company owns 70 percent of S Company. P's ending inventory includes $100,000 of unconfirmed intercompany profit on merchandise purchased from S. After applying the lower-of-cost-or-market test, P's auditors insist that the inventory acquired from S be written down by $20,000.

Required: Compute the effect on consolidated net income assuming that (1) the LCM loss is charged to the purchasing affiliate in consolidation and (2) the LCM loss is charged to the selling affiliate in consolidation.

E9.10 Refer to E9.2. P and S Companies file separate income tax returns and face marginal income tax rates of 40 percent. Prepare only the working paper entries at the end of 19X7 for the income tax effects on the unconfirmed intercompany profits.

E9.11 Refer to E9.3. Assuming that Portland and Salem file separate income tax returns and face income tax rates of 40 percent, prepare the working paper entries at December 31, 19X4, for the income tax effects only.

E9.12 P Company and its 60-percent-owned subsidiary, S Company, both face income tax rates of 40 percent. Income tax expense of $800,000 and $200,000 has been accrued on the separate books of P and S, respectively. At the end of the current year, P's ending inventory reflects intercompany profit of $100,000 on goods purchased from S, while S's ending inventory includes goods purchased from P which reflect P's gross margin of $40,000. S declared no dividends during the year.

Required: Compute consolidated income tax expense and prepare the necessary working paper eliminations. Assume that the indefinite reversal criteria apply.

Problems

P9.1 Eliminating Entries—Various Intercompany Transactions On October 1, 19X0, the Arba Company acquired a 90 percent interest in the common stock of the Braginetz Company on the open market for $750,000; the book value was $712,500 at that date. Since the excess could not be attributed to the undervaluation of any specific assets, Arba reported $37,500 of consolidated goodwill on its consolidated balance sheet at September 30, 19X1. During fiscal 19X2, it was decided that the consolidated goodwill should be amortized in equal amounts over 10 years beginning with fiscal 19X2. Arba uses the equity method.

On October 1, 19X1, Arba purchased new equipment for $14,500 from Braginetz. The equipment cost Braginetz $9,000 and had an estimated life of 10 years as of October 1, 19X1. Arba uses the sum-of-the-years'-digits depreciation method for both financial and income tax reporting.

During fiscal 19X3, Arba made merchandise sales to Braginetz of $100,000; the merchandise was priced at 25 percent above Arba's cost. Braginetz still owed Arba $17,500 on open account and had 20 percent of this merchandise in inventory at September 30, 19X3.

On August 1, 19X3, Braginetz borrowed $30,000 from Arba by issuing twelve $2,500, 9 percent, 90-day notes. Arba discounted four of the notes at its bank with recourse on August 31 at 6 percent. Braginetz reported net income from its own operations of $200,000 in fiscal 19X3.

Required:

1. What criteria could influence Arba in its decision to include or exclude Braginetz as a subsidiary in consolidated financial statements? Explain.
2. Prepare a schedule to compute Arba's equity method accrual for fiscal 19X3. Ignore income taxes.
3. For each of the following items, give the elimination entry (including explanation) that should be made on the working paper for the preparation of the indicated consolidated statement(s) at September 30, 19X3. Ignore income taxes throughout.
   a. For the consolidated goodwill—to prepare all consolidated statements. Goodwill amortization did not appear on consolidated statements in fiscal 19X1.
   b. For the equipment—(1) to prepare only a consolidated balance sheet, and (2) to prepare all consolidated statements.
   c. For the intercompany merchandise transactions—to prepare all consolidated statements.
   d. For the note transactions—to prepare only a consolidated balance sheet.

P9.2 Intercompany Transfers of Depreciable Assets Pert Corporation acquired 80 percent of the Smart Company 10 years ago. In the intervening years, Pert and Smart have engaged in several intercompany transfers of depreciable assets. Pert's controller is beginning the process of preparing consolidated statements for the current year ended December 31, 19X8. As the new assistant controller, you have been asked to develop the working paper eliminations for the following group of intercompany transactions. Pert uses the equity method to account for its investment in Smart. All depreciation is allocated according to the straight-line method.

Transaction No.	Date	Original Cost	Accumulated Depreciation	Transfer Price	Remaining Life	Upstream (U) Downstream (D)
1	6/30/X2	$100,000	$ 20,000	$160,000	8 years	D
2	1/2/X4	450,000	300,000	200,000	10	U
3	1/1/X7	600,000	360,000	200,000	5	D

Required:

1. Prepare the needed working paper eliminations for consolidation at December 31, 19X8. All computations must be in good form.
2. Assume that the item in Transaction 2 was sold externally on January 1, 19X8, for $400,000. Prepare the working paper eliminations needed for Transaction 2 at December 31, 19X8, reflecting the sale to an outside party during 19X8.

P9.3 Consolidated Income Statement—Pooling of Interests The Pow Company and the Sow Company united in a pooling of interests several years ago as Pow exchanged its own shares for 95 percent of the outstanding stock of Sow. Pow recorded its share of Sow's retained earnings at that time. Condensed income statements for the two companies are given below. Pow uses the equity method to account for its investment in Sow.

	Pow	Sow
Sales.	$25,000,000	$10,000,000
Other Income	1,200,000	500,000
Income from Sow	895,000	—
Total Revenue.	$27,095,000	$10,500,000
Cost of Goods Sold	$19,000,000	$ 7,600,000
Operating Expenses	4,100,000	1,800,000
Other Expenses	800,000	300,000
Total Expenses	$23,900,000	$ 9,700,000
Net Income.	$ 3,195,000	$ 800,000
Retained Earnings, Jan. 1	15,700,000	6,200,000
Dividends	(1,000,000)	(400,000)
Retained Earnings, Dec. 31	$17,895,000	$ 6,600,000

Additional information:

1. Pow's *beginning* inventory included $400,000 of intercompany profit on goods purchased from Sow, and Sow's *ending* inventory included $200,000 of intercompany profit on purchases of $3,000,000 from Pow.
2. Sow's Other Expenses balance includes a loss of $100,000 on an intercompany sale of land to Pow.
3. Pow's Other Income balance reflects a $250,000 gain on a sale of machinery to Sow at the beginning of the year. At date of sale, the machinery had a remaining life of 5 years; it is being depreciated by the straight-line method.
4. Several years ago, Pow had recorded a gain of $60,000 on land sold to Sow for $280,000. Sow sold the land externally during the year for $390,000. The current gain is reflected in Sow's Other Income account.

Required:

1. Prepare a schedule to calculate Pow's equity method accrual.
2. Prepare a consolidated statement of income and retained earnings for Pow and Sow.

P9.4 Equity Method Accrual—Various Intercompany Transactions and Taxes The Silver Company, an 80-percent-owned subsidiary of Platinum, Inc., reported net income from its own operations of $600,000. Both firms face a 40 percent marginal tax rate and use straight-line depreciation and amortization. As the new assistant controller at Platinum, you have been asked to compute Platinum's equity method accrual and are given the following information:

1. A summary of unconfirmed intercompany inventory profits is as follows:

	Platinum	Silver
Intercompany Profits in Ending Inventory	$200,000	$80,000
Intercompany Profits in Beginning Inventory	150,000	90,000

2. On January 2, the beginning of the accounting period, Silver sold a piece of equipment to Platinum for $320,000. The net book value to Silver had been $240,000; the equipment had a remaining useful life of 5 years at January 2.
3. When Platinum purchased Silver 3 years ago, it paid a purchase premium of $100,000. Allocation of the $100,000 consisted of a $150,000 decrease to Silver's Long-Term Debt account and a $50,000 decrease to Silver's Patents account. At date of acquisition, the debt had a maturity date 6 years in the future, and the revalued patent had a remaining economic life of 10 years.

4. During the year in which the acquisition took place, Platinum recognized a gain of $180,000 on a sale of land to Silver. Silver still owns the land.

5. Silver declared dividends of $400,000 during the year. Its undistributed earnings are assumed to be permanently reinvested.

Required: Prepare a schedule to compute the equity method accrual to be made by Platinum at the end of the current year.

P9.5 Calculation of Consolidated Retained Earnings Philip Corporation acquired 75 percent of Samson Corporation's common stock for $200,000 over book value on January 2, 19X1. Samson's assets and liabilities were all fairly stated except for certain depreciable assets (remaining life, 5 years) which were undervalued by $120,000. Philip amortizes all intangibles over the maximum period allowed.

During the 4 years following the acquisition, Samson reported total net income of $4,000,000 and paid out $2,400,000 in dividends. In addition, the following intercompany transactions occurred:

1. During 19X1, Samson sold land carried on its books at $40,000 to Philip for $56,000. Philip still owns the land.

2. Early in 19X2, Philip sold a patent recorded at $10,000 to Samson for $80,000. Samson currently holds the patent and is amortizing it over a 10-year period.

3. Over the years since acquisition, total intercompany merchandise sales amounted to $2,800,000, reflecting an average markup of 40 percent over cost. Unconfirmed intercompany profits in the December 31, 19X4, ending inventories of Philip and Samson are $60,000 and $85,000, respectively.

Required:

1. Prepare a schedule showing the calculation of consolidated retained earnings at December 31, 19X4. Philip's retained earnings from its own operations is $4,750,000.

2. If the amount originally paid for the 75 percent interest in Samson was $1,900,000 and the equity method is being used, determine what the balance in the investment account should be at December 31, 19X4.

P9.6 Equity Accrual and Eliminating Entries—Intercompany Asset Transfers On January 2, 19X7, P Company acquired 80 percent of S Company's voting stock for $1,000,000 and carries the investment at equity. The resulting purchase premium of $200,000 was allocated entirely to assets being depreciated over a remaining life of 5 years by the straight-line method. S reported net income of $100,000 and $130,000 in 19X7 and 19X8, respectively, paying out 50 percent of each period's earnings in dividends. In addition, the following intercompany transactions occurred:

1. Upstream intercompany merchandise sales of $150,000 made during 19X7 resulted in $20,000 of intercompany profits in P's inventory at December 31, 19X7. There were no intercompany profits in P's inventory at December 31, 19X8.
2. Downstream intercompany merchandise sales of $132,000 made during 19X8 resulted in $12,000 of intercompany profits in S's inventory at December 31, 19X8.
3. On January 5, 19X8, P sold to S for $30,000 some equipment that it had manufactured at a cost of $24,000. The equipment is being depreciated by the straight-line method over a remaining life of 6 years.

Required:

1. Prepare a schedule to compute P's equity method accrual for 19X8.
2. Prepare all working paper eliminations made in consolidation at December 31, 19X8.

P9.7 Equity Accrual and Eliminating Entries—Intercompany Asset Transfers, Services, and Receivables/Payables On January 2, 19X3, P Company acquired 80 percent of S Company's voting common stock for $1,300,000. The investment is carried at equity. The resulting purchase premium of $100,000 was allocated entirely to goodwill, which is being amortized over the maximum period permitted by *APBO 17*. S reported net income of $150,000 and $200,000 in 19X3 and 19X4, respectively, paying out 40 percent of each period's earnings in dividends. In addition, the following intercompany transactions occurred:

1. On March 5, 19X3, S sold a parcel of land to P for $50,000; the land had originally cost $40,000. P continues to own the land.
2. During 19X4, P and S recorded intercompany merchandise sales of $250,000, an amount equal to cost plus 25 percent. S's *beginning* inventory included $25,000 of intercompany merchandise (from prior years' sales), while P's *ending* inventory included $40,000 of intercompany merchandise.
3. On January 2, 19X4, S sold a piece of machinery to P for $60,000 and recorded a gain of $20,000. Accumulated depreciation on the machinery amounted to $30,000 on January 2. The machinery is being depreciated by the straight-line method over its remaining life of 5 years.
4. P billed S $15,000 for computer services during the year. The out-of-pocket costs incurred by P in supplying these services amounted to $10,000. On December 31, 19X4, the unpaid portion of these intercompany services amounted to $2,000.

Required:

1. Prepare a schedule to compute P's equity method accrual for 19X4.
2. Prepare the working paper eliminations made in consolidation at December 31, 19X4.

P9.8 Condensed Consolidated Financial Statement Working Paper—Intercompany Inventory Transactions P Company and S Company, a 90-percent-owned subsidiary, engage in extensive intercompany transactions involving raw materials, component parts, and completed products. P acquired its interest in S several years ago at book value, and carries the investment account at equity. Intercompany sales for 19X6 and the unconfirmed intercompany profits in the beginning and ending inventories of both companies are summarized below:

	P Company	S Company
Intercompany Profit in Inventory, Jan. 1, 19X6	$ 100,000	$ 60,000
Intercompany Sales to Affiliate	2,200,000	3,700,000
Intercompany Profit in Inventory, Dec. 31, 19X6	80,000	75,000

Prior to consolidation at December 31, 19X6, the separate condensed financial statements of the two companies are as shown in Exhibit 9.7.

Exhibit 9.7 **P and S Companies: Financial Statements at December 31, 19X6, to Be Used in P9.8**

STATEMENTS OF INCOME AND RETAINED EARNINGS
FOR THE YEAR ENDED DECEMBER 31, 19X6

	P Company	S Company
Sales	$15,000,000	$6,000,000
Income from S	813,000	—
Total Revenue	$15,813,000	$6,000,000
Cost of Goods Sold:		
Beginning Inventory	$ 2,000,000	$ 950,000
Purchases	9,000,000	3,200,000
Ending Inventory	(1,950,000)	(980,000)
	$ 9,050,000	$3,170,000
Operating Expenses	4,150,000	1,930,000
Total Expenses	$13,200,000	$5,100,000
Net Income	$ 2,613,000	$ 900,000
Beginning Retained Earnings	6,700,000	2,300,000
Dividends	(1,000,000)	(400,000)
Ending Retained Earnings	$ 8,313,000	$2,800,000

CONDENSED BALANCE SHEETS AT DECEMBER 31, 19X6

ASSETS	P Company	S Company
Inventory	$ 1,950,000	$ 980,000
Investment in S	3,453,000	—
Other Assets	10,810,000	5,120,000
Total Assets	$16,213,000	$6,100,000

LIABILITIES AND STOCKHOLDERS' EQUITY		
Liabilities	$ 4,900,000	$2,100,000
Capital Stock	3,000,000	1,200,000
Retained Earnings	8,313,000	2,800,000
Total Liabilities and Stockholders' Equity	$16,213,000	$6,100,000

Required:

1. Prepare a schedule to show how the equity method accrual was calculated.
2. Prepare a consolidated financial statement working paper for P and S at December 31, 19X6.

P9.9 Consolidated Financial Statement Working Paper The Plato Company owns 90 percent of the Socrates Company. Socrates was acquired for a price $500,000 greater than its book value on January 2, 19X3. The entire

---

Exhibit 9.8 | **Plato Company and Socrates Company: Financial Statements at December 31, 19X9, to Be Used in P9.9**

STATEMENTS OF INCOME AND RETAINED EARNINGS
FOR THE YEAR ENDED DECEMBER 31, 19X9

	Plato	Socrates
Sales	$10,000,000	$4,000,000
Income from Socrates	253,500	—
Total Revenue	$10,253,500	$4,000,000
Cost of Goods Sold:		
Beginning Inventory	$ 2,100,000	$ 510,000
Purchases	7,800,000	3,100,000
Ending Inventory	(2,000,000)	(530,000)
	$ 7,900,000	$3,080,000
Operating Expenses	1,600,000	640,000
Total Expenses	$ 9,500,000	$3,720,000
Net Income	$ 753,500	$ 280,000
Beginning Retained Earnings	4,043,000	1,200,000
Dividends	(400,000)	(100,000)
Ending Retained Earnings	$ 4,396,500	$1,380,000

BALANCE SHEETS AT DECEMBER 31, 19X9

ASSETS	Plato	Socrates
Cash and Receivables	$ 1,700,000	$ 490,000
Inventory	2,000,000	530,000
Investment in Socrates	1,596,500	—
Plant Assets	8,000,000	2,100,000
Accumulated Depreciation	(2,000,000)	(500,000)
Total Assets	$11,296,500	$2,620,000

LIABILITIES AND STOCKHOLDERS' EQUITY		
Current Liabilities	$ 1,900,000	$ 340,000
Noncurrent Liabilities	4,000,000	800,000
Capital Stock	1,000,000	100,000
Retained Earnings	4,396,500	1,380,000
Total Liabilities and Stockholders' Equity	$11,296,500	$2,620,000

$500,000 was allocated to goodwill and is being amortized over 20 years according to the straight-line method. On January 2, 19X7, Plato sold a depreciable asset to Socrates for $200,000. The asset originally cost $300,000 and had been fully depreciated by Plato, yet, due to a shift in consumption patterns, the asset was believed to have an economic life of 4 more years as of January 2, 19X7. Socrates uses sum-of-the-years'-digits depreciation.

Socrates regularly sells merchandise to Plato for further processing and external sale. In 19X9, Plato's beginning and ending inventories reflected intercompany profits on purchases from Socrates of $30,000 and $45,000, respectively. Intercompany sales during 19X9 were $1,400,000. Separate financial statements for the two companies at December 31, 19X9, are shown in Exhibit 9.8.

Required:

1. Prepare a schedule to show how the equity method accrual of $253,500 was computed.
2. Prepare a consolidated financial statement working paper for Plato and Socrates at December 31, 19X9.

P9.10 **Consolidated Trial Balance Working Paper** Following are the preclosing trial balances of P Company and its 80-percent-owned subsidiary, S Company, at December 31, 19X4:

Account	P Company	S Company
Cash and Receivables	$ 2,000,000	$ 1,100,000
Inventory	1,500,000	800,000
Investment in S	2,930,000	—
Plant Assets	9,600,000	5,200,000
Accumulated Depreciation	(2,800,000)	(1,400,000)
Current Liabilities	(1,900,000)	(700,000)
Noncurrent Liabilities	(3,000,000)	(1,000,000)
Capital Stock	(1,000,000)	(500,000)
Retained Earnings	(6,226,000)	(3,000,000)
Dividends	800,000	200,000
Sales	(15,000,000)	(7,000,000)
Income from S	(704,000)	—
Purchases	10,000,000	5,000,000
Operating Expenses	3,800,000	1,300,000
	$ 0	$ 0
Ending Inventory	$ 1,200,000	$ 1,000,000

Additional information:

1. P uses the equity method to account for the investment in S.

2. P recorded a gain of $150,000 on land sold to S during 19X3. S continues to hold the land.

3. A summary of intercompany merchandise transactions is as follows:

	P Company	S Company	Total
Intercompany Profits in Inventory, Jan. 1, 19X4	$ 80,000	$ 200,000	$ 280,000
Intercompany Sales of Merchandise during 19X4.	2,000,000	1,000,000	3,000,000
Intercompany Profits in Inventory, Dec. 31, 19X4.	50,000	240,000	290,000

4. Unpaid invoices on intercompany sales amounted to $375,000 at December 31, 19X4.

Required: Prepare a consolidated trial balance working paper.

P9.11 Consolidated Financial Statement Working Paper—Intercompany Transactions and Taxes Preclosing trial balances of the Power Company and its 60-percent-owned subsidiary, the Sour Company, at December 31, 19X0, are as shown here:

Account	Power	Sour
Cash and Receivables	$ 960,000	$ 700,000
Inventory	1,000,000	500,000
Investment in Sour	1,192,000	—
Plant Assets.	7,200,000	4,270,000
Accumulated Depreciation.	(2,100,000)	(1,600,000)
Current Liabilities	(820,000)	(420,000)
Noncurrent Liabilities	(2,600,000)	(1,600,000)
Capital Stock	(500,000)	(200,000)
Retained Earnings.	(3,200,000)	(1,300,000)
Sales	(8,000,000)	(3,200,000)
Income from Sour	(92,000)	—
Gain on Sale of Land	(100,000)	—
Purchases.	5,000,000	2,100,000
Operating Expenses.	1,300,000	550,000
Income Tax Expense	760,000	200,000
	$ 0	$ 0
Ending Inventory	$ 1,100,000	$ 450,000

Additional information:

1. The Investment in Sour account reflects a purchase premium of $200,000, entirely attributable to goodwill amortizable over a remaining life of 20 years.

2. Power recognized a gain of $100,000 on land sold to Sour.

3. Power's ending inventory includes $50,000 of unconfirmed intercompany profits on goods acquired from Sour. Total intercompany sales were $600,000 during 19X0.

4. Sour declared no dividends during the year; the indefinite reversal criteria apply.
5. Both companies' Income Tax Expense accounts relate to their own operations; the marginal income tax rate is 40 percent.

Required: Prepare a consolidated financial statement working paper for Power and Sour.

P9.12 Computation of Consolidated Income Tax Expense   Percy Corporation owns 80 percent of the Stetson Company. Both firms file separate income tax returns and face a marginal tax rate of 60 percent. The following information relates to their operations during 19X5.

1. Percy reported pretax book income of $1,200,000 from its own operations. Unconfirmed intercompany profits in Percy's beginning and ending inventories amounted to $70,000 and $80,000, respectively.
2. Percy's beginning retained earnings includes a $40,000 pretax gain recognized on a prior period transfer of land to Stetson. The land is still owned by Stetson.
3. Stetson reported pretax book income of $400,000 from its own operations and declared dividends of $100,000 during 19X5. The indefinite reversal criteria do not apply.
4. Stetson began buying merchandise from Percy during 19X5. Its ending inventory included goods marked up $25,000 by Percy. During 19X5, Stetson recognized a loss of $50,000 on land sold to Percy.
5. Stetson leased equipment from Percy during 19X5. Total intercompany billings were $200,000.

Required: Prepare a schedule to compute consolidated income tax expense for Percy and Stetson in 19X5.

Chapter 10 Consolidated Financial Statements: Intercompany Transactions II

In this chapter, we complete our study of intercompany transactions in consolidated statements. After considering the consolidation problems created by one affiliate holding bonds issued by another affiliate and the problems arising from intercompany leasing arrangements, we present a comprehensive example incorporating various intercompany transactions and a consolidated financial statement working paper. The chapter ends with a discussion of consolidation issues relating to subsidiary companies that have preferred stock as well as common stock outstanding.

Intercompany Bondholdings

Study of the consolidation techniques called for when intercompany bondholdings are present can become very involved. Following the single entity concept, when the bonds of one affiliate are held by another affiliate, no external relationship exists insofar as the consolidated entity is concerned (that is, transactions regarding the bondholding are internal). If the bonds are acquired directly from the issuing affiliate, the purchaser's *investment in bonds* will equal the issuer's *bond liability*. Each year the intercompany debt and related interest expense can be cleanly and simply eliminated. The only requirement is that both companies use the same method to amortize any offsetting discount or premium on the bonds. As the following illustration shows, such a simple situation presents no accounting complications.

Suppose P Company owns 80 percent of S Company. On January 1, 19X3, P issues $1,000,000 par value bonds for $950,000. The bonds pay 10 percent interest annually and mature in 20 years. S acquires 40 percent of the bond issue directly from P. Therefore, $400,000 par value bonds are held by an affiliate and are viewed as being **constructively retired** from a consolidated point of view. The accounts relative to this intercompany bondholding at January 1, 19X3, are as follows:

P Company		**S Company**	
Bonds Payable (Par)	$400,000	Investment in Bonds (Par) . . .	$400,000
Discount on Bonds Payable. . .	(20,000)	Discount on Investment in Bonds	(20,000)
Net Bond Liability	$380,000	Net Bond Investment	$380,000

Both companies amortize their discounts by the straight-line method. In consolidation at December 31, 19X3, the intercompany bondholding and the intercompany interest revenue and expense must be eliminated. The three working paper entries that follow accomplish this:

CONSOLIDATED FINANCIAL STATEMENT WORKING PAPER

Bonds Payable   400,000
    Investment in Bonds   400,000
To eliminate the par value of the intercompany bonds.

Discount on Investment in Bonds   19,000
    Discount on Bonds Payable.   19,000
To eliminate the unamortized discounts on the intercompany
bondholding; $19,000 = $20,000 - $20,000/20.

Interest Revenue   41,000
    Interest Expense   41,000
To eliminate the interest revenue and expense on the
intercompany bonds; $41,000 = (.1 × $400,000) + $20,000/20.

These eliminations are repeated at each subsequent consolidation point as long as the bonds are held internally. While the annual interest and par value of the intercompany bondholding are unchanged in future years, the unamortized discounts decline by $1,000 (= $20,000/20) each year. At December 31, 19X4, for example, the first and third working paper entries above would be made in the same amounts. In the second entry, however, the unamortized discounts would have decreased to $18,000 [= $20,000 - 2($20,000/20)]. We now turn to a more intricate set of circumstances.

Intercompany Bonds Acquired in the Open Market

When bonds are acquired directly from the issuing company, their price equals the proceeds received by the issuer. Thus if the bonds are issued at a discount from par, they will be purchased at an equal discount; the intercompany bond accounts will be equal and offsetting. Unfortunately, this is not normally the case if the bonds are acquired in the open market after they were originally issued. Changes in interest rates affect the present value of the cash payments promised by the bonds and thus also affect bond prices. Therefore, a dramatic increase in interest rates can cause bonds originally issued at a premium to subsequently sell at a discount. Similarly, a decline in interest rates can cause bonds originally issued at a discount to sell at a premium.

If interest rates have changed since the bonds were issued, problems will arise when consolidated statements are prepared following the purchase of intercompany bonds in the open market. The two major problems are:

1. Because of interest rate changes since date of issue, the *investment in bonds* will not equal the carrying value of the *bond liability*. This produces a *consolidated gain (loss)* if the investment in bonds is less than (greater than) the bond liability.

2. As a consequence of this first problem, the *interest expense* recorded by the *issuing affiliate* will *differ* from the *interest revenue* recorded by the *purchasing affiliate*. Even though the amount of coupon interest paid equals the amount received, *different amounts of premium or discount amortization* cause the intercompany interest expense and revenue amounts to be unequal.

Nature of the Gain or Loss on Retirement of Consolidated Debt. When one affiliate acquires the bonds of another, the acquisition has the same effect as retirement of the bonds by the selling firm from the point of view of the consolidated firms (or, we say that the bonds have been *constructively retired*). If the cost of the bonds is less than the issuing affiliate's bond liability, a *consolidated gain* arises. In contrast, if the investment in bonds exceeds the bond liability, a *consolidated loss* is incurred. Once the amount of gain or loss is determined, the accountant must decide to what extent it should accrue to the issuing and purchasing affiliates. Four alternative treatments have been proposed to answer this question.

1. **Allocate entirely to issuing affiliate.** This position rests on the notion that when companies are under common control, the affiliate purchasing the bonds is acting as an *agent* for the issuing affiliate. Hence the entire gain or loss should be attributed to the issuing affiliate. We see no basis, however, for allocating to the issuing affiliate the portion of the gain or loss to be realized by the purchasing affiliate over time.

2. **Allocate entirely to purchasing affiliate.** Under this interpretation, it is the purchasing affiliate's investment which led to the constructive retirement of the bonds. In our opinion, this is adequate justification of attributing the difference between par and the cost of the bonds to the purchasing affiliate; however, we see no basis for allocating to the purchaser the issuer's unamortized discount or premium.

3. **Allocate entirely to controlling interest.** Parent company management controls its subsidiaries and therefore is responsible for decisions involving material investments, debt issues, and debt retirements. Hence, it could be argued that the entire gain or loss accrues to the parent. This certainly does follow if the parent is the issuing company and the bonds actually are retired or if the purchasing affiliate is a wholly owned subsidiary. Otherwise, the minority interest shares in the gain or loss as it is realized over time. If a minority interest is present, allocation of the entire gain or loss to the controlling interest seems to be at odds with the facts.

4. **Allocate between the issuing and purchasing affiliates.** We believe this to be the most consistent treatment of gain or loss on constructive retirement

of consolidated debt. It recognizes the *fact that both affiliates will typically record a discount or premium and will realize a gain or loss as the bonds are held to maturity.* If a partially owned subsidiary is involved, the minority interest will clearly absorb some portion of the gain or loss due to discount or premium amortization over time.

In our view, the first three treatments described are not consistent with the fact acknowledged in the fourth treatment. Therefore, in our illustrations, *both affiliates share in the gain or loss to the extent of their respective discounts or premiums.* Moreover, if a partially owned subsidiary is involved, Minority Interest in Net Income is affected. When there are *offsetting* premiums or discounts such that there is no *net* gain or loss, the minority interest nevertheless absorbs its share of the gain or loss attributable to the subsidiary.

The treatment of intercompany bondholdings in consolidation can therefore be summarized as follows:

Because they are held inside the affiliated group, intercompany bonds are considered to be *constructively retired* and are eliminated. In the year of acquisition, a consolidated gain (loss) arises if the net bond liability is greater than (less than) the net investment in bonds. This gain or loss is attributed to the affiliates according to their recorded premium or discount. It is recognized and booked over time through discount or premium amortization on the affiliates' books. At each subsequent consolidation point, P's portion of the consolidated gain or loss not yet so recognized must be removed from the Investment in S account (it was originally entered via the equity method). S's unrecognized portion must be entered in its beginning retained earnings. Finally, the unamortized premium and discount and current interest expense and revenue on intercompany bonds must be eliminated.

Before proceeding to specific eliminating entries, we note one very important difference between intercompany bondholdings and other transactions generating intercompany gains and losses. In the other intercompany transactions, the gains or losses have been recorded by the affiliates as part of their own operations; *at consolidation the unconfirmed portion is eliminated.* An intercompany bondholding, however, gives rise to a gain or loss which will not be recorded by the affiliates, except through P's equity method accrual. Since the equity accrual is eliminated in consolidation, the gain or loss related to the intercompany bondholding *must be recorded on the working paper at the first consolidation point after the bonds are acquired internally.*

Eliminations When the Bonds Are Acquired. To introduce the eliminations, assume that the bonds are acquired on December 31, 19X1, and consolidated statements are prepared immediately. (This assumption allows us to sidestep, for now, the complications created by premium/discount amortization after acquisition.) Our presentation incorporates the following facts:

1. The bonds were originally issued at a premium over par. When acquired in the open market, however, they were selling at a discount under par.
2. The issuing affiliate has its bond liability recorded in two accounts: Bonds Payable for the par value and an adjunct account having a credit balance, Premium on Bonds Payable, for the unamortized balance of the proceeds in excess of par.
3. The purchasing affiliate has its bond investment recorded in two accounts: Investment in Bonds for the par value and a contra account having a credit balance, Discount on Investment in Bonds, for the discount from par.

In a situation such as this, we eliminate the par value of the intercompany bonds and eliminate the unamortized premium and discount separately, thereby simplifying the elimination process.

We now present the eliminations to be made when the bonds are first acquired within the affiliated group at December 31, 19X1.

CONSOLIDATED FINANCIAL STATEMENT WORKING PAPER

Bonds Payable XXX
    Investment in Bonds   XXX
To eliminate the par value of the intercompany bonds.

Premium on Bonds Payable XXX
Discount on Investment in Bonds. XXX
    Gain on Retirement of Consolidated Debt   XXX
To eliminate the premium and discount on intercompany bonds and to
recognize a gain attributable to the constructive retirement of the debt.
The gain equals the excess of bond liability over bond investment; in
effect, less money was spent to acquire (and retire) the bonds than
was owed by the issuing affiliate.

To illustrate, suppose that on December 31, 19X1, Pinto Corporation purchases $100,000 par value bonds issued by its 80-percent-owned subsidiary, Stallion Corporation. The bonds pay 8 percent interest annually on December 31 and were acquired in the open market for $95,000, reflecting a current market yield of approximately 9.3 percent. They mature in 5 years, on December 31, 19X6. Stallion had an unamortized premium of $10,000 related to the bonds recorded on its books. Both companies use the straight-line method of amortizing bond discounts and premiums. These data are summarized as follows:

Pinto		**Stallion**	
Investment in Bonds (Par). . . .	$100,000	Bonds Payable (Par)	$100,000
Discount on Investment in Bonds	(5,000)	Premium on Bonds Payable. . .	10,000
Net Bond Investment	$ 95,000	Net Bond Liability	$110,000

From the foregoing, we can make two observations:

1. P's bond investment ($95,000) does not equal S's bond liability ($110,000).
2. P's annual interest revenue will not equal S's annual interest expense; $9,000 (= $8,000 + $5,000/5) does not equal $6,000 (= $8,000 − $10,000/5).

At the end of 19X1, when Pinto records its equity method accrual, it must reflect its share of the intercompany gain on constructive retirement of consolidated debt. The total gain is $15,000 (= $110,000 − $95,000), of which $5,000 (the discount) is allocated directly to Pinto and $10,000 (the premium) to Stallion. If Stallion earns $50,000 in 19X1, Pinto makes the following accrual under the equity method:

BOOKS OF PINTO CORPORATION

Investment in S	53,000	
Income from S		53,000

To record Pinto's 80 percent share of Stallion's net income $40,000 (= .8 × $50,000) plus Pinto's portion of the gain on intercompany bonds ($5,000) plus 80 percent of Stallion's portion of the gain on intercompany bonds $8,000 (= .8 × $10,000).

Preparation of consolidated financial statements then occurs. The working paper entries made to prepare the statements are as follows:

CONSOLIDATED FINANCIAL STATEMENT WORKING PAPER

Income from S	53,000	
Investment in S		53,000

To eliminate the equity method accrual and restate the investment account to its balance at Jan. 1, 19X1.

Bonds Payable	100,000	
Investment in Bonds		100,000

To eliminate the intercompany bonds at par value.

Premium on Bonds Payable.	10,000	
Discount on Investment in Bonds	5,000	
Gain on Retirement of Consolidated Debt.		15,000

To eliminate the discount and premium on intercompany bonds and establish the gain on constructive retirement of the intercompany bonds.

In 19X1, the Minority Interest in Net Income would be $12,000—20 percent of Stallion's reported net income of $50,000 plus 20 percent of $10,000, Stallion's portion of the gain on constructive retirement of the intercompany bonds.

Impact of Intercompany Bondholdings on the Equity Method Accrual. In order to understand the working paper entries required to eliminate intercompany bondholdings, it is necessary to grasp the dual role played here by the equity method. To simplify the discussion, we assume that the intercompany bondholding resulted in *gains* being attributed to both P and S.

1. P's equity method accrual made during the year the bonds are acquired includes the gain attributable to itself *plus* its share (α) of the gain attributable to S. This was just illustrated in Pinto's 19X1 equity method accrual of $53,000. Therefore, in that year of acquisition, both the Investment in S and the net income of P include P's share of the total consolidated gain. At the

same time, S's net income does not include its portion of the gain, nor does it include P's portion of the gain.

2. At consolidation points *following* the date the bonds are acquired, the books of P and S both reflect their current year amortization of premium and discount on the intercompany bondholding. This amortization of premium and discount represents partial recognition of the consolidated gain previously recorded by P under the equity method (in No. 1). Consequently, P's share of these annual amounts of premium and discount amortization are charged *against* the equity method accrual in postacquisition years *so that the total gain is counted only once*.

Put another way, the total consolidated gain arising out of the intercompany bondholding consists of the affiliates' unamortized discount and premium on the intercompany bonds when the bonds are acquired. P's share of the gain is recorded as part of the equity method accrual in the year the bonds are acquired. On the working paper in that year, the total gain is recognized and allocated to consolidated net income (P's share) and the minority interest in net income (the minority's share of S's portion of the gain). After the bonds are acquired, both P and S recognize a portion of the gain on their books each year as P's discount and S's premium on the bonds are amortized. If the periodic discount and premium amortization are not eliminated from the equity method accruals (and on the working papers) in subsequent years, the total gain will be counted in income twice—once in the year the bonds are acquired internally and a second time through periodic discount and premium amortization by P and S.

In sum, at any consolidation point following the year in which the bonds are acquired, the Investment in S account will include P's share of the total consolidated gain not yet recorded by the affiliates through discount and premium amortization. Working paper entries are necessary to adjust the investment account and the retained earnings of S to permit clean eliminations and to avoid recognizing the consolidated gain twice.

Eliminations in Subsequent Years. As we have seen, the affiliates involved in the intercompany bondholding recognize their portions of the total gain over time through amortization of the discount and premium on their own books. Consistent application of the equity method leads to differences between the investment account and the retained earnings of S. For these reasons, the following must be accomplished at each subsequent consolidation point:

1. *Par value* of the intercompany bondholding must be eliminated.
2. The *unamortized premium and discount* as of the end of the current year must be eliminated; Nos. 3 and 4 below achieve this.
3. *Intercompany interest expense and revenue* must be eliminated. Since the recorded amounts represent the coupon payment plus or minus the current discount and premium amortization, the elimination reverses the current year's amortization and adjusts the discount and premium to their beginning-of-year balances.

4. One of these beginning-of-year balances (S's unamortized premium) is *S's portion of the gain* not yet recognized via the amortization process; it is eliminated and allocated to the beginning retained earnings of S. The other balance (P's unamortized premium) is *P's portion of the gain* not yet recognized via the amortization process; its elimination goes to reduce the investment account.

As indicated in No. 1 above, the entry used at acquisition to eliminate the par value of the intercompany bondholding is also used at each subsequent consolidation point. We do not repeat that entry here. Rather, we shall provide a general form of the **bond elimination entry** needed to eliminate intercompany interest and the premium and discount, and to deal with the portion of the gain not recorded by the individual companies. Assume that S originally issued the bonds at a premium and P subsequently acquired them at a discount.

CONSOLIDATED FINANCIAL STATEMENT WORKING PAPER

Interest Revenue.	Coupon plus current discount amortization
Discount on Investment in Bonds	Unamortized discount at end of year
Premium on Bonds Payable . .	Unamortized premium at end of year
Retained Earnings—S, Jan. 1	Unamortized premium at beginning of year
Investment in S	Unamortized discount at beginning of year
Interest Expense.	Coupon less current premium amortization

To eliminate the unamortized discount and premium on the intercompany bonds and the intercompany interest revenue and expense.

This general form of the bond elimination entry is appropriate whether *straight-line* or *effective-interest* amortization of premiums and discounts is used. The principles embodied in the eliminating entry are as follows:

1. Each affiliate's unamortized premium or discount on the intercompany bonds at the *end* of the current year is part of the total intercompany bondholding and must be eliminated.
2. The periodic intercompany interest revenue and expense as recorded by the affiliates are eliminated. The difference between the coupon amount and the interest revenue or expense is the amount of total gain or loss recorded via periodic discount or premium amortization by each affiliate during the year.
3. The portion of the total gain or loss which has *not* been recorded on the affiliates' books via periodic discount or premium amortization in prior years is also dealt with in consolidation. This is the amount of unamortized discount or premium at the *beginning* of the current year (the amortized portion

has been recorded in the affiliates' books by inclusion in prior years' interest revenue and expense). The Investment in S account is adjusted by the portion pertaining to P, and Retained Earnings—S is adjusted by the portion pertaining to S.

An *alternative approach* to the bond elimination process would *partition* the above bond elimination entry into three smaller entries, as follows:

CONSOLIDATED FINANCIAL STATEMENT WORKING PAPER

Interest Revenue. . . . . Coupon portion of intercompany interest

    Interest Expense. . . . .   Coupon portion of intercompany interest

To eliminate that portion of the intercompany interest revenue and expense represented by the annual coupon on the intercompany bonds.

Interest Revenue. . . . . Current discount amortization

Discount on Investment in Bonds . Unamortized discount at end of year

    Investment in S . . . .   Unamortized discount at beginning of year

To eliminate the unamortized discount on the intercompany bond investment and the portion of intercompany interest revenue represented by the current discount amortization, and remove the total from the investment account.

Interest Expense. . . . . Current premium amortization

Premium on Bonds Payable . . . . Unamortized premium at end of year

    Retained Earnings—S, Jan. 1 . .   Unamortized premium at beginning of year

To eliminate the unamortized premium on the intercompany bond liability and the portion of intercompany interest expense represented by the current premium amortization (a *decrease* to interest expense), and add the total to the beginning retained earnings of S.

Continuing with the Pinto and Stallion example, we give the bond elimination entry made in consolidation at December 31, 19X2. We assume that both companies use straight-line amortization so that $1,000 (= \$5,000/5) of Pinto's discount and $2,000 (= \$10,000/5) of Stallion's premium have been amortized during the year.

CONSOLIDATED FINANCIAL STATEMENT WORKING PAPER

```
Interest Revenue ($8,000 + $1,000) . . . . . . . . . . . . . . . .   9,000
Discount on Investment in Bonds ($5,000 − $1,000) . . . . . . . .   4,000
Premium on Bonds Payable ($10,000 − $2,000) . . . . . . . . . .   8,000
    Retained Earnings—S, Jan. 1, 19X2 . . . . . . . . . . . . . .            10,000
    Investment in S. . . . . . . . . . . . . . . . . . . . . . . .             5,000
    Interest Expense ($8,000 − $2,000) . . . . . . . . . . . . . .             6,000
To eliminate the unamortized discount and premium on the
intercompany bondholding at December 31, 19X2, and the
intercompany interest revenue and expense recorded by the
companies during 19X2.
```

Under the *alternative approach* described above, the following three working paper entries are needed:

CONSOLIDATED FINANCIAL STATEMENT WORKING PAPER

```
Interest Revenue . . . . . . . . . . . . . . . . . . . . . . . . . .   8,000
    Interest Expense . . . . . . . . . . . . . . . . . . . . . . . .             8,000

Interest Revenue . . . . . . . . . . . . . . . . . . . . . . . . . .   1,000
Discount on Investment in Bonds . . . . . . . . . . . . . . . . .   4,000
    Investment in S. . . . . . . . . . . . . . . . . . . . . . . . .             5,000

Interest Expense . . . . . . . . . . . . . . . . . . . . . . . . . .   2,000
Premium on Bonds Payable . . . . . . . . . . . . . . . . . . . .   8,000
    Retained Earnings—S, Jan. 1, 19X2 . . . . . . . . . . . . . .            10,000
```

Impact on Equity Method Accrual in Subsequent Year. To illustrate how amortization of the discount and premium on intercompany bonds affects the equity method accrual, let us take a typical subsequent year, 19X2. In 19X2, $3,000 of gain will be recorded by the affiliates as they amortize the bond discount ($1,000) and premium ($2,000), thereby increasing interest revenue and decreasing interest expense, respectively. As we have previously stated, this amortization must be eliminated in consolidation of financial statements to avoid counting the $3,000 twice—once in beginning consolidated retained earnings and again in current period consolidated net income.

Under the one-line consolidation concept, Pinto Corporation must incorporate those eliminations affecting consolidated net income in the equity method accrual. Assume that Stallion earned $30,000 in 19X2. Pinto's share is $24,000 (= .8 × \$30,000). Stallion's income, however, includes $2,000 of premium amortization which will be eliminated. Pinto's share of this is $1,600 (= .8 × \$2,000); the other $400 will be charged against the minority interest in net income in consolidation [the Minority Interest in Net Income for 19X2 will be $5,600 (= .2 × \$30,000 − \$400)]. In addition, Pinto's bond discount amortization of $1,000 will also be eliminated (the entire amount relates to Pinto).

If these were the only intercompany items affecting the equity method accrual, Pinto would record $21,400 (= $24,000 − $1,600 − $1,000) of income from Stallion in 19X2. After 5 years of reducing the equity method accrual by $2,600, Pinto's $13,000 share of the total $15,000 gain on retirement of intercompany debt will have been removed from the investment account. Pinto will have recorded $5,000 of interest revenue on its books through the periodic discount amortization. Stallion will have recorded $10,000 of reductions to interest expense on its books through the periodic premium amortization, $2,000 of which relates to the minority interest. The total $15,000 gain will have been counted only once.

Bond Eliminations Made in the Years Remaining until Maturity. Starting with 19X2, then, the first year after the intercompany bonds are acquired, bookkeeping entries made by Pinto and Stallion affect the working paper eliminations as follows:

1. The discount and premium are reduced each year by $1,000 and $2,000, respectively, as they are amortized.
2. Retained earnings of Stallion begin to reflect Stallion's portion of the gain as $2,000 of bond premium is amortized each year.
3. The Investment in S account is reduced by $1,000 each year, as elimination of the $1,000 bond discount amortization is reflected in the equity method accrual.

The eliminating entries made in consolidation at the end of each of the 5 years remaining to maturity after the bonds were acquired (including 19X2) are presented in Exhibit 10.1. After these eliminating entries have been made, the following consolidated results are obtained:

1. The intercompany bondholdings, including premium and discount, have vanished.
2. Intercompany interest revenue and expense are gone.
3. The portion of the gain directly attributable to P and previously recorded under the equity method has been removed from the Investment in S account. Furthermore, the unrecorded portion of the gain attributable to S is now part of S's retained earnings. The Investment in S account still includes P's share of S's portion of the gain and can be eliminated cleanly.

Intercompany Leasing

Leasing arrangements between affiliates represent another category of intercompany transaction. Although there is virtually an infinite variety of such arrangements, they all provide for the *lessor* (owner of the property) to transfer *use* of the property to the *lessee* (user of the property) in return for a series of cash payments. Accounting for leases is prescribed in *SFAS 13*[1] and the many

Exhibit 10.1 **Working Paper Eliminations for Intercompany Bondholdings in Years Subsequent to Acquisition by Pinto Corporation**

	12/31/X2		12/31/X3	
	Debit	Credit	Debit	Credit
1. Bonds Payable.	100,000		100,000	
Investment in Bonds.		100,000		100,000
2. Interest Revenue.	9,000		9,000	
Discount on Investment in Bonds	4,000		3,000	
Premium on Bonds Payable	8,000		6,000	
Retained Earnings—S, Jan. 1.		10,000		8,000
Investment in S		5,000		4,000
Interest Expense.		6,000		6,000

	12/31/X4		12/31/X5		12/31/X6	
	Debit	Credit	Debit	Credit	Debit	Credit
1. Bonds Payable	100,000		100,000		100,000	
Investment in Bonds.		100,000		100,000		100,000
2. Interest Revenue . . .	9,000		9,000		9,000	
Discount on Investment in Bonds	2,000		1,000		—	
Premium on Bonds Payable.	4,000		2,000		—	
Retained Earnings— S, Jan. 1		6,000		4,000		2,000
Investment in S . . .		3,000		2,000		1,000
Interest Expense . .		6,000		6,000		6,000

1. To eliminate the intercompany bonds at par.
2. To eliminate the unamortized premium and discount on intercompany bonds and the intercompany interest expense and revenue.

amendments thereto and is discussed in standard intermediate accounting texts. Our objective here is to ignore complications and indicate how the principal lease categories as defined by the FASB are treated in consolidation when both lessor and lessee are affiliated corporations. These categories are (1) operating leases and (2) capital leases, including direct financing leases and sales-type leases.

Throughout most of the following discussion, we are not concerned with whether the parent or the subsidiary is the lessor or the lessee or whether a minority interest exists. These matters become critical in our discussion only in the case of a sales-type lease.

---

[1]Financial Accounting Standards Board, *Statement of Financial Accounting Standards No. 13*, "Accounting for Leases" (Stamford, CT: FASB, 1976); CT § L10.

Intercompany Operating Leases

An **operating lease** is viewed as a pure rental agreement in which the lessor retains most of the rights, risks, and rewards of ownership. The lessor records Rent Revenue and the lessee records Rent Expense each period. In consolidation, the intercompany rent revenues and expenses are eliminated as well as the inter-company receivables and payables for rent due but unpaid. Because there are no unconfirmed intercompany profits in an operating lease arrangement, neither the parent's equity accrual nor the minority interest in net income is affected.

Intercompany Capital Leases

In contrast, a **capital lease,** usually characterized by a long noncancelable series of payments, is viewed as a transfer of substantially all of the rights, risks, and rewards of ownership to the lessee, even though title to the property has not passed. Upon inception of a capital lease, the *lessee* records an asset (generally titled *Leasehold*) and a liability (generally titled *Capitalized Lease Obligation*) for the present value of the minimum lease payments required during the lease term. The *leasehold* is depreciated according to the lessee's normal depreciation policy (assumed here to be straight-line) over the term of the lease.

The *capitalized lease obligation* is amortized by the **effective interest method,** whereby each lease payment is allocated between interest expense and principal reduction. Treatment by the lessor depends on whether the capital lease is a direct financing lease or a sales-type lease.

Direct Financing Leases. A **direct financing lease** is viewed as a transaction in which the lessor finances the asset it transfers to the lessee. No gain is recognized by the lessor upon inception; the lessor's return is the interest implicit in the lease payments. Rather, the *undiscounted sum* of the minimum lease payments required is recorded as a receivable by the lessor, the property account is credited for the book value of the leased asset, and the difference is recorded as Unearned (or Deferred) Interest Revenue. The difference between the receivable and the un-earned revenue is the present value of the lease payments and should equal the lessee's capitalized lease obligation. The lessor amortizes the net receivable by the effective interest method, which produces amounts of interest revenue and principal reduction equal to those recorded by the lessee. We now illustrate the recording of a direct financing lease by lessor and lessee and the related consoli-dation procedures.

Assume that a 3-year intercompany capital lease is entered on January 2, 19X7, with annual payments of $42,725 to be made at the end of each year. The leased asset was constructed by the lessor and has a fair value equal to its book value of $90,000. Discounted at the desired internal rate of return of 20 percent, the present value of the three payments is $90,000 (= $2.1065 \times \$42,725$), an amount equal to the book value of the leased asset. The lessee records straight-line depreciation of $30,000 (= \$90,000/3$) per year.

The resulting intercompany debt will be amortized by both the lessor (net lease receivable) and lessee (capitalized lease obligation) according to the following schedule:

Year	(1) Beginning Principal Balance	(2) Interest Expense .2 × (1)	(3) Payment	(4) = (3) − (2) Principal Reduction	(5) = (1) − (4) Ending Principal Balance
19X7	$90,000	$18,000	$ 42,725	$24,725	$65,275
19X8	65,275	13,055	42,725	29,670	35,605
19X9	35,605	7,120	42,725	35,605	—
		$38,175	$128,175	$90,000	

During 19X7, the leasing affiliates record the following entries, assuming *direct financing lease* treatment by the lessor:

BOOKS OF LESSOR

1/2/X7

Lease Receivable. . .	128,175	
Asset		90,000
Unearned Interest		
Revenue		38,175

12/31/X7

Cash	42,725	
Lease Receivable. .		42,725
Unearned Interest		
Revenue	18,000	
Interest Revenue . .		18,000

BOOKS OF LESSEE

1/2/X7

Leasehold.	90,000	
Capitalized Lease		
Obligation		90,000

12/31/X7

Interest Expense . . .	18,000	
Capitalized Lease		
Obligation.	24,725	
Cash		42,725
Depreciation		
Expense	30,000	
Accumulated		
Depreciation . . .		30,000

In consolidation at December 31, 19X7, we must eliminate (1) the intercompany debt represented by the present value of the remaining lease payments and (2) the intercompany interest revenue and expense.

CONSOLIDATED FINANCIAL STATEMENT WORKING PAPER

Capitalized Lease Obligation ($90,000 − $24,725)	65,275	
Unearned Interest Revenue ($38,175 − $18,000).	20,175	
Lease Receivable ($128,175 − $42,725)		85,450

To eliminate the intercompany lease obligation. Note that the *net* lease receivable, $65,275 (= $85,450 − $20,175), equals the capitalized lease obligation.

Interest Revenue	18,000	
Interest Expense		18,000

To eliminate the intercompany interest revenue and expense.

There is no unconfirmed intercompany profit to be eliminated, as none was recorded by the lessor. Similarly, there is no effect on the parent's equity accrual or on the minority interest in net income. On the consolidated balance sheet, the Leasehold and related Accumulated Depreciation should be reported in the appropriate asset category of the lessor and not as leased property.

Sales-Type Leases. The lessor treats a **sales-type lease** as an outright sale financed by a form of debt. Assume that the leased property has no residual value at the end of the lease term. The lessor records a gain equal to the difference between the property's book value and its fair value (normally equal to the present value of the lease payments). The receivable is recorded at the undiscounted sum of the required lease payments, and unearned interest revenue results as in the direct financing type lease. The lessor amortizes its net receivable via the effective-interest method and records the same periodic interest *revenue* and principal reduction as the lessee's interest *expense* and principal reduction.

In consolidation, we now have the added problem of intercompany profit—the gain recorded by the lessor. As before, the gain is assumed confirmed as the lessee (purchaser) depreciates the leased property. The unconfirmed portion must be eliminated. Moreover, the equity method accrual is affected and, if the lease was upstream (*subsidiary* is the *lessor*), the minority interest in net income is affected.

To illustrate this additional complication in a sales-type lease, we can modify the preceding example by assuming that while the fair market value of the leased asset is $90,000 (equal to the present value of the lease payments), the cost to the lessor was $75,000. Thus the lessor will record a gain of $15,000 (= $90,000 − $75,000) at inception of the lease, as shown below. All other entries made by the lessor and lessee in the direct financing lease example are the same.

BOOKS OF LESSOR

1/2/X7

Lease Receivable	128,175	
Asset		75,000
Gain on Sale.		15,000
Unearned Interest Revenue		38,175

The lessee's depreciation expense, previously given as $30,000 (= $90,000/3), is now *larger* than the $25,000 (= $75,000/3) depreciation to which the lessor would be entitled had it retained and depreciated the leased property. This annual difference of $5,000 represents partial confirmation of the intercompany gain. If the lease was upstream and the subsidiary was partially owned, the parent's 19X7 equity accrual would be reduced by its proportionate share of $10,000 (= $15,000 − $5,000), the unconfirmed gain at the end of 19X7.

This unconfirmed intercompany gain requires the following eliminating entries in 19X7 in addition to those given in the direct financing case:

CONSOLIDATED FINANCIAL STATEMENT WORKING PAPER

Gain on Sale 15,000
   Leasehold.   15,000
To eliminate the intercompany gain recognized by the lessor.

Accumulated Depreciation. 5,000
   Depreciation Expense.   5,000
To eliminate the annual excess depreciation expense recorded by
the lessee. This is the portion of the intercompany gain confirmed
during 19X7.

If the lease had been upstream by a partially owned subsidiary, the minority interest in net income would be reduced by the minority's proportionate share of the $10,000 unconfirmed intercompany gain at the end of 19X7.

This completes our discussion of intercompany leasing. Consolidation procedures related to intercompany revenue/expense, bondholdings, and transfers of depreciable assets are all relevant here. Lease accounting contains many complexities resulting from executory costs, residual values, sale-leaseback transactions, and leveraged leasing. Although these can complicate the consolidation process, the principles just discussed continue to apply.

A Comprehensive Illustration of the Consolidation Process

This section of the chapter integrates the various aspects of the consolidation process by means of a comprehensive illustration. It incorporates accounting for the original business combination, some representative intercompany transactions, and a consolidated financial statement working paper. Income tax effects are not considered.

P Company acquired 80 percent of S Company's outstanding common stock several years ago on December 31, 19X1, for $2,400,000. When the stock was acquired, S's stockholders' equity was $2,500,000, and the book values of S's assets and liabilities approximated their fair values with one exception. A factory owned by S had an estimated fair value of $500,000; it was recorded on S's books at a net book value of $300,000. The factory had an estimated remaining life of 10 years when the acquisition was made by P. Determination and allocation of the purchase premium implicit in the acquisition price are given in Exhibit 10.2.

We are now beginning the preparation of consolidated financial statements at December 31, 19X4, 3 years after the stock acquisition on December 31, 19X1. P accounts for its investment in S by the equity method and amortizes the goodwill on the straight-line basis over 40 years. The following information regarding intercompany transactions is provided:

1. P sold merchandise to S for $125,000 during 19X4; the cost to P was $100,000. Of this $125,000 of merchandise purchased from P, $30,000 remained in the ending inventory of S. The unconfirmed intercompany profit

Exhibit 10.2 **P and S Companies: Schedule for Determining and Allocating the Purchase Premium Arising in the Stock Acquisition on December 31, 19X1**

Cost of Acquisition $2,400,000
Book Value of Net Assets or Stockholders' Equity Acquired (80%):
Capital Stock. $1,200,000
Retained Earnings   800,000

Total Book Value of S Company (80%) $2,000,000
Purchase Premium . . . . $ 400,000

Assets and Liabilities of S Company	Fair Value	Book Value	Fair Value less Book Value	Allocation Based on P's Interest (80%)
Cash and Receivables . . .	$ 550,000	$ 550,000	—	—
Inventory.	750,000	750,000	—	—
Land	600,000	600,000	—	—
Buildings and Equipment, Net .	2,500,000	2,300,000	$200,000	$160,000
Current Liabilities. .	(672,000)	(672,000)	—	—
Bonds Payable, 8%	(1,000,000)	(1,000,000)	—	—
Premium on Bonds Payable	(28,000)	(28,000)	—	—
	$ 2,700,000	$ 2,500,000	$200,000	$160,000

Goodwill. 240,000
Total Purchase Premium $400,000

is $6,000. Furthermore, S's beginning inventory included $1,000 of intercompany profits on purchases from P during 19X3, which were not confirmed at December 31, 19X3.

2. During 19X3, S transferred a parcel of land (Parcel #1) to P for $48,000. The original cost was $38,000; S recorded a gain of $10,000. P still owns the land at December 31, 19X4.

3. During 19X4, S transferred another parcel of land (Parcel #2) to P for $60,000. The original cost was $35,000; S recorded a gain of $25,000.

4. On December 31, 19X2, P sold some equipment to S for $112,000. Immediately prior to the sale, the equipment and related accumulated depreciation accounts showed $200,000 and $120,000, respectively. Thus the net book value was $80,000 at time of sale, and P recorded a gain of $32,000. Previous depreciation expense had been $10,000 annually; the equipment had a remaining useful life of 8 years at December 31, 19X2. Annual excess depreciation will therefore be $4,000 (= $32,000/8).

5. On January 1, 19X4, P acquired all of the outstanding bonds of S for $924,180. The bonds have a par value of $1,000,000, pay 8 percent interest annually on December 31, and mature on December 31, 19X8. The yield to

maturity on the bonds at January 1, 19X4, was 10 percent, as indicated in the following calculations:

Present Value of $1,000,000, to Be Received in 5 Years (Dec. 31, 19X8),
Discounted at 10%; .62092 × $1,000,000 . . . . $620,920
Present Value of Five Annual Interest Payments of $80,000 (= .08 ×
$1,000,000), Discounted at 10%; 3.79079 × $80,000 303,260
Price Paid by P Company $924,180

When the bonds were acquired on January 1, 19X4, S's books showed an unamortized premium on bonds payable of $20,000. This reflects $8,000 of premium amortization since S was acquired on December 31, 19X1 ($4,000 in 19X2 and $4,000 in 19X3). P Company recorded a discount on investment in bonds of $75,820 (= $1,000.000 − $924,180). Thus at January 1, 19X4, the total gain on constructive retirement of consolidated debt was $95,820, of which $75,820 pertained to P and $20,000 to S. The gain will be recorded by both companies over the 5 years remaining to maturity as the discount and premium are amortized at the straight-line annual rates of $15,164 (= $75,820/5) and $4,000 (= $20,000/5), respectively.

S paid dividends of $200,000 and reported net income of $500,000 in 19X4. Upon receipt of this information, P determines the accrual required under the equity method and records it. Exhibit 10.3 explains how the accrual is computed. Note that the 19X4 equity accrual does *not* reflect elimination of the intercompany gains on the 19X3 land transfer (Parcel #1), $10,000, and the 19X2 equipment transfer, $32,000. Those gains were subtracted from the equity accruals in 19X3 and 19X2, respectively. The equity method entries made by P are given below:

BOOKS OF P COMPANY

Investment in S 430,456
  Income from S   430,456
To record income from S accrued under the equity method.

Cash 160,000
  Investment in S   160,000
To record the receipt of dividends from S according to the equity method.

After the equity method entries are made at December 31, 19X4, the Investment in S account has a balance of $2,909,456. Exhibit 10.4 on page 477 shows how this amount is determined. The calculation reflects consistent application of the equity method since acquisition on December 31, 19X1, and assumes that S's retained earnings increased by $400,000 between December 31, 19X1, and December 31, 19X3 (January 1, 19X4).

Working Paper Eliminations

Complete financial statement data for P Company and S Company appear a little later in the chapter on the consolidated financial statement working paper in Ex-

Exhibit 10.3	P and S Companies: Schedule for Computing the Equity Method Accrual for the Year Ended December 31, 19X4

P's Share of S's Reported Net Income (.8 ×
$500,000) $400,000
Less Amortization of Purchase Premium:
  Additional Depreciation Expense on P's Share of
  Factory ($160,000/10). $(16,000)
  Amortization of Goodwill ($240,000/40) . . . .   (6,000)   (22,000)
Less P's Downstream Unconfirmed Intercompany
  Inventory Profits of $6,000 (= .2 × $30,000;
  Markup is 20% of Selling Price) at Dec. 31,
  19X4. . . . .   (6,000)
Plus P's Downstream Intercompany Inventory Profits
  of $1,000 in Beginning (Jan. 1, 19X4) Inventory
  Assumed Confirmed in 19X4   1,000
Less 80% of S's Unconfirmed Profit of 19X4
  Upstream Intercompany Sale of Land (Parcel
  #2) to P (.8 × $25,000) . . . .   (20,000)
Plus Excess Depreciation Expense of $4,000 on
  Downstream Intercompany Sale of Equipment to
  S at Dec. 31, 19X2 . . . .   4,000[a]
Plus Gain on Constructive Retirement of
  Intercompany Bonds:

	100%	80%	
Amount Attributable to P			
($1,000,000 − $924,180)	$ 75,820	—	
Less P's Amortization of Discount in 19X4			
($75,820/5) included in P's 19X4			
Interest Income	(15,164)	—	
Amount Attributable to S ($1,020,000 −			
$1,000,000)	—	$ 16,000	
Less S's Amortization of Premium in 19X4			
($20,000/5) Reflected in S's 19X4 Interest			
Expense	—	(3,200)	
	$ 60,656	$ 12,800	73,456
Net Equity Method Accrual			$430,456

[a]This is the portion of P's gain confirmed in 19X4 [$4,000 = ($112,000/8) − $10,000].

hibit 10.7. We first explain the working paper entries in our discussion, then show their impact on the completed working paper and prepare formal consolidated financial statements. Numbers assigned to the working paper entries in the narrative also appear on the working paper in Exhibit 10.7 for ease in cross-reference.

Elimination of the Equity Method Entries. Under the equity method, P increases its Investment in S by its share of S's reported net income adjusted for intercompany items arising in consolidation. Dividends received from S during the year reduce the Investment in S balance. Since the effects of these entries are

---

Exhibit 10.4   **P and S Companies: Analysis of the Investment in S Account at December 31, 19X4**

Acquisition Cost at Dec. 31, 19X1.	$2,400,000
P's Share of Growth in S's Retained Earnings from Dec. 31, 19X1, to Jan. 1, 19X4 [.8($1,400,000 − $1,000,000)]	320,000
Less Amortization of Purchase Premium in 19X2 and 19X3 [2 × $16,000 (factory) + 2 × $6,000 (goodwill)]	(44,000)
Less Gain on P's Downstream Intercompany Sale of Equipment Removed from Equity Method Accrual in 19X2	(32,000)
Plus Excess Depreciation Expense of $4,000 on Equipment Sold Downstream by P Added to Equity Method Accrual in 19X3	4,000[a]
Less 80% of S's Gain on Upstream Intercompany Sale of Land (Parcel #1) Removed from Equity Method Accrual in 19X3 (.8 × $10,000)	(8,000)
Less P's Downstream Unconfirmed Intercompany Profit in S's Ending (Dec. 31, 19X3) Inventory Removed from Equity Method Accrual in 19X3	(1,000)
Balance in Investment in S at Jan. 1, 19X4	$2,639,000
Plus Equity Method Accrual for 19X4 (Exhibit 10.3)	430,456
Less Dividends Received from S in 19X4 (.8 × $200,000)	(160,000)
Balance in Investment in S at Dec. 31, 19X4	$2,909,456

[a]This is the portion of P's gain confirmed in 19X3.

---

duplicated in consolidation, we eliminate them, thereby adjusting the Investment in S to its balance at the beginning of the year.

CONSOLIDATED FINANCIAL STATEMENT WORKING PAPER
(1)

Income from S	430,456	
Dividends—S		160,000
Investment in S		270,456

To eliminate the equity method entries recorded by P, thereby adjusting the investment account to its Jan. 1, 19X4, balance.

Elimination of the Intercompany Transactions. As we have seen, proper use of the equity method treats P's equity in the earnings of S as a one-line consolidation. Thus the equity method accrual is not based simply on a fraction of S's reported net income; it must be adjusted for those items which affect consolidated statements. In this process, differences develop over time between the balance in the Investment in S account and the book value of S's underlying stockholders' equity. Therefore, before we are able to eliminate the beginning-of-year Investment in S balance, we must adjust it and the beginning retained earnings of S for the items producing these differences. Only in this way can a clean elimination of the investment account be made. At the same time, however, note that P's retained earnings equal consolidated retained earnings—each period's equity method accrual reflects all the items which affect the computation of consolidated net income.

Intercompany Inventory Transactions. Three eliminating entries are necessary to remove all intercompany inventory transactions. The first eliminates total intercompany sales of merchandise. The second removes unconfirmed intercompany profit from the ending inventory. The third transfers the intercompany profit in the beginning inventory to current income and increases the Investment in S account, thus replacing an item never removed from S's beginning retained earnings.

CONSOLIDATED FINANCIAL STATEMENT WORKING PAPER

(2)

Sales	125,000	
Purchases		125,000
To eliminate intercompany sales and purchases		

(3)

Inventory, Dec. 31 (Income Statement)	6,000	
Inventory (Balance Sheet)		6,000
To eliminate unconfirmed intercompany profit in ending inventory, consistent with the confirmation principle. Consolidated inventories are reduced and cost of goods sold increased.		

(4)

Investment in S	1,000	
Inventory, Jan. 1 (Income Statement)		1,000
To remove the unconfirmed intercompany profit from the beginning inventory and decrease cost of goods sold. This amount was eliminated in computing last year's equity method accrual and must now be added to the investment account.		

Intercompany Sales of Land. Two eliminations are needed to remove the gains recorded by S in 19X3 and 19X4 and reduce the land account to its original acquisition cost:

CONSOLIDATED FINANCIAL STATEMENT WORKING PAPER

(5)

Retained Earnings—S, Jan. 1	10,000	
Land		10,000
To eliminate the unconfirmed gain on the 19X3 intercompany sale of land (Parcel #1).		

(6)

Gain on Sale of Land	25,000	
Land		25,000
To eliminate the unconfirmed gain on the 19X4 intercompany sale of land (Parcel #2).		

Intercompany Sale of Equipment. This transaction took place 2 years ago, on December 31, 19X2. The gain originally recorded by P and eliminated in the equity method accrual was $32,000. Each year, $\frac{1}{8}$ of that gain, or $4,000, is realized by P as the equipment depreciates; $4,000 is the excess depreciation generated by the intercompany transaction. The $4,000 is included each year in the equity method accrual. At each consolidation point, then, the portion of the gain *not yet realized* by P via the annual depreciation represents a difference between the investment account and S's retained earnings and must be added to the investment account. Also, on the working paper we eliminate the excess depreciation and restate the asset and related accumulated depreciation accounts to their original acquisition cost balances.

CONSOLIDATED FINANCIAL STATEMENT WORKING PAPER

(7)

Investment in S	28,000	
Accumulated Depreciation.	4,000	
Equipment		32,000

To eliminate the excess depreciation recorded in 19X3, reduce the equipment account to its net book value at date of intercompany sale, and add the intercompany gain unconfirmed in prior years to the investment account.

(8)

Accumulated Depreciation.	4,000	
Depreciation Expense.		4,000

To eliminate the annual excess depreciation expense recorded by S Company in 19X4.

(9)

Equipment	120,000	
Accumulated Depreciation		120,000

To restate the equipment and accumulated depreciation accounts to their original acquisition cost basis ($120,000 was the amount of accumulated depreciation of date of sale).

Intercompany Bondholding. Here we eliminate the intercompany bondholding and establish the gain on constructive retirement of consolidated debt. As previously stated, the consolidated gain consists of P's discount on the bond investment of $75,820 and S's premium on the bonds payable of $20,000 on January 1, 19X4, when the bonds were acquired. We also eliminate the intercompany interest revenue and expense. Intercompany interest revenue of $95,164 is the coupon of $80,000 ($= .08 \times \$1,000,000$) *plus* one-fifth of the discount on the bond investment, $15,164 ($= \$75,820/5$). Similarly, intercompany interest expense of $76,000 is the coupon of $80,000 *minus* one-fifth of the premium on the bonds payable, $4,000 ($= \$20,000/5$).

CONSOLIDATED FINANCIAL STATEMENT WORKING PAPER

(10)

Bonds Payable	1,000,000	
Investment in Bonds		1,000,000

To eliminate the par value of the intercompany bonds.

(11)

Premium on Bonds Payable.	16,000	
Discount on Investment in Bonds	60,656	
Interest Revenue	95,164	
Interest Expense		76,000
Gain on Retirement of Consolidated Debt.		95,820

To eliminate the unamortized premium ($16,000 = $20,000 − $4,000) and discount ($60,656 = $75,820 − $15,164) on intercompany bonds acquired on Jan. 1, 19X4, and the intercompany interest (net of premium and discount amortization), and to establish the gain on constructive retirement of consolidated debt.

Elimination of the Investment in S Account. Since 80 percent of S's outstanding shares are now held internally by P, we eliminate the Investment in S against the stockholders' equity of S to avoid counting these items twice. The investment account balance at the beginning of 19X4, after the preceding eliminations, is $2,668,000, including the unamortized purchase premium of $356,000 [= $400,000 − 2($22,000)]. Exhibit 10.5 presents an analysis of how those eliminations affect the investment account and why a balance of $2,668,000 is needed for a clean elimination. We now make the elimination and establish both the unamortized purchase premium and the minority interest at January 1, 19X4:

CONSOLIDATED FINANCIAL STATEMENT WORKING PAPER

(12)

Capital Stock—S	1,500,000	
Retained Earnings—S, Jan. 1, 19X4	1,390,000	
Purchase Premium	356,000	
Investment in S.		2,668,000
Minority Interest in S		578,000

To eliminate the Investment in S against the stockholders' equity of S Company and establish the unamortized purchase premium and minority interest in S, all as of Jan. 1, 19X4.

Allocation and Amortization of Purchase Premium. Once the unamortized purchase premium has been established in the working paper, it must be allocated to the assets of S Company, and the current year depreciation and amortization must be recorded. As of January 1, 19X4, 2 years have expired since the stock acquisition. Hence, our allocation of the purchase premium must reflect 2 years' amortization applied to the original values given in Exhibit 10.2. The net book value of the portion attributable to the factory is down by $32,000—2 years' annual depreciation of $16,000—while the original goodwill of $240,000 has an unamortized balance of $228,000 at January 1, 19X4. We now record the allocation and current amortization of the purchase premium:

Exhibit 10.5 **Analysis of the Effect of Intercompany Profit Eliminations on the Investment in S and Equivalence between the Adjusted Balance of $2,668,000 and P Company's Share of S Company's Stockholders' Equity**

INVESTMENT IN S

Balance, Dec. 31, 19X4	2,909,456	(1) Equity method entries	270,456
(4) Profit in Jan. 1, 19X4,			
inventory	1,000		
(7) Unconfirmed gain on			
equipment sale	28,000		

Adjusted balance, Jan. 1, 19X4   2,668,000

Stockholders' Equity of S Company, Jan. 1, 19X4:
Capital Stock $1,500,000
Retained Earnings. 1,400,000
Unconfirmed Gain on Land Sale (5) . . . . (10,000)
$2,890,000
P's Share (.8 × $2,890,000) $2,312,000
Unamortized Purchase Premium at Jan. 1, 19X4 356,000
Investment Account Balance Needed for Clean Elimination $2,668,000

CONSOLIDATED FINANCIAL STATEMENT WORKING PAPER
(13)

Buildings and Equipment 160,000
Goodwill. 228,000
    Accumulated Depreciation 32,000
    Purchase Premium 356,000
To allocate the unamortized purchase premium at Jan. 1, 19X4.

(14)

Operating Expenses 22,000
    Accumulated Depreciation 16,000
    Goodwill 6,000
To record current year amortization of the purchase premium.
Depreciation on the portion allocated to the factory equals
$16,000 (= $160,000/10) and amortization of goodwill is $6,000
(= $240,000/40).

Recording the Minority Interest in Net Income. Two of the intercompany transactions affect the minority interest in net income. *First,* the $25,000 gain recorded by S on the upstream sale of land to P has been eliminated in consolidation. The minority should be charged for 20 percent of this amount, or $5,000, under the principle of proportional allocation of intercompany profit eliminations. *Second,* the unamortized premium on the bonds of S now held by P represents S's portion of the gain on retirement of consolidated debt. This amount was $20,000 at Jan-

Exhibit 10.6	P and S Companies: Determination of the Minority Interest in Net Income, 19X4

Reported Net Income of S Company $500,000
Elimination of Unconfirmed Intercompany Gain on Upstream Sale of Land
    (Parcel #2) . . . . (25,000)
Unamortized Premium on Intercompany Bonds When Constructively Retired at
    Jan. 1, 19X4 (S Company's Portion of the Gain on Retirement
    of Consolidated Debt) 20,000
Partial Realization of the Gain through Premium Amortization in 19X4 . . . . . . (4,000)
Adjusted Net Income of S Company $491,000
Minority Interest (.2 × $491,000) . . . . $ 98,200

uary 1, 19X4, but $4,000 of the premium was amortized during 19X4 and is reflected in S's net income. The minority is entitled to 20 percent of the remaining $16,000, or $3,200. The computation of minority interest in net income appears in Exhibit 10.6; the eliminating entry is as follows:

CONSOLIDATED FINANCIAL STATEMENT WORKING PAPER
(15)

Minority Interest in Net Income 98,200
    Dividends—S 40,000
    Minority Interest in S 58,200
To record the minority's interest in S Company's adjusted net
income and eliminate the minority's share of S Company's
dividends.

The completed consolidated financial statement working paper is presented in Exhibit 10.7.

Explanations of Working Paper Entries, for Use with Exhibit 10.7

(1) To eliminate the equity method entries made by P in 19X4.
(2) To eliminate intercompany merchandise sales.
(3) To eliminate unconfirmed intercompany profit in ending inventory.
(4) To remove unconfirmed intercompany profit from the beginning inventory and increase the Investment in S accordingly.
(5) To eliminate the unconfirmed gain on intercompany sale of land in 19X3 and reduce the land account to original acquisition cost.
(6) To eliminate the unconfirmed gain on intercompany sale of land in 19X4 and reduce the land account to original acquisition cost.
(7) To eliminate excess depreciation recorded in prior years, reduce the equipment account to its net book value on date of intercompany sale, and add the unrealized portion of the gain to the investment account.
(8) To eliminate the annual excess depreciation expense recorded by S in 19X4.
(9) To restate the equipment and accumulated depreciation accounts to their original acquisition cost basis.
(10) To eliminate the par value of the intercompany bonds.
(11) To eliminate the unamortized premium and discount on the intercompany bonds and the intercompany interest and establish the gain on retirement of consolidated debt.
(12) To eliminate the Investment in S against the stockholders' equity of S and establish the unamortized purchase premium and the minority interest in S, all as of Jan. 1, 19X4.
(13) To allocate the unamortized purchase premium at Jan. 1, 19X4.
(14) To record amortization of the purchase premium for 19X4.
(15) To record the minority's interest in S's adjusted net income and eliminate the minority's share of S's dividends.

Exhibit 10.7 **P and S Companies: Consolidated Financial Statement Working Paper for the Year Ended December 31, 19X4**

	P Company	S Company (80%)	Adjustments and Eliminations				Consolidated
				Dr.		Cr.	
INCOME STATEMENT							
Sales	6,000,000	2,800,000	(2)	125,000			8,675,000
Income from S	430,456	—	(1)	430,456			—
Interest Revenue	95,164	—	(11)	95,164			—
Gain on Sale of Land	—	25,000	(6)	25,000			—
Gain on Ret. of Cons. Debt .	—	—			(11)	95,820	95,820
Inventory, 12/31/X4	1,000,000	670,000	(3)	6,000			1,664,000
Total Credits	7,525,620	3,495,000		681,620		95,820	10,434,820
Inventory, 1/1/X4	1,040,000	620,000			(4)	1,000	1,659,000
Purchases	2,800,000	1,350,000			(2)	125,000	4,025,000
Operating Expenses	1,860,000	949,000	(14)	22,000	(8)	4,000	2,827,000
Interest Expense	300,000	76,000			(11)	76,000	300,000
Total Debits	6,000,000	2,995,000		22,000		206,000	8,811,000
Minority Interest in Net Income	—	—	(15)	98,200			(98,200)
Net Inc.—to Ret. Earn. Stmt.	1,525,620	500,000		801,820		301,820	1,525,620
RETAINED EARNINGS STATEMENT							
Retained Earnings, 1/1/X4—P.	2,492,000	—					2,492,000
Retained Earnings, 1/1/X4—S.	—	1,400,000	(5)	10,000			—
			(12)	1,390,000			
Net Income—from Inc. Stmt.	1,525,620	500,000		801,820		301,820	1,525,620
Dividends—P	(400,000)	—					(400,000)
Dividends—S	—	(200,000)			(1)	160,000	—
					(15)	40,000	
Ret. Earn., 12/31/X4— to Bal. Sht.	3,617,620	1,700,000		2,201,820		501,820	3,617,620
BALANCE SHEET							
Cash and Receivables . . .	950,000	700,000					1,650,000
Inventory	1,000,000	670,000			(3)	6,000	1,664,000
Investment in S	2,909,456	—	(4)	1,000	(1)	270,456	—
			(7)	28,000	(12)	2,668,000	
Investment in Bonds	1,000,000	—			(10)	1,000,000	—
Discount on Inv. in Bonds . .	(60,656)	—	(11)	60,656			—
Land	1,000,000	800,000			(5)	10,000	1,765,000
					(6)	25,000	
Buildings and Equipment . .	6,000,000	3,600,000	(9)	120,000	(7)	32,000	9,848,000
			(13)	160,000			
Accumulated Depreciation . .	(3,221,180)	(832,000)	(7)	4,000	(13)	32,000	(4,213,180)
			(8)	4,000	(9)	120,000	
					(14)	16,000	
Purchase Premium	—	—	(12)	356,000	(13)	356,000	—
Goodwill	—	—	(13)	228,000	(14)	6,000	222,000
Total	9,577,620	4,938,000		961,656		4,541,456	10,935,820
Current Liabilities	960,000	722,000					1,682,000
Bonds Payable	3,000,000	1,000,000	(10)	1,000,000			3,000,000
Premium on Bonds Payable .	—	16,000	(11)	16,000			—
Capital Stock—P.	2,000,000	—					2,000,000
Capital Stock—S.	—	1,500,000	(12)	1,500,000			—
Ret. Earn.—from Retained Earnings Statement . . .	3,617,620	1,700,000		2,201,820		501,820	3,617,620
Minority Interest in S	—	—			(12)	578,000	636,200
					(15)	58,200	
Total	9,577,620	4,938,000		4,717,820		1,138,020	10,935,820
				5,679,476		5,679,476	

Formal Consolidated Financial Statements

To complete this example, we have prepared formal consolidated financial statements from the consolidated account balances on the working paper in Exhibit 10.7. The consolidated statement of income and retained earnings appears in Exhibit 10.8. Cost of goods sold consists of the beginning inventory of $1,659,000 plus purchases of $4,025,000 less ending inventory of $1,664,000. Finally, the consolidated balance sheet is presented in Exhibit 10.9.

Subsidiaries with Preferred Stock

Preferred stock may be issued by companies that are already controlled by another company as well as by those that might become subsidiaries in the future. The two major issues that arise when consolidating a subsidiary that has outstanding preferred stock are indicated below:

1. How is the stockholders' equity of the subsidiary to be apportioned among the preferred and common stockholders? This apportionment affects the elimination of the common stockholders' interest, the minority interest in common stock, *and,* when preferred shares are held externally, the minority interest in preferred stock.
2. If the parent company acquires some or all of the subsidiary's preferred stock, how is any difference between cost and book value of the preferred to be treated in consolidation? How is the Investment in Preferred to be accounted for?

Note that the parent's equity method accrual relating to its investment in the subsidiary's common stock is based on the subsidiary's income available to common shareholders (*after* preferred dividends are deducted).

Establishing the Correct Book Value of the Preferred Stockholders' Interest

Preferred stock has priority over common stock in regard to dividends and to proceeds in liquidation. Regardless of the market value of the preferred stock, the preferred stockholders' interest in the subsidiary is often not adequately measured by the amount shown for Preferred Stock on the subsidiary's balance sheet. The preferred stock may be recorded at par value, yet its call price or liquidation value may exceed par value. In the event the stock is purchased by call or retired in a liquidation of the corporation, the par value does not measure the claim of the preferred shareholders.

Preferred stock issues may be cumulative, participating, or both. **Cumulative** preferred stock requires that payment of preferred dividends which had not

Exhibit 10.8 **P and S Companies: Consolidated Statement of Income and Retained Earnings for the Year Ended December 31, 19X4**

P COMPANY AND S COMPANY
CONSOLIDATED STATEMENT OF INCOME AND RETAINED EARNINGS
FOR THE YEAR ENDED DECEMBER 31, 19X4

Sales	$8,675,000
Gain on Retirement of Consolidated Debt	95,820
Total Revenues	$8,770,820
Cost of Goods Sold	$4,020,000
Operating Expenses	2,827,000
Interest Expense	300,000
Total Expenses	$7,147,000
Minority Interest in Net Income of S	$ 98,200
Consolidated Net Income	$1,525,620
Retained Earnings, Jan. 1, 19X4	2,492,000
Dividends	(400,000)
Retained Earnings, Dec. 31, 19X4	$3,617,620

Exhibit 10.9 **P and S Companies: Consolidated Balance Sheet at December 31, 19X4**

P COMPANY AND S COMPANY
CONSOLIDATED BALANCE SHEET
DECEMBER 31, 19X4

ASSETS

Cash and Receivables	$ 1,650,000
Inventory	1,664,000
Total Current Assets	$ 3,314,000
Land	$ 1,765,000
Buildings and Equipment	9,848,000
Less Accumulated Depreciation	(4,213,180)
Goodwill	222,000
Total Noncurrent Assets	$ 7,621,820
Total Assets	$10,935,820

LIABILITIES AND STOCKHOLDERS' EQUITY

Current Liabilities	$ 1,682,000
Bonds Payable	3,000,000
Total Liabilities	$ 4,682,000
Minority Interest in S Company	$ 636,200
Capital Stock	2,000,000
Retained Earnings	3,617,620
Total Stockholders' Equity	$ 6,253,820
Total Liabilities and Stockholders' Equity	$10,935,820

been paid in prior years and those for the current year be made before any profits can be distributed to common stockholders. Preferred stock that is **participating** shares any profit distributions in excess of preferred dividends with the common stockholders in an agreed-upon ratio. Since participating preferred stock is rarely encountered today, we shall assume that preferred stock in our examples is cumulative but not participating.

If the preferred stock is *cumulative,* the preferred stockholders' interest is increased by the amount of any preferred dividends in arrears. This arrearage is not normally recorded in the accounts of the issuing company.

By properly stating the equity of preferred stockholders, the minority interest in preferred, if any, can be correctly measured. This is necessary because preferred stockholders' equity is *not a residual.* Similarly, the minority interest in preferred reflects the preferences inherent in preferred stock. In this sense, it differs from the true residual nature of minority interest in common stock.

Before turning to a numerical example, consider whether call price or liquidation value should be used to measure the claims of preferred stockholders, aside from any dividend arrearage. The **call price** or **redemption price** gives the amount to which preferred stockholders are entitled if the issuing corporation as a going concern purchases or calls the preferred stock. The use of call price to measure the claims of preferred stockholders could therefore be justified by the *going concern assumption* which underlies financial accounting.

In contrast, preferred stock's **liquidation value** indicates the claim of preferred stockholders when the corporation is in liquidation. It has practical meaning only in the event of a liquidation and has no relevance to a going concern. Its use to measure the claims of preferred stockholders is derived from the notion that *only* in the event of liquidation do preferred stockholders have a *claim* on the corporation's net assets as opposed to the *right* to receive a given sum of money if their stock is redeemed by the corporation.

> In our judgment, a going concern should use *call* or *redemption price* when establishing the preferred shareholders' interest in consolidation. When a preferred stock issue does not specify a call price but does indicate a liquidation value in excess of par, the liquidation value should be used.

To illustrate, suppose the Parsons Company owns 80 percent of the Stone Company's outstanding common stock. Stone's stockholders' equity at January 1, 19X4, is given here:

10 Percent Cumulative, Nonparticipating Preferred Stock, $100 Par Value, Redemption Price $103, Liquidation Value $105	$1,000,000
Additional Paid-In Capital—Preferred	150,000
Common Stock, Par Value $1	1,000,000
Additional Paid-In Capital—Common	2,700,000
Retained Earnings	5,000,000
Total Stockholders' Equity	$9,850,000

Note: Preferred dividends for the prior 2 years are in arrears.

We now compute the proper book value of the preferred stockholders' equity and indicate the needed working paper adjustment. Since all preferred shares are held externally, this amount will appear as Minority Interest in Stone—Preferred on the consolidated balance sheet.

Total Redemption Price of Preferred Stock (10,000 × $103). $1,030,000
Dividends in Arrears (10% of Par Value for 2 Years; .1 × $1,000,000 × 2) . . .   200,000
Corrected Book Value of Preferred Shareholders' Interest $1,230,000
Less Amount Recorded by Stone ($1,000,000 + $150,000) 1,150,000
Working Paper Adjustment Required . . . . $ 80,000

This required adjustment has the effect of earmarking $80,000 of Stone's retained earnings for the preferred stockholders. The adjustment is made only on the consolidated financial statement working paper, does not affect the accounts of Stone, and is part of the working paper entry which reclassifies the corrected book value of the preferred stock as Minority Interest in Preferred.

CONSOLIDATED FINANCIAL STATEMENT WORKING PAPER

Retained Earnings—Stone   80,000
Preferred Stock 1,000,000
Additional Paid-In Capital—Preferred   150,000
   Minority Interest in Stone—Preferred   1,230,000
To establish the book value of the preferred stockholders'
equity in Stone Company by earmarking $80,000 of Stone's
retained earnings and to reclassify Stone's preferred stock
held outside the affiliation as Minority Interest in Stone—
Preferred. *Note:* A single account could be used to identify
the total minority interest in Stone, including both common
and preferred.

In this case, the Additional Paid-In Capital—Preferred (APIC—P) is part of the preferred stockholders' interest because it, plus the par value, is less than the call price. It is not always true that the APIC—P "belongs" to the preferred stockholders. If par plus APIC—P is more than the call or redemption value, some of that APIC—P is actually part of the common stockholders' interest.

Suppose that, in addition to the prior 2 years' preferred dividends being in arrears, the *current* year's preferred dividends are also in arrears. On the working paper, the amount of the current year's preferred dividends would be included in the Minority Interest in Net Income; it would not be charged to Stone's beginning retained earnings.

Treatment at Date of Business Combination. In determining the book value of the common stockholders' equity acquired at the date of a business combination, the parent must consider the proper amount of the preferred stockholders' interest. If the common stockholders' equity is decreased when the correct book value of the preferred stock is established, the purchase premium (discount) is increased (decreased). Assuming a purchase premium was paid to acquire the common stock in the example just given, the purchase premium is increased by $80,000.

Parent's Investment in the Subsidiary's Preferred Stock

When the parent company acquires some or all of the subsidiary's preferred stock, the following two issues arise:

1. If the cost of the preferred shares differs from their book value, properly computed, how is the difference treated in consolidation?
2. How should the parent account for the investment in preferred on its books?

Difference between Cost and Book Value of Investment in Preferred Stock. To simplify the discussion, consider only the case of an *excess* of cost over book value. This implies a *purchase premium* on the investment in preferred stock. An analysis of the debt-equity characteristics of preferred stock and an understanding of why the market prices of preferred stocks change will help show how this purchase premium should be treated in consolidation.

Preferred stock is neither pure debt nor pure equity. It does carry a specific dividend rate, but there is no contractual agreement specifying that the firm *must* pay the stated dividend or *must* redeem the shares at a specified time. In terms of debt instruments, preferred stock is not like a conventional bond, but it is close to a *consol* or *perpetual bond*. Consols have occasionally been issued by the British and Canadian governments. A consol's price equals the present value of the stated interest payments in perpetuity. As the market rate of interest (the rate used to discount the interest payments) changes, the price of the consol moves inversely to the change.

Moreover, most preferred stocks, especially the cumulative and nonparticipating issues, are quite different from common equity. There is a stated dividend rate, similar to a stated interest rate. Passing the preferred dividend does not remove the preferred dividend obligation. Finally, preferred stock is not a residual. Its priority is lower than bonds but higher than common stock.

We believe that the fixed dividend characteristic of preferred stock suggests that changes in its price are due primarily to changes in the market rate of interest. Whether the firm's net assets are undervalued or overvalued has little relevance, except insofar as firm-specific risk influences the discount rate.

Suppose Parsons acquired 2,000 of Stone's preferred shares at a cost of $300,000 on January 1, 19X4. In the last section, we found the book value per preferred share to be $123 (= $1,230,000/10,000). The book value of the 2,000 shares is $246,000, and a purchase premium of $54,000 (= $300,000 − $246,000) arises. From a consolidated point of view, these 2,000 preferred shares are retired. Since the purchase premium is the result of a change in market yields and not of undervalued assets, it should not be allocated to the assets and liabilities of Stone.[2]

---

[2] In the case of *convertible* preferred stock or preferred stock that *participates* in the earnings available to common shareholders, it may be that the preferred stock price behaves more like equity than like debt. If so, the purchase premium or discount on an investment in preferred should be treated in the same way as a purchase premium or discount on an investment in common.

The purchase premium on preferred has all the characteristics of a *loss*. One approach is to assign the loss to the consolidated income statement, as in the case of intercompany debt. Another is to view the internally held preferred stock as retired treasury stock and to charge the loss against the parent's additional paid-in capital. We support the latter position.

> In our judgment, *retirement of preferred stock held internally* for the purposes of consolidation is more like the *retirement of treasury stock* than the retirement of debt. Any purchase premium (discount) on the preferred should be charged (credited) to additional paid-in capital.

This leads to the following working paper entries. The first entry establishes the correct value of the preferred stock, and the second eliminates the investment in preferred.

CONSOLIDATED FINANCIAL STATEMENT WORKING PAPER

Retained Earnings—Stone	80,000	
Additional Paid-In Capital—Preferred		80,000
To establish the correct book value of the preferred		
stockholders' equity in Stone Company by reducing Stone's		
retained earnings. APIC—P now has a balance of $230,000.		
Preferred Stock	1,000,000	
Additional Paid-In Capital—Preferred	230,000	
Additional Paid-In Capital—Common (Parsons)	54,000	
Investment in Stone—Preferred.		300,000
Minority Interest in Stone—Preferred		984,000
To eliminate the investment in preferred against the preferred		
stock of Stone, charging the purchase premium against		
consolidated additional paid-in capital and reclassifying the		
remaining 8,000 preferred shares as minority interest;		
$984,000 (= 8,000 × $123).		

Cumulative Preferred Stock and the Consolidated Income Statement. Current dividends on preferred stock of a subsidiary which is held outside the affiliated group become a component of the Minority Interest in Net Income and therefore represent a deduction in computing consolidated net income. In the Stone Company example, 80 percent of Stone's preferred stock is owned by outsiders. Each year, the dividends of $80,000 (= .8 × .1 × $1,000,000) on those shares are charged against consolidated net income and credited to Preferred Stock whether or not they were actually declared. The cumulative feature reduces the amount of earnings available for distribution to common stockholders; declaration is not required to achieve this reduction.

This is a departure from conventional treatment of preferred dividends. In the single firm case, preferred dividends are not accrued and charged against income available to the common stockholders unless they have been declared. The consolidation case is different because all dividends on S's cumulative preferred

Exhibit 10.10 **Parsons Company and Subsidiary Stone Company: Consolidated Financial Statement Working Paper for the Year Ended December 31, 19X4**

	P Company	S Company (80%)	Adjustments and Eliminations Dr.	Adjustments and Eliminations Cr.	Consolidated
INCOME STATEMENT					
Sales.	50,000,000	20,000,000			70,000,000
Income from Stone.	420,000	—	(1) 420,000		—
Inventory, Dec. 31, 19X4 . .	8,000,000	5,000,000			13,000,000
Total Credits.	58,420,000	25,000,000	420,000		83,000,000
Inventory, Jan. 1, 19X4. . . .	7,500,000	4,800,000			12,300,000
Purchases.	35,000,000	15,000,000			50,000,000
Operating Expenses	13,920,000	4,600,000			18,520,000
Total Debits	56,420,000	24,400,000			80,820,000
Minority Interest in Net Income	—	—	(5) 180,000		(180,000)
Net Income—to Retained Earnings Statement . . .	2,000,000	600,000	600,000		2,000,000
RETAINED EARNINGS STATEMENT					
Ret. Earn., Jan. 1, 19X4—P	10,000,000	—			10,000,000
Ret. Earn., Jan. 1, 19X4—S	—	5,000,000	(2) 80,000 (4) 4,920,000		—
Net Income—from Inc. Stmt.	2,000,000	600,000	600,000		2,000,000
Dividends—P	(1,000,000)	—			(1,000,000)
Dividends—S	—	—			
Ret. Earn., Dec. 31, 19X4— to Balance Sheet	11,000,000	5,600,000	5,600,000		11,000,000
BALANCE SHEET					
Cash and Receivables . . .	5,884,000	3,000,000			8,884,000
Inventory	8,000,000	5,000,000			13,000,000
Invest. in Stone—Common .	7,296,000	—		(1) 400,000 (4) 6,896,000	—
Invest. in Stone—Preferred .	320,000	—		(1) 20,000 (3) 300,000	—
Land	4,000,000	2,000,000			6,000,000
Buildings and Equipment . .	13,000,000	9,000,000			22,000,000
Accumulated Depreciation. .	(2,500,000)	(1,550,000)			(4,050,000)
Total	36,000,000	17,450,000		7,616,000	45,834,000
Current Liabilities	8,000,000	4,000,000			12,000,000
Other Liabilities	12,000,000	3,000,000			15,000,000
Preferred Stock—Stone. . .	—	1,150,000	(3) 1,230,000	(2) 80,000	—
Common Stock—Parsons . .	5,000,000	—	(3) 54,000		4,946,000
Common Stock—Stone. . .	—	3,700,000	(4) 3,700,000		—
Ret. Earn.—from Retained Earnings Statement . . .	11,000,000	5,600,000	5,600,000		11,000,000
Minority Interest in Stone . .	—	—		(3) 984,000 (4) 1,724,000 (5) 180,000	2,888,000
Total	36,000,000	17,450,000	10,584,000	2,968,000	45,834,000
			10,584,000	10,584,000	

Explanations of Working Paper Entries

(1) To eliminate the equity method entries made by Parsons during 19X4.
(2) To establish the correct book value of Stone's preferred stock as of Jan. 1, 19X4.
(3) To eliminate the investment in preferred against Stone's preferred stock, charge the purchase premium of $54,000 against Parson's common stock (APIC), and establish the minority interest in preferred, all as of Jan. 1, 19X4; $984,000 ($= .8 \times $1,230,000$).
(4) To eliminate the investment in common against the common stockholders' equity of Stone and establish the minority interest in common, all as of Jan. 1, 19X4; $1,724,000 [$= .2($4,920,000 + $3,700,000)$].
(5) To record the minority interest in net income for 19X4; $80,000 ($= .8 \times $100,000$), preferred; $100,000 [$= .2($600,000 - $100,000)$], common.

stock not held by P, whether declared or not, reduce the amount of S's retained earnings available for distribution to the controlling common stockholders. The charge in the consolidated income statement signifies this reduction.

If the parent accounts for its investment in the subsidiary's preferred using the *equity method*—which follows from P's control over S's preferred dividend policy—P's equity method accrual will include the preferred dividends attributable to the shares owned by P. The Investment in Preferred will be increased by the amount of the preferred dividends and will be decreased when the preferred dividends are actually declared. Thus the Investment in Preferred will move in tandem with the book value of the preferred stockholders' equity after the previously discussed working paper entry establishing the correct book value is made.

Use of the *cost method* to account for the investment in preferred will require that the investment account be restated to the equity basis as of the beginning of the current year. At each consolidation point, another working paper entry will be needed to reflect P's share of any dividend arrearage in the Investment in Preferred account. This is similar to the working paper entry required when the investment in common is carried at cost (as was discussed in Chapter 8).

Preferred Stock: A Numerical Example

To illustrate these preferred stock matters on a consolidated financial statement working paper, consider the Parsons and Stone data just discussed. Parsons's investment in Stone's common was at book value at a time when no dividend arrearages existed on the preferred stock but the redemption price was $103 per share. This excess of $30,000 [$= ($103 - $100)10,000$] was allocated to the preferred stock in determining the book value of the common equity acquired.

On January 1, 19X4, Parsons acquired the 2,000 shares (20 percent interest) of Stone's preferred stock for $300,000; the investment is carried at equity. Stone earned $600,000 from its own operations in 19X4, of which $100,000, representing the current year's preferred dividend, is allocated to the preferred stockholders. Parsons's equity method accrual is therefore $420,000, consisting of $400,000 [$= .8($600,000 - $100,000)$] for the common and $20,000 ($= .2 \times $100,000$) for the preferred.

At consolidation on December 31, 19X4, we assume that 3 years of preferred dividends are in arrears—the current year *and* the 2 prior years. There were no intercompany transactions in 19X4, and Stone declared no common dividends.

The completed consolidated financial statement working paper is presented in Exhibit 10.10 on page 490. All detailed financial statement data are assumed.

Summary of Key Concepts

When the bonds of one affiliate are acquired by another affiliate, the resulting **intercompany asset and liability** must be **eliminated** when consolidated statements are prepared. If the bonds are acquired on the **open market,** the carrying value of the purchaser's **bond investment** will normally differ from the carrying value of the issuer's **bond liability.** Thus the **constructive retirement** of the intercompany bondholding in consolidation produces a **consolidated gain or loss** on retirement of intercompany debt.

The **total consolidated gain or loss** consists of the sum of the **premium** or **discount** related to the intercompany bondholding which is recorded on each company's books. Since each company systematically amortizes its premium or discount, the gain or loss is recognized by the companies through interest expense and revenue over the time remaining to maturity.

At the **first consolidation point** following the acquisition of intercompany bonds, the **total consolidated gain or loss** on retirement of the intercompany bondholding is recognized in the consolidated income statement. Any premium or discount amortization by the respective companies after acquisition of the bonds is part of the total gain or loss and must not be counted twice. In this book, we allocate the consolidated gain or loss between the affiliates according to the unamortized premium or discount at the date the bonds were acquired internally.

Under the **one-line consolidation concept** of *APBO 18,* the parent company will record its share of the total gain or loss in the equity method accrual made in the year the bonds are acquired. In subsequent years, P's share of the periodic premium or discount amortization recorded by the companies is charged **against** the equity method accrual in order that the total gain not be counted twice.

The effects of intercompany bondholdings on the equity method accrual create a discrepancy between the balance in the Investment in S and P's share of S's stockholders' equity. At each subsequent consolidation point, this discrepancy must be removed by (1) eliminating P's unconfirmed portion of the gain or loss (P's unamortized discount or premium at the beginning of the year) from the investment account and (2) allocating S's unconfirmed portion of the gain or loss (S's unamortized premium or discount at the beginning of the year) to Retained Earnings—S.

When **intercompany leasing arrangements** exist, their effects must be eliminated in consolidation. The intercompany debt and interest related to the lease must be removed. In a **sales-type** lease, the lessor's unconfirmed gain resulting from transfer of the property is also eliminated.

When a subsidiary has **preferred stock outstanding,** the correct book value of the preferred stock must be established on the working paper. If the preferred stock is cumulative and dividends are in arrears, common shareholders' equity must be reduced. A similar approach is required when the call or redemption price of the preferred exceeds the par value plus additional paid-in capital attributable to the preferred shareholders. Each year, on the **consolidated income statement,** consolidated net income must be **charged for the dividends** on cumulative preferred stock held externally.

The parent company may own some (or all) of the subsidiary's preferred stock. If so, the **Investment in Preferred** would normally be carried at **equity,** being increased by the periodic preferred dividend amount and decreased as preferred dividends are actually declared. A purchase premium or discount will exist if the amount paid for the preferred shares differs from their book value. While this **purchase premium or discount** ultimately represents a gain or loss to the consolidated entity, we believe that it should be **credited or debited to Additional Paid-In Capital in consolidation.** This treatment follows from the treatment accorded to the retirement of treasury stock, which we feel is analogous to the retirement of internally held preferred stock in consolidation.

Questions

Q10.1 When the bonds in an intercompany bondholding are acquired directly from the issuing company, consolidation problems are minimized. Explain why.

Q10.2 Briefly describe the two major problem areas which typically arise when the bonds of one affiliate are acquired in the open market by another affiliate.

Q10.3 Most unconfirmed intercompany gains or losses are recorded on the selling affiliate's books; in consolidation they must be *eliminated*. The gain or loss on an intercompany bondholding, however, is somewhat different. Explain the nature of the difference and how the consolidation procedures deal with it.

Q10.4 When the bonds of an affiliate are acquired in the open market, a consolidated gain or loss attributable to the constructive retirement of the intercompany bonds often arises. Criticize the position taken in the text that allocates this gain or loss between the purchaser and issuer of the bonds.

Q10.5 In the year a gain arises from the constructive retirement of intercompany bonds, the equity method accrual is *increased* by the parent's share. Yet in subsequent years, the equity method accrual is *decreased* by a portion of the original increase. Explain what is happening here and why.

Q10.6 The one-line consolidation concept of *APBO 18* requires some working paper entries which may seem unusual. Specifically, a gain on constructive retirement of an intercompany bondholding generally means that the Investment in S is *credited* at subsequent consolidation points. Carefully explain what is happening here.

Q10.7 In most intercompany bondholding situations, intercompany interest expense differs from intercompany interest revenue. How should this difference be interpreted? To what is the sum of these periodic differences equal?

Q10.8 Describe the ways in which the minority interest in net income can be affected in an intercompany bondholding.

Q10.9 What are the circumstances in which intercompany leasing arrangements may affect consolidated net income, the minority interest in net income, and the equity method accrual? Briefly describe these circumstances.

Q10.10 While reviewing a consolidated financial statement working paper, you notice the following working paper entry:

```
Minority Interest in Net Income . . . . . . . . . . . . . . . . . . . . . . .   XXX
    Preferred Stock—S (or Dividends—S) . . . . . . . . . . . . . . .             XXX
```

Indicate the purpose of such an entry.

Q10.11 Criticize the position taken by the authors regarding the treatment of purchase premium or discount arising on an investment in a subsidiary's preferred stock.

Q10.12 Suppose P Company carries its investment in S Company's preferred stock at cost rather than at equity. How would consolidation procedures differ under the cost method?

Exercises

E10.1 P Company owns 90 percent of S Company's outstanding common stock. On January 3, 19X6, S acquired $100,000 par value of P's 8 percent annual coupon bonds for $80,000. The bonds mature in 10 years and are carried on P's books at $110,000, reflecting an unamortized premium of $10,000. Both companies use the straight-line method of amortization, and P's investment in S's common stock is carried at equity.

Required:

1. Prepare the working paper eliminations made in consolidation at December 31, 19X6, relative to the intercompany bondholding.
2. Repeat No. 1 for consolidation at December 31, 19X7.

E10.2 On January 1, 19X7, Solid Corporation purchased $2,000,000 par value of bonds issued several years ago by its parent company, PBR, Inc., for $2,200,000. The bonds pay 11 percent annually and mature 10 years after January 1, 19X7. PBR's books show the carrying value of this bond liability to be $2,080,000. Both companies amortize bond premiums and discounts by the straight-line method.

Required: Prepare the working paper entries relative to the intercompany bondholding when consolidated statements are prepared at December 31, 19X7, and December 31, 19X8. Assuming that PBR owns 70 percent of Solid's stock, also give the effect on the Minority Interest in Net Income during the 2 years.

E10.3 On December 31, 19X7, P Company acquired $200,000 par value bonds of S Company, an 80-percent-owned affiliate, for $185,000. S was carrying these bonds on its books at $208,000. The bonds pay 10 percent interest annually and mature in 10 years. S reported net income of $125,000 in 19X7.

Required:

1. Compute P's equity method accrual at December 31, 19X7, and prepare the working paper eliminations on that date relative to the intercompany bondholding.
2. Repeat No. 1 for the year ended December 31, 19X8, assuming S reported net income of $60,000 in 19X8. Both companies use straight-line amortization.

E10.4 On December 31, 19X3, the Sampson Company acquired $1,000,000 face value of the Petersen Company's 12 percent annual bonds for $1,122, 888. The bonds mature in 10 years, and the price reflects a 10 percent yield to maturity. At date of issue, the bonds were sold to yield 15 percent. Sampson is wholly owned by Peterson, and the book value of Petersen's bond liability is $849,432.

Required:

1. Give the working paper eliminations required at December 31, 19X3, and December 31, 19X4, assuming that the straight-line method of premium and discount amortization is used by both companies.
2. Repeat No. 1 except assume that both companies use the effective interest method of premium and discount amortization.

E10.5 P Company owns 80 percent of S Company's stock (carried at equity) and 60 percent of S Company's outstanding 10 percent bonds. Data relative to the intercompany bondholding are as follows:

P COMPANY

Investment in Bonds (Par) Made on Dec. 31, 19X1	$ 6,000,000
Discount on Investment in Bonds at Dec. 31, 19X1	(639,390)
Net Investment In Bonds	$ 5,360,610

S COMPANY

Bonds Payable (Par), 10% Interest Paid Annually on Dec. 31 and
Maturing in 9 years on Dec. 31, 19Y0 . . . . $10,000,000
Premium on Bonds Payable at Dec. 31, 19X1   1,249,388
Total Bond Liability $11,249,388

When originally issued by S, the bonds yielded 8 percent. At the time they were acquired by P, however, their price had fallen, reflecting a yield to maturity on December 31, 19X1, of 12 percent.

Required:

1. Give the working paper entries required to eliminate the effects of the intercompany bondholding at consolidation on December 31, 19X1, and December 31, 19X2. Both companies use the straight-line method to amortize the discount and premium.
2. Repeat No. 1 except assume that both companies use the effective interest method of discount and premium amortization.
3. Explain how the minority interest in S is affected at December 31, 19X1, (a) when the straight-line method is used and (b) when the effective interest method is used.

E10.6 On December 31, 19X3, the Scythe Company took out a 20-year, $100,000 mortgage from the Second National Bank of Odon. The equal annual mortgage payments are based on a 10 percent interest rate and are made at the end of each year. One year later, when Scythe is acquired by Pond corporation, Pond purchases the mortgage from the bank at an amount which provides Pond with a 12 percent internal rate of return on the mortgage. Both companies amortize premiums and discounts on long-term notes by the effective interest method. Pond accounts for its investment in Scythe using the equity method.

Required: Assuming Scythe is wholly owned by Pond, give the working paper eliminations relative to the above intercompany loan which would be made at December 31, 19X4, 19X5, and 19X6. Show all computations.

E10.7 On January 2, 19X5, P Company leased some equipment to its 80-percent-owned subsidiary, S Company. The lease is noncancelable and runs for a 5-year term, the useful life of the equipment. Annual payments of $14,916 are to be made at the end of each year. Discounted at the lessor's interest rate of 15 percent, the present value of the payments is $50,000, an amount equal to the carrying value of the equipment on the lessor's books. Both companies use straight-line depreciation.

Required:

1. Prepare the working paper eliminations relative to the intercompany lease to be made at the end of 19X5. Assume direct-financing treatment by the lessor.
2. Repeat No. 1 at December 31, 19X6.

E10.8 Jackson Corporation purchased 100 percent of K-TEL's common stock at book value for $1,000,000 on January 1, 19X5. Simultaneously, Jackson purchased all of K-TEL's outstanding bonds for $56,000. The bonds pay 10 percent annually, mature in 5 years, and are carried at $46,000 on K-TEL's balance sheet on December 31, 19X4. K-TEL's unamortized discount is $4,000.

Required: Assume that K-TEL reports net income of $100,000 in 19X5, 19X6, and 19X7, and that Jackson carries its investment at equity. Prepare an analysis showing how the working paper entries made in consolidation at December 31, 19X5, 19X6, and 19X7, achieve the equivalence between the investment account and K-TEL's stockholders' equity that is needed for clean eliminations.

E10.9 P Company owns 80 percent of S Company's outstanding common stock. Included in S's capital structure are 1,000,000 outstanding shares of 8 percent, $100 par value cumulative preferred stock. The preferred shares have a call price of $102 and have a 2-year dividend arrearage (including the current year).

Required: Prepare the needed working paper eliminations relative to the preferred stock when consolidated statements are prepared at the end of the current year.

E10.10 Punch Corporation acquired 70 percent of Stun Company's outstanding common stock for $1,000,000. The book value of Stun's common stockholders' equity at date of acquisition was $1,000,000. In addition, Stun had 5,000 shares of preferred stock with par value of $500,000 outstanding. The preferred has a stated dividend rate of 12 percent, has a call price of $101, and is 3 years in arrears on dividends.

Required: Compute the purchase premium paid by Punch on its investment in Stun's common stock. Show all calculations.

E10.11 The stockholders' equity section of Steedle Corporation's balance sheet is shown here:

10 Percent Cumulative, Nonparticipating Preferred Stock,	
$200 Par Value, Liquidation Value $208	$ 2,000,000
Additional Paid-In Capital—Preferred	270,000
Common Stock, Par Value $10	500,000
Additional Paid-In Capital—Common	4,800,000
Retained Earnings	7,900,000
Total Stockholders' Equity . . . .'	$15,470,000

Pundit, Inc., owns 90 percent of Steedle's common stock and 10 percent of Steedle's preferred stock. Steedle's board of directors has just voted to omit the current year's preferred dividend for the first time in 20 years.

Required: Show how Steedle's preferred stock will appear on the consolidated balance sheet. All computations must be in good form.

E10.12 Selected account balances from the books of P Company and its subsidiary, S Company, appear as follows:

P COMPANY

Investment in S (Common; 80%) $5,800,000
Investment in S (Preferred; 40%) 300,000

S COMPANY

Common Stock, $1 Par Value. . . . . $ 100,000
10 Percent Cumulative Preferred Stock, $100 Par Value,
    Call Price $105, Liquidation Price $102 800,000
Additional Paid-In Capital 2,400,000
Retained Earnings. 4,000,000

Assume that the above account balances existed at the *beginning* of the current year, the day that P purchased the common and preferred shares. This year's preferred dividend has not yet been declared, and there is no prior arrearage. The fair values of S's net assets, both individually and collectively, approximate their book values. No intercompany transactions occurred during the year. Both investment accounts are carried at equity.

Required: Prepare the working paper eliminations needed to consolidate P and S at the *end* of the current year. Show all computations.

Problems

P10.1 **Consolidated Financial Statement Working Paper—Complex Purchase Premium and Intercompany Transactions** On June 30, 19X9, Linskey, Inc., purchased 100 percent of the outstanding common stock of Cresswell Corporation, paying $3,605,000 cash and Linskey's common stock valued at $4,100,000. At the date of purchase, the book and fair values of Cresswell's assets and liabilities were as follows:

	Book Value	Fair Value
Cash.	$ 160,000	$ 160,000
Accounts Receivable, Net	910,000	910,000
Inventory.	860,000	1,025,186
Furniture, Fixtures, and Machinery, Net	3,000,000	2,550,000
Building	9,000,000	7,250,000 (net)
Accumulated Depreciation—Building.	(5,450,000)	—
Intangible Assets, Net	150,000	220,000
	$8,630,000	
Accounts Payable	$ 580,000	580,000
Note Payable	500,000	500,000
5% Mortgage Note Payable	4,000,000	3,710,186
Common Stock	2,900,000	—
Retained Earnings	650,000	—
	$ 8,630,000	

By year-end, December 31, 19X9, the net balance of Cresswell's accounts receivable at June 30, 19X9, had been collected; the inventory on hand at June 30, 19X9, had been charged to cost of goods sold; the accounts payable at June 30, 19X9, had been paid; and the $500,000 note had been paid.

As of June 30, 19X9, Cresswell's furniture, fixtures, and machinery, and its building had estimated remaining lives of 8 and 10 years, respectively. All intangible assets had estimated remaining lives of 20 years. All depreciation and amortization is to be computed using the straight-line method.

As of June 30, 19X9, the 5 percent mortgage note payable had eight equal annual payments remaining with the next payment due in one year. The fair value of the note was based on a 7 percent rate. The discount of $289,814 (= \$4,000,000 - \$3,710,186)$ will be amortized using the effective-interest method.

Prior to June 30, 19X9, there were no intercompany transactions between Linskey and Cresswell; however, during the last 6 months of 19X9, the following intercompany transactions occurred:

1. Linskey sold $400,000 of merchandise to Cresswell. The cost of the merchandise to Linskey was $360,000. Of this merchandise, $75,000 (at billed prices) remained on hand at December 31, 19X9.
2. On December 31, 19X9, Cresswell purchased $300,000 of Linskey's $7\frac{1}{2}$ percent bonds payable in the market for $312,500, including $22,500 of accrued interest. Linskey had issued $1,000,000 of these 20-year $7\frac{1}{2}$ percent bonds payable on January 1, 19X2, for $960,000.
3. Many of the management functions of the two companies have been consolidated since the merger. Linskey charges Cresswell a $30,000-per-month management fee.
4. At December 31, 19X9, Cresswell owes Linskey 2 months' management fees and $18,000 for merchandise purchases.

Financial statements of Linskey and Cresswell at December 31, 19X9, appear in Exhibit 10.11. Linskey has not recorded the equity method accrual for the last six months of 19X9. It may be ignored in your solution.

Linskey's profit and loss figures are for the 12-month period, while Cresswell's are for the last 6 months. You may assume that both companies made all the adjusting entries required for separate financial statements unless an obvious discrepancy exists. Income taxes should not be considered in your solution. Round all computations to the nearest dollar.

Required: Prepare a consolidated financial statement working paper for Linskey and its subsidiary, Cresswell, for the year ended December 31, 19X9. Provide computations in good form where appropriate to support entries. *(AICPA adapted)*

P10.2 Consolidated Financial Statement Working Paper—Purchase Premium and Intercompany Transactions On April 1, 19X3, Jared, Inc., purchased

Exhibit 10.11	**Linskey, Inc., and Cresswell Corporation: Financial Statements at December 31, 19X9, to Be Used in P10.1**

STATEMENTS OF INCOME AND RETAINED EARNINGS
FOR THE YEAR ENDED DECEMBER 31, 19X9

	Linskey	**Cresswell**
Sales	$26,000,000	$ 6,000,000
Management Service Revenue	180,000	—
Total Revenue	$26,180,000	$ 6,000,000
Cost of Goods Sold:		
Beginning Inventory	$ 2,000,000	$ 1,000,500
Purchases	18,031,000	3,959,000
Ending Inventory	(2,031,000)	(1,009,500)
	$18,000,000	$ 3,950,000
Selling, General, and Administrative Expenses	3,130,000	956,000
Depreciation Expense.	3,701,000	600,000
Interest Expense	662,000	100,000
Management Service Expense	—	180,000
Amortization Expense.	—	3,750
Total Expenses.	$25,493,000	$ 5,789,750
Net Income	$ 687,000	$ 210,250
Beginning Retained Earnings	2,167,500	650,000
Ending Retained Earnings	$ 2,854,500	$ 860,250

BALANCE SHEETS AT DECEMBER 31, 19X9

ASSETS	**Linskey**	**Cresswell**
Cash	$ 507,000	$ 200,750
Accounts Receivable, Net.	1,890,000	817,125
Interest Receivable	—	22,500
Inventory	2,031,000	1,009,500
Furniture, Fixtures, and Machinery	4,200,000	3,000,000
Buildings	17,000,000	9,000,000
Accumulated Depreciation	(8,000,000)	(6,050,000)
Intangible Assets, Net.	—	146,250
Investment in Subsidiary	7,705,000	—
Investment in Linskey $7\frac{1}{2}$% Bonds	—	300,000
Discount on Investment in $7\frac{1}{2}$% Bonds.	—	(10,000)
Total Assets	$25,333,000	$ 8,436,125

LIABILITIES AND STOCKHOLDERS' EQUITY		
Accounts Payable.	$ 1,843,000	$ 575,875
Interest Payable	200,500	100,000
Mortgage Notes Payable	6,786,500	4,000,000
Bonds Payable, $7\frac{1}{2}$%.	1,000,000	—
Discount on $7\frac{1}{2}$% Bonds Payable	(24,000)	—
Bonds Payable, $8\frac{1}{4}$%.	3,900,000	—
Common Stock	8,772,500	2,900,000
Retained Earnings	2,854,500	860,250
Total Liabilities and Stockholders' Equity	$25,333,000	$ 8,436,125

100 percent of the common stock of the Munson Manufacturing Company for $5,850,000. At the date of purchase, the book and fair values of Munson's assets and liabilities were as follows:

	Book Value	Fair Value
Cash and Receivables	$1,093,000	– $1,093,000
Inventories	1,000,000	872,000
Land.	1,560,000	2,100,000
Machinery and Equipment.	7,850,000	6,600,000 (net)
Accumulated Depreciation.	(3,250,000)	—
Other Assets	140,000	50,000
	$8,393,000	
Current Liabilities	$ 515,000	515,000
Other Liabilities	750,000	750,000
Subordinated Debentures—7%	5,000,000	5,000,000
Capital Stock	1,122,000	—
Retained Earnings.	1,006,000	—
	$8,393,000	

Additional information:

1. By December 31, 19X3, the following transactions had occurred:
   a. The balance of Munson's net accounts receivable at April 1, 19X3, had been collected.
   b. The inventory on hand at April 1, 19X3, had been charged to cost of sales. Munson used a perpetual inventory system in accounting for inventories.
   c. Prior to 19X3, Jared had purchased at face value $1,500,000 of Munson's 7 percent subordinated debentures. These debentures mature on October 31, 19X9, with interest payable annually on October 31.
   d. As of April 1, 19X3, the machinery and equipment had an estimated remaining life of 6 years. Munson uses the straight-line method of depreciation. Munson's depreciation expense calculation of $588,750 (included in Operating Expenses) for the 9 months ended December 31, 19X3, was based upon the old depreciation rates.
   e. The other assets consist entirely of long-term investments made by Munson and do *not* include any investment in Jared.
   f. During the last 9 months of 19X3, the following intercompany inventory transactions occurred between Jared and Munson:

	Jared to Munson	Munson to Jared
Net Sales	$158,000	$230,000
Included in Purchaser's Inventory at Dec. 31, 19X3 .	36,000	12,000
Balance Unpaid at Dec. 31, 19X3 .	16,800	22,000

Jared sells merchandise to Munson at cost. Munson sells merchandise to Jared at regular selling price, including a normal gross profit margin of 35 percent of selling price. There were *no* intercompany sales between the two companies prior to April 1, 19X3.

Exhibit 10.12 | **Jared, Inc., and Munson Manufacturing Company: Financial Statements at December 31, 19X3, to Be Used in P10.2**

STATEMENTS OF INCOME AND RETAINED EARNINGS
FOR THE YEAR ENDED DECEMBER 31, 19X3

	Jared	Munson
Sales	$18,200,000	$ 5,760,000
Income from Munson	514,700	—
Interest Revenue	105,000	1,700
Total Revenue	$18,819,700	$ 5,761,700
Cost of Goods Sold:		
Beginning Inventory	$ 3,000,000	$ 1,000,000
Purchases	10,804,000	3,342,000
Ending Inventory	(3,204,000)	(1,182,000)
	$10,600,000	$ 3,160,000
Operating Expenses	4,551,500	1,652,650
Interest Expense	806,000	269,400
Total Expenses	$15,957,500	$ 5,082,050
Net Income	$ 2,862,200	$ 679,650
Beginning Retained Earnings	12,683,500	1,006,000
Ending Retained Earnings	$15,545,700	$ 1,685,650

BALANCE SHEETS AT DECEMBER 31, 19X3

ASSETS	Jared	Munson
Cash and Receivables	$ 3,580,000	$ 1,983,400
Inventory	3,204,000	1,182,000
Investment in Munson	6,364,700	—
Investment in Bonds	1,500,000	—
Land	4,000,000	1,560,000
Buildings	1,286,000	—
Accumulated Depreciation—Buildings	(372,000)	—
Machinery and Equipment	15,875,000	4,600,000
Accumulated Depreciation—Machinery and Equipment	(6,301,000)	(588,750)
Other Assets	413,000	140,000
Total Assets	$29,549,700	$ 8,876,650

LIABILITIES AND STOCKHOLDERS' EQUITY		
Current Liabilities	$ 1,364,000	$ 319,000
Other Liabilities	10,000,000	750,000
Subordinated Debentures, 7%	—	5,000,000
Capital Stock	2,640,000	1,122,000
Retained Earnings	15,545,700	1,685,650
Total Liabilities and Stockholders' Equity	$29,549,700	$ 8,876,650

2. Accrued interest on intercompany debt is recorded by both companies in their respective Accounts Receivable and Accounts Payable accounts.
3. Jared's policy is to amortize intangible assets over a 20-year period.
4. Separate financial statements for Jared and Munson at December 31, 19X3, are shown in Exhibit 10.12.
5. Jared's revenue and expense figures are for the 12-month period, while Munson's are for the last 9 months of 19X3. You may assume that both companies made all the adjusting entries required for separate financial statements unless stated to the contrary. Round all computations to the nearest dollar. Ignore income taxes.

Required:

1. Prepare a schedule to determine and allocate the purchase premium arising in the acquisition of Munson's stock.
2. Prepare a schedule to show how the equity method accrual was computed.
3. Prepare formal eliminating entries with explanations and supporting calculations in good form.
4. Complete a consolidated financial statement working paper for Jared and Munson at December 31, 19X3. Show any supporting computations in good form. *(AICPA adapted)*

P10.3 Consolidated Financial Statement Working Paper—Purchase Premium and Intercompany Transactions On January 2, 19X6, P Company acquired 80 percent of S Company's voting common stock for $140,000; S's stockholders' equity amounted to $150,000 on that date (of which $100,000 was retained earnings), and the fair values of its assets and liabilities approximated their book values. The investment account is carried at equity and P always elects the maximum amortization period for intangible assets.

Additional Information:

1. P sells merchandise to S at 25 percent over cost. Intercompany sales amounted to $100,000 during 19X7. Intercompany profits included in S's beginning and ending inventories amounted to $8,000 and $6,000, respectively.
2. On March 4, 19X6, S sold land to P for $30,000 and recorded a gain of $8,000. P continued to own the land.
3. P acquired some used shop equipment from S on January 3, 19X7, for $25,000. A gain of $5,000 was recognized and is included in S's Sales account. The equipment is expected to last another 5 years and will be depreciated by the straight-line method.
4. On January 3, 19X7, P spent $51,000 for $50,000 par value bonds issued by S at par. The bonds pay 10 percent interest annually and mature in 5 years on December 31, 19Y1. Interest for 19X7 has been paid.

Exhibit 10.13	**P and S Companies: Financial Statements at December 31, 19X7, to Be Used in P10.3**

STATEMENTS OF INCOME AND RETAINED EARNINGS
FOR THE YEAR ENDED DECEMBER 31, 19X7

	P Company	S Company
Sales	$ 900,400	$610,000
Income from S	37,500	—
Interest Revenue	4,800	—
Total Revenue	$ 942,700	$610,000
Cost of Goods Sold:		
Beginning Inventory	$100,000	$ 80,000
Purchases	500,000	400,000
Ending Inventory	(120,000)	(70,000)
	$ 480,000	$410,000
Operating Expenses	180,000	140,000
Interest Expense	—	10,000
Total Expenses	$ 660,000	$560,000
Net Income	$ 282,700	$ 50,000
Beginning Retained Earnings	300,000	130,000
Dividends	(80,000)	(60,000)
Ending Retained Earnings	$ 502,700	$120,000

BALANCE SHEETS AT DECEMBER 31, 19X7

ASSETS	P Company	S Company
Cash and Receivables	$ 313,100	$210,000
Inventory	120,000	70,000
Investment in S	138,600	—
Investment in Bonds	50,800	—
Land	60,000	40,000
Buildings and Equipment	450,000	250,000
Accumulated Depreciation	(90,000)	(50,000)
Total Assets	$1,042,500	$520,000

LIABILITIES AND STOCKHOLDERS' EQUITY		
Current Liabilities	$ 239,800	$190,000
Other Liabilities	200,000	160,000
Capital Stock	100,000	50,000
Retained Earnings	502,700	120,000
Total Liabilities and Stockholders' Equity	$1,042,500	$520,000

5. Financial statements for P and S as of December 31, 19X7, appear in Exhibit 10.13.

Required: Prepare a consolidated financial statement working paper for P Company and S Company as of December 31, 19X7.

P10.4 Consolidated Financial Statement Working Paper—Intercompany Transactions The trial balances of Preston Corporation and Stanton Corporation as of March 31, 19X6, the close of their current fiscal year, appear in Exhibit 10.14. Assume that each company's individual books are correct and reflect all necessary adjustments unless it is otherwise apparent.

Additional information:

1. Preston acquired 80 percent of the outstanding common stock of Stanton on April 1, 19X4, for a cash price of $240,000. At that time, it was estimated that a certain parcel of land was undervalued by $56,000. Stanton's Capital Stock and Retained Earnings accounts on the trial balance are unchanged since April 1, 19X4. The investment in Stanton is carried at equity.

2. Stanton declared and paid dividends of $5,000 in January 19X6. During the year ended March 31, 19X5, Stanton had zero profit and paid no dividends.

3. Intercompany sales of merchandise during the year were as follows. Preston sold Stanton merchandise at a price of $96,000, while Stanton sold Preston merchandise at a price of $65,000 (of which $10,000 had not yet been paid at March 31, 19X6). At the beginning and end of the current year, Preston's inventories of intercompany merchandise (bought from Stanton) were $26,000 and $13,000, respectively. Stanton's inventories (bought from Preston) were $12,000 and $18,000.

xhibit 10.14 **Preston Corporation and Stanton Corporation: Trial Balances at March 31, 19X6, to Be Used in P10.4**

Account	Preston	Stanton
Cash	$ 75,000	$ 80,000
Accounts Receivable	120,000	65,000
Inventories	70,000	90,000
Investment in Stanton	274,040	—
Advance to Stanton	25,000	—
Plant Assets	500,000	315,000
Accumulated Depreciation	(180,000)	(55,000)
Current Liabilities	(90,000)	(30,000)
Advance from Preston	—	(25,000)
Bonds Payable	(400,000)	(200,000)
Capital Stock	(250,000)	(150,000)
Retained Earnings	(106,520)	(50,000)
Sales	(720,000)	(377,000)
Purchases	610,000	275,000
Operating Expenses	55,000	42,000
Other Revenue	(20,000)	(15,000)
Other Expense	35,000	30,000
Dividends	20,000	5,000
Income from Stanton	(17,520)	—
	$ 0	$ 0
Ending Inventory	$ 80,000	$ 75,000

Preston's selling price reflects a 20 percent markup over cost, while Stanton's sales reflect a 30 percent markup over cost.

4. On August 8, 19X4, Preston sold land having a book value of $30,000 to Stanton at a price of $50,000.

5. On October 1, 19X5, Stanton sold equipment to Preston for $60,000. The equipment had a net book value of $48,000 and a remaining life of 6 years on that date. The gain was recorded in Other Revenue.

6. On April 1, 19X5, Preston acquired 25 percent of Stanton's outstanding bonds for $48,000, debiting this amount to its Investment in Subsidiary account. The total bond issue had a par value of $200,000 and was issued by Stanton 10 years prior to April 1, 19X5. The bonds pay 7 percent interest annually on March 31 and mature 20 years from the issue date. Preston used the straight-line method to amortize the discount during the current year.

Required: Prepare a consolidated financial statement working paper for Preston and Stanton for the year ended March 31, 19X6. Formal eliminating entries and financial statements are not required, but each working paper entry should be numbered and a brief explanation provided. Supporting computations should be in good form. Ignore income taxes and assume that all depreciation and amortization (40 years for goodwill) is allocated on the straight-line basis.

P10.5 Consolidated Financial Statement Working Paper—Incomplete Equity Method Following are the trial balances of Pierce Corporation and Stanley Corporation as of March 31, 19X6, the close of the fiscal year. Assume that each company's individual books are correct and include all necessary adjustments unless it is otherwise apparent. Assume that any depreciation and amortization are allocated on a straight-line basis.

Account	Pierce	Stanley
Cash	$ 50,000	$ 30,000
Accounts Receivable	120,000	15,000
Interest and Dividends Receivable.	24,000	—
Inventories	95,000	40,000
Investment in Stanley	309,600	—
Investment in Bonds.	94,000	—
Plant Assets.	406,000	488,000
Accumulated Depreciation.	(240,000)	(78,000)
Current Liabilities	(40,000)	(18,000)
Interest and Dividends Payable	—	(32,000)
Bonds Payable	—	(200,000)
Capital Stock	(550,000)	(150,000)
Retained Earnings.	(133,400)	(80,000)
Sales	(750,000)	(350,000)
Purchases.	585,000	275,000
Operating Expenses.	104,000	82,000
Other Revenue	(70,000)	(42,000)
Dividends	30,000	20,000
Income from Stanley	(34,200)	—
	$ 0	$ 0
Ending Inventory	$ 80,000	$ 45,000

Additional information:

1. Pierce acquired 90 percent of Stanley's common stock on April 1, 19X3, for a cash price of $270,000. At that time, Stanley's stockholders' equity accounts were:

Capital Stock. $150,000
Retained Earnings   50,000

It was further estimated that certain equipment having a 10-year remaining life was undervalued by $20,000 and that land was undervalued by $80,000 on Stanley's books.

2. An analysis of Pierce's Investment in Subsidiary account shows the following:

4/1/X3	Original Investment	$270,000
3/31/X4	Share of Stanley's $10,000 Income, Less Adjustment	
	for Depreciation on Revaluation of Equipment	7,200
3/31/X5	Share of Stanley's $20,000 Income, Less Adjustment	
	for Depreciation on Revaluation of Equipment	16,200
3/31/X6	Share of Stanley's $40,000 Income, Less Adjustment	
	for Depreciation on Revaluation of Equipment	34,200
3/31/X6	Share of $20,000 Dividend Declared by Stanley on	
	3/31.	(18,000)
	Balance	$309,600

3. Pierce sold merchandise to Stanley during the year in the amount of $125,000. This price reflects a 25 percent markup over cost. Stanley had $25,000 of intercompany merchandise in its inventory at both the beginning and end of the year.

4. Pierce charges Stanley $3,000 per month for administrative services. Pierce credits the Other Revenue account, and Stanley charges Operating Expenses. Two months' charges are unpaid at year-end.

5. On April 1, 19X5, Stanley sold Pierce a building for $190,000. The building originally cost $200,000 and had a net book value of $168,000 when it was sold. On April 1, 19X5, the building had a remaining useful life of 11 years.

6. On April 2, 19X5, Pierce acquired one-half of Stanley's outstanding 20-year bonds at a price of $94,000. The bonds had been issued 14 years before at their par value. They pay 6 percent interest annually on April 1; current year discount amortization has not been recorded.

Required: Prepare a consolidated financial statement working paper for Pierce and Stanley for the year ended March 31, 19X6. Formal eliminating entries and financial statements are not required, but each working paper entry should be numbered and a brief explanation provided. Supporting computations should be in good form.

P10.6 Consolidated Financial Statement Working Paper—Pooling and Intercompany Sales-Type Lease Pinson Corporation merged with Stanky Cor-

Exhibit 10.15	**Pinson Corporation and Stanky Corporation: Financial Statements at December 31, 19X1, to Be Used in P10.6**

INCOME STATEMENTS
FOR THE YEAR ENDED DECEMBER 31, 19X1

	Pinson	Stanky
Sales	$5,000,000	$1,200,000
Income from Stanky	158,500	—
Interest Revenue	—	12,000
Gain on Sale of Equipment	—	20,000
Total Revenue	$5,158,500	$1,232,000
Cost of Goods Sold:		
Beginning Inventory	$ 320,000	$ 175,000
Purchases	3,400,000	800,000
Ending Inventory	(300,000)	(190,000)
	$3,420,000	$ 785,000
Interest Expense	12,000	—
Depreciation Expense	25,000	—
Other Expenses	1,023,000	247,000
Total Expenses	$4,480,000	$1,032,000
Net Income	$ 678,500	$ 200,000

RETAINED EARNINGS STATEMENTS
FOR THE YEAR ENDED DECEMBER 31, 19X1

	Pinson	Stanky
Beginning Retained Earnings	$1,750,000	$ 400,000
Net Income	678,500	200,000
Dividends	(300,000)	(80,000)
Ending Retained Earnings	$2,128,500	$ 520,000

BALANCE SHEETS AT DECEMBER 31, 19X1

ASSETS	Pinson	Stanky
Inventory	$ 300,000	$ 190,000
Lease Receivable	—	98,769
Leasehold, Net	75,000	—
Investment in Stanky	536,500	—
Other Assets	4,088,500	711,231
Total Assets	$5,000,000	$1,000,000

LIABILITIES AND STOCKHOLDERS' EQUITY		
Capitalized Lease Obligation	$ 79,077	$ —
Unearned Interest Revenue	—	19,692
Other Liabilities	2,292,423	360,308
Capital Stock	500,000	100,000
Retained Earnings	2,128,500	520,000
Total Liabilities and Stockholders' Equity	$5,000,000	$1,000,000

poration, a 90-percent-owned subsidiary, several years ago in a pooling of interests. On January 1, 19X1, Stanky leased equipment with a 4-year life to Pinson for a noncancelable term of 4 years. The annual payments of $32,923, discounted at Stanky's borrowing rate of 12 percent, have a present value of $100,000. Payments are due at the end of each year. Stanky had constructed the equipment at a cost of $80,000 and recognized a gain of $20,000 at inception of the lease. Both companies use straight-line depreciation. In addition, Stanky's ending inventory included $8,000 of unconfirmed intercompany profit on $120,000 of goods purchased from Pinson. Condensed financial statements for the two companies at December 31, 19X1, are given in Exhibit 10.15.

Required:

1. Prepare a schedule showing how the equity method accrual was calculated.
2. Prepare a consolidated financial statement working paper as of December 31, 19X1.

P10.7 Reconstructing Eliminations—Intercompany Bondholding and Leases
Selected data from the separate financial statements of two affiliated companies and the consolidated statements are given below. Both companies use straight-line amortization and depreciation over 5 years and the same discount rate, 12 percent.

	P Company	S Company (80%)	Consolidated
Investment in 10% Bonds (Par) . .	$ 500,000	—	—
Discount on Investment in Bonds. .	(40,000)	—	—
Bonds Payable, 10% (Par).	—	$(800,000)	$(300,000)
Premium on Bonds Payable	—	(80,000)	30,000
Gain on Retirement of Consolidated			
Debt	—	—	(112,500)
Interest Expense	—	60,000	22,500
Lease Receivable	—	138,705	—
Capitalized Lease Obligation	(105,324)	—	—
Interest Expense	15,000	—	—
Gain on Sale of Asset	—	(22,000)	—
Depreciation Expense	25,000	—	20,600

Required: Reconstruct the working paper eliminations made in consolidation in connection with the intercompany bondholding and the intercompany sales-type lease.

P10.8 Intercompany Leasing Goldstein, Inc., acquired 80 percent of Wharton Corporation's common stock several years ago and uses the equity method. On January 2, 19X4, the two companies engaged in the following leasing transactions:

Lease No.	Type of Lease	Lessor	Annual Payment	Terms of Lease	Leased Property Type	Book Value to Lessor
1	Operating	Wharton	$25,000	5 years	Office space	—
2	Direct financing	Goldstein	71,475	4 years	Equipment	$200,000
3	Sales-type	Wharton	71,475	4 years	Land	150,000
4	Sales-type	Goldstein	71,475	4 years	Equipment	120,000

Both companies use an incremental borrowing rate of 16 percent in their lease transactions. Equipment is depreciated over the lease term by the straight-line method (no salvage value). Payments are made at the end of each year.

Required:

1. Prepare the eliminating entries relative to the intercompany lease transactions in consolidation as of December 31, 19X4.
2. Repeat No. 1 in consolidation as of December 31, 19X5.
3. How do these transactions affect the equity method accrual and the minority interest in net income in 19X4 and 19X5?

P10.9 Consolidated Financial Statement Working Paper—Preferred Stock: Equity Method Parent, Inc., purchased for $151,000 cash 100 percent of the common stock and 20 percent of the 5 percent noncumulative, nonparticipating preferred stock of Subsidiary Manufacturing Corporation on June 30, 19X1. At that date, Subsidiary's stockholders' equity was as follows: 5,000 shares of $10 par value preferred stock, $50,000; 100,000 shares of $1 par value common stock, $100,000; and retained earnings, $41,000. The total purchase price was recorded as Investment in Subsidiary, which is being carried at equity. The fair values of the assets, liabilities, and preferred stock did not differ materially from their book values. At December 31, 19X1, Parent and Subsidiary prepared consolidated financial statements.

Transactions between Parent and Subsidiary during the year ended December 31, 19X2, follow:

1. On January 3, 19X2, Parent sold land with an $11,000 book value to Subsidiary for $15,000. Subsidiary made a $3,000 down payment and signed an 8 percent mortgage note payable in 12 equal quarterly payments of $1,135, including interest, beginning March 31, 19X2.
2. Subsidiary produced equipment for Parent under two separate contracts. The first contract, which was for office equipment, was begun and completed during the year at a cost to Subsidiary of $17,500. Parent paid $22,000 cash for the equipment on April 17, 19X2. The second contract was begun on February 15, 19X2, but will not be completed until May 19X3. Subsidiary has incurred $45,000 costs as of December 31, 19X2, and anticipates an additional $30,000 cost to complete the $95,000 contract. Subsidiary accounts for all contracts under the percentage-of-completion method of accounting. Parent has

made no entry on its books for this uncompleted contract as of December 31, 19X2.

3. On December 1, 19X2, Subsidiary declared a 5 percent cash dividend on its preferred stock, payable on January 15, 19X3, to stockholders of record as of December 14, 19X2.

4. Parent sells merchandise to Subsidiary at an average markup of 12 percent of cost. During the year, Parent charged Subsidiary $238,000 for merchandise purchased, of which Subsidiary paid $211,000. Subsidiary has $11,200 of this merchandise on hand at December 31, 19X2.

Parent depreciates all its equipment over a 10-year estimated economic life with no salvage value. Parent takes a half-year's depreciation in year of purchase.

Both companies have made all of the adjusting entries required for separate financial statements unless an obvious discrepancy exists. Their separate financial statements for the year ended December 31, 19X2, appear in Exhibit 10.16.

Required:

1. Prepare a schedule to compute the equity method accrual.

2. Prepare a consolidated financial statement working paper for Parent and Subsidiary for the year ended December 31, 19X2. Formal statements and journal entries are not required. Round all computations to the nearest dollar. *(AICPA adapted)*

P10.10 Consolidated Financial Statement Working Paper—Intercompany Bonds and Preferred Stock The trial balances of Pawn Corporation and its 80-percent-owned subsidiary, the Standish Company, at December 31, 19X3, are given in Exhibit 10.17. Pawn acquired these common shares and 20 percent of Standish's outstanding cumulative preferred shares on January 1, 19X1, for $1,990,400 and $200,000, respectively. On January 1, 19X1, Pawn's common shareholders' equity accounts amounted to $2,000,000; the preferred stock was $600,000. No dividends have been declared on the preferred stock since 19X0. Also on January 1, 19X1, Pawn purchased one half of Standish's $4,000,000 par value outstanding bonds for $1,800,000. The bonds mature 10 years after the date they were acquired; straight-line amortization has been used by both companies. No other intercompany transactions occurred between the two companies during 19X3. Any purchase premium attributable to the investment in common is goodwill amortized over 40 years.

Required: Prepare a consolidated financial statement working paper for Pawn and Standish for the year ended December 31, 19X3.

P10.11 Computing Consolidated Retained Earnings—Intercompany Transactions and Preferred Stock P Company owns 80 percent of S Company's

Exhibit 10.16 **Parent, Inc., and Subsidiary Manufacturing Corporation: Financial Statements at December 31, 19X2, to Be Used in P10.9**

STATEMENTS OF INCOME AND RETAINED EARNINGS
FOR THE YEAR ENDED DECEMBER 31, 19X2

	Parent	Subsidiary
Sales	$1,800,000	$ —
Earned Revenues on Contracts	—	1,289,000
Interest Revenue	20,000	—
Gain on Sale of Land	4,000	—
Income from Subsidiary	21,525	—
Total Revenue	$1,845,525	$1,289,000
Cost of Sales	$1,155,000	—
Cost of Earned Revenue on Contracts	—	$ 852,000
Selling, General, and Administrative Expenses	497,000	360,000
Interest Expense	49,000	32,000
Total Expenses	$1,701,000	$1,244,000
Net Income	$ 144,525	$ 45,000
Beginning Retained Earnings	147,811	49,500
Dividends	—	(2,500)
Ending Retained Earnings	$ 292,336	$ 92,000

BALANCE SHEETS AT DECEMBER 31, 19X2

ASSETS	Parent	Subsidiary
Cash	$ 43,000	$ 31,211
Accounts Receivable	119,000	53,000
Costs and Estimated Earnings in Excess of Billings on Uncompleted Contracts	—	87,100
Dividends Receivable	500	—
Mortgage Receivable	8,311	—
Unsecured Notes Receivable	18,000	—
Inventories	217,000	117,500
Land	34,000	42,000
Plant and Equipment, Net	717,000	408,000
Investment in Subsidiary Corporation	180,525	—
Total Assets	$1,337,336	$ 738,811

LIABILITIES AND STOCKHOLDERS' EQUITY		
Accounts Payable	$ 203,000	$ 97,000
Dividends Payable	—	2,500
Mortgages Payable	592,000	397,311
Preferred Stock	—	50,000
Common Stock	250,000	100,000
Retained Earnings	292,336	92,000
Total Liabilities and Stockholders' Equity	$1,337,336	$ 738,811

| Exhibit 10.17 | **Pawn Corporation and Standish Company: Financial Statements at December 31, 19X3, to Be Used in P10.10** |

STATEMENTS OF INCOME AND RETAINED EARNINGS
FOR THE YEAR ENDED DECEMBER 31, 19X3

	Pawn	Standish
Sales	$11,000,000	$ 6,005,000
Income from Standish	316,000	—
Interest Revenue	180,000	—
Total Revenue	$11,496,000	$ 6,005,000
Cost of Goods Sold:		
Beginning Inventory	$ 3,250,000	$ 2,400,000
Purchases	5,800,000	4,200,000
Ending Inventory	(3,100,000)	(2,600,000)
	$ 5,950,000	$ 4,000,000
Operating Expenses	2,000,000	1,200,000
Interest Expense	—	305,000
Total Expenses	$ 7,950,000	$ 5,505,000
Net Income	$ 3,546,000	$ 500,000
Beginning Retained Earnings	10,000,000	3,000,000
Dividends	(400,000)	—
Ending Retained Earnings	$13,146,000	$ 3,500,000

BALANCE SHEETS AT DECEMBER 31, 19X3

ASSETS	Pawn	Standish
Cash and Receivables	$ 2,601,600	$ 1,805,000
Inventory	3,100,000	2,600,000
Investment in Standish—Common (Equity)	3,598,400	—
Investment in Standish—Preferred (Cost)	200,000	—
Investment in Bonds	1,860,000	—
Plant Assets, Net	7,300,000	5,300,000
Total Assets	$18,660,000	$ 9,705,000
LIABILITIES AND STOCKHOLDERS' EQUITY		
Current Liabilities	$ 3,514,000	$ 1,000,000
Bonds Payable, 8%, Annual Coupons	—	4,105,000
Preferred Stock, 10%, Par Value $100, Call Price $102	—	600,000
Capital Stock	2,000,000	500,000
Retained Earnings	13,146,000	3,500,000
Total Liabilities and Stockholders' Equity	$18,660,000	$ 9,705,000

common stock and 10 percent of its preferred stock. Both investments were acquired on January 1, 19X4, for $5,000,000 and $200,000, respectively. Because certain accounting records on the computer have been ''lost,'' you must reconstruct the correct balance in consolidated retained earnings as of December 31, 19X5.

Additional information:

1. On January 1, 19X4, S's common shareholders' equity amounted to $5,000,000, and its assets and liabilities were recorded at amounts which approximated their fair values.
2. S's preferred stock consists of 20,000 shares of $100 par value 10 percent cumulative preferred stock. The stock has a call price of $105. Dividends have always been declared on a timely basis except for the 19X4 and 19X5 dividends which were omitted.
3. P's policy is to amortize intangibles over 40 years.
4. On January 1, 19X5, P sold a machine to S for $200,000. The machine had a remaining life of 5 years and a net book value of $120,000 on that date.
5. P's January 1, 19X5, and December 31, 19X5, inventories include intercompany profits of $25,000 and $15,000, respectively, on goods purchased from S.
6. On December 31, 19X5, P acquired all of S's outstanding 10 percent bonds for $860,000. The bonds have par value of $800,000, mature in 10 years, and were recorded by S at $780,000. Both companies amortize their premiums and discounts by the straight-line method.
7. During 19X4–19X5, P reported income from its own operations of $2,000,000 (excluding intercompany dividends) and declared dividends of $900,000.
8. During 19X4–19X5, S reported income from its own operations of $800,000. No dividends were declared during 19X4–19X5.
9. On January 1, 19X4, the retained earnings of P and S were $10,000,000 and $3,000,000, respectively.

Required: Compute consolidated retained earnings at December 31, 19X5. Show all computations.

P10.12 Consolidated Stockholders' Equity Calculations—Preferred Stock
Nickles, Inc., a manufacturer of restaurant and kitchen equipment, was incorporated 30 years ago. Its stock is closely held. You have been assigned to analyze certain transactions affecting a portion of the income statement and the stockholders' equity section of Nickles and its subsidiaries. In this assignment, income taxes and earnings per share calculations are to be ignored.

The stockholders' equity section of the balance sheet at September 30, 19X1, and the income statement for the year then ended follow. At that time, Nickles held no investments in other corporations.

STOCKHOLDERS' EQUITY

$1 Cumulative Preferred Stock, Par Value $15 per Share; Shares Authorized 500,000; Issued and Outstanding 4,000	$ 60,000
Common Stock, $10 Par Value per Share; Shares Authorized 1,000,000; Issued and Outstanding 110,000	1,100,000
Retained Earnings	622,000
Total Stockholders' Equity	$1,782,000

INCOME STATEMENT

Sales $1,050,000
Cost of Goods Sold   725,000
Gross Operating Income . . . . $ 325,000
Selling, General, and Administrative Expenses   135,000
Net Income . . . . $ 190,000

Additional information:

1. On May 1, 19X1, an empty warehouse with a book and fair market value of $145,000 was completely destroyed by fire. Though the building was insured, the insurance company refused to pay for the loss. Nickles immediately instigated litigation, and management was confident of winning; hence, no provision was made for a possible loss in fiscal 19X1. The trial was completed October 5, 19X2, finding for the insurance company.

2. The 4,000 shares of preferred stock were issued for cash at incorporation, and no other preferred shares have been issued prior to fiscal 19X2. No dividends have been declared on the common stock prior to fiscal 19X2.

3. Nickles's capital stock transactions during fiscal 19X2 were:

    a. Preferred stock: On September 30, 19X2, 8,000 shares were issued to the stockholders of Wixon, Inc., to acquire 100 percent of the outstanding common stock of the corporation, whose fiscal year ends September 30. The fair value of Wixon at acquisition was $140,000.

    b. Common stock:
    January 17, 19X2—Sold 4,500 shares for cash to Horace Edwards at $25 per share.
    May 5, 19X2—Sold 5,500 shares for cash to James Morgan at $25 per share.
    September 14, 19X2—Purchased dissident stockholder Edwards's 4,500 shares at $27 per share. The shares are to be held as treasury shares and accounted for at cost. (Edwards violently opposed Nickles's expansion program. It was necessary to pay a $2 premium to eliminate his interest.)
    September 28, 19X2—Contracted with Charles Trenton for the sale of 10,000 previously unissued shares at $25 per share to be issued when purchase price is fully paid. At September 30, only $195,000 had been paid. Trenton agreed to pay the balance on or before November 3, 19X2.
    September 30, 19X2—Issued 51,000 previously unissued shares to the stockholders of Acme, Inc., in exchange for 100 percent of the outstanding common stock of the corporation, whose fiscal year ends September 30.

4. Dividends declared by Nickles during fiscal 19X2 were:

    a. Preferred stock—A cash dividend of $1 per share was declared on May 15, 19X2, for shares of record on May 27, 19X2, and paid on June 12, 19X2. There were no dividends in arrears on preferred stock at September 30, 19X2.

b. Common stock—A cash dividend of $1.25 per share and a 2 percent common stock dividend were declared on September 15, 19X2, for shares of record on September 27, 19X2, payable October 10, 19X2.

5. Data on Acme and Wixon:

a. Both corporations are authorized to issue only no-par-value common stock. Data applicable at September 30, 19X0 and 19X2, (no change) follow:

	Acme	Wixon
Shares Authorized.	50,000	25,000
Shares Issued and Outstanding	34,000	2,500
Dollar Balance in the Common Stock Account.	$631,000	$105,000

b. An analysis of retained earnings (deficit) for the 2 years ended September 30, 19X2, follows:

	Acme	Wixon
Balance Sept. 30, 19X0	$(147,000)	$ 32,000
Net Income (Loss) for the Year Ended:		
Sept. 30, 19X1[a]	112,000	(15,000)
Sept. 30, 19X2	125,000	(6,000)
Balance Sept. 30, 19X2	$ 90,000	$ 11,000

[a]Also net operating income (loss).

c. Prior to September 30, 19X2, Acme and Wixon have never had any intercompany transactions with Nickles or with each other.

6. Nickles's unconsolidated net income (also net operating income) was $215,000 for the year ended September 30, 19X2.

7. You have previously determined that the acquisitions of Acme and Wixon must be accounted for as a pooling of interests and a purchase, respectively.

Required:

1. Prepare a comparative consolidated statement of income beginning with net operating income and arriving at net income for the years ended September 30, 19X2 and 19X1. This statement should be supported by a schedule calculating consolidated net operating income.

2. Assuming consolidated net income of $405,000 and $240,000 for the years ended September 30, 19X2 and 19X1, respectively, prepare a comparative stockholders' equity section of the consolidated balance sheet for the years ended September 30, 19X2 and 19X1. This statement should be supported by the following schedules presented in the order given:

a. Changes in preferred stock account.
b. Changes in common stock account.
c. Calculation of number of shares to be issued for common stock dividend.
d. Calculation of paid-in capital in excess of par.
e. Changes in retained earnings. *(AICPA adapted)*

Chapter 11 Consolidated Financial Statements: Special Topics

In this chapter, we examine some additional topics in consolidated financial statements which may be encountered in practice. The two principal areas developed are (1) changes in the parent's ownership interest in the subsidiary and (2) complex ownership relationships among the affiliated companies. Although other consolidation issues—such as intercompany transactions and preferred stock—may be present in an actual situation, for the most part we assume such complications away in this chapter.

Changes in the Parent's Ownership Interest

To this point, our discussions and examples of business combinations and consolidated financial statements involved one-time acquisitions of controlling interest. This was done in order to avoid additional complexities when control is achieved after a series of purchases or when the parent's ownership interest changes. In practice, of course, the world is not so neatly ordered. Our objective in this section is to deal with some of these problems. Some theoretical issues as well as technical issues will arise. We begin with a discussion of consolidation issues when control is achieved after a series of purchases.

Control Achieved in a Series of Purchases

When an acquiring company achieves a controlling interest in a subsidiary after two or more acquisitions of stock, the mechanics of allocating purchase premiums and discounts become more complex. The original guidance provided in *ARB 51* is presented below:

> If two or more purchases are made over a period of time, the earned surplus of the subsidiary at acquisition should generally be determined on a step-by-step basis; *however, if small purchases are made over a period time and then a purchase is*

made which results in control, the date of the latest purchase, as a matter of convenience, may be considered the date of acquisition.[1] (Emphasis added.)

Times have changed since *ARB 51* was published in 1959. The guidance quoted above was expressive of a concern over eliminating the correct amount of the subsidiary's retained earnings in consolidation. This is not a burning issue today. Rather, concern has turned to determination of the appropriate time(s) for estimating the fair values of the subsidiary's assets and liabilities. When *ARB 51* was published, most unconsolidated intercorporate investments were carried at *cost.* Today, substantial intercorporate investments are carried at *equity,* reflecting the one-line consolidation concept of *APBO 18.* Under *APBO 18,* once an investor company's position in the investee's voting stock passes 20 percent (or less, if substantial influence over the investee's affairs can be demonstrated), the equity method is to be used, estimates of fair values made, and goodwill established and amortized. It seems that if small purchases are made over a period of time, the acquiring company must enter the equity method range and fair values will be established before control is actually achieved. The issue was specifically addressed in an unofficial 1973 AICPA accounting interpretation of *APBO 17:*

> When a company in a series of purchases on a step-by-step basis acquires either a subsidiary which is consolidated or an investment which is accounted for under the equity method, the company should identify the cost of each investment, the fair value of the underlying assets acquired and the goodwill for each step purchase.[2]

For these reasons, we believe that the old "convenience" provision of *ARB 51* governing the date of acquisition when control is achieved after a series of small purchases is no longer relevant. Note that a step acquisition can occur only in a purchase combination. In a pooling, control must be achieved in a single "acquisition" of at least 90 percent of the stock. If any further acquisitions are made to buy out the minority interest, however, these subsequent acquisitions are treated as purchases. We now illustrate the mechanics of a step acquisition in which the acquiring company uses the equity method.

To illustrate, consider the following data. The Puck Company acquires an 80 percent interest in the Stick Company after three purchases spanning two years. Stick Company has 100,000 outstanding shares. Details concerning the acquisitions follow:

---

[1]Committee on Accounting Procedure, *Accounting Research Bulletin No. 51,* "Consolidated Financial Statements" (New York: AICPA, 1959), par. 10; CT § C51.111.

[2]American Institute of Certified Public Accountants, *Unofficial Interpretation No. 2 of APB Opinion No. 17,* "Goodwill in a Step Acquisition" (New York: AICPA, 1973); CT § I60.504.

DATA FOR THREE BLOCKS OF STOCK PURCHASED IN A STEP ACQUISITION

Acquisition Date	Percent Acquired	Cost of Shares	Net Assets of Stick		Stick Net Income	
			Fair Value	Book Value	Year	Amount
5/1/X1	25%	$180,000	$500,000	$400,000	19X1	$ 60,000
4/1/X2	20	190,000	600,000	470,000	19X2	120,000
10/1/X2	35	400,000	700,000	530,000		

Note: No dividends were paid by Stick during 19X1 and 19X2; Stick's income is earned evenly throughout the year.

In analyzing the purchase premium paid at each step, we assume that any which is allocated to Stick's net assets will be depreciated on the straight-line basis over 10 years. Any remaining purchase premium is evidence of goodwill, which is to be amortized over 40 years. Determination and allocation of the purchase premium at each step are summarized in the following schedule:

DETERMINATION AND ALLOCATION OF THE PURCHASE PREMIUMS IN A STEP ACQUISITION

Acquisition Date	(1) Cost of Shares	(2) Book Value of Net Assets Acquired	(3) [(1) − (2)] Purchase Premium	Net Assets of Stick		(6) [(4) − (5)] (FV − BV)	(7) Puck's Interest	(8) [(3) − (7)] Goodwill
				(4) Fair Value	(5) Book Value			
5/1/X1	$180,000	$100,000 (25%)	$ 80,000	$500,000	$400,000	$100,000	$ 25,000 (25%)	$ 55,000
4/1/X2	190,000	94,000 (20%)	96,000	600,000	470,000	130,000	26,000 (20%)	70,000
10/1/X2	400,000	185,500 (35%)	214,500	700,000	530,000	170,000	59,500 (35%)	155,000
	$770,000	$379,500	$390,500				$110,500	$280,000

Our next concern involves computing the equity method accrual made by Puck in each year. This is given in Exhibit 11.1. Then we calculate the unamortized purchase premium to be included in consolidated assets on the first consolidated balance sheet prepared at December 31, 19X2.

To keep track of the unamortized purchase premium which will be included in consolidated assets, it is helpful to prepare a schedule which separates the portions attributable to identifiable assets and to goodwill. Such a schedule giving information for the Puck and Stick case is summarized next:

SCHEDULE OF UNAMORTIZED PURCHASE PREMIUM

Acquisition Date	Identifiable Assets				Goodwill			
	5/1/X1	4/1/X2	10/1/X2	Total	5/1/X1	4/1/X2	10/1/X2	Total
Acquired: 19X1	$25,000	—	—	$ 25,000	$55,000	—	—	$ 55,000
Amort.: 19X1	(1,650)	—	—	(1,650)	(921)	—	—	(921)
Bal., 12/31/X1	$23,350	—	—	$ 23,350	$54,079	—	—	$ 54,079
Acquired: 19X2	—	$26,000	$59,500	85,500	—	$70,000	$155,000	225,000
	$23,350	$26,000	$59,500	$108,850	$54,079	$70,000	$155,000	$279,079
Amort.: 19X2	(2,500)	(1,950)	(1,488)	(5,938)	(1,375)	(1,313)	(969)	(3,657)
Bal., 12/31/X2	$20,850	$24,050	$58,012	$102,912	$52,704	$68,687	$154,031	$275,422

This schedule will be updated annually.

| Exhibit 11.1 | **Puck and Stick Companies: Computation of Equity Method Accruals for the Years Ended December 31, 19X1 and 19X2** |

19X1

Puck's Share of Stick's Net Income [.25 × $60,000 × ($8/12$)]	$10,000
Less Amortization of Purchase Premium:	
Additional Depreciation ($25,000/10) × ($8/12$)	$ 1,650
Amortization of Goodwill ($55,000/40) × ($8/12$).	921
Total Purchase Premium Amortization	$ 2,571
Net Equity Method Accrual for 19X1.	$ 7,429

19X2

Puck's Share of Stick's Net Income:	
May 1, 19X1, Acquisition (.25 × $120,000)	$30,000
Apr. 1, 19X2, Acquisition [.20 × $120,000 × ($9/12$)]	18,000
Oct. 1, 19X2, Acquisition [.35 × $120,000 × ($3/12$)]	10,500
Total Share of Stick's 19X2 Net Income	$58,500
Less Amortization of Purchase Premium:	
Additional Depreciation:	
May 1, 19X1, Acquisition ($25,000/10)	$ 2,500
Apr. 1, 19X2, Acquisition [($26,000/10) × ($9/12$)].	1,950
Oct. 1, 19X2, Acquisition [($59,500/10) × ($3/12$)].	1,488
Amortization of Goodwill:	
May 1, 19X1, Acquisition ($55,000/40)	1,375
Apr. 1, 19X2, Acquisition [($70,000/40) × ($9/12$)].	1,313
Oct. 1, 19X2, Acquisition [($155,000/40) × ($3/12$)]	969
Total Purchase Premium Amortization	$ 9,595
Net Equity Method Accrual for 19X2.	$48,905

Whenever the parent's investment in a particular subsidiary reflects two or more blocks of stock acquired at different times, a record is needed to keep their book values separate. If some of the shares are ultimately sold, the correct book value is needed to determine gain or loss. A schedule like the following enables the accountant to identify the book values of the various blocks of stock. It too will be updated annually.

SCHEDULE OF CARRYING VALUES OF STOCK PURCHASES
IN A STEP ACQUISITION

Acquisition Date	Block A (25%) 5/1/X1	Block B (20%) 4/1/X2	Block C (35%) 10/1/X2	Total
Cost of Acquisition .	$180,000	$190,000	$400,000	$770,000
Equity Accrual: 19X1	7,429	—	—	7,429
Dividends: 19X1. . .	—	—	—	—
	$187,429	$190,000	$400,000	$777,429
Equity Accrual: 19X2	26,125	14,737	8,043	48,905
Dividends: 19X2. . .	—	—	—	—
Balance: Dec. 31,				
19X2	$213,554	$204,737	$408,043	$826,334

To illustrate consolidation in the Puck and Stick step-acquisition case, we prepare the eliminating entries made in consolidation at the end of 19X2, after the full 80 percent interest has been acquired.

CONSOLIDATED FINANCIAL STATEMENT WORKING PAPER

Income from Stick. 48,905
   Investment in Stick   48,905
To reverse the current year's equity method accrual.

After this entry is made, the investment account has a balance of $777,429 ($= \$826,334 - \$48,905$), which equals the total cost of the three blocks of stock, $770,000, plus the 19X1 equity accrual, $7,429. Since two of these three blocks were purchased *during* the year, however, reversal of the equity method accrual does not adjust the investment account to its beginning-of-year balance. The normal clean elimination against Stick's beginning stockholders' equity, after reclassification of the unamortized purchase premium, is not yet possible. This is because total investment cost reflected in the investment account includes some **preacquisition earnings,** Puck's shares of Stick's net income attributable to the 19X2 intrayear acquisitions and earned *prior* to these acquisitions. (If needed, refer to the Business Combinations during an Accounting Period section in Chapter 8 to review the preacquisition earnings concept).

In developing the investment elimination as of the beginning of the year, therefore, two matters must be considered. *First,* Stick's stockholders' equity on January 1, 19X2, is $440,000, consisting of $400,000 on May 1, 19X1 (when Block A was acquired) plus Stick's net income for the next 8 months of 19X1, $40,000 ($= \frac{8}{12} \times \$60,000$). The investment account includes 80 percent of this $440,000. *Second,* the investment account also includes the shares of Stick's 19X2 net income attributable to the 19X2 intrayear acquisitions and earned prior to these acquisitions. These shares amount to $37,500, consisting of $6,000 [$= (.20 \times \frac{3}{12} \times \$120,000)$] for Block B from January to March plus $31,500 [$= (.35 \times \frac{9}{12} \times \$120,000)$] for Block C from January to September. Thus a clean elimination will include Preacquisition Earnings of $37,500, as shown next. If all acquisitions had occurred at the beginning of an accounting period, preacquisition earnings (and dividends) would not need to be considered.

CONSOLIDATED FINANCIAL STATEMENT WORKING PAPER

Preacquisition Earnings 37,500
Identifiable Assets. 108,850
Goodwill. 279,079
Stockholders' Equity—Stick. 440,000
   Investment in Stick   777,429
   Minority Interest in Stick   88,000
To eliminate the investment account against the stockholders'
equity of Stick, allocate the unamortized purchase premium,
and establish the minority interest on a pro forma basis as of
Jan. 1, 19X2.

Cost of 10 Percent Acquisition $30,000
Less 10 Percent of 19X5 Dividends. . . . . (500)
Plus 10 Percent of 19X5 Income, $1,000 (= .1 × $10,000) less Purchase Premium
(Goodwill) Amortization of $100 (= $4,000/40) 900
Less 10 Percent of 19X6 Dividends. . . . . (700)
Plus 10 Percent of 19X6 Income, $2,000 (= .1 × $20,000) less Purchase Premium
(Goodwill) Amortization of $100 (= $4,000/40) 1,900
Balance at Dec. 31, 19X6, under the Equity Method $31,600

Thus the investment account must be increased by $1,600 (= $31,600 − $30,000) on January 2, 19X7. Similarly, Investor's Retained Earnings account must be increased by $1,600. Dividend income of $1,200 (= $500 + $700) was recorded but Investor's share of Investee's earnings during 19X5 and 19X6, $3,000 [= .1($10,000 + $20,000)], less goodwill amortization of $200 (= 2 × $4,000/40), amounted to $2,800. The difference of $1,600 (= $2,800 − $1,200) is Investor's share of Investee's *undistributed income* less implied goodwill amortization in 19X5 and 19X6. To record the 30 percent acquisition and retroactive application of the equity method to the 10 percent block, Investor makes the following entries:

BOOKS OF INVESTOR COMPANY

1/2/X7

Intercorporate Investments 180,000
    Cash 180,000
To record acquisition of 30 percent of the shares of Investee
Company.

Intercorporate Investments 1,600
    Retained Earnings 1,600
To restate the investment account in order to reflect retroactive
application of the equity method to the initial 10 percent block of
shares acquired.

Investor's accounting for this intercorporate investment in 19X7 and subsequent years will reflect the equity method applied to the entire 40 percent interest.

Transactions Involving the Subsidiary's Shares

Although accounting theory tends to stress substance (the actual outcome of transactions) over form (the way in which the result was achieved), the form of a transaction involving the subsidiary's shares may influence its accounting treatment. From the standpoint of the affiliated group, different transactions involving the subsidiary's shares which have the same economic end result can be accounted for differently. Consider the following three ways in which the subsidiary's shares could be sold outside the affiliated group:

1. The parent could reduce its ownership interest by selling some of the subsidiary's shares which it owns to outsiders.

2. The parent could reduce its ownership interest by instructing the subsidiary to sell previously unissued shares to outsiders.
3. The parent could reduce its ownership interest by instructing the subsidiary to sell treasury shares to outsiders.

All of these transactions involve a reduction in the parent's ownership interest. If the shares are sold for more than their book value, consolidated stockholders' equity will increase even though the controlling interest's ownership percentage has decreased. Is the increase in consolidated stockholders' equity an income item or a capital item? Does it depend on whether the parent or the subsidiary sold the shares? In our judgment, current accounting practice in this area can be inconsistent, as the following numerical example illustrates.

P Company owns 8,000 of S Company's 10,000 outstanding common shares, for an ownership interest of 80 percent. P carries the shares at equity, $80,000. No purchase premium or discount exists. The stock currently sells in the market for $30 a share.

Case 1: P Company sells 1,000 of the shares it owns for $30,000. Since the book value of those shares was $10,000, P's shareholders have realized an increase in their equity of $20,000 (= $30,000 − $10,000), and they now own 70 percent of S's outstanding shares.

Case 2: S Company issues 1,429 shares for $42,870 (= $30 × 1,429), increasing S's stockholders' equity to $142,870 (= $100,000 + $42,870).[3] The portion of S's stockholders' equity now owned by P is 70 percent (= 8,000/11,429), and it has a book value of $100,000 (= .7 × $142,870). P's shareholders have realized an increase in their equity of $20,000 (= $100,000 − $80,000).

In our judgment, Cases 1 and 2 are fundamentally identical. Yet, current accounting practice would treat the Case 1 "gain" as *income* and, although some might object, would often treat the Case 2 "gain" as a capital transaction and record it as *additional paid-in capital*. It would be argued that in Case 1 P has realized income on the sale of an investment and in Case 2 S has sold its own stock—a capital transaction—and P has realized no income.

We believe that these accounting treatments are inconsistent. From the viewpoint of the parent company, *both* transactions provide income to its shareholders. On the other hand, from the standpoint of the total entity, *neither* transaction provides income—the parent's sale of the subsidiary's shares is, in effect, a sale of treasury stock.

A major contributing factor to the treatment of subsidiary stock issues (Case 2) as capital transactions is a position that had been taken by the SEC: "No profits

---

[3]Given that the 8,000 shares presently owned by P are to represent a 70 percent ownership interest after the new issue, the additional number of shares is determined as follows: Define X as the total number of shares of S outstanding after the new issue. Then,

$$.7 = 8,000/X$$
$$.7X = 8,000$$
$$X = 11,429.$$

This represents an increase of 1,429 shares over the 10,000 originally outstanding.

on the person's own equity securities, or profits of its affiliates on their own equity securities, shall be included under this caption [*profits on securities*]."[4]

It is widely acknowledged that sound accounting theory relies on substance, not form. Unfortunately, these inconsistent accounting treatments can arise in practice because form is being stressed over substance. We favor treating the gains arising in both Case 1 and Case 2 as income in consolidated statements because the economic position of the controlling interest has been improved by a completed market transaction. Our position is consistent with the *parent theory* of consolidated statements, whereas the capital transaction approach follows from the *entity theory*. Either approach consistently followed is preferable to the inconsistency that currently can exist in practice.

This inconsistency is likely to disappear in the future. In a 1980 *Issues Paper*, "Accounting in Consolidation for Issuances of a Subsidiary's Stock," the Accounting Standards Division of the AICPA recommended that such gains (or losses) be recognized in the consolidated income statement. Moreover, in *Staff Accounting Bulletin No. 51*, "Accounting for Sales of Stock by Subsidiary Company," the SEC modified its position by permitting companies to report such gains as separate nonoperating line items in their consolidated income statements.[5] Treatment as capital transactions is no longer required by the SEC. The gains (or losses) must result from direct sales of previously unissued stock which is not part of a broader corporate reorganization.

We now illustrate the accounting for (1) a sale of part of the parent's ownership interest in the subsidiary and (2) a sale of additional shares by the subsidiary, which also reduces the parent's ownership interest. Transactions in which the subsidiary purchases or sells treasury stock are, in substance, quite similar to the transactions in Cases 1 and 2 above. We shall briefly illustrate and comment on them later in the section.

Parent Sells Shares of Subsidiary to Outsiders. The two major issues of interest when the parent sells a portion of its holdings of the subsidiary's stock are:

1. Establishing the book value of the interest sold.
2. Adjusting the purchase premium or discount.

Book Value of Shares Sold. Use of the equity method by the parent enables it to account for the current book value of its interests in the subsidiary. If the shares are sold *during* an accounting period, the change in book value since the beginning of the accounting period must be estimated. An adjustment may be necessary at year-end if subsequent information calls for a revision in that estimate. When the parent's investment in the subsidiary consists of two or more separate blocks of shares, management must decide which shares have been sold. Since one share

---

[4]Louis H. Rappaport, *SEC Accounting Practice and Procedure*, 3rd ed. (New York: Ronald Press, 1972), p. 18.28.
[5]Securities and Exchange Commission, *Staff Accounting Bulletin No. 51*, "Accounting for Sales of Stock by Subsidiary Company" (Washington: SEC, Mar. 29, 1983).

of a company's stock is indistinguishable from another, identifying the particular shares sold becomes difficult. *Specific identification* of shares sold is not really possible unless an entire block is disposed. The use of *first-in, first-out* (FIFO) is a reasonable though arbitrary policy for identifying shares sold. Another approach involves computing the *average book value* of all shares owned and assumes that shares chosen at random are sold. In our judgment, the last approach has the most conceptual appeal because of the identical nature of the shares. If it is used, there is no need to keep track of the separate book value of each block of shares.

Purchase Premium (Discount) Adjustment. If the carrying value of the shares sold includes a purchase premium, the amount of unamortized purchase premium remaining in the investment account is reduced. Subsequent allocation and amortization of the purchase premium on consolidated financial statement working papers are affected because some portion of the purchase premium has been "sold." The adjustment process is most vividly illustrated when a *particular*, rather than *average*, block of stock is sold. Therefore, we shall use the data developed in the Puck and Stick example here, employing FIFO rather than specific identification, to identify the particular block of stock assumed sold.

Suppose that on December 31, 19X2, the Puck Company sells 10,000 shares of the Stick Company stock for $105,422. This is 10 percent of Stick's outstanding stock and is assumed to be taken from Puck's first acquisition of 25,000 shares made on May 1, 19X1 (that is, Block A). After the sale, the 15,000 shares remaining in that initial acquisition represent 15 percent of Stick's outstanding shares. An analysis of the components of Block A before and after the sale is given below:

ANALYSIS OF BLOCK A (25,000 SHARES) ACQUIRED ON MAY 1, 19X1

	Share of S's Stockholders' Equity	Unamortized Purchase Premium		Total Book Value
		Identifiable Assets	Goodwill	
12/31/X2 (before Sale)	$140,000	$20,850	$ 52,704	$213,554
Sale of 10,000 shares.	(56,000)[a]	(8,340)[a]	(21,082)[a]	(85,422)[a]
12/31/X2 (after Sale)	$ 84,000	$12,510	$ 31,622	$128,132

[a]This amount is 40 percent (= 10,000/25,000) of the before-sale balance.

Thus the 10,000 shares sold had a book value of $85,422, and a gain of $20,000 (= $105,422 − $85,422) resulted. Puck records the sale as follows, and the gain shows up on the consolidated income statement for the year ended December 31, 19X2:

BOOKS OF PUCK COMPANY

Cash 105,422
    Investment in Stick   85,422
    Gain on Sale of Investment.   20,000
To record the sale of 10,000 shares of Stick Company stock for
$105,422, thereby reducing our ownership interest to 70 percent.

The following analysis of the total purchase premium shows the unamortized balance at December 31, 19X2 (*after* 19X2 amortization) reduced by the portion sold.

COMPONENTS OF THE UNAMORTIZED PURCHASE PREMIUM

	Amount Allocated to		Total Unamortized
	Identifiable Assets	**Goodwill**	**Purchase Premium**
Balance, 80% Interest	$102,912[a]	$275,422[a]	$378,334[a]
Portion Sold, 10% Interest (from Block A Acquired May 1, 19X1).	(8,340)[b]	(21,082)[c]	(29,422)
Balance, 70% Interest	$ 94,572	$254,340	$348,912

[a]Net of 19X2 amortization.
[b]$8,340 = $20,850(10,000/25,000).
[c]$21,082 = $52,704(10,000/25,000).

Working paper entries achieve the ending balances shown—$94,572 and $254,340—by first allocating the purchase premium before 19X2 amortization and then entering the 19X2 amortization. The balances of Identifiable Assets, Goodwill, and Investment in Stick needed to allocate the purchase premium and eliminate the investment account are calculated below:

COMPONENTS OF THE INVESTMENT IN STICK ACCOUNT
(SUBSIDIARY SHARES SOLD BY PARENT)

		Unamortized Purchase Premium		
	Equity in Stick's Net Assets	**Identifiable Assets**	**Goodwill**	**Total**
Balance before 19X2 Equity Method Entries (80% Interest).	$389,500[a]	$108,850	$279,079	$777,429
Portion Sold.	(56,000)	(8,340)	(21,082)	(85,422)
Balance to Be Eliminated (70% Interest).	$333,500	$100,510	$257,997	$692,007

[a]$389,500 = (.8 × $440,000) + $37,500 (preacquisition earnings).

The first working paper entry, which allocates the unamortized purchase premium, eliminates the investment account, and establishes the Minority Interest in Stick as of January 1, 19X2, is given next. Because the minority interest is 30 percent of Stick's stockholders' equity at December 31, it is entered at its pro forma amount as of January 1, 19X2, $132,000 (= .3 × $440,000).

CONSOLIDATED FINANCIAL STATEMENT WORKING PAPER

Preacquisition Earnings	25,500	
Identifiable Assets.	100,510	
Goodwill.	257,997	
Stockholders' Equity—Stick	440,000	
Investment in Stick		692,007
Minority Interest in Stick		132,000

To eliminate the investment account against the stockholders' equity of Stick, allocate the unamortized purchase premium, and establish the minority interest on a pro forma basis as of Jan. 1, 19X2.

Some additional words of explanation are in order here. Preacquisition Earnings, which had been $37,500 before the sale, is reduced by $12,000, which is the 10 percent of Stick's 19X2 net income "sold" on December 31, 19X2. In effect, this $12,000 is moved from Preacquisition Earnings to Minority Interest in Net Income. The latter, shown in the working paper entry below, is entered at the end-of-year minority ownership percentage of 30 percent on a pro forma basis for the entire year. Thus the Minority Interest in Net Income is now $36,000 (= .3 × $120,000) rather than the $24,000 (= .2 × $120,000) given in the previous example before the stock sale. Note that if the 10 percent stock sale had been the *only* stock transaction during the year (that is, if there had been no stock acquisitions), the $12,000 would appear as an "other income" item in the consolidated income statement. This is necessary to offset the additional $12,000 added to Minority Interest in Net Income to produce the 30 percent pro forma amount.

The remaining eliminations enter the 19X2 purchase premium amortization and the change in the minority interest on the working paper.

CONSOLIDATED FINANCIAL STATEMENT WORKING PAPER

Operating Expenses.	9,595	
Identifiable Assets.		5,938
Goodwill.		3,657

To recognize purchase premium amortization for 19X2. These amounts include amortization for 19X2 on the portion of the premium sold because it was held all year. After 19X2, purchase premium amortization will be lower.

Minority Interest in Net Income	36,000	
Minority Interest in Stick.		36,000

To record the change in the minority interest on a pro forma basis for the entire year; $36,000 = .3 × $120,000.

In the consolidated balance sheet at December 31, 19X2, the unamortized purchase premium consists of Identifiable Assets of $94,572 (= $100,510 − $5,938) and Goodwill of $254,340 (= $257,997 − $3,657). The Minority Interest in Stick is $168,000 (= $132,000 + $36,000). This is 30 percent of Stick's ending stockholders' equity of $560,000.

Subsidiary Issues Additional Shares to Outsiders. Sales of its own stock by a subsidiary is handled in the usual way on the subsidiary's books. In consolidation, however, two additional matters must be considered:

1. Establishing the book value of the parent's new ownership interest.
2. Adjusting the purchase premium or discount.

Book Value of Ownership Interest. If the additional stock issued by the subsidiary is at a price *other than book value* of the shares issued, the monetary value of the ownership interest in the investment account must be adjusted. The amount of the adjustment is the controversial ''gain or loss'' discussed earlier. No entry is made by P when the new shares are issued at book value. In this case, the decline in the percentage of shares owned by the parent is exactly offset by the percentage of increase in the stockholders' equity of the subsidiary.

Purchase Premium (Discount) Adjustment. The decline in the fraction of subsidiary shares owned by the parent following an issue of subsidiary shares to outsiders is equivalent to the sale of a portion of the parent's ownership interest. As was the case with the sale by the parent, any purchase premium or discount must be reduced in proportion to the decrease in ownership interest. This will be necessary even if there is no gain or loss; the portion of the purchase premium ''sold'' will have been replaced by an increase in the subsidiary's stockholders' equity.

To illustrate this type of transaction and contrast it directly with the sale of shares by the parent, we assume that Stick issues an additional 14,286 shares of stock in the market on December 31, 19X2. This increases the number of shares outstanding to 114,286 (= 100,000 + 14,286), of which the 80,000 shares owned by Puck represent a 70 percent (= 80,000/114,286) interest. All shares are purchased by outside interests at an average price of $10.542, for a total of $150,603 (= 14,286 × $10.542). The book value of Stick's stockholders' equity now stands at $710,603. Recall that as of October 1, 19X2, the date the third block of Stick's stock was acquired, the net assets of Stick amounted to $530,000. Following our assumption that Stick's income is earned evenly throughout the year, 25 percent of the 19X2 net income of $120,000 was earned in the last 3 months of 19X2 and the book value of Stick's stockholders' equity prior to the issue of securities was $560,000. Adding the proceeds from the issue brings the book value up to $710,603.

Puck now owns 70 percent (= 80,000/114,286) of Stick's outstanding shares, and 70 percent of Stick's stockholders' equity is now $497,422 (= .7 × $710,603). The net effect of this new security issue will be to increase the Investment in Stick account balance by $20,000. An entry will be made recording the $20,000 either as a *gain* to Puck—to be consistent with the outright sale of shares by Puck—or as *additional paid-in capital* to Puck, following the old SEC rule. As can be seen from the following analysis, the $20,000 is the difference between two partially offsetting effects on the investment account. *First,* the monetary amount of Puck's interest in Stick, now 70 percent, has risen by $49,422 [= $497,422 − .8($560,000)]. *Second,* a portion of the purchase premium associated with Block A, $29,422 [= ($20,850 + $52,704)(10,000/25,000)], is assumed sold.

COMPONENTS OF THE INVESTMENT IN STICK ACCOUNT (SUBSIDIARY ISSUES NEW SHARES)

	Equity in Stick's Net Assets	Purchase Premium		Total
		Identifiable Assets	Goodwill	
Balance before 19X2 Equity Method Entries (80% Interest)	$389,500	$108,850	$279,079	$777,429
New Stock Issued	49,422	(8,340)	(21,082)	20,000
	$438,922	$100,510	$257,997	$797,429
19X2 Equity Accrual	58,500	(5,938)	(3,657)	48,905
Balance, Dec. 31, 19X2, after Stock Issue	$497,422	$ 94,572	$254,340	$846,334

At December 31, 19X2, Puck makes the following entry on its books to record the net increase in the monetary value of the investment account:

BOOKS OF PUCK COMPANY

Investment in Stick 20,000
 Gain (or Additional Paid-In Capital) 20,000
To record the net increase in the Investment in Stick generated by
the issue of additional shares by Stick Company in the open market
at more than their book value (to Stick).

When the consolidated balance sheet is prepared at December 31, 19X2, the unamortized purchase premium will be allocated as shown below. Working paper entries achieve the net result—$94,572 and $254,340—in the same way as shown when Puck sold the shares itself.

COMPONENTS OF THE UNAMORTIZED PURCHASE PREMIUM

	Amount Allocated to:		Total Unamortized Purchase Premium
	Identifiable Assets	Goodwill	
Balance, 80% Interest	$102,912[a]	$275,422[a]	$378,334[a]
Portion "Sold," 10% Interest (from Block A)	(8,340)[b]	(21,082)[c]	(29,422)
Balance, 70% Interest	$ 94,572	$254,340	$348,912

[a]Net of 19X2 amortization.
[b]$8,340 = $20,850(10,000/25,000).
[c]$21,082 = $52,704(10,000/25,000).

Except for the investment elimination, which is given below, other working paper entries are the same as previously described when Puck had sold the shares itself. After the issue of the additional shares by Stick, its stockholders' equity is $710,603 and the pro forma beginning-of-year balance in the investment account is $797,429 (= $777,429 + $20,000). Because Stick's capital stock has changed during the year, we shall eliminate the investment account against Stick's beginning stockholders' equity of $440,000, plus the stock proceeds of $150,603, a total of $590,603.

CONSOLIDATED FINANCIAL STATEMENT WORKING PAPER

Preacquisition Earnings	25,500	
Identifiable Assets.	100,510	
Goodwill.	257,997	
Stockholders' Equity—Stick	590,603	
Investment in Stick		797,429
Minority Interest in Stick		177,181

To eliminate the investment account against the stockholders' equity of Stick, allocate the unamortized purchase premium, and establish the minority interest on a pro forma basis as of Jan. 1, 19X2.

After consolidation, the Minority Interest in Stick will be $213,181 (= .3 × $710,603, Stick's stockholders' equity after the stock issue), consisting of the $177,181 entered above plus the change in the minority interest of $36,000 (= .3 × $120,000).

The case we have illustrated involves the issue of stock by the subsidiary to outsiders only. It is reasonable to expect that the parent company will often acquire some of those shares. If so, the transaction becomes a combination of (1) an additional acquisition of stock by the parent and (2) an issue of subsidiary stock to outsiders. It must be analyzed accordingly and is not discussed further or illustrated here.

Subsidiary Transactions in Treasury Stock. Sales of treasury stock by a subsidiary create no new problems. The effects of such transactions on the investment account are analyzed and treated as if they arose from sales of unissued stock by the subsidiary.

Purchases of treasury stock from outsiders by the subsidiary decrease the number of shares outstanding and increase the parent's ownership interest. There are three possibilities:

1. Treasury shares acquired at book value have no effect on the investment account. The decrease in the subsidiary's stockholders' equity is exactly offset by the increase in the parent's ownership percentage.
2. Treasury shares acquired at *more* than book value reduce the subsidiary's stockholders' equity by more than the increase in the parent's ownership percentage. Although the balance in the investment account will fall, it is difficult to justify recognizing a loss on what is, in effect, a purchase. Hence, the debit will be to Additional Paid-In Capital. An alternative procedure, which has some merit, calls for leaving the investment account balance undisturbed and increasing the unamortized purchase premium by the amount of the decrease in equity. Our preference is to charge Additional

Exhibit 11.2	Effects of Stick's Acquisition of 11,111 Treasury Shares at Alternative Prices of $5.60, $5.00, and $6.20 per Share

STOCKHOLDERS' EQUITY OF STICK COMPANY

	Without Purchase of Treasury Stock	With Purchase of 11,111 Shares of Treasury Stock		
		At $5.60	At $5.00	At $6.20
Stockholders' Equity, before..........	$560,000	$560,000	$560,000	$560,000
Less Treasury Stock. . .	—	(62,222)	(55,555)	(68,888)
Stockholders' Equity, after..........	$560,000	$497,778	$504,445	$491,112
Puck's Percentage Interest	.8	.9^a	.9^a	.9^a
Puck's Share	$448,000	$448,000	$454,000	$442,000
Increase (Decrease). . .	—	—	$ 6,000^b	$ (6,000)^c

^{a}9 = 80,000/88,889.
^{b}$6,000 = $454,000 − $448,000.
^{c}$(6,000) = $442,000 − $448,000.

Paid-In Capital for the difference, on the grounds that the acquisition of treasury stock should not increase an amortizable asset.

3. Treasury shares acquired at *less* than book value have the opposite effect, reducing the subsidiary's stockholders' equity by less than the increase in the parent's ownership percentage. In this case, the balance in the investment account rises. To avoid recognizing a gain on a purchase, we suggest crediting Additional Paid-In Capital. As before, we believe that this treatment is preferable to a reduction in the unamortized purchase premium which offsets the increase in equity and leaves the investment account balance unchanged.

To illustrate these three possibilities, we return to our Puck and Stick example. At December 31, 19X2, Puck owns 80 percent of Stick's 100,000 outstanding common shares. The book value of Stick's stockholders' equity per share is $5.60 (= $560,000/100,000). The effects of purchases of 11,111 shares of treasury stock at prices of $5.60, $5.00, and $6.20 are illustrated in Exhibit 11.2. By reducing the number of shares outstanding to 88,889 (= 100,000 − 11,111), Puck's percentage interest increases to 90 percent (= 80,000/88,889). Investment elimination entries following the treasury stock purchase at the three alternative prices are given in Exhibit 11.3.

Complex Affiliation Relationships

Our last set of special topics deals with the preparation of consolidated statements when affiliation relationships are more intricate than those **direct holdings** (par-

Exhibit 11.3	Investment Eliminations Following Purchase of Treasury Shares at Alternative Prices of $5.60, $5.00, and $6.20 per Share

	$5.60		$5.00		$6.20	
	Debit	Credit	Debit	Credit	Debit	Credit
Preacquisition Earnings[a]	49,500		49,500		49,500	
Identifiable Assets	108,850		108,850		108,850	
Goodwill	279,079		279,079		279,079	
Stockholders' Equity—Stick[b] . .	377,778		384,445		371,112	
Investment in Stick[c]		777,429		783,429		771,429
Minority Interest in Stick[d] . .		37,778		38,445		37,112

[a]Stick's purchase of treasury stock increased Puck's ownership interest by 10 percent. Preacquisition earnings of $49,500 (= $37,500 + $12,000) is increased by 10 percent of Stick's 19X2 net income, $12,000.
[b]These amounts are Stick's stockholders' equity at Jan. 1, 19X2, $440,000, reduced by the cost of the treasury shares in each case (e.g., $377,778 = $440,000 − $62,222).
[c]When the treasury shares are acquired at prices not equal to book value, the investment account is adjusted by Puck's share of the difference in each case (e.g., $783,429 = $777,429 + $6,000).
[d]This is 10 percent of Stick's stockholders' equity in each case (e.g., $37,778 = .1 × $377,778).

ent's direct ownership of controlling interest in a subsidiary) studied to this point. The basic types of affiliation relationships are diagramed in Figure 11.1 where α_{ij} refers to the percentage of Company j's common stock owned by Company i. For example, α_{PS} indicates the percentage of S Company's common stock owned by P Company.

Indirect holdings arise when the parent company's controlling interest in a subsidiary enables the parent to control a second subsidiary even though it owns few or none of the second subsidiary's shares directly. The main problems generated by indirect holdings relate to the interpretation of a purchase premium or discount and the order in which the procedures for preparing consolidated financial statements are carried out. **Mutual holdings** occur when one or more subsidiaries own stock in the parent or in each other. Such shares are not shown as outstanding in a consolidated balance sheet.[6] The principal conceptual problem arises when there is a minority interest in a parent-subsidiary mutual holding. In this case, there are two acceptable alternative treatments which result in different consolidated statements.

Indirect Holdings

The first issue to be addressed is the interpretation of the purchase premium or discount in an indirect holding. Note that the **father-son-grandson (FSG)** and **connecting affiliate (CA)** configurations have one thing in common—one subsidiary's interest in the second subsidiary enables the parent to control the second

---

[6]The subsidiaries' shares are, as usual, eliminated in consolidation. Similarly, *ARB 51* states that "shares of the parent held by a subsidiary should not be treated as outstanding stock in the consolidated balance sheet." Committee on Accounting Procedure, *ARB 51*, par. 13; CT § C51.114.

Figure 11.1	Basic Types of Affiliation Relationships

Direct Holdings

One Subsidiary

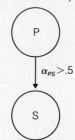

Several Subsidiaries

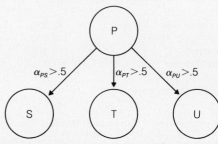

Indirect Holdings

Father-Son-Grandson

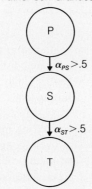

Connecting Affiliates

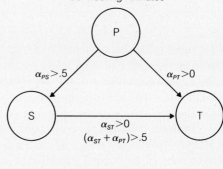

Mutual Holdings

Parent and Subsidiary

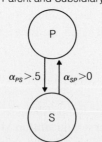

Connecting Affiliates

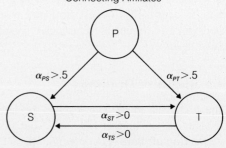

subsidiary. In the FSG case, P controls T because P controls S and S controls T. In the CA case, P controls T because P controls S *and* P and S *together* have a controlling interest in T.

Suppose we have an FSG affiliation in which P controlled S *before* S acquires its controlling interest in T. Any purchase premium arising when S acquires T is allocated in the usual way across T's assets and liabilities, with any residual being assigned to goodwill. Modify this to the situation where P acquires S *after* S acquired its controlling interest in T. Assuming that P pays a purchase premium for its interest in S (and through S its interest in T), the accountant's allocation problem has a new dimension. There are now three possible explanations for this purchase premium:

1. The fair value of S Company's net assets, *excluding the Investment in T,* may exceed their book value.
2. The fair value of T's net assets may exceed the amount reflected in the Investment in T on S Company's books.
3. Net assets of both S and T may be fairly stated and the premium is evidence of purchased goodwill.

Of course, any given purchase premium may easily represent a combination of these three factors. When consolidating P, S, and T, the net assets of S may require revaluation, the net assets of T may require revaluation beyond that implied by S's investment in T, and goodwill may be present as well. Before we illustrate these points with a numerical example, observe that the same situation may hold in the CA case. If P acquires S *after* S acquired its minority interest in T, a portion of P's purchase premium in S may be attributable to an excess of fair value over book value of T's assets. This can be complicated further if P acquires its interest in T at a time different from when the interest in S is acquired.

To illustrate some of these possibilities, assume that two companies, S and T, have the following condensed balance sheet data at December 31, 19X3:

BALANCE SHEET DATA AS OF DECEMBER 31, 19X3

	S Company		T Company	
	Book Value	Fair Value	Book Value	Fair Value
Various Assets	$8,200,000	$10,000,000	$3,000,000	$4,000,000
Liabilities	$4,200,000	3,000,000	$2,000,000	2,000,000
Stockholders' Equity	4,000,000	—	1,000,000	—
Total	$8,200,000		$3,000,000	

S Acquires T. On December 31, 19X3, S Company acquires a 70 percent interest in T Company ($\alpha_{ST} = .7$) for $1,800,000 in cash. The book value of 70 percent of T's stockholders' equity is $700,000 (= .7 × $1,000,000), and a purchase premium of $1,100,000 (= $1,800,000 − $700,000) results. Allocation of this purchase premium is as follows:

ALLOCATION OF PURCHASE PREMIUM PAID WHEN S COMPANY ACQUIRES 70 PERCENT OF T COMPANY AT DECEMBER 31, 19X3

Assets and Liabilities of T Company	Fair Value	Book Value	Fair Value Less Book Value	Allocation Based on S's Interest (70%)
Various Assets	$ 4,000,000	$ 3,000,000	$1,000,000	$ 700,000
Liabilities	(2,000,000)	(2,000,000)	—	—
	$ 2,000,000	$ 1,000,000	$1,000,000	$ 700,000
Goodwill				400,000
Total Purchase Premium				$1,100,000

The straight-line method will be used to depreciate the write-up of the various assets over 10 years and the goodwill over 40 years. Consolidating the balance sheets of S and T at December 31, 19X3, requires the following combined working paper entry:

CONSOLIDATED FINANCIAL STATEMENT WORKING PAPER

Various Assets—T	700,000	
Goodwill	400,000	
Stockholders' Equity—T	1,000,000	
Investment in T		1,800,000
Minority Interest in T		300,000

To allocate the purchase premium, eliminate the Investment in T against the stockholders' equity of T, and establish the minority interest in T as of Dec. 31, 19X3.

During 19X4, S and T report income from their own operations and make dividend payments as follows:

	Year Ended December 31, 19X4	
	S Company	T Company
Net Income from Own Operations	$1,200,000	$500,000
Dividends Declared and Paid	400,000	200,000

S's equity method accrual is computed in the following schedule:

S COMPANY AND T COMPANY
SCHEDULE TO DETERMINE THE EQUITY METHOD ACCRUAL
FOR THE YEAR ENDED DECEMBER 31, 19X4

S's Share of T's Net Income (.7 × $500,000)	$350,000
Less Amortization of Purchase Premium:	
Additional Depreciation ($700,000/10)	$ 70,000
Amortization of Goodwill ($400,000/40)	10,000
Total Amortization	$ 80,000
Net Equity Method Accrual for 19X4	$270,000

Therefore, at December 31, 19X4, S's Investment in T account has a balance of $1,930,000 (= $1,800,000 + $270,000 − $140,000), reflecting the $140,000 (= .7 × $200,000) of T's dividends received by S. Condensed balance sheet data at December 31, 19X4, for companies S and T are given here:

BALANCE SHEET DATA AS OF DECEMBER 31, 19X4

	S Company		T Company	
	Book Value	**Fair Value**	**Book Value**	**Fair Value**
Various Assets	$ 9,200,000	$10,000,000	$3,600,000	$5,000,000
Investment in T.	1,930,000	—	—	—
Total	$11,130,000		$3,600,000	
Liabilities	$ 6,060,000	4,500,000	$2,300,000	2,300,000
Stockholders' Equity	5,070,000	—	1,300,000	—
Total	$11,130,000		$3,600,000	

S's stockholders' equity of $5,070,000 consists of the $4,000,000 balance at December 31, 19X3, plus S's 19X4 net income from its own operations of $1,200,000 plus the 19X4 equity method accrual of $270,000 minus dividends paid during 19X4 of $400,000.

P Acquires S. On December 31, 19X4, P Company acquires an 80 percent interest in S Company for $7,200,000 cash. Since the book value of S's stockholders' equity is $5,070,000, a purchase premium of $3,144,000 [= $7,200,000 − .8($5,070,000)] was paid for the 80 percent interest. In analyzing the acquisition of S, P's management may also have considered the differences between fair and book values of the assets and liabilities of T. Therefore, we have two alternative approaches to analyzing and allocating the purchase premium paid to acquire the 80 percent interest in S.

Allocate Only to S. Allocation of the purchase premium among the assets (except the Investment in T) and liabilities of S and goodwill yields the following results:

ALLOCATION OF PURCHASE PREMIUM PAID
WHEN P ACQUIRES 80 PERCENT OF S AT DECEMBER 31, 19X4
(FAIR VALUE OF T IGNORED)

Assets and Liabilities of S Company	Fair Value	Book Value	Fair Value Less Book Value	Allocation Based on P's Interest (80%)
Various Assets	$10,000,000	$ 9,200,000	$ 800,000	$ 640,000
Liabilities	(4,500,000)	(6,060,000)	1,560,000	1,248,000
	$ 5,500,000	$ 3,140,000	$2,360,000	$1,888,000
Goodwill				1,256,000
Total Purchase Premium				$3,144,000

This procedure leaves the Investment in T undisturbed and, if a consolidated balance sheet were prepared immediately, the various assets of S would be increased by $640,000, the liabilities decreased by $1,248,000, and goodwill increased by $1,256,000. Allocation of S's purchase premium in T will, as before, result in an increase in $700,000 in T's assets and $400,000 in goodwill before deduction of $80,000 in depreciation and amortization expense for the current year.

Allocate to S and T. Using the alternative approach, we would first allocate the purchase premium to the assets and liabilities of S, in accordance with the 80 percent interest owned by P. Any remaining purchase premium would then be allocated among the assets and liabilities of T and goodwill. The portion of P's purchase premium attributable to the increase in fair value of S's 70 percent interest in T is transferred from the Investment in S account to the Investment in T account on the working paper. The previous allocation left us with $1,256,000 in goodwill. After the allocation shown next, in which an additional $350,000 is allocated to the identifiable assets of T Company, only $906,000 remains as goodwill.

ALLOCATION OF PURCHASE PREMIUM PAID
WHEN P ACQUIRES 80 PERCENT OF S AT DECEMBER 31, 19X4
(FAIR VALUE OF T RECOGNIZED)

Assets and Liabilities of T Company	Fair Value	Book Value	Fair Value Less Book Value	Allocation Based on S's Interest (70%)
Various Assets	$ 5,000,000	$ 3,600,000	$1,400,000	$ 980,000
Liabilities	(2,300,000)	(2,300,000)	—	—
	$ 2,700,000	$ 1,300,000	$1,400,000	$ 980,000
Amount Already Included in Investment in T ($700,000 − $70,000 Depreciation)				(630,000)
Write-Up of Investment in T				$ 350,000
Amount Attributed to Undervaluation of S's Assets and Liabilities				1,888,000
Goodwill Included in Price Paid by P				906,000
Total Purchase Premium				$3,144,000

If in fact the price paid for the interest in S reflected a premium attributable to the undervalued net assets of T, then allocating the total premium to S and T would best reflect the facts. Nevertheless, some accountants would prefer to allocate the entire amount to S on the grounds that there is only *indirect evidence* in support of the needed revaluations of T's assets and liabilities. In other words, it may be very difficult to determine whether the excess premium represents purchased goodwill or recognition of undervalued net assets held by T. We do not share this view; careful estimates of the fair values of T's assets and liabilities should be as reliable as those made for the assets and liabilities of S.

We illustrate the preparation of consolidated balance sheets of P, S, and T on a working paper prepared for this purpose in Exhibit 11.4. Balance sheet data for P are assumed and are independent of other examples. Note that S's purchase premium in T is dependent on the allocation of P's purchase premium in S. To facilitate consolidation, the purchase premiums should be dealt with early in the consolidation process, and the allocation of P's purchase premium in S should precede allocation of S's purchase premium in T.

Consolidating the Income Statements in an Indirect Holding. Consolidation of income statements in the case of an indirect holding is not complicated by special problems, but the order in which working paper adjustments affecting income statement items are made is important. At year-end, S will determine and book its equity method accrual from T. S's share of T's reported net income will be adjusted by any purchase premium amortization and unconfirmed intercompany profits. Once this is accomplished, P's equity method accrual from S—which will reflect P's share of S's equity accrual from T—can be computed and booked by P.

Moving to the consolidated financial statement working paper, note that the effects of any working paper entries to remove unconfirmed intercompany profits from the income of T affect the minority interest in T's net income. Similarly, since S's stockholders own a portion of T's income, working paper adjustments to T's income also affect the minority interest in S's net income. Hence working paper entries affecting the income statement items of S and T normally precede entries affecting the income statement items of P and S.

Consolidation of S and T on the working paper is outlined in the following steps. Subsequent consolidation of P and S is handled in the usual way on the same working paper.

1. Reverse the equity method entries, thereby adjusting the Investment in T to its beginning-of-year balance.
2. Eliminate any intercompany revenues, expenses, and unconfirmed profits from the appropriate income statement and balance sheet accounts.
3. If P's acquisition of S called for further revaluation of T's assets and liabilities, adjust the Investment in T by removing the amount of P's purchase premium attributable to T from the Investment in S [see Entry (1) in Exhibit 11.4].
4. Reclassify and allocate the purchase premium—as adjusted in No. 3— among the assets and liabilities of T.
5. Record the purchase premium amortization for the year.
6. Eliminate the Investment in T against the stockholders' equity of T and establish the minority interest in T, all as of the beginning of the year.
7. Record the minority's share of T's adjusted net income and eliminate the minority's share of T's dividends.

Mutual Holdings

Mutual holdings arise when one or more subsidiaries own stock in the parent or in each other. Those ownership relationships are also known as **bilateral** or **reciprocal holdings.** None of the affiliates' shares held by other members of the group are treated as outstanding in the consolidated balance sheet. Although this consolidated result is achieved in all mutual holding situations, acceptable alternative treatments can lead to different consolidated statements when a partially owned subsidiary owns some of the parent's stock.

Exhibit 11.4 P, S, and T Companies: Consolidated Balance Sheet Working Paper at December 31, 19X4 (Indirect Holding)

ASSETS	P Company	S Company	T Company	Adjustments and Eliminations Dr.	Adjustments and Eliminations Cr.	P, S, and T Consolidated
Various Assets	30,000,000	9,200,000	3,600,000	(3) 980,000 (6) 640,000		44,420,000
Investment in S (80%)	7,200,000	—	—		(1) 350,000 (5) 2,794,000 (7) 4,056,000	—
Investment in T (70%)	—	1,930,000	—	(1) 350,000	(2) 1,370,000 (4) 910,000	—
Purchase Premium—T				(2) 1,370,000	(3) 1,370,000	—
Purchase Premium—S				(5) 2,794,000	(6) 2,794,000	—
Goodwill				(3) 390,000 (6) 906,000		1,296,000
Total Assets	37,200,000	11,130,000	3,600,000	15,048,000	15,048,000	45,716,000
LIABILITIES AND STOCKHOLDERS' EQUITY						
Liabilities	12,000,000	6,060,000	2,300,000	(6) 1,248,000		19,112,000
Stockholders' Equity—P	25,200,000	—	—			25,200,000
Stockholders' Equity—S	—	5,070,000	—	(7) 5,070,000		—
Stockholders' Equity—T	—	—	1,300,000	(4) 1,300,000		—
Minority Interest in S	—	—	—		(7) 1,014,000	1,014,000
Minority Interest in T	—	—	—		(4) 390,000	390,000
Total Liabilities and Stockholders' Equity	37,200,000	11,130,000	3,600,000	15,048,000	15,048,000	45,716,000

Explanations of Working Paper Entries

(1) To increase Investment in T by amount of P's purchase premium in S attributable to T.
(2) To reclassify purchase premium related to T; $1,020,000 ($= $1,100,000 - $80,000$) of the $1,370,000 is the unamortized portion of the purchase premium paid by S; $350,000 is S's share (70 percent) of the further increase in the fair value of T's assets imputed from P's investment in S.
(3) To allocate the total purchase premium related to T; the $980,000 allocated to various assets consists of the original $700,000 less one year's depreciation of $70,000 plus the $350,000 imputed from P's investment in S; the balance is unamortized goodwill.
(4) To eliminate the Investment in T against the stockholders' equity of T and establish the Minority Interest in T; $390,000 $= .3($1,300,000)$.
(5) To reclassify the purchase premium attributable to P's investment in S; $2,794,000 $= $3,144,000 - $350,000$.
(6) To allocate the portion of P's purchase premium related to the investment in S to the assets and liabilities of S and to goodwill.
(7) To eliminate the Investment in S against the stockholders' equity of S and establish the Minority Interest in S; $1,014,000 $= .2($5,070,000)$.

We now analyze consolidation of the four basic mutual holding configurations, beginning with those situations in which no minority interest is present.

Parent and Subsidiary: No Minority Interest. In the first mutual holding case we consider, the subsidiary is wholly owned. This case is diagramed below; it is the simplest because there is no minority interest.

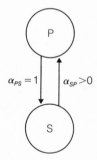

The treatment in consolidation is straightforward and follows from the facts of the case. *First,* the shares of P owned by S are, in consolidation, held internally. Hence, they are treated as *treasury shares* by reclassifying the Investment in P as Treasury Stock on the consolidated financial statement working paper. Note that, had the parent reacquired the shares instead of the subsidiary, the same result would be achieved.

Second, P owns all of the shares of S, and thus all of S's earnings accrue to the controlling interest, the shareholders of P. Therefore, even though S owns some of P's shares, and conceptually S's net income should include a pro rata share of P's net income under the equity method, any attempt at allocation would be unnecessary and superfluous. For these reasons, the Investment in P should be carried at *cost,* not equity, on S's books. Intercompany dividends received by S would be recorded as dividend income and would be eliminated against P's Dividends account on the working papers. To illustrate this case, consider the following situation.

On January 1, 19X1, P Company acquired all of S Company's outstanding shares for $340,000. One day later, S acquired 20 percent of P's outstanding shares at a cost of $150,000. There were purchase premiums involved in both cases, as shown below:

	P Company	S Company
Cost of Investment in	$150,000	$340,000
Retained Earnings, Jan. 1, 19X1	$400,000	$200,000
Capital Stock, Jan. 1, 19X1	200,000	100,000
Total Stockholders' Equity, Jan. 1, 19X1	$600,000	$300,000
α_{SP}	.20	—
α_{PS}	—	1.00
Purchase Premium	$ 30,000^a	$ 40,000^b

^{a}$30,000 = $150,000 − .2($600,000).
^{b}$40,000 = $340,000 − 1($300,000).

Since the shares of P held by S are considered to be treasury stock in consolidation, the purchase premium of $30,000 paid by S remains as part of the cost of the treasury stock and is not allocated and amortized. We assume that the purchase premium of $40,000 paid by P is entirely attributable to goodwill, which will be amortized over 40 years.

For the year ended December 31, 19X1, P and S reported the following summary data:

	P Company	S Company
Income from Own Operations.	$131,000	$75,000
Dividends Paid	80,000	20,000
Intercompany Merchandise Sales.	40,000	—
Unconfirmed Profit in Ending Inventory	—	5,000

The equity method accrual made at December 31, 19X1, by P was $69,000, as shown in the following schedule:

P COMPANY AND S COMPANY
SCHEDULE TO COMPUTE THE EQUITY METHOD ACCRUAL
FOR THE YEAR ENDED DECEMBER 31, 19X1

P's Share of S's Net Income from Its Own Operations (1 × $75,000) . . $75,000
Less Amortization of Purchase Premium (Goodwill, $40,000/40) . . . . . (1,000)
Less P's Unconfirmed Intercompany Inventory Profit . . . . (5,000)
Net Equity Method Accrual $69,000

Consolidation of P and S at December 31, 19X1, is given in the working paper displayed in Exhibit 11.5 on page 546. Detailed balance sheet and income statement data are assumed. The balance of $389,000 in the Investment in S account reflects original cost of $340,000 plus the equity method accrual of $69,000 less S's dividends of $20,000. Note that P's retained earnings, $520,000, do not equal consolidated retained earnings, $536,000. This deviation from the equity method requirement of equality is caused by the elimination of the $16,000 of P's dividends received by S. The alternative procedure which achieves equality by increasing the Investment in S and decreasing P's Dividends on P's books is not used in this text because it overstates P's retained earnings.

Connecting Affiliates: No Minority Interest. In a situation involving **connecting affiliates** with no minority interest, there are two subsidiaries controlled by the same parent company, and each owns some of the other subsidiary's shares. None of the parent's shares are held by the subsidiaries.

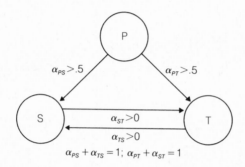

$$\alpha_{PS} + \alpha_{TS} = 1; \ \alpha_{PT} + \alpha_{ST} = 1$$

The *treasury stock* interpretation is not relevant here, since none of the parent's shares are held by the subsidiaries and, in consolidation, all of the subsidiaries' paid-in capital is eliminated. Hence, only the parent's outstanding common stock appears on the consolidated balance sheet. Since there is no minority interest (that is, $\alpha_{PS} + \alpha_{TS} = 1$; $\alpha_{PT} + \alpha_{ST} = 1$), all of the subsidiaries' earnings accrue to P, the controlling interest, and no allocation of these earnings is required. The subsidiaries' investments in each other are carried at *cost*, and intercompany dividends are eliminated in consolidation by debiting Dividend Revenue and crediting Dividends—S and Dividends—T on the working paper.

It would not be unusual if the amount paid by one subsidiary to acquire the shares of another reflected a purchase premium or discount. Any such purchase premium or discount must be reclassified, allocated, and amortized in consolidation, *just as if the parent company had acquired the shares directly.* Again, we argue that substance should govern rather than form; it makes no difference whether the parent or a subsidiary acquires the shares. A numerical example follows.

Suppose that P Company acquired 80 percent of the shares of S Company and 70 percent of the shares of T Company on January 2, 19X2. Two years later, on January 2, 19X4, S acquired the remaining 30 percent of T's shares, and T acquired the remaining 20 percent of S's shares. Details of the acquisitions are as follows:

Exhibit 11.5 **P and S Companies: Consolidated Financial Statement Working Paper for the Year Ended December 31, 19X1**

	P Company (20%)	S Company (100%)	Adjustments and Eliminations		Consolidated
INCOME STATEMENT			Dr.	Cr.	
Sales	800,000	300,000	(3) 40,000		1,060,000
Income from S.	69,000	—	(1) 69,000		—
Dividend Revenue	—	16,000	(2) 16,000		—
Inventory, Dec. 31, 19X1	120,000	40,000	(4) 5,000		155,000
Total Credits.	989,000	356,000	130,000		1,215,000
Inventory, Jan. 1, 19X1	100,000	35,000			135,000
Purchases.	400,000	140,000		(3) 40,000	500,000
Operating Expenses	289,000	90,000	(8) 1,000		380,000
Total Debits	789,000	265,000	1,000	40,000	1,015,000
Net Income—to Ret. Earn. Stmt. .	200,000	91,000	131,000	40,000	200,000
RETAINED EARNINGS STATEMENT					
Ret. Earnings, Jan. 1, 19X1—P .	400,000	—			400,000
Ret. Earnings, Jan. 1, 19X1—S .	—	200,000	(6) 200,000		—
Net Income—from Income Stmt. .	200,000	91,000	131,000	40,000	200,000
Dividends—P	(80,000)	—		(2) 16,000	(64,000)
Dividends—S	—	(20,000)		(1) 20,000	—
Ret. Earnings, Dec. 31, 19X1— to Balance Sheet	520,000	271,000	331,000	76,000	536,000
BALANCE SHEET					
Cash and Receivables	241,000	116,000			357,000
Inventory	120,000	40,000		(4) 5,000	155,000
Investment in S (100%).	389,000	—		(1) 49,000	—
				(6) 340,000	
Investment in P (20%)	—	150,000		(5) 150,000	—
Land	100,000	75,000			175,000
Buildings and Equipment	380,000	180,000			560,000
Accumulated Depreciation. . . .	(100,000)	(20,000)			(120,000)
Purchase Premium.	—	—	(6) 40,000	(7) 40,000	—
Goodwill	—	—	(7) 40,000	(8) 1,000	39,000
Total	1,130,000	541,000	80,000	585,000	1,166,000
Current Liabilities	200,000	75,000			275,000
Other Liabilities	210,000	95,000			305,000
Treasury Stock	—	—	(5) 150,000		(150,000)
Capital Stock—P.	200,000	—			200,000
Capital Stock—S.	—	100,000	(6) 100,000		—
Ret. Earn.—from Ret. Earn. Stmt.	520,000	271,000	331,000	76,000	536,000
Minority Interest in S	—	—			—
Total	1,130,000	541,000	581,000	76,000	1,166,000
			661,000	661,000	

Explanations of Working Paper Entries

(1) To eliminate the equity method entries made by P in 19X1.
(2) To eliminate intercompany dividends received by S.
(3) To eliminate intercompany merchandise sales.
(4) To eliminate unconfirmed intercompany profit in ending inventory.
(5) To reclassify the Investment in P as Treasury Stock.
(6) To eliminate the Investment in S and establish the unamortized purchase premium.
(7) To allocate the unamortized purchase premium at Jan. 1, 19X1.
(8) To record amortization of the purchase premium for 19X1.

	S Company	T Company
Price Paid by P on Jan. 2, 19X2, to Acquire		
Shares of	$530,000	$400,000
Book Value of P's Share of Net Assets	400,000 (80%)	350,000 (70%)
Purchase Premium Paid by P to Acquire	$130,000	$ 50,000
Price Paid by S on Jan. 2, 19X4, for Remaining		
Shares of	—	$200,000
Price Paid by T on Jan. 2, 19X4, for Remaining		
Shares of	$300,000	—
Book Value of Remaining Share of Net Assets at		
Jan. 2, 19X4	220,000 (20%)	192,000 (30%)
Purchase Premium Paid on Jan. 2, 19X4	$ 80,000	$ 8,000

All purchase premiums are assumed attributable to land and are not amortized. During 19X4, the only intercompany transactions involved the payment of dividends; net income and dividend activity for 19X4 are summarized below:

	P Company	S Company	T Company
Income from Own Operations	$300,000	$180,000	$140,000
Dividends Paid	200,000	100,000	40,000

The consolidated financial statement working paper for the year ended December 31, 19X4, is given in Exhibit 11.6. The detailed financial statement data are assumed.

P's equity accruals include all of the subsidiaries' income from their own operations to produce the equality between P's net income and retained earnings and their respective consolidated amounts required by the equity method. Even though the subsidiaries have investments in each other, there is no minority interest and the equity accruals should reflect all of their income from their own operations, as will consolidated net income.

An alternative approach is to allocate the subsidiaries' income among them in order to provide them with equity method accruals, and base P's equity method accrual on the reported net incomes of the subsidiaries, which now include their shares of each other's income. This is the so-called **traditional allocation method** and is equivalent to accounting for the subsidiaries' investments in each other on the *equity* rather than the *cost* basis. This allocation method is used in later examples where mutual holdings have minority interests present. When this alternative is followed, the net income and ending retained earnings of P will equal the consolidated amounts.

Exhibit 11.6   **P Company and Subsidiaries S and T Companies: Consolidated Financial Statement Working Paper for the Year Ended December 31, 19X4**

	P Company	S Company (80%, 20%)	T Company (70%, 30%)	Adjustments and Eliminations Dr.	Cr.	Consolidated
INCOME STATEMENT						
Sales	1,000,000	600,000	400,000			2,000,000
Income from S	180,000	—	—	(1) 180,000		—
Income from T.	140,000	—	—	(2) 140,000		—
Dividend Revenue	—	12,000	20,000	(3) 12,000		—
				(4) 20,000		
Inventory, Dec. 31, 19X4. . .	150,000	110,000	80,000			340,000
Total Credits.	1,470,000	722,000	500,000	352,000		2,340,000
Inventory, Jan. 1, 19X4 . . .	160,000	105,000	83,000			348,000
Purchases	500,000	300,000	200,000			1,000,000
Operating Expenses	190,000	125,000	57,000			372,000
Total Debits	850,000	530,000	340,000			1,720,000
Net Inc.—to Ret. Earn. Stmt. .	620,000	192,000	160,000	352,000		620,000
RETAINED EARNINGS STATEMENT						
Ret. Earn., Jan. 1, 19X4—P .	2,600,000	—	—			2,600,000
Ret. Earn., Jan. 1, 19X4—S .	—	800,000	—	(7) 640,000		—
				(8) 160,000		
Ret. Earn., Jan. 1, 19X4—T .	—	—	390,000	(9) 273,000		—
				(10) 117,000		
Net Inc.—from Inc. Stmt . . .	620,000	192,000	160,000	352,000		620,000
Dividends—P	(200,000)	—	—			(200,000)
Dividends—S	—	(100,000)	—		(1) 80,000	—
					(4) 20,000	
Dividends—T	—	—	(40,000)		(2) 28,000	—
					(3) 12,000	
Ret. Earn., Dec. 31, 19X4—to Balance Sheet	3,020,000	892,000	510,000	1,542,000	140,000	3,020,000
BALANCE SHEET						
Inventory	150,000	110,000	80,000			340,000
Other Assets	2,368,000	952,000	490,000			3,810,000
P's Investment in S (80%) . .	1,110,000	—	—		(1) 100,000	—
					(5) 130,000	
					(7) 880,000	
T's Investment in S (20%) . .	—	—	300,000		(5) 80,000	—
					(8) 220,000	
P's Investment in T (70%) . .	610,000	—	—		(2) 112,000	—
					(5) 50,000	
					(9) 448,000	
S's Investment in T (30%) . .	—	200,000	—		(5) 8,000	—
					(10) 192,000	
Land	450,000	330,000	180,000	(6) 268,000		1,228,000
Purchase Premium	—	—	—	(5) 268,000	(6) 268,000	—
Total	4,688,000	1,592,000	1,050,000	536,000	2,488,000	5,378,000
Liabilities	1,168,000	400,000	290,000			1,858,000
Capital Stock—P.	500,000	—	—			500,000
Capital Stock—S.	—	300,000	—	(7) 240,000		—
				(8) 60,000		
Capital Stock—T.	—	—	250,000	(9) 175,000		—
				(10) 75,000		
Ret. Earn.—from Ret. Earn. Stmt.	3,020,000	892,000	510,000	1,542,000	140,000	3,020,000
Total	4,688,000	1,592,000	1,050,000	2,092,000	140,000	5,378,000
				2,628,000	2,628,000	

Explanations of Working Paper Entries

(1) To eliminate the equity method entries made by P in connection with its investment in S during 19X4.
(2) To eliminate the equity method entries made by P in connection with its investment in T during 19X4.
(3) To eliminate intercompany dividends received by S from T.
(4) To eliminate intercompany dividends received by T from S.
(5) To reclassify the purchase premiums reflected in the intercompany investments.
(6) To allocate the purchase premium entirely to land.
(7) To eliminate P's investment in S.
(8) To eliminate T's investment in S.
(9) To eliminate P's investment in T.
(10) To eliminate S's investment in T.

Parent and Subsidiary: Minority Interest Present. The following diagram of the affiliation relationship indicates that, although the parent controls the subsidiary, the subsidiary is not wholly owned.

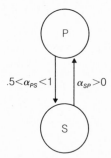

As previously indicated, shares of the parent held by a subsidiary are not to be treated as outstanding in the consolidated balance sheet. The cost of such shares is eliminated or reclassified as treasury stock on the working paper, depending on the context. We have seen that when no minority interest is present, it is convenient to carry the subsidiary's investment in the parent at *cost* and simply eliminate the subsidiary's intercompany dividend revenue and any other intercompany transactions on the working paper.

In the present case, however, existence of a minority interest in the subsidiary can complicate the consolidation process when income statement data are consolidated. Two alternative acceptable approaches are found in practice; each normally leads to different consolidated results.

Treasury Stock Method. The **treasury stock method** is simply an extension of the treasury stock approach encountered when there is no minority interest present. It is supported by an early position taken by the American Accounting Association:

> Shares of the controlling company's capital stock owned by a subsidiary should be treated in consolidation as treasury stock. Any subsequent acquisition or sale by a

subsidiary should likewise be treated in the consolidated statements as though it had been the act of the controlling company.[7]

Under this approach, the minority interest in the subsidiary's net income includes a pro rata share of any dividend revenue from the parent. The intercompany dividends are, of course, eliminated on the working paper, but the minority interest in net income is based on the subsidiary's reported net income, which reflects the intercompany dividend revenue. In applying the equity method, the parent company accrues its share of the subsidiary's net income from its own operations excluding the minority share of intercompany dividend revenue. An identical result is achieved by determining the parent's share of the subsidiary's reported net income and then subtracting all the intercompany dividend revenue.

To illustrate, suppose P Company owns 90 percent of S Company (α_{PS} = .9), and S Company owns 10 percent of P Company (α_{SP} = .1). P and S had net incomes from their own operations of $131,000 and $75,000, respectively. During the year, P paid $80,000 in dividends and S paid $20,000. The following schedule shows how the equity method accrual is determined:

P COMPANY AND S COMPANY
SCHEDULE TO COMPUTE THE EQUITY METHOD ACCRUAL

P's Share of S's Net Income from Its Own Operations (.9 × $75,000) . .	$67,500
Less Minority's Share of P's Dividends Received by S (.1 × $8,000). . .	(800)
Net Equity Method Accrual	$66,700
or	
P's Share of S's Reported Net Income [.9($75,000 + $8,000)].	$74,700
Less Intercompany Dividends Received by S (.1 × $80,000).	(8,000)
Net Equity Method Accrual	$66,700

Under this approach, consolidated net income is $197,700 (= $131,000 + $66,700), and the minority interest in S's net income is $8,300 [= .1 × ($75,000 + $8,000)] for a total of $206,000 (= $131,000 + $75,000) income from the two companies' own operations.

Traditional Allocation Method. The **traditional allocation method** involves application of the equity method to *both* P and S. Hence the combined earnings of P and S from their own operations must be allocated between the two companies and, subsequently, between the controlling and minority interests. P's total earnings under the equity method depend in part on S's earnings. But because S owns some of P's shares, S's earnings (and the minority interest in S's earnings) also depend on P's earnings. Thus the earnings of P and S are interdependent (and the relationship is circular in nature) because each is influenced by the other.

Proper allocation of combined earnings between the controlling and minority

---

[7]Committee on Accounting Concepts and Standards, *Accounting and Reporting Standards for Corporate Financial Statements* (Columbus: AAA, 1957), 44.

interests calls for computation of the net incomes of P and S on an equity basis. Determination of these equity basis incomes is facilitated by the use of simultaneous equations which take into account the interdependence between P and S. The following general relationships are used:

$P^* = $ P Company's net income on an equity basis.

$S^* = $ S Company's net income on an equity basis.

$Y_P = $ Net income of P from its own operations.

$Y_S = $ Net income of S from its own operations.

$\alpha_{PS} = $ Percentage of S's shares owned by P.

$\alpha_{SP} = $ Percentage of P's shares owned by S.

We can express P* and S* as follows.

$$P^* = Y_P + \alpha_{PS}S^* \quad \text{and} \quad S^* = Y_S + \alpha_{SP}P^*.$$

Note that $(P^* + S^*) > (Y_P + Y_S)$ because some income is double counted. The solutions, denoted P^* and S^*, are *tentative* and will be reduced to reflect the controlling and minority interests in these equity basis incomes. By substitution, we have

$$P^* = Y_P + \alpha_{PS}(Y_S + \alpha_{SP}P^*)$$

$$(1 - \alpha_{PS}\alpha_{SP})P^* = Y_P + \alpha_{PS}Y_S$$

$$P^* = \frac{Y_P + \alpha_{PS}Y_S}{(1 - \alpha_{PS}\alpha_{SP})},$$

$$S^* = Y_S + \alpha_{SP}(Y_P + \alpha_{PS}S^*)$$

$$(1 - \alpha_{SP}\alpha_{PS})S^* = Y_S + \alpha_{SP}Y_P$$

$$S^* = \frac{Y_S + \alpha_{SP}Y_P}{(1 - \alpha_{SP}\alpha_{PS})}.$$

Since α_{SP} of P's shares are owned by S, only $(1 - \alpha_{SP})$ of P^*, P Company's net income on an equity basis, pertains to the controlling interest. Similarly, since α_{PS} of S's shares are owned by the controlling interest, only $(1 - \alpha_{PS})$ of S^*, S Company's net income on an equity basis, pertains to the minority interest.

Using the facts from our last example, suppose P owns 90 percent of S (α_{PS} = .9) and S owns 10 percent of P (α_{SP} = .1). The net incomes of P and S from their own operations, Y_P and Y_S, respectively, are \$131,000 and \$75,000.

$P*$ = P Company's net income on an equity basis.

$S*$ = S Company's net income on an equity basis.

$$P* = \frac{\$131,000 + .9(\$75,000)}{[1 - (.9)(.1)]} = \frac{\$198,500}{.91} = \boxed{\$218,132.}$$

$$S* = \frac{\$75,000 + .1(\$131,000)}{[1 - (.1)(.9)]} = \frac{\$88,100}{.91} = \boxed{\$96,813.}$$

Note that $P* + S* = \$314,945$, while the net incomes of P and S from their own operations total $206,000 (= $131,000 + $75,000). Since the total of the income shares attributable to the controlling and minority interests *must equal* $206,000, we adjust $P*$ and $S*$ as follows:

P's Net Income on an Equity Basis ($P*$). $218,132
Less Amount Attributable to S (.1 × $218,132). 21,813
    Controlling Interest's Share of Combined Income. . . . . $196,319[a]
S's Net Income on an Equity Basis ($S*$). . . . . $ 96,813
Less Amount Attributable to P (.9 × $96,813) 87,132
    Minority Interest's Share of Combined Income . . . . $ 9,681[b]
Combined Net Incomes of P and S from Their Own Operations $206,000

[a]$(1 - \alpha_{SP}) = (1 - .1) = .9; \$196,319 = .9(\$218,132).$
[b]$(1 - \alpha_{PS}) = (1 - .9) = .1; \$9,681 = .1(\$96,813).$

Consider the equity method accruals which now will be recorded by both companies. First we consider P's equity method accrual:

P COMPANY AND S COMPANY
SCHEDULE TO COMPUTE P COMPANY'S EQUITY METHOD ACCRUAL
$(\alpha_{PS} = .9, \alpha_{SP} = .1)$

P's Share of S's Equity Basis Net Income (.9 × $96,813) . . . . $ 87,132
Less S's Share of P's Equity Basis Net Income (.1 × $218,132) . . . . (21,813)
Net Equity Method Accrual Made by P . . . . $ 65,319
    or
Controlling Interest's Share of Combined Income $196,319
Less P's Income from Its Own Operations 131,000
Net Equity Method Accrual Made by P . . . . $ 65,319

We now give the entries made by P to record the dividends received from S during the year and the equity method accrual:

BOOKS OF P COMPANY

Cash	18,000	
Investment in S		18,000

To record intercompany dividends received from S; $18,000 (= .9 × $20,000).

Investment in S	65,319	
Income from S		65,319

To record income from S accrued under the equity method.

The equity method accrual for S equals $21,813, as shown in the following schedule.

P COMPANY AND S COMPANY
SCHEDULE TO COMPUTE S's EQUITY METHOD ACCRUAL
$(\alpha_{PS} = .9, \alpha_{SP} = .1)$

S's Share of P's Equity Basis Net Income (.1 × $218,132)	$21,813
or	
S's Equity Basis Net Income	$96,813
Less S's Income from Its Own Operations	75,000
Net Equity Method Accrual Made by S	$21,813

Entries made during the year by S to record the dividends received from P and the equity method accrual are given below:

BOOKS OF S COMPANY

Cash	8,000	
Investment in P		8,000

To record intercompany dividends received from P; $8,000 (= .1 × $80,000).

Investment in P	21,813	
Income from P		21,813

To record income from P accrued under the equity method.

A Numerical Comparison. We now prepare working papers to contrast the *treasury stock* and *traditional allocation* methods of consolidating mutual holdings. On January 1, 19X1, P acquired 90 percent of S's stock for $306,000, while S acquired 10 percent of P's stock for $80,000. The book value of the S shares acquired was $270,000 (90 percent of the total book value of $300,000), while the 10 percent interest in P had a book value of $60,000. The purchase premium of $36,000 (= $306,000 − $270,000) paid by P is attributable to land. S also paid a purchase premium of $20,000 (= $80,000 − $60,000). Treatment of S's purchase premium in consolidation depends on the method being used.

1. Under the *treasury stock method,* the purchase premium is included in the Investment in P account, which is reclassified as Treasury Stock. The working paper reflecting this method appears in Exhibit 11.7. Note that P's re-

Exhibit 11.7 **P and S Companies: Consolidated Financial Statement Working Paper for the Year Ended December 31, 19X1 (Treasury Stock Method)**

	P Company (10%)	S Company (90%)	Adjustments and Eliminations Dr.	Cr.	Consolidated
INCOME STATEMENT					
Sales	800,000	300,000			1,100,000
Income from S.	66,700	—	(1) 66,700		—
Dividend Revenue	—	8,000	(2) 8,000		—
Inventory, Dec. 31, 19X1	120,000	40,000			160,000
Total Credits.	986,700	348,000	74,700		1,260,000
Inventory, Jan. 1, 19X1	100,000	35,000			135,000
Purchases.	400,000	140,000			540,000
Operating Expenses	289,000	90,000			379,000
Total Debits	789,000	265,000			1,054,000
Minority Interest in Net Income .	—	—	(6) 8,300		8,300
Net Income—to Ret. Earn. Stmt.	197,700	83,000	83,000		197,700
RETAINED EARNINGS STATEMENT					
Ret. Earn., Jan. 1, 19X1—P. . . .	400,000	—			400,000
Ret. Earn., Jan. 1, 19X1—S. . . .	—	200,000	(4) 200,000		—
Net Inc.—from Inc. Stmt.	197,700	83,000	83,000		197,700
Dividends—P	(80,000)	—		(2) 8,000	(72,000)
Dividends—S	—	(20,000)		(1) 18,000	—
				(6) 2,000	
Ret. Earn., Dec. 31, 19X1—to Balance Sheet	517,700	263,000	283,000	28,000	525,700
BALANCE SHEET					
Cash and Receivables	273,000	178,000			451,000
Inventory	120,000	40,000			160,000
Investment in S (90%)	354,700	—		(1) 48,700	—
				(4) 306,000	
Investment in P (10%)	—	80,000		(3) 80,000	—
Land	100,000	75,000	(5) 36,000		211,000
Buildings and Equipment	380,000	180,000			560,000
Accumulated Depreciation. . . .	(100,000)	(20,000)			(120,000)
Purchase Premium			(4) 36,000	(5) 36,000	—
Total	1,127,700	533,000	72,000	470,700	1,262,000
Current Liabilities	200,000	75,000			275,000
Other Liabilities	210,000	95,000			305,000
Treasury Stock	—	—	(3) 80,000		(80,000)
Capital Stock—P.	200,000	—			200,000
Capital Stock—S.	—	100,000	(4) 100,000		—
Ret. Earn.—from Ret. Earn. Stmt.	517,700	263,000	283,000	28,000	525,700
Minority Interest in S	—	—		(4) 30,000	36,300
				(6) 6,300	
Total	1,127,700	533,000	463,000	64,300	1,262,000
			535,000	535,000	

Explanations of Working Paper Entries

(1) To eliminate the equity method entries made by P in 19X1.
(2) To eliminate intercompany dividends received by S.
(3) To reclassify the Investment in P as Treasury Stock.
(4) To eliminate the Investment in S, establish the purchase premium and minority interest, all as of the beginning of the year.
(5) To allocate the unamortized purchase premium at 1/1/X1.
(6) To record the change in the minority interest in S during 19X1.

---

tained earnings, $517,700, are $8,000 less than consolidated retained earnings, $525,700, because P's dividends received by S are eliminated in consolidation. As stated in the discussion relating to Exhibit 11.5, when the issue first arose, we reject the alternative procedure which would eliminate the $8,000 of dividends on P's books because it leads to an overstatement of P's retained earnings.

2. Under the *traditional allocation method*, the stock of P held by S is assumed to be *constructively retired*. Hence, the Investment in P will be eliminated on the working paper against the stockholders' equity of P. Since the retirement of stock cannot generate gain or loss, the purchase premium is debited to P's Additional Paid-In Capital account. In our example, the caption "Capital Stock" includes the additional paid-in capital. This method is illustrated in a working paper presented in Exhibit 11.8. Again, we observe that P's retained earnings, $516,319, differ from consolidated retained earnings, $484,319, by $32,000 in the present case. This is due to two factors. *First,* P's dividends received by S, $8,000, are eliminated in consolidation but not on P's books. We have already discussed the reason for this. *Second,* in consolidation, the Investment in P is eliminated against P's capital stock and retained earnings, thereby reducing consolidated retained earnings by $40,000. We see no economic justification for eliminating the $40,000 of retained earnings on P's books. Only by decreasing P's retained earnings, in this way, by $40,000 accompanied by an increase of $8,000 for the reduced dividends, can the equity method equality requirement be satisfied. We cannot justify "forcing" equality in this way.

We previously pointed out that the two methods lead to different amounts of consolidated net income. This can be seen clearly from the working papers. Note also that consolidated retained earnings differ under the two methods. This difference in consolidated retained earnings arises because (1) consolidated net income under each method differs and (2) the portion of P's retained earnings owned by S is eliminated in the traditional allocation method. Of somewhat lesser importance is the fact that consolidated paid-in capital is also affected by the method being used.

Authors' Conclusion. We have observed that in a parent/subsidiary mutual holding situation, two acceptable alternative accounting treatments can lead to materially different results. In our example, consolidated retained earnings under the

Exhibit 11.8   **P and S Companies: Consolidated Financial Statement Working Paper for the Year Ended December 31, 19X1 (Traditional Allocation Method)**

	P Company (10%)	S Company (90%)	Adjustments and Eliminations Dr.	Cr.	Consolidated
INCOME STATEMENT					
Sales.	800,000	300,000			1,100,000
Income from S.	65,319	—	(1) 65,319		—
Income from P.	—	21,813	(2) 21,813		—
Inventory, Dec. 31, 19X1 . . .	120,000	40,000			160,000
Total Credits.	985,319	361,813	87,132		1,260,000
Inventory, Jan. 1, 19X1	100,000	35,000			135,000
Purchases.	400,000	140,000			540,000
Operating Expenses	289,000	90,000			379,000
Total Debits	789,000	265,000			1,054,000
Minority Interest in Net Income .	—	—	(6) 9,681		(9,681)
Net Inc.—to Ret. Earn. Stmt. . .	196,319	96,813	96,813		196,319
RETAINED EARNINGS STATEMENT					
Ret. Earn., Jan. 1, 19X1—P. . .	400,000	—	(3) 40,000		360,000
Ret. Earn., Jan. 1, 19X1—S. . .	—	200,000	(4) 200,000		—
Net Inc.—from Inc. Stmt.	196,319	96,813	96,813		196,319
Dividends—P	(80,000)	—		(2) 8,000	(72,000)
Dividends—S	—	(20,000)		(1) 18,000	—
				(6) 2,000	
Ret. Earn., Dec. 31, 19X1—to Balance Sheet	516,319	276,813	336,813	28,000	484,319
BALANCE SHEET					
Cash and Receivables	273,000	178,000			451,000
Inventory	120,000	40,000			160,000
Investment in S (90%)	353,319	—		(1) 47,319	—
				(4) 306,000	
Investment in P (10%)	—	93,813		(2) 13,813	—
				(3) 80,000	
Land	100,000	75,000	(5) 36,000		211,000
Buildings and Equipment	380,000	180,000			560,000
		(20,000)			(120,000)
Accumulated Depreciation. . . .	(100,000)				
Purchase Premium			(4) 36,000	(5) 36,000	—
Total	1,126,319	546,813	72,000	483,132	1,262,000
Current Liabilities	200,000	75,000			275,000
Other Liabilities	210,000	95,000			305,000
Capital Stock—P.	200,000	—	(3) 40,000		160,000
Capital Stock—S.	—	100,000	(4) 100,000		—
Ret. Earn.—from Ret. Earn. Stmt.	516,319	276,813	336,813	28,000	484,319
Minority Interest in S				(4) 30,000	37,681
				(6) 7,681	
Total	1,126,319	546,813	476,813	65,681	1,262,000
			548,813	548,813	

Explanations of Working Paper Entries

(1) To eliminate the equity method entries made by P in 19X1.
(2) To eliminate the equity method entries made by S in 19X1.
(3) To eliminate the Investment in P against the stockholders' equity of P. The implicit purchase premium of $20,000 is charged against the APIC of P which is included in Capital Stock—P.
(4) To eliminate the Investment in S and establish the purchase premium and minority interest, all as of the beginning of the year.
(5) To allocate the unamortized purchase premium to Land.
(6) To record the change in the minority interest in S during 19X1.

treasury stock method amounted to $525,700, or about $8\frac{1}{2}$ percent more than the $484,319 reported by the traditional allocation method. We conclude that the **treasury stock method** is more appropriate, for the following reasons:

1. From the standpoint of the controlling interest, any shares of P held by S have all of the characteristics of treasury stock.
2. Use of the equity method for S's investment in P seems improper in most situations. The entire equity method concept is based on the notion that the *investor* can exercise significant influence over the *investee*.[8] This will hardly be true in the present case, for P (the investee) *controls* S (the investor). Of course, one can conceive of circumstances in which the minority shareholders in S are also large holders of P's stock. In such a situation, the equity method—and the traditional allocation method—may well be appropriate.

Connecting Affiliates: Minority Interest Present. In the case diagramed below (involving connecting affiliates and minority interest), we observe that, while the subsidiaries own some shares in each other, they do not hold any of the parent's shares. As a result, the treasury stock approach is not applicable, and the traditional allocation method must be used for S and T.

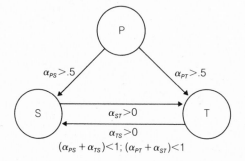

Notice that one could argue against use of the equity method by S and T on the grounds that their investments in each other are minimal compared to P's clear

---

[8]See Accounting Principles Board, *Opinion No. 18,* "The Equity Method of Accounting for Investments in Common Stock" (New York: AICPA, 1971), par. 12; CT § 182.104.

control over both subsidiaries. P's control over S and T, however, is reflected both by its *direct* interest in S and T and by its *indirect* interest in the subsidiaries' mutual holdings. Hence, P's equity accrual and the controlling interest's share of total earnings are influenced by the circularity between S and T. Consider a numerical example.

All acquisitions of stock are assumed to have occurred at January 1, 19X1. We recognize that purchase premiums or discounts paid by S or T are treated as if the parent had made the acquisition, but, to simplify the analysis, we ignore these items in our example. Data for the example are summarized here:

	P Company	S Company	T Company
Interest in S Company	$\alpha_{PS} = .8$	—	$\alpha_{TS} = .1$
Interest in T Company	$\alpha_{PT} = .7$	$\alpha_{ST} = .2$	—
Net Income from Own Operations	$300,000	$180,000	$150,000
Dividends Paid	200,000	100,000	40,000
Intercompany Merchandise Sales	90,000	60,000	50,000
Unconfirmed Intercompany Inventory Profit in Net Income	8,000	10,000	5,000

We have included unconfirmed intercompany profits to show how they are handled under the traditional allocation method. As long as the treatment of intercompany profits set forth in this text is used (100 percent elimination, proportionately against the controlling and minority interests), these profits can be deducted directly from income from own operations before solving the simultaneous equations. We first solve for the equity basis incomes of S and T and then use these tentative solutions to compute P's equity method accrual and the minority interest in net income. Note the reductions made for unconfirmed intercompany profits.

$$S^* = (\$180,000 - \$10,000) + .2T^*.$$

$$T^* = (\$150,000 - \$5,000) + .1S^*.$$

$$S^* = \frac{\$170,000 + .2(\$145,000)}{[1 - (.2)(.1)]} = \frac{\$199,000}{.98} = \boxed{\$203,061.}$$

$$T^* = \frac{\$145,000 + .1(\$170,000)}{[1 - (.1)(.2)]} = \frac{\$162,000}{.98} = \boxed{\$165,306.}$$

Since P's net income from its own operations is $292,000 (= $300,000 − $8,000), total income to be allocated among the controlling and minority interests is $607,000 (= $292,000 + $170,000 + $145,000). This allocation is as follows:

P's Net Income on an Equity Basis (Consolidated Net Income); $292,000 + .8S^* + .7T^* = $292,000 + .8($203,061) + .7 ($165,306)	$570,163
Minority Interest in Net Income of S; $.1S^* = .1($203,061)	20,306
Minority Interest in Net Income of T; $.1T^* = .1($165,306)	16,531
Combined Net Income less Unconfirmed Intercompany Profits	$607,000

Exhibit 11.9   **Computation of Equity Method Accruals**

P COMPANY, S COMPANY, AND T COMPANY
SCHEDULE TO COMPUTE THE EQUITY METHOD ACCRUALS
MADE BY P, S, AND T
$(\alpha_{PS} = .8, \alpha_{PT} = .7, \alpha_{ST} = .2, \alpha_{TS} = .1)$

P COMPANY

P's Share of S's Equity Basis Net Income (.8 × $203,061)	$162,449
P's Share of T's Equity Basis Net Income (.7 × $165,306)	115,714
Less Unconfirmed Intercompany Profit Recorded by P	(8,000)
Net Equity Method Accrual Made by P Company	$270,163

S COMPANY

S's Share of T's Equity Basis Net Income (.2 × $165,306)	$ 33,061
Less Unconfirmed Intercompany Profit Recorded by S	(10,000)
Net Equity Method Accrual Made by S Company	$ 23,061

T COMPANY

T's Share of S's Equity Basis Net Income (.1 × $203,061)	$ 20,306
Less Unconfirmed Intercompany Profit Recorded by T	(5,000)
Net Equity Method Accrual Made by T Company	$ 15,306

Note: For P, $570,163 = $300,000 + $270,163; for S, $203,061 = $180,000 + $23,061; for T, $165,306 = $150,000 + $15,306.

Computation of the equity method accruals for the three companies is shown in Exhibit 11.9. A working paper to consolidate P, S, and T is presented in Exhibit 11.10. Detailed financial statement data are assumed.

Conclusion

This completes our study of consolidated financial statements. In Chapters 7–11, we have stressed substance over form and have been guided by the single entity concept. Although a group of affiliated corporations consists of several legal entities, the fact that the group is under common control creates a new accounting entity, an area of economic activity of interest to the controlling shareholders. Thus all transactions and other intercompany relationships between members of the affiliated group are eliminated in consolidation.

Summary of Key Concepts

When the parent achieves its controlling interest by a series of smaller purchases, the purchase premium or discount related to **each block of stock** must be determined and allocated among the assets and liabilities of S and to goodwill. To do

Exhibit 11.10 **P, S, and T Companies: Consolidated Financial Statement Working Paper for the Year Ended December 31, 19X1**

	P Company	S Company (80%, 10%)	T Company (70%, 20%)	Adjustments and Eliminations Dr.		Adjustments and Eliminations Cr.		Consolidated
INCOME STATEMENT								
Sales.	1,000,000	600,000	400,000	(5)	200,000			1,800,000
P's Income from S.	154,449	—	—	(1)	154,449			—
P's Income from T.	115,714	—	—	(2)	115,714			—
S's Income from T.	—	23,061	—	(3)	23,061			—
T's Income from S.	—	—	15,306	(4)	15,306			—
Inventory, Dec. 31, 19X1	150,000	110,000	80,000	(6)	23,000			317,000
Total Credits	1,420,163	733,061	495,306		531,530			2,117,000
Inventory, Jan. 1, 19X1	160,000	105,000	83,000					348,000
Purchases.	500,000	300,000	200,000			(5)	200,000	800,000
Operating Expenses	190,000	125,000	47,000					362,000
Total Debits	850,000	530,000	330,000				200,000	1,510,000
Minority Int. In Net Inc. of S	—	—	—	(13)	20,306			(20,306)
Minority Int. in Net Inc. of T	—	—	—	(14)	16,531			(16,531)
Net Inc.—to Ret. Earn. Stmt..	570,163	203,061	165,306		568,367		200,000	570,163
RETAINED EARNINGS STMT.								
Ret. Earn., Jan. 1, 19X1—P	2,600,000	—	—					2,600,000
Ret. Earn., Jan. 1, 19X1—S	—	800,000	—	(7)	640,000			—
				(8)	80,000			
				(11)	80,000			
Ret. Earn., Jan. 1, 19X1—T	—	—	400,000	(9)	280,000			—
				(10)	80,000			
				(12)	40,000			
Net Inc.—from Inc. Stmt.	570,163	203,061	165,306		568,367		200,000	570,163
Dividends—P	(200,000)	—	—					(200,000)
Dividends—S	—	(100,000)	—			(1)	80,000	—
						(4)	10,000	
						(13)	10,000	
Dividends—T	—	—	(40,000)			(2)	28,000	—
						(3)	8,000	
						(14)	4,000	
Ret. Earn., 12/31/X1—to Bal. Sht.	2,970,163	903,061	525,306		1,768,367		340,000	2,970,163
BALANCE SHEET								
Inventory	150,000	110,000	80,000			(6)	23,000	317,000
Other Assets	3,023,000	1,348,000	880,000					5,251,000
P's Investment in S (80%)	954,449	—	—			(1)	74,449	—
						(7)	880,000	
T's Investment in S (10%)	—	—	115,306			(4)	5,306	—
						(8)	110,000	
P's Investment in T (70%)	542,714	—	—			(2)	87,714	—
						(9)	455,000	
S's Investment in T (20%)	—	145,061	—			(3)	15,061	—
						(10)	130,000	
Total	4,670,163	1,603,061	1,075,306				1,780,530	5,568,000
Liabilities	1,200,000	400,000	300,000					1,900,000
Capital Stock—P	500,000	—	—					500,000
Capital Stock—S	—	300,000	—	(7)	240,000			—
				(8)	30,000			
				(11)	30,000			
Capital Stock—T	—	—	250,000	(9)	175,000			—
				(10)	50,000			
				(12)	25,000			
Ret. Earn.—from Ret. Earn. Stmt.	2,970,163	903,061	525,306		1,768,367		340,000	2,970,163
Minority Interest in S	—	—	—			(11)	110,000	120,306
						(13)	10,306	
Minority Interest in T	—	—	—			(12)	65,000	77,531
						(14)	12,531	
Total	4,670,163	1,603,061	1,075,306		2,318,367		537,837	5,568,000
					2,318,367		2,318,367	

Explanations of Working Paper Entries

(1) To eliminate the equity method entries made by P in connection with its investment in S during 19X1.
(2) To eliminate the equity method entries made by P in connection with its investment in T during 19X1.
(3) To eliminate the equity method entries made by S in connection with its investment in T during 19X1.
(4) To eliminate the equity method entries made by T in connection with its investment in S during 19X1.
(5) To eliminate intercompany sales and purchases.
(6) To eliminate unconfirmed intercompany profit in ending inventory.
(7) To eliminate P's investment in S.
(8) To eliminate T's investment in S.
(9) To eliminate P's investment in T.
(10) To eliminate S's investment in T.
(11) To establish the minority interest in S at Jan. 1, 19X1.
(12) To establish the minority interest in T at Jan. 1, 19X1.
(13) To record the change in the minority interest in S during 19X1.
(14) To record the change in the minority interest in T during 19X1.

---

so, the fair values of S's identifiable assets and liabilities at the dates the several blocks are acquired must be estimated.

Care must be taken to insure that **consistent accounting treatment** is afforded those various transactions in the **subsidiary's shares** that have **identical effects** on the economic position of the **controlling interest.** We believe that if the controlling interest's position is improved following the issue of additional shares by the subsidiary, a consolidated gain should be recognized just as if P had sold at a gain shares of S which P owned.

A new dimension of the problem of allocating a purchase premium arises when P acquires a company that **already** has its own subsidiary, T. In this type of **indirect holding,** the accountant is faced with the dilemma of whether to attribute some of P's purchase premium or discount in the acquisition of S to the assets and liabilities of T. If the fair values of T's assets and liabilities are to be considered in the purchase premium allocation, the premium is *first* allocated among the assets and liabilities of S. Any **remaining** unallocated premium, which otherwise would be classified as goodwill, is *then* allocated among the assets and liabilities of T.

A **mutual holding** arises when one or more subsidiaries own stock in the parent or in each other. Any shares of the parent held by a subsidiary are treated as **treasury stock** in consolidation. We believe that subsidiary investments in shares of the parent should be carried at *cost,* although a case could be made for use of the equity method when a minority interest exists.

The **treasury stock method** is the preferred consolidation method in a parent/ subsidiary mutual holding for two principal reasons. *First,* from the viewpoint of the controlling interest, any shares of P held by S have all of the characteristics of treasury stock. *Second,* use of the equity method for S's investment in P seems inappropriate in most situations.

The **traditional allocation method** *may* be used in a parent/subsidiary mutual holding with minority interest present and *must* be used in a connecting affiliate mutual holding when a minority interest is present. A computational problem arises in allocating the affiliates' total income to the controlling and minority interests in these cases. The mutual holding creates a situation in which one company's equity accrual from another company is also dependent on the second company's equity accrual from the first. This interdependence or circularity is best dealt with by the use of simultaneous equations.

The existence of **unconfirmed intercompany profits** is easily handled under the traditional allocation method as long as consolidation policy calls for elimination of 100 percent of the intercompany profit proportionately against the controlling and minority interests. Such unconfirmed intercompany profits are simply deducted from the selling companies' incomes from their own operations before solving the simultaneous equations.

Questions

Q11.1 P Company may obtain control over S Company after several blocks of S's stock are purchased over time. Generally accepted accounting principles seem to suggest that, in such situations, "the date of the latest purchase, as a matter of convenience, may be considered the date of acquisition." How would you comment on this suggestion?

Q11.2 During 19X3, the Investor Company doubled its holdings of the Investee Company's stock by purchasing an additional 15 percent of the stock. In addition to recording the cost of the second 15 percent block, Investor made the following entry:

Intercorporate Investments 9,000
   Retained Earnings   9,000

What did Investor accomplish in the above entry?

Q11.3 Briefly explain the nature of the accounting problems which arise when P sells a portion of its holdings of S's stock.

Q11.4 We believe that if the economic position of the controlling interest is improved by the sale of some of S's shares—either by P or by S—the resulting gain should flow through the consolidated income statement. How might you criticize this approach?

Q11.5 Suppose S reacquired its own stock for a total of $30,000, $10,000 less than its book value. As a result, P's ownership interest increased from 70 percent to 80 percent. What entry would be made by P using the treatment recommended in the text?

Q11.6 Suppose a subsidiary purchases treasury stock in the open market (not from its parent) at an amount different from its book value. Describe the adjusting entry made by the parent when this occurs.

Q11.7 The father-son-grandson (FSG) type of indirect holding is a common ownership configuration. Suppose P paid $5,000,000 for an 80 percent interest in S. The estimated fair value of S's identifiable assets less liabilities was $4,000,000 at date of acquisition. Discuss the conceptual difference in accounting for this combination under two alternatives: (1) S controls no subsidiaries, and (2) S controls two subsidiaries, T Company and U Company.

Q11.8 Why is the order of consolidation important in an indirect holding?

Q11.9 In the connecting affiliation involving P, S, and T with no minority interest, alternative accounting treatments can cause P's net income and retained earnings to differ from their respective consolidated amounts, even if P uses the equity method. Explain how this situation can arise.

Q11.10 Explain the basic consolidation problem often encountered in a mutual holding situation with minority interest present.

Q11.11 "In a mutual holding involving a partially owned subsidiary, application of either the treasury stock method or the traditional allocation method will yield identical amounts of minority interest in net income." How would you comment on this statement?

Q11.12 The chapter presents formulas for the computation of P^* and S^*, *tentative* measurements of the net incomes of P and S on equity basis. Why are these solutions tentative, and how must they be adjusted so that they are no longer tentative?

Exercises

E11.1 P Company acquired control of S Company by purchasing two large blocks of S's stock. The details are as follows:

Acquisition Date	Percent Acquired	Cost of Shares	Net Assets of S Company Fair Value	Book Value	Net Income (Dividends) of S for the Year	
1/2/X8	25%	$ 300,000	$1,100,000	$1,000,000	$100,000	$(40,000)
1/2/X9	60	1,000,000	1,400,000	1,060,000	150,000	(60,000)

S's undervalued assets are being depreciated by the straight-line method over a remaining life of 10 years at date(s) of acquisition. P's policy is to amortize intangibles over 20 years.

Required:

1. Prepare a schedule to determine and allocate the purchase premiums reflected in the acquisition prices paid by P.
2. Prepare a schedule to compute the equity method accruals recorded by P in 19X8 and 19X9.

E11.2 Information pertaining to Marvel Corporation's acquisition of Nunn Corporation's stock is summarized on page 564:

Date	Percent Acquired	Cost	Nunn's Stockholders' Equity	Year	Nunn Net Income	Dividends
1/1/X2	25%	$400,000	$1,400,000	19X2	$160,000	$60,000
1/1/X3	50	900,000	1,500,000	19X3	200,000	80,000

Book values of Nunn's identifiable assets and liabilities approximated their fair values. Marvel amortizes intangibles over a 10-year period.

Required: Prepare the working paper entries made in consolidation at December 31, 19X3, including reversal of Marvel's equity method entries.

E11.3 The Norwood Company purchased 50 percent of Sanly Company's stock for $1,000,000 on December 31, 19X7, and an additional 30 percent for $573,000 on July 1, 19X8. Sanly's net assets (all fairly valued) amounted to $1,800,000 on December 31, 19X7. During 19X8, Sanly reported net income of $200,000 and paid dividends of $120,000, with equal amounts occurring before and after July 1. When the second block of stock was purchased on July 1, one of Sanly's buildings (21-year life) was undervalued by $70,000. Goodwill is amortized over 40 years.

Required: Compute Norwood's equity method accrual for 19X8 and prepare the eliminating entries made in consolidation at December 31, 19X8.

E11.4 On January 2, 19X4, The Investor Company purchased 10 percent of the outstanding shares of The Investee Company for $100,000, implying a purchase premium of $10,000. The premium was attributed to undervalued depreciable assets owned by Investee which are being depreciated by the straight-line method over a remaining life of 5 years. During 19X4 and 19X5, Investee reported the following:

Year	Net Income	Dividends
19X4	$ 70,000	$30,000
19X5	100,000	40,000

Investor increased its ownership of Investee stock by purchasing another 20 percent for $350,000 on January 2, 19X6.

Required: Prepare the entry made by Investor on January 2, 19X6, to retroactively apply the equity method to its investment in Investee.

E11.5 P Company owns 80,000 of S Company's 100,000 outstanding shares of common stock. An analysis of the investment account appears below:

INVESTMENT IN S COMPANY

1/1/X2

Original Acquisition Cost:
Book Value of Shares Acquired	$800,000
Purchase Premium (Goodwill—12-Year Life)	60,000

19X2

P's Share of S's Dividends (.8 × $40,000). . . . .   (32,000)

12/31/X2

P's Equity Method Accrual:
  P's Share of S's Net Income (.8 × $100,000) $80,000
  Goodwill amortization ($60,000/12) . . . . (5,000)   75,000

12/31/X2

Balance $903,000

Required: Assume that P sells 10,000 of the shares for $130,000 on January 1, 19X3. Prepare the entry to record the sale and the investment elimination made in consolidation at December 31, 19X3.

E11.6 Petri Corporation owns 60,000 of Storrs Company's 100,000 shares of outstanding common stock. The balance in the Investment in S, carried at equity, is $1,400,400, including an unamortized purchase premium of $200,000. Storrs' Company's stock currently sells for $35 per share.

Required: Given the current price at which Storrs's shares are selling, the controlling interest believes that now might be a good time to realize $60,000 of the unrealized holding gains attributable to its investment in Storrs's shares. To achieve this desired result, determine how many shares must be (1) sold by Petri or (2) issued by Storrs.

E11.7 Carol Corporation owns 90,000 of Jones Company's 100,000 outstanding common shares. At January 1, 19X4, the investment account balance of $1,890,000 reflects an unamortized purchase premium (goodwill—remaining life, 10 years) of $90,000. On that date, Jones issues 12,500 new shares in the open market for $300,000; none are acquired by Carol.

Required: Prepare the journal entry made by Carol to record these events and prepare the investment elimination to be made in consolidation at December 31, 19X4.

E11.8 Pidgeon Corporation owns 90 percent of Starling Company's 100,000 outstanding common shares. The investment account is carried at equity, has a balance at December 31, 19X4, of $1,700,000, and reflects an unamortized purchase *discount* of $100,000. Starling is contemplating the purchase of 5,263 shares of treasury stock.

Required: Determine the effects on the dollar amount of Pidgeon's investment in Starling if the treasury shares are purchased at (1) $22 per share, (2) $20 per share, and (3) $18 per share.

E11.9 At December 31, 19X1, condensed balance sheet data for S Company and T Company are as follows:

	S Company		T Company	
	Book Value	**Fair Value**	**Book Value**	**Fair Value**
Various Assets.	$2,000,000	$2,400,000	$1,100,000	$1,300,000
Investment in T (80%) .	480,000	—	—	—
	$2,480,000		$1,100,000	
Liabilities.	$ 800,000	710,000	$ 500,000	540,000
Stockholders' Equity . .	1,680,000	—	600,000	—
	$2,480,000		$1,100,000	

S had acquired its interest in T several years before, when the book values of T's assets and liabilities equaled their fair values. On December 31, 19X1, P Company acquired 90 percent of S's outstanding shares for a total cash price of $2,200,000. This price was based, in part, on a careful analysis of the fair values of T's assets and liabilities as well as those of S.

Required: Prepare a schedule to determine and allocate P's purchase premium in S among the assets and liabilities of S and T.

E11.10 The Sue-Anne Company acquired 60 percent of Theo Corporation's common stock several years ago at book value. All of Theo's identifiable assets and liabilities were fairly stated at date of acquisition. The investment account, carried at equity, has a balance of $2,400,000 at December 31, 19X7. Sue-Anne's stockholders' equity amounts to $5,000,000 on that date.

In a business combination consummated on December 31, 19X7, the Pauli Company purchased 80 percent of Sue-Anne's stock for $4,400,000. All identifiable assets and liabilities were fairly valued except that a parcel of land owned by Sue-Anne was undervalued by $200,000 and one of Theo's buildings was undervalued by $100,000.

Required: Prepare the working paper entries made if a consolidated balance sheet is prepared on December 31, 19X7. The price paid by Pauli was influenced by the fair values of property owned by both Sue-Anne and Theo.

E11.11 P Company, S Company, and T Company are related in a connecting affiliation, diagramed here:

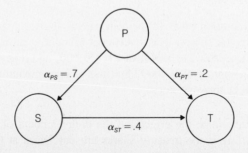

The three companies' condensed statements of income and retained earnings from their own operations for the year ended December 31, 19X6, appear as follows. Although P carries its investments in S and T at equity, the current year's equity accruals have not been made.

	P Company	S Company	T Company
Sales.	$10,000,000	$5,000,000	$4,000,000
Cost of Goods Sold	5,500,000	3,000,000	2,000,000
Operating Expenses	3,000,000	1,400,000	1,600,000
Net Income.	$ 1,500,000	$ 600,000	$ 400,000
Retained Earnings, Jan. 1, 19X6. . .	8,000,000	2,000,000	1,900,000
Dividends Declared.	500,000	300,000	200,000
Retained Earnings, Dec. 31, 19X6 . .	$ 9,000,000	$2,300,000	$2,100,000

Required: Prepare a condensed consolidated statement of income and retained earnings for 19X6. There were no purchase premiums or discounts and no intercompany transactions.

E11.12 P Company owns 100 percent of S Company's stock. S recently purchased 20 percent of P's stock in the open market on July 1 for $2,000,000. The book value of those shares was $1,800,000 at time of purchase. Following the acquisition by S, P declared $100,000 in dividends. During the current year, P reported net income of $340,000 from its own operations, earned evenly throughout the year.

Required: Prepare the working paper entries relative to S's investment in P's stock necessary for consolidation at December 31.

E11.13 Companies P, S, and T are related in a connecting affiliation, diagramed here:

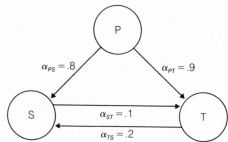

Information relative to these investments is summarized below:

	S Company	T Company
Price Paid by P on Dec. 31, 19X7, to		
Acquire Shares of	$4,000,000	$2,000,000
Book Value of P's Share of Net Assets at Acquisition . .	3,500,000	1,800,000
Price Paid by S on Dec. 31, 19X8,		
for Remaining Shares of	—	200,000
Price Paid by T on Dec. 31, 19X8,		
for Remaining Shares of	1,000,000	—
Book Value of Remaining Share of Net Assets at		
Dec. 31, 19X8	950,000	240,000

Any purchase premiums are attributed to goodwill amortizable over 20 years. Purchase discounts are allocated to depreciable assets with a remaining life of 10 years at acquisition. Neither S nor T engaged in any capital transactions after 19X7. P carries its investments in S and T at equity.

Required: From the information given, prepare the working paper eliminations necessary to consolidate the financial statements of P, S, and T at December 31, 19X9.

E11.14 P Company owns 90 percent of S Company and S Company owns 20 percent of P Company. During the current year, P earned $500,000 from its own operations and paid dividends of $200,000. S earned $300,000 from its own operations and paid dividends of $100,000.

Required: Compute consolidated net income and the minority interest in net income under (1) the treasury stock method and (2) the traditional allocation method.

E11.15 Akron, Inc., owns 80 percent of the capital stock of the Benson Company and 70 percent of the capital stock of Cashin, Inc. Benson owns 15 percent of the capital stock of Cashin. Cashin, in turn, owns 25 percent of the capital stock of Akron. These ownership relationships are illustrated in the diagram below:

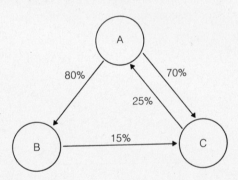

Net income of each corporation from its own operations follows:

Akron	$190,000
Benson	170,000
Cashin	230,000

Required: For each multiple choice item that follows, select the correct answer. Ignore all income tax considerations. The following notations relate to Items 1 through 4:

A_e = Akron's net income on an equity basis.

B_e = Benson's net income on an equity basis.

C_e = Cashin's net income on an equity basis.

1. The equation, in a set of simultaneous equations, which computes A_e is:
   a. $A_e = .75(190,000 + .8B_e + .7C_e)$.
   b. $A_e = 190,000 + .8B_e + .7C_e$.
   c. $A_e = .75(190,000) + .8(170,000) + .7(230,000)$.
   d. $A_e = .75(190,000) + .8B_e + .7C_e$.

2. The equation, in a set of simultaneous equations, which computes B_e is:
   a. $B_e = 170,000 + .15C_e - .75A_e$.
   b. $B_e = 170,000 + .15C_e$.
   c. $B_e = .2(170,000) + .15(230,000)$.
   d. $B_e = .2(170,000) + .15C_e$.

3. Cashin's minority interest in net income is:
   a. $.15(230,000)$.
   b. $230,000 + .25A_e$.
   c. $.15(230,000) + .25A_e$.
   d. $.15C_e$.

4. Benson's minority interest in net income is:
   a. 34,316.
   b. 25,500.
   c. 45,755.
   d. 30,675.
   (AICPA adapted)

E11.16 The following information relates to the P, S, and T affiliation:

	P Company	S Company	T Company
Ownership Interest of P Company in. . . .	—	.7	.8
Ownership Interest of S Company in. . . .	—	—	.1
Ownership Interest of T Company in. . . .	—	.2	—
Net Income from Own Operations of. . . .	$100,000	$70,000	$40,000

Required: Compute consolidated net income and the minority interest in net income for the P, S, and T affiliation, using the traditional allocation method as appropriate.

Problems

P11.1 Consolidated Financial Statement Working Paper after Sale of Partial Interest Prune Corporation owns 60 percent of the outstanding common stock of the Squash Company, having held an 80 percent interest through June 30, 19X7, the current year. A gain of $50,000 was recognized on the sale, based on January 1, 19X7, book value, and was recorded as Other Income. The 20 percent interest was sold for $169,750. The original acquisition of the 80 percent interest occurred on January 2, 19X2, at a transaction price of $400,000, $160,000 more than the portion of Squash's stockholders' equity acquired. The $160,000 was allocated to depreciable assets with a 10-year life ($120,000) and to goodwill amortized over 40 years ($40,000).

On April 20, 19X7, Squash sold a parcel of land to Prune and recorded a gain of $20,000. Later in the year, Squash sold merchandise costing $50,000 to Prune for $75,000. This sale occurred on October 15 and, as of December 31, 19X7, one-half of the merchandise was still on hand and it had not been paid for. Squash makes semiannual dividend payments of $10,000 on February 15 and August 15 of each year. Its net income is earned evenly throughout the year.

Exhibit 11.11	Prune Corporation and Squash Company: Financial Statements at December 31, 19X7, to Be Used in P11.1

STATEMENTS OF INCOME AND RETAINED EARNINGS

	Prune	Squash
Sales	$2,100,000	$1,400,000
Income from Squash	140,125	—
Other Income	50,000	20,000
Total Revenue	$2,290,125	$1,420,000
Cost of Goods Sold:		
Beginning Inventory	$ 200,000	$ 120,000
Purchases	1,100,000	700,000
Ending Inventory	(230,000)	(100,000)
	$1,070,000	$ 720,000
Operating Expenses	500,000	450,000
Total Expenses	$1,570,000	$1,170,000
Net Income	$ 720,125	$ 250,000
Beginning Retained Earnings	828,000	380,000
Dividends	(100,000)	(20,000)
Ending Retained Earnings	$1,448,125	$ 610,000

BALANCE SHEETS

ASSETS	Prune	Squash
Cash and Receivables	$ 477,750	$ 180,000
Inventory	230,000	100,000
Investment in Squash	485,375	—
Plant Assets	1,300,000	720,000
Accumulated Depreciation	(270,000)	(130,000)
Total Assets	$2,223,125	$ 870,000

LIABILITIES AND STOCKHOLDERS' EQUITY	Prune	Squash
Current Liabilities	$ 275,000	$ 160,000
Noncurrent Liabilities	400,000	—
Capital Stock	100,000	100,000
Retained Earnings	1,448,125	610,000
Total Liabilities and Stockholders' Equity	$2,223,125	$ 870,000

Separate financial statements for the two companies at December 31, 19X7, are given in Exhibit 11.11.

Required: Prepare a consolidated financial statement working paper for Prune and Squash at December 31, 19X7.

P11.2 Consolidated Balance Sheet Working Paper—Step Acquisition; Incomplete Equity Method The December 31, 19X8, postclosing trial balances of the Major Corporation and its two subsidiaries are as shown in Exhibit 11.12.

Exhibit 11.12 **Postclosing Trial Balances of Major Corporation and Subsidiaries at December 31, 19X8, to Be Used in P11.2**

ASSETS	Major Corporation	Minor Corporation	Mode Corporation
Cash	$ 100,000	$ 75,000	$ 95,000
Accounts Receivable	158,200	210,000	105,000
Inventories.	290,000	90,000	115,000
Advance to Minor Corporation	17,000		
Dividends Receivable	24,000		
Property, Plant, and Equipment . . .	777,600	325,000	470,000
Allowance for Depreciation	(180,000)	(55,000)	(160,000)
Investment in Minor Corporation:			
6% Bonds	23,800		
Common Stock	308,600		
Investment in Mode Corporation:			
Preferred Stock	7,000		
Common Stock	196,000		
Totals	$1,722,200	$645,000	$ 625,000
LIABILITIES AND STOCKHOLDERS' EQUITY			
Accounts Payable	$ 170,000	$ 96,000	$ 86,000
Notes Payable	45,000	14,000	44,000
Bonds Payable	285,000	150,000	125,000
Discount on Bonds Payable	(8,000)	(12,000)	
Dividends Payable	22,000	30,000	
Preferred Stock, $20 Par	400,000		
Mode Corporation			50,000
Common Stock, $10 Par	600,000		
Minor Corporation		250,000	
Mode Corporation			200,000
Retained Earnings	208,200		
Minor Corporation		117,000	
Mode Corporation			120,000
Totals	$1,722,200	$645,000	$ 625,000

Additional information:

1. The investment in Minor Corporation stock by Major Corporation is composed of the following items:

Date	Description	Amount
4/1/X7	Cost of 5,000 Shares of Minor Corporation Stock . . .	$ 71,400
12/31/X7	20% of the Dividends Declared in December 19X7 by Minor Corporation.	(9,000)
12/31/X7	20% of the 19X7 Net Income of Minor Corporation . .	12,000
7/1/X8	Cost of 15,000 Shares of Minor Corporation Stock . .	226,200
12/31/X8	80% of the Dividends Declared in December 19X8 by Minor Corporation.	(24,000)
12/31/X8	80% of the 19X8 Net Income of Minor Corporation . .	32,000
12/31/X8	Total.	$308,600

2. Major Corporation acquired 250 shares of noncumulative fully participating preferred stock for $7,000 and 14,000 shares of common stock for $196,000 (their book value) of the Mode Corporation on January 2, 19X8. Mode had a net income of $20,000 in 19X8 and did not declare any dividends. Under the fully participating provision, Mode's common and preferred shareholders have interests in current and retained earnings equal to the ratios of common stock ($200,000) and preferred stock ($50,000) to total contributed capital ($250,000), respectively.

3. Mode's inventory includes $22,400 of merchandise acquired from Minor for which no payment has been made. Minor charged Mode an amount 40 percent above its own cost for the merchandise.

4. Major acquired in the open market twenty-five $1,000 face-value, 6 percent bonds of Minor for $21,400 on January 5, 19X5. The Minor bonds mature in 2 years, on December 31, 19Y0. Interest is paid each June 30 and December 31.

5. The three corporations are all in the same industry, and their operations are similar. Major exercises control over the boards of directors of both Minor and Mode and has installed new principal officers in both.

Required: Prepare a consolidated balance sheet working paper as of December 31, 19X8, for Major Corporation and its subsidiaries. The consolidation is to be accounted for as a purchase. Formal financial statements and journal entries are not required. Supporting computations should be in good form. *(AICPA adapted)*

P11.3 Intrayear Step Acquisition—Eliminations and Consolidated Calculations
Phydeaux Corporation now owns a controlling interest in the Styx Company and uses the equity method of accounting. Three blocks of stock were acquired over a period of 18 months; the related data are as follows:

Acquisition Date	Percent Acquired	Cost of Shares	Net Assets of Styx	
			Fair Value	Book Value
1/3/X4	25%	$500,000	$1,800,000	$1,600,000
1/5/X5	20	600,000	2,400,000	2,000,000
7/2/X5	30	900,000	2,500,000	2,300,000

Net Income and Dividends of Styx

Year	Net Income	Dividends
19X4	$450,000	$ 50,000
19X5	830,000	230,000

Styx's undervalued assets are being depreciated by the straight-line method at an annual rate of 20 percent. Phydeaux amortizes intangibles over the maximum period allowable by *APBO 17*. Phydeaux's retained earnings from its own operations at December 31, 19X4, amounted to $7,200,000. During 19X5, Phydeaux earned $1,500,000 from its own operations and declared dividends of $800,000. All earnings and dividends occur evenly during each year.

Required:

1. Compute the balance in the investment account at December 31, 19X5.
2. Compute consolidated net income for 19X5 and consolidated retained earnings at December 31, 19X5.
3. Give the working paper eliminations made in consolidation at December 31, 19X5. Use the preacquisition earnings approach where appropriate.

P11.4 Sale of Subsidiary's Stock—Working Paper Eliminations The Page Company owns 80 percent of Swann Corporation's 100,000 shares of outstanding common stock. An analysis of the Investment in Swann on January 1, 19X9, appears below:

Book Value of Shares Owned	$2,000,000
Unamortized Purchase Premium:	
Equipment (Remaining Life, 5 Years)	160,000
Goodwill (Remaining Life, 20 Years)	400,000
Balance of Investment in Swann, Jan. 1, 19X9	$2,560,000

During 19X9, Swann reported net income of $280,000 and paid dividends of $112,000.

Required:

1. Assume that on January 1, 19X9, Page sells 10,000 shares of Swann stock in the open market for $350,000 and records a gain of $30,000.

Compute Page's equity method accrual and prepare all eliminations made in consolidation at December 31, 19X9.

2. Assume that on January 1, 19X9, Swann issues sufficient new shares to reduce Page's interest to 70 percent and produce the $30,000 gain. Prepare the investment elimination made in consolidation at December 31, 19X9.

P11.5 Consolidated Balance Sheet—Indirect Holding Condensed balance sheets at January 2, 19X6, for three affiliated companies are given below:

ASSETS	Q Company	R Company	S Company
Current Assets	$2,100,000	$1,780,000	$ 900,000
Investment in R (75%)	2,600,000	—	—
Investment in S (60%)	—	820,000	—
Other Assets, Net	4,200,000	2,300,000	1,300,000
Total Assets	$8,900,000	$4,900,000	$2,200,000
LIABILITIES AND STOCKHOLDERS' EQUITY			
Current Liabilities	$1,200,000	$ 700,000	$ 550,000
Other Liabilities	2,700,000	1,400,000	450,000
Capital Stock	1,000,000	800,000	400,000
Retained Earnings	4,000,000	2,000,000	800,000
Total Liabilities and Stockholders' Equity	$8,900,000	$4,900,000	$2,200,000

Additional information:

1. R Company acquired its interest in S Company 2 years ago when all of S's identifiable assets and liabilities were fairly stated. Goodwill resulting from the acquisition is being amortized over a 12-year period. The investment account is carried at equity.
2. Q Company acquired its interest in R Company on January 2, 19X6, taking R's interest in S into account. On that date, R's Other Assets are undervalued by $200,000 and its Other Liabilities are undervalued by $160,000. Moreover, S's Current Assets are undervalued by $80,000 and its Other Assets are undervalued by $300,000.

Required:

1. Prepare the working paper entries needed to consolidate the balance sheets of Q, R, and S on January 2, 19X6.
2. Prepare a formal consolidated balance sheet.

P11.6 Mutual Holding—Connecting Affiliates with Minority Interest Present Companies P, S, and T are affiliated according to the relationship diagramed on page 575.

P, S, and T reported income from their own operations of $900,000, $200,000, and $500,000, respectively. No dividends were declared during the year. P's beginning and ending inventories included unconfirmed inter-

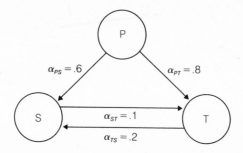

company profits on goods purchased from S of $30,000 and $40,000, respectively. T's net income included a gain of $50,000 on a sale of land to S. S still owned the land at year-end.

Required:

1. Compute consolidated net income and the minority interest in net income.
2. Prepare a schedule to determine the equity method accruals of P, S, and T.

P11.7 Mutual Holding—Working Paper Eliminations P Company owns 80 percent of S Company and S Company owns 20 percent of P Company. During the current year, P earned $800,000 from its own operations and paid dividends of $300,000. S earned $500,000 from its own operations and paid dividends of $200,000. Balances in the investment and stockholders' equity accounts of the affiliates are given below. There were no capital transactions during the year.

	P Company	S Company
Investment in S (Equity), Dec. 31.	$2,602,857	—
Investment in P (Equity), Dec. 31.	—	$1,925,714
Capital Stock, Jan. 1.	2,000,000	800,000
Retained Earnings, Jan. 1	6,000,000	2,000,000

All of S's identifiable assets and liabilities were fairly stated when the acquisition was made by P. At the beginning of the current year, the implicit goodwill of $200,000 had a remaining life of 10 years.

Required:

1. Using the *traditional allocation method,* compute consolidated net income and prepare all consolidation elimination entries, including reversal of current year equity method entries.
2. Repeat No. 1 using the *treasury stock method.* The Investment in S (Equity) will now have a balance of $2,648,000 and the Investment in P (Cost) will now have a balance of $1,000,000.

P11.8 Derive Expressions for P^*, S^*, and T^* in a Complex Mutual Holding
Consider the following ownership configuration:

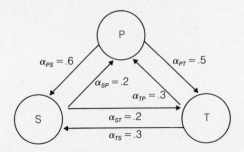

Required: Derive formulas to compute P^*, S^*, and T^*. Explain how P^*, S^*, and T^* must be adjusted in order that the total net income of the group be allocated between the controlling and minority interests on the equity basis.

Part THREE Special Topics in Financial Reporting

Part Two addressed the issues involved in accounting and reporting for multiple corporate entities. Part Three continues discussion of the corporate entity, addressing three special topics in financial reporting. Chapter 12 deals with two special dimensions of corporate reports: the presentation of information on components of the entity's activities (segment reporting) and the presentation of information for portions of the reporting year (interim reporting). Chapter 13 then surveys the accounting and reporting requirements of the Securities and Exchange Commission (SEC).

Segment reporting involves issues of entity identification (determining the segments to be reported) and revenue/cost allocation among segments. Interim reporting also involves allocation issues, as transactions must be assigned to one or more interim reporting periods.

In Chapter 13, we discuss the organization and operation of the SEC, its accounting and reporting requirements for both annual and quarterly reports, and its role in corporate governance. Numerous excerpts are presented from reports filed with the SEC.

Chapter 12 Segment and Interim Reporting

Chapters 5 through 11 focused on the preparation of financial statements for business firms with several components. Certain procedures are required to combine or consolidate the firm with its branches or subsidiaries on the grounds that the appropriate reporting entity is the *total enterprise*. Furthermore, "the basic time period for which financial statements are presented is one year," according to *APBS 4*.[1] Traditionally, the most prevalent financial reporting model called for the issuance of total enterprise statements at annual intervals. However, increases in the complexity of firms, improvements in communications technology, and the growing sophistication of investors and analysts have led to modifications in the traditional financial reporting model. For many firms, annual consolidated statements are no longer sufficient to meet the information needs of users and regulatory agencies. This chapter addresses two major dimensions of accounting's response to this problem: *segment reporting* and *interim reporting*.

The Entity Question

The total enterprise continues to be the principal reporting entity, yet the increased diversity of operations within a business firm often means that total enterprise statements provide insufficient information about this diversity. Recall that the third merger movement discussed in Chapter 6 was characterized by large numbers of *conglomerate* mergers. Such business combinations often brought totally unrelated business operations under common control in an effort to diversify business risks. As a consequence, however, traditional financial statements portrayed the *total* financial position and results of operations of the business units in the firm but revealed nothing about the *components* of the total. Similarly, enterprise-wide financial ratios are weighted averages of the underlying individual ratios and may bear no resemblance to the individual ratios—some may be much higher and others much lower.

---

[1]Accounting Principles Board, *Statement No. 4,* "Basic Concepts and Accounting Principles Underlying Financial Statements of Business Enterprises" (New York: AICPA, 1970), par. 194.

To assist statement users in understanding these complex business enterprises, the notion of reporting information about the components of the enterprise became popular. These components, labeled **business segments,** have become quasi-entities in their own right. As a result, generally accepted accounting principles have come to require **segment reporting,** the disclosure of extensive supplementary information on these business segments in the firm's financial statements or notes thereto. The major source of these requirements is *SFAS 14,* which we examine in a subsequent section.[2]

A related issue concerns the time frame covered by financial reports. The demand for more timely financial statement information, which could be processed and acted on quickly by investors and others, has been accompanied by growth in the incidence of **interim reporting.** Even though interim reports cover the total enterprise, they are typically released at quarterly intervals as the year between annual reports unfolds. Interim reports are less complete than annual reports and are generally unaudited. As we shall see, generally accepted accounting principles do not require interim reporting, but *APBO 28* governs the preparation and disclosure of interim information if the firm releases it.[3]

Figure 12.1 shows the relationship between annual total enterprise financial statements, the supplementary business segment data that accompany them, and the interim data released quarterly during the year.

Segment Reporting: A Disclosure Issue

Demand for segment reports by investors and analysts is motivated by two separate yet related factors. In considering these factors, the reader should note that **segment reporting** provides information relating to lines of business, areas of geographical activity, export sales, and major customers.

1. Better forecasts of total enterprise earnings are possible when the various components of earnings are known. Different product lines and industry activities have different growth rates and varying degrees of susceptibility to general economic conditions. Relating forecasts of these factors to specific segments of a firm's operations can produce more meaningful earnings forecasts for the firm as a whole.

2. Modern investment theory is heavily concerned with both the risk and return of alternative investments. The earnings forecast mentioned above is one key element in the analysis of returns. At the same time, however, adequate segment data can also assist the analyst in evaluating the riskiness of investing in a particular company. This is accomplished through an understanding of the firm's capital commitments to various industry activities and foreign operations.

---

[2]Financial Accounting Standards Board, *Statement of Financial Accounting Standards No. 14,* "Financial Reporting for Segments of a Business Enterprise" (Stamford, CT: 1976); CT § S20.
[3]Accounting Principles Board, *Opinion No. 28,* "Interim Reporting" (New York: AICPA, 1973); CT § I73.

Figure 12.1	**Enterprise, Segment, and Interim Financial Reports**

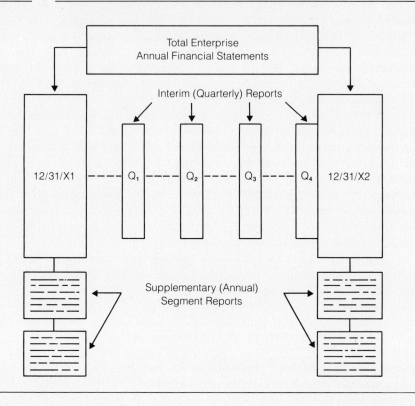

The FASB alluded to these factors in its statement of the purpose of segment information in *SFAS 14:*

> The purpose of the information . . . about an enterprise's operations in different industries and different areas of the world and about the extent of its reliance on export sales or major customers is to assist financial statement users in analyzing and understanding the enterprise's financial statements by permitting better assessment of the enterprise's past performance and future prospects.[4]

Segment information as presently disclosed is supplementary in nature and is intended not to replace total enterprise financial statements but rather to enhance the interpretability of those statements.

Problem Areas in Segment Reporting

Accounting information generally lacks the precision suggested by the assignment of specific numbers of dollars to specific items, transactions, and events. Esti-

---

[4]Financial Accounting Standards Board, *Statement No. 14,* par. 75.

mates, allocations, and other subjective judgments lie behind those numbers. Total enterprise reporting tends to be less subjective in this respect than segment reporting. Financial statements of the total enterprise reflect the relationship and performance of that enterprise relative to external parties and markets. The transactions entered into by the firm and recorded and reflected in the accounts are, for the most part, the result of arm's-length negotiations with outsiders. Furthermore, allocation decisions tend to relate to *time periods* only, as in the case of depreciation and amortization. In contrast, segment reporting in any detail tends to require disclosure of some *internal* transactions *among* the firm's segments as well as the segments' transactions with outsiders. Of equal concern is the need to allocate many costs incurred on behalf of two or more segments of the business among those segments in order to generate certain segment information. This is the familiar joint cost or common cost allocation problem which inevitably entails arbitrary judgments by those performing the allocations.

For these reasons, segment reports are of doubtful value when used for comparison with (1) similar segments in other firms and (2) free-standing firms in the same line of business. We now proceed to discuss problems arising from internal transactions and common cost allocations. Later we shall see how the existing segment reporting requirements have tried to cope with these difficulties.

Pricing Internal Transfers. We know that when combined or consolidated statements are prepared, transactions among the components of the firm are eliminated. Thus the pricing of internal transfers may affect internal perfomance measurements but not the firm's external financial statements. In developing income statement information for the segments of a business enterprise, however, internal pricing issues assume importance when the segment data are reported externally. Internal prices, known as **transfer prices,** affect the reported revenues of the selling segments and the reported costs of the purchasing segments.

The **transfer pricing problem** is a major stumbling block to optimal management and control within a decentralized corporation. In its purest form, a decentralized firm is one with several autonomous divisions under the common control of corporate headquarters. Most decision-making authority is concentrated at the divisional level. The divisions may do business with each other as well as in the open market, and divisional managers are supposed to react to internal prices no differently than they react to external market prices. In practice, one finds the following bases for transfer prices:

1. Variable cost of production.
2. Full cost of production, including allocated fixed overhead.
3. Full cost plus a percentage markup.
4. "Market" prices.

A transfer pricing system which uses external competitive market prices to price internal transfers is probably the best. Unfortunately, competitive prices do not always exist, due to market imperfections. And there may be no external market prices at all for certain manufactured products, especially subassemblies or specialized parts. Finally, determination of "market" prices is complicated by the facts that list prices are not necessarily transaction prices and that prices are often dependent upon order size and freight cost absorption. The reasons for placing quotation marks around "market," then, are that several comparable but different market prices may exist or no truly comparable external price may be available. When no external market price exists, transfer prices based on variable or marginal costs of production generally lead to the correct internal decisions.

Although the transfer pricing problem is most crucial in internal decision making, it also has implications for externally reported segment information. Under *SFAS 14,* business segments report revenue and profitability information which reflects sales to outside customers and to other segments within the firm. Hence, such information is influenced by the sales and purchases among business units within the firm which are not completed market transactions. Methods for pricing internal transfers may vary from company to company, making comparisons among segments difficult. Even disclosure of the method used may not be of much help, as can be seen from the following excerpt from an annual report of Norton Simon, Inc.: "Intersegment sales are recorded at fair value adjusted for quantity and production efficiencies." Readers are left to their own imaginations to determine precisely what that statement means.

Common Cost Allocations. Common costs incurred on behalf of two or more segments in a diversified firm can be a significant problem if (1) the common costs are material and (2) the segment reports reflect a common cost allocation. All common costs, however, are not the same, and several categories can be listed: (1) corporate services, (2) corporate administration, and (3) corporate taxes.

Corporate Services. The **corporate services** category includes common costs incurred by corporate departments which provide services to the several operating divisions. Examples include personnel, accounting, data processing, and printing and reproduction departments. These kinds of costs are related to divisional activities and requests for services. Hence, they often can be allocated in a sensible way at year-end or be charged to the divisions on an ongoing basis.

Corporate Administration. Expenses of operating corporate headquarters; compensation of corporate managers, staff, and support personnel; and directors' fees fall into the category of **corporate administration.** Other costs which would be included in this category for purposes of allocation are interest expense and institutional advertising. These costs are further removed from divisional activities and, indeed, the divisions have little control over how much of such "services" they "use." Allocations of corporate administrative costs are coarser than those related to corporate services. Such gross measurements as assets, sales, investment, employment, and gross profits by segment are employed to allocate corporate administrative costs. One single allocation base, such as assets, is often not sufficient, so various combinations of these bases may be used. Alternatively, some costs may be allocated on one basis and other costs on other bases.

Corporate Taxes. If segment income statements are to reflect a share of corporate taxes, care must be taken not to determine that share by a general allocation scheme. External financial statement users are concerned about the segments affected by special tax treatments. Therefore, the best approach is to estimate the tax expense for each segment as if it were standing alone.

Users' Evaluation of Common Cost Allocation Bases. Mautz's 1967 survey of financial analysts revealed substantial diversity with respect to analysts' *preferences* for allocation bases and the *acceptability* of those bases to the analysts, as shown below:[5]

	Percent of Financial Analysts Indicating:	
Basis of Common Cost Allocation	a Preference for the Basis	the Basis Would Be Acceptable
Sales or Gross Revenue.	18.4%	25.8%
Assets Employed	29.5	28.1
Benefits Received	24.9	19.2
Net Income before Common Costs	21.8	23.8
Other	5.4	3.1
	100.0%	100.0%

These data lead one to wonder whether analysts perceived little difference among the major bases or whether the allocations were likely to be disregarded no matter what basis was used. On this point, these analysts did feel that when common costs amount to 10 percent or more of segment revenue, profit figures reflecting common cost allocations tend to lose their significance.

Allocations Based on Sales: A Special Danger. We believe it is worth illustrating a particular danger that can arise when material amounts of common cost are allocated to segments based on their sales or total revenue. As the ratio of total common costs to total traceable segment costs increases, the use of sales as a basis for allocating common costs tends to *equalize* segment profit margin ratios. Consider a company with three identifiable segments. Segments X, Y, and Z have sales revenues of $140,000, $270,000, and $160,000, respectively. Total costs are $400,000, and we will vary the common portion of those costs from zero up to $400,000; the portion of traceable costs will therefore be decreasing from $400,000 to zero. After determining segment costs and profits for several intermediate traceable cost/common cost combinations, we will compute segment profit margins (profit/sales) and plot them on a graph. This analysis is given in Exhibit 12.1.

In Exhibit 12.1, traceable costs were chosen to illustrate very diverse profit/sales ratios (Case 1). The main point of Exhibit 12.1 is that, as allocated common costs become a large portion of total costs, use of sales revenue to allocate these costs across products or business segments drives profit margin ratios toward

---

[5]Robert K. Mautz, *Financial Reporting by Diversified Companies* (New York: Financial Executives Research Foundation, 1968), 120.

Exhibit 12.1	**Effect on Segment Profit Margins of Using Sales as the Basis for Allocating Common Costs to Segments**

		Segment		
DATA FOR ILLUSTRATION	X	Y	Z	Total
Sales Revenue	$140,000	$270,000	$160,000	$570,000
Sales/Total Sales*	.245	.474	.281	1.000
CASE 1: $0 COMMON COSTS (0%)				
Sales	$140,000	$270,000	$160,000	$570,000
Traceable Costs	140,000	180,000	80,000	400,000
Common Costs	0	0	0	0
Profit	$ 0	$ 90,000	$ 80,000	$170,000
Profit/Sales	0	.333	.500	.298
CASE 2: $100,000 COMMON COSTS (25%)				
Sales	$140,000	$270,000	$160,000	$570,000
Traceable Costs	105,000	135,000	60,000	300,000
Common Costs	24,500	47,400	28,100	100,000
Profit	$ 10,500	$ 87,600	$ 71,900	$170,000
Profit/Sales	.075	.324	.450	.298
CASE 3: $200,000 COMMON COSTS (50%)				
Sales	$140,000	$270,000	$160,000	$570,000
Traceable Costs	70,000	90,000	40,000	200,000
Common Costs	49,000	94,800	56,200	200,000
Profit	$ 21,000	$ 85,200	$ 63,800	$170,000
Profit/Sales	.150	.316	.399	.298
CASE 4: $300,000 COMMON COSTS (75%)				
Sales	$140,000	$270,000	$160,000	$570,000
Traceable Costs	35,000	45,000	20,000	100,000
Common Costs	73,500	142,200	84,300	300,000
Profit	$ 31,500	$ 82,800	$ 55,700	$170,000
Profit/Sales	.224	.307	.349	.298
CASE 5: $400,000 COMMON COSTS (100%)				
Sales	$140,000	$270,000	$160,000	$570,000
Traceable Costs	0	0	0	0
Common Costs	98,000	189,600	112,400	400,000
Profit	$ 42,000	$ 80,400	$ 47,600	$170,000
Profit/Sales	.300	.298	.298	.298

*These percentages are used to allocate the firmwide common costs among the three segments.

Exhibit 12.1   Continued

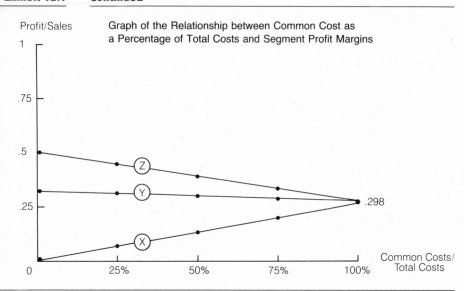

Profit/Sales — Graph of the Relationship between Common Cost as a Percentage of Total Costs and Segment Profit Margins

equality. This is best seen in Case 5 of Exhibit 12.1, where all costs are charged to the segments in proportion to their sales revenue, leading to equal profit/sales ratios. The effect of such an allocation scheme applied when common costs are significant is to destroy the usefulness of segment profitability data.

Segment Reporting under *SFAS 14*

To conform to generally accepted accounting principles, public companies must disclose the information required by *SFAS 14*. Nonpublic companies need not provide these disclosures. A **nonpublic** company is either a company whose debt or equity securities are not publicly traded or a company which is not required to file financial statements with the SEC. Other segment reporting requirements affect certain reports submitted to the SEC and the Federal Trade Commission (FTC). The FTC program is somewhat outside the mainstream of financial reporting. Indeed, one of its major purposes is to assess the degree of competition in American industries. For an analysis of this program, see the study by Benston.[6]

SFAS 14 calls for disaggregated information to be prepared and reported for each reportable segment in accordance with the same accounting principles underlying the aggregate information. Requirements for information and rules for determining reportable segments in the following three categories will be discussed in turn.

---

[6]George J. Benston, "FTC's Line of Business Program: A Benefit-Cost Analysis," in H.J. Goldschmid, ed., *Government Information Needs and Business Disclosure* (New York: McGraw-Hill, 1978).

1. Operations in different industries.
2. Foreign operations and export sales.
3. Major customers.

Operations in Different Industries. The principal industry-related information to be disclosed for the firm's reportable industry segments is:

1. *Sales* to unaffiliated customers, total sales to other segments of the firm, and the basis for pricing the sales to other segments.
2. *Operating profit or loss* net of traceable expenses and the *corporate service* type of expenses mentioned earlier in the chapter. Corporate administrative expenses, domestic and foreign income taxes, extraordinary items, minority interest in net income, and other items listed in paragraphs 10(d) and 24 of *SFAS 14* are not to be allocated in computing segment operating profit.
3. *Identifiable assets,* including both assets used exclusively in particular segments and those used jointly by two or more segments where a reasonable allocation of the jointly used assets can be made. Intersegment advances shall *not* be counted as identifiable assets unless they are made by a *finance segment*. Interest income from intersegment advances made by a finance segment shall be included in the finance segment's operating profit.
4. *Depreciation, depletion, and amortization expense* (in total).
5. *Capital expenditures*—additions to property, plant, and equipment.
6. *Equity method investment in and income of vertically integrated investees* and the geographical areas in which these investees operate.
7. *Effects of changes in accounting principles on segment operating profits.*

Determining Reportable Industry Segments. SFAS 14 provides both guidance to assist management in identifying industry segments and significance tests to assure that management identifies neither too few nor too many segments. Approaches adopted by the federal government to classify business activities, such as the Standard Industrial Classification (SIC) and Enterprise Standard Industrial Classification (ESIC) systems, are mentioned in paragraph 12 of *SFAS 14*. These systems, however, often bear little relationship to the organization of business operations. As a result, the selection of industry segments is generally based on the judgment of the company's management.

The basic approach is to start with a firm's *profit centers,* generally the smallest units of business activity selling to customers outside the firm, and to group the products and services of these profit centers along industry lines. For example, a company's profit centers for production and sales of spark plugs, instrument panels, and windshield wiper blades may be designated as a segment in the automobile parts industry. When possible, industry segmentation should incorporate the worldwide operations of the enterprise. If some or all of an enterprise's foreign operations cannot be broken down by industry segments, those foreign operations will constitute an industry segment themselves and the types of industry operations involved will be disclosed.

Only *significant* industry segments need be reported. Unless the firm has a single dominant segment, however, *sufficient industry segments* must be identified so that *combined sales* to unaffiliated customers of reportable segments is at least *75 percent* of the firm's total sales to unaffiliated customers (the "75 percent test"). Generally, the number of reportable segments should not exceed ten.

A single **dominant segment** exists when that segment accounts for at least 90 percent of the revenue, operating profit or loss, and identifiable assets of all the firm's industry segments. Also, no other industry segment within that firm can meet any of the significance tests indicated below. Whatever industry such a firm's operations are concentrated in must be identified.

Satisfaction of *any one* of the following **significance tests** (paragraph 15 of *SFAS 14*) by an industry segment indicates that it is sufficiently significant to be reported separately. In applying these significance tests, we have assumed away any unconfirmed intersegment profits in inventory, land, and so on. If there were unconfirmed intercompany profits, they would *not* be removed from the segments' operating profit and identifiable asset amounts. In reconciling to the consolidated totals, however, the unconfirmed intercompany profits would be eliminated in Tests 2 and 3 below, just as intersegment revenue is eliminated in Test 1 below.

1. The segment's **total revenue**—intersegment sales plus external sales—is at least 10 percent of the combined total revenue of all the company's industry segments. Note that *combined total revenue* includes intersegment sales and hence differs from *consolidated revenue*.

   Example:

		Segment					
	W	X	Y	Z	Combined	Elimination	Consolidated
External Sales	$6,000	$80,000	$10,000	$ 5,000	$101,000	—	$101,000
Intersegment Sales	3,000	—	2,000	20,000	25,000	$(25,000)	—
Total Revenue	$9,000	$80,000	$12,000	$25,000	$126,000	$(25,000)	$101,000

   Result: Segments X and Z are reportable because their total revenues of $80,000 and $25,000 are at least 10 percent of combined total revenue of $126,000, as shown in the third row of the example. Segments W and Y are not reportable under the revenue test.

2. The segment's **operating profit or loss,** in absolute value, is at least 10 percent of the *greater* of the absolute value of (a) the combined operating profit of profitable segments or (b) the combined operating loss of loss segments.

   Example:

		Segment			Corporate Revenue	
	W	X	Y	Z	(Expense)	Consolidated
Operating Profit (Loss)	$ 3,000	$30,000	$(4,000)	$(1,000)	—	$28,000
Other Revenue (Expense)	7,000	(6,000)	—	—	$(8,500)	(7,500)
Total Income before Taxes	$10,000	$24,000	$(4,000)	$(1,000)	$(8,500)	$20,500

Result: As indicated in the first row of the example, Segments X and Y are reportable because the absolute values of their operating profit or loss of $30,000 and $4,000 are at least 10 percent of the combined operating profit of $33,000 (=$3,000 + $30,000). The combined operating profit of $33,000 exceeds the absolute value of combined operating losses of $5,000. Segments W and Z are not reportable under the operating profit or loss test.

3. The segment's **identifiable assets** are at least 10 percent of the combined identifiable assets of all the company's industry segments.

Example:

	Segment W	Segment X	Segment Y	Z	Combined	Corporate Assets	Elimination	Consolidated
Identifiable Assets . . .	$120,000	$280,000	$80,000	$50,000	$530,000	$75,000	—	$605,000
Intersegment Advances .	8,000	—	5,000	25,000	38,000	10,000	$(48,000)	—
Total Assets	$128,000	$280,000	$85,000	$75,000	$568,000	$85,000	$(48,000)	$605,000

Result: Segments W, X, and Y are reportable because the first row of the example shows that their identifiable assets of $120,000, $280,000, and $80,000 are at least 10 percent of combined identifiable assets of $530,000. Segment Z is not reportable under the identifiable assets test.

Since each industry segment is significant in at least one test, *all* must be reported separately. Note that in these examples, the *75 percent test* is of no concern because the $80,000 external sales of Segment X alone make up more than 75 percent of combined external sales of $101,000.

Financial information is to be presented in dollar terms (percentages are optional), and revenue, operating profit or loss, and identifiable assets are to be reconciled to the consolidated totals. We illustrate these disclosures and reconciliations in Exhibit 12.2 with an excerpt from a recent annual report of McKesson Corporation.

Comments on the Industry Disclosure Requirements. *SFAS 14* has compromised in the troubling area of common costs (see definition of operating profit or loss above). Major categories of corporate expenses are not to be allocated to segments, although other common costs more closely related to segments' activities must be allocated.

The transfer pricing issue has been only partially accommodated. Each segment must disclose both its total sales to other segments and the basis for pricing those sales. This is an inadequate approach to the problems created by intersegment transfers large enough to be considered material. Such transfers are both sales *and* purchases, yet there are no requirements to (1) disclose each segment's internal purchases and (2) disclose the amounts of intersegment sales and pur-

Exhibit 12.2	Example of Industry Segment Disclosures under *SFAS 14:* McKesson Corporation

SEGMENTS OF BUSINESS

The company's principal business activities are grouped into four industry segments.

The Drug & Health Care Group includes the largest nationwide distributor of ethical and proprietary drugs, toiletries and sundries serving retail drugstore and hospital pharmacy customers from its distribution centers. It also markets a broad range of computer services to retailers.

The Beverage Group combines the Wine & Spirits Group with the Water Division. Previously, the Water Division was part of the now discontinued Foods Group. The Beverage Group is the largest wholesale distributor of wine and spirits in the United States, representing most U.S. distillers, importers and wineries in one or more markets. Sales are made to liquor stores, restaurants, bars and other establishments from its distribution centers. Certain brands of alcoholic beverages are imported and marketed throughout the country. In addition, the group is a major supplier of processed water for consumer use in the western and Sunbelt states.

The Chemical Group is the largest independent full-line distributor of chemicals in the United States. It handles a broad line of industrial and specialty chemicals through a national network of distribution facilities. This group also specializes in reclaiming and recycling chemicals, principally solvents.

The Development Group acquires and manages growth-oriented businesses. Its results primarily reflect Armor All Products, a maker of automotive and household appearance-protection products.

Revenues include net sales, interest income, pre-tax gains on disposition of assets and miscellaneous revenues. Sales between segments are not significant. No material part of the company's business is dependent upon a single or a very few customers.

Operating profit is total revenues less cost of sales and operating expenses. Operating expenses do not include interest and corporate expenses or taxes on income.

Identifiable assets are those assets used in the operations of each segment. Corporate assets are principally cash, receivables, investments and net assets of discontinued operations.

	1984	1983	1982
Revenues		**(Thousands of Dollars)**	
Drug & Health Care.	$2,466,847	$2,135,116	$1,870,213
Beverage	1,057,932	1,002,640	975,446
Chemical	632,806	603,276	628,207
Development	118,291	86,870	74,133
Total	$4,275,876	$3,827,902	$3,547,999
Operating Profit			
Drug & Health Care.	$ 60,069	$ 61,188	$ 54,743
Beverage	49,592	45,963	50,347
Chemical	11,242	14,907	21,416
Development	27,304	13,537	12,353
Total	148,207	135,595	138,859
Interest	(19,247)	(26,928)	(25,028)
Corporate.	(12,458)	(3,841)	(1,544)
Income before Taxes on Income	$ 116,502	$ 104,826	$ 112,287

(continued on next page)

Exhibit 12.2 **Continued**

Identifiable Assets—at Year-End	1984	1983	1982
	(Thousands of Dollars)		
Drug & Health Care	$ 586,395	$ 467,967	$ 427,499
Beverage	285,211	279,771	264,634
Chemical	167,536	156,156	150,798
Development	·115,049	71,377	56,165
Total	1,154,191	975,271	899,096
Corporate	257,113	373,204	406,246
Total	$1,411,304	$1,348,475	$1,305,342
Depreciation and Amortization			
Drug & Health Care	$ 8,877	$ 6,658	$ 5,481
Beverage	13,615	12,231	9,906
Chemical	5,691	5,652	4,768
Development	2,388	1,585	1,435
Capital Expenditures			
Drug & Health Care	$ 19,435	$ 18,345	$ 17,475
Beverage	17,885	20,814	22,341
Chemical	6,209	7,152	12,305
Development	7,706	3,916	227

chases between *each pair* of industry segments. As a result, the financial statement reader cannot determine the total impact of internal transactions on each segment when three or more segments are reported. Although one can ascertain the extent to which each segment makes *sales* to internal and external customers, one cannot determine the amount of *purchases* made by each segment from internal and external suppliers. This is important because, in our judgment, when either substantial intersegment sales or purchases are present it becomes difficult to evaluate true segment profitability.

Foreign Operations and Export Sales. Foreign operations generally face risks different from those of domestic operations. To appreciate the extent of foreign operations, the following information is to be disclosed for domestic operations in total[7] and for the various significant foreign geographical areas (segments).

1. *Sales* to unaffiliated customers, total sales to other geographical segments, and the basis for pricing the sales to other geographical segments.
2. *Operating profit or loss* as previously defined *or* net income *or* another measure of profitability *between* operating profit or loss and net income.
3. *Identifiable assets* as previously defined.

---

[7]The firm need not report separate information about domestic operations if domestic sales to unaffiliated customers and domestic identifiable assets are less than 10 percent of the consolidated amounts.

Export Sales. When domestic sales to unaffiliated customers in foreign countries *(export sales)* amount to 10 percent or more of consolidated sales to unaffiliated customers, the firm's *domestic operations* must report export sales separately. They must be reported in total and by geographical areas deemed appropriate by management.

Determining Foreign Geographical Segments. There are two stages involved in determing whether information about foreign operations must be disclosed and, if disclosure is necessary, how many geographical segments must be identified.

1. Information about foreign operations must be disclosed if *either* sales by foreign operations to unaffiliated customers are at least 10 percent of consolidated revenue *or* assets identified with the foreign operations are at least 10 percent of consolidated assets.
2. If foreign operations are conducted in two or more geographical areas (countries or groups of countries), more than one geographical segment must be reported if a segment's sales to unaffiliated customers or identifiable assets are at least 10 percent of the consolidated amounts. That is, the segment(s) meeting the 10 percent test must be reported separately from the others; the others may be combined for reporting purposes.

The financial information must be presented in dollars; percentages are optional. Foreign geographical segments are to be identified and the sales, profitability, and identifiable assets of each segment shall be reconciled to the consolidated totals. These disclosures and reconciliations are illustrated in Exhibit 12.3, using General Foods Corporation.

Major Customers. To alert investors to the possible dependence of a firm on one or more large customers, the following information about major customers must be disclosed, even if the firm need not disclose industry or foreign segment information.

1. If at least 10 percent of consolidated revenue is derived from a single customer (or group of customers under common control), the firm must disclose that fact and the revenue from each such major customer.
2. If at least 10 percent of consolidated revenue is derived from the federal government, a state government, or a local government (each would be considered a major customer), the firm must so indicate and disclose the revenue from each.

In both cases, the industry segments making the sales to major commercial and governmental customers must be identified. Names of specific customers, however, need not be revealed. Examples of such disclosures appear in Exhibit 12.4 on page 596.

Authors' Comments on *SFAS 14*. Disclosure of segment information in external reports is necessary if complex, diversified firms are to satisfy any reasonable standard of full disclosure. We have seen that some inherent conceptual problems—transfer pricing and common cost allocations—can limit the usefulness of

Exhibit 12.3 **Example of Foreign Operations Disclosures under *SFAS 14*:**
General Foods Corporation

GEOGRAPHICAL AREAS

United States operations include the Packaged Convenience Foods, Basic Foods & Baked Goods and Coffee & Food Service sectors, the domestic operations of Oscar Mayer and U.S. exports. Other geographic areas contain the balance of the General Foods International sector and Oscar Mayer's international operations.

Earnings of non-consolidated affiliates (primarily joint ventures) are included in "Unallocated Expenses, Net."

United States: Fiscal 1984 net sales increased 7.3 per cent, with the full year results of Entenmann's being a major contributing factor.

Operating earnings increased 6.2 per cent over fiscal 1983, primarily due to the impact of Entenmann's, plus earnings gains in several other Packaged Grocery Product businesses and Oscar Mayer. Fiscal 1983 operating earnings increased 8.0 per cent as a result of Louis Rich turkey volume increases, reduced operating costs and more focused development spending.

Europe: Fiscal 1984 net sales were 3.1 per cent lower than fiscal 1983, principally due to translation. Operating earnings were down 27.0 per cent, due to competitive activity which constrained margins and the impact of translation. Fiscal 1983 operating earnings were down 2.7 per cent from fiscal 1982, reflecting lower margins and the impact of translation.

Canada: Net sales and operating earnings from the Packaged Grocery Products businesses increased, based on strong volume gains. Overall net sales and operating earnings were down slightly as the absence of sales and earnings from certain food service businesses, sold in 1983, more than offset these advances.

Other International: Fiscal 1984 net sales decreased 25.0 per cent from the prior year, due to lower volume and the impact of translation.

Both Latin America and Asia/Pacific contributed to the year-to-year operating earnings improvement of 25.1 per cent. In fiscal 1983, operating earnings increased 38.4 per cent, due to the absence of losses from low-return businesses and higher earnings in Latin America.

Unallocated Expenses, Net decreased by $10.0 million, or 6.6 per cent, in fiscal 1984, due to gains on property sales and the absence of one-time relocation costs incurred in fiscal 1983.

Total Identifiable Assets increased by $80.3 million in fiscal 1984, principally from the increase in net fixed assets.

(Millions of Dollars)

	F1984	F1983	F1982	F1981	F1980
Net Sales					
United States	$6,876.0	$6,407.5	$6,263.6	$4,560.5	$4,339.6
Europe	999.6	1,031.3	1,156.5	1,230.0	854.1
Canada	500.8	520.0	532.6	510.0	473.0
Other International	223.4	297.6	398.4	300.8	292.9
Total Net Sales	$8,599.8	$8,256.4	$8,351.1	$6,601.3	$5,959.6
Operating Earnings					
United States	$ 602.0	$ 566.9	$ 525.1	$ 431.8	$ 439.4
Europe	33.7	46.1	47.4	35.4	11.7
Canada	44.4	45.5	40.8	34.9	39.7
Other International	35.1	28.1	20.3	29.5	14.0
Total Operating Earnings	$ 715.2	$ 686.6	$ 633.6	$ 531.6	$ 504.8
Provision for Loss on Restructured Operations	—	—	$ 64.1	—	—
Interest, Net.	$ 92.6	$ 90.0	110.3	$ 22.0	$ 7.4
Other	49.3	61.9	41.6	37.0	27.5
Unallocated Expenses, Net.	$ 141.9	$ 151.9	$ 216.0	$ 59.0	$ 34.9
Earnings from Continuing Operations before Income Taxes	$ 573.3	$ 534.7	$ 417.6	$ 472.6	$ 469.9
Identifiable Assets:					
United States	$2,993.3	$2,870.9	$2,442.1	$1,762.5	$1,678.0
Europe	550.7	548.3	590.8	547.4	597.4
Canada	210.2	219.0	220.7	231.6	221.1
Other International	125.6	161.3	227.3	175.6	160.6
Total Identifiable Assets	$3,879.8	$3,799.5	$3,480.9	$2,717.1	$2,657.1
Unallocated Assets	552.0	510.1	379.8	412.7	321.4
Total Assets.	$4,431.8	$4,309.6	$3,860.7	$3,129.8	$2,978.5

Exhibit 12.4	Examples of *SFAS 14* Major Customer Disclosures

LOCKHEED CORPORATION, which reported sales of $3,485 million in 1978 and $3,348 million in 1977, disclosed the following:

By customer category, sales to the U.S. Government totaled $1,968 million in 1978 and $2,076 million in 1977, and to foreign governments $998 million in 1978 and $749 million in 1977 excluding sales to foreign airlines that are owned by their respective governments of $174 million in 1978 and $162 million in 1977. Sales to one foreign government including sales to its national airline totaled $515 million in 1978 and $418 million in 1977.

WESTINGHOUSE ELECTRIC CORPORATION disclosed the following:

The largest single customer of the Corporation is the United States Government and its agencies, whose purchases accounted for 10.8 per cent of total consolidated sales in 1977 and 10.2 per cent in 1976. Of these purchases, 22 per cent in 1977 and 18 per cent in 1976 were made from Power Systems, 4 per cent in 1977 and 4 per cent in 1976 from Industry Products, and 71 per cent in 1977 and 74 percent in 1976 from Public Systems. In addition, Other Income includes fees generated through United States Government-owned Westinghouse-operated facilities.

---

segment data when intersegment transactions and common costs are material. *SFAS 14* presents a reasonable compromise on these conceptual issues, requiring disclosures that enable the careful reader to estimate the limitations in a given segment report. Unfortunately, we believe that the *Statement* suffers from two additional flaws as it relates to firms with significant intersegment transactions:

1. Disclosure of the volume of intersegment sales *and* purchases between each pair of selling and buying segments is not required but should be, so the reader can ascertain the degree of interdependence among the various segments. Remember that intersegment transactions are *not* market transactions, even though transfer prices may be based on market prices. Furthermore, it would be useful to know which of the segments are most heavily influenced by the behavior of other segments.

2. Meaningful selection of reportable segments is made more difficult by the failure to include the volume of intersegment transactions as a significance criterion. In this case, however, the significance test would be in the opposite direction. For example, if the volume of intersegment transactions is at least 10 percent, the segment should *not* be separately reported. Recall our earlier reference to the annual report of Norton Simon, Inc. In that report, we are told that ''operating results of the packaging segment are affected by the volume of intersegment transactions.'' Of the six segments reported that year, packaging ranked second in operating profit and third in terms of the ratio of operating profit to sales. Fully *40 percent* of packaging's sales were to other segments in the firm. Our proposed significance test would require that packaging be combined with another segment and not be reported separately.

Interim Reporting: Accounting Theory and Disclosure Issues

Whereas segment reporting involves disaggregating information of the reporting *entity* into relevant areas of economic activity, interim reporting concerns a breakdown of information for the annual reporting *period* into shorter periods. Allocations are a problem in segment reporting because some costs benefit more than one business segment. In **interim reporting,** we seek to divide the annual reporting period into several reporting periods of shorter duration. But many costs incurred benefit more than one interim period and allocations may also be a problem here. This part of the chapter addresses these and other problems associated with interim reporting as they relate to conceptual issues, generally accepted accounting principles and actual practice.

The Problem

Although not *required* by generally accepted accounting principles, interim reports have been issued by major companies for years. The New York Stock Exchange requires listed companies to release interim information, and the SEC calls for registrants to file Form 10-Q, a quarterly report to the SEC. There are, however, accounting rules regarding the form, content, and principles underlying interim reports released to investors. The rules simply specify that *if* interim information is reported, *then* these principles and practices are to be followed. Official pronouncements setting forth these guidelines include *APBO 28,*[8] *SFAS 3,*[9] and *IFAS 18.*[10] Interim reporting, however, continues to be a controversial subject because of the difficulties created by the fundamental problem in interim reporting, that is, defining *the nature of the interim reporting period.*

> When contemplating the measurement of earnings for an interim period, one must decide whether the interim period is to be viewed as an *integral* but subordinate portion of a longer period—the year— or as a *discrete* reporting period, standing on its own and unaffected by the other interim periods within the year.

These are the polar positions regarding the nature of the interim reporting period. Adoption of one or the other provides an overall orientation for more detailed

---

[8]Accounting Principles Board, *Opinion No. 28;* CT § 173.

[9]Financial Accounting Standards Board, *Statement of Financial Accounting Standards No. 3,* "Reporting Accounting Changes in Interim Financial Statements" (Stamford, CT: FASB, 1974); CT § I73.135–.141.

[10]Financial Accounting Standards Board, *Interpretation of Financial Accounting Standards No. 18,* "Accounting for Income Taxes in Interim Periods" (Stamford, CT: FASB, 1977); CT § I73.111–.130.

interim reporting rules. Accommodating the characteristics of some items, however, may require that an intermediate position be accepted.

The Integral Position. The **integral position** views the interim reporting period as an integral part of the annual reporting period and avoids many strange results that would otherwise occur. For example, major maintenance costs undertaken early in the year but benefiting the entire year are charged against each of the four quarterly periods on a pro rata basis. Bonuses determined in the last quarter of the year are estimated and charged proportionately against the four quarterly periods. However, other problems arise in connection with intrayear impairment of LIFO layers and income taxes. They will be discussed later.

The FASB Discussion Memorandum on interim reporting identifies the following characteristics of the *integral position:*

1. Interim period profit margins are reasonably constant throughout the year.
2. Expenses are allocated to interim periods on the basis of annual estimates of revenues and costs.
3. Inaccuracies in those estimates require adjustments in subsequent interim periods.
4. Earnings fluctuate less than under other approaches if those estimates are reasonably accurate.
5. Components of financial statements, such as assets, liabilities, revenues, expenses, and earnings are defined differently for interim periods than for annual periods.
6. Unforeseen events, such as catastrophic losses, gains or losses from discontinued segments of a business, and settlements of major litigation are not allocated to all periods but are recognized when they occur.[11]

The major thrust of the integral view is to estimate "annual" operating expenses—not those costs traceable to specific production and sales in particular interim periods—and allocate them to the quarterly periods on some basis of activity. The result is to smooth earnings over the four quarterly periods; the principal reporting period is the entire year.

The *integral position* seems consistent with the view that the *primary function of interim reports is prediction*. Quarterly reports are progress reports between annual closing dates and, as such, should be helpful in predicting future quarterly and annual results. The smoothing of interim income achieved by allocating annual items to quarterly periods on some activity basis aids in the prediction effort. On the other hand, there is some cost in terms of reduced objectivity because the estimates, allocations, and accruals called for under the integral view involve subjective judgments.

---

[11]Financial Accounting Standards Board, Discussion Memorandum, "Interim Financial Accounting and Reporting" (Stamford, CT: FASB, 1978), iv.

The Discrete Position. The **discrete position** sees each interim period standing on its own, reporting what occurred in that period, unaffected by accountants' subjective judgments regarding estimates and allocations of "annual" expenses. In principle, the quarterly interim report becomes a miniannual report, covering 3 months rather than 12.

Characteristics of the *discrete position* identified in the FASB Discussion Memorandum are:

1. Expense recognition standards do not change with the length of the reporting period.
2. Interim reporting requires no estimates or allocations different from those required for annual reporting.
3. Components of financial statements such as assets, liabilities, expenses, and earnings are defined in the same way as they are for annual statements.
4. The shorter the reporting period, the more likely it is that seasonal influences and discretionary costs will cause fluctuations in period-to-period earnings.[12]

Those who favor the discrete position believe that quarterly reporting periods are principal reporting periods, fundamentally different from annual periods only in the amount of time spanned. They make no special claims for the discrete period view except to observe that it requires no resources devoted to making the estimates, accruals, deferrals, and adjustments prescribed by the integral position and needs fewer subjective judgments.

In contrast to the predictive role envisioned by the integral position, the *discrete position* sees the *major function of interim reports as historical.* Under the discrete view, whatever usefulness is possessed by annual reports is also possessed by interim reports. Such reports may be helpful in prediction only insofar as any objectively determined historical record is helpful. No special effort should be made to improve the predictive ability of interim reports at the expense of objectivity.

A Numerical Example Comparing the Two Positions. To illustrate the differences in interim earnings that can arise under these two polar approaches, we concentrate on two items that would be handled differently in interim reports prepared under the integral and discrete views:

1. Maintenance costs are incurred in the first quarter but benefit the entire year.
2. Quantity purchase discounts are realized in the fourth quarter but depend on the purchases made in all four quarters.

Suppose the Johnson Company projects the following activity and cost levels during the year's four quarterly periods:

---

[12]Ibid., iv–v.

	Quarter 1	Quarter 2	Quarter 3	Quarter 4
Units Produced and Sold.	40,000	60,000	30,000	80,000
Unit Selling Price.	$2.00	$2.25	$2.30	$2.30
Traceable Costs per Unit.	$1.00	$1.10	$1.20	$1.20
Major Maintenance.	$50,000	—	—	—
Credit for Quantity Purchase Discounts	—	—	—	$(20,000)

Exhibit 12.5 gives condensed quarterly income statements under the integral and discrete views, assuming that all projected amounts come to be realized. Allocation of the major maintenance and quantity purchase discounts across the four quarters under the integral position is based on the percentage of total units produced and sold in each quarter.

We can see how one's view of the nature of the interim period affects the accounting information produced. Note that the pattern of quarterly income portrayed in the graph under the integral approach is smoother or less variable than under the discrete approach. In this case, the differences are due to large annual items, the maintenance costs and purchase discounts. Supporters of the integral view might also allocate fixed overhead costs which occur uniformly during the year to the four quarters based on some measure of quarterly activity. If this is done, differences appear even if there are no annual items.

Evaluation of the Integral and Discrete Positions. We believe that by reporting on the past, financial statements provide information helpful in judging the future. Interim reports should also serve this purpose, although the future may be interpreted more narrowly as the time when annual financial statements are prepared. Similarly, the timeliness of interim reports has particular value if the reports are capable of revealing any changes or turning points in the firm's performance. The *integral position* as it relates to the interim reporting period seems most consistent with these objectives. Our objection to the *discrete position* is that in reporting each interim period's information just as it occurs, without making adjustments and allocations, the discrete view may distort the quarterly results. The seasonal nature of a firm's business ought to be made clear in the interim reports, but the lumpiness of many annual expenses can conceal such seasonality. Charging such expenses entirely against the quarterly period when they are incurred may cause quarterly earnings to behave randomly or in some other pattern unrelated to underlying seasonal influences.

We hasten to add, however, that in favoring the integral approach we would allocate only *annual items*. Fixed costs incurred uniformly throughout the year should be reported as incurred and not be shifted to other quarterly periods by an allocation scheme related to quarterly sales or some other measure of activity. Such allocations could lead to a different picture of seasonality than actually exists.

Therefore, the integral position seems to us to provide the most useful frame of reference within which detailed interim reporting principles can be developed. On specific items, however, intermediate or compromise positions may be appropriate.

Exhibit 12.5   **Comparison of the Integral and Discrete Approaches to Interim Reporting**

THE JOHNSON CORPORATION
CONDENSED QUARTERLY INCOME STATEMENTS

INTEGRAL APPROACH	Quarter 1	Quarter 2	Quarter 3	Quarter 4	Total
Sales.	$ 80,000	$135,000	$ 69,000	$184,000	$468,000
Traceable Costs	$ 40,000	$ 66,000	$ 36,000	$ 96,000	$238,000
Maintenance Costs[a]	9,500	14,500	7,000	19,000	50,000
Quantity Purchase Discount Credit[a] . . .	(3,800)	(5,800)	(2,800)	(7,600)	(20,000)
Total Expenses.	$ 45,700	$ 74,700	$ 40,200	$107,400	$268,000
Income before Taxes	$ 34,300	$ 60,300	$ 28,800	$ 76,600	$200,000
Deferred Costs at End of Period	$ 40,500	$ 26,000	$ 19,000	—	—
Accrued Income at End of Period	(3,800)	(9,600)	(12,400)	$ (20,000)	—

DISCRETE APPROACH	Quarter 1	Quarter 2	Quarter 3	Quarter 4	Total
Sales.	$ 80,000	$135,000	$ 69,000	$184,000	$468,000
Traceable Costs	$ 40,000	$ 66,000	$ 36,000	$ 96,000	$238,000
Maintenance Costs.	50,000	—	—	—	50,000
Quantity Purchase Discount Credit. . . .	—	—	—	(20,000)	(20,000)
Total Expenses.	$ 90,000	$ 66,000	$ 36,000	$ 76,000	$268,000
Income (Loss) before Taxes.	$(10,000)	$ 69,000	$ 33,000	$108,000	$200,000
Deferred Costs at End of Period	—	—	—	—	—
Accrued Income at End of Period	—	—	—	—	—

Graph of Quarterly Income (Loss)
before Taxes under the
Integral and Discrete Approaches

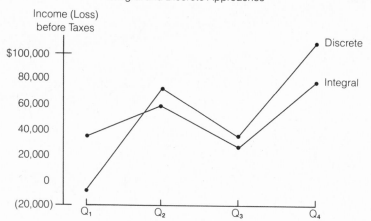

[a]Allocation of these items based on the following percentages: $Q_1 = 19\%$; $Q_2 = 29\%$; $Q_3 = 14\%$; $Q_4 = 38\%$.

Income Taxes in Interim Reports

Reporting income taxes in interim reports is a particularly thorny problem for two reasons:

1. The corporate tax rate schedule is progressive, and the marginal tax rate can change from quarter to quarter.
2. The effective tax rate may differ from the statutory rate and, furthermore, may change from period to period as investment tax credits are earned, or as permanent differences arise.

If the interim reporting period is viewed as an *integral* portion of a longer period, the year, the firm estimates its effective tax rate for the entire year and applies that rate to income before taxes in each quarter. This practice smooths income tax expense for the year over the four quarters and removes fluctuations in net income due to tax items which arise in individual interim periods but are meaningful only within the context of a full year.

In contrast, viewing the interim period as a *discrete* reporting period normally gives different results. Quarterly income tax expense is based on developments in each quarter rather than over the entire year. For example, suppose a firm's quarterly pretax income is fairly constant, and large investment tax credits are earned in the third quarter. Income tax expense in the third quarter could fall, even though pretax income is constant, and net income would appear to jump.

These two approaches to accounting for income taxes in interim periods are illustrated in Exhibit 12.6. The smoothing of quarterly income tax expense under the integral approach permits the quarterly results to accurately reflect the firm's stable, nonseasonal operations.

Using LIFO in Interim Periods

Accounting for inventories under the LIFO cost-flow assumption gives rise to another issue in the context of interim reporting. When physical inventories at interim reporting dates change, and LIFO is being used, should the changes be accounted for within the context of the (estimated) year-end LIFO inventory or be based on the actual change occurring at the end of the interim period? In short, how should LIFO layers added or deleted at interim dates be valued? The question is important because its answer affects both cost of goods sold and net income for the interim period.

The question assumes even greater practical importance when LIFO layers include very old low costs. Suppose inventory at the end of a quarterly period *falls,* but the firm plans to replace it by year-end. Should cost of goods sold for the interim period reflect the old costs of the temporarily impaired LIFO layer(s)? Is it misleading to do so when the impairment will be restored later in the year?

The Integral Position on LIFO. As one might expect, the integral position sup-

Exhibit 12.6	Accounting for Income Taxes in Interim Periods

DATA FOR ILLUSTRATION

The West Corporation predicts income before taxes of $50,000 in each of the four quarterly periods during the next calendar year. Furthermore, it expects to earn $20,000 in investment credits on property placed in service in June. Under current law, West faces the following U.S. corporate income tax schedule:

Income	Marginal Tax Rate
First $25,000	15%
Second $25,000	18
Third $25,000	30
Fourth $25,000	40
Over $100,000	46

Condensed quarterly income statements for the integral and discrete approaches are as follows:

INTEGRAL APPROACH	Quarter 1	Quarter 2	Quarter 3	Quarter 4	Total
Income before Taxes	$50,000	$50,000	$50,000	$50,000	$200,000
Income Tax Expense[a]	12,937	12,937	12,938	12,938	51,750
Net Income	$37,063	$37,063	$37,062	$37,062	$148,250

DISCRETE APPROACH	Quarter 1	Quarter 2	Quarter 3	Quarter 4	Total
Income before Taxes	$50,000	$50,000	$50,000	$50,000	$200,000
Income Tax Expense	8,250[b]	(2,500)[c]	23,000[d]	23,000[d]	51,750
Net Income	$41,750	$52,500	$27,000	$27,000	$148,250

[a]Effective tax rate for the year is 25.875% = [.15($25,000) + .18($25,000) + .30(25,000) + .40($25,000) + .46($100,000) − $20,000]/$200,000.
[b]$8,250 = .15($25,000) + .18($25,000).
[c]($2,500) = .3($25,000) + .4($25,000) − $20,000.
[d]$23,000 = .46($50,000).

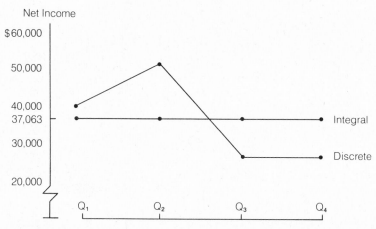

Graph of Quarterly Net Income
under the
Integral and Discrete Approaches

ports the notion that it is not the change in *interim* inventory that is important; it is the change in the *annual* inventory that counts. Under this concept, the estimated annual change in inventory is allocated to the interim periods on a systematic and rational basis, perhaps on the basis of interim sales.

The Discrete Position on LIFO. If each interim period is considered to be a discrete reporting period, standing alone, the principles and procedures used to determine LIFO inventory at year-end are also used at the end of each interim period. While no estimates or allocations are called for here, the total income reported for the four quarters may not equal annual net income, a troubling result. To see this, suppose a LIFO layer in the beginning inventory is used up at June 30 but is fully replenished by the end of the year, December 31. Impairment of the layer at June 30 would be reflected in the second quarter's reported net income, yet, because the layer was not impaired at December 31, annual net income would be unaffected. This leads to a discrepancy between annual net income and the sum of the quarterly net incomes.

An Intermediate Position on LIFO. One way to avoid the discrepancy that might result under the discrete approach to LIFO also limits the smoothing effect of inventory changes when the integral position is applied. This intermediate position calls for charging cost of goods sold for the current replacement cost of any LIFO layers used during the year but expected to be replenished by the end of the year. An expected annual change in the LIFO inventory, however, is not estimated and allocated to the quarterly periods.

To illustrate the alternative treatments of LIFO inventory, we have prepared a numerical example in Exhibit 12.7. Since the example focuses on the temporary impairment of a LIFO layer, and not on a change in the annual LIFO inventory, the integral and intermediate positions provide the same results. Note the $20,000 difference between the total quarterly gross profit reported under the discrete approach and the annual gross profit. On the annual basis, the LIFO inventory is unchanged. The ending inventory implied by the discrete approach, however, includes a new layer of 10,000 units valued at current cost of $6. Thus the year-end inventory under the discrete approach is $20,000 higher and cost of goods sold $20,000 lower than either would be if LIFO were simply applied on an annual basis.

Alternative approaches are available to account for the excess of current cost over LIFO cost of temporarily impaired LIFO layers. In the third quarter, the 10,000 units sold from inventory were charged to cost of goods sold at their current cost of $60,000 rather than their LIFO inventory cost of $40,000. The $20,000 difference is accounted for in interim periods as a reduction to inventory or as a deferred credit such as Interim Inventory Allowance. In the fourth quarter, when the sold LIFO layer is replenished, the LIFO cost of $40,000 is restored to the inventory, not the current replacement cost of $60,000. The following adjusting journal entries made at the end of Quarters 3 and 4 would accomplish this in a periodic inventory system:

Exhibit 12.7   **Alternative Treatments of Temporary Impairment of LIFO Layer in Interim Reports**

DATA FOR ILLUSTRATION

The Webster Corporation uses LIFO and begins the year with an inventory of $90,000, consisting of the following LIFO layers: (1) 10,000 units @ $4, (2) 10,000 units @ $3, and (3) 10,000 units @ $2. Quarterly sales and purchases occur according to the following schedule:

	Quarter 1	Quarter 2	Quarter 3	Quarter 4
Sales.	40,000 @ $10	40,000 @ $10	50,000 @ $10	40,000 @ $10
Purchases	40,000 @ $6	40,000 @ $6	40,000 @ $6	50,000 @ $6

Notice that sales exceed purchases by 10,000 units in Quarter 3, while purchases exceed sales by 10,000 units in Quarter 4. Units in inventory are used in Quarter 3, but they are replenished in Quarter 4. From an annual point of view, the beginning and ending inventories valued at LIFO are identical. Condensed quarterly income statements under the integral and discrete approaches and a condensed annual income statement are as follows:

INTEGRAL APPROACH

	Quarter 1	Quarter 2	Quarter 3	Quarter 4	Total
*Sales	$ 400,000	$ 400,000	$ 500,000	$ 400,000	$ 1,700,000
Cost of Goods Sold	(240,000)	(240,000)	(300,000)[a]	(240,000)	(1,020,000)
Gross Profit	$ 160,000	$ 160,000	$ 200,000	$ 160,000	$ 680,000

DISCRETE APPROACH

	Quarter 1	Quarter 2	Quarter 3	Quarter 4	Total
Sales	$ 400,000	$ 400,000	$ 500,000	$ 400,000	$ 1,700,000
Cost of Goods Sold	(240,000)	(240,000)	(280,000)[b]	(240,000)	(1,000,000)
Gross Profit	$ 160,000	$ 160,000	$ 220,000	$ 160,000	$ 700,000

ANNUAL STATEMENT

Sales (170,000 @ $10)	$ 1,700,000
Cost of Goods Sold (170,000 @ $6)	(1,020,000)
Gross Profit	$ 680,000

[a]Valued at current replacement cost; the LIFO layer temporarily "used" is ignored.
[b]Consists of 40,000 units at current replacement cost of $6 ($240,000) plus the most recent LIFO layer of 10,000 units with a LIFO cost of $4 ($40,000).

QUARTER 3

Cost of Goods Sold 60,000
   Inventory   40,000
   Interim Inventory Allowance (or Inventory).   20,000
To charge Cost of Goods Sold for the current cost of the goods
sold from inventory and record the excess over LIFO cost in an
allowance until the LIFO layer is replenished. Cost of Goods Sold
of $300,000 = $90,000 + $240,000 − [$90,000 − ($40,000 +
$20,000)].

QUARTER 4

Inventory 40,000
Interim Inventory Allowance (or Inventory). 20,000
   Cost of Goods Sold   60,000
To restore the replenished LIFO layer to Inventory at its LIFO cost,
remove the allowance, and adjust the Cost of Goods Sold
accordingly. Cost of Goods Sold of $240,000 = [$90,000 −
($40,000 + $20,000)] + $300,000 − $90,000.

This interim inventory allowance can fluctuate during the interim periods in order to provide the needed amounts of cost of goods sold. At year-end, when the firm knows exactly what LIFO layers have been replenished and what the annual cost of goods sold is, the allowance is closed out and fourth quarter cost of goods sold adjusted accordingly. If the actual cost of replacing the LIFO layers differs from the estimated cost at date of impairment, the difference is reflected in cost of goods sold in the period in which replacement occurs.

Interim Reporting under *APBO 28*

APBO 28 provides most of the authoritative guidance governing the principles and practices to be used in developing interim financial information.[13] Specific provisions involving income taxes and accounting changes have been amended and are discussed following this overview of *APBO 28*.

APBO 28. This *Opinion* was issued in response to the great diversity existing in interim reporting practices. Its objective was to clarify the application of generally accepted accounting principles to interim reports and to prescribe minimum disclosures for publicly traded companies choosing to issue interim reports. Early in the *Opinion,* the board "concluded that each interim period should be viewed primarily as an *integral part of an annual period.*"[14] Much of the *Opinion* is devoted to describing how annual reporting principles and practices must be modified in order to conform to the integral position. As previously indicated, *APBO 28* does *not* impose a requirement for the disclosure of interim information as *SFAS 14* did for segment information. Rather, if the decision is made to issue

---

[13]Accounting Principles Board, *Opinion No. 28;* CT § 173.
[14]Ibid., par. 9; CT § 173.103; emphasis added.

Exhibit 12.8	Principal Requirements of *APBO 28*

1. Revenue from products sold or services rendered should be recognized as earned during an interim period on the same basis as that followed for the full year.
2. Those costs and expenses that are associated directly with or allocated to the products sold or to the services rendered for annual reporting purposes (including, for example, material costs, wages and salaries and related fringe benefits, manufacturing overhead, and warranties) should be similarly treated for interim reporting purposes. The following exceptions relate to interim inventory valuation:
   a. Companies often use methods to estimate interim inventories which differ from the methods used at annual inventory dates. These companies should disclose the method used at the interim date and any significant adjustments which result from reconciliations with the annual physical inventory.
   b. Companies using LIFO may encounter temporary impairment of base period inventories which are expected to be replaced by the end of the annual period. In such cases, neither interim inventories nor cost of sales should reflect this temporary impairment; cost of sales should indicate the expected cost of replacing the liquidated LIFO base.
   c. Inventory losses from market declines should not be deferred beyond the interim period in which the decline occurs unless they are temporary and can reasonably be expected to be restored by the end of the annual period.
   d. For companies using standard cost systems, variances that are planned and expected to be absorbed by the end of the annual period should ordinarily be deferred at interim reporting dates.
3. Costs and expenses other than product costs should be charged to income in interim periods as incurred or be allocated among interim periods on the basis of an estimate of time expired, benefit received, or activity associated with the periods.
4. To avoid the possibility that interim results with material seasonal variations may be taken as fairly indicative of the estimated results for a full fiscal year, businesses should disclose the seasonal nature of their activities and consider supplementing their interim reports with information for twelve-month periods ended at the interim date for the current and preceding years.
5. At the end of each interim period, the company should make its best estimate of the effective tax rate expected to be applicable for the full fiscal year. The rate so determined should be used in providing for income taxes on a current year-to-date basis.
6. Extraordinary items should be disclosed separately and included in the determination of net income by the interim period in which they occur.
7. When publicly traded companies report summarized financial information to their security holders at interim dates (including reports on fourth quarters), the following data should be reported, as a minimum:
   a. Sales or gross revenues, provision for income taxes, extraordinary items (including related income tax effects), cumulative effect of a change in accounting principles or practices, and net income.
   b. Primary and fully diluted earnings per share data for each period presented.
   c. Seasonal revenue, cost, or expenses.
   d. Significant changes in estimates or provisions for income taxes.
   e. Disposal of a segment of a business and extraordinary, unusual, or infrequently occurring items.
   f. Contingent items.
   g. Changes in accounting principles or estimates.
   h. Significant changes in financial position.

Source: Accounting Principles Board, *Opinion No. 28*, "Interim Financial Reporting" (New York: AICPA, 1973); CT § I73; Copyright © 1973 by the American Institute of Certified Public Accountants, Inc.

interim information, it should conform with the provisions of *APBO 28*, even though the information is not audited. The principal requirements of *APBO 28* are summarized in Exhibit 12.8.

Note that these requirements relate almost entirely to income statement information; no mention is made of information normally included in balance sheets and statements of changes in financial position. Indeed, the *Opinion* provides no guidance as to the form and content of interim financial *statements*. It deals with interim financial *information* disclosed in an unspecified format. The minimum disclosure requirements for publicly traded companies are listed in Item 7 of Exhibit 12.8. Again, this is not a requirement that publicly traded companies issue interim reports; rather it provides guidelines for minimum disclosures by those publicly traded companies that do report on an interim basis.

Consider some ways in which *APBO 28*'s provisions are consistent with the integral position:

1. Temporary impairment of LIFO layers expected to be replenished by year-end should not be reflected in interim cost of sales or inventories (paragraph 14.b). Permanent impairment of LIFO layers in interim periods and inventory increases should be recognized in those interim periods. Interim income is not to be smoothed by an allocation of expected inventory change to the interim periods. This is the *intermediate position* on LIFO previously discussed rather than the pure integral position.

2. Inventory losses resulting from application of the lower-of-cost-or-market principle should not be recognized in the interim period if they are viewed as being restored by year-end (paragraph 14.c).

3. Costs and expenses not associated with revenue *may* be expensed as incurred, or, if more than one interim period is benefited, the cost or expense *may* be allocated among the periods benefited (paragraph 15). This provision undercuts an important feature of the integral view—namely, that costs benefiting more than one interim period *must* be allocated. *APBO 28* does not preclude allocation but does not require it either. Paragraph 16 offers some examples of costs that might or might not be allocated, such as quantity discounts based on annual sales volume, property taxes, and advertising costs clearly benefiting more than one interim period.

4. Income tax expense in interim periods will be based on the firm's best estimate of its annual effective tax rate (paragraph 19). If the estimate of the effective tax rate is revised in a period, that period's income tax expense equals the year-to-date income tax expense (the new rate times the year-to-date pretax income) minus total income tax expense reported in prior interim periods. The following table illustrates computation of income tax expense in interim periods:

Period	Pretax Income Current Period	Year-to-Date	Estimated Annual Effective Tax Rate	Income Tax Expense Year-to-Date	Total Prior Periods	Current Period
Q_1	$150,000	$150,000	42%	$ 63,000	—	$ 63,000
Q_2	120,000	270,000	44	118,800	$ 63,000	55,800
Q_3	130,000	400,000	38	152,000	118,800	33,200
Q_4	160,000	560,000	41	229,600	152,000	77,600
	$560,000					$229,600

Exhibit 12.9 Extract from Quaker Oats Oats Interim Report

QUAKER OATS COMPANY
SECOND QUARTER REPORT
DECEMBER 31, 1984
(IN MILLIONS OF DOLLARS)

ASSETS	1984	1983
Current Assets:		
Cash and Marketable Securities	$ 116.3	$ 21.6
Receivables, Net	315.5	328.5
Inventories:		
Finished Goods	269.0	202.2
Grains and Materials	103.8	125.4
Supplies	30.4	18.5
Inventories	$ 403.2	$ 346.1
Other Current Assets	31.2	73.5
Current Assets	$ 866.2	$ 769.7
Other Receivables and		
Investments	19.0	20.8
Property, Plant, and Equipment	1,054.5	1,075.2
Less: Accumulated Depreciation	362.7	316.5
Properties, Net	$ 691.7	$ 758.7
Intangible Assets	121.5	80.0
	$1,698.4	$1,629.2

LIABILITIES AND SHAREHOLDERS' EQUITY	1984	1983
Current Liabilities:		
Short-Term Debt	$ 111.4	$ 184.7
Current Portion of Long-Term		
Debt	2.0	6.4
Trade Accounts Payable	171.7	161.0
Other Current Liabilities	225.0	210.3
Current Liabilities	$ 510.1	$ 562.4
Long-Term Debt	189.9	184.8
Other Liabilities	59.8	44.3
Deferred Income Taxes	164.1	123.6
Redeemable Preference Stock,		
without Par Value, $100		
Stated Value, $9.56		
Cumulative	38.0	40.6
Common Shareholders' Equity:		
Common Stock, $5 Par Value,		
Authorized 100,000,000		
Shares: Issued 41,994,698		
Shares	210.0	105.0
Additional Paid-In Capital	.2	24.4
Reinvested Earnings	655.8	651.5
Cumulative Exchange Adjustment	(110.4)	(79.1)
	$ 755.6	$ 701.8
Treasury Common Stock, at		
Cost: 1,142,430 Shares and		
1,774,324 Shares,		
Respectively	(19.1)	(28.3)
Common Shareholders' Equity	$ 736.5	$ 673.5
	$1,698.4	$1,629.2

5. Attempts should be made to estimate certain year-end adjustments in order that each interim period bear a reasonable portion of the expected annual amount (paragraph 17). Some examples are bad debt expense, inventory shrinkage, and year-end bonuses.

Accounting Changes in Interim Reports. The original provisions in *APBO 28* called for reporting any accounting changes made during the year in the appropriate interim periods and required that the accounting treatment of those changes conform to *APBO 20*. Unfortunately, a problem arose with respect to the treatment of *cumulative effect* accounting changes adopted in other than the first interim period. The problem concerned a potential discrepancy between interim income statements and balance sheets issued *prior* to a cumulative-effect accounting change which were restated in interim periods *after* the change. In order to remedy this, *SFAS 3*[15] provides that the cumulative effect of a change in accounting principles be recognized only in the first quarter. If the change occurs in another quarter, the cumulative effect of the change on retained earnings at the beginning of the first quarter shall be included in (restated) first quarter net income. Other interim reports issued prior to the occurrence of the change are to be restated to reflect the new accounting principle.

Examples of Interim Reports. Substantial diversity in interim reporting continues to exist. Some companies mail small pamphlets to stockholders containing selected data and no financial statements. Other companies develop elaborate brochures, complete with a full set of financial statements and notes. We reproduce portions of three of the latter type of interim report in Exhibits 12.9, 12.10, and 12.11. Exhibit 12.9, on page 609, illustrates an interim balance sheet, and Exhibit 12.10 shows an income statement and statement of changes in financial position. Exhibit 12.11, on page 613, illustrates segment reporting in an interim statement, thereby illustrating both topics in the chapter.

Authors' Evaluation of *APBO 28*. Any evaluation of *APBO 28* must take into account the controversy over the nature of the interim reporting period. Insofar as accounting principles are concerned, the *Opinion* reflects a reasonable intermediate position embodying elements of both the integral and discrete views. These issues are not settled, however, and interim reporting continues to be an active item on the FASB's agenda. The Discussion Memorandum mentioned previously uses 126 pages to analyze all aspects of the various issues.

Our major concerns with *APBO 28* relate primarily to disclosure rather than accounting principles. In the area of accounting principles, we believe that annual items of expense or revenue *must* be allocated to the quarterly periods benefited. *APBO 28* says such items *may* be allocated. While we see no need to require firms to issue interim reports, we do believe that the format of interim reports, when issued, ought to be comparable across firms. Such an objective probably

---

[15]Financial Accounting Standards Board, *Statement No. 3;* CT § 173.135–173.137.

Exhibit 12.10	Extract from DuPont Interim Report

E. I. DUPONT DE NEMOURS AND COMPANY
FIRST QUARTER REPORT
MARCH 31, 1984

CONSOLIDATED INCOME STATEMENT[a]

(Dollars in Millions, Except per Share)	1984	1983
Sales	$9,253	$8,597
Other Income	77	89
Total	$9,330	$8,686
Cost of Goods Sold and Other Expenses	$7,012	$6,886
Selling, General and Administrative Expenses	489	486
Depreciation, Depletion and Amortization	434	428
Exploration Expenses, Including Dry Hole Costs and Impairment of Unproved Properties	93	106
Interest and Debt Expense	138	152
Total	$8,166	$8,058
Earnings before Income Taxes	$1,164	$ 628
Provision for Income Taxes	791	425
Net Income	$ 373	$ 203
EARNINGS PER SHARE OF COMMON STOCK[b]	$ 1.55	$ .85
DIVIDENDS PER SHARE OF COMMON STOCK	$ .70	$ .60

CONSOLIDATED STATEMENT OF CHANGES IN FINANCIAL POSITION[a]

	Three Months Ended March 31	
(Dollars in Millions)	1984	1983
CASH PROVIDED BY OPERATIONS		
Net Income	$ 373	$ 203
Depreciation, Depletion and Amortization	434	428
Increase (Decrease) in Deferred Income Taxes—Noncurrent	58	(4)
Dry Hole Costs and Impairment of Unproved Properties	50	66
Other Noncash Charges and Credits—Net	138	36
Cash Flow from Operations—before Changes in Working Capital	$1,053	$ 729
Decrease (Increase) in Working Capital*	(208)	(421)
Cash Provided by Operations	$ 845	$ 308
Dividends Paid to Stockholders	$ (170)	$ (145)
INVESTMENT ACTIVITIES		
Capital Expenditures	$ (663)	$ (605)
Proceeds from Sale of Assets to Petro-Lewis	—	569
Miscellaneous—Net	(44)	39
Cash Provided by (Used for) Investment Activities	$ (707)	$ 3

(continued on next page)

Exhibit 12.10	Continued

FINANCING ACTIVITIES

Net Decrease in Borrowings and Capital Lease Obligations	$ (25)	$ (141)
Common Stock Issued in Connection with Compensation and		
Benefit Plans.	32	30
Cash provided by (Used for) Financing Activities.	$ 7	$ (111)

INCREASE (DECREASE) IN CASH AND MARKETABLE SECURITIES . . . . $ (25) $ 55

*Excluding cash and marketable securities, and short-term borrowings and capital lease obligations.

NOTES TO FINANCIAL STATEMENTS

(Dollars in Millions)

(a) These statements are unaudited, but reflect all adjustments that, in the opinion of management, are necessary to provide a fair statement of the results for the periods covered. Certain reclassifications of 1983 data have been made to conform to 1984 classifications.

(b) Average shares outstanding. Earnings per share are calculated on the basis of average number of common shares outstanding. Three Months Ended March 31, 1984— 239,187,665.

Exhibit 12.11	Industry Segment Performance Information in Interim Report

E. I. DUPONT DE NEMOURS AND COMPANY
FIRST QUARTER REPORT
MARCH 31, 1984

Industry Segment Performance

The following text and accompanying table compare first quarter industry segment results with the first quarter of 1983:

- Income of the Biomedical Products segment was down 17 percent, primarily reflecting lower sales for medical X-ray products, the effects of hospital cost containment programs which impacted sales of consumables for the "aca" discrete clinical analyzer, and planned increases in pharmaceuticals research and marketing expenditures.
- Industrial and Consumer Products segment income was up $37 million primarily due to strong electronic sales and continued strong performance for specialty products, such as "Corian" building products. The company's cost containment programs also contributed to the improvement.
- Fibers segment income increased 82 percent as a result of higher demand for all product lines and lower cost. Shipments as a percent of capacity reached 81 percent compared to 73 percent a year ago.
- Income for the Polymer Products segment was up $40 million on an increase in sales of 18 percent. This improvement reflects steady growth in demand for specialty polymers due to continued recovery in consumer durables, especially in the automotive market.
- Agricultural and Industrial Chemicals segment income rose 39 percent on a 13 percent increase in sales. The improvement is principally due to strong gains achieved by agricultural chemicals reflecting worldwide volume increases and lower costs. Titanium dioxide also achieved worldwide volume increases, and prices improved.

Exhibit 12.11   Continued

- Income of the Petroleum Exploration and Production segment was 60 percent higher. The improvement is due to higher domestic natural gas volumes and higher crude oil volumes.
- Petroleum Refining, Marketing and Transportation segment income was up 80 percent, reflecting higher domestic refined product margins and volumes, partially offset by lower international margins.
- Income of the Coal segment was up 26 percent due to higher margins and increased volume.

Consolidated Industry Segment Information
(Dollars in Millions)

Sales	1984	1983
Biomedical Products	$ 260	$ 274
Industrial and Consumer Products	671	603
Fibers	1,203	1,074
Polymer Products	917	779
Agricultural and Industrial Chemicals	989	876
Petroleum Exploration and Production (Excludes Intersegment Transfers)[a]	507	498
Petroleum Refining, Marketing and Transportation[b]	4,295	4,140
Coal	411	353
Total	$9,253	$8,597

After-Tax Operating Income		
Biomedical Products	$ 20	$ 24
Industrial and Consumer Products	55	18
Fibers	102	56
Polymer Products	66	26
Agricultural and Industrial Chemicals	71	51
Petroleum Exploration and Production	120	75
Petroleum Refining, Marketing and Transportation	27	15
Coal	49	39
Total	$ 510	$ 304
Interest and General Corporate Expenses Net of Tax[c]	(137)	(101)
Net Income	$ 373	$ 203

[a]Intersegment transfers excluded from sales were $842 for first quarter 1984 and $575 for first quarter 1983.
[b]Sales data include $1,693 for first quarter 1984 and $1,618 for first quarter 1983 for crude oil sales at the approximate cost of the crude oil to the segment.
[c]Includes exchange gains of $7 in 1984 and $48 in 1983.

---

implies a complete set of interim financial statements, condensed in a standard way. Unaudited statements should be clearly labeled as *unaudited*. Explanatory notes to the statements are needed. Specifically, one of these notes should describe accounting policies followed in preparing the interim financial information. Such a note would include a reference to *APBO 28* and give some indication of the nature and extent of the accruals, estimates, deferrals, and adjustments reflected in the interim information. We believe that these modifications to present interim reporting practices would improve the overall quality of interim reporting.

Summary of Key Concepts

Segment reporting refers to the disclosure of financial information along **lines of business** and **geographical areas.** To provide such information, companies must break down information along those lines in their combined or consolidated financial statements. The principal pronouncement in this area is *SFAS 14,* which also requires that **information about major customers** be reported.

Any attempt at segment reporting must consider the **pricing of internal transfers** and the **allocation of common costs** among segments. If segments must report revenue from sales to internal and external customers, the revenue from internal customers is based on prices that are not the result of completed market transactions. Allocations of the costs of shared facilities or other jointly used resources inject a degree of **arbitrariness** into financial data which reflect them.

Management is responsible for **identifying reportable segments** according to several criteria which make it difficult to report either too many segments or too few. These criteria employ data on segment revenue, operating profit or loss, and identifiable assets to establish the significance of a potentially reportable segment. Generally, a potentially reportable segment having at least 10 percent of the sum of any of the criteria items for all such segments is significant enough to be reported separately.

Interim reporting is concerned with the regular issuance of financial statements covering **time periods of less than one year.** A fundamental issue in interim reporting is whether to treat the interim period as part of a larger period—the **integral position**—or as a **separate,** identifiable, and complete reporting period— the **discrete position.**

The **integral approach** reflects the position that items such as income taxes, year-end bonuses, quantity discounts, and investment tax credits are meaningful only within the context of a full year and should be **allocated among the interim periods.** In contrast, proponents of the **discrete position** reject any additional allocations beyond those normally made for annual periods.

Accounting for **income taxes** and **LIFO inventories** is particularly **troublesome** under the **discrete approach** to interim reporting. The progressive nature of the corporation income tax, losses in interim periods, and the uneven flow of tax credits during the year all lead one to question the usefulness of interim income tax expense based **only** on the events of that interim period. The seasonal aspects of many businesses might result in **temporary impairment of LIFO layers** which will be replenished by the end of the annual period. Interim cost-of-goods-sold amounts reflecting the impairment of old LIFO layers which are not impaired at year-end seem questionable.

APBO 28 provides guidance for the preparation and disclosure of interim financial information but **does not require** that companies issue interim reports. It reflects the APB's conclusion that an **interim period** does not stand alone and is properly viewed as an **integral part of an annual period.** The treatment of annual items, particularly income taxes and LIFO cost of goods sold, in interim reports is based on the best estimates of them for the entire annual period.

Questions

Q12.1 What is segment reporting, and why are many financial statement users interested in it?

Q12.2 Describe the major conceptual problems inherent in any segment reporting scheme. Evaluate the ways in which *SFAS 14* deals with these problems.

Q12.3 In one of its annual reports, Ford Motor Company stated that "the company and its consolidated subsidiaries comprise a vertically integrated business operating primarily in a single industry segment consisting of the manufacture, assembly and sale of cars and trucks and related parts and accessories." In effect, Ford reported no supplementary information for *industry* segments. Later in the report, Ford noted that it sold 2,322,902 cars and 1,301,172 trucks in North America during the year. Does Ford really have a single dominant segment? Comment.

Q12.4 One of the significance tests employed in identifying reportable industry segments relates to segments' identifiable assets. *SFAS 14* does not count intersegment advances as identifiable assets unless made by a finance segment. What is the purpose of this rule? Does it seem consistent with the inclusion of intersegment revenue in applying the total revenue significance test?

Q12.5 We have taken the position that *SFAS 14* is seriously flawed because it pays too little attention to the volume of intersegment transactions in determining reportable segments and in selecting information to be disclosed. Do you agree? Explain.

Q12.6 For each of the following items, indicate whether it should be included in the operating profit or loss of a segment:
    a. Allocated general corporate expenses.
    b. Common costs allocated on a reasonable basis.
    c. Domestic and foreign income taxes.
    d. Extraordinary items.
    e. Interest expense (assuming the segment's operations are not principally of a financial nature).
    f. Intersegment sales.
    g. Loss on discountinued operations.
    h. Revenue earned at the corporate level.
    i. Traceable operating costs.

Q12.7 A well-known accountant once observed that "accountants know the limitations of quarterly or other very short-term financial statements, but persons to whom the reports are addressed cannot be depended upon to treat them with adequate caution.'' To what limitations is the accountant referring? Why do you think that concern is expressed about users' ability to properly interpret interim statements?

Q12.8 Interim reporting continues to be a controversial subject because of the alternative ways in which accountants view the nature of the interim reporting period. Describe these alternative views, and indicate why each of them is likely to require modification before being accepted by the profession.

Q12.9 Suppose a corporation expected to earn taxable income of $1,000,000 evenly over the calendar year and to receive investment tax credits of $50,000 for property placed in service during the month of May. The flow-through method of accounting for investment tax credits is used. Calculate the effective tax rate reported by the corporation in its second quarter interim report under the integral and discrete views of the interim reporting period. Use the tax rate schedule given in Exhibit 12.6.

Q12.10 The use of LIFO requires special consideration in discussions of interim reporting, yet no particular concern is expressed over the use of FIFO. Why?

Q12.11 *APBO 28* provides that costs and expenses (other than product costs) incurred in one interim period but benefiting more than one interim period *may* (not *must*) be allocated among the interim periods benefited. Do you agree with this position? Explain.

Q12.12 The computation of a company's third quarter provision for income taxes should be based upon earnings for which of the following periods? Defend your choice by explaining why the others are inappropriate.
   a. The quarter at an expected annual effective income tax rate.
   b. The quarter at the statutory rate.
   c. To date at an expected annual effective income tax rate less prior quarters' provisions.
   d. To date at the statutory rate less prior quarters' provisions.
   (AICPA adapted)

Exercises

E12.1 The following summary data have been gathered for the Carson Company's industry segments:

	Industry Segment (Amounts in Millions)				
	A	B	C	D	E
Sales to Unaffiliated					
Customers	$400	$700	$200	$1,400	$1,000
Intersegment Sales	100	300	200	400	—
Operating Profit (Loss)	(50)	60	(30)	500	200
Identifiable Assets	300	800	200	1,500	900

Required: Identify the reportable industry segments for the Carson Company, and indicate all significance tests which were satisified by each reportable segment.

E12.2 Management of Manchester Corporation is trying to decide how many of the company's industry segments must be separately reported under *SFAS 14*. Revenue data for the various segments are as shown below. Divisional operating profit or loss and identifiable assets show the same pattern.

		Industry Segment				
	A	B	C	D	E	F
Sales to Unaffiliated						
Customers . . .	$4,000	$3,000	$1,000	$1,200	$ 800	$1,100
Intersegment						
Sales	1,000	500	100	—	500	—
Total Sales. . . .	$5,000	$3,500	$1,100	$1,200	$1,300	$1,100

Required: Indicate how these industry segments are to be reported in accordance with *SFAS 14* and explain why.

E12.3 Hines Corporation annually reports operating profit of industry segments in its supplementary financial information. The following information is available for 19X1:

	Sales	Traceable Costs
Segment A	$ 750,000	$450,000
Segment B	500,000	225,000
Segment C	250,000	125,000
	$1,500,000	$800,000

Expenses in addition to those above are as follows:

Indirect Operating Expenses	$240,000
General Corporate Expenses	180,000
Interest Expense	96,000

Hines allocates common costs based on the ratio of a segment's sales to total sales. What should be the operating profit for Segment B for 19X1? (*AICPA adapted*)

E12.4 During the course of your audit of Abbott Corporation, you ask the client's personnel to develop the necessary supplementary disclosures under *SFAS 14*. After several days' hard work, the assistant controller returns with the following list of data. Confused by some of the provisions of the *Statement,* the assistant asks you which of the items indicated below are to be disclosed under *SFAS 14*.

1. Abbott does business in several industries, and none of its industry segments transact with other segments in the firm. Total sales and

identifiable assets are $580,000,000 and $400,000,000, respectively. Amounts for the three largest segments are shown below:

	Segment A	Segment B	Segment C
Sales	$264,000,000	$200,000,000	$50,000,000
Identifiable Assets	180,000,000	120,000,000	65,000,000

2. Abbott operates in the United States and in foreign countries. Its domestic operations recorded sales of $65,000,000 to customers in Europe and South America. The foreign operations themselves generated $175,000,000 in sales on $130,000,000 in assets. Breaking the foreign operations down by geographical area yields the following:

Geographical Area	Sales	Identifiable Assets
Europe	$60,000,000	$38,000,000
Asia	20,000,000	10,000,000
South America	50,000,000	37,000,000
Australia	45,000,000	45,000,000

3. Sales to Abbott's major customers appear as follows:

Customer	Sales
U.S. Department of Defense	$61,000,000
U.S. Auto Companies (Equally Divided among GM, Ford, and Chrysler)	65,000,000
Qantas Airlines (Privately Owned)	20,000,000
Ministry of Defense, U.K.	40,000,000
Office of the Admiralty, U.K.	20,000,000
Air Brazil (Privately Owned)	24,000,000

Required: Identify which of the above information is to be reported separately under the various provisions of *SFAS 14*. Give reasons for your answers.

E12.5 Russell, Inc., is a diversified company. All of its industry segments are profitable. A condensed version of Russell's consolidated income statement for 19X3 follows:

Sales	$100,000,000
Equity in Income of Unconsolidated Subsidiaries	17,700,000
Interest Income	4,000,000
Total Revenue	$121,700,000
Cost of Goods Sold	$ 60,000,000
Selling Expenses	15,000,000^a
General and Administrative Expenses	8,000,000^b
Interest Expense	2,000,000
Income Tax Expense	15,000,000
Minority Interest in Net Income	2,800,000
Total Expenses	$102,800,000

Income from Continuing Operations	$ 18,900,000
Gain on Sale of ASAP Division, Net of Taxes of $1,000,000	1,500,000
Income before Extraordinary Loss	$ 20,400,000
Extraordinary Loss, Net of Taxes of $450,000	1,250,000
Net Income	$ 19,150,000

[a]Includes $1,900,000 of corporate advertising.
[b]Includes $2,200,000 of corporate administrative expenses.

Required: Using the concept of operating profit employed in *SFAS 14*, prepare a schedule to determine the combined operating profit of all of Russell's reportable industry segments. Total intersegment sales during the year amounted to $8,000,000. There are no unconfirmed intercompany inventory profits.

E12.6 The Mill Company is a diversified firm with four reportable industry segments. Mill's controller has identified $10,000,000 of costs not directly traceable to the individual segments. The historical behavior of these cost categories shows fairly high correlation between the levels of these costs and the operating activity of the segments.

Cost Categories	**Amounts**
Computer Center	$5,000,000
Industrial Relations and Personnel Department	2,000,000
Central Purchasing Department	3,000,000

Data for the four segments follow:

Segment	**Sales**	**Traceable Costs**	**Employees**	**Identifiable Assets**
A	$60,000,000	$38,000,000	600	$34,000,000
B	15,000,000	10,000,000	100	15,000,000
C	30,000,000	22,000,000	1,000	20,000,000
D	45,000,000	30,000,000	300	40,000,000

Required: Prepare a schedule to allocate the common costs among the four segments for purposes of complying with *SFAS 14*. Give reasons to support the allocation bases you choose.

E12.7 The unaudited quarterly statements of income issued by many corporations to their stockholders are usually prepared on the same basis as annual statements, the statement for each quarter reflecting the transactions of that quarter.

Required:

1. Why do problems arise in using such quarterly statements to predict the income (before extraordinary items) for the year? Explain.
2. Discuss the ways in which quarterly income can be affected by the

behavior of the costs recorded in a Repairs and Maintenance of Factory Machinery account.

3. Do such quarterly statements give management opportunities to manipulate the results of operations for a quarter? If so, explain or give an example. *(AICPA adapted)*

E12.8 Interim financial reporting has become an important topic in accounting. There has been considerable discussion about the proper method of reporting results of operations at interim dates. Accordingly, the Accounting Principles Board issued *APBO 28* to clarify some aspects of interim financial reporting.

Required:

1. Discuss generally how revenue should be recognized at interim dates and specifically how revenue should be recognized for industries subject to large seasonal fluctuations in revenue and for long-term contracts using the percentage-of-completion method at annual reporting dates.
2. Discuss generally how product and period costs should be recognized at interim dates. Also discuss how inventory and cost of goods sold may be afforded special accounting treatment at interim dates.
3. Discuss how the provision for income taxes is computed and reflected in interim financial statements. *(AICPA adapted)*

E12.9 Many corporations issue quarterly financial statements. In general, the accounting concepts underlying these interim statements are the same as those underlying annual statements. However, certain concepts are modified in the development of interim statements because to treat the fiscal quarter as an independent accounting period might limit the usefulness of the interim statements to management, investors, and the public.

Required:

1. On what matters does the knowledgeable reader attempt to draw conclusions from interim financial statements? (Assume the statements are reliable, even though they are unaudited.)
2. An objective of income presentation should be the avoidance of any practice that is adopted for the purpose of equalization of reported income. Discuss the modifications, if any, of this generally accepted principle that would be made in developing interim income statements with regard to:
   a. Sales.
   b. Manufacturing costs, including over- or underabsorbed overhead.
   c. Selling expenses, including advertising.
   (AICPA adapted)

E12.10 The Bailey Company, a calendar-year corporation, has the following income before income tax provision and estimated effective annual income tax rates for the first three quarters of 19X9:

Quarter	Income before Income Tax Provision	Estimated Effective Annual Tax Rate at End of Quarter
First.	$60,000	40%
Second	70,000	40
Third	40,000	45

Calculate the amount of Bailey's income tax provision in its interim income statement for the third quarter. *(AICPA adapted)*

E12.11 The Greer Company issues quarterly reports to stockholders. Below we present annual estimates of income and related tax items and actual quarterly results for 19X2. The initial estimate prepared at the end of the first quarter is revised in each subsequent quarter. At the end of the fourth quarter, the actual annual results are used as the basis for the fourth quarter's results.

	Quarter 1	Quarter 2	Quarter 3	Quarter 4
Estimated Annual Taxable Income	$600,000	$650,000	$610,000	$620,000[a]
Estimated Annual Tax Credits.	10,000	11,000	16,000	15,000[a]
Actual Quarterly Taxable Income	160,000	160,000	150,000	150,000

[a]Actual for the year.

Required: Compute the amount of income tax expense reported by Greer in each of its four quarterly reports according to the provisions of *APBO 28,* using the rate schedule given in Exhibit 12.6. Carry the calculation of effective tax rates to tenths of 1 percent.

E12.12 Ross Corporation expects to sustain an operating loss of $100,000 for the full year ending December 31, 19X3. Ross operates entirely in one jurisdiction where the tax rate is 40 percent. Anticipated tax credits for 19X3 total $10,000. No permanent differences are expected. Realization of the full tax benefit of the expected operating loss and realization of anticipated tax credits are assured beyond any reasonable doubt because they will be carried back. For the first quarter ended March 31, 19X3, Ross reported an operating loss of $20,000. How much of a tax benefit should Ross report for the interim period ended March 31, 19X3? *(AICPA adapted)*

E12.13 Inventory quantities at the Mascoma Company change considerably during the year, due to the seasonal nature of Mascoma's business. Mascoma uses LIFO, and, because the company is growing rapidly, management fully expects that ending inventory quantities will exceed those in the beginning inventory. Selected interim and annual financial data for the Mascoma Company are given below:

	12/31/X0	3/31/X1	6/30/X1	9/30/X1	12/31/X1
LIFO Layers at Reporting Dates, at original LIFO cost.	(1) $400,000 (2) 600,000 (3) 500,000	(1) $ 400,000 (2) 600,000 (3) 200,000	(1) $ 400,000 (2) 300,000	(1) $ 400,000 (2) 600,000 (3) 300,000	(1) $ 400,000 (2) 600,000 (3) 500,000 (4) 200,000
Merchandise Purchases during the Quarter . .	—	3,000,000	2,400,000	3,200,000	3,600,000
Current Cost of Replacing Impaired Part of LIFO Layer(s) at Time of Original Impairment. . .	—	(3) 400,000	(3) 700,000 (2) 500,000	(3) 300,000	

Required: Compute quarterly cost of goods sold according to (1) *APBO 28* and (2) the discrete approach to interim reporting, and compare the quarterly totals with annual cost of goods sold. Comment on any troubling aspects of the results in the discrete case.

Problems

P12.1 Issues in Segment Reporting Many accountants and financial analysts contend that companies should report financial data for segments of the enterprise.

Required:

1. What does financial reporting for segments of a business enterprise involve?
2. Identify the reasons for requiring financial data to be reported by segments.
3. Identify the possible disadvantages of requiring financial data to be reported by segments.
4. Identify the accounting difficulties inherent in segment reporting. *(AICPA adapted)*

P12.2 Provisions of *SFAS 14*

1. In order to properly understand current generally accepted accounting principles with respect to accounting for and reporting upon segments of a business enterprise, as stated by the Financial Accounting Standards Board in *SFAS 14,* it is necessary to be familiar with certain unique terminology. With respect to segments of a business enterprise, explain the following terms:

a. Industry segment.

b. Revenue.

c. Operating profit and loss.

d. Identifiable assets.

2. A central issue in reporting on industry segments of a business enterprise is the determination of which segments are reportable.

   a. What are the tests to determine whether or not an industry segment is reportable?

   b. What is the test to determine if enough industry segments have been separately reported upon and what is the guideline on the maximum number of industry segments to be shown? *(AICPA adapted)*

P12.3 **Evaluation of Segment Report**   The Airguide Company is having an independent audit by CPAs for the first time this year. It must comply with *SFAS 14,* and, in connection therewith, the assistant controller provides you with the following draft of an industry segment report for Airguide:

	Division A	Division B	Division C	Total
Sales	$110,000	$ 220,000	$ 550,000	$ 880,000
Cost of Goods Sold . . .	(80,000)	(125,000)	(300,000)	(505,000)
Gross Profit	$ 30,000	$ 95,000	$ 250,000	$ 375,000
Variable Selling and Administrative				
Expenses	(20,000)	(20,000)	(100,000)	(140,000)
Fixed Selling and Administrative				
Expenses	(5,000)	(40,000)	(50,000)	(95,000)
Corporate Administrative				
Expenses	(5,000)	(10,000)	(25,000)	(40,000)
Operating Profit before Taxes.	$ 0	$ 25,000	$ 75,000	$ 100,000
Income Tax Expense . .	0	(10,000)	(30,000)	(40,000)
Operating Profit	$ 0	$ 15,000	$ 45,000	$ 60,000

In speaking with the assistant controller, you determine the following additional information:

1. Division A sells only to Division B, while Divisions B and C sell to customers outside the firm.

2. Corporate administrative expenses were allocated to the divisions based on sales.

3. Divisional income tax expense is based on Airguide's firmwide effective corporate income tax rate.

Required: Using the information given, explain whether the proposed segment report conforms with the requirements of *SFAS 14.* If necessary, recast the report in a format which would be acceptable under *SFAS 14. (Adapted from a problem prepared by Clyde P. Stickney)*

P12.4 Presentation of Industry Segment Information The MacDonald Company has four reportable industry segments. The following data have been gathered for these segments:

	Industry W	Industry X	Industry Y	Industry Z
External Sales	$40,000	$20,000	$15,000	$30,000
Internal Sales	1,500	—	2,000	1,000
Traceable Costs.	30,000	15,000	10,000	20,000
Allocated Joint Costs . . .	3,000	2,000	1,000	4,000
Identifiable Assets.	38,000	19,000	12,000	27,000
Depreciation Expense[a] . .	4,000	2,000	1,300	2,200
Capital Expenditures . . .	5.000	3,000	2,000	4,000
Allocated Income Taxes. .	1,200	400	1,000	1,100
Share of Corporate Interest Expense	400	200	150	300

[a]Included in Traceable Costs above.

Additional information:

1. General corporate administrative expenses were $12,000.
2. Dividend income from nonequity investments was $5,000.
3. Corporate assets not identified with any segment amounted to $18,000.

Required: Prepare a report of supplementary financial information for MacDonald's industry segments as required by *SFAS 14*.

P12.5 Presentation of Geographical Segment Information Webster, Inc., has extensive business operations in the United States and in two distinct foreign geographical areas. Financial information for these three geographical segments is summarized here:

	United States	Foreign Area A	Foreign Area B
External Sales	$120,000	$40,000	$20,000
Transfers between Geographical Areas	10,000	—	6,000
Traceable Costs	75,000	30,000	12,000
Allocated Joint Costs.	15,000	5,000	2,000
Share of Corporate Administrative Expenses. .	12,000	3,000	1,500
Share of Equity Method Income	6,000	2,000	1,000
Depreciation Expense[a]. . . .	9,000	4,000	3,000
Identifiable Assets	100,000	35,000	15,000
Capital Expenditures.	30,000	10,000	5,000
Allocated Income Taxes . . .	20,000	2,000	4,800
Allocated Interest Income . .	5,000	2,700	1,200

[a]Included in Traceable Costs above.

Additional information:

1. U.S. operations made sales of $25,000 to unaffiliated customers in Europe.
2. General corporate assets, not identified with any segment, amounted to $27,000.

Required: Prepare a report of supplementary financial information for the geographical segments identified by Webster as required by *SFAS 14*.

P12.6 Using Quarterly Data to Predict Annual Income The controller of Navar Corporation wants to issue to stockholders quarterly income statements that will be predictive of expected annual results. He proposes to allocate all fixed costs for the year among quarters in proportion to the number of units expected to be sold in each quarter, stating that the annual income can then be predicted through use of the following equation:

$$\text{Annual income} = \text{Quarterly income} \times \frac{100\%}{\text{Percent of unit sales applicable to quarter}}.$$

Navar expects the following activity for the year:

	Units	Average per Unit	Amount (in Thousands)
Sales Revenue:			
First Quarter	500,000	$2.00	$1,000
Second Quarter	100,000	1.50	150
Third Quarter.	200,000	2.00	400
Fourth Quarter	200,000	2.00	400
	1,000,000		$1,950
Costs to Be Incurred:			
Variable:			
Manufacturing		$ .70	$ 700
Selling and Administrative		.25	250
		$ .95	$ 950
Fixed:			
Manufacturing			$ 380
Selling and Administrative			220
			$ 600
Income before Income Taxes.			$ 400

Required: Ignoring income taxes, complete the following:

1. Assuming that Navar's activities do not vary from expectations, will the controller's plan achieve his objective? If not, how can it be modified to do so? Explain and give illustrative computations. Be sure to prepare quarterly income statements under the controller's plan *and*, if you suggest a modification, under the modified plan.

2. How should the effect of variations of actual activity from expected activity be treated in Navar's quarterly income statements?
3. What assumption has the controller made in regard to inventories? Discuss. *(AICPA adapted)*

P12.7 Multiple Choice Questions on Interim Reporting

1. Which of the following is an inherent difficulty in the determination of the results of operations on an interim basis?
   a. Cost of sales reflects only the amount of product expense allocable to revenue recognized as of the interim date.
   b. Depreciation on an interim basis is a partial estimate of the actual annual amount.
   c. Costs expensed in one interim period may benefit other periods.
   d. Revenues from long-term construction contracts accounted for by the percentage-of-completion method are based on annual completion, and thus interim estimates may be incorrect.

2. In considering interim financial reporting, how did the Accounting Principles Board conclude that such reporting should be viewed?
   a. As a "special" type of reporting that need *not* follow generally accepted accounting principles.
   b. As useful only if activity is evenly spread throughout the year so that estimates are unnecessary.
   c. As reporting for a basic accounting period.
   d. As reporting for an integral part of an annual period.

3. For annual reporting purposes, the Storrar Company appropriately accounts for revenues from long-term construction contracts under the percentage-of-completion method. In December 19X5, for budgeting purposes, Storrar estimated that these revenues would be $1,600,000 for 19X6. Favorable business conditions occurred in October 19X6, and, as a result, Storrar recognized revenues of $2,000,000 for the year ended December 31, 19X6. If the percentage-of-completion method had been used for the quarterly income statements on the same basis followed for the year-end income statement, revenues would have been as follows:

Three months ended Mar. 31, 19X6	$ 300,000
Three months ended June 30, 19X6	400,000
Three months ended Sept. 30, 19X6	200,000
Three months ended Dec. 31, 19X6	1,100,000
Total	$2,000,000

What amount of revenues from long-term construction contracts should be reflected in Storrar's quarterly income statement for the 3 months ended December 31, 19X6?
   a. $500,000.
   b. $800,000.
   c. $1,100,000.
   d. $2,000,000.

4. In January 19X7, Hunter, Inc., estimated that its year-end bonus to executives would be $240,000 for 19X7. The actual amount paid for the year-end bonus for 19X6 was $224,000. The estimate for 19X7 is subject to year-end adjustment. What amount of expense, if any, should be reflected in Hunter's quarterly income statement for the 3 months ended March 31, 19X7?
  a. $0.
  b. $56,000.
  c. $60,000.
  d. $240,000.

5. On January 1, 19X6, Perry, Inc., paid property taxes of $40,000 on its plant for the calendar year 19X6. In March 19X6, Perry made its annual major repairs to its machinery, which cost $120,000. These repairs will benefit the entire calendar year's operations. How should these expenses be reflected in Perry's quarterly income statements?

	Three Months Ended (19X6)		
Mar. 31	**June 30**	**Sept. 30**	**Dec. 31**
a. $ 22,000	$46,000	$46,000	$46,000
b. 40,000	40,000	40,000	40,000
c. 70,000	30,000	30,000	30,000
d. 160,000	0	0	0

6. A $420,000 inventory loss from market decline occurred in April 19X6. The Manny Company recorded this loss in April 19X6 after its March 31, 19X6, quarterly report was issued. None of this loss was recovered by the end of the year; how should it be reflected in Manny's quarterly income statements?

	Three Months Ended (19X6)		
Mar. 31	**June 30**	**Sept. 30**	**Dec. 31**
a. $ 0	$ 0	$ 0	$420,000
b. 0	140,000	140,000	140,000
c. 0	420,000	0	0
d. 105,000	105,000	105,000	105,000

7. A company that uses the LIFO method of inventory pricing finds at an interim reporting date that there has been a partial liquidation of the base period inventory level. The decline is considered temporary, and the partial liquidation will be replaced prior to year-end. The amount shown as inventory at the interim reporting date should:
  a. *Not* give effect to the LIFO liquidation, and cost of sales for the interim reporting period should include the expected cost of replacement of the liquidated LIFO base.
  b. Be shown at the actual level, and cost of sales for the interim reporting period should reflect the decrease in the LIFO base period inventory level.
  c. *Not* give effect to the LIFO liquidation, and cost of sales for the interim reporting period should reflect the decrease in the LIFO base period inventory level.

d. Be shown at the actual level, and the decrease in inventory level should *not* be reflected in the cost of sales for the interim reporting period.

8. The Doll Company estimates the cost of its physical inventory at March 31, 19X2, for use in an interim financial statement. The rate of markup on cost is 25 percent. The following account balances are available:

Inventory, Mar. 1, 19X2	$160,000
Purchases during March	86,000
Purchase Returns	4,000
Sales during March	140,000

The estimate of the cost of inventory at March 31 would be:
   a. $137,000.
   b. $130,000.
   c. $112,000.
   d. $102,000.
   e. None of the above.

9. The Q Company prepares monthly income statements. A physical inventory is taken only at year-end; hence, month-end inventories must be estimated. All sales are made on account. The rate of markup on cost is 50 percent. The following information relates to the month of June 19X3:

Accounts Receivable, June 1, 19X3	$10,000
Accounts Receivable, June 30, 19X3	15,000
Collection of Accounts Receivable during June 19X3	25,000
Inventory, June 1, 19X3	18,000
Purchases of Inventory during June 19X3	16,000

The estimated cost of the June 30, 19X3, inventory would be:
   a. $12,000.
   b. $14,000.
   c. $19,000.
   d. $22,000.
      (AICPA adapted)

P12.8 Disclosure and Treatment of Items in Interim Reports The Anderson Manufacturing Company, a California corporation listed on the Pacific Coast Stock Exchange, budgeted activities for 19X5 as follows:

	Amount	• Units
Net Sales	$6,000,000	1,000,000
Cost of Goods Sold	3,600,000	1,000,000
Gross Margin	$2,400,000	
Selling, General, and Administrative Expenses	1,400,000	
Operating Earnings	$1,000,000	
Nonoperating Revenues and Expenses	0	
Earnings before Income Taxes	$1,000,000	
Estimated Income Taxes (Current and Deferred)	550,000	
Net Earnings	$ 450,000	
Earnings per Share of Common Stock	$ 4.50	

Anderson has operated profitably for many years and has experienced a seasonal pattern of sales volume and production similar to the following ones forecast for 19X5. Sales volume is expected to follow a quarterly pattern of 10, 20, 35, and 35 percent, respectively, because of the seasonality of the industry. Also, due to production and storage capacity limitations, it is expected that production will follow a pattern of 20, 25, 30, and 25 percent per quarter, respectively.

At the conclusion of the first quarter of 19X5, the controller of Anderson has prepared and issued the interim report for public release as shown below:

	Amount	Units
Net Sales	$ 600,000	100,000
Cost of Goods Sold	360,000	100,000
Gross Margin.	$ 240,000	
Selling, General, and Administrative Expenses.	275,000	
Operating Loss.	$ (35,000)	
Loss from Warehouse Fire.	(175,000)	
Loss before Income Taxes.	$(210,000)	
Estimated Income Taxes.	0	
Net Loss.	$(210,000)	
Loss per Share of Common Stock	$ (2.10)	

The following additional information is available for the first quarter just completed but was not included in the public information released:

1. The company uses a standard cost system in which standards are set at currently attainable levels on an annual basis. At the end of the first quarter, there was underapplied fixed factory overhead (volume variance) of $50,000 that was treated as an asset at the end of the quarter. Production during the quarter was 200,000 units, of which 100,000 were sold.

2. The selling, general, and administrative expenses were budgeted on a basis of $900,000 fixed expenses for the year plus $0.50 variable expenses per unit of sales.

3. The warehouse fire loss met the conditions of an extraordinary loss. The warehouse had an undepreciated cost of $320,000; $145,000 was recovered from insurance on the warehouse. No other gains or losses are anticipated this year from similar events or transactions, nor has Anderson had any similar losses in preceding years; thus the full loss will be deductible as an ordinary loss for income tax purposes.

4. The effective income tax rate, for federal and state taxes combined, is expected to average 55 percent of earnings before income taxes during 19X5. There are no permanent differences between pretax accounting earnings and taxable income.

5. Earnings per share were computed on the basis of 100,000 shares of capital stock outstanding. Anderson has only one class of stock issued, no long-term debt outstanding, and no stock option plan.

Required:

1. Without referring to the specific situation described above, list and explain the standards of disclosure for interim financial data (published interim financial reports) for publicly traded companies.
2. Identify the weaknesses in form and content of Anderson's interim report without reference to the additional information.
3. For each of the five items of additional information, indicate the preferable treatment for each item for interim reporting purposes, and explain why that treatment is preferable. *(AICPA adapted)*

P12.9 Preparation of Quarterly Income Statements After carefully planning its operations for the coming year, West Corporation prepared the forecast of results for the four quarters in the year as shown below:

	Quarter 1	Quarter 2	Quarter 3	Quarter 4
Sales.	$10,000,000	$8,000,000	$12,000,000	$15,000,000
Interest Received on Investments	—	80,000	—	80,000
Cost of Goods Sold (at Standard)	6,000,000	4,800,000	7,200,000	9,000,000
Fixed Overhead Volume Variance	—	120,000 (U)	—	120,000
Labor Efficiency Variance.	—	100,000 (F)	—	—
Material Price Variance.	100,000 (F)	—	50,000 (U)	—
Other Selling Expenses.	1,000,000	800,000	1,200,000	1,500,000
Annual Advertising Campaign	900,000	—	—	—
Annual Sales Quantity Discounts	—	—	—	500,000
Executive Bonuses.	—	—	—	900,000
Annual Maintenance Program	600,000	—	—	—
Provision for Bad Debts (1% of Sales)	—	—	—	450,000
Investment Tax Credits.	140,000	—	160,000	—
Other General and Administrative Expenses	1,100,000	1,000,000	1,000,000	1,200,000

Additional information:

1. West uses a standard cost system in its manufacturing operations. Its standards represent currently attainable expectations and are reviewed and adjusted, if necessary, shortly after the end of each year. The favorable labor efficiency variance is expected to result from the temporary shutdown of less efficient equipment during the second quarter. Market forecasts of prices of several raw materials used in production are expected to generate the material price variances shown. All standard cost variances are charged or credited to cost of goods sold.
2. The Adco Advertising Agency has been retained to develop radio and television commercials which will be broadcast throughout the year. Adco will be paid in full on March 15.
3. Sales quantity discounts and executive bonuses are both tied to gross sales.
4. The annual maintenance work on the office building is performed during the first quarter of each year.
5. Other general and administrative expenses are incurred uniformly throughout the year except for payment of the annual insurance pre-

mium ($100,000) in the first quarter and recognition of other prepayment amortization of $200,000 for the year in the fourth quarter.

6. Market value of the company's inventory is expected to fall below cost by $160,000 during the second quarter. Management anticipates that $90,000 of this will be recouped by the end of the year.

7. Semiannual payments of interest on bonds held for investment occur on June 30 and December 31.

8. West faces a combined federal, state, and city statutory income tax rate of 60 percent.

9. The company had 1,000,000 shares of common stock outstanding during the year.

10. The flow-through method of accounting is used for investment tax credits.

Required: Assuming that actual results do not deviate from the estimates given above, prepare for West a schedule of quarterly income statements in accordance with *APBO 28*. Show all supporting calculations.

P12.10 Interim Report and Disclosures Carllock Corporation, a publicly traded company, is preparing the interim financial data which it will issue to its stockholders at the end of the first quarter of the 19X7–19X8 fiscal year. Carllock's financial accounting department has compiled the following summarized revenue and expense data for the first quarter of the year:

Sales	$10,000,000
Cost of Goods Sold	6,000,000
Variable Selling Expenses	300,000
Fixed Selling Expenses	500,000

Included in the fixed selling expenses was the single lump-sum payment of $400,000 for television advertisements for the entire year.

Required:

1. Carllock must issue its quarterly financial statements in accordance with generally accepted accounting principles regarding interim financial reporting.

   a. Explain whether Carllock should report its operating results for the quarter as if the quarter were a separate reporting period in and of itself or if the quarter were an integral part of the annual reporting period.

   b. State how the sales, cost of goods sold, and fixed selling expenses would be reflected in Carllock's quarterly report prepared for the first quarter of the 19X7–19X8 fiscal year. Briefly justify your presentation.

2. What financial information, as a minimum, must Carllock disclose to its stockholders in its quarterly reports? *(CMA adapted)*

P12.11 Reporting Transactions in Interim Statements The following statement is an excerpt from paragraphs 9 and 10 of *APBO 28:*

Interim financial information is essential to provide investors and others with timely information as to the progress of the enterprise. The usefulness of such information rests on the relationship that it has to the annual results of operations. Accordingly, the Board has concluded that each interim period should be viewed primarily as an integral part of the annual period.

In general, the results for each interim period should be based on the accounting principles and practices used by an enterprise in the preparation of its latest annual financial statements unless a change in an accounting practice or policy has been adopted in the current year. However, the Board has concluded that certain accounting principles and practices followed for annual reporting purposes may require modification at interm reporting dates so that the reported results for the interim period may better relate to the results of operations for the annual period.

Required: Listed below are six independent cases depicting how accounting facts might be reported on an individual company's interim financial reports. For each case, state whether the method proposed to be used for interim reporting would be acceptable under generally accepted accounting principles applicable to interim financial data. Support each answer with a brief explanation.

1. The Coe Company was reasonably certain that it would have an employee strike in the third quarter. As a result, it shipped heavily during the second quarter but plans to defer recognition of those sales that were in excess of the normal sales volume. The deferred sales will be recognized as sales in the third quarter when the strike is in progress. Management thinks this is more nearly representative of normal second and third quarter operations.

2. The Day Company takes a physical inventory at year-end for annual financial statement purposes. Inventory and cost of sales reported in the interim quarterly statements are based on estimated gross profit rates, because a physical inventory would result in a cessation of operations. Day does have reliable perpetual inventory records.

3. The Ball Company is planning to report one fourth of its pension expense each quarter.

4. The Fragle Company wrote inventory down to reflect lower of cost or market in the first quarter of 19X5. At year-end the market exceeds the original acquisition cost of this inventory. Consequently, management plans to write the inventory back up to its original cost as a year-end adjustment.

5. The Good Company realized a large gain on the sale of investments at the beginning of the second quarter. The company wants to report one third of the gain in each of the remaining quarters.

6. The Jay Company has estimated its annual audit fee. The company plans to prorate this expense equally over all four quarters. *(CMA adapted)*

P12.12 Interim Reports and Accounting Changes The Locke Company is a publicly held manufacturing company whose fiscal year ends March 31. On December 1, 19X1, after several months of discussion and analysis, the management of Locke decided, for financial reporting purposes, to change from accelerated depreciation to straight-line depreciation and to increase the warranty expense accrual. These revisions are to be effective immediately, but they will not affect tax accounting procedures.

The table below presents the accelerated depreciation for the past two quarters and the estimated amount for the third quarter of the current fiscal year as reported for financial statement purposes. The table also presents the recalculated figures for the same periods under the straight-line method. The accumulated depreciation as of April 1, 19X1, amounted to $980,000 under the accelerated depreciation method but would have been only $700,000 if straight-line depreciation had been used.

Fiscal Quarter, Fiscal Year Mar. 31, 19X2	Accelerated Depreciation (Actual Amount Used for Financial Reporting Purposes)	Straight-Line Depreciation (Recalculated Amounts)
First (Apr. 1–June 30, 19X1)	$62,000	$50,000
Second (July 1–Sept. 30, 19X1)	58,000	50,000
Third (Oct. 1–Dec. 31, 19X1), Est.	55,000	50,000

Locke has a one-year warranty on its products. Management has been accruing warranty expense at the rate of 1 percent of net sales. The balance of the accrued warranty account as of April 1, 19X1, was $47,000. The data presented in the following table show the actual warranty accruals and expenditures for the past six quarters and the estimates for the current third quarter. Actual warranty expenditures have exceeded the accrual for the past three quarters and are expected to exceed the accrual for future quarters if a 1 percent accrual rate continues to be used. Consequently, management has decided to increase the accrual rate to 1.25 percent of net sales effective with the third quarter of the current year.

Fiscal Quarter,	Accrued Warranty Expenses at 1%	Actual Warranty Expenditures
Fiscal Year Mar. 31, 19X1		
First (Apr. 1–June 30, 19X0).	$40,000	$32,000
Second (July 1–Sept. 30, 19X0)	42,000	35,000
Third (Oct. 1–Dec. 31, 19X0)	45,000	42,000
Fourth (Jan. 1–Mar. 31, 19X1).	35,000	44,000
Fiscal year Mar. 31, 19X2		
First (Apr. 1–June 30, 19X1).	43,000	47,000
Second (July 1–Sept. 30, 19X1)	46,000	55,000
Third (Oct. 1–Dec. 31, 19X1), Est..	50,000	58,000

The estimated financial results and related earnings per share for the third quarter and for the 9 months ending December 31 for the current fiscal year are shown below. The third quarter and 9-month data presented for the current fiscal year were compiled before the two accounting revisions were implemented. The company has issued only common stock and has no dilutive securities. One million shares of common stock have been outstanding for the past 2 years. Locke is subject to a 40 percent income tax rate.

	Fiscal Year Ending Mar. 31, 19X2	
	Third quarter (Oct. 1–Dec. 31, 19X1)	Nine months (Apr. 1–Dec. 31, 19X1)
Income before Extraordinary Items	$600,000	$1,500,000
Extraordinary Loss, Net of Related Income Tax Effect	400,000	1,000,000
Net Income	$200,000	$ 500,000
Earnings per Share:		
Earnings before Extraordinary Loss	$.60	$1.50
Extraordinary Loss	.40	1.00
Net Earnings	$.20	$ .50

Required:

1. Discuss the disclosure requirements for current and prior year data which Locke would need to make in its interim financial statements as a consequence of the change in depreciation method and increase in warranty expense accrual.

2. Locke will prepare and distribute to its stockholders interim financial statements at the end of the third quarter of the current fiscal year. These statements will present the third quarter and year-to-date data following generally accepted accounting procedures. Present the financial results and related earnings per share data as they would appear in the interim financial statements issued at the end of the third quarter; these should reflect the change in depreciation method and increase in warranty expense accrual. Explain your presentation completely and show supporting calculations. *(CMA adapted)*

Chapter 13   The SEC and Its Role in Financial Reporting

The stock market crash of 1929 led to considerable discussion as to what role the federal government should play in regulating the issuance and trading of securities. Several years of debate led to the passage of the Securities Act of 1933 and the Securities Exchange Act of 1934. The latter act established the Securities and Exchange Commission (SEC). These actions, however, did not end the debate over the federal government's role in regulating the securities markets; that discussion still continues, as evidenced by several well-known congressional hearings in recent years.

Organization and Operation of the SEC

The **Securities Act of 1933** deals primarily with the issuance of new securities. It regulates the public offering of securities, prohibiting (subject to certain exemptions) the offering and sale of securities unless they are registered with the government, and prohibits fraudulent or deceptive practices in the offering or sale of securities.

The **Securities Exchange Act of 1934** deals with trading in securities once they have been issued and are outstanding. This act authorizes the establishment, by the government, of reporting and disclosure requirements for publicly owned corporations, and it prohibits deceptive and manipulative practices in the purchase or sale of securities. In addition, this law established the Securities and Exchange Commission and granted it jurisdiction over the securities markets.

While the 1933 and 1934 Acts are the primary focus of our discussion, there are many other laws which relate to the securities markets. The **Trust Indenture Act of 1940** deals with the issuance of bonds. It requires a formal trust agreement *(indenture)* specifying the rights of the bondholders, and provides for the appointment, by the issuing company, of an independent trustee to represent the bondholders. The **Investment Company Act of 1940** regulates investment companies, such as mutual funds. The **Investment Advisers Act of 1940** provides that those who provide paid advice to the public concerning securities must register with the SEC. The activities of such advisers are also regulated; for example, they may not receive a share of the gains in their clients' portfolios. The **Securities Investor Protection Act of 1970** created the Securities Investor Protection Corp. (SIPC), which insures customer accounts held by brokers. These and other laws add additional dimensions to the basic structure provided by the 1933 and 1934 Acts.

Definition of Security

The Securities Act of 1933 established a broad definition of the meaning of *security*. It described a security as:

> . . . any note, stock, treasury stock, bond, debenture, evidence of indebtedness, certificate of interest or participation in any profit-sharing agreement, collateral-trust certificate, preorganization certificate or subscription, transferable share, investment contract, voting trust certificate, certificate of deposit for a security, fractional undivided interest in oil, gas, or other mineral rights, or, in general, any interest or instrument commonly known as a "security," or any certificate of interest or participation in, temporary or interim certificate for, receipt for, guarantee of, or warrant or right to subscribe or to purchase, any of the foregoing.[1]

The law provided several categories of securities that are exempt from the registration and reporting rules (although other provisions, such as the antifraud rules, generally apply to these securities). Among the exempt securities are:

1. Securities issued or guaranteed by federal, state, or local government.
2. Securities issued or guaranteed by a bank or savings and loan association (these are, however, subject to the provisions of the 1934 act).
3. Commercial paper, that is, short-term notes (original maturity not exceeding 9 months) issued for working capital purposes.
4. Securities issued by nonprofit organizations (these also are subject to the provisions of the 1934 act).

Subsequent legislation and litigation has clarified the status of other financial instruments. The basic question to be addressed in deciding that a financial instrument is a "security" is whether "the person invests his money in a common enterprise and is led to expect profits solely from the efforts of the promoter or a third party."[2] Thus interests in real estate condominiums, interests in oil drilling programs, variable annuities (where the return depends on the performance of a portfolio of securities), and commodity option contracts have all been held to be "securities." On the other hand, bank certificates of deposit, savings and loan "shares," life insurance policies, and notes representing ordinary bank loans are not "securities." The definition of a security is a very broad one, and therefore many financial transactions will fall under the jurisdiction of the securities laws.

---

[1]Securities Act of 1933, Sec. 2(1).
[2]SEC v. W. J. Howey Co., 328 U.S. 293(1946).

Structure of the SEC

The SEC is the agency responsible for the administration and enforcement of the federal securities laws. The SEC consists of 5 commissioners, appointed by the president for 5-year terms. The commission is supported by a staff of about 2,000 employees; the staff position best known to accountants is that of Chief Accountant of the SEC.

The SEC is organized into several divisions. The **Division of Corporation Finance** examines and processes all documents (registration statements, periodic reports, etc.) filed with the SEC. In general, it administers the disclosure requirements of the securities laws. This division is also involved in matters concerning proxy statements, insider trading, and tender offers. The **Division of Enforcement** handles enforcement of the securities laws. It investigates possible violations, and makes recommendations to the Justice Department concerning prosecution. The **Division of Corporate Regulation,** among other activities, is involved in reorganization and bankruptcy proceedings involving public companies. The **Division of Market Regulation** oversees the operations of the securities markets and the trading of securities; it also administers the provisions of the Investment Advisers Act. Finally, the **Division of Investment Management Regulation** has oversight and investigative responsibilities concerning investment companies and dealers.

The **Chief Accountant** is the SEC's expert on accounting and auditing matters, advising on these topics, supervising the preparation of pronouncements, and investigating questionable accounting and auditing practices. The Chief Accountant also serves as the link between the SEC and the accounting profession, expressing the SEC's views via speeches, papers, and appearances before standard-setting groups.

Information on accounting matters comes from the SEC in various ways, both formal and informal. Among these are:

1. Formal rules, such as *Financial Reporting Releases* (FRR) [prior to 1982 these were known as *Accounting Series Releases* (ASR)], which are formal pronouncements analogous to Statements of the FASB, and *Staff Accounting Bulletins* (SAB), which are similar to Interpretations. By law, the SEC has the power to establish accounting and reporting standards for companies whose securities are under its jurisdiction. The FRRs therefore may be viewed as the highest-ranking authoritative source of accounting principles for publicly held companies.
2. Forms for presenting reports, plus instructions for the nature and detail of disclosures, as presented in Regulation S-K, Regulation S-X, and the General Rules.
3. Private rulings to companies concerning the treatment of a particular transaction. Referred to as ''no-action and interpretation letters,'' these rulings indicate that the SEC will not object if a transaction is handled in the proposed manner. Such rulings frequently relate to the accounting treatment of a merger or acquisition.

4. Reports of cases that have been decided, whether by administrative proceeding or by the courts. Included are the **Accounting and Auditing Enforcement Releases** (AAER), which report disciplinary or other enforcement actions against accountants. These matters were previously included in Accounting Series Releases. Thus, the topics previously covered in the ASRs are now covered in two series: accounting pronouncements in the FRR and enforcement matters in the AAER.

5. Informal statements by commissioners or top staff (such as the chief accountant). These statements, often in the form of speeches or written releases, convey informally the views of key individuals on certain matters. This is often a format used to express views on matters being considered by the FASB or the accounting profession.

In the following sections, we discuss some of the accounting and reporting requirements of the SEC, its regulation of corporate activity and governance, the procedures for the registration of new securities, and the role of the SEC in the total process of setting accounting standards.

Periodic Reporting Requirements

The reporting and disclosure requirements of the SEC cover all companies that have securities listed on a national securities exchange, along with all companies that have more than 500 stockholders and more than $3,000,000 in assets. About 3,000 listed companies and several thousand unlisted (over-the-counter) companies are subject to the SEC's reporting and disclosure rules.

Prior to 1982, separate disclosure systems existed under the two major securities acts. The disclosure system under the 1933 act (which regulates new issuances) was oriented toward companies making public offerings of their securities. The disclosure system under the 1934 act, however, emphasized up-to-date disclosure of current information about companies whose securities were already publicly traded. Each system had its own set of requirements and reports. In 1982, a new **Integrated Disclosure System** was introduced. Major efforts were made to standardize the disclosures required by the 1933 and 1934 acts, and to bring financial statement data published in annual reports to shareholders into conformity with those required by the SEC, along with other changes and simplifications. As a result, the reporting and disclosure standards discussed in the subsequent sections generally apply to all SEC reports.

The principal reports to the SEC are the annual report (Form 10-K), quarterly reports (Form 10-Q), and special reports (Form 8-K) that are filed for any month in which certain specified events occur. The contents of these reports are largely governed by two sets of regulations: **Regulation S-X** covers accounting and financial statement requirements for both annual and quarterly reports, and **Regulation S-K** covers all other disclosures.

| Exhibit 13.1 | Structure and Contents of Form 10-K |

Item	Description
Part I	
1	Description of the business
2	Description of properties
3	Legal proceedings involving the company
4	Submission of matters to a vote of stockholders
Part II	
5	Market price of common stock, dividends, and related stockholder matters
6	Selected financial data
7	Management's discussion and analysis of financial condition and results of operations
8	Financial statements and supplementary financial information
9	Disagreements with accountants on accounting and financial disclosure
Part III	
10	Directors and executive officers
11	Executive compensation and transactions with executives
12	Security ownership by certain beneficial owners and by management
13	Certain relationships and related-party transactions
Part IV	
14	Exhibits
Signatures	

The Annual Report

The **annual report** to the SEC—**Form 10-K**—is an extensive document presenting both financial statements and a variety of disclosures and descriptive information. Exhibit 13.1 presents the structure of Form 10-K. Note that financial statements comprise only one of the 14 categories of information; financial disclosures and a variety of nonfinancial information account for the remainder.

In the interest of standardizing reporting and disclosure, the new Integrated Disclosure System requires that the annual report to stockholders must conform to SEC requirements as set forth in Regulation S-X. Previously, the annual report might differ from the 10-K, provided the differences were not substantial and were disclosed in a note to the financial statements. In addition, inclusion of other SEC-required disclosures into the annual report to stockholders is encouraged. Such information may then simply be incorporated into the 10-K by reference to the annual report. **Incorporation by reference** means that the data already appear, in the required form, in the annual report to shareholders. In presenting a particular item in the 10-K (or other report to the SEC), specific reference is made to the location of the information in the annual report. For example, the following disclosure appeared in General Electric's 10-K for the year ended December 31, 1984:

Item 8. Financial Statements and Supplementary Data

Incorporated by reference to report of independent certified public accountants, financial statements, summary of significant accounting policies, notes to financial statements, quarterly dividend and stock market information, and operations by quarter for 1984 and 1983 appearing on pages 26, 28, 30, 37, 38 through 49, and 57 of the GE Annual Report to Share Owners for the fiscal year ended December 31, 1984.

The 10-K must be filed with the SEC within 90 days of the end of the year. It must also be filed with the exchange on which the stock is traded, and, in addition, copies must be made available to company stockholders upon request.

The 10-K must be signed by the company, its principal executive officer, its principal financial officer, its principal accounting officer (usually the controller), and a majority of the board of directors. This requirement illustrates the broad responsibility of officers and directors for proper reporting and disclosure.

The accounting, reporting, and disclosure requirements for preparing the 10-K are set forth in Regulations S-X and S-K. We now consider some of the major features of these regulations.

Regulation S-K

Exhibit 13.1 set forth the structure of Form 10-K. Item 8 (financial statements and supplementary financial information) is governed by Regulation S-X; the other 13 items are governed by Regulation S-K. In this section, we briefly discuss the content of many of these 13 items. This discussion indicates the broad range of information required by the SEC, extending far beyond what is commonly found in the annual financial report to stockholders.

Description of Business. This item presents a narrative description of the business, including its principal products or services, the major markets it serves, and its primary methods of distribution. Any significant organizational developments since the beginning of the year are reported, such as mergers or acquisitions, or bankruptcy proceedings. In addition, financial information about industry segments, foreign and domestic operations, and export sales is presented. Accounting standards governing these disclosures were presented in Chapter 12.

Exhibit 13.2 presents an illustration of this item, drawn from the 10-K of the Parker Pen Company for the year ended February 29, 1984. Note that the industry segment data is incorporated by reference to the company's annual report to stockholders (which is not reproduced here).

Description of Property. This item contains descriptions of the location and general character of the company's principal plants, oil, gas, or other mineral deposits, and other physical properties. Property descriptions may be extremely brief, as illustrated by the disclosure of General Electric in its 10-K for the year ended December 31, 1984 (shown in Exhibit 13.3 on page 642). Exhibit 13.4, on page 643, shows a more detailed description by the Huffy Corporation for the year ended June 29, 1984.

Exhibit 13.2	Description of Business (Parker Pen Company)

Item 1. Business

(a) General Development of Business

The Parker Pen Company was incorporated in 1892 as a manufacturer and marketer of high quality writing instruments.

On March 1, 1976, the Company acquired an 80 percent interest with purchases of additional interest since that date as follows: December 31, 1977, 5 percent; May 31, 1980, 5.52 percent; June 23, 1981, .53 percent; June 1, 1982, 5.2 percent; December 31, 1982, 2.25 percent for a total of 98.5 percent interest as of February 29, 1984, in Manpower, Inc., the principal business of which is to provide temporary help services to business, professional and service organizations, government agencies and others in the United States and abroad. The Company also has less significant operations in the manufacture and distribution of leisure and recreation clothing and packaging materials. During 1982 the Company announced the formation of a joint venture, First Deposit Corporation, to develop and market innovative consumer financial services. Subsequent to February 29, 1984, the Company sold its interest in this joint venture to Capitol Holding Corporation, Louisville, Kentucky.

(b) (d) Financial Information About Industry Segments and Financial Information About Foreign and Domestic Operations and Export Sales

The Company's major industry segments are writing instruments and related products and temporary help services. Information as to Industry Segments and Foreign and Domestic operations can be found on page 26 of the Company's annual report to Stockholders for the year ended February 29, 1984, a copy of which is attached hereto. Except for those portions thereof incorporated by reference in this Form 10K, the annual report to Stockholders is furnished for the information of the Commission but is not deemed filed as part of this report.

(c) Narrative Description of Business

Parker writing instruments include a range of quality fountain pens, roller-ball pens, ball pens, soft tip pens, and mechanical pencils aimed at the appropriate markets. A number of models are offered, utilizing intricately engraved designs, lacquered surfaces and a variety of materials, including all-plastic, plastic and metal, all-metal, silver and gold. In addition, Parker manufactures and supplies ink under the Super Quink trade name, ball pen, roller-ball, cartridge pencil and soft tip pen refills, and fountain pen ink cartridges. These products are marketed under the Parker and Eversharp trade names. Parker products are marketed in virtually every country of the free world. A majority of the Company's total consolidated sales of writing instruments represent sales to foreign markets or sales by Parker's foreign subsidiaries.

Manpower, Inc., a pioneer in the growing service industry has 1,050 offices in 31 countries with more than 600,000 temporary employees. This makes it one of the largest employers in the world. Of these offices, 477 are part of an independent licensee system in which participants pay a percentage of receipts for the right to use the Manpower name and operating system. Temporary help employees range from highly skilled professional and technical specialists to secretarial-clerical generalists and unskilled labor. Approximately 60% of Manpower's sales and license fees are from foreign subsidiaries and foreign licensees.

The writing instrument segment of the Company uses a number of different raw materials in the manufacturer of its tangible products. These raw materials are available from several sources, and it is believed that the Company is not dependent on one source.

The Company has various patents and patent applications. However, the Company does not believe any material part of its business is dependent on any one patent or a group of patents. The service mark "Manpower" has been federally registered under U.S. Service Mark Registration No. 921701 issued October 5, 1971 and will remain in effect for twenty years, subject to renewal as provided by law.

The Company's writing instrument and temporary help services segments are not considered to be highly seasonal.

(Continued on the next page)

Exhibit 13.2 **Continued**

Neither of the Company's segments is dependent on a single customer or a few customers.

Products of the Company's writing instrument segment are sold direct to retailers, distributors, and wholesalers. These products are standard and are generally supplied from inventory. Consequently backlogs are not a major factor.

Writing instrument segment products are sold in highly competitive markets in which numerous domestic and foreign companies compete. Parker is known as a manufacturer of quality writing instruments and the name is recognized worldwide. Manpower, the temporary help segment, is recognized as the world's largest company in this highly competitive field.

The Company spent an estimated $3,517,000 in fiscal 1984, $3,175,000 in fiscal 1983, and $2,803,000 in fiscal 1982 on Writing Instrument Group research and development on new product development, improvement of existing products and improved processes.

The Company does not expect that compliance with Federal, State and local requirements respecting environmental quality will materially affect the earning power or competitive position of the business or cause material changes.

The Company had a total of approximately 5,485 permanent employees at the end of fiscal 1984.

Exhibit 13.3 **Description of Properties (General Electric Company)**

Item 2. Properties

Manufacturing operations are carried on at approximately 217 manufacturing plants located in 33 states in the United States and Puerto Rico and some 116 manufacturing plants located in 24 other countries.

Legal Proceedings. This item describes, in some detail, significant legal proceedings involving the company. This disclosure is usually more detailed than that presented in the annual report to stockholders. Exhibits 13.5 and 13.6 illustrate these disclosures. The McKesson Corporation disclosure for the year ended March 31, 1984, in Exhibit 13.5, deals with environmental and product liability issues. The Cessna Aircraft Company disclosure for the year ended September 30, 1984, shown in Exhibit 13.6, on page 644, deals primarily with antitrust matters.

Stock Prices and Dividends. Data in this item indicate the approximate number of stockholders of the company and the principal markets in which the stock is traded. The high and low stock price for each quarter of the past 2 years is presented, along with the amount and frequency of dividends during the past 2 years. Companies are also encouraged to make a statement of expectation that dividends will or will not be paid in the near future. These disclosures are illustrated in Exhibit 13.7, on page 645, drawn from Bethlehem Steel Corporation's 10-K for the year ended December 31, 1984.

Exhibit 13.4 | **Description of Properties (Huffy Corporation)**

Location	Description	Sq. Ft.	Owned or Expiration Date of Lease		Annual Rental
Miamisburg, Ohio	Executive offices and display facilities	47,000	Owned		—
Celina, Ohio	Bicycles	822,000	n(1)	1994	$406,070
Denver, Colorado	Juvenile products	80,000	n(2)	1988	$202,993
Milwaukee, Wisconsin	Basketball, exercise and physical fitness equipment	175,000	Owned		—
Ponca City, Oklahoma	Unused plant	408,000	n(3)	2010	$935,616

n(1)   Subject to option to renew at reduced rentals for an additional 10-year period and an option to purchase at varying prices. In addition, the Company has leased, with purchase option, a 68-acre tract of land immediately adjacent to its leased plant in Celina, at an annual rental of $6,766; this lease also expires in 1994.

n(2)   Subject to a renewal option for an additional term of 10 years at a rent to be determined, but in no event in excess of 150 percent of current rental. Subject also to an option to purchase during the last four months of the prime term for $2,534,813.

n(3)   Subject to an option to purchase at any time after April 1, 1989, for the unamortized balance due on the industrial revenue bonds issued by the lessor to finance the facility.

The Recreational and Leisure Time Products industry segment utilizes the Celina, Ohio; Milwaukee, Wisconsin; and Miamisburg, Ohio, properties, and previously utilized the Ponca City, Oklahoma, property. All of the Company's facilities are in good condition and are considered suitable for the purposes for which they are used. The Milwaukee and Denver facilities are operated on a full one-shift basis, while additional shift operations are scheduled as needed to meet seasonal requirements. The Celina facility is normally operated on a full two-shift basis, with third-shift operations scheduled as needed to meet seasonal requirements. Manufacturing operations at the Ponca City facility were terminated in July, 1983, and the machinery and equipment has been transferred to the Celina, Ohio, and other facilities. Efforts are underway to sell or lease the Ponca City facility. In connection with the discontinuance by the Company in 1975 of the outdoor power equipment line, American Motors Corporation assumed the lease on the Company's Richmond, Indiana, outdoor power equipment plant and purchased various major items of equipment during fiscal 1976. The Company became a guarantor of the lease obligation along with Walter Kidde & Company, Inc., which assigned the lease to the Company in 1968.

Exhibit 13.5 | **Legal Proceedings (McKesson Corporation)**

Item 3. Legal Proceedings

The company is subject to various claims and other pending and possible legal actions arising out of the conduct of the company's business including legal actions for damages and investigations relating to governmental laws and regulations (including contingent liability under the Multiemployer Pension Plan Amendments Act of 1980, environmental matters, and investigations concerning the existence of possible violations of federal or state liquor laws); is subject to personal injury and product liability claims; and has the usual contractor's obligations

(Continued on the next page)

Exhibit 13.5   Continued

for completion of contracts and the usual seller's obligations incurred in connection with sales of realty assets.

As a result of past operations of its Chemical Group, and the 1981 acquisition of Inland Chemical Corporation, the company may become a party to certain legal proceedings, known to be contemplated by the United States Environmental Protection Agency under the Comprehensive Environmental Response Compensation and Liability Act of 1980 (the "Superfund" law), which proceedings, if any, would seek payment or reimbursement of costs required for cleanup of various abandoned hazardous waste storage and disposal sites. Management does not consider these proceedings in the aggregate to be material.

In March 1983, a class action in the Hawaii state court was filed against a subsidiary of the company, and certain of its former employees, arising primarily out of a recall of milk products distributed on the island of Oahu, ordered by the Hawaii Department of Health in March 1983, due to allegedly excessive levels of the pesticide heptachlor found in samples of the products and which plaintiffs allege were contaminated with excessive levels of heptachlor from 1980 to 1982. Plaintiffs seek (1) reimbursement for all monies paid for the purchase of milk over an unspecified time period; (2) separate funds to register and monitor the health of all babies conceived or born on Oahu since October 2, 1980, to pay for medical expenses for any illnesses attributable to the heptachlor in the products, and to provide for risk assessment study of the probable health effects of heptachlor; (3) actual damages in an unspecified amount; (4) treble damages under the Hawaii statute governing unfair or deceptive trade practices; (5) punitive damages of $1,000 per plaintiff for what plaintiffs estimate to be more than 250,000 persons; and (6) attorney's fees. Certification of the class has been denied by the trial court. The company is a party to other suits that have also been filed on the basis of the same occurrences.

There is considerable uncertainty inherent in any litigation or governmental proceeding and the evaluation of individual matters is necessarily dependent on the historical experience of the company and others in similar circumstances and the stage of the litigation or proceeding. The company, based upon the opinion of its General Counsel, believes that adequate provision has been made for probable losses. In cases where losses (or the imposition of other sanctions, such as liquor license suspensions or revocations) are possible but not probable, it is the company's belief that their ultimate resolution will not have a material adverse effect on the company's consolidated financial position or the results of its consolidated operations.

Exhibit 13.6   Legal Proceedings (Cessna Aircraft Company)

Item 3. Legal Proceedings

The business of the Company, and in particular, its aircraft business, routinely results in claims and lawsuits being asserted against the Company. The Company is presently a defendant in a number of lawsuits involving product liability claims, some of which involve substantial sums. Some of such claims are uninsured and others, if successful, could be subject to deductible provisions of insurance contracts or determined not to be covered by insurance. In one of the product liability suits a verdict has been rendered against the Company in the amount of $4.3 million compensatory damages, plus prejudgment interest, and $24 million punitive damages which the Company is appealing. The compensatory damages are covered by insurance and it is the Company's position that the punitive damages are also covered, but the Company's insurers disagree.

In addition to litigation relating to its products, the Company is a defendant in two suits alleged to have arisen under the federal antitrust laws. One such case does not involve material claims. The other case, White Industries, Inc., vs. The Cessna Aircraft Company et al., was filed in the United States District Court for the Western District of Missouri in 1972 and

Exhibit 13.6   Continued

involves alleged violations of the Robinson-Patman Act and the Sherman Act. In that case, purportedly brought on behalf of a class of all authorized Cessna dealers in the United States for the period from April 14, 1968, through June 5, 1974, including two separate subclasses, the plaintiff is alleging that class members sustained damages in excess of $30,000,000 (before trebling as required by the federal antitrust laws) as the result of paying more for airplanes than the Company's independent wholesale distributors paid. Although the case has been certified as a class action, in August 1983, the Court granted the Company's motion for partial decertification of the litigating class and entered an order limiting the litigating class to only Cessna dealers served by company zones and dismissing the Cessna dealers served by independent distributors. In the Plaintiff's Offer of Proof Concerning Damages, approximately $20 million of the total alleged damages were attributable to claims of such independent distributors' dealers.

Trial of this action before United States District Court Judge Ross T. Roberts commenced on March 6, 1984, and trial was held up to and including May 11, 1984. During the course of the trial, the Court ordered that the trial be bifurcated and that the parties first address the issue of liability as to the individual plaintiffs, White Industries, Inc., and Carthage Airways, Inc.

On May 11, 1984, plaintiffs completed their case respecting the individual plaintiffs and the Company moved the Court for judgment in favor of the Company. The Court recessed the trial for the purpose of considering the Company's motion and to reconsider the Company's motion to decertify the class action, presented prior to trial, in the light of the evidence adduced at trial.

The Company, after consultation with its counsel, also believes that it has various substantial defenses to the claims.

While the outcome of such pending litigation cannot be predicted with certainty, the Company does not believe the ultimate outcome of any such litigation will, individually or in the aggregate, have a material adverse effect on its consolidated financial position.

Exhibit 13.7   Market for Common Stock (Bethlehem Steel Corporation)

Item 5. Market for the Registrant's Common Stock and Related Security Holder Matters

As of January 31, 1985, there were 46,544,364 shares of the Common Stock of Bethlehem outstanding held by 92,171 stockholders of record. The principal market for Bethlehem's Common Stock is the New York Stock Exchange; such Stock is also listed on the Midwest Stock Exchange. Dividends are paid quarterly, and Bethlehem knows of no restrictions on its present or future ability to pay dividends. In accordance with previously announced policies, increases and decreases in the quarterly dividend rate will be determined by the Board of Directors on the basis of attained results and the business outlook. The following table sets forth, for the periods indicated, the high and low sales prices of Bethlehem's Common Stock as reported in the consolidated transaction reporting system, and the dividends paid thereon.

	1984			1983		
	Sales Prices		Dividends	Sales Prices		Dividends
	High	Low	Paid	High	Low	Paid
January–March	$29.50	$22.50	$0.15	$24.125	$19.00	$0.15
April–June	27.625	18.625	0.15	26.125	20.75	0.15
July–September	20.375	16.125	0.15	26.125	20.125	0.15
October–December . . .	19.375	14.25	0.15	28.50	22.125	0.15
			$0.60			$0.60

(Continued on the next page)

Exhibit 13.7   Continued

On January 30, 1985, the Board of Directors of Bethlehem declared a dividend of $.10 per share of Common Stock, payable March 10 to holders of record on February 8. This represents a reduction of $.05 in the quarterly dividend. The reduction was made in view of the significant losses incurred by Bethlehem in the fourth quarter and for 1984 as a whole and because another significant loss is expected for the first quarter of 1985.

Selected Financial Data. Summaries of financial data are presented to highlight trends in the company's financial condition and operating results. These summaries include, for each of the past 5 years, at least the following:

Net sales or operating revenues.

Income or loss from continuing operations.

Income or loss per share from continuing operations.

Total assets.

Long-term obligations and redeemable preferred stock.

Cash dividends declared per common share.

Companies may add additional items that they believe are informative with respect to trends in their financial condition and operating results. Inflation-related disclosures would be an example of such an item.

Management's Discussion and Analysis. A major disclosure is a discussion and analysis by management of the company's financial condition and operating results, with particular emphasis on the company's liquidity and capital resources.

Liquidity is the ability of the company to generate adequate amounts of cash to meet its needs. Any known commitments or events that will significantly affect liquidity, or any major uncertainties that, if realized, will significantly affect liquidity should be identified. If significant liquidity problems exist, there should be discussion of actions (or proposed actions) to remedy the problems.

Capital resources involve both sources of long-term funding and expenditures on long-term assets. Major commitments or plans for capital expenditures, such as plant expansions, acquisition of pollution control equipment, or energy-saving investments, should be described. Trends or anticipated changes in the sources of long-term capital—debt, equity, and off-balance-sheet forms of financing—should also be discussed.

With respect to **operations,** any unusual or infrequent events or transactions that materially affected income should be disclosed. Trends or uncertainties that may significantly affect revenues—whether favorably or unfavorably—should be discussed, along with events that are expected to change the relationship between costs and revenues.

These disclosures are often very extensive and detailed. A relatively brief example, drawn from the 10-K of Denny's, Inc., for the year ended June 29, 1984, is reproduced in Exhibit 13.8. An excerpt from the 10-K of Delta Air Lines,

Exhibit 13.8	Management's Discussion and Analysis (Denny's, Inc.)

Item 7. Management's Discussion and Analysis of Financial Condition and Results of Operations

The following comments address the principal variations in results of operations over the most recent fiscal.years. This information should be read in conjunction with the information appearing on pages 6 through 16 of the Company's Annual Report.

Denny's Restaurants

Revenues increased as a result of opening new restaurants and increasing average unit sales volume. Over the past three fiscal years the Company has opened 217 domestic restaurants with 95 openings in 1984, 68 in 1983 and 54 in 1982. In line with the policy of closing lower volume units which no longer conform to current standards, five units were closed in 1984 and ten were closed in 1983. Of the 217 units opened over the past three years only 40 percent were conventional ground-up construction and the remaining 60 percent were conversions of restaurants acquired from others. Because of the favorable terms on the purchase of competitors' units, capital costs are reduced. In addition, such restaurants have an existing sales base from which we can build. Average sales of Company-operated restaurants increased from $907,000 in 1982 (52 Weeks) to $941,000 in 1983 (52 Weeks) to $1,000,000 in 1984 (53 Weeks). Gains in average units sales were the result of increased food and beverage sales as well as increases in menu prices.

In 1984, operating margins increased to 9.8 percent, up from 9.5 percent in both 1983 and 1982. The gain in 1984 is principally due to lower food costs.

Winchell's

Donut house revenues increased in 1984 as a result of real increases in product sold and price increases. This is the first major real traffic increase in a number of years, primarily because of the new discount program being offered on purchases of a dozen or more donuts. Average sales per donut house increased from $184,000 in 1982 (52 Weeks) to $194,000 in 1983 (52 Weeks) to $217,000 in 1984 (53 Weeks). The number of new domestic donut houses opened has equaled the number of donut houses closed over the past three years so that at the end of each of the past three fiscal years there have been 836 domestic donut houses in operation.

Operating income was up only 2 percent on sales increases of 11 percent. The fluctuation in operating margins from 8.1 percent in 1982 to 8.8 percent in 1983 to 8.1 percent in 1984 is primarily the result of changes in commodity costs.

El Pollo Loco

Results of operations reflect activity for the period since October, 1983, when El Pollo Loco was acquired.

El Pollo Loco provides the Company with an entry into the fast-food chicken segment which is less labor-intensive than other operations and shows good growth potential. At the current fiscal year-end 20 units were in operation of which six were company operated and 14 were franchises. Twenty-five company-operated units are scheduled to open during fiscal 1983 in California, Texas, and Arizona. Approximately ten of these will be conversions from existing Del Taco units.

The loss from operations of $819,000 is primarily the result of increased levels of expenditures to support planned unit expansion. Such expenditures include management training, computer systems development, preparation of operating manuals, and headquarters staffing.

Distribution and Production

Distribution and Production revenues exclude intercompany sales of $310,884,000 in 1984, $278,732,000 in 1983 and $252,379,000 in 1982. Intercompany sales represented 83.0 percent, 83.6 percent, and 83.0 percent of total sales for the three years, respectively. Operating margins and pricing are substantially the same for both intercompany and outside sales.

(Continued on the next page)

Exhibit 13.8 **Continued**

Revenues increased in 1984 over the prior two years because of increased outside sales activity. The Company anticipates additional outside customers in 1985, which will provide a broader revenue base.

Operating margins were 3.8 percent, 4.6 percent, and 4.7 percent in 1984, 1983, and 1982, respectively. The decrease in 1984 margins is a result of higher warehousing and distribution costs.

International

International revenues consist primarily of royalties based on revenues of licensees received under agreement with several foreign companies.

Revenue increases over the past three years result primarily from an increase in the number of restaurants and donut houses operated by the Company's foreign licensees. Operating income increased to $1.8 million from $1.3 million in 1983. Operating income was $1.8 million in 1982.

Foreign licensees opened 35 Denny's and 11 Winchell's in 1984 for a total of 232 restaurants and 29 donut houses. In 1983, there were 197 restaurants and 20 donut houses; at the end of 1982, there were 181 and 14, respectively.

Beginning in 1985, the international operations will be reorganized so that responsibility for foreign affiliations will reside in each domestic division. The International division will continue to be responsible for the development of international markets and for the liaison with management of foreign licensees.

Expenses Not Allocated to Divisions

There have been no significant variations in corporate general and administrative expenses, which were .95 percent of total revenues in 1982, .82 percent in 1983 and 1.0 percent in 1984. Due to improved cost identification systems, general and administrative expenses for 1984 include approximately $1,630,000 which previously would have been allocated to the Divisions.

Company contributions to the employee profit-sharing plan are based on domestic earnings from operations. As defined in the plan, they were 6 percent of income in each period.

All Company interest, including that related to mortgages and capital leases of divisions, is included in interest expense. The increase in interest expense in 1984 is a result of a greater number of capital leases and a full-year effect of interest relating to the Company's $9\frac{1}{2}$ percent convertible subordinated debentures which were issued in the second quarter of 1983. Because of slightly lower cash balances, interest income dropped 7.6 percent in 1984.

The Company's effective income tax rate of 42.0 percent did not change from 1983. In 1982 the rate was 44.7 percent. Investment tax credits, state taxes, and other factors which affect the provision for income tax remained at comparable levels in 1984 relative to 1983.

Financial Condition and Liquidity

The Company's financial condition and liquidity at June 29, 1984, reflect a continuing trend of strength and improvement.

Shareholders' equity was $301 million in 1984, representing 52.3 percent of total capitalization. This compares to $263 million and 48.1 percent in the prior year.

Working capital provided from operations in 1984 exceeded $100 million for the first time in the Company's history, reaching $104 million. In relation to capital expenditures, cash flow covered 96 percent of new additions for the year. In 1982, working capital from operations were $38 million or 84 percent of capital additions. The continued high level of cash flow will benefit the Company in 1985 as increased capital expansion takes place in the Restaurant Division and El Pollo Loco.

Cash and short-term investments were $95 million at the end of 1984 and $102 million in June 1983, representing 57.4 percent and 60.0 percent of current assets, respectively. The ratio of current assets to current liabilities was 1.40 at the end of 1984 compared to 1.66 and 1.42 at the end of 1983 and 1982, respectively.

Inc., for the year ended June 30, 1984, is presented in Exhibit 13.9. This excerpt, dealing with the cost and consumption of jet fuel, illustrates the detailed operating data that are often presented.

Disagreements with Accountants. One area of concern in recent years has been the extent to which firms replace their outside auditors because of disagreements over accounting or financial disclosure matters. A change of accountants would be a special event calling for separate reporting on Form 8-K, which would also indicate whether disagreement on a matter of accounting principles or financial statement disclosures existed between the company and the former auditors. If such an 8-K has been filed within the past 24 months, the annual 10-K must disclose, for the transactions or events under dispute, the difference between the company's reporting method and that proposed by the former auditors.

Directors and Executive Officers. The company's directors, executive officers, and certain other key employees are identified, and their business experience is described. In addition, any family relationships among directors and executive officers is disclosed, along with any involvement of directors or executive officers in certain legal proceedings.

Management Remuneration and Transactions. This item describes various as-

---

Exhibit 13.9	**Excerpt from Management's Discussion and Analysis (Delta Air Lines, Inc.)**

Fuel

Delta obtains most of its jet fuel pursuant to contracts with petroleum refiners, and also purchases jet fuel in the spot market. Although Delta is currently able to obtain adequate supplies of jet fuel and does not anticipate a significant reduction in jet fuel availability, political disruptions in the oil-producing countries and other unpredictable events may result in fuel supply shortages in the future. Such shortages could have a materially adverse effect on Delta's business.

The following table shows Delta's jet fuel costs and consumption for fiscal years 1980–1984.

Fiscal Year	Fuel Consumption in Millions of Gallons	Total Cost in Millions of Dollars	Average Price per Gallon	Percent of Operating Expenses
1980	1,141.9	$ 857.2	75.07 cents	29.9%
1981	1,118.3	1,070.1	95.68	31.9
1982	1,078.4	1,078.0	99.97	29.7
1983	1,086.5	999.2	91.96	26.1
1984	1,106.0	938.2	84.83	23.2

Priced declined during fiscal 1984 from 85.06 cents per gallon in the first quarter to 84.04 cents per gallon in the fourth quarter. Fuel efficiency improved 4 percent over the previous fiscal year, from 44.10 available seat miles per gallon in fiscal 1983 to 46.05 available seat miles per gallon in fiscal 1984.

Exhibit 13.10	Security Ownership (MGM Grand Hotels, Inc.)

Item 12. Security Ownership of Certain Beneficial Owners and Management

Shown below is certain information as of November 1, 1984, with respect to beneficial ownership (as that term is defined in the federal securities laws) of shares of Common Stock by the only person or entity who is known to MGM Grand to be the beneficial owner of more than 5 percent of MGM Grand's Common Stock, by each of its directors and by all directors and officers of MGM Grand as a group.

Beneficial Owner	Amount and Nature of Beneficial Ownership $n(1)$, $n(2)$	Percent of Class $n(3)$
Kirk Kerkorian. . . . . $n(4)$ 15,739,173		69.4%
4045 Spencer Street		
Las Vegas, Nevada		
James D. Aljian $n(5)$	31,013	
Alvin Benedict	143,897	
Fred Benninger.	4,303	
Barrie K. Brunet.	61,272	
Cary Grant	5,000	
Peter M. Kennedy	667	
Frank E. Rosenfelt $n(5)$	11,190	
Bernard J. Rothkopf	78,793	
Walter M. Sharp $n(5)$	1,000	
Robert Van Buren	1,000	
All directors and officers as a group (14 persons)	386,766	

$n(1)$ Subject to applicable community property and similar statutes.

$n(2)$ The number of shares of Common Stock shown as beneficially owned includes 5,882 shares and 158,840 shares, respectively, which persons in the group have the right to acquire within 60 days following November 1, 1984, through the conversion of convertible debentures and through the exercise of employee stock options, and 4,320 shares which have been allocated to the accounts of persons in the group under the 1983 Employee Stock Ownership Plan as well as an earlier employee stock ownership plan terminated in 1980.

$n(3)$ The number of shares of Common Stock beneficially owned by each director represents less than 1 percent of the outstanding shares and by all directors and officers as a group represents less than 2 percent of the outstanding shares.

$n(4)$ Of these shares 14,709,747 are held by Tracinda Corporation ("Tracinda"), which is wholly owned by Mr. Kerkorian. MGM Grand is informed that Tracinda has a line of credit agreement pursuant to which certain loans have been, and in the future may be, made to it. These loans bear interest payable quarterly at the bank's reference rate on the first $100,000,000 and ½ percent above such reference rate thereafter. Said loans are secured, in part, by a pledge of the shares of MGM Grand Common Stock and Preferred Stock owned by Tracinda. Excluded are 2,200,000 shares of Preferred Stock which Tracinda has promised or intends to promise to donate to various charities. The line of credit agreement contains various covenants by Tracinda, including that the pledged collateral at all times have a market value equal to the greater of 200 percent of the amounts borrowed or applicable margin requirements. Any event of default under the agreement which results in a foreclosure upon the pledged securities might result in a change in Mr. Kerkorian's control position with respect to MGM Grand. Tracinda made a Tender Offer for up to 5,000,000 shares of Common Stock and 2,000,000 shares of Preferred Stock of MGM Grand that expired on October 31, 1984. The Offer was not conditioned upon any minimum number of shares being tendered. As a result of the Tender Offer, Tracinda has advised MGM Grand that it has acquired 4,287,734 shares of Common Stock and 859,098 shares of Preferred Stock. Said shares of common stock are reflected in the above table.

$n(5)$ Messrs. Aljian, Rosenfelt and Sharp also beneficially own 20,000, 15,071 and 24,934 shares, respectively, of Series A Redeemable Preferred Stock (nonvoting) of MGM Grand. These persons have sole investment power with respect to such shares. Such ownership, which constitutes all of such shares held by directors and officers, totals less than 1 percent of the outstanding shares of such issue.

pects of the compensation of officers and directors. The total compensation of all officers and directors as a group is disclosed, along with the number of such individuals. In addition, the names and amount of compensation (if over $60,000) of the five highest-paid officers and directors is disclosed. Narrative descriptions of deferred compensation plans, pension and profit-sharing plans, stock option plans, and the like are presented, as well as any proposed changes in the compensation of officers and directors. Finally, management indebtedness to the company and other transactions with management (if over $60,000) are disclosed.

Security Ownership. This item discloses the holdings of major stockholders and management of the company. Exhibit 13.10 illustrates this disclosure. It is taken from the 10-K of MGM Grand Hotels, Inc., for the year ended August 31, 1984.

Regulation S-X

Regulation S-X governs the form and content of financial statements. This regulation is actually a collection of pronouncements, generally initially issued as Financial Reporting Releases (previously Accounting Series Releases). It is, together with FASB Statements, the body of accounting and reporting principles to be followed for SEC reports.

Regulation S-X is organized into several Articles, as outlined in Exhibit 13.11. Of major concern are Articles 4 and 5, which present accounting and reporting rules that are broadly applicable to most companies; Article 10, which deals with interim reports; and Article 12, which deals with the disclosure of detailed information in the form of schedules to be included in the 10-K. Many of the other sections are concerned with accounting and reporting issues appropriate to particular industry types.

In most cases, the SEC accounting rules are the same as Generally Accepted Accounting Principles as issued by the FASB and its predecessors. FRR Section 101 provides that pronouncements of the FASB are automatically accepted by the SEC, unless the SEC issues its own pronouncement on the particular subject. Historically, most accounting standard setting has been done directly by the private sector with SEC oversight rather than by the SEC itself. The SEC has accepted and encouraged this procedure, except in a few cases where the SEC has acted first to spur the private standard-setting body into action on some pressing matter.

General Accounting and Reporting Rules. Article 4 of Regulation S-X deals with selected accounting and reporting matters that are applicable to companies in general, independent of their industry. It provides for the usual form, order, and terminology. Some examples of its treatment of various items are presented in the following paragraphs.

Current assets and current liabilities are defined in terms of the usual one-year criterion. If the normal operating cycle is longer than one year, normal industry practice may be followed with respect to including items of longer duration. If such longer-term items are included, there should be explanation provided,

Exhibit 13.11	Contents of Regulation S-X

Article	Contents
1	Application of Regulation S-X
2	Qualifications and reports of accountants
3	General instructions as to financial statements
3A	Consolidated and combined financial statements
4	Rules of general application
5	Commercial and industrial companies
5A	Companies in the development stage
6	Registered investment companies
6A	Employee stock purchase, savings, and similar plans
7	Insurance companies other than life insurance
8	Committees issuing certificates of deposit
9	Bank holding companies
10	Interim financial statements
11	Pro forma financial statements
12	Form and content of schedules

along with an estimate of the amount not realizable or payable within one year. If such items extend over several years, there should be disclosure of the amounts maturing each year, and the related interest rates.

With respect to the presentation of income tax expense, SEC rules go beyond the tax allocation requirements of GAAP. Timing differences whose effect exceeds 5 percent of the total tax expense are to be separately identified. In addition, a reconciliation is to be provided between the amount actually reported as income tax expense and the amount computed by multiplying the income before tax by the statutory federal tax rate.

Significant transactions with related parties are to be disclosed. The disclosure should cover:

The nature of the relationship.

A description of the transactions.

The dollar volume of the transactions.

Amounts due to or from related parties, and terms of settlement.

Amount of investment in related parties.

These rules encompass the related party disclosures set forth in SAS 6 ("Related Party Transactions").[3] They also require that there be separate information presented on subsidiaries and on transactions between parent and subsidiary. Material related party items (receivables, payables, revenue, expense, gain or loss, or cash flows) must appear on the face of the respective financial statement, not merely in the notes.

---

[3]Auditing Standards Executive Committee, *Statement on Auditing Standards No. 6,* "Related Party Transactions" (New York: AICPA, 1975).

Schedules of Information. The schedule requirements of Regulation S-X provide for considerable detail on a number of items. In general, schedules are required on the following items:

1. Marketable securities and other investments.
2. Amounts receivable from related parties and underwriters, promoters, and employees other than related parties.
3. Condensed financial information of the parent company.
4. Noncurrent debt of and to related parties.
5. Property, plant and equipment.
6. Accumulated depreciation, depletion and amortization of property, plant and equipment.
7. Guarantees of other issuers' securities.
8. Valuation and qualifying accounts.
9. Short-term borrowings.
10. Supplemental income statement information.
11. Real estate and accumulated depreciation.
12. Mortgage loans.
13. Other investments.

Exhibits 13.12 through 13.15 illustrate selected schedules (specifically, Schedules 2, 5, 8, and 9 in the above list). These are drawn from the 10-K of General Foods Corporation for the year ended March 31, 1984. Three years of data are usually presented; we have reproduced only one year (not always the most current year) in the interest of space. Exhibit 13.12 presents receivables from officers and employees, showing details in the change in the balance of this account. Exhibit 13.13 shows details of changes in the property, plant, and equipment accounts. Valuation accounts, such as the allowance for bad debts and other reserves, are illustrated in Exhibit 13.14. Finally, Exhibit 13.15, on page 655, presents details

---

Exhibit 13.12 **Schedule of Amounts Receivable from Related Parties (General Foods Corporation)**

GENERAL FOODS CORPORATION AND SUBSIDIARIES
SCHEDULE II—AMOUNTS RECEIVABLE FROM OFFICERS AND EMPLOYEES
(In Thousands)

FISCAL YEAR ENDED MARCH 31, 1984

	Balance at Beginning of Period	Additions	Amounts Collected	Balance at End of Period
Various Officers and Employees. . . .	$1,828	$808	$461	$2,175 (1)

(1)   At March 31, 1984, real estate mortgage loans were outstanding to three officers and eleven employees. The loans were made in connection with company-requested transfers and are payable upon sale of the residence. The loan to one officer bears interest at 11.625 percent; the remaining loans are noninterest-bearing, but the company will share in any gain realized when the residences are sold.

Exhibit 13.13	Schedule of Property, Plant, and Equipment (General Foods Corporation)

GENERAL FOODS CORPORATION AND SUBSIDIARIES
SCHEDULE V—PROPERTY, PLANT AND EQUIPMENT
(In Thousands)

FISCAL YEAR ENDED APRIL 2, 1983

	Balance at Beginning of Period	Additions at Cost		Deductions		Balance at End of Period
		Capital Expenditures	Businesses Acquired (2)	Disposals/ Retirements	Other (1)	
Land	$ 74,259	$ 1,398	$ 6,080	$ 9,743	$ 3,011	$ 68,983
Buildings.	666,946	124,547	35,036	37,525	12,386	776,618
Machinery and Equipment	1,294,389	204,241	71,712	76,049	25,545	1,468,748
Construction Work in Progress.	138,252	(64,126)	2,712	2,214	5,334	69,290
Totals	$2,173,846	$266,060	$115,540	$125,531	$46,276	$2,383,639

(1) Principally foreign currency translation adjustments.
(2) Principally Entenmann's, Inc.

Exhibit 13.14	Schedule of Valuation Accounts (General Foods Corporation)

GENERAL FOODS CORPORATION AND SUBSIDIARIES
SCHEDULE VIII—VALUATION AND QUALIFYING ACCOUNTS
(In Thousands)

FISCAL YEAR ENDED APRIL 3, 1982

	Balance at Beginning of Period	Additions		Deductions		Balance at End of Period
		Charged to Costs and Expenses	Other	Businesses Sold	Other	
Allowance for Doubtful Accounts	$17,616	$4,094	$2,098 (3)	$ 2,699	$3,174 (1) 1,127 (2)	$16,808
Reserve for Discontinued Fast-Food Operations	$13,476	—	—	12,547	$ 929 (3)	—

(1) Receivables written off against related reserves.
(2) Principally foreign currency translation adjustments.
(3) Charges written off against related reserves.

on short-term borrowings, including the weighted average interest rate for both the ending balance and for the entire year.

The Quarterly Report

Firms that are required to file an annual report with the SEC are also required to file a **quarterly report,** known as **Form 10-Q.** This report must be filed within

Exhibit 13.15 **Schedule of Short-Term Borrowings (General Foods Corporation)**

GENERAL FOODS CORPORATION AND SUBSIDIARIES
SCHEDULE IX—SHORT-TERM BORROWINGS
(In Thousands)

FISCAL YEAR ENDED MARCH 31, 1984

	Balance at End of Period	Weighted Average Interest Rate	Maximum Amount Outstanding during the Period	Average Amount Outstanding during the Period	Weighted Average Interest Rate during the Period
Commercial Paper	$ 39,860	10.0%	$ 39,860	$ 18,772	8.8%
Notes Payable to Banks, Primarily by International Subsidiaries.	144,500	9.9	251,639	206,100	10.9

45 days after the end of each of the first three quarters of the company's fiscal year; a fourth quarter report need not be filed.

APBO 28 and *IFAS 18* are the primary sources of accounting principles for interim reports; these were discussed in detail in Chapter 12. The SEC further requires that the quarterly operating data be presented in the annual report and, while these data need not be audited, they must at least be reviewed by the independent accountants.

Quarterly reports are typically considerably shorter than the annual report. Form 10-Q contains the financial statements (balance sheet, income statement, and statement of changes in financial position) for the current quarter and for the corresponding quarter of the previous year. The statements themselves may have fewer categories as compared to the annual statements. On the balance sheet, for example, a major caption (e.g., Receivables) is needed only if the item exceeds 10 percent of total assets or if the item has changed by more than 25 percent from the latest year-end balance. If these tests are not met, the caption may be combined with others as long as the general format of the statements is maintained (e.g., current items may not be combined with noncurrent items).

Selected other disclosures are also included in the 10-Q. A major disclosure is management's discussion and analysis. Other disclosures include any legal proceedings during the quarter, changes in the company's securities, defaults on senior securities, and matters reported via Form 8-K during the quarter. The extensive financial disclosures found in the annual report are not required on a quarterly basis. Exhibit 13.16 reproduces the entire Form 10-Q for the H. J. Heinz Company for the quarter ended October 31, 1984, except that the details of the financial statements have been omitted in the interests of space. By comparison to the quarterly report to stockholders discussed in Chapter 12, note that the 10-Q is much more detailed.

Exhibit 13.16	Complete Form 10-Q (H. J. Heinz Company)

SECURITIES AND EXCHANGE COMMISSION
WASHINGTON, D.C. 20549

FORM 10-Q
Quarterly Report Under Section 13 or 15(d) of the
Securities Exchange Act of 1934

FOR QUARTER ENDED: October 31, 1984

COMMISSION FILE NUMBER: 1–3385

H. J. HEINZ COMPANY

PENNSYLVANIA
(State or other jurisdiction of
incorporation or organization)

25–0542520
(I.R.S. Employer Identification Number)

600 Grant Street, Pittsburgh, Pennsylvania
(Address of principal executive offices)

15219
(Zip Code)

REGISTRANT'S TELEPHONE NUMBER, INCLUDING AREA CODE: (412) 237–5757

Indicate by check mark whether the registrant (1) has filed all reports required to be filed by Section 13 or 15(d) of the Securities Exchange Act of 1934 during the preceding 12 months (or for such shorter period that the registrant was required to file such reports), and (2) has been subject to such filing requirements for the past 90 days. YES X NO

The number of shares of the Registrant's Common Stock, par value $1.00 per share, outstanding as of December 7, 1984, was 68,063,331 shares.

PART 1—FINANCIAL INFORMATION

Item 1. Financial Statements

H. J. HEINZ COMPANY AND CONSOLIDATED SUBSIDIARIES
CONSOLIDATED STATEMENT OF INCOME

Six Months Ended	Six Months Ended
October 31, 1984	October 26, 1983
FY 1985	FY 1984

[Details Omitted]

H. J. HEINZ COMPANY AND CONSOLIDATED SUBSIDIARIES
CONSOLIDATED STATEMENT OF INCOME

Three Months Ended	Three Months Ended
October 31, 1984	October 26, 1983
FY 1985	FY 1984

[Details Omitted]

Exhibit 13.16 **Continued**

H. J. HEINZ COMPANY AND CONSOLIDATED SUBSIDIARIES
CONSOLIDATED STATEMENT OF INCOME

October 31, 1984   May 2, 1984
FY 1985   FY 1984

[Details Omitted]

H. J. HEINZ COMPANY AND CONSOLIDATED SUBSIDIARIES
CONSOLIDATED STATEMENT OF CHANGES IN FINANCIAL POSITION

Six Months Ended   Six Months Ended
October 31, 1984   October 26, 1983
FY 1985   FY 1984

[Details Omitted]

H. J. HEINZ COMPANY AND CONSOLIDATED SUBSIDIARIES
NOTES TO CONSOLIDATED FINANCIAL STATEMENTS

(1) The Management's Discussion and Analysis of Financial Condition and Results of Operations which follows these notes contains additional information on the results of operations and the financial position of the Registrant. Those comments should be read in conjunction with these notes. The Registrant's annual report on Form 10-K for the fiscal year ended May 2, 1984, includes additional information about the Registrant, its operations, and its financial position and should be read in conjunction with this quarterly report on Form 10-Q.

(2) The results for the interim periods are not necessarily indicative of the results to be expected for the full fiscal year due to the seasonal nature of the Registrant's business.

(3) In the opinion of management, all adjustments (none of which were other than normal recurring accruals) necessary to a fair statement of the results of these interim periods have been included.

(4) The composition of inventories at the balance sheet dates was as follows:

	October 31, 1984	May 2, 1984
	(Thousands of Dollars)	
Finished Goods and Work-in-Process	$557,412	$494,095
Ingredients and Packaging Material	235,384	206,136
	$792,796	$700,231

(5) As of October 31, 1984, there were 4,150,834 shares of common stock reserved for conversion of convertible preferred stock outstanding, for outstanding options, and for the granting of options under the company's stock option plans.

(6) The provision for income taxes consists of provisions for federal, state, U.S. possessions, and foreign income taxes. The Registrant operates in an international environment with significant operations in various locations outside the United States. Accordingly, the consolidated income tax rate is a composite rate reflecting the earnings in the various locations and the applicable tax rates.

Item 2. Management's Discussion and Analysis of Financial Condition and Results of Operations

RESULTS OF OPERATIONS
SIX MONTHS ENDED OCTOBER 31, 1984, AND OCTOBER 26, 1983

Sales were $2,061.7 million for the current six-month period, an increase of $114.2 million, or 5.9 percent, over the comparable period of last year. Improved sales volume

(Continued on the next page)

Exhibit 13.16 **Continued**

throughout the company contributed to the increase. Lower average exchange rates used in translation of foreign-currency-denominated sales adversely affected reported sales for the period by approximately $83 million.

The gross profit margin increased to 38.6 percent in the current six-month period from 37.9 percent in the same period of the prior year. The improvement is due to volume gains in some of the Company's higher profit margin products and lower raw fish costs at Star-Kist.

Operating expenses were $540.2 million in the current six-month period, an increase of $29.5 million, or 5.8 percent. Heavy marketing spending in support of the company's major brands accounted for a major portion of this increase. In addition, other operating expenses increased as a result of the higher sales volume.

Operating income increased $28.9 million or 12.7 percent to $255.9 million in the current period. The improvement in operating income resulted from unit volume gains and good operating performances throughout the company.

Interest income increased $3.0 million over the prior year's first six months to $16.0 million in the current period. The increase results from higher average short-term investments combined with higher average interest rates. Interest expense increased $5.4 million to $26.3 million in the current period because of both higher interest rates and higher average borrowings.

The provision for income taxes in the current period was $100.8 million, an increase of $10.3 million over the same period of the prior year. The increase resulted from higher earnings in the current year, as the effective tax rate for the current period was 41.6 percent, compared with 42.2 percent in the prior period.

Results of Operations
Three Months Ended October 31, 1984, and October 26, 1983

Sales for the second quarter of the current year were $1,040.3 million, an increase of $33.2 million, or 3.3 percent, over the second quarter of the prior year. Higher unit volume on a worldwide basis, partially offset by lower average exchange rates used in translation of foreign-currency-denominated sales, was primarily responsible for this improvement.

Gross profit was $397.7 million in the second quarter of the current year, an increase of $19.4 million, or 5.1 percent, over last year's second quarter, reflecting the higher sales volume.

Operating income increased $10.8 million, or 9.4 percent. Operating expenses increased $8.6 million, or 3.3 percent, reflecting higher marketing spending and higher volume-related operating expenses.

Interest income in the second quarter of the current year was $8.4 million as compared with $6.8 million a year ago, reflecting both the increase in average short-term investments and higher average interest rates. Interest expense was $14.1 million in the current year's second quarter compared with $10.6 million last year. This increase was due to both higher interest rates and higher average borrowings in the current period.

The provision for taxes in the second quarter of the current period was $48.9 million and represented an effective tax rate of 41.2 percent. This compares with $44.9 million and 41.8 percent for the comparable period of last year.

Liquidity and Financial Position

Cash and short-term investments were $334.8 million at the end of the second quarter of the current year. Cash and short-term investments have increased $22.9 million from a year ago and $24.1 million during the first six months of the current fiscal year. Current debt was $257.0 million at the end of the second quarter, an increase of $88.5 million from a year ago. This increase includes the effect of $70.0 million in repurchases of the company's common stock.

Exhibit 13.16   Continued

Funds generated from operations were $205.2 million in the six months ended October 31, 1984, compared wtih $185.6 million for the comparable period of the prior year. These funds generally are sufficient to cover operating requirements.

Short-term borrowings were higher at the end of the second quarter than at the end of the previous fiscal year because of increased receivables related to sales volume and increased inventories related to seasonal crop purchases. The seasonal period generally runs through January, at which time borrowing requirements begin to ease.

PART 2—OTHER INFORMATION

Item 1. Legal Proceedings

Nothing to report under this item.

Item 2. Changes in Securities

Nothing to report under this item.

Item 3. Defaults upon Senior Securities

Nothing to report under this item.

Item 4. Submission of Matters to a Vote of Security Holders

Nothing to report under this item.

Item 5. Other Information

Nothing to report under this item.

Item 6. Exhibits and Reports on Form 8-K

(a) Exhibits required to be furnished by Item 601 of Regulation S-K are listed below and are filed as a part hereof. Documents not designated as being incorporated herein by reference are filed herewith. The paragraph number corresponds to the exhibit number designated in Item 601 of Regulation S-K.

11. Computation of net income per share

(b) Reports on Form 8-K
No reports on Form 8-K were filed during the quarter ended October 31, 1984.

Signature:

Pursuant to the requirements of the Securities Exchange Act of 1934, the Registrant has duly caused this report to be signed on its behalf by the undersigned thereunto duly authorized.

H. J. Heinz Company
(Registrant)

By K. M. von der Heyden
   Senior Vice President—Finance and Chief Financial Officer
   (Principal Financial and Accounting Officer)
   Date: December 12, 1984
By Alvin J. Catz
   Corporate Controller
   Date: December 12, 1984

(Continued on the next page)

Exhibit 13.16 **Continued**

Exhibits:
Exhibit 11

H. J. HEINZ COMPANY AND CONSOLIDATED SUBSIDIARIES
COMPUTATION OF NET INCOME PER SHARE

	Six Months Ended	
	October 31, 1984 FY 1985	October 26, 1983 FY 1984
Net Income.	$141,710	$123,911
Preferred Dividends.	153	214
Net Income Applicable to Common Stock.	$141,557	$123,697
Average Common Shares Outstanding and Common Stock Equivalents	68,768	70,488
Net Income per Share	$2.06	$1.75

Fully diluted net income per share has not been shown since it differs by less than 3 percent from primary net income per share.

All amounts in thousands except per-share amounts.

Special Reports

Regular reports by firms are issued annually (Form 10-K) and quarterly (Form 10-Q). In addition, a **special report (Form 8-K)** is required when certain specified events occur. These events include a major acquisition or disposition, initiation or settlement of major nonroutine legal matters, default by the company on a debt obligation, or a change of auditors. Form 8-K must be filed within 15 days of any of these occurrences.

Corporate Activity and Governance

In addition to corporate accounting, there has been considerable interest in recent years in corporate accountability. The way the corporation conducts its affairs and the way it relates to its stockholders are important aspects of **corporate accountability.** The SEC has played an important role, both directly and indirectly, in setting guidelines for corporate activity and governance.

One of its indirect influences was on the Foreign Corrupt Practices Act of 1978. Besides proscribing certain activities in the conduct of international transactions, this act also contains requirements that management maintain accurate books and records (so that any illegal transactions are not hidden) and maintain an adequate system of internal control (to reduce the occurrence of such transactions). These two provisions had been originally proposed by the SEC in 1977, as amendments to Regulation S-X.

A number of other matters of corporate activity and governance have been addressed in recent years. In the following sections, we briefly discuss audit committees, insider trading, proxy statements, and tender offers.

Audit Committees

The board of directors plays an important role in the governance of the corporation. The board, representing the stockholders, oversees the activities of management. To strengthen the independence of the board, the SEC requires that the identity of each director (or nominee for director) be disclosed, along with any relationship the individual has with the company (e.g., whether the director is also a member of management or is the corporation's banker or attorney). Although there are no requirements, there is encouragement that there be a number of "outside" (independent) directors. In addition, companies are encouraged to have committees on the board of directors, such as a compensation committee and an audit committee. The **audit committee** is responsible for seeing that management fulfills its responsibilities with respect to accounting, reporting, and control. It monitors the financial accounting and reporting system as well as the audit functions, both internal and external. The exact relationships vary among companies. The audit committee may be responsible for hiring the independent auditor, and the auditor may report to it. The internal audit department may be responsible to the audit committee or it may be responsible to management. At a minimum, the internal audit department should be able to have direct access to the audit committee for special problems, and the committee should be able to use the internal audit department for special investigations. The audit committee also must interact with top management on financial accounting, reporting, and control issues. Although the SEC does not require audit committees, the New York Stock Exchange does. All domestic companies listed on the New York Stock Exchange must have an audit committee composed solely of "outside directors" (i.e., directors who are independent of management).

Other committees of the board may also exist. For example, a **compensation committee** would be responsible for making recommendations regarding salaries and benefits for top management. Exhibit 13.17 presents a description of the duties of the audit committee and the compensation committee of Sears, Roebuck and Co.

Insider Trading

Insider trading is purchase or sale of the company's stock by those individuals who have access to information that is not yet available either to those with whom they are dealing or to the market in general. An "insider" is a company officer, director, major stockholder, or anyone else who receives information directly from a corporate source. A major objective of the securities laws has been to promote full disclosure of information to all participants in the market. Trading by insiders having access to special knowledge is at variance with this objective. Although it is impossible to completely prevent use of inside knowledge, there are rules that help to constrain it. One rule requires that officers, directors, and stockholders

Exhibit 13.17	Description of Audit and Compensation Committees (Sears, Roebuck and Co.)

The Audit Committee meets periodically with the Company's internal auditors and its independent public accountants to review their reports concerning (i) their examination of the financial statements and of the internal accounting control systems of the Company and its subsidiaries, (ii) their recommendations for strengthening internal controls and improving operating procedures, and (iii) compliance by Company personnel with Company policies relating to various governmental laws and regulations dealing with ethics, conflicts of interest and disbursements of corporate funds. The Committee also makes recommendations to the Board of Directors regarding the independent public accountants to be appointed as the Company's auditors.

The Compensation Committee makes recommendations to the Board of Directors with respect to the compensation and benefits to be paid to officers and performs other duties prescribed by the Board with respect to employee stock option plans and benefit programs.

---

who own more than 10 percent of a class of securities, whether directly or indirectly, must report any of their transactions in these securities to the SEC. This report is a public record, and hence serves to disclose any insider transaction that does occur. A second rule permits the company, or a stockholder acting on behalf of the company, to sue to recover any profit earned by an insider from in-and-out trading (purchase-sale or sale-purchase) within a 6-month period.

The insider trading rules are a part of a broader set of rules known as the **antifraud provisions.** These provide, in both the 1933 and 1934 acts, regulations concerning fraud, deceit, and manipulative practices with respect to the issuance or trading of securities. The corporation cannot issue false or misleading statements about the company or its stock. Underwriters of a stock issue cannot artificially stimulate demand or hold back stock in order to profit from a price rise. Various kinds of corporate mismanagement are also prohibited, such as issuing corporate stock for less than adequate compensation. These provisions have also been used to attack mergers or acquisitions when they are not in the interest of minority shareholders.

Insider trading is a very complex and unsettled subject, one that is currently the subject of many legal proceedings.

Proxy Statements

Proxy statements are communications to shareholders of matters for stockholder action, such as the election of directors, the appointment of an auditor, a change in the corporate charter or bylaws, the issuance of new securities, or the approval of a merger. The proxy statement discloses these matters to the stockholder, and advises the stockholder of the procedure for voting. In many cases, voting occurs at the annual meeting of stockholders. Since many stockholders are unable to attend this meeting, their voting right (''proxy'') is often solicited by management. Typically, the stockholder may mark the proxy as to how he or she wishes to vote on the major items. An illustration of a proposal for stockholder action,

Exhibit 13.18	Proposal in Proxy Statement (Polaroid Corporation)

PROPOSAL TO RATIFY APPOINTMENT OF INDEPENDENT AUDITORS

The Board of Directors recommends a vote FOR the following resolution:

"RESOLVED, that the appointment by the Board of Directors of the Company of Peat, Marwick, Mitchell & Co., independent public accountants, to audit the books and accounts of the Company and its subsidiaries for the year ending December 31, 1984, be and hereby is approved, ratified and confirmed."

The affirmative vote of the holders of a majority of the Company's Common Stock represented and voting at the Annual Meeting will be necessary for adoption of the foregoing Resolution.

During the year ended December 31, 1983, Peat, Marwick, Mitchell & Co. performed audit services and certain nonaudit services for the company and its subsidiaries. The audit services included the examination of the consolidated financial statements of the Company and its subsidiaries, the review of certain related reports filed with the Securities and Exchange Commission and limited reviews of the Company's unaudited quarterly financial reports.

Total fees paid by the Company for professional services rendered by Peat, Marwick, Mitchell & Co. in 1983 amounted to about $1.6 million.

Representatives of Peat, Marwick, Mitchell & Co. will be present at the Annual Meeting, will be provided an opportunity to make a statement if they should so desire and will be available to respond to appropriate questions. The Board of Directors recommends a vote FOR the Proposal.

drawn from the March 19. 1984, proxy statement of Polaroid Corporation, is presented in Exhibit 13.18.

The proxy statement also provides a mechanism for action on stockholder proposals that are not supported by management. Notice of such a proposal must be given to the company at least 90 days prior to the mailing of the proxy statement. The proposal must be personally presented at the annual meeting by a stockholder. Virtually any proposal can be offered, except one that has already been rejected by the stockholders within the past 5 years. Exhibit 13.19 presents such a proposal, drawn from the June 18, 1984, proxy statement of McKesson Corporation.

In addition, the proxy statement contains a variety of detailed information on nonvoting matters, such as committees of the board, legal matters, management compensation plans (including the amount of compensation paid to top management), and related-party transactions.

Registration of New Securities

The Securities Act of 1933 is primarily concerned with the registration of new securities. The act provides that (subject to a few exemptions) no security may be offered or sold to the public unless it is registered with the SEC. Achieving registration does not mean that the SEC passes judgment on the merits of the security; rather, it means only that certain disclosure requirements have been satisfied. The

Exhibit 13.19	**Stockholder Proposal in Proxy Statement (McKesson Corporation)**

STOCKHOLDER PROPOSAL

Mr. Lewis D. Gilbert, of 1165 Park Avenue, New York, N.Y., 10028, who is the record owner of 10 shares of Common Stock and who states that he represents an additional family interest of 130 shares of Common Stock, has notified the Corporation that he will cause the following resolution to be introduced from the floor at the Annual Meeting:

"RESOLVED that the stockholders of McKesson Corporation, assembled in annual meeting in person and by proxy, hereby request the board of directors to take the steps necessary to provide that each director own at least 100 shares of the Corporation's stock.

Reasons

"The last proxy statement disclosed that Dr. Ezra Solomon owned no stock in the company."

"Directors ought to be willing to own at least 100 shares in the company or they should not run for office."

"The Securities and Exchange Commission recently changed the rules to require $1000 ownership of stock for proponents of a resolution. It is logical, therefore, for directors to own at least 100 shares in the company."

"If you agree, please mark your proxy for this resolution; otherwise it is automatically cast against it, unless you have marked to abstain."

The affirmative vote of a majority of the votes cast at the annual meeting will, if a quorum is present, be required to adopt this resolution.

The Board of Directors recommends a vote AGAINST this resolution for the following reasons:

The Corporation always seeks the most qualified individuals to serve upon its Board of Directors. Over the years, McKesson directors have been selected on the basis of demonstrated achievements in their chosen fields, experience in dealing with a wide variety of complex issues, and for their general business or professional knowledge. Ownership of a certain number of shares of stock has no bearing on those qualities and should not, in our opinion, be a consideration in the selection of directors. We believe that a decision to make a financial investment in the Corporation is one that should be left to the judgment of each director, based on personal circumstances.

In considering this proposal, we ask you to note that even without a specific requirement, each McKesson director has exercised his or her individual judgment and currently owns at least 100 shares of McKesson Common Stock.

Proxies solicited by the Board of Directors will, therefore, be voted AGAINST this resolution unless a vote for or abstention with respect to the resolution is specifically indicated.

---

act also sets forth the registration procedure and establishes liabilities for misstatements or omissions.

A prospective issuer must file a **registration statement,** consisting of two parts: (1) a **prospectus,** a copy of which must be furnished to each purchaser of the security, and (2) other information and exhibits, which must be publicly available (though these need not be supplied to each investor). A registration statement "becomes effective" 20 days after it is filed. In effect, the SEC (specifically, the

Division of Corporation Finance) has 20 days to review the statement to see if it meets disclosure requirements; various formal and informal means exist for dealing with incomplete or inaccurate registration statements. Once the registration statement becomes effective, the issuer may sell the securities to the public.

Form S-1 is the basic form for the registration of new issues. Under the Integrated Disclosure System, firms that already file 10-K's may file a simpler Form S-2 or S-3 when issuing new securities. The logic here is that, since information about such companies is already available to the market, less additional information is needed than would be needed for the company going public for the first time.

Financial data presented in a registration statement include a balance sheet dated within 90 days of filing, income statements and statements of changes in financial position for the past 3 years, summaries of operations for the past 5 years, and various other schedules and disclosures. Such data must be accompanied by an auditor's report, at least through the end of the last fiscal year. The period from the last audited statement to the date of the registration statement is generally covered by an accountant's review report.

There are two major exemptions to the registration requirements. One exemption is for small offerings; there have been various rules as to the maximum dollar size and number of investors that are allowed under this provision. The second exemption is for "private placements," that is, issuance of securities to a single investor, usually an institutional investor (e.g., an insurance company or pension fund).

The flow of the typical issuance is:

$$\text{Issuer} \rightarrow \text{Underwriter} \rightarrow \text{Dealer} \rightarrow \text{Public.}$$

An underwriter agrees to handle a security issue under one of two types of arrangement. (1) A "firm commitment" underwriting means that the underwriter buys the entire issue at a fixed price, and it is responsible for selling the issue to dealers, who will in turn sell it to the public. The underwriter bears the risk that the issue will not find market acceptance at the asking price. (2) A "best efforts" underwriting means that the underwriter sells as many shares as possible, receiving a commission based on sales. The issuing company bears the risk of nonacceptance in the market.

The SEC and Accounting Standards

While the SEC has the statutory authority to set accounting standards for companies under its jurisdiction, it has historically left the bulk of this task to private-sector standard setting bodies—the FASB and its predecessors. Many of the accounting-related ASRs issued over the years dealt with disclosure requirements for public companies rather than accounting measurement issues. Over the last 15 years, however, the SEC has played a much more active role in standard-setting. Sometimes this has taken the form of issuing a pronouncement on a topic where the FASB has failed to act. In the mid-1970s, there was much discussion about the need for disclosure of the impact of inflation on financial statements. The FASB debated this matter for some time, and finally seemed to be moving toward a pronouncement requiring supplemental disclosure of price-level-adjusted data. At this point, the SEC intervened and issued ASR 190 in 1976, requiring disclosure of replacement cost data. By this action, the SEC clearly indicated its opposition to the FASB's proposal. The FASB proposal was withdrawn, and finally in 1979 SFAS 33 was issued, calling for the disclosure of *both* price-level-adjusted and replacement cost data. Following the issuance of SFAS 33, the SEC rescinded ASR 190.

SEC action may take other forms. In the early 1970s, the issue of whether to capitalize interest during construction was an important accounting issue in certain industries. In 1974, the SEC issued ASR 163, placing a moratorium on the adoption of this accounting practice until such time as the FASB took a position. Finally, in 1979, SFAS 34 was issued, whereupon ASR 163 was rescinded.

In recent years, the SEC, primarily through the Chief Accountant, has become a much stronger force in accounting standard setting. In some cases, the actual or threatened issuance of an SEC pronouncement has been used; in other cases, the position of the Commission has been conveyed through public speeches, papers, and presentations at standard-setting hearings. Clearly, the SEC is, and will remain, a very active participant in the standard-setting process.

Summary of Key Concepts

The Securities Act of 1933 regulates the issuance of new securities. The Securities Exchange Act of 1934 regulates the trading of securities and also established the **Securities and Exchange Commission.** The SEC is responsible for the administration and enforcement of the federal securities laws.

The SEC has authority to establish accounting and reporting principles for publicly held companies. Although it relies heavily on the private sector (FASB) for standard setting, it does issue its own pronouncements—**Financial Reporting Releases (FRR)** and **Staff Accounting Bulletins (SAB).**

Companies under SEC jurisdiction file annual reports **(Form 10-K)** and quarterly reports **(Form 10-Q).** They also file special reports **(Form 8-K)** when certain events occur. The contents of these reports are largely governed by **Regulation S-X,** which covers accounting and financial statement requirements, and **Regulation S-K,** which covers all other disclosures.

Besides its role in accounting and reporting, the SEC has also played an important role in corporate governance. It provides proxy statement requirements, encourages audit committees, and regulates insider trading.

Questions

Q13.1 Distinguish the major purpose of the Securities Act of 1933 from the major purpose of the Securities Exchange Act of 1934.

Q13.2 What companies must file reports with the SEC?

Q13.3 How does Form 10-K relate to the annual report to stockholders?

Q13.4 Distinguish between Regulation S-K and Regulation S-X.

Q13.5 What are the broad topics covered by "management's discussion and analysis"?

Q13.6 What has been the impact of the Integrated Disclosure System on the filing of reports with the SEC?

Q13.7 What is a "proxy statement"?

Q13.8 What is the function of an underwriter?

Exercises

E13.1 Each of the following multiple choice questions deals with the federal securities laws and the organization, structure, and authority of the SEC.

1. Assuming that all other criteria regarding the issuing organization and its "security" are met, which one of the following is *not* a "security" under the jurisdiction of the SEC?
   a. A trust certificate.
   b. A municipal bond.
   c. An oil drilling venture participation unit.
   d. A limited partnership share.
   e. A subordinated debenture.

2. Which one of the following is the act that gives the SEC the ultimate power to suspend trading of a security, delist a security, and prevent brokers and dealers from working in the securities market?
   a. Securities Investor Protection Act of 1970.
   b. Securities Act of 1933.
   c. Securities Exchange Act of 1934.
   d. Investment Company Act of 1940.
   e. Investment Advisers Act of 1940.

3. The Securities and Exchange Commission is organized into several divisions and principal offices. Which of the following is the organizational unit that reviews registration statements, annual reports, and proxy statements that are filed with the Commission?
   a. Office of the Chief Accountant.
   b. Division of Corporation Finance.
   c. Division of Enforcement.
   d. Division of Market Regulation.
   e. Office of the Comptroller.

4. The Securities and Exchange Commission (SEC) was established in 1934 to help regulate the United States securities market. Which of the following statements is true concerning the SEC?

a. The SEC prohibits the sale of speculative securities.

b. The SEC regulates only securities offered for public sale.

c. Registration with the SEC guarantees the accuracy of the registrant's prospectus.

d. The SEC's initial influence and authority has diminished in recent years as the stock exchanges have become more organized and better able to police themselves.

e. The SEC's powers are broad with respect to enforcement of its reporting requirements as established in the 1933 and 1934 acts but narrow with respect to new reporting requirements because these require confirmation by the Congress.

(CMA adapted)

E13.2 Each of the following multiple choice questions deals with the federal securities laws and the organization, structure, and authority of the SEC.

1. Which of the following are *not* requirements imposed by the Securities Exchange Act of 1934 and its amendments?

   a. Proxy solicitation requirements.

   b. Prospectus requirements.

   c. Insider trading requirements.

   d. Tender offer requirements.

   e. Accounting, recordkeeping, and internal control requirements.

2. The Securities Exchange Act of 1934 specifies the types of companies that must report periodically to the SEC. Which one of the following types of companies is *not* required to report to the SEC under this act?

   a. Banks and carriers subject to the Interstate Commerce Act.

   b. Companies whose securities are listed on the National Securities Exchanges.

   c. Companies whose securities are traded over the counter, if those companies have total assets in excess of $3 million and 500 or more stockholders.

   d. Companies whose securities are traded over the counter that voluntarily elect to comply with the reporting requirements even though they have total assets less than $3 million and less than 500 stockholders.

   e. Companies with over 300 stockholders of a class of securities that are registered under the Securities Act of 1933.

3. Which of the following is *not* a purpose of the Securities Exchange Act of 1934?

   a. To establish federal regulation over securities exchanges and markets.

   b. To prevent unfair practices on securities exchanges and markets.

   c. To discourage and prevent the use of credit in financing excessive speculation in securities.

   d. To approve the securities of corporations that are to be traded publicly.

   e. To control unfair use of information by corporate insiders.

4. The SEC prescribes certain qualifications for accountants before it will accept their certification of financial reports. Which one of the following qualifications had been prescribed by the SEC?
   a. The CPA must be from a regional or national firm of CPAs.
   b. The CPA must be independent of the management of the filing company.
   c. The CPA must be in practice a minimum of 5 years.
   d. The CPA must have audited the filing company for each of the preceding 2 years.
   e. The CPA must have legal counsel.
5. Which of the following is a category *not* registered by the SEC?
   a. Securities brokers who deal in over-the counter markets.
   b. Securities brokers who deal only in interstate markets.
   c. Public accounting firms.
   d. Securities exchanges.
   e. Securities of publicly traded companies.
   (CMA adapted)

E13.3 Each of the following multiple choice questions deals with the reporting requirements of the SEC.

1. Which of the following is the one item of discussion that is considered optional by the SEC in "Management's Discussion and Analysis of Financial Condition and Results of Operations" included in Form 10-K and the annual shareholders' report?
   a. Projections or other forward-looking information.
   b. Favorable and unfavorable trends.
   c. The effects of inflation and changing prices.
   d. Causes of material changes in financial statements as a whole.
   e. Capital resources and liquidity.
2. Nonfinancial statement disclosures are specified in which of the following?
   a. Regulation S-K.
   b. Financial Reporting Releases.
   c. Staff Accounting Bulletins.
   d. Accounting and Auditing Enforcement Releases.
   e. Regulation S-X.
3. Which one of the following items is *not* required by the SEC in either the Securities Act of 1933 or the Securities Exchange Act of 1934?
   a. Identification of directors and executive officers with the principal occupation and employer of each.
   b. Line-of-business or product-line report for the last 5 fiscal years.
   c. Identification of the principal market in which the securities of the firm are traded.
   d. Range of market prices and dividends for each quarter of the 2 most recent fiscal years.
   e. Comfort letter to the underwriter and legal counsel from the company's independent accountant.

4. The underlying concept of the Security and Exchange Commission's (SEC) integrated disclosure program recognizes which of the following?

   a. The need for more detailed regulatory requirements to maintain separate generally accepted accounting principles and SEC disclosures.

   b. That no basic information can be described as common to the annual report and the 10-K.

   c. The efficient capital markets concept, i.e., that widely followed companies produce information for the public in various forms resulting in less need for a specific disclosure format.

   d. Recent actions to provide oversight of the SEC by the senior technical committees of professional organizations.

   e. The elimination of the need for an unqualified auditor's opinion on financial statements filed with the SEC.

5. SEC regulations provide for a procedure known as *incorporation by reference*. Which of the following best illustrates the concept of *incorporation by reference?*

   a. A partnership is incorporated by reference to the U.S. Tax Code.

   b. The incorporation of a proprietorship or partnership.

   c. Inclusion of information on officers' remuneration in Form 10-K by reference to the same information in the proxy statement to shareholders.

   d. Footnote reference to market data per share since incorporation.

   e. Footnote disclosure that financial statements are incorporated into the annual report by reference from Form 10-K.

6. The SEC requires Form 8-K to be filed with the Commission within 15 days after the end of the month in which a significant event transpired. However, financial statements accompany Form 8-K only under certain conditions. Which of the following events requires financial statements to accompany Form 8-K?

   a. A material default on a senior security.

   b. A write-down, write-off, or abandonment of assets, where such assets represent more than 15 percent of total assets.

   c. An acquisition in which the acquired company represents more than 15 percent of total assets or revenues of the registering company.

   d. An increase or decrease of more than 5 percent in any class of outstanding security.

   e. A change in the registrant's certifying accountants.

   (CMA adapted)

E13.4 Each of the following multiple choice questions deals with the reporting requirements of the SEC.

1. A significant event affecting a company registered under the Securities and Exchange Act of 1934 should be reported on which of the following?

a. Form 10-K.
b. Form 10-Q.
c. Form S-1.
d. Form 8-K.
e. Form 11-K.

2. The primary intent of the Integrated Disclosure Rules issued by the Securities and Exchange Commission (SEC) is which of the following?

a. To reduce the influence of SEC regulations in public financial reporting.

b. To replace generally accepted accounting principles with Regulation S-X.

c. To replace Regulation S-X with generally accepted accounting principles.

d. To minimize the differences between published financial reports and financial reports filed on Form 10-K.

e. To integrate the materiality criteria of Regulation S-X with generally accepted accounting principles.

3. The Management Discussion and Analysis section of Form 10-K has been revised by the SEC's Integrated Disclosure System. The revised Management and Discussion section does *not* require a description of which of the following?

a. Factors affecting financial condition as well as the results of operations.

b. Factors affecting international markets and currency exchange.

c. Factors that are likely to increase or decrease liquidity materially.

d. Material commitments for capital expenditures, including the purpose of and source of financing for such commitments.

e. The impact of inflation and changing prices on net sales and revenues and on income from continuing operations.

4. Which one of the following is a required disclosure in the annual reports of companies registered with the Securities and Exchange Commission?

a. Audited balance sheets for the last 4 years.

b. Audited summary of earnings for the last 10 years.

c. Identification of registrar and transfer agent.

d. Identification of significant research projects.

e. Range of market prices of the common stock of the registrant for each quarter of the last 2 years.

5. The Securities and Exchange Commission has substantially increased the disclosure requirements on Form 10-Q quarterly reports to the point where all but one of the following items must be disclosed. Select the item which need *not* be filed with the quarterly 10-Q.

a. Signature of either the chief financial officer or chief accounting officer.

b. Management analysis of reasons for material changes in the amount of revenue and expense items from one quarter to the next.

c. In case of a change in accounting principle, a letter indicating that the public accountant believes the new principle is preferable for measuring business operations.

d. Income statements for the most recent quarter, the equivalent quarter from the preceding year, and year-to-date data for both years.

e. A statement by the public accountant that he has reviewed the financial data in Form 10-Q and that all necessary adjustments are reflected in the statements.

(CMA adapted)

E13.5 Each of the following mulitple choice questions deals with the reporting requirements of the SEC.

1. Which of the following describes Regulation S-X?
   a. Specifies the information that can be incorporated by reference from the annual report into the registration statement filed with the SEC.
   b. Specifies the regulations and reporting requirements of proxy solicitations.
   c. Provides the basis for generally accepted accounting principles.
   d. Specifies the general form and content requirements of financial statements filed with the SEC.
   e. Provides explanations and clarifications of changes in accounting or auditing procedures used in reports filed with the SEC.

2. The SEC integrated disclosure of financial information sets forth criteria for conditions for "Management Discussion and Analysis of Financial Conditions and Results of Operations." Which of the following is one of these criteria?
   a. Forward-looking information is encouraged but not required to be disclosed.
   b. A discussion of financial conditions for the most recent 7 fiscal years is to be included.
   c. Information on the effects of inflation is to be provided only when the registrant is already subject to the reporting requirements of *SFAS 33*, "Financial Reporting and Changing Prices."
   d. An analysis of income from foreign operations is to be included even if such operations are not material to the results of the firm.
   e. Identification of all equity security investments in defense contracts and oil and gas subsidiaries are to be included whether or not such investments are material to the overall financial statements and operations.

3. The board of directors of the Mally Company has 11 seats, all of which are currently filled with outside directors. The company's top management consists of the following administrative offices:

President (chief executive officer)

Secretary

Vice-President—Marketing

Vice-President—Engineering

Vice-President—Finance (chief financial officer)

Controller (chief accounting officer)

What is the minimum number of signatures needed to file Form 10-K under the Integrated Disclosure Rules of the SEC?

a. Two.

b. Six.

c. Eight.

d. Nine.

e. Fourteen.

4. Within 15 days after the occurrence of any event which is of material importance to the stockholders, a company must file a Form 8-K Information Report with the Securities and Exchange Commission to disclose the event. Which of the following is an example of the type of event required to be disclosed?

   a. Salary increases to the officers.

   b. A contract to continue to employ the same certified public accounting firm as in the prior year.

   c. A change in projected earnings per share from $12.00 to $12.11 per share.

   d. The purchase of bank certificates of deposit.

   e. The acquisition of a large subsidiary other than in the ordinary course of business.

5. Which one of the following items is not required to be included in a company's periodic 8-K report filed with the SEC when significant events occur?

   a. Acquisition or disposition of a significant amount of assets.

   b. Instigation or termination of material legal proceedings other than routine litigation incidental to the business.

   c. Change in certifying public accountant.

   d. Election of new vice-president of finance to replace the retiring incumbent.

   e. Default in the payment of principal, interest, or sinking fund installment.

   (CMA adapted)

E13.6 Each of the following multiple choice questions deals with matters of corporate governance.

1. Formation and meaningful utilization of an audit committee of the board of directors is required of publicly traded companies that are subject to the rules of which of the following?

   a. Securities and Exchange Commission.

   b. Financial Accounting Standards Board.

      c. New York Stock Exchange.

      d. National Association of Securities Dealers.

      e. SEC Practice Section of the American Institute of Certified Public Accountants' Division of Firms.

  2. The Securities and Exchange Commission's antifraud rules prohibit trading on the basis of inside information of a business corporation's stock by which of the following?

      a. Officers.

      b. Officers and directors.

      c. All officers, directors, and stockholders.

      d. Officers, directors, and beneficial holders of 10 percent of the corporation's stock.

      e. Anyone who bases his or her trading activities on inside information.

  (CMA adapted)

E13.7 Each of the following multiple choice questions deals with the role of the SEC in establishing accounting and reporting standards.

  1. The role of the Securities and Exchange Commission regarding financial accounting for public companies is that the SEC does which of the following?

      a. Promulgates generally accepted accounting principles.

      b. Adopts pronouncements of the Financial Accounting Standards Board in every case.

      c. Regularly adopts requirements that conflict with the pronouncements of the Financial Accounting Standards Board.

      d. Makes regulations and rules pertaining to filings with the SEC but not to annual or quarterly reports to shareholders.

      e. Makes regulations and rules pertaining more to disclosure outside the financial statements than to the setting of accounting measurement principles.

  2. Financial Reporting Releases (FRR), called Accounting Series Releases (ASR) prior to 1982, issued by the SEC do which of the following?

      a. Provide the basis for generally accepted accounting principles.

      b. Specify the regulations and reporting requirements of proxy solicitations.

      c. Provide explanations, interpretations, and procedures used by the SEC in administering the federal securities laws.

      d. Specify the general form and content requirements of financial statements filed with the SEC.

      e. Provide explanations and clarifications of changes in accounting or auditing procedures used in reports filed with the SEC.

  3. Staff Accounting Bulletins issued by the SEC do which of the following?

a. Specify the information that can be incorporated by reference from the annual report into the registration statement filed with the SEC.

b. Specify the regulations and reporting requirements of proxy solicitations.

c. Provide explanations, interpretations, and procedures used by the SEC in administering the federal securities laws.

d. Specify the general form and content requirements of financial statements filed with the SEC.

e. Provide explanations and clarifications of changes in accounting or auditing procedures used in reports filed with the SEC.

4. Financial Reporting Releases (FRRs) and Staff Accounting Bulletins (SABs) are two pronouncements issued by the Securities and Exchange Commission (SEC). How do FRRs and SABs differ?

a. FRRs are part of the 1934 Securities Exchange Act while SABs are not part of that act.

b. SABs represent official rules of the SEC while FRRs do not.

c. SABs pertain to the 1933 Securities Act while FRRs pertain to the 1934 Securities Exchange Act.

d. SABs represent amendments to Regulation S-X while FRRs do not represent such amendments.

e. FRRs represent requirements applicable to the form and content of financial statements filed with the SEC while SABs represent accounting interpretations followed by the SEC.

5. Two interesting and important topics concerning the Securities and Exchange Commission are the role the commission plays in the development of accounting principles and the impact the SEC has had and will continue to have on the accounting profession and business in general. Which of the following statements concerning the SEC's authority relative to accounting practice is *false?*

a. The SEC has the statutory authority to regulate and to prescribe the form and content of financial statements and other reports it receives.

b. Regulation S-X of the SEC is the principal source relating to the form and content of financial statements to be included in registration statements and financial reports filed with the SEC.

c. The SEC has little, if any, authority over disclosures in corporate annual reports mailed to shareholders with proxy solicitations. Here, the type of information disclosed and the format to be used are left to the discretion of management.

d. If the SEC disagrees with some presentation in the registrant's financial statements but the principles used by the registrant have substantial authoritative support, the SEC often will accept footnotes to the statements in lieu of correcting the statements to the SEC view, provided the SEC has not previously expressed its opinion on the matter in published material.

e. The SEC has reserved the right to rule against a registrant even if the registrant follows principles having substantial authoritative support, as well as to determine which accounting principles have substantial authoritative support.

(CMA adaped)

E13.8 Each of the following multiple choice questions deals with the registration of new security issues with the SEC.

1. In the registration and sale of new securities issues, the SEC:
   a. Endorses the investment merit of a security by allowing its registration to ''go effective.''
   b. Provides a rating of the investment quality of the security.
   c. May not allow the registration to ''go effective'' if it judges the security's investment risk to be too great.
   d. Allows all registrations to ''go effective'' if the issuing company's external accountant is satisfied that disclosures and representations are not misleading.
   e. Does not make any guarantees regarding the material accuracy of the registration statement.

2. In cases of false or misleading disclosure in a registration statement that the SEC has allowed to become effective in conjunction with the public sale of securities, investors have the potential for legal recourse (e.g., damage suits) against all of the following *except:*
   a. The Securities and Exchange Commission.
   b. The issuing entity.
   c. The underwriter (managing broker) of the sale.
   d. The issuing entity's legal counsel.
   e. The issuing entity's external accountant.

3. Which of the following is *not* required for the registration statements filed under the Securities Act of 1933?
   a. Nature and history of the issuer's business.
   b. Description of the securities being registered.
   c. Estimate of the net proceeds and the uses to which such proceeds will be put.
   d. Financial forecasts for the next 2 fiscal years.
   e. Salaries and security holdings of officers and directors.

4. The 1933 Securities Act provides for a 20-day waiting period between the filing and the effective date of the registration. During this waiting period the registrant is prohibited from engaging in which of the following activities?
   a. Preparing any amendments to the registration statement.
   b. Announcing the prospective issue of the securities being registered.
   c. Accepting offers to purchase the securities being registered from potential investors.
   d. Placing an advertisement indicating by whom orders for the securities being registered will be accepted.

e. Issuing a prospectus in preliminary form.

5. Before turning over the proceeds of a securities offering to a registrant, the underwriters frequently require a "comfort letter" from the public accountant. The purpose of the "comfort letter" is which of the following?

   a. To remove the public distrust of a red herring by converting the letter into a prospectus.

   b. To find out if the public accountant found any adverse financial change between date of audit and the effective date of the securities offering.

   c. To gain comfort from the public accountant's audit of the stub period financial statements contained in the registration statement.

   d. To meet Securities and Exchange Commission regulations requiring the public accountant to give his opinion as an expert on the financial statements of the registrant.

   e. To conform to New York Stock Exchange (NYSE) member requirements that a comfort letter from a public accountant be obtained prior to public sale of securities.

   (CMA adapted)

Problems

P13.1 Nature and Operations of the SEC The U.S. Securities and Exchange Commission (SEC) was created in 1934 and consists of 5 commissioners and a staff of approximately 2,000. The SEC professional staff is organized into five divisions and several principal offices. The primary objectives of the SEC are to support fair securities markets and to foster enlightened shareholder participation in major corporate decisions. The SEC has a significant presence in financial markets and corporation-shareholder relations and has the authority to exert significant influence on entities whose actions lie within the scope of its authority. The SEC chairman has identified enforcement cases and full disclosure filings as major activities of the SEC.

Required:

1. The SEC must have some "license" to exercise power. Explain where the SEC receives its authority.

2. Discuss in general terms the major ways in which the SEC (a) supports fair securities markets, and (b) fosters enlightened shareholder participation in major corporate decisions.

3. The major responsibilities of the SEC's Division of Corporation Finance include full disclosure filings. Describe the means by which the SEC attempts to assure the material accuracy and completeness of registrants' financial disclosure filings.

   (CMA adapted)

P13.2 Annual Reports to Stockholders and Form 10-K The SEC has encouraged managements of public companies to disclose more information in the shareholders' annual report. As a consequence, a significant amount of the information required in the SEC's Form 10-K now appears in published annual reports. At the same time, the SEC has attempted to make the annual financial reporting process simpler and more efficient, through its new integrated disclosure system.

Required:

1. Identify the major classes of information that must be included in both the annual report to shareholders and Form 10-K filed with the SEC.
2. The Integrated Disclosure System is intended to simplify the annual reporting process with the SEC by expanding the ability to incorporate by reference.
   a. Define what is meant by *incorporating by reference* and identify the documents that are involved when incorporating by reference.
   b. Explain how the Integrated Disclosure System should reduce managements' efforts in filing annual reports with the SEC.
   c. Explain the SEC's principal reasons for making the changes in the annual reporting process.
   d. Identify and explain potential problems that the integrated disclosure system could have on the annual reporting process from the aspect of users of financial information.
   (CMA adapted)

P13.3 Annual Reports to Stockholders and Form 10-K The Jerford Company is a well-known manufacturing company with several wholly owned subsidiaries. The company's stock is traded on the New York Stock Exchange, and the company files all appropriate reports with the Securities and Exchange Commission, Jerford's financial statements are audited by a public accounting firm.

Jerford's Annual Report to Stockholders for the year ended December 31, 1974, contained the following phrase in boldface type: **The Company's 10-K is available upon written request.**

Required:

1. What is Form 10-K, who requires that the form be completed, and why is the phrase "The Company's 10-K is available upon written request" shown in the annual report?
2. What information not normally included in the company's annual report could be ascertained from the 10-K?
3. Indicate three items of financial information that are often included in annual reports that are not required for the 10-K. *(CMA adapted)*

P13.4 Quarterly Reports to the SEC In order to aid in integrating quarterly reports to shareholders with Form 10-Q, the Securities and Exchange Commission issued *Accounting Series Release (ASR) 286* in February 1981. The ASR modifies and expands the financial information content of the previous Form 10-Q disclosures. Specific guidelines are set forth in the ASR as to what information must be included on Form 10-Q.

Required:

1. Corporations are required by the SEC to file a Form 10-Q.
   a. What is Form 10-Q, and how often is it filed with the SEC?
   b. Explain why the SEC requires corporations to file Form 10-Q.
2. Discuss the disclosure requirements now pertaining to Form 10-Q with specific regard to the following:
   a. Condensed balance sheet.
   b. Condensed income statement.
   c. Condensed statements of changes in financial position.
   d. Management's discussion and analysis of the interim period(s).
   e. Footnote disclosures.
   (CMA adapted)

P13.5 Audit Committees An early event leading to the establishment of audit committees as regular subcommittees of boards of directors occurred in 1940 as part of the consent decree relative to the McKesson-Robbins scandal. An audit committee composed of outside directors was required as part of the consent decree.

Another major development affecting audit committees occurred in June 1978 when the New York Stock Exchange required all domestic listed members to establish and maintain an audit committee composed solely of directors independent of management. By June 1979 the Securities and Exchange Commission had issued an interpretive release, *ASR 264,* which dealt with the scope of services by independent accountants. Although the ASR is now rescinded because the SEC believes the ASR is no longer necessary, the ASR had advised audit committees, boards of directors, and managements about factors that should be considered in determining whether to engage their independent accountants to perform nonaudit services.

Despite the increasing interest in audit committees and the official actions taken as described above, no specific role, duties, or liabilities have been established for them by the SEC, the NYSE, or any of the accounting organizations. Nevertheless, a commonly accepted set of duties and expectations has developed for the conduct and performance of audit committees.

Required:

1. Explain the role the audit committee generally assumes with respect to the annual audit conducted by the company's external auditors.
2. Identify duties other than those associated with the annual audit that might be assigned to the audit committee by the board of directors.

3. Discuss the relationship that should exist between the audit committee and a company's internal audit staff.
4. Explain why board members appointed to serve on the audit committee should be outside (independent of management) board members. *(CMA adapted)*

P13.6 Audit Committees The establishment and use of audit committees by corporations is not a recent phenomenon. The Securities and Exchange Commission first recommended their creation in 1940 in response to the McKesson & Robbins, Inc., investigation. Although there was some support for the concept, the recommendation did not result in the actual formation of many audit committees by corporations. However, support for audit committees was renewed in the 1970s, especially as a result of the concerns of the SEC and the New York Stock Exchange. In 1977 the SEC approved a rule originally proposed by the NYSE which required all domestic companies listing their common stock on the NYSE to establish independent audit committees by July 1, 1978.

Corporations are establishing audit committees. While commonly accepted guidelines have not been formalized, the duties and responsibilities are emerging through an evolutionary process.

Required:

1. Identify the basic responsibilities a corporation's audit committee are most likely to assume.
2. Identify and discuss the probable benefits that can result from establishing audit committees by corporations. *(CMA adapted)*

P13.7 Proxy Statements The Securities and Exchange Commission has the authority to regulate proxy solicitation. This authority is derived from the Securities and Exchange Act of 1934 and is closely tied to the disclosure objective of this act. Regulations established by the SEC require that a proxy statement be mailed by a corporation's management to each shareholder shortly before the annual shareholders meeting.

Required:

1. Explain the purpose of proxy statements.
2. Identify four types of events or actions for which proxy statements normally are solicited.
3. Identify the conditions that must be met in order to have a dissident shareholder proposal included in a proxy statement. *(CMA adapted)*

P13.8 Registration of New Securities Ensign Corporation is a manufacturing firm with ten domestic plants. Increased demand for the company's products and a near full capacity production have caused management to decide to build a new plant. The plant expansion is to be financed by a public issue of $10,000,000 of long-term bonds. Before the issue can be sold to the public, a registration statement will have to be filed with the Securities and

Exchange Commission using a Form S-1. Ensign Corporation's financial statements have been certified by the corporation's independent accountants for many years.

Required:

1. Several parties are involved in the preparation, filing, and approval of the registration statement. In this procedure, briefly indicate the responsibility of (1) Ensign Corporation's management, (2) Ensign's independent accountants, and (3) the Securities and Exchange Commission.

2. Indicate the general types of financial information and statistical data that would be disclosed in the schedules and reports included in the registration statement and the time period(s) to which this information and data must refer. *(CMA adapted)*

P13.9 **Role of the SEC in Standard Setting** The development of accounting theory and practice has been influenced directly and indirectly by many organizations and institutions. Two of the most important institutions have been the Financial Accounting Standards Board (FASB) and the Securities and Exchange Commission (SEC).

The FASB is a relatively new, independent body that was established in 1972 as a result of the recommendation of the Study Group on Establishment of Accounting Principles (commonly referred to as the Wheat Committee). The FASB is composed of seven persons who represent the field of public accounting and fields other than public accounting.

The SEC is a governmental regulatory agency that was created in 1934 to administer the Securities Act of 1933 and the Securities and Exchange Act of 1934. These acts and the creation of the SEC resulted from the widespread collapse of business and the securities markets in the early 1930s.

Required:

1. What official role does the SEC have in the development of financial accounting theory and practice?

2. What is the interrelationship between the FASB and SEC with respect to the development and establishment of financial accounting theory and practices? *(CMA adapted)*

Part FOUR Accounting for International Operations

The continuing growth in world trade and the increasing significance of foreign operations to U.S. corporations lead us to devote two chapters to the area of international operations. Our primary objective in these chapters is to present the United States' generally accepted accounting principles as they relate to foreign currency transactions and the translation of foreign currency financial statements. A related objective of considerable importance is to present these matters not in isolation but within the context of business practices in import/export transactions and recent changes in the international monetary system. In addition, we offer an overview of accounting principles around the world.

We begin Chapter 14 with a discussion of foreign exchange rates and the economic environment which produces them. The spot and forward markets are explained, and their use is related to the widespread business practice of hedging foreign currency transactions. A frame of reference is therefore provided within which the accounting rules germane to forward contracts can be considered. The chapter then proceeds to explain the accounting for import and export transactions, foreign borrowing and lending, and related operations in the forward market for foreign currencies.

Chapter 15 discusses the extent of U.S. firms' business operations abroad and deals specifically with the accounting standards governing the translation of foreign currency financial statements. Financial statements of branches and subsidiaries located in foreign lands must be translated or converted into dollar equivalents before they can be included in U.S. firms' combined or consolidated financial statements. Several translation methods are compared, but current generally accepted accounting principles are emphasized. Exchange gains and losses which are produced by the translation process are carefully explained and related to similar items arising out of the foreign currency transactions discussed in Chapter 14.

To show the diversity of accounting principles and practices around the world, we compare different societal orientations toward accounting and illustrate the wide variety of accounting practices in selected areas. Finally, we conclude Chapter 15 with an introduction to the international environment of accounting.

Chapter 14   Accounting for Foreign Currency Transactions

This is the first of two chapters that deal with the subject of accounting for international operations, concentrating on the need of U.S. companies to report their international operations in U.S. dollars. These chapters address the following two aspects of accounting for international operations.

First, in Chapter 14, the appropriate accounting for the *foreign currency transactions* of U.S. firms is studied. These transactions include *import and export dealings* with foreign suppliers and customers, *borrowing and lending* in foreign currencies, and various *hedging* (risk-neutralizing) transactions. Regarding such transactions, a recent annual report of R. J. Reynolds Industries noted:

> The Company has operations in many countries, with foreign currency gains and losses in about 40 currencies. . . . The Company also has significant exposure to foreign exchange transactions, such as sales, purchases, and debt service. . . . The Company closely monitors its economic exposure to foreign currency exchange rate fluctuations and various actions are taken to minimize the net earnings effects. . . . Additionally, the Company engages in hedging activities to minimize the potential losses on cash flows denominated in foreign currencies.[1]

The problem common to all such transactions—*their dollar equivalent changes as the value of the foreign currency changes*—is studied in detail in this chapter.

Second, Chapter 15 focuses on the complex reporting issues present when a U.S. company has business operations abroad. All foreign entities which are branches, divisions, or subsidiaries of U.S. firms maintain their books in units of foreign currency, not in dollars. The need for *translation of foreign currency statements* therefore exists in order that the financial affairs of these foreign entities can be reported in dollars as part of the U.S. parent company's financial statements. In an annual report of W. R. Grace & Co., for example, the following observation was made:

---

[1]R. J. Reynolds Industries, *Annual Report,* 1983, 33.

Net foreign exchange losses of $122 million in 1983 and $7.3 million in 1982 were primarily the result of exchange losses incurred in hyperinflationary countries and, in particular for 1983, reflected the devaluation of the Brazilian cruzeiro and the Argentine peso.[2]

The main source of generally accepted accounting principles in this area is *SFAS 52*, "Foreign Currency Translation."[3] Since much of the content of *SFAS 52* pertains to translation of foreign currency financial statements—the controversial subject of Chapter 15—we shall discuss the developments which produced the *Statement* in detail in Chapter 15. While *SFAS 52* has modified the treatment of some foreign currency transactions, its provisions in this area are generally consistent with those of its predecessor, *SFAS 8*.[4] As background information essential to an understanding of accounting for international operations, a description of the operation of foreign exchange markets and the relationship between the spot and forward markets is presented, along with some important history of the international monetary system.

Foreign Exchange Rates and Markets

Accounting for, reporting, and analyzing the financial affairs of multinational corporations are complicated by the fact that, worldwide, the accounts are denominated in various currencies. Just as Ford's subsidiary in the United Kingdom keeps its accounts in pounds sterling, the U.K. currency, Volkswagen's automobile assembly plant in New Stanton, Pennsylvania, records its transactions in dollars. Yet both Ford and Volkswagen must express their financial statements in a single currency, in order that the amounts reported will be based on a common monetary measuring unit. Each company is an *accounting entity* and will use its own reporting currency as the appropriate measuring unit. The process of restating or translating foreign currency amounts into units of domestic currency employs *foreign exchange rates*. Foreign exchange rates are themselves the results of various sets of forces operating within the *international monetary system*. To set the stage for our discussion of accounting for foreign currency transactions by U.S. firms, we now define foreign exchange rates, describe the operation of foreign exchange markets, and review the international monetary system.

Foreign Exchange Rates

Foreign exchange rates are *prices*. They are not, however, prices for automobiles, television sets, or bananas. Rather:

---

[2]W. R. Grace & Co., *Annual Report,* 1983, 51.
[3]Financial Accounting Standards Board, *Statement of Financial Accounting Standards No. 52,* "Foreign Currency Translation" (Stamford, CT: FASB, 1981); CT § F60.
[4]Financial Accounting Standards Board, *Statement of Financial Accounting Standards No. 8,* "Accounting for the Translation of Foreign Currency Transactions and Foreign Currency Financial Statements" (Stamford, CT: FASB, 1975).

A **foreign exchange rate** is the price of a unit of one country's currency expressed in units of another country's currency.

Foreign currencies, like commodities, are traded in markets. Business transactions made with foreign companies by U.S. firms are often *denominated in the foreign currency,* meaning that they must be settled in the foreign currency and not in dollars. In such situations, the U.S. firm must sell or purchase foreign currency in order to settle these transactions. Similarly, foreign companies must sell or purchase dollars to settle any transactions with U.S. firms that are *denominated in dollars.* Each case demonstrates that even transactions across national borders are within the boundaries of an accounting entity, and these must be stated in units of the entity's reporting currency. Buyers and sellers of foreign currencies use the foreign exchange markets for these purposes.

Foreign currencies are traded on both **spot markets** and **forward** (or **futures**) **markets.** Transactions involving *immediate delivery* of the foreign currency are executed at **spot rates.** In contrast, many business dealings require that foreign currency be bought or sold at some later date. To satisfy these demands, prices for futures—**forward rates**—in many foreign currencies are also quoted. A typical quotation of both spot and forward foreign exchange rates is shown below. Readers should consult the financial pages of the *Wall Street Journal* or the *New York Times* for current rate quotations.

FOREIGN EXCHANGE RATES

France (Franc)	U.S. $ Price	Foreign Currency Price per U.S. $
Spot Rate	$.1039	F9.6250
30-day Forward	.1037	9.6430
90-day Forward	.1034	9.6712
180-day Forward	.1030	9.7087

The preceding foreign exchange rates are expressed in both the direct and indirect forms. The *direct form* gives the dollar price of one unit of foreign currency (the left-hand column), while the *indirect form* shows the foreign currency price of one dollar (the right-hand column). Consider first the spot rate for the French franc (F). At the time of this quotation, $.1039/F was the dollar price for immediate delivery of francs (the direct form). Similarly, F9.6250/$ was the franc price for immediate delivery of dollars (the indirect form). Forward (or futures) rates are also listed for the French franc. In this case, the dollar *(direct)* price for delivery of francs in 180 days was $.1030/F. A discussion of the reasons for the differences typically existing between spot and forward rates follows our discussion of hedging.

Hedging. The forward (futures) markets in foreign currencies serve many of the same purposes as the commodities futures markets. In both sets of markets, the intent of nonspeculative traders is to guarantee the prices at which transactions will be consummated at a time to come by entering into contracts establishing those prices today. This process is known as **hedging.** The risk that the dollar value of a foreign currency will change is inherent in agreements to accept or deliver that foreign currency at a later date. This risk can be removed by contracting today, at a known price, to sell or purchase the foreign currency on the later date.

As an example, consider an American firm importing worsted wool fabric from the United Kingdom. In order to set selling prices to permit sufficient profit, the firm's management must know costs. Suppose the fabric is to be delivered and payment made in 90 days. The agreed price of the fabric is denominated in the U.K. currency, pounds sterling (£), and set at £100,000. Relevant foreign exchange quotations are as follows:

United Kingdom (Pound)	U.S. $ Price ($/£)	Foreign Currency Price (£/$)
Spot Rate	$1.90	£.526
30-day Forward	1.89	.529
90-day Forward	1.88	.532
180-day Forward	1.85	.541

The pattern of forward rates indicates that the market expects the dollar to appreciate relative to the pound or that differences in U.S. and U.K. interest rates exist. At the spot rate, the fabric costs $190,000 (= 100,000 × $1.90); a 90-day futures contract changes the cost to $188,000 (= 100,000 × $1.88). By purchasing pounds forward (that is, for delivery in) 90 days, the actual dollar price of the fabric is fixed at $188,000. In this way, the commitment to deliver £100,000 is *hedged*. Should the firm elect not to hedge this foreign currency commitment, it must purchase pounds on the spot market in 90 days. If the forward contract is purchased at $1.88/£ the U.S. firm will gain, so long as the spot rate in 90 days is greater than $1.88. On the other hand, if the spot rate acutally *declines* below $1.88 in 90 days, say to $1.80, the firm incurs an opportunity loss of $8,000 [= ($1.88 − $1.80) × 100,000]. By fixing the price for delivery in 90 days, the hedging process removes the chance of gain as well as loss.

Why Forward Rates Differ from Spot Rates. Forward rates differ from spot rates for two reasons:

1. Market-makers expect the spot rate to change in the future, perhaps because of economic forecasts or upcoming political developments. If, for example, the U.S. demand for Japanese automobiles is expected to decrease and the value of the dollar relative to the Japanese yen is expected to increase, the forward rate for yen may be lower than the spot rate.
2. Investors observe that interest rates and expected rates of inflation differ between countries and, through the practice of covered interest arbitrage, explained next, cause the observed difference between spot and forward foreign exchange rates.

Covered Interest Arbitrage. The practice of **covered interest arbitrage** takes place when investors (1) react to higher interest rates abroad by purchasing foreign investments and (2) protect themselves against adverse exchange rate movements by *covering* their foreign investments with forward contracts to sell the foreign currency when the investments mature. It is the major reason why some currencies sell at a premium and others at a discount in the forward market. Suppose that interest rates on 180-day certificates of deposit are 4 percent per 180-day period in the United States and 5 percent in West Germany. In a free market, American investors in search of a higher yield will move their funds from dollars into deutsche marks (DM) and purchase certificates of deposit issued by banks in West Germany. To hedge against the foreign exchange risk associated with converting DM back into dollars, investors will *cover* their investment (now *denominated* in DM) by *selling* DM forward for dollars with delivery in 180 days. These forward sales of DM produce a downward pressure on the 180-day forward rate for DM until the discount on DM sold forward 180 days approximately equals the interest rate differential of 1 percent. At this point, U.S. investors stop moving their funds from dollars into DM because the West German interest rate advantage has been offset by a decline in the dollar value of DM when the investments mature in 180 days. Therefore, in New York 180-day futures in DM would sell at a discount of approximately 1 percent from the spot rate, while in Frankfurt 180-day futures in dollars would sell at a premium of approximately 1 percent.

> In general, if the *foreign interest rate exceeds the U.S. interest rate,* the spot rate is higher than the forward rate, and forward contracts sell at a *discount* from the spot rate. Similarly, if the *U.S. interest rate exceeds the foreign interest rate,* the forward rate is higher than the spot rate, and forward contracts sell for a *premium* over the spot rate.

To illustrate the interplay between spot and forward exchange rates and interest rate differentials, consider the investment of $10,000 in Exhibit 14.1. The interest rate differential of 1 percent is acted upon by covered interest arbitragers to create the necessary equilibrating discount in the forward rate for deutsche marks in New York and premium in the forward rate for dollars in Frankfurt. Investing the $10,000 in a U.S. certificate of deposit generates $10,400 (= 1.04 × $10,000) in 6 months. Converting dollars to deutsche marks at the spot rate of $.5/DM permits an investment of DM20,000 (=$10,000/$.5) in West Germany. This investment provides DM21,000 (= 1.05 × DM20,000) in 6 months. If deutsche marks had been sold forward to hedge the foreign currency conversion, the DM21,000 provided by the investment would also be worth $10,400 (≈DM21,000/DM2.0194).

Maintaining Consistency among Foreign Exchange Rates. The structure of foreign exchange rates is kept consistent by a group of traders known as **arbitragers.** When inconsistencies in the structure of exchange rates appear, the prospect of immediate and risk-free gains will motivate arbitragers to buy and sell the appropriate currencies until the inconsistencies are removed. For example, **two-point**

Exhibit 14.1   The Effects of Covered Interest Arbitrage

FOREIGN EXCHANGE RATES

	Spot	6-Month Futures
New York	$.5/DM	$.4952/DM
Frankfurt	DM2/$	DM2.0194/$

INTEREST RATES PER 6-MONTH PERIOD

6-Month Certificates of Deposit (CD)

4%	Differential = 1%
5%	

CASE 1: DOMESTIC INVESTMENT

Time 0	Six Months Later
Investor in New York invests $10,000 in a 6-month CD.	CD matures, producing $10,400 (= 1.04 × $10,000).

CASE 2: FOREIGN INVESTMENT COVERED WITH A FORWARD CONTRACT

Time 0	Six Months Later
a. Investor in New York converts $10,000 into DM20,000 (=$10,000/$.5) and invests in a 6-month CD.	a. CD matures, producing DM21,000 (= 1.05 × DM20,000).
b. Investor in New York enters a 6-month forward contract to convert DM into dollars (at $.4952/DM) when the West German CD matures.	b. Forward contract matures and the DM21,000 from the CD are converted into $10,400 (≈ 21,000 × $.4952).

CONCLUSION

In both cases, the investor ends up with $10,400. The fact that the 6-month forward rate of $.4952 is approximately 1 percent lower than the spot rate offsets the fact that 6-month CD rates in Frankfurt are 1 percent higher than in New York.

---

arbitrage removes any difference between the exchange rates for the same currency on two different markets. Suppose that in New York the rate $/£ = 2.000 and in London $/£ = 2.006. Arbitragers would quickly purchase pounds with dollars in New York and sell the pounds for dollars in London until both rates equalize and the arbitrage gains disappear.

A more intricate scheme involves **three-point arbitrage.** This technique exploits inconsistencies existing among the exchange rates of three currencies and, by so doing, removes them. To see this, consider the following set of foreign exchange quotations:

In New York	In Tokyo
$/£ = 2.00	Yen/£ = 410
$/Yen = .005	

Alert traders would observe that a pound could be bought for $2 in New York and exchanged for 410 yen in Tokyo. The 410 yen could each be sold for $.005 in New York for a total of $2.05, a gain of $.05 per pound purchased. Holding the rate in Tokyo constant, arbitragers in New York might purchase pounds with dollars and cause the price of pounds to gradually rise, perhaps to $2.0295. At the same time, the arbitragers could sell yen for dollars in New York until the price of yen fell to $.00495, thereby eliminating any further gains from arbitraging. Alternatively, the same result would be achieved by bidding up the dollar price of pounds to $2.05, holding the other rates constant. Whatever new exchange rates result, however, they too will be kept consistent with the rates in other markets and for other currencies by arbitragers.

In the contemporary world economy, foreign exchange rates are generally the result of free market forces. Some of the underlying factors affecting exchange rates are relative rates of inflation, relative interest rates, and the terms of trade (or international commodity exchange ratios) between countries. As these conditions change, the foreign exchange rates change. Economists refer to this as a system of **floating** or **flexible exchange rates.** It was not always so. During most of the post-World War II period, exchange rates were generally *fixed* under the terms of an international agreement. The established set of exchange rates was maintained (or *pegged)* by central banks as they purchased and sold foreign currencies in the foreign exchange markets.

We believe that the study of accounting for international operations is enriched by an understanding of the international monetary system, an important part of the international environment. Accordingly, the next section is devoted to a discussion of developments in the international monetary system.

The International Monetary System

The growth in the world economy and the relative international economic stability experienced since World War II followed, in large measure, from negotiations undertaken near the end of the war. Determined to create an orderly international economic environment after the war, representatives of the Western allied powers met at Bretton Woods, New Hampshire, in the summer of 1944 to fashion the elements of a sound international monetary system. The USSR did not participate. Renowned British economist John Maynard Keynes played an important role at the conference.

The exchange rate instability experienced between World War I and World War II had been attributed, rightly or wrongly, to freely floating exchange rates and the abuses perpetrated by international speculators. The desire for stability in the short run and flexibility in the long run led the Bretton Woods conferees to adopt what has been termed an **adjustable peg system.** Currency exchange rates were set, by agreement, in terms of the U.S. dollar. The value of the dollar, in turn, was tied to gold; the official price of gold was set at $35 per ounce. The discipline in the system was that the dollar was freely convertible into gold. In other words, if the dollar became overvalued, making an ounce of gold worth more than $35, foreigners would convert their dollars into gold at the U.S. Treasury. This would deplete the finite U.S. gold reserves, exactly what eventually happened.

The other countries which subscribed to the Bretton Woods agreements were to attempt to maintain the values of their currencies (in dollars) within 1 percent of the par or pegged exchange rate. Therefore, if the exchange rate for a particular currency began to move above or below the allowable 1 percent deviation from par, that country's central bank was obliged to intervene in the foreign exchange market. The home currency was purchased with dollars or another acceptable international reserve (such as gold) to raise the exchange rate; to lower the exchange rate, the home currency was sold.

To assist countries facing temporary shortages of international reserves, the International Monetary Fund (IMF) was established as an integral part of the Bretton Woods agreements. Member countries can borrow specified quantities of international reserves from the IMF to tide them over transitory deficits in international payments. The resources of the IMF consist of mandatory contributions made by member countries.

Flexibility in the system was to be achieved by permitting countries to change the official rate by as much as 10 percent without approval of the International Monetary Fund. IMF approval was required for larger changes in the official exchange rate. An increase in the official peg was termed a **devaluation,** while a reduction in the official peg implied **revaluation.** To see this, observe that by raising the price of a foreign currency in terms of the home currency, the home currency *loses value.* That is, after the increase in the exchange rate, the home currency has been devalued because more units of it are needed to acquire the foreign currency. In the United States, the dollar would be devalued by raising the dollar price of gold. Concurrently, a devaluation of one currency means that at least one other currency experiences a revaluation. In November 1967, the British pound sterling was devalued by the United Kingdom from \$2.80 to \$2.40. The effects of this action on the exchange rate between dollars and pounds were:

	In New York (\$/£)	In London (£/\$)
Before the Sterling Devaluation	\$2.80	£.357
After the Sterling Devaluation	2.40	.417

Note that, under the Bretton Woods agreements, the ability of a country to defend its currency in the face of a declining exchange rate was directly influenced by that country's supply of international reserves, including borrowing rights from the IMF. In contrast, keeping the exchange rate from rising usually generated an expanding domestic money supply which created inflationary pressures.

The Fatal Flaw

The problem with an adjustable peg system is that when the rate becomes more difficult to maintain through intervention, the direction of the forthcoming change in the official exchange rate is clear and "bear speculators are then presented with that rare, and greatly desired phenomenon, a 'sure thing'."[5] Under the Bretton Woods system, a large adjustment in the exchange rate occurred in a single discrete step. As the underlying economic conditions gradually changed, the ex-

---

[5]Frank Graham, "Achilles' Heels in Monetary Standards," *American Economic Review* (March 1940), 19.

change rate was not allowed to change accordingly. Eventually, as the central bank intervened more and more in the foreign exchange market, a forthcoming change in the official peg, usually a devaluation, was signaled. Speculators would sell large amounts of the suspect currency and short sales would increase. The central bank became the buyer of last resort and often engaged in extremely costly counterspeculative policies. In connection with the devaluation of the British pound mentioned earlier, on November 17, 1967, the Bank of England lost $250 million. This amount was expended to support the pound in the face of a massive speculative outflow of that currency. Deliberations regarding a devaluation were shrouded in secrecy, and announcements were made when markets were closed, typically on weekends or holidays.

Unfortunately, this fundamental problem was aggravated by the general unwillingness of governments to adjust the peg frequently. Devaluations were seen as assaults on national pride. Hence, the crises, when they came, were massive and abrupt.

The requirement that central banks intervene in foreign exchange markets to support their currencies often created problems in domestic economic policy. Government intervention in the economy has grown in significance since World War II, so that the conflicting use of policy tools to achieve policy objectives had not been forecast by the Bretton Woods conferees. As an example, suppose a particular country were confronted with both excessive domestic unemployment and an international deficit. Domestic monetary policy would likely be expansionary, leading to a larger money supply and lower interest rates to combat unemployment. Yet just the opposite would be called for to cope with the international deficit. High interest rates attract the international investment funds which would help alleviate the international deficit. Such conflicts in economic policy were often caused by the need to support the official exchange rate.

The Evolution of Flexible Exchange Rates

As time passed, changes in international economic relations simply outgrew the capability of the pegged exchange rate system to accommodate them.

> It is not possible to date precisely the end of the international monetary system established at Bretton Woods in 1944. Different aspects of the system died at different times. And the basic principles of international financial cooperation on which the Bretton Woods system was based never died at all.
>
> There is general agreement that the final end of the adjustably pegged par value exchange rate system established at Bretton Woods was marked by the initiation of generalized floating of exchange rates by the major industrial countries following the second devaluation of the dollar in early 1973. But many who viewed the gold convertibility of the dollar as the linchpin of the system would point to the formal termination of the convertibility of official dollar holdings into gold in August 1971 as the symbolic death date of the system. Still others would point out that, de facto, the unfettered gold convertibility of the dollar as envisioned at Bretton Woods had already ended years before.[6]

---

[6]Thomas D. Willett, *Floating Exchange Rates and International Monetary Reform* (Washington, DC: American Enterprise Institute for Public Policy Research, 1977), 1.

Essentially untouched by the devastation of World War II, the United States emerged as the major economic power in the free world. It had most of the free world's supply of gold, and its currency, the dollar, was in great demand throughout the world as an international medium of payment. As the countries of the world were rebuilt, with significant aid from the United States through such programs as the Marshall Plan, American economic dominance began to decline. The flow of dollars abroad became a flood in the late 1960s as the persistent balance of payments[7] deficits which began in the late 1950s grew substantially larger. The dollar shortage had become a glut; conversion of dollars into gold had reduced the United States gold reserve to a low of $10.2 billion in 1971 from a high of $24.6 billion in 1949.

In August 1971, President Nixon reacted to the growing crisis of confidence in the dollar. Anticipating the record balance of payments deficit in 1971 (which amounted to $29.7 billion on the official reserve transactions balance), the president unilaterally suspended convertibility of the dollar into gold as one of several economic policy initiatives announced on August 15, 1971. Subsequent appreciation of major foreign currencies led to an increase in the official price of gold to $38 per ounce in December 1971. A second devaluation of the dollar in February 1973 raised the official price of gold to $42 per ounce.

Serious negotiations for the reform of the international monetary system began in earnest in 1972 and reached their culmination in Kingston, Jamaica, on January 7 and 8, 1976. At the Jamaica meetings, representatives of the 128 member nations of the International Monetary Fund ratified amendments to the IMF's Articles of Agreement, officially sanctioning flexible or floating exchange rates as the basis for our international monetary system. As Nobel laureate economist Milton Friedman had suggested many years before,

> Our problem is not to solve *a* balance of payments problem. It is to solve *the* balance of payments problem by adapting a mechanism that will enable free market forces to provide a prompt, effective, and automatic response to changes in conditions affecting international trade.[8]

This movement away from pegged exchange rates has led to a new international economic environment, one in which foreign exchange rates constantly fluctuate principally in response to market forces. The system that emerged from the Jamaica meetings, however, is not a pure floating-rate system. Some countries attempt to peg their currencies to the currency of an important trading partner, such as the U.S. dollar or the British pound. In other situations, central banks occasionally intervene in the foreign exchange markets to promote orderly markets, rather than to support specific currencies. This mixed system is often referred to as a "dirty float."

Indeed, foreign exchange rates *have* changed substantially since the early 1970s, with the dollar losing ground against some of the major currencies during the 1970s. To indicate the extent of this change, we reproduce in Figure 14.1 a

---

[7]The *balance of payments* refers to the net flow of funds in or out of a particular country. A deficit occurs when the quantity of funds flowing out exceeds the quantity flowing in.

[8]Milton Friedman, *Capitalism and Freedom* (Chicago: University of Chicago Press, 1962), 67.

Figure 14.1   **Indexes of Foreign Currency Price of the U.S. Dollar (May 1970 = 100)**

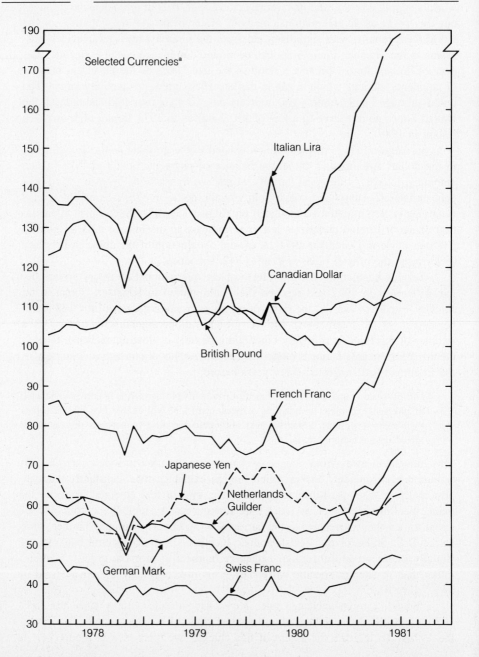

Source: U.S. Department of Commerce, Bureau of Economic Analysis, *Survey of Current Business* (September 1981), 43.

plot of the movements in several foreign exchange rates from 1977 to 1981. The exchange rates are expressed in the *indirect* form (foreign currency/$) as ratios of the rates existing in May 1970.

First, notice that all of the exchange rates are volatile. *Second,* observe that the dollar lost ground against several of the major currencies during the 1970s. These currencies—the French franc and the German mark, for example—have *revalued* against the dollar because the price of dollars in those currencies has declined, although the dollar has strengthened beginning in 1980. For example, at the end of 1979, the West German deutsche mark price of dollars was about half that prevailing in May 1970 (the index had fallen from 100 to about 50) but had risen to about two-thirds of the May 1970 price by the end of 1980.

Exchange rate movements in this new economic environment have affected the international operations of corporations and have made the accounting for those international operations more complex. We begin our study of these accounting matters with a thorough examination of accounting for foreign currency transactions entered into by U.S. corporations.

Accounting for Foreign Currency Transactions

Accounting problems resulting from various transactions involving foreign currencies are examined in the remainder of this chapter. *Import/export* transactions are considered first, then those which involve *borrowing and lending abroad.* We also discuss the accounting for *forward contracts* used to hedge such transactions, used as economic hedges of net investments in foreign entities, and used in speculation.

The principal source of accounting problems faced by U.S. firms transacting in foreign currencies is the need to deal in units of foreign currency while maintaining books of account in dollars. If the foreign currency transaction is *denominated* (must be settled) in units of foreign currency, it must also be *measured* in dollars for inclusion in the U.S. company's accounting records. As these transactions are studied, the following general statement of the accounting treatment should be kept in mind:

> Assets and liabilities denominated in a foreign currency are generally carried at their current dollar equivalents—they are restated from foreign currency units into dollars at the current spot rate when recorded, when settled, and at intervening balance sheet dates. As the spot rate changes, the resulting revaluation to a current dollar equivalent produces an **exchange gain or loss** which enters the U.S. firm's income statement, except in the case of certain hedging transactions.

Import/Export Transactions

Import/export transactions would present no particular accounting problem *if* all sales, purchases, payments, and receipts were made in dollars. Such an unlikely situation would mean that our international customers and suppliers did business in terms of the dollar, a currency foreign to *them.*

The basic problem caused by the need to transact in a foreign currency may be summarized as follows:

> When a transaction is denominated in a foreign currency, its value in dollars is determined by the appropriate foreign exchange rate. The *passage of time* between the inception of the transaction and its ultimate settlement with cash *allows the dollar value of the unsettled balance to change as the appropriate foreign exchange rate changes.*

Therefore, if a U.S. company makes a credit sale abroad and the transaction price is stated in units of foreign currency, the dollar value of the account receivable may change before payment is received in the foreign currency and converted into dollars. Similarly, when a U.S. company purchases goods from abroad on account at a price denominated in foreign currency units, the dollar amount owed may change before dollars are converted into the foreign currency and payment is made. These changes in the dollar value of receivables and payables generate gains and losses to the U.S. firm which must be recognized at settlement and at intervening balance sheet dates. Since the ultimate settlement of these transactions involves the *conversion* of dollars into foreign currency or foreign currency into dollars, we label them **transaction gains or losses** (or **transaction adjustments**). This is one of two general types of *exchange gain or loss.* The other type, discussed in Chapter 15, arises when foreign currency financial statements are *translated* into dollars.

Separate identification and reporting of transaction gains and losses as accounting events *apart* from the related sale (revenue) or purchase (expense) transactions has been referred to as the **two transaction approach.** The alternative **single transaction approach** views a transaction denominated in a foreign currency as incomplete until settled. Any intervening transaction gain or loss is used to adjust the dollar basis of the revenue or expense transaction and is not reported separately. The FASB specifically rejected this single transaction view by observing that "the exchange exposure in a purchase or sale transaction whose price is denominated in a foreign currency stems not from the purchase or sale itself but from a delay in payment or receipt of the equivalent dollars."[9] No transaction gain or loss can occur if the sale or purchase is settled immediately. To accommodate the two transaction approach, the following three accounting procedures are used:

1. Record the transaction in dollars, determined by restating the foreign currency invoice price into dollars using the appropriate foreign exchange spot rate.
2. Record a transaction gain or loss when the transaction is settled if the number of dollars received or paid differs from that originally recorded at date of transaction in No. 1.

---

[9]Financial Accounting Standards Board, *Statement No. 8,* par. 114.

3. If the transaction has not been settled at a balance sheet date, record a transaction gain or loss on the existing receivable or payable by adjusting it to the dollar equivalent implied by the spot rate at the balance sheet date.

Observe the two objectives of these procedures. *First,* recognition is given to changes in value of receivables and payables attributable to movements in the exchange rate. *Second,* this recognition is based on accrual accounting and is not deferred until eventual settlement if a balance sheet date occurs prior to settlement.

We now illustrate the accounting for import and export transactions with the following series of events:

1. On October 16, 19X1, Acme International purchased lamb's wool at an invoice price of 17,000 New Zealand dollars ($NZ17,000) from a New Zealand rancher. The exchange rate was $.92/$NZ. Payment was to be made on December 16, 19X1.

10/16/X1

Purchases.	15,640	
Accounts Payable.		15,640

To record the purchase of wool from New Zealand; $15,640 = $.92 × 17,000.

2. On December 16, 19X1, Acme purchased 17,000 New Zealand dollars at an exchange rate of $.93/$NZ and transmitted them to the rancher's bank in New Zealand.

12/16/X1

Transaction Loss	170	
Accounts Payable.		170

To recognize the transaction loss on the account payable; $170 = ($.93 − $.92)17,000.

Foreign Currency	15,810	
Cash		15,810

To purchase sufficient foreign currency to pay off the New Zealand rancher; $15,810 = $.93 × 17,000.

Accounts Payable.	15,810	
Foreign Currency		15,810

To record payment of the liability to the New Zealand rancher; $15,810 = $15,640 + $170.

Consider the transaction loss recorded in event 2. Acme had a liability to the New Zealand rancher denominated in New Zealand dollars. Since the exchange rate had risen (so that it took more U.S. dollars to purchase New Zealand dollars), the dollar value of the liability had increased, and Acme had incurred a transaction loss. The loss was accounted for separately from the cost of the merchandise under the *two transaction approach.*

3. On December 20, 19X1, Acme purchased worsted wool fabrics from a British mill for 40,000 pounds sterling (£40,000), when the exchange rate was $2/£. Payment was due on January 20, 19X2.

12/20/X1

Purchases. 80,000
  Accounts Payable.   80,000
To record the purchase of wool fabric from Great Britain; $80,000
= $2 × 40,000.

4. On December 22, 19X1, Acme sold a quantity of deluxe wool blankets to a Canadian concern for 9,800 Canadian dollars ($CN9,800). The exchange rate was $.97/$CN. Acme's terms are 60 days, net.

12/22/X1

Accounts Receivable 9,506
  Sales.   9,506
To record the sale of blankets to Canada; $9,506 = $.97 × 9,800.

5. On December 29, 19X1, Acme purchased buttons valued at 10,000 pesos (P10,000) from a Mexican manufacturer. The exchange rate was $.05/P; a check was mailed immediately.

12/29/X1

Purchases 500
  Cash   500
To record the cash purchase of buttons from Mexico; $500 = $.05 ×
10,000.

6. Financial statements were prepared at December 31, 19X1, and the following adjusting entries were made. Relevant exchange rates were $1.96/£ and $.985/$CN.

12/31/X1

Accounts Payable. 1,600
  Transaction Gain   1,600
To record the transaction gain accrued on the liability to the British
mill; $1,600 = ($2.00 − $1.96)40,000. The dollar value of this
liability has decreased to $78,400(= $1.96 × 40,000).

Accounts Receivable 147
  Transaction Gain   147
To record the transaction gain accrued on the receivable from
Canada; $147 = ($.985 − $.97)9,800. The dollar value of this asset
has increased to $9,653 (= $.985 × 9,800).

Contrast the two transaction gains accrued at December 31, 19X1, in Event 6.

Since the exchange rate for pounds sterling had declined, the dollar value of Acme's liability had declined accordingly, and a transaction gain resulted. Although the exchange rate of Canadian dollars had risen at year-end, it also generated a transaction gain. This is because Acme had a receivable denominated in Canadian dollars. As the value of Canadian dollars rose, so did the U.S. dollar value of Acme's receivable from the Canadian firm.

7. Acme paid its obligation to the British mill on January 20, 19X2. The exchange rate was $1.93/£.

1/20/X2

Accounts Payable   1,200
   Transaction Gain   1,200
To recognize the transaction gain on the account payable; $1,200 = ($1.96 − $1.93)40,000.

Foreign Currency   77,200
   Cash   77,200
To record the purchase of foreign currency to pay off the British mill; $77,200 = $1.93 × 40,000.

Accounts Payable   77,200
   Foreign Currency   77,200
To record payment of the liability to Great Britain; $77,200 = $80,000 − $1,600 − $1,200.

8. On February 20, 19X2, payment was received from the Canadian customer on the sale of the blankets. The exchange rate was $.91/$CN.

2/20/X2

Transaction Loss   735
   Accounts Receivable   735
To recognize the transaction loss on the receivable; $735 = ($.985 − $.91)9,800.

Foreign Currency   8,918
   Accounts Receivable   8,918
To record receipt of foreign currency from Canada in payment of the receivable; $8,918 = $.91 × 9,800 = $9,506 + $147 − $735.

Cash   8,918
   Foreign Currency   8,918
To record sale of the Canadian currency for U.S. dollars.

To summarize, accounts receivable and accounts payable arising in international transactions are often denominated in a foreign currency and are recorded at the dollar equivalent of a fixed quantity of foreign currency. As the exchange rate changes, the dollar equivalent also changes. The effects of changing exchange rates on these dollar equivalents and the resulting transaction gains and losses are as follows:

EFFECTS OF CHANGING EXCHANGE RATES
ON RECEIVABLES AND PAYABLES
DENOMINATED IN FOREIGN CURRENCIES
AND RESULTING TRANSACTION GAINS AND LOSSES

Account	Change in Exchange Rate (\$ Price of Foreign Currency)	
	Increase	Decrease
Accounts Receivable (A/R)	A/R increases; gain	A/R decreases; loss
Accounts Payable (A/P)	A/P increases; loss	A/P decreases; gain

Using Forward Contracts to Hedge Import and Export Transactions

We indicated earlier in the chapter how foreign exchange rates have fluctuated in recent years. One result of these fluctuations has been a growing recognition by managers that their foreign currency transactions have to be *hedged*. Hedging, as previously defined, involves contracting in the forward market to purchase or to sell foreign currency at a specified time in the future for a fixed price. In this way, managers neutralize the impact of changing exchange rates on their foreign currency commitments.

Contracting for future delivery of a foreign currency can involve either *forward contracts*—individual contracts negotiated with dealers—or *futures contracts*—contracts with standardized terms, including margin deposits, traded on organized exchanges. Since *SFAS 52* prescribes the same accounting treatment for forward and futures contracts in foreign currencies, we concentrate on forward contracts in the ensuing discussion. An introduction to the characteristics of and accounting for futures contracts *not* involving foreign currencies appears in the appendix to this chapter.

Because the accounting for forward contracts is complex, our discussions and illustrations related to hedging are primarily devoted to forward contracts used for this purpose. Other foreign currency transactions, such as foreign loans and investments in foreign debt securities, can also function as hedges. If they do, accounting for the exchange gains or losses on such transactions parallels the forward contract case.

These forward contracts are recorded when entered, although no money actually changes hands until the contracts are settled. If the company must pay some cash upon inception of the contract as evidence that performance is intended, it is reported as a *deposit* in the current asset section of the company's balance sheet. We begin our discussion by examining a forward purchase contract.

Forward Purchase Contracts. A **forward purchase contract** would be used by an *importer*. Such a contract gives the importer the right to purchase foreign currency at a specified time in the future for a known price. When the importer's obligations to foreign suppliers come due, the needed amount of foreign currency will be available at a price agreed upon in advance. For accounting purposes, three components of a forward purchase transaction are important:

1. The *liability* to the foreign exchange broker, denoted *Due to Exchange Broker*. It is recorded at the agreed-upon dollar value of the foreign currency to be purchased; that is, the quantity of foreign currency translated at the applicable *forward rate*. Since the rate is fixed by the contract, the liability is denominated in dollars and is unaffected by changes in the exchange rate and generates no transaction gain or loss.

2. The *forward purchase contract* itself, representing the receivable for the foreign currency. It is recorded at the current value of the foreign currency to be purchased; that is, the quantity of foreign currency translated at the *spot rate*. This asset is denominated in units of the foreign currency and is based upon the current translated value of the foreign currency; its dollar value will change with the *spot rate* and transaction gains and losses will occur.

3. The *premium or discount on the forward purchase contract,* the difference between the current and future values of the foreign currency to be purchased. As mentioned previously, it generally is attributable to interest rate differentials and represents a revenue or expense to the firm. Amortization of this premium or discount is accounted for separately from any transaction gain or loss on the forward purchase contract.

For example, suppose that goods costing £1,000 are purchased from a British supplier on October 1 when the spot rate is $2.10/£. Payment in pounds is due in 30 days. Because this liability (account payable) is denominated in pounds, it is *exposed* to risk of exchange rate movements. To hedge this **exposed liability** to the British supplier, a forward purchase contract calling for the broker to deliver £1,000 in 30 days is entered on October 1. If the 30-day forward rate is $2.20/£, the *liability to the exchange broker* is fixed at $2,200 (= $2.20 × 1,000) and will not be affected by subsequent movements in the exchange rate. Thus the £1,000 needed to pay the British supplier will be purchased for $2,200. Translating the £1,000 at the spot rate of $2.10 gives us the current value of the receivable for the foreign currency, $2,100 (= $2.10 × 2,000), which we call the *forward purchase contract*. Since the foreign currency was purchased in the forward market for *more* than the current spot rate, a *premium on the forward purchase contract* of $100 [= ($2.20 − $2.10)1,000] results. The entries recording (1) the purchase of goods and (2) the forward purchase contract on October 1 are given below:

October 1

Purchases	2,100	
Accounts Payable		2,100
To record the purchase of goods from Britain; $2,100 = $2.10 × 1,000.		

Forward Purchase Contract ($2.10 × 1,000)	2,100	
Premium on Forward Contract [($2.20 − $2.10)1,000]	100	
Due to Exchange Broker ($2.20 × 1,000)		2,200
To record the forward purchase contract entered to hedge the payable to the British supplier.		

On October 31, when the forward contract is settled and the British supplier is paid with the £1,000 received from the broker, the spot rate is $2.14/£. The following entries made on October 31 show the accrual of the transaction gain on the forward purchase contract and the settlement of the contract:

October 31

Forward Purchase Contract	40	
Transaction Gain.		40
To recognize the transaction gain accrued on the forward contract; $40 = ($2.14 - $2.10)1,000.		
Due to Exchange Broker.	2,200	
Cash.		2,200
To record payment to foreign exchange broker.		
Foreign Currency.	2,140	
Forward Purchase Contract		2,140
To record receipt of the foreign currency from the broker; $2,140 = $2.14 × 1,000 = $2,100 + $40.		
Expense—Premium Amortization	100	
Premium on Forward Contract.		100
To amortize the premium on the forward contract.		

At this point, the forward contract is settled, the importer has the £1,000 from the broker, and the premium has been expensed. We now recognize the transaction loss on the account payable and record payment of the £1,000 to the British supplier:

October 31

Transaction Loss.	40	
Accounts Payable		40
To recognize the transaction loss accrued on the account payable; $40 = ($2.14 - $2.10)1,000.		
Accounts Payable	2,140	
Foreign Currency		2,140
To record payment of the liability to the British supplier; $2,140 = $2.14 × 1,000 = $2,100 + $40.		

Note that the transaction gain on the forward contract exactly offsets the transaction loss on the account payable, as would be expected with a perfect hedge. In retrospect, however, the hedge was not profitable. Even though the transaction loss of $40 was avoided, a premium of $100 was paid to do so. In other words $2,200 was paid for £1,000 which could have been purchased on October 31 for $2,140, or purchased on October 1 for $2,100.

Forward Sale Contracts. *Exporters* use **forward sale contracts** to permit the sale of foreign currency at a specified time in the future for a known price. As foreign customers remit payments in foreign currency to the exporter, the foreign currency can be converted to prearranged quantities of dollars by using forward sale contracts. These contracts also have three components of importance for accounting.

1. The *receivable* from the foreign exchange broker, designated *Due from Exchange Broker*. It consists of the agreed-upon dollar value of the foreign currency to be sold. This is the quantity of foreign currency translated at the applicable *forward rate*. The receivable is denominated in dollars, is unaffected by any change in the exchange rate, and generates no transaction gain or loss.
2. The *forward sale contract* itself, representing the obligation (account payable) to deliver the foreign currency. It is denominated in units of the foreign currency and is recorded at the current dollar equivalent of the currency to be sold; its dollar value changes with the *spot rate* and transaction gains and losses will occur.
3. *The premium or discount on the forward contract,* i.e., the difference between the current and future values of the currency to be sold. As before, this is generally attributable to interest rate differentials and is accounted for separately from any transaction adjustment on the forward sale contract.

For example, suppose that goods were *sold* to a British customer on December 1 at a price stated in pounds, £1,000, when the spot rate is $2.10/£. Payment in pounds will be received in 30 days. Because this asset (account receivable) is denominated in pounds, it is exposed to risk of exchange rate movements. To hedge this **exposed asset,** the receivable from the British customer, a forward sale contract calling for delivery of £1,000 to the broker in 30 days is entered on December 1. If the 30-day forward rate is $2.20/£, the *receivable from the exchange broker* is fixed at $2,200 ($= \$2.20 \times 1,000$) and will not be affected by subsequent movements in the exchange rate. Thus the £1,000 received from the British customer will be sold for $2,200. Translating the £1,000 at the spot rate of $2.10 gives us the current value of the payable for the foreign currency, $2,100 ($= \$2.10 \times 1,000$), which we call the *forward sale contract*. Since the foreign currency was sold in the forward market for *more* than the current spot rate, a *premium on the forward sale contract* of $100 [$= (\$2.20 - \$2.10)1,000$] results. The entries recording (1) the sale of goods and (2) the forward sale contract on December 1 are given below:

December 1

Accounts Receivable. 2,100
    Sales 2,100
To record the sale of goods to Britain; $2,100 = $2.10 × 1,000.

Due from Exchange Broker ($2.20 × 1,000). 2,200
    Premium on Forward Contract [($2.20 − $2.10)1,000]. 100
    Forward Sale Contract ($2.10 × 1,000) 2,100
To record the forward sale contract entered to hedge the receivable from the British customer.

On December 31, the British customer pays the £1,000, which is then delivered to the broker in settlement of the forward contract. The spot rate has risen to $2.14/£. Because the receivable must be collected before the forward contract can be settled in this case, the first two entries made on December 31 relate to the transaction gain on the account receivable and the collection of the receivable:

December 31

Accounts Receivable	40	
Transaction Gain		40
To recognize the transaction gain accrued on the account receivable; $40 = (\$2.14 - \$2.10)1,000.$		
Foreign Currency	2,140	
Accounts Receivable		2,140
To record collection of the receivable from the British customer; $2,140 = \$2.14 \times 1,000 = \$2,100 + \$40.$		

Now that the receivable has been collected, £1,000 is available for delivery to the broker. We accrue the transaction loss on the forward contract and settle the contract:

December 31

Transaction Loss	40	
Forward Sale Contract		40
To recognize the transaction loss accrued on the forward contract; $40 = (\$2.14 - \$2.10)1,000.$		
Forward Sale Contract	2,140	
Foreign Currency		2,140
To record delivery of the foreign currency to the broker; $2,140 = \$2.14 \times 1,000 = \$2,100 + \$40.$		
Cash	2,200	
Due from Exchange Broker		2,200
To record the $2,200 received from the broker.		
Premium on Forward Contract	100	
Revenue—Premium Amortization		100
To amortize the premium on the forward contract.		

Note that the transaction loss on the forward contract exactly offsets the transaction gain on the account receivable, as would be expected with a perfect hedge. Unlike the purchase case, however, this hedge did turn out to be profitable. Even though the transaction gain of $40 was neutralized, a premium of $100 was received. In other words, $2,200 was received for £1,000 which could have been sold on December 31 for only $2,140.

Determining Whether a Discount or Premium Exists on a Forward Contract.
To assist in identifying a premium or discount on a forward contract, the following rules may be used:

Case	Type of Contract	Forward Rate (FR) $\geq$ Spot Rate (SR)	Discount/ Premium	Income Statement Effect
1	Forward sale	FR < SR	Discount	Expense
2	Forward purchase	FR < SR	Discount	Revenue
3	Forward sale	FR > SR	Premium	Revenue
4	Forward purchase	FR > SR	Premium	Expense

For example, if the foreign currency is sold forward and the forward rate is *less than* the current spot rate (Case 1), the currency is sold at a *discount* from the current spot rate. Alternatively, if the foreign currency is purchased forward and the forward rate is *greater than* the current spot rate (Case 4), the currency is purchased at a *premium* over the current spot rate.

Hedging an Identifiable Foreign Currency Commitment. Many transactions are preceded by the issuance of purchase orders or other contractual agreements. Accordingly, forward contracts may be entered before the transaction occurs and is recorded. There may be a further period of time after the transaction is recorded until settlement, and the forward contract often remains in effect during this period to hedge the liability exposed to exchange rate risk. If the contract was entered into *before* a transaction denominated in the foreign currency is recorded and meets the conditions described below, it is considered a **hedge of an identifiable foreign currency commitment.** Should the contract remain in effect (or be entered into) *after* a payable or receivable transaction denominated in the foreign currency is recorded, it is then treated as a **hedge of an exposed asset or liability position.** These situations are depicted as follows for a *forward purchase contract:*

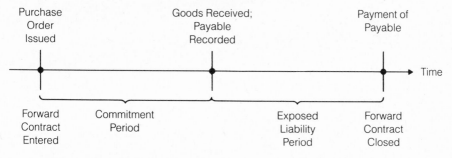

$SFAS\ 52$ specifies the accounting for the transaction gains and losses and for the premium or discount on the forward contract. The forward contract is *a hedge of an identifiable foreign currency commitment* if both of the following conditions are met:

1. The contract is designated as, and is effective as, a hedge of a foreign currency commitment.[10]
2. The foreign currency commitment is firm.

---

[10]Par. 21 of *SFAS 52* (CT § F60.130) permits the contract to exceed the amount of the foreign currency commitment if it is necessary to hedge the commitment on an aftertax basis.

The forward contract need not be in the currency being committed. Under *SFAS 52,* contracts in currencies *economically linked to* (that is, moving in tandem with) the currency being committed can function as hedges as long as the conditions above are satisfied. Moreover, other foreign currency transactions such as loans or investments can serve as hedges of identifiable foreign currency commitments. Treatment of exchange gains and losses on such other transactions parallels the forward contract case. A foreign currency transaction will be treated as a hedge here and elsewhere in the chapter only if it is an *effective hedge,* a determination made *after* the foreign currency transaction is entered. An **effective hedge** is one that achieves its stated purpose. That is, the transaction gain or loss accruing on the hedge is opposite from the transaction gain or loss accruing on the foreign currency position or commitment being hedged. For example, if the foreign currency position being hedged produces a transaction *loss* and the hedge produces a transaction *gain,* the hedge is *effective.*

Hedging a Foreign Currency Purchase Commitment. Note that for the importer an identifiable foreign currency commitment is based on a purchase order issued prior to the actual receipt of the goods. Any transaction gain or loss accruing on the forward contract during the commitment period is *deferred* until the payable to the foreign supplier is booked. In effect, the forward contract is viewed as an integral part of the purchase transaction. At the time the purchase is recorded, the deferred transaction gain or loss is included in the dollar basis of the purchase transaction. After this, transaction gains and losses on both the forward contract and the payable are recorded but are offsetting. The premium or discount may either be deferred until the transaction is recorded or be amortized proportionately over the life of the contract. If it is deferred until the transaction is recorded, the portion pertaining to the commitment period is used to adjust the dollar basis of the transaction, as entered in the Purchases (or Inventory) account.

Say, for example, that on August 10, 19X2, Acme issues a purchase order to Queens, Ltd., a U.K. exporter, to purchase fabric valued at £100,000; the spot rate is $1.80/£. Delivery of the fabric in the United States is expected on November 30, 19X2, and payment is due on January 10, 19X3. This future payment of £100,000 is an identifiable foreign currency commitment, and Acme elects to hedge it by purchasing £100,000 for delivery on January 10, 19X3. The *commitment period,* however, runs from August 10, 19X2, to November 30, 19X2, a period of $3\frac{2}{3}$ months. With a 5-month forward rate of $1.83/£, the forward contract results in a premium of $3,000, which Acme elects to defer. Since the purchase order for the fabric does not generate an accounting entry, the only entry made during the *commitment period* recognizes the forward contract, as shown below:

8/10/X2

Forward Purchase Contract ($1.80 × 100,000)	180,000	
Premium on Forward Contract [($1.83 − $1.80)100,000]	3,000	
Due to Exchange Broker ($1.83 × 100,000)		183,000

To record the forward purchase contract engaged in to hedge
the identifiable foreign currency commitment to Queens, Ltd.

Hedging the Exposed Liability Position. The commitment period expires once the fabric is received and the purchase transaction is recorded. After the purchase and related payable are recorded, the forward contract acts as a *hedge of an exposed liability position*—the account payable. Because the payable is denominated in pounds, its dollar value changes as the $/£ exchange rate changes. Thus the payable is *exposed* to foreign exchange rate risk.

At the time the purchase and related payable are recorded, the accountant must also record the deferred transaction adjustment accrued on the forward purchase contract during the commitment period. Then, Purchases must be adjusted by (1) the deferred transaction adjustment on the forward purchase contract and (2) the portion of the premium on the forward purchase contract pertaining to the commitment period. The spot rate at November 30, 19X2, is $1.82/£. The entries are:

11/30/X2

Forward Purchase Contract.	2,000	
Deferred Transaction Gain		2,000
To record as deferred the transaction gain accrued on the forward purchase contract during the commitment period; $2,000 = ($1.82 − $1.80)100,000.		
Purchases.	182,000	
Accounts Payable.		182,000
To record the purchase of fabric from Queens, Ltd., in the United Kingdom; $182,000 = $1.82 × 100,000.		
Deferred Transaction Gain	2,000	
Purchases		2,000
To adjust the dollar basis of Purchases recorded by the accrued transaction gain on the forward exchange contract during the commitment period.		
Purchases.	2,200	
Premium on Forward Contract		2,200
To adjust the dollar basis of purchases recorded by the portion of the premium on the forward contract pertaining to the commitment period.		

The third and fourth entries record the adjustments to the Purchases account. Purchases are decreased by the deferred transaction gain of $2,000 which accrued on the forward purchase contract during the commitment period. The commitment period covered $3\frac{2}{3}$ months of the 5-month forward purchase contract. Since the premium represents an implied interest cost, $2,200 \{= [(3\frac{2}{3})/5] \times \$3,000\}$ is recorded as an increase in Purchases. In sum, Purchases is increased by $200 (= $2,200 − $2,000).

At December 31, 19X2, a financial reporting date, both the payable to Queens, Ltd., and the forward purchase contract are still outstanding. The forward purchase contract is now hedging an exposed liability position. The spot rate has risen to $1.84/£ at December 31 from $1.82/£ on November 30. In the next two entries, the transaction adjustments on these items are accrued.

12/31/X2

Transaction Loss	2,000	
Accounts Payable		2,000

To record the transaction loss accrued on the liability to Queens, Ltd., $2,000 = ($1.84 − $1.82) 100,000.

Forward Purchase Contract	2,000	
Transaction Gain		2,000

To record the transaction gain accrued on the forward purchase contract for £100,000; $2,000 = ($1.84 − $1.82)100,000.

Note that the transaction loss on the account payable is offset by the transaction gain on the forward purchase contract. Amortization of the premium for December 19X2 (part of the exposed liability period) is as follows:

12/31/X2

Expense—Premium Amortization	600	
Premium on Forward Contract		600

To amortize one-fifth of the premium related to Dec. 19X2; $600 = .2 × $3,000.

On January 10, 19X3, the forward purchase contract matures, and the payable to Queens, Ltd., becomes due. The spot rate is $1.835/£. The next six entries record the closing out of the forward purchase contract, amortization of the remaining premium, disbursement of the foreign currency to Queens, Ltd., and accrual of the offsetting transaction loss and gain on the forward purchase contract and the account payable.

1/10/X3

Transaction Loss	500	
Forward Purchase Contract		500

To recognize the transaction loss accrued on the forward purchase contract since Dec. 31, 19X2; $500 = ($1.84 − $1.835)100,000.

Due to Exchange Broker	183,000	
Cash		183,000

To record payment to foreign exchange broker

Foreign Currency	183,500	
Forward Purchase Contract		183,500

To record receipt of the foreign currency from the broker; $183,500 = $1.835 × 100,000.

Expense—Premium Amortization	200	
Premium on Forward Contract		200

To expense the remaining premium on the forward contract; $200 = $3,000 − ($2,200 + $600).

Accounts Payable	500	
Transaction Gain		500

To recognize the transaction gain accrued on the account payable since Dec. 31, 19X2: $500 = ($1.84 − $1.835) 100,000.

Accounts Payable 183,500
    Foreign Currency   183,500
To record payment of the liability to Queens, Ltd.; $183,500 =
$180,000 + $2,000 + $2,000 − $500.

In sum, the importer uses the hedging process to fix the dollar amount of the liability to the foreign supplier at $183,000. Of the $3,000 premium, $2,200 went to increase Purchases and the other $800 was expensed. Had the hedging not taken place in the above example, Acme would have lost $3,500 [= ($1.835 − $1.80)100,000] due to the adverse exchange rate movement from the time the purchase was negotiated to final payment. Since it paid a premium of $3,000 to avoid this loss, the hedging saved Acme $500 (= $3,500 − $3,000). The decrease in Purchases from the contemplated amount of $183,000 to the recorded amount of $182,200 (= $182,000 − $2,000 + $2,200) was offset by the remaining premium amortization of $800(= $600 + $200).

Hedging a Foreign Currency Sale Commitment. In the sale case, the exporter will be receiving foreign currency and contracts to sell it for dollars to a broker at a specified time in the future for a given price. When the contract is entered before the exporter records the foreign sale and the conditions specified in *SFAS 52* are met, any transaction gain or loss which accrues during the commitment period is deferred and generates an adjustment to the dollar basis of the sale transaction. The premium or discount may be amortized proportionately over the life of the forward contract or be deferred. If the premium or discount is deferred, that portion relating to the commitment period is used to adjust the dollar basis of the sale transaction. When the contract remains in force after the sale is recorded until the receivable is subsequently collected, it becomes a *hedge of an exposed asset position*—in this case, the receivable. During this time, the remaining premium or discount is amortized. Any transaction gain or loss accruing on the forward sale contract is now recognized at a financial reporting date and is not deferred. The commitment period and the exposed asset period for a forward sale contract are depicted below:

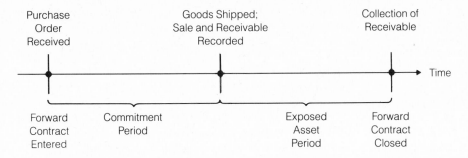

We illustrate the accounting for a forward sale contract with an example in which the sale and collection take place simultaneously. Therefore, the forward sale contract will be hedging only the foreign currency commitment; there will be no exposed asset to be hedged following the sale.

Acme International negotiated a sale of wool coats to Corsin, a Canadian retailer, on October 21, 19X2. Corsin is to pay on January 19, 19X3, when the coats are delivered (and the sale is recorded). The sale price was stated in Canadian dollars ($CN) and amounted to $CN50,000. On October 21, 19X2, the spot rate was $.96/$CN. Simultaneously, Acme sold $CN50,000 for future delivery on January 19, 19X3, at a forward rate of $.94/$CN. Acme elects to *amortize* the discount of $1,000 over the life of the contract. Since the discount is not deferred, no portion of it will be used to adjust the dollar value of the sale transaction. Subsequent spot rates were $.965/$CN on December 31, 19X2, and $.93/$CN on January 19, 19X3. Note that the balance sheet date of December 31, 19X2, falls during the commitment period, after 71 days of the 90-day commitment period have expired. The entries recording these events follow:

10/21/X2

Due from Exchange Broker ($.94 × 50,000)	47,000	
Discount on Forward Contract [($.96 − $.94)50,000]	1,000	
Forward Sale Contract ($.96 × 50,000).		48,000

To record the forward sale contract engaged in to hedge the identifiable foreign currency committment with Corsin.

12/31/X2

Deferred Transaction Loss	250	
Forward Sale Contract		250

To record the transaction loss accrued on the forward sale contract for $CN50,000; $250 = ($.965 − $.96)50,000.

Expense—Discount Amortization	789	
Discount on Forward Contract.		789

To amortize the portion of the discount relating to 19X2; $789 = (71/90)$1,000.

1/19/X3

Accounts Receivable	46,500	
Sales		46,500

To record the sale of wool coats to Corsin of Canada; $46,500 = $.93 × $CN50,000.

Foreign Currency	46,500	
Accounts Receivable		46,500

To record receipt of the foreign currency ($46,500 = $.93 × 50,000) from Corsin.

Forward Sale Contract	1,750	
Deferred Transaction Gain		1,750

To recognize the deferred transaction gain which accrued on the forward sale contract since Dec. 31, 19X2; $1,750 = ($.965 − $.93)50,000.

Forward Sale Contract	46,500	
Foreign Currency		46,500

To record disbursement of the foreign currency to the broker; $46,500 = $48,000 + $250 − $1,750.

Cash	47,000	
Due from Exchange Broker		47,000
To record payment received from the foreign exchange broker.		

Deferred Transaction Gain	1,750	
Deferred Transaction Loss		250
Sales		1,500
To adjust the dollar basis of recorded sales by the net deferred transaction gain ($1,500 = $1,750 − $250) accrued on the forward contract during the commitment period. In the example, the entire 3-month life of the contract is the commitment period.		

Expense—Discount Amortization	211	
Discount on Forward Contract.		211
To expense the remaining discount on the forward contract in 19X3; $211 = (19/90)$1,000.		

Here the exporter used the hedging process to fix the dollar amount to be received from the foreign customer at $47,000. The $1,000 discount was expensed, $789 in 19X2 and $211 in 19X3. If hedging had not been undertaken, Acme would have lost $1,500 [= ($.96 − $.93)50,000]. Because this loss was avoided, Acme actually saved $500 (= $1,500 − $1,000) by using the forward market. The increase in Sales from the contemplated amount of $47,000 to the recorded amount of $48,000 (= $46,500 + $1,500) was offset by the discount amortization of $1,000.

In this example, the forward contract expired when the transaction was recorded at the end of the commitment period. The account receivable was collected immediately, so there was no exposed asset position to be hedged. If the receivable was not collected immediately and the forward sale contract extended beyond the transaction date, offsetting transaction gains and losses would continue to accrue. Finally, the remaining period of the forward sale contract would absorb a portion of the discount amortization.

Foreign Lending and Borrowing Transactions

The growth in the volume of international capital flows indicates that substantial investment funds move across national boundaries. U.S. companies may engage in the following investment transactions requiring foreign currency conversions:

1. Investment in securities of foreign companies, banks, and governments.
2. Borrowing from foreign lenders.
3. Direct investment in branches and subsidiaries abroad.

Of these three, direct investment in branches and subsidiaries abroad is the most complex. These investment funds provide a basis for setting up a business operation, acquiring assets, and incurring debts in the foreign country. The problem associated with the translation of these items for inclusion in U.S. company financial statements are addressed in Chapter 15.

Loans and investments in securities of foreign entities often require the U.S.

firm to convert dollars into the foreign currency to acquire the security and then convert the foreign currency into dollars when the security matures or is sold. Similarly, borrowing from abroad may mean that the U.S. firm borrows a quantity of foreign currency, converts it into dollars for use domestically and later purchases sufficient foreign currency to repay the amount borrowed.

When an interest-bearing investment or note payable is denominated in a foreign currency, what exchange rate should the U.S. firm use to translate the foreign interest income or expense? Theoretically, the average exchange rate in effect while the foreign interest is accruing should be used. In contrast, the receivable, payable, or collection or disbursement of cash when the accrued interest is recorded is translated at the current exchange rate. Taken together, these practices will result in a discrepancy between the revenue or expense and the asset or liability when exchange rates are fluctuating. We avoid this by translating accrued *interest income and expense at the current exchange rate when the interest is recorded.* If interest receivable or interest payable is recorded, it will be subject to transaction gains or losses due to subsequent movements in the exchange rate.

Since all such transactions expose the U.S. firm to the risk of changes in the exchange rate, they may either (1) require a hedge to offset the risk or (2) serve as a hedge to offset the risk on another foreign currency transaction. Our illustration will involve (1) above in which investment in a foreign interest-bearing security requires a forward contract to hedge the exchange rate risk. Thus we can concurrently illustrate the accounting for the forward contract serving as a hedge of an exposed net asset position.

In the preceding section, we discussed accounting for forward contracts used to hedge individual import and export transactions. A forward contract entered prior to recording the import or export transaction was viewed as a hedge of an *identifiable foreign currency commitment.* We saw how the commitment period expired once the transaction was recorded. If payment takes place at a date subsequent to recording the transaction (as it did in our forward purchase contract example), treatment of the related forward exchange contract changes. The contract is now being used to hedge an exposed asset or liability. Any accrued transaction gains or losses are recognized currently and any premium or discount on the forward contract is amortized and not deferred.

This latter treatment applies to *all hedges* which are neither hedges of identifiable foreign currency commitments *nor* economic hedges of a net investment in a foreign entity (this is discussed later). Most forward contracts used to hedge any exposed net asset or net liability position fall into this category. Thus the items being hedged need not be assets or liabilities related to individual transactions. We illustrate this with a foreign lending transaction—investment in a foreign interest-bearing security—although it applies equally to trade receivables and payables, as in the preceding section.

Hedging an Exposed Net Asset or Exposed Net Liability Position. Foreign lending and borrowing transactions will, on an individual basis or in the aggregate, result in an **exposed net asset position** or an **exposed net liability position.** Furthermore, a U.S. company's business operations abroad may involve exposure to exchange rate risk because its monetary assets denominated in the foreign currency exceed its monetary liabilities, or vice versa. **Monetary assets and liabilities** in this context refer to cash, claims to cash, and obligations to disburse cash which are denominated in the foreign currency. These items must represent fixed quantities of foreign currency and are not susceptible to price changes; only movements in the exchange rate cause their dollar equivalents to change.

Consistent with our previous discussion, forward contracts and other foreign currency transactions are carried at their current dollar equivalents. When these transactions are used to hedge an exposed net asset or liability position, the following accounting treatment is required:

1. Accrued transaction gains or losses are to be recognized currently in income and not deferred. Current recognition serves to offset the transaction gain or loss on the item being hedged.
2. A premium or discount on a forward contract *must* be amortized to operations over the life of the contract.

As an example, we consider a U.S. investment in a foreign bank certificate of deposit and a forward sale contract to hedge an exposed net asset position, which includes the certificate of deposit. Although investment in the bank certificate of deposit contributes to the exposed net asset position, there need be no particular link between the investment and the forward contract. All we assume is that the company has sufficient asset exposure abroad to justify the forward contract.

On August 15, 19X2, Acme International purchases a 90-day certificate of deposit from a Swiss bank. The certificate has a face value of 1,000,000 Swiss francs (SF1,000,000), costs $600,000 (the spot rate is $.60/SF), and pays interest at an annual rate of 10 percent. Concurrently, Acme hedges an exposed net asset position by selling SF2,000,000 forward for delivery on February 11, 19X3; the forward rate is $.63/SF. The entries to record these transactions are:

8/15/X2

Temporary Investments	600,000	
Cash		600,000
To record the purchase of a Swiss certificate of deposit with face value of SF1,000,000 (the spot rate is $.60/SF).		

Due from Exchange Broker ($.63 × 2,000,000).	1,260,000	
Premium on Forward Contract [($.63 − $.60)2,000,000] .		60,000
Forward Sale Contract ($.60 × 2,000,000)		1,200,000
To record the forward sale contract engaged in to hedge an exposed net asset position.		

On November 13, 19X2, Acme receives SF1,025,000 [= SF1,000,000 + .1(SF1,000,000)/4] when the certificate of deposit matures; the spot rate is $.59/SF. The following three entries record the transaction adjustment on the certificate, recognize receipt of the foreign currency from the Swiss bank, and record the conversion of the Swiss francs into dollars. If the books are closed on November 13, 19X2, the accrued transaction gain on the forward contract would also be recognized, thereby offsetting the transaction loss on the temporary investments.

11/13/X2

Transaction Loss	10,000	
Temporary Investments		10,000

To recognize the transaction loss accrued on the certificate of deposit; $10,000 = (\$.60 - \$.59)1,000,000$.

Foreign Currency ($\$.59 \times 1,025,000$)	604,750	
Temporary Investments ($\$600,000 - \$10,000$)		590,000
Interest Income ($\$.59 \times 25,000$)		14,750

To record the foreign currency (SF1,025,000) received at maturity of the certificate of deposit and record the interest income based on the exchange rate when the interest is recorded.

Cash	604,750	
Foreign Currency		604,750

To record the exchange of SF1,025,000 for $604,750.

Acme closes its books on December 31, 19X2, at which time it records the transaction adjustment accrued on the forward contract and amortizes the portion of the premium relating to 19X2. The spot rate is $.62/SF. Note that the transaction loss on the forward sale contract is not deferred—it offsets the transaction gain on the exposed net asset position which it is hedging (not recorded here).

12/31/X2

Transaction Loss	40,000	
Forward Sale Contract		40,000

To record the transaction loss accrued on the forward sale contract in 19X2; $40,000 = (\$.62 - \$.60)2,000,000$.

Premium on Forward Contract	46,000	
Revenue—Premium Amortization		46,000

To amortize the portion of the premium relating to 19X2; $46,000 = (138/180)\$60,000$.

Finally, the forward contract is settled on February 11, 19X3, when the spot rate is $.635/SF. The following entries recognize the transaction adjustment accrued since December 31, 19X2, settlement of the contract, and amortization of the remaining premium:

2/11/X3

Transaction Loss	30,000	
Forward Sale Contract		30,000

To recognize the transaction loss accrued on the forward sale contract since Dec. 31, 19X2; $30,000 = (\$.635 - \$.62)2,000,000$.

Forward Sale Contract	1,270,000	
Foreign Currency		1,270,000

To record disbursement of foreign currency assumed to be on hand to the broker; $1,270,000 (=\$.635 \times 2,000,000)$.

```
Cash . . . . . . . . . . . . . . . . . . . . . . . . . . . . . .   1,260,000
    Due from Exchange Broker . . . . . . . . . . . . . . . .                 1,260,000
To record payment from the foreign exchange broker.

Premium on Forward Contract . . . . . . . . . . . . . .      14,000
    Revenue—Premium Amortization. . . . . . . . . . . .                        14,000
To amortize the portion of the premium relating to 19X3;
$14,000 = (42/180)$60,000.
```

The above entries deal only with the forward contract. Since it is hedging an exposed net asset position (not recorded here), the transaction loss of $30,000 is offset by the transaction gain on the exposed net asset position. This gain, which has not been recorded here, arises because the increase in the spot rate to $.635/SF produces an increase in the dollar equivalent of the exposed net asset position.

Economic Hedge of a Net Investment in a Foreign Entity

SFAS 52 also recognizes as hedges those forward contracts or other foreign currency transactions undertaken to neutralize the effect of exchange rate movements on a U.S. firm's investment in a foreign branch, an equity investee, or a subsidiary. If a hedge is so designated and is effective, it is viewed as an **economic hedge of a net investment in a foreign entity.** Accounting treatment of the transaction gain or loss on such "economic hedges" depends on the **functional currency** of the foreign entity (the currency in which the foreign entity generates most of its net cash flows), a concept discussed in detail in Chapter 15. Briefly, if the *functional currency* of the foreign entity is the *U.S. dollar,* the transaction gain or loss on the hedge is included in net income; if the hedge is a forward contract, any premium or discount is amortized over the life of the contract.

In contrast, if the *functional currency* of the foreign entity is a *foreign currency,* the transaction gain or loss on the hedge is carried directly to a separate component of stockholders' equity, bypassing periodic net income. If the hedge is a forward contract, any premium or discount may be amortized over the life of the contract *or* may be carried directly to the special component of stockholders' equity.

Use of Forward Contracts for Speculation

Forward contracts engaged in for hedging purposes represent defensive measures to protect against exchange rate movements adversely affecting the firm's foreign currency exposure. In contrast, firms may often sell or purchase foreign currency forward for **speculative purposes**—to gain from anticipated changes in the exchange rate. Suppose Acme's management believed that, despite the 180-day forward rate of $.63/SF, the spot rate for Swiss francs would be $.57/SF in 180 days. To speculate, Acme might sell 5,000,000 Swiss francs forward for delivery in 180 days. Such a contract would be for $3,150,000 (= $.63 × 5,000,000). If Acme is right, in 180 days it will be able to purchase SF5,000,000 for $2,850,000 (=$.57 × 5,000,000) to cover the forward sale and realize a gain of $300,000. Should the spot rate in 180 days be above $.63/SF, of course, Acme will incur a loss. *SFAS 52* provides the following accounting rules for such speculative forward contracts:

1. Both the amount due to or from the exchange broker and the forward exchange contract are recorded at the *forward* rate. As a result, neither discount nor premium is separately measured.
2. Transaction gains and losses are to be based on the difference between the forward rate specified in the contract and the forward rate for the period remaining until settlement and are to be recorded currently.

Note the contrast with the accounting rules governing hedges. Forward exchange contracts used for hedging are measured using the current spot rate; speculative contracts are measured using the forward rate for the remaining period in the contract. Transaction gains and losses for hedges derive from movements in the spot rate; for speculations, they derive from movements in the forward rates. Finally, any discount or premium is explicitly accounted for in the hedge and implicitly in the speculative contract.

To illustrate, suppose Acme decides to speculate in the Dutch guilder (G) by purchasing, on November 1, 19X2, G8,000,000 for delivery in 90 days. Acme will cover the contract by selling guilders in the spot market on January 29, 19X3. Relevant exchange rates ($/G) are as follows:

Date	Spot Rate	Forward Rate
November 1, 19X2	$.500	$.470 (90-day)
December 31, 19X2	.495	.465 (30-day)
January 29, 19X3	.462	—

Acme records the events relating to this speculative forward contract as follows:

11/1/X2

Forward Purchase Contract	3,760,000	
Due to Exchange Broker		3,760,000

To record a forward purchase contract calling for delivery of G8,000,000 in 90 days at the forward rate of $.47/G; $3,760,000 = $.47 × 8,000,000.

12/31/X2

Transaction Loss	40,000	
Forward Purchase Contract		40,000

To recognize the transaction loss accrued on the forward contract, $40,000 = ($.47 − $.465)8,000,000, and to revalue it based on the 30-day forward rate.

1/29/X3

Transaction Loss	24,000	
Forward Purchase Contract		24,000

To recognize the transaction loss accrued on the forward purchase contract since Dec. 31, 19X2; $24,000 = ($.465 − $.462)8,000,000.

```
Foreign Currency . . . . . . . . . . . . . . . . . . . . . .  3,696,000
   Forward Purchase Contract. . . . . . . . . . . . . . . .              3,696,000
To record receipt of the foreign currency from the broker;
$3,696,000 = $.462 × 8,000,000 = $3,760,000 −
$40,000 − $24,000.

Due to Exchange Broker . . . . . . . . . . . . . . . . . .  3,760,000
   Cash . . . . . . . . . . . . . . . . . . . . . . . . . . . .              3,760,000
To record payment to the foreign exchange broker.

Cash . . . . . . . . . . . . . . . . . . . . . . . . . . . . .  3,696,000
   Foreign Currency . . . . . . . . . . . . . . . . . . . . .              3,696,000
To record sale of the G8,000,000 in the spot market
at $.462/G.
```

We can see clearly that the total transaction loss recognized in the accounts, $64,000 ($= \$40,000 + \$24,000$), equals the net cash loss of $64,000 ($= \$3,760,000 - \$3,696,000$) from the speculative activity. Note that had a discount been recorded at November 1, 19X2, when the forward contract was entered, the total loss would still be $64,000. The discount would have a credit balance of $240,000 [$= (\$.50 - \$.47)8,000,000$], but the forward purchase contract would have produced a transaction loss of $304,000 [$= (\$.50 - \$.462)8,000,000$], exactly $64,000 more than the revenue effect of the discount amortization.

Summary of Accounting for Forward Exchange Contracts

In all forward contracts, the account *Due to (from) Exchange Broker* is denominated in dollars. It fixes the number of dollars to be paid to (or received from) the exchange broker based on the appropriate forward rate when the contract is signed. Consequently, it does not move with the exchange rate and does not generate transaction gains and losses. It is the account *Forward Exchange Contract* which is denominated in the foreign currency. Its dollar value does change with the exchange rate and transaction gains and losses accrue to it. In the published financial statements, these two accounts generally are offset against each other and only the net amount is shown as a current asset or liability in the balance sheet.

The accounting treatments prescribed for forward exchange contracts by *SFAS 52* are summarized in Exhibit 14.2. These rules may seem unnecessarily complex. Nevertheless, the underlying rationale appears reasonable. Since the hedge of an identifiable foreign currency commitment is an integral part of the entire transaction, it is appropriate to defer transaction gains and losses until the transaction is recorded. Other hedges may not be related to specific transactions and may contain an element of speculation. Hence the transaction gains and losses on other hedges are recognized currently, but a portion of the premium or discount is deferred via the amortization process when the contract's life spans more than one accounting period. Finally, speculative contracts have as their main product the generation of gains or losses from movements in exchange rates. These transaction gains and losses are recognized currently as they occur with no deferral at

Exhibit 14.2 Summary of Accounting for Forward Exchange Contracts

Purpose of Contract	Balance Sheet Valuation		Treatment of Transaction Gain or Loss	Treatment of Discount or Premium
	Amount Due to (from) Broker	Forward Exchange Contract		
To hedge an identifiable foreign currency commitment.	Fixed at the dollar equivalent of the foreign currency translated at the forward rate.	Varies with the dollar equivalent of the foreign currency translated at the spot rate.	Deferred during the commitment period until the transaction is recorded;[a] used to adjust the dollar basis of the recorded transaction.	Deferred during the commitment period or amortized over the life of the contract. If deferred, the portion pertaining to the commitment period is used to adjust the dollar basis of the recorded transaction. Any remaining amount is amortized over the contract's remaining life.
To hedge an exposed net asset or net liability position.	Fixed at the dollar equivalent of the foreign currency translated at the forward rate.	Varies with the dollar equivalent of the foreign currency translated at the spot rate.	Recognized in income currently as it accrues; not deferred.	Amortized over the life of the contract.
Economic hedge of a net investment in a foreign entity.	Fixed at the dollar equivalent of the foreign currency translated at the forward rate.	Varies with the dollar equivalent of the foreign currency translated at the spot rate.	Recognized in income currently as it accrues if functional currency is U.S. dollar; carried directly to separate component of stockholders' equity if functional currency is a foreign currency.	Amortized over the life of the contract if functional currency is U.S. dollar; amortized over the life of the contract or carried directly to separate component of stockholders' equity if functional currency is a foreign currency.
Speculation.	Fixed at the dollar equivalent of the foreign currency translated at the forward rate.	Varies with the dollar equivalent of the foreign currency translated at the forward rate for the remaining life of the contract.	Recognized in income currently as it accrues; not deferred.	Included as part of gain or loss but not recognized separately.

Note: The notes to this exhibit are at the top of page 719.

[a]Paragraph 21 of *SFAS 52* states that deferral of transaction losses on forward contracts is not appropriate if deferral could lead to recognition of losses in subsequent periods. For example, if the loss exceeds the expected gross profit (less costs of sale or disposal) on a sale transaction that has been hedged, it should *not* be deferred until that sale transaction is complete.

Source: Financial Accounting Standards Board, *Statement of Financial Accounting Standards No. 52*, "Foreign Currency Translation" (Stamford, CT: FASB, 1981, pars. 17–21; CT § F60.124–127.

---

all, and there is no separate measurement of the premium or discount on a speculative forward contract.

This completes our discussion of accounting for foreign currency transactions. These transactions produce assets or liabilities on the U.S. company's books which are denominated in foreign currencies. Even though some variations apply to certain forward contracts, the general accounting for foreign currency transactions may be summarized as follows:

1. Record the asset or liability when it arises, using the current spot rate.
2. Adjust the carrying value of the asset or liability to its current dollar equivalent when it is settled and at any intervening balance sheet dates by using the spot rates at these dates.
3. Recognize the transaction gain or loss arising in No. 2 in current income, except in the case of certain hedges.

In the next chapter, we address the problems associated with the need to translate the foreign currency financial statements of foreign entities into dollars for inclusion in U.S. accounting reports, and we consider the international environment of accounting.

Summary of Key Concepts

The price of one currency in terms of another is called a **foreign exchange rate.** The **spot rate** is the price for immediate delivery of the foreign currency. Delivery at a specified time in the future can be contracted at the appropriate **forward** or **futures rate** with a foreign exchange broker or dealer.

Import/export transactions and borrowing and lending abroad by domestic companies often generate **receivables and payables denominated in a foreign currency.** As the exchange rate rises (falls), the number of dollars ultimately to be received or paid increases (decreases). These changes in the dollar equivalents of these receivables and payables generate **transaction gains and losses** (or **transaction adjustments**) which are recognized by the domestic company as they occur.

Forward exchange contracts (and other foreign currency transactions) are often used to **hedge** the risk of gain or loss from movements in the exchange rate as explained above. When the contract covers some time after a transaction has been negotiated but before it is recorded, it hedges an **identifiable foreign currency commitment.** If the contract remains in effect after the transaction is recorded, it hedges an **exposed asset (liability) position.** Many forward contracts cover both the commitment and exposed periods.

When the forward rate is greater than (less than) the current spot rate, there will be a premium (discount) on the forward contract. The **premium or discount** may be deferred during **the commitment period** or **amortized over the entire life of the contract.** The amount deferred during the commitment period should be proportional to the total life of the contract and is used to adjust the dollar basis of the transaction. The balance is amortized over the remaining life of the contract.

Transaction gains and losses accrue to the forward purchase (sale) contract, **not** to the amount due to (from) the exchange broker. The net transaction adjustment accruing during the **commitment period** is **deferred** and is used to adjust the dollar basis of the transaction. **Once the transaction is recorded,** an exposed liability or asset position results. **Further** transaction gains or losses accruing to the forward contract **are recognized as they occur.**

A forward contract or other foreign currency transaction may serve as an **economic hedge of a net investment in a foreign entity.** If the foreign entity's **functional currency is the U.S. dollar,** transaction gains and losses are recognized in **income currently;** any **premium or discount** on a forward contract is amortized. If the **functional currency is a foreign currency,** transaction adjustments are carried directly to **stockholders' equity;** any premium or discount on a forward contract may be carried to **stockholders' equity** or be **amortized.**

A forward purchase (sale) contract may be entered solely in anticipation of an increase (decrease) in the spot rate, that is, for **speculative reasons.** In such cases, there is **no hedging,** no separate measurement of premium or discount, and all transaction gains and losses are recognized currently as they accrue.

Appendix to Chapter 14   Accounting for Futures Contracts

In this chapter we discussed extensively the accounting for forward contracts in foreign currencies as a natural component of accounting for foreign currency transactions. Because of the dramatic growth in other forms of futures trading and the emergence of accounting standards, however, this appendix provides an introductory examination of accounting for futures contracts *not* involving foreign currencies. Whereas *SFAS 52* prescribes accounting standards for foreign currency forward contracts (or futures), *SFAS 80,* ''Accounting for Futures Contracts,''[11] from which the definition below was taken, proposes accounting standards for all futures contracts *other than* those involving foreign currencies—principally *commodity futures* and *interest rate futures.* Nevertheless, the terminology and the accounting can easily be related to the foreign currency case. The FASB defines a **futures contract** as follows:

> A legal agreement between a buyer or seller and the *clearinghouse* of a *futures exchange* . . . in the United States and . . . in other countries. . . . (a) They obligate the purchaser (seller) to accept (make) delivery of a *standardized quantity* of a commodity or financial instrument at a *specified date* or during a specified period, or they provide for *cash settlement rather than delivery,* (b) they *effectively can be canceled before the delivery date* by entering into an offsetting contract for the same commodity or financial instrument, and (c) all changes in value of open contracts are *settled on a regular basis,* usually daily. [Emphasis added][12]

A futures contract can be closed out without delivery by entering an identical contract. Indeed, actual delivery is rarely intended and occurs infrequently. Changes in market value are settled in cash on a daily basis.

In contrast, foreign currency forward contracts are usually made with dealers in foreign exchange and are tailored to fit the needs of the transacting entity. Delivery of the subject currency is intended and does occur. Changes in market value of a forward contract constitute accounting events, but cash is not actually transferred until the contract matures and the currency is delivered.

Commodity futures, which involve contracting for future delivery of specified fungible commodities such as agricultural products and precious metals, were mentioned early in the chapter. They have been in existence for well over 100 years. **Interest rate futures,** however, have essentially developed within the last decade. ''An interest rate futures contract is a contract to make or take delivery of a certain type of interest-bearing security at some future time. The price that will be received (or paid) is based on the price of the particular futures contract when a trade is executed.''[13] That is, the price of the futures contract, when entered, fixes the price to be received or paid for the securities.

U.S. Treasury bills and bonds and Eurodollar deposits are the most common interest rate futures. Prices are normally stated as an index, a percentage of 100 or face value, which reflects *annual* yield. Thus if the futures price is 89, one of the above securities will be delivered at a *discount yield* of 11 ($= 100 - 89$).

---

[11]Financial Accounting Standards Board, *Statement of Financial Accounting Standards No. 80,* ''Accounting for Futures Contracts'' (Stamford, CT: FASB, 1984).

[12]Ibid., par. 15.

[13]Larry M. Walther, ''Commodity Futures: What the Accountant Should Know,'' *Journal of Accountancy* (March, 1982), 78.

Transacting in Futures Contracts

Futures contracts rarely result in actual delivery. Rather, those entities transacting in the futures markets settle (close) their position at some time during the term of the contract by entering an offsetting position. Actual sale of the commodities or securities generally takes place in cash or spot markets. An entity using futures contracts traded on an organized exchange encounters two types of accounting events prior to settlement of the contract:

1. An *initial margin deposit*—cash or government securities—must be paid to the broker upon inception of the contract. The margin deposit ranges from less than 1 percent of face value on some interest rate futures contracts to over 10 percent on some commodity futures. This is not a commission or transaction cost; rather, it represents a performance bond.
2. At the end of each trading day, the clearinghouse values each outstanding contract at the closing price. The contract is thereby "marked to market" and the entity must either deposit additional funds with the broker—a realized loss—or receive cash or a credit to its account from the broker—a realized gain—for the change in the value of the contract. The amount deposited, however, cannot fall below the applicable *maintenance margin*.

If the entity has a *long* position (it is a *purchaser* of futures), an increase in price produces a gain and a decrease in price produces a loss. The entity could choose to close out its long position by selling its long contract and lock in the realized gain or loss. Similarly, if the entity has a *short* position (it is a *seller* of futures), an increase in price produces a loss and a decrease in price produces a gain. Here the entity could close out its short position by purchasing a long contract, again locking in the realized gain or loss.

For example, suppose an entity purchases commodity futures (goes *long*) for 100,000 units at $7.50 per unit and sells (goes *short*) $1,000,000 face value interest rate futures (91-day Treasury bills) at 88. At the close of the next trading day, the commodity futures are selling at $7.60 per unit and the interest rate futures have increased to 88.5. The entity realizes a *gain* of $10,000 [= ($7.60 − $7.50) 100,000] on the commodity futures (it would receive an additional $.10 per unit if it sold the long contract to close out its long position). At the same time, the entity realizes a *loss* of $5,000 [= (.88 − .885) $1,000,000] on the interest rate futures (it would have to pay an additional $.005 per dollar if it purchased a long contract to close out its short position).

Accounting Standards

With the basic economics in mind, we now consider the fundamental accounting issue relating to treatment of the realized gain or loss on a futures contract. Should it be recognized in income immediately or should it be deferred? *SFAS 80* provides for *immediate recognition in income, unless* the contract is an *effective hedge* of one of the following:

1. An *existing exposure* (ownership of or liability to deliver the commodity).
2. A *firm commitment* (legally enforceable obligation to make or accept delivery of the commodity).
3. An *anticipated transaction* (performance is intended and expected but not legally enforceable).

An **effective hedge** arises if the item to be hedged exposes the entity to price or interest rate risk and the futures contract reduces that exposure and is designated as a hedge.[14] The entity must expect high correlation between the market value of the futures contract and the fair value or interest rate on the hedged item.

Even in these cases, however, *if the hedged item is carried at market,* with concurrent recognition of changes in market values in income as gains or losses, changes in the market value of the futures contract serving as the hedge will also be *recognized currently in income.* Accounting treatment of realized gains and losses on hedges of items not carried at market value may be summarized as follows:

1. *Existing exposure:* Gain or loss adjusts the carrying value of the hedged item, whether carried at cost or lower of cost or market.
2. *Firm commitment:* Gain or loss is deferred and adjusts the dollar basis of the transaction occurring when the commitment is fulfilled.
3. *Anticipated transaction:* Gain or loss is deferred and adjusts the dollar basis of the related subsequent transaction when it occurs.

While the accounting for Nos. 2 and 3 above is identical (both are similar to the hedge of an identifiable foreign currency commitment discussed in the chapter), No. 3 represents a rather broad hedging concept and is the subject of considerable controversy. Paragraph 9 of *SFAS 80* discusses two conditions, both of which must be met if a futures contract related to an anticipated transaction is to be treated as a hedge with concurrent deferral of realized gains and losses. These conditions specify (1) that the significant characteristics and expected terms of the anticipated transaction be identified and (2) that it be probable that the anticipated transaction will occur.

Unlike the accounting for foreign currency forward contracts prescribed in *SFAS 52*—requiring that the dollar amount of the entire contract be recorded at inception—*SFAS 80* requires that for other futures contracts only the margin deposit with the broker be recorded at inception. The reason for this difference is that because delivery is presumed in the foreign currency case, the accounts should reflect the dollar amount of the entire contract. In contrast, other futures contracts are normally closed out prior to the delivery date; only the margin deposit is significant.

---

[14]*SFAS 80,* op. cit., par. 4.

Illustrations of Accounting for Futures Contracts

We conclude this appendix with a series of examples demonstrating how the provisions of *SFAS 80* are applied. In each example, the futures contract is closed out prior to delivery. Brokerage commissions and other transaction costs are ignored.

Example 1: Hedge of an Exposed Asset Position. An entity owns 100,000 units of a commodity carried in Inventory at cost, $800,000. The commodity will be sold in the normal course of business in 90 days, and the entity wishes to guarantee the current 90-day futures price of $900,000. Thus it sells commodity futures (goes *short*) for delivery in 90 days for $900,000. A margin deposit of $60,000 is recorded as follows:

```
Margin Deposit with Broker . . . . . . . . . . . . . . . . . .    60,000
  Cash . . . . . . . . . . . . . . . . . . . . . . . . . . . .              60,000
To record the initial margin deposit on the sale of $900,000 in
commodity futures.
```

By the end of the next accounting period, we assume that the futures price has decreased to $850,000 and that the company decides to close out the futures contract and lock in the realized gain of $50,000 (= $900,000 − $850,000). Since this is a hedge of an *existing exposure,* the realized gain *reduces the carrying value of the hedged inventory*. When the inventory is sold, this reduced carrying value will be charged to Cost of Goods Sold and the gain recognized as a component of gross profit.

```
Margin Deposit with Broker . . . . . . . . . . . . . . . . . .    50,000
  Inventory . . . . . . . . . . . . . . . . . . . . . . . . . .            50,000
To adjust the carrying value of the hedged inventory by the gain
realized on the futures contract.

Cash . . . . . . . . . . . . . . . . . . . . . . . . . . . . . .  110,000
  Margin Deposit with Broker . . . . . . . . . . . . . . . . .            110,000
To record receipt of cash from the broker, including the $60,000
initial margin, when the futures contract is closed out.
```

Example 2: Hedge of a Firm Liability Commitment. An entity contracts with a financing syndicate to issue (roll over) $1,000,000 face value of commercial paper every 90 days. The current annual interest rate on such issues is 12 percent; on U.S. Treasury bills it is 10.5 percent. The yield on Treasury bills is highly correlated with the yield on the entity's commercial paper. To hedge against the possibility that interest rates will rise in 90 days, the entity sells (goes *short*) $1,000,000 face value of 91-day Treasury bill (interest rate) futures at 89.5 (= 100 − annual discount yield of 10.5 percent) and deposits $2,500 cash with the broker as margin:

Margin Deposit with Broker 2,500
    Cash   2,500
To record the initial margin deposit on the sale of $1,000,000
face value 91-day Treasury bill futures.

At the end of the 90-day period, the futures price has risen to 92.3 and the entity has realized a loss of $7,000 [= (.895 − .923) $1,000,000/4] because these are 91-day Treasury bills and the futures price reflects *annual* yields. The entity closes out its short position and rolls over its commercial paper:

Deferred Loss on Futures Contract 7,000
    Cash   7,000
To record the realized loss on the futures contract, deferring
it pending issue of the new commercial paper, and transfer
$7,000 cash to the broker.

Cash 2,500
    Margin Deposit with Broker   2,500
To record receipt of the initial margin deposit from the broker
when the futures contract is closed out. In effect, the $7,000
transferred to the broker above is the incremental cost of
offsetting the short position entered at 89.5 with a long
position entered at 92.3.

Short-Term Notes Payable (Old) 1,000,000
    Short-Term Notes Payable (New).   1,000,000
To roll over the commercial paper.

Discount on Short-Term Notes Payable (New) 7,000
    Deferred Loss on Futures Contract   7,000
To reclassify the deferred loss on the futures contract entered
to hedge the new notes payable as a *discount* on those new
notes payable.

In addition to coupon interest on the new commercial paper, the $7,000 discount on the liability will be amortized to interest expense over the 90-day term of the commercial paper. Note that at 92.3, Treasury bills have an annual yield of 7.7 percent (= 100 − 92.3). Assuming that the 1.5 percent (= 12 percent − 10.5 percent) spread between the entity's commercial paper and Treasury bills still holds, the new commerical paper will pay interest at the rate of 9.2 percent (= 7.7 percent + 1.5 percent). The $7,000 loss is exactly offset by the reduced interest on the new issue, $7,000 [= (.12 − .092) $1,000,000/4]. Effectively, the old 12 percent rate has been maintained for another 90-day period. Had the hedge *not* been undertaken, however, the interest cost on the new commercial paper would be only 9.2 percent. Thus the hedge could be criticized, even though it was effective.

In contrast, if interest rates had risen, the futures price would have fallen. This would have produced a *gain* on the futures contract which will be offset by the increased interest the entity must pay on the new commercial paper.

Example 3: Hedge of an Anticipated Purchase. A jewelry manufacturer is planning its silver requirements over the next several months. The entity anticipates an increase in the demand for silver jewelry with a concurrent upward movement in the price of silver. Although it is not contractually required to supply silver jewelry to its customers, the entity expects to do so because it fears loss of customers if it does not supply the jewelry ordered at competitive prices. Therefore, to guarantee a supply of silver at relatively favorable prices, the entity purchases (goes *long*) 20,000 ounces of silver bullion for delivery in 90 days at $7.70 per ounce and makes a margin deposit of $20,000 cash with the broker:

Margin Deposit with Broker	20,000	
Cash		20,000
To record the initial margin deposit of $20,000 on the purchase of $154,000 (= $7.70 × 20,000) of silver futures.		

Over the next 3 months, the futures price increases to $7.90 per ounce, as the entity had predicted. A gain of $4,000 [= ($7.90 − $7.70) 20,000] has been realized. The entity closes out its long position and, several days later, purchases the silver it needs on the spot market for $7.88 per ounce. These events are recorded as follows:

Margin Deposit with Broker	4,000	
Deferred Gain on Futures Contract		4,000
To record the gain on the futures contract, which increases the deposit with the broker, and defer it pending completion of the anticipated transaction.		
Cash	24,000	
Margin Deposit with Broker		24,000
To record receipt of cash from the broker, including the initial $20,000 deposit, when the futures contract is closed out.		
Inventory	157,600	
Cash		157,600
To record the purchase of 20,000 ounces of silver bullion at $7.88 per ounce on the spot market.		
Deferred Gain on Futures Contract	4,000	
Inventory		4,000
To adjust the carrying value of the silver bullion just purchased— the anticipated transaction has occurred—by the deferred gain on the futures contract.		

Note that the hedge effectively locked in the price of $7.70 per ounce. Even though a gain was realized, it was offset by the higher current cost of the actual silver purchase.

Concluding Remarks

Strategies involving futures contracts can become very complex and often involve combinations of long and short positions as well as various types of hedging and speculative activities. Similarly, the accounting for such transactions can become complex.[15] Moreover, the accounting standards are evolving. Areas of controversy relate to anticipated transactions and treatment of realized gains and losses on futures contracts which hedge items carried at lower of cost or market.

Questions

Q14.1 What is the major change that took place in the international monetary system during the 1970s? Briefly explain why this change took place.

Q14.2 Those U.S. firms engaged in transactions denominated in currencies other than the dollar generally have additional decisions to make. Describe the basic cause of these extra decisions. What can management do to deal with this problem?

Q14.3 The Barber Corporation is considering developing some overseas markets for its products. Credit and payment policies for overseas customers are two of several matters being considered. You have been engaged by Barber to explain the accounting implications of export transactions as well as to give general advice on the subject to Barber's controller. What special risks would be faced by Barber in overseas markets? What kinds of general information should be considered in formulating credit and payment policies for foreign customers?

Q14.4 Describe the *hedging* process and identify its costs and benefits.

Q14.5 Suppose that interest rates on 6-month certificates of deposit are 12 percent in the United States and 10 percent in the United Kingdom. Based on this information alone, would you expect pounds sterling to be delivered in 6 months to sell at a premium over or discount from the spot rate? Explain.

Q14.6 A manager once remarked that "all of these accounting problems related to import/export transactions and forward contracts represent unnecessary complications. Denominating all foreign transactions of domestic firms in units of domestic currency would render these problems irrelevant." Is the manager's analysis correct? Explain.

Q14.7 If a forward contract is entered to hedge an identifiable foreign currency commitment, transaction gains and losses accruing during the commitment period are deferred and used to adjust the dollar basis of the transaction. What is the logic behind this rule?

---

[15]For additional reading, see Arthur Andersen & Co., *Accounting for Interest Rate Futures Transactions* (Chicago: Arthur Andersen & Co., 1982); William C. Rupert, "Accounting for Financial and Commodity Futures," *Highlights of Financial Reporting Issues* (Stamford, CT: FASB, Sept. 19, 1983); and Paul Munter, Donald J. Clancy, and Tommy Moores, "Accounting for Futures Contracts," *CPA Journal* (March 1985), 18–25.

Q14.8 The Armen Company has outstanding receivables, denominated in pounds sterling (£), of £1,000,000. If Armen sells £1,000,000 forward for delivery in 30 days when the receivables are to be collected, is this likely to be an *effective hedge?* Why or why not?

Q14.9 The Camel Company purchases 1,000,000 deutsche marks (DM) for delivery in 6 months at the forward rate of $.57/DM, recognizing a liability to the exchange broker of $570,000. As the weeks and months pass, both the spot and forward rates for deutsche marks fluctuate. How is Camel's liability to the exchange broker affected as the exchange rates move up and down?

Q14.10 *SFAS 52* requires that the premium or discount on a forward contract entered to hedge an exposed asset or liability position be amortized to operations over the life of the contract. Comment on the propriety of this treatment.

Q14.11 Accounting for a forward contract entered for speculative purposes calls for valuation of the forward exchange contract at the forward rate for the remaining life of the contract. No premium or discount is separately measured, even though one will typically exist. Explain why you feel this rule is consistent or inconsistent with accounting for forward contracts entered for nonspeculative reasons.

Q14.12 *SFAS 52* introduced the concept of a foreign currency transaction entered into to serve as an "economic hedge of a net investment in a foreign entity." Explain this concept and indicate how transaction adjustments accruing to such hedges are treated.

Exercises

E14.1 The Eastern Merchandise Company imports a variety of items for resale to U.S. retailers. During one month it made the following purchases (on credit) and payments:

Country	Amount	Currency	Spot Rate at Purchase	Spot Rate at Payment
Australia	15,000	Australian Dollar	$1.100	$1.130
Finland.	42,000	Markka	.260	.250
Indonesia.	730,000	Rupiah	.002	.003
Turkey	80,000	Lira	.060	.060

Required: Give the journal entries made by Eastern to record the above purchase and payment transactions.

E14.2 Western Exports sells many different items abroad. During one month it made the following sales (on credit) and collections:

Country	Amount	Currency	Spot Rate at Sale	Spot Rate at Collection
Austria	25,000	Schilling	$ .074	$ .082
Greece	400,000	Drachma	.028	.025
Iraq	300,000	Dinar	.014	.017
South Africa	10,000	Rand	1.150	1.140

Required: Give the journal entries made by Western to record the above sale and collection transactions.

E14.3 Walsh Corporation imports raw materials from foreign countries and exports finished goods to customers throughout the world. Information regarding four such transactions, all denominated in units of foreign currency (FC), is given below:

Transaction	Amount (FC)	Spot Rate at Transaction Date	Spot Rate at Payment Date
1. (Import)	30,000	$1.10	$1.15
2. (Import)	100,000	.30	.28
3. (Export)	50,000	.97	.93
4. (Export)	40,000	.16	.17

Required: Prepare the journal entries made by Walsh to record the above on the transaction date and on the payment date.

E14.4 On September 15, 19X3, the Haskell Company agreed to purchase 5,000 radios from a South Korean company for a total invoice price of 12,000,000 won (W). The radios are received on October 15 and payment made on November 14. Concurrently, on September 15, 19X3, Haskell purchased W12,000,000 for delivery on November 14, 19X3. Haskell's accounting practice is to defer a premium or discount on a forward contract during the commitment period. Relevant exchange rates ($/W) are as follows:

	9/15/X3	10/15/X3	11/14/X3
Spot Rate	$.002	$.0021	$.0022
Sixty-Day Forward Rate	.00185	—	—

Required: Prepare the journal entries made by Haskell on September 15, 19X3, October 15, 19X3, and November 14, 19X3.

E14.5 On December 1, 19X1, Diversified Industries purchased merchandise from a Belgian firm, at a price of 32,000 francs, payable in 60 days. Diversified also sold merchandise to a firm in Uruguay, at a price of 40,000 pesos, to be collected in 60 days. No forward exchange contracts were used. The following exchange rates existed:

Date	$/Franc	$/Peso
Dec. 1, 19X1	$.029	$.220
Dec. 31, 19X1	.032	.225
Jan. 29, 19X2	.033	.207

Required: Determine the amount of exchange gain or loss to be reported by Diversified Industries in its 19X1 and 19X2 income statements. Show all calculations.

E14.6 On August 18, 19X9, the Cup-of-Kava Company imports 6,000 bags of coffee from a Brazilian grower. The invoice price is for 20,000,000 cruzeiros, payable in cruzeiros on October 31, 19X9. Cup-of-Kava immediately enters into a forward exchange contract for delivery of 20,000,000 cruzeiros on October 31, 19X9. The forward rate specified in the contract is $.072. The spot rate on August 18, 19X9, is $.07. On October 31, 19X9, the spot rate is $.069.

Required:

1. Calculate the discount or premium on the forward exchange contract.
2. Calculate the exchange gain or loss incurred by Cup-of-Kava.
3. Calculate the exchange gain or loss that would have been incurred if Cup-of-Kava had not hedged by entering into the forward exchange contract.

E14.7 The Livingstone Company, a calendar-year corporation, manufactures various kinds of filter materials. On April 15, 19X4, Livingstone received an order from a diamond-mining company in South Africa for a large quantity of reusable filters to be used in the dust masks of diamond miners. The total price in rands (R) was R12,000. Livingstone planned on shipping the filters on April 30, 19X4, and payment is to be received in rands on May 15, 19X4. Upon receipt of the purchase order, Livingstone immediately sells R12,000 for delivery in 30 days. The firm's practice is to amortize any premium or discount on a forward contract over the life of the contract. Relevant exchange rates ($/R) are shown below:

	4/15/X4	4/30/X4	5/15/X4
Spot Rate	$1.15	$1.16	$1.19
Thirty-Day Forward Rate	1.18	—	—

Required: Prepare the journal entries made by Livingstone on April 15, 19X4, April 30, 19X4, and May 15, 19X4.

E14.8 On April 1, 19X1, Hoover Corporation placed an order for 8,000 cameras with a West German firm. The invoice price is 1,600,000 deutsche marks (DM). To protect itself against adverse movements in the exchange rate, Hoover immediately enters into a forward contract for delivery of DM 1,600,000 on July 1, 19X1, the date payment is to be made. The forward rate specified in the contract is $.486. The spot rate on April 1, 19X1, is $.50; it increases to $.51 on July 1, 19X1. It is $.503 on June 1, 19X1, when the cameras are delivered.

Required:

1. Identify the type of forward contract (purchase or sale) entered into by Hoover.
2. Based on the information given, are interest rates higher or lower in West Germany than in the United States?
3. Give the entry made to record the forward contract on April 1, 19X1.
4. Calculate the exchange gain or loss incurred by Hoover.
5. Calculate the exchange gain or loss that would have been incurred by Hoover had the camera transaction not been hedged.

E14.9 The Carolina Company's books reflected the following receivables (payables) denominated in foreign currency (FC) units prior to closing on December 31. The spot rates at December 31 are also given.

Item	Amount $	FC	Spot Rate ($/FC)
1.	$ 100,000	FC1,000,000	$ .09
2.	180,000	225,000	.82
3.	(500,000)	(400,000)	1.30
4.	(50,000)	(200,000)	.24

Required: Prepare the adjusting entry recorded by Carolina at December 31. Show all calculations.

E14.10 To take advantage of high short-term interest rates, Carlton Enterprises purchased a 1,000,000 deutsche mark (DM) 6-month certificate of deposit from a West German bank for $500,000 on October 1, 19X8. The annual interest rate is 15 percent. Exchange rates ($/DM) at December 31, 19X8, and March 31, 19X9, are $.52 and $.465, respectively.

Required:

1. Prepare the journal entries recorded by Carlton on October 1, 19X8, December 31, 19X8, and March 31, 19X9.
2. Was this a good investment? Explain with calculations.

E14.11 The Williams Company has a wholly owned subsidiary in Uruguay. The subsidiary's net assets in *new pesos* (NP, the currency of Uruguay), amount to NP35,000,000. At a time when the spot rate is $.02/NP, Williams wishes to hedge its investment in this foreign entity.

Required:

1. For the hedge to be effective, should Williams borrow NP (or sell NP forward) or invest in NP (or purchase NP forward)? Why?

2. Assume Williams undertakes such a hedge by entering into a forward contract at $.019/NP calling for delivery of NP20,000,000 in 90 days. Prepare the journal entry to record the forward contract as an effective hedge.

3. If the books are closed in 45 days when the spot rate is $.0194/NP, calculate the transaction adjustment and indicate the accounting treatment for it and the discount on the forward contract.

E14.12 Fallon Associates is a firm making markets in certain foreign currencies. On December 15, 19X6, Fallon's net speculative position in the forward market consisted of (1) an agreement to purchase 2,000,000 Hong Kong dollars ($H) in 60 days and (2) an agreement to sell 5,000,000 Singapore dollars ($S) in 30 days. Relevant exchange rates are given below:

	12/15/X6	12/31/X6	1/14/X7	2/13/X7
Forward Rate for Remaining Life of Contract ($/$H)	$.2108	$.2101	—	$.2112[a]
Forward Rate for Remaining Life of Contract ($/$S)	.4619	.4620	.4610[a]	—

[a]Spot rate.

Required: Prepare the journal entries made by Fallon on December 15, 19X6, December 31, 19X6, January 14, 19X7, and February 13, 19X7.

Problems

P14.1 Accounting for Forward Contracts—Hedging and Speculation Futura Corporation, a calendar-year corporation, is an active trader in foreign exchange, both for purposes of hedging its international activities and for outright speculation. In particular, it had several transactions in the futures market for rands (R), the currency of South Africa, during 19X7. Relevant exchange rates ($/R) are shown below:

	11/1/X7	12/31/X7	1/29/X8
Spot Rate	$1.15	$1.17	$1.19
Thirty-Day Futures	1.13	1.16	1.20
Sixty-Day Futures	1.11	1.15	1.21
Ninety-Day Futures	1.09	1.14	1.22

On November 1, 19X7, Futura entered into the following forward contracts. The contracts were settled on January 29, 19X8.

1. Sold R100,000 forward to hedge a forthcoming sale to a South African firm; the sale price of R100,000 has been negotiated although delivery and collection will not take place until January 29, 19X8.

2. Purchased R200,000 forward to hedge the exposed net liability position of its South African branch.
3. Sold R100,000 forward in anticipation of a fall in the spot rate.

Required:

1. Prepare the journal entries made by Futura on November 1, 19X7, December 31, 19X7, and January 29, 19X8. Assume that Futura defers the premium or discount on a forward contract when permitted to do so under *SFAS 52*.
2. Comment on the specific use of the forward market by Futura in the problem.

P14.2 Computation of Exchange Gain or Loss Wheelstick Corporation, incorporated in the state of Delaware, is active in the import/export business. An analysis of Wheelstick's receivables, payables, and other assets (liabilities) prior to adjustment at December 31, 19X2, disclosed the following:

RECEIVABLES

U.S. Customers	$ 100,000
Belgian Customers (300,000 Francs)	9,000
Indian Customers (120,000 Rupees)	14,400
Saudi Arabian Customers (90,000 Riyal)	27,000
Exchange Broker (Forward Sale Contract for 300,000 Francs)	9,300
Total Receivables	$ 159,700

PAYABLES

U.S. Suppliers	$ (47,000)
Ecuadorian Suppliers (600,000 Sucre)	(24,000)
Mexican Suppliers (500,000 Pesos)	(19,000)
Exchange Broker (Forward Purchase Contract for 500,000 Pesos)	(20,000)
Total Payables	$(110,000)

OTHER ASSETS (LIABILITIES)

Trademarks	$ 75,000
Forward Purchase Contract (500,000 Pesos)	19,000
Forward Sale Contract (300,000 Francs)	(9,000)
Total Other Assets (Liabilities)	$ 85,000

Spot rates for the above currencies at December 31, 19X2, are:

Currency	Exchange Rate
Belgian Francs	$.036
Rupees	.125
Riyal	.287
Sucre	.042
Mexican Pesos	.035

Required: Prepare a schedule to compute the exchange gain or loss recognized by Wheelstick in 19X2. Record the needed adjusting entries.

P14.3 Recording International Transactions The following international transactions were entered into during 19X3 by CONNCO, an American corporation:

1. April 1, 19X3: Purchased a 6-month (182-day) certificate of deposit from the Bank of England—face value, £1,000,000; interest rate, 12 percent per annum; cost, $2,000,000.
2. June 15, 19X3: Entered into a firm commitment to purchase goods from Italy which will be resold in the United States. The invoice price was 40,000,000 lira, delivery and payment were to be made in 60 days, and the spot rate is $.0014. Concurrently, 40,000,000 lira were purchased in the forward market for delivery in 60 days at the forward rate of $.0012.
3. August 14, 19X3: The transactions in No. 2 were settled; the spot rate was $.0015.
4. September 1, 19X3: Agricultural products priced at 30,000 riyal were sold to a concern in Iraq when the spot rate was $3.44. Payment was to be received in 90 days.
5. September 28, 19X3: The certificate of deposit purchased in Transaction 1 matured, and the pounds were converted into dollars at an exchange rate of $2.02.
6. October 15, 19X3: After considering the worsening political situation in Thailand, CONNCO's management decided to sell 50,000,000 baht forward 90 days in order to hedge the exposed net asset position of the Bangkok branch. The spot and 90-day futures rates were $.05 and $.044, respectively.
7. November 30, 19X3: The receivable in Transaction 4 was collected and the riyal were converted to dollars at a spot rate of $3.47.
8. December 31, 19X3: The books were closed and made ready for the preparation of financial statements. The spot rate for baht was $.046, and the 15-day futures rate is $.045.

Required:

1. Prepare the journal entries made by CONNCO to record its international transactions during 19X3. Amortize any discount or premium arising on a forward contract.
2. Compare the exchange gain or loss recognized on Transaction 6 with the amounts to be recognized had the forward contract been entered into for the other reasons identified in *SFAS 52*.

P14.4 Recording Hedged Import and Export Transactions International Molding Machinery, Inc., produces plastic molding machinery. During November 19X1, it purchased raw materials and sold finished goods abroad as explained below:

1. On November 7, 19X1, a special steel alloy was purchased from a Japanese company—invoice price 6,000,000 yen, payable in 60 days.

The spot rate was $.0041. International immediately entered into a forward contract to purchase 6,000,000 yen on January 6, 19X2; the forward rate was $.004. When International's books were closed on December 31, 19X1, the spot rate was $.0045; it is $.005 on January 6, 19X2.

2. On November 28, 19X1, some machinery was sold to a Venezuelan firm—invoice price 180,000 bolivar, payment to be received on January 27, 19X2. The spot rate was $.233. To hedge this transaction, International signed a forward contract to sell 180,000 bolivar on January 27, 19X2, at a forward rate of $.236. The spot rate was $.227 on December 31, 19X1, when International's books were closed and is $.236 on January 27, 19X2.

Required: Prepare the journal entries made by International on November 7, 19X1, November 28, 19X1, December 31, 19X1, January 6, 19X2, and January 27, 19X2.

P14.5 Hedging a Foreign Currency Commitment—Effects on Income On October 1, 19X2, Ellis Corporation agreed to sell 50,000 electric motors to a Swiss customer for 500,000 Swiss francs (SF). Delivery is to be made on November 30, 19X2, and payment to be received on January 31, 19X3. Concurrently, Ellis sold SF500,000 forward for delivery on January 31, 19X3, for a total contract price of $249,000. Ellis closes its books annually on December 31.

Required:

1. Prepare all dated journal entries relative to the sale and the forward contract during 19X2 and 19X3. Ellis elects to defer any premiums or discounts on forward contracts during the commitment period. Relevant spot rates are as follows:

	Spot Rate ($/SF)
Oct. 1, 19X2	$.45
Nov. 30, 19X2	.48
Dec. 31, 19X2	.47
Jan. 31, 19X3	.51

2. Suppose Ellis had elected to amortize the premium or discount on the forward contract during the commitment period. How would Ellis's income be affected in 19X2? In 19X3? Explain.

P14.6 Recording a Hedged Foreign Loan The Roderick Company borrowed 50,000 pounds (£) from a London bank on December 16, 19X1. The £50,000 were immediately converted to dollars for use in the United States and are scheduled to be repaid with interest of £500 on January 15, 19X2. To hedge the risk of an unfavorable change in the exchange rate, Roderick purchased £50,500 for delivery on January 15, 19X2. Roderick's accounting period ends on December 31, 19X1. Exchange rates ($/£) on the various dates are as follows:

	12/16/X1	12/31/X1	1/15/X2
Spot Rate.	$2.10	$2.08	$2.05
Thirty-day Forward Rate	2.13	—	—

Required: Prepare the journal entries made by Roderick on December 16, 19X1, December 31, 19X1, and January 15, 19X2.

P14.7 Analyzing the Performance of an Import/Export Department William Johnston manages the import/export department of Bush Specialty Products. Because of the complexities of foreign currency transactions and the continual changes in exchange rates, Bush's management is having difficulty determining exactly how Johnston's operation is performing. You have been called in as a consultant to give advice on this performance-evaluation task.

After you discuss the problem with Mr. Johnston, he produces the summary of his department's activities shown in Exhibit 14.3. The letters

---

Exhibit 14.3 **Bush Specialty Products: Summary of Import/Export Department Activities to Be Used in P14.7**

IMPORT TRANSACTIONS

Quantity—Part No.	Unit Cost (FC)	Spot Rate When Purchased	Spot Rate When Paid	Unit Selling Price
2,000—K14.	6.4	$ .83	$ .80	$ 7.75
17,000—KR08	10.0	.49	.58	6.00
5,000—L16.	8.2	1.13	1.22	10.00
10,000—M290	25.2	.37	.32	9.20

EXPORT TRANSACTIONS

Quantity—Part No.	Unit Selling Price (FC)	Spot Rate When Sold	Spot Rate When Collected	Unit Cost
14,000—A24.	8.4	$ .27	$ .29	$ 1.98
6,000—DD2	12.5	2.00	1.92	24.00
20,000—A27.	10.0	1.10	1.16	8.90
1,000—B23.	14.6	.63	.58	8.50

FORWARD CONTRACTS

Quantity of FC Purchased (Sold)	Average Spot Rate at Inception	Average Forward Rate at Inception	Average Spot Rate at Maturity	Purpose of Contract
210,000	$.57	$.62	$.59	Hedge
(300,000)	.88	.90	.87	Hedge
1,000,000	.28	.25	.22	Speculation
(1,000,000)	.75	.74	.85	Speculation

FC identify foreign currency units, and exchange rates are defined as $/FC. Premiums and discounts on forward contracts are always amortized over the contracts' lives, never deferred.

Required:

1. Prepare, in good form, schedules to calculate the profit contribution or loss realized by the import/export department.
2. Write a short memorandum to top management regarding your findings. Should Mr. Johnston be fired? Explain.

P14.8 Adjusting Entries at Balance Sheet Date You have been engaged to audit the books of Warner Corporation as of December 31, 19X7. Because assets and liabilities recorded by Warner but denominated in foreign currencies have required extensive audit adjustments in the past, you look sharply at the schedule prepared by Warner's controller. It appears in Exhibit 14.4.

Exhibit 14.4   **Schedule of Warner Corporation's Assets and Liabilities to Be Used in P14.8**

ACCOUNTS RECEIVABLE

Domestic Customers	$ 25,000,000
Australian Customers (2,000,000 Australian Dollars)	2,280,000
Norwegian Customers (5,000,000 Krone)	1,000,000
Peruvian Customers	1,900,000
Spanish Customers (10,000,000 Pesetas)	200,000
ABC Foreign Exchange Specialists (10,000,000 Drachma)	300,000
Union Bank Foreign Exchange Department (10,000,000 Pesetas)	210,000
Total Accounts Receivable	$ 30,890,000

ACCOUNTS PAYABLE

Domestic Suppliers	$(15,000,000)
Brazilian Suppliers (4,000,000 Cruzeiros)	(200,000)
Colombian Suppliers (6,000,000 Pesos)	(180,000)
Dutch Suppliers (10,000,000 Guilders)	(5,000,000)
Swedish Suppliers	(800,000)
BR Foreign Exchange Service (5,000,000 Rupees)	(500,000)
Union Bank Foreign Exchange Department (10,000,000 Guilders)	(5,500,000)
Total Accounts Payable	$(27,180,000)

OTHER ASSETS (LIABILITIES)

Note Payable, Nippon Bank, Japan (200,000,000 Yen)	$ (1,000,000)
Forward Purchase Contract (5,000,000 Rupees)	500,000
Forward Purchase Contract (10,000,000 Guilders)	4,800,000
Forward Sale Contract (10,000,000 Drachma)	(300,000)
Forward Sale Contract (10,000,000 Pesetas)	(190,000)
Total Other Assets (Liabilities)	$ 3,810,000

Spot rates at December 31, 19X7, are as follows:

Currency	Rate	Currency	Rate
Australian Dollar	$1.200	Pesetas	$ .020
Cruzeiro	.060	Pesos	.032
Drachma	.028[a]	Rupees	.102[a]
Guilder	.490	Yen	.006
Krone	.190		

[a]Forward rates for remaining terms of speculative contracts are $.025 and $.11 for drachma and rupees, respectively.

Required: Prepare the necessary adjusting entries for Warner Corporation as of December 31, 19X7. Support with calculations in good form.

P14.9 Reconstructing Transaction Adjustments On December 1, 19X5, Mackley Corporation recorded the following foreign currency transactions, all denominated in foreign currencies. The spot rate on December 1, 19X5, is $1/FC and the 60-day forward rate is $1.10/FC.

1. Sold goods to a foreign customer—FC1,000,000.
2. Sold FC1,000,000 forward to be delivered on January 31, 19X6.
3. Ordered goods which are delivered on December 31, 19X5—FC500,000—and purchased FC500,000 forward for delivery on January 31, 19X6.
4. Invested FC2,000,000 in a foreign 6-month certificate of deposit paying 12 percent per annum.

On December 31, 19X5, the following adjusted balances were included in Mackley's accounting records:

	Dr. (Cr.)
Accounts Receivable	$1,060,000
Premium on Forward Contracts	(25,000)
Accounts Payable	(530,000)
Temporary Investments	2,120,000
Purchases (Merchandise)	525,000

Required: Reconstruct all adjusting entries (transaction gains and losses, premium amortization, etc.) related to the transactions in Nos. 1–4 above, which were recorded by Mackley as of December 31, 19X5. Assume that all such adjustments have been made, not only those implicit in the selected December 31 balances reported here.

P14.10 Evaluation of Domestic and Foreign Investments The treasurer of Enormo Corporation is always on the lookout for short-term, high-yielding investments. Six-month low-risk domestic investments currently yield 12 percent per annum. Two foreign investments of comparable risk are presented:

1. A 6-month certificate of deposit issued by the Bank of England has a coupon rate of 14 percent per annum. Spot and 6-month forward exchange rates are $2.00 and $2.03, respectively.
2. A 6-month certificate of deposit issued by the Bundesbank in West Germany carries a coupon rate of 8 percent per annum. Spot and 6-month forward rates are $.50 and $.55, respectively.

Required:

1. Assuming that Enormo has $1,000,000 to invest, cannot tolerate exchange rate risk, and wants to maximize the number of dollars at the end of 6 months, analyze the three alternative investments and make a recommendation. Support your analysis with calculations.
2. Do you expect the results in the first requirement to be maintained over time? Holding everything constant except the forward rates for pounds and deutsch marks, calculate the forward exchange rates which should prevail under the theory of covered interest arbitrage.

P14.11 Accounting for Futures Contracts *(Appendix)* Daley, Inc., engages in futures trading on a regular basis. Its books are closed on June 30 of each year. On June 1, 19X6, it enters the following futures contracts. In each case, an initial margin deposit of $10,000 is made.

1. Purchases 10,000 units of commodity futures at $10 per unit specifying delivery in 90 days. Daley has a liability (recorded as Deferred Revenue) to supply the commodity (which it plans to purchase on the spot market) in 90 days to a customer. The customer has already paid in full—$150,000.
2. Sells 100,000 units of commodity futures at $5 per unit for delivery in 120 days. Daley has a firm commitment to purchase the commodity from a supplier in 90 days and to resell it 30 days later.
3. As part of its cash management activities, Daley regularly invests in 91-day Treasury bills. It recently purchased $1,000,000 face value of these bills and, fearing lower interest rates when it "rolls over" these short-term investments, it purchases $1,000,000 face value Treasury bill futures to be delivered in 91 days at 90. This price locks in an annual discount yield of 10 $(= 100 - 90)$ percent on the new Treasury bills, equivalent to a quarterly discount yield of 2.5 $(= 10/4)$ percent.

Required:

1. Prepare the journal entries made on June 1, on June 30 when the futures in the first contract are selling at $11 per unit, and on August 29 when the long position is closed out at $11.50 per unit.
2. Prepare the journal entries made on June 1, on June 30 when the futures in the second contract are selling at $4.80 per unit, on August 29 when the futures are selling for $4.75 per unit and the commodity

is purchased at a total cost of $460,000, and on September 28 when the short position is closed out at $4.77 per unit.

3. Prepare the journal entries made on June 1, on June 30 when the Treasury bill futures in the third contract are selling at 91, and on August 29 when the old Treasury bills mature and the new ones are delivered. On August 29, Daley's futures contract is selling at 91.5.

P14.12 Accounting for Futures Contracts *(Appendix)* The Davis Company grows soybeans and processes them into soybean meal for eventual sale to a variety of manufacturing concerns. The company currently owns 10,000 tons of soybean meal, carried in inventory at cost of $1,100,000. Soybean meal is currently trading on the spot markets for $150 per ton; 3-month futures are selling for $163 per ton. Davis expects to sell the 10,000 tons in 90 days. On August 1, 19X5, Davis sells 10,000 tons of soybean meal futures to be delivered on October 30, 19X5, at the $163-per-ton price. The price of Davis's futures contracts has advanced to $167 per ton on September 30, when the books are closed for interim reporting purposes. Davis closes out its short position on October 28, 19X5, when the price is $161 per ton.

Required:

1. Assuming that Davis deposits $75,000 margin with the broker on August 1, prepare the journal entries it makes on August 1, on September 30, and on October 28.
2. If Davis sells the soybean meal in the spot market on November 2, 19X5, for $158.50 per ton, calculate its net cash gain or loss from the sale, taking into account the hedging transaction.

Chapter 15 Translating Foreign Currency Financial Statements

Our discussion in Chapter 14 focused on the structure of foreign exchange markets and how those markets are used by U.S. firms to facilitate various transactions involving foreign currency. Generally accepted accounting principles governing foreign currency transactions were explained in detail.

Another major accounting problem arises when U.S. firms have branches, divisions, or subsidiaries operating in foreign countries. When a U.S. company prepares its financial statements, the foreign currency financial statements of these overseas business units must be translated into dollars for inclusion in the U.S. statements. This is necessary so that all amounts are expressed in a common unit of measurement, the dollar. The various methods of translating these data are studied first in this chapter. In the latter part of the chapter, the diversity of accounting principles and practices around the world and the development of international accounting standards are discussed.

Growth in International Operations of U.S. Corporations

An important economic characteristic of the post-World War II period is the expanded scope of domestic corporations' activities in foreign markets. Many corporations domiciled in the United States, Japan, West Germany, and the United Kingdom, for example, all now have extensive foreign operations.

A recent study reported that the number of foreign subsidiaries owned by 180 manufacturing corporations domiciled in the United States increased from 2,196 at the end of 1950 to 11,198 at the end of 1975.[1] During this 25-year period, 13,795 foreign subsidiaries were established, and 4,793 subsidiary relationships were terminated. The U.S. parent corporations held a majority owner-

---

[1] Joan P. Curhan, William H. Davidson, and Rajan Suri, *Tracing the Multinationals* (Cambridge, MA: Ballinger Publishing Company, 1977), 19–20.

ship interest in 78 percent of these subsidiaries. These data provide some indication of the relative scope of U.S. corporations' activities abroad as well as the dynamic character of these activities.

Import/export business, foreign manufacturing facilities, investments in foreign corporations, and obligations to foreign suppliers of capital are all indicative of the growing reliance of business on foreign markets. Although the expansion of world trade, coinciding with the reconstruction of areas devastated by World War II, has obviously contributed to the current importance of international business activities, the *structure* of international funds flows has also been a significant factor. Whereas international operations were once characterized primarily by the import and export of goods among countries, international flows of *capital* now heavily influence relations among countries.

This changing character of the world economy has meant new challenges for corporate managements, professional accountants, and financial analysts. These challenges have developed as the multinational operations of domestic corporations have grown and as the international monetary system has evolved from a fixed exchange-rate regime to one in which exchange rates fluctuate as conditions in foreign exchange markets change.

The Multinational Corporate Entity

Consider a diversified conglomerate corporation domiciled in the United States, such as LTV or Gulf & Western. Two major problems faced by the managements of such firms are (1) controlling wide-ranging, geographically diverse operations and (2) measuring the performance of the various divisions or subsidiaries included in the conglomerates. The fundamental managerial issue of centralization versus decentralization and accounting concerns such as transfer pricing schemes and cost allocation techniques are familiar. Indeed, the discussion of segment reporting presented in Chapter 12 emphasized the importance of these accounting matters on subfirm performance measurement. In addition to these, the following difficulties are common to multinational operations:

1. Corporate headquarters frequently separated from foreign operations by great geographical distances.
2. Books of account maintained in units of various currencies.
3. Interest rates, inflation rates, and growth rates which vary widely across countries.
4. Political conditions and economic institutions which differ among nations.
5. Language and other cultural barriers to effective communication.
6. Alternative sets of accounting principles and reporting standards around the globe.

Considering such obstacles to smooth operation, we can begin to grasp the dimensions of the planning, organizing, and control problems which confront top managements of multinational enterprises. Such problems must also be considered by the accountant who will define the boundaries of the reporting entity appropriate in a multinational enterprise.

The Entity Concept in Multinational Corporations

We have already indicated that many public reporting and disclosure issues in accounting are tied to questions concerning the entity appropriate in the circumstances. For accounting purposes, the corporation is separate from its shareholders. In consolidated statements, treatment of minority interest often differs from that of the controlling interest. *SFAS 14* requires the entity known as the *firm* to identify those *segments* which also appear to have the characteristics of a proper accounting entity. Finally, governmental and nonprofit units will later be seen to consist of several entities. What, then, is the appropriate entity or group of entities for accounting and reporting purposes of the multinational corporation?

The multinational corporation having foreign subsidiaries is a case in point. The Ford Motor Company manufactures and sells automobiles at numerous locations outside the United States. Currently, Ford issues worldwide consolidated financial statements. An alternative reporting posture would be for Ford not to consolidate its foreign subsidiaries and divisions but to report them as long-term investments and include their separate financial statements in the notes. Such a posture has an advantage. Ford's owners and creditors would have a better understanding of the financial status of the various pieces included in their ownership interest. At the same time, however, their view of the big picture with respect to Ford would be clouded. Ford stockholders have an interest in the *totality* of Ford's operations. Their interests are not divisible among the pieces of Ford spread around the world.

Therefore, the entity concept appropriate for reporting the status of the stockholders' and creditors' interests in multinational enterprises is generally one which includes the foreign operations. As we shall see later in the chapter, however, there are circumstances which create exceptions to this general rule. When effective control over the assets of domestically owned foreign subsidiaries is in jeopardy, a less inclusive entity definition may be warranted.

Translating Foreign Currency Financial Statements

We now turn to the accounting problems associated with the translation of foreign currency financial statements into financial statements based on dollar equivalents. These statements reflect the assets, liabilities, revenues, and expenses of *foreign entities*—branches, divisions, and subsidiaries—*owned by U.S. companies*. This chapter thus addresses the need to include these foreign operations in the financial statements of U.S. companies; Chapter 14 addressed accounting for individual foreign currency transactions of U.S. companies.

The discussion in Chapter 14 indicated that recent changes in the international monetary system have resulted in the replacement of pegged, or fixed, foreign exchange rates with flexible, or floating, rates. Foreign exchange rates now change as the underlying relationships between the supply and demand of the various currencies change.

The constant and unpredictable fluctuations in exchange rates can cause translated account balances to become obsolete quickly. The fact that exchange rates do move up *and* down differentiates this problem from a similar one caused by domestic inflation. As a result, the inclusion of exchange gains and losses arising in the translation process in current income may be responsible for excessive and unwarranted instability in reported earnings.

In Chapter 14, we described the *exchange gains and losses* produced by transactions involving the actual conversion to and from foreign currencies. In such exchange conversion cases, we saw how increases in the dollar equivalents of foreign currencies directly affect the economic position of the firm. Today, there is little controversy over including transaction gains and losses in the U.S. income statement. Controversy does exist, however, over including in income the exchange gains and losses resulting from the translation of foreign statements. To sharpen the distinction between exchange gains and losses arising from foreign currency *transactions* and those arising in the translation of foreign *statements* we label the latter *translation gains and losses* (or *translation adjustments*).

Translation Gains and Losses

As foreign exchange rates change, **translation gains and losses** (or **translation adjustments**) arise when some accounts are translated at the *current rate* and others at *historical rates*. Those accounts translated at the current rate change in dollar equivalents, whereas those translated at historical rates remain fixed in dollar equivalents.

> The **current exchange rate** is the spot rate at the end of a reporting period. It is the rate in existence on the balance sheet date. A **historical exchange rate** is a past spot rate, in existence when a particular transaction occurred.

Unlike *transaction* gains and losses, *translation* gains and losses may have little economic significance. For example, suppose the London branch of a U.S. company purchases merchandise from a U.K. supplier on credit. The resulting payable will be liquidated with pounds sterling generated from business in the United Kingdom. If the exchange rate ($/£) *increases,* the dollar equivalent of the payable rises, but the quantity of pounds required to discharge it does not change. Has the U.S. firm incurred a loss when this happens? Probably not, yet prior to *SFAS 52* accounting practice would always record a translation loss at year-end when the statements of the London branch are translated into dollars.

A similar situation occurs when plant assets are acquired in the foreign country with debt denominated in that foreign currency. The debt is to be retired with foreign currency generated in normal business operations. If the exchange rate ($/£) *falls,* fewer dollars would be required to retire the debt. Has the U.S. firm now realized a gain? Prior to *SFAS 52,* accounting practice would always record one at translation time, although management does not intend to use dollars to retire the debt. In cases such as these, there are neither actual nor intended conversions of foreign currency, and the U.S. firm is only affected indirectly, if at all. Thus it seems to us that *translation* gains and losses may not have the same economic significance as *transaction* gains and losses. This point is reflected in the provisions set forth in *SFAS 52* that are intended to link accounting treatment of translation adjustments to their economic consequences.

Translation gains and losses arise because all approaches to translating foreign currency financial statements translate some accounts at the current rate and other accounts at historical rates. Determining those accounts to be translated at the current rate and those to be translated at historical rates is the most controversial issue in accounting for international operations. The most important provisions of *SFAS 52* relate to this issue and, in part, were adopted to overcome the severe criticism leveled at the previous rules embodied in *SFAS 8*. To develop an appreciation of the translation problem, we offer a discussion and comparison of the four principal approaches to translating foreign currency financial statements. We then provide a detailed explanation of the two translation methods permitted by *SFAS 52*.

Approaches to Translating Foreign Currency Financial Statements

The various approaches differ in their selection of accounts to be translated at current and historical rates. Four major approaches may be identified—current/ noncurrent, monetary/nonmonetary, temporal, and current rate. *Only the temporal and current rate translation methods are acceptable today.* We discuss each in the approximate chronological order of their acceptability in practice.

Current/Noncurrent Method. The **current/noncurrent method** is described in Chapter 12 of *ARB 43*[2] and incorporates the following dichotomy. *Current assets* and *current liabilities* are to be translated at the *current rate* in effect at the balance sheet date. Other assets and liabilities, as well as the stockholders' equity accounts, are all *noncurrent* and are translated at the *historical rates* in existence when those items originated. There seems to be no stated theoretical basis for the current/noncurrent dichotomy, although the method itself suggests a rationale. Current assets and liabilities are, by definition, either cash or items that are relatively close to being converted to cash or to being liquidated with cash. Being denominated in units of foreign currency, like cash, they are exposed to the effects of movements in the exchange rate. Hence, it could be argued that translation at the current rate best expresses the dollar equivalents of these ''near cash'' items.

Revenues and expenses which occur evenly over the year are translated at average spot rates. Uneven revenue and expense flows should be translated at the rates in effect when they occur. Alternatively, a weighted average rate could be used for all revenue and expense items, except those representing amortization of balance sheet accounts which are translated at historical rates. For example, de-

---

[2]Committee on Accounting Procedure, *Accounting Research Bulletin No. 43,* ''Restatement and Revision of Accounting Research Bulletins'' (New York: AICPA, 1953).

preciation expense is translated at the historical rate used to translate the related asset.

The current/noncurrent method predominated in practice until the 1960s. In that decade, the monetary/nonmonetary method increased in favor because it remedied some logical inconsistencies in the current/noncurrent method. Present accounting principles do not permit use of the current/noncurrent method.

Monetary/Nonmonetary Method. Hepworth, in his classic work, *Reporting Foreign Operations,* points out some flaws in the current/noncurrent method.[3] He first questions translation of inventory (a current asset) at the current rate on the grounds that it is not a clearly defined foreign currency value—as are cash and receivables—but rather a *potential* foreign currency value. That is, since inventory is not a claim to a fixed quantity of foreign currency, it is more like plant assets (translated at historical rates) than cash (translated at the current rate).

Hepworth's second concern is with translation of long-term debt at historical rates under the current/noncurrent method. He argues that long-term debt, like accounts payable, is a contractual obligation to disburse a fixed number of foreign currency units. Although the disbursement will take place in the future, the current rate better reflects the dollar equivalent of the foreign currency obligation than a past rate.

Observe that both of Hepworth's objections cited above derive from a common theme: current exchange rates should be used to translate those items which represent cash or contractual claims to receive or disburse cash. Other items, which do not represent fixed quantities of foreign currency, should be translated at historical rates. This approach to the translation problem is known as the **monetary/nonmonetary method.** *Monetary assets and liabilities* are measured in fixed quantities of foreign currency; their dollar value changes only if the exchange rate changes. These are to be translated at the *current rate. Nonmonetary assets and liabilities* (all others) are therefore properly translated at the appropriate *historical rates.* Translation of revenues and expenses under the monetary/nonmonetary method is the same as under the current/noncurrent method.

The monetary/nonmonetary approach was widely used in practice during the late 1960s and early 1970s, prior to the adoption of *SFAS 8. APBO 6*(1965)[4] amended *ARB 43* to allow translation of long-term receivables and payables at the current exchange rate, thereby effectively granting permission to use the monetary/nonmonetary approach. Publication of *SFAS 8* in 1975 required firms to translate according to the *temporal method,* a method which closely approximates the monetary/nonmonetary method when applied to the historical cost accounting model. Today, the pure monetary/nonmonetary method is not used.

---

[3]Samuel R. Hepworth, *Reporting Foreign Operations* (Ann Arbor: University of Michigan, Bureau of Business Research, 1956).

[4]Accounting Principles Board, *Opinion No. 6,* "Status of Accounting Research Bulletins" (New York: AICPA, 1965), par. 18.

Temporal Method. The **temporal method** of translation was comprehensively developed by Lorensen in *Accounting Research Study No. 12*.[5] It is based on two fundamental principles:

1. Translation changes the unit of measurement.
2. Translation changes no other accounting principle.

Thus foreign currency translation is, like constant-dollar accounting, viewed as an arithmetic technique designed to convert disparate measurement units to a common one. Valuation or other attributes of the items being translated are not (and should not be) affected by the translation process. The appendix to this chapter provides a formal explanation of the relationship between the foreign currency translation process and constant-dollar restatements.

Lorensen proceeds to establish that the major attribute of assets and liabilities which accountants measure is the **money price.** *APB Statement No. 4* refers to money prices as "ratios at which money and other resources are or may be exchanged."[6] It follows that the *date* at which an item's money price is measured should govern the date of the foreign exchange rate used to translate the item. This notion of dating the money price measured and using the foreign exchange rate on the same date to translate the money price is known as the **temporal principle of translation.** Lorensen summarizes its meaning as follows:

> Money and receivables and payables measured at the amounts promised should be translated at the foreign exchange rate in effect at the balance sheet date. Assets and liabilities measured at money prices should be translated at the foreign exchange rate in effect at the dates to which the money prices pertain.[7]

Thus assets and liabilities valued at current prices, such as monetary items and inventory carried at market, are translated at the current rate; those valued at past prices, such as plant assets and inventory carried at cost, are translated at historical rates. The temporal method is the translation method that had been required by *SFAS 8* in all cases. It is now required only in certain cases under *SFAS 52*. At the present time, the temporal method is very similar to the monetary/nonmonetary method. This is due to the GAAP requirement that most nonmonetary items be carried at past prices representing historical or acquisition cost. Note that if current value accounting were to become accepted, assets such as buildings and equipment, which are both noncurrent and nonmonetary, would be translated at the current rate under the temporal method because they would be valued at current money prices. Translation of revenues and expenses denominated in a

---

[5]Leonard Lorensen, *Accounting Research Study No. 12*, "Reporting Foreign Operations of U.S. Companies in U.S. Dollars" (New York: AICPA, 1972).

[6]Accounting Principles Board, *Statement No. 4*, "Basic Concepts and Principles Underlying Financial Statements of Business Enterprises" (New York: AICPA, 1970), par. 70.

[7]Lorensen, op. cit., 19.

foreign currency under the temporal method involves using the foreign exchange rates in effect when the money prices measuring revenues and expenses occurred. This is really no different from the approach used in both the current/noncurrent and monetary/nonmonetary methods to translate most revenues and expenses. Revenues and expenses occurring evenly over the year are translated at average exchange rates for the year under all three methods. Depreciation and amortization are translated at whatever rates are used to translate the related assets or liabilities.

Current Rate Method. During the 1970s, professional societies of chartered accountants in England, Wales, and Scotland proposed the **current rate method,** derived from the older ''closing rate method.'' This method called for translating most balance sheet and income statement accounts at the current exchange rate as of the balance sheet date. The current rate method represents a significant departure from traditional U.S. accounting principles and practice. Nevertheless, a version of it was adopted by the FASB in *SFAS 52* to be used in certain situations. Under the version set forth in *SFAS 52,* all assets and liabilities are to be translated at the current rate. Historical rates are used to translate stockholders' equity accounts, and the average rate for the period is used to translate income statement accounts, including depreciation and cost of goods sold.

At first glance it might seem that use of the current rate method would eliminate the translation adjustment. Unfortunately, such is not the case. A translation adjustment still arises because, while assets and liabilities are translated at the current rate, stockholders' equity accounts are translated at historical rates and income statement accounts at an average rate.

Comparison of the Four Translation Approaches. In order to better explain the differences between these methods and to differentiate their diverse accounting results, we have prepared four exhibits. The first, Exhibit 15.1, contrasts the use of current versus historical rates to translate specific financial statement items. Although the monetary/nonmonetary method often approximates the temporal method, Exhibit 15.1 points out major differences. For example, nonmonetary items carried at current market (inventory, investments, and warranty obligations) are translated at the current rate under the temporal method but at historical rates under the monetary/nonmonetary method.

The underlying data for a numerical example which contrasts the four foreign currency translation methods are presented in Exhibit 15.2. Our objective in this illustration is to clearly differentiate the accounting results of the four methods. This can be done using an uncomplicated situation with few transactions. Before applying these four methods to the data in Exhibit 15.2, however, we shall discuss calculation of the translation adjustment.

Calculation of the Translation Adjustment. At one level, the translation adjustment is simply a *plug*. It is the amount required in the translated income statement which, through its inclusion in retained earnings, brings the balance sheet into balance. It is at another level, however, that one is able to grasp what actually is happening in the translation process. A central concept is the *exposed position*.

Exhibit 15.1	Exchange Rates Used by Four Translation Methods to Translate Selected Financial Statement Items

BALANCE SHEET	Current/ Noncurrent	Monetary/ Nonmonetary	Temporal	Current Rate
Cash and Receivables	C	C	C	C
Inventory at Cost	C	H	H	C
Inventory at Market	C	H	C	C
Investments at Cost	H	H	H	C
Investments at Market	H	H	C	C
Plant Assets	H	H	H	C
Accounts Payable	C	C	C	C
Deferred Taxes	H	H	H, C^a	C
Long-Term Debt	H	C	C	C
Obligations under Warranties, Current (at current prices)	C	H	C	C
Capital Stock	H	H	H	H
Retained Earnings	^{b}	^{b}	^{b}	^{b}
INCOME STATEMENT				
Sales Revenue	A	A	A	A
Variable Expenses	A	A	A	A
Fixed Expenses	H, A^c	H, A^c	H, A^c	A

Legend and Notes

C = Current Rate; H = Historical rate; A = Average rate during the year.
^{a}The rate(s) applied to translate deferred taxes are those used to translate the items giving rise to the timing differences; both historical and current rates may be included. See Lorensen, *ARS 12*, 28; and *SFAS 8*, pars. 50–52. Deferred taxes are translated at the current rate under *SFAS 52*.
^{b}"Translated" retained earnings is a residual, consisting of current rates of previous periods.
^{c}Fixed expenses such as depreciation and amortization are translated at the same historical rates as the related assets. Other fixed expenses which involve current outlays, such as rent and property taxes, are translated at the average rate during the year.

For accounting purposes, a firm's **exposed position** is the difference between its assets and liabilities denominated in the foreign currency which are to be translated at the *current rate*.

The exposed position under each of the four translation methods discussed above is defined as follows:

Translation Method	Definition of Exposed Position
Current/Noncurrent	Current assets − Current liabilities
Monetary/Nonmonetary	Monetary assets − Monetary liabilities
Temporal	Assets measured at current money prices − Liabilities measured at current money prices
Current Rate	Total assets − Total liabilities

Exhibit 15.2   **Data for Foreign Currency Translation Illustration**

MULTIPLE METHODS, INC.

Balance Sheet as of January 1, 19X1	June 30, 19X1	December 31, 19X1
Cash. . . . . £ 50	Exchange Rate $1.60/£	$1.44/£
Inventory		
(2 Widgets @ £50) 100	Transaction . . 1. Sell 1 widget for £120.	1. Record straight-line depreciation on furniture, £10.
Furniture		
(5-Year Life). . . . . __50__	2. Replace widget for £80.	2. Close books and prepare financial statements.
£200		
Contributed Capital £200	3. Pay other expenses of £30.	
Note: The exchange rate on Jan. 1, 19X1, is $2.00/£	4. Accrue current warranty liability of £20 (current price of estimated warranty service).^{a}	

^{a}The warranty liability pertains to services expected to be rendered during 19X2. As such, it is a current liability, and, although it reflects the current cost of providing warranty service, it is not an obligation for a fixed amount of foreign currency.

    The exposed position generates the translation gain or loss caused by movements in the exchange rate. The exposed position at any balance sheet date, the *ending* exposed position, is translated at the current rate. Increases and decreases which occurred in the exposed position during the year just ended are, under double entry accounting, also reflected in accounts which are translated at historical or average rates. The beginning exposed position is implicitly translated at the beginning-of-period current rate, which now is a historical rate. An approach to computing the translation adjustment is presented in Exhibit 15.3. The top panel illustrates the general procedure, and the bottom panel applies the general procedure to the temporal method using our illustrative data from Multiple Methods, Inc.

    To further analyze a portion of the translation gain or loss, consider the inventory sale and purchase transactions from our example in Exhibit 15.2. In the *current/noncurrent* and *current rate methods,* the *purchase* of inventory with cash has no net effect on the exposed position because neither net current assets nor net assets have changed. Both the increase in inventory and the £80 decrease in cash are translated at the current rate of $1.44/£, and no *translation gain or loss* results. Under the *monetary/nonmonetary and temporal methods,* however, the purchase of inventory for £80 reduces the amount of net monetary assets which

Exhibit 15.3	Schedule to Compute the Translation Adjustment

GENERAL APPROACH

	FC	Exchange Rate ($/FC)	$
Exposed Position, Jan. 1 . .	x	Rate on Jan. 1: a	ax
		Rate(s) When Increases	
Plus Increases	y	Occurred: b	by
		Rate(s) When Decreases	
Less Decreases	(z)	Occurred: c	(cz)
Exposed Position,			
Dec. 31	x + y − z		$ax + by − cz$ (1)

Current Rate on Dec. 31: d $\quad -d(x + y - z)$ (2)

Translation Adjustment (Gain if <0, Loss if >0) $\longrightarrow$ $\underline{(1) - (2)}$

TEMPORAL METHOD EXAMPLE FOR MULTIPLE METHODS, INC.

	£	$/£	$
Exposed Position, Jan. 1 (Net Assets Carried at Current			
Money Prices; Cash of £50)	£ 50	$2.00	$ 100.0
Plus Increase: Sales	120	1.60	192.0
Less Decreases:			
Purchase of Inventory.	(80)	1.60	(128.0)
Payment of Expenses.	(30)	1.60	(48.0)
Recognition of Warranty Expense (Liability).	(20)	1.60	(32.0)
Exposed Position, Dec. 31	£ 40		$ 84.0
		1.44 →	−57.6
Translation Adjustment (Loss).			$ 26.4

will be translated at the current rate of $1.44/£, while creating a nonmonetary asset (inventory) which will be translated at the historical rate of $1.60/£. This generates a *translation gain* of $12.8 [=($1.60 − $1.44)80] because the exchange rate moved against pounds sterling during the year and £80 fewer were affected by the declining exchange rate (£/$). These effects are summarized in journal entry format below.

	Current/Noncurrent and Current Rate Methods				Monetary/Nonmonetary and Temporal Methods			
	£		$		£		$	
	Dr.	Cr.	Dr.	Cr.	Dr.	Cr.	Dr.	Cr.
Inventory	80		115.2		80		128	
Cash		80		115.2		80		115.2
Translation Gain		—		—		—		12.8

Notes: $115.2 = $1.44 × 80; $128 = $1.60 × 80; $12.8 = ($1.60 − $1.44)80.

The effect of the inventory sale for £120 is opposite to that of the purchase, yet the same result is produced in all four translation methods. In each case, the

Exhibit 15.4 **Illustration of Four Methods of Translating Foreign Currency Financial Statements (Year Ended December 31, 19X1) for Multiple Methods, Inc.**

	£	Current/Noncurrent $/£	$	Monetary/Nonmonetary $/£	$	Temporal $/£	$	Current Rate $/£	$
BALANCE SHEET									
Cash	£ 60	1.44 (C)	$ 86.4	1.44 (C)	$ 86.4	1.44 (C)	$ 86.4	1.44 (C)	$ 86.4
Inventory, Unit 2	50	1.44 (C)	72.0	2.00 (H)	100.0	2.00 (H)	100.0	1.44 (C)	72.0
Inventory, Unit 3	80	1.44 (C)	115.2	1.60 (H)	128.0	1.60 (H)	128.0	1.44 (C)	115.2
Furniture, Net	40	2.00 (H)	80.0	2.00 (H)	80.0	2.00 (H)	80.0	1.44 (C)	57.6
Total Assets	£230		$ 353.6		$ 394.4		$ 394.4		$ 331.2
Warranty Liability, Current	£ 20	1.44 (C)	$ 28.8	1.60 (H)	$ 32.0	1.44 (C)	28.8	1.44 (C)	28.8
Contributed Capital	200	2.00 (H)	400.0	2.00 (H)	400.0	2.00 (H)	400.0	2.00 (H)	400.0
Retained Earnings	10	—	(75.2)	—	(37.6)	—	(34.4)	—	(97.6)
Total Equities	£230		$ 353.6		$ 394.4		$ 394.4		$ 331.2
INCOME STATEMENT									
Sales	£120	1.60 (A)	$ 192.0	1.60 (A)	$ 192.0	1.60 (A)	$ 192.0	1.60 (A)	$ 192.0
Cost of Goods Sold	(50)	2.00 (H)	(100.0)	2.00 (H)	(100.0)	2.00 (H)	(100.0)	1.60 (A)	(80.0)
Warranty Expense	(20)	1.60 (A)	(32.0)	1.60 (A)	(32.0)	1.60 (A)	(32.0)	1.60 (A)	(32.0)
Other Expenses	(30)	1.60 (A)	(48.0)	1.60 (A)	(48.0)	1.60 (A)	(48.0)	1.60 (A)	(48.0)
Depreciation Expense	(10)	2.00 (H)	(20.0)	2.00 (H)	(20.0)	2.00 (H)	(20.0)	1.60 (A)	(16.0)
Translation Adjustment	—		(67.2)		(29.6)		(26.4)		(113.6)^i
Net Income (Loss)	£ 10		$ (75.2)		$ (37.6)		$ (34.4)		$ (97.6)

COMPUTATION OF TRANSLATION ADJUSTMENT	£	ER	$	£	ER	$	£	ER	$	£	ER	$
Exposed Position, Jan. 1, 19X1	150^a	2.0	$ 300.0	50^c	2.0	$ 100.0	50^e	2.0	$ 100.0	200^g	2.0	$ 400.0
Plus: Sale of Inventory	120	1.6	192.0	120	1.6	192.0	120	1.6	192.0	120	1.6	192.0
Less: Purchase of Inventory	—		—	(80)	1.6	(128.0)	(80)	1.6	(128.0)	—	—	—
Payment of Expenses	(30)	1.6	(48.0)	(30)	1.6	(48.0)	(30)	1.6	(48.0)	(30)	1.6	(48.0)
Recognition of Cost of Goods Sold	(50)	2.0	(100.0)	—		—	—		—	(50)	1.6	(80.0)
Recognition of Depreciation Expense	—		—	—		—	—		—	(10)	1.6	(16.0)
Recognition of Warranty Expense (Liability)	(20)	1.6	(32.0)	—		—	(20)	1.6	(32.0)	(20)	1.6	(32.0)
Exposed Position, Dec. 31, 19X1	170^b		$ 312.0	60^d		$ 116.0	40^f		$ 84.0	210^h		$ 416.0
	↓ 1.44 →		−244.8	↓ 1.44 →		−86.4	↓ $1.44 →		−57.6	↓ 1.44 →		−302.4
Translation Adjustment (Loss)			$ 67.2			$ 29.6			$ 26.4			$ 113.6

[a]150 = Cash (50) + Inventory (100); net current assets.
[b]170 = Cash (60) + Inventory (130) − Warranty Liability, Current (20).
[c]50 = Cash (50); net monetary assets.
[d]60 = Cash (60).
[e]50 = Cash (50); net assets carried at current money prices.
[f]40 = Cash (60) − Warranty Liability, Current (20).
[g]200 = Capital Stock (200); net assets.
[h]210 = Capital Stock (200) + Retained Earnings (10).
[i]Under *SFAS 52*, the translation adjustment is entered directly in stockholders' equity; it is *not* included in the income statement.

Note: The exchange rate of $1.60/£ on June 30, 19X1, represents both the average rate for the year and the historical rate insofar as the purchase of Inventory: Unit 3 and the creation of the Warranty Liability. Current, are concerned.

---

exposed position—net current assets, net monetary assets,[8] or net assets, depending on the context—is increased. The £120 cash will be translated at the current rate of $1.44/£. At the same time, £120 of sales revenue to be translated at the historical (average) rate of $1.60/£ is recognized. This produces a *translation loss* of $19.2 $[=($1.60 − $1.44)120]$ because the £120 was held during a year in which its dollar equivalent declined. These effects are also shown in journal entry format:

	All Four Translation Methods			
	£		**$**	
	Dr.	**Cr.**	**Dr.**	**Cr.**
Cash	120		172.8	
Translation Loss	—		19.2	
Sales.		120		192

Notes: $172.8 = 1.44×120; $192 = 1.60×120; $19.2 = ($1.60 − $1.44)120$.

We can now sum up the explanation for these translation gains and losses as follows:

> Translation gains and losses arise because the *current rate* is used to translate the *ending exposed position*, while the *beginning exposed position* and all *changes* during the current year are translated at *historical* (or *average*) *rates*.

We now apply the four translation methods just discussed to the illustrative data from Exhibit 15.2. The translated results appear in Exhibit 15.4. The upper part of Exhibit 15.4 presents translated balance sheets and income statements. Note the dramatically different results reported under the four methods. Translated assets (equities) range from $331.2 to $394.4, which is 19 percent higher. The

---

[8]Net monetary assets *is* the exposed position under the monetary/nonmonetary method; it is a large part of the exposed position under the temporal method.

translated net *loss* is $97.6 under the current rate method, almost three times the net loss reported under the temporal method. We shall see shortly, however, that when the current rate method is used under *SFAS 52,* the translation adjustment does *not* enter current income.

The lower part of Exhibit 15.4 shows how the translation adjustment is calculated under each of the four methods. In examining these calculations, please refer to Exhibit 15.3 for a review of the general approach and the temporal method computation.

Translation under *SFAS 52*

Following a 3-year period of deliberation, research, and public hearings, the FASB issued *SFAS 52,* "Foreign Currency Translation," in December 1981. It superseded *SFAS 8, SFAS 20, IFAS 15,* and *IFAS 17,* and in paragraph 4 embraced the following "objectives of translation":

1. Provide information that is generally compatible with the expected economic effects of a rate change on the enterprise's cash flow and equity.
2. Reflect in consolidated statements the financial results and relationships of the individual consolidated entities as measured in their *functional currencies* in conformity with U.S. generally accepted accounting principles.

These objectives seem to have a decision orientation in that they call for reported information to be consistent with the underlying economic developments of interest to decision makers. Thus they follow the general objectives of financial reporting given in the FASB's first *Concepts Statement.*[9]

The Functional Currency

The specific translation methodology used in *SFAS 52* for a particular foreign entity follows from determination of that entity's *functional currency.* An entity's **functional currency** is the currency of the primary economic environment in which the entity operates and generates net cash flows.[10] It may be either the foreign entity's local currency, another foreign currency, or the U.S. dollar (the reporting currency).

Appendix A of *SFAS 52* identifies several salient economic indicators which should be considered both individually and collectively when the functional currency is determined. They are summarized in Exhibit 15.5. Another factor might be the hedging practices of the foreign entity. If the entity regularly hedges its foreign currency commitments and positions in dollars, a case could be made for designating the dollar as the entity's functional currency.[11] In any event, deter-

---

[9]Financial Accounting Standards Board, *Statement of Financial Accounting Concepts No. 1,* "Objectives of Financial Reporting by Business Enterprises" (Stamford, CT: FASB, 1978).
[10]Financial Accounting Standards Board, *Statement No. 52,* par. 5; CT § F60.104.
[11]Deloitte Haskins & Sells, *Foreign Currency Translation—Issues and Answers* (New York: Deloitte Haskins & Sells, 1981), 3–4.

Exhibit 15.5 **Economic Indicators Which Influence Determination of the Functional Currency**

	Functional Currency Probably Is:	
Economic Indicators	**Local or Other Foreign Currency**	**Parent's Currency ($)**
Cash Flow	Cash flows are primarily in the foreign currency and do not directly impact the parent's cash flows.	Cash flows impact the parent's cash flows on a current basis and are readily available for remittance to the parent company.
Sales Price	Selling prices are determined primarily by local competition or governmental regulation, and not by short-term changes in exchange rates.	Selling prices are primarily determined by worldwide competition or international prices and respond to short-term changes in exchange rates.
Sales Market	Active sales market for the entity's products is primarily local.	Sales market for the entity's products is primarily in the parent's country *or* sales contracts are denominated in the parent's currency.
Expense	Costs of labor, materials, and so forth are primarily local costs.	Costs of labor, materials, and so forth are primarily costs for components obtained from the parent's country.
Financing	Financing is primarily denominated in the local currency and is serviced by foreign currency cash flows generated in the foreign country.	Financing is primarily from dollar-denominated obligations *or* parent company funds are needed to service debt obligations.
Intercompany Transactions and Arrangements	Volume of intercompany transactions is low, resulting in minimal relationship between the operations of the foreign entity and the parent.	Volume of intercompany transactions is high, resulting in substantial relationship between the operations of the foreign entity and the parent.

Source: Financial Accounting Standards Board, *Statement of Financial Accounting Standards No. 52* (Stamford, CT: FASB, 1981), par. 42; CT §F60.110.

mination of the functional currency is essentially a matter of fact. The functional currency is changed only when significant new economic facts and circumstances clearly indicate that a different functional currency is warranted. Although selection of the functional currency is not viewed as something to be manipulated, it is not considered a choice between alternative accounting principles and a change in the functional currency does *not* call for disclosure of the cumulative effect of the change in earnings as would otherwise be required under *APBO 20*.[12]

After sorting out all the relevant factors, determination of the functional currency can generally be summarized as follows:

1. A foreign entity with operations which are relatively self-contained and integrated within the country in which it is located would normally use the *local currency* of that country as its functional currency.
2. A foreign entity whose operations are a direct and integral component or extension of a U.S. parent company's operations would normally use the *U.S. dollar* as its functional currency.
3. A foreign entity located in one foreign country but generating most of its cash flows in the currency of another foreign country would normally use the *currency of the other foreign country* as its functional currency.
4. A foreign entity located in a country with a highly inflationary economy—cumulative inflation of 100 percent or more over a 3-year period—*must use the U.S. dollar* as its functional currency (paragraph 11 of *SFAS 52*).

Notice the role played by the entity concept in determination of the functional currency. If the foreign operations are mere extensions of the domestic entity, then the functional currency of the foreign entity is *identical* to the reporting currency of the domestic parent, and dollar measurement is the key to evaluating the financial results of the foreign entity. This is clearly a single-entity orientation. In contrast, if the foreign operations are substantially independent of the domestic entity, then the functional currency of the foreign entity is *different* from the reporting currency of the domestic parent. While the foreign results are ultimately reported in dollars, foreign functional currency measurement is the key to evaluating the financial results of the foreign entity. Here there is more of a multiple-entity orientation.

Translation Methodologies

After the foreign entity's functional currency is determined, translation under *SFAS 52* is conceptually the two-step process appearing below:

1. *Remeasure* the entity's local currrency (LC) statements into its functional currency (FC).
2. *Translate* the functional currency (FC) statements into the reporting currency, the U.S. dollar.

---

[12]Accounting Principles Board, *Opinion No. 20*, "Accounting Changes" (New York: AICPA, 1971), par. 8; CT § A06.106.

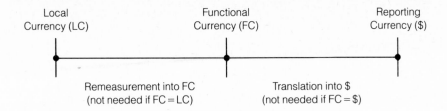

Note, however, that *one* of these two steps is *already complete* if the entity's functional currency is either its *local currency* (LC) or the *U.S. dollar*. Only when the entity's functional currency is neither its local currency nor the U.S. dollar are two separate numerical calculations required, as shown below:

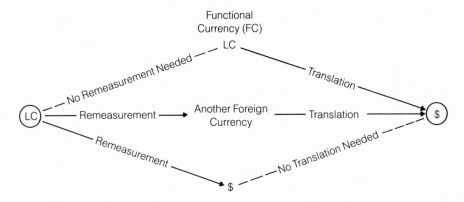

The following three situations can therefore be identified:

Case 1. If the *foreign entity's functional currency is its local (home) currency,* its accounts will be translated into dollars by the *current rate method.* Translation gains and losses are *deferred;* they bypass the income statement and are entered directly into a separate component of stockholders' equity. We refer to this separate component as the "Equity Adjustment from Foreign Currency Translation." If the foreign entity is sold or liquidated, the accumulated translation adjustment (balance in the "Equity Adjustment" account) is recognized in earnings as part of the gain or loss from the sale or liquidation. In the event that *part* of the parent's ownership interest in the foreign entity is sold, a pro rata portion of the accumulated translation adjustment shall be recognized in measuring the gain or loss on the sale.[13]

Case 2. If the *foreign entity's functional currency is the dollar,* its accounts are *remeasured* in the functional currency (the dollar) by a procedure essentially the

---

[13]Financial Accounting Standards Board, *Interpretation of Financial Accounting Standards No. 37,* "Accounting for Translation Adjustments upon Sale of Part of an Investment in a Foreign Entity" (Stamford, CT: FASB, 1983), par. 2; CT § F60.120.

same as the *temporal method*. After the accounts are remeasured in dollars, no further translation is necessary and the translation gain or loss resulting from the remeasurement process is included in consolidated net income.

Case 3. If the *foreign entity's functional currency is another foreign currency,* the accounts are (1) *remeasured* in the other foreign currency by the *temporal method* and the remeasured account balances are then (2) *translated* into dollars using the *current rate method* as specified in *SFAS 52*. Note that in this case the translation adjustment arising in the temporal remeasurement process will be translated into dollars and included in consolidated net income, while the translation gain or loss produced by the current rate translation process itself is carried directly to stockholders' equity.

The above relationship between the functional currency determination and the current rate and temporal methods follows from a basic objective of *SFAS 52: preservation of the foreign entity's financial results and relationships as expressed in its functional currency.* When the entity's functional currency is either the U.S. dollar or another foreign currency, the local currency statements are *remeasured* in the functional currency via the *temporal method.* This is the most precise way of simulating the entity's transactions as if they all had been consummated in the

Exhibit 15.6	Translation Approach under *SFAS 52*			
Functional Currency of Foreign Entity	Input to Translation or Remeasurement Process	Translation or Remeasurement Method	Output of Translation or Remeasurement Process	Treatment of Translation Adjustment
Local Foreign Currency	Local currency units	Current rate method (translation)	U.S. dollars	Carried directly to "Equity Adjustment from Foreign Currency Translation" in stockholders' equity; bypasses income statement
U.S. Dollars	Local currency units	Temporal method (remeasurement)	U.S. dollars	Included in consolidated or combined net income
Another Foreign Currency:				
Step 1	Local currency units	Temporal method (remeasurement)	Foreign functional currency units	Included in foreign functional currency income (input to Step 2)
Step 2	Foreign functional currency units	Current rate method (translation)	U.S. dollars	Translation adjustment from Step 1 (now measured in U.S. dollars) included in consolidated or combined net income; translation adjustment from Step 2 carried directly to "Equity Adjustment from Foreign Currency Translation" in stockholders' equity and bypasses income statement

functional currency. *Translation* into dollars via the *current rate method*—which multiplies all assets and liabilities by one constant (the current rate) and all revenues and expenses by another constant (the average rate)—preserves the functional currency results and relationships reasonably well. The FASB's decision to use the U.S. dollar as the functional currency of foreign entities located in highly inflationary economies was a pragmatic one. It reflects the belief that because a highly inflationary local currency is unable to serve as a store of value, its use as a functional measuring unit is questionable.

Application of the above translation principles is summarized in Exhibit 15.6. If remeasurement is called for, *SFAS 52* requires that historical rates be used for the specific accounts listed in Exhibit 15.7, following the temporal method. The current rate is used for other balance sheet accounts and the average rate for the year is used for other income statement accounts in the remeasurement process.

Illustration of the *SFAS 52* Translation Process

The example below illustrates several aspects of the translation and remeasurement processes. Companies were permitted to switch from *SFAS 8* to *SFAS 52* in their 1981 annual reports but must follow *SFAS 52* in fiscal years beginning on or after December 15, 1982. This change was significant for the many companies

---

Exhibit 15.7   Accounts to Be Remeasured Using Historical Exchange Rates

---

Marketable Securities Carried at Cost:
  Equity Securities
  Debt Securities Not Intended to Be Held until Maturity
Inventories Carried at Cost
Prepaid Expenses Such as Insurance, Advertising, and Rent
Property, Plant, and Equipment
Accumulated Depreciation on Property, Plant, and Equipment
Patents, Trademarks, Licenses, and Formulas
Goodwill
Other Intangible Assets
Deferred Charges and Credits, except Deferred Income Taxes and Policy Acquisition Costs
     for Life Insurance Companies
Deferred Income
Common Stock
Preferred Stock Carried at Issuance Price
Revenues and Expenses Related to Nonmonetary Items, Such as:
  Cost of Goods Sold
  Depreciation of Property, Plant, and Equipment
  Amortization of Intangible Items Such as Goodwill, Patents, Licenses, etc.
  Amortization of Deferred Charges or Credits except Deferred Income Taxes and Policy
     Acquisition Costs for Life Insurance Companies

Source: Financial Accounting Standards Board, *Statement of Financial Accounting Standards No. 52,* "Foreign Currency Translation" (Stamford, CT: FASB, 1981), Appendix B; CT § F60.147.

---

which determined that some or all of their foreign entities have foreign functional currencies. In such cases, the current rate method applies under *SFAS 52*. The temporal method of *SFAS 8* continues to apply under *SFAS 52* for those foreign entities having the U.S. dollar as their functional currency. Some U.S. companies, of course, find that certain of their foreign entities have foreign functional currencies and others use the U.S. dollar as their functional currency. These companies will use the current rate method for some of their foreign entities and the temporal method for others.

Determining the Initial Balance in the Equity Adjustment Account. As long as *SFAS 8* was in force, the temporal method was used and there was no equity adjustment account. The switch to the current rate method required by *SFAS 52* for entities with foreign functional currencies created differences between the last *SFAS 8* translated balance sheet and the first *SFAS 52* translated balance sheet. These differences were caused by translating at the current rate those assets and liabilities that had been translated at historical rates under *SFAS 8*. The *net difference*—the difference between net assets translated according to *SFAS 52* and *SFAS 8*—is the initial balance in the equity adjustment account. It is needed to link the last *SFAS 8* balance sheet to the first *SFAS 52* balance sheet. Once established, the balance in the equity adjustment account will increase (decrease) by the annual translation gain (loss) arising under the current rate method of translation. To illustrate the calculation of this initial balance, we consider the following condensed balance sheet of the Overseas Company at January 1, 19X1, measured in units of local currency (LC). Management of the company's U.S. parent has determined that the Overseas Company's *local currency (LC)* is its *functional currency* and adopts *SFAS 52* as of January 1, 19X1.

OVERSEAS COMPANY
BALANCE SHEET AT JANUARY 1, 19X1

ASSETS		LIABILITIES AND STOCKHOLDERS' EQUITY	
Cash and Receivables . . .	LC1,000,000	Liabilities	LC2,000,000
Inventory and Plant Assets .	3,000,000	Capital Stock	800,000
		Retained Earnings	1,200,000
		Total Liabilities and	
Total Assets.	LC4,000,000	Stockholders' Equity . . .	LC4,000,000

Following *SFAS 52*, the assets and liabilities of Overseas at January 1, 19X1, are translated at the current rate on January 1, 19X1, assumed to be $2/ LC. The difference between net assets translated in this way and the net assets translated according to *SFAS 8* on January 1, 19X1, is the *initial balance* of the Equity Adjustment from Foreign Currency Translation account, the separate component of stockholders' equity used when the current rate method is applied. For purposes of this illustration, assume that Inventory and Plant Assets were acquired when the exchange rate was $1.90/LC and the Capital Stock was issued when the

Exhibit 15.8 **Comparative Translation to Determine the Initial Equity Adjustment Account Balance at January 1, 19X1, for the Overseas Company (Functional Currency: Local Currency)**

	Current Rate Method *(SFAS 52)*			Temporal Method *(SFAS 8)*	
ASSETS	LC	$/LC	$	$/LC	$
Cash and Receivables	LC1,000,000	$2.00	$2,000,000	$2.00	$2,000,000
Inventory and Plant Assets	3,000,000	2.00	6,000,000	1.90	5,700,000
Total Assets.	LC4,000,000		$8,000,000		$7,700,000
LIABILITIES AND STOCKHOLDERS' EQUITY					
Liabilities	LC2,000,000	2.00	$4,000,000	2.00	$4,000,000
Capital Stock	800,000	1.75	1,400,000	1.75	1,400,000
Retained Earnings	1,200,000	(1)	2,300,000	(1)	2,300,000
Equity Adjustment from Foreign Currency Translation . .	—	(2)	300,000	—	—
Total Liabilities and Stockholders' Equity	LC4,000,000		$8,000,000		$7,700,000

(1) Retained Earnings is a plug.
(2) $300,000 = net assets translated under the current rate method, $4,000,000 (= $8,000,000 − $4,000,000) minus net assets translated under *SFAS 8*, $3,700,000 (= $7,700,000 − $4,000,000); equivalently, $300,000 = ($2.00 − $1.90)3,000,000, the difference between Inventory and Plant Assets translated at the current and historical rates.

exchange rate was $1.75/LC. This comparative translation process used to determine the initial $300,000 balance in the equity adjustment account appears in Exhibit 15.8.

Applying *SFAS 52* after Adoption. Continuing with our example of the Overseas Company, we now illustrate the application of *SFAS 52* as of December 31, 19X1, one year after the switch to *SFAS 52* occurred. Data related to the Overseas Company's operations during 19X1 are given in Exhibit 15.9 on page 763.

Translation of the Overseas Company's 19X1 financial statements and supporting schedules appears in Exhibit 15.10 on page 764. Case 1 illustrates *translation under the current rate method* (functional currency is the local currency). Case 2 illustrates *remeasurement under the temporal method* (functional currency is the U.S. dollar). You may wish to compare these translation processes to the previous illustration involving Multiple Methods, Inc., in Exhibits 15.2—15.4.

To see how successful the current rate method is in preserving the financial results and relationships as expressed in the functional currency, consider the following computation of some typical financial ratios for Overseas Company in 19X1:

		U.S. Dollars ($)	
	(1)	(2)	(3)
	Functional	Current Rate	
Ratio	Currency: (LC)	Method	Temporal Method
Net Income/Sales. . . .	.140 (= 700/5,000)	.140 (= 1,435/10,250)	.145 (= 1,485/10,250)
Net Income/Average			
Total Assets	.169 [= 700/(4,000 + 4,300)/2]	.169 [= 1,435/(8,000 + 9,030)/2]	.183 [= 1,485/(7,700 + 8,555)/2]
Net Income/Average			
Stockholders' Equity .	.333 [= 700/(2,000 + 2,200)/2]	.333 [= 1,435/(4,000 + 4,620)/2]	.379 [= 1,485/(3,700 + 4,145)/2]
Liabilities/Total			
Assets	.488 (= 2,100/4,300)	.488 (= 4,410/9,030)	.515 (= 4,410/8,555)
Liabilities/Stockholders'			
Equity	.955 (= 2,100/2,200)	.955 (= 4,410/4,620)	1.064 (= 4,410/4,145)

Although the ratios computed in Columns (1) and (2) will not always be identical, they will be very similar if the exchange rate is relatively stable. In most cases, ratios computed in Columns (1) and (3) will differ by more than those in (1) and (2) because of the potentially large number of different exchange rates used in temporal method translation.

Disclosures

Under *SFAS 52*, companies must disclose the aggregate transaction gain or loss reflected in net income for the period, including any translation gain or loss produced by *remeasuring* foreign currency financial statements into the functional currency. In addition, an analysis of changes in the Equity Adjustment from Foreign Currency Translation account during the period shall be disclosed in a note to the financial statements, in a separate financial statement, or as part of a statement of changes in stockholders' equity. If a change in the exchange rate after the balance sheet data are recorded but before the statements are issued has a significant effect on unsettled foreign currency transactions, that fact and the magnitude of the effect are also to be disclosed.

An example of a particularly informative disclosure appears in Note 14 to the financial statements in the 1983 annual report of CBS. In the note, which is reproduced below, the reference to "gains and losses from certain hedges" relates to transaction adjustments accruing to *economic hedges of net investments in foreign entitites*, which we discussed in Chapter 14.

14. FOREIGN CURRENCY TRANSLATION

The accounting for foreign currency translation conforms to Statement of Financial Accounting Standards No. 52. Generally, adjustments for currency exchange rate changes are excluded from net income for those fluctuations that do not have an impact on cash flow.

Net income included foreign currency losses of $15.9 million, $5.1 million and $5.4 million for 1983, 1982 and 1981, respectively.

An analysis of the changes to the "Foreign currency fluctuations" component of shareholders' equity is as follows:

Exhibit 15.9	Data Related to Applying *SFAS 52* to the Overseas Company during 19X1

THE OVERSEAS COMPANY
STATEMENT OF INCOME AND RETAINED EARNINGS
FOR THE YEAR ENDED DECEMBER 31, 19X1

Sales	LC5,000,000
Cost of Sales and Depreciation	(2,600,000)
Current Operating Expenses	(1,700,000)
Net Income	LC 700,000
Retained Earnings, Jan. 1	1,200,000
Dividends	(500,000)
Retained Earnings, Dec. 31	LC1,400,000

THE OVERSEAS COMPANY
BALANCE SHEET AT DECEMBER 31, 19X1

ASSETS

Cash and Receivables	LC1,200,000
Inventory and Plant Assets	3,100,000
Total Assets	LC4,300,000

LIABILITIES AND STOCKHOLDERS' EQUITY

Liabilities	LC2,100,000
Capital Stock	800,000
Retained Earnings	1,400,000
Total Liabilities and Stockholders' Equity	LC4,300,000

Additional information:

1. The exchange rate is $2.10/LC at December 31, 19X1. The weighted average exchange rate during 19X1 was $2.05/LC. Dividends were declared when the exchange rate was $2.08/LC.

2. LC2,700,000 of inventory and plant assets were purchased during 19X1 at the average exchange rate of $2.05/LC. Cost of Sales and Depreciation are derived from some inventory and plant assets on hand at January 1, 19X1, and from some 19X1 purchases. The average historical exchange rate related to the inventory sold and to depreciation is $2.00/LC.

	Year Ended December 31		
	1983	**1982**	**1981**
	(Dollars in Thousands)		
Balance at Beginning of Year	$(50,795)	$(15,456)	$ 10,940
Translation Adjustments, and Gains and Losses from Certain Hedges and Intercompany Balances, Net.	(551)	(35,454)	(26,861)
Income Taxes Related to Hedges and Intercompany Balances Included Above	(64)	115	465
Balance at End of Year	$(51,410)	$(50,795)	$(15,456)

Exhibit 15.10   **Overseas Company: Translation under *SFAS 52* for the Year Ended December 31, 19X1 (Functional Currency: Local Currency in Case 1 and U.S. Dollar in Case 2)**

STATEMENT OF INCOME AND RETAINED EARNINGS

	LC	Case 1: Current Rate Method $/LC	$	Case 2: Temporal Method $/LC	$
Sales	LC5,000,000	$2.05	$10,250,000	$2.05	$10,250,000
Cost of Sales and					
Depreciation	(2,600,000)	2.05	(5,330,000)	2.00	(5,200,000)
Current Operating Expenses . . .	(1,700,000)	2.05	(3,485,000)	2.05	(3,485,000)
Translation Loss	—	—	—	(2)^a	(80,000)
Net Income	LC 700,000		$ 1,435,000		$ 1,485,000
Retained Earnings, Jan. 1	1,200,000	—	2,300,000	—	2,300,000
Dividends	(500,000)	2.08	(1,040,000)	2.08	(1,040,000)
Retained Earnings, Dec. 31 . . .	LC1,400,000		$ 2,695,000		2,745,000

BALANCE SHEET

ASSETS

	LC		$		$
Cash and Receivables	LC1,200,000	2.10	$ 2,520,000	2.10	$ 2,520,000
Inventory and Plant Assets. . . .	3,100,000	2.10	6,510,000	(3)^a	6,035,000
Total Assets	LC4,300,000		9,030,000		8,555,000

LIABILITIES AND STOCKHOLDERS' EQUITY

	LC		$		$
Liabilities.	LC2,100,000	2.10	$ 4,410,000	2.10	$ 4,410,000
Capital Stock.	800,000	1.75	1,400,000	1.75	1,400,000
Retained Earnings	1,400,000	—	2,695,000	—	2,745,000
Equity Adjustment from Foreign					
Currency Translation.	—	(1)^a	525,000	—	—
Total Liabilities and Stockholders'					
Equity	LC4,300,000		$ 9,030,000		$ 8,555,000

^{a}The supporting schedule appears below (1) or on the facing page (2) and (3).

(1) ANALYSIS OF EQUITY ADJUSTMENT FROM FOREIGN CURRENCY TRANSLATION (CURRENT RATE METHOD)

	LC	Dr. (Cr.) $/LC	$
Balance, Jan. 1, 19X1 (Exhibit 15.8)	—	—	$ (300,000)
19X1 Translation Adjustment:			
Exposed Position (Net Assets), Jan. 1, 19X1	LC2,000,000	$2.00	$ 4,000,000
Plus: Net Income in 19X1	700,000*	2.05	1,435,000
Less: Dividends Declared.	(500,000)	2.08	(1,040,000)
Exposed Position (Net Assets), Dec. 31, 19X1	LC2,200,000		$ 4,395,000
	└——————→ 2.10 →		−4,620,000
Net 19X1 Translation Adjustment (Gain)			$ (225,000)
Balance, Dec. 31, 19X1			$ (525,000)

*The revenues and expenses which make up net income represent individual increases and decreases to the exposed position. Since they are all translated at the same average rate of $2.05/LC, a single entry for net income will suffice.

Exhibit 15.10 **Continued**

(2) PROOF OF TRANSLATION LOSS (TEMPORAL METHOD)

	LC	$/LC	$
Exposed Position, Jan. 1, 19X1	LC(1,000,000)*	$2.00	$ (2,000,000)
Plus: Sales	5,000,000	2.05	10,250,000
Less: Purchase of Inventory and Plant Assets	(2,700,000)	2.05	(5,535,000)
Less: Payment of Current Operating Expenses	(1,700,000)	2.05	(3,485,000)
Less: Dividends Declared	(500,000)	2.08	(1,040,000)
Exposed Position, Dec. 31, 19X1	LC (900,000)*		$ (1,810,000)
		2.10 →	− (1,890,000)
Translation loss			$ 80,000

*The exposed position under the temporal method is Cash and Receivables minus Liabilities; at January 1, 19X1, it is (LC1,000,000) = LC1,000,000 − LC2,000,000 and at December 31, 19X1, it is (LC900,000) = LC1,200,000 − LC2,100,000.

(3) ANALYSIS OF INVENTORIES AND PLANT ASSETS (TEMPORAL METHOD)

	LC	$/LC	$
Balance, Jan. 1, 19X1 (Exhibit 15.8)	LC3,000,000	$1.90	$ 5,700,000
Amount Purchased	2,700,000	2.05	5,535,000
Inventory Sold and Depreciation Expense	(2,600,000)*	2.00*	(5,200,000)
Balance, Dec. 31, 19X1	LC3,100,000		$ 6,035,000

*Includes portions from January 1, 19X1, balance and from 19X1 purchases; average exchange rate related to inventory sold and depreciation is $2.00/LC.

Other Foreign Currency Translation Matters

The preceding section discussed and illustrated the principal concepts and methods underlying translation of foreign statements pursuant to *SFAS 52*. Additional issues are discussed below.

Business Combinations

When a foreign entity's assets are acquired and its liabilities assumed in a business combination, these items must be translated into dollars for inclusion in the U.S. parent's financial statements. Both the foreign entity's functional currency and the method of accounting—purchase or pooling of interests—used by the parent are important.

At date of business combination, the spot rate is used unless the functional currency is the U.S. dollar and the combination is accounted for as a pooling of interests. In this situation, translation (remeasurement) is accomplished via the temporal method, and historical rates in existence prior to the business combination are used as appropriate.

All *purchase combinations* call for use of the spot rate at date of business combination to translate *fair values* of assets acquired, liabilities assumed, and purchased goodwill and, in a stock acquisition, the *book value* of the foreign entity's stockholders' equity. In a *pooling* involving a foreign entity with a foreign functional currency, the *book values* of all assets, liabilities, and stockholders' equity accounts are translated at the spot rate at date of business combination.

When consolidated statements are prepared *after date of business combination,* the *current rate method* applies to entities with *foreign* functional currencies. If the entity's functional currency is the U.S. dollar, the temporal method is used; in a purchase, the spot rate at date of business combination becomes the historical rate for purposes of remeasuring the entity's stockholders' equity in existence at date of business combination.

Translated *minority interest* in a partially owned foreign subsidiary is the minority's pro rata share of the subsidiary's stockholders' equity translated or remeasured as outlined above. It will also include the portion of the accumulated Equity Adjustment attributable to the minority interest. These rules are summarized in Exhibit 15.11.

Exhibit 15.11 **Translation of Assets Acquired, Liabilities Assumed, and Stockholders' Equity in a Business Combination**

Method of Accounting	Functional Currency	Translation Rate/Method		Accounting Basis to Be Translated
		Date of Business Combination	Subsequent to Business Combination	
Purchase	Foreign currency	Spot rate	Current rate method	Fair values of assets acquired, liabilities assumed, and purchased goodwill; book value of stockholders' equity
Pooling of Interests	Foreign currency	Spot rate	Current rate method	Book values of assets acquired, liabilities assumed, and stockholders' equity
Purchase	U.S. dollar	Spot rate	Temporal method utilizing spot rate at date of business combination as historical rate for those items in existence at date of business combination	Fair values of assets acquired, liabilities assumed, and purchased goodwill; book value of stockholders' equity
Pooling of Interests	U.S. dollar	Temporal method	Temporal method utilizing same historical rates as used at date of business combination	Book values of assets acquired, liabilities assumed, and stockholders equity

Equity Investments

The financial statements of a foreign equity investee are to be translated (or re-measured) into dollars according to *SFAS 52* before the equity method accrual is booked. When the *current rate method* is used, the portions of any purchase premium reflected in the original purchase price that are allocable to undervalued assets of the investee or to goodwill are to be translated at the ending current rate, but the weighted average current rate for the period is used to translate the purchase premium amortization reflected in the equity method accrual. In making the accrual, the investor should also adjust its investment account for its share of the changes in the investee's Equity Adjustment from Foreign Currency Translation account, if any, and include its share in the investor's Equity Adjustment account. If the investee's statements are *remeasured* using the *temporal method,* purchase premium amortization is based on the exchange rate when the shares were acquired. Moreover, the equity method accrual includes the investor's share of the investee's translation gain or loss through its inclusion in the investee's remeasured net income.

Income Tax Effects

Exchange gains and losses enter into taxable income when receivables or payables are *settled* and conversion from or to foreign currency takes place. If reported exchange gains or losses exceed the amount currently taxable, deferred taxes must be provided on timing differences. Many translation gains or losses, however, are actually permanent differences. To the extent that the timing differences are large, the *aftertax* exchange gain or loss may be significantly different from the *pretax* amount. Yet these tax effects need not be specifically disclosed. This is one reason why attempting to evaluate the economic significance of reported exchange gains or losses may be a hazardous undertaking.

Application of the Lower-of-Cost-or-Market Rule

Specific application of the lower-of-cost-or-market (LCM) rule depends on whether the foreign entity's books are maintained in the functional currency. Different financial outcomes can occur. If the entity's functional currency is its home (local) currency, no special problems arise. On the entity's books, functional currency losses associated with inventory write-downs to market are recognized and then translated into dollars at the current exchange rate on the balance sheet date. The reduced functional-currency carrying value of the inventory is translated into dollars at the current rate.

The LCM process is more complex when the foreign entity's books are *not* maintained in its functional currency. This will be the case when the entity's functional currency is the U.S. dollar or another foreign currency. In such situations, LCM is applied in the following steps:

1. Remeasure the inventory at cost (in the home currency) into the functional

currency using the historical exchange rate(s) between the functional currency and the home currency when the inventory was acquired.

2. Remeasure the inventory at market (in the home currency) into the functional currency using the current exchange rate.

3. When $(1) < (2)$, remeasured market exceeds remeasured cost. No write-down is needed in the functional currency statements, and any write-down reflected in the home currency statements is reversed prior to the remeasurement process.

4. When $(1) > (2)$, remeasured cost exceeds remeasured market and a loss equal to $(1) - (2)$ is recognized in the functional currency statements. If a write-down has already been made in the home currency financial statements, it is reversed prior to the remeasurement process. After reversal, the inventory at cost is remeasured into the functional currency and then is written down by $(1) - (2)$.

These rules are illustrated in the following examples:

1. A unit of inventory owned by a U.K. subsidiary was purchased when the price was £10 and the exchange rate was \$2.00/£. At year-end, market in the United Kingdom is £12 and the exchange rate is \$1.50/£. No write-down in the foreign statements is required (£12 > £10).

   a. If the pound is the functional currency, no LCM write-down is needed (£12 > £10) and the translated inventory is reported at \$15 (= 10 × \$1.50).

   b. If the U.S. dollar is the functional currency, remeasured historical cost of \$20 (= 10 × \$2) exceeds remeasured market of \$18 (= 12 × \$1.50). Thus a loss of \$2 (= \$20 − \$18) is recognized in the remeasured (dollar) statements and the inventory is reported at \$18.

2. Use the facts in Example 1, except that at year-end market in the United Kingdom is £9 and the exchange rate is \$2.50/£. This produces a loss of £1 (= £10 − £9), which is recognized in the foreign currency statements.

   a. If the £ is the functional currency, this £1 loss remains and becomes \$2.50 when translated into dollars. Inventory, now at market, is reported at \$22.50 (= 9 × \$2.50).

   b. If the functional currency is the U.S. dollar, we compare remeasured historical cost of \$20 with remeasured market of \$22.50 (= 9 × \$2.50). Since \$22.50 > \$20, no loss is recognized in the functional currency statements and the £1 loss in the foreign statements is reversed prior to remeasurement into dollars. Inventory, now at cost, is reported at \$20.

3. Now assume that at year-end market in the United Kingdom is £9 and the exchange rate is \$1.50/£. The foreign statements show a loss of £1.

   a. If the functional currency is the pound, this £1 loss remains and becomes \$1.50 when translated into dollars. Inventory, now at market, is reported at \$13.50 (= 9 × \$1.50).

   b. If the U.S. dollar is the functional currency, comparison of remeasured cost with remeasured market produces a functional currency loss of \$6.50

$[= (10 \times \$2) - (9 \times \$1.50)]$. The £1 loss in the foreign statements is reversed prior to remeasurement and inventory at cost is remeasured into $\$20 (= 10 \times \$2)$. The loss of $\$6.50$ is now recognized and inventory is reported in the functional currency statements at remeasured market, $\$13.50 [= \$20 - \$6.50 = (9 \times \$1.50)]$.

Foreign Branches and Subsidiaries

Translation of foreign currency financial statements is required when the operations of foreign branches and subsidiaries are to be included in the U.S. financial statements of the parent company. The foreign accounts are generally translated according to the rules presented in the previous sections. Issues related to reporting these foreign operations and including them in U.S. combined or consolidated statements are discussed below.

Reporting on Foreign Operations. *ARB 43* expresses concern over the inclusion of translated foreign operations in U.S. company statements.[14] Given the inherent riskiness of foreign operations—distant geographical locations subject to foreign sovereign states—extreme care should be taken in reporting earnings in excess of amounts received in cash or available in cash for unrestricted transmission to the United States. Similarly, uncertainty with respect to the ultimate realization of other foreign assets is an issue to be resolved in determining the propriety of combined or consolidated statements which include translated foreign assets and liabilities.

ARB 43 also identifies four possible ways of reporting information related to foreign subsidiaries or branches:

(a) To exclude foreign subsidiaries from consolidation and to furnish (1) statements in which only domestic subsidiaries are consolidated and (2) as to foreign subsidiaries, a summary in suitable form of their assets and liabilities, their income and losses for the year, and the parent company's equity therein. The total amount of investments in foreign subsidiaries should be shown separately, and the basis on which the amount was arrived at should be stated. If these investments include any surplus of foreign subsidiaries and such surplus had previously been included in consolidated surplus, the amount should be separately shown or earmarked in stating the consolidated surplus in the statements here suggested. The exclusion of foreign subsidiaries from consolidation does not make it acceptable practice to include intercompany profits which would be eliminated if such subsidiaries were consolidated.

(b) To consolidate domestic and foreign subsidiaries and to furnish in addition the summary described in (a) (2) above.

(c) To furnish (1) complete consolidated statements and also (2) consolidated statements for domestic companies only.

(d) To consolidate domestic and foreign subsidiaries and to furnish in addition parent company statements showing the investment in and income from foreign subsidiaries separately from those of domestic subsidiaries.[15]

---

[14]Committee on Accounting Procedure, *ARB 43*, Chap. 12; CT § C51.105.
[15]Ibid., CT § C51.106. Copyright © 1953 by the American Institute of Certified Public Accountants, Inc.

Translation of Reciprocal Accounts. Both home office/branch accounting and parent/subsidiary accounting involve the use of **reciprocal accounts.** Reciprocal accounts are those that have equal and offsetting balances on the home/branch books or the parent/subsidiary books. Such accounts are *eliminated* when combined or consolidated financial statements are prepared. The simplest approach to translating reciprocal accounts in the foreign statements is to use the dollar balances from the reciprocal accounts on the home office or parent company's books as the translated balances.

In the *home office/branch* situation, the following reciprocal accounts are affected:

1. Investment in Branch (Dr.)/Home Office (Cr.).
2. Shipments from Home Office (Dr.)/Shipments to Branch (Cr.), Overvaluation of Branch Inventory (Cr.).
3. Remittances to Home Office (Dr.)/Remittances from Branch (Cr.).

Observe that translating in this way removes the built-in check possessed by the reciprocal accounts in domestic home office/branch settings. The home office must now obtain a complete list of transactions recorded in the branch's reciprocal accounts and reconcile the reciprocal accounts. Since the translated foreign balance will by definition equal the U.S. dollar balance, there is no automatic way of determining whether all intrafirm transactions have been recorded properly on both sets of books.

Similarly, the preparation of consolidated financial statements in the *parent/subsidiary* setting requires that reciprocal intercompany accounts be eliminated. As in the home office/branch case, intercompany accounts in the foreign statements are given translated balances equal to the dollar balances of the offsetting accounts on the parent's books. Where intercompany sales, purchases, receivables, and payables are concerned, the foreign subsidiary must inform the parent of the transactions it recorded. Only in this way can the parent reconcile the offsetting accounts without separate translation of each entry made by the foreign subsidiary.

Preparation of Consolidated Statements. The basic consolidation procedure involves elimination of the investment account against the translated stockholders' equity (including the Equity Adjustment account) of the foreign subsidiary. *At the date of business combination,* the investment account reflects the parent's portion of the subsidiary's translated stockholders' equity, as well as a purchase premium or discount in the purchase case. Once any purchase premium or discount is reclassified and allocated on the working paper, a clean elimination is possible.

For example, suppose that Domestic Corporation pays $4,200,000 cash for 80 percent of the common stock of the Overseas Company, the entity in Exhibits 15.8, 15.9, and 15.10. The Overseas Company's stockholders' equity at January 1, 19X1, translated at the $2/LC spot rate, amounts to $4,000,000 [= $2(800,000 + 1,200,000)], and a *purchase premium* of $1,000,000 [= $4,200,000 − (.8 × $4,000,000)] results. If we also assume that the Overseas Company's inventory and plant assets have an estimated fair value of LC3,400,000 (their book value is LC3,000,000), the purchase premium is allocated as follows:

```
Inventory and Plant Assets [.8 × $2(3,400,000 − 3,000,000)] . . . . . . . . .    $  640,000
Goodwill . . . . . . . . . . . . . . . . . . . . . . . . . . . . . . . . . . .       360,000
Total Purchase Premium  . . . . . . . . . . . . . . . . . . . . . . . . . . .    $1,000,000
```

Preparation of a consolidated balance sheet at date of business combination—January 1, 19X1—requires the following working paper entries:

CONSOLIDATED FINANCIAL STATEMENT WORKING PAPER

```
Inventory and Plant Assets . . . . . . . . . . . . . . . . .    640,000
Goodwill. . . . . . . . . . . . . . . . . . . . . . . . . .    360,000
    Investment in Overseas Company . . . . . . . . . . . .                 1,000,000
To reclassify and allocate the purchase premium.

Capital Stock—Overseas Company ($2 × 800,000) . . . .  1,600,000
Retained Earnings—Overseas Company ($2 × 1,200,000).  2,400,000
    Investment in Overseas Company . . . . . . . . . . .                  3,200,000
    Minority Interest in Overseas Company . . . . . . . . .                 800,000
To eliminate the investment account ($3,200,000 =
$4,200,000 − $1,000,000) against the stockholders' equity
of the Overseas Company and establish the minority
interest [800,000 = .2 × ($1,600,000 + $2,400,000)], all
as of Jan. 1, 19X1.
```

At consolidation points *after date of business combination,* the procedures discussed in Chapters 8–11 are used. If the equity method is employed, the investment account is updated each year to reflect the parent's portion of the change in the translated book value of the subsidiary's stockholders' equity. Moreover, use of the current rate method results in a currently translated unamortized purchase premium; the change in the translated amount is entered in the Equity Adjustment account. When the parent employs the cost method to account for investments in foreign subsidiaries, a working paper entry is necessary to adjust the investment account to the equity basis, as described in Chapter 8. In all cases, the Minority Interest in S will reflect the minority's portion of the translated book value of the subsidiary's stockholders' equity, including the Equity Adjustment, when reclassified on the working paper.

Continuing with the above example involving the Overseas Company, we work through consolidation at December 31, 19X1, one year after date of acquisition. Domestic Corporation uses the *equity method.* The Overseas Company's *functional currency* is assumed to be the *local currency* in *Case 1* and the *U.S. dollar* in *Case 2.*

First, consider Domestic's 19X1 *equity accrual.* Domestic's share of the Overseas Company's translated net income is reduced by purchase premium amortization. We assume that 25 percent of the original allocation to inventory and plant assets has been sold or depreciated and that the goodwill is being amortized over 10 years. The equity accrual is calculated in the schedule below.

DOMESTIC CORPORATION
SCHEDULE TO DETERMINE THE EQUITY METHOD ACCRUAL
FOR THE YEAR ENDED DECEMBER 31, 19X1

	Case 1 (Current Rate Method)	Case 2 (Temporal Method)
Share of Overseas Company's Net Income (1)	$1,148,000	$1,188,000
Less Amortization of Purchase Premium:		
Cost of Sales and Depreciation (2)	$ 164,000	$ 160,000
Amortization of Goodwill (3)	36,900	36,000
	$ 200,900	$ 196,000
Net Equity Method Accrual for 19X1	$ 947,100	$ 992,000

(1) These amounts are 80 percent of the respective translated net incomes calculated in Exhibit 15.10; $1,148,000 = .8 × $1,435,000, $1,188,000 = .8 × $1,485,000.
(2) These amounts reflect translation at the average rate of $2.05/LC and the historical rate of $2.00/LC, respectively; $164,000 = .8 × $2.05(3,400,000 − 3,000,000)/4; $160,000 = .8 × $2.00(3,400,000 − 3,000,000)/4.
(3) These amounts reflect translation at the average rate of $2.05/LC and the historical rate of $2.00/LC, respectively; goodwill in local currency is LC180,000 (= 360,000/2); $36,900 = $2.05 × 180,000/10; $36,000 = $2.00 × 180,000/10.

In applying the equity method, we first record Domestic's share of the Overseas Company's dividends, translated at the $2.08 rate when the dividends were declared. We then record the 19X1 equity accrual and, in a separate entry under *Case 1,* adjust the investment account for Domestic's share of the change in the Overseas Company's Equity Adjustment account. In this case, the change consists of the translation adjustment of $225,000 calculated under the current rate method (see Exhibit 15.10).

BOOKS OF DOMESTIC CORPORATION

	Case 1 (Current Rate Method)	Case 2 (Temporal Method)
Cash	832,000	832,000
Investment in Overseas Company	832,000	832,000
To record Domestic's share of Overseas Company's dividends; $832,000 = .8 × $2.08 × 500,000.		
Investment in Overseas Company	947,100	992,000
Income from Overseas Company	947,100	992,000
To record Domestic's 19X1 equity method accrual.		

```
Investment in Overseas Company . . . . . .   180,000              No entry
   Equity Adjustment from Foreign Currency
      Translation . . . . . . . . . . . . . . .              180,000
To record Domestic's share of the change in
Overseas Company's Equity Adjustment
account; $180,000 = .8 × $225,000.
```

We now turn to consolidation at the end of 19X1. The equity method entries will be reversed but, in Case 1, the entry for Domestic's share of the change in the Equity Adjustment account will not be reversed. This is necessary so that the Equity Adjustment account on the Overseas Company's translated balance sheet can be eliminated in consolidation. We illustrate below the working paper entries relating to the purchase premium, elimination of the investment account, and change in the minority interest.

CONSOLIDATED FINANCIAL STATEMENT WORKING PAPER

	Case 1 (Current Rate Method)		Case 2 (Temporal Method)	
Income from Overseas Company	947,100		992,000	
Dividends—Overseas Company		832,000		832,000
Investment in Overseas Company		115,100		160,000
To reverse the 19X1 equity method entries, thereby adjusting the Investment Account to its beginning-of-year balance, except for Domestic's share of the change in the Equity Adjustment account.				
Inventory and Plant Assets	672,000		640,000	
Goodwill	378,000		360,000	
Investment in Overseas Company		1,000,000		1,000,000
Equity Adjustment from Foreign Currency				
Translation		50,000		—
To reclassify and allocate the unamortized purchase premium as of Jan. 1, 19X1. In Case 1, the unamortized amounts are translated at the Dec. 31, 19X1, current rate. The effect of the changing exchange rate is entered in the Equity Adjustment account; $50,000 = ($2.10 − $2.00) LC500,000, where LC500,000 [= $1,000,000/($2.00/LC)] is the original purchase premium measured in units of foreign currency.				
Capital Stock—Overseas Company.	1,600,000		1,600,000	
Retained Earnings, 1/1/X1—Overseas Company .	2,400,000		2,400,000	
Equity Adjustment—Overseas Company	225,000		—	
Investment in Overseas Company		3,380,000		3,200,000
Minority Interest in Overseas Company.		845,000		800,000
To eliminate the investment account against the stockholders' equity of the Overseas Company and establish the 20 percent minority interest. The eliminated investment account balances are determined as follows:				

(Continued on the next page)

	Case 1	Case 2
Cost of the Investment, 1/1/X1	$4,200,000	$4,200,000
19X1 Intercompany Dividends	(832,000)	(832,000)
19X1 Equity Accrual	947,100	992,000
19X1 Equity Adjustment Entry	180,000	—
Balance per Books, 12/31/X1	$4,495,000	$4,360,000
Reversal of Equity Method Entries	(115,100)	(160,000)
Reclassification of Purchase Premium	(1,000,000)	(1,000,000)
Eliminated Balances	$3,380,000	$3,200,000

CONSOLIDATED FINANCIAL STATEMENT WORKING PAPER

		Case 1			Case 2
Minority Interest in Net Income	287,000			297,000	
Dividends—Overseas Company		208,000			208,000
Minority Interest in Overseas Company		79,000			89,000

To record the change in the minority interest during 19X1. The minority's interest in the Overseas Company's net income is 20 percent of the respective translated amounts of $1,435,000 and $1,485,000 (see Exhibit 15.10).

		Case 1			Case 2
Cost of Sales and Depreciation	164,000			160,000	
Amortization Expense	36,900			90,000	
Equity Adjustment from Foreign Currency Translation	4,900			—	
Inventory and Plant Assets		168,000			160,000
Goodwill		37,800			90,000

To record purchase premium amortization for 19X1, as reflected in the schedule to determine the equity method accrual. In Case 1, the amortization is translated at the average rate of $2.05/LC, whereas the asset accounts are translated at the current rate of $2.10/LC; the difference is charged to the Equity Adjustment account.

Intercompany Transactions. Transaction gains and losses on **foreign currency intercompany transactions** are normally included in net income. Under *SFAS 52*, however, if any intercompany transactions are deemed to be of a "long-term investment" nature (i.e., settlement is not anticipated in the foreseeable future), the related transaction adjustments are not reported in income but are carried directly to the Equity Adjustment from Foreign Currency Translation account and are included in the analysis of the changes in that account.

Elimination of *unconfirmed intercompany profits* under *SFAS 52* is based on the exchange rates in effect when the intercompany transactions took place. Subsequent changes in the exchange rate do not affect the amount of intercompany profit to be eliminated. Instead, they accrue on the consolidated balance of the unsold or unused items after removal of the dollar amount of intercompany profit determined when the transfer took place.

Concluding Remarks. As the above illustration demonstrates, consolidation of a foreign subsidiary can be complex when the current rate method is used (Case 1). Not only must the foreign subsidiary's Equity Adjustment account be dealt with, but the parent company also needs to consider the way in which the fluctuating exchange rate affects translation of purchase premium allocations and amortization. Thus the *Equity Adjustment from Foreign Currency Translation* appearing in consolidated statements consists of the parent's share of the foreign subsidiary's Equity Adjustment account, translation adjustments related to the purchase premium and its amortization, transaction adjustments accrued on "long-term" intercompany transactions, and transaction adjustments on "economic hedges of net investments in foreign entities" (Chapter 14).

Use of the current rate method, with concurrent creation of the Equity Adjustment account, will also complicate preparation of the consolidated statement of changes in financial position (SCFP). Although not illustrated in this chapter, material changes in "funds"—cash or working capital—and in nonfund assets and liabilities attributed to movements in exchange rates must be disclosed in the SCFP.

Summary of Foreign Currency Translation

SFAS 52 represents a major change in accounting for international operations. In effect, it recognizes that the nature of a U.S. company's economic exposure to the risks of foreign operations depends in large measure on the nature of the foreign business activity. Flexibility is permitted so that the current rate method can be used when the parent's exposed position is best represented by its net investment in the foreign entity and its economic exposure is a direct function of the viability of the foreign entity's operations. Alternatively, the temporal method of *SFAS 8* is retained to account for those foreign entities closely related to the U.S. parent and where the parent's economic exposure is more closely tied to the individual monetary assets and liabilities of the foreign entity.[16]

SFAS 52 offers a new solution to a very complex fundamental problem. Fluctuating exchange rates are the result of many factors, and they contribute to the inherent difficulty of devising a reporting scheme which adequately reflects the economics of foreign operations. Only time will tell how successful *SFAS 52* will be in overcoming the alleged weaknesses of *SFAS 8*.

International Accounting Standards

Reporting international operations is complicated by the fact that accounting principles and practices vary widely across countries. Not only is the accounting function in the multinational firm affected, the task faced by investors attempting to compare and evaluate alternative investment opportunities around the world is extremely difficult. In this section, we discuss the dimensions of the problem and review the development of international accounting standards.

---

[16]For a critical evaluation of *SFAS 52,* see James A. Largay III, "*SFAS 52:* Expediency or Principle?," *Journal of Accounting, Auditing and Finance* (Fall, 1983), 44–53.

Exhibit 15.12	Some Examples of the Variability in Accounting Worldwide

19. ACCOUNTING POLICIES

A change in accounting principles or methods without a change in circumstances is accounted for by restatement of financial informaiton currently presented in respect of prior periods.

FIXED ASSETS—LEASES 52.

The amount and period of commitments under long-term leases for future years are disclosed.

19. ACCOUNTING POLICIES

Required	Insisted upon	Predominant practice	Minority practice	Rarely or not found	Not accepted	Not permitted	SOURCE	Country
						■	LEG	Argentina
			■					Australia
						■	LEG	Austria
		■						Bahamas
						■	LEG	Belgium
		■						Bermuda
			■					Bolivia
		■						Botswana
■							LEG	Brazil
		■						Canada
			■					Chile
						■	LEG	Colombia
			■					Costa Rica
			■					Denmark
				■				Dominican Rep.
		■						Ecuador
			■					El Salvador
			■					Fiji
			■					France
						■	LEG	Germany
			■					Greece
			■					Guatemala
			■					Honduras
■							HKSA	Hong Kong
			■					India
		■						Iran
■							SSAP 6	Ireland, Rep. of
		■						Italy
			■					Ivory Coast
■							SSAP 3	Jamaica
				■				Japan
	■							Jersey, Channel Is.
	■							Kenya
						■	ASR	Korea
		■						Malawi
		■						Malaysia
			■					Morocco
						■	CPC A7	Mexico
		■						Netherlands
■							SSAP 7	New Zealand
						■	CN 6	Nicaragua
	■							Nigeria
		■						Norway
			■					Pakistan
		■						Panama
			■					Paraguay
		■						Peru
			■					Philippines
			■					Portugal
			■					Senegal
	■							Singapore
						■	GAAP 3	South Africa
			■					Spain
				■				Sweden
						■	LEG	Switzerland
■							GAAP	Taiwan
		■						Trinidad and Tobago
■							SSAP 6	United Kingdom
						■	APB 20	United States
			■					Uruguay
						■	AC	Venezuela
						■	LEG	Zaire
		■						Zambia
■							RM 4	Zimbabwe Rhodesia

FIXED ASSETS—LEASES 52.

Country	Required	Insisted upon	Predominant practice	Minority practice	Rarely or not found	Not accepted	Not permitted	SOURCE
Argentina					■			
Australia					■			
Austria					■			
Bahamas			■					
Belgium					■			
Bermuda	■							3065
Bolivia					■			
Botswana					■			
Brazil	■							LEG
Canada	■							3065
Chile					■			
Colombia			■					
Costa Rica			■					
Denmark					■			
Dominican Rep.	■							
Ecuador			■					
El Salvador			■					
Fiji		■						
France					■			
Germany					■			
Greece					■			
Guatemala			■					
Honduras			■					
Hong Kong					■			
India					■			
Iran		■						
Ireland, Rep. of	■							
Italy		■						
Ivory Coast					■			
Jamaica					■			
Japan					■			
Jersey, Channel Is.					■			
Kenya					■			
Korea	■							ASR
Malawi					■			
Malaysia					■			
Morocco					■			
Mexico	■							CPC C6
Netherlands	■							LEG
New Zealand		■						
Nicaragua			■					
Nigeria			■					
Norway	■							LEG
Pakistan			■					
Panama			■					
Paraguay					■			
Peru	■							CNSEV
Philippines	■							LEG
Portugal					■			
Senegal					■			
Singapore					■			
South Africa					■			
Spain					■			
Sweden					■			
Switzerland					■			
Taiwan		■						
Trinidad and Tobago			■					
United Kingdom			■					
United States	■							FAS 13
Uruguay					■			
Venezuela	■							AC
Zaire					■			
Zambia					■			
Zimbabwe Rhodesia					■			

Exhibit 15.12   **Continued**

BUSINESS COMBINATIONS 246.
When, in a business combination accounted for as a purchase, the consideration is an issue of shares, their fair value is determined by reference either to the value of the underlying net assets acquired or to the market value of the shares issued, whichever is more clearly evident.

FOREIGN CURRENCIES 252.
In translating foreign currency financial statements, the closing exchange rate is applied to all assets and liabilities.

Required	Insisted upon	Predominant practice	Minority practice	Rarely or not found	Not accepted	Not permitted	SOURCE		Required	Insisted upon	Predominant practice	Minority practice	Rarely or not found	Not accepted	Not permitted	SOURCE
		■						Argentina					■			
	■							Australia			■					
						■	LEG	Austria							■	LEG
		■						Bahamas				■				
		■						Belgium					■			
■							1580	Bermuda							■	1650
			■					Bolivia					■			
		■						Botswana			■					
		■						Brazil					■			
■							1580	Canada							■	1650
	■							Chile				■				
			■					Colombia			■					
		■						Costa Rica				■				
		■						Denmark			■					
	■							Dominican Rep.					■			
			■					Ecuador					■			
		■						El Salvador					■			
			■					Fiji			■					
■							LEG	France			■					
						■	LEG	Germany				■				
		■						Greece			■					
		■						Guatemala				■				
		■						Honduras					■			
	■							Hong Kong			■					
NOT APPLICABLE								India			■					
			■					Iran					■			
	■							Ireland, Rep. of			■					
		■						Italy				■				
			■					Ivory Coast			■					
			■					Jamaica							■	SSAP 7
		■						Japan			■					
			■					Jersey, Channel Is.			■					
		■						Kenya			■					
		■						Korea						■		
		■						Malawi				■				
		■						Malaysia			■					
		■						Morocco					■			
			■					Mexico					■			
		■						Netherlands			■					
		■						New Zealand				■				
		■						Nicaragua				■				
			■					Nigeria					■			
		■						Norway			■					
			■					Pakistan					■			
			■					Panama						■		
			■					Paraguay			■					
		■						Peru						■		
		■						Philippines				■				
			■					Portugal					■			
			■					Senegal			■					
		■						Singapore			■					
■							LEG	South Africa				■				
						■	LEG	Spain			■					
			■					Sweden				■				
			■					Switzerland			■					
		■						Taiwan						■		
		■						Trinidad and Tobago			■					
	■							United Kingdom			■					
■							APB 16	United States							■	FAS 8
			■					Uruguay	■							BCCU 1
		■						Venezuela				■				
			■					Zaire					■			
			■					Zambia				■				
		■						Zimbabwe Rhodesia			■					

Source: Price Waterhouse, *International Survey of Accounting Principles and Reporting Practices,* Butterworths (Canada), Scarborough, Ontario, 1979.

Diversity in Accounting Principles and Practices throughout the World

We begin by providing some evidence regarding the lack of uniformity in accounting around the globe.[17] The extents to which selected accounting practices are generally accepted in various countries are tabulated in Exhibit 15.12. Note that there are relatively few countries in which a given accounting matter is *required*. Furthermore, the extent of acceptability of any individual item tends to range all the way from *required* to *not permitted*.

At first glance, it might appear that the diversity illustrated in Exhibit 15.12 is the outcome of some unspecified random process. Upon reflection, however, it becomes apparent that the existence of alternative patterns of development in accounting leads both to diversity and to similarities in accounting across countries. Choi and Mueller identify four approaches or orientations to accounting development which provide starting points for analyzing the differences and similarities in accounting around the world.[18]

1. A **macroeconomic orientation** results in accounting systems of individual units in the economy designed to interface closely with national programs, goals, and information requirements. One implication of a macroeconomic orientation involves accounting principles. For example, income smoothing might be encouraged in order that fluctuations in the national income and product accounts and, hence, in reported business cycles, be dampened. Moreover, a macroeconomic orientation could lead to the design of accounting systems and reports along the lines dictated by governmental central planning activities.

2. In contrast, a **microeconomic orientation** has as its focal points individual firms and other economic entities. Under such an orientation, accounting and reporting tend to have a distinct managerial flavor. Information is structured to facilitate good (if not optimal) decisions relating to the prosperity of the firm. Replacement cost accounting and line-of-business reporting are examples of what might flow from a microeconomic orientation to accounting.

3. Another approach views accounting as an **independent discipline,** for which conventions, principles, and procedures are derived primarily from experience in the world of business affairs. Development of a theoretical structure grounded in scientific disciplines from which logical rules of behavior can be deduced is difficult for accounting to achieve. The evolution of generally accepted accounting principles in the United States is representative of the independent discipline approach. The realization convention and historical cost valuation illustrate the pragmatic—perhaps expedient—

---

[17]In addition to the reference provided in Exhibit 15.12, a detailed and comprehensive analysis of comparative accounting principles and practice can be found in American Institute of Certified Public Accountants, *Professional Accounting in 30 Countries* (New York: AICPA, 1975).

[18]Frederick D. S. Choi and Gerhard G. Mueller, *International Accounting* (Englewood Cliffs, NJ: Prentice-Hall, 1984), Chapter 2.

process from which rules in the independent discipline of accounting emerge.

4. Choi and Mueller also identify a stress on **uniform rules** as an approach to accounting development. This orientation emphasizes the importance of administrative fiat; detailed regulations prescribing uniform systems, reports, and accounting treatments; and the resulting comparability of reported information. The uniformity might be limited to particular industries or might encompass all entities in an economy. We tend to see uniform accounting in regulated industries and, from the relatively uniform perspective of the tax code, in all industries. A specific example of the influence of uniformity on accounting in the United States appears in *SFAS 2*, which prescribes a single accounting treatment for research and development costs.

Note that the development of accounting in the United States is not exclusively the result of any of the four approaches mentioned above. Rather, it has elements of all. The microeconomic and independent discipline approaches are probably dominant, although increasing emphasis is being placed on uniform rules.

Efforts to Achieve Standardization. Attempts aimed at standardizing accounting principles and practices are underway both nationally and internationally. Groups like the FASB and AICPA in the United States and the Canadian Institute of Chartered Accountants (CICA) in Canada are examples of private organizations which have national standardization as one of their objectives. In France, however, the government and the tax laws are most influential in shaping accounting principles and promoting standardization. Through its *Plan Comptable Général,* French accounting principles and practice are highly standardized. The *Plan* includes a detailed uniform chart of accounts adaptable to all industries, complete with definitions and regulations comparable to those of prescribed accounting systems for regulated industries in the United States.

Regional groups working toward standardization across national boundaries include the Confederation of Asian and Pacific Accountants (CAPA), the Inter-American Accounting Association (IAA; composed primarily of Spanish-speaking Western Hemisphere nations) and the Union Européenne des Experts Comptables Economiques (UEC). Membership in the UEC includes most of the member countries of the European Economic Community, or "Common Market," as well as other European nations.

Member nations of the European Economic Community (EEC)[19] are also active in developing accounting principles. The EEC Commission periodically issues directives relating to companies in the common market. The directives are part of the EEC's program to harmonize company laws; those that deal with accounting matters are briefly summarized below. They are currently in various stages of implementation.

The *Fourth Directive* (1978) specifies in detail the form and content of fi-

---

[19]The member nations of the EEC are Belgium, Denmark, France, Greece, Republic of Ireland, Italy, Luxembourg, the Netherlands, United Kingdom, and West Germany.

nancial statements and the requirements for disclosure. Consistency, the going-concern concept, and accrual accounting are among the basic concepts provided for. Various valuation methods are prescribed, and a number of options which may be elected by the EEC member nations are provided. As of June, 1983, only three of the EEC member nations had implemented this directive.

Consolidated financial statements are called for in the *Seventh Directive* (1983) as being appropriate when one company is under the *dominant influence* of another, even though a controlling degree of ownership does not exist. Furthermore, the directive states that independent companies within the EEC which are controlled by an enterprise *outside* the EEC should be consolidated. It specifies consolidation principles, mechanics, and disclosure requirements.[20] The *Seventh Directive* also presents various options available to EEC member nations. Its full impact will not be felt until some time in the future because (1) consolidated statements are not required until 1990 and (2) many of the presentation provisions and valuation rules prescribed by the *Fourth Directive* (which has only been partially implemented) are incorporated in the *Seventh Directive*.

The *Eighth Directive* establishes minimum qualifications for outside auditors of companies in the EEC. It was first proposed in 1978, revised in 1979, and is currently being negotiated by EEC member nations.

In addition to the organizations previously mentioned, the Accountants International Study Group (AISG), consisting of representatives of professional accounting organizations in Canada, the United Kingdom, and the United States, was active from the late 1960s through the late 1970s. Its mission was not to promulgate international accounting standards; rather, it produced a series of studies dealing with various accounting topics of concern to the three countries. To bring them to the reader's attention, a complete list is provided in Exhibit 15.13. They are available from the American Institute of Certified Public Accountants.

International Accounting Standards Committee

We have seen that there are many accounting organizations which have an interest in studying international accounting issues and promoting communication and cooperation among accountants in many countries. Among these groups, the **International Accounting Standards Committee (IASC)** stands out for its breadth of membership and its promulgation of quasi-authoritative worldwide accounting standards. The IASC was founded on June 29, 1973, by the leading professional accounting associations of Australia, Canada, France, Germany, Japan, Mexico, the Netherlands, the United Kingdom and Ireland, and the United States. Today, more than 60 countries are members. The IASC has been and continues to be active in issuing official pronouncements known as **International Accounting**

---

[20]See Sharon M. McKinnon and Alan D. H. Newham, ed., *The Seventh Directive* (Brentford, England: Kluwer Publishing Limited, Arthur Young International, 1984) for a comprehensive discussion of the *Seventh Directive* and background material on all of the EEC directives and other efforts to promote harmonization of accounting principles and practices around the world.

Exhibit 15.13 *Accountants International Studies* **by the Accountants International Study Group**

Study No.	Title	Date
1	Accounting and Auditing Approaches to Inventories	1968
2	The Independent Auditor's Reporting Standards	1969
3	Using the Work and Report of Another Auditor	1969
4	Accounting for Corporate Income Taxes	1971
5	Reporting by Diversified Companies	1972
6	Consolidated Financial Statements	1973
7	The Funds Statement.	1973
8	Materiality in Accounting	1974
9	Extraordinary Items, Prior Period Adjustments, and Changes in Accounting Principles	1974
10	Published Profit Forecasts	1975
11	International Financial Reporting	1975
12	Glossary of Accounting Terms	1975
13	Accounting for Goodwill	1975
14	Interim Financial Reporting	1975
15	Going Concern Problems.	1976
16	Independence of Auditors	1977
17	Audit Committees.	1977
18	Accounting for Pension Costs	1977
19	Revenue Recognition.	1978
20	Related Party Transactions.	1978

Standards (IAS).[21] Before a list of the standards currently in force is presented, two matters must be made clear:

1. The IASC *cannot require* the accounting profession in any country to adhere to its standards. Rather, the focus is on voluntary cooperation and on the good-faith efforts pledged by member countries to promote the worldwide acceptance and observance of the standards.
2. The intention of the IASC is to concentrate on essentials and not to make the International Accounting Standards so complex and detailed that they cannot be effectively applied throughout the world.

A list of the International Accounting Standards in force as of June 1, 1984, appears in Exhibit 15.14.

Summary of Key Concepts

Corporations now do business abroad within the context of an international monetary system characterized by **flexible** or **floating exchange rates.** These con-

---

[21]For more information relating to the IASC, its organization, structure, and operating procedures, see American Institute of Certified Public Accountants, *AICPA Professional Standards* (New York: AICPA, 1984), Volume B; AC § 9000.

Exhibit 15.14   **International Accounting Standards in Force as of June 1, 1984**

Standard No.	Title	Date
1	Disclosure of Accounting Policies	1975
2	Valuation and Presentation of Inventories in the Context of the Historical Cost System	1975
3	Consolidated Financial Statements	1976
4	Depreciation Accounting	1976
5	Information to Be Disclosed in Financial Statements	1976
7	Statement of Changes in Financial Position	1977
8	Unusual and Prior Period Items and Changes in Accounting Policies	1978
9	Accounting for Research and Development Activities	1978
10	Contingencies and Events Occurring after the Balance Sheet Date	1978
11	Accounting for Construction Contracts	1979
12	Accounting for Taxes on Income	1979
13	Presentation of Current Assets and Current Liabilities	1979
14	Reporting Financial Information by Segment	1981
15	Information Reflecting the Effects of Changing Prices (supersedes *IAS 6,* originally issued in 1978)	1981
16	Accounting for Property, Plant, and Equipment	1982
17	Accounting for Leases	1982
18	Revenue Recognition	1982
19	Accounting for Retirement Benefits in the Financial Statements of Employers	1983
20	Accounting for Government Grants and Disclosures of Government Assistance	1983
21	Accounting for the Effects of Changes in Foreign Exchange Rates	1983
22	Accounting for Business Combinations	1983
23	Capitalization of Borrowing Costs	1984

NOTE: The complete texts of the above International Accounting Standards, along with explanations and dicussions of differences with U.S. GAAP, may be found in American Institute of Certified Public Accountants, *AICPA Professional Standards* (New York: AICPA, 1984), Volume B; AC § 9000.

stantly changing exchange rates make the tasks of accounting and reporting foreign operations more difficult.

Domestic corporations with branches, divisions, and subsidiaries abroad must translate the accounts of those business units into dollars for inclusion in the U.S. financial statements. Most of the translation methods devised to accomplish this use the **current exchange rate** at the balance sheet date to translate some accounts and **historical exchange rates** to translate other accounts.

The four major approaches to this translation process are the **current/noncurrent, monetary/nonmonetary, temporal,** and **current rate** methods. Translation rules in *SFAS 52* depend on the foreign entity's **functional currency**—the currency of the principal economic environment in which the entity generates net cash flows.

The **current rate method** is used when the functional currency is a **foreign currency;** the **temporal method** is used when the functional currency is the **U.S. dollar.** Each method defines an exposed position consisting of accounts to be translated at the current rate; other accounts are translated at historical rates.

Fluctuating exchange rates produce a translation gain or loss which normally differs across methods. This translation adjustment arises because the exposed position is translated at the current rate, while many changes in the exposed position are translated at historical rates. The translation adjustment is carried directly to a special component of **stockholders' equity** when the functional currency is a **foreign currency** (the current rate method is used). In contrast, when the functional currency is the **U.S. dollar** (the temporal method is used), the translation gain or loss is included in **current earnings.**

The **dollar balances of home office reciprocal accounts** are generally used as the translated balances of the **offsetting reciprocal accounts at foreign branches.** In parent/subsidiary accounting, foreign intercompany accounts should be translated at the dollar balances of the parent's offsetting accounts.

Translation of a foreign subsidiary's assets and liabilities differs under the **purchase** and **pooling of interests** methods. If **purchase accounting** is used, the **spot rate at date of business combination** is used to translate the subsidiary's assets and liabilities in existence at date of business combination. This is also true under pooling, if the functional currency is a foreign currency. Otherwise, the book values of the subsidiary's accounts at date of business combination are carried forward, and whatever historical rates existed when those account balances arose are to be used.

Significant differences exist among accounting principles and practices around the world. Factors contributing to these differences include the social, economic, and political conditions and institutions in various countries as well as the different ways that accounting has developed in those countries. Organizations such as the **International Accounting Standards Committee (IASC)** seek to promote uniformity in accounting principles and practices internationally. The **standards issued by the IASC,** however, are **not mandatory** and rely on good faith and cooperation for their implementation.

Appendix to
Chapter 15

The Relationship between Foreign Currency Translation and Constant-Dollar Accounting

A study of the process of translating foreign currency financial statements into units of domestic currency reveals its similarity to constant-dollar, or general price-level restatements. Some elements common to both techniques are:

1. A change in the measuring unit, either from one currency to another or from historical dollars to current dollars.
2. A distinction between current and historical items.
3. A special gain or loss arising out of the translation or restatement process.

Use of the monetary/nonmonetary approach to foreign currency translation provides the most direct comparison with constant-dollar restatements. Both methods distinguish between monetary and nonmonetary items and treat each category differently. The simplest case is one in which a firm is organized at the beginning of the year and engages in no transactions during the year. At year-end, we prepare either translated or restated financial statements, depending on the method being analyzed. We begin with the fundamental accounting equation:

$$\text{Assets } (A) = \text{Liabilities } (L) + \text{Stockholders' Equity } (SE).$$

Recognizing that both assets and liabilities have monetary (M) and nonmonetary (N) components, we have

$$MA + NA = ML + NL + SE$$

or

$$MA - ML = NL - NA + SE. \tag{1}$$

Foreign Currency Translation

Define R as the percentage change between the ending (e) and beginning (b) foreign exchange rates; $R = (R_e/R_b) - 1$ and $R_e = R_b(1 + R) = R_b + R_bR$. Thus R_b is the *historical rate,* and R_e is the *current rate.* The following manipulations of Equation 1 provide the translated foreign currency accounts. We first multiply the ending exchange rate by each of the account categories in Equation 1:

$$R_eMA - R_eML = R_eNL - R_eNA + R_eSE. \tag{2}$$

In foreign currency translation, the monetary items are translated at the current rate by multiplying them by R_e. The nonmonetary items are translated at the historical beginning-of-period rate, in this case R_b. We now expand the right-hand side of Equation 2, after replacing R_e with $R_b + R_bR$,

$$R_eMA - R_eML = R_bNL + R_bRNL - R_bNA - R_bRNA + R_bSE + R_bRSE,$$

and group the *potential change* in the translated nonmonetary items $[R_bR(NL - NA + SE)]$ on the right:

$$R_eMA - R_eML = R_bNL - R_bNA + R_bSE + R_bR(NL - NA + Se) \qquad (3)$$

Since the historical exchange rate R_b is used to translate the nonmonetary items, their translated amounts do not change. Therefore, this potential change in the translated nonmonetary items must equal the effect of a change in the exchange rate on the translated monetary items.

Using Equation 1, we substitute *(MA − ML)* for *(NL − NA + SE)* and group the terms as follows:

$$R_e(MA - ML) = R_b(NL - NA + SE) + R_bR(MA - ML). \qquad (4)$$

The quantity $\boldsymbol{R_bR(MA - ML)}$ in Equation 4 is the **translation gain or loss.** It is the exact amount by which the translated monetary items change as the exchange rate moved from R_b to R_e. If $R_bR(MA - ML)$ is positive, we have a *gain*. In contrast, if $R_bR(MA - ML)$ is negative, we have a *loss*.

Constant-Dollar Restatement

Define P as the percentage change between the ending *(e)* and beginning *(b)* general price levels as measured by the Consumer Price Index, Gross National Product Implicit Price Deflator, or some other broad-based index; $P = (P_e/P_b) - 1$ and $P_e = P_b(1 + P) = P_b + P_bP$. Thus P_b is the *historical price level* and P_e is the *current price level*. Again using our fundamental accounting equation (as arranged in Equation 1), the year-end constant-dollar restatement is based on the following:

$$(P_e/P_b)MA - (P_e/P_b)ML = (P_e/P_b)NL - (P_e/P_b)NA + (P_e/P_b)SE. \qquad (5)$$

Since monetary items are *not* restated in constant-dollar accounting, we expand the left-hand side of Equation 4, after replacing P_e with $P_b + P_bP$,

$$(P_b/P_b)MA + (P_bP/P_b)MA - (P_b/P_b)ML - (P_bP/P_b)ML$$
$$= (P_e/P_b)NL - (P_e/P_b)NA + (P_e/P_b)SE,$$

or

$$MA + PMA - ML - PML = (P_e/P_b)NL - (P_e/P_b)NA + (P_e/P_b)SE,$$

and transfer the *potential restatement* of the monetary items $[P(MA - ML)]$ to the right-hand side:

$$MA - ML = (P_e/P_b)NL - (P_e/P_b)NA + (P_e/P_b)SE - P(MA - ML).$$

Since there is no restatement of monetary items under constant-dollar accounting, their restated amounts do not change. Therefore, the potential restatement in the monetary items must equal the effect of a change in the general price level on the restated nonmonetary items.

The quantity $P(MA - ML)$ is the familiar **purchasing power gain or loss** on monetary items. It represents the amount by which monetary items should have changed in the face of a changing price level, but didn't. In a period of rising prices, if $(MA - ML) > 0$, then $P(MA - ML)$ is positive, a *loss*. If $(MA - ML) < 0$, then $P(MA - ML)$ is negative, a *gain*.

Compare the *translation gain or loss*, $R_b R(MA - ML)$ with the *purchasing power gain or loss*, $P(MA - ML)$. These are the *special gains or losses* mentioned in the introduction to this appendix. *First,* note that net monetary items are inside the parentheses. In foreign currency translation, their dollar equivalents *are* affected by movements in the exchange rate, whereas in constant-dollar restatement their dollar equivalents are *not* affected by movements in the general price level but their *purchasing power* equivalents are. *Second,* the terms outside the brackets represent percentage changes (in foreign currency translation, R_b is used to translate the foreign currency amounts of MA and ML into dollars; in constant-dollar restatement, MA and ML are already stated in dollars). Under double entry accounting, $R_b R(MA - ML)$ is needed to offset the change in the translated amount of monetary items (translated nonmonetary items do not change), and $P(MA - ML)$ is needed to offset the change in the restated amount of nonmonetary items (restated monetary items do not change).

Moving to a multiperiod, multitransaction setting complicates but does not change the above relationships. It simply requires the replacement of P or R with a set of P_t and R_t, where t identifies the time that a transaction occurred and hence the change in price level or exchange rate since that time. In the foreign currency translation case, use of one of the other three translation methods merely affects the way balance sheet items are grouped in Equation 1 and the components of the exposed position on the left-hand side.

A Numerical Example

At the beginning of the year, a firm is formed with account balances as shown in the following table. No transactions take place during the year, and beginning and ending exchange rates and price levels are also given in the table. The account balances are measured in either units of foreign currency or beginning-of-year dollars, depending on the context.

$$
\begin{array}{ll}
MA = 1{,}000 & R_b = 1.00 \\
NA = 2{,}000 & R_e = 1.10 \\
ML = 800 & R = .10 \\
NL = 400 & P_b = 100 \\
SE = 1{,}800 & P_e = 110 \\
& P = .10
\end{array}
$$

Exhibit 15.15   **Translated/Restated Balance Sheets**

Translated Foreign Currency Balance Sheet		**Restated Constant-Dollar Balance Sheet**	
Monetary Assets		Monetary Assets	
$(1,000 \times 1.10)$	1,100	$(1,000 \times 1.00)$	1,000
Nonmonetary Assets		Nonmonetary Assets	
$(2,000 \times 1.00)$	2,000	$(2,000 \times 1.10)$	2,200
Total Assets.	3,100	Total Assets.	3,200
Monetary Liabilities (800×1.10) .	880	Monetary Liabilities (800×1.00) .	800
Nonmonetary Liabilities		Nonmonetary Liabilities	
(400×1.00)	400	(400×1.10)	440
Stockholders' Equity		Stockholders' Equity	
$(1,800 \times 1.00)$	1,800	$(1,800 \times 1.10)$	1,980
Translation Gain	20[a]	Purchasing Power Loss	(20)[b]
Total Liabilites and Stockholders'		Total Liabilities and Stockholders'	
Equity	3,100	Equity	3,200

[a]$20 = .1(400 - 2,000 + 1,800)$.
[b]$20 = .1(1,000 - 800)$.

The end-of-period translated/restated balance sheets are given in Exhibit 15.15.

A careful look at these balance sheets reveals both a fundamental similarity and a fundamental difference between the two methods when they are applied to identical data. As expected, the similarity is that the exchange translation gain and the purchasing power loss are equal in absolute value but have opposite signs. In this example, net monetary items $(MA - ML)$ equals net monetary assets (debit balance) of $200. Concurrently, net nonmonetary items $(NL - NA + SE)$ indicates net nonmonetary equities (credit balance) of $200. In the translation case, the gain of $20 represents the amount by which the net monetary assets in foreign currency *increased* in translated value; it is added to owners' equity. In contrast, the purchasing power loss of $20 in constant-dollar accounting arose because the net monetary assets *did not increase* in the face of inflation, which sapped their value; it is deducted from owners' equity.

The differences between the translated and restated balances occur because the nonmonetary items are translated at the lower historical rate but are restated at the higher current general price level. Moreover, since the nonmonetary items are larger than the monetary items, total *restated* assets and equities exceed total *translated* assets and equities.

Questions

Q15.1 Briefly discuss the nature of the financial accounting problems peculiar to multinational corporations.

Q15.2 Why is it necessary for domestic companies to translate the accounts of their overseas branches, divisions, and subsidiaries?

Q15.3 How has the historical-cost accounting model influenced the methods most frequently used to translate foreign currency financial statements?

Q15.4 Compare the effect on the translation gain or loss associated with translation of inventory at the current rate (under the current/noncurrent method) and at the historical rate (under the temporal method) when exchange rates are (1) rising and (2) falling.

Q15.5 Compare the effect on the translation gain or loss associated with translation of long-term debt at the historical rate (under the current/noncurrent method) and at the current rate (under the temporal method) when exchange rates are (1) rising and (2) falling.

Q15.6 This text has drawn a distinction between *transaction* gains and losses and *translation* gains and losses. What is the basis for the distinction? As a financial statement user, would you prefer separate disclosure of both types of exchange gains and losses? Explain.

Q15.7 What is an entity's "functional currency"? Explain its role in the translation process under *SFAS 52*.

Q15.8 Distinguish between *remeasurement* and *translation*. How is the exchange gain or loss produced by remeasurement and translation reported in the financial statements of a U.S. company?

Q15.9 It is recommended that translation of the reciprocal accounts of foreign branches be accomplished by using the dollar balances in the related reciprocal accounts at the domestic home office. What are the advantages and disadvantages of this procedure?

Q15.10 Explain how the minority interest in a partially owned foreign subsidiary should be translated by its U.S.-based parent for purposes of preparing consolidated financial statements.

Q15.11 Explain the approach and rationale for the translation of the assets and liabilities of foreign subsidiaries for inclusion in consolidated financial statements when the business combination was accounted for (1) as a purchase and (2) as a pooling of interests.

Q15.12 Describe the role of the International Accounting Standards Committee (IASC). What obstacles does it face?

Exercises

E15.1 In each of the following independent situations, give the appropriate translated amount under (a) the current/noncurrent method and (b) the temporal method.

1. On January 1, 19X8, the Ben Company formed a foreign subsidiary. On February 15, 19X8, Ben's subsidiary purchased 100,000 local currency (LC) units of inventory. LC25,000 of the original inventory purchased on February 15, 19X8, made up the entire inventory on December 31, 19X8. The exchange rates were LC2.2 to $1 from January 1, 19X8, to June 30, 19X8, and LC2 to $1 from July 1, 19X8, to December 31, 19X8. What is the translated inventory balance of Ben's foreign subsidiary at December 31, 19X8?

2. The France Company owns a foreign subsidiary with LC2,400,000 of property, plant, and equipment before accumulated depreciation at December 31, 19X8. Of this amount, LC1,500,000 were acquired on January 1, 19X6, when the rate of exchange was LC1.5 to $1, and LC900,000 were acquired on January 1, 19X7, when the rate of exchange was LC1.6 to $1. The rate of exchange in effect at December 31, 19X8, was LC1.9 to $1. The weighted average of exchange rates in effect during 19X8 was LC1.8 to $1. Assuming that the property, plant, and equipment are depreciated using the straight-line method over a 10-year period with no salvage value, how much depreciation expense relating to the foreign subsidiary's property, plant, and equipment should be charged in France's income statement for 19X8? Calculate the translated balances of property, plant, and equipment and accumulated depreciation at December 31, 19X8. *(AICPA adapted)*

E15.2 On September 10, 19X6, the Globe Trading Company advanced $30,000 to its representative in Bogota, Colombia, to establish a small sales office. The representative, Mr. Moreno, converted the $30,000 into 1,000,000 pesos (P) and opened a bank account in Bogota. No formal accounting system is established in Bogota. At December 31, 19X6, Mr. Moreno submitted the following report to Globe:

	Pesos
Funds Received on Sept. 10, 19X6.	1,000,000
Payments:	
Purchase of Equipment on Sept. 10	270,000
Office Rent.	70,000
Secretary's Salary	120,000
Telephone and Other Expenses	100,000
Total Payments	560,000
Cash (Pesos) on Hand, Dec. 31, 19X6.	440,000

The exchange rate was $.033/P on December 31, 19X6, and averaged $.031/P during the period from September 10 to December 31, 19X6.

Required:

1. Assuming the functional currency is the U.S. dollar, prepare a schedule to compute the translation gain or loss related to the Bogota sales office in 19X6.

2. Repeat No. 1 but assume the functional currency is the peso.
3. Suppose Globe treats the $30,000 as an advance. Give the journal entries which would be made by Globe on September 10 and on December 31, when Globe's books are closed and the accounts of the Bogota branch are included in Globe's financial statements. Consider both functional currency alternatives.

E15.3 U.S. Industries has a subsidiary in Switzerland. The subsidiary's financial statements are maintained in Swiss francs (SF). Exchange rates ($/SF) for selected dates are as follows:

Jan. 1, 19X4	$.75	Jan. 1, 19X6	$.68
Jan. 1, 19X5	.70	Dec. 31, 19X6	.65

Required: Assuming the functional currency of the Swiss subsidiary is the U.S. dollar, calculate the correct dollar amount for each of the following items appearing in the subsidiary's trial balance at December 31, 19X6:

1. Cash in Bank, SF400,000.
2. Inventory on LIFO basis, SF300,000. The inventory cost consists of SF100,000 acquired in January 19X4 and SF200,000 acquired in January 19X6.
3. Machinery and Equipment, SF1,100,000. A review of the records indicates that the company bought equipment costing SF500,000 in January 19X4 (20 percent of this was sold in January 19X6) and additional equipment costing SF700,000 in January 19X5. Ignore accumulated depreciation.
4. Depreciation Expense on machinery and equipment, SF110,000 (depreciated over 10 years, straight-line basis).

E15.4 The following data relate to Sterling, Limited, located in the city of Liverpool, England. Sterling is controlled by a U.S. company.

Net Monetary Assets (Liabilities), Jan. 1, 19X1	£ 70,000
Acquisition of Plant Assets for Debt, Feb. 15, 19X1	100,000
Purchase of Inventory Made Evenly during 19X1	350,000
Collection of Receivables Outstanding at Jan. 1, 19X1	270,000
Sales Made Evenly during 19X1	600,000
Cost of Goods Sold	330,000
Depreciation of Assets Acquired When the Exchange Rate Was $1.80/£	40,000
Operating Expenses (Excluding Depreciation and Amortization), Incurred Evenly during 19X1	120,000
Refinancing or "Rollover" of Commercial Paper	80,000

Exchange rates ($/£) during 19X1 were as follows:

Jan. 1, 19X1	$1.90	Average for 19X1	$1.97
Feb. 15, 19X1	1.95	Dec. 31, 19X1	2.01

Required:

1. Assuming that Sterling's functional currency is the U.S. dollar, prepare a schedule to compute the translation adjustment for Sterling during 19X1.
2. Repeat No. 1 but assume that Sterling's functional currency is the pound and that net assets on January 1, 19X1, amounted to £120,000.

E15.5 The following transactions were recorded by the Larson Company's subsidiary in Finland during 19X3. The Finnish currency is the markka (M).

	Amount (M)	Exchange Rate ($/M)
Purchase of Inventory.	4,000,000	$.30
Proceeds from Sale of Equipment	500,000	.33
Book Value of Equipment Sold	350,000	.40[a]
Sales	5,000,000	.33[b]
Cost of Goods Sold.	3,000,000	.29[a]
Issue of Long-Term Debt for Cash	1,000,000	.35
Amortization of Prepayments	100,000	.34[a]

[a]Exchange rates when assets sold or amortized were acquired by the Finnish subsidiary.
[b]The average exchange rate during 19X3.

Required: The exchange rate ($/M) at December 31, 19X3, is $.36. Assuming the functional currency is (1) the U.S. dollar and (2) the markka, calculate the effect of each of the above transactions on the translation gain or loss reported by Larson in 19X3.

E15.6 On January 1, 19X1, *SFAS 52* is adopted by the Bainbridge Company. Its wholly owned South African subsidiary has net assets of 5,000,000 rands (R), which translate into $5,500,000 under *SFAS 8* and $5,100,000 under *SFAS 52*. The rand is the functional currency. At the end of 19X1, the South African subsidiary reported net income of R500,000; it had declared dividends of R100,000 on April 15, 19X1, when the exchange rate was $1.10/R. The weighted average exchange rate during the year was $1.05/R and the current rate stood at $1.03/R on December 31, 19X1. Except for the dividends, there were no capital transactions during the year.

Required: Prepare an analysis of Bainbridge's Equity Adjustment account during 19X1 as it relates to the South African subsidiary.

E15.7 On January 2, 19X9, Maddox Corporation, headquartered in the United States, opened a branch in Mexico City. An initial investment of $100,000 was made on that date; the exchange rate was $.10/peso. During 19X9, the following cash transactions occurred at the Mexico City branch. All amounts are in pesos (P).

Legal Expenses of Organizing the Branch (Jan. 2; 5-Year Life).   30,000
Purchase of Office Equipment (Apr. 1; 10-Year Life)   100,000
Sales   1,200,000
Merchandise Purchases   900,000
Operating Expenses   300,000

The exchange rate was $.11/P in April when the office equipment and P200,000 of merchandise were purchased. Sales, other merchandise purchases, and operating expenses were assumed to have been made or incurred at an average exchange rate of $.12/P. At year-end, the exchange rate had risen to $.15/P and the ending inventory (LIFO) amounted to P200,000. All depreciation and amortization is straight-line.

Required: Prepare a balance sheet and income statement for the Mexico City branch as of December 31, 19X9, in dollars, the branch's functional currency. Show all calculations, especially those supporting the translation gain or loss.

E15.8 Oliver Corporation adopted *SFAS 52* on January 1, 19X2. On that date, the net assets of its foreign subsidiary amounted to FC20,000,000 and to $15,000,000 when translated according to the temporal method; the exchange rate was $.80/FC. During 19X2, the foreign subsidiary reported net income of FC2,500,000 and paid dividends of FC1,000,000. No other changes in owners' equity occurred. The subsidiary's functional currency is the foreign currency.

Required: Prepare an analysis of the Equity Adjustment account for 19X2. Relevant exchange rates were: $.78/FC (average); $.765/FC (dividend declaration date); $.76/FC (December 31, 19X2).

E15.9 The Thode Company established a branch in Saudi Arabia on January 1, 19X6, when the exchange rate was $.28/Riyal (R). Of Thode's initial $5,000,000 investment, $2,800,000 was used to acquire plant assets (10-year life) and $1,400,000 was used to acquire inventory. The remaining amount was initially held as cash by the branch.

During 19X6, the branch reported net income of R2,000,000. It remitted R4,000,000 to Thode's home office in the United States on September 30, when the exchange rate was $.255/R. No other transactions occurred between the branch and the home office. The branch's condensed income statement appears below:

Sales R8,500,000
Cost of Goods Sold . . . . (4,000,000)   (1)
Depreciation Expense . . . . (1,000,000)   (2)
Other Expenses . . . . (1,500,000)
Net Income R2,000,000

(1) R3,000,000 was from original inventory; the balance had been acquired evenly throughout the year from local sources.
(2) Relates solely to plant assets acquired on Jan. 1, 19X6.

The average exchange rate during the year was $.265/R. On the balance sheet date, it was $.25/R.

Required:

1. Assuming the functional currency is the riyal, translate the branch's income statement into dollars and prepare an analysis of the branch's Equity Adjustment account during 19X6.
2. Assuming the functional currency is the U.S. dollar, remeasure the branch's income statement into dollars. Disregard the translation adjustment.

E15.10 The Dhia Products Company was incorporated in the state of Florida to do business as a manufacturer of medical supplies and equipment. Since incorporating, Dhia has doubled in size about every 3 years and is now considered one of the leading medical supply companies in the country.

During January 19X1, Dhia established a subsidiary, Ban, Ltd., in the emerging nation of Shatha. Dhia owns 90 percent of the outstanding capital stock of Ban; the remaining 10 percent is held by Shatha citizens, as required by Shathan constitutional law. The investment in Ban, accounted for by Dhia by the equity method, represents about 18 percent of the total assets of Dhia at December 31, 19X4, the close of the accounting period for both companies.

Required:

1. What criteria should Dhia use in determining whether it would be appropriate to prepare consolidated financial statements with Ban for the year ended December 31, 19X4? Explain.
2. Independent of your answer to No. 1, assume it has been appropriate for Dhia and Ban to prepare consolidated financial statements for each year 19X1 through 19X4. But before consolidated financial statements can be prepared, the individual account balances in Ban's December 31, 19X4, adjusted trial balance must be translated into the appropriate number of U.S. dollars. For each of the ten accounts listed, taken from Ban's adjusted trial balance, specify what exchange rate (for example, average exchange rate for 19X4 or current exchange rate at December 31, 19X4) should be used to translate the account balances into dollars, according to *SFAS 52*. Your answer must consider that Ban's functional currency could be either the U.S. dollar or Shatha's local currency. Assign letters *a* through *j* to your answers, to correspond with each account in the following list:
   a. Cash in Shatha National Bank.
   b. Trade Accounts Receivable (all from 19X4 revenues).
   c. Supplies Inventory (all purchased during the last quarter of 19X4).
   d. Land (purchased in 19X1).
   e. Short-Term Note Payable to Shatha National Bank.

f. Capital Stock (no par or stated value and all issued in January 19X1).

g. Retained Earnings, January 1, 19X4.

h. Sales Revenue.

i. Depreciation Expense (on buildings).

j. Salaries Expense.

(AICPA Adapted)

E15.11 Kasha, Limited, is located in India and is owned by Caldwell, Inc., a U.S. corporation. The lower-of-cost-or-market rule is being applied to Kasha's inventory for inclusion in Caldwell's consolidated financial statements. The inventory consists of four different categories of merchandise. Items within each category are similar. Data on cost, market, and average exchange rates when the goods were acquired by Kasha are given below. The current exchange rate is $.12.

Category	Cost (Rupees)	Average Exchange Rate When Acquired	Current Market (Rupees)
A	5,000,000	$.14	6,500,000
B	10,000,000	.11	9,900,000
C	8,000,000	.18	12,000,000
D	2,000,000	.10	1,600,000

Required: Assuming the functional currency is the U.S. dollar, compute the dollar value of each category of inventory that will be reflected in Caldwell's consolidated balance sheet and the dollar amount of the write-down to market included in the consolidated income statement for each category of inventory.

E15.12 Following is the condensed balance sheet of the Cheung Company at September 15, 19X8. On that date, Wint Corporation, headquartered in Chicago, acquired 90 percent of Cheung's outstanding stock in exchange for its own stock valued at $2,000,000. Both book value and fair value data are given in units of foreign currency (FC).

ASSETS	Book Value (FC)	Fair Value (FC)
Current Assets	3,000,000	3,400,000
Noncurrent Assets	5,000,000	6,000,000
Total Assets	8,000,000	

LIABILITIES AND STOCKHOLDERS' EQUITY

	Book Value (FC)	Fair Value (FC)
Current Liabilities	2,000,000	2,000,000
Noncurrent Liabilities	2,000,000	2,600,000
Stockholders' Equity	4,000,000	—
Total Liabilities and Stockholders' Equity	8,000,000	

The exchange rate at September 15, 19X8, is $.40/FC. The noncurrent assets and noncurrent liabilities (mostly long-term debt) were acquired (incurred) at average exchange rates of $.45 and $.50, respectively. Cheung's current assets and liabilities are monetary items except for inventory of FC1,000,000, acquired when the exchange rate was $.42. Capital stock of FC2,000,000 was issued when the exchange rate was $.45.

Required:

1. Assuming the purchase method of accounting and Cheung's functional currency to be the foreign currency, give the eliminating entries made on a consolidated balance sheet working paper prepared at September 15, 19X8. Show all calculations.
2. Assuming the pooling of interests method of accounting and Cheung's functional currency to be the U.S. dollar, repeat No. 1.

Problems

P15.1 Remeasuring a Condensed Trial Balance—Equity Method Accrual
The trial balance of Valiant Corporation, a small Swedish company, is given below. Its functional currency is the U.S. dollar. The account balances are for the year ended December 31, 19X4, and are measured in krone (K), the Swedish currency.

Account	Amount (K) Dr. (Cr.)
Cash	240,000
Accounts Receivable	400,000
Allowance for Uncollectible Accounts	(40,000)
Plant and Equipment, Net	2,000,000
Accounts Payable	(200,000)
Notes Payable	(600,000)
Capital Stock	(400,000)
Retained Earnings, Jan. 1, 19X4	(1,160,000)
Sales	(1,200,000)
Depreciation Expense	320,000
Other Expenses	640,000
	0

Valiant Corporation was formed, and its stock issued, when the exchange rate was $.20/K. The plant assets were acquired and the notes payable executed when the exchange rate was $.25/K. Sales and Other Expenses occurred evenly during 19X4. The remeasured (dollar) balance of Valiant's January 1 retained earnings was $150,000. Exchange rates in 19X4 were as follows:

Time	Rate ($/K)
Jan. 1, 19X4	$.30
Average for 19X4	.33
Dec. 31, 19X4	.35

Required:

1. Remeasure Valiant's trial balance into dollars.
2. Prepare a remeasured income statement and balance sheet for Valiant.
3. If Domestic Corporation, a U.S. firm, owned 70 percent of Valiant's outstanding stock, prepare the journal entry made by Domestic to record the equity method accrual at December 31, 19X4. There were no intercompany transactions and no purchase premium or discount.

P15.2 Translating a Condensed Trial Balance—Equity Method Accrual Refer to Problem P15.1. Repeat the requirements of P15.1, assuming the krone (K) is the functional currency. In No. 2, also prepare an analysis of the Equity Adjustment account.

P15.3 Translating Selected Accounts On January 1, 19X1, the Franklin Company formed a foreign subsidiary which issued all of its currently outstanding common stock on that date. Selected captions from the balance sheets, all of which are shown in units of local currency (LC), are as follows:

	December 31	
ACCOUNTS RECEIVABLE	**19X2**	**19X1**
(Net of Allowance for Uncollectible Accounts of LC2,200 at Dec. 31, 19X2, and LC2,000 at Dec. 31, 19X1)	LC40,000	LC35,000
INVENTORIES, AT COST	80,000	75,000
PROPERTY, PLANT, AND EQUIPMENT (Net of Accumulated Depreciation of LC31,000 at Dec. 31, 19X2, and LC14,000 at Dec. 31, 19X1)	163,000	150,000
LONG-TERM DEBT	100,000	120,000
COMMON STOCK Authorized 10,000 Shares, Par Value LC10 per Share, Issued and Outstanding 5,000 Shares at Dec. 31, 19X2 and Dec. 31, 19X1	50,000	50,000

Additional information:

1. Exchange rates are as follows:

	LC/$1
Jan. 1, 19X1–July 31, 19X1	2
Aug. 1, 19X1–Oct. 31, 19X1	1.8
Nov. 1, 19X1–June 30, 19X2	1.7
July 1, 19X2–Dec. 31, 19X2	1.5
Average Monthly Rate for 19X1	1.9
Average Monthly Rate for 19X2	1.6

2. An analysis of the accounts receivable balance is as follows:

ACCOUNTS RECEIVABLE   **19X2**   **19X1**

Balance at Beginning of Year	LC37,000	—
Sales (LC36,000 per Month in 19X2 and LC31,000 per Month in 19X1)	432,000	LC372,000
Collections.	(423,600)	(334,000)
Write-Offs (May 19X2 and Dec. 19X1).	(3,200)	(1,000)
Balance at Year-End.	LC42,200	LC 37,000

ALLOWANCE FOR UNCOLLECTIBLE ACCOUNTS

Balance at Beginning of Year	LC 2,000	
Provision for Uncollectible Accounts	3,400	LC 3,000
Write-Offs (May 19X2 and Dec. 19X1).	(3,200)	(1,000)
Balance at Year-End.	LC 2,200	LC 2,000

3. An analysis of inventories, for which the FIFO inventory method is used, is as follows:

                                                                    19X2   **19X1**

Inventory at Beginning of Year.	LC 75,000	—
Purchases (June 19X2 and June 19X1)	335,000	LC375,000
Goods Available for Sale.	410,000	375,000
Inventory at Year-End	80,000	75,000
Cost of Goods Sold	LC330,000	LC300,000

4. On January 1, 19X1, Franklin's foreign subsidiary purchased land for LC24,000 and plant and equipment for LC140,000. On July 4, 19X2, additional equipment was purchased for LC30,000. Plant and equipment is being depreciated on a straight-line basis over a 10-year period with no salvage value. A full year's depreciation is taken in the year of purchase.

5. On January 15, 19X1, 7 percent bonds with a face value of LC120,000 were sold. These bonds mature on January 15, 19X7, and interest is paid semiannually on July 15 and January 15. Bonds with a face value of LC20,000 were retired on January 14, 19X2.

Required: Prepare a schedule remeasuring the selected captions above into U.S. dollars (the functional currency) at December 31, 19X2, and December 31, 19X1, respectively. Show supporting computations in good form. *(AICPA adapted)*

P15.4 Remeasuring a Foreign Subsidiary's Trial Balance Wiend Corporation acquired Dieck Corporation on January 1, 19X5, by the purchase at book value of all outstanding capital stock. Dieck is located in a Central American country whose monetary unit is the peso (P). Dieck's accounting records were continued without change; trial balances, in pesos, at the purchase date and at December 31, 19X6, are shown in Exhibit 15.16.

Exhibit 15.16	Trial Balance Data to Be Used in P15.4

DIECK CORPORATION
TRIAL BALANCE (IN PESOS)
JANUARY 1, 19X5

	Debit	Credit
Cash	P 3,000	
Accounts Receivable	5,000	
Inventory	32,000	
Machinery and Equipment	204,000	
Accumulated Depreciation		P 42,000
Accounts Payable		81,400
Capital Stock		50,000
Retained Earnings		70,600
Total	P244,000	P244,000

DIECK CORPORATION
TRIAL BALANCE (IN PESOS)
DECEMBER 31, 19X6

	Debit	Credit
Cash	P 25,000	
Accounts Receivable	20,000	
Allowance for Uncollectible Accounts		P 500
Due from Wiend	30,000	
Inventory, Dec. 31, 19X6	110,000	
Prepayments	3,000	
Machinery and Equipment	210,000	
Accumulated Depreciation		79,900
Accounts Payable		22,000
Income Taxes Payable		40,000
Notes Payable		60,000
Capital Stock		50,000
Retained Earnings		100,600
Sales—Domestic		170,000
Sales—Foreign		200,000
Cost of Sales	207,600	
Depreciation Expense	22,400	
Selling and Administrative Expenses	60,000	
Gain on Sale of Assets		5,000
Income Tax Expense	40,000	
Total	P728,000	P728,000

Additional information:

1. All Dieck's export sales are made to its parent company and are accumulated in the account, Sales—Foreign. The balance in the Due from Wiend account is the total of unpaid invoices. All foreign sales are billed in U.S. dollars. The reciprocal accounts on the parent com-

change rate is LC3 to $1. Which of the following journal entries should Marvin make to record the collection of this receivable?

	Debit	Credit
a. Cash	300,000	
Accounts Receivable		300,000
b. Cash	300,000	
Exchange Loss	15,000	
Accounts Receivable		315,000
c. Cash	300,000	
Deferred Exchange Loss	15,000	
Accounts Receivable		315,000
d. Cash	315,000	
Accounts Receivable		315,000

2. The Clark Company owns a foreign subsidiary which had net income for the year ended December 31, 19X5, of 4,800,000 local currency (LC) units, which was appropriately translated into $800,000. On October 15, 19X5, when the rate of exchange was LC5.7 to $1, the foreign subsidiary paid a dividend to Clark of LC2,400,000. The dividend represented the net income of the foreign subsidiary for the 6 months ended June 30, 19X5, during which time the weighted average of exchange rates was LC5.8 to $1. The rate of exchange in effect at December 31, 19X5, was LC5.9 to $1. What rate of exchange should be used to translate the dividend for the December 31, 19X5, financial statements?

   a. LC5.7/$1.
   b. LC5.8/$1.
   c. LC5.9/$1.
   d. LC6.0/$1.

3. Certain balance sheet accounts in a foreign subsidiary of the Brogan Company at December 31, 19X7, have been translated into U.S. dollars as follows:

	Translated at:	
	Current Rates	Historical Rates
Marketable Equity Securities Carried at Cost	$100,000	$110,000
Marketable Equity Securities Carried at Current Market Price	120,000	125,000
Inventories Carried at Cost	130,000	132,000
Inventories Carried at Net Realizable Value	80,000	84,000
	$430,000	$451,000

Assuming the functional currency is the U.S. dollar, what amount should be shown in Brogan's balance sheet at December 31, 19X7, as a result of the above information?

   a. $430,000.

    b. $436,000.

    c. $442,000.

    d. $451,000.

4. On January 1, 19X6, the Ace Company formed a foreign subsidiary. On February 15, 19X6, Ace's subsidiary purchased 175,000 local currency (LC) units of inventory. LC50,000 of the original inventory purchased on February 15, 19X6, made up the entire inventory on December 31, 19X6. The exchange rates were LC2.2 to $1 from January 1, 19X6, to June 30, 19X6, and LC2 to $1 from July 1, 19X6, to December 31, 19X6. If the functional currency is the local currency, the December 31, 19X6, inventory balance for Ace's foreign subsidiary should be translated into which of the following U.S. dollar amounts?

    a. $23,077.

    b. $22,727.

    c. $23,810.

    d. $25,000.

5. The Dease Company owns a foreign subsidiary with 3,600,000 local currency LC units of property, plant, and equipment before accumulated depreciation at December 31, 19X5. Of this amount, LC2,400,000 were acquired in 19X3, when the rate of exchange was LC1.6 to $1, and LC1,200,000 were acquired in 19X4, when the rate of exchange was LC1.8 to $1. The rate of exchange in effect at December 31, 19X5, was LC2 to $1. The weighted average of exchange rates in effect during 19X5 was LC1.92 to $1. Assuming that the property, plant, and equipment are depreciated using the straight-line method over a 10-year period with no salvage value, and that the U.S. dollar is the functional currency, how much depreciation expense relating to the foreign subsidiary's property, plant, and equipment should be charged in Dease's income statement for 19X5?

    a. $180,000.

    b. $187,500.

    c. $200,000.

    d. $216,667.

6. The Witter Company owns a foreign subsidiary with 4,800,000 local currency (LC) units of property, plant, and equipment before accumulated depreciation at December 31, 19X4. Of this amount, LC3,000,000 were acquired in 19X2, when the rate of exchange was LC1.5 to $1, and LC1,800,000 were acquired in 19X3, when the rate of exchange was LC1.6 to $1. The rate of exchange in effect at December 31, 19X4, was LC1.9 to $1. The weighted average of exchange rates in effect during 19X4 was LC1.8 to $1. Assuming that the property, plant, and equipment are depreciated using the straight-line method over a 10-year period with no salvage value, and that the local currency is the functional currency, how much depreciation ex-

pense relating to the foreign subsidiary's property, plant, and equipment should be charged in Witter's income statement for 19X4?

a. $252,632.

b. $266,667.

c. $300,000.

d. $312,500.

7. The Lochlann Company purchased with U.S. dollars all the outstanding common stock of the Dey Company, a Canadian corporation. The functional currency is the Canadian dollar. At the date of purchase, a portion of the investment account was appropriately allocated to goodwill. One year later, after an exchange rate increase (U.S. dollars have become less valuable), the goodwill should be shown in the consolidated balance sheet at what amount?

a. An increased amount, less amortization.

b. The same amount, less amortization.

c. A lesser amount, less amortization.

d. An increased or lesser amount depending on management policy, less amortization.

8. If a parent company bills all sales to a foreign subsidiary in terms of dollars and is to be repaid in the same number of dollars, the Purchases account on the subsidiary's trial balance will be converted to U.S. dollars by using:

a. The average exchange rate for the period.

b. The exchange rate at the beginning of the period.

c. The exchange rate at the end of the period.

d. The amount shown in the parent's accounts for sales to the subsidiary.

(AICPA adapted)

P15.7 Multiple Choice Questions on Foreign Currency Translation

1. How should exchange gains and losses resulting from translating foreign currency financial statements into U.S. dollars be accounted for when the functional currency is the foreign currency?

a. Included as an ordinary item in net earnings for the period in which the rate changes.

b. Included as an extraordinary item in net earnings for the period in which the rate changes.

c. Included under a special caption in stockholders' equity.

d. Included as an ordinary item in net earnings for gains, but deferred for losses.

2. A material loss arising from the devaluation of the currency of a country in which a corporation was conducting foreign operations through a branch whose functional currency is the U.S. dollar would be reflected in the company's year-end financial statements as:

a. An asset to be subsequently offset against gains from foreign currency revaluations.

b. A factor in determining earnings before extraordinary items in the year during which the loss occurred.

c. An extraordinary item on the earnings statement of the year during which the loss occurred.

d. A prior period adjustment, unless the operations of the foreign branch had begun during the year in which the loss occurred.

3. A change in the foreign currency exchange rate between the date a transaction occurred and the date of the current financial statements gives rise to an exchange gain or loss if the functional currency is the U.S. dollar and:

a. The asset or liability being translated is carried at a current money price.

b. The asset or liability being translated is carried at a price from a past purchase or sale exchange.

c. The revenue or expense item relates to an asset or liability that is translated at historical rates.

d. The revenue or expense item relates to a deferred asset or liability shown on a previous statement of financial position.

4. The Seed Company had a receivable from a foreign customer which is payable in the customer's local currency. On December 31, 19X6, this receivable was appropriately included in the accounts receivable section of Seed's balance sheet at $450,000. When the receivable was collected on January 4, 19X7, Seed converted the local currency of the foreign customer into $440,000. Seed also owns a foreign subsidiary (whose functional currency is the foreign currency) in which exchange gains of $45,000 resulted as a consequence of translation in 19X7. What amount, if any, should be included as an exchange gain or loss in Seed's 19X7 consolidated income statement?

a. $0.

b. $10,000 exchange loss.

c. $35,000 exchange gain.

d. $45,000 exchange gain.

5. The Fore Company had a $30,000 exchange loss resulting from the translation of the accounts of its wholly owned foreign subsidiary (whose functional currency is the U.S. dollar) for the year ended December 31, 19X8. Fore also had a receivable from a foreign customer which was payable in the customer's local currency. On December 31, 19X7, this receivable for 500,000 local currency (LC) units was appropriately included in the accounts receivable section of Fore's balance sheet at $245,000. When the receivable was collected on February 5, 19X8, the exchange rate was LC2 to $1. What amount should be included as the total exchange gain or loss in the 19X8 consolidated income statement of Fore Company and its wholly owned foreign subsidiary as a result of the above?

a. $5,000 exchange gain.

b. $20,000 exchange loss.

c. $25,000 exchange loss.

d. $30,000 exchange loss.

6. When preparing combined or consolidated financial statements for a domestic and a foreign company, account balances expressed in the foreign currency must be translated into the domestic currency. The objective of the translation process is to obtain currency valuations that:

a. Are conservative.

b. Reflect current monetary equivalents.

c. Are in conformity with domestic generally accepted accounting principles and reflect financial results and relationships as measured in the functional currency.

d. Reflect the translated account at its unexpired historical cost.

7. The year-end balance of accounts receivable on the books of a foreign subsidiary should be translated by the parent company for consolidation purposes at the:

a. Historical rate.

b. Current rate.

c. Negotiated rate.

d. Forward rate.

8. When translating an amount for fixed assets shown on the statement of financial position of a foreign subsidiary whose functional currency is a foreign currency, the appropriate rate of translation is the:

a. Current exchange rate.

b. Average exchange rate for the current year.

c. Historical exchange rate.

d. Average exchange rate over the life of each fixed asset.

(AICPA adapted)

P15.8 Translating under Temporal and Current Rate Methods; Analysis of Equity Adjustment On January 1, 19X3, the U.K. branch of U.S. International Corporation had the following condensed balance sheet, in pounds (£):

ASSETS		LIABILITIES AND OWNERS' EQUITY	
Cash and Receivables.	£2,000	Accounts Payable	£2,100
Inventory (LIFO)	2,200	Long-Term Debt	1,200
Plant Assets	1,600	Home Office	2,100
Accumulated Depreciation . . .	(400)		
	£5,400		£5,400

The exchange rate on January 1, 19X3, was $2/£. Inventory and Plant Assets at January 1 were acquired when the exchange rate was $1.80/£. Plant assets costing £200 were purchased during the year when the exchange rate was $2.15/£. No depreciation was taken on these assets in 19X3, and no transactions between the home office and branch occurred during 19X3. At the end of 19X3, the branch reported the following trial balance, in pounds:

Account	Dr. (Cr.)
Cash and Receivables	£2,660
Inventory (LIFO)	2,500
Plant Assets	1,800
Accumulated Depreciation	(560)
Accounts Payable	(2,200)
Long-Term Debt	(1,100)
Home Office	(2,100)
Sales	(4,000)
Cost of Goods Sold	2,000
Depreciation Expense	160
Other Operating Expenses	840
	£ 0

The exchange rate when the new LIFO layer was acquired was $2.05/£. Goods Sold were purchased at an average exchange rate of $2.12/£. Sales and Other Operating Expenses occurred evenly over the year. At year-end, the exchange rate stood at $2.20/£; the average for the year was $2.10/£.

Required:

1. Translate the trial balance in accordance with the temporal method (functional currency is the U.S. dollar). The translated balance of "Home Office" on January 1, 19X3, was $3,520.
2. Repeat No. 1 using the current rate method (functional currency is the pound) and the $3,520 translated balance of "Home Office" at January 1, 19X3.
3. Prepare a schedule to calculate the translation adjustment arising in No. 1. Describe the accounting treatment of this item.
4. Assuming that *SFAS 52* was adopted on January 1, 19X3, and the current rate method is being used as in No. 2, prepare an analysis of the Equity Adjustment from Foreign Currency Translation account for 19X3.

P15.9 Translating Branch Accounts and Preparing Combined Trial Balance Working Paper The Copra Trading Company established a foreign branch office in Arpoc Cay in 19X0 to purchase local products for resale by the home office and to sell company products. The branch's functional currency is the U.S. dollar.

You were engaged to examine the company's financial statements for the year ended December 31, 19X7, and engaged a chartered professional accountant in Arpoc to examine the branch office accounts. He reported that the branch accounts were fairly stated in pesos, the local currency, except for a franchise fee, and that any possible adjustments required by home office accounting procedures were not recorded. Trial balances for both the branch office and home office appear in Exhibit 15.17.

Exhibit 15.17   Trial Balance Data to Be Used in P15.9

COPRA TRADING COMPANY AND BRANCH OFFICE
TRIAL BALANCES
AT DECEMBER 31, 19X7

DEBITS	Branch Office (in Pesos)	Home Office (in Dollars)
Cash	P 110,000	$ 90,000
Trade Accounts Receivable.	140,000	160,000
Branch Current Account	—	10,000
Inventory, Jan. 1	80,000	510,000
Prepaid Expenses	10,000	18,000
Fixed Assets	1,000,000	750,000
Deferred Marketing Research.	—	12,000
Purchases	488,889	3,010,000
Purchases from Home	711,111	—
Purchases from Branch.	—	140,000
Operating and General Expenses	190,000	680,000
Depreciation Expense	100,000	50,000
Total Debits	P2,830,000	$5,430,000
CREDITS		
Allowance for Depreciation	P 650,000	$ 350,000
Current Liabilities.	220,000	240,000
Home Office Current Account.	50,000	—
Long-Term Debt	230,000	200,000
Capital Stock	—	300,000
Retained Earnings, Jan. 1	—	142,500
Sales	1,057,778	4,035,000
Sales to Branch	—	120,000
Sales to Home	622,222	—
Overvaluation of Branch Inventory	—	42,500
Total Credits	P2,830,000	$5,430,000

Your examination disclosed the following information:

1. The peso was devalued on July 1, 19X7, from 4 pesos per $1 to 5 pesos per $1. The former rate of exchange had been in effect for 10 years. Branch ending inventory and prepaid expenses were acquired after the devaluation.
2. Sales to the branch are marked up 33⅓ percent and shipped F.O.B. home office. Branch sales to the home office are made at branch cost.
3. The branch had a beginning and ending inventory on hand valued at 80,000 pesos, of which one-half at each date had been purchased from the home office. The home office had an inventory at December 31, 19X7, valued at $520,000.
4. The Deferred Marketing Research account is the unamortized portion of a $15,000 fee paid in January 19X6 to a U.S. firm for continuing

marketing research for the branch. Currency restrictions prevented the branch from paying the fee, which was paid by the home office. The home office charges the branch $3,000 annually during the 5-year amortization period, and the branch records the expense.

5. The branch incurred its long-term indebtedness in 19X2 to finance its most recent purchase of fixed assets.

6. The government of Arpoc imposes a franchise fee of 10 pesos per 100 pesos of net income of the branch in exchange for certain exclusive trading rights granted. The fee is payable each May 1 for the preceding calendar year's trading rights and had not been recorded by the branch at December 31, 19X7.

Required: Prepare a combined trial balance working paper for Copra and its foreign branch office with all amounts stated in U.S. dollars. Your working paper should have captions for Branch Trial Balance (pesos), Translation Rate, Branch Trial Balance (dollars), Home Office Trial Balance, Adjustments and Eliminations, and Combined Trial Balance. Ending inventories must be included and supporting computations must be in good form. Number the working paper adjusting and eliminating entries. *(AICPA adapted)*

P15.10 Translating Financial Statements under Four Alternative Translation Methods The SA Company was organized in Mexico on December 31, 19X1, with a capital stock issue that yielded 1,000,000 pesos (P). The exchange rate was $.10/P. Transactions engaged in during 19X2 and the relevant exchange rates are shown below:

	January 5, 19X2	June 30, 19X2	December 31, 19X2
Exchange rate:	$.10/P	$.12/P	$.15/P
Transactions:	1. Buy 2,000 wood carvings at P200 each.	1. Sell 1,000 carvings for P300,000.	1. Record straight-line depreciation on office equipment.
	2. Purchase office equipment (10-year life) for P200,000.	2. Buy 1,500 carvings for P360,000.	2. Write-down the carvings bought on June 30 to market of P320,000.
		3. Pay rent of P30,000.	3. Close books and prepare financial statements.

Required: Using a schedule like the one presented in Exhibit 15.4 in the chapter, prepare translated balance sheets and income statements under the current/noncurrent, monetary/nonmonetary, temporal, and current rate (functional currency is the peso) translation methods. Show the calculation of the translation adjustment in each of the four methods.

P15.11 Preparing Consolidated Financial Statements with Purchased Foreign Subsidiary On January 1, 19X4, the Phillips Company acquired 80 percent of the outstanding shares of Standard, Ltd., a U.K. firm, for $10,000,000 cash. At the end of 19X4, the two companies presented the condensed financial statements appearing in Exhibit 15.18.

At date of acquisition, the exchange rate was $2/£. Standard's inventory and buildings were undervalued by £100,000 and £500,000, respectively. All of the undervalued inventory was sold during the year, and the buildings are being depreciated over a 20-year life. Other relevant information is as follows:

1. The exchange rate at December 31, 19X4, was $2.30/£.
2. Standard's sales and other operating expenses occurred evenly during the year. The average exchange rate was $2.15/£.
3. Standard's inventory and goods sold were acquired when the exchange rate was $2.10/£.
4. Standard's plant assets were acquired when the exchange rate was $1.80/£.
5. Phillips's policy is to amortize intangibles over 40 years.
6. Phillips carries its Investment in Standard at equity. However, the eq-

---

Exhibit 15.18   **Phillips Company and Standard, Ltd.: Condensed Financial Statements to Be Used in P15.11**

BALANCE SHEETS

ASSETS	Phillips ($)	Standard (£)
Cash and Receivables	$ 7,680,000	£ 3,000,000
Inventory	4,000,000	3,000,000
Property, Plant, and Equipment, Net	12,000,000	5,000,000
Investment in Standard	8,320,000	—
Total Assets	$32,000,000	£11,000,000

LIABILITIES AND STOCKHOLDERS' EQUITY		
Current Liabilities	$ 8,000,000	£ 4,000,000
Long-Term Debt	4,000,000	1,000,000
Capital Stock	10,000,000	2,000,000
Retained Earnings	10,000,000	4,000,000
Total Liabilities and Stockholders' Equity	$32,000,000	£11,000,000

STATEMENTS OF INCOME AND RETAINED EARNINGS

	Phillips ($)	Standard (£)
Sales	$30,000,000	£10,000,000
Cost of Goods Sold	$20,000,000	£ 6,000,000
Depreciation Expense	1,000,000	500,000
Other Operating Expenses	5,000,000	2,000,000
	$26,000,000	£ 8,500,000
Net Income	$ 4,000,000	£ 1,500,000
Dividends Declared and Paid	(2,000,000)	(1,000,000)
Increase in Retained Earnings	$ 2,000,000	£ 500,000

uity method accrual for 19X4 has not been booked and can be disregarded in this problem. Intercompany dividends, paid when the exchange rate was $2.10, were credited to the investment account.

Required: Assuming that the pound is the functional currency, prepare a consolidated balance sheet and a consolidated statement of income and retained earnings for Phillips and Standard. Neither a working paper nor formal working paper entries are required. All supporting computations should be in good form.

P15.12 Translating Postcombination Balance Sheets under Pooling and Purchase; Analysis of Equity Adjustment Marcus Corporation acquired all of the outstanding stock of Blatt, Ltd., a U.K. company, on December 31, 19X4, for stock worth $1,200,000. On that date, the exchange rate was $2.00/£. Blatt's condensed balance sheet as of December 31, 19X4, is given below:

ASSETS		LIABILITIES AND STOCKHOLDERS' EQUITY	
Cash and Receivables . . .	£ 600,000	Current Liabilities.	£ 400,000
Inventory (FIFO)	250,000	Long-Term Debt	300,000
Plant Assets, Net.	350,000	Capital Stock.	200,000
Patents.	100,000	Retained Earnings	400,000
	£1,300,000		£1,300,000

Blatt was organized on June 15, 19X1, when the exchange rate was $2.10/£. The capital stock was issued and £200,000 (net) of plant assets was acquired on that date. The remaining net plant assets were acquired and the long-term debt issued when the exchange rate was $2.05/£. Blatt acquired the patents when the exchange rate was $1.90/£.

Required:

1. Translate Blatt's condensed balance sheet into dollars for inclusion in Marcus's consolidated statements on December 31, 19X4. Assume that the combination was accounted for as a *pooling of interests* and that the U.S. dollar is the functional currency.
2. Repeat No. 1 assuming that the combination was accounted for as a *purchase* and that the pound is the functional currency.
3. Blatt reported net income of £100,000 and paid dividends of £60,000 during 19X5. There were no other changes in Blatt's stockholders' equity. The average exchange rate during 19X5 was $2.10/£ and the dividends were declared when the exchange rate was $2.06/£. Prepare an analysis of the Equity Adjustment account during 19X5 assuming that the acquisition of Blatt had been accounted for by the purchase method, that the exchange rate on December 31, 19X5, is $2.02/£, and that the pound is the functional currency.

Part FIVE **Governmental and Nonprofit Entities**

The growth of the government and nonprofit sectors and their increasing importance in our economy lead us to devote three chapters to accounting for these entities. Our primary objective is to highlight the areas in which accounting and reporting for government and nonprofit entities differ from accounting and reporting for corporate business entities.

Because local government is the level most often encountered in accounting practice, Chapters 16 and 17 are devoted to a detailed coverage of this subject. Recently, local governmental accounting has experienced changes in accounting and reporting standards; these new standards are discussed and illustrated. Each of the numerous accounting entities that exist in local government is considered. In Chapter 18, attention is given to the nongovernment, nonprofit entity. Although many types of nonprofit organizations exist, voluntary health and welfare organizations, colleges, and hospitals are given primary attention. Many of the accounting and reporting practices for these three types apply equally to other types of nonprofit organizations. Again, recent developments in this area of accounting are considered.

As we shall discuss, governmental and nonprofit entities use a wide variety of accounting procedures, ranging from business-type, profit-oriented accounting to various versions of fund accounting. There are key differences in emphasis between governmental/nonprofit accounting and business accounting. In general, governmental and nonprofit accounting emphasizes management's accountability for the use of resources, whereas business accounting emphasizes management's performance on behalf of stockholders. Also, in governmental and nonprofit accounting, the entity is generally subdivided into several components, and each is reported separately; the concept of consolidation is typically not used. In business accounting, a single report for the entire firm is common, including the consolidation of other majority-owned entities. As accounting standards for governmental and nonprofit organizations continue to develop, however, these differences are likely to narrow.

Chapter 16 Accounting and Reporting for Routine Activities of Local Government

Government, at all levels, is an increasingly important segment of the economy. As the scope and diversity of governmental services and programs expand, so too does the importance of governmental accounting and reporting. Governmental accounting and reporting practices differ from those of commercial enterprises. Legal considerations, organizational objectives, and decentralization of control over resources create special reporting needs of governmental units.

In this chapter, we consider the accounting aspects of the normal operating activities of local government. These activities are recorded and reported by the general and special revenue funds, which are studied in detail. The chapter ends with a discussion of the special sets of accounts used for fixed assets and long-term debt.

Accounting by Local Government

Since the level of government most frequently served by accountants is the local government, we concentrate on this subject. The term **governmental unit** will therefore refer to a local governmental unit. The accounting concepts and procedures discussed apply equally to towns, cities, counties, school districts, water districts, fire protection districts, and other local governmental units.

The Entity

Although a governmental unit, such as a town, may appear to be a single entity, this is often not the case. We may find additional legal entities either within a governmental unit or overlapping it. For example, a school district may be a legally separate entity from a city or town, and the two may or may not geographically coincide. A municipality may contain "special districts"—legally separate entities which provide a particular service such as sewers, sidewalks, street lighting, or fire protection to a particular area. Each of these units—the city, the town, the school district, the fire district—constitutes a separate legal entity. Each is likely to have its own taxing authority, ability to issue debt, and other powers. Each legal entity will also issue its own financial statements.

Initially, we focus on the legal entity as the one whose activities must be accounted for and reported to the taxpayers or other constituencies. *Within each legal entity, however, the concept of economic entity dominates.* In corporate accounting, the entity concept led to presentation of consolidated financial statements (one economic entity) for several corporations (separate legal entities). Conversely, following the economic entity concept in governmental accounting may lead to division of one legal entity (the governmental unit) into several economic or accounting entities called **funds.**

The notion of an economic entity differs for business and local government. In the corporate context, the presence of common control over the affairs of several entities leads to the conclusion that one economic entity exists. In the context of local government, management control is influenced to a great extent by legal considerations. When several legal entities coexist within a geographical area, there may be no common managerial control. The mayor of a city, for example, may have little or no control over a legally separate school district. Even within a single legal entity such as a city, not all control rests in the hands of management; laws of various types also exert considerable control. For example, a city's financial management may be influenced by:

1. The city charter.
2. Local ordinances.
3. State laws affecting city operations.
4. State or federal laws affecting the use of particular resources
   (for example, the federal revenue-sharing laws).
5. Bond covenants.

Although legal considerations are not lacking in the corporate world, they are present and influential to a much greater degree in government.

Legislation and regulations define the ways in which resources may be spent, thus providing much of the legal control over governmental entities. It may be stipulated that resources derived from local property taxes be spent in certain ways, resources derived from a bond issue in other ways, and resources from federal revenue sharing in yet other ways. One of the responsibilities of the management of local government is to ensure that resources are spent in the legally prescribed manners. This responsibility is often referred to as **stewardship,** meaning that management is entrusted with these resources by the community and must carry out certain specified responsibilities with respect to their use.

As a result of the stewardship concept, a single legal entity in local government is likely to be organized into several accounting entities.

> Each entity, called a **fund,** is defined as a fiscal and accounting entity with a self-balancing set of accounts recording cash and other financial resources, together with all related liabilities and residual equities or balances, and changes therein, which are segregated for the purpose of carrying on specific activities or attaining certain objectives in accordance with special regulations, restrictions, or limitations.[1]

In short, a fund is a set of resources that may be used for certain specified purposes or activities of the governmental unit. The fact that there are different economic purposes and constraints related to resources results in the presence of several entities. Accounting focuses on these separate *entities*. The financial report of a governmental unit contains financial statements for each entity (fund) of the unit. In the local government context, therefore, the entity concept leads to the presentation of multiple sets of financial statements for a single legal entity, whereas in the corporate context, the entity principle leads to a single set of statements for multiple legal entities.

The Eight Standard Funds

The affairs of a governmental unit may be organized into eight economic entities or funds. In a given local governmental unit, some or all of these **eight standard funds** will exist. We shall briefly describe each in terms of the source of its financial resources and the activities and purposes for which its resources are used. A city government is used as an example.

1. **General fund**—accounts for the basic services provided by city government, through the use of general revenue.
   a. Resources are derived from property taxes, sales taxes, general state aid, fees, fines, and so on.
   b. Resources are used for city administration, police, fire protection, courts, streets, parks, sanitation, and so on.
2. **Special revenue funds**—account for selected basic operations of the city, funded from special revenue sources.
   a. Resources are derived from state or federal aid for specific purposes (for example, federal revenue-sharing funds, which are limited to certain activities such as public safety); taxes levied for a certain purpose (for example, a school tax levied by a city), grants, and so on.
   b. Resources are used for the particular operations which are specified by the revenue source, as illustrated above.
3. **Capital projects funds**—account for the financing and construction or acquisition of major capital assets.

---

[1]National Council on Governmental Accounting, *Statement 1,* "Governmental Accounting and Financial Reporting Principles" (Chicago: Municipal Finance Officers Association of the United States and Canada, 1979), 2.

a. Resources are derived primarily from proceeds of bond issues for specific projects; other sources may include state or federal aid, or allocation of general revenues (from general fund).

b. Resources are used for construction or acquisition of buildings, major equipment, or public improvements such as roads, bridges, and sewer systems.

4. **Special assessment funds**—account for public improvements financed by specific assessments on property owners.

a. Resources are derived from assessments on property owners who are served by the improvement, and allocation of general revenues (from general fund).

b. Resources are used for construction or acquisition of improvements such as sewers, sidewalks, or street lighting.

5. **Debt service funds**—account for the payment of principal and interest on the general long-term debt of the city.

a. Resources are generally derived from transfers from other funds (the general fund or the capital projects fund) and from interest earned.

b. Resources are used for payment of interest and principal; in some cases, resources are accumulated (and invested) in anticipation of future principal payments.

6. **Enterprise funds**—account for certain business activities of a city in which goods or services are sold to the public, such as a city water department or a municipal golf course.

a. Resources are derived from amounts charged to customers.

b. Resources are used for operating expenses of the enterprise.

7. **Internal service funds**—account for central services provided to other departments of the city; for example, a central supply unit which buys supplies in large quantities and issues them to various departments, a central vehicle maintenance shop, or a central computer center.

a. Resources are derived from charges to other city departments, that is, transfers from other funds.

b. Resources are used for operating expenses of the central service activities.

8. **Trust and agency funds**—account for resources collected by the city on behalf of another entity and resources held by the city under a trust agreement.

a. Resources are derived from collections on behalf of other entities, such as income taxes withheld from employees, and amounts received to be held in trust and used for a specific purpose, such as an endowment for the public library.

b. Resources are used for transmittal of amounts collected to other entities, and for expenditures in accord with trust agreements.

These eight funds encompass all the activities of a city government. One (and only one) general fund will always exist. In the case of each of the other fund types, none, one, or several may exist. For example, if a city has no construction

Exhibit 16.1	Fund Structure of a School District	
Fund	**Resources Derived from**	**Resources Used for**
General	School tax; local, state, and federal aid; fees.	Administration, instruction, transportation, maintenance, debt service.
Special Revenue	Special state or federal aid (for example, Head Start Program)	Instruction and other costs related to specified program.
Capital Projects	Bond issues; state or federal aid, or transfers from general fund.	Construction, acquisition or renovation of school buildings; major equipment purchases (for example, fleet of buses).
Enterprise	Charges to customers of cafeteria, bookstore, and other enterprises; may be supplemented from other sources (for example, state aid for school lunch program).	Operating expenses of cafeteria, bookstore, or other enterprises.
Special Assessments	(Usually not applicable to a school district)	
Debt Service	Transfers from general or capital projects funds.	Payment of principal and interest.
Trust and Agency	Collections for others (for example, taxes withheld); gifts for specified purposes (for example, scholarship funds).	Transmittal of amounts collected; payment of scholarships.
Internal Service	Transfers from other funds for central services.	Costs of central services.

projects underway, a capital projects fund may not exist. On the other hand, if three projects are currently under construction, the city may use three capital projects funds or combine all three projects in one capital projects fund.

To further illustrate how the activities are structured into these eight funds, Exhibit 16.1 presents the fund structure of a typical school district. As noted earlier, some governmental units may not need all eight funds. There will, however, always be a general fund; this fund accounts for the basic operations of the governmental unit.

In summary, a local government consists of several economic entities. We next consider the general accounting principles applicable to these entities; later the typical financial statements for these entities are presented.

Accounting Principles for Local Government

As is the case with business accounting, accounting principles for local governments have developed from several sources. While many principles and procedures have evolved from practice over the years, formal pronouncements also play a role. Four major sources of pronouncements on accounting principles for local government exist: (1) the Governmental Accounting Standards Board, (2) the National Council on Governmental Accounting, (3) the American Institute of Certified Public Accountants, and (4) state governments.

Governmental Accounting Standards Board. A Governmental Accounting Standards Board (GASB) was established in 1984, as another wing of the Financial Accounting Foundation (the parent organization of the FASB). The GASB issues authoritative standards on accounting and financial reporting by state and local governmental entities, while the FASB issues authoritative standards for all other entities. At this writing, the GASB is in its beginning stages.

National Council on Governmental Accounting. Prior to the formation of the GASB, the National Council on Governmental Accounting (NCGA) had been the major standard-setting organization in the field of governmental accounting. The NCGA is sponsored and supported by the Municipal Finance Officers Association of the United States and Canada, a professional organization. For many years, the NCGA's book, *Governmental Accounting, Auditing, and Financial Reporting* (often referred to as *GAAFR* or the "blue book"), served as the leading source of accounting principles for state and local government.[2] In 1979, *GAAFR* was restructured to become a series of official pronouncements. *Statement 1,* "Governmental Accounting and Financial Reporting Principles,"[3] covered the broad principles that underlie governmental accounting. A total of seven statements, one concepts statement, and eleven interpretations were issued by the NCGA. These were reconfirmed as authoritative by GASB *Statement 1.*

Other Sources. Although the NCGA was the major source of principles for governmental accounting, it was not the only source. In 1974, the American Institute of Certified Public Accountants issued an audit guide entitled *Audits of State and Local Governmental Units.* In addition to establishing auditing standards, this document set forth accounting principles applicable to state and local governments. The principles set forth in this audit guide were influential in leading to some of the 1979 revisions in *GAAFR.* The audit guide, along with its amendments issued in the form of Statements of Position by the AICPA, was also reconfirmed as authoritative by GASB *Statement 1.*

Another source of accounting requirements is law or regulation. A state may specify certain accounting rules for all local governmental units within the state. In New York State, for example, the State Department of Audit and Control has numerous accounting requirements to be followed by counties, cities, towns, school districts, and other units within the state. A possible future source of accounting principles for local governments is the SEC. Local governments have

---

[2]Municipal Finance Officers Association of the United States and Canada, *Governmental Accounting, Auditing, and Financial Reporting* (Chicago: MFOA, 1968). A revision was issued in 1980 but was not deemed an authoritative pronouncement.

[3]National Council on Governmental Accounting, *Statement 1,* "Governmental Accounting and Financial Reporting Principles" (Chicago: MFOA, 1979).

been exempt from the reporting requirements of the securities laws. In recent years, however, concern over the solvency of municipalities has increased, accompanied by calls for registration and reporting requirements for municipal securities. Some municipalities have voluntarily issued formal prospectuses in response to these concerns. Increased regulation in this area appears likely.

Types of Accounting for Funds

Differing characteristics of the economic entities in a local government require different types of accounting. In particular, business accounting, fiduciary accounting, and fund accounting are employed.

Business Accounting. Two of the eight funds—the enterprise fund and the internal service fund—conduct business activities and are sometimes referred to as **proprietary funds.** They sell goods and services either to the public or to units of the government. It is reasonable, therefore, that accrual accounting be applied to these funds as it is to commercial firms. Thus, for these two funds, the accounting procedures are already familiar. These funds will be discussed further in Chapter 17.

Fiduciary Accounting. The trust and agency funds hold and manage resources on behalf of others and are referred to as **fiduciary funds.** These resources may be amounts collected for transmittal to others or amounts held under some sort of formal trust agreement, to be used in a certain manner. Because fiduciary responsibilities exist, trust and agency funds generally use the same fiduciary accounting procedures presented in Chapter 4 for trusts and estates. We examine the application of fiduciary accounting to the trust and agency funds in Chapter 17.

Fund Accounting. The remaining five funds (general, special revenue, capital projects, special assessments, and debt service) are referred to as **governmental funds** and use a type of accounting known as **fund accounting.** The following sections discuss the various characteristics of this type of accounting and provide the basis for illustrating accounting for routine activities of local government in the general and special revenue funds.

Principles of Fund Accounting

Revenues and Expenditures. Fund accounting is concerned with changes in the resources available to each fund. Thus the focus is on accounting for the revenues and expenditures of each fund. In business accounting, revenues are amounts earned from the sale of goods and services. In fund accounting, **revenues** are inflows of resources, with no requirement that they be generated from the services provided by the government. Taxes, fees, and state aid all constitute revenues in fund accounting, but transfers from another fund and amounts borrowed are not considered revenues.

Since fund accounting is concerned with changes in resources, we are concerned with reporting **expenditures** (outflows of resources) rather than *expenses* (costs consumed in generating revenue or in delivering the current period's goods and services). In fund accounting, payments for labor, materials, equipment, and repayment of long-term debt all constitute expenditures.

Basis of Accounting. The emphasis on revenues and expenditures suggests that fund accounting would use cash basis rather than accrual basis accounting. In fact, an in-between approach, known as a **modified accrual basis** (sometimes called a *modified cash basis*) **of accounting** is used.

Under the modified accrual approach, revenues are recognized when they become *measurable* and *available* (collectible within the current period or soon enough thereafter to be used to meet obligations of the current period). Some revenue items of a local government are assessed and collected in a manner that makes them subject to accrual, while others are not. Property taxes, for example, are accrued because (1) the total amount is known, since it is levied by the local government, (2) collection usually occurs within a short time, and (3) uncollectible amounts can be reasonably estimated. In many cases, grants from the state or federal government are also accrued. There are many revenue items of a local government that cannot be measured and recorded until they are actually collected; the cash basis is used for these items. Examples include traffic fines and sales and income taxes.

Generally, all expenditures are recorded on the accrual basis. The major exception is interest on general long-term debt and on special assessment fund debt. This interest is not accrued but is recorded when paid. Thus the modified accrual approach may be summarized as follows:

1. Revenues are recorded when they become measurable and available; this results in the use of the accrual basis for some items and the cash basis for other items.
2. All expenditures except certain interest payments are recorded on the accrual basis.

Budgetary Accounts. Accounting serves an important control function in local government—namely, to aid in ensuring that resources are spent in compliance with legal requirements. Legal restrictions on spending are usually expressed in the form of a **budget,** which prescribes both the total amount of spending allowed and the amounts in each expense category. A budget may be adopted by legislative/executive action (for example, passage by a city council and acceptance by a mayor) or by popular vote, as is the case with many school district budgets. Typically, any change in the total budget must be approved in the same way, while changes within the budget (transfers among budget components) usually require less formal approval (for example, a school board may approve budget transfers).

To aid in control of revenues and expenditures, *the budget is recorded in the accounts.* At the beginning of the year, the budgeted revenues and budgeted expenditures are entered in **budgetary accounts.** As actual revenues are received and resources are expended during the year, comparison with the budget is made regularly. This comparison helps to ensure that, in each category of the budget, actual spending does not exceed the authorized amount. Recording of budget data in the accounts is one of the key aspects of fund accounting and one of the major ways in which governmental accounting differs from corporate accounting. In governmental situations, the budget is more than a managerial plan; it is a legal constraint. The budget establishes a legal spending limit, which must not be exceeded. Recording the budget, and regularly comparing actual expenditures to the budget, aids management in complying with the limits on its spending authority. Because of this constraint, it is important to know at any one time not only the amount actually spent to date and the amount of unpaid bills, but also the amount of outstanding spending commitments. Any commitment to spend is a potential charge against the budget; to aid in the control of expenditures, spending commitments (purchase orders) are recorded in the accounts.

Recording Purchase Orders. Expenditures are recorded on the accrual basis in fund accounting; hence both paid and unpaid invoices are recorded. We must, however, go beyond this to record outstanding spending commitments—contracts and purchase orders for goods and services yet to be delivered. When a purchase order is issued, the municipality commits some of its limited spending authority. If no record is kept, the danger exists that the government will overcommit itself and exceed the legal spending authority. Thus purchase orders and other legally binding commitments for spending, known as **encumbrances** or **obligations,** are recorded in the accounts. Recording encumbrances is another significant difference between governmental accounting and corporate accounting.

Fund Balance. Because a local government does not have owners, no stockholders' (or owners') equity is present. The equivalent of owners' equity in fund accounting is known simply as the **fund balance.** This account signifies the difference between the assets and liabilities of the entity. Portions of the fund balance are often "reserved" to signify a restriction on the spending of resources. Thus total fund balance will consist of an *unreserved* portion, which signifies that assets are available for future spending, and one or more *reserved* portions or *reserves,* which signifies some limitation on the ability to spend.

Accounting for Fixed Assets and Long-Term Debt. For those entities in which fund accounting is used, fixed assets and long-term debt are generally absent from the balance sheet. These items are accounted for in special sets of accounts known as the **general fixed asset account group** and the **general long-term debt account group.** These two account groups are separate from the various funds and may contain items originating in several funds. They are not considered funds, since they have no resources to spend and no activities to carry out. These account groups will be fully discussed later in this chapter.

Budget Formulation

The general and special revenue funds, two of the five funds which use fund accounting, require the recording of budget information in the accounts. The process of recording budget information is straightforward. However, the formulation of the budget may be a lengthy and difficult process.

Unlike business budgeting, which begins with a sales forecast, the budget formulation process in local government usually begins with *expenditure planning*. Activities and programs for the coming year are planned and their cost is estimated. When a tentative expenditure budget is complete, the revenue budget is prepared. First it must be decided whether the budget is to be balanced or is to provide for an increase or decrease in the fund balance. Then revenues from all sources other than the local property tax are estimated. Property taxes are the residual revenue and are planned in an amount necessary to achieve the required total revenue. If the resulting amount to be raised via property tax is unacceptable (for example, too large an increase is needed to achieve the total revenue), the process recycles until expenditures consistent with an acceptable level of property taxation are determined.

To illustrate, assume that the Wilford School District is formulating its general fund budget for 19X1–19X2. A detailed expenditure budget is prepared, which may be summarized as follows:

Central Administration	$ 480,000
Instruction	3,900,000
Operation and Maintenance	770,000
Transportation	600,000
Debt Service	850,000
Total Appropriations	$6,600,000

Next, a list of revenue sources other than the property tax is prepared:

State Aid	$2,000,000
Share of Local Sales Tax	400,000
Fees	200,000
Federal Aid	500,000
Total before Property Tax	$3,100,000

Assuming that the budget is to be balanced, $3,500,000 must be raised via property taxes. If this is deemed acceptable, a proposed tax rate is then calculated. Suppose that the assessed value of taxable property within the Wilford School District is $58,450,230. The tax rate is determined as follows:

$$\text{Tax rate} = \frac{\text{Amount to be raised by property tax}}{\text{Assessed value of taxable property}}$$

$$= \frac{\$3,500,000}{\$58,450,230}$$

$$= .05988.$$

Tax rates are commonly expressed as a rate per $1,000 of assessed valuation. Thus the rate for the Wilford School District would be $59.88 per $1,000 of assessed value, or 59.88 mills. Ideally, in setting the tax rate, the estimated percentage of uncollectible taxes should be taken into account. This would require than an amount greater than $3,500,000 be levied, so that expected collections are $3,500,000. For example, if 2 percent of the property tax levy is expected to be uncollectible, $3,571,428 (=$3,500,000/.98) must be levied in order to have expected revenue of $3,500,000. In many cases, however, the property tax levy is not adjusted for collectibility.

Budget approval must generally follow a specified legal process. A common process calls for a proposed budget to be presented by the executive (for example, mayor or school board president) of the local government to the legislative body for its approval. Ultimately, the budget approved by the legislature may differ from the proposed budget. The approved budget is then subject to acceptance or veto by the executive. Some jurisdictions provide that the executive must accept or veto the budget in its entirety; others permit veto of specific items in the budget. Another budget approval process used in some school districts requires that a budget be formulated by a school board and presented to the voters for acceptance or rejection. In either case, the process continues until a budget is accepted.

The General Fund

Once the budget is formulated and approved, the accounting process begins. We first consider the general fund, which accounts for the routine operations of a local government funded by general revenues.

Accounting for the General Fund

As mentioned above, the five governmental funds (general, special revenue, capital projects, special assessments, and debt service) use procedures known as *fund accounting*. We begin by illustrating these procedures for the general fund.

Budget Entry. The budget is recorded in the accounts to aid in controlling expenditures. A budget has two elements: planned revenues and planned expenditures. If the budget is *balanced*, these two amounts are equal, and the budget is recorded as:

```
Estimated Revenues . . . . . . . . . . . . . . . . . . . . . . . . . . . . . . . . . . .   XX
    Appropriations. . . . . . . . . . . . . . . . . . . . . . . . . . . . . . . . . . . .         XX
```

Estimated revenues is debited because it represents the expected inflow of resources to the fund (roughly analogous to receivables). Similarly, *Appropriations* (meaning budgeted expenditures) is credited because it represents the expected outflow of resources from the fund (roughly analogous to payables). To illustrate, assume that expenditures of $800,000 are budgeted, and revenues are also expected to be $800,000. The budget entry would be:

```
Estimated Revenues . . . . . . . . . . . . . . . . . . . . . . . .   800,000
    Appropriations . . . . . . . . . . . . . . . . . . . . . . . . . .            800,000
To record budget for the year.
```

It is not necessary that the budget be balanced in a particular fiscal period. A local government may plan to spend *less* than its anticipated revenue and thus to increase the net assets of the fund (which is called the *fund balance*). In this circumstance, the budget entry would show a credit to the fund balance. If revenues were expected to amount to $810,000, while expenditures were budgeted at $800,000, the unit is planning to increase its unreserved fund balance by $10,000 by spending less than it receives. The budget entry would be:

```
Estimated Revenues . . . . . . . . . . . . . . . . . . . . . . .    810,000
    Appropriations . . . . . . . . . . . . . . . . . . . . . . .               800,000
    Fund Balance—Unreserved  . . . . . . . . . . . . . . . .                    10,000
To record budget for the year and planned increase in fund
balance.
```

The fund balance—the equity account in governmental accounting—may be designated as *reserved* or *unreserved*. A *reserved fund balance* (analogous to appropriated retained earnings in corporate accounting) signifies a limitation on the ability to spend assets of the fund. Various examples of reserved fund balances will be presented as we progress. An *unreserved fund balance,* on the other hand, signifies the existence of assets which are expendable in carrying out the fund's activities. The above budget entry signifies that a $10,000 increase in expendable assets is anticipated for the period.

Alternatively, a local government may plan to spend *more* than its anticipated revenue, using resources accumulated in previous periods. The budget entry in this case would have a debit to the fund balance. If revenues were expected to amount to only $785,000, while expenditures were budgeted at $800,000, the unit is planning to decrease its fund balance by spending more than it receives this year. The budget entry would be:

```
Estimated Revenues . . . . . . . . . . . . . . . . . . . . . . .    785,000
Fund Balance—Unreserved. . . . . . . . . . . . . . . . . . .         15,000
    Appropriations . . . . . . . . . . . . . . . . . . . . . . .               800,000
To record budget for the year and planned decrease in fund
balance.
```

Note that after the budget is recorded, the fund balance account shows the expected *year-end balance*. In the preceding example, where budgeted revenues were $785,000 and budgeted expenditures were $800,000, assume that the fund balance at the beginning of the year was $500,000. After the budget is recorded, the fund balance is $485,000. If the budgeted figures are achieved, $485,000 will be the amount of the fund balance at the end of the year.

Recording Property Tax Revenues. Under the modified accrual approach used in fund accounting, some revenues are recorded on the accrual basis, while others are recorded on the cash basis. The general forms of the entries are:

```
Receivables . . . . . . . . . . . . . . . . . . . . . . . . . . . . . . . .    XX
    Revenues . . . . . . . . . . . . . . . . . . . . . . . . . . . . . . . .         XX
```

for revenues recorded on the accrual basis and

Cash	XX	
Revenues.		XX

for revenues recorded on the cash basis. Note that the account Revenues signifies the actual amount of revenues, as distinct from the budgeted amount recorded in the Estimated Revenues account.

In our presentation, and in practice, *control accounts* are generally used for revenues and expenditures. All revenue transactions in the fund are credited to a single account (called *Revenues*). A subsidiary ledger is also maintained, containing accounts for each type of revenue. The total of the detailed accounts in the subsidiary ledger must equal the balance in the Revenues control account. Expenditures, discussed in the next section, are handled in the same manner.

Property tax revenue is a major example of a case where the accrual basis is used, because the amount of revenue can be estimated with reasonable accuracy and the probability of collection is very high. The amount of the tax levy, less an appropriate allowance for uncollectibles, should be recorded as revenue in the following manner:

Taxes Receivable—Current	XX	
Allowance for Uncollectible Taxes—Current.		XX
Revenues		XX

The amount credited to Revenues is the *net amount* which the local government expects to collect. The net amount is recorded because it reflects the amount of spendable resources expected to be available. Property tax collections, which are a major source of revenue for most local governments, may not occur until after a few months of the fiscal year have elapsed. To provide operating cash for the period from the beginning of the fiscal year until collection, local governments often issue **tax anticipation notes.** These are short-term borrowings that are repaid from tax collections.

After a period of time has passed, the uncollected taxes will change from current to delinquent status. This balance should be reclassified to a Taxes Receivable—Delinquent account with a corresponding allowance for uncollectibles. The reclassification entries would be:

Taxes Receivable—Delinquent	XX	
Taxes Receivable—Current.		XX
Allowance for Uncollectible Taxes—Current.	XX	
Allowance for Uncollectible Taxes—Delinquent		XX

It is common to **fully reserve** delinquent taxes, which means that the amount of the allowance for uncollectibles should equal the amount of delinquent taxes receivable. To accomplish this, it may be necessary to adjust the amount of revenues originally recorded to bring the original estimate of uncollectible taxes into agreement with the delinquent amount.

To illustrate, assume that a city levies a property tax of $3,000,000, which is expected to be 95 percent collectible. The initial entry is:

```
Taxes Receivable—Current. . . . . . . . . . . . . . . .  3,000,000
    Allowance for Uncollectible Taxes—Current . . . . . . .          150,000
    Revenues. . . . . . . . . . . . . . . . . . . . . . . .        2,850,000
To record tax levy.
```

If $2,800,000 is collected, and the unpaid amounts are officially declared delinquent, the entries are:

```
Cash . . . . . . . . . . . . . . . . . . . . . . . . . .  2,800,000
    Taxes Receivable—Current. . . . . . . . . . . . . .            2,800,000
To record collections of property taxes.

Taxes Receivable—Delinquent . . . . . . . . . . . . . .    200,000
    Taxes Receivable—Current. . . . . . . . . . . . . .              200,000
To reclassify unpaid taxes.

Allowance for Uncollectible Taxes—Current. . . . . . . .   150,000
Revenues . . . . . . . . . . . . . . . . . . . . . . . .    50,000
    Allowance for Uncollectible Taxes—Delinquent . . . . . .         200,000
To reclassify allowance for uncollectible taxes and increase it
to $200,000.
```

Note that the last entry fully reserves the delinquent taxes by adjusting the allowance to be equal to the amount of delinquent taxes. To increase the allowance to $200,000, Revenues (originally recorded as $2,850,000) must be reduced by $50,000. This adjustment has the effect of correcting the original entry to record the tax levy, so that Revenues shows the amounts actually collected and the Allowance for Uncollectible Taxes balance equals the amount of delinquent taxes receivable. Had the collections exceeded the amount originally entered as revenues, resulting in delinquent taxes being less than the allowance for uncollectible taxes, the adjusting entry would increase (credit) revenues and decrease (debit) the allowance.

If delinquent taxes are fully reserved, no revenue from these particular tax levies is anticipated. The criteria for accrual of revenue require that collection occur within a short time and the degree of collectibility be capable of reasonable estimation. These criteria are not met in the case of delinquent taxes. The collection process may take a long time, and its success is highly uncertain. As a result, revenue from delinquent taxes is not accrued. Any collections which do occur are recorded as revenues at time of collection. For example, a $10,000 collection of delinquent taxes would be recorded as:

```
Cash . . . . . . . . . . . . . . . . . . . . . . . . . .  10,000
Allowance for Uncollectible Taxes—Delinquent . . . . . . . . .  10,000
    Taxes Receivable—Delinquent . . . . . . . . . . . . . . .          10,000
    Revenues . . . . . . . . . . . . . . . . . . . . . . . .           10,000
To record collection of delinquent taxes.
```

In effect, revenues from delinquent taxes are recorded on the cash basis.

After additional time passes, delinquent taxes may become tax liens. **Tax liens** are legal claims against the taxed property, which may be satisfied by forcing sale of the property. Reclassification to a Tax Liens Receivable account, with a corresponding allowance for uncollectibles, should be made. Again, it is common to fully reserve tax liens. The entries are similar to those illustrated above for reclassifying taxes receivable from current to delinquent.

Purchase of Goods and Services. As discussed earlier, purchase orders or contracts for goods and services are recorded in fund accounting so that all commitments of resources are reflected in the accounts. Commitments in the form of outstanding purchase orders are known in local government as *encumbrances*. At the time a purchase order is placed, the following entry is made:

```
Encumbrances . . . . . . . . . . . . . . . . . . . . . . . . . . . . . . . . . . .   XX
     Fund Balance—Reserved for Encumbrances . . . . . . . . . . . . . .          XX
```

The debit to Encumbrances represents a commitment of the fund's limited spending authority; it will become an expenditure when the goods or services are delivered. The credit to Fund Balance—Reserved for Encumbrances represents a restriction on the fund balance. It signifies that, because of this commitment, the freedom to spend resources of the fund has been reduced. It is not a liability because the goods and services have not yet been delivered. The encumbrance entry is a temporary one. It is recorded when the purchase order is issued and is reversed when the goods or services are delivered.

When goods or services are received, an expenditure is recorded, following the modified accrual approach. If an encumbrance was previously recorded when these goods or services were ordered, we first reverse that entry:

```
Fund Balance—Reserved for Encumbrances . . . . . . . . . . . . . . .   XX
     Encumbrances. . . . . . . . . . . . . . . . . . . . . . . . . . . . . . . .          XX
```

The reversal signifies that the purchase order is no longer outstanding. The expenditure is then recorded:

```
Expenditures . . . . . . . . . . . . . . . . . . . . . . . . . . . . . . . . . . .   XX
     Vouchers Payable. . . . . . . . . . . . . . . . . . . . . . . . . . . . . . .          XX
```

Recall that *expenditures* merely signifies an outflow of resources. This is different from the concept of *expenses* used in corporate accounting, which signifies a consumption of resources in the process of earning revenue. Expenditures is a control account: individual accounts for particular expenditure items are maintained in a subsidiary ledger. Also, the term *vouchers payable* is commonly used in place of the term *accounts payable* in fund accounting.

For example, assume that a city places an order for office supplies on March 18, with the expected cost of the supplies being $18,500. To formally record this commitment, the following entry is made on March 18:

```
Encumbrances . . . . . . . . . . . . . . . . . . . . . . . . . . .  18,500
    Fund Balance—Reserved for Encumbrances . . . . . . . . . .        18,500
To record purchase order for office supplies.
```

This entry signifies that $18,500 of the office supplies budget has been committed. Suppose that the office supplies budget is $42,000 and that $8,000 has previously been spent. Recording the encumbrance of $18,500 on March 18 tells the management of the city that only $15,500 of the office supplies budget still remains:

```
Original Budget for Office Supplies . . . . . . . . . . . . . . . . . . . . . . . .  $42,000
Expended to Date . . . . . . . . . . . . . . . . . . . . . . . . . . . . . . . . . .    8,000
  Unexpended Balance . . . . . . . . . . . . . . . . . . . . . . . . . . . . . . .  $34,000
Outstanding Purchase Order. . . . . . . . . . . . . . . . . . . . . . . . . . . .    18,500
Uncommitted Balance . . . . . . . . . . . . . . . . . . . . . . . . . . . . . . . .  $15,500
```

Continuing the example, assume that on June 3 the office supplies ordered on March 18 are delivered, accompanied by an invoice for $18,650. Two entries are required: (1) the previously recorded encumbrance must be reversed, and (2) the expenditure must be recorded.

```
Fund Balance—Reserved for Encumbrances . . . . . . . . . . .  18,500
    Encumbrances . . . . . . . . . . . . . . . . . . . . . . . . . . .      18,500
To reverse encumbrance entry; goods delivered.

Expenditures . . . . . . . . . . . . . . . . . . . . . . . . . . . . .  18,650
    Vouchers Payable. . . . . . . . . . . . . . . . . . . . . . . . .        18,650
To record cost of office supplies.
```

It is not necessary that the amount of the encumbrance and the amount of the expenditure be equal. At the time the purchase order was placed, the exact cost of the goods or services may not have been determinable, and so an estimate may have been used. Note that the reversing entry is based on the amount previously encumbered ($18,500), while the expenditure entry is based on the actual cost ($18,650).

Two special problems with respect to accounting for materials and supplies merit further discussion. One is the presence of inventories, discussed below; the other is the existence of outstanding purchase orders at year-end, discussed in the section on closing entries.

Inventories. Two methods of inventory accounting exist for governmental funds: the purchases method, which treats inventory items as expenditures when *purchased,* and the consumption method, which treats inventory items as expenditures when *used*.

Under the **purchases method,** the cost of materials and supplies is charged to Expenditures as they are purchased, without regard to their consumption during the current period. Recall that a major objective of fund accounting is to account for the spending of resources as prescribed by a budget. Once materials and supplies have been purchased, spending authority has been used, and this important fact is recorded by debiting Expenditures. Whether the materials or supplies are currently consumed is of little importance insofar as spending authority is concerned.

Despite having recorded the purchase as an expenditure, it is still desirable to report on the financial statements the amount of materials and supplies in inventory at year-end. To accomplish this without changing the expenditure accounting for the purchase requires the following entry to establish the inventory:

Inventory	XX	
Fund Balance—Reserved for Inventory		XX

The Fund Balance—Reserved for Inventory account signifies that a portion of the fund's assets is no longer available for appropriation and expenditure. The inventory is an asset which can be used but cannot be expended to acquire goods and services. The reserve appears as part of the fund balance section on the balance sheet.

To illustrate, suppose that during the year supplies are purchased at a cost of $210,000. An encumbrance is recorded when the supplies are ordered. Upon delivery, the encumbrance is reversed and the purchase is recorded as:

Expenditures	210,000	
Vouchers Payable		210,000
To record purchase of supplies.		

Assume that, at year-end, supplies costing $33,000 remain in inventory. The year-end entry to establish the inventory is:

Inventory	33,000	
Fund Balance—Reserved for Inventory		33,000
To record inventory at year-end.		

In subsequent years, inventory changes are easily recorded. Suppose that at the end of the following year, the inventory has decreased to $28,000. The year-end adjusting entry to reduce the inventory balance and the corresponding reserve by $5,000 is:

Fund Balance—Reserved for Inventory	5,000	
Inventory		5,000
To adjust inventory to current year-end balance of $28,000.		

Under the **consumption method,** inventory is viewed as a spendable or consumable asset, similar to cash. Consequently, Inventory is debited at time of purchase, and Expenditures is debited only as the inventory is used. Disregarding the encumbrances, the entries under this approach are:

```
Inventory . . . . . . . . . . . . . . . . . . . . . . . . . . . . . . . . . . . XX
    Vouchers Payable. . . . . . . . . . . . . . . . . . . . . . . . . . . .          XX
To record purchase of supplies.

Expenditures . . . . . . . . . . . . . . . . . . . . . . . . . . . . . . . . . XX
    Inventory . . . . . . . . . . . . . . . . . . . . . . . . . . . . . . . .          XX
To record use of supplies.
```

No reserve account is needed. If such a reserve is established, however, it is created by debiting the Fund Balance—Unreserved.

Interfund Transactions. Transactions among funds are common in local government. These transactions are of various types, each with its own accounting treatment. We shall discuss five types of **interfund transactions.**

Loans or **advances** are temporary transfers from one fund to another, with repayment expected. These are recorded as receivables or payables by the funds involved. Special account titles are used: Due from _____ Fund and Due to ___ Fund. Temporary interfund transfers may be used to provide initial financing for a particular activity. For example, suppose a particular project in the special revenue fund is to be supported by a federal grant. To provide for costs incurred prior to the actual receipt of the grant, the local government might advance $8,000 from the general fund to the special revenue fund. This transaction would be recorded in the general fund as:

```
Due from Special Revenue Fund. . . . . . . . . . . . . . . . . . 8,000
    Cash. . . . . . . . . . . . . . . . . . . . . . . . . . . . . . . . . .          8,000
To record advance to special revenue fund.
```

A parallel entry is required on the books of the special revenue fund:

```
Cash . . . . . . . . . . . . . . . . . . . . . . . . . . . . . . . . . . . . 8,000
    Due to General Fund . . . . . . . . . . . . . . . . . . . . . . . .          8,000
To record advance from general fund.
```

Reimbursements occur when Fund A pays an expenditure properly applicable to Fund B, and Fund B subsequently repays Fund A. Assuming Fund A originally recorded the payment as an expenditure, the reimbursement is recorded as an expenditure by Fund B and as a reduction of expenditures by Fund A. For example, suppose that the general fund paid $4,000 for supplies which are properly chargeable to a special revenue fund project and recorded:

```
Expenditures . . . . . . . . . . . . . . . . . . . . . . . . . . . . . . . . 4,000
    Cash. . . . . . . . . . . . . . . . . . . . . . . . . . . . . . . . . . .          4,000
To record purchase of supplies for special revenue fund project.
```

Subsequently, the special revenue fund reimburses the general fund for the supplies. The entry for the special revenue fund is:

```
Expenditures. . . . . . . . . . . . . . . . . . . . . . . . . . . . . . . .   4,000
  Cash. . . . . . . . . . . . . . . . . . . . . . . . . . . . . . . . . .            4,000
To record reimbursement to general fund for supplies.
```

The entry for the general fund is:

```
Cash. . . . . . . . . . . . . . . . . . . . . . . . . . . . . . . . . .   4,000
  Expenditures. . . . . . . . . . . . . . . . . . . . . . . . . . . .            4,000
To record reimbursement from special revenue fund.
```

Note that following the reimbursement the expenditure is recorded in the proper fund, and there is no net effect on the general fund.

Quasi-external transactions are transactions which, if they involved an external party rather than another fund, would be treated as revenues or expenditures. The same accounting treatment applies when the transaction occurs between two funds. For example, if the general fund purchases supplies from an outside vendor, an expenditure is recorded by the general fund. If the supplies are purchased from an internal service fund, the accounting is identical: an expenditure is recorded by the general fund (and revenue is recorded by the internal service fund). Other examples of transactions of this type include:

1. Contributions to a pension trust fund.
2. Payments in lieu of property taxes by an enterprise fund.
3. Payments to an enterprise fund for utility services provided to city buildings.

Residual equity transfers occur when resources of a permanent equity nature are transferred from one fund to another. For example, if a city establishes an internal service fund, the initial equity of the fund might be provided by a transfer of general fund resources. Residual equity transfers are accounted for as direct changes in beginning fund balances.

Operating transfers involve legally authorized transfers of resources from the fund receiving the revenues to the fund which will make the expenditures. Unlike residual equity transfers, operating transfers are spent by the receiving fund in carrying on its activities rather than serving as permanent equity. Operating transfers occur when resources of one fund (usually the general fund) are used to make expenditures in another fund. Some examples are:

1. Debt payments (principal and interest) on long-term debt originally incurred by the general or capital projects funds are commonly made with general fund resources. Money would be transferred from the general fund (operating transfer out) to the debt service fund (operating transfer in).
2. A business activity of the local government such as the water department might be partially subsidized by general fund resources, which would be transferred to the enterprise fund.
3. A construction project might be financed in part by a bond issue and in part by general fund resources transferred to the capital projects fund.

Operating transfers are not considered revenues and expenditures. They are reported as Other Financing Sources (Uses) in the financial statements.

Closing Entries. When closing entries are prepared at the end of the reporting period, both the *budgetary* accounts and the *actual* accounts must be closed. All closing entries are made to the Fund Balance. While a single combined closing entry is possible, use of two closing entries—one for revenues and the other for expenditures—aids in understanding the process.

As noted earlier, the fund balance of a government entity usually consists of an unreserved portion and one or more reserves. Closing entries are made to the unreserved portion. To close revenues, we must close both Estimated Revenues (debit balance) and Revenues (credit balance) to the Unreserved Fund Balance. This may result in either a debit or a credit to Unreserved Fund Balance. A debit results if actual revenues are less than budgeted:

```
Revenues . . . . . . . . . . . . . . . . . . . . . . . . . . . . . . . . . . .  XX
Fund Balance—Unreserved . . . . . . . . . . . . . . . . . . . . . . . .  XX
    Estimated Revenues . . . . . . . . . . . . . . . . . . . . . . . . . . .          XX
```

If actual revenues exceed the budget, Unreserved Fund Balance is credited.

If, at the end of the period, there are no outstanding purchase orders, we close Expenditures (debit balance) and Appropriations (credit balance) to the Unreserved Fund Balance. In the case where actual expenditures are less than the amount budgeted, the entry is:

```
Appropriations . . . . . . . . . . . . . . . . . . . . . . . . . . . . . . . .  XX
    Expenditures . . . . . . . . . . . . . . . . . . . . . . . . . . . . . . .           XX
    Fund Balance—Unreserved . . . . . . . . . . . . . . . . . . . . . . .           XX
```

If actual expenditures exceed the budget, Unreserved Fund Balance is debited.

To illustrate, assume that budgeted revenues were $785,000 and budgeted expenditures were $800,000, and that actual revenues amounted to $787,000, while actual expenditures amounted to $791,000. The closing entries would be:

```
Revenues . . . . . . . . . . . . . . . . . . . . . . . . . . . . . .  787,000
    Estimated Revenues . . . . . . . . . . . . . . . . . . . . . . .          785,000
    Fund Balance—Unreserved . . . . . . . . . . . . . . . . . .            2,000
To close revenues and estimated revenues to fund balance.

Appropriations . . . . . . . . . . . . . . . . . . . . . . . . . . .  800,000
    Expenditures . . . . . . . . . . . . . . . . . . . . . . . . . . .          791,000
    Fund Balance—Unreserved . . . . . . . . . . . . . . . . . .            9,000
To close expenditures and appropriations to fund balance.
```

As a result of these entries, the fund balance is increased by $11,000, because actual revenues exceeded the budget by $2,000, and actual expenditures were $9,000 less than planned. Recall that the budget entry at the beginning of the year was:

```
Estimated Revenues . . . . . . . . . . . . . . . . . . . . . . .  785,000
Fund Balance—Unreserved . . . . . . . . . . . . . . . . . . .   15,000
    Appropriations . . . . . . . . . . . . . . . . . . . . . . . . . .          800,000
To record budget for the year and planned decrease in fund balance.
```

While the fund balance was expected to decrease by $15,000, it actually decreased by only $4,000:

	Budget	Actual	Variance
Revenues	$ 785,000	$ 787,000	$ (2,000)
Expenditures	(800,000)	(791,000)	(9,000)
Change in Fund Balance	$ (15,000)	$ (4,000)	$(11,000)

Note that the $15,000 debit to the fund balance in the budget entry and the $11,000 total credits to the fund balance in the closing entries together account for the $4,000 decrease during the year.

Outstanding Encumbrances at Year-End. At the end of the fiscal year, it is likely that there will be some purchase orders outstanding for goods or services which have been ordered but have not yet been received. Assume that purchase orders amounting to $27,000 were issued late in 19X1 and were still outstanding at year-end. At time of issue, the entry was:

Encumbrances	27,000	
Fund Balance—Reserved for Encumbrances		27,000
To record purchase orders.		

The treatment of outstanding encumbrances at year-end and the treatment of the related expenditure in the subsequent year depend on whether the accounting system follows a legal or GAAP approach.

Under a **legal approach,** the budget is viewed in legal terms, namely as the authority to *commit* (encumber) the governmental unit's resources during a period of time. Thus an encumbrance—a commitment to spend—constitutes a charge against the annual budget, irrespective of when the expenditure occurs. In terms of their effect on spending authority, outstanding encumbrances are equivalent to expenditures; that is, they are closed to the fund balance and are included in the **budgetary comparison** statements. In the succeeding year, the expenditures related to year-end encumbrances are recorded separately and are charged against the reserve portion of fund balance rather than against the subsequent year's budget.

Using the legal approach, the $27,000 of encumbrances outstanding at the end of 19X1 would be reflected in the closing entry as follows:

Appropriations	XX	
Fund Balance—Unreserved		XX
Expenditures		XX
Encumbrances		27,000

Closing the encumbrances at the end of 19X1 signifies that they are charged against the 19X1 budget. Note that the reserve account (Fund Balance—Reserved for Encumbrances) remains and will appear on the general fund balance sheet. This account carries over into 19X2 to signify that there are some transactions relating to the 19X1 budget yet to be completed. The goods and services will be

received in 19X2 but will not be charged against the 19X2 budget. Various accounting procedures exist to properly record this situation; we shall illustrate one.
At the beginning of 19X2, the reserve account should be reclassified to signify
that it involves purchase orders of the prior year:

```
Fund Balance—Reserved for Encumbrances . . . . . . . . . . . 27,000
    Fund Balance—Reserved for Encumbrances (Prior Year). . . .          27,000
To reclassify purchase orders outstanding at beginning of 19X2.
```

When the goods and services ordered in 19X1 are received in 19X2 at a cost of
$26,600, a separate expenditures account is used:

```
Expenditures—Prior Year Encumbrances . . . . . . . . . . . . . 26,600
    Vouchers Payable. . . . . . . . . . . . . . . . . . . . . . . .          26,600
To record invoices for goods and services ordered in 19X1.
```

At the end of 19X2, an additional closing entry is required, to close the prior year
encumbrances and related expenditures to the fund balance:

```
Fund Balance—Reserved for Encumbrances (Prior Year). . . . . 27,000
    Expenditures—Prior Year Encumbrances . . . . . . . . . . . .          26,600
    Fund Balance—Unreserved. . . . . . . . . . . . . . . . . . .             400
To close encumbrances carried over from 19X1 and related
expenditures.
```

The $400 credit to fund balance is in effect a correction of the 19X1 closing entry.
That entry closed $27,000 of encumbrances against the fund balance. However,
the actual charge for these goods and services was only $26,600. The entry to
close 19X2 revenues, expenditures, and encumbrances would be unaffected by the
above transactions.

Alternatively, under a **GAAP approach,** the budget is viewed in terms of
modified accrual accounting—the authority to spend (use) the governmental unit's
resources during a period of time. Budgetary comparison statements compare expenditures recorded during the year (which do *not* include outstanding encumbrances) with a budget figure that indicates authority to spend during the year.
Thus a GAAP budget—one that measures authority to *spend* during the current
year—consists of the current year's legal budget *plus* prior year appropriations
carried over to the current year in the form of outstanding encumbrances.

Using the GAAP approach, the $27,000 of encumbrances outstanding at the
end of 19X1 is reflected in the closing entry as follows:

```
Appropriations. . . . . . . . . . . . . . . . . . . . . . . . . . . . XX
    Fund Balance—Unreserved. . . . . . . . . . . . . . . . . . .          XX
    Expenditures . . . . . . . . . . . . . . . . . . . . . . . . . .          XX
    Encumbrances . . . . . . . . . . . . . . . . . . . . . . . . .          27,000
```

Again, the reserve account remains. However, the $27,000 of encumbrances does
not appear on the 19X1 statement of revenues, expenditures, and changes in fund
balance or on the 19X1 budgetary comparison statements.

In 19X2, the $27,000 encumbrance is restored to the accounts, in effect
reversing part of the 19X1 closing entry:

Encumbrances 27,000
   Fund Balance—Unreserved.   27,000
To restore encumbrances carried over from 19X1.

The subsequent expenditure is recorded in the same manner as all other 19X2 expenditures. At year-end, total expenditures for 19X2 include the $26,600 related to the carryover encumbrance. In the budgetary comparison statements for 19X2, total expenditures for 19X2 are then compared to a budget figure consisting of the 19X2 legal budget plus the carryover appropriation of $27,000.

The GAAP approach would automatically be used if encumbered appropriations lapse at year-end. In such a case, outstanding encumbrances must be reappropriated in the subsequent year's budget, and hence would be part of that year's expenditures. If encumbered appropriations do not lapse, either approach may be used.

The two methods may be summarized as follows. Assume for convenience that an encumbrance is outstanding at the end of 19X1.

1. Under the *legal approach,* the encumbered amount is treated as if it were an expenditure of 19X1:
   a. It is closed to the fund balance in 19X1.
   b. It is included in comparing budget to actual for 19X1.
   c. When the actual expenditure occurs in 19X2, it is recorded separately from 19X2 expenditures and is closed against the carried-over reserve for encumbrances.
   d. It does not affect the comparison of budget to actual for 19X2.

2. Under the *GAAP approach* the encumbered amount is carried into 19X2:
   a. It is temporarily closed to the fund balance at the end of 19X1, but this entry is reversed in 19X2.
   b. It is *not* included in comparing budget to actual for 19X1.
   c. When the actual expenditure occurs in 19X2, it is included with all other 19X2 expenditures.
   d. In comparing budget to actual for 19X2, the encumbered amount from 19X1 is added to the 19X2 budget.

Wherever possible, the GAAP approach should be used for financial statement presentation. The presentation of budgeted and actual expenditures under this approach is consistent with accrual accounting, which focuses on the time at which an expenditure is incurred. However, if state law specifies the legal approach (for example, in reporting by a municipality to the state government), this approach would be used, and audited financial statements would disclose the method of accounting being used.

Financial Statements for the General Fund

Financial statements for the general fund typically include a balance sheet; a statement of revenues, expenditures, and changes in fund balance; and a budgetary comparison statement.

Balance Sheet. The *balance sheet* of the general fund has the following format:

Assets	Liabilities
Cash	Vouchers payable
Short-term investments	Due to other funds
Taxes receivable, less allowance for uncollectible taxes	**Fund Balance**
Other receivables	Reserved for encumbrances
Due from other funds	Reserved for inventories
Inventories	Unreserved
Total Assets	Total Liabilities and Fund Balance

The balance sheet is unclassified. Fixed assets and long-term debt are excluded from the balance sheet and are recorded in separate account groups. Thus the assets of the general fund are limited to those which are able to be spent or otherwise consumed during the next fiscal period in carrying on the fund's activities. Similarly, the liabilities of the general fund are limited to claims that will be paid during the next fiscal year.

Exhibit 16.2 presents a simple balance sheet for the general fund of a city. Note that only current assets are shown; these are the resources available for use in carrying on the particular activities of this fund. Note also that the total fund

---

Exhibit 16.2   **Illustration of General Fund Balance Sheet**

CITY OF NORWOOD
BALANCE SHEET—GENERAL FUND
JUNE 30, 19X8

ASSETS

Cash	$ 51,000
Short-Term Investments, at Cost	1,850,000
Accounts Receivable (Net of $300 Allowance for Uncollectible Accounts)	1,200
Due from Other Governments	1,040,800
Total Assets	$2,943,000

LIABILITIES AND FUND BALANCE

Liabilities:	
Vouchers Payable	$ 239,000
Due to Other Funds	170,000
Total Liabilities	$ 409,000
Fund Balance:	
Reserved for Encumbrances	$2,265,000
Unreserved	269,000
Total Fund Balance	$2,534,000
Total Liabilities and Fund Balance	$2,943,000

balance includes the reserve for encumbrances, which signifies that purchase orders were outstanding at year-end.

Statement of Revenues, Expenditures, and Changes in Fund Balance. The *statement of revenues, expenditures, and changes in fund balance* for the general fund summarizes all transactions affecting the *total fund balance* during the reporting period. The format of the statement is as follows:

> Revenues (Classified)
> − Expenditures (Classified)
> = Excess of Revenues over (under) Expenditures
> +/− Other Financing Sources (Uses) (such as proceeds of bond issues and transfers to or from other funds)
> = Excess of Revenues and Other Sources over (under) Expenditures and Other Uses
> + Fund Balance—Beginning of Period
> = Fund Balance—End of Period

Exhibit 16.3 **Illustration of General Fund Statement of Revenues, Expenditures, and Changes in Fund Balance**

CITY OF NORWOOD
STATEMENT OF REVENUES, EXPENDITURES, AND CHANGES
IN FUND BALANCE—GENERAL FUND
FOR THE FISCAL YEAR ENDED JUNE 30, 19X8

REVENUES

Taxes	$6,453,000
Licenses and Permits	800,000
Charges for Services	1,500,000
Miscellaneous Revenues	879,000
Total Revenues	$9,632,000

EXPENDITURES

General Government	$1,508,000
Public Safety	3,600,000
Health and Welfare	730,000
Education	3,080,000
Total Expenditures	$8,918,000
Excess of Revenues over (under) Expenditures	$ 714,000

OTHER FINANCING SOURCES (USES)

Operating Transfers In	$ 670,000
Operating Transfers Out	(850,000)
Total Other Financing Sources (Uses)	$ (180,000)
Excess of Revenues and Other Sources over Expenditures and Other Uses	$ 534,000
Fund Balance—July 1, 19X7	2,000,000
Fund Balance—June 30, 19X8	$2,534,000

The fund balance referred to in this statement is the *total* fund balance, including the reserved portions. Exhibit 16.3 illustrates the statement of revenues, expenditures, and changes in fund balance.

Revenues are classified by *source*. For the general fund, major sources of revenue include taxes, intergovernmental revenues, licenses and permits, charges for services, and fines. Various types of expenditure classification also exist. For financial statement purposes, expenditures are often classified by character and function. Classification by *character* hinges on the time period(s) which the expenditures benefit. Common character classifications are *current expenditures, capital outlays,* and *debt service.* Classification by *function* identifies groups of related activities designed to accomplish a particular service or regulatory responsibility. Examples of functions are general government, public safety, education, highways, sanitation, health, and recreation. Other financing sources and uses include proceeds of long-term debt issues and operating transfers to or from the general fund. As noted earlier, residual equity transfers are reported as a change to the beginning fund balance.

Exhibit 16.4   **Illustration of General Fund Budgetary Comparison Statement**

CITY OF NORWOOD
STATEMENT OF REVENUES, EXPENDITURES, AND CHANGES
IN FUND BALANCE—BUDGET AND ACTUAL—GENERAL FUND
FOR THE FISCAL YEAR ENDED JUNE 30, 19X8

	Budget	Actual	Variance—Favorable (Unfavorable)
REVENUES			
Taxes	$6,461,000	$6,453,000	$ (8,000)
Licenses and Permits	975,000	800,000	(175,000)
Charges for Services	1,604,000	1,500,000	(104,000)
Miscellaneous Revenues	866,000	879,000	13,000
Total Revenues	$9,906,000	$9,632,000	$(274,000)
EXPENDITURES			
General Government	$1,764,000	$1,508,000	$ 256,000
Public Safety	3,334,000	3,600,000	(266,000)
Health and Welfare	839,000	730,000	109,000
Education	2,886,000	3,080,000	(194,000)
Total Expenditures	$8,823,000	$8,918,000	$ (95,000)
Excess of Revenues over (under) Expenditures	$1,083,000	$ 714,000	$(369,000)
OTHER FINANCING SOURCES (USES)			
Operating Transfers In	$ 665,000	$ 670,000	$ 5,000
Operating Transfers Out	(850,000)	(850,000)	—
Total Other Financing Sources (Uses)	$ (185,000)	$ (180,000)	$ 5,000
Excess of Revenues and Other Sources over Expenditures and Other Uses	$ 898,000	$ 534,000	$(364,000)
Fund Balance—July 1, 19X7	2,000,000	2,000,000	—
Fund Balance—June 30, 19X8	$2,898,000	$2,534,000	$(364,000)

Budgetary Comparison Statements. In addition to the statement of revenues, expenditures, and changes in fund balance discussed above, a parallel statement showing the comparison between budget and actual data is presented. The format of the budgetary comparison statement (formally called the **statement of revenues, expenditures, and changes in fund balance—budget and actual**) is identical to the format of the statement of revenues, expenditures, and changes in fund balance, except that three columns of numbers are presented:

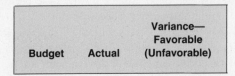

Budget	Actual	Variance—Favorable (Unfavorable)

An illustration of a budgetary comparison statement appears in Exhibit 16.4 on page 839. Note that the convention here differs from cost accounting. In cost accounting, favorable variances are commonly enclosed in parentheses, while in governmental accounting, parentheses are used for unfavorable variances.

Comprehensive Illustration of General Fund Accounting and Reporting

Ranford County maintains its general fund on a calendar-year basis. On January 1, 19X2, the accounts of the general fund had the following balances:

RANFORD COUNTY
TRIAL BALANCE
JANUARY 1, 19X2

Accounts	Debit	Credit
Cash	$ 80,000	
Taxes Receivable—Delinquent	15,000	
Due from Special Revenue Fund	10,000	
Supplies Inventory	5,000	
Vouchers Payable		$ 5,000
Fund Balance—Unreserved		83,000
Fund Balance—Reserved for Supplies Inventory		5,000
Fund Balance—Reserved for Encumbrances		2,000
Allowance for Uncollectible Taxes—Delinquent		15,000
	$110,000	$110,000

The 19X2 general fund budget included revenues from the following sources:

Property Taxes (Expected to Be 95% Collectible)	$200,000
State Aid	30,000
Fees and Licenses	8,000
Charges for Services	12,000
Miscellaneous	5,000

Expenditures for 19X2 were estimated to be:

General Services. $180,000
Supplies   18,000
Maintenance   14,000
Miscellaneous   6,000

In addition, the county decided to establish an internal service fund to purchase supplies used by the general fund and the special revenue fund. A permanent transfer of $20,000 from the general fund was authorized to enable the internal service fund to purchase an inventory base. For the first year of operation the general fund plans to subsidize $8,000 of the operating costs of the internal service fund.

Transactions during the Year. The events and transactions occurring during the year were recorded as follows:

1. The budget was recorded on January 2 as:

Estimated Revenues.	255,000	
Appropriations		246,000
Fund Balance—Unreserved		9,000

To record 19X2 budget as follows:
Revenues from:

Property taxes	$200,000
State aid	30,000
Fees and licenses	8,000
Charges for services	12,000
Miscellaneous revenues	5,000
Total revenues.	$255,000

Appropriations for:

General services	$180,000
Supplies	18,000
Maintenance	14,000
Capital transfer to internal service fund	20,000
Operating transfer to internal service fund . . .	8,000
Miscellaneous	6,000
Total appropriations	$246,000

2. Taxes were levied:

Taxes Receivable—Current.	200,000	
Allowance for Uncollectible Taxes—Current		10,000
Revenues.		190,000

To record property tax levy, estimated to be 95% collectible.

3. The county received $30,000 in state aid:

Cash	30,000	
Revenues.		30,000

To record aid received from state government.

4. Delinquent taxes of $4,000 were received; the remainder of 19X1 taxes were reclassified as tax liens:

Cash	4,000	
Allowance for Uncollectible Taxes—Delinquent	4,000	
Taxes Receivable—Delinquent		4,000
Revenues		4,000

To record collection of delinquent taxes.

Tax Liens Receivable	11,000	
Allowance for Uncollectible Taxes—Delinquent	11,000	
Allowance for Uncollectible Tax Liens		11,000
Taxes Receivable—Delinquent		11,000

To reclassify uncollected delinquent taxes as tax liens and to fully reserve tax liens.

5. The internal service fund was established, and the $28,000 authorized was transferred from the general fund:

Fund Balance—Unreserved	20,000	
Cash		20,000

To record permanent capital transfer to establish the internal service fund.

Operating Transfers Out	8,000	
Cash		8,000

To record authorized subsidy of internal service fund operating costs.

6. Ranford County follows the GAAP approach for recording encumbrances outstanding at year-end. For the miscellaneous amounts encumbered for $2,000 but not received in 19X1, the bill received in 19X2 was $1,800. The bill was paid in cash.

Encumbrances	2,000	
Fund Balance—Unreserved		2,000

To restore encumbrances carried over from 19X1.

Fund Balance—Reserved for Encumbrances	2,000	
Encumbrances		2,000

To reverse encumbrances.

Expenditures	1,800	
Cash		1,800

To record expenditures.

7. Revenues were received as follows: $8,500 from fees and licenses, $11,800 from charges for services, and $5,300 from miscellaneous sources:

Cash	25,600	
Revenues		25,600

To record revenues.

8. Supplies of $18,000 were ordered from the internal service fund:

```
Encumbrances . . . . . . . . . . . . . . . . . . . . . . . . . .    18,000
    Fund Balance—Reserved for Encumbrances . . . . . . . .              18,000
To record supplies ordered.
```

9. Expenditures of cash were $6,200 for miscellaneous purchases and $40,000 for general services. For maintenance $14,000 was encumbered; for general services, $135,000.

```
Expenditures . . . . . . . . . . . . . . . . . . . . . . . . . .    46,200
    Cash . . . . . . . . . . . . . . . . . . . . . . . . . . . . .          46,200
To record cash expenditures.

Encumbrances . . . . . . . . . . . . . . . . . . . . . . . . .    149,000
    Fund Balance—Reserved for Encumbrances . . . . . . . .              149,000
To encumber resources for goods and services ordered.
```

10. Supplies were received and the internal service fund was paid cash of $18,000. Ranford County follows the *purchases method* of accounting for inventory.

```
Fund Balance—Reserved for Encumbrances . . . . . . . . . .    18,000
    Encumbrances . . . . . . . . . . . . . . . . . . . . . . . .              18,000
To reverse encumbrances.

Expenditures . . . . . . . . . . . . . . . . . . . . . . . . . .    18,000
    Cash . . . . . . . . . . . . . . . . . . . . . . . . . . . . .          18,000
To record payment for supplies.
```

11. Current taxes of $183,000 were collected:

```
Cash . . . . . . . . . . . . . . . . . . . . . . . . . . . . . .    183,000
    Taxes Receivable—Current. . . . . . . . . . . . . . . . .              183,000
To record collection of current taxes.
```

12. Bills for goods and services ordered and received were as follows: maintenance, $14,000 and general services, $137,000. The total vouchers paid in 19X2 amounted to $152,000.

```
Fund Balance—Reserved for Encumbrances . . . . . . . . . .    149,000
    Encumbrances . . . . . . . . . . . . . . . . . . . . . . . .              149,000
To reverse encumbrances.

Expenditures . . . . . . . . . . . . . . . . . . . . . . . . . .    151,000
    Vouchers Payable . . . . . . . . . . . . . . . . . . . . . .              151,000
To record expenditures.

Vouchers Payable. . . . . . . . . . . . . . . . . . . . . . . .    152,000
    Cash . . . . . . . . . . . . . . . . . . . . . . . . . . . . .          152,000
To record payment of vouchers outstanding.
```

13. Goods to be used in providing general services were ordered late in December but were not received in 19X2. The anticipated price of the goods was $1,300.

Encumbrances	1,300	
Fund Balance—Reserved for Encumbrances		1,300
To encumber resources for goods ordered.		

14. Cash of $10,000 was received from the special revenue fund as repayment of a loan made in 19X1:

Cash	10,000	
Due from Special Revenue Fund		10,000
To record repayment of loan.		

15. At year-end, a count of supplies showed inventory costing $7,000 was on hand:

Supplies Inventory	2,000	
Fund Balance—Reserved for Supplies Inventory		2,000
To adjust supplies inventory and reserve account from $5,000 beginning balance to $7,000 ending balance.		

16. Taxes uncollected at year-end were classified delinquent and fully reserved:

Revenues	7,000	
Taxes Receivable—Delinquent	17,000	
Allowance for Uncollectible Taxes—Current	10,000	
Taxes Receivable—Current		17,000
Allowance for Uncollectible Taxes—Delinquent		17,000
To reclassify uncollected taxes as delinquent and fully reserved and to reduce revenues by the amount uncollected in excess of the estimated uncollectibles.		

The preclosing trial balance for Ranford County at December 31, 19X2, appears as follows:

RANFORD COUNTY
PRECLOSING TRIAL BALANCE
DECEMBER 31, 19X2

Account	Debit	Credit
Cash	$ 86,600	
Taxes Receivable—Delinquent	17,000	
Tax Liens Receivable	11,000	
Supplies Inventory	7,000	
Encumbrances	1,300	
Expenditures	217,000	
Operating Transfers Out	8,000	
Estimated Revenues	255,000	

Vouchers Payable.		$ 4,000
Revenues.		242,600
Appropriations.		246,000
Allowance for Uncollectible Taxes—Delinquent		17,000
Allowance for Uncollectible Tax Liens.		11,000
Fund Balance—Reserved for Supplies Inventory		7,000
Fund Balance—Reserved for Encumbrances		1,300
Fund Balance—Unreserved.		74,000
	$602,900	$602,900

The county's subsidiary records show the detail of the revenues and expenditure accounts as follows:

REVENUES

Property Taxes.	$187,000
State Aid.	30,000
Fees and Licenses.	8,500
Charges for Services.	11,800
Miscellaneous	5,300
Total Revenues	$242,600

EXPENDITURES

General Services.	$177,000
Maintenance.	14,000
Supplies	18,000
Miscellaneous	8,000
Total Expenditures.	$217,000

Closing entries at December 31, 19X2, are as follows:

Revenues.	242,600	
Fund Balance—Unreserved.	12,400	
Estimated Revenues		255,000
To close revenues.		

Appropriations.	246,000	
Operating Transfers Out		8,000
Expenditures		217,000
Encumbrances		1,300
Fund Balance—Unreserved		19,700
To close expenditures, encumbrances, and operating transfers.		

The financial statements for the general fund of Ranford County can now be prepared. The balance sheet appears as Exhibit 16.5 on page 846.

Note that the delinquent taxes receivable and tax liens receivable have both been fully reserved, signifying that no revenues are anticipated from these sources.

The statement of revenues, expenditures, and changes in the general fund balance is presented in Exhibit 16.6 on page 847. The *total* fund balance (unreserved fund balance plus the reserves) appears on this statement. Since the purchases method was used for the supplies inventory, all purchases of supplies dur-

Exhibit 16.5	Balance Sheet of Ranford County

RANFORD COUNTY
BALANCE SHEET—GENERAL FUND
DECEMBER 31, 19X2

ASSETS

Cash	$86,600
Taxes Receivable—Delinquent (net of $17,000 allowance for uncollectible taxes) . .	—
Tax Liens Receivable (net of $11,000 allowance for uncollectible tax liens)	—
Supplies Inventory.	7,000
Total Assets.	$93,600

LIABILITIES AND FUND BALANCE

Liabilities:	
Vouchers Payable.	$ 4,000
Total Liabilities	$ 4,000
Fund Balance:	
Reserved for Supplies Inventory	$ 7,000
Reserved for Encumbrances	1,300
Unreserved	81,300
Total Fund Balance.	$89,600
Total Liabilities and Fund Balance.	$93,600

ing the year are included in expenditures. The effect of the inventory increase, which increases the total fund balance, is shown under the caption "Other Financing Sources (Uses)."

The budgetary comparison statement for Ranford County appears in Exhibit 16.7 on page 848.

The Special Revenue Fund

The special revenue fund is also used to account for operating activities of a local government. It is distinguished from the general fund in that the revenues (usually from state or federal grants) are directed to very specific activities or projects. For example, a local government might receive grants to provide a summer youth employment program, a drug abuse control program, and downtown redevelopment. In addition to special project grants, other restricted-use money such as federal revenue sharing, block grants, and urban renewal programs is handled in the special revenue fund. It is not unusual for hundreds of such programs to exist in a single local government. Thus the special revenue fund is likely to consist of several separate funds, many of which will further require detailed subsidiary records by project.

The special revenue fund involves many of the same types of activities as the general fund. The difference between the two lies in their sources of revenue. Revenue for the general fund comes from general sources such as property taxes,

Exhibit 16.6	**Statement of Revenues, Expenditures, and Changes in Fund Balance of Ranford County**

RANFORD COUNTY
STATEMENT OF REVENUES, EXPENDITURES, AND
CHANGES IN FUND BALANCE—GENERAL FUND
FOR THE FISCAL YEAR ENDED DECEMBER 31, 19X2

REVENUES:

Property Taxes	$187,000
State Aid	30,000
Fees and Licenses	8,500
Charges for Services	11,800
Miscellaneous	5,300
Total Revenues	$242,600

EXPENDITURES:

General Services	$177,000
Maintenance	14,000
Supplies	18,000
Miscellaneous	8,000
Total Expenditures	$217,000
Excess of Revenues over Expenditures	$ 25,600

OTHER FINANCING SOURCES (USES):

Increase in Supplies Inventory	$ 2,000
Operating Transfers Out	(8,000)
Total Other Financing Sources (Uses)	$ (6,000)
Excess of Revenues and Other Sources over Expenditures and Other Uses	$ 19,600
Fund Balance—Jan. 1	$ 90,000[a]
Less: Residual Equity Transfer	20,000
Adjusted Fund Balance—Jan. 1	$ 70,000
Fund Balance—Dec. 31	$ 89,600

[a]Unreserved Fund Balance	$83,000
Reserved for Supplies Inventory	5,000
Reserved for Encumbrances	2,000
	$90,000

fees, and unrestricted state aid. The local government is free to allocate this revenue among its various operating activities as it wishes. In the special revenue fund, on the other hand, each item of revenue is restricted to use for specified activities.

Because the special revenue fund involves the same type of activities as the general fund, the same accounting procedures are followed. Moreover, the financial statements of the special revenue fund parallel those of the general fund; that is, a balance sheet; statement of revenues, expenditures, and changes in fund balance; and budgetary comparison statement are presented. If several special revenue funds exist, *combining* balance sheets and statements of revenues, expendi-

Exhibit 16.7	Budgetary Comparison Statement for Ranford County

RANFORD COUNTY
STATEMENT OF REVENUES, EXPENDITURES, AND CHANGES
IN FUND BALANCE—BUDGET AND ACTUAL—GENERAL FUND
FOR THE FISCAL YEAR ENDED DECEMBER 31, 19X2

	Budget	Actual	Variance—Favorable (Unfavorable)
REVENUES:			
Property Taxes	$200,000	$187,000	$(13,000)
State Aid	30,000	30,000	—
Fees and Licenses	8,000	8,500	500
Charges for Services	12,000	11,800	(200)
Miscellaneous	5,000	5,300	300
Total Revenues	$255,000	$242,600	$(12,400)
EXPENDITURES:			
General Services	$180,000	$177,000	$ 3,000
Maintenance	14,000	14,000	—
Supplies	18,000	18,000	—
Miscellaneous	6,000	8,000	(2,000)
Total Expenditures	$218,000	$217,000	$ 1,000
Excess of Revenues over (under) Expenditures	$ 37,000	$ 25,600	$(11,400)
OTHER FINANCING SOURCES (USES):			
Increase in Supplies Inventory	$ —	$ 2,000	$ 2,000
Operating Transfers Out	(8,000)	(8,000)	—
Total Other Financing Sources (Uses)	$ (8,000)	$ (6,000)	$ 2,000
Excess of Revenues and Other Sources over Expenditures and Other Uses	$ 29,000	$ 19,600	$ (9,400)
Fund Balance—Jan. 1	$ 90,000	$ 90,000	—
Less: Residual Equity Transfer	20,000	20,000	
Adjusted Fund Balance—Jan. 1	$ 70,000	$ 70,000	—)
Fund Balance—Dec. 31	$ 99,000	$ 89,600	$ (9,400)

tures, and changes in fund balances are presented. These combining statements show the data for each fund as well as the total for all special revenue funds. The format of combining statements is illustrated in Exhibits 16.8 and 16.9 (on page 850). Combining statements are not typically presented in the case of budgetary comparison statements because the format is unwieldy. If more detail beyond the combined budgetary comparison statement is desired, statements may be presented for each individual special revenue fund.

Accounting for Fixed Assets

The various funds which comprise a local government account for fixed assets in different ways. Proprietary funds (enterprise and internal service funds) and fidu-

Exhibit 16.8   **Illustration of Combining Balance Sheet**

NAME OF GOVERNMENTAL UNIT
COMBINING BALANCE SHEET—
ALL SPECIAL REVENUE FUNDS
DECEMBER 31, 19X2

ASSETS	Parks	State Gasoline Tax	Motor Vehicle License	Parking Meter	Juvenile Rehabilitation	Totals Dec. 31, 19X2	Dec. 31, 19X1
Cash	$39,525	$22,460	$ 5,420	$16,260	$17,720	$101,385	$ 91,459
Investments, at Cost.	16,200	—	—	15,000	6,000	37,200	25,000
Receivables:							
Taxes Receivable—							
Delinquent (Net of							
Allowance for							
Uncollectibles of $500).	2,500	—	—	—	—	2,500	—
Accounts Receivable (Net of							
Allowance for							
Uncollectibles of $800).	3,300	—	—	—	—	3,300	2,700
Accrued Interest	25	—	—	—	—	25	—
Due from State Government	—	47,250	28,010	—	—	75,260	62,400
Inventory of Supplies, at Cost	1,100	990	702	1,066	1,332	5,190	5,190
Total Assets	$62,650	$70,700	$34,132	$32,326	$25,052	$224,860	$186,749
LIABILITIES AND FUND BALANCES							
Liabilities:							
Vouchers Payable.	$10,000	$11,220	$ 4,260	$ 3,220	$ 5,150	$ 33,850	$ 23,414
Contracts Payable.	12,500	4,000	—	1,800	—	18,300	12,300
Judgments Payable .	2,000	—	—	—	—	2,000	—
Due to General Fund	2,000	—	—	—	—	2,000	—
Total Liabilities	$26,500	$15,220	$ 4,260	$ 5,020	$ 5,150	$ 56,150	$ 35,714
Fund Balances:							
Reserved for							
Encumbrances	$14,000	$16,500	$10,000	$ 500	$ 5,500	$ 46,500	$ 12,550
Reserved for Inventory of							
Supplies	1,100	990	702	1,066	1,332	5,190	5,190
Unreserved.	21,050	37,990	19,170	25,740	13,070	117,020	133,295
Total Fund Balances.	$36,150	$55,480	$29,872	$27,306	$19,902	$168,710	$151,035
Total Liabilities and Fund							
Balances.	$62,650	$70,700	$34,132	$32,326	$25,052	$224,860	$186,749

Source: Reproduced with permission from National Council on Governmental Accounting, *Statement 1*, "Governmental Accounting and Financial Reporting Principles" (Chicago: Municipal Finance Officers Association of the United States and Canada, 1979), 41. © Copyright 1979 by Municipal Finance Officers Association of the United States and Canada.

ciary funds (trust and agency funds) include fixed assets on their balance sheets. The five governmental funds, on the other hand, exclude fixed assets from their balance sheets. The emphasis in fund accounting is on reporting of revenues and expenditures. The balance sheet of an entity using fund accounting focuses on financial assets—those which can be expended in a subsequent period—and does not list fixed assets, which cannot be expended. However, some accounting and reporting of fixed assets is desirable. To maintain accountability for these assets,

Exhibit 16.9 Illustration of Combining Statement of Revenues, Expenditures, and Changes in Fund Balance

NAME OF GOVERNMENTAL UNIT
COMBINING STATEMENT OF REVENUES, EXPENDITURES, AND CHANGES
IN FUND BALANCES—ALL SPECIAL REVENUE FUNDS
FOR THE FISCAL YEAR ENDED DECEMBER 31, 19X2

	Parks	State Gasoline Tax	Motor Vehicle License	Parking Meter	Juvenile Rehabilitation	Totals Year Ended December 31, 19X2	December 31, 19X1
REVENUES:							
Taxes.	$189,300	$ —	$ —	$ —	$ —	$ 189,300	$ 168,400
Intergovernmental Revenues	—	422,500	201,000	79,100	207,600	831,100	749,990
Charges for Services	—	—	—	—	—	79,100	71,420
Miscellaneous Revenues	70,700	—	—	600	325	71,625	63,614
Total Revenues	$260,000	$422,500	$201,000	$79,700	$207,925	$1,171,125	$1,053,424
EXPENDITURES:							
Public Safety	$ —	$ —	$199,400	$80,900	$199,700	$ 480,000	$ 414,040
Highways and Streets	—	417,000	—	—	—	417,000	346,414
Culture and Recreation	256,450	—	—	—	—	256,450	238,419
Total Expenditures	$256,450	$417,000	$199,400	$80,900	$199,700	$1,153,450	$ 998,873
Excess of Revenues over (under) Expenditures	$ 3,550	$ 5,500	$ 1,600	$ (1,200)	$ 8,225	$ 17,675	$ 54,551
Fund Balances—Jan. 1.	32,600	49,980	28,272	28,506	11,677	151,035	96,484
Fund Balances—Dec. 31	$ 36,150	$ 55,480	$ 29,872	$27,306	$ 19,902	$ 168,710	$ 151,035

Source: Reproduced with permission from National Council on Governmental Accounting, *Statement 1*, "Governmental Accounting and Financial Reporting Principles" (Chicago: Municipal Finance Officers Association of the United States and Canada, 1979), 42. © Copyright 1979 by Municipal Finance Officers Association of the United States and Canada.

records should be kept, showing the nature and cost[4] of each item of land, buildings, equipment, and improvements owned by the governmental unit. To provide information to financial statement users, a report on the investment in fixed assets is needed. What results is a separate set of records known as an **account group.** Thus, the **general fixed assets account group** is a set of records which account for the fixed assets acquired by a local government through its general, special revenue, capital projects, special assessments, and debt service funds.[5]

General Fixed Assets Account Group

The general fixed assets account group consists of two types of accounts. First, there are the asset accounts, showing the major classifications of fixed assets owned by a local government. Typical classifications are:

Land

Buildings

Improvements (for example, streets, bridges, sewer systems)

Construction in Progress (costs of uncompleted projects)

Equipment

These accounts are used to record the cost of the assets. Second is a set of accounts showing the sources of the fixed assests, that is, the specific funds through which the assets were acquired. These accounts are titled:

Investment in General Fixed Assets—General Fund

Investment in General Fixed Assets—Special Revenue Fund

Investment in General Fixed Assets—Capital Projects Fund

Investment in General Fixed Assets—Special Assessments Fund

If fixed assets are acquired by donation (for example, roads deeded to a town by a developer or a building turned over to a city by the federal government), an Investment in General Fixed Assets—Donations account is used. The sole function of the general fixed assets account group is to provide a record of fixed assets acquired by certain funds; it has no expendable resources and thus cannot by itself acquire fixed assets. It is not a fund, only a set of accounts showing the amounts and sources of fixed assets.

Accounting for Fixed Asset Transactions

An acquisition of fixed assets by a fund using fund accounting requires two sets of entries: one is made by the fund itself to record the use of resources to acquire

---

[4]If cost cannot be determined, it should be estimated, as in the case of assets which are constructed by the unit's own employees. Donated fixed assets are recorded at estimated fair market value at the time of donation.

[5]These are the five governmental funds. The debt service fund would not be expected to acquire fixed assets so, as a practical matter, we are concerned with the fixed assets acquired by only four funds.

the assets, and one is made by the general fixed assets account group to record the acquisition of the assets and the source of the resources used to acquire them. For example, assume that highway equipment costing $400,000 is purchased by the general fund. The entry made in the *general fund* records the expenditure of resources:

```
Expenditures . . . . . . . . . . . . . . . . . . . . . . . . . . . . .  400,000
   Vouchers Payable  . . . . . . . . . . . . . . . . . . . . . .              400,000
To record purchase of highway equipment.
```

Since fixed asset records are not maintained in the general fund, an entry must also be made in the *general fixed assets account group* as follows:

```
Equipment  . . . . . . . . . . . . . . . . . . . . . . . . . . . . .  400,000
   Investment in General Fixed Assets—General Fund . . . . .              400,000
To record purchase of highway equipment by general fund.
```

Depreciation of fixed assets is *not* recorded in governmental funds and thus is not shown in the general fixed assets accounts. The emphasis in fund accounting is on the expenditure of resources, not on the use of physical assets. This aspect of fund accounting has long been a center of controversy; many argue that depreciation should be recorded in governmental funds to better enable determination of the costs of governmental services. To date, however, this position has not been adopted.

A sale or other disposition of fixed assets also requires two sets of entries. Assume that old highway equipment, previously acquired with $150,000 of state grant funds (through the special revenue fund), is now sold for $30,000, with the proceeds going to the general fund. The entry in the *general fund* is:

```
Cash . . . . . . . . . . . . . . . . . . . . . . . . . . . . . . .  30,000
   Revenues. . . . . . . . . . . . . . . . . . . . . . . . . . . .              30,000
To record proceeds from sale of equipment.
```

The entry in the *general fixed assets account group* removes the previously recorded cost of the equipment:

```
Investment in General Fixed Assets—Special Revenue Fund. .  150,000
   Equipment  . . . . . . . . . . . . . . . . . . . . . . . . . . .              150,000
To record disposition of equipment originally purchased by
special revenue fund.
```

Note that since the fixed assets have no book value in the general fund, no gain or loss is recognized. In the general fund, we simply record the proceeds as revenues.

Financial Statements for General Fixed Assets

The major financial statement for the general fixed assets account group is a balance-sheet-type statement called a **statement of general fixed assets.** The format of this statement is:

General Fixed Assets	Investment in General Fixed Assets
Land	General Fund
Buildings	Special Revenue Fund
Improvements	Capital Projects Fund
Equipment	Special Assessments Fund

An example is presented in Exhibit 16.10. In addition, a statement detailing the changes in general fixed assets during the year may be presented, as shown in Exhibit 16.11.

Accounting for Long-Term Debt

As was the case with fixed assets, long-term debt is accounted for in various ways by local governments. Proprietary and fiduciary funds present long-term debt on their own balance sheets. In addition, the balance sheet of the special assessments fund presents the long-term debt issued to finance its activities. For the other four governmental funds,[6] long-term debt is excluded from the balance sheet and presented in a separate set of accounts known as the **general long-term debt account group.** As was the case with general fixed assets, this account group is used solely to provide a record of outstanding debt; *it does not engage in actual transactions.*

Exhibit 16.10   **Illustration of Statement of General Fixed Assets**

CITY OF ANDERSON
STATEMENT OF GENERAL FIXED ASSETS
GENERAL FIXED ASSET GROUP OF ACCOUNTS
DECEMBER 31, 19X8

GENERAL FIXED ASSETS

Land	$ 40,000,000
Buildings	196,000,000
Improvements	19,000,000
Equipment	43,000,000
Total	$298,000,000

INVESTMENT IN GENERAL FIXED ASSETS FROM

General Fund	$103,000,000
Special Revenue Funds	50,000,000
Capital Projects Funds	142,000,000
Special Assessments Funds	3,000,000
Total	$298,000,000

---

[6]Again, the debt service fund is unlikely to issue long-term debt, and thus we are concerned only with debt issued by the general, special revenue, and capital projects funds.

Exhibit 16.11 | **Illustration of Statement of Changes in General Fixed Assets**

CITY OF ANDERSON
STATEMENT OF CHANGES IN GENERAL FIXED ASSETS
GENERAL FIXED ASSETS GROUP OF ACCOUNTS
FOR THE YEAR ENDED DECEMBER 31, 19X8

	Land	Buildings	Improvements	Equipment	Total
General Fixed Assets, Jan. 1, 19X8	$39,100,000	$187,150,000	$13,370,000	$37,500,000	$277,120,000
ADDITIONS					
Expenditures from:					
General Fund	$ —	$ 50,000	$ —	$ 4,300,000	$ 4,350,000
Special Revenue Fund	600,000	600,000	30,000	700,000	1,930,000
Capital Projects Fund	300,000	8,600,000	3,600,000	500,000	13,000,000
Special Assessments Fund . . .	—	—	2,000,000	—	2,000,000
Total Additions	$ 900,000	$ 9,250,000	$ 5,630,000	$ 5,500,000	$ 21,280,000
	$40,000,000	$196,400,000	$19,000,000	$43,000,000	$298,400,000
DISPOSITIONS					
Capital Projects Fund	—	400,000	—	—	400,000
General Fixed Assets, Dec. 31, 19X8	$40,000,000	$196,000,000	$19,000,000	$43,000,000	$298,000,000

General Long-Term Debt Account Group

The primary account of the long-term debt group is the long-term liability account. This may be a single account (for example, Bonds Payable) or separate accounts for various classes of debt such as term bonds, serial bonds, and so forth.

To meet the requirements for a double entry system, accounts are provided to designate the amount of resources which will be required to pay the liabilities. There are two accounts of this type:

1. *Amounts Available for Repayment of Long-Term Debt.* This account indicates the amount of resources which have already been set aside, usually in the debt service fund, for the eventual repayment of long-term debt.
2. *Amounts to Be Provided for Repayment of Long-Term Debt.* This account indicates the amount of resources which must be set aside in future years.

Accounting for Long-Term Debt Transactions

Issuance of long-term debt requires two sets of entries: one in the fund issuing the debt and spending the proceeds and one in the general long-term debt account group. For example, assume that $3,000,000 of long-term bonds are issued by the capital projects fund to finance the construction of a new school building. The receipt of proceeds of the bond issue is recorded by the *capital projects fund* as:

Cash	3,000,000	
Bond Proceeds		3,000,000

To record proceeds of bond issue for school construction.

As was mentioned previously, bond proceeds are not considered revenue; rather, they are included in "other financing sources" on the statement of revenues, expenditures, and changes in fund balance. This point will be illustrated further in Chapter 17, when the capital projects fund is discussed. In addition to the entry in the capital projects fund, a record of the bond liability and the amount of resources needed in the future to repay the liability is entered in the *general long-term debt account group* as:

```
Amount to Be Provided for Repayment of Bonds . . . . . .  3,000,000
   Bonds Payable . . . . . . . . . . . . . . . . . . . . . .           3,000,000
To record bonds issued by capital projects fund.
```

The general long-term debt account group records only the *amount of principal* of the debt. Interest obligations are not shown, nor are any premium or discount on the original issue. Accounting for premiums and discounts is discussed in Chapter 17.

As resources are set aside in the debt service fund for eventual repayment of the bonds, an entry is needed in the general long-term debt account group to signify that resources are *available* (rather than needing *to be provided* in the future). For example, assume that in a given year $150,000 was appropriated in the general fund budget as a transfer to the debt service fund, to be invested for future debt principal repayments. The entry in the *general fund* is:

```
Operating Transfers Out . . . . . . . . . . . . . . . . . .  150,000
   Cash . . . . . . . . . . . . . . . . . . . . . . . . . . .            150,000
To record transfer to debt service fund.
```

The *debt service fund* records the receipt of the transfer as:

```
Cash . . . . . . . . . . . . . . . . . . . . . . . . . . . .  150,000
   Operating Transfer In . . . . . . . . . . . . . . . . . . .            150,000
To record transfer from general fund for future debt principal
payments.
```

Finally, the entry in the *general long-term debt account group* is:

```
Amount Available for Repayment of Bonds . . . . . . . . . . .  150,000
   Amount to Be Provided for Repayment of Bonds . . . . . . .            150,000
To record resources set aside for future principal payments.
```

Repayment of long-term debt also requires two sets of entries. Assume that $500,000 of long-term bonds mature this year, and that resources have been accumulated in the debt service fund for the retirement of these bonds. The entry in the *debt service fund* is:

```
Expenditures . . . . . . . . . . . . . . . . . . . . . . . .  500,000
   Cash . . . . . . . . . . . . . . . . . . . . . . . . . . .            500,000
To record payment of principal of matured bonds.
```

Exhibit 16.12	Illustration of Statement of General Long-Term Debt

BLACKSTONE COUNTY
STATEMENT OF GENERAL LONG-TERM DEBT
JUNE 30, 19X7

Amount Available for Repayment of Serial Bonds . . . . $ 453,000
Amount to Be Provided for Repayment of Serial Bonds 9,184,000
Total $9,637,000
Serial Bonds Payable $9,637,000

The entry in the *general long-term debt account group* is:

Bonds Payable 500,000
    Amount Available for Repayment of Bonds   500,000
To record retirement of matured bonds.

Financial Statement for General Long-Term Debt

A **statement of general long-term debt** presents information on long-term debt at year-end. This statement presents *Bonds Payable* on the credit side, and the two accounts *Amount Available for Repayment of Long-Term Debt* and *Amount to Be Provided for Repayment of Long-Term Debt* on the debit side. An example of such a statement is presented in Exhibit 16.12.

Summary of Key Concepts

A **local governmental unit** is made up of several economic entities known as **funds.** Eight standard types of funds and two account groups exist, some or all of which may be used by a particular local governmental unit.

The general, special revenue, capital projects, special assessments, and debt service funds are known as **governmental funds** and use a method of accounting known as **fund accounting.** Fund accounting is characterized by use of the **modified accrual basis** for recording revenues and expenditures, and by inclusion of budgetary accounts.

The enterprise and internal service funds are known as **proprietary funds** because they are used to conduct business-type activities. **Accrual accounting** is used for proprietary funds.

The trust and agency funds are known as **fiduciary funds** and generally use fiduciary accounting principles.

The general fund usually requires a formal **budget determination process,** resulting in the calculation of a property tax rate.

Under the **modified accrual method of accounting,** certain revenues of the general fund are accrued, while others are recorded on the cash basis. In particular, property tax revenues are recorded on the accrual basis, with an allowance for uncollectible taxes.

Inventories may be accounted for either by the **purchases method,** which recognizes the expenditure at time of purchase, or by the **consumption method,** which recognizes the expenditure at time of use.

Alternative treatments also exist for **encumbrances outstanding at year-end.** Under the **legal approach,** encumbrances and expenditures both constitute charges against the current annual budget. Under the **GAAP approach,** expenditures are compared to a modified accrual budget, which is the annual budget plus carryover appropriations.

Various types of **interfund transactions** exist, each having distinct accounting treatment. **Operating transfers** must be distinguished from revenue and expenditure transactions.

Financial statements presented for the general fund include a **balance sheet,** a **statement of revenues, expenditures, and changes in fund balance,** and a **budgetary comparison statement.**

Fixed assets acquired by the general fund and by other governmental funds are recorded in the **general fixed assets account group.**

Long-term debt incurred by the general fund and by all other governmental funds except the special assessments fund is recorded in the **general long-term debt account group.**

Questions

Q16.1 "Within each legal entity, the concept of economic entity dominates." Explain the meaning of this statement in terms of financial statement reporting for local government.

Q16.2 In accounting for the activities of local governmental units, three types of accounting are followed: business accounting, fiduciary accounting, and fund accounting. How can you justify the use of three types of accounting in one legal entity?

Q16.3 Select the best answer for each of the following questions:

1. Under the modified accrual method of accounting used by a local governmental unit, which of the following would be a revenue most susceptible to accrual?
   a. Income taxes.
   b. Business licenses.
   c. Property taxes.
   d. Sales taxes.

    2. Within a local governmental unit, two funds that are accounted for in a manner similar to a business entity are:

    a. General and debt service.

    b. Enterprise and general.

    c. Enterprise and trust and agency.

    d. Internal service and enterprise.

    3. When used in fund accounting, the term *fund* usually refers to:

    a. A sum of money designated for a special purpose.

    b. A liability to other governmental units.

    c. The equity of a municipality in its own assets.

    d. A fiscal and accounting entity having a set of self-balancing accounts.

    (AICPA adapted)

Q16.4 Briefly describe the budgeting process of a governmental unit.

Q16.5 Why are balance sheets of the governmental funds which use fund accounting unclassified as to current and noncurrent items?

Q16.6 Why are delinquent taxes often fully reserved? What effect does this procedure have on the balance sheet?

Q16.7 Explain the difference between temporary and permanent interfund transfers and give an example of each type.

Q16.8 What is the effect on the fund balance of each of the following? (Answer "increase," "decrease," or "no effect.")

    1. Budgeted expenditures exceed budgeted revenues.

    2. Budgeted revenues exceed budgeted expenditures.

    3. Actual revenues equal budgeted revenues.

    4. Actual expenditures exceed budgeted expenditures.

Q16.9 Select the best answer for each of the following questions:

    1. Which of the following accounts is a budgetary account?

    a. Vouchers Payable.

    b. Expenditures.

    c. Encumbrances.

    d. Fund Balance.

    2. A town issues purchase orders of $630,000 to vendors and suppliers. Which of the following entries should be made to record this transaction?

	Debit	Credit
a. Encumbrances	630,000	
Fund Balance—Reserved for Encumbrances		630,000
b. Expenditures	630,000	
Vouchers Payable		630,000
c. Expenses	630,000	
Accounts Payable		630,000

d. Fund Balance—Reserved for Encumbrances 630,000
　　 Encumbrances . . . . 　　　 630,000

3. If a credit was made to the fund balance in the process of recording a budget for a local governmental unit, it can be assumed that:
   a. Budgeted expenditures exceed actual revenues.
   b. Actual expenditures exceed budgeted expenditures.
   c. Budgeted revenues exceed budgeted expenditures.
   d. Budgeted expenditures exceed budgeted revenues.
   (AICPA adapted)

Q16.10 Select the best answer for each of the following multiple choice questions:

1. A city's general fund budget for the forthcoming fiscal year shows estimated revenues in excess of appropriations. The initial effect of recording this will result in an increase in:
   a. Taxes receivable.
   b. Fund balance—unreserved.
   c. Fund balance—reserved for encumbrances.
   d. Encumbrances.

2. In the current year, what would be the effect on the general fund balance of recording a $15,000 purchase for a new fire truck out of general fund resources, for which a $14,600 encumbrance had been recorded in the general fund in the previous year, using the legal approach?
   a. Reduce the general fund balance by $15,000.
   b. Reduce the general fund balance by $14,600.
   c. Reduce the general fund balance by $400.
   d. Have no effect on the general fund balance.

3. In preparing the general fund budget of Brockton City for the forthcoming fiscal year, the city council appropriated a sum greater than expected revenues. This action of the council will result in:
   a. A cash overdraft during the fiscal year.
   b. An increase in encumbrances by the end of that fiscal year.
   c. A decrease in the fund balance.
   d. An increase in the fund balance.
   (AICPA adapted)

Q16.11 Select the best answer for each of the following multiple choice questions:

1. Which of the following should be accrued as revenues by the general fund of a local government?
   a. Sales taxes held by the state which will be remitted to the local government.
   b. Parking meter revenues.
   c. Sales taxes collected by merchants.
   d. Income taxes currently due.

2. Which of the following types of revenue would generally be recorded directly in the general fund of a governmental unit?
   a. Receipts from a city-owned parking structure.
   b. Property taxes.
   c. Interest earned on investments held for retirement of employees.
   d. Revenues of internal service funds.
   (AICPA adapted)

Q16.12 Select the best answer for each of the following multiple choice questions:

1. Authority granted by a legislative body to make expenditures and to incur obligations during a fiscal year is the definition of an:
   a. Appropriation.
   b. Estimated revenue.
   c. Encumbrance.
   d. Expenditure.
2. What type of account is used to earmark the fund balance to liquidate the contingent obligations for goods ordered but not yet received?
   a. Appropriations.
   b. Encumbrances.
   c. Expenditures.
   d. Fund balance—reserved for encumbrances.
3. The Fund Balance—Reserved for Encumbrances (Prior Year) account represents amounts recorded by a governmental unit for:
   a. Anticipated expenditures in the next year.
   b. Anticipated expenditures for which purchase orders were made in the prior year but disbursement will be in the current year.
   c. Excess expenditures in the prior year that will be offset against the current year budgeted amounts.
   d. Unanticipated expenditures of the prior year that become evident in the current year.
   (AICPA adapted)

Q16.13 The following was recorded in the general fund when equipment originally purchased by the special revenue fund was sold. What other journal entry was made in the governmental unit's accounts?

```
Cash . . . . . . . . . . . . . . . . . . . . . . . . . . . . . . . . 6,000
  Revenues . . . . . . . . . . . . . . . . . . . . . . . . . . . . .        6,000
To record sale of equipment originally purchased for $7,500.
```

Q16.14 The following was recorded in the general long-term debt account group. What other journal entry was made in the governmental unit's accounts?

```
Bonds Payable . . . . . . . . . . . . . . . . . . . . . . . . . . 850,000
  Amount to Be Provided for Repayment of Bonds . . . . . . .          850,000
To record payment of matured bonds by general fund.
```

Q16.15 What does the account entitled "Amount Available for Repayment of Long-Term Debt" represent, and where does it appear?

Exercises

E16.1 Following are several common activities or financial events in which a local government may participate:

1. Operations of a public library receiving the majority of its support from property taxes levied for that purpose.
2. Proceeds of a federal grant made to assist in financing the future construction of an adult training center.
3. Operations of a municipal swimming pool receiving the majority of its support from charges to users.
4. Monthly remittance to an insurance company of the lump sum of hospital/surgical insurance premiums collected as payroll deductions from employees.
5. Activities of a central motor pool which provides and services vehicles for the use of municipal employees on official business.
6. Activities of a municipal employee retirement plan which is financed by equal employer and employee contributions.
7. Collections of property taxes for the benefit of local sanitary, park, and school districts. The collections are periodically remitted to these units.
8. Activities of a street improvement project which is being financed by requiring each owner of property facing the street to pay a proportionate share of the total cost.
9. Activities of a central print shop offering printing services at cost to various city departments.
10. Transactions of a municipal police retirement system.
11. Activities of a municipal golf course which receives three-fourths of its total revenue from a special tax levy.
12. Self-supporting activities of government that are provided on a user-charge basis.
13. Activities of a data-processing center established to service all agencies within a governmental unit.

Required: For each of the above, indicate the type of fund in which the activity should be recorded by a local government and the type of accounting (business, fiduciary, or fund) that should be followed. *(AICPA adapted)*

E16.2 Each of the following transactions relates to a city government:

1. A sinking fund is set up to accumulate and invest resources for the retirement of a general bond issue which matures in 10 years.

2. The city receives a $50,000 grant from the federal government to institute a meal delivery program for senior citizens.

3. New curbing is being installed in a section of the city. The residents of that section will have an additional charge on their property tax bill during each of the next 10 years to pay the cost of the curbing.

4. To remedy a flooding problem, the city plans a new drainage system in the southern part of the city. It is decided that this project will be financed by a general bond issue rather than by tax assessments to property owners.

5. The city establishes a retirement fund for its fire fighters. Each year, 8 percent of the fire fighters' wages is set aside by the city. The city administers the investment of funds and the payment of benefits.

6. Same as No. 5, except that the city pays a premium to an insurance company, which is fully responsible for investment of funds and benefit payments.

7. The city has set up a computer services division to handle payroll and other functions for all city agencies. Each agency is billed by the computer services division for the work done for that agency.

8. Fifteen new police cars are purchased, as provided in the general budget.

9. State aid funds are received. These funds may be used for any of the general operations of the city.

10. The city deducts federal income taxes from its employees' wages and periodically remits them to the federal government.

Required: Identify the fund in which each of the above would be recorded.

E16.3 The Anderson School District, an independent governmental unit, maintains several funds to account for its many activities. Following are several transactions:

1. Construction of a new library for the school district. Bonds were issued to finance the construction.

2. Receipt of a grant from the state to finance purchase of books for the new library.

3. Operating costs for the school cafeterias. Charges to students and faculty for food provide 85 percent of the operating costs.

4. Costs of operating and maintaining the school bus fleet, which are met by general school tax revenues.

5. Income from investments which were donated to the school district by a wealthy citizen. Investment income is used to provide scholarships to needy students.

6. Costs of operating school bookstores. Bookstores derive revenues from sale of books and stationery supplies and are self-sufficient.

7. Salaries for faculty and administration, which are paid out of general school tax revenues.

Required: Identify the fund in which each of the above would be recorded.

E16.4 Legal requirements of Woten County set the maximum property tax rate at $60 per $1,000 of assessed value. Assessed value of taxable property within the county is $600,000,000. In preparing the county's general fund budget, appropriations of $40,000,000 were anticipated. State and federal aid to Woten County will be $13,000,000.

Required:

1. What is the maximum amount Woten County could receive from property tax revenues?
2. If the county plans a balanced budget, what will the tax rate be?

E16.5 The following information relates to actual revenues and expenditures for the town of Greenwood:

REVENUES	Actual	Over (under) Budget
Property Taxes.	$3,000,000	$150,000
Fines.	6,000	6,000
Intergovernmental	12,000	0
Sale of Services	500,000	(75,000)
Miscellaneous	4,000	(1,000)
EXPENDITURES		
Services	2,050,000	55,000
Supplies	500,000	(76,000)
Other.	950,000	32,000

Required:

1. What budget entry was made at the beginning of the year?
2. If the fund balance *before* the budget entry was $2,100,000, what is the fund balance after year-end closing entries?

E16.6 The following related entries were recorded in sequence in the general fund of a municipality:

Encumbrances	12,000	
Fund Balance—Reserved for Encumbrances		12,000
Fund Balance—Reserved for Encumbrances	12,000	
Encumbrances		12,000
Expenditures	12,350	
Vouchers Payable.		12,350

Required: From the information given, answer the following multiple choice questions:

1. The sequence of entries indicates that:
   a. An adverse event was foreseen and a reserve of $12,000 was created; later the reserve was canceled and a liability for the item was acknowledged.
   b. An order was placed for goods or services estimated to cost $12,000; the actual cost was $12,350, for which a liability was acknowledged upon receipt.
   c. Encumbrances were anticipated but later failed to materialize and were reversed. A liability of $12,350 was incurred.
   d. The first entry was erroneous and was reversed; an unrelated liability of $12,350 was recorded.
2. Assuming the legal approach to encumbrance accounting was followed, the entries:
   a. Occurred in the same fiscal period.
   b. Did not occur in the same fiscal period.
   c. Could have occurred in the same fiscal period, but it is impossible to be sure of this.
   d. Would reflect the equivalent of a prior period adjustment had the entity concerned been one operated for profit.
3. If the encumbrance equaled the appropriation for the items in the entries, what effect would the third entry have on the fund balance during closing?
   a. Increase the fund balance.
   b. Decrease the fund balance.
   c. Not affect the fund balance.
   d. Not affect the fund balance but affect the budget of the following fiscal period.
4. Entries similar to those for the general fund may also appear on the books of the municipality's:
   a. General fixed assets account group.
   b. General long-term debt account group.
   c. Trust fund.
   d. Special revenue fund.
   (AICPA adapted)

E16.7 On July 10, Marchville levied property taxes of $2,500,000. Based on past experience, city management estimated that the city would be unable to collect 4 percent of the taxes. Taxes were due September 30, but $800,000 was received before that date from taxpayers taking advantage of the 1 percent discount for early payment. Marchville treats discounts given as a reduction of revenues.

On January 1, outstanding taxes due of $150,000 were declared delinquent and were fully reserved. By the end of the fiscal year, 40 percent of the delinquent taxes had been collected. There were no taxes receivable, either current or delinquent, at the beginning of the fiscal year.

Actual expenditures were $2,000,000, the same amount as appropriations. All expenditures were cash transactions. The budget entry included $2,400,000 of estimated revenues. After the budget entry, the fund balance was $472,000.

Required:

1. Prepare the journal entries to record the property tax transactions.
2. State the balance sheet accounts and their respective balances relating to the property tax levy and collections as of the end of the fiscal year. Assume that the cash balance at the beginning of the fiscal year was $93,000.

E16.8 A year-end count of materials and supplies at Mooreland City showed inventories on hand totaling $63,000. A similar count at the end of the previous year revealed inventories of $57,000. During the year, the city purchased materials and supplies of $160,500.

Required: Prepare the journal entries relating to inventory during the year, including any year-end adjustments, under each of the following assumptions:

1. The accounting focus is on expenditures for rather than consumption of inventories. The financial statements reflect year-end inventory balances.
2. The accounting focus is on consumption of inventories, viewing inventory as a spendable asset.

E16.9 The Newberry County budget for the 19X7 fiscal year included estimates of revenues of $3,501,000 and appropriations of $3,449,000.

Required: Prepare the closing entries for 19X7 under each of the following independent assumptions:

1. Actual revenues and expenditures equaled estimates.
2. Actual revenues were as expected, but actual expenditures exceeded estimates by $22,000.
3. Actual revenues of $3,500,000 equaled actual expenditures.
4. The net effect of the closing entries on the fund balance was zero. Actual revenues were $3,576,000.

E16.10 The December 31, 19X0, balance sheet for the special revenues fund of Burnville showed $19,000 reserved for encumbrances. This figure represented $11,000 encumbered for office equipment and $8,000 for supplies. Early in 19X1, the equipment and supplies were delivered and bills received for $11,700 and $7,950, respectively.

Required: Prepare the journal entries for 19X1 relating to these events, using (1) the legal approach and (2) the GAAP approach.

E16.11 Interfund transfers of the general fund of North Weston City for 19X7 were:

	Transfers In	Transfers Out
1. To the special revenue fund to permit initial expenditures under a project to be fully supported by a federal grant		$18,000
2. To a special assessments fund as the city's contribution to a street lighting project		25,000
3. From the capital projects fund, unspent proceeds of a bond issue	$ 7,000	
4. To the enterprise fund as city's cost of services provided		12,000
5. To the internal service fund to temporarily finance a purchase of supplies		35,000
6. From the special revenue fund to repay advance	18,000	

Required: What accounts will appear on the 19X7 general fund balance sheet as a result of these transfers?

E16.12 The preclosing trial balance for the general fund of Graystone is given below:

Cash	$ 350,000
Taxes Receivable—Current	80,000
Allowance for Uncollectible Taxes—Current	(45,000)
Estimated Revenues	1,300,000
Expenditures	1,050,000
Expenditures—Prior Year Encumbrances	42,000
Encumbrances	30,000
Due from Other Funds	12,000
	$2,819,000
Vouchers Payable	$ 180,000
Due to Other Funds	21,000
Revenues	1,400,000
Appropriations	1,100,000
Fund Balance—Reserved for Encumbrances	30,000
Fund Balance—Reserved for Encumbrances (Prior Year)	45,000
Fund Balance—Unreserved	43,000
	$2,819,000

Additional information:

1. At year-end, all uncollected taxes are deemed delinquent. Delinquent taxes are fully reserved.
2. A physical count of inventory revealed $25,000 of supplies on hand. Graystone discloses inventory available in the body of its financial statement.

Required:

1. Prepare all year-end adjusting and closing entries for the general fund of Graystone.
2. Prepare a year-end balance sheet for the general fund of Graystone.

E16.13 The following information relates to activities of the city of Wilsondale:

1. Wilsondale ordered 15 police cars on February 15 at an expected total cost of $120,000. On April 28, the cars were delivered. The amount of the invoice was $123,500. Payment was made by the general fund on June 10.
2. On June 30, the city paid a semiannual interest payment of $130,000 and a principal payment of $75,000 on general obligation bonds. Payment was made from the general fund.

Required: Prepare all necessary entries which the city of Wilsondale should make with respect to the above transactions. Identify for each entry the particular fund or account group in which the entry is being made.

E16.14 The Salinas City Statement of General Fixed Assets as of the beginning of the fiscal year follows:

SALINAS CITY
STATEMENT OF GENERAL FIXED ASSETS
JULY 1, 19X0

GENERAL FIXED ASSETS		**INVESTMENTS IN GENERAL FIXED ASSETS**	
Land	$ 150,000	General Fund	$1,450,000
Buildings	1,000,000	Capital Projects Fund . . .	500,000
Equipment	800,000		
Total	$1,950,000	Total	$1,950,000

During October 19X0, the city purchased a warehouse for $375,000, of which 40 percent was attributable to the land. The city began construction of a civic center in 19X0. The entire project was estimated to cost $800,000. By June 30, 19X1, $200,000 had been expended on the project, which was estimated to be one-fifth complete.

Old equipment originally costing $20,000 was scrapped, and new equipment was purchased for $35,000 early in 19X1.

Required: Prepare the General Fixed Assets portion of the June 30, 19X1, statement of general fixed assets for Salinas City.

E16.15 The village of Jamesville acquired the following fixed assets during 19X3:

1. Snow removal equipment was purchased by the general fund at a cost of $58,000.

2. A delivery van was purchased by the internal service fund at a cost of $8,300.
3. A building was purchased for $220,000 by the capital projects fund to serve as a youth center. The purchase was financed by a 20-year bond issue.
4. Sewer lines were extended to an undeveloped section of the village at a cost of $700,000. This cost will eventually be paid by the property owners through special tax assessments. To cover the actual construction cost, bonds were issued by the special assessment fund.

Required: Prepare the entries needed in the village of Jamesville's general fixed assets accounts to reflect the above acquisitions.

E16.16 The county of Edgewater had the following transactions involving long-term debt during 19X6:

1. A $2,000,000 bond issue by the capital projects fund provided money for construction of new streets and bridges.
2. A $1,500,000 bond issue by the water authority (an enterprise fund) provided money for replacement of water mains.
3. A $3,300,000 bond issue by the special assessments fund provided money for improvements to the sewage treatment plant.
4. $100,000 of principal and $120,000 of interest was paid by the general fund on bonds issued in 19X4 for construction of a fire station.
5. Of the bond proceeds described in No. 1, $80,000 was not spent on the project and was transferred to the debt service fund to be used for principal payments on the bonds in future years.

Required: Prepare the entries needed in the general long-term debt accounts of the county of Edgewater.

Problems

P16.1 Property Tax Levy In February 19X6, the city of Greenville began planning its budget for the fiscal year beginning July 1, 19X6. The following information was available:

General Fund Balance, Jan. 1, 19X6	$ 352,000
Estimated Receipts from Property Taxes (Jan. 1, 19X6–June 30, 19X6)	2,222,000
Estimated Revenue from Investments (Jan. 1, 19X6–June 30, 19X7)	442,000
Estimated Proceeds from Sale of General Obligation Bonds in August 19X6	3,000,000
	$6,016,000
Estimated Expenditures (Jan. 1, 19X6–June 30, 19X6)	$1,900,000
Proposed Appropriations (July 1, 19X6–June 30, 19X7)	4,300,000
	$6,200,000

Additional information:

1. The general fund balance required by the city council for July 1, 19X7, is $175,000.
2. Property tax collections are due in March and September of each year. During the month of February 19X6, estimated expenditures are expected to exceed available funds by $200,000. Pending collection of property taxes in March 19X6, this deficiency will have to be met by the issuance of 30-day tax anticipation notes of $200,000 at an estimated interest rate of 9 percent per annum.
3. The proposed general obligation bonds will be issued by the city water fund (an enterprise fund) and will be used for the construction of a new water pumping station.

Required: Prepare a statement as of January 1, 19X6, calculating the property tax levy required for the city of Greenville general fund for the fiscal year ending June 30, 19X7. *(AICPA adapted)*

P16.2 **Simple Fund Accounting for Local Government**   The rural township of Barnesville provides a minimum of services to residents, all of which are accounted for in one fund. The budget approved by the town council at the beginning of the fiscal year 19X3 included expected revenues of $13,000 in taxes and $15,000 of anticipated expenditures. Cash on hand at the beginning of the year was $5,000. The fund balance was $5,000.

During the year, the following occurred:

1. Taxes of $12,050 were collected.
2. A community member died and left $2,000 to the township with no restrictions on the use of the money.
3. Cash expenditures for services provided (including labor, gasoline, and miscellaneous expenses) were $12,680.
4. Purchase orders were approved as follows: typewriter, $250; office supplies, $420; shop supplies, $340; tires, $325.
5. The office supplies bill was for $410. The shop supplies bill was for $360. The bill for tires totaled $325. All bills were paid.
6. At the end of the fiscal year, the typewriter had not been received or billed.

Required:

1. Make all the journal entries for the fund of the township of Barnesville, including closing entries.
2. Compute the fund balance as of the end of the fiscal year.

P16.3 **Recording Transactions and Closing Entries**   The January 1, 19X7, balance sheet for the single fund of the village of Owen is as follows:

VILLAGE OF OWEN
FUND BALANCE SHEET
JANUARY 1, 19X7

Cash	$30,000	Vouchers Payable.	$43,000
Receivables.	20,000	Fund Balance	7,000
		Total Liabilities and Fund	
Total Assets.	$50,000	Balance.	$50,000

Transactions for the village during 19X7 were:

1. The village council approved a budget estimating revenues of $41,000 in property taxes and $10,000 in user charges. Property taxes are accrued on Owen's books. The budget authorized expenditures of $51,000.
2. Receivables of $18,500 from last year were collected. Of the 19X7 tax levy, $26,500 was collected.
3. Encumbrances of $50,300 were recorded. On December 31, 19X7, purchase orders of $13,000 were outstanding.
4. Bills received exceeded the amounts encumbered by $200.
5. Checks for $44,000 were mailed in payment of vouchers. No payments were made without vouchers.
6. User charges of $11,000 were collected.

Required:

1. Prepare journal entries to record the transactions for the village of Owen during 19X7.
2. Prepare closing entries at December 31, 19X7, for the village of Owen.

P16.4 General Fund—Entries and Financial Statements The township of Wyatt finances its operations from revenues provided by property taxes, water distribution, fines levied by the municipal court, and interest on savings accounts.

Wyatt maintains only a general fund. The following information is available for the year ended December 31, 19X6:

1. General fund account balances on January 1, 19X6, were:

Cash in Savings Account.	$ 620,000
Cash in Checking Accounts	384,800
Cash on Hand (Undeposited).	1,600
Water Department Supplies	36,400
Accounts Receivable—Water Customers.	36,700
Fund Balance—Unreserved	1,043,100
Fund Balance—Reserved for Supplies . . . . :	36,400

2. The budget for 19X6 adopted by the township commission and the

transactions relating to the budget (with all current bills vouchered and paid on December 31, 19X6) for the year were:

	Budget	Actual
Property Taxes	$267,500	$267,500
Water Department Costs	665,000	643,600[a]
Township Constable and Court Fees Paid by Township	100,000	95,500[a]
Water Revenues	300,000	320,600[b]
Court Fines	125,000	110,250
Commissioners' Salaries and Expenses	60,000	54,700[a]
Interest on Savings Accounts	20,000	22,400
Miscellaneous Expenses	12,000	26,100[a]

[a]Cash expenditures.
[b]Billings.

3. All property taxes were collected.
4. A count of cash on December 31, 19X6, determined that there was $2,500 on hand that was not deposited until January 2, 19X7.
5. All outstanding water bills on January 1, 19X6, were collected during 19X6. All billings for water during 19X6 were paid with the exception of statements totaling $22,300, which were mailed to customers the last week of December.
6. All water department supplies were consumed during the year on the repair of water mains.

Required:

1. Prepare 19X6 journal entries for the township of Wyatt.
2. Prepare a balance sheet and a statement of revenues, expenditures, and changes in fund balance for Wyatt's general fund. *(AICPA adapted)*

P16.5 Special Revenue Fund In 19X4, Grand City established a special revenue fund to account for the addition of an aquarium to the city zoo. Work on the aquarium was scheduled to begin in January 19X5. Appropriations were not recorded until 19X5. Financing for the project was to be provided as follows:

From Federal Grant to Be Received in March 19X5	$ 90,000
From 19X4 General Fund Revenue	45,000
From 19X5 General Fund Revenue	45,000
	$180,000

The special revenue fund balance sheet for December 31, 19X4, was:

GRAND CITY SPECIAL REVENUE FUND
BALANCE SHEET
DECEMBER 31, 19X4

ASSETS		LIABILITIES AND FUND BALANCE	
Cash.	$ 13,000	Fund Balance	$135,000
Investments	32,000		
Accounts Receivable (Federal			
Grant)	90,000		
	$135,000		$135,000

During 19X5, the following occurred:

1. An appropriation of $180,000 was made for the project.
2. A contract for $175,000 for the addition to the aquarium was signed. Work was started, completed, and billed for $175,000.
3. Cash from the general fund and federal grant was received as scheduled.
4. Investments yielded $1,800 in revenues, $200 less than anticipated.
5. Vouchers remaining to be paid at year-end totaled $8,000.
6. Any remaining resources were reclassified for transfer to the general fund.

Required:

1. What was the 19X4 budget entry?
2. Prepare all 19X5 journal entries for the special revenue fund.
3. Prepare the balance sheet for the special revenue fund as of December 31, 19X5.

P16.6 General Fund—Adjustments and Statements The books for the town of Fountain Inn are maintained by an inexperienced bookkeeper. All transactions were recorded in the town's general fund for the fiscal year ended June 30, 19X6. The bookkeeper prepared the following trial balance:

TOWN OF FOUNTAIN INN
GENERAL FUND TRIAL BALANCE
JUNE 30, 19X6

Accounts	Debit	Credit
Cash.	$ 12,900	
Accounts Receivable.	1,200	
Taxes Receivable, Current	8,000	
Tax Anticipation Notes Payable		$ 15,000
Appropriations		350,000
Expenditures.	344,000	
Estimated Revenues	290,000	
Revenues		320,000
Town Property	16,100	

Bonds Payable.	36,000	
Fund Balance		23,200
Total	$708,200	$708,200

Additional information:

1. The accounts receivable balance was due from the town's golf course, representing an advance made by the general fund. Accounts for the municipal golf course operated by the town are maintained in a separate enterprise fund.

2. The total tax levy for the year was $280,000, of which $10,000 was abated during the year. The town's tax collection experience in recent years indicates an average loss of 5 percent of the net tax levy for uncollectible taxes. At year-end, all taxes receivable are considered delinquent.

3. On June 30, 19X6, the town retired at face value 4 percent general obligation serial bonds totaling $30,000. The bonds were issued on July 1, 19X4, in the total amount of $150,000. Interest paid during the year was also recorded in the Bonds Payable account.

4. At the beginning of the year, the town council authorized a supply room with an inventory not to exceed $10,000. During the year, supplies totaling $12,300 were purchased and charged to Expenditures. The physical inventory taken at June 30 disclosed that supplies totaling $8,400 were used.

5. Expenditures for 19X6 included $2,600 applicable to purchase orders issued in the prior year. Outstanding purchase orders at June 30, 19X6, not recorded in the accounts, amounted to $4,100. The GAAP approach is used for outstanding encumbrances.

6. The amount of $8,200, due from the state for the town's share of state gasoline taxes, was not recorded in the accounts.

7. Equipment costing $7,500 was removed from service and sold for $900 during the year, and new equipment costing $17,000 was purchased. These transactions were recorded in the Town Property account.

Required:

1. Prepare the adjusting and closing entries for the general fund of Fountain Inn and any corresponding entries to the general fixed assets and general long-term debt groups of accounts. Assume that general fixed assets and general long-term debt accounts were properly maintained in prior years.

2. Prepare a balance sheet and statement of changes in fund balance for Fountain Inn's general fund. *(AICPA adapted)*

P16.7 Reconstructing Journal Entries Balance sheets for the city of Golden's special revenue fund appear as shown on page 874.

CITY OF GOLDEN
SPECIAL REVENUE FUND
BALANCE SHEETS
JUNE 30, 19X1 AND 19X0

ASSETS	19X1	19X0
Cash	$ 39,000	$ 10,000
Investments	140,000	200,000
Due from General Fund	50,000	—
Due from Federal Government	—	150,000
	$229,000	$360,000

LIABILITIES AND FUND BALANCE		
Vouchers Payable	$ 87,000	$180,000
Fund Balance—Reserved for Encumbrances	—	75,000
Fund Balance—Unreserved	142,000	105,000
	$229,000	$360,000

The budget entry made in July 19X0 was:

Estimated Revenues	50,000	
Fund Balance—Unreserved	13,000	
Appropriations		63,000
To record budget.		

Bills for the June 30, 19X0, encumbrances were $3,000 less than the amount committed. There were no unanticipated revenues. The legal approach is used for outstanding encumbrances.

Required: Reconstruct the journal entries for the year ended June 30, 19X1, for Golden's special revenue fund.

P16.8 Statement of Revenues, Expenditures, and Changes in Fund Balance Information concerning Dalton City's 19X1 general fund revenues and expenditures is given below:

	Budgeted Amount	Actual Amount
Property Taxes	$432,000	$425,000
Licenses—Revenue	30,000	32,000
Permits—Revenue	37,500	35,000
Share of State Tax	60,000	58,000
Sale of Equipment	—	8,000
Interest Revenue	4,500	4,200
Gifts	—	7,000
General Government Expenditures	180,000	172,000
Public Safety Expenditures	105,000	106,000
Highway Expenditures	75,000	68,000
Health Services Expenditures	68,000	72,000
Education Expenditures	150,000	141,000

At year-end, the following amounts were encumbered:

For General Government.	$6,000
For Public Safety.	500
For Health Services	1,000
	$7,500

Required:

1. Property taxes are assessed at a rate of $48 per $1,000 assessed value. What is the assessed value of the taxable property in Dalton City?
2. What tax rate would give Dalton City a balanced budget?
3. Prepare a statement of revenues, expenditures, and changes in fund balance—budget and actual—for the Dalton City general fund.

P16.9 General Fund and Account Groups—Corrections and Adjustments
During the fiscal year ending June 30, 19X7, all transactions of Salleytown were recorded in the general fund due to the inexperience of the town's bookkeeper. The trial balance of Salleytown's general fund is as follows:

SALLEYTOWN
GENERAL FUND TRIAL BALANCE
JUNE 30, 19X7

Accounts	Debit	Credit
Cash.	$ 16,800	
Short-Term Investments	40,000	
Accounts Receivable.	11,500	
Taxes Receivable—Current	30,000	
Tax Anticipation Notes Payable		$ 50,000
Appropriations		400,000
Expenditures.	382,000	
Estimated Revenue	320,000	
Revenues		360,000
General Property.	85,400	
Bonds Payable.	52,000	
Fund Balance		127,700
	$937,700	$937,700

The following information is also available:

1. The accounts receivable of $11,500 includes $1,500 due from the town's water utility. Accounts for the municipal water utility operated by the town are maintained in a separate fund.
2. The balance in Taxes Receivable—Current is now considered delinquent, and the town estimates that $24,000 will be uncollectible.
3. On June 30, 19X7, the town retired, at face value, 6 percent general obligation serial bonds totaling $40,000. The bonds were issued on July 1, 19X2, at face value of $200,000. Interest and principal paid during the year ended June 30, 19X7, were charged to Bonds Payable.
4. During the year, supplies totaling $128,000 were purchased and

charged to Expenditures. The town conducted a physical inventory of supplies on hand at June 30, 19X7, and this physical count disclosed that supplies totaling $84,000 were used. The purchases method is used.

5. Expenditures for the year ended June 30, 19X7, included $11,200 applicable to purchase orders issued in the prior year. Outstanding purchase orders at June 30, 19X7, not recorded in the accounts, amounted to $17,500. The legal approach is used.

6. On June 28, 19X7, the state revenue department informed the town that its share of a state-collected, locally shared tax would be $34,000.

7. During the year, equipment with a book value of $7,900 was removed from service and sold for $4,600. In addition, new equipment costing $90,000 was purchased. The transactions were recorded in General Property.

8. During the year, 100 acres of land were donated to the town for use as an industrial park. The land had a value of $125,000. No recording of this donation has been made.

Required:

1. Prepare the formal reclassification, adjusting, and closing journal entries for the general fund as of June 30, 19X7.

2. Prepare the formal adjusting journal entries for the general long-term debt group of accounts and the general fixed assets group of accounts as of June 30, 19X7. Assume that proper entries were made in prior years. *(AICPA adapted)*

P16.10 General Fund—Comprehensive The following summary of transactions was taken from the accounts of the West Columbia School District General Fund *before* the books had been closed for the fiscal year ended June 30, 19X5:

	Postclosing Balances June 30, 19X4	Preclosing Balances June 30, 19X5
Cash	$400,000	$ 700,000
Taxes Receivable	150,000	170,000
Allowance for Uncollectible Taxes	(40,000)	(70,000)
Estimated Revenues	—	3,000,000
Expenditures	—	2,842,000
Expenditures—Prior Year	—	58,000
Encumbrances	—	91,000
	$510,000	$6,791,000
Vouchers Payable	$ 80,000	$ 408,000
Due to Other Funds	210,000	142,000
Fund Balance—Reserved for Encumbrances	60,000	151,000
Fund Balance—Unreserved	160,000	180,000
Revenues from Taxes	—	2,800,000
Miscellaneous Revenues	—	130,000
Appropriations	—	2,980,000
	$510,000	$6,791,000

Additional information:

1. A Taxes Receivable—Delinquent account is not used.
2. The estimated taxes receivable for the year ended June 30, 19X5, were $2,870,000, and taxes collected during the year totaled $2,810,000.
3. An analysis of the transactions in the Vouchers Payable account for the year ended June 30, 19X5, follows:

	Debit (Credit)
Current Expenditures	$(2,700,000)
Expenditures—Prior Year	(58,000)
Vouchers for Payment to Other Funds	(210,000)
Cash Payments during Year	2,640,000
Net Change	$ (328,000)

4. During the year, the general fund was billed $142,000 for services performed on its behalf by other city funds.
5. On May 2, 19X5, commitment documents were issued for the purchase of new textbooks at a cost of $91,000. The GAAP approach is used.

Required: Based on the data presented above, reconstruct the original detailed journal entries that were required to record all transactions for the fiscal year ended June 30, 19X5, including the recording of the current year's budget. Prepare closing entries at June 30, 19X5. *(AICPA adapted)*

P16.11 General Fund—Comprehensive Data relating to the general fund of the Pilotsville School District are as follows:

PILOTSVILLE SCHOOL DISTRICT
GENERAL FUND
BALANCE SHEET
DECEMBER 31, 19X6

ASSETS		**LIABILITIES AND FUND BALANCE**	
Cash	$36,600	Vouchers Payable	$22,000
Taxes Receivable—Current		Due to Enterprise Fund	7,000
(Net of $8,000 Allowance for		Fund Balance:	
Uncollectible Taxes)	42,000	Reserved for Encumbrances	4,600
Inventory	17,000	Reserved for Inventory	17,000
		Unreserved	45,000
	$95,000		$95,600

Additional information:

1. The 19X7 budget included $287,000 in expected revenue, all from property taxes, and a $6,000 planned decrease in the fund balance. The tax levy was for $300,000.
2. Tax collections during 19X7 were:

19X6 Taxes . . . . $ 45,000
19X7 Taxes   238,000
                                                                        $283,000

Remaining 19X6 taxes were written off.

3. Taxes due at year-end are not considered delinquent but are 16 percent reserved.

4. Old school desks were sold for $800. The desks had originally cost $1,200.

5. New desks were purchased for $2,000. Neither transaction regarding the desks had been anticipated in the budget.

6. Vandalism to the schools resulted in $3,000 of unexpected repair and cleanup costs.

7. Actual total expenditures by the general fund were $291,000.

8. Supplies on hand at year-end totaled $13,000.

9. Although no vouchers payable were outstanding at the end of 19X7, $7,000 had been encumbered for goods ordered but not yet received. The GAAP approach is used.

10. The 19X6 encumbrance for $4,600 was canceled when the goods ordered were found to be defective.

11. Cash of $7,000 was transferred to the enterprise fund.

Required:

1. Prepare all the 19X7 journal entries for the school district's general fund.

2. Prepare a 19X7 balance sheet and a statement of revenues, expenditures, and changes in fund balance for the general fund.

P16.12 Acquisition and Disposition of Fixed Assets At January 1, 19X3, the town of Bakersville compiled a current listing of its fixed assets and the means by which they were acquired. The fixed assets are shown below:

LAND	**Cost**
Site of Town Hall	$ 17,000
Site of Town Garage and Services Building	48,000
Town Park and Wildlife Preserve	160,000

BUILDINGS	
Town Hall	775,000
Garage	380,000
Services Building	625,000
Park Buildings.	63,000

EQUIPMENT	
Office Equipment	116,000
Highway Equipment	843,000
Park Equipment	102,000
Other Equipment	477,000

IMPROVEMENTS

Streets	1,755,000
Sewers and Drainage	2,416,000
Park	288,000

The land and buildings, except for those related to the park, were financed by general obligation bonds through the capital projects fund. The park land was donated by a corporation which has a large plant in Bakersville. The town then applied for and received a state grant of $250,000 to develop the park. The cost of sewers and drainage was financed by assessments to property owners. All other fixed asset costs were paid from general fund appropriations.

During 19X3, the following transactions occurred:

1. Highway equipment purchased 10 years ago at a cost of $62,000 was sold for $18,000.
2. New highway equipment costing $77,000 was purchased. An appropriation for this amount was included in the general fund budget.
3. A bond issue of $510,000 was approved to finance the construction of a youth center. Construction will begin in early 19X4.
4. Office equipment costing $2,000 was stolen and has not yet been replaced.
5. The town received a $40,000 federal grant to expand the wildlife preserve. It used the grant plus $5,000 of general fund resources to buy 200 acres of land adjoining the present site.

Required:

1. Record the transactions in the general fixed assets account group for 19X3.
2. Prepare a statement of general fixed assets as of December 31, 19X3, and a statement of changes in general fixed assets for the year.

Chapter 17 Accounting and Reporting for Nonroutine Activities of Local Government

Six funds—capital projects, special assessments, debt service, enterprise, internal service, and trust and agency—account for activities other than the routine operations of a governmental unit. Many of these activities are normal functions of government such as building schools, operating recreational facilities, and administering retirement benefits. However, they are outside the routine operating activities accounted for by the general and special revenue funds.

Recall that various types of accounting procedures are followed by these six funds. Capital projects, special assessments, and debt service funds follow fund accounting. Enterprise and internal service funds follow business accounting. Trust and agency funds follow fiduciary accounting. Each of the six and its respective accounting procedures are discussed in turn in this chapter.

Budget Formulation

Budget formulation for the six funds considered in this chapter is less involved than was the case for the general fund. Proprietary and fiduciary funds do not record budgets in the accounts and may not even require that formal budgets be adopted. Governmental funds other than the general and special revenue funds may or may not be required to prepare and record budgets, and the process of formulating and approving the budget may not be as complex as it was for the general fund. In the case of a debt service fund, for example, the budget is primarily dictated by required payments of principal and interest on debt. Thus the budget may be easily formulated by management and may not require legislative or voter approval. Budgets for the capital projects or special assessments funds, on the other hand, typically require more formal approval. The activities of these funds involve construction or acquisition of capital assets, which are usually financed by bond issues. Because these activities are discretionary, the process of formulating and approving a budget is in effect a decision as to whether these activities should be undertaken.

The Capital Projects Fund

Governmental units may finance the acquisition or construction of fixed assets in various ways. The purpose of the assets and the means of financing their purchase or construction affect the accounting and reporting for these activities. Four principal alternatives exist:

1. Relatively small acquisitions, such as a purchase of a parcel of land or items of equipment, are often financed via the budget of the general (or special revenue) fund. The acquisition expenditure is recorded in the general fund, and the asset is recorded in the general fixed assets accounts.

2. Assets acquired by a proprietary fund (an enterprise or internal service fund) are fully accounted for by that fund. For example, if the city water division issues bonds and constructs a new pumping station, the transactions, the bond liability, and the assets are all recorded in the enterprise fund.

3. Assets financed by assessments to property owners, such as sidewalks or sewers, are accounted for in a special assessments fund. The receipt of proceeds from bond issues, the expenditures for construction, the collection of the assessments from the property owners, and the bond liability and subsequent payments thereon are all reported by the special assessments fund. The assets, however, are recorded in the general fixed assets accounts.

4. Asset acquisitions or construction projects which do not fall into any of the above categories are typically handled through a capital projects fund. Bonds are usually issued to provide the financing. The transactions relating to the acquisition or construction are recorded in the capital projects fund. The assets are recorded in the general fixed assets accounts, and the bond liability is recorded in the general long-term debt accounts.

Acquisition or construction accounted for in capital projects funds may initially be financed by a temporary advance from another fund and by short-term financing known as **bond anticipation notes,** which are short-term loans from a bank or other financial institution. When the long-term bonds are issued, these temporary loans are repaid. As will be discussed later, any bond proceeds not used for the project, along with any bond premium, are then used for debt service on the bond issue. Thus the typical cash flow of a capital projects fund may be summarized as follows:

Sources of Cash	Uses of Cash
Advances from other funds Bond anticipation notes	Construction costs
Bond proceeds	Repay advances and bond anticipation notes Construction costs Interest and principal on bonds
Bond premium, if any	Interest and principal on bonds

Accounting for the Capital Projects Fund

To illustrate the accounting procedures for a capital projects fund, we shall follow through a typical project. Assume that Lake City decides to construct a new fire station. A bond issue of $500,000 is authorized to meet the expected cost of construction. If a budget entry is recorded, it appears as follows:

```
Bonds Authorized—Unissued. . . . . . . . . . . . . . . . .  500,000
    Appropriations . . . . . . . . . . . . . . . . . . . . . . .           500,000
    To record approval of project (construction of fire station).
```

Note that **Bonds Authorized—Unissued** is an *estimated revenues* account, signifying that the source of resources for the project will be the issuance of bonds.

Initial resources for the project might be temporarily advanced from another fund. This permits work to begin prior to the issuance of the bonds. Assume that, in our example, $12,000 is advanced from the general fund. The entry in the capital projects fund is:

```
Cash . . . . . . . . . . . . . . . . . . . . . . . . . . . . .  12,000
    Due to General Fund . . . . . . . . . . . . . . . . . . . .           12,000
    To record advance from general fund.
```

A parallel entry is made in the general fund.

Suppose that bids are taken for the construction of the fire station, and a contract for $495,000 is awarded to the qualified low bidder. This constitutes an encumbrance, which is recorded as:

```
Encumbrances . . . . . . . . . . . . . . . . . . . . . . . . .  495,000
    Fund Balance—Reserved for Encumbrances . . . . . . . . .           495,000
    To record award of contract for construction of fire station.
```

Bonds are often not issued until the project is complete or nearly complete. In some cases, mortgage bonds are issued, with the property constructed serving as security for the debt. Such bonds are typically not issued until the construction is complete. In other cases, the city may delay issuing the bonds in anticipation of more favorable interest rates in the future. In either case, temporary financing is needed. This temporary financing often takes the form of *bond anticipation notes*. Assume that Lake City borrows $400,000 in this way to meet construction costs of the fire station. The entry is:

```
Cash . . . . . . . . . . . . . . . . . . . . . . . . . . . . .  400,000
    Bond Anticipation Notes Payable . . . . . . . . . . . . . .           400,000
    To record temporary financing for fire station.
```

Cash not required immediately may be invested in certificates of deposit or other short-term investments:

```
Temporary Investments . . . . . . . . . . . . . . . . . . . .  175,000
    Cash . . . . . . . . . . . . . . . . . . . . . . . . . . . .           175,000
    To record purchase of certificate of deposit.
```

Assume that $200,000 of vouchers are received, representing payments due for partial completion of the contract. Encumbrances are reversed and expenditures are recorded:

```
Fund Balance—Reserved for Encumbrances . . . . . . . . . .  200,000
    Encumbrances . . . . . . . . . . . . . . . . . . . . . . .           200,000
To reverse encumbrances for amount billed by contractor.

Expenditures . . . . . . . . . . . . . . . . . . . . . . . . . .  200,000
    Vouchers Payable  . . . . . . . . . . . . . . . . . . . . .           200,000
To record billing from contractor.
```

Contracts of this type often provide that a portion of each billing may be withheld by the city until the project is completed and passes inspection. This is known as a **retainage,** which helps protect the city against failure of the contractor to complete the project or against deficiencies which need to be remedied. If the Lake City contract provides for a 20 percent retainage, the contractor will be paid $160,000, recorded as follows:

```
Vouchers Payable. . . . . . . . . . . . . . . . . . . . . . . .  160,000
    Cash . . . . . . . . . . . . . . . . . . . . . . . . . . . . .           160,000
To record payment to contractor, less 20% retainage of $40,000
(= .2 × $200,000).
```

If desired, a separate account for Vouchers Payable—Retainage could be used. Later, when the project is completed and the contractor submits a second (final) bill for $298,000, the following entries are made:

```
Fund Balance—Reserved for Encumbrances . . . . . . . . . .  295,000
    Encumbrances . . . . . . . . . . . . . . . . . . . . . . .           295,000
To reverse balance of encumbrances on project.

Expenditures . . . . . . . . . . . . . . . . . . . . . . . . . .  298,000
    Vouchers Payable  . . . . . . . . . . . . . . . . . . . . .           298,000
To record billing from contractor.
```

To pay the contractor, Lake City liquidates the temporary investments and records $6,000 of earned interest:

```
Cash . . . . . . . . . . . . . . . . . . . . . . . . . . . . . .  181,000
    Temporary Investments. . . . . . . . . . . . . . . . . . . .           175,000
    Revenues. . . . . . . . . . . . . . . . . . . . . . . . . . .             6,000
To record liquidation of temporary investments and interest
earned.
```

Legal provisions specify how the interest earned on the temporary investments may be spent. In our example, Lake City may not use the $6,000 to meet construction costs but may apply it toward the interest on the bond anticipation notes. In other words, construction costs are limited to the $500,000 originally authorized.

The contractor is paid, with 20 percent retained by the city until the building passes final inspection:

```
Vouchers Payable. . . . . . . . . . . . . . . . . . . . . . . . .   238,400
    Cash . . . . . . . . . . . . . . . . . . . . . . . . . . . .              238,400
To record payment to contractor, less 20% retainage of $59,600
(= .2 × $298,000).
```

Assume now that the bonds are issued. The face amount of the bonds is $500,000, but they are issued at a premium such that Lake City receives $510,000. Bond proceeds and bond premium are not considered revenues or liabilities of the fund. Rather, they are classified as other financing sources and are reported as such on the statement of revenues, expenditures, and changes in fund balance. Thus the entry is:

```
Cash . . . . . . . . . . . . . . . . . . . . . . . . . . . . . .   510,000
    Bond Proceeds . . . . . . . . . . . . . . . . . . . . . . . .            500,000
    Bond Premium . . . . . . . . . . . . . . . . . . . . . . . .              10,000
To record issuance of $500,000 bonds for $510,000.
```

Again, legal provisions dictate how the $10,000 premium may be spent. Generally, the premium cannot be spent on construction costs of the project. The project was authorized for $500,000, and this authorization cannot be increased by the expedient of issuing bonds at a premium. Since a premium results from the fact that the bonds bear an interest rate higher than the market rate, any premium must normally be applied toward repayment of the principal and interest on the bonds. Thus a bond premium is usually transferred to the debt service fund. Bond discounts rarely occur in this context. If bonds were issued at a discount, the proceeds would be less than the amount authorized for the project, causing a potential cash shortage. To avoid this problem, the interest rate on the bonds is set high enough so that no discount results.

The proceeds of the face amount of the bond issue are used to pay off the bond anticipation notes, to repay the advance from the general fund, and to pay remaining amounts due the contractor. After the city officials have approved the completed project, they authorize payment of the retainages to the contractor. These events are recorded as follows:

```
Bond Anticipation Notes Payable . . . . . . . . . . . . . . .   400,000
Expenditures . . . . . . . . . . . . . . . . . . . . . . . . . .     6,500
    Cash . . . . . . . . . . . . . . . . . . . . . . . . . . . .             406,500
To record repayment of bond anticipation notes, plus interest of
$6,500.

Due to General Fund . . . . . . . . . . . . . . . . . . . . . .    12,000
    Cash . . . . . . . . . . . . . . . . . . . . . . . . . . . .              12,000
To repay advance from general fund.

Vouchers Payable. . . . . . . . . . . . . . . . . . . . . . . .    99,600
    Cash . . . . . . . . . . . . . . . . . . . . . . . . . . . .              99,600
To record payment of retainages to contractor ($40,000 +
$59,600).
```

The project is complete, but the capital projects fund shows a cash balance of $11,500, representing $10,000 of bond premium and $1,500 of unspent bond proceeds. Laws or regulations usually specify that unspent bond proceeds, like the bond premium, must be transferred to the debt service fund to be used for repayment of the bonds. Thus we transfer the cash balance and close the accounts:

Operating Transfers Out	11,500	
Cash		11,500
To transfer balance to debt service fund.		
Revenues.	6,000	
Bond Proceeds	500,000	
Bond Premium	10,000	
Bonds Authorized—Unissued.		500,000
Fund Balance—Unreserved		16,000
To close revenues, bond proceeds, and bond premium.		
Appropriations.	500,000	
Fund Balance—Unreserved.	4,500	
Expenditures		504,500
To close expenditures ($504,500 = $200,000 + $298,000 + $6,500).		
Fund Balance—Unreserved.	11,500	
Operating Transfers Out		11,500
To close operating transfers out.		

Capital projects often take more than one year to complete. Because the budget is usually established at the outset for the entire project, some modification must be made to the annual closing process. The following rules for closing entries exist when the project is not complete:

1. Close Estimated Revenues only to the extent of actual Revenues and close Bonds Authorized—Unissued only to the extent of Bond Proceeds. There will be no debit or credit to Fund Balance.
2. Close Appropriations only to the extent of Expenditures and Encumbrances. There will be no debit or credit to Fund Balance.

To illustrate, assume that in January 19X1 a capital project is authorized, and the following budget entry is recorded:

Bonds Authorized—Unissued	1,000,000	
Appropriations		1,000,000
To record approval of project.		

Suppose that during 19X1 $400,000 of bonds were issued at par, that expenditures on the project were $280,000, and that $40,000 in encumbrances were outstanding. At the end of 19X1, the project is not yet complete. Closing entries at December 31, 19X1, are:

Bond Proceeds	400,000	
Bonds Authorized—Unissued.		400,000
To close bond proceeds.		

```
Appropriations. . . . . . . . . . . . . . . . . . . . . . . . . .   320,000
   Expenditures . . . . . . . . . . . . . . . . . . . . . . . . . .            280,000
   Encumbrances . . . . . . . . . . . . . . . . . . . . . . . . .              40,000
To close expenditures and encumbrances.
```

Note that no entries are made to fund balance and that $600,000 of bonds authorized but unissued and $680,000 of appropriations remain on the books for 19X2. At the beginning of 19X2, one additional entry is required to restore the open encumbrances to the accounts:

```
Encumbrances . . . . . . . . . . . . . . . . . . . . . . . . . .   40,000
   Fund Balance—Unreserved. . . . . . . . . . . . . . . . . .               40,000
To restore encumbrances closed at Dec. 31, 19X1.
```

Each capital project has a limited life. Once the project is completed and all bills are paid, any remaining resources are transferred (usually to the debt service fund). A governmental unit may, at any one time, have several projects underway. The capital projects fund, therefore, often consists of several individual project funds. Alternatively, if several projects are included in one fund, subsidiary records must be kept by project.

Interaction with Other Funds and Account Groups

Generally, activities carried on in the capital projects fund affect other funds and account groups. The interactions contained in the Lake City illustration are typical:

1. Cash was advanced from the general fund to the capital projects fund and subsequently repaid.
2. Excess cash left in the capital projects fund at the conclusion of construction was transferred to the debt service fund.
3. A building was constructed, requiring an entry in the general fixed assets account group.
4. Bonds were issued, requiring an entry in the general long-term debt account group.

The entries made in the other funds and account groups to reflect these interactions are presented in the following sections.

General Fund. The entries for the advance and subsequent repayment are straightforward:

```
Due from Capital Projects Fund. . . . . . . . . . . . . . . . .   12,000
   Cash . . . . . . . . . . . . . . . . . . . . . . . . . . . . .            12,000
To record advance to capital projects fund.

Cash . . . . . . . . . . . . . . . . . . . . . . . . . . . . . .   12,000
   Due from Capital Projects Fund. . . . . . . . . . . . . . .               12,000
To record repayment of advance.
```

Debt Service Fund. The transfer of bond premium and unspent appropriations from the capital projects fund is considered an operating transfer to the debt service fund. It is a legally authorized transfer of resources generated in one fund to another fund, where they will be spent, namely, for the payment of interest and principal on the bonds by the debt service fund. The entry is:

```
Cash . . . . . . . . . . . . . . . . . . . . . . . . . . . . . . .    11,500
    Operating Transfers In . . . . . . . . . . . . . . . . . .              11,500
To record transfer from capital projects fund.
```

General Fixed Assets Account Group. The cost of the new fire station must be recorded in the general fixed asset accounts. The cost would normally be recorded as $498,000, the amount paid to the contractor. Recall that an additional $6,500 was spent by the capital projects fund as interest on the bond anticipation notes. Although an argument can be made for the inclusion of interest as a cost of the building, common practice is to exclude it. The entry is:

```
Buildings . . . . . . . . . . . . . . . . . . . . . . . . . . .    498,000
    Investment in General Fixed Assets from
        Capital Projects Fund. . . . . . . . . . . . . . . . .              498,000
To record cost of new fire station.
```

If a capital project is only partially complete at year-end, an entry to a Construction in Progress account should be made. For example, assume that a highway project was partially complete at the end of 19X1, with a cost to date of $900,000. This would be recorded in the general fixed asset accounts as:

```
Construction in Progress . . . . . . . . . . . . . . . . . .    900,000
    Investment in General Fixed Assets from
        Capital Projects Fund. . . . . . . . . . . . . . . . .              900,000
To record 19X1 costs of highway project.
```

Suppose that the highway project is completed in 19X2 at an additional cost of $273,000. The entries in the general fixed asset accounts would be:

```
Construction in Progress . . . . . . . . . . . . . . . . . .    273,000
    Investment in General Fixed Assets from
        Capital Projects Fund. . . . . . . . . . . . . . . . .              273,000
To record 19X2 costs of highway project.

Improvements. . . . . . . . . . . . . . . . . . . . . . . . .  1,173,000
    Construction in Progress . . . . . . . . . . . . . . . . .            1,173,000
To record completion of highway project.
```

Entries to Construction in Progress may be made as individual expenditures are incurred during the period, or the account may be updated at financial statement dates. The latter approach, illustrated above, is probably more common in practice.

General Long-Term Debt Account Group. While the proceeds from the issuance of bonds were recorded by the capital projects fund, the bond liability must be recorded in the general long-term debt accounts. At the time the bonds were issued, the following entry was made:

```
Amount to Be Provided for Repayment of Bonds . . . . . . . .   500,000
    Bonds Payable . . . . . . . . . . . . . . . . . . . . . . .             500,000
To record issuance of bonds by capital projects fund for
construction of fire station.
```

Note that the premium was not recorded in the general long-term debt accounts.

Subsequently, $11,500 was transferred from the capital projects fund to the debt service fund, to be used for payment of principal and interest on the bonds. If this money will be used for interest, no entry should be made in the general long-term debt accounts. If, however, this money will be used for principal payments, this availability of resources must be reflected in the general long-term debt accounts as follows:

```
Amount Available for Repayment of Bonds . . . . . . . . . . . .   11,500
    Amount to Be Provided for Repayment of Bonds . . . . . . . .             11,500
To record resources available in debt service fund.
```

Recall that the general long-term debt accounts show the amount of resources which must be provided in future budgets in order to repay the debts. As resources are actually set aside for this purpose, they are recorded as an "amount available" and the "amount to be provided" account is reduced.

Financial Statements for the Capital Projects Fund

A balance sheet and a statement of revenues, expenditures, and changes in fund balance are commonly presented for the capital projects fund. The balance sheet of a capital projects fund would include items such as the following:

Cash	Vouchers Payable
Temporary Investments	Contracts Payable
Due from Other Funds	Due to Other Funds
	Fund Balance:
	Reserved for Encumbrances
	Unreserved

If budgetary accounts are recorded and the project is incomplete, Bonds Authorized—Unissued also appears in the asset section and Appropriations appears in the fund balance section. In the Lake City illustration, the project was completed, the accounts were closed, and the fund balance was transferred to the debt service fund. Thus the balance sheet accounts all have zero balances.

The statement of revenues, expenditures, and changes in fund balance of a

Exhibit 17.1	Illustration of Statement of Revenues, Expenditures, and Changes in Fund Balance for Capital Projects Fund

LAKE CITY
STATEMENT OF REVENUES, EXPENDITURES,
AND CHANGES IN FUND BALANCE—CAPITAL PROJECTS FUND
FOR THE YEAR ENDED DECEMBER 31, 19X0

REVENUES

Interest Earned . . . . $ 6,000

EXPENDITURES

Capital Outlay. $498,000
Interest—Temporary Financing 6,500 504,500
    Excess of Revenues over (under) Expenditures . . . . $(498,500)

OTHER FINANCING SOURCES (USES)

Bond Proceeds and Premium $510,000
Operating Transfers Out . . . . (11,500) 498,500
    Excess of Revenues and Other Sources over (under)
      Expenditures and Other Uses . . . . $ 0

Fund Balance—Jan. 1 0

Fund Balance—Dec. 31 . . . . $ 0

capital projects fund follows the format illustrated earlier for the general fund. The statement for the Lake City example appears in Exhibit 17.1.

In many cases, several capital projects funds exist at any one time. Thus a combining balance sheet and a combining statement of revenues, expenditures, and changes in fund balance are presented. Combining statements show the accounts for each capital projects fund, along with totals for all such funds.

The Special Assessments Fund

Improvements constructed by government which benefit a limited, identifiable geographical area often are financed, at least in part, by the property owners benefited. For example, installation of sidewalks in a neighborhood is often financed by assessments to property owners in that neighborhood. Projects of this nature—streets, sidewalks, sewers, street lighting—are accounted for in a special assessments fund.

To ease the financial burden on the assessed parties, assessments are often spread over several years. Because funds to pay for the project will not be available immediately, financing is needed initially to pay the costs of the project. Bonds are often issued for this purpose. Thus the typical cash flow of a special assessments fund appears as follows:

Sources of Cash	Uses of Cash
Bond proceeds	Construction costs
Collection of assessments	Interest and principal on bonds

Recall that in the capital projects fund, bond proceeds are recorded as a source of financing. This is not the case in the special assessments fund. The resources of a special assessments fund come from the assessments and any other permanent means of financing, such as a nonrepayable contribution from the general fund. The bond proceeds are recorded as a *liability* by the special assessments fund; repayment will also be recorded in this fund. The debt service fund and the general long-term debt account group are *not* used in accounting for the issuance and repayment of special assessment bonds.

Accounting for the Special Assessments Fund

To illustrate the accounting procedures for a special assessments fund, assume that Lake City is installing new street lights in a certain area. The lights are expected to cost $100,000. A 10-year serial bond issue will provide funds for construction, and residents of the affected area are to be assessed $140,000 over 10 years. A serial bond issue is, in effect, a series of individual bond issues, each due in a different year. In our example, $10,000 of bonds mature in one year, $10,000 in 2 years, and so forth. The assessments collected each year are used to pay the principal of bonds maturing that year and the interest on all outstanding bonds.

Authorization of the project may or may not be recorded. If it is, the budget entry appears as:

```
Improvements Authorized . . . . . . . . . . . . . . . . . . . . .  100,000
    Appropriations  . . . . . . . . . . . . . . . . . . . . . . . . . . .              100,000
To record approval of project (new street lighting).
```

Suppose that 6 percent, 10-year serial bonds in the amount of $100,000 are issued at a $1,000 premium. As was the case in the capital projects fund, any bond premium is generally devoted to debt repayment rather than to providing additional resources for construction. Since both construction *and* debt service are handled by the special assessments fund, it may be convenient to establish two cash accounts to enhance control. Thus the issuance of the bonds is recorded as:

```
Cash—Construction. . . . . . . . . . . . . . . . . . . . . . .  100,000
Cash—Debt Service . . . . . . . . . . . . . . . . . . . . . .    1,000
    Bonds Payable . . . . . . . . . . . . . . . . . . . . . . . . . .              100,000
    Bond Premium . . . . . . . . . . . . . . . . . . . . . . . . . .                1,000
To record issuance of 10-year, 6 percent serial bonds at 101.
```

Bids are taken on the project and a contract is awarded for $97,000. This is recorded as an encumbrance:

```
Encumbrances . . . . . . . . . . . . . . . . . . . . . . . .    97,000
    Fund Balance—Reserved for Encumbrances . . . . . . . . .          97,000
To record award of contract for street lighting.
```

The assessment of $140,000 is levied, payable over a 10-year period. As discussed earlier, this item constitutes a revenue to the special assessments fund and is recorded as:

```
Special Assessments Receivable—Current . . . . . . . . . . .    14,000
Special Assessments Receivable—Deferred . . . . . . . . . .   126,000
    Revenue . . . . . . . . . . . . . . . . . . . . . . . . .          140,000
To record assessments levied.
```

Disagreement exists over the timing of recognition of revenue from special assessments. In the above entry, revenue from the 10 years of assessments is recognized currently, to match against the current expenditures for the improvement project. An alternative view is that the amount of future assessments should be recorded initially as deferred revenue, and recognized as the assessments become due. At this writing, the matter awaits resolution by the GASB; we shall use the immediate-recognition approach in subsequent illustrations and problems.

Some months later, the contract is completed, billed, and paid. The following entries are then recorded:

```
Fund Balance—Reserved for Encumbrances . . . . . . . . . .    97,000
    Encumbrances . . . . . . . . . . . . . . . . . . . . . . .          97,000
To reverse encumbrances.

Expenditures . . . . . . . . . . . . . . . . . . . . . . . . .    97,000
    Vouchers Payable . . . . . . . . . . . . . . . . . . . . . .          97,000
To record cost of completed street lighting.

Vouchers Payable. . . . . . . . . . . . . . . . . . . . . . . .    97,000
    Cash—Construction . . . . . . . . . . . . . . . . . . . . .          97,000
To record payment of contract.
```

Since the project is complete, the remaining $3,000 from the bond proceeds is available for repayment of the bonds:

```
Cash—Debt Service . . . . . . . . . . . . . . . . . . . . . .     3,000
    Cash—Construction . . . . . . . . . . . . . . . . . . . . .           3,000
To reallocate remaining construction cash to be used for debt
service.
```

Assume that at year-end the annual assessment is collected in full and the required payment on the serial bonds is made:

```
Cash—Debt Service . . . . . . . . . . . . . . . . . . . . . . .    14,000
    Special Assessments Receivable—Current. . . . . . . . . .              14,000
To record collection of current year assessments.

Bonds Payable . . . . . . . . . . . . . . . . . . . . . . . . .    10,000
Expenditures . . . . . . . . . . . . . . . . . . . . . . . . .     6,000
    Cash—Debt Service . . . . . . . . . . . . . . . . . . . . .            16,000
To record payment of annual interest and $10,000 of principal on
bonds.
```

Closing entries can now be made in the usual manner, closing actual revenues against budgeted revenues (Improvements Authorized) and actual expenditures against appropriations:

```
Revenues. . . . . . . . . . . . . . . . . . . . . . . . . . . .   140,000
Bond Premium . . . . . . . . . . . . . . . . . . . . . . . . .     1,000
    Improvements Authorized. . . . . . . . . . . . . . . . . .            100,000
    Fund Balance—Unreserved  . . . . . . . . . . . . . . . .               41,000
To close revenues and bond premium.

Appropriations. . . . . . . . . . . . . . . . . . . . . . . . .   100,000
Fund Balance—Unreserved. . . . . . . . . . . . . . . . . .         3,000
    Expenditures . . . . . . . . . . . . . . . . . . . . . . . .           103,000
To close expenditures.
```

A fund balance of $38,000 remains. Although construction is complete, the fund will be active for 9 more years, collecting the assessments and paying the principal and interest on the bonds. No further revenues are likely to be generated, but further expenditures (interest) will be incurred, gradually reducing the fund balance. Once the activities of the fund are completed (that is, once the bonds are paid), legal requirements govern the disposition of any remaining fund balance. The final year assessment could be reduced, effectively returning any fund balance to the property owners, or the balance could be transferred to the general fund. Similarly, legal guidelines would be followed if the fund had a deficiency, as might occur if some assessments prove uncollectible.

Interaction with Other Funds and Account Groups

Transactions by a special assessments fund have limited interaction with other funds and account groups. The general fund becomes involved if it provides temporary financing or if a portion of the cost of the improvements is funded through the general fund budget. In addition, the cost of the improvements must be recorded in the general fixed assets account group. For the Lake City illustration, the entry in the *general fixed assets account group* is:

```
Improvements. . . . . . . . . . . . . . . . . . . . . . . . . .    97,000
    Investment in General Fixed Assets—Special
        Assessments Fund . . . . . . . . . . . . . . . . . . . .           97,000
To record cost of street lighting.
```

Since the special assessments fund records its own bond liability and handles its own debt service, there is no interaction with either the debt service fund or the general long-term debt account group.

Financial Statements for the Special Assessments Fund

A balance sheet and a statement of revenues, expenditures, and changes in fund balance are presented for the special assessments fund. The balance sheet typically contains the following items:

Cash—Construction	Vouchers Payable
Cash—Debt Service	Contracts Payable
Special Assessments Receivable	Special Assessments Bonds Payable
	Fund Balance:
	Reserved for Encumbrances
	Unreserved

The unreserved fund balance is often designated for use for debt service, and may be so indicated on the balance sheet. For the Lake City illustration, the balance sheet is as follows:

LAKE CITY
SPECIAL ASSESSMENTS FUND
BALANCE SHEET
DECEMBER 31, 19X0

Cash—Debt Service	$ 2,000
Special Assessments Receivable	126,000
	$128,000
Bonds Payable	$ 90,000
Fund Balance:	
Unreserved—Designated for Debt Service	38,000
	$128,000

The statement of revenues, expenditures, and changes in fund balance follows the format previously discussed. For the Lake City illustration, the statement appears as follows:

LAKE CITY
SPECIAL ASSESSMENTS FUND
STATEMENT OF REVENUES, EXPENDITURES,
AND CHANGES IN FUND BALANCE
FOR THE YEAR ENDED DECEMBER 31, 19X0

REVENUES

Special Assessments Levied		$140,000

EXPENDITURES

Capital Outlay	$97,000	
Debt Service—Interest	6,000	103,000
Excess of Revenues over Expenditures		$ 37,000

OTHER FINANCING SOURCES (USES)

Bond Premium 1,000
  Excess of Revenues and Other Sources over Expenditures and
    Other Uses . . . . $ 38,000

Fund Balance—Jan. 1 0
Fund Balance—Dec. 31 . . . . $ 38,000

As was the case with capital projects funds, several special assessments funds may exist, in which case combining statements are also presented.

The Debt Service Fund

Accounting treatment of long-term debt in governmental accounting depends in part on the source of cash used for repayment, the entity (fund) making the payment, and the fund incurring the debt. Debt may be recorded in the accounts of the originating fund or in the general long-term debt account group. The primary role of the debt service fund is to receive cash from other funds and to use it either (1) to make current payments of principal and interest to debtholders or (2) to invest resources which are to be used for future principal payments.

A summary of the treatment of debt in governmental accounting is presented in Exhibit 17.2. Long-term debt incurred by an enterprise, internal service, trust and agency, or special assessments fund is recorded as a liability in those funds rather than in the general long-term debt accounts. Resources to repay the debt are generated by the operations of the related funds. Thus payments of principal and interest are usually made directly by those funds to the bondholders. The debt

---

Exhibit 17.2 **Accounting for Long-Term Debt by Various Funds**

Long-Term Debt Incurred by	Where Liability Is Recorded	Source of Resources to Repay Debt	Payment Made from
Special assessments fund	Special assessments fund	Assessments on property owners	Special assessments fund
Enterprise or internal service fund	Specific fund (enterprise or internal service)	Revenues from operations	Specific fund
Trust fund	Trust fund	Income of trust fund	Trust fund
General, special revenue, or capital projects fund	General long-term debt accounts	Provision in general fund budget Special tax levies Bond premium Proceeds of bond issue not spent on project	Debt service fund

service fund is not used for payments on such debt, unless the governmental unit deems it particularly convenient to make all debt payments from a single fund. In such a case, the enterprise, internal service, trust and agency, and special assessments funds would transfer money to the debt service fund, which in turn would pay the bondholders.

Long-term debt incurred by the general, special revenue, and capital projects funds is recorded as a liability in the general long-term debt accounts. Resources to repay the debt come primarily from the general fund budget, although special tax levies for debt retirement are also possible. As was illustrated earlier in the chapter, some resources for debt payment may be provided by bond premiums and unspent appropriations on capital projects. Payments on debt incurred by the general, special revenue, and capital projects funds are typically made through the debt service fund. In the following discussion, we assume the most common case—that the debt service fund handles payments on *general obligation debt* only and not on the debt of the special assessments, enterprise, internal service, and trust and agency funds. The typical components of a debt service fund's cash flow are shown next:

Sources of Cash	Uses of Cash
Transfers from general fund (budgetary appropriations for debt service) Transfers from special revenue fund (proceeds of any special tax levies for debt service) Transfers from capital projects fund (bond premium and unspent appropriations) Earnings on investments Liquidation of investments	Current payments of interest and principal on general obligation debt Investment for future principal payments

Accounting for the Debt Service Fund

Because the debt service fund employs fund accounting techniques, a budget for estimated revenues and appropriations *may* be recorded in the accounts but does not have to be, since the budget is usually the result of managerial design rather than a legal approval process. Resources of a debt service fund come from transfers from other funds and earnings on investments. Two estimated revenue accounts are used: **Required Additions** signifies the amount of transfers to be made from the general or special revenue funds (transfers from the capital projects fund are difficult to estimate and thus are often not budgeted), and **Required Earnings** signifies the estimated income from investments. Since the debt service fund is used to accumulate resources for future debt payment, annual appropriations usually differ from annual estimated revenues. In years in which resources are being accumulated toward future debt payments, appropriations will be less than estimated revenues; in years in which an accumulation is expended, appropriations will exceed estimated revenues.

To illustrate the sequence of entries, assume that Lake City establishes a debt service fund to make annual interest payments on a 5 percent, $500,000 general obligation bond issue and to accumulate resources for the future retirement of principal. A transfer of $50,000 to the debt service fund is appropriated in the general fund budget, and investment income for the year is estimated to be $2,700. The only planned expenditure is the $25,000 interest payment on the bonds. The budget entry for the debt service fund is:

```
Required Additions  . . . . . . . . . . . . . . . . . . . . . . . .  50,000
Required Earnings. . . . . . . . . . . . . . . . . . . . . . . . . .   2,700
    Appropriations. . . . . . . . . . . . . . . . . . . . . . . .            25,000
    Fund Balance—Unreserved. . . . . . . . . . . . . . . . .                 27,700
To record budget.
```

Assume that early in the year the $50,000 transfer is received from the general fund and is immediately invested in time deposits, government bonds, or other appropriate securities.

```
Cash . . . . . . . . . . . . . . . . . . . . . . . . . . . . . . . .  50,000
    Operating Transfers In . . . . . . . . . . . . . . . . . . . .            50,000
To record transfer from general fund.

Investments . . . . . . . . . . . . . . . . . . . . . . . . . . . .  50,000
    Cash . . . . . . . . . . . . . . . . . . . . . . . . . . . . . .          50,000
To record purchase of investments.
```

Later in the year, the interest payment on the bonds becomes due. Securities which had cost $24,000 are liquidated for $25,000, and the interest payment is made:

```
Cash . . . . . . . . . . . . . . . . . . . . . . . . . . . . . . . .  25,000
    Investments . . . . . . . . . . . . . . . . . . . . . . . . . .           24,000
    Revenues . . . . . . . . . . . . . . . . . . . . . . . . . . . .           1,000
To record liquidation of securities costing $24,000.

Expenditures . . . . . . . . . . . . . . . . . . . . . . . . . . .  25,000
    Cash . . . . . . . . . . . . . . . . . . . . . . . . . . . . . .          25,000
To record payment of bond interest.
```

If, at year-end, interest accrued on investments is $1,500, and $11,500 of bond premium and unspent appropriations are transferred from the capital projects fund, the following entries are made:

```
Investments . . . . . . . . . . . . . . . . . . . . . . . . . . . .   1,500
    Revenues . . . . . . . . . . . . . . . . . . . . . . . . . . . .           1,500
To record earnings on investments.

Cash . . . . . . . . . . . . . . . . . . . . . . . . . . . . . . . .  11,500
    Operating Transfers In . . . . . . . . . . . . . . . . . . . .            11,500
To record transfer from capital projects fund.
```

Despite the use of the modified accrual method for all governmental funds, interest on long-term debt is *not* accrued by the debt service fund. Rather it is recorded as an expenditure in the year in which the payment is made. Year-end closing entries are:

Operating Transfers In	61,500	
Revenues	2,500	
Required Additions		50,000
Required Earnings		2,700
Fund Balance—Unreserved.		11,300
To close revenues and operating transfers in.		

Appropriations.	25,000	
Expenditures		25,000
To close expenditures.		

After the closing entries, the accounts show cash of \$11,500, investments of \$27,500, and an unreserved fund balance of \$39,000. The unreserved fund balance is designated for debt service.

Interaction with Other Funds and Account Groups

Several transactions of a debt service fund involve other funds and account groups. The two major interactions are: (1) transfers to the debt service fund must be recorded by the fund making the transfer and (2) the accumulation of resources available for repayment of debt must be noted in the general long-term debt accounts.

In our illustration, there were two transfers to Lake City's debt service fund. The transfer from the *general fund* is recorded on the general fund books as:

Operating Transfers Out.	50,000	
Cash		50,000
To record transfer of appropriated contribution to debt service fund.		

Similarly, the entry for the transfer from the *capital projects fund* is recorded in that fund as:

Operating Transfers Out.	11,500	
Cash		11,500
To record transfer of bond premium and unspent appropriations to debt service fund.		

At year-end, the debt service fund had accumulated \$39,000. If this amount will be used for the future repayment of bond principal, it is recorded in the *general long-term debt account group* as:

Amount Available for Repayment of Bonds	39,000	
Amount to Be Provided for Repayment of Bonds		39,000
To record amounts available in debt service fund.		

Financial Statements for the Debt Service Fund

A balance sheet and a statement of revenues, expenditures, and changes in fund balance are typically presented for the debt service fund. The balance sheet for the Lake City illustration appears as follows:

LAKE CITY
DEBT SERVICE FUND
BALANCE SHEET
DECEMBER 31, 19X0

Cash	$11,500	Fund Balance:
Investments	27,500	Unreserved—Designated for Debt
	$39,000	Service $39,000

The statement of revenues, expenditures, and changes in fund balance appears as shown below:

LAKE CITY
DEBT SERVICE FUND
STATEMENT OF REVENUES, EXPENDITURES,
AND CHANGES IN FUND BALANCE
FOR THE YEAR ENDED DECEMBER 31, 19X0

REVENUES

Earnings on Investments.	$ 2,500

EXPENDITURES

Debt Service—Interest.	25,000
Excess of Revenues over (under) Expenditures.	$(22,500)

OTHER FINANCING SOURCES (USES)

Operating Transfers In.	61,500
Excess of Revenues and Other Sources over (under) Expenditures and Other Uses.	$ 39,000
Fund Balance—Jan. 1.	0
Fund Balance—Dec. 31.	$ 39,000

The Enterprise and Internal Service Funds

Enterprise funds are used to account for governmental operations that are financed and operated in a manner similar to private business enterprise, that is, where the costs of providing goods or services to the general public on a continuing basis are to be recovered primarily through user charges. In addition, an enterprise fund may be used in any circumstance where income determination is appropriate for capital maintenance, public policy, management control, accountability, or other purposes.[1] Typical activities for which enterprise funds are used include:

---

[1]National Council on Governmental Accounting, *Statement 1,* ''Governmental Accounting and Financial Reporting Principles'' (Chicago: Municipal Finance Officers Association of the United States and Canada, 1979), 7.

1. Utilities—municipal water, gas, and electricity.
2. Sanitation—sewer systems.
3. Recreational facilities—golf courses, marinas, swimming pools, tennis courts, and stadiums.
4. Commercial facilities—airports, ports, and farmers' markets.
5. Transportation facilities—bus, rapid transit, and toll bridges.
6. Public hospitals and health clinics.
7. Public housing projects.

In addition to user charges, these activities are often subsidized by general governmental revenues. The principal source of revenue usually determines whether the activity is accounted for in an enterprise fund or in the general fund. If the majority of the activity's revenue is generated by charges to users, the activity should be accounted for in an enterprise fund; otherwise, it should be accounted for in the general fund.

Internal service funds account for goods or services provided by one department or agency of the governmental unit to another, on a cost reimbursement basis.[2] Centralized service functions are the most common examples, including activities such as:

1. Central maintenance and repair services.
2. Central vehicle pool.
3. Central supply facilities.
4. Central print shop.
5. Central computer services.

Such activities are centralized so that cost savings may be realized through more efficient use of equipment, volume purchasing, and other economies of scale. The internal service fund pays the cost of operating the central service facility and sets user charges so as to produce sufficient revenues to recover costs.

Accounting and Reporting for Enterprise and Internal Service Funds

Enterprise funds and internal service funds employ the same accounting practices as do business entities. This means that they use full accrual accounting, distinguish between capital and expense items, and recognize depreciation on fixed assets.

The financial statements of enterprise and internal service funds are patterned after the financial statements of a business firm. The balance sheet has the same accounts and structure as a business balance sheet, with a minor exception in the equity section. While an enterprise or internal service fund has no capital stock and no stockholders, it is likely to have contributed capital, usually from

---

[2]Ibid.

the general fund. Thus there will be differences in terminology, but not in substance. Typical owners' equity items are shown below:

Business Firm	Enterprise or Internal Service Fund
Stockholders' Equity: Common Stock Paid-In Capital Retained Earnings	Fund Balance: Capital Contributed by General Fund Retained Earnings

In addition, a statement of revenues, expenses, and changes in retained earnings and a statement of changes in financial position are presented. These also are very similar to the business counterparts. They are illustrated in Exhibits 17.4 and 17.5, following the discussion of trust funds. Because the same statement format is used by both enterprise or internal service funds and trust and agency funds, a single set of illustrations suffices.

The Trust and Agency Funds

Trust and agency funds, while commonly combined, consist of two distinct elements: trust funds and agency funds. Although both involve resources collected, held, and paid out by the unit acting as a fiduciary, there are differences in terms of the purpose and duration of the fiduciary responsibility.

Agency Funds

Agency funds account for situations in which the governmental unit acts as collection agent for another entity. The two most common situations are employee deductions and tax collections. Deductions of various types (for example, federal and state taxes, health insurance, retirement contributions, union dues, payroll savings) are taken from the earnings of employees and periodically remitted on behalf of the employees to appropriate entities. In the case of tax collections, one governmental unit may collect taxes on behalf of another. For example, a state may collect income taxes or sales taxes on behalf of a city or county. A county may collect property taxes on behalf of other legal entities (cities, towns, or special districts) within its jurisdiction. In both situations, the resources are likely to be held for only a short time by the agency fund.

Accounting for Agency Funds. The majority of transactions of an agency fund fall into two categories: collection and payment. The entries for these two transaction types are straightforward. A collection requires a debit to cash and a credit to an appropriate liability account; a payment requires a debit to the liability and a credit to cash. Since most transactions involve the creation or settlement of a liability, we rarely find revenues or expenditures in an agency fund, and consequently an agency fund has little or no fund balance.

Trust Funds

Trust funds are used when the governmental unit holds, manages, and spends resources under terms of a trust agreement. Two general types exist. One type, often called a **nonexpendable trust fund,** requires that the principal be maintained intact and that the income be spent for a particular purpose. Examples include an endowment fund for the public library or a scholarship fund for students. The other type, called an **expendable trust fund,** does not maintain a distinction between principal and income; all resources of the fund may be spent for the specified purpose. A retirement (pension) fund is a common example. The fund receives resources from the local government, perhaps from the employees, and from earnings on investments. These resources are then used to pay retirement benefits. Note that, in contrast to agency funds, both types of trust funds normally hold resources for long periods of time.

Accounting for Trust Funds. Nonexpendable trust funds use the principles of fiduciary accounting outlined in Chapter 4. Distinction must be maintained between principal and income, resulting in reserved and unreserved fund balance accounts. To illustrate, assume that Lake City receives a $25,000 gift from a wealthy citizen, with the provision that the money be invested and income be used to purchase books for the library. The gift is credited to revenue and is closed to a reserved fund balance account to indicate the restriction on its spending. The entries are:

```
Cash . . . . . . . . . . . . . . . . . . . . . . . . . . . . . . . . . . .  25,000
    Revenues . . . . . . . . . . . . . . . . . . . . . . . . . . . . . .              25,000
To record endowment for library.

Investments . . . . . . . . . . . . . . . . . . . . . . . . . . . . . .  25,000
    Cash . . . . . . . . . . . . . . . . . . . . . . . . . . . . . . . .              25,000
To record investment of library endowment funds.
```

Assume that during the remainder of the year $1,300 is earned on the investments, and $1,050 is spent to acquire library books.

```
Cash . . . . . . . . . . . . . . . . . . . . . . . . . . . . . . . . . .  1,300
    Revenues . . . . . . . . . . . . . . . . . . . . . . . . . . . . . .              1,300
To record earnings on investments.

Expenditures . . . . . . . . . . . . . . . . . . . . . . . . . . . . .  1,050
    Cash . . . . . . . . . . . . . . . . . . . . . . . . . . . . . . . .              1,050
To record purchase of library books.
```

Closing entries would show an increase in the reserved fund balance of $25,000 and an increase in the unreserved fund balance of $250. Since the latter amount can be spent, it must be distinguished from the nonexpendable portion of the balance.

```
Revenues . . . . . . . . . . . . . . . . . . . . . . . . . . . . . 26,300
  Expenditures . . . . . . . . . . . . . . . . . . . . . . . . .          1,050
  Fund Balance—Reserved for Endowment. . . . . . . . . . . .          25,000
  Fund Balance—Unreserved. . . . . . . . . . . . . . . . . .              250
To close revenues and expenditures.
```

Expendable trust funds may require only a single unreserved fund balance account or may also use reserves to signify the purpose for which the resources are held. In a pension fund, for example, an account entitled "Fund Balance—Reserved for Retirement Pensions" may be used. Transactions in an expendable trust fund typically involve revenues, expenditures, and investment activities. These present few accounting problems. Consider, for example, a fire fighters' pension fund administered by a city. Employer contributions, employee contributions, and earnings on investments are all recorded as revenues. Payment of benefits to retirees or refunds of contributions to individuals leaving the system are recorded as expenditures.

Financial Statements for Trust and Agency Funds

Balance sheets are presented for both trust funds and agency funds. Beyond this, the statements differ. Since agency funds have few, if any, revenue and expenditure transactions, and hence little or no fund balance, a statement of revenues, expenditures, and changes in fund balance is not used. Rather, a **statement of changes in assets and liabilities** is used to show the agency fund's activity during the year. This statement is illustrated in Exhibit 17.3.

Trust funds, like proprietary funds, measure net income and changes in financial position. The statement of revenues, expenses, and changes in fund balance is illustrated in Exhibit 17.4 (on page 904), and the statement of changes in financial position is illustrated in Exhibit 17.5 (on page 905).

The Comprehensive Annual Financial Report

The principal financial report of a local governmental unit is known as a **comprehensive annual financial report (CAFR).** Two broad types of financial statements are included in the CAFR. One type is combined statements. **Combined statements,** as the name suggests, bring together information on several funds. The purpose is to provide an overview of the financial affairs of the governmental unit by combining some or all of the economic entities that comprise the unit. The following combined statements are presented:

1. Combined balance sheet covering all funds and account groups.
2. Combined statement of revenue, expenditures, and changes in fund balance for all *governmental* funds.
3. Budgetary comparison statements for the *general* and *special revenue* funds, and for any other *governmental* funds for which annual budgets have been legally adopted.
4. Combined statement of revenues, expenses, and changes in retained earnings for all *proprietary* funds.

Exhibit 17.3	**Agency Fund Statement of Changes in Assets and Liabilities**

NAME OF GOVERNMENTAL UNIT
COMBINING STATEMENT OF CHANGES IN ASSETS
AND LIABILITIES—ALL AGENCY FUNDS
FOR THE FISCAL YEAR ENDED DECEMBER 31, 19X2

	Balance Jan. 1, 19X2	Additions	Deductions	Balance Dec. 31, 19X2
SPECIAL PAYROLL FUND				
ASSETS				
Cash.	$ 6,000	$ 40,900	$ 43,550	$ 3,350
LIABILITIES				
Vouchers Payable	$ 6,000	$ 40,900	$ 43,550	$ 3,350
PROPERTY TAX FUND				
ASSETS				
Cash.	$ 25,800	$ 800,000	$ 725,000	$100,800
Taxes Receivable (Net of Allowances for Uncollectibles)	174,200	1,205,800	800,000	580,000
Total Assets	$200,000	$2,005,800	$1,525,000	$680,800
LIABILITIES				
Due to Other Taxing Units:				
County	$180,000	$1,085,220	$ 652,500	$612,720
Special District	20,000	120,580	72,500	68,080
Total Liabilities.	$200,000	$1,205,800	$ 725,000	$680,800
STUDENT ACTIVITY FUND				
ASSETS				
Cash.	$ 1,600	$ 1,900	$ 1,650	$ 1,850
LIABILITIES				
Due to Student Groups	$ 1,600	$ 1,900	$ 1,650	$ 1,850
TOTALS—ALL AGENCY FUNDS				
ASSETS				
Cash.	$ 33,400	$ 842,800	$ 770,200	$106,000
Taxes Receivable (Net of Allowance for Uncollectibles)	174,200	1,205,800	800,000	580,000
Total Assets	$207,600	$2,048,600	$1,570,200	$686,000
LIABILITIES				
Vouchers Payable	$ 6,000	$ 40,900	$ 43,550	$ 3,350
Due to Other Taxing Units	200,000	1,205,800	725,000	680,800
Due to Student Groups	1,600	1,900	1,650	1,850
Total Liabilities.	$207,600	$1,248,600	$ 770,200	$686,000

Exhibit 17.4 | **Proprietary and Trust Funds Statements**

NAME OF GOVERNMENTAL UNIT
COMBINED STATEMENT OF REVENUES, EXPENSES, AND CHANGES IN
RETAINED EARNINGS/FUND BALANCES
ALL PROPRIETARY FUND TYPES AND SIMILAR TRUST FUNDS
FOR THE FISCAL YEAR ENDED DECEMBER 31, 19X2

	Proprietary Fund Types		Fiduciary Fund Types		Totals (Memorandum Only)	
	Enterprise	Internal Service	Nonexpendable Trust	Pension Trust	Dec. 31, 19X2	Dec. 31, 19X1
Operating Revenues:						
Charges for Services	$ 672,150	$88,000	$ —	$ —	$ 760,150	$ 686,563
Interest	—	—	2,480	28,460	30,940	26,118
Contributions	—	—	—	160,686	160,686	144,670
Gifts	—	—	45,000	—	45,000	—
Total Operating Revenues	$ 672,150	$88,000	$ 47,480	$ 189,146	$ 996,776	$ 857,351
Operating Expenses:						
Personal Services	$ 247,450	$32,500	—	—	$ 279,950	$ 250,418
Contractual Services	75,330	400	—	—	75,730	68,214
Supplies	20,310	1,900	—	—	22,210	17,329
Materials	50,940	44,000	—	—	94,940	87,644
Heat, Light, and Power	26,050	1,500	—	—	27,550	22,975
Depreciation	144,100	4,450	—	—	148,550	133,210
Benefit Payments	—	—	—	21,000	21,000	12,000
Refunds	—	—	—	25,745	25,745	13,243
Total Operating Expenses	$ 564,180	$84,750	—	$ 46,745	$ 695,675	$ 605,033
Operating Income	$ 107,970	$ 3,250	$ 47,480	$ 142,401	$ 301,101	$ 252,318
Nonoperating Revenues (Expenses):						
Operating Grants	$ 55,000	—	—	—	$ 55,000	$ 50,000
Interest Revenue	3,830	—	—	—	3,830	3,200
Rent	5,000	—	—	—	5,000	5,000
Interest Expense and Fiscal Charges	(92,988)	—	—	—	(92,988)	(102,408)
Total Nonoperating Revenues (Expenses)	$ (29,158)	—	—	—	$ (29,158)	$ (44,208)
Income before Operating Transfers	$ 78,812	$ 3,250	$ 47,480	$ 142,401	$ 271,943	$ 208,110
Operating Transfers In (Out)	—	—	(2,530)	—	(2,530)	(2,120)
Net Income	$ 78,812	$ 3,250	$ 44,950	$ 142,401	$ 269,413	$ 205,990
Retained Earnings/Fund Balances—Jan. 1.	2,088,544	6,550	139,100	1,040,800	3,274,994	3,069,004
Retained Earnings/Fund Balances—Dec. 31	$2,167,356	$ 9,800	$184,050	$1,183,201	$3,544,407	$3,274,994

Source: Reproduced with permission from National Council for Governmental Accounting, *Statement 1*, "Governmental Accounting and Financial Reporting Principles" (Chicago: Municipal Finance Officers Association of the United States and Canada, 1979), 36. © Copyright 1979 by Municipal Finance Officers Association of the United States and Canada.

---

5. Combined statement of changes in financial position for all *proprietary* funds.

Fiduciary funds are typically included either with the governmental funds (in No. 2) or the proprietary funds (in Nos. 4 and 5), although a separate combined statement may be prepared for the fiduciary funds.

Exhibit 17.5 Statement of Changes in Financial Position—Proprietary and Trust Funds

NAME OF GOVERNMENTAL UNIT
COMBINED STATEMENT OF CHANGES IN
FINANCIAL POSITION—ALL PROPRIETARY FUND TYPES AND SIMILAR TRUST FUNDS
FOR THE FISCAL YEAR ENDED DECEMBER 31, 19X2

	Proprietary Fund Types		Fiduciary Fund Types		Totals (Memorandum Only)	
	Enterprise	Internal Service	Nonexpendable Trust	Pension Trust	Dec. 31, 19X2	Dec. 31, 19X1
SOURCES OF WORKING CAPITAL						
Operations:						
Net Income	$ 78,812	$ 3,250	$44,950	$142,401	$ 269,413	$ 205,990
Items Not Requiring (Providing) Working Capital: Depreciation	144,100	4,450	—	—	148,550	133,210
Working Capital Provided by Operations	$ 222,912	$ 7,700	$44,950	$142,401	$ 417,963	$ 339,200
Cash from Revenue Bond Construction Account	127,883	—	—	—	127,883	743,800
Contributions	672,666	—	—	—	672,666	—
Total Sources of Working Capital	$1,023,461	$ 7,700	$44,950	$142,401	$1,218,512	$1,083,000
USES OF WORKING CAPITAL						
Acquisition of Property, Plant, and Equipment	$ 324,453	$ 7,000	—	—	$ 331,453	$ 842,812
Retirement of General Obligation Bonds	50,000	—	—	—	50,000	50,000
Retirement of Revenue Bonds Payable	52,000	—	—	—	52,000	48,000
Repayment of Advance from General Fund	—	10,000	—	—	10,000	10,000
Net Decrease in Other Current Liabilities Payable from Restricted Assets	8,946	—	—	—	8,946	4,318
Net Increase in Other Restricted Assets	1,624	—	—	—	1,624	414
Total Uses of Working Capital	$ 437,023	$ 17,000	—	—	$ 454,023	$ 955,544
Net Increase (Decrease) in Working Capital	$ 586,438	$ (9,300)	$44,950	$142,401	$ 764,489	$ 127,456
ELEMENTS OF THE NET INCREASE (DECREASE) IN WORKING CAPITAL						
Cash	$ 119,276	$(20,300)	$ 4,310	$ 20,121	$ 123,407	$ 796,412
Investments	—	—	45,640	118,341	163,981	(84,286)
Receivables (Net of Allowances for Uncollectibles)	(5,570)	—	(5,000)	—	(10,570)	2,396
Due from Other Funds	(6,000)	(8,000)	—	2,189	(11,811)	(4,923)
Inventory of Supplies	11,250	14,000	—	—	25,250	(3,414)
Prepaid Expenses	460	—	—	—	460	520
Vouchers Payable	(72,471)	5,000	—	—	(67,471)	(42,427)
Contracts Payable	551,653	—	—	1,750	553,403	(525,400)
Accrued Liabilities	(12,160)	—	—	—	(12,160)	(11,422)
Net Increase (Decrease) in Working Capital	$ 586,438	$ (9,300)	$44,950	$142,401	$ 764,489	$ 127,456

Source: Reproduced with permission from National Council for Governmental Accounting. *Statement 1*, "Governmental Accounting and Financial Reporting Principles" (Chicago: Municipal Finance Officers Association of the United States and Canada, 1979), 38. © Copyright 1979 by Municipal Finance Officers Association of the United States and Canada.

A *combined* statement is different from a *consolidated* statement. A consolidated statement is based on the principle that one economic entity exists. To prepare a consolidated statement, transactions and relationships among the component entities are eliminated. For a combined statement, however, no eliminations are made. Several economic entities continue to exist but are reported together.

The second broad type of financial statement included in the CAFR is individual or combining statements. **Individual statements** are presented for the two *account groups*—general fixed assets and general long-term debt—and for any of the eight fund types containing only *one* fund account. **Combining statements** are presented where the governmental unit has *more than one* fund of a given type. For example, if three capital projects funds exist, a combining statement would show the accounts of each of the three along with totals.

In addition to these two sets of statements, the CAFR contains the independent auditor's report, notes to the financial statements, schedules providing further details on statement data, and statistical information, such as 10-year summaries of key accounting and tax data.

Thus the comprehensive annual financial report resolves the problem of presenting financial data on a governmental unit consisting of numerous economic entities by presenting two sets of statements. Combined statements focus on the overall status of the governmental unit, while individual and combining statements focus on the individual entities.

Disclosure

Disclosure by local government has lagged significantly behind disclosure by business firms. A research study[3] published in 1976 by Coopers & Lybrand and the University of Michigan, covering 46 cities, reported that compliance with then-existing disclosure requirements was seriously deficient. Selected findings of this study are as follows:

Disclosure Requirement	Percent of Cities Not Complying
Disclosure of any excess of value of vested pension benefits over annual pension fund resources plus accruals	76%
Disclosure of accrued vacation and sick leave by employees	84
Disclosure of information on noncapitalized lease commitments	93
Disclosure of significant accounting policies	46

The revision of *GAAFR* in 1979 clarified the disclosure requirements for local government. Disclosure involves three components of the CAFR: notes to the financial statements, narrative information, and statistical tables. Notes to the financial statements must contain information necessary for fair presentation at the combined statements level, such as:

---

[3]Coopers & Lybrand and The University of Michigan, *Financial Disclosure Practices of the American Cities: A Public Report* (New York: Coopers & Lybrand, 1976), 30–33.

1. Summary of significant accounting policies.
2. Pension plan obligations.
3. Accumulated unpaid employee benefits.
4. Debt service requirements to maturity.
5. Contingent liabilities and commitments such as noncapitalized leases and construction contracts.
6. Interfund receivables and payables.
7. Material violations of finance-related legal or contractual provisions.

Narrative information includes a description of the nature and purpose of the various funds, and such other information as may be required to understand the individual or combining statements. Statistical tables typically cover several years and include nonaccounting data. Examples of statistical tables include:

1. General government expenditures by function and revenues by source—last 10 years.
2. Property tax levies and collections—last 10 years.
3. Assessed property values and tax rates—last 10 years.
4. Legal debt limit.
5. Demographic statistics.

Summary of Key Concepts

The nonroutine activities of a local government are handled through six special entities: the capital projects, special assessments, debt service, enterprise, internal service, and trust and agency funds.

The **capital projects, special assessments,** and **debt service funds** are **governmental funds.** They use the modified accrual basis of accounting and the other fund accounting procedures. However, budgetary accounting is less important for these funds than for the general and special revenue funds.

The **enterprise** and **internal service funds** are **proprietary funds.** Their transactions, accounting, and financial statements closely parallel those for business firms.

The **trust and agency funds** are **fiduciary funds.** A combination of fiduciary accounting and fund accounting is employed.

Many transactions affect more than one fund or account group. Consideration of these **interactions** is very important in governmental accounting.

The **comprehensive annual financial report** of a local governmental unit presents both **combined statements,** which give an overview of the financial affairs of the entire governmental unit, and **individual or combining statements** for each fund type and account group.

Appendix to
Chapter 17

Accounting by State and Federal Governments

Accounting by State Government

Accounting and reporting principles for state government are less well developed than those for local government. There are many fewer units—50 states compared to thousands of counties, cities, towns, villages, and school districts. While local government reports are routinely submitted to the states, states are not required to report to the federal government. Each state's financial report is directed to the citizens of the state. Moreover, a given state's system has evolved from its particular laws, regulations, and historical practices. As a result, there is considerable variety in state accounting and reporting. In an effort to move toward uniformity, the Council of State Governments has been collecting information on current practices[4] and working on the development of suggested accounting practices for state government.[5]

State government accounting tends to be similar to local government accounting. There is no separate body of generally accepted accounting principles for state government. The fund system and related accounting principles described in this chapter are generally applicable to state government. Several of the recommendations of the State Government Accounting Project were adopted by the NCGA and incorporated into its pronouncements. Therefore, we shall not discuss the mechanics of accounting and reporting at the state level. We shall, however, briefly discuss the entity issue.

As is the case in local government, state government consists of a variety of subunits. In addition to the usual offices and agencies of the executive, legislative, and judicial branches of the state, there are also various boards, institutions (such as state hospitals and universities), and authorities (such as bridge or port authorities). Some of these may be semiautonomous in that their management possesses such powers as the ability to issue bonds. For financial reporting purposes, it must be determined whether each of these subunits is a separate entity or a component of the state entity. The Council of State Governments offers this entity definition:

---

[4]Relmond Van Daniker and Kay Pohlmann, *Inventory of Current State Government Accounting and Reporting Practices* (Lexington, KY: Council of State Governments, 1980).
[5]Relmond P. Van Daniker and Kay T. Pohlmann, *Preferred Accounting Practices for State Governments* (Lexington, KY: Council of State Governments, 1983).

The reporting entity for general purpose financial reports of state government requires the inclusion of any governmental department, agency, institution, commission, or other governmental organization for which the elected state officials have oversight responsibility. Oversight responsibility is derived from the state's power and includes, but is not limited to: selection of governing authority, designation of management, ability to significantly influence operations, accountability for fiscal matters, or scope of public service. Oversight responsibility, in general, implies that a governmental unit is dependent on another and the dependent unit should be disclosed in the financial reports as part of the other entity.[6]

If at least one of the five indicators of state oversight responsibility mentioned in the above definition is clearly present, the unit in question will be considered as part of the state for reporting purposes.

Accounting by the Federal Government

Accounting at the federal level differs in several ways from state and local government accounting. In this section, we discuss the financial organization and operations of the federal government and illustrate the recording of transactions by a governmental agency.[7]

Financial Organization

As is generally true of government at any level, the budgeting process is the first step in the sequence of financial operations for the federal government. The executive branch prepares a budget request and submits it to Congress. Following hearings and deliberation, Congress adopts a budget, which the president may sign or veto. This process involves both a general budget resolution and individual appropriation bills (budgets for individual activities). Once a budget is approved, various agencies are involved in its administration and other aspects of the financial management of the government. We shall briefly discuss each agency.[8]

Office of Management and Budget. The Office of Management and Budget (OMB) was established in 1970 as the successor to the Bureau of the Budget. Its major functions are:

1. To assist the president in the preparation of the budget and the formulation of the fiscal program of the government.
2. To supervise and control administration of the budget.
3. To assist the president in his effort to develop and maintain effective gov-

---

[6]Ibid., 39.

[7]For an extensive coverage of federal government accounting, see Cornelius E. Tierney, *Handbook of Federal Accounting Practices* (Reading, MA: Addison-Wesley, 1982).

[8]The agency descriptions are drawn from "Financial Management Functions in the Federal Government," published by the Joint Financial Management Improvement Program (sponsored by various federal agencies), August 1979.

ernment by reviewing the organizational structures and management procedures of the executive branch to assure that they are capable of producing the intended results.

4. To evaluate the performance of federal programs and to serve as a catalyst in the effort to improve interagency and intergovernmental cooperation and coordination.

5. To assist the president by clearing and coordinating departmental advice on proposed legislation and recommendations for presidential action on bills passed by Congress.

6. To assist in the consideration, clearance, and, where necessary, the preparation of executive orders and proclamations.

7. To help develop regulatory reform proposals and programs for paperwork reduction.

8. To keep the president advised of the progress of activities by agencies with respect to those proposed, actually initiated, and completed. This, together with the relative timing of interagency activities, is necessary to assure that programs are coordinated and that money appropriated by Congress is spent effectively, with the least possible overlapping and duplication.

9. To provide overall direction of procurement policies, regulations, and procedures for executive agencies.

The OMB is headed by a director, a position which is viewed as cabinet level.

Department of the Treasury. The Department of the Treasury has existed since 1789. Its head, the Secretary of the Treasury, has general responsibility for managing the government's finances. These responsibilities fall into two main areas: financial and accounting. In operating the federal financial system, the Department of the Treasury's major functions are:

1. As the nation's treasurer, the department receives and disburses funds. Bank accounts are maintained at the Federal Reserve Bank and at thousands of private banks throughout the country.

2. The department is the agency responsible for borrowing money necessary to meet operating obligations and for coordinating the debt activities of various federal agencies.

3. The department is the federal government's banker. Although it operates through the private and Federal Reserve banks, checks are actually drawn on the U.S. Treasury. In addition, reconciliation functions are performed by the Treasury Department.

4. The department is responsible for the physical production of money. It operates the Bureau of Engraving and Printing, which produces paper currency, and the Bureau of the Mint, which produces coin.

In addition to these financial functions, the Treasury maintains central accounting records on the government's financial transactions. These central accounts do not constitute a complete general ledger of all the government's assets and liabilities; rather they reflect those assets and liabilities directly related to cash operations (receipts, expenditures, borrowings, and so on). The accounts are maintained on the basis of reports from agencies as to deposits made and checks issued, and reports from the Federal Reserve system and other banks as to deposits received and checks paid. The Treasury also maintains subsidiary records for each federal agency.

The Treasury prepares certain financial reports which relate to the operations of the government as a whole. The major reports are:

1. Daily Treasury Statement, showing cash and public debt transactions.
2. Monthly Statement of the Public Debt of the United States.
3. Monthly Treasury Statement of Receipts and Outlays of the United States Government, which includes the budget surplus or deficit.
4. Annual Treasury Combined Statement of Receipts, Expenditures, and Balances of the United States Government.

Office of Personnel Management. The Office of Personnel Management (OPM) was established in 1978 to assume some of the functions formerly performed by the Civil Service Commission. The OPM has broad responsibility for managing the personnel function within the federal government, including responsibility for:

1. Recruitment and examination of prospective employees.
2. Management of the federal compensation and fringe benefit system.
3. Employee relations, merit programs, discipline, affirmative action programs, and other areas of labor–management relations.

Other than its involvement in benefit programs such as retirement, life insurance, and health benefits, the OPM has limited involvement in financial management functions.

General Services Administration. The General Services Administration (GSA) was created in 1949 to provide property management services for the federal government. Its major functions include:

1. Planning, acquisition, and management of public buildings.
2. Inventory management.
3. Management of the government's transportation equipment (for example, interagency motor pool).
4. Management of the government's data-processing and communications services.

Thus the GSA is responsible for management of and reporting on the government's noncash assets.

General Accounting Office. The General Accounting Office (GAO) was established in 1921 as an agency of Congress. Whereas the four agencies discussed previously are part of the executive branch of government, the GAO is an independent agency within the legislative branch.

Under the direction of the comptroller general, the GAO has the following principal functions:

1. Auditing the programs, activities, and financial transactions of the federal government and its agencies. Included in a GAO audit are examination of accounting records, examination of compliance with laws and regulations, reviews of the efficiency and economy of operations, and evaluation of the effectiveness of programs in light of desired results and legislative objectives.
2. Establishing accounting principles, standards, and procedures for the federal government and reviewing agency accounting systems.
3. Undertaking special studies for congressional committees or individual members of Congress.
4. Settling claims by and against the federal government and collecting accounts owed to the government.

Congressional Budget Office. The Congressional Budget Office (CBO) was formed in 1974 to provide Congress with budget-related information and analyses of alternative fiscal, budgetary, and programmatic policies. The CBO does not have direct management responsibilities; it is concerned with budgetary estimates and analysis.

Cost Accounting Standards Board. The Cost Accounting Standards Board (CASB) was established in 1970 to create uniform and consistent cost accounting policies in the federal government. Its major impact is on government contractors, who must follow the standards set by the CASB in any cost-plus or cost-reimbursement contracts with the federal government. Individual federal agencies must ensure that their contracts with external parties comply with the board's standards and procedures. The CASB actively issued standards for about 10 years, then became inactive. Consideration is currently being given to resuming the work of the board.

Fund Accounts

The accounts of the federal government are organized into several fund types. **General fund accounts** are used for receipts from general taxing and operating sources which are not dedicated to specific purposes and for expenditures arising from congressional authorization to spend general revenues. **Special fund accounts** are used for receipts earmarked by law for a specific purpose. **Revolving fund accounts** are used when there is a continuing cycle of operations, with continuing authority to spend receipts. **Management fund accounts** are used for intragovernmental activities. All of the above involve resources which are derived from the government's general taxing and revenue powers and from its business operations. In addition, **trust fund accounts** and **deposit fund accounts** are used where the federal government holds funds as a trustee or custodian.

Rather than illustrate the entire range of fund accounting for the federal government, we focus primarily on the accounting records maintained by a typical federal agency. Most often, an agency is included within the general fund, although it could be included elsewhere. For our discussions, we assume a general fund agency.

Financial Operations of a Federal Agency

Suppose that the Federal Seaweed Control Agency is appropriated $3,000,000 in the federal budget for the fiscal year 19X5–19X6 passed by Congress and signed by the president. This **appropriation** by Congress must undergo two more steps before the agency may spend resources. The executive branch, as represented by the Office of Management and Budget, must apportion the funds to the department in which the agency is located. This **apportionment** of funds is often done on a quarterly basis, to control the timing of spending by the agency. Moreover, some of the appropriated amount may not be apportioned; it may be held in reserve to cover unanticipated events. In our example, suppose the OMB apportions the $3,000,000 appropriation as follows:

First Quarter	$ 650,000
Second Quarter	700,000
Third Quarter	800,000
Fourth Quarter	700,000
Total Apportionment	$2,850,000
Reserve	150,000
Total Appropriation	$3,000,000

One further step remains: the agency head must allot the resources to operating officials. If, for example, there were several programs within the agency, the **allotment** would divide the resources among the various programs. At this point, the operating officials are able to obligate resources—to make spending commitments or **obligations** (these were called *encumbrances* in the local government context).

Budget Entries. Because three steps are involved in providing spending authority to the agency—Congress, the OMB, and the agency head—three budget entries are needed. The first entry by the agency records the appropriation by Congress:

Fund Balance with U.S. Treasury	3,000,000	
Unapportioned Appropriations.		3,000,000
To record appropriation by Congress.		

This entry signifies that the agency can potentially draw on $3,000,000 from the Treasury to pay its bills. Note, however, that this appropriation is as yet unapportioned by the OMB.

The second entry by the agency records the apportionment by the OMB for the first quarter of the year:

Unapportioned Appropriations.	650,000	
Unallotted Apportionments		650,000
To record first quarter apportionment by OMB.		

Subsequent apportionments are recorded later in the year, at the beginning of each quarter.

The third entry records the allotment by the agency head. On the assumption that $200,000 is allotted to Program A and $450,000 to Program B, the entry is:

```
Unalloted Apportionments.  . . . . . . . . . . . . . . . . . . . .   650,000
    Unobligated Allotments—Program A . . . . . . . . . . . . .             200,000
    Unobligated Allotments—Program B . . . . . . . . . . . . .             450,000
To record allotments to programs for first quarter.
```

As a result of these three budget entries, the manager of Program A has $200,000 of first-quarter spending authority, and the manager of Program B has $450,000.

Transaction Entries. As was discussed for local government accounting, an entry is made when a legal commitment to spend resources occurs. These commitments, known as **obligations** in federal accounting, arise from purchase orders, contracts, and the like. Suppose that, during July 19X5, Program A incurs obligations of $76,150. At the end of July, the general ledger of the agency is updated by the following entry:

```
Unobligated Allotments—Program A . . . . . . . . . . . . . . .   76,150
    Unliquidated Obligations . . . . . . . . . . . . . . . . . . . . .            76,150
To record obligations incurred during July.
```

When recorded obligations are reversed, they are said to be **liquidated.** Suppose that, during July, obligations of $41,150 are liquidated, resulting in expenditures of $41,600. The following entries are made in the general ledger:

```
Unliquidated Obligations. . . . . . . . . . . . . . . . . . . . . .   41,150
    Unobligated Allotments—Program A . . . . . . . . . . . . .            41,150
To record obligations liquidated during July.

Unobligated Allotments—Program A . . . . . . . . . . . . . . .   41,600
    Expended Appropriations . . . . . . . . . . . . . . . . . . . .            41,600
To record expenditure of appropriations during July.
```

In addition to maintaining a record of commitments of allotted funds, a record of the details of expenditures must also be maintained. The $41,600 of actual expenditures of the agency is now recorded as:

```
Inventories  . . . . . . . . . . . . . . . . . . . . . . . . . . . . .       250
Equipment. . . . . . . . . . . . . . . . . . . . . . . . . . . . . .       100
Expenses . . . . . . . . . . . . . . . . . . . . . . . . . . . . . .    29,250
Work in Process. . . . . . . . . . . . . . . . . . . . . . . . . . .    12,000
    Accounts Payable—Government Agencies . . . . . . . . . . .             9,850
    Accounts Payable—Other. . . . . . . . . . . . . . . . . . . .            31,750
To record accrued expenditures for July.
```

When payment is made from the Treasury, it is recorded by the agency as:

```
Accounts Payable—Government Agencies . . . . . . . . . . . .     9,850
Accounts Payable—Other. . . . . . . . . . . . . . . . . . . . .    31,750
    Fund Balance with U.S. Treasury . . . . . . . . . . . . . . .            41,600
To record payment of accounts payable.
```

From this brief illustration, we see that the procedure for recording transactions at the federal level is similar to that at the local level. Budget entries are used to record spending authority, commitments are recorded, and expenditures are recorded on an accrual basis.

Financial Reporting. While agency reports may vary somewhat depending on the purposes and activities of the agency, they will generally include:

1. A balance sheet which sets forth the assets and liabilities of the agency, and the equity of the U.S. government. Unlike local government reporting, all assets—including fixed assets—are presented.
2. An operating statement showing the revenues and costs associated with the agency's programs and activities.
3. A statement of sources and applications of funds.

Other reports, such as comparisons of budgeted and actual expenditures and reports on the status of appropriations may also be included.

Questions

Q17.1 In governmental accounting, the budget for a fund may be entered in the accounting records. Briefly explain the purpose of this entry. For which of the eight fund types is a budget entry usually made?

Q17.2 A governmental unit may have several capital projects underway simultaneously. How must the accounting records and financial statements of the capital projects fund be structured so as to properly reflect this situation?

Q17.3 Improvement projects undertaken by a governmental unit may be financed by general revenues or by assessments to property owners. What criterion is often used in determining the source of financing for improvements?

Q17.4 The general fund of Taylor City transferred $15,000 to a special assessment fund. Under what assumptions would each of the following entries be made in the general fund?

```
1. Due from Special Assessments Fund . . . . . . . . . . . . .  15,000
     Cash. . . . . . . . . . . . . . . . . . . . . . . . . . . . . . . .          15,000
2. Expenditures . . . . . . . . . . . . . . . . . . . . . . . . . . .  15,000
     Cash. . . . . . . . . . . . . . . . . . . . . . . . . . . . . . . .          15,000
```

Q17.5 Where should the liability for special assessment bonds which carry a secondary pledge of a municipality's general credit be recorded? *(AICPA adapted)*

Q17.6 Describe the major differences that exist in the purpose of accounting and financial reporting and in the types of financial reports for a large city when compared to those for a large industrial corporation. *(AICPA adapted)*

Q17.7 Why are inventories often ignored in accounting for local government units? *(AICPA adapted)*

Q17.8 Most general municipal debt is repaid by using general fund resources. Why is a debt service fund frequently used, rather than simply recording these payments as expenditures in the general fund?

Q17.9 Distinguish between an expendable and a nonexpendable trust fund. What are the major accounting differences between the two types?

Q17.10 Select the best answers for each of the following multiple choice questions:

1. Premiums received on general obligation bonds are generally transferred to what fund or group of accounts?
   a. Debt service.
   b. General long-term debt.
   c. General.
   d. Special revenue.
2. A statement of changes in financial position is prepared for which fund?
   a. Enterprise.
   b. General.
   c. Special assessment.
   d. Agency.
3. Cash secured from property tax revenue was transferred for the eventual payment of principal and interest on general obligation bonds. The bonds had been issued when land was acquired several years ago for a city park. Upon the transfer, an entry would *not* be made in which of the following?
   a. Debt service fund.
   b. General fixed assets group of accounts.
   c. General long-term debt group of accounts.
   d. General fund.
   (AICPA adapted)

Q17.11 Select the best answers for each of the following multiple choice questions:

1. An account for expenditures does *not* appear in which fund?
   a. Capital projects.
   b. Enterprise.
   c. Special assessment.
   d. Special revenue.
2. Which account represents the equity of a nonenterprise fund?
   a. Net assets.
   b. Fund balance.
   c. Reserves.
   d. Unencumbered balance.
3. When should revenues from interest on assessments receivable be recorded in a special assessments fund?
   a. When legally due.
   b. When assessed.

c. When collected in cash.

d. When the amount is known.

(AICPA adapted)

Q17.12 Select the best answers for each of the following multiple choice questions:

1. Which governmental fund would account for its fixed assets in a manner similar to a business organization?
   a. Enterprise.
   b. Capital projects.
   c. General fixed assets group of accounts.
   d. General.

2. A city realized large capital gains and losses on securities in its library endowment fund. In the absence of specific instructions from the donor or state statutory requirements, the general rule of law holds that these amounts should be charged or credited to:
   a. General fund income.
   b. General fund principal.
   c. Trust fund income.
   d. Trust fund principal.

3. Of the items listed below, those most likely to have parallel accounting procedures, account titles, and financial statements are:
   a. Special revenue funds and special assessment funds.
   b. Internal service funds and debt service funds.
   c. The general fixed assets group of accounts and the general long-term debt group of accounts.
   d. The general fund and special revenue funds.

4. A city should use a capital projects fund to account for:
   a. Structures and improvements constructed with the proceeds of a special assessment.
   b. Proceeds of a bond issue to be used to acquire land for city parks.
   c. Construction in progress on the city-owned electric utility plant, financed by an issue of revenue bonds.
   d. Assets to be used to retire bonds issued to finance an addition to the city hall.

   (AICPA adapted)

Q17.13 *(Appendix)* Compare the recording of the budget by local government with that by a federal agency.

Q17.14 *(Appendix)* Compare the recording of purchase orders by local government with that by a federal agency.

Q17.15 *(Appendix)* Identify the agency that performs each of the following financial management activities in the federal government:

1. Auditing.
2. Budgetary administration.
3. Budgetary analysis for Congress.

4. Budgetary planning for the president.
5. Cash management.
6. Debt management.
7. Employee benefits.
8. Establishing accounting standards for government agencies.
9. Establishing accounting standards for government contractors.
10. Management of fixed assets.
11. Management of inventories.
12. Settlement of claims.

Exercises

E17.1 On January 14, 19X1, the city of Waterport authorized a $750,000 bond issue for the purchase of a building to be used as a community center. On May 3, the bonds were issued at par, and on June 1, the building was purchased and paid for. On November 1, the general fund paid the semiannual interest of $30,000 on the bonds.

Required: Record all necessary entries for the above information. Identify the fund or account group for each entry.

E17.2 The town of Kaley recently completed construction of a recreational facility which was accounted for in a capital projects fund. Bonds were issued at the onset of the project to finance construction. Legal constraints prevented use of the $800 premium on the bonds toward construction costs. The premium has not yet been transferred to the debt service fund. Temporary investments of bond proceeds yielded a 3 percent return, or $2,424.

Kaley awarded the construction contract for the facility to the lowest bidder. The contract called for a 15 percent retainage. Kaley's books show $11,550 due the contractor pending final inspection. All other amounts due the contractor have been remitted.

Required:

1. What was the face value of the bonds issued?
2. What was the amount of the contract awarded?
3. What was the original authorization for the project?
4. What is the fund balance after closing entries?

E17.3 At the beginning of fiscal year 19X2, Waller Town established a central supplies storehouse to service its several funds. The general fund contributed $25,000 (nonrefundable) to aid in the establishment of the supplies storehouse. It was agreed that the storehouse would charge other funds for the purchase price of supplies plus 15 percent. During the year, the storehouse purchased $18,000 of supplies, paid operating expenses of $1,500, and billed other funds for $17,250. All accounts have been settled except $2,000 remaining to be collected from the general fund for supplies billed.

Required:

1. Prepare the balance sheet for the central supplies storehouse at the end of fiscal 19X2.
2. State any effects of the transactions on the financial statements of the general fund of Waller Town. Assume the general fund bought supplies for $6,000 and used only $5,500 worth of supplies.

E17.4 In March 19X3, a resident of Randall City died, leaving her entire estate to the Randall City School District. The will specified that proceeds from the liquidation of the estate were to be invested, and investment income was to be used to provide scholarships for needy high school students. Three students were to be selected each year by the school superintendent. At the date of the donor's death, the fair market value of the estate was estimated to be $103,000. In December, the estate was liquidated, realizing $105,000. Administrative costs of the estate in 19X3 were $4,000. The net proceeds were then transferred to the school district and were invested in appropriate securities.

In 19X4, income from investments was $7,000. Administrative costs (all related to income) were $250. The first scholarships were awarded in 19X4 for a total of $5,000.

Required: Record the events described above in an appropriate fund. Include closing entries.

E17.5 The questions below apply to the funds and account groups for Ranchville. Assuming each situation is independent of the others, select the best answer to each question.

1. Ranchville's water utility, which is an enterprise fund, submits a bill for $9,000 to the general fund for water service supplied to city departments and agencies. Submission of this bill results in:
   a. Creation of balances which will be eliminated on the city's combined balance sheet.
   b. Recognition of revenue by the water utility fund and of an expenditure by the general fund.
   c. Recognition of an encumbrance by both the water utility fund and the general fund.
   d. Creation of a balance which will be eliminated on the city's combined statement of revenues, expenditures, and changes in fund balances.
2. The water utility transferred land and a building to the general city administration for public use at no charge to the city. On the water utility books, the land was carried at $4,000 and the building at a cost of $30,000, on which $23,000 depreciation had been recorded. In the year of the transfer, what would be the effect of the transaction?
   a. Reduce retained earnings of the water utility by $11,000 and increase the fund balance of the general fund by $11,000.

    b. Reduce retained earnings of the water utility by $11,000 and increase the total assets in the general fixed assets group by $11,000.

    c. Reduce retained earnings of the water utility by $11,000 and increase the total assets in the general fixed assets group by $34,000.

    d. Have no effect on a combined balance sheet for the city.

3. The following information applies to the water utility fund:

Prepaid Insurance Paid in December 19X6	$ 43,000
Depreciation for 19X6	129,000
Provision for Doubtful Accounts for 19X6	14,000

What amount should be reflected in the statement of revenues and expenses (income statement) of the Ranchville water utility fund for the above items?

    a. $(43,000).

    b. $0.

    c. $129,000.

    d. $143,000.

4. What will be the balance sheet effect of recording $50,000 of depreciation in the accounts of the water utility?

    a. Reduce total assets of the utility fund and the general fixed assets group by $50,000.

    b. Reduce total assets of the utility fund by $50,000 but have no effect on the general fixed assets group.

    c. Reduce total assets of the general fixed assets group by $50,000 but have no effect on assets of the utility fund.

    d. Have no effect on total assets of either the utility fund or the general fixed assets group.

5. Ranchville has approved a special assessments project in accordance with applicable laws. Total assessments of $500,000, including 10 percent for the city's share of the cost, have been levied. The levy will be collected from property owners in ten equal annual installments commencing with the current year. Recognition of the approval and levy will result in entries of:

    a. $500,000 in the special assessments fund and $50,000 in the general fund.

    b. $450,000 in the special assessments fund and $50,000 in the general fund.

    c. $50,000 in the special assessments fund and $50,000 in the general fund.

    d. $50,000 in the special assessments fund and no entry in the general fund.

6. Ranchville's debt service fund (for principal of term bonds) recorded required additions and required earnings of $15,000 and $7,000, respectively, for the fiscal year. The actual revenues and interest earnings were $16,000 and $6,500, respectively. What is the amount of

actual additions and earnings to be recorded in the debt service fund and in the general long-term debt account group, respectively?

   a. $22,500 and $22,000.

   b. $22,000 and $22,000.

   c. $22,500 and $22,500.

   d. $22,500 and no entry.

7. Ranchville serves as collecting agency for the local independent school district and for a local fire district. For this purpose, Ranchville has created a single agency fund and charges the other entities a fee of 1 percent of the gross amounts collected. The service fee is treated as general fund revenue. During the latest fiscal year, a gross amount of $268,000 was collected for the independent school district and $80,000 for the fire district. As a consequence of the foregoing, Ranchville's general fund should:

   a. Recognize receipts of $348,000.

   b. Recognize receipts of $344,520.

   c. Record revenue of $3,480.

   d. Record encumbrances of $344,520.

8. When Ranchville realized $1,020,000 from the sale of a $1,000,000 bond issue, the entry in its capital projects fund was

```
Cash . . . . . . . . . . . . . . . . . . . . . .   1,020,000
     Bond Proceeds . . . . . . . . . . . . . .               1,000,000
     Premium on Bonds . . . . . . . . . . . .                   20,000
```

Recording the transaction in this manner indicates that:

   a. The $20,000 cannot be used for the designated purpose of the fund but must be transferred to another fund.

   b. The full $1,020,000 can be used by the capital projects fund to accomplish its purpose.

   c. The nominal rate of interest on the bonds is below the market rate for bonds of such term and risk.

   d. A safety factor is being set aside to cover possible contract defaults on the construction.

   (AICPA adapted)

E17.6 Often an entry on the books of one fund triggers corresponding entries in other funds of the governmental unit.

Required: Record any entries to other funds or account groups that correspond to the entries below. Identify the fund or account group for each entry made.

   1. *General Fund*

```
Cash. . . . . . . . . . . . . . . . . . . . . . .   12,000
     Due from Capital Projects Fund . . . . . . . . . .          12,000
     To record repayment of advance.
```

2. *Capital Projects Fund*

Bond Premium.	8,000	
Cash		8,000
To transfer bond premium to debt service fund to be used for future repayment of principal.		

3. *Special Assessments Fund*

Cash.	40,000	
Bonds Payable		40,000
To record issuance of bonds at par.		

4. *Special Assessments Fund*

Expenditures.	40,000	
Vouchers Payable.		40,000
To record final payment for improvements contract totaling $100,000.		

5. *Enterprise Fund*

Cash.	18,000	
Capital Contributed from General Fund		18,000
To record transfer from general fund.		

E17.7 Name the fund(s) or group(s) of accounts which correctly answers each of the following questions:

1. An actuarial deficiency would appear in which fund?
2. "Excess of Net Billings to Departments over Costs" would appear as a caption in the financial statement of which fund?
3. Which type of fund can be either expendable or nonexpendable?
4. The account "Investment in Fixed Assets" appears where?
5. To provide for retirement of general obligation bonds, a city invests a portion of its receipts from general property taxes in marketable securities. Where should this investment activity be recorded?
6. Depreciation expense is recorded in which fund(s) or group(s) of accounts?
7. Where should the liability for general obligation bonds issued for the benefit of a municipal electric company and serviced by its earnings be recorded?

(AICPA adapted)

E17.8 List *all* the funds or groups of accounts in which each of the following situations requires accounting recognition:

1. Part of the general obligation bond proceeds from a new issue was used to pay for the cost of a new city hall as soon as construction was

completed. The remainder of the proceeds was transferred to repay the debt.

2. Equipment in general governmental service that had been constructed 10 years before by a capital projects fund was sold. The receipts were accounted for as unrestricted revenue.

3. Cash was received from a special tax levy to retire and pay interest on general obligation bonds issued to finance the construction of a new city hall.

4. Fixed assets were acquired by a central purchasing and supplies department organized to serve all municipal departments.

5. Several years ago a city provided for the establishment of a sinking fund to retire an issue of general obligation bonds. This year, the city made a $50,000 contribution to the sinking fund from general revenues and realized $15,000 in revenue from securities in the sinking fund. The bonds due this year were retired.

6. A municipal electric utility paid $150,000 out of its earnings for new equipment.

7. A municipality issued general obligation serial bonds to finance the construction of a fire station.

8. Expenditures of $200,000 were made during the year on the fire station in No. 7.

9. A municipal electric utility issued bonds to be repaid from its own operations.

(AICPA adapted)

E17.9 During 19X1, the city of Reyland acquired a variety of assets.

Required: For each transaction listed below, identify any *asset accounts* debited at the time of the transaction. Specify the funds or account groups used.

1. Supplies of $800 were purchased by an internal service fund.

2. Early in the year, the general fund purchased supplies of $800. No inventory account is maintained by the general fund.

3. Sidewalks were installed at the expense of neighborhood property owners. Cost of installation was $4,000.

4. The city pool facility, which is financed by user charges, bought pool-cleaning equipment for $450.

5. An ambulance garage was constructed by the capital projects fund for $80,000.

6. An ambulance was purchased by the general fund for $35,000.

E17.10 On January 1, a governmental unit issued 7 percent bonds at par for $70,000. On June 30, semiannual interest became due and was paid.

Required: Make all the appropriate entries for January 1 and June 30 given the following independent assumptions. Explanations are not required. Identify each fund or account group affected.

1. The bonds were issued to finance special assessment construction.
2. The bonds were issued to finance city court expansion. General fund resources are transferred to debt service at the beginning of each year to finance annual interest charges.
3. The bonds were issued to finance city operations. General fund resources are transferred to debt service at the beginning of each year to finance annual interest charges.
4. The bonds were issued by a self-supporting city utility.
5. The bonds were issued by a police retirement fund.

E17.11 Select the best answer for each of the following multiple choice questions:

1. When a capital project is financed entirely from a single bond issue, and the proceeds of the bond issue equal the par value of the bonds, the capital projects fund would record this transaction by debiting cash and crediting:
   a. Bond proceeds.
   b. Fund balance.
   c. Appropriations.
   d. Bonds payable.
2. Which of the following accounts could be included in the balance sheet of an enterprise fund?

	Fund Balance—Reserved for Encumbrances	Revenue Bonds Payable	Retained Earnings
a.	No	No	Yes
b.	No	Yes	Yes
c.	Yes	Yes	No
d.	No	No	No

3. Fixed assets utilized in a city-owned utility are accounted for in which of the following?

	Enterprise Fund	General Fixed Assets Group of Accounts
a.	No	No
b.	No	Yes
c.	Yes	No
d.	Yes	Yes

4. Which of the following funds of a governmental unit would use the general long-term debt account group to account for unmatured general long-term liabilities?
   a. Special assessment.
   b. Trust.
   c. Internal service.
   d. Debt service.
5. Which of the following funds of a governmental unit recognizes rev-

enues and expenditures under the same basis of accounting as the general fund?
   a. Debt service.
   b. Enterprise.
   c. Internal service.
   d. Nonexpendable pension trust.
6. Which of the following funds of a governmental unit would include retained earnings in its balance sheet?
   a. Expendable pension trust.
   b. Internal service.
   c. Special revenue.
   d. Capital projects.
7. Which of the following requires the use of the encumbrance system?
   a. Special assessment fund.
   b. Debt service fund.
   c. General fixed assets group of accounts.
   d. Enterprise fund.
8. Which of the following funds of a governmental unit would use the general long-term debt account group to account for unmatured general long-term liabilities?
   a. Special assessment.
   b. Capital projects.
   c. Trust.
   d. Internal service.
9. Which of the following funds of a governmental unit uses the same basis of accounting as an enterprise fund?
   a. Special revenue.
   b. Internal service.
   c. Expendable trust.
   d. Capital projects.
10. Which of the following funds of a governmental unit could use the general fixed assets account group to account for fixed assets?
   a. Internal service.
   b. Enterprise.
   c. Trust.
   d. Special assessment.
   (AICPA adapted)

E17.12 Select the best answer for each of the following multiple choice questions:

Nos. 1 and 2 are based on the following information:
The following events relating to the city of Albury's debt service funds occurred during the year ended December 31, 19X1:

Debt principal matured	$2,000,000
Unmatured (accrued) interest on outstanding debt at Jan. 1, 19X1	50,000
Interest on matured debt	900,000
Unmatured (accrued) interest on outstanding debt at Dec. 31, 19X1	100,000
Interest revenue from investments	600,000

Cash transferred from general fund for retirement of debt principal 1,000,000
Cash transferred from general fund for payment of interest due 900,000

All principal and interest due in 19X1 were paid on time.

1. What is the total amount of expenditures that Albury's debt service funds should record for the year ended December 31, 19X1?
   a. $900,000.
   b. $950,000.
   c. $2,900,000.
   d. $2,950,000.
2. How much revenue should Albury's debt service funds record for the year ended December 31, 19X1?
   a. $600,000.
   b. $1,600,000.
   c. $1,900,000.
   d. $2,500,000.

Nos. 3 and 4 are based on the following information:
During the year ended December 31, 19X1, Leyland City received a state grant of $500,000 to finance the purchase of buses, and an additional grant of $100,000 to aid in the financing of bus operations in 19X1. Only $300,000 of the capital grant was used in 19X1 for the purchase of buses, but the entire operating grant of $100,000 was spent in 19X1.

3. If Leyland's bus transportation system is accounted for as part of the city's general fund, how much should Leyland report as grant revenues for the year ended December 31, 19X1?
   a. $100,000.
   b. $300,000.
   c. $400,000.
   d. $500,000.
4. If Leyland's bus transportation system is accounted for as an enterprise fund, how much should Leyland report as grant revenues for the year ended December 31, 19X1?
   a. $100,000.
   b. $300,000.
   c. $400,000.
   d. $500,000.
5. The village of Ariel issued the following bonds during the year ended June 30, 19X1:

Revenue bonds to be repaid from admission fees
   collected by the Ariel Zoo enterprise fund $200,000
General obligation bonds issued for the Ariel water
   and sewer enterprise fund which will service the debt 300,000

How much of these bonds should be accounted for in Ariel's general long-term debt account group?

a. $0.
b. $200,000.
c. $300,000.
d. $500,000.

Nos. 6 and 7 are based on the following information:
On December 31, 19X1, Madrid Township paid a contractor $2,000,000 for the total cost of a new firehouse built in 19X1 on township-owned land. Financing was by means of a $1,500,000 general obligation bond issue sold at face amount on December 31, 19X1, with the remaining $500,000 transferred from the general fund.

6. What should be reported on Madrid Township's 19X1 financial statements for the capital project fund?
   a. Revenues, $1,500,000; expenditures, $1,500,000.
   b. Revenues, $1,500,000; other financing sources, $500,000; expenditures, $2,000,000.
   c. Revenues, $2,000,000; expenditures, $2,000,000.
   d. Other financing sources, $2,000,000; expenditures, $2,000,000.
7. What should be reported on Madrid Township's 19X1 financial statements for the general fund?
   a. Expenditures, $500,000.
   b. Other financing uses, $500,000.
   c. Revenues, $1,500,000; expenditures, $2,000,000.
   d. Revenues, $1,500,000; other financing uses, $2,000,000.
   (AICPA adapted)

E17.13 *(Appendix)* The Wildlife Preservation Commission, an agency of the federal government, was included in the annual budget passed by Congress for funding of $4,000,000 for the 19X1–19X2 fiscal year. The Office of Management and Budget authorized the commission to spend $1,200,000 during the first quarter of the year. The chief commissioner of the agency divided this spending authority as follows:

Western Region Programs	$650,000
Central Region Programs	200,000
Eastern Region Programs	350,000

Required: Prepare the budget entries that should be recorded by the Wildlife Preservation Commission at July 1, 19X1, the beginning of the first quarter.

Problems

P17.1 **Transaction Recording—Various Funds** The following transactions represent practical situations frequently encountered in accounting for municipal governments. Each transaction is independent of the others.

1. The city council of Bernardville adopted a budget for the general operations of the city government during the new fiscal year. Revenues

were estimated at $695,000. Legal authorizations for budgeted expenditures were $650,000.

2. Taxes of $160,000 were levied for the special revenue fund of Millstown. One percent was estimated to be uncollectible.

3. **a.** On July 25, 19X3, office supplies estimated to cost $2,390 were ordered for the city manager's office of Bullersville. Bullersville, which operates on the calendar year, does not maintain an inventory of such supplies.

   b. The supplies ordered on July 25 were received on August 9, 19X3, accompanied by an invoice for $2,500.

4. On October 10, 19X3, the general fund of Washingtonville repaid to the utility fund a loan of $1,000 plus $40 interest. The loan had been made earlier in the fiscal year.

5. A prominent citizen died and left 10 acres of undeveloped land to Harper City for a future school site. The donor's cost of the land was $55,000. The fair value of the land was $85,000.

6. **a.** On March 6, 19X3, Dahlstrom City issued 4 percent special assessment bonds payable March 6, 19X8, at face value of $90,000. Interest is payable annually. Dahlstrom City, which operates on the calendar year, will use the proceeds to finance a curbing project.

   b. On October 29, 19X3, the full $84,000 cost of the completed curbing project was accrued. Also, appropriate closing entries were made with regard to the project.

7. **a.** Conrad Thamm, a citizen of Basking Knoll, donated common stock valued at $22,000 to the city under a trust agreement. Under the terms of the agreement, the principal amount is to be kept intact; use of income from the stock is restricted to financing academic college scholarships for needy students.

   b. On December 14, 19X3, dividends of $1,100 were received on the stock donated by Mr. Thamm.

8. **a.** On February 23, 19X3, the town of Lincoln, which operates on the calendar year, issued 4 percent general obligation bonds with a face value of $300,000 payable February 23, 19Y3, to finance the construction of an addition to the city hall. Total proceeds were $308,000. The bond premium is immediately transferred to the debt service fund.

   b. On December 31, 19X3, the addition to the city hall was officially approved, the full cost of $297,000 was paid to the contractor, and appropriate closing entires were made with regard to the project. (Assume that no entries have been made with regard to the project since February 23, 19X3.) Remaining cash is transferred to the debt service fund.

Required: For each transaction, prepare the necessary journal entries for all of the funds and groups of accounts involved. No explanation of the journal entries is required. Use the following headings for your solution:

Transaction Number	Journal Entries	Dr.	Cr.	Fund or Group of Accounts

In the far right column, indicate in which fund or group of accounts each entry is to be made, using the code shown below:

Funds:
General . . . . G
Special revenue . . . . SR
Capital projects . . . . CP
Debt service . . . . DS
Special assessments. . . . . SA
Enterprise . . . . E
Internal service. . . . . IS
Trust and agency . . . . TA
Groups of accounts:
General fixed assets . . . . GFA
General long-term debt . . . . LTD

(AICPA adapted)

P17.2 Transaction Recording—Various Funds The fiscal year for the city of Cran ended on June 30, 19X7. An examination of the accounts on that date revealed the following:

1. On December 31, 19X6, the city paid $115,000 from the general fund to establish a central garage to service its vehicles, with $67,500 being applicable to the building, which has an estimated life of 25 years, $14,500 to land, and $33,000 to machinery and equipment which has an estimated life of 15 years. A $12,200 cash contribution was received by the garage from the general fund on the same date.

2. The garage maintains no records, but a review of deposit slips and canceled checks revealed the following:

Collections for Services to City Departments Financed from the
General Fund $30,000
Office Salaries 6,000
Utilities 700
Mechanics' Wages 11,000
Materials and Supplies 9,000

3. The garage had uncollected billings of $2,000 from the general fund, accounts payable for materials and supplies of $500, and an inventory of materials and supplies of $1,500 at June 30, 19X7.

4. On June 30, 19X7, the city issued $200,000 in special assessment bonds at par to finance a street improvement project estimated to cost $225,000. The project is to be funded by a $15,000 levy against the city (payable in fiscal year 19X7–19X8) and $210,000 against property owners (payable in five equal annual installments beginning Oc-

tober 1, 19X7). The levy was made on June 30. A $215,000 contract was let for the project on July 2, 19X7, but work has not begun.

5. On July 1, 19X5, the city issued $400,000 in 30-year, 6 percent general obligation term bonds of the same date at par and awarded a contract for $397,500 for the construction of a public health center. Construction was completed and the contractors fully paid a total of $397,500 in fiscal year 19X6–19X7. (Assume that no expenditures were recorded in 19X5–19X6).

6. For the health center bonds, the city sets aside general fund revenues sufficient to cover interest (payable semiannually on July 1 and January 1 of each year) and $5,060 to provide for the retirement of bond principal, the latter transfer being made at the end of each fiscal year and invested at the beginning of the next. These investments earned $304, the exact amount budgeted, during fiscal year 19X6–19X7. This $304 was received in cash and will be invested at the beginning of the next year.

Required: Assume that appropriate entries were made in the general fund. Prepare the necessary entries for the year ended June 30, 19X7, for all other funds and account groups. Do not prepare closing entries. *(AICPA adapted)*

P17.3 Capital Projects Fund In a special election held on July 1, 19X7, the voters of the city of Nicknar approved a $10,000,000 issue of 6 percent general obligation bonds maturing in 19Z7. The proceeds of this sale will be used to help finance the construction of a new civic center. The total cost of the project was estimated at $15,000,000. The remaining $5,000,000 will be financed by an irrevocable state grant which has been awarded. A capital projects fund was established to account for this project and was designated the "civic center construction fund."

The following transactions occurred during the fiscal year beginning July 1, 19X7, and ending June 30, 19X8:

1. On August 1, the general fund loaned $500,000 to the civic center construction fund for defraying engineering and other expenses.

2. Preliminary engineering and planning costs of $320,000 were paid to Akron Engineering Company. There had been no encumbrance for this cost.

3. On December 1, the bonds were sold at 101. The premium on bonds was transferred to the debt service fund to be used for future payment of bond principal.

4. On March 15, a contract for $12,000,000 was entered into with Candu Construction Company for the major part of the project.

5. Orders were placed on March 23 for materials estimated to cost $55,000.

6. On April 1, a partial payment of $2,500,000 was received from the state.

7. The materials that were previously ordered were received on June 7 at a cost of $51,000, and payment was made.
8. On June 15, a progress billing of $2,000,000 was received from Candu Construction for work done on the project. According to the terms of the contract, the city will withhold 6 percent of any billing until the project is completed.
9. The general fund was repaid the $500,000 previously loaned.

Required: Based on the transactions presented above:

1. Prepare journal entries to record the transactions in the civic center construction fund for the period July 1, 19X7, through June 30, 19X8, and the appropriate closing entries at June 30, 19X8.
2. Prepare a balance sheet for the civic center construction fund as of June 30, 19X8. *(AICPA adapted)*

P17.4 Capital Projects Fund During the fiscal year ended June 30, 19X2, the city of Westgate authorized the construction of a new library and sale of general obligation term bonds to finance the construction of the library. The authorization imposed the following restrictions: (1) construction cost was not to exceed $5,000,000, and (2) the annual interest rate was not to exceed 8½ percent. The city does not record project authorizations, but other budgetary accounts are maintained. The following transactions relating to the financing and constructing of the library occurred during the fiscal year ended June 30, 19X3:

1. On July 1, 19X2, Westgate issued $5,000,000 of 30-year 8 percent general obligation bonds for $5,100,000. The semiannual interest payment dates are December 31 and June 30. The premium of $100,000 was transferred to the library debt service fund.
2. On July 3, 19X2, the library capital projects fund invested $4,900,000 in short-term commercial paper. These purchases were at face value with no accrued interest. Interest on cash invested by the library capital projects fund must be transferred to the library debt service fund. During the fiscal year ending June 30, 19X3, estimated interest to be earned is $140,000.
3. On July 5, 19X2, Westgate signed a contract with F&A Construction Company to build the library for $4,980,000.
4. On January 15, 19X3, the library capital projects fund received $3,040,000 from the maturity of short-term notes purchased on July 3. The cost of these notes was $3,000,000. The interest of $40,000 was transferred to the library debt service fund.
5. On January 20, 19X3, F&A Construction Company properly billed the city $3,000,000 for work performed on the new library. The contract calls for 10 percent retention until final inspection and acceptance of the building. The library capital projects fund paid F&A $2,700,000.

6. On June 30, 19X3, the library capital projects fund made the proper adjusting entries (including accrued interest receivable of $103,000) and closing entries.

Required:

1. Prepare journal entries to record the six preceding sets of facts in the library capital projects fund. Do not record journal entries in any other fund or group of accounts.
2. Prepare in good form a balance sheet for the City of Westgate—Library Capital Projects Fund as of June 30, 19X3. *(AICPA adapted)*

P17.5 Capital Projects and Debt Service Funds The information below relates to the construction of a new recreation building in the city of Lander.

19X0 Transactions

1. A bond issue in the amount of $1,000,000 was authorized by vote on March 1, 19X0, to provide funds for the construction. The bonds are to be repaid, in 20 annual installments, from a debt service fund, with the first installment due on March 1, 19X1.
2. An advance of $80,000 was received from the general fund to make a deposit on the land contract of $120,000. The deposit was made.
3. Bonds having a face value of $900,000 were sold for cash at 102. Since the cost of the land was much less than anticipated, the city decided to postpone sale of the remaining bonds.
4. Contracts amounting to $780,000 were awarded to the lowest bidder for the construction of the recreation center.
5. The temporary advance from the general fund was repaid, and the balance on the land contract was paid.
6. The architect certified that work in the amount of $640,000 had been completed, and bills for that amount were received.
7. Vouchers paid by the treasurer relative to the completed work amounted to $620,000.
8. The bond premium was transferred to the debt service fund.

19X1 Transactions

9. Due to engineering modifications in the construction plans, the contract was revised to $880,000. The remaining bonds were sold at 101.
10. The recreation center was completed and billed at a further cost of $230,000. The building passed final inspection.
11. The treasurer paid all bills.
12. The cash balance remaining was transferred to the debt service fund.

Interest on the bond issue is paid directly from the general fund. Transfers from the general fund to the debt service fund were $25,000 in 19X0 and $30,000 in 19X1. All cash was invested in certificates of deposit which yielded interest of $1,000 in 19X0 and $800 in 19X1. Expected investment income was $1,000 in each year. The first installment on the bonds ($45,000) was paid when due.

Required:

1. Prepare the journal entries for the recreation center fund for 19X0 and 19X1.
2. Prepare the balance sheet for the recreation center fund on December 31, 19X0.
3. Prepare the journal entries for the debt service fund and the general long-term debt account group for 19X0 and 19X1.

P17.6 Special Assessments Fund Early in 19X1, the town of Jacobs authorized widening of streets and installation of curbs in a residential area known as Woodside. The project was expected to cost $400,000 and to be financed by $50,000 from the 19X1 general fund budget and $350,000 from Woodside residents. Residents were assessed for equal principal payments over 10 years plus interest on bonds as due. Ten-year, 6 percent bonds with a face value of $350,000 were issued at par on July 1, 19X1. Interest is due on December 31 and June 30. Proceeds from the bonds not currently needed to finance construction and proceeds of the assessments after payment of interest were invested in appropriate securities. Assessments to residents for interest are to be reduced by the prior year's earnings on investments.

Regarding the street improvement project, the following occurred:

1. Investments yielded $8,000 in 19X1 (collected in 19X2) and $18,000 in 19X2 (collected in 19X3). The balance in the cash account was $40,000 on December 31, 19X1, and $30,000 on December 31, 19X2.
2. Project costs of $400,000 were encumbered at the start of the project.
3. Construction costs billed in 19X1 were $150,000, of which $20,000 was not paid at year-end.
4. The improvement project was completed in 19X2 at a total cost of $400,000. All amounts due the contractor were paid.
5. Of the 19X1 assessment, $15,000 was not collected until 19X2. All 19X2 assessments were collected when due.

Required:

1. Prepare a schedule showing assessments due for 19X1 and 19X2.
2. Prepare 19X1 and 19X2 balance sheets for the special assessments street improvement fund.
3. What other funds or account groups are affected by the street improvement project?

P17.7 Internal Service Fund The city of Merlot operates a central garage through an internal service fund to provide garage space and repairs for all city-owned and operated vehicles. The central garage fund was established by a contribution of $200,000 from the general fund on July 1, 19X1, at which time the building was acquired. The after-closing trial balance at June 30, 19X3, was as follows:

	Debit	Credit
Cash	$150,000	
Due from General Fund	20,000	
Inventory of Materials and Supplies	80,000	
Land	60,000	
Building	200,000	
Allowance for Depreciation—Building		$ 10,000
Machinery and Equipment	56,000	
Allowance for Depreciation—Machinery and Equipment		12,000
Vouchers Payable		38,000
Contribution from General Fund		200,000
Retained Earnings		306,000
	$566,000	$566,000

The following information applies to the fiscal year ended June 30, 19X4:

1. Materials and supplies were purchased on account for $74,000.
2. The inventory of materials and supplies at June 30, 19X4, was $58,000, which agreed with the physical count taken.
3. Salaries and wages paid to employees totaled $230,000, including related fringe benefit costs.
4. A billing was received from the enterprise fund for utility charges totaling $30,000, and was paid.
5. Depreciation of the building was recorded in the amount of $5,000. Depreciation of the machinery and equipment amounted to $8,000.
6. Billings to other departments for services rendered to them were as follows:

General Fund	$262,000
Water and Sewer Fund	84,000
Special Revenue Fund	32,000

7. Unpaid interfund receivable balances at June 30, 19X4, were as follows:

General Fund	$ 6,000
Special Revenue Fund	16,000

8. Vouchers payable at June 30, 19X4, were $14,000.

Required:

1. For the period July 1, 19X3, through June 30, 19X4, prepare journal entries to record all of the transactions in the central garage fund accounts.

2. Prepare closing entries for the central garage fund at June 30, 19X4. *(AICPA adapted)*

P17.8 Agency Fund In compliance with a newly enacted state law, Dial County assumed the responsibility of collecting all property taxes levied within its boundaries as of July 1, 19X5. A composite property tax rate per $1,000 of net assessed valuation was developed for the fiscal year ending June 30, 19X6, and is presented below:

Dial County General Fund	$ 60
Eton City General Fund	30
Bart Township General Fund.	10
Composite Tax Rate	$100

All property taxes are due in quarterly installments, and when collected they are distributed to the governmental units represented in the composite rate. In order to administer collection and distribution of such taxes, the county has established a tax agency fund.

Additional information:

1. In order to reimburse the county for estimated administrative expenses of operating the tax agency fund, the tax agency fund is to deduct 2 percent from the tax collections each quarter for Eton City and Bart Township. The total amount deducted is to be remitted to the Dial County general fund.

2. Current year tax levies to be collected by the tax agency fund are as follows:

	Gross Levy	Estimated Amount to Be Collected
Dial County	$3,600,000	$3,500,000
Eton City	1,800,000	1,740,000
Bart Township.	600,000	560,000
	$6,000,000	$5,800,000

3. As of September 30, 19X5, the tax agency fund had received $1,440,000 in first-quarter payments. On October 1, this fund made a distribution to the three governmental units.

Required: For the period July 1, 19X5, through October 1, 19X5, prepare journal entries to record the transactions described above for the following funds:

Dial County tax agency fund.

Dial County general fund.

Eton City general fund.

Bart Township general fund.

Your solution should be organized as follows:

	Dial County Tax Agency Fund		Dial County General Fund		Eton City General Fund		Bart Township General Fund	
Accounts	Debit	Credit	Debit	Credit	Debit	Credit	Debit	Credit

(AICPA adapted)

P17.9 Budgeting for Various Funds The Laurens city council passed a resolution requiring a yearly cash budget by fund for the city beginning with its fiscal year ending September 30, 19X3. The city's financial director has prepared a list of expected cash receipts and disbursements, but he is having difficulty subdividing them by fund. The list is given in Exhibit 17.6.

The financial director provides you with the following additional information:

1. A bond issue was authorized in 19X2 for the construction of a civic center. Future civic center revenues are to account for 20 percent of the repayment of debt. The remainder is to come from general property taxes.

2. A bond issue was authorized in 19X2 for additions to the library. The debt is to be paid from general property taxes.

3. General obligation bonds are paid from general property taxes collected by the general fund.

4. Ten percent of the total annual school taxes represents an individually voted tax for payment of bonds, the proceeds of which were used for school construction.

5. In 19X0, a wealthy citizen donated rental property to the city. Net income from the property is to be used to assist in operating the library. The net cash increase attributable to the property is transferred to the library on September 30 of each year.

6. All sales taxes are collected by the city; the state receives 85 percent of these taxes. The state's portion is remitted at the end of each month.

7. Payment of the street construction bonds is to be made from assessments previously collected from the respective property owners. The proceeds from the assessments were invested and the principal of $312,000 will earn $15,000 interest during the coming year.

8. In 19X2, a special assessment in the amount of $203,000 was made on certain property owners for sewer construction. During fiscal 19X3, $50,000 of this assessment is expected to be collected. The remainder of the sewer cost is to be paid from a $153,000 bond issue to be sold in fiscal 19X3. Future special assessment collections will be used to pay principal and interest on the bonds.

9. All sewer and sanitation services are provided by a separate enterprise fund.

10. The federal grant is for fiscal 19X3 school operations.

11. The proceeds remaining at the end of the year from the sale of civic center and library bonds are to be invested.

Required: Prepare a budget of cash receipts and disbursements by fund for the year ending September 30, 19X3. All interfund transactions of cash are to be included. *(AICPA adapted)*

Exhibit 17.6   **Cash Receipts and Disbursements, to Be Used in P17.9**

CASH RECEIPTS		CASH DISBURSEMENTS	
Taxes:		General Government. . . .	$ 671,000
General Property.	$ 685,000	Public Safety.	516,000
School	421,000	Schools	458,000
Franchise	223,000	Sanitation	131,000
	$1,329,000	Library	28,000
Licenses and Permits:		Rental Property	17,500
Business Licenses	$ 41,000	Parks.	17,000
Automobile Inspection			$1,838,500
Permits	24,000	Debt Service:	
Building Permits	18,000	General Obligation Bonds	$ 618,000
	$ 83,000	Street Construction	
Intergovernmental Revenue:		Bonds	327,000
Sales Tax	$1,012,000	School Bonds	119,000
Federal Grants.	128,000	Sewage Disposal Plant	
State Motor Vehicle Tax .	83,500	Bonds	37,200
State Gasoline Tax . . .	52,000		$1,101,200
State Alcoholic Beverage		Investments	$ 358,000
Licenses.	16,000	State Portion of Sales Tax .	$ 860,200
	$1,291,500	Capital Expenditures:	
Charges for Services:		Sewer Construction	
Sanitation Fees	$ 121,000	(Assessed Area). . . .	$ 114,100
Sewer Connection Fees .	71,000	Civic Center Construction	73,000
Library Revenues	13,000	Library Construction . . .	36,000
Park Revenues	2,500		$ 223,100
	$ 207,500	Total Disbursements	$4,381,000
Bond Issues:			
Civic Center	$ 347,000		
General Obligation	200,000		
Sewer	153,000		
Library	120,000		
	$ 820,000		
Other:			
Proceeds from the Sale			
of Investments	$ 312,000		
Sewer Assessments . . .	50,000		
Rental Revenue	48,000		
Interest Revenue.	15,000		
	$ 425,000		
Total Receipts	$4,156,000		

Exhibit 17.7	Trial Balance for City of Hayes, to Be Used in P17.10

CITY OF HAYES
GENERAL FUND TRIAL BALANCE
JUNE 30, 19X9

DEBITS

Cash	$ 127,180
Cash for Construction	174,000
Taxes Receivable—Current	8,000
Assessments Receivable—Deferred	300,000
Inventory of Materials and Supplies	36,000
Improvements Authorized	365,000
Estimated Revenues	3,785,000
Encumbrances	360,000
Expenditures	4,290,000
Total Debits	$9,445,180

CREDITS

Vouchers Payable	$ 69,090
Bonds Payable	300,000
Premium on Bonds	3,000
Fund Balance—Reserved for Inventory	36,000
Fund Balance—Reserved for Encumbrances	360,000
Appropriations	4,440,000
Interest Revenue	21,000
Fund Balance—Unreserved	106,090
Revenues	4,110,000
Total Credits	$9,445,180

P17.10 General and Special Assessments Funds The trial balance of the general fund of the city of Hayes is given in Exhibit 17.7. Transactions were recorded in the general fund rather than establishing special-purpose funds.

The following additional information is available:

1. A physical inventory taken on June 30, 19X9, showed that materials and supplies with a cost of $37,750 were on hand at that date. Materials and supplies purchased during the year were correctly charged as expenditures.

2. Current taxes are now considered delinquent, and it is estimated that $5,500 of such taxes will be uncollectible. Revenues equal to gross taxes receivable were previously recorded.

3. On June 25, 19X9, the state revenue department informed the city that its share of a state-collected, locally shared tax would be $75,000.

4. New equipment for the police department was acquired at a cost of $90,000 and was properly recorded as an expenditure in the general fund.

5. During the year, 100 acres of land were donated to the city for use as an industrial park. The land had a value of $250,000. No entry has been made.

6. The city council authorized the paving and widening of certain streets at an estimated cost of $365,000, which included an estimated $5,000 cost for planning and engineering to be paid from the general fund. The remaining $360,000 was to be financed by a $10,000 contribution from the city in later years and $350,000 by assessments against property owners, payable in seven equal installments. A $5,000 appropriation was made for the city's share at the time the annual budget was recorded, and the total $365,000 was also recorded as an appropriation. The following information is also relevant to the street improvement project:

a. Property owners paid in full the $50,000 annual installment plus an additional $21,000 assessment for bond interest.

b. Special assessment bonds of $300,000 were authorized and sold at a premium of $3,000. The bond premium is to be used for interest payments.

c. The city's $15,000 share was recorded as an expenditure during the year. The $5,000 for planning and engineering fees was paid; the $10,000 contribution was not paid. Construction began July 5, 19X8, and the contractor has been paid $200,000 under the contract for construction which calls for performance of the work at a total cost of $360,000. This $360,000 makes up the balance in the Reserve for Encumbrances.

d. The Cash for Construction account was used for all receipts and disbursements relative to the project. It is made up of the proceeds of the bond issue and collection of assessment installments and interest minus payments to the contractor.

Required: Prepare a working paper to adjust the account balances at June 30, 19X9, and to distribute them to the appropriate funds or account groups. Do not make closing entries. Formal financial statements are not required. (*AICPA adapted*)

P17.11 Comprehensive Fund Accounting The balance sheet presented below was prepared by the city of Bayside's bookkeeper:

CITY OF BAYSIDE
BALANCE SHEET
JUNE 30, 19X6

ASSETS

Cash	$ 160,000
Taxes Receivable—Current	32,000
Supplies on Hand	8,000
Marketable Securities	250,000
Land	1,000,000
Buildings	7,000,000
Total Assets	$8,450,000

LIABILITIES AND FUND BALANCE

Vouchers Payable.	$ 42,000
Bonds Payable	3,000,000
Fund Balance—Reserved for Supplies Inventory	8,000
Fund Balance—Unreserved.	5,400,000
Total Liabilities and Fund Balance.	$8,450,000

Additional information:

1. An analysis of the fund balance account disclosed the following:

Fund Balance, June 30, 19X5		$2,100,000
Add:		
Donated Land	$ 800,000	
Federal Grant-in-Aid	2,200,000	
Creation of Endowment Fund	250,000	
Excess of Actual Tax Revenue over Estimated Revenue.	24,000	
Excess of Appropriations Closed Out over Expenditures and Encumbrances	20,000	
Net Income from Endowment Funds.	10,000	3,304,000
		$5,404,000
Deduct:		
Excess of Cultural Center Operating Expenses over Income		4,000
Fund Balance, June 30, 19X6		$5,400,000

2. In July 19X5, land appraised at a fair market value of $800,000 was donated to the city for a cultural center which was opened on April 15, 19X6. Building construction expenditures for the project were financed from a federal grant-in-aid of $2,200,000 and from an authorized 10-year $3,000,000 issue of 7 percent general obligation bonds sold at par on July 1, 19X5. Interest is payable on December 31 and June 30. The fair market value of the land and the cost of the building are included in the Land and the Fixed Assets accounts, respectively.

3. The cultural center receives no direct state or city subsidy for current operating expenses. A cultural center endowment fund was established by a gift of marketable securities having a fair market value of $250,000 at date of receipt. The endowment principal is to be kept intact. Income is to be applied to any operating deficit of the center.

4. It is anticipated that $7,000 of the 19X5–19X6 tax is uncollectible.

5. The physical inventory of supplies on hand at June 30, 19X6, amounted to $12,500.

6. Unfilled purchase orders for the general fund at June 30, 19X6, totaled $5,000.

7. On July 1, 19X5, an all-purpose building was purchased for $2,000,000. Of the purchase price, $200,000 was allotted to the land. The purchase had been authorized under the budget for the year ended June 30, 19X6.

Required: Prepare a working paper showing adjustments and distributions to the proper funds or groups of accounts. The working paper should have the following column headings:

1. Balance per Books
2. Adjustments—Debit
3. Adjustments—Credit
4. General Fund
5. City Cultural Center Endowment Fund:
   Principal
   Income
6. General Fixed Assets Group of Accounts
7. General Long-Term Debt Group of Accounts

Number all adjusting entries. Formal journal entries are not required. Supporting computations should be in good form. *(AICPA adapted)*

P17.12 Comprehensive Fund Accounting The village of Dexter was recently incorporated and began financial operations on July 1, 19X8, the beginning of its fiscal year.

The following transactions occurred during this first fiscal year, July 1, 19X8, to June 30, 19X9:

1. The village council adopted a budget for general operations during the fiscal year ending June 30, 19X9. Revenues were estimated at $400,000. Legal authorizations for budgeted expenditures were $394,000.
2. Property taxes were levied in the amount of $390,000; it was estimated that 2 percent of this amount would prove to be uncollectible. These taxes are available as of the date of levy to finance current expenditures.
3. During the year a resident of the village donated marketable securities valued at $50,000 to the village under the terms of a trust agreement. The terms of the trust agreement stipulated that the principal amount is to be kept intact; use of revenue generated by the securities is restricted to financing college scholarships for needy students. Revenue earned and received on these marketable securities amounted to $5,500 through June 30, 19X9.
4. A general fund transfer of $5,000 was made to establish an internal service fund to provide for a permanent investment in inventory.
5. The village decided to install lighting in the village park, and a special assessment project was authorized to install the lighting at a cost of $75,000. The appropriation was formally recorded.
6. The assessments were levied for $72,000, with the village contributing $3,000 out of the general fund. All assessments were collected during the year, including the village's contribution.
7. A contract for $75,000 was let for the installation of the lighting. At June 30, 19X9, the contract was completed but not approved. The

contractor was paid all but 5 percent, which was retained to ensure compliance with the terms of the contract. Encumbrances and other budgetary accounts are maintained.

8. During the year the internal service fund purchased various supplies at a cost of $1,900.

9. Cash collections recorded by the general fund during the year were as follows: property taxes, $386,000; licenses and permits, $7,000.

10. The village council decided to build a village hall at an estimated cost of $500,000 to replace space occupied in rented facilities. The village does not record project authorizations. It was decided that general obligation bonds bearing interest at 6 percent would be issued. On June 30, 19X9, the bonds were issued at their face value of $500,000, payable in 20 years. No contracts have been signed for this project and no expenditures have been made.

11. A fire truck was purchased for $15,000 and the voucher approved and paid by the general fund. This expenditure was previously encumbered for $15,000.

Required: Prepare journal entries to record each of the above transactions in the appropriate fund(s) or group of accounts of the village of Dexter for the fiscal year ended June 30, 19X9. Use the following funds and groups of accounts:

General Fund.

Capital Projects Fund.

Special Assessment Fund.

Internal Service Fund.

Trust Fund.

General Long-Term Debt Group of Accounts.

General Fixed Assets Group of Accounts.

Closing entries are not required. *(AICPA adapted)*

P17.13 Federal Agency Accounting *(Appendix)* The International Cultural Commission is an agency of the State Department which sends U.S. cultural programs to perform in foreign countries and invites foreign cultural programs to perform in the United States. For the fiscal year beginning July 1, 19X3, the commission submitted the following budget to Congress:

Cultural Export Program:		
Administrative Salaries	$700,000	
Other Administrative Costs	600,000	
Program Costs	350,000	$1,650,000
Cultural Import Program:		
Administrative Salaries	$550,000	
Other Administrative Costs	400,000	
Program Costs	200,000	1,150,000

General Administration:
Salaries $300,000
Other Costs 520,000   820,000
Total Budgeted Costs. $3,620,000

Congress approved a budget of $3,820,000, adding $100,000 to the authorized program costs of each program. The OMB apportioned one-half of the final budget to the commission on July 1, and one-half on January 1, 19X4. On each date, the chief commissioner allotted the budgeted amounts to the three unit managers.

Expenditures were obligated, liquidated, and accrued during the year as follows:

	July 1–December 31, 19X3			January 1–June 30, 19X4		
	Obligated	Accrued Expenditures	Obligations December 31	Obligated	Accrued Expenditures	Obligations June 30
General Administration:						
Salaries	$135,000	$120,000	$15,000	$150,000	$165,000	$ 0
Other	240,000	180,000	70,000	265,000	310,000	20,000
Export Program:						
Administrative Salaries	320,000	300,000	20,000	360,000	370,000	0
Other Admin. Costs . .	280,000	260,000	35,000	280,000	300,000	15,000
Program Costs	220,000	140,000	90,000	175,000	250,000	45,000
Import Program:						
Administrative Salaries	250,000	230,000	10,000	250,000	250,000	0
Other Admin. Costs . .	190,000	150,000	50,000	170,000	220,000	25,000
Program Costs	100,000	30,000	80,000	130,000	70,000	110,000

Actual payments recorded by the Treasury were $1,350,000 for July 1–December 31, 19X3, and $1,900,000 for January 1–June 30, 19X4.

Required:

1. Prepare journal entries to record the budget and the transactions of the International Cultural Commission for the year.
2. Prepare closing entries at June 30, 19X4. Assume that any amounts obligated as of year-end are carried forward and that unobligated spending authority lapses.
3. Prepare a balance sheet as of June 30, 19X4.
4. Prepare a statement comparing the commission's budgeted and actual expenditures for the year (include outstanding obligations in actual expenditures).

Chapter 18 Accounting and Reporting by Nonprofit Organizations

Business firms and governmental units constitute two of the three major types of economic entities in our society. The third type is nonprofit organizations, which are important providers of human services (health care, education, and so forth). From an accounting viewpoint, nonprofit organizations bear some similarity to both business firms and governmental units. This chapter presents a brief overview of accounting and reporting by nonprofit organizations in general, with detailed illustration and discussion of three major forms: voluntary health and welfare organizations, colleges, and hospitals.

Nonprofit organizations have the following characteristics:

1. Significant amounts of the organizations' resources are received from providers who neither expect to receive repayment nor expect to receive economic benefits proportionate to the resources provided.
2. The primary operating purposes of the organization are something other than providing goods or services at a profit.
3. There are no ownership interests that can be sold, transferred, or redeemed, or that convey entitlement to a share of resources in the event the organization is liquidated.[1]

These characteristics could apply to governmental units as well as nongovernmental nonprofit organizations. The two differ in their means of support: governmental units typically have taxing power as a means of compelling support, whereas nongovernmental organizations depend on voluntary contributions and user charges to provide resources. In this chapter, we use the term **nonprofit organizations** more narrowly, to mean private (nongovernmental) organizations only. The accounting principles discussed, however, are generally applicable across dif-

---

[1]Financial Accounting Standards Board, *Statement of Financial Accounting Concepts No. 4,* "Objectives of Financial Reporting by Nonbusiness Organizations" (Stamford, CT: FASB, 1980), par. 6.

ferent forms of ownership. Hospital accounting and financial reporting, for example, do not differ greatly among government-operated hospitals, private nonprofit hospitals, and proprietary hospitals.

Nonprofit organizations are numerous in today's society and include the following types:

1. Hospitals.
2. Colleges, universities, and other educational organizations.
3. Voluntary health and welfare organizations, such as the Red Cross and United Way.
4. Churches and other religious organizations.
5. Philanthropic foundations, such as the Ford Foundation.
6. Professional organizations, such as the American Institute of Certified Public Accountants.
7. Trade organizations, such as the National Association of Retail Merchants.
8. Labor organizations, such as the United Auto Workers.
9. Civic and community groups, such as the League of Women Voters.
10. Social and fraternal organizations, such as a Veterans of Foreign Wars post.
11. Membership benefit organizations, such as the American Automobile Association.

Among these types of nonprofit organizations, we may identify three major approaches to the generation of financial resources and the provision of services:

1. Organizations which derive their support from voluntary contributions rather than user charges and offer their services to the public in general. Voluntary health and welfare organizations, churches, foundations, and civic groups tend to fall into this category.
2. Organizations which derive most of their support from user charges and offer services to the public in general. Hospitals and colleges tend to fall into this category.
3. Organizations which derive most of their support from member dues and provide services primarily to their members. Professional, trade, labor, social, and membership benefit organizations fall into this category.

Given these three different approaches, we may expect some differences in accounting and reporting practices. However, since such differences tend to be minor, there is sufficient similarity among the three that we may discuss accounting and reporting for nonprofit organizations in general.

Sources of Accounting Principles

Accounting principles for nonprofit organizations have developed over time, drawing from both business and governmental accounting practices. A **fund structure** is typically employed, dividing the organization into several accounting entities, as is the case in governmental accounting. However, many of the characteristics of fund accounting are not used by nonprofit organizations. Budgetary and encumbrance accounting and the modified accrual approach to revenue recognition are typically *not used* in nonprofit accounting. We shall discuss these matters more fully in subsequent sections.

To date, no one authoritative body has emerged as the leader in standard setting for nonprofit organizations. For many years, the main standard-setting groups of the accounting profession (the APB, FASB, etc.) have concentrated on accounting standards for business firms and have largely ignored the nonprofit sector. Only recently has the FASB begun to deal with this area. As a result, many of the accounting principles for nonprofit organizations have developed informally through practice. However, three groups have played some formal role in the development of these accounting principles.

Industry Groups

Several groups have published materials which set forth accounting principles and procedures for a particular type of nonprofit organization. For example:

1. The United Way of America's *Accounting and Financial Reporting* presents information on general accounting principles, financial reporting, and financial control. It serves as a guide not only for member agencies of the United Way but also for other human service organizations.
2. The American Hospital Association has published a series of booklets dealing with accounting and financial management issues in hospitals. These are used extensively by hospitals throughout the country.
3. The National Association of College and University Business Officers has published a book entitled *College and University Business Administration*. Its recommendations on accounting for educational institutions have been widely adopted.

American Institute of Certified Public Accountants

The American Institute of Certified Public Accountants has issued a series of audit guides dealing with certain types of nonprofit organizations. While primarily designed to set standards for auditing these organizations, the guides also set forth the accounting and reporting principles which should be followed. Existing audit guides cover hospitals, colleges and universities, and voluntary health and welfare organizations.

Financial Accounting Standards Board

The Financial Accounting Standards Board has recently begun to consider the area of nonprofit organizations. Its initial effort was a statement of concepts[2] entitled "Objectives of Financial Reporting by Nonbusiness Organizations" issued in 1980. This statement identifies the factors that affect financial reporting by non-

---

[2]Ibid.

profit organizations and establishes objectives that will serve as the foundation for subsequent adoption of specific accounting principles.

The concepts statement identifies three broad objectives for financial reporting by nonprofit organizations. *First,* financial information should be useful in making resource allocation decisions. Among the users of financial information who make resource allocation decisions are contributors, lenders, suppliers, members, governing or oversight bodies, and managers. These users make decisions on the amount of resources provided to the organization or on the allocation of existing resources among alternative activities. *Second,* financial information should be useful in evaluating the services provided by the organization and in determining its ability to continue to provide these services. *Third,* financial information should be useful in assessing the performance of management. As these objectives eventually lead to specific accounting standards, one may expect that nonprofit accounting will use many of the principles of commercial accounting (such as expense accounting rather than expenditure accounting). For the present, however, nonprofit accounting is very similar to governmental accounting.

Fund Entities

The activities of nonprofit organizations, like those of local governments, are organized into funds for purposes of accounting and reporting. Depending on the nature and complexity of the organization, there may be a single fund or there may be several. Since many different types of organizations fall into the broad category of nonprofit organizations, considerable variation in the specific titles of funds exists. We can, however, identify the *general types of funds* that are often found in nonprofit accounting. In subsequent sections, we shall discuss how these general types are employed in several specific types of nonprofit organizations.

Unrestricted Operating Fund

An **unrestricted operating fund,** also commonly called an **unrestricted current fund** or **general current fund,** is analogous to the general fund of a local governmental unit. This fund accounts for the organization's day-to-day operating activities which are funded by resources having no restriction on their use. In other words, unrestricted fund assets may be spent, at the discretion of management, for *any* activity of the organization. Such resources may come from voluntary contributions, user charges, unrestricted grants for operating purposes, and so on. Expenditures are made from the unrestricted operating fund to cover the costs of the primary services or activities of the organization.

Restricted Operating Fund

A **restricted operating fund,** also called a **restricted current fund,** is analogous to the special revenue fund of a local government. Expenditures from this fund are also made for the day-to-day operating activities or services of the organization. In this case, however, use of the fund's resources has been restricted by their provider to certain operating activities. Such resources typically come from grants or contributions. For example, a hospital may receive a grant for a research program, or a church may receive a contribution for its missionary work.

Plant Fund

The **plant fund** of a nonprofit organization, also called a **land, building, and equipment fund,** accounts for various aspects of the investment in land, buildings, and equipment. A plant fund is often a complex entity consisting of several subfunds; it may contain some or all of the following:

1. Unexpended resources which are to be used for the *acquisition* of land, buildings, or equipment (hereafter called plant assets). This component is analogous to the capital projects fund of a local government.
2. Resources set aside for the *renewal or replacement* of plant assets. When expended, the costs may be capitalized as additional plant assets or may be expensed. The resources of this component are usually transfers from operating funds set aside by management for future needs. There is no counterpart to this component in local governmental accounting.
3. Resources set aside for the *payment of interest and principal* on indebtedness related to past acquisitions of plant assets. This component is analogous to the debt service fund of a local government.
4. Information relating to *amounts already invested in plant assets* and the *unpaid balance of related indebtedness*. This component is analogous to both the general fixed assets and the general long-term debt account groups of a local government.

Endowment Fund

The **endowment fund** accounts for resources which the organization holds for the generation of income and is analogous to a trust fund of a local government. A *permanent endowment* consists of resources provided by outside donors or agencies who have stipulated that the principal is to be maintained indefinitely and is to be invested so as to produce income which often must be spent in a specified way. A *term endowment* is similar, except that at some point the principal may be spent. A *quasi-endowment* (also called *funds functioning as endowment*) consists of resources which the management of the organization has set aside to be retained and invested for certain purposes. In this case, any restrictions are imposed by management rather than by an outside donor and thus can be easily modified in the future.

Agency Fund

The **agency fund** of a nonprofit organization, also called a **custodian fund,** like the agency fund of a local government, accounts for resources held by the organization as a custodian or fiscal agent. For example, if a college holds the resources of student clubs and organizations, these resources would be recorded in an agency fund.

Loan Fund

A **loan fund,** found primarily in educational organizations, accounts for loans outstanding and resources available for lending to employees, students, and so on. A loan fund is usually said to be *revolving,* that is, the interest and principal payments on current loans provide the resources for future loans. The initial capital needed to establish the fund is typically provided either by outside gifts or by allocation of internal resources. As a revolving, self-sustaining fund which primarily serves individuals within the organization, a loan fund is somewhat similar to an internal service fund of a local government.

Annuity Fund

An **annuity fund** accounts for resources acquired by a nonprofit organization in exchange for a promise to make specified payments to designated individuals for a given period of time. Many types of nonprofit organizations offer annuities as a means of deferred fund-raising. For example, assume an individual contributes $50,000 to a religious organization. In return, the organization agrees to pay the individual $4,000 annually for life. The organization invests the $50,000 and uses the income (and, if necessary, some of the principal) to make the annual payments. Upon the donor's death, the remaining funds become available to the organization for other uses. Annuity terms may vary from those in the above example; payments may be made to an individual other than the donor, or the payments may be for a specified number of years rather than for life.

Annuity agreements are attractive to both donors and organizations. Donors assure themselves (or others) of a specified income, while also assuring that the remaining funds will eventually go to the charity of their choice. In addition, there may be tax advantages to transferring assets to a charity while living rather than after death via bequest. From the organization's point of view, annuity agreements enable them to attract sizable contributions, even though it may be several years until the resources become available for the organization's programs.

A variation of an annuity agreement is a life income agreement. Such an agreement provides that *all* income earned on the contributed resources be paid annually to the donor for life. Under a life income agreement, therefore, the annual payment may vary, while under an annuity agreement the annual payment is fixed. Life income agreements may be recorded in the annuity fund or in a separate **life income fund.**

Annuity funds and life income funds have no direct counterparts in local governmental accounting. They are, however, similar to trust funds.

Financial Statements

Financial statements of a nonprofit organization parallel those of a local government. A *balance sheet* presents the assets, liabilities, and fund balance of a particular fund. A *statement of revenues, expenditures (or expenses), and changes in fund balance* reports the activities of the period. The exact format and content of these statements varies somewhat among different funds and different organizational types. They are illustrated for the various nonprofit organizations we consider in the following sections.

Voluntary Health and Welfare Organizations

Voluntary health and welfare organizations are very prevalent in our society. These organizations provide a wide variety of services, either to individuals or to broader segments of society, in the areas of health, social welfare, and community services. A brief list drawn from the multitude of services and organizations illustrates the pervasiveness and diversity of this category:

1. Health education and research (for example, the American Heart Association).
2. Disaster relief (for example, the American Red Cross).
3. Alcoholism and drug abuse counseling (for example, Alcoholics Anonymous).
4. Family counseling (for example, Planned Parenthood).
5. Social development (for example, Boys' Club).
6. Services to the handicapped (for example, Goodwill Industries).

Voluntary health and welfare organizations are primarily supported by contributions, either to individual organizations or to "umbrella" organizations such as the United Way.

Accounting Principles

For many years, no formal pronouncements on accounting principles existed for voluntary health and welfare organizations. Practices were adapted from other areas of nonprofit accounting, such as hospitals and educational institutions. In 1964, the National Health Council and the National Social Welfare Assembly jointly published a guide entitled *Standards of Accounting and Financial Reporting for Voluntary Health and Welfare Organizations*. Known as the "black book," this guide came to be widely accepted as an authoritative source. Subsequently, the United Way of America published an accounting manual for use by its member agencies, incorporating the principles set forth in the black book. These principles were also the basis for an industry audit guide entitled *Audits of Voluntary Health and Welfare Organizations* published in 1966 by the AICPA and revised in 1973. Thus three primary sources of accounting principles and practices by voluntary health and welfare organizations currently exist: the black book, the United Way manual, and the AICPA audit guide.

Types of Funds

The various types of funds employed by nonprofit organizations in general were discussed earlier in the chapter. The funds commonly found in voluntary health and welfare organizations are:

1. Unrestricted current fund.
2. Restricted current fund.
3. Plant fund (which includes unexpended resources for acquisition or replacement, net investment in fixed assets, and liabilities related to these assets).
4. Endowment fund.
5. Agency fund.

Loan funds and annuity funds are usually not found in voluntary health and welfare organizations; they will be illustrated in the section on colleges and universities.

The following sections illustrate accounting and reporting for the current, plant, and endowment funds. For each, entries will be presented, leading to a balance sheet and a statement of revenues, expenses, and changes in fund balance. In addition, a *statement of functional expenses* will be illustrated. This statement presents detail on the expenses connected with each activity of the organization, without regard to the fund in which the transactions occurred.

Comprehensive Illustration

The Northeastern Heart Society supports research, education, and public awareness programs on the prevention of heart disease. Its resources are primarily generated from contributions, bequests, and grants. Its activities for the year ended December 31, 19X3, have been organized into four funds, which are discussed in the following sections.

Unrestricted Current Fund. At January 1, 19X3, the balance sheet of the unrestricted current fund showed the following:

Cash	$117,000	Vouchers Payable	$ 33,000
Pledges Receivable (Net of $16,000 Allowance for Uncollectibles)	64,000	Fund Balance	148,000
	$181,000		$181,000

Contributions pledged during 19X3 amounted to $1,300,000, of which $1,150,000 was collected during the year. In addition, $67,000 of the pledges outstanding at January 1 was collected; the balance was written off. The society provides an allowance for uncollectibles equal to 20 percent of pledges outstanding at year-end. Revenue of $46,000 was earned from programs which the society conducted for employee groups of various corporations. The entries to record the above transactions are:

Pledges Receivable	1,300,000	
Revenue—Contributions		1,300,000
To record pledges during 19X3.		
Cash	1,150,000	
Pledges Receivable		1,150,000
To record collections of current pledges.		

```
Cash . . . . . . . . . . . . . . . . . . . . . . .        67,000
    Pledges Receivable. . . . : . . . . . . . . .                   67,000
To record collections of prior year pledges.

Allowance for Uncollectible Pledges. . . . . . . . . . . .   13,000
    Pledges Receivable. . . . . . . . . . . . . . . . . .            13,000
To write off uncollected pledges from 19X2 ($13,000 =
$80,000 - $67,000).

Revenue—Contributions . . . . . . . . . . . . . . . . .   27,000
    Allowance for Uncollectible Pledges . . . . . . . . . .          27,000
To adjust allowance to 20% of year-end balance.

Cash . . . . . . . . . . . . . . . . . . . . . . .        46,000
    Revenue—Program Services . . . . . . . . . . . . . .             46,000
To record revenue from educational programs.
```

Cash expenditures for 19X3 amounted to $1,255,000, as follows:

```
Research. . . . . . . . . . . . . . . . . . . . . . . . . . . . . . . .  $  400,000
Public Awareness Programs . . . . . . . . . . . . . . . . . . . . . . .     350,000
Corporate Programs . . . . . . . . . . . . . . . . . . . . . . . . . .       35,000
General Administration . . . . . . . . . . . . . . . . . . . . . . . . .    195,000
Fund-Raising. . . . . . . . . . . . . . . . . . . . . . . . . . . . . .     175,000
Transfer to Plant Fund . . . . . . . . . . . . . . . . . . . . . . . . .    100,000
                                                                         $1,255,000
```

Vouchers payable increased from $33,000 to $48,000; all unpaid vouchers at beginning and end of year relate to general administration costs. Entries to record the above are:

```
Expenses—Research. . . . . . . . . . . . . . . . . . . . .  400,000
Expenses—Public Programs . . . . . . . . . . . . . . . . .  350,000
Expenses—Corporate Programs . . . . . . . . . . . . . . .    35,000
Expenses—General Administration . . . . . . . . . . . . .   210,000
Expenses—Fund-Raising. . . . . . . . . . . . . . . . . . .  175,000
    Cash . . . . . . . . . . . . . . . . . . . . . . . . . .            1,155,000
    Vouchers Payable . . . . . . . . . . . . . . . . . . . .               15,000
To record expenses for 19X3.

Transfer to Plant Fund . . . . . . . . . . . . . . . . . . .  100,000
    Cash . . . . . . . . . . . . . . . . . . . . . . . . . .              100,000
To record transfer to plant fund.
```

Financial statements for the unrestricted current fund at December 31, 19X3, are presented in Exhibit 18.1.

Restricted Current Fund. During 19X3, the society received a federal grant of $200,000 to expand its public awareness programs into smaller communities where it had not previously been active. The grant period expires on March 31, 19X4; by the end of 19X3, $143,000 had been spent on the project. A restricted current fund was established to account for the grant. Financial statements at year-end appeared as shown in Exhibit 18.2.

Exhibit 18.3	Endowment Fund Financial Statements

NORTHEASTERN HEART SOCIETY
ENDOWMENT FUND
BALANCE SHEET
DECEMBER 31, 19X3

Cash	$ 11,400	Fund Balance:	
Investments	728,500	Principal	$733,500
		Income	6,400
	$739,900		$739,900

NORTHEASTERN HEART SOCIETY
ENDOWMENT FUND
STATEMENT OF REVENUES, EXPENSES,
AND CHANGES IN FUND BALANCE
FOR THE YEAR ENDED DECEMBER 31, 19X3

REVENUES

Bequests	$10,000	
Contributions	3,500	
Investment Income	80,000	$ 93,500

EXPENSES

Scholarships	75,000
Excess of Revenues over Expenses	$ 18,500
Fund Balance—Beginning of Year	721,400
Fund Balance—End of Year	$739,900

gage will be obtained, and the building loan will be paid off. During 19X3, $240,000 was spent on construction costs, and $28,000 of interest was paid on the loan. Investment of excess cash balances in time deposits yielded $7,700 in interest revenue; the society's board of directors has authorized the use of this money for unanticipated construction costs. Depreciation on office equipment of $3,000 was charged to general administration.

The above information was recorded in the plant fund by the following entries:

Cash—Construction	50,000	
Cash—Debt Service	50,000	
Transfer from Unrestricted Current Fund		100,000
To record transfer from unrestricted current fund.		
Cash—Construction	300,000	
Loan Payable		300,000
To record building loan.		
Construction in Progress	240,000	
Cash—Construction		240,000
To record construction costs on building.		

```
Interest Expense . . . . . . . . . . . . . . . . . . . . . . . . .   28,000
    Cash—Debt Service . . . . . . . . . . . . . . . . . . . . .           28,000
To record interest paid on loan.

Cash—Construction. . . . . . . . . . . . . . . . . . . . . . .    7,700
    Interest Revenue . . . . . . . . . . . . . . . . . . . . . .            7,700
To record interest earned on time deposits.

Expenses—General Administration . . . . . . . . . . . . . .      3,000
    Accumulated Depreciation—Equipment. . . . . . . . . . .              3,000
To record depreciation on office equipment.
```

The financial statements for 19X3 appear as shown in Exhibit 18.4.

Statement of Functional Expenses. The Northeastern Heart Society incurred expenses in each of its four funds. To more easily assess the total cost of its pro-

---

Exhibit 18.4 | **Plant Fund Financial Statements**

NORTHEASTERN HEART SOCIETY
PLANT FUND
BALANCE SHEET
DECEMBER 31, 19X3

Cash—Construction . . .		$117,700	Loan Payable.	$300,000
Cash—Debt Service . . .		22,000	Fund Balance:	
Land		20,000	Expended	41,000
Equipment	$30,000		Unexpended	79,700
Accumulated Depreciation	9,000	21,000		
Construction in Progress		240,000		
		$420,700		$420,700

NORTHEASTERN HEART SOCIETY
PLANT FUND
STATEMENT OF REVENUES, EXPENSES
AND CHANGES IN FUND BALANCE
FOR THE YEAR ENDED DECEMBER 31, 19X3

REVENUES

Interest.		$ 7,700

EXPENSES

General Administration.	$ 3,000	
Interest.	28,000	31,000
Excess (Deficiency) of Revenues over Expenses		$ (23,300)

OTHER CHANGES IN FUND BALANCE

Transfer from Unrestricted Current Fund.	100,000
Excess of Revenues and Other Changes Over Expenses	$ 76,700
Fund Balance—Beginning of Year.	44,000
Fund Balance—End of Year	$120,700

Exhibit 18.5	Statement of Functional Expenses

NORTHEASTERN HEART SOCIETY
STATEMENT OF FUNCTIONAL EXPENSES
FOR THE YEAR ENDED DECEMBER 31, 19X3

	Program Services			Supporting Services		
	Research	Public Programs	Corporate Programs	General Administration	Fund-Raising	Total Expenses
Salaries	$ 65,000	$160,000	$22,000	$110,000	$ 20,000	$ 377,000
Employee Benefits	15,000	30,000	4,000	20,000	5,000	74,000
Payroll Taxes	7,000	15,000	2,000	10,000	2,000	36,000
Total Personnel Costs	$ 87,000	$205,000	$28,000	$140,000	$ 27,000	$ 487,000
Professional Fees	0	0	0	0	70,000	70,000
Supplies	45,000	23,000	0	10,000	10,000	88,000
Telephone	10,000	50,000	0	10,000	25,000	95,000
Postage	10,000	30,000	0	5,000	5,000	50,000
Occupancy Costs	15,000	15,000	5,000	20,000	5,000	60,000
Equipment Rental and Maintenance	35,000	20,000	0	15,000	0	70,000
Printing and Publications	20,000	90,000	0	0	30,000	140,000
Travel	40,000	40,000	2,000	0	3,000	85,000
Conferences and Meetings	35,000	20,000	0	10,000	0	65,000
Research Grants	103,000	0	0	0	0	103,000
Scholarship Awards	75,000	0	0	0	0	75,000
Interest	0	0	0	28,000	0	28,000
Total before Depreciation	$475,000	$493,000	$35,000	$238,000	$175,000	$1,416,000
Depreciation	0	0	0	3,000	0	3,000
Total Expenses	$475,000	$493,000	$35,000	$241,000	$175,000	$1,419,000

grams and supporting services, a **statement of functional expenses** is prepared. This statement presents expenses by object classification (salaries, supplies, telephone, etc.) for each function of the organization (research, public programs, etc.). Which fund incurred the expense is unimportant for the purposes of this statement. The statement of functional expenses for the Northeastern Heart Society is shown in Exhibit 18.5.

Important Accounting Issues

The accounting procedures used to record transactions of voluntary health and welfare organizations (and other nonprofit organizations) are similar to those illustrated for local government. However, several special considerations exist, as will be discussed in the following sections.

Investments. A voluntary health and welfare organization may invest endowment and other restricted resources on a long-term basis and may invest unrestricted resources on a temporary basis. Accounting questions arise in regard to the basis for carrying these investments on the balance sheet and the treatment of investment income, gains, and losses.

Three methods for presenting investments on the balance sheet are considered acceptable: *cost, market,* and *lower of cost or market.* The same method should be used for all funds. If the cost basis is used, market value should also be disclosed, and vice versa.

The treatment of investment income, gains, and losses involves legal as well as accounting issues. The questions are (1) whether gains and losses are expendable as income or are considered part of principal, and (2) whether *expendable* gains and losses and investment income earned by restricted or endowment funds may be spent for *unrestricted* uses. The usual answers to these questions are summarized as follows:

Fund Type	Investment Income	Gains	Losses
Unrestricted Fund	Unrestricted	Unrestricted	Unrestricted
Restricted Fund	Restricted unless legally available for unrestricted	Restricted unless legally available for unrestricted	Restricted
Endowment Fund	Unrestricted unless restricted by donor	Addition to principal unless donor or state law permits otherwise	Subtraction from principal unless donor or state law permits otherwise

If the cost method is used, only realized gains and losses are recorded. Under the market method, both realized and unrealized gains and losses are recorded. Under the lower-of-cost-or-market method, realized gains, realized and unrealized losses, and unrealized loss recoveries are recorded. The references to *gains* and *losses* in the above table thus must be interpreted in accordance with the method of accounting being used.

To facilitate the management of investments, a nonprofit organization may decide to combine the investments of several funds into a single portfolio or **investment pool.** Records must be maintained so that the equity of each fund in the pool can be determined. For example, assume that three funds originally contributed a total of $90,000 to an investment pool as follows:

Fund	Contribution	Original Equity Percentage
A	$40,000	44.44%
B	35,000	38.89
C	15,000	16.67
	$90,000	100.00%

Whenever a change in the composition of the pool occurs—a fund invests or withdraws—new equity percentages should be calculated based on *current market values.* Assume that the investments in the pool have increased in value to $150,000 and that Fund C will invest an additional $100,000. The calculation of revised equity percentages proceeds as follows:

Fund	Original Equity Percentage	Allocation of Current Value	Value after Investment	Revised Equity Percentage
A	44.44%	$ 66,667	$ 66,667	26.67%
B	38.89	58,333	58,333	23.33
C	16.67	25,000	125,000	50.00
	100.00%	$150,000	$250,000	100.00%

If the market method were used to account for investments, each fund would report according to the above data. For example, the balance sheet of Fund A would show investments having a market value of $66,667 and a cost of $40,000.

Fixed Assets. Fixed assets of a voluntary health and welfare organization available for use in carrying out the organization's programs are recorded in the plant fund. *Purchased assets* are recorded at *cost,* and *donated assets* are recorded at *fair market value.* If a donated asset has a restricted use which prevents its disposition or use in certain programs, it is recorded in the restricted fund rather than the plant fund.

Depreciation practices vary widely. Some organizations record depreciation; others do not. Depreciation may be recorded on assets which are to be maintained and replaced out of operating revenues but not on assets which are to be maintained and replaced by contributions and grants. Ideally, depreciation on all assets should be recognized, so that the cost of the organization's programs and services is not understated.

Donations. Donations—of cash, goods, and services—often constitute the major source of support for voluntary health and welfare organizations. Donations may be received directly or indirectly through a parent or umbrella agency. Any restrictions placed on the use of the donated resources will determine the fund to be used.

Fund-raising activities by a nonprofit organization often result in promises of contributions known as **pledges.** Pledges of cash should be recorded as receivables on the accrual basis, with an allowance for uncollectible pledges based on past collection experience and the organization's collection practices (many organizations feel that public relations considerations prevent aggressive collection practices). For example, assume that a local Association for the Blind chapter holds an annual telethon on June 1, 19X1, to raise funds for the fiscal year beginning on that date. Callers to the telethon pledge $350,000 to the association, mostly in small amounts of $10 to $50. Past experience suggests that 30 percent of these pledges will not be collected. The organization should record:

```
Pledges Receivable. . . . . . . . . . . . . . . . . . . . . . 350,000
    Allowance for Uncollectible Pledges  . . . . . . . . . . . .        105,000
    Revenue from Contributions  . . . . . . . . . . . . . . . .        245,000
    To record pledges net of estimated amount uncollectible.
```

In this example, resources from the pledges are expected to be available within the current year and are considered to be current revenues. If the pledge is such that the normal collection period extends beyond the current year, a deferred revenue account should be used. For example, suppose a foundation awards a grant of $7,500 to the Association for the Blind, payable over 3 years, to support a special project. This would be recorded as:

```
Grants Receivable . . . . . . . . . . . . . . . . . . . . . . . . . . . . . 7,500
    Revenue from Grants . . . . . . . . . . . . . . . . . . . . . . . . .        2,500
    Deferred Revenue . . . . . . . . . . . . . . . . . . . . . . . . . .        5,000
To record pledge of 3-year grant from foundation.
```

Donations of significant amounts of goods should be recorded at fair market value, if a clear basis for determining market value exists and if the goods are used in the organization's programs. For example, suppose medicine with a fair market value of $4,000 is donated to a health organization by a pharmaceutical company, and is used in a free clinic program. The entry would be:

```
Expenses—Free Clinic Program . . . . . . . . . . . . . . . . . . 4,000
    Revenue from Contributions . . . . . . . . . . . . . . . . . . .        4,000
To record donation of medicine.
```

On the other hand, goods whose value is difficult to determine, such as donations of used clothing to a social welfare agency, are usually not recorded.

Donations of services present a similar situation; some are recorded, others are not. Donated services are recorded if they meet the following conditions:

1. The services are a normal part of the organization's programs.
2. In the absence of volunteers, the services are performed by salaried personnel.
3. The organization controls the use and duties of volunteers.
4. There is a clearly measurable basis for the value of the services.

Many services do not meet these criteria and thus are generally not recorded. Examples include volunteers who provide auxiliary services which otherwise would not be provided and solicitors in fund-raising campaigns.

Colleges and Universities

Accounting and reporting for institutions of higher education is subject to some degree of variation because of the different "ownerships" which exist. Colleges and universities may be run by state government (as is, for example, Michigan State University), city government (as is City University of New York), or state and local government (the community colleges in New York State are jointly supported by the state and the county), or they may be private nonprofit institutions (as is Lehigh University). Profit-making organizations, such as proprietary business and secretarial schools, also exist. Our discussion here will focus primarily on *private nonprofit institutions*. Accounting for government-operated institutions involves a combination of accounting principles for colleges and universities with those for governmental units. Similarly, accounting for proprietary schools involves a combination of college and business accounting.

Accounting Principles

Accounting principles for colleges and universities are derived from two major sources. One is the work of professional education groups. The National Association of College and University Business Officers (NACUBO) through its Accounting Principles Committee and the American Council on Education have been especially influential. The other source is the accounting profession, which set forth accounting principles in an industry audit guide entitled *Audits of Colleges and Universities,* published by the AICPA in 1973. The audit guide was heavily influenced by the previous work of the American Council on Education and NACUBO.

Types of Funds

All of the fund types discussed earlier in the chapter are commonly found in college and university accounting. These are: unrestricted current fund, restricted current fund, plant fund, endowment fund, agency fund, loan fund, and annuity and life income funds.

Current Funds. Current funds (both unrestricted and restricted) account for the operating activities of the institution. Revenues of current funds are produced by:

1. Student tuition and fees. These should be reported at gross amount. Scholarships, tuition waivers, and similar reductions are considered expenses.
2. Government aid, grants, and contracts.
3. Gifts and private grants.
4. Endowment income.
5. Sales and services of educational departments, such as publications and testing services.
6. Revenues of auxiliary enterprises, such as food service, residence halls, campus store, and athletics.

Expenditures of current funds include such items as:

1. Instruction.
2. Research.
3. Extension and public service programs.
4. Libraries.
5. Student aid.
6. Student services (such as admissions, financial aid, and guidance).
7. Operation and maintenance of physical facilities.
8. General and administrative expenses.
9. Operating costs of auxiliary enterprises.

10. Transfers, whether voluntary or mandatory, to loan fund, plant fund (for example, for replacement of assets or for debt service), endowment funds, and others.

Entries for these normal, day-to-day operating transactions are not illustrated, as they are similar to those presented for voluntary health and welfare organizations.

Financial statements for current funds consist of a balance sheet, a statement of revenues, expenses and other changes, and a statement of changes in fund balances. Each statement is subdivided into unrestricted and restricted categories. The balance sheet is illustrated in Exhibit 18.6. Note that it contains only current assets and liabilities; long-term assets and liabilities are presented in the plant fund. The statement of revenues, expenses, and other changes is illustrated in Exhibit 18.7.

Plant Funds. As discussed earlier in the case of a voluntary health and welfare organization, the plant fund may have several subcategories, including:

1. Unexpended plant funds, representing resources still to be spent on construction or acquisitions in process.
2. Renewal and replacement funds, representing resources contributed or set aside for these purposes.
3. Retirement of indebtedness funds, representing resources set aside for debt payments.
4. Investment in plant, representing the cost of assets and any related long-term debt.

Financial statements include a balance sheet and a statement of changes in fund balance. The balance sheet is illustrated in Exhibit 18.8 (on page 964). A state-

---

Exhibit 18.6   **Current Funds Balance Sheet**

MOUNTAIN STATE UNIVERSITY
CURRENT FUNDS
BALANCE SHEET
JUNE 30, 19X6

ASSETS			LIABILITIES AND FUND BALANCES		
Unrestricted:			Unrestricted:		
Cash	$353,000		Accounts Payable . .	$140,000	
Investments	608,000		Accrued Liabilities . .	81,000	
Accounts Receivable,			Student Deposits . . .	200,000	
Net	277,000		Due to Other Funds .	100,000	$ 521,000
Inventories	82,000		Fund Balance		820,000
Prepaid Expenses . .	21,000				
Total Unrestricted .		$1,341,000	Total Unrestricted .		$1,341,000
Restricted:			Restricted:		
Cash	$170,000		Accounts Payable . .	$ 35,000	
Investments	205,000		Fund Balance	340,000	
Total Restricted . .		375,000	Total Restricted . .		375,000
Total Current Funds . .		$1,716,000	Total Current Funds . .		$1,716,000

Exhibit 18.7 **Current Funds Statement of Revenues, Expenses, and Other Changes**

MOUNTAIN STATE UNIVERSITY
CURRENT FUNDS
STATEMENT OF REVENUES, EXPENSES, AND OTHER CHANGES IN
FUND BALANCE
FOR THE YEAR ENDED JUNE 30, 19X6

	Unrestricted	Restricted	Total
Revenues			
Student Tuition and Fees.	$3,000,000		$ 3,000,000
State Aid and Grants.	4,000,000		4,000,000
Gifts and Private Grants	800,000	$ 700,000	1,500,000
Endowment Income	200,000	500,000	700,000
Auxiliary Enterprises	1,200,000		1,200,000
Total Revenues	$9,200,000	$1,200,000	$10,400,000
Expenses			
Instruction	$2,700,000		$ 2,700,000
Research.	600,000	$ 300,000	900,000
Libraries	300,000	100,000	400,000
Student Services	250,000		250,000
Operation and Maintenance	900,000		900,000
Administration	700,000		700,000
Student Aid.	750,000	700,000	1,450,000
Auxiliary Enterprises	1,150,000		1,150,000
Total Expenses	$7,350,000	$1,100,000	$ 8,450,000
Transfers			
Debt Service	1,500,000		1,500,000
Equipment Replacement	150,000		150,000
Total Expenses and Transfers . . .	$9,000,000	$1,100,000	$10,100,000
Net Increase in Fund Balance	$ 200,000	$ 100,000	$ 300,000

ment of changes in fund balance, for both current funds and plant funds, is presented in Exhibit 18.9 (on page 965).

Loan Funds. Loan funds exist to provide loans to students or employees of the educational institution. Outstanding loans are carried as receivables, with an appropriate allowance for uncollectibles. Interest revenue on loans is usually recorded when collected rather than as it accrues.

To illustrate, suppose that McKinley College transfers $100,000 from its unrestricted operating fund to establish a loan fund for its students. The transfer is recorded by the loan fund as:

```
Cash . . . . . . . . . . . . . . . . . . . . . . . . . . . . .  100,000
   Fund Balance. . . . . . . . . . . . . . . . . . . . . . . .           100,000
To establish loan fund by transfer from unrestricted operating
fund.
```

Exhibit 18.8	Plant Funds Balance Sheet

MOUNTAIN STATE UNIVERSITY
PLANT FUNDS
BALANCE SHEET
JUNE 30, 19X6

ASSETS

Unexpended:	
Cash	$ 73,000
Investments	288,000
Total Unexpended.	$ 361,000
Renewal and Replacement:	
Cash	$ 18,000
Investments	440,000
Due from Other Funds.	30,000
Total Renewal and Replacement	$ 488,000
Retirement of Indebtedness:	
Cash	$ 12,000
Investments	48,000
Due from Other Funds.	70,000
Total Retirement of Indebtedness.	$ 130,000
Investment in Plant:	
Land.	$ 100,000
Land Improvements	2,400,000
Buildings.	57,820,000
Equipment	22,051,000
Library Books.	3,644,000
Total Investment in Plant.	$86,015,000
Total Plant Funds	$86,994,000

LIABILITIES AND FUND BALANCE

Unexpended:	
Accounts Payable.	$ 117,000
Fund Balance.	244,000
Total Unexpended.	$ 361,000
Renewal and Replacement:	
Fund Balance—Restricted	$ 105,000
Fund Balance—Unrestricted	383,000
Total Renewal and Replacement	$ 488,000
Retirement of Indebtedness:	
Fund Balance—Restricted	$ 15,000
Fund Balance—Unrestricted	115,000
Total Retirement of Indebtedness.	$ 130,000
Investment in Plant:	
Bonds Payable	$10,000,000
Mortgage Payable.	8,300,000
	$18,300,000
Net Investment in Plant	67,715,000
Total Investment in Plant.	$86,015,000
Total Plant Funds	$86,994,000

During the first year, $28,000 is loaned to students, and $2,000 of interest and $3,000 of principal are collected. At year-end, 3 percent of the outstanding balance is estimated to be uncollectible, and $1,200 of interest revenue has accrued. Entries for the year are as follows:

Loans Receivable.	28,000	
Cash		28,000
To record loans made.		
Cash	5,000	
Loans Receivable.		3,000
Revenues.		2,000
To record collections.		
Bad Debt Expense	750	
Allowance for Doubtful Accounts		750
To record allowance for estimated uncollectibles.		

Note that no entry is made for the accrued interest; interest revenue is recognized on a cash basis.

Exhibit 18.9   Statement of Changes in Fund Balances

MOUNTAIN STATE UNIVERSITY
STATEMENT OF CHANGES IN FUND BALANCE
FOR THE YEAR ENDED JUNE 30, 19X6

	Current Funds			Plant Funds		
	Unrestricted	Restricted	Unexpended	Renewal and Replacement	Indebtedness	Investment in Plant
Revenues and Other Additions:						
Revenues	$ 9,200,000	$1,200,000	$ 20,000	$ 50,000	$ 5,000	
Bond Proceeds			3,000,000			
Plant Additions						$ 3,320,000
Retirement of Indebtedness						200,000
Total Revenues and Additions	$ 9,200,000	$1,200,000	$3,020,000	$ 50,000	$ 5,000	$ 3,520,000
Expenses and Other Deductions:						
Expenses	$ 7,350,000	$1,100,000	$2,870,000	$ 450,000		
Plant and Equipment					$1,550,000	
Principal and Interest						
Plant Retirements						$ 70,000
Total Expenses and Deductions	$ 7,350,000	$1,100,000	$2,870,000	$ 450,000	$1,550,000	$ 70,000
Transfers among Funds:						
Debt Service	$(1,500,000)				$1,500,000	
Equipment Replacement	(150,000)			$ 150,000		
Total Transfers	$(1,650,000)			$ 150,000	$1,500,000	
Net Increase (Decrease) for Year	$ 200,000	$ 100,000	$ 150,000	$(250,000)	$ (45,000)	$ 3,450,000
Fund Balance, Beginning of Year	620,000	240,000	94,000	633,000	160,000	64,265,000
Fund Balance, End of Year	$ 820,000	$ 340,000	$ 244,000	$ 383,000	$ 115,000	$67,715,000

Following the closing entries, the balance sheet for the loan fund appears as shown below:

MCKINLEY COLLEGE
LOAN FUND
BALANCE SHEET
JUNE 30, 19X0

Cash	$ 77,000	Fund Balance	$101,250
Loans Receivable (Net of $750 Allowance for Doubtful Accounts)	24,250		
	$101,250		$101,250

Annuity and Life Income Funds. One means of fund-raising by colleges and universities (and by some other nonprofit organizations such as churches and religious groups) is the annuity or life income agreement. A donor contributes a sum of money or other resources to the institution. In exchange, the institution agrees to make periodic payments, either to the donor or to other specified individuals, for a period of time. The time period may be a fixed number of years or may be the lifetime of the beneficiary. At the termination of the agreement period, any remaining resources are typically available to the institution for restricted or unrestricted use. If the periodic payment is a fixed amount, the agreement is called an **annuity;** if the payment is defined as the amount of income earned on the contributed assets, it is a **life income agreement.**

In the case of annuity funds, the contributed assets are recorded at either donor's cost or, preferably, fair market value. The present value of the annuity payments should be calculated and recorded as a liability. The difference is recorded as fund balance. It is not appropriate to merely debit assets and credit fund balance, as would be done for endowment funds.

Life income funds, on the other hand, are treated in a manner similar to endowment funds. The future payments to beneficiaries are equal to future income, and thus no present value exists for the liability.

To illustrate, suppose that an elderly alumnus, who has a life expectancy of 9 years, donates $50,000 to McKinley College under an *annuity agreement* whereby he is to receive $7,000 annually for life. It is determined that a 10 percent discount rate is appropriate. The present value of the liability is calculated as: $7,000 \times$ present value of an ordinary annuity of (9 years, 10%) = $7,000 \times$ 5.759 = $40,313. The contribution is recorded as:

Cash	50,000	
Annuity Payable		40,313
Annuity Fund Balance		9,687
To record contribution and corresponding annuity agreement.		

Suppose further that $40,000 was invested at 12 percent, and $10,000 remained in a savings account at 6 percent. Entries for the first year are as follows:

Investments 40,000
   Cash   40,000
To record investment of $40,000 at 12%.

Cash 5,400
   Annuity Fund Balance.   5,400
To record income for year from investments ($4,800) and from
savings account ($600).

Annuity Payable. 2,968
Annuity Fund Balance. 4,032
   Cash   7,000
To record annuity payment and corresponding reduction in liability.

In the third entry above, the reduction in the liability was calculated as follows:

Original liability (present value of $7,000 for 9 years at 10%: $7,000 × 5.759) . . . $40,313
Liability after one year (present value of $7,000 for 8 years at 10%:
   $7,000 × 5.335) 37,345
Reduction in liability . . . . $ 2,968

This calculation is analogous to the use of the effective-interest method for long-term debt. The balance sheet of the annuity fund appears as follows:

MCKINLEY COLLEGE
ANNUITY FUND
BALANCE SHEET
JUNE 30, 19X0

Cash . . . . $ 8,400   Annuity Payable. $37,345
Investments. 40,000   Fund Balance 11,055
                          $48,400 $48,400

If the same contribution were made under a *life income agreement,* no initial liability would be calculated. The donor is entitled to receive whatever income is generated each year. Assuming the same facts as above, the entries for a life income fund would be:

Cash 50,000
   Life Income Fund Balance   50,000
To record contribution under life income agreement.

Investments 40,000
   Cash   40,000
To record investment of $40,000 at 12%.

Cash 5,400
   Life Income Payable   5,400
To record income for year from investments and from savings
account and corresponding obligation to donor.

Life Income Payable. 5,400
   Cash   5,400
To record payment of current income to donor per agreement.

The balance sheet would appear as:

MCKINLEY COLLEGE
LIFE INCOME FUND
BALANCE SHEET
JUNE 30, 19X0

Cash	$10,000	Fund Balance	$50,000
Investments	40,000		
	$50,000		$50,000

If an organization has both annuity and life income agreements, a combined balance sheet is often presented.

Important Accounting Issues

Colleges and universities follow accrual accounting. The accounting practices with respect to investments and donations are generally similar to those discussed for voluntary health and welfare organizations. Other issues are discussed below.

Depreciation. Depreciation of plant assets is not reported in the current funds, since these funds emphasize cash expenditures rather than operating expenses. Depreciation may or may not be recorded in the plant fund. If it is, it appears as depreciation expense on the statement of changes in fund balance and as accumulated depreciation on the balance sheet.

Gains on Investments. The question of whether gains on endowment investments constitute principal or income is particularly relevant to colleges and universities. Endowment income is a significant portion of the budget for many private educational institutions. The treatment of gains influences the investment policies of the institution; if gains are not spendable, the institution is likely to invest in securities promising high current interest or dividend income rather than in securities with low current income but good future growth potential. Such an investment policy may act against the institution's long-run interests; investment in growth securities may be desirable to help offset the effects of inflation on the endowment. If a growth-oriented investment policy is followed and gains are not spendable, however, current budget problems may result.

The question of the treatment of gains has been widely debated in recent years. The traditional view that interest and dividends are spendable income but that gains are not is based on a fiduciary viewpoint with respect to endowments. Under this point of view, the organization does not *own* its endowment, but rather *administers it as a trustee* on behalf of the beneficiaries of the organization. Thus the endowment is viewed as a trust, and fiduciary accounting principles are applied, requiring a separation of principal and income and treatment of gains as a part of principal. The opposing view holds that considering an endowment as a trust is inappropriate. The organization is the absolute owner of the endowment, and corporate accounting principles, which do not involve a separation of principal and income, should apply.

A compromise position has emerged, known as a **total return approach,** which permits some spending of gains but also attempts to protect the principal. Traditional yield (interest and dividends) plus net gains equals the total investment return. A *spending rate* is established (5 percent is commonly used) and is applied to the market value of the portfolio (or, to minimize fluctuations, a multiyear average portfolio value). This portion of the return is available for current use; the remainder becomes part of principal. The logic of assigning a portion of the total return to principal is based on protection of principal from inflation and future losses. For example, assume that a college's portfolio has a market value of $3,000,000 and produces a total return for the year of $283,000 (consisting of interest, dividends, and net gains). If a 5 percent spending rate is used, $150,000 ($= \$3,000,000 \times 5\%$) is available for current use and $133,000 ($= \$283,000 - \$150,000$) is added to principal. This approach removes the motivation to invest solely in securities having high current yield, but still provides for protection (growth) of principal. In recent years, several states have adopted legislation permitting some version of the total return approach. Thus there is a trend toward eliminating or reducing the limitations on the spending of gains. This continues to be a subject of controversy.

Hospitals

As was the case with colleges and universities, hospitals may be government, private nonprofit, or proprietary organizations. Thus aspects of governmental or business accounting may be present. Our focus in this discussion is on the voluntary (that is, private nonprofit) hospitals, although many of the accounting principles apply also to government or proprietary hospitals. Similarly, many of the accounting principles apply to health care institutions other than hospitals, such as rehabilitation centers and nursing homes.

Accounting Principles

Accounting principles for hospitals derive from two major sources. The American Hospital Association has issued several publications relating to accounting, cost determination, and internal control by hospitals. The AICPA has published a *Hospital Audit Guide* which discusses accounting principles for hospitals.

Types of Funds

The various funds employed by a voluntary hospital fall into two major categories: unrestricted and restricted funds. Other funds might be present in certain circumstances. For example, a teaching hospital (one which educates doctors or nurses in addition to providing patient services) may have funds common to educational institutions, such as a loan fund.

Unrestricted Funds. Unrestricted funds account for resources that are not externally restricted and are available for general operating and capital activities at the discretion of management.

Assets of unrestricted funds include current assets (cash, receivables, inventories, and so on) and also noncurrent assets—primarily property, plant, and equipment, and *board-designated funds*. Board-designated funds are resources (usually cash and investments) set aside by the hospital's governing board for specific purposes or projects, thereby making them unavailable for current use. These funds are considered unrestricted since no *external* restriction exists.

Liabilities of unrestricted funds include both current liabilities and long-term debt. The fund balance may be subdivided into components (operating, board-designated, and plant). A typical balance sheet for a hospital's unrestricted fund is shown in Exhibit 18.10.

Unrestricted fund revenues come from patient services and other operating and nonoperating sources. Patient service revenue is recorded on an accrual basis, using the hospital's established rates, and consists of:

Exhibit 18.10   **Unrestricted Fund Balance Sheet**

COMMUNITY HOSPITAL
UNRESTRICTED FUND
BALANCE SHEET
DECEMBER 31, 19X3

ASSETS		**LIABILITIES AND FUND BALANCE**	
Current:		Current:	
Cash	$ 74,000	Notes Payable	$ 100,000
Receivables (Net of $140,000		Current Installments	
Estimated Uncollectibles		of Long-Term Debt	125,000
and Allowances)	463,000	Accounts Payable	87,000
Due from Restricted Funds	100,000	Accrued Expenses	59,000
Inventories	131,000	Due from Restricted Funds	60,000
	$ 768,000		$ 431,000
Other:		Long-Term Debt:	
Board-Designated Funds:		Bonds Payable	$2,000,000
Cash	$ 50,000	Mortgage Payable	1,100,000
Investments	300,000		$3,100,000
	$ 350,000		
		Fund Balance:	
Property, Plant, and		Operations	$ 337,000
Equipment	$5,477,000	Board-Designated	350,000
Less: Accumulated		Plant	1,044,000
Depreciation	1,333,000		$1,731,000
	$4,144,000		
		Total Liabilities and	
Total Assets	$5,262,000	Fund Balance	$5,262,000

1. Revenue from daily patient services such as room, board, and general nursing, medical, and surgical services.
2. Revenue from other medical services such as operating room and emergency room.
3. Revenue from ancillary services such as blood bank, laboratory, pharmacy, and anesthesiology.

These revenues are initially recorded at gross amounts. However, full rates may not be collected from all patients. Thus gross revenues should be reduced by the following allowances:

1. Charity allowances—full or partial reductions in charges for indigent patients.
2. Courtesy allowances—reductions in charges for employees, clergy, and so on.
3. Contractual adjustments—differences between a hospital's rate and the rate established by contractual agreements with third-party payers such as Blue Cross.
4. Allowance for uncollectible accounts.

Other operating revenue includes sales to patients and others of nonmedical goods

---

Exhibit 18.11   **Unrestricted Fund Statement of Revenues and Expenses**

COMMUNITY HOSPITAL
UNRESTRICTED FUND
STATEMENT OF REVENUES AND EXPENSES
FOR THE YEAR ENDED DECEMBER 31, 19X3

Patient Service Revenue.	$5,887,000	
Less: Allowances and Uncollectible Accounts	955,000	
Net Patient Service Revenue		$4,932,000
Other Operating Revenue		312,000
Total Operating Revenue		$5,244,000
Operating Expenses:		
Nursing Services	$1,643,000	
Other Professional Services	1,317,000	
General Services	1,338,000	
Administrative	521,000	
Interest	290,000	
Depreciation	282,000	
Total Operating Expenses.		5,391,000
Loss from Operations		$ (147,000)
Nonoperating Revenue		
Unrestricted Gifts and Bequests	$ 67,000	
Unrestricted Income from Endowment Funds	102,000	
Income and Gains from Board-Designated Funds . . .	40,000	
Total Nonoperating Revenue		209,000
Excess of Revenues over Expenses		$ 62,000

Exhibit 18.12 | **Unrestricted Fund Statement of Changes in Fund Balance**

COMMUNITY HOSPITAL
UNRESTRICTED FUND
STATEMENT OF CHANGES IN FUND BALANCE
FOR THE YEAR ENDED DECEMBER 31, 19X3

Balance at Beginning of Year.	$1,519,000
Excess of Revenues over Expenses	62,000
Transferred from Plant Replacement and Expansion Funds to Finance Expenditures for New Equipment.	210,000
Transferred to Plant Replacement and Expansion Funds to Reflect Third-Party Payer Revenue Restricted to Plant and Equipment Replacement .	(60,000)
Balance at End of Year.	$1,731,000

and services (such as telephone calls, gift shop, cafeteria, and parking lot), revenue from educational programs, and gifts or grants for specified purposes. Nonoperating revenue includes such items as unrestricted gifts, unrestricted income from endowments, and donated services. A statement of revenues and expenses is illustrated in Exhibit 18.11 (on page 971). Other statements which may be presented for the unrestricted fund include a statement of changes in fund balance (Exhibit 18.12) and a statement of changes in financial position.

Exhibit 18.13 | **Restricted Funds Balance Sheet**

COMMUNITY HOSPITAL
RESTRICTED FUNDS
BALANCE SHEET
DECEMBER 31, 19X3

SPECIFIC PURPOSE FUNDS

Cash	$ 13,000	Due to Unrestricted Fund . . .	$ 100,000
Investments	177,000	Fund Balance	170,000
Grants Receivable	80,000		
	$ 270,000		$ 270,000

PLANT REPLACEMENT AND EXPANSION FUNDS

Cash	$ 15,000	Fund Balance	$ 904,000
Investments	774,000		
Due from Unrestricted Fund. .	60,000		
Pledges Receivable, Net of Estimated Uncollectibles . .	55,000		
	$ 904,000		$ 904,000

ENDOWMENT FUNDS

		Fund Balance:	
Cash	$ 21,000	Permanent Endowment . . .	$ 942,000
Investments	1,136,000	Term Endowment.	215,000
	$1,157,000		$1,157,000

Restricted Funds. Hospitals commonly receive gifts, bequests, and grants subject to restricted use. These resources are categorized as restricted funds. Three major types of restriction exist:

1. Resources to be used for specific operating purposes, such as research or a particular clinic. These resources are usually referred to as **specific-purpose funds.**
2. Resources to be used for acquisition of plant assets **(plant replacement and expansion funds).**
3. Resources for permanent or limited-term endowment **(endowment funds).**

When these resources are to be used for their specified purpose, they are transferred first to the unrestricted fund, from which the expenditure is made. Thus expenses rarely appear on the financial statements of restricted funds.

A balance sheet for restricted funds is illustrated in Exhibit 18.13 and a statement of changes in fund balances is shown in Exhibit 18.14. A statement of revenues and expenses is usually not presented.

Exhibit 18.14   **Restricted Funds Statement of Changes in Fund Balance**

COMMUNITY HOSPITAL
RESTRICTED FUNDS
STATEMENT OF CHANGES IN FUND BALANCES
FOR THE YEAR ENDED DECEMBER 31, 19X3

SPECIFIC PURPOSE FUNDS

Balance at Beginning of Year.	$ 152,000
Restricted Gifts and Bequests	101,000
Research Grants	40,000
Income from Investments.	20,000
Transferred to Unrestricted Fund (Other Operating Revenue).	(143,000)
Balance at End of Year.	$ 170,000

PLANT REPLACEMENT AND EXPANSION FUNDS

Balance at Beginning of Year.	$ 882,000
Restricted Gifts and Bequests	107,000
Income from Investments.	65,000
Transferred from Unrestricted Funds (Third-Party Payer Revenue Restricted to Plant and Equipment Replacement)	60,000
Transferred to Unrestricted Fund for New Equipment.	(210,000)
Balance at End of Year.	$ 904,000

ENDOWMENT FUNDS

Balance at Beginning of Year.	$1,026,000
Restricted Gifts and Bequests	97,000
Net Gain on Sale of Investments	34,000
Income from Investments.	102,000
Transferred to Unrestricted Fund	(102,000)
Balance at End of Year.	$1,157,000

Important Accounting Issues

Again, many of the accounting issues discussed earlier, especially those with respect to investments and donations, apply to hospitals. Additional issues are discussed below. One aspect that affects much of hospital accounting is the need for *extensive cost accounting*. Most nonprofit organizations pay little attention to cost accounting, but for hospitals it is essential. A large percentage of a hospital's patient service revenues are paid not by the patients themselves, but by **third-party payers**—Blue Cross, Medicare, Medicaid, and private insurance plans. Because many of these pay on a cost-reimbursement basis, hospitals generally attempt to determine the *full cost* (not variable cost) of their services. The need for costing affects many other accounting procedures.

Depreciation. Property, plant, and equipment and related liabilities are included in the unrestricted fund. Thus the plant fund for a hospital differs from plant funds for other nonprofit organizations. A hospital plant fund typically contains *only* resources set aside for expansion or replacement of plant.

Depreciation is recorded and is included in operating expenses of the unrestricted fund. Recording of depreciation is essential if all costs of providing services are to be recognized.

Cost Finding. As mentioned earlier, much of a hospital's revenue is based on cost reimbursement for services rendered. **Cost finding** is the process of first segregating all direct costs by cost centers, and then allocating overhead costs to the revenue-producing operations of the hospital. Various methods of cost allocation may be employed, ranging from direct allocation to step methods to simultaneous equation methods. These methods are typically covered in cost accounting courses and are not discussed here.

Malpractice Costs. Potential claims for negligence or malpractice constitute a major financial risk for hospitals. If this risk is fully covered by insurance, the cost is included in operating expenses in the form of insurance premiums. It is not unusual, however, for hospitals to not be fully covered by external insurance. The increased frequency of malpractice claims in recent years has driven insurance rates up substantially, and has caused some insurers to withdraw from the market. Hospitals have reacted in various ways to this problem. Some have become self-insured by discontinuing their insurance coverage, and bearing the full risk of future claims. Many hospitals bear some risk by purchasing policies with high deductible amounts. Other hospitals have, as a group, formed captive insurance companies; in such cases, premium costs are often not known until after the fact, when claims and operating costs are known. In each of these cases where the hospital bears some risk, whether in the form of absence of insurance, high deductibles, or retrospective premiums from captive insurance companies, the provisions of *SFAS 5* concerning accrual and/or disclosure of loss contingencies apply.[3]

---

[3]Financial Accounting Standards Board, *Statement No. 5;* CT § C59.105–C59.114.

Overview of Nonprofit Accounting

Accounting for nonprofit organizations involves a combination of the principles and procedures used by local government with those used by business. This chapter has discussed one type which is supported primarily by voluntary contributions and two types which are supported in large part by user charges. While many other types of nonprofit organizations exist, their accounting and reporting tend to parallel that discussed for voluntary health and welfare organizations, colleges, or hospitals. Because of the comparative lack of standard setting by a single body, procedures developed by various industry groups are widely used.

Summary of Key Concepts

Nonprofit organizations have an objective other than providing goods and services at a profit. Resource providers do not expect direct benefits, and there are no equity interests.

A **fund structure** is commonly used for nonprofit organizations. The fund structure has some similarities to and some differences from the fund structure for local government. Of particular note is the **plant fund,** which possesses characteristics of a local government's capital projects fund, debt service fund, general fixed assets account group, and general long-term debt account group all in one fund. Also, the **loan fund** and the **annuity fund** of a nonprofit organization have no counterparts in governmental accounting.

Financial statements for a nonprofit organization typically consist of a **balance sheet** and a **statement of revenues, expenditures, and changes in fund balance.**

Investments of nonprofit organizations may be valued using the **cost, market,** or **lower-of-cost-or-market method.** Treatment of investment income, gains, and losses depends on the nature of the fund holding the investments. The question of whether **gains** constitute **principal or income** is an important and unresolved issue.

Accounting for **donations** is typically on the accrual basis for **cash donations,** with revenue deferred if the cash will not be available until a subsequent year. **Donations of goods and services** may not be recorded at all under certain circumstances; when such donations are recorded, fair market value is used.

Cost determination, while important to virtually all nonprofit organizations, is particularly vital to hospitals because of third-party reimbursements. **Cost allocation,** including recognition of depreciation, is important in hospital accounting.

Questions

Q18.1 Compare the objectives and sources of revenues of (1) local government and (2) nonprofit organizations.

Q18.2 Explain the difference between restricted and unrestricted funds in nonprofit accounting. What counterparts do these funds have in governmental accounting?

Q18.3 What is the purpose of a loan fund? How are resources for the fund provided?

Q18.4 What is the accounting treatment for debt incurred for construction by a nonprofit organization? Contrast this treatment to that by a local government.

Q18.5 Why are liabilities recorded in an annuity fund but not in a life income fund?

Q18.6 Hospital volunteers visit patients daily, selling newspapers, magazines, and other patient needs. Proceeds from the sales go to the hospital. How should the volunteers' services be recorded?

Q18.7 What fund would a college use to record each of the following: (1) borrowing $100,000 for construction currently in progress, (2) making a $30,000 mortgage payment, and (3) recording the donation of laboratory equipment from a scientific company?

Q18.8 An important accounting issue for nonprofit organizations is the treatment of gains from sale of endowment fund investments. What effect does the accounting treatment have on the investment behavior of portfolio managers?

Q18.9 The total return approach may be said to provide a compromise answer to the question of the spendability of investment gains. Explain.

Q18.10 Select the best answer for each of the following multiple choice questions:

    1. A reason for a voluntary health and welfare organization to adopt fund accounting is that:
    a. Restrictions have been placed on certain of its assets by donors.
    b. It provides more than one type of program service.
    c. Fixed assets are significant.
    d. Donated services are significant.

    2. A voluntary health and welfare organization received a pledge from a donor in 19X1 specifying that the amount pledged be used in 19X3. The donor paid the pledge in cash in 19X2. The pledge should be accounted for as:
    a. A deferred credit in the balance sheet at the end of 19X1, and as revenue in 19X2.
    b. A deferred credit in the balance sheet at the end of 19X1 and 19X2, and as revenue in 19X3.
    c. Revenue in 19X1.
    d. Revenue in 19X2, with no deferred credit in the balance sheet at the end of 19X1.

    (AICPA adapted)

Q18.11 Select the best answer for each of the following multiple choice questions:

1. Which of the following receipts is properly recorded in the restricted current fund by a university?
   a. Tuition.
   b. Student laboratory fees.
   c. Housing fees.
   d. Research grants.
2. What is the recommended method of accounting to be used by colleges and universities?
   a. Cash.
   b. Modified cash.
   c. Restricted accrual.
   d. Accrual.
3. In the loan fund of a college or university, each of the following types of loans would be found *except:*
   a. Student.
   b. Staff.
   c. Building.
   d. Faculty.
   (AICPA adapted)

Q18.12 The following multiple choice questions refer to the accounts of a large nonprofit hospital which properly maintains four funds: current unrestricted, current restricted, endowment, and plant. For each question, select the best answer.

1. The endowment fund consists of several small endowments, each for a special purpose. The hospital treasurer has determined that it would be legally possible and more efficient to pool the assets and allocate the resultant revenue. The soundest basis on which to allocate revenue after assets are pooled and to comply with the special purposes of each endowment would be to:
   a. Determine market values of securities or other assets comprising each endowment at the time of transfer to the pool and credit revenue to each endowment on that pro rata basis.
   b. Determine book value of each endowment at the time of transfer to the pool and credit revenue to each endowment on that pro rata basis.
   c. Apportion future revenue in the moving-average ratio in which the various endowments have earned revenue in the past.
   d. Ask the trustee who administers the pooled assets to make the determination, since the trustee is in a position to know which assets are making the greatest contribution.
2. How should charity service, contractual adjustments, and bad debts be classified in the statement of revenues and expenses for the hospital?
   a. All three should be treated as expenses.

    b. All three should be treated as deductions from patient service revenues.

    c. Charity service and contractual adjustments should be treated as revenue deductions, and bad debts should be treated as an expense.

    d. Charity service and bad debts should be treated as expenses, and contractual adjustments should be treated as a revenue deduction.

3. To assure the availability of money for improvement, replacement, and expansion of plant, it would be most desirable for the hospital to:

    a. Use accelerated depreciation to provide adequate funds for eventual replacement.

    b. Use the retirement or replacement system of depreciation to provide adequate funds.

    c. Sell assets at the earliest opportunity.

    d. Transfer cash from the current unrestricted fund to the plant fund in amounts at least equal to the periodic depreciation charges.

(AICPA adapted)

Exercises

E18.1 Funds X and Y of the VHW Organization, a voluntary health and welfare organization, pool their idle resources for investment purposes. At the beginning of the year, each fund contributed $30,000 to the pool. During the year, the value of the investments increased 10 percent. At the end of the year, Fund X withdrew $5,000 from the investment pool and Fund Y contributed $7,000. The net addition was immediately invested.

Required:

1. Compute the percentage of equity in the investment pool held by each fund at year-end after the transactions described above.

2. What amount would be presented under the "Investments" caption on the end-of-year balance sheet for each fund if VHW uses the cost method for reporting investments? If VHW uses the market method?

E18.2 Hopeville Retreat is a nonprofit organization that counsels former drug addicts in readjusting to productive community life. Donations provide the major support for Hopeville Retreat. During 19X2, the following gifts were received by the organization:

1. Cash from fund-raising campaign, $25,000.
2. Cash from rehabilitated clients of the organization, $10,000.
3. Clothing donated by a local department store. Cost to the store was $2,800; market value was $3,600.
4. A television set, valued at $300, donated by a private citizen.
5. Medicine used for drug withdrawal symptoms, donated by a pharmaceutical company. Cost of drugs was $3,000; market value was $5,000.

6. Secretarial and bookkeeping services for necessary paperwork and record-keeping performed by volunteers, valued at $7,000.
7. Door-to-door fund solicitation time donated by local high school students. The organization estimates this service to be worth $2,800 when valued using minimum wage rates.
8. Free radio announcements of the fund-raising campaign given by a local radio station. The normal charge for advertisements of comparable length is $400.

Required: For each gift, indicate at what amount the donation would be recorded on the books of Hopeville Retreat.

E18.3 The following items relate to a voluntary health and welfare organization:

1. A gift of cash is received with no stipulations as to use.
2. The organization borrows money to finance construction of a new office building.
3. Money is collected and held for distribution to an unaffiliated organization.
4. Money is collected and held for distribution to the beneficiaries of one of the organization's programs.
5. An automobile is donated for use in transporting officials on organization business.
6. Depreciation is computed on the automobile in No. 5.
7. General revenues are set aside to repay the loan in No. 2.
8. Used toys are collected for holiday distribution to needy children.

Required: For each item, identify the type of fund in which the event or activity should be recorded.

E18.4 The First Baptist Church of Lawton has followed a policy of recording gross pledges to its missionary fund as revenues and writing off uncollected pledges in the year following the pledge. In 19X9, the church decided to establish an allowance for uncollectible pledges based on pledges and collections for the first 5 years of the fund. Data pertaining to the missionary fund appear below:

Year	Pledged	Collected	
19X3	$1,000	$ 600	
19X4	1,500	110	(19X3 pledges)
		1,200	(19X4 pledges)
19X5	1,200	150	(19X4 pledges)
		960	(19X5 pledges)
19X6	3,000	2,550	(19X6 pledges)
19X7	2,500	2,000	(19X7 pledges)
19X8	2,800	250	(19X7 pledges)
		2,000	(19X8 pledges)

Required:

1. Establish an allowance for uncollectible pledges and correct the church's books as of the beginning of 19X9. Uncollected 19X8 pledges have not yet been written off. All uncollected pledges for years prior to 19X8 have been written off.
2. During 19X9, $3,000 was pledged. Of the $2,500 which was collected that year, $400 applied to 19X8 pledges. The remaining 19X8 pledges were written off. Record the 19X9 transactions related to pledges.

E18.5 The following items relate to a nonprofit college:

1. An alumna donates cash for purchase of library books.
2. An alumna donates cash, stipulating that income generated by investment of the cash be paid to the donor during the donor's lifetime. At the donor's death, the gift and all future income belongs to the college.
3. An alumna donates cash, stipulating that income generated by investment of the cash be used for student scholarships. The principal is to remain intact.
4. A gymnasium is constructed.
5. Salaries to faculty are paid.
6. Loans are made to faculty members.
7. Student activity fees for student organizations are collected with tuition payments.
8. Depreciation on the gymnasium is computed.

Required: For each item, identify the type of fund in which the event or activity should be recorded.

E18.6 Canton College, a nonprofit organization, maintains the following funds:

Unrestricted current fund.

Restricted current fund—scholarships.

Plant fund.

Agency fund.

Loan fund.

Required: For each of the transactions below, specify the fund(s) affected and record the journal entry. Explanations may be omitted.

1. The school's general fund-raising campaign generates pledges of $80,000. Past history shows pledges to be 90 percent collectible.
2. A previously recorded pledge for scholarship money is received ($7,000).
3. An employee borrows $1,000 from the school and signs a note for repayment within one year.
4. Student activity fees of $6,000 are transferred to student organizations.

5. Salaries of $20,000 are paid to employees. An accrual had not been recorded.
6. A loan of $11,000 is taken to buy audiovisual equipment.
7. An $800 scholarship is awarded.

E18.7 On January 1, 19X0, Patricia Dahlene gave Stokely College $100,000 in cash with the provision that the cash be invested in income-producing securities. Actuarial estimates set Dahlene's life expectancy at 15 years from the date of the gift. The annual discount rate associated with the arrangements outlined below is 8 percent.

Required: Specify the fund affected and record Patricia Dahlene's gift on the college's books under each of the following *independent* arrangements:

1. The college is to pay Patricia Dahlene $7,500 every December 31 of her remaining life. If earnings of the principal are insufficient to meet the payments, then the principal is to be depleted. Any earnings exceeding the required payment can be spent by the college without restriction. Gains and losses on principal assets must be added to (deducted from) principal. Upon Dahlene's death, remaining resources become available to the college with no restriction as to use.
2. The college is to pay Patricia Dahlene all earnings of the principal for life. Any gains and losses pertaining to principal assets are treated as income and therefore affect payments to the donor. Upon Dahlene's death, remaining resources become available to the college with no restrictions as to use.

E18.8 Davis College's plant fund had the following balance sheet at June 30, 19X7:

DAVIS COLLEGE
PLANT FUND
BALANCE SHEET
JUNE 30, 19X7

Cash	$ 70,000	Mortgage Payable	$4,600,000
Land	400,000	Fund Balance	2,020,000
Buildings	3,700,000		
Equipment	2,450,000		
	$6,620,000		$6,620,000

During the year ended June 30, 19X8, the following transactions occurred:

1. Resources in the amount of $500,000 were transferred from the unrestricted current fund.
2. Resources in the amount of $80,000 were transferred from the restricted current fund and spent on the purchase of audiovisual equipment.
3. Interest of $330,000 and principal of $200,000 were paid on the mortgage.

4. The college does not record depreciation on its assets.

Required: Prepare the balance sheet and the statement of revenues, expenses, and changes in fund balance for the plant fund for the year ended June 30, 19X8.

E18.9 The following multiple choice questions deal with college and university accounting. Select the best answer for each.

1. Which of the following should be used in accounting for not-for-profit colleges and universities?
   a. Fund accounting and accrual accounting.
   b. Fund accounting but not accrual accounting.
   c. Accrual accounting but not fund accounting.
   d. Neither accrual accounting nor fund accounting.

2. Which of the following is utilized for current expenditures by a not-for-profit university?

	Unrestricted Current Funds	Restricted Current Funds
a.	No	No
b.	No	Yes
c.	Yes	No
d.	Yes	Yes

3. Tuition waivers for which there is no intention of collection from the student should be classified by a not-for-profit university as:

	Revenue	Expenditures
a.	No	No
b.	No	Yes
c.	Yes	Yes
d.	Yes	No

(AICPA adapted)

E18.10 The following multiple choice questions deal with college and university accounting. Select the best answer for each.

1. During the years ended June 30, 19X1 and 19X2, Sonata University conducted a cancer research project financed by a $2,000,000 gift from an alumnus. This entire amount was pledged by the donor on July 10, 19X0, although he paid only $500,000 at that date. The gift was restricted to the financing of this particular research project. During the 2-year research period, Sonata's related gift receipts and research expenditures were as follows:

	Year Ended June 30	
	19X1	19X2
Gift receipts	$1,200,000	$ 800,000
Cancer research expenditures	900,000	1,100,000

How much gift revenue should Sonata report in the restricted column of its statement of current funds revenues, expenditures, and other changes for the year ended June 30, 19X2?

a. $0.

b. $800,000.

c. $1,100,000.

d. $2,000,000.

2. On January 2, 19X2, John Reynolds established a $500,000 trust, the income from which is to be paid to Mansfield University for general operating purposes. The Wyndham National Bank was appointed by Reynolds as trustee of the fund. What journal entry is required on Mansfield's books?

	Debit	Credit
a. Memorandum Entry Only		
b. Cash	500,000	
Endowment Fund Balance		500,000
c. Nonexpendable Endowment Fund	500,000	
Endowment Fund Balance		500,000
d. Expendable Funds	500,000	
Endowment Fund Balance		500,000

3. For the fall semester of 19X1, Cranbrook College assessed its students $2,300,000 for tuition and fees. The net amount realized was only $2,100,000 because of the following revenue reductions:

Refunds occasioned by class cancellations and student withdrawals .	$ 50,000
Tuition remissions granted to faculty members' families	10,000
Scholarships and fellowships	140,000

How much should Cranbrook report for the period for unrestricted current funds revenues from tuition and fees?

a. $2,100,000.

b. $2,150,000.

c. $2,250,000.

d. $2,300,000.

(AICPA adapted)

E18.11 The following multiple choice questions deal with hospital accounting. Select the best answer for each.

1. Depreciation should be recognized in the financial statements of:

a. Proprietary (for-profit) hospitals only.

b. Both proprietary (for-profit) and not-for-profit hospitals.

c. Both proprietary (for-profit) and not-for-profit hospitals, only when they are affiliated with a college or university.

d. All hospitals, as a memorandum entry not affecting the statement of revenues and expenses.

2. A gift to a voluntary not-for-profit hospital that is not restricted by the donor should be credited directly to:

a. Fund balance.
b. Deferred revenue.
c. Operating revenue.
d. Nonoperating revenue.

3. Donated medicines which normally would be purchased by a hospital should be recorded at fair market value and should be credited directly to:
a. Other operating revenue.
b. Other nonoperating revenue.
c. Fund balance.
d. Deferred revenue.

4. An unrestricted pledge from an annual contributor to a voluntary not-for-profit hospital made in December 19X1 and paid in cash in March 19X2 would generally be credited to:
a. Nonoperating revenue in 19X1.
b. Nonoperating revenue in 19X2.
c. Operating revenue in 19X1.
d. Operating revenue in 19X2.
(AICPA adapted)

E18.12 The following multiple choice questions deal with hospital accounting. Select the best answer for each.

1. Glenmore Hospital's property, plant, and equipment (net of depreciation) consists of the following:

Land	$ 500,000
Buildings	10,000,000
Movable equipment	2,000,000

What amount should be included in the restricted fund grouping?
a. $0.
b. $2,000,000.
c. $10,500,000.
d. $12,500,000.

2. During the year ended December 31, 19X1, Melford Hospital received the following donations stated at their respective fair values:

Employee services from members of a religious group	$100,000
Medical supplies from an association of physicians. These supplies were restricted for indigent care, and were used for such purpose in 19X1	30,000

How much revenue (both operating and nonoperating) from donations should Melford report in its 19X1 statement of revenues and expenses?
a. $0.
b. $30,000.
c. $100,000.
d. $130,000.

3. On July 1, 19X1, Lilydale Hospital's board of trustees designated $200,000 for expansion of outpatient facilities. The $200,000 is expected to be expended in the fiscal year ending June 30, 19X4. In Lilydale's balance sheet at June 30, 19X2, this cash should be classified as a:
   a. Restricted current asset.
   b. Restricted noncurrent asset.
   c. Unrestricted current asset.
   d. Unrestricted noncurrent asset.
   (AICPA adapted)

Problems

P18.1 Journal Entries and Financial Statements The Southside Counseling Center was established on January 10, 19X1, to provide a variety of counseling services to community residents, including alcoholism, drug abuse, and marital and family counseling. The Center's initial resources were provided by the county government in the form of a $100,000 capital grant. Of this sum, $50,000 was designated for building and equipment, and $25,000 was designated for the establishment of a special program for counseling parolees; the remaining funds were unrestricted. The following transactions occurred during 19X1:

1. Contributions of $80,000 were received through the local United Way campaign, and an additional $13,000 was received in direct contributions. Of the direct contributions, $1,000 was for the parolees' program and $3,000 was for the building fund; the remaining $9,000 (of which $4,000 was in the form of pledges, expected to be 75 percent collectible) was unrestricted.
2. Operating expenses for the year were $93,000, of which $85,000 had been paid by year-end.
3. The special parolees' program had not yet begun as of December 31, 19X1. All resources dedicated to this program have been invested in short-term securities. Investment income for the year was $2,000.
4. The Center purchased a building for $220,000 ($180,000 is owed on the mortgage at year-end) and equipment for $24,000 (of which $14,000 is owed on a 3-year note).

Required:

1. Prepare journal entries to record the transactions for 19X1. Identify the fund for each entry.
2. Prepare a balance sheet and a statement of changes in fund balance for each fund.

P18.2 Investment Pools Modern Families is a voluntary health and welfare organization that specializes in family counseling. Three of the organization's funds (family planning, FP; marriage counseling, MC; and single parenting,

SP) were financed by grants from donors who restricted the use of the gifts. The resources of the funds not required for current operations are combined in an investment pool. On January 1, 19X7, the date of the investment pool's establishment, the following contributions were made:

FP $40,000
MC 20,000
SP 40,000

These monies were invested in securities as follows:

Security A: 100 shares at $80 each.

Security B: 270 shares at $100 each.

Security C: 1,000 shares at $30 each.

Security D: 500 shares at $70 each.

Dividends received on the securities were distributed pro rata rather than being reinvested.

During 19X7, the following occurred:

1. On June 30, SP contributed $20,600 to the investment pool, FP withdrew $20,600, and MC withdrew $5,760. Shares of Security D were sold to finance the net withdrawal.
2. On September 30, FP contributed $17,000 and SP withdrew $9,400. The net cash inflow was invested in Security D.
3. Market values of the securities fluctuated as follows:

	March 31	June 30	September 30	December 31
Security A	$ 90	$94	$94	$90
Security B	100	98	97	98
Security C	30	30	30	33
Security D	70	72	76	76

Required:

1. Determine the equity percentage in the investment pool of each fund as of January 1, March 31, June 30, September 30, and December 31.
2. Determine the amount each fund would present as investments on its respective December 31, 19X7, balance sheet if Modern Families follows the cost method of accounting for investments.
3. Determine the amount each fund would present as investments on its respective December 31, 19X7, balance sheet if Modern Families follows the market method of accounting for investments.
4. Determine the amount each fund would present as investments on its respective December 31, 19X7, balance sheet if Modern Families follows the lower-of-cost-or-market method of accounting for investments.

P18.3 Journal Entries and Statements Several years ago, a group of civic-minded merchants in the city of Albury organized the "Committee of 100" for the purpose of establishing a community sports club, a nonprofit sports organization for local youth. Each of the Committee's 100 members contributed $1,000 towards the club's capital, and in turn received a participation certificate. In addition, each participant agreed to pay dues of $200 a year for the club's operations. All dues have been collected in full by the end of each fiscal year ending March 31. Members who have discontinued their participation have been replaced by an equal number of new members through transfer of the participation certificates from the former members to the new ones. Following is the club's trial balance at April 1, 19X2:

	Debit	Credit
Cash	$ 9,000	
Investments (at Market, Equal to Cost)	58,000	
Inventories	5,000	
Land	10,000	
Building	164,000	
Accumulated Depreciation—Building		$130,000
Furniture and Equipment	54,000	
Accumulated Depreciation—Furniture and Equipment		46,000
Accounts Payable		12,000
Participation Certificates (100 at $1,000 each)		100,000
Cumulative Excess of Revenue over Expenses		12,000
	$300,000	$300,000

Transactions for the year ended March 31, 19X3, were as follows:

1. Collections from Participants for Dues. $20,000
2. Snack Bar and Soda Fountain Sales 28,000
3. Interest and Dividends Received 6,000
4. Additions to Voucher Register:
   House Expenses 17,000
   Snack Bar and Soda Fountain Expenses 26,000
   General and Administrative Expenses 11,000
5. Vouchers Paid 55,000
6. Assessments for Future Capital Improvements (Assessed on Mar. 20, 19X3; None Collected by Mar. 31, 19X3; Deemed 100% Collectible during Year Ending Mar. 31, 19X4) 10,000
7. Unrestricted Bequest Received 5,000

Adjustment data:

1. Investments are valued at market, which amounted to $65,000 at March 31, 19X3. There were no investment transactions during the year.
2. Depreciation for the year: building—$4,000, furniture and equipment—$8,000.
3. Allocation of depreciation: house expenses—$9,000, snack bar and soda fountain—$2,000, general and administrative—$1,000.

4. Actual physical inventory at March 31, 19X3, was $1,000, and pertains to the snack bar and soda fountain.

Required: On a functional basis:

1. Record the transactions and adjustments in journal entry form for the year ended March 31, 19X3. Omit explanations.
2. Prepare an all-inclusive activity statement for the year ended March 31, 19X3. *(AICPA adapted)*

P18.4 Cost of Services The following data are available concerning the Somerset Blood Bank, a nonprofit organization:

1. Blood is furnished to the blood bank by volunteers and when necessary by professional donors. During the year, 2,568 pints of blood were taken from volunteers and professional blood donors.
2. Volunteer donors who give blood to the bank can draw against their accounts when necessary. An individual who requires a blood transfusion has the option of paying for the blood used at $25 per pint or replacing it at the blood bank. Hospitals purchase blood at $8 per pint.
3. The Somerset Blood Bank has a reciprocal arrangement with a number of other blood banks that permits a member who requires a transfusion in a different locality to draw blood from the local blood bank against his account in Somerset. The issuing blood bank charges a set fee of $14 per pint to the home blood bank.
4. If blood is issued to hospitals but is not used and is returned to the blood bank, there is a handling charge of $1 per pint. Only hospitals are permitted to return blood. During the year, 402 pints were returned. The blood being returned must be in usable condition.
5. Blood can be stored for only 21 days and then must be discarded. During the year, 343 pints were outdated. This is a normal rate of loss.
6. The blood bank sells serum and supplies at cost to doctors and laboratories. These items are used in processing blood and are sold at the same price that they are billed to the blood bank. No blood bank operating expenses are allocated to the cost of sales of these items.
7. Inventories of blood are valued at the sales price to hospitals. The sales price to hospitals was increased on July 1, 19X1. The inventories are as shown below:

	Pints	Sales Price	Total
June 30, 19X1	80	$6	$480
June 30, 19X2	80	8	640

8. The financial statements are shown in Exhibits 18.15 and 18.16.

Exhibit 18.15   **Balance Sheet for the Somerset Blood Bank, to Be Used in P18.4**

SOMERSET BLOOD BANK
BALANCE SHEET

ASSETS	June 30, 19X1	June 30, 19X2
Cash	$ 2,712	$ 2,093
U.S. Treasury Bonds	15,000	16,000
Accounts Receivable—Sales of Blood:		
Hospitals	1,302	1,448
Individuals	425	550
Inventories:		
Blood	480	640
Supplies and Serum	250	315
Furniture and Equipment, less Depreciation	4,400	4,050
Total Assets	$24,569	$25,096
LIABILITIES AND FUND BALANCE		
Accounts Payable—Supplies	$ 325	$ 275
Fund Balance	24,244	24,821
Total Liabilities and Fund Balance	$24,569	$25,096

Required:

1. Prepare a statement of the total expense of taking and processing blood. Use the accrual basis.
2. Prepare a schedule computing (a) the number of pints of blood sold and (b) the number of pints withdrawn by members.
3. Prepare a schedule computing the expense per pint of taking and processing the blood that was used. *(AICPA adapted)*

P18.5 **Budgeting for a College** Crosby College, a nonprofit school, is developing its budget for the upcoming 19X1–19X2 academic year. The following data relate to the current academic year (19X0–19X1):

	Lower Division (Freshman/Sophomore)	Upper Division (Junior/Senior)
Average Number of Students per Class	25	20
Average Salary of Faculty Members	$24,000	$24,000
Average Number of Credit Hours Carried Each Year per Student	33	30
Enrollment, Including Scholarship Students	2,000	1,360
Average Faculty Teaching Load in Credit Hours per Year (8 Classes of 3 Credit Hours)	24	24

Additional information:

1. For 19X1–19X2, lower division enrollment is expected to increase by 10 percent, while the upper division's enrollment is expected to re-

Exhibit 18.16	**Statement of Cash Receipts and Disbursements for the Somerset Blood Bank, to Be Used in P18.4**

SOMERSET BLOOD BANK
STATEMENT OF CASH RECEIPTS AND DISBURSEMENTS
FOR THE YEAR ENDED JUNE 30, 19X2

Balance, July 1, 19X1:
Cash in Bank			$ 2,712
U.S. Treasury Bonds			15,000
Total			$17,712
Receipts:			
From Hospitals:			
Hillcrest Hospital	$7,702		
Good Samaritan Hospital	3,818	$11,520	
Individuals		6,675	
From Other Blood Banks.		602	
From Sales of Serum and Supplies		2,260	
Interest on Bonds		525	
Gifts and Bequests.		4,928	
Total Receipts.			26,510
Total to Be Accounted for			$44,222
Disbursements:			
Laboratory Expense:			
Serum.	$3,098		
Salaries	3,392		
Supplies.	3,533		
Laundry and Miscellaneous	277	$10,300	
Other Expenses and Disbursements:			
Salaries	$5,774		
Dues and Subscriptions	204		
Rent and Utilities	1,404		
Blood Testing	2,378		
Payments to Other Blood Banks for Blood			
Given to Members Away from Home	854		
Payments to Professional Blood Donors	2,410		
Other Expenses	1,805		
Purchase of U.S. Treasury Bond	1,000	15,829	
Total Disbursements			26,129
Balance, June 30, 19X2:.			$18,093
Cash in Bank			$ 2,093
U.S. Treasury Bonds			16,000
Total			$18,093

main stable. Faculty salaries will be increased by a standard 8 percent, and additional merit increases to be awarded to individual faculty members will be $150,000 for the lower division and $135,000 for the upper division.

2. The current budget is $384,000 for operation and maintenance of plant and equipment; this includes $180,000 for salaries and wages. Experience of the past 3 months suggests that the current budget is realistic

but that expected increases for 19X1–19X2 are 8 percent in salaries and wages and $18,000 in other expenditures for operation and maintenance of plant and equipment.

3. The budget for the remaining expenditures for 19X1–19X2 is as follows:

Administrative and General	$280,000
Library	220,000
Health and Recreation	150,000
Athletics	240,000
Insurance and Retirement	330,000
Interest	96,000

4. The college expects to award 15 free-tuition scholarships to lower division students and 10 to upper division students. Tuition is $44 per credit hour, and no other fees are charged.

5. Budgeted revenues for 19X1–19X2 are as follows:

Endowments	$342,000
Net Income from Auxiliary Services	500,000
Athletics	460,000

The college's remaining source of revenue is an annual support campaign held during the spring.

Required:

1. Compute by division (a) the expected enrollment, (b) the total credit hours to be carried, and (c) the number of faculty members needed for 19X1–19X2.
2. Compute the budget for 19X1–19X2 faculty salaries by division.
3. Compute the 19X1–19X2 tuition revenue budget by division.
4. Compute the amount that must be raised during the annual support campaign in order to cover the 19X1–19X2 expenditures budget.

P18.6 Multifund Balance Sheets The bookkeeper for the Jacob Vocational School resigned on March 1, 19X8, after preparing the general ledger trial balance and analysis of cash as of February 28, 19X8. These statements appear in Exhibits 18.17 and 18.18.

At the end of the fiscal year, August 31, 19X8, an examination of the records showed the following:

1. D. E. Marcy donated 100 shares of Trans, Inc., stock in September 19X7 with a market value of $110 per share at the date of donation. The terms of the gift provide that the stock and any income thereon are to be retained intact. At any date designated by the board of directors, the assets are to be liquidated and the proceeds used to assist the school's director in acquiring a personal residence. The school will not retain any financial interest in the residence.

2. E. T. Pearce donated 6 percent bonds in September 19X7 with par and market values of $150,000 at the date of donation. Annual payments of $3,500 are to be made to the donor during his lifetime. Earnings in excess of these payments are to be used for current operations in the following fiscal year. Upon the donor's death, the fund is to be used to construct a school cafeteria.

Exhibit 18.17   **Trial Balance for the Jacob Vocational School, to be Used in P18.6**

JACOB VOCATIONAL SCHOOL
GENERAL LEDGER TRIAL BALANCE
FEBRUARY 28, 19X8

DEBITS

Cash for Current Operations.	$258,000
Cash for Restricted Current Uses	30,900
Stock Donated by D. E. Marcy	11,000
Bonds Donated by E. T. Pearce.	150,000
Building	33,000
Land.	22,000
General Current Operating Expenses	38,000
Faculty Recruitment Expenses	4,100
Total.	$547,000

CREDITS

Mortgage Payable on Fixed Assets	$ 30,000
Income from Gifts for General Operations	210,000
Income from Gifts for Restricted Uses.	196,000
Student Fees	31,000
Fund Balances	80,000
Total.	$547,000

Exhibit 18.18   **Analysis of Cash for the Jacob Vocational School, to be Used P18.6**

JACOB VOCATIONAL SCHOOL
ANALYSIS OF CASH
FOR THE 6 MONTHS ENDED FEBRUARY 28, 19X8

Unrestricted Cash for Current Operations:			
Balance, Sept. 1, 19X7		$ 80,000	
Add: Student Fees	$ 31,000		
Gift of W. L. Jacob.	210,000	241,000	
		$321,000	
Deduct: General Current Operating			
Expenses.	$ 38,000		
Payment on Land and Building . . .	25,000	63,000	$258,000
Cash for Restricted Uses:			
Gift of W. L. Jacob for Faculty Recruitment		$ 35,000	
Less: Faculty Recruitment Expenses		4,100	30,900
Checking Account Balance, Feb. 28, 19X8 . .			$288,900

3. No transactions have been recorded on the school's books since February 28, 19X8. An employee of the school prepared the following analysis of the checking account for the period from March 1 through August 31, 19X8:

```
Balance, Mar. 1, 19X8. . . . . . . . . .                               $288,900
Deduct: General Current Operating
            Expenses. . . . . . . . . . .     $14,000
            Purchase of Equipment. . . . . .    47,000     $61,000
            Less: Student Fees. . . . . . . .                8,000
                  Net Expenses . . . . . . .               $53,000
            Payment for Director's Residence  $11,200
            Less: Sale of 100 Shares of Trans,
                  Inc., Stock . . . . . . . .   10,600         600        53,600
                  Total . . . . . . . . . . . . .                        $235,300
Add: Interest on 6% Bonds . . . . . . .                    $ 9,000
     Less: Payments to E. T. Pearce . . .                    3,500         5,500
Balance, Aug. 31, 19X8 . . . . . . . . .                                 $240,800
```

Required: Prepare August 31, 19X8, balance sheets for the four funds of Jacob Vocational School: unrestricted current fund, restricted current fund, plant fund, and annuity fund. *(AICPA adapted)*

P18.7 **University Accounting—Noncurrent Funds** Baxter University is a private nonprofit institution. In addition to various routine transactions in its restricted and unrestricted current funds, Baxter had the following activity during the year ended June 30, 19X4:

1. A loan fund was established by transferring $75,000 from the unrestricted current fund and $20,000 from endowment fund income. During the year, $32,000 was loaned to students; there were no principal repayments during the year. Five percent of the loans are expected to be uncollectible. Interest earned on the loans was $2,000, of which $1,300 was received in cash. In addition, interest of $5,200 was earned on the unexpended cash, which is maintained in interest-bearing bank accounts.

2. At July 1, 19X3, the plant fund showed:

```
Land . . . . . . . . . . . . . . . . . . . . . . . . . . . . . . . . $   100,000
Buildings . . . . . . . . . . . . . . . . . . . . . . . . . . . . .    12,200,000
Equipment . . . . . . . . . . . . . . . . . . . . . . . . . . . . .     6,600,000
Mortgage Payable . . . . . . . . . . . . . . . . . . . . . . . .       (3,000,000)
Cash for Replacements. . . . . . . . . . . . . . . . . . . . . .           30,000
```

During the year, $78,000 was transferred from the unrestricted current fund for equipment replacement. In addition, $100,000 in principal and $210,000 in interest on the mortgage was paid by the unrestricted current fund. Plant fund resources of $83,000 were spent for new equipment; old equipment which had cost $46,000 was retired, with no proceeds.

3. An annuity fund was established in July 19X3, as two alumni made substantial contributions to the university in exchange for a guaranteed annual payment. One, who has a life expectancy of 10 years, contributed $40,000 and is to receive $4,800 annually. The other, who has a life expectancy of 12 years, contributed $75,000 and is to receive $8,400 annually (first payment for each annuity is June 30, 19X4). Baxter uses an 8 percent rate to account for the annuities. Interest earned on invested funds during the year was $13,000.

4. At July 1, 19X3, Baxter's endowment fund had cash of $10,000 and investments of $284,000. The fund balance—principal was $250,000. During the year, securities which had cost $61,000 were sold for $78,000, and all proceeds were reinvested. Baxter attributes all gains and losses to principal. Interest and dividends of $22,000 were received, along with $15,000 in new principal contributions. In addition to the transfer to the loan fund, $25,000 of income was spent for faculty research grants.

Required:

1. Prepare journal entries to record transactions for the year.
2. For each fund, prepare a balance sheet and a statement of revenues, expenses, and changes in fund balance.

P18.8 University Accounting Presented in Exhibit 18.19 is the current funds balance sheet of Mayville University as of the end of its fiscal year ended June 30, 19X7.

The following transactions occurred during the fiscal year ended June 30, 19X8:

1. On July 7, 19X7, a gift of $100,000 was received from an alumnus. The alumnus requested that one-half of the gift be used for the purchase of books for the university library and the remainder be used for the establishment of a scholarship fund. The alumnus further requested that the income generated by the scholarship fund be used annually to award a scholarship to a qualified disadvantaged student. On July 20, 19X7, the board of trustees resolved that the resources of the newly established scholarship fund would be invested in savings certificates. On July 21, 19X7, the savings certificates were purchased.

2. Revenue from student tuition and fees applicable to the year ended June 30, 19X8, amounted to $1,900,000. Of this amount, $66,000 was collected in the prior year, and $1,686,000 was collected during the year ended June 30, 19X8. In addition, at June 30, 19X8, the university had received cash of $158,000, representing fees for the session beginning July 1, 19X8.

3. During the year ended June 30, 19X8, the university had collected $349,000 of the outstanding accounts receivable at the beginning of the year. The balance was determined to be uncollectible and was

Exhibit 18.19 **Current Funds Balance Sheet, to Be Used in P18.8**

MAYVILLE UNIVERSITY
CURRENT FUNDS BALANCE SHEET
JUNE 30, 19X7

ASSETS

Current Funds—Unrestricted:
Cash. $210,000
Accounts Receivable—
Student Tuition and Fees,
less Allowance for Doubtful
Accounts of $9,000 341,000

State Appropriations 75,000
Receivable. $626,000

Current Funds—Restricted:
Cash. . . . . $ 7,000
Investments 60,000
$ 67,000
Total Current Funds $693,000

LIABILITIES AND FUND BALANCES

Current Funds—Unrestricted:
Accounts Payable . . . . . $ 45,000
Deferred Revenues 66,000
Fund Balance 515,000
$626,000

Current Funds—Restricted:
Fund Balances. 67,000

Total Current Funds $693,000

written off against the allowance account. At June 30, 19X8, the allowance account was increased to $11,000.

4. Interest charges of $6,000 were earned and collected on late student-fee payments.

5. The state appropriation was received. An additional unrestricted appropriation of $50,000 was made by the state but had not been paid to the university as of June 30, 19X8.

6. An unrestricted gift of $25,000 cash was received from alumni of the university.

7. During the year, pre-19X7 investments of $21,000 were sold for $26,000. Investment income amounting to $1,900 was also received. Gains and losses on the sale of investments by the restricted current fund are considered to be restricted. Gains and losses on the sale of investments by the endowment fund are treated as adjustments of principal.

8. During the year, unrestricted operating expenses of $1,777,000 were recorded. At June 30, 19X8, $59,000 of these expenses remained unpaid.

9. Restricted cash of $13,000 was spent for authorized purposes during the year.

10. The accounts payable at June 30, 19X7, were paid during the year.

11. During the year, $7,000 interest was earned and received on the savings certificates purchased in accordance with the board of trustees' resolution discussed in No. 1.

Required:

1. Prepare journal entries to record in summary the above transactions for the year ended June 30, 19X8. Each journal entry should be numbered to correspond with the transaction described above. Your answer sheet should be organized as follows:

Exhibit 18.20   **Statements of Revenues and Expenses for General Medical Institute, to Be Used in P18.9**

THE GENERAL MEDICAL INSTITUTE
COMPARATIVE STATEMENTS OF REVENUES AND EXPENSES
FOR THE YEARS ENDED OCTOBER 31, 19X3 AND 19X2

REVENUE FROM SERVICES RENDERED	19X3	19X2	Increase (Decrease)
Services to Patients	$360,000	$304,000	$ 56,000
Less: Free Services	36,000	38,000	(2,000)
Net Revenue from Services Rendered	$324,000	$266,000	$ 58,000
OPERATING EXPENSES			
Departmental Expenses:			
Medical Services	$ 32,700	$ 29,300	$ 3,400
Medicine and Supplies	14,600	10,500	4,100
Nursing Services	89,900	76,200	13,700
Therapy Services	34,300	31,300	3,000
Dietary	40,700	37,100	3,600
Housekeeping and Maintenance	37,300	29,500	7,800
Administration and Other	33,700	23,400	10,300
General Expenses:			
Rental of Leased Premises (Net)	—	3,100	(3,100)
Depreciation—Building and Equipment	9,900	8,300	1,600
Provision for Uncollectible Accounts	5,400	3,500	1,900
Interest Expense	6,500	—	6,500
Loss on Sale of Equipment	2,000	—	2,000
Other	16,200	6,500	9,700
Total Expenses	$323,200	$258,700	$ 64,500
Excess of Revenues from Services Rendered over Operating Expenses	$ 800	$ 7,300	$ (6,500)
OTHER INCOME (EXPENSES)			
Research	$ (13,300)	$ (13,200)	$ (100)
Gain on Sale of Investments	18,600	3,500	15,100
Investment Income	16,500	13,300	3,200
Contributions	10,300	14,800	(4,500)
Grant from Government Designated for Expansion	335,000	—	335,000
Miscellaneous	2,700	1,500	1,200
Total Other Income	$369,800	$ 19,900	$349,900
Excess of Revenues over Expenses	$370,600	$ 27,200	$343,400

	Current Funds				Endowment Fund	
	Unrestricted		Restricted			
Accounts	Debit	Credit	Debit	Credit	Debit	Credit

2. Prepare a statement of revenues, expenditures, and changes in fund balance for the year ended June 30, 19X8. *(AICPA adapted)*

P18.9 Sources and Uses of Cash The General Medical Institute is a nonprofit corporation without capital stock, and it accounts for its activities in a single fund. Its comparative financial statements appear as Exhibits 18.20 and 18.21.

Additional information:

1. Accounts receivable—patients are stated net of the allowance for doubtful accounts, which amounted to $10,000 at October 31, 19X2,

---

Exhibit 18.21 **Balance Sheets for General Medical Institute, to Be Used in P18.9**

THE GENERAL MEDICAL INSTITUTE
COMPARATIVE BALANCE SHEETS
OCTOBER 31, 19X3 AND 19X2

ASSETS	19X3	19X2	Increase (Decrease)
Cash.	$ 28,600	$ 18,500	$ 10,100
Accounts Receivable—Patients (Net) . . .	75,500	55,500	20,000
Investments (Cost).	413,100	463,100	(50,000)
Prepaid Expenses	2,200	1,600	600
Land, Building, Equipment (Net)	327,200	333,700	(6,500)
Construction in Progress.	793,800	—	793,800
Total Assets	$1,640,400	$872,400	$768,000
LIABILITIES AND FUND BALANCE			
Accounts Payable—Construction	$ 110,800	—	$110,800
Less: Receivables from Government			
Agencies	80,000	—	80,000
Accounts Payable—Construction (Net) . .	$ 30,800	—	$ 30,800
Accounts Payable—Current Operations . .	11,800	$ 10,200	1,600
Mortgage Payable	365,000	—	365,000
Total Liabilities	$ 407,600	$ 10,200	$397,400
Fund Balance:			
Balance, Nov. 1	$ 862,200	$835,000	$ 27,200
Excess of Revenues over Expenses for			
Year	370,600	27,200	343,400
Balance, Oct. 31	$1,232,800	$862,200	$370,600
Total Liabilities and Fund Balance	$1,640,400	$872,400	$768,000

and $14,600 at October 31, 19X3. During the year, bad debts totaling $800 were written off.

2. The research activities are net of research grants aggregating $10,000. Included as a research expense is depreciation of $6,600 on special research equipment.

3. During 19X3, the construction of a new building was begun. The estimated cost of the building and equipment is $1,000,000. The expansion is being financed as follows:

Grant from Government	$ 335,000
Mortgage (Repayment to Begin upon Completion of Building)	500,000
Special Features Installed at the Request of Government Agencies and to Be Paid for by the Agencies	80,000
Institute Funds	85,000
Total	$1,000,000

4. New therapy equipment costing $15,000 was purchased in 19X3 and replaced therapy equipment with a book value of $5,000 which was sold for $3,000.

5. To obtain additional cash for working capital, investments with a cost of $50,000 were sold during July.

Required: Prepare a statement accounting for the increase in cash for the year ended October 31, 19X3, to be included in the annual report of the General Medical Institute. The statement should set forth information concerning cash applied to or provided by:

1. Operations.
2. Research activities.
3. Acquisitions of assets.
4. Other sources of funds.

(AICPA adapted)

P18.10 Hospital Break-Even Analysis Melford Hospital operates a general hospital, but rents space and beds to separately owned entities rendering specialized services such as pediatric and psychiatric care. Melford charges each separate entity for common services such as patients' meals and laundry, and for administrative services such as billings and collections. Space and bed rentals are fixed charges for the year, based on bed capacity rented to each entity.

Melford charged the following costs to pediatrics for the year ended June 30, 19X2:

	Patient Days (Variable)	Bed Capacity (Fixed)
Dietary	$ 600,000	—
Janitorial	—	$ 70,000
Laundry	300,000	—

Laboratory	450,000	—
Pharmacy.	350,000	—
Repairs and Maintenance.	—	30,000
General and Administrative	—	1,300,000
Rent	—	1,500,000
Billings and Collections	300,000	—
Total	$2,000,000	$2,900,000

During the year ended June 30, 19X2, pediatrics charged each patient an average of $300 per day, had a capacity of 60 beds, and had revenue of $6,000,000 for 365 days. In addition, pediatrics directly employed the following personnel:

	Annual Salaries
Supervising Nurses.	$25,000
Nurses	20,000
Aides.	9,000

Melford has the following minimum departmental personnel requirements based on total annual patient days:

Annual Patient Days	Aides	Nurses	Supervising Nurses
Up to 21,900	20	10	4
21,901 to 26,000	26	13	4
26,001 to 29,200	30	15	4

These staffing levels represent full-time equivalents. Pediatrics always employs only the minimum number of required full-time equivalent personnel. Salaries of supervising nurses, nurses, and aides are therefore fixed within ranges of annual patient days.

Pediatrics operated at 100 percent capacity on 90 days during the year ended June 30, 19X2. It is estimated that during these 90 days the demand exceeded capacity by more than 20 patients. Melford has an additional 20 beds available for rent for the year ending June 30, 19X3. Such additional rental would increase pediatrics' fixed charges based on bed capacity.

Required:

1. Calculate the minimum number of patient days required for pediatrics to break even for the year ending June 30, 19X3, if the additional 20 beds are not rented. Patient demand is unknown, but assume that revenue per patient day, cost per patient day, cost per bed, and salary rates will remain the same as for the year ended June 30, 19X2.

2. Assume that patient demand, revenue per patient day, cost per patient day, cost per bed, and salary rates for the year ending June 30, 19X3, will remain the same as for the year ended June 30, 19X2. Prepare a

schedule of increase in revenue and increase in costs for the year ending June 30, 19X3, in order to determine the net increase or decrease in earnings from the additional 20 beds if pediatrics rents this extra capacity from Melford. *(AICPA adapted)*

P18.11 Hospital Accounting—Insurance Reimbursements   Grady Hospital completed its first year of operation as a qualified institutional provider under the health insurance (HI) program for the aged and wishes to receive maximum reimbursement for its allowable costs from the government. The following financial, statistical, and other information is available:

1. The hospital's charges and allowable costs for departmental inpatient services were as shown below:

Departments	Charges for HI Program Beneficiaries	Total Charges	Total Allowable Costs
Inpatient Routine Services (Room, Board, Nursing)	$425,000	$1,275,000	$1,350,000
Inpatient Ancillary Service Departments:			
X-ray	$ 56,000	$ 200,000	$ 150,000
Operating Room	57,000	190,000	220,000
Laboratory	59,000	236,000	96,000
Pharmacy	98,000	294,000	207,000
Other	10,000	80,000	88,000
Total Ancillary	$280,000	$1,000,000	$ 761,000
Totals	$705,000	$2,275,000	$2,111,000

2. For the first year, the reimbursement settlement for inpatient services may be calculated at the option of the provider under either of the following apportionment methods:
   a. *The departmental RCC (ratio of cost centers) method* provides for listing on a departmental basis the ratios of beneficiary inpatient charges to total inpatient charges, with each departmental beneficiary inpatient charge ratio applied to the allowable total cost of the respective department.
   b. *The combination method (with cost finding)* provides that the cost of routine services be apportioned on the basis of the average allowable cost per day for all inpatients applied to total inpatient days of beneficiaries. The residual part of the provider's total allowable cost attributable to ancillary (nonroutine) services is to be apportioned in the ratio of the beneficiaries' share of charges for ancillary services to the total charges to all patients for such services.
3. Statistical and other information:
   a. Total inpatient days for all patients—20,000.
   b. Total inpatient days applicable to HI beneficiaries (600 aged patients whose average length of stay was 12.5 days)—7,500.
   c. A fiscal intermediary acting on behalf of the government's Medi-

care program negotiated a fixed allowance rate of $90 per inpatient day subject to retroactive adjustment as a reasonable cost basis for reimbursement of covered services to the hospital under the HI program. Interim payments based on an estimated 500 inpatient days per month were received during the 12-month period subject to an adjustment for the provider's actual cost experience.

Required:

1. Prepare schedules computing the total allowable cost of inpatient services for which the provider should receive payment under the HI program and the remaining balance due for reimbursement under each of the following methods:
   a. Departmental RCC method.
   b. Combination method (with cost finding).
2. Under which method should Grady Hospital elect to be reimbursed for its first year under the HI program, assuming the election can be changed for the following year with the approval of the fiscal intermediary? Why?
3. Grady Hospital wishes to compare its charges to HI program beneficiaries with published information on national averages for charges for hospital services. Compute the following (show your computations):
   a. The average total hospital charge for an HI inpatient.
   b. The average charge per inpatient day for HI inpatients.
   (AICPA adapted)

P18.12 Hospital Cost Accounting Bowman Hospital, a nonprofit organization, is preparing a preliminary budget for the year ending June 30, 19X2. Projections for room requirements for inpatients by type of service are as follows:

Type of Patient	Total Patients Expected	Average Number of Days in Hospital		Percent of Regular Patients Selecting Types of Service		
		Regular	Medicare	Private	Semiprivate	Ward
Medical	2,100	7	17	10%	60%	30%
Surgical	2,400	10	15	15	75	10

Of the patients served by the hospital, 10 percent are expected to be Medicare patients, all of whom are expected to select semiprivate rooms. Both the number and proportion of Medicare patients have increased over the past 5 years. Daily rentals per patient are: $80 for a private room, $70 for a semiprivate room, and $50 for a ward.

Operating room charges are based on man-minutes (number of minutes the operating room is in use multiplied by number of personnel assisting in the operation). The per man-minute charges are $.26 for inpatients and $.44 for outpatients. Studies for the current year show that operations on inpatients are broken down as follows:

Type of Operation	Number of Operations	Average Number of Minutes per Operation	Average Number of Personnel Required
A	800	30	4
B	700	45	5
C	300	90	6
D	200	120	8
	2,000		

The same proportion of inpatient operations is expected for the next fiscal year, and 180 outpatients are expected to use the operating room. Outpatient operations average 20 minutes and require the assistance of three persons.

Budgeted expenses for the year ending June 30, 19X2, by departments, are:

General Services:
Maintenance of Plant . . . . $ 100,000
Operation of Plant. 55,000
Administration. 195,000
All Others 384,000
Revenue-Producing Services:
Operating Room 136,880
All Others 2,200,000
$3,070,880

The following information is provided for cost allocation purposes:

	Square Feet	Salaries
General Services:		
Maintenance of Plant	12,000	$ 80,000
Operation of Plant	28,000	50,000
Administration	10,000	110,000
All Others	36,250	205,000
Revenue-Producing Services:		
Operating Room	17,500	30,000
All Others	86,250	605,000
	190,000	$1,080,000

Basis of Allocations:
Maintenance of plant—salaries.
Operation of plant—square feet.
Administration—salaries.
All other general service costs—8% to operating room, 92% to other revenue-producing departments.

Required: Prepare schedules showing the computation of each of the following:

1. The number of patient days (number of patients multiplied by average stay in hospital) expected by type of patient and service.

2. The total number of man-minutes expected for operating room services for inpatients and outpatients. For inpatients, show the breakdown of total operating room man-minutes by type of operation.
3. Expected gross revenue from room charges.
4. Expected gross revenue from operating room services.
5. Cost per man-minute for operating room services. Use the step-down method of cost allocation (costs of the general service departments are allocated in the following order: maintenance of plant, operation of plant, administration, all others). *(AICPA adapted)*

Index